The Modern Law of Evidence

Tenth Edition

ADRIAN KEANE LL.B

of the Inner Temple, Barrister,
Professor of Law, The City Law School,
City University London,
Former Dean of the Inns of Court School of Law

PAUL McKEOWN LL.B, LL.M

of Lincoln's Inn, Barrister,
Senior Lecturer, The City Law School,
City University London

OXFORD
UNIVERSITY PRESS

OXFORD
UNIVERSITY PRESS

Great Clarendon Street, Oxford, OX2 6DP,
United Kingdom

Oxford University Press is a department of the University of Oxford.
It furthers the University's objective of excellence in research, scholarship,
and education by publishing worldwide. Oxford is a registered trade mark of
Oxford University Press in the UK and in certain other countries

Seventh edition 2008
Eighth edition 2010
Ninth edition 2012

Impression: 1

Published in the United States of America by Oxford University Press
198 Madison Avenue, New York, NY 10016, United States of America

British Library Cataloguing in Publication Data
Data available

Library of Congress Control Number: 2013952971

ISBN 978-0-19-968434-2

Printed in Italy by
L.E.G.O. S.p.A.—Lavis TN

PREFACE TO THE TENTH EDITION

The law of evidence continues to develop apace. That is the primary justification for this new tenth edition a bare two years after the appearance of the ninth. In that period, the new material that we have drawn upon includes some 180 reported cases and some 36 articles written by lawyers, both academic and in practice, as well as those from other disciplines. However, it is not just the volume of this material that justifies a new edition, but also its importance. The work has been updated to cover, for example:

- *The Judicial College Bench Checklist: Young Witness Cases* and the Advocacy Training Council's Report, *Raising the Bar: The handling of vulnerable witnesses, victims and defendants in court*, both designed to enable vulnerable witnesses to give their 'best evidence';
- the decision of the Grand Chamber of the European Court of Human Rights in *Al-Khawaja and Tahery v UK* and the Court of Appeal decision *R v Riat*, on hearsay;
- the Court of Appeal decision *R v Phillips*, on bad character evidence where co-accused run 'cut-throat' defences;
- the Court of Appeal decision in *R v Alexander*, on visual identification by Facebook;
- the Justice and Security Act 2013, Parliament's controversial response to the Supreme Court decision in *Al Rawi v Security Service*, enabling civil courts to order a closed material procedure in the case of material the disclosure of which would damage the interests of national security;
- the Court of Appeal decision *R v E*, on the cross-examination of children;
- the Court of Appeal decision *R v Chinn*, on memory refreshing; and
- the Privy Council decision *Tido v R*, on dock identifications.

Between the writing of this new edition and its production, and thereafter, there are bound to be yet more developments in the law. It is for that reason that this book is accompanied by an Online Resource Centre, which contains updates to the text, a list of useful weblinks and examples of how some of the legal principles are applied in practice. As to this tenth edition, we have attempted to state the law, accurately, as at 1 September 2013. There is one exception: our references to the Criminal Procedure Rules are to the 2013 version, which comes into force on 7 October 2013.

We remain grateful to OUP, for being so helpfully supportive and efficient, and to our readers, both here and around the world, for their use of this work and their constructive feedback.

Paul dedicates his work on this edition to his sister Maria, who died in November 2011.

Adrian Keane
Paul McKeown
September 2013

OUTLINE CONTENTS

DETAILED CONTENTS

TABLE OF STATUTES

Page references in **bold** indicate that the text is reproduced in full. References to the ECHR are tabled under Sch 1 to the Human Rights Act 1998.

TABLE OF STATUTORY INSTRUMENTS

TABLE OF CODES, CODES OF PRACTICE, AND PRACTICE DIRECTIONS

TABLE OF CASES

xxviii

TABLE OF CASES

University Centre Library
The Hub at Blackburn College

Customer ID: ******90

Title: The modern law of evidence. (Tenth edition.)
ID: BB60244
Due: Thu, 22 Feb 2018

Total items: 1
08/02/2018 15:52

Please retain this receipt for your records
Contact Tel. 01254 292165

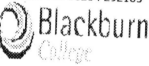

Introduction

Key issues

- What is 'evidence' and 'the law of evidence'?

- Typically, the parties to litigation dispute the facts. What are the factors that operate to prevent the court from looking at *all* the evidence that could assist in discovering where the truth lies?

- What human factors can operate to prevent the court from discovering where the truth lies?

- Are there any good reasons to restrict the evidence taken into account *more* when the tribunal of fact is a jury or lay justices than when it is a professional judge?

- Should the law of evidence be codified or allowed to continue to evolve by way of common law development and piecemeal statutory reform?

Evidence is information by which facts tend to be proved, and the law of evidence is that body of law and discretion regulating the means by which facts may be proved in both courts of law and tribunals and arbitrations in which the strict rules of evidence apply.[1] It is adjectival rather than substantive law and overlaps with procedural law.

At the risk of oversimplification, the broad governing principle underlying the English law of evidence can be stated in no more than nine words: all relevant evidence is admissible, subject to the exceptions.

Truth and the fact-finding process

In most litigation, the parties will dispute the facts. In an ideal world, perhaps, the court inquiring into those facts would take account of all evidence which is relevant to the dispute, that is all evidence that logically goes to prove or disprove the existence of those facts, and would thereby get to the truth of the matter.[2] In the real world, however, a variety of factors operate to restrict the evidence taken into account. First, there are practical constraints inherent in the fact-finding process and common to all legal systems: considerations of time and cost and the need for finality to litigation.[3] Second, under the English adversarial system of trial, whatever its undoubted merits, the court itself cannot undertake a search for relevant evidence but must reach its decision solely on the basis of such evidence as is presented by the parties.[4] Third, there is the law of evidence itself, much of which comprises rules which exclude relevant evidence for a variety of different reasons. For example, evidence may be insufficiently relevant or of only minimal probative force; it may give rise to a multiplicity of essentially subsidiary issues, which could distract the court from the main issue; it may be insufficiently reliable or unreliable; its potential for prejudice to the party against whom it is introduced may be out of all proportion to its probative value on behalf of the party introducing it; its disclosure may be injurious to the national interest; and so on. Thus the court may aspire to the ascertainment of the truth, but at the end of the day it must come to a decision and settle the dispute even if the evidence introduced is inadequate or inconclusive.

The risk that the court will not get to the truth of the matter is heightened by virtue of the fact that litigation is, of course, a human endeavour and therefore will, in one way or another, provide scope for differences of opinion, error, deceit, and lies. Thus judges, who are called upon to decide what evidence is relevant and to be taken into account, may take different views about whether one fact is relevant to prove or disprove another. As to the parties to litigation, they are hardly impartial and may well be more concerned with winning their case than in assisting to establish the truth. As to the fact-finders, they are most likely to use inferential reasoning to supplement the evidence in the case and fill the gaps in it, which may

---

[1] The strict rules of evidence do not apply, for example, to civil claims which have been allocated to the small claims track (see CPR r 27.8) or at hearings before employment tribunals (see r 41, Sch 1, Employment Tribunals (Constitution and Rules of Procedure) Regulations 2013, SI 2013/1237).

[2] In support of the view that trials should be a search for the truth, see the Government's White Paper, *Justice for All*, Cm 563 (2002) at 32 and Lord Justice Auld's *Review of the Criminal Courts of England and Wales*, HMSO, 2001, para 154, ch 10.

[3] See Morgan, *Introduction to the American Law Institute Model Code of Evidence* (Philadelphia, 1942) 3–4.

[4] However, in criminal cases, the judge does have the power, albeit a power to be exercised most sparingly, to call a witness not called by either side: see Ch 5, under **Witnesses in criminal cases**, **The witnesses to be called**.

involve the creation of non-existent facts.[5] Finally, there are the witnesses who, if not telling the truth, will either be lying or mistaken. As to mistakes, there is obvious scope for error, not only in their observation of events, but also in their memory of it and in their recounting of those events in court.[6] There is also the risk that witnesses may give truthful but unreliable evidence of facts which have been created by parties involved in the legal process, a classic example being evidence of a false confession produced during the interrogation of a suspect.[7]

The development of the law

The largely exclusionary ethos of the modern law of evidence reflects its common law history. Many of the rules evolved at a time when the tribunal of fact comprised either jurors or lay justices to whom the judges adopted a paternalistic and protective attitude, excluding relevant evidence such as hearsay evidence, evidence of character, and the opinion evidence of non-experts on the basis that lay persons might overvalue its weight and importance, or even treat it as conclusive. A typical example is evidence of the accused's previous convictions or of his disposition towards wrongdoing which, to an extent, remains inadmissible because of fears that it might influence jurors disproportionately against the accused and distract their attention from other evidence tending to prove his guilt or innocence. Distrust of the jury probably had little to do with the origin of the rule against hearsay evidence, but much to do with the delay in the growth of exceptions to that rule. Historically, the judges also suffered from an ingrained fear of the deliberate concoction or manufacture of evidence by the parties to litigation and their witnesses. This accounted for the general ban on statements made out of court by a witness and consistent with his present testimony (the rule against previous consistent or self-serving statements). In large measure, it also explained why an out-of-court statement, even if it could be shown to be of virtually indisputable reliability, was generally excluded as evidence of the truth of its contents under the rule against hearsay. The dread of manufactured evidence went much further than the exclusion of specific kinds of evidence: it also meant that whole classes of persons were treated as incompetent to give evidence at all. For example, the incompetence of persons with a pecuniary or proprietary interest in the outcome of the proceedings, including the parties themselves in civil cases, was not fully abolished until the mid-nineteenth century, and it was not until the Criminal Evidence Act 1898 that the accused and his spouse were entitled, in all criminal cases, to give evidence on oath. Another factor which contributed to the largely exclusionary nature of the law of evidence in criminal proceedings stemmed from an understandable desire, at a time when the dice were unfairly loaded against the accused, to offer some judicial protection against injustice. Trials were often conducted with indecent haste, accused persons enjoyed far less legal representation, and convictions could be questioned only on narrow legal grounds.[8]

In civil cases, nowadays, trial is usually by a judge sitting alone who is perfectly capable, by virtue of her training, qualifications, and experience, of attaching no more weight to an item of evidence than the circumstances properly allow. In criminal cases, the scales can no longer

[5] See generally Pennington and Hastie, 'The story model for juror decision making' in Hastie (ed), *Inside the Juror* (Cambridge, 1993).
[6] See Keane, 'The Use at Trial of Scientific Findings relating to Human Memory' [2010] Crim LR 19.
[7] See McConville, Sanders, and Leng, *The Case for the Prosecution* (London, 1991).
[8] See Criminal Law Revision Committee, 11th Report, *Evidence (General)*, Cmnd 4991 (1972), paras 21 ff.

be said to be unfairly loaded against the accused, especially since the coming into force of the Human Rights Act 1998. No doubt, it remains necessary to prevent some material being placed before juries on the grounds of irretrievable prejudice against the accused, but the quality of juries and lay magistrates has greatly improved and it is questionable whether they are incapable, given clear and proper judicial direction, of properly evaluating the weight and reliability of some relevant evidence which continues to be excluded, such as evidence of the previous consistent statements of witnesses.

Over the years, there has been much statutory reform, sometimes significant, including in particular the enactments designed to bring domestic law into line with the European Convention on Human Rights. Statutory reform has done much to reduce the number of restrictions on the admissibility of relevant evidence, to rationalize and clarify the law, to enhance the discretionary powers of the judge, and to remove some of the more anomalous and unnecessary discrepancies between the rules in civil and criminal cases. Reform, however, has been piecemeal, sporadic, slow, and usually limited to one specific area of the law, with little or no consideration of the impact of change on other related areas of the subject. The current law of evidence, therefore, may be likened to a machine which has been constructed on common law principles by judicial engineers, but which is subject to periodic alteration by parliamentary mechanics, who variously remove or redesign parts or bolt on new parts. The judges oil and maintain the machine, and continually seek to refine, modify, and develop it to meet the continually changing needs it is designed to serve. But there are constraints and limitations. Developments can only occur in relation to the specific issues brought before the judges by litigants, some of which are slow to surface.[9] Moreover, in relation to the issues that do surface, the basic framework of the law may be so unprincipled or out of line with con-temporary needs or moral and social values that the judges, bound by *stare decisis* or saddled with antiquated legislation, can only act on a 'make do and mend' basis and put out a call for parliamentary assistance.[10] Whether the call is answered, however, is something of a lottery, with the odds improving if the proposals are based on, or supported by, the recommendations of a law reform agency. Some proposals, however, are simply unacceptable to the government of the day or too dull to win votes, being technical or relating to the quality rather than the content of the law.

Speaking generally, statutory reform has done much to improve the civil rules across a range of subjects. Additionally, and as a result of Lord Woolf's review of the procedural rules in the civil courts,[11] the Civil Procedure Act 1997 provided for the creation of the Civil Procedure Rules (CPR) (and supplementary Practice Directions). The rules, which replaced the former Rules of the Supreme Court and County Court Rules, and which may modify the rules of evidence,[12] constituted the most radical reform of the ethos and procedure of civil litigation since the Supreme Court of Judicature Act 1875.[13] The jury is still out on whether

---

[9] For example, it was only in the early 1990s that the courts were first asked to give detailed consideration to the applicability, in criminal proceedings, of the general doctrine of public interest immunity.

[10] For example, there have been repeated judicial requests for reform of the privilege against self-incrimination. See also the comments in *C v DPP* [1995] 2 All ER 43, HL, concerning the presumption of *doli incapax*, subsequently abolished by statute.

[11] *Access to Justice, Final Report* (HMSO, 1996).

[12] See Civil Procedure Act 1997, Sch 1, para 4.

[13] See also the Family Procedure Rules 2010, SI 2010/2955, which provide a separate code of procedure, including evidence rules, for family proceedings.

they render the civil justice system as a whole more 'accessible, fair, and efficient',[14] but concerning the law of evidence, they have done much to simplify and rationalize the relevant procedural rules.[15]

Parliament has also rationalized and improved many of the criminal rules. The most recent of the major reforms, the Criminal Justice Act 2003, has brought about radical change in relation to hearsay evidence and evidence of bad character. The provisions are premised on a welcome new confidence that fact-finders can be trusted to evaluate evidence correctly, reflecting the view in Lord Justice Auld's *Review of the Criminal Courts of England and Wales* that 'the English law of criminal evidence should, in general, move away from technical rules of inadmissibility to trusting judicial and lay fact finders to give relevant evidence the weight it deserves'.[16] As to the procedural rules, the Criminal Procedure Rules 2005[17] represented the first steps towards the creation of a new consolidated and comprehensive criminal procedure code of the kind recommended by Lord Justice Auld in his *Review*. Although, initially, the rules merely consolidated and adopted all the pre-existing rules of court, r 1.1 sets out a new overriding objective of the code that criminal cases be dealt with justly. Under r 3.2, the court must further the overriding objective by actively managing the case, which includes ensuring that evidence, whether disputed or not, is presented in the shortest and clearest way; and under r 3.3, each party must (a) actively assist the court in fulfilling its duty under r 3.2, without, or if necessary with, a direction; and (b) apply for a direction if needed to further the overriding objective.[18] There is some evidence, however, that the rules have given rise to a number of practical problems and that defence lawyers may have difficulties reconciling their ethical obligations to the accused with their enhanced duties to the court.[19]

'It would be unfortunate', it has been said, 'if the law of evidence was allowed to develop in a way which was not in accordance with the common sense of ordinary folk',[20] not least, one might add, because it has to be used and understood not only by professional judges, but also by part-time judges, lay magistrates, jurors and, increasingly, the police. Recent developments give some cause for cautious optimism. Looking at the law of evidence overall, however, there are strong grounds for believing that fairness, coherence, clarity, and accessibility will only come, not from common law development coupled with piecemeal statutory intervention, but from codification.

ADDITIONAL READING

Coen, 'Hearsay, bad character and trust in the jury: Irish and English contrasts' (2013) 17 E&P 250.

Dwyer, ed, *The Civil Procedure Rules Ten Years On* (Oxford, 2009).

[14] See Civil Procedure Act 1997, s 1(3).

[15] See generally Dwyer, ed, *The Civil Procedure Rules Ten Years On* (Oxford, 2009).

[16] Para 78. See also, generally, Coen, 'Hearsay, bad character and trust in the jury: Irish and English contrasts' (2013) 17 E&P 250.

[17] SI 2005/384. See now the Criminal Procedure Rules 2013, SI 2013/1554.

[18] All participants in criminal cases must follow and apply the rules, which are not mere guidance. Compliance is compulsory and the word 'must' means must. See Leveson LJ, *Essential case management: applying the Criminal Procedure Rules* (2009) at <www.judiciary.gov.uk/publications-and-reports/protocols/criminal-protocols/applying-criminal-procedure-rules>.

[19] Garland and McEwan, 'Embracing the overriding objective: difficulties and dilemmas in the new criminal climate' (2012) 16 E&P 233.

[20] Per Lawton LJ in *R v Chandler* [1976] 1 WLR 585, CA at 590.

Garland and McEwan, 'Embracing the overriding objective: difficulties and dilemmas in the new criminal climate' (2012) 16 E&P 233.

Keane, 'The Use at Trial of Scientific Findings relating to Human Memory' [2010] Crim LR 19.

McConville et al, *The Case for the Prosecution* (London, 1991).

Pennington and Hastie, 'The story model for juror decision making' in Hastie (ed), *Inside the Juror* (Cambridge, 1993).

Research Board of the British Psychological Society, *The Guidelines on Memory and the Law* (2008).

Twining, *Rethinking Evidence* (Oxford, 1990).

and to comment adversely might work injustice, since there might be a good reason but one which it would be unfair to disclose to the jury. Moreover, there might be an issue between the prosecution and defence as to whether a witness was available. There was no simple answer and much depended upon the judge's sense of fairness. (2) The dangers of making adverse comments, and failing to warn the jury not to speculate, are the paramount considerations. (3) On the other hand, now that a defendant's failure to disclose his case in advance can be the subject of comment, the case for permitting comment on an absent witness may be stronger. (4) If the judge comments on a failure to call a witness, a reference to the burden of proof may be appropriate. (5) A judge who is proposing to make a comment should first invite submissions from counsel in the absence of the jury.

Concerning the failure of the spouse of an accused to testify, comment by the *prosecution* was prohibited by proviso (b) to s 1 of the Criminal Evidence Act 1898. The Criminal Law Revision Committee proposed the lifting of this prohibition,[44] a proposal rejected by Parliament. Re-enacting the relevant parts of the proviso, s 80A of the Police and Criminal Evidence Act 1984 provides that the failure of the wife or husband or civil partner of a person charged in any proceedings to give evidence in the proceedings shall not be made the subject of any comment by the prosecution. Under proviso (b), it was held that where counsel for the prosecution does make an adverse comment on the failure of the accused to call his spouse to give evidence on his behalf, it is the duty of the trial judge, depending upon the circumstances of each case, to remedy that breach in his summing-up, especially when the accused is a man of good character and this is central to his defence.[45] It may be assumed that a breach of s 80A should be remedied in the same way.

Section 80A applies only to the prosecution. In appropriate circumstances, therefore, the *judge* may comment on the failure of the spouse or civil partner of the accused to testify. However, if the judge, in the exercise of his discretion, does decide to make a comment, he must, save in exceptional circumstances, do so with a great deal of circumspection.[46] The same degree of circumspection would also seem to be required in the case of comment on failure to call cohabitees, who are not covered by s 80A.[47]

A breach of s 80A is unlikely to result in a successful appeal if the judge, in summing up, makes appropriate and suitable comments on the failure of the spouse to testify: the error made by counsel is subsumed in the summing-up.[48]

Failure to provide samples
Under s 23(1) of the Family Law Reform Act 1969, if, in any civil proceedings in which the paternity of any person falls to be determined, the court directs a party to undergo a blood test and that party fails to obey the direction, the court may draw such inferences as appear proper in the circumstances.[49] Similarly, s 62(10) of the Police and Criminal Evidence Act 1984 provides that where an accused has refused without good cause the taking from him of an intimate body sample the court, in determining whether there is a case to answer, and the court or jury, in determining whether he is guilty of the offence charged, 'may draw such inferences from

---

[44] Cmnd 4991 (1972), para 154.
[45] *R v Naudeer* [1984] 3 All ER 1036, CA. See also *R v Dickman* (1910) 5 Cr App R 135 and *R v Hunter* [1969] Crim LR 262, CA.
[46] Per Purchas LJ in *R v Naudeer* [1984] 3 All ER 1036, CA at 1039.
[47] See *R v Weller* [1994] Crim LR 856, CA.
[48] See *R v Whitton* [1998] Crim LR 492, CA.
[49] See *McVeigh v Beattie* [1988] 2 All ER 500.

the refusal as appear proper'. Section 62 is considered further in Chapter 14, together with the inferences that may be drawn, pursuant to statute, from an accused's silence or conduct.

Lies

Lies told by an accused, on their own, do not prove that a person is guilty of any crime.[50] However, evidence of such post-offence behaviour may indicate a consciousness of guilt.[51] In appropriate circumstances, lies may be relied upon by the prosecution as evidence supportive of guilt, as in *R v Goodway*[52] in which the accused's lies to the police as to his whereabouts at the time of the offence were used in support of the identification evidence adduced by the prosecution.[53] It was held that whenever a lie told by an accused is relied on by the Crown, or may be used by the jury to support evidence of guilt, as opposed merely to reflecting on his credibility (and not only when it is relied on as corroboration or as support for identification evidence), a direction—often referred to as a *Lucas* direction[54]—should be given to the jury that: (1) the lie must be deliberate and must relate to a material issue; (2) they must be satisfied that there was no innocent motive for the lie, reminding them that people sometimes lie, for example, in an attempt to bolster up a just cause, or out of shame or a wish to conceal disgraceful behaviour; and in cases where the lie is relied upon as corroboration;[55] (3) the lie must be established by evidence other than that of the witness who is to be corroborated.[56] It was also said, however, that such a direction need not be given where it is otiose, as indicated in *R v Dehar*,[57] ie where the rejection of the explanation by the accused almost necessarily leaves the jury with no choice but to convict as a matter of logic. An example is *R v Barsoum*,[58] where the lie related to the presence of another person, M, at the scene of the crime and if M was present, B was entitled to be acquitted, but if M was an invention it automatically followed that B must be guilty.[59] Where a direction is given, it should also make the point that the lie must be admitted or proved beyond reasonable doubt.[60] At a trial for murder in which the only issue is provocation, and the accused's lie is a statement that he never had any contact with the victim, the jury should be directed that the lie can support the case of murder if they are sure that it was told to conceal the fact of murder, rather than connection with the death, ie to avoid responsibility for murder rather than a provoked killing.[61]

[50] *R v Strudwick* (1993) 99 Cr App R 326, CA at 331.

[51] As to the relevance to *mens rea* of the post-offence behaviour of flight, or flight without hesitation, see *R v White* 2011 SCC 13, with commentary by Pattenden in (2011) 15 E&P 261.

[52] [1993] 4 All ER 894, CA.

[53] In civil proceedings, also, a party's lies may diminish his credibility and make it harder for him to prove his case: see *MA (Somalia) v Secretary of State for the Home Department* [2011] 2 All ER 65, SC.

[54] See *R v Lucas* [1981] QB 720, CA.

[55] See Ch 8.

[56] Applied in *R v Taylor* [1994] Crim LR 680, CA. If a lie is relied on merely to attack credibility, a direction may be appropriate in exceptional circumstances, as when the lie figures largely in the case and the jury may think that the accused must be guilty because he lied: *R v Tucker* [1994] Crim LR 683, CA.

[57] [1969] NZLR 763, NZCA.

[58] [1994] Crim LR 194, CA.

[59] Cf *R v Wood* [1995] Crim LR, CA, where the accused may have been influenced by panic or confusion and therefore guilt was not the only possible explanation for the lies he told. But see also *R v Saunders* [1996] 1 Cr App R 463, CA at 518–19, where it was held that a direction was not required, the accused having explained his lies on the basis that he was confused and under pressure, and the judge having dealt with that explanation fairly in his summing-up.

[60] *R v Burge* [1996] 1 Cr App R 163, CA.

[61] *R v Taylor* [1998] Crim LR 822, CA. See also *R v Reszpondek* [2010] EWCA Crim 2358 at [19].

term does not of itself express the element of experience which is so significant of its operation in law, and possibly elsewhere. It is sufficient to say, even at the risk of etymological tautology, that relevant (i.e. logically probative or disprobative) evidence is evidence which makes the matter which requires proof more or less probable.[90]

In *R v Randall*[91] Lord Steyn cited and applied the statement appearing in the fifth edition of this book that 'relevance is a question of degree determined, for the most part, by common sense and experience'. R and G were tried together on a charge of murder. Each raised a cut-throat defence, blaming the other for the infliction of the fatal injuries. Both therefore lost the protection of s 1 of the Criminal Evidence Act 1898[92] and were asked questions about their previous convictions and bad character. R had relatively minor convictions for driving offences and disorderly behaviour. G had a bad record, including convictions for burglary, the most recent being for burglary committed by a gang in which G had been armed with a screwdriver. G also admitted in cross-examination that at the date of the killing he was on the run from the police, having been involved in a robbery committed by a gang, all the robbers having been armed with knives. The House of Lords held that the evidence of G's propensity to use and threaten violence was relevant not only in relation to the truthfulness of his evidence, but also because the imbalance between that history and the antecedent history of R tended to show that the version of events put forward by R was more probable than that put forward by G.

Examples of irrelevance and insufficient relevance

Examples of evidence sufficiently relevant to prove or disprove a fact in issue have already been given under the rubric of circumstantial evidence which, it will be recalled, is a term used to refer to evidence of *relevant* facts. Consideration may now be given to some examples of evidence which has been excluded on the grounds of irrelevance or insufficient relevance. *Holcombe v Hewson*[93] concerned an alleged breach of covenant by the defendant, a publican, to buy his beer from the plaintiff, a brewer. The plaintiff, in order to rebut the defence that he had previously supplied bad beer, intended to call publicans to give evidence that he had supplied them with good beer. Excluding this evidence, Lord Ellenborough said:

> We cannot here enquire into the quality of different beer furnished to different persons. The plaintiff might deal well with one, and not with the others. Let him call some of those who frequented the defendant's house, and there drank the beer which he sent in...

In *Hollingham v Head*[94] the defendant, in order to defeat an action for the price of goods sold and delivered, sought to establish that the contract was made on certain special terms by evidence that the plaintiff had entered into contracts with other customers on similar terms. The evidence was held to be inadmissible on the grounds that it would have afforded no reasonable inference as to the terms of the contract in dispute.[95] On a charge of manslaughter against

---

[90] Concerning the role of probability theory in legal proceedings, see Eggleston, *Evidence, Proof and Probability* (2nd edn, London, 1983).

[91] [2004] 1 All ER 467 at 474.

[92] See now Criminal Justice Act 2003, s 101.

[93] (1810) 2 Camp 391, KB.

[94] (1858) 27 LJCP 241.

[95] Evidence of 'similar facts' is not invariably excluded, however: see, eg, *Hales v Kerr* [1908] 2 KB 601, DC and the other cases on the point in Ch 15.

a doctor, expert evidence may be adduced as to the doctor's skill as shown by his treatment of the case under investigation, but evidence of his skilful treatment of other patients on other occasions must be excluded.[96] Evidence that after an accident the defendants to a negligence action altered and improved their practice has no relevance to the question whether the accident was caused by their negligence: 'Because the world gets wiser as it gets older, it was not therefore foolish before.'[97]

Where two criminal trials arise out of the same transaction, evidence of the outcome of the first will generally be inadmissible, because irrelevant, at the second; some exceptional feature is needed before it is considered relevant.[98] This is the position, *a fortiori*, where the earlier trial related to a different event.[99] It has been said that the rationale for the 'rule' is that the evidence amounts to nothing more than evidence of the opinion of the first jury,[100] but taken alone that would be a reason for never admitting evidence of a previous verdict. The true rationale, in the case of an earlier acquittal, is that in most cases it is not possible to be certain why a jury acquitted.[101] The 'exception' to the rule is where there is a clear inference from the verdict that the jury rejected a witness's evidence, on the basis that they did not believe him, as opposed to thinking that he was mistaken, and the witness's credibility is directly in issue in the second trial.[102] An example is where an officer who has given evidence of an admission in a trial resulting in an acquittal by virtue of which his evidence can be shown to have been disbelieved, faces an allegation, in a subsequent trial, that he has fabricated an admission.[103] Another example is where the prosecution allege that as part of a joint enterprise, A and B, one after the other, raped C; A and B are tried separately; the prosecution case against each man depends almost entirely on the evidence of C and therefore the jury have to decide which side is lying; and A is tried first and acquitted.[104]

In *R v Sandhu*[105] it was held that, insofar as an offence of strict liability involves no proof of *mens rea*, evidence of motive, intention, or knowledge on the part of the accused is inadmissible because irrelevant to the issue of his guilt and merely prejudicial to him.[106]

Another, but controversial, example of irrelevance is to be found in the decision of the House of Lords in *R v Blastland*.[107] The appellant B was charged with the buggery and murder of a boy. At the trial B admitted that he had met the boy and engaged in homosexual activity with him

---

[96] *R v Whitehead* (1848) 3 Car&Kir 202.

[97] Per Bramwell B in *Hart v Lancashire & Yorkshire Rly Co* (1869) 21 LT 261.

[98] *Hui Chi-ming v R* [1991] 3 All ER 897, PC. See also, concerning the admissibility, at a retrial, of the first jury's acquittal on some counts and failure to agree on others, *R v H* (1989) 90 Cr App R 440, CA; *R v Greer* [1994] Crim LR 745, CA; *R v Scott* [1994] Crim LR 947, CA; and, generally, Choo, 'The Notion of Relevance' [1993] Crim LR 114.

[99] *R v Terry* [2005] 2 Cr App R 118, CA at [34].

[100] *Hui Chi-ming v R* [1991] 3 All ER 897, PC.

[101] *R v Deboussi* [2007] EWCA Crim 684. The rule also seems to apply in the case of an acquittal based on a judge's ruling that there is insufficient evidence for the case to go to the jury: *R v Hudson* [1994] Crim LR 920, CA. As to the relevance and admissibility of previous convictions as evidence of the facts on which they were based, see Ch 21.

[102] *R v Deboussi* [2007] EWCA Crim 684.

[103] *R v Edwards* [1991] 2 All ER 266, CA. See also *R v Hay* (1983) 77 Cr App R 70, CA and *R v Cooke* (1986) 84 Cr App R 286, CA.

[104] *R v Deboussi* [2007] EWCA Crim 684.

[105] [1997] Crim LR 288, CA.

[106] See also, applying *R v Sandhu, R v Byrne* [2002] 2 Cr App R 311.

[107] [1986] AC 41, HL, applied in *R v Williams* [1998] Crim LR 494, CA. See also *R v Kearley* [1992] 2 AC 228, HL (see Ch 10); and *R v Akram* [1995] Crim LR 50, CA.

but said that when he saw another man nearby, who might have witnessed what he had done, he panicked and ran away. B gave a description of the other man which corresponded closely to M and alleged that M must have committed the offences charged. At the trial there were formal admissions[108] by the prosecution. Some related to M's movements on the evening in question and others showed that M had been investigated by the police after the murder and had been known to engage in homosexual activities in the past with adults but not children. The defence sought leave to call a number of witnesses to elicit from them that, before the victim's body had been found, M had made statements to them that a boy had been murdered. The trial judge held this evidence to be inadmissible. B was convicted on both counts. Before the House of Lords, the appellant submitted that, although the statements made by M were inadmissible hearsay if tendered for the truth of any fact stated, they were admissible, as original evidence, if tendered to prove the state of mind of their maker, ie to show M's knowledge of the murder before the body had been found.[109] Lord Bridge, giving the judgment of the House, held that original evidence of this kind is only admissible if the state of mind in question 'is either itself directly in issue at the trial or is of direct and immediate relevance to an issue which arises at the trial'. The issue at the trial was whether B had committed the crimes and what was relevant to that issue was not the fact of M's knowledge but how he had come by it; since he might have done so in a number of different ways, there was no rational basis on which the jury could be invited to draw an inference as to the source of that knowledge or conclude that he rather than B was the offender. The evidence, therefore, had been properly rejected. The flaw in this reasoning, it is submitted, is the unwarranted introduction of the requirement that the evidence be 'of direct and immediate' relevance. The evidence was no less relevant than the evidence relating to M's movements which was thought to have been properly admitted, albeit neither item, by itself, could show that M, rather than B, was the offender.[110]

It is submitted that an unnecessarily strict approach to relevance was also taken in *R v T (AB)*.[111] The complainant alleged that A, the appellant, B, and C had each sexually abused her. There was no suggestion that they had acted in concert or that any one of them was aware of the abuse of either of the others. B admitted the allegations against him, but died before his trial, and C pleaded guilty to counts of indecent assault. It was held that evidence of B's admission and of C's guilty plea was inadmissible because irrelevant to the issues of whether A had abused the complainant and that while it was 'tempting' to say that it was relevant to the issue of her credibility, evidence is inadmissible simply to bolster credibility because this would be a form of 'oath helping' which has never been a permissible ground for admitting evidence.

---

[108] See under **Facts open to proof or disproof**, **Facts in issue**, in this chapter. There were also a number of *informal* admissions, M having successively made and withdrawn admissions of his own guilt of the offences in question, but these were properly rejected by the trial judge as inadmissible hearsay: see *R v Turner* (1975) 61 Cr App R 67, CA.

[109] See under **The varieties of evidence**, **Hearsay evidence**, in this chapter.

[110] Contrast the approach taken in *Wildman v R* [1984] 2 SCR 311 (Supreme Court of Canada) and *R v Szach* (1980) 23 SASR 504 (Supreme Court of South Australia). See also *R v Gadsby* [2006] Crim LR 631, CA, where it was held, obiter, that evidence may be relevant if capable of increasing (or diminishing) the probability of facts indicating that some other person committed the crime, eg, evidence that a person with the opportunity of committing the crime had a propensity to do so; and *R v Greenwood* [2005] Crim LR 59, CA, where it was held that an accused charged with murder is entitled to seek to establish that a third party had a motive to murder the victim.

[111] [2007] 1 Cr App R 43, CA.

Evidence of demeanour may be relevant, depending on the circumstances. For example, in the case of an accused charged with murder, the evidence of an experienced physician that the accused was calm and uninterested when the baby was found to be dead may be relevant, but not evidence of the fact that the accused did not appear emotional at the funeral, because 'outward appearances at a funeral home offer no reliable barometer of one's grief'.[112] The demeanour of the victim of a crime immediately after its commission may be relevant and admissible to support his or her account, by analogy with the principle of *res gestae*.[113] However, it is submitted that the *res gestae* conditions[114] do not have to be met: the evidence is not hearsay. Similarly, the condition in *R v Keast*[115] seems unduly restrictive. In that case, it was held that unless there is some concrete basis for regarding long-term demeanour and state of mind of an alleged victim of sexual abuse as confirming or disproving the occurrence of such abuse, it cannot assist a jury bringing their common sense to bear on who is telling the truth.[116]

On a charge of causing death by dangerous driving, evidence that the accused took cocaine shortly before the accident is relevant, even without evidence as to the amount taken,[117] but evidence that the accused took drink will not be relevant without evidence to show that the amount taken would adversely affect a driver.[118] The reasoning for the distinction appears to be based on the dubious generalization that a modest dose of cocaine has a greater capacity to impair driving ability than a modest intake of alcohol.[119] Much, it is submitted, should turn on both the timing and the amounts.

In criminal proceedings, evidence to bolster the credibility of a prosecution witness is generally inadmissible, but evidence of a specific disposition will be admissible if relevant to an issue in the case. Examples of such relevance include: in a sexual case, the defence being consent, evidence of the complainant's disposition to resist pre-marital sexual intimacy;[120] in a case of murder, the defence being self-defence, evidence of the deceased's non-violent disposition;[121] and evidence of non-racist disposition in rebuttal of an allegation of racist abuse forming an integral part of a defence of self-defence.[122]

There are occasions when the effect of evidence, albeit technically admissible, is likely to be so slight that it is wiser not to adduce it, particularly if, in a criminal trial, there is any danger that its admission will have an adverse effect on the fairness of the proceedings.[123] Evidence of marginal relevance may also be excluded on the grounds that it would lead to a multiplicity of subsidiary issues which, in addition to distracting the court from the main issue,[124] might

[112] *R v MT* [2004] OJ No 4366 (Ont. CA).
[113] *R v Townsend* [2003] EWCA Crim 3173.
[114] See Ch 12.
[115] [1998] Crim LR 748, CA.
[116] See also, applying *R v Keast* [1998] Crim LR 748, CA, *R v Venn* [2003] EWCA Crim 236.
[117] *R v Pleydell* [2006] 1 Cr App R 212, CA, applied in *R v Ashworth* [2012] EWCA Crim 1064.
[118] *R v McBride* (1961) 45 Cr App R 262, followed in *R v Thorpe* [1972] 1 WLR 342.
[119] See *R v Pleydell* [2006] 1 Cr App R 212, CA at [27] and [28].
[120] *R v Amado-Taylor* [2001] EWCA Crim 1898.
[121] *R v RG* [2002] EWCA Crim 1056.
[122] *R v Lodge* [2013] EWCA Crim 987. See also *R v Q* [2011] All ER (D) 210 (Jun).
[123] Per Lord Lane CJ in *R v Robertson; R v Golder* [1987] 3 All ER 231 at 237, CA in relation to the admissibility of evidence under the Police and Criminal Evidence Act 1984, s 74 (see Ch 21). See also *R v Williams* [1990] Crim LR 409, CA.
[124] See per Byrne J in *R v Patel* [1951] 2 All ER 29 at 30.

involve the court in a protracted investigation[125] or a difficult and doubtful controversy of precisely the same kind as that which the court has to determine.[126] Similarly, questioning of a witness may be disallowed if it is no more than a fishing expedition.[127] In *Agassiz v London Tramway Co*[128] the plaintiff, a passenger in an omnibus, claimed damages for serious personal injuries arising out of a collision allegedly caused by the driver's negligence. The action was dismissed for want of evidence as to how the accident had happened. After the accident, the conductor, in reply to the suggestion of another passenger that the driver's conduct should be reported, said: 'Sir, he has been reported, for he has been off the points five or six times today; he is a new driver.' Kelly CB held that this evidence was properly excluded, since it neither related to the conduct of the driver at the relevant time nor explained the actual cause of the collision, but merely gave rise to a multiplicity of sideissues.

Relevance of possession of money or drugs paraphernalia in offences relating to drugs
On charges of possession of drugs with intent to supply, there is a difficult distinction to be drawn between evidence which is relevant to the intention to supply the drug found, and evidence which, although of some relevance to that issue, is unduly prejudicial because it relates to past dealing or dealing generally. It is submitted that on the question of admissibility, rather than relevance, some of the reported cases must now be read subject to ss 98–113 of the Criminal Justice Act 2003, which govern admissibility of evidence of the accused's bad character.[129] In *R v Batt*,[130] a charge of possession of cannabis resin with intent to supply, the Court of Appeal did not question the admissibility in evidence of B's possession of weights and scales (on which there were traces of cannabis resin), but held that evidence of the discovery of £150 in an ornamental kettle in her house was inadmissible because it had nothing to do with intent to supply in future the drugs found, but had a highly prejudicial effect as 'a hallmark of a propensity to supply generally, or a hallmark of the fact that there had been a past supply, or that the money will be used in future to obtain cannabis for future supply'.

However, it seems that *Batt* has not laid down any general principle that evidence of possession of money is never admissible on a charge of possession with intent to supply, and on one view the decision in that case turned upon the fact that the trial judge had failed to direct the jury as to how they could properly use the evidence of the possession of money.[131] In *R v Wright*[132] it was held that drug traders needed to keep by them large sums of cash and therefore evidence of the

---

[125] See per Rolfe B in *A-G v Hitchcock* (1847) 1 Exch 91 at 105 and per Willes J in *Hollingham v Head* (1858) 27 LJCP 241 at 242: 'litigants are mortal…'.

[126] Per Lord Watson in *Metropolitan Asylum District Managers v Hill* (1882) 47 LT 29, HL, where a majority of the House was of the opinion, without deciding the point, that in considering the effect of a smallpox hospital on the health of local residents, evidence of the effect of similar hospitals in other localities on their residents would be admissible. See also *Folkes v Chadd* (1782) 3 Doug KB 157.

[127] *R v Haddock* [2011] EWCA Crim 303!

[128] (1872) 21 WR 199.

[129] See Ch 17. However, it has been said that if the evidence would have been admissible before the 2003 Act, it would be 'highly artificial' to require the prosecution to apply to admit it under the Act: *R v Graham* [2007] EWCA Crim 1499. See further, Ormerod [2010] Crim LR 307–9.

[130] [1994] Crim LR 592, CA.

[131] See *R v Morris* [1995] 2 Cr App R 69, CA, and *R v Nicholas* [1995] Crim LR 942, CA. Alternatively, it should be regarded as a case confined to its own facts, remembering that £150 was too small, and its hiding place too unremarkable, to be the hallmark of present and active drug dealing: *R v Okusanya* [1995] Crim LR 941, CA.

[132] [1994] Crim LR 55, CA.

discovery of £16,000 could have given rise to an inference of dealing and tended to prove that the drugs found were for supply. This approach was followed in *R v Gordon*,[133] where it was held that although evidence as to past deposits in, and withdrawals from, savings accounts was irrelevant, because it could only found an inference of past drug dealing, evidence of the discovery of £4,200 in G's home was admissible ('cash for the acquisition of stock for present active drug dealing must be relevant to a count of possession with intent to supply'), subject to an appropriate direction on any possible innocent explanations for the presence of the cash.[134] The jury should be directed that they should regard the finding of the money as relevant only if they reject any innocent explanation for it put forward by the accused, but that if they conclude that the money indicates not merely past dealing, but an ongoing dealing in drugs, they may take into account the finding of it, together with the drugs, in considering whether intent to supply has been proved.[135] The jury should also be directed not to treat such evidence as evidence of propensity, ie not to pursue the line of reasoning that, by reason of past dealing, the accused is likely to be guilty of the offence charged.[136]

At one stage, it was thought that where *possession* of drugs is in issue, evidence of possession of money or drugs paraphernalia can never be relevant to that issue.[137] However, in *R v Guney*[138] the Court of Appeal, declining to follow the earlier authorities, held that although evidence of possession of a large sum of cash or enjoyment of a wealthy lifestyle does not, on its own, prove possession, there are numerous sets of circumstances in which it may be relevant to that issue, not least to the issue of knowledge as an ingredient of possession. The issue in that case was whether the accused was knowingly in possession of some 5 kilos of heroin or whether it had been 'planted', and the defence conceded that if possession were to be proved, then it would be open to the jury to infer intent to supply. It was held that, in all the circumstances, evidence of the finding of nearly £25,000 in cash in the wardrobe of the accused's bedroom, in close proximity to the drugs, was relevant to the issue of possession.[139]

The exclusionary rules

Evidence must be sufficiently relevant to be admissible, but sufficiently relevant evidence is only admissible insofar as it is not excluded by any rule of the law of evidence or by the exercise of judicial discretion. The consequence, of course, is that some relevant evidence is excluded. Thus although statutes make provision for the admissibility of various categories of hearsay, not *all* relevant hearsay is admissible.[140] Relevant evidence, including highly relevant evidence, may also be withheld as a matter of public policy on the grounds that its

[133] [1995] 2 Cr App R 61, CA. See also *R v Morris* [1995] 2 Cr App R 69, CA.

[134] Concerning the accounts, cf *R v Okusanya* [1995] Crim LR 941, CA. But see also *R v Smith (Ivor)* [1995] Crim LR 940, CA: evidence that £9,000 had been deposited in S's account in recent months, of which £2,100 was unexplained by various legitimate transactions, was admissible (subject to an appropriate direction).

[135] *R v Grant* [1996] 1 Cr App R 73, CA; see also *R v Green* [2009] EWCA Crim 1688 (a case of conspiracy to supply drugs); and cf *R v Antill* [2002] EWCA Crim 2114. However, the judge is not tied to this or any other particular form of words: *R v Malik* [2000] Crim LR 197, CA.

[136] See *R v Simms* [1995] Crim LR 304, CA, and *R v Lucas* [1995] Crim LR 400, CA.

[137] See *R v Halpin* [1996] Crim LR 112, CA and *R v Richards* [1997] Crim LR 499, CA.

[138] [1998] 2 Cr App R 242.

[139] Applied in *R v Griffiths* [1998] Crim LR 567, CA. See also *R v Edwards* [1998] Crim LR 207, CA and *R v Scott* [1996] Crim LR 652, CA.

[140] See generally Chs 10–13.

production and disclosure would jeopardize national security or would be injurious to some other national interest.[141] The opinion evidence of a non-expert is generally regarded as being insufficiently relevant to a subject not calling for any particular expertise but, whatever its degree of relevance, is generally excluded on the basis that the tribunal of fact might be tempted simply to accept the opinion proffered rather than draw its own inferences from the facts of the case.[142] These and other exclusionary rules make up much of the law of evidence and are considered throughout this book.

Multiple admissibility

Where evidence is admissible for one purpose, but inadmissible for another, it remains admissible in law for the first purpose (although it may be excluded by the exercise of judicial discretion). For example, an out-of-court statement may be inadmissible for the purpose of proving the truth of its contents, being inadmissible hearsay, but admissible, as original evidence, for the purpose of proving that the statement was made. The principle has been described, somewhat misleadingly, as one of 'multiple admissibility';[143] 'limited admissibility' might be a better tag. Where it applies, the judge is often required to warn the jury of the limited purpose for which the evidence has been admitted.[144] The risk that the jury may misunderstand or ignore such a warning is felt to be more than outweighed by the greater mischief that would be occasioned if the evidence were to be excluded altogether.[145]

Conditional admissibility

An item of evidence, viewed in isolation, may appear to be irrelevant and therefore inadmissible. Taken together with, or seen in the light of, some other item of evidence, its relevance may become apparent. Evidence, however, can only be given at a trial in piecemeal fashion, and it may be difficult to adduce the second item of evidence before the first. In order to overcome this difficulty, the first item of evidence may be admitted conditionally or *de bene esse*. If, viewed in the light of evidence subsequently adduced, it becomes relevant, it may be taken into account. If, notwithstanding the evidence subsequently adduced, it remains irrelevant, it must be disregarded. The operation of the principle may be illustrated by reference to the admissibility of accusations made in the presence of the accused, the relevance of which may depend on evidence, subsequently adduced, of the accused's reaction to them. An accusation made in the presence of the accused upon an occasion on which he might reasonably be expected to make some observation, explanation, or denial is, in certain circumstances, admissible in evidence against him, provided that a foundation for its admission is laid by proof of facts from which, in the opinion of the judge, a jury might reasonably draw the inference that the accused, by his answer, whether given by word, conduct, or silence, acknowledged the truth of the accusation made. The accusation may be admitted in

---

[141] See Ch 19.

[142] See Ch 18.

[143] Wigmore, *A Treatise on the Anglo-American System of Evidence* (3rd edn, Boston, 1940) I, para 13.

[144] For example, where a confession, admissible as evidence of the truth of its contents by way of exception to the hearsay rule, implicates both its maker and a co-accused, but is inadmissible against the co-accused, the trial judge is duty bound to impress upon the jury that it can be used only against its maker and not against the co-accused: *R v Gunewardene* [1951] 2 KB 600, CCA (see Ch 13). Cf *R v Randall* [2004] 1 All ER 467, HL at 478 (see Ch 17).

[145] See per Tindall CJ in *Willis v Bernard* (1832) 8 Bing 376 at 383.

evidence, however, even where the evidential foundation has not been laid, provided that, if evidence is *not* subsequently adduced from which it can be inferred that the accused did acknowledge the truth of the accusation made, the judge directs the jury to disregard the accusation altogether.[146]

The best evidence rule

The so-called best evidence rule, at one time thought to be a fundamental principle of the law of evidence, is now applied so rarely as to be virtually extinct. The eighteenth-century case of *Omychund v Barker*,[147] suggests that it was an inclusionary rule, allowing for the admissibility of the best evidence available that a party to litigation could produce. The rule, however, was rarely used in this way, and as an inclusionary doctrine of general application certainly finds no place in the modern law of evidence. The authorities show that the rule was normally treated as being of an exclusionary nature, preventing the admissibility of evidence where better was available.[148] As an exclusionary principle, however, the rule is now virtually defunct. The rule that a party seeking to rely upon the contents of a document must adduce primary evidence of the contents, secondary evidence being admissible only exceptionally,[149] is sometimes said to be the only remaining instance of the best evidence rule,[150] notwithstanding that it pre-dates the best evidence rule, but in *Springsteen v Flute International Ltd*[151] it was held, in this context, that it could be said with confidence that the best evidence rule, long on its deathbed, had finally expired. Prior to that decision, the rule did make a rare appearance in *R v Quinn and R v Bloom*.[152] The accused, two club proprietors, were charged with keeping a disorderly house. The charge arose out of certain allegedly indecent striptease acts performed at their clubs. One of the accused sought to put in evidence a film made three months after the events complained of and showing what the performers actually did, together with evidence that the performances shown in the film were identical with those in question. The Court of Criminal Appeal held that this evidence had been properly excluded. Ashworth J, giving the judgment of the court, said:

> it was admitted that some of the movements in the film (for instance, that of a snake used in one scene) could not be said with any certainty to be the same movements as were made at the material time...this objection goes not only to weight, as was argued, but to admissibility: it is not the best evidence.[153]

---

[146] Per Lords Atkinson and Reading in *R v Christie* [1914] AC 545, HL at 554 and 565 respectively.

[147] (1745) 1 Atk 21 at 49.

[148] See, eg, *Chenie v Watson* (1797) Peake Add Cas 123, where oral evidence relating to the condition of a material object was excluded on the grounds that the object itself ought to have been produced for inspection by the court; and *Williams v East India Co* (1802) 3 East 192, where circumstantial evidence was excluded because direct evidence was available. Both cases have, on the point in question, been reversed: as to the former, see now *R v Francis* (1874) LR 2 CCR 128 and *Hocking v Ahlquist Bros Ltd* [1944] KB 120 (which are considered in Ch 9); as to the latter, see now *Dowling v Dowling* (1860) 10 ICLR 236.

[149] See Ch 9.

[150] See, eg, per Lord Denning MR in *Garton v Hunter* [1969] 2 QB 37, CA at 44 and per Ackner LJ in *Kajala v Noble* (1982) 75 Cr App R 149, CA at 152.

[151] [2001] EMLR 654, CA.

[152] [1962] 2 QB 245.

[153] Cf *R v Thomas* [1986] Crim LR 682, a case of reckless driving in which a video recording of the route taken by the accused was admitted to remove the need for maps and still photographs and to convey a more accurate picture of the roads in question.

Although out-of-court demonstrations and re-enactments are admissible as a variety of real evidence,[154] the court held that a reconstruction made privately for the purpose of constituting evidence at a trial is inadmissible.[155]

The best evidence rule is of no more than marginal contemporary significance, but where a party fails to make use of the best evidence available and relies upon inferior evidence, the absence of the best evidence or the party's failure to account for its absence may always be the subject of adverse judicial comment. The inferior evidence may be slighted or ignored on the grounds that it lacks weight.[156] For example, in *Post Office Counters Ltd v Mahida*,[157] a debt action, it was held that the claimant company, which relied upon secondary evidence of documents submitted to it by the defendant, having itself destroyed the originals, had failed to prove the debts in question.

Weight

The weight of evidence is its cogency or probative worth in relation to the facts in issue. The assessment of the weight of evidence is in large measure a matter of common sense and experience, dependent upon a wide variety of factors such as: (i) the extent to which it is supported or contradicted by other evidence adduced; (ii) in the case of direct testimony, the demeanour, plausibility, and credibility of the witness and all the circumstances in which she claims to have perceived a fact in issue; and (iii) in the case of hearsay, all the circumstances from which any inference can reasonably be drawn as to the accuracy or otherwise of the out-of-court statement including, for example, whether the statement was made contemporaneously with the occurrence or existence of the facts stated and whether its maker had any incentive to conceal or misrepresent the facts.[158] Weight, like relevance, is a question of degree: at one extreme, an item of evidence may be of minimal probative value in relation to the facts in issue; at the other extreme, it may be virtually conclusive of them. Where the evidence adduced by a party in relation to a fact in issue is, even if uncontradicted, so weak that it could not reasonably justify a finding in his favour, it is described as 'insufficient evidence'. Where the evidence adduced by a party is so weighty that it could reasonably justify a finding in his favour, it is described as 'prima facie evidence'. Somewhat confusingly, however, this term is also used to describe evidence adduced by a party which is, in the absence of contradictory evidence, so weighty that it does justify a finding in his favour. 'Conclusive evidence' might be thought to denote the weightiest possible evidence. In fact, the term refers to evidence which, irrespective of its weight, concludes the fact in issue: the fact ceases to be in issue and is not even open to contradictory proof because the court must find the fact to have been proved.[159]

The issue of the weight to be attached to an item of evidence is related to, but distinct from, the issue of its admissibility. The weight of evidence is a question of fact, its admissibility a question of law. Thus, in a jury trial, the judge decides whether an item of evidence is relevant

[154] See, eg, *Buckingham v Daily News Ltd* [1956] 2 QB 534, CA: a demonstration of the way in which a worker cleaned the blades of a rotary press in a printing house.
[155] Cf *Li Shu-ling v R* [1988] 3 All ER 138, PC: a video recording of a re-enactment of the crime by the accused may be admitted in evidence as a confession (see Ch 13).
[156] See per Lord Coleridge CJ in *R v Francis* (1874) LR 2 CCR 128.
[157] [2003] EWCA Civ 1583.
[158] See Civil Evidence Act 1995, s 4 (see Ch 11).
[159] See, eg, Criminal Justice Act 1967, s 10(1) (see Ch 22) and Civil Evidence Act 1968, s 13(1) (see Ch 21).

and admissible and, if the evidence is admitted, the jury decides what weight, if any, to attach to it. It does not follow from this, however, that the weight of evidence is solely the concern of the tribunal of fact. For a variety of different purposes, the judge must also form a view as to the weight of evidence. In determining admissibility, he must consider whether evidence is sufficiently relevant and this will depend, to some extent, on his assessment of its weight. In examining the evidence adduced to establish preliminary facts, which, it will be recalled, must be proved as a condition precedent to the admissibility of certain items of evidence, the weight of the evidence should be taken into account. As we shall see, a judge should withdraw an issue from the tribunal of fact where a party has adduced 'insufficient evidence' in support of that issue. As we shall also see, the judge has a discretion to exclude certain items of evidence and, for these purposes also, may have regard to, inter alia, the weight of the evidence in question. Last, and by no means least, in his summing-up the judge is entitled to comment upon the cogency of the evidence admitted, provided that he does not usurp the jury's function as the tribunal of fact.[160]

The functions of the judge and jury

The division of functions between tribunal of law and tribunal of fact, which dates from a time when jury trial was the norm in both civil and criminal proceedings, has left a deep impression on the modern law of evidence, even as it now applies in cases tried without a jury.

Questions of law and fact

The resolution of disputes in courts of law gives rise to questions of fact, or questions of law, and often both. In jury trials, the general rule is that questions of law are decided by the judge and questions of fact by the jury. This is not as straightforward a division as it may appear at first blush, because some questions of 'fact' for the jury, for example the issue of dishonesty in theft and related offences, may be considered to be as much questions of law as of fact, and some questions of 'law' for the judge, for example the existence or non-existence of preliminary facts, are essentially questions of fact.[161]

Questions of law for the judge include those relating to the substantive law, the competence of a person to give evidence as a witness, the admissibility of evidence, the withdrawal of an issue from the jury, and the way in which he should direct the jury on both the substantive law and the evidence adduced.[162] Questions of fact for the jury include those relating to the credibility of the witnesses called, the weight to be attached to the evidence adduced and ultimately, of course, the existence or non-existence of the facts in issue.

In trials on indictment without a jury, ie complex fraud cases and trials where there is a real danger of jury tampering, the judge decides all questions of both law and fact and, if the accused is convicted, must give a judgment which states the reasons for the conviction.[163] In

---

[160] *R v O'Donnell* (1917) 12 Cr App R 219; *R v Canny* (1945) 30 Cr App R 143.

[161] See generally Glanville Williams, 'Law and Fact' [1976] Crim LR 472 and Allen and Pardo, 'Facts in Law and Facts of Law' (2003) 7 E&P 153.

[162] The judge may choose to reduce his directions of law, or some of them, into writing. It is increasingly the practice to provide a written direction on the central legal issue or the 'steps to verdict'. Any such written directions should be discussed with counsel before being finalized. For the relevant factors in deciding whether to prepare written directions, see *R v Thompson* [2011] 2 All ER 83, CA at [13].

[163] Criminal Justice Act 2003, s 48(3) and (5).

the case of a trial by lay justices, the bench decides all questions of both law and fact, but on questions of law, including the law of evidence, questions of mixed law and fact, and matters of practice and procedure, should give heed to the advice of its clerk or legal adviser.[164] Theoretically in the same position, district judges (magistrates' courts) tend to decide questions of law as well as fact. In civil cases tried by a judge sitting alone, the judge decides all questions of both law and fact.

Although questions of fact are generally decided by the jury, the judicial function includes the investigation of preliminary facts (for the purpose of determining the admissibility of evidence), the assessment of the sufficiency of evidence (for the purpose of deciding whether to withdraw an issue from the jury), and the evaluation of evidence adduced (for the purpose of commenting upon the matter to the jury in summing up). Each of these matters is considered separately in this chapter. Additionally, there is a variety of special cases in which questions of fact are also capable of being questions of law or are treated as being questions of law or for some other reason fall to be decided, wholly or in part, by the judge. They include the following.[165]

The construction of ordinary words

The modern authorities are in a state of disarray on the important question whether, in criminal cases, the construction of ordinary statutory words is a question for the tribunal of fact. The leading authority on the point, *Brutus v Cozens*,[166] expressly supports an affirmative answer. The appellant, during the annual tennis tournament at Wimbledon, had gone on to No 2 Court while a match was in progress, blown a whistle, and thrown leaflets around. He was charged with using insulting behaviour whereby a breach of the peace was likely to be occasioned under s 5 of the Public Order Act 1986. The magistrates dismissed the information on the grounds that the appellant's behaviour was not insulting. On a case stated, the question was whether, on the facts found, the decision was correct in law. This assumed that the meaning of the word 'insulting' in s 5 was a matter of law. Allowing the appellant's appeal against the decision of the Divisional Court, the House of Lords rejected this assumption. Lord Reid said:[167]

> The meaning of an ordinary word of the English language is not a question of law. The proper construction of a statute is a question of law.[168] If the context shows that a word is used in an unusual sense the court will determine in other words what that unusual sense is. But here there

---

[164] For the duties of the clerk or legal adviser, see para 55, *Consolidated Criminal Practice Direction* and r 37.14(2), Criminal Procedure Rules 2013, SI 2013/1554.

[165] Other examples relate to defamation, in respect of which the judge decides whether the writing in question is capable of the defamatory meaning alleged and, if so, the jury then decides whether it does constitute a libel (*Nevill v Fine Arts & General Insurance Co Ltd* [1897] AC 68, HL) and manslaughter by gross negligence, in respect of which the existence of a duty of care or a duty to act is a question of law, but the jury has to decide whether the facts establish the existence of the duty (*R v Evans* [2009] 1 WLR 1999, CA).

[166] [1973] AC 854.

[167] [1973] AC 854 at 861.

[168] See also *R v Spens* [1991] 4 All ER 421, CA: it is for the judge to construe binding agreements between parties, and all forms of parliamentary and local government legislation, including codes which sufficiently resemble legislation as to require such construction, eg the City Code on Takeovers and Mergers; and cf *R v Adams* [1993] Crim LR 525, CA, and *R v Morris* [1994] Crim LR 596, CA. However, if the legislation contains ordinary straightforward words, no judicial interpretation of them is required: *R v Pouladian-Kari* [2013] EWCA Crim 158.

is in my opinion no question of the word 'insulting' being used in any unusual sense. It appears to me…to be intended to have its ordinary meaning. It is for the tribunal which decides the case to consider, not as law but as fact, whether in the whole circumstances the words of the statute do or do not as a matter of ordinary usage of the English language cover or apply to the facts which have been proved. If it is alleged that the tribunal has reached a wrong decision then there can be a question of law but only of a limited character. The question would normally be whether their decision was unreasonable in the sense that no tribunal acquainted with the ordinary use of language could reasonably reach that decision.

Applying this dictum in *R v Feely*,[169] Lawton LJ held that whereas the word 'fraudulently' which was used in s 1(1) of the Larceny Act 1916 had acquired a special meaning as a result of case law, the word 'dishonestly' as used in s 1(1) of the Theft Act 1968 was an ordinary word in common use. Accordingly, it was a question of fact for the jury and required no direction by the judge as to its meaning.[170]

In *DPP v Stonehouse*[171] the question whether acts are sufficiently proximate to the intended complete offence to rank as an attempt, was treated as a question of fact. This was justified by Lord Diplock on the grounds that the concept of proximity is a question of degree on which the opinion of reasonable men may differ and as to which the legal training and experience of a judge does not make his opinion more likely to be correct than that of a non-lawyer.[172]

Lord Reid's dictum, however, although never expressly disowned, has largely been ignored. As one commentator has observed, the number of cases when *Cozens v Brutus* ought to have been cited but was not 'are as the sands of the sea'.[173] This disregard extends to the House of Lords itself. In *Metropolitan Police Comr v Caldwell*,[174] for example, 'recklessly' was held to be an ordinary word, but given a legal definition. A similar approach has been taken in relation to the word 'supply' in s 5(3) of the Misuse of Drugs Act 1971[175] and the word 'discharge' in s 5(1)(b) of the Firearms Act 1968.[176] The need for such legal definition of ordinary words stems from the potential diversity of interpretation by jurors, and indeed judges, and the concomitant risk of inconsistent verdicts, and for these reasons, it is submitted, Lord Reid's dictum should continue to be ignored until it is expressly repudiated.

In civil cases tried with a jury, there is old authority to support the view that the meaning of ordinary words is a question of construction for the judge.[177]

---

[169] [1973] QB 530, CA.

[170] See also *R v Harris* (1986) 84 Cr App R 75, CA: the words 'knowledge or belief' are words of ordinary usage and therefore, in most cases of handling stolen goods contrary to the Theft Act 1968, s 22(1), all that need be said to a jury is to ask whether the prosecution has established receipt, knowing or believing that the goods were stolen; *R v Jones* [1987] 2 All ER 692, CA: whether a person is 'armed' while being concerned in the illegal importation of cannabis contrary to the Customs and Excise Management Act 1979, s 86; *Chambers v DPP* [1995] Crim LR 896, DC: 'disorderly behaviour' contrary to the Public Order Act 1986, s 5; and *R v Kirk* [2006] Crim LR 850, CA: 'indecent or obscene' under the Postal Services Act 2000, s 85(4).

[171] [1978] AC 55, HL.

[172] [1978] AC 55 at 69. See now the Criminal Attempts Act 1981, s 4(3).

[173] Elliott, '*Brutus v Cozens*; Decline & Fall' [1989] Crim LR 323 at 324.

[174] [1982] AC 341, HL.

[175] *R v Maginnis* [1987] AC 303, HL.

[176] *Flack v Baldry* [1988] 1 All ER 673, HL.

[177] Per Parke B in *Neilson v Harford* (1841) 8 M&W 806 at 823.

Corroboration

In the now rare cases in which a conviction cannot be based on uncorroborated evidence, it is for the judge to direct the jury as to what evidence is capable, in law, of amounting to corroboration and for the jury to decide whether that evidence does, in fact, constitute corroboration.[178]

Foreign law

In the courts of England and Wales, questions of foreign law, that is questions relating to the law of any jurisdiction other than England and Wales, are issues of fact to be decided, on the evidence adduced, by the judge. Section 15 of the Administration of Justice Act 1920 provides that:

> Where for the purposes of disposing of any action or other matter which is being tried by a judge with a jury in any court in England or Wales it is necessary to ascertain the law of any other country which is applicable to the facts of the case, any question as to the effect of the evidence given with respect to that law shall, instead of being submitted to the jury, be decided by the judge alone.

This provision applies to criminal proceedings only,[179] but has been re-enacted, in relation to High Court proceedings and County Court proceedings, by s 69(5) of the Senior Courts Act 1981 and s 68 of the County Courts Act 1984 respectively. Foreign law is usually proved by the evidence of an appropriately qualified expert, who may refer to foreign statutes and decisions, or by the production of a report of a previous decision by an English court of superior status on the point of foreign law in question.[180] Where necessary, the judge must determine the point by deciding between the conflicting opinion evidence of the expert witnesses.[181]

Questions of reasonableness

What is reasonable is a question of fact and therefore normally decided by the jury. In some civil cases, however, it must be decided by the judge on the basis of facts which, if not agreed, have been ascertained by the jury. In an action for malicious prosecution, for example, it is the function of the jury to ascertain the facts, if disputed, which operated on the mind of the prosecutor, and the function of the judge, on the basis of the facts thus ascertained, to decide whether the prosecutor did or did not have reasonable and probable cause for commencing the prosecution in question.[182]

Perjury

The offence of perjury is committed where a person lawfully sworn as a witness or interpreter in a judicial proceeding wilfully makes a statement *material* in that proceeding which he knows to be false or does not believe to be true.[183] Section 1(6) of the Perjury Act 1911 provides that 'the

[178] *R v Tragen* [1956] Crim LR 332; *R v Charles* (1976) 68 Cr App R 334n, HL; and *R v Reeves* (1979) 68 Cr App R 331, CA. See generally Ch 8.
[179] *R v Hammer* [1923] 2 KB 786, CCA.
[180] See Ch 18. For the circumstances in which judicial notice may be taken of points of foreign law, see Ch 22.
[181] See, eg, *Re Duke of Wellington, Glentanar v Wellington* [1947] Ch 506.
[182] *Herniman v Smith* [1938] AC 305, HL, applied, in relation to the tort of procuring the grant of a search warrant falsely, maliciously, and *without reasonable and probable cause*, in *Reynolds v Metropolitan Police Comr* (1984) 80 Cr App R 125, CA.
[183] Perjury Act 1911, s 1(1).

question whether a statement on which perjury is assigned was material is a question of law to be determined by the court of trial'.

Autrefois acquit and convict

An accused charged with an offence which is the same as an offence in respect of which he has previously been acquitted or convicted or an offence in respect of which he could on some previous indictment have been lawfully convicted, may tender a special plea in bar of *autrefois acquit* or *convict* in order to quash the indictment. Where such a plea is tendered, it is for the judge to decide the issue, without empanelling a jury.[184]

The *voir dire*, or trial within a trial

Preliminary facts, as we have seen, must be proved as a condition precedent to the admissibility of certain items of evidence. For example, where the prosecution propose to adduce evidence of a confession made by the accused and the defence object to its admissibility on the grounds that it was or may have been obtained by oppression of the accused, or in consequence of something said or done which was likely, in the circumstances, to render unreliable any confession which might be made by him in consequence thereof, the court shall not allow the confession to be admitted except insofar as the prosecution prove to the court that the confession was not obtained by such means.[185] Proof of due search for the original of a lost document, on the contents of which a party seeks to rely, is a condition precedent to the admissibility of a copy of that document.[186] Similarly, it may become necessary to show that a person is competent to give evidence as a witness or that a witness is privileged from answering a particular question. Questions of this kind are matters of law for the judge. The preliminary facts may be agreed or assumed, but where they are in dispute it is for the judge to hear evidence and adjudicate upon them.[187] The witnesses give their evidence on a special form of oath known as a *voir dire*. The hearing before the judge is called a hearing on the *voir dire* or a 'trial within a trial'.

In general, disputes about the admissibility of evidence in civil proceedings are best resolved by the judge at trial rather than at a separate preliminary hearing, because at such a hearing the judge will usually be less well informed and such a hearing can cause unnecessary costs and delays.[188]

In the Crown Court

In the Crown Court, questions of admissibility, including those involving the hearing of evidence on the *voir dire*, are usually determined in the absence of the jury because of the

---

[184] Criminal Justice Act 1988, s 122.

[185] Police and Criminal Evidence Act 1984, s 76(2) (see Ch 13).

[186] *Brewster v Sewell* (1820) 3 B&Ald 296 (see Ch 9).

[187] However, where the preliminary facts are identical with the facts in issue, the condition precedent is held to be established if the judge is satisfied that there is *sufficient evidence* of it to go before the jury. For example, if a party seeks to adduce a tape recording in evidence, the question of whether it is genuine and original being ultimately for the determination of the jury, the judge need satisfy himself by no more than prima facie evidence that the tape is genuine and original and therefore competent to be considered by the jury: *R v Robson, R v Harris* [1972] 1 WLR 651; cf *R v Stevenson* [1971] 1 WLR (see Ch 4). See also *Stowe v Querner* (1870) LR 5 Exch 155 and per Lord Penzance in *Hitchins v Eardley* (1871) LR 2 P&D 248. However, it has also been said that the judge must reach a definite decision on the preliminary fact in question: see per Lord Denman CJ in *Doe d Jenkins v Davies* (1847) 10 QB 314.

[188] *Stroude v Beazer Homes Ltd* [2005] EWCA Civ 265.

impossibility of deciding such questions without some reference either to the disputed evidence, which in the event may be ruled inadmissible, or to other material prejudicial to the accused. Thus where the prosecution propose to adduce a certain item of evidence and counsel for the defence intends to make a submission that it is inadmissible, that intention will be conveyed to the prosecution either at the Plea and Case Management Hearing or immediately before the trial commences so that the evidence is not referred to in the presence of the jury, whether in the prosecution opening speech or otherwise. The prosecution will adduce their evidence in the normal way but at that point in time when the evidence would otherwise be admitted, counsel will intimate to the judge that a point of law has arisen which falls to be decided in the absence of the jury and the jury will be told to retire.[189] Whether or not the jury, on returning to court, hear the disputed evidence, depends, of course, on the judge's ruling on its admissibility. In *R v Reynolds*[190] Lord Goddard CJ was of the opinion that the determination of preliminary facts in the absence of the jury is confined to exceptional cases, such as those relating to the admissibility of a confession, where it is almost impossible to prevent some reference to the terms of the confession.[191] However, the modern practice is to ask the jury to retire whenever there is a risk of them being exposed to material which might be ruled inadmissible or which, in any event, would be likely to prejudice the accused.[192] The modern position, therefore, is probably accurately reflected in r 104(c) of the United States Federal Rules, which provides that hearings on the admissibility of confessions shall always be conducted in the absence of the jury and that hearings on other matters shall be so conducted when the interests of justice require.

In criminal proceedings in the magistrates' court

In *F (an infant) v Chief Constable of Kent*[193] Lord Lane CJ observed that since the function of the *voir dire* is to allow the arbiter of law to decide a legal point in the absence of the arbiter of fact, in proceedings before magistrates, where the justices are judges of both fact and law, there can be no question of a trial within a trial. In that case, it was held that once the question of the admissibility of a confession has been decided as a separate issue, the magistrates having heard evidence on the preliminary facts and having ruled in favour of admissibility, it is unnecessary for the evidence about the confession to be repeated later in the trial proper. Lord Lane CJ also held that it was impossible to lay down any general rule as to when a question of admissibility should be taken in a summary trial or as to when the magistrates should announce their decision on it, every case being different. This flexible approach was reiterated in *R v Epping and Ongar Justices, ex p Manby*,[194] where the accused contested the admissibility of certain documentary evidence tendered by the prosecution and sought leave to have the question resolved as a preliminary issue. The magistrates refused and admitted the evidence as providing a prima facie case for the accused to deal with later, if he saw fit. The Divisional

[189] Occasionally it is necessary to determine admissibility immediately after the jury has been empanelled, eg, where the evidence of a confession is so crucial to the prosecution case that, without reference to it, their case cannot even be opened: see *R v Hammond* [1941] 3 All ER 318.
[190] [1950] 1 KB 606.
[191] See further Ch 13, under **The *voir dire*.**
[192] See *R v Deakin* [1994] 4 All ER 769, CA.
[193] [1982] Crim LR 682, DC.
[194] [1986] Crim LR 555, DC.

Court held that the justices had not erred: within statutory constraints, they should determine their own procedure.

Section 78 of the 1984 Act, whereby a criminal court has a discretion to exclude evidence on which the prosecution propose to rely on the grounds that it would have an adverse effect on the fairness of the proceedings,[195] is not a statutory constraint for these purposes and accordingly does not entitle an accused to have an issue of admissibility settled as a preliminary issue in a trial within a trial.[196]

In *Halawa v Federation Against Copyright Theft*[197] it was held that the duty of a magistrate, on an application under s 78, is either to deal with it when it arises or to leave the decision until the end of the hearing, the objective being to secure that the trial is fair and just to both sides. Thus, in some cases there will be a trial within a trial in which the accused is given the opportunity to exclude the evidence before he is required to give evidence on the main issues (because, if denied that opportunity, his right to remain silent on the main issues is impaired); but in most cases the better course will be for the whole of the prosecution case to be heard, including the disputed evidence, before any trial within a trial is held. In order to decide, the court may ask the accused the extent of the issues to be addressed by his evidence in the trial within a trial—a trial within a trial might be appropriate if the issues are limited, but not if it is likely to be protracted, raising issues which will have to be re-examined in the trial proper.

Where justices resolve to exclude, under s 78, evidence of statements made by an accused, they should consider, after seeking the views of the parties, whether the substantive hearing— if there still is one—should be conducted by a differently constituted bench.[198]

Section 76(2) of the 1984 Act[199] is a statutory constraint and an exception to the generally flexible approach. In *R v Liverpool Juvenile Court, ex p R*[200] the Divisional Court held that if, in a summary trial, the accused, before the close of the prosecution case, represents to the court that a confession was or may have been obtained by the methods set out in s 76(2), the magistrates are required to hold a trial within a trial, in which the accused is entitled to give evidence relating to the issue of admissibility, and are also required to make their ruling on admissibility before or at the end of the prosecution case.[201] In such a case, an alternative contention based on s 78 would also be examined at the same trial within a trial, at the same time.[202]

Applicability of the rules of evidence

Somewhat surprisingly, given the importance of the matter, there is little authority on the question whether the tribunal of law, whether judge or magistrates, in deciding what evidence

---

[195] See under **Judicial discretion, Exclusionary discretion, Criminal cases,** in this chapter.

[196] *Vel v Owen* [1987] Crim LR 496, DC.

[197] [1995] 1 Cr App R 21, DC.

[198] *DPP v Lawrence* [2008] 1 Cr App R 147, CA, *per curiam* at 153–4.

[199] See under **The functions of the judge and jury, The *voir dire*, or trial within a trial,** in this chapter.

[200] [1987] 2 All ER 668, DC.

[201] A trial within a trial will only take place before the close of the prosecution case if a representation is made pursuant to s 76(2). If no such representation is made, the accused may raise the question of the admissibility or weight of the confession at any subsequent stage of the trial. However, at this later stage in the proceedings, although the court retains an inherent jurisdiction to exclude the confession, as well as the power to exclude by virtue of s 78, it is not required to embark on a trial within a trial: see per Russell LJ at 672–3.

[202] *Halawa v Federation Against Copyright Theft* [1995] 1 Cr App R 21, per Ralph Gibson LJ at 33.

is admissible for the purpose of proving or disproving disputed preliminary facts, is bound by the rules of evidence which apply at the trial proper,[203] including those relating to oaths and affirmations.[204] Under the United States Federal Rules,[205] the judge is only bound by those rules of evidence which concern privilege.

The sufficiency of evidence

The obligation on a party to adduce sufficient evidence on a fact in issue to justify a finding on that fact in his favour is referred to as 'the evidential burden'.[206] A party discharges an evidential burden borne by him by adducing sufficient evidence for the issue in question to be submitted to the jury (tribunal of fact). Whether there is sufficient evidence is a question of law for the judge. If the party has adduced enough evidence to justify, *as a possibility*, a favourable finding by the jury, the judge leaves it to them to decide whether or not the issue has been proved; if the evidence is insufficient, the judge withdraws the issue from the jury, whatever their view of the matter, directing them either to return a finding on that issue in favour of the other party or, in appropriate circumstances, to return a verdict on the whole case in favour of the other party. For example, in criminal proceedings, the evidential burden in relation to most common law defences is borne by the accused. If the accused, on a charge of assault, fails to adduce sufficient evidence of, say, self-defence, the judge will withdraw that issue from the jury, directing them that it must be taken as proved against the accused.[207] The prosecution normally bear the evidential burden in relation to all those facts essential to the Crown case. If the prosecution fail to adduce sufficient evidence in relation to an essential element of the offence, they fail not only on that issue, but also in the whole case and the judge will direct the jury to acquit.

Submission of no case to answer in the Crown Court

In criminal cases tried with a jury, the defence, after the prosecution have adduced all their evidence and closed their case, may make a submission of no case to answer.[208] If there is no evidence that the alleged crime has been committed by the accused, no evidence of an essential ingredient of that offence, or no corroborative evidence where corroboration is required as a matter of law, the submission will be upheld. Likewise, if the judge comes to the conclusion that the Crown's evidence, taken at its highest, is such that a jury properly directed could not

[203] In the case of statutory exceptions to the hearsay rule, it has been held that preliminary facts call for proof by admissible evidence: see per Lord Mustill, obiter, in *Neill v North Antrim Magistrates' Court* [1992] 4 All ER 846, HL, at 854, applied in *R v Belmarsh Magistrates' Court, ex p Gilligan* [1998] 1 Cr App R 14, DC and *R v Wood and Fitzsimmons* [1998] Crim LR 213, CA. But cf *R v Foxley* [1995] 2 Cr App R 523, CA. See also *Edwards v Brookes (Milk) Ltd* [1963] 1 WLR 795, QBD.

[204] See *R v Greer* [1998] Crim LR 572, CA, and contrast *R v Jennings* [1995] Crim LR 810, CA.

[205] Rule 104(a).

[206] The meaning of this term is considered fully in Ch 4.

[207] See Ch 4.

[208] The submission should be made in the absence of the jury and, if the trial proceeds thereafter, should not be referred to by the judge in his summing-up: see *R v Smith and Doe* (1986) 85 Cr App R 197, CA, and, in the case of visual identification evidence, *R v Akaidere* [1990] Crim LR 808, CA (see Ch 8). See also *Crosdale v R* [1995] 2 All ER 500, PC: if the judge rejects the submission, the jury need know nothing about the decision—no explanation is required; and if the judge rules in favour of the submission on some charges but not on others, all the jury need be told is that the decision was taken for legal reasons—any further explanation will risk potential prejudice.

properly convict on it, it is his duty to stop the case.[209] However, where the Crown's evidence is such that its strength or weakness depends on the view to be taken of a witness's reliability, or other matters which are, generally speaking, within the jury's province, and where on one view of the facts there is evidence on which a jury could properly conclude that the accused is guilty, the submission will fail; the judge should give brief reasons to enable the defence to understand why the submission has failed,[210] then the accused should call his evidence in the usual way and the case should go before the jury.[211] Cases in which the evidence is purely circumstantial are not in a special category; the judge should not withdraw the case from the jury simply because the proved facts do not exclude every reasonable inference besides that of guilt,[212] but should ask the simple question, looking at all the evidence with appropriate care: is there a case on which a jury properly directed could convict?[213] Nor should the test be altered for offences—whether or not sexual offences—alleged to have been committed some years ago.[214]

The judge also has a power to withdraw a case from the jury at any time after the close of the prosecution case, even as late as the end of the defence case, and whether or not a submission of no case to answer has been made at the end of the prosecution case. This is a power to be very sparingly exercised and only if the judge is satisfied that no jury properly directed could safely convict.[215] However, it is not open to a judge to entertain a submission of no case before the close of the prosecution case, because it is only at that stage that it is known what the evidence actually is and until then the most that can be known is what it is expected to be.[216] A ruling may be made at an earlier stage, where it is admitted or agreed what the outstanding

[209] See, eg, *R v Bland* (1987) 151 JP 857, CA, where the only evidence that the accused had assisted a man in the commission of an offence was that she was living with him at a time when he possessed and dealt in drugs. Cf *R v Suurmeijer* [1991] Crim LR 773, CA; *R v McNamara* [1998] Crim LR 278, CA; and *R v Berry* [1998] Crim LR 487, CA. A submission of no case will succeed where the only evidence against an accused is evidence of a DNA match on an item of clothing found at the scene of the crime: *R v Grant* [2008] EWCA Crim 1890, followed in *R v Ogden* [2013] EWCA Crim 1294.

[210] *R v Powell* [2006] All ER (D) 146 (Jan).

[211] See generally per Lord Lane CJ in *R v Galbraith* [1981] 1 WLR 1039, CA; cf *R v Beckwith* [1981] Crim LR 646. The Royal Commission on Criminal Justice recommended replacement of the rule in *R v Galbraith* by a new power for the judge to withdraw from the jury an issue or the whole case if he considers the evidence too weak or demonstrably unsafe or unsatisfactory: see para 42, ch 4, *Report of the Royal Commission on Criminal Justice*, Cm 2263 (1993). For the correct approach in cases where the issue is mistaken identity, see *R v Turnbull* [1977] QB 224, CA and *Daley v R* [1993] 4 All ER 86, PC (see Ch 8). See also, where a case against an accused is based wholly or partly on an 'unconvincing' hearsay statement, the Criminal Justice Act 2003, s 125 (see Ch 10). Where a judge improperly rejects a defence submission of no case to answer, a conviction may be set aside on appeal on the grounds that he made a wrong decision on a question of law. As to the position on appeal in cases where, subsequent to the improper rejection of the submission, evidence was given entitling the jury to convict, see *R v Power* [1919] 1 KB 572; and contrast *R v Abbott* [1955] 2 QB 497 and *R v Juett* [1981] Crim LR 113, CA.

[212] *R v Morgan* [1993] Crim LR 870, CA; *R v P* [2008] 2 Cr App R 68, CA.

[213] *R v P* [2008] 2 Cr App R 68, CA. Thus although account may be taken of the fact that a prosecution witness gave evidence in some respects inconsistent with the inferential case being advanced by the prosecution, that could not, by itself, be determinative of a submission of no case to answer: *R v Goring* [2011] EWCA Crim 2.

[214] *R v F(S)* [2011] 2 Cr App R 393, CA.

[215] *R v Brown* [2002] 1 Cr App R 46, CA.

[216] *R v N Ltd* [2009] 1 Cr App R 56, CA. Nor does the judge have power to prevent the prosecution from calling evidence and to direct an acquittal on the basis that he thinks that a conviction is unlikely: *Attorney General's Reference (No 2 of 2000)* [2001] 1 Cr App R 503.

prosecution evidence will be, but any direction to return a not guilty verdict should normally await the end of the prosecution case unless, of course, the Crown bows to the ruling and offers no further evidence. Similarly, before the calling of any evidence, the parties may agree that it would be helpful for the judge to rule on the question whether, on agreed, admitted, or assumed facts, the offence charged will be made out, with a view either to the Crown offering no evidence or to the accused considering whether to plead guilty.[217]

Submission of no case to answer in criminal proceedings in the magistrates' court

In criminal cases tried by magistrates, the position is not entirely clear. The test, contained in a Practice Direction, used to be that a submission of no case may be properly made and upheld (1) when there has been no evidence to prove an essential ingredient of the offence alleged;[218] or (2) when the evidence adduced by the prosecution has been so discredited as a result of cross-examination or is so manifestly unreliable that no reasonable tribunal could safely convict on it.[219] This Practice Direction was revoked[220] but not replaced. There can be no doubt that the first limb of the Practice Direction remains good law. As to the second limb, it is submitted that it should continue to apply, on the basis that the magistrates are the tribunal of fact as well as law. Thus although it has been said that questions of credibility, except in the clearest of cases, should not normally be taken into account by justices on a submission of no case,[221] if magistrates conclude that the prosecution evidence has been so discredited or is so manifestly unreliable that they cannot safely convict on it in any event, there can be no point in allowing the case to continue.

Submission of no case to answer in civil proceedings

In civil cases tried by a judge sitting alone, a defendant can submit that there is no case to answer at the close of the claimant's case, but in most cases the judge will only rule on the submission if the defendant elects not to call evidence.[222] In *Benham Ltd v Kythira Investments Ltd*[223] the Court of Appeal, after reviewing the authorities, held that there were two disadvantages of entertaining a submission of no case to answer without putting the defendant to his or her election. First, it interrupted the trial and required the judge to make up his mind as to the facts on the basis of one side's evidence only, applying the lower test of a prima facie case, with the result that, if he rejected the submission, he had to make up his mind afresh in the light of further evidence and on the application of a different test. Second, if the judge acceded to a submission of no case, his judgment might be reversed on appeal, with all the expense and inconvenience of resuming or retrying the action. The court concluded that rarely, if ever, should a judge trying a civil action without a jury entertain a submission of no case, although it conceded that 'conceivably', as Mance LJ had suggested in *Miller v Margaret Cawley*,[224]

---

[217] See *R v N Ltd* [2009] 1 Cr App R 56, CA at 66.
[218] See, eg, *Chief Constable of Avon and Somerset Constabulary v Jest* [1986] RTR 372, DC.
[219] *Practice Direction (Submission of No Case)* [1962] 1 WLR 227.
[220] *Practice Direction (Criminal Proceedings: Consolidation)* [2002] 1 WLR 2870.
[221] *R v Barking and Dagenham Justices, ex p DPP* (1995) 159 JP 373, DC, in which it was held that the prosecutor should be given the opportunity to reply to the submission or, where the magistrates are minded to dismiss the case of their own motion, to address the court.
[222] *Alexander v Rayson* [1936] 1 KB 169, CA at 178.
[223] [2003] EWCA Civ 1794, followed in *Graham v Chorley Borough Council* [2006] EWCA Civ 92.
[224] [2002] All ER (D) 452.

there may be some flaw of fact or law of such a nature as to make it entirely obvious that the claimant's case must fail, and the determination at that stage may save significant costs. The decision, it is submitted, is unnecessarily inflexible, especially in the light of the wide powers of case management under the Civil Procedure Rules, which should enable a court to consider a submission with or without putting the defendant to his election. In some cases, albeit rare, there will be grounds for contending that the claimant has no reasonable prospect of success whether or not the defendant gives evidence, as when the judge forms the view that the claimant is not a reliable witness of fact and that the position will not change even if the defendant calls evidence.[225]

In civil cases tried with a jury, the judge has a discretion whether to rule on a submission of no case to answer without requiring the defendant to elect to call no evidence[226] and a submission may also be made, after all the evidence has been adduced, that there is insufficient evidence to go before the jury.[227] The test would appear to be the same test as is used in criminal jury trials,[228] namely whether the evidence, taken at its highest, is such that a jury properly directed could not properly reach a necessary factual conclusion.[229]

The summing-up

At a trial on indictment, after the conclusion of all the evidence and closing speeches by counsel, the judge must sum up the case to the jury. In addition to directing them on the substantive law and reminding them of the evidence that has been given, the judge must also explain a number of evidential points.[230] Many directions will reflect or be based upon the guidance given in the Crown Court Bench Book.

The judge should begin with a direction as to which party bears the obligation to prove what facts and the standard of proof required to be met before they are entitled to conclude that those facts have been proved.[231] He should remind the jury of the evidence adduced by the prosecution and defence[232] and refer to any defence which that evidence

---

[225] See *Mullan v Birmingham City Council* (1999) The Times, 29 July, QBD.

[226] *Young v Rank* [1950] 2 KB 510.

[227] *Grinsted v Hadrill* [1953] 1 WLR 696, CA. In civil cases, with or without a jury, if the judge rejects a submission of no case to answer, albeit improperly, and the defendant subsequently adduces evidence and is found liable, the Court of Appeal may consider all of the evidence adduced, including that of the defendant: *Payne v Harrison* [1961] 2 QB 403, CA.

[228] See *R v Galbraith* [1981] 1 WLR 1039, CA (see n 211).

[229] See *Alexander v Arts Council of Wales* [2001] 4 All ER 205, CA per May LJ at [37].

[230] It would be helpful if prosecuting counsel made a checklist of the directions on the law which they considered the trial judge ought to give and drew the attention of the judge to any failure on his part to give an essential direction before the jury retired: per Watkins LJ in *R v Donoghue* (1987) 86 Cr App R 267, CA.

[231] See *R v McVey* [1988] Crim LR 127. See also, as to burden of proof, *R v Donoghue* (1987) 86 Cr App R 267, and as to standard of proof, *R v Edwards* (1983) 77 Cr App R 5 and *R v Bentley (Deceased)* [2001] 1 Cr App R 307, CA. Where the prosecution case depends solely on the identification of a single witness, it is particularly important to give a general clear and simple direction on burden and standard: *R v Lang-Hall* (1989) The Times, 24 Mar, CA. In cases involving injuries to a very small child, any temptation on the part of the jury to succumb to emotion should be countered by a very clear direction on the burden of proof: *R v Bowditch* [1991] Crim LR 831, CA.

[232] *R v Tillman* [1962] Crim LR 261. See also *R v Gregory* [1993] Crim LR 623, CA, and cf *R v Sargent* [1993] Crim LR 713, CA. It may be that, in a straightforward case, failure to sum up on the facts is not necessarily a fatal defect (*R v Attfield* (1961) 45 Cr App R 309), but in the majority of cases it is clearly desirable that the judge should do so (*R v Brower* [1995] Crim LR 746, CA).

discloses,[233] even if it has not been relied upon by defence counsel.[234] He should also explain, where necessary, that the onus of disproving certain defences, such as self-defence, rests on the prosecution. Depending on the nature of the case and the evidence called, it may be necessary: (i) to give a warning on or to explain the requirement for corroboration, indicating the meaning of that word and pointing out the evidence capable in law of amounting to corroboration; (ii) to direct on any relevant presumptions of law, making it clear, where necessary, that if the jury are satisfied that certain matters are proved, they *must* find that other matters are proved; (iii) to warn of the special need for caution, where the case against the accused depends wholly or substantially on the correctness of identification, before convicting in reliance on the correctness of the identification or identifications; and (iv) to explain that certain items of evidence can only be used for certain restricted purposes.[235]

The judge is entitled to comment on the plausibility and credibility of the witnesses and the weight of the evidence. He may do so in strong or emphatic terms provided that he also makes it clear that, apart from whatever he says about the law, the jury are in no way bound by any view of his own about the evidence which he may have appeared to express.[236] The specimen direction of the Judicial Studies Board, concerning comments by the judge on the evidence, used to include the following passage: 'If I mention or emphasize evidence that you regard as unimportant, disregard that evidence. If I do not mention evidence that you regard as important, follow your own view and take that evidence into account.' Such a direction is best given at the start of the summing-up, especially if the judge is minded to express strong views on the evidence.[237]

The judge should never give an express indication of his own disbelief in relation to the evidence of a witness, especially the evidence of an accused, even in a case in which the evidence warrants incredulity;[238] and on certain matters, such as the accused's failure to call a particular witness,[239] the judge is restricted in the comments that he may properly make.

If a judge is satisfied that there is no evidence before the jury which could justify them in convicting the accused and that it would be perverse for them to do so, it is his duty to

[233] *R v Badjan* (1966) 50 Cr App R 141. The judge is under no duty to build up a defence for an accused who has elected not to testify, but need only remind the jury of any relevant matter contained in pre-trial statements and interviews with the police and the assistance, if any, provided by the Crown's witnesses: *R v Hillier* (1992) 97 Cr App R 349, CA. See also *R v Curtin* [1996] Crim LR 831, CA. If the accused has said nothing in police interviews and adduces no evidence to refute, qualify, or explain the case against him, the judge is under no duty to remind the jury of the defence case: *R v Briley* [1991] Crim LR 444, CA.

[234] *R v Porritt* (1961) 45 Cr App R 348. See also *R v Bennett* [1995] Crim LR 877, CA and *R v Williams* (1994) 99 Cr App R 163, CA. The duty only arises, however, if there is a reasonable possibility of the jury finding in favour of the defence, and not where the matter is merely fanciful and speculative: *R v Johnson* [1994] Crim LR 376, CA.

[235] See under **Relevance and admissibility, Multiple admissibility**, in this chapter.

[236] It is undesirable for judges to make comments which place police witnesses in any special category or which may lead a jury to think that there will be adverse consequences for police officers if a verdict of not guilty is returned: *R v Harris* [1986] Crim LR 123, CA. Nor should the prosecution suggest that an acquittal will ruin a prosecution witness: *R v Gale* [1994] Crim LR 208, CA. If the witness refers in his evidence to the consequences of his evidence being disbelieved, the judge should direct the jury that their verdict should not be influenced by such a consideration: *R v Gale*. See also *Mears v R* (1993) 97 Cr App R 239, PC.

[237] See *R v Everett* [1995] Crim LR 76, CA.

[238] *R v Iroegbu* (1988) The Times, 2 Aug, CA. See also *R v Winn-Pope* [1996] Crim LR 521, CA, *R v Farr* [1999] Crim LR 506, CA, and *Michel v R* [2010] 1 Cr App R 359, PC.

[239] *R v Gallagher* [1974] 1 WLR 1204, CA.

direct them to acquit. Equally, a judge may withdraw a defence from the jury if there is no evidence whatever to support it. However, if there is evidence before the jury to support a defence, albeit no reasonable jury, properly directed, could acquit, which would be a perverse verdict, the judge has no power to direct them to convict, because the jury alone have the right to decide that the accused is guilty. In *DPP v Stonehouse*,[240] from which this principle derives, the trial judge had directed the jury that if they were satisfied that the accused had falsely staged his death by drowning, dishonestly intending that claims should be made and money obtained by his wife under policies on his life with insurance companies, that would constitute the offence of attempting to obtain property by deception. This amounted to a withdrawal from the jury of the question of fact of whether the accused's conduct was sufficiently proximate to the complete offence. A majority of the House of Lords held that this was a misdirection, being of the opinion that even where a reasonable jury properly directed on the law must on the facts reach a guilty verdict, the trial judge should still leave issues of fact to the jury. However, since no reasonable jury could have had the slightest doubt that the facts proved did establish the attempt charged, it was further held that no miscarriage of justice could have resulted from the direction. The proviso to s 2(1) of the Criminal Appeal Act 1968 was applied and the conviction affirmed.[241]

In exceptional cases, a court may rule that an explanation advanced by an accused is incapable in law of amounting to a defence of 'good reason' or 'reasonable excuse' if, on a proper construction of the Act in question, it would be inconsistent with the essential nature and purpose of the offence for the explanation to be capable of amounting to the defence.[242] However, in *R v Wang*,[243] the House of Lords confirmed that there are no circumstances in which a judge is entitled to direct a jury to convict and that no distinction is to be drawn between cases in which a burden lies on the defence and those in which the burden lies solely on the Crown, because that distinction is inconsistent with the rationale of the majority in *DPP v Stonehouse*, which is that no matter how inescapable a judge may consider a conclusion to be, in the sense that any other conclusion would be perverse, it remains his duty to leave the decision to the jury and not to dictate what the verdict should be. The jury therefore retain the power to return a perverse verdict, a power which has been memorably exercised from time to time.[244] This is viewed by some as a blatant affront to the legal process,[245] but by others as a means of controlling oppressive state prosecutions and ensuring that the law conforms to the layman's idea of justice.[246]

Where there has been a direction to convict and the decision as to guilt was not in reality made by the jury at all, a conviction will be quashed, but an appeal may be dismissed, notwithstanding a direction to convict, if the jury were left to make a decision and retired to do so and the evidence of guilt was overwhelming.[247]

---

[240] [1978] AC 55, HL.

[241] See also per Lloyd LJ in *R v Gent* [1990] 1 All ER 364, CA at 367 and cf per May LJ in *R v Thompson* [1984] 3 All ER 565, CA at 571, approved in *R v Gordon* (1987) 92 Cr App R 50n, CA.

[242] *R v Asmeron* [2013] 2 Cr App R 209, CA at [22], citing *R v Kelleher* [2013] EWCA Crim 3525 by way of example.

[243] [2005] 2 Cr App R 8, HL.

[244] See, eg, *R v Ponting* [1985] Crim LR 318.

[245] See Auld LJ's *Review of the Criminal Courts of England and Wales: Report* (2001), paras 99–108.

[246] See Lord Devlin, 'The Conscience of the Jury' (1991) 107 LQR 398.

[247] See *R v Kelleher* [2003] EWCA Crim 3525, approved in *R v Caley-Knowles* [2007] 1 Cr App R 197, CA.

Many of the rules governing the way in which a judge should sum up rest on largely uninvestigated assumptions about the way in which jurors analyse and evaluate evidence. Section 8 of the Contempt of Court Act 1981 operates to prevent research involving real juries and therefore research within the jurisdiction has been confined to simulated and shadow juries, who obviously do not meet real parties and are not responsible for making real decisions. However, the research, together with research projects undertaken elsewhere with real jurors, has shed much light on the extent to which jurors understand, recall, and apply directions on such matters as the standard of proof and the use to which character evidence may be put. It also indicates that 'jurors routinely fail to comprehend fully the directions they are supposed to apply'[248] and the need for clearer guidance for juries at the start of the trial, for the use of simpler language, and for greater use of written material in what remains a predominantly oral process.[249]

Judicial discretion

If all evidence was either legally admissible or legally inadmissible, the law of evidence would be more certain. The price of such increased certainty, however, would be a rigidity that would do nothing to promote the integrity of the judicial process because it would sometimes occasion injustice by the exclusion of highly relevant evidence or the admission of evidence that would be unduly prejudicial or unfair to one of the parties. This can be avoided if the judge, over and above his general duty to rule on the admissibility of evidence as a matter of law, has a discretionary power to admit legally inadmissible evidence and to exclude legally admissible evidence. The former, inclusionary discretion, is virtually non-existent in English law. The latter, exclusionary discretion may be exercised in civil cases in favour of either party and in criminal cases in favour of the accused.

Inclusionary discretion

Despite the absence of express authority on the point, it seems clear that at common law, in both civil and criminal cases, a judge has no discretionary power to admit legally inadmissible evidence. In *Sparks v R*[250] the accused, a white man aged 27, was convicted of indecently assaulting a girl. At the trial, the judge held that evidence by the girl's mother to the effect that shortly after the assault her daughter had said 'it was a coloured boy' was inadmissible. The child gave no evidence at the trial. The Privy Council held that the evidence had been properly excluded as hearsay evidence which came within no recognized exception to the rule against hearsay in criminal cases.[251] It seems clear that Lord Morris, who delivered the opinion of the Privy Council, was operating on the assumption that where evidence is inadmissible as a matter of law, there is no inclusionary discretion.[252]

---

[248] L Ellison and V E Munro, 'Getting to (not) guilty: examining jurors' deliberative processes in, and beyond, the context of a mock rape trial' (2010) 30(1) *Legal Studies* 74 at 95 and n 80.

[249] See Young, 'Summing-up to Juries in Criminal Cases—What Jury Research says about Current Rules and Practice' [2003] Crim LR 665, which refers to much of the relevant literature.

[250] [1964] AC 964, PC.

[251] The appeal was allowed on different grounds.

[252] [1964] AC 964 at 978. See also per Lord Reid in *Myers v DPP* [1965] AC 1001 at 1024.

Exclusionary discretion

Civil cases

Prior to the introduction of the Civil Procedure Rules, a judge in a civil case had no discretionary power to exclude evidence that would otherwise be admissible as a matter of law. There was an exception, arguably, in the case of information given and received under the seal of confidence. On one view, the judge had a wide discretion to permit a witness, whether or not a party to the proceedings, to refuse to disclose information where disclosure would be a breach of some ethical or social value and non-disclosure would be unlikely to result in serious injustice in the case in which it was claimed.[253] In *D v National Society for the Prevention of Cruelty to Children*[254] Lords Hailsham and Kilbrandon were of the opinion that such a discretionary power did exist, but Lords Simon and Edmund-Davies disagreed. Lord Simon was of the view that although the judge could exercise a considerable 'moral authority' on the course of a trial, by which he could either seek to persuade counsel not to ask the question or gently guide the witness to overcome his reluctance to answer it, when 'it comes to the forensic crunch...it must be law not discretion which is in command'.[255]

CPR r 32.1(2) has introduced a general exclusionary discretion in civil cases.[256] Rule 32.1 provides as follows:

(1) The court may control the evidence by giving directions as to—
    (a) the issues on which it requires evidence;
    (b) the nature of the evidence which it requires to decide those issues; and
    (c) the way in which the evidence is to be placed before the court.
(2) The court may use its power under this rule to exclude evidence that would otherwise be admissible.
(3) The court may limit cross-examination.

When the court decides to exercise its power to exclude evidence under r 32.1(2), as when exercising any other power given to it by the rules, it must seek to give effect to the 'overriding objective',[257] which is to enable the court 'to deal with cases justly'.[258] Rule 1.1(2) provides as follows:

(2) Dealing with a case justly includes, so far as is practicable—
    (a) ensuring that the parties are on an equal footing;
    (b) saving expense;
    (c) dealing with the case in ways which are proportionate—
        (i)   to the amount of money involved;
        (ii) to the importance of the case;
        (iii) to the complexity of the issues; and
        (iv) to the financial position of each party;
    (d) ensuring that it is dealt with expeditiously and fairly; and
    (e) allotting to it an appropriate share of the court's resources, while taking into account the need to allot resources to other cases.

---

[253] 16th Report of the Law Reform Committee, *Privilege in Civil Proceedings*, Cmnd 3472 (1967), para 1.
[254] [1978] AC 171.
[255] [1978] AC 171 at 239.
[256] Including claims allocated to the small claims track: CPR r 27.2(1).
[257] CPR r 1.2.
[258] CPR r 1.1(1).

Rule 32.1(1) invests the court with extraordinarily wide powers, whereby it can override the views of the parties as to which issues call for evidence, the nature of the evidence appropriate to decide the issues, and the way in which the evidence should be given, eg in documentary form rather than orally.

Rule 32.1(2) also confers extremely wide powers: subject to r 1.1, there are no express limitations as to the extent of the power or the manner of its exercise.[259] As we have seen, civil courts already have the common law power to exclude evidence of marginal relevance.[260] In theory r 32.1(2) allows the court to exclude evidence even if plainly relevant, but it has been said that the more relevant the evidence is, the more reluctant the court is likely to be to exercise its discretion to exclude and that the power to exclude under r 32.1(2) should be exercised with great circumspection.[261] However, r 32.1(2) can be used to exclude peripheral material which is not essential to the just determination of the real issues between the parties[262] and, in appropriate circumstances, evidence that has been obtained illegally or improperly.[263] It can also be used, it is submitted, to restrict the number of witnesses and exclude superfluous evidence.

At common law, the judge has a discretion to prevent any questions in cross-examination which in his opinion are unnecessary, improper, or oppressive. Cross-examination, it has been held, should be conducted with restraint and a measure of courtesy and consideration to the witness.[264] Rule 32.1(3) supplements the common law powers of the judge and may be used to impose limits on the time permitted for cross-examination.[265] It may also be used to limit cross-examination about a witness's previous convictions. Thus although a witness may be asked about his convictions even where the offence is not one of dishonesty, in order to attack his credit,[266] r 32.1(3) gives the judge a discretion as to which previous convictions can be put. However, where sitting with a jury, he should be more hesitant to exercise the discretion because it is for the jury to decide what weight to give to such matters in relation to a witness's credibility.[267]

Because circumstances vary infinitely, it is submitted that it would be undesirable for the courts to go beyond the wording of r 1.1(2) with a view to providing additional guidance as to the way in which the discretion under r 32.1(2) and (3) should be exercised. It is further submitted that exercise of the discretionary powers should only be impugned on appeal if perverse in the *Wednesbury* sense,[268] ie where the court makes a decision which no reasonable tribunal could have reached.

Criminal cases

That a judge in a criminal trial has a discretion to exclude legally admissible evidence tendered by the prosecution has been accepted for some time[269] and was confirmed by the House

---

[259] *Grobbelaar v Sun Newspapers Ltd* (1999) The Times, 12 Aug, CA.

[260] See under **Relevance and admissibility**, in this chapter.

[261] *Great Future International Ltd v Sealand Housing Corporation* (2002) LTL 25 July.

[262] See *McPhilemy v Times Newspapers Ltd* [1999] 3 All ER 775, CA.

[263] See Ch 3, under **Discretion, Civil cases**.

[264] See *Mechanical and General Inventions Co Ltd v Austin* [1935] AC 346 at 360 and generally Ch 7, under **Cross-examination, The permitted form of questioning in cross-examination**.

[265] *Rall v Hume* [2001] 3 All ER 248.

[266] See Ch 7, under **Cross-examination, The permitted form of questioning in cross-examination**.

[267] *Watson v Chief Constable of Cleveland Police* [2001] EWCA Civ 1547.

[268] *Associated Provincial Picture Houses Ltd v Wednesbury Corpn* [1948] 1 KB 223, CA.

[269] See, eg, *R v Christie* [1914] AC 545, HL.

of Lords in *R v Sang*.[270] The House was of the unanimous albeit obiter view[271] that the judge, as a part of his inherent power and overriding duty in every case to ensure that the accused receives a fair trial, always has a discretion to refuse to admit legally admissible evidence if, in his opinion, its prejudicial effect on the minds of the jury outweighs its true probative value.[272] Exercise of the discretion is a subjective matter,[273] each case turning on its own facts and circumstances.[274] The judge must balance on the one hand the prejudicial effect of the evidence against the accused on the minds of the jury and on the other its weight and value having regard to the purpose for which it is adduced. Where the former is out of all proportion to the latter, the judge should exclude it. In one sense, of course, all relevant evidence adduced by the prosecution is prejudicial to the accused and the greater its probative value, the greater its prejudicial effect. In some cases, however, there will be a serious risk that the jury will attach undue weight to an item of evidence which is, in reality, of dubious reliability or of no more than trifling or minimal probative value, and in these circumstances the judge should exclude. In the words of Roskill J in *R v List*:[275]

> A trial judge always has an overriding duty in every case to secure a fair trial, and if in any particular case he comes to the conclusion that, even though certain evidence is strictly admissible, yet its prejudicial effect once admitted is such as to make it virtually impossible for a dispassionate view of the crucial facts of the case to be thereafter taken by the jury, then the trial judge, in my judgment, should exclude that evidence.

The case law on the basis of which the House of Lords in *R v Sang* came to its conclusion shows the discretion operating in a number of different sets of circumstances in relation to particular kinds of evidence. Their Lordships, however, were of the firm view that the cases were no more than examples of the exercise of a single discretion of general application and not of several specific or limited discretions.[276] Moreover, it was recognized that the existing cases were not the only ones in which the discretion could be exercised. Lord Salmon said:[277]

> I recognize that there may have been no categories of cases, other than those to which I have referred, in which technically admissible evidence proffered by the Crown has been rejected by the court on the ground that it would make the trial unfair. I cannot, however, accept that a judge's undoubted duty to ensure that the accused has a fair trial is confined to such cases. In my opinion the category of such cases is not and never can be closed except by statute.

There has been much scope for exercise of the discretion in relation to otherwise admissible evidence of the accused's bad character. For example, where the accused became liable to

---

[270] [1980] AC 402.

[271] A view affirmed by Lord Roskill in *Morris v Beardmore* [1981] AC 446, HL at 469.

[272] This 'fair trial' discretion may be exercised not only in the case of evidence the prejudicial effect of which outweighs its probative value, but also in the case of evidence obtained from the accused, after the commission of the offence charged, by improper or unfair means: see per Lords Diplock, Fraser, and Scarman at 436, 450, and 456 respectively. See Ch 3.

[273] Per Lord Fraser at 450.

[274] Per Lord Scarman at 456. See also per Lord Guest in *Selvey v DPP* [1970] AC 304 at 352: 'If it is suggested that the exercise of this discretion may be whimsical and depend on the individual idiosyncrasies of the judge, this is inevitable where it is a question of discretion.'

[275] [1966] 1 WLR 9 at 12.

[276] Per Lords Scarman and Fraser at 452 and 447 respectively.

[277] At 445. See also per Lord Dilhorne at 438.

cross-examination about his previous convictions and bad character under s 1(3)(ii) of the Criminal Evidence Act 1898, ie where the nature or conduct of the defence was such as to involve imputations on the character of the prosecutor or witnesses for the prosecution (see now s 101(1)(g) of the Criminal Justice Act 2003), the judge could exercise his discretion to disallow it.

> He may feel that even though the position is established in law, still the putting of such questions as to the character of the accused person may be fraught with results which immeasurably outweigh the result of questions put by the defence and which make a fair trial of the accused person almost impossible.[278]

There is also scope for exercise of the discretion in relation to hearsay. In *Grant v The State*[279] it was said to be clear that the judge in a criminal trial has an overriding discretion to exclude evidence judged to be unfair to the accused in the sense that it will put him at an unfair disadvantage or deprive him unfairly of the ability to defend himself, and that conscientiously exercised it affords the accused an important safeguard where statute permits the admission of hearsay.

A judge can also exercise his discretion to exclude evidence otherwise admissible under s 27(3) of the Theft Act 1968. Under s 27(3), where a person is charged with handling stolen goods and evidence is given of his possession of the goods, evidence that he has within the five years preceding the date of the offence charged been convicted of theft or handling stolen goods is admissible to prove that he knew or believed the goods to be stolen. The trial judge has a discretion to disallow the admission of such evidence, albeit strictly admissible, if, on the facts of the particular case, there is a risk of injustice. This may occur, for example, where possession is in issue in the case and it will be difficult, therefore, for the jury to appreciate that the evidence is relevant not to that issue but only to the issue of guilty knowledge.[280]

The discretion can also be used to exclude an out-of-court accusation directed at the accused which is admissible in evidence against him because by his conduct or demeanour it is possible to infer that he accepted, in whole or in part, the truth of the accusation made. Again, in these circumstances, the judge may exercise his discretion to exclude where the prejudicial effect of the evidence in the minds of the jury is out of all proportion to its true evidential value.[281]

It remains to note two matters of general importance relating to the exercise of the discretion now under discussion. First, the discretion may only be exercised to exclude evidence on which the prosecution, as opposed to any co-accused, proposes to rely. There is no discretion to exclude, at the request of one co-accused, evidence tendered by another. This principle, and the description of it appearing in the third edition of this work, were approved by the Privy Council in *Lobban v R*.[282] In that case L and R were charged with three murders. R, under caution, made a 'mixed' statement, ie a statement which contained

---

[278] Per Singleton J in *R v Jenkins* (1945) 31 Cr App R 1 at 15, approved in *Selvey v DPP* [1970] AC 304, HL.

[279] [2006] 2 WLR 835, PC.

[280] *R v List* [1966] 1 WLR 9, Assizes, a decision under the Larceny Act 1916, s 43(1), which was repealed by the Theft Act 1968 but re-enacted, with some modification, in s 27(3). The decision was approved in *R v Herron* [1967] 1 QB 107, CCA. See further Ch 17.

[281] See per Lord Moulton in *R v Christie* [1914] AC 545, HL at 559.

[282] [1995] 2 All ER 602, PC.

admissions as well as an exculpatory explanation. An integral part of the exculpatory explanation implicated L by name. The prosecution tendered R's statement for the truth of its
contents against R—it was no evidence against L. Counsel for L submitted that the trial
judge should have exercised his discretion to edit R's statement so as to exclude the parts
which implicated L on the basis that the prejudice to L by allowing the whole statement
to be admitted outweighed the relevance of the disputed material to the defence of R. The
Privy Council held that no such discretion existed—counsel's submission, if accepted,
would result in a serious derogation of an accused's liberty to defend himself by such legitimate means as he thinks it wise to employ. It was held that the discretionary power applies
only to evidence on which the prosecution propose to rely. Although R's statement was
tendered by the prosecution, the disputed material supported R's defence and the prosecution were not entitled to rely on it as evidence against L. Thus, although a trial judge has a
discretion to exclude or edit evidence tendered by the prosecution which is wholly inculpatory and probative of the case against one co-accused on the ground that it is unduly
prejudicial against another co-accused, there is no discretion to exclude the exculpatory
part of a 'mixed' statement on which one co-accused wishes to rely on the grounds that it
implicates another. One remedy to the latter situation is to order separate trials, but if that
is not done then the interests of the implicated co-accused must be protected by the most
explicit direction by the judge to the effect that the statement of the one co-accused is not
evidence against the other.[283]

The second matter of general importance is that, because exercise of the discretion is, as
we have seen, a subjective matter, each case turning on its own peculiar facts, it is difficult
to appeal successfully against a judge's decision not to exclude. Thus although an appellate
court will interfere with exercise of the discretion if there is no material on which the trial
judge could properly have arrived at his decision, or where he has erred in principle,[284] it is
not enough that the appellate court thinks that it would have exercised the discretion differently. However, the appellate courts have from time to time set out guidelines for exercise
of the discretion in relation to various types of evidence.[285] This assists judges. It also assists
defence counsel in advising and deciding tactics, to predict whether the discretion will be
exercised.

The discretionary common law power to exclude evidence on the basis that its prejudicial
effect outweighs its probative value has now been supplemented by s 78(1) of the Police and
Criminal Evidence Act 1984, which provides that:

the court may refuse to allow evidence on which the prosecution propose to rely to be given if
it appears to the court that, having regard to all the circumstances, including the circumstances
in which the evidence was obtained, the admission of the evidence would have such an adverse
effect on the fairness of the proceedings that the court ought not to admit it.

[283] But see also *R v Thompson* [1995] 2 Cr App R 589, CA: without a discretion to exclude evidence which is relevant
and therefore admissible in relation to an accused but inadmissible and prejudicial in relation to a co-accused, the
only safeguard is the cumbersome device of separate trials. The court observed that this seemed undesirable and that
it might be preferable to allow a discretion where the prejudice is substantial and the evidence is of only limited
benefit to the accused.
[284] See per Viscount Dilhorne in *Selvey v DPP* [1970] AC 304, HL at 342 and per Lord Lane CJ in *R v Powell* [1986]
1 All ER 193, CA at 197.
[285] See, eg, per Lawton LJ in *R v Britzman; R v Hall* [1983] 1 All ER 369, CA at 373–4.

Section 78(1) is of general application. Other statutory provisions empower a criminal court to exclude, in the exercise of its discretion, specific varieties of otherwise admissible evidence.[286]

Although s 78(1) is formally cast in the form of a discretion ('the court may'), the objective criterion whether 'admission…would have such an adverse effect on the fairness of the proceedings' in truth imports a judgment whether, in the light of the criterion of fairness, the court ought to admit the evidence.[287]

A simple example of the application of s 78(1) is *R v O'Connor*.[288] B and C were jointly charged in one count with having conspired to obtain property by deception. B pleaded guilty and C not guilty. The evidence of B's conviction was then admitted at the trial of C under s 74 of the 1984 Act to prove that B had committed the offence charged. The Court of Appeal held that the conviction should have been excluded under s 78 because evidence of B's admission of the offence charged might have led the jury to infer that C in his turn must have conspired with B.[289] Another straightforward illustration is furnished by *R v Ibrahim*,[290] a rape case in which it was held that the hearsay statements of the complainant, who had died by the time of the trial, should have been excluded under s 78: the statements were central to the Crown's case, but could not be shown to be reliable, and the complainant, a heroin addict, was potentially a very unreliable witness.

Section 78(1) operates without prejudice to the discretionary common law power to exclude. Section 82(3) of the 1984 Act provides that 'Nothing in this Part of this Act shall prejudice any power of a court to exclude evidence (whether from preventing questions from being put or otherwise) at its discretion'. The terms of s 78(1) are clearly wide enough to apply to items of prosecution evidence already subject to the common law discretion[291]—and the weighing of probative value against prejudicial effect can be an important factor in exercising the discretion under s 78(1)[292]—but s 78(1) is not confined to such cases.

Section 78(1) directs the court, when considering exercise of the discretion, to have regard to all the circumstances, 'including the circumstances in which the evidence was obtained'. Thus, although it is clear that s 78(1) can be applied by a court in the absence of any illegality or impropriety,[293] the chief importance of the subsection lies in its potential for the exclusion of evidence illegally or improperly obtained. That topic is considered in Chapter 3.

Applications to exclude evidence in reliance on s 78(1) should be made before the evidence is adduced: the section applies to evidence on which the prosecution 'propose' to rely.[294]

---

[286] See, in the case of hearsay, the Criminal Justice Act 2003, s 126 (see Ch 10), which expressly preserves the general power to exclude under s 78; and in the case of evidence of the bad character of the accused, the Criminal Justice Act 2003, s 101(3) (see Ch 17), which also, it seems, provides protection additional to s 78(1): see *R v Highton* [2005] 1 WLR 3472.

[287] Per Lord Steyn in *R v Hasan* [2005] 2 AC 467, HL at [53]. See also per Auld LJ in *R v Chalkley and Jeffries* [1998] 2 All ER 155, CA at 178.

[288] (1986) 85 Cr App R 298, CA.

[289] See further Ch 21, where additional cases on the issue are considered.

[290] [2012] 2 Cr App R 420, CA.

[291] See *Matto v Crown Court at Wolverhampton* [1987] RTR 337, DC, per Woolf LJ at 346: '[s 78] certainly does not reduce the discretion of the court to exclude unfair evidence which existed at common law. Indeed, in my view in any case where the evidence could properly be excluded at common law, it can certainly be excluded under s 78.'

[292] Per Lord Lane CJ in *R v Quinn* [1990] Crim LR 581, CA.

[293] *R v Samuel* [1988] QB 615, CA; *R v O'Leary* (1988) 87 Cr App R 387, CA at 391; and *R v Brine* [1992] Crim LR 122, CA.

[294] *R v Sat-Bhambra* (1988) 88 Cr App R 55, CA.

Proof of birth, death, age, convictions and acquittals

Birth and death

The normal and easiest way of proving a person's birth or death is by (a) producing to the court a certified copy of an entry in the register of births (deaths),[295] which is admissible under an exception to the hearsay rule[296] and admissible, therefore, as evidence of the truth of its contents; *and* (b) adducing some evidence to identify the person whose birth (death) is in question with the person named in the birth (death) certificate.[297] Proof of birth or death may also be effected by the testimony of someone present at the time of birth (death), by hearsay statements admissible under either the Criminal Justice Act 2003 or the Civil Evidence Act 1995[298] or, in proceedings in which a question of pedigree is directly in issue, by a declaration as to pedigree made by a deceased blood relation or spouse of a blood relation.[299] A person's death may also be proved in reliance on the presumption of death, which is considered in Chapter 22, or by the testimony of someone who saw the corpse and was capable of identifying it as that of the person whose death is in question.

Age

The date of a person's birth being contained in his or her birth certificate, the normal way of proving a person's age is by (a) producing to the court a certified copy of an entry in the register of births, which, as we have seen, is admissible as evidence of the truth of its contents; *and* (b) adducing some evidence identifying the person whose age is in question with the person named in the birth certificate. A person's age may also be proved by the testimony of someone present at the time of his or her birth, by inference from his or her appearance,[300] by hearsay statements admissible by statute, and by declarations as to pedigree.

Convictions and acquittals

Section 73 of the Police and Criminal Evidence Act 1984, which superseded a variety of outdated statutory provisions, provides for the proof of convictions and acquittals by means of a certificate signed by an appropriate court officer together with evidence identifying the person whose conviction (acquittal) is in question with the person named in the certificate. It provides as follows:

(1) Where in any proceedings[301] the fact that a person has in the United Kingdom or any other member State[302] been convicted or acquitted of an offence otherwise than by a Service court

---

[295] See the Births and Deaths Registration Act 1953, s 34.

[296] See generally Chs 10–12.

[297] See also the Evidence (Foreign, Dominion and Colonial Documents) Act 1933, s 1, whereby an Order in Council may be made providing for the proof by authorized copy of extracts from properly kept public registers kept under the authority of the law of the country in question and recognized by the courts of that country as authentic records. Concerning births (deaths) on board ship, see the Merchant Shipping (Returns of Births and Deaths) Regulations 1979, made under the Merchant Shipping Act 1970, s 75.

[298] See Chs 10 and 11 respectively.

[299] See Ch 12.

[300] See, eg, the Children and Young Persons Act 1933, s 99 and the Criminal Justice Act 1948, s 80(3).

[301] 'Proceedings' means criminal proceedings including proceedings before a court-martial or Courts-Martial Appeal Court.

[302] ie other EU member states.

is admissible in evidence, it may be proved by producing a certificate of conviction or, as the case may be, of acquittal relating to that offence, and proving that the person named in the certificate as having been convicted or acquitted of the offence is the person whose conviction or acquittal of the offence is to be proved.

(2) For the purposes of this section a certificate of conviction or of acquittal—

(a) shall, as regards a conviction or acquittal on indictment, consist of a certificate, signed by the proper officer of the court where the conviction or acquittal took place, giving the substance and effect (omitting the formal parts) of the indictment and of the conviction or acquittal; and

(b) shall, as regards a conviction or acquittal on a summary trial, consist of a copy of the conviction or of the dismissal of the information, signed by the proper officer of the court where the conviction or acquittal took place or by the proper officer of the court, if any, to which a memorandum of the conviction or acquittal was sent; and

(c) shall, as regards a conviction or acquittal by a court in a member State (other than the United Kingdom), consist of a certificate, signed by the proper officer of the court where the conviction or acquittal took place, giving details of the offence, of the conviction or acquittal, and of any sentence;and a document purporting to be a duly signed certificate of conviction or acquittal under this section shall be taken to be such a certificate unless the contrary is proved.

(3) In subsection (2) above 'proper officer' means—

(a) in relation to a magistrates' court in England and Wales, the designated officer for the court;

(b) in relation to any other court in the United Kingdom, the clerk of the court, his deputy or any other person having custody of the court record; and

(c) in relation to any court in another member State ('the EU court'), a person who would be the proper officer of the EU court if that court were in the United Kingdom.

The section contains a saving for 'any other authorised manner of proving a conviction or acquittal'.[303] The issue of identity in s 73(1) is a question of fact for the jury.[304] In *Pattison v DPP*[305] the following general principles were said to apply when s 73(1) is relied on by the prosecution to prove the conviction of an accused.

(a) Identity must be proved to the criminal standard.

(b) This may be effected by a formal or informal admission,[306] by evidence of fingerprints, or by the evidence of someone present in court at the time.

(c) There is no prescribed means of proof: identity can be proved by any admissible evidence, for example a match between the personal details of the accused and those on the certificate.

(d) Even if the personal details, such as the name, are not uncommon, a match will be sufficient for a prima facie case.

(e) The failure of the accused to give any contradictory evidence can be taken into account and may give rise to an adverse inference under section 35(2) of the Criminal Justice and Public Order Act 1994.[307]

---

[303] Section 73(4).

[304] *R v Burns* [2006] 1 WLR 1273, CA and *R v Lewendon* [2006] 2 Cr App R 294, CA.

[305] [2006] 2 All ER 317, QBD.

[306] As to the former, see Criminal Justice Act 1967, s 10 (see Ch 22); as to the latter, see Ch 13.

[307] See Ch 14.

ADDITIONAL READING

Aitken and Taroni, 'Fundamentals of Statistical Evidence—a Primer for Legal Professionals' (2008) 12 E&P 181.

Anderson and Twining, *Analysis of Evidence* (London and Boston, 1991).

Choo, 'The Notion of Relevance' [1993] Crim LR 114.

Eggleston, *Evidence, Proof and Probability* (2nd edn, London, 1983).

Elliott, '*Brutus v Cozens*; Decline and Fall' [1989] Crim LR 323.

Grove, *The Juryman's Tale* (London, 1998).

Heaton-Armstrong et al (eds), *Analysing Witness Testimony* (London, 1999).

Pundik, 'The epistemology of statistical evidence' (2011) 15 E&P 117.

Wigmore, *The Principles of Judicial Proof* (2nd edn, Boston, 1931) 17–31.

Young, 'Summing-up to Juries in Criminal Cases—What Jury Research Says about Current Rules and Practice' [2003] Crim LR 665.

Evidence obtained by illegal or unfair means

3

Key issues

- When and why should relevant evidence obtained illegally, improperly, or unfairly be admitted at trial?

- When and why should relevant evidence obtained illegally, improperly, or unfairly be excluded at trial?

- Should the law of evidence admit or exclude relevant evidence obtained by (a) torture; (b) inhuman or degrading treatment; (c) entrapment; and (d) undercover operations?

- Should decisions on the above issues be governed by rules of law or the exercise of judicial discretion?

- When and why should the law of evidence, in dealing with the above issues, differentiate between criminal and civil cases?

This chapter concerns the circumstances in which relevant evidence can be excluded, as a matter of law or discretion, on the grounds that it was obtained illegally, improperly, or unfairly. It also considers a related matter, the circumstances in which criminal proceedings should be stayed as an abuse of the court's process where a trial would undermine public confidence in the criminal justice system and bring it into disrepute.

Evidence may be obtained illegally, for example by a crime, tort, or breach of contract, or in contravention of statutory or other provisions governing the powers and duties of the police or others involved in investigating crime. Evidence may also be obtained by other improper or unfair means, for example by trickery, deception, bribes, threats, or inducements. At one extreme, the view could be taken that evidence which is relevant and otherwise admissible should not be excluded because of the means by which it was obtained, whether illegal, improper, or unfair; to exclude it would, in some cases, result in injustice, including the acquittal of the guilty. On this view, all evidence which is necessary to enable justice to be done would be admitted; and those responsible for the illegality or impropriety could be variously prosecuted (in the case of crime), sued (in the case of actionable wrongs), or disciplined (in the case of conduct amounting to breach of some statutory, professional, or other code of conduct). The view at the other extreme would be that illegally or improperly obtained evidence should always be excluded; to admit it might encourage the obtaining of evidence by such means or at any rate bring the administration of justice into disrepute. On this view, all such evidence would be excluded, even if this would sometimes result in injustice, including the guilty going free, in order that those responsible for the illegality or impropriety are in future compelled to respect, and deterred from invading, the civil liberties of the citizen.

The modern law of evidence in this country represents a compromise between these two extreme views. Thus although at common law there is a general rule of law that relevant and otherwise admissible evidence should not be excluded because of the means by which it was obtained, there are both exceptions to the rule and discretionary powers to exclude.[1] It is useful, before turning to consider the exceptions and discretionary powers, to consider first the theoretical principles for exclusion.

Principles for exclusion

There are four principles that may be used to justify the exclusion of evidence obtained illegally or unfairly. The first is the reliability principle—which would be better described as the unreliability principle—under which evidence should be excluded where its reliability has been impaired, or the accused's ability to test its reliability has been impaired, by reason of the way in which it was obtained. The second is the integrity principle, under which the court excludes evidence to disassociate itself from the way in which it was obtained and to maintain the integrity of the criminal justice process. The third is the disciplinary principle, under which the court excludes evidence obtained illegally or improperly to 'discipline' the police and discourage them from obtaining evidence in such a way. The fourth is the 'rights-based' or 'protective' principle, under which the court excludes evidence obtained in breach of the rights that suspects have been granted. This principle is probably no different, except in name,

---

[1] For an interesting analysis of the question whether to admit illegally obtained evidence and the shortcomings of the exclusionary principle, see Zuckerman, *The Principles of Criminal Evidence* (Oxford, 1989) Ch 16. See also Mirfield, *Silence, Confessions and Improperly Obtained Evidence* (Oxford, 1997).

from the remedial principle, under which evidence is excluded as a 'remedy' for breach of the rights of the suspect.

These four principles overlap in their operation, so that to use one may well be to give effect to another. Thus, for example, to use the reliability or rights-based principle, and not the disciplinary principle, may nonetheless have the effect of 'disciplining' the police.

Law

Staying proceedings as an abuse of process

In English law, it is well established that the powers of a court to stay proceedings as an abuse of its process may be exercised in two categories of case.[2] The first, which is beyond the proper scope of this book, is where it will be impossible to give the accused a fair trial. The second, which is clearly underpinned by the integrity principle, was described by Sir John Dyson SCJ in *R v Maxwell*[3] in the following terms:

> In the second category of case, the court is concerned to protect the integrity of the criminal justice system. Here a stay will be granted where the court concludes that in all the circumstances a trial will 'offend the court's sense of justice and propriety' (per Lord Lowry in *R v Horseferry Road Magistrates' Court, ex p Bennett* [1993] 3 All ER 138 at 161, [1994] 1 AC 42 at 74) or will 'undermine public confidence in the criminal justice system and bring it into disrepute' (per Lord Steyn in *R v Latif, R v Shahzad* [1996] 1 All ER 353 at 360, [1996] 1 WLR 104 at 112).

The second category calls for a balancing exercise. Some of the factors that are frequently taken into account when carrying out the exercise are: the seriousness of any violation of the rights of the accused or a third party; whether the police have acted in bad faith or maliciously, or with an improper motive; whether the misconduct was committed in circumstances of urgency, emergency, or necessity; the availability or otherwise of a direct sanction against the person responsible for the misconduct; and the seriousness of the offence with which the accused is charged.[4] In *Warren v Attorney General for Jersey*[5] Lord Dyson held that how the discretion will be exercised will depend on the particular circumstances of the case; that in abduction and entrapment cases, the court will generally conclude that the balance favours a stay,[6] but rigid classifications are undesirable; and that whether a stay should be granted will not always, or even in most cases, be necessarily determined by the test of whether, but for an abuse of executive power, the accused would never have been before the court at all. A stay may be justified where intrusive covert surveillance has interfered significantly with an accused's right to legal professional privilege.[7]

The general rule of law

Where proceedings have not been stayed as an abuse of process, then, subject to exceptions, the rules of English *law* make no provision for the exclusion of relevant evidence on the grounds that it was obtained illegally or improperly. The general rule of law is accurately

---

[2] *R v Beckford* [1996] 1 Cr App R 94.

[3] [2011] 1 WLR 1837, SC.

[4] Choo, *Abuse of Process and Judicial Stays of Criminal Proceedings* (2nd edn, New York, 2008) 132, endorsed as a 'useful summary' by Lord Dyson in *Warren v Attorney General for Jersey* [2012] AC 22, PC at [25].

[5] [2012] AC 22, PC.

[6] As to entrapment cases, see further, in this chapter, under **Discretion, Criminal cases: section 78 of the Police and Criminal Evidence Act 1984, Entrapment and undercover operations**.

[7] *R v Turner* [2013] EWCA Crim 642 at [28].

represented by the following words of Crompton J in *R v Leatham*:[8] 'It matters not how you get it; if you steal it even, it would be admissible in evidence.' Thus evidence remains admissible in law if obtained by the use of agents provocateurs,[9] or by invasion of privacy,[10] or by the unlawful search of persons[11] or premises.[12]

The exceptions

Theft of privileged documents in court

One exception to the general rule concerns privileged documents. Although there is a general rule allowing secondary evidence of privileged documents to be adduced, even though obtained illegally or improperly,[13] a party to litigation who obtains by a trick documents belonging to the other party and brought into court by him will not be permitted to adduce copies of those documents, because the public interest in the ascertainment of truth in litigation is outweighed by the public interest that litigants should be able to bring their documents into court without fear that they may be filched by their opponents.[14]

Improperly obtained confessions

A second exception relates to a confession made by an accused that was or may have been obtained by oppression or in consequence of anything said or done which was likely, in the circumstances, to render unreliable any confession which might be made by him in consequence thereof.[15] Oppression, for these purposes, is defined to include torture,[16] in respect of which there is a broader common law exclusionary principle.

Evidence obtained by torture

In *A v Secretary of State for the Home Department (No 2)*[17] it was held that as a matter of constitutional principle evidence obtained by torture may not lawfully be admitted against a party to proceedings in a British court, irrespective of where, or by whom, or on whose authority the torture was inflicted. Such evidence falls to be excluded both at common law and in accordance with the European Convention on Human Rights, which takes account of the United Nations Convention Against Torture and Other Cruel, Inhuman or Degrading Treatment or Punishment 1987.[18] Article 15 of the Torture Convention requires states to ensure that statements made as a result of torture shall not be invoked as evidence in any proceedings.

---

[8] (1861) 8 Cox CC 498 at 501.

[9] *R v Sang* [1980] AC 402, HL.

[10] *R v Khan (Sultan)* [1997] AC 558, HL.

[11] See *Jones v Owens* (1870) 34 JP 759 and *Kuruma, Son of Kaniu v R* [1955] AC 197, PC.

[12] See *Jeffrey v Black* [1978] QB 490.

[13] See per Parke B in *Lloyd v Mostyn* (1842) 10 M&W 478, applied by Lindley MR in *Calcraft v Guest* [1898] 1 QB 759, CA at 764 (see Ch 20).

[14] *ITC Film Distributors v Video Exchange Ltd* [1982] Ch 431. Cf *R v Tompkins* (1977) 67 Cr App R 181, CA (see Ch 20).

[15] Police and Criminal Evidence Act 1984 (the 1984 Act), s 76(2) (see Ch 13). See also the Regulation of Investigatory Powers Act 2000, s 17, which renders inadmissible evidence which tends to suggest the commission of an offence of intentional interception, at any place in the United Kingdom, of any communication in the course of its transmission by means of a public postal service or by means of a public telecommunication system.

[16] The 1984 Act, s 76(8).

[17] [2005] 3 WLR 1249, HL.

[18] See per Lord Bingham at [51] and [52]. The definition of torture for these purposes appears to be that adopted in the Criminal Justice Act 1988, s 134, namely the infliction of severe pain or suffering by a public official in the performance or purported performance of his official duties: see per Lord Hoffmann at [97].

In reaching this decision, some of their Lordships relied explicitly upon the integrity principle.[19] However, their Lordships declined to accept that the exclusionary rule should extend beyond torture to inhuman or degrading treatment, a distinction that is difficult to justify. As one commentator has observed: '... if torture evidence is an affront to civilised values, so too will [sic] evidence procured by inhuman treatment, albeit to a lesser extent'.[20]

Difficult distinctions have also been drawn, in the European jurisprudence, between cases of torture and cases of inhuman or degrading treatment. In *Jalloh v Germany*[21] the Grand Chamber of the European Court of Human Rights held that evidence obtained by torture should be automatically excluded. The court expressly left open the question whether there should also be automatic exclusion for evidence obtained by inhuman or degrading treatment, but on the facts held that the admission of such evidence did violate the accused's rights under Art 6.[22] In *Gäfgen v Germany*[23] it was held that incriminating real evidence recovered as a direct result of torture should always be excluded, but if it is obtained as a result of statements obtained by inhuman treatment, it may be admitted, provided that it is not necessary to secure a conviction.

There is an argument for the exclusion of evidence obtained as a result of secret detention, but it is not as strong as in the case of torture, there being no equivalent of Art 15 of the Torture Convention.[24]

Discretion

Civil cases

Prior to the introduction of the Civil Procedure Rules, such authority as there was suggested that in civil proceedings there was no discretion to exclude evidence obtained illegally or improperly.[25]

Under CPR r 32.1(2) the court may now exclude evidence that would otherwise be admissible and, in deciding whether to do so, must seek to give effect to the overriding objective of enabling the court to deal with cases justly.[26] It is submitted that, in appropriate circumstances, therefore, the court may exercise the discretionary power to exclude evidence which, although relevant, has been obtained illegally or improperly. In *Jones v University of Warwick*,[27] a claim for damages for personal injuries, the defendant was allowed to introduce a video of the claimant obtained by trespass and in breach of Art 8 of the European Convention on Human Rights (the right of respect for private and family life). Inquiry agents acting for the defendant's insurers had gained access to the claimant's home by deception and had filmed her without her knowledge. It was held that the court should consider two

---

[19] See per Lord Hoffmann at [87] and per Lord Carson at [150].

[20] Rasiah, '*A v Secretary of State for the Home Department (No 2)*: Occupying the Moral High Ground?' (2006) 69 MLR 995 at 1003.

[21] (2007) 44 EHRR 32.

[22] See also *R v Ahmed* [2011] EWCA Crim 184.

[23] Application No 22978/05, 30 June 2008, [2010] Crim LR 865, ECHR.

[24] Per Richards LJ, obiter, in *XX v Secretary of State for the Home Department* [2012] 4 All ER 692, CA at [39].

[25] See per Lord Denning MR in *Helliwell v Piggott-Sims* [1980] FSR 582.

[26] See Ch 2, under **Judicial discretion**, **Exclusionary discretion**, **Civil cases**.

[27] [2003] 1 WLR 954, CA.

conflicting public interests, on the one hand the achieving of justice in the particular case and on the other, considering the effect of its decision upon litigation generally, the risk that if the improper conduct goes uncensored, improper practices of the type in question will be encouraged. The weight to be attached to each public interest will vary according to the circumstances. The significance of the evidence will differ as will the gravity of the breach of Art 8, and the decision will depend on all the circumstances. In the case before it, the Court of Appeal held that the conduct of the insurers was not so outrageous that the defence should be struck out and that it would be artificial and undesirable to exclude the evidence, which would involve the instruction of fresh medical experts from whom relevant evidence would have to be concealed. However, it was also held that the conduct of the insurers was improper and unjustified and that the trial judge should take it into account when deciding the appropriate order for costs.[28]

Criminal cases—common law

That a judge, in criminal proceedings, has a discretionary power to exclude otherwise admissible evidence on the grounds that it was obtained improperly or unfairly was, until *R v Sang*,[29] only clearly established in relation to evidence of admissions and confessions. The power to exclude, as a matter of discretion, an otherwise admissible admission or confession is a large and complex topic which is considered separately in Chapter 13. Admissions and confessions apart, there was also an unbroken series of dicta from a variety of impressive sources to suggest that in criminal proceedings the trial judge also has a general discretion to exclude evidence tendered by the prosecution which has been obtained oppressively, improperly, or unfairly[30] or as a result of the activities of an agent provocateur.[31] However, despite these weighty dicta, this discretion was rarely exercised. A very rare reported example is *R v Payne*[32] where the accused, charged with drunken driving, agreed to a medical examination to see if he was suffering from any illness or disability on the understanding that the doctor would not examine him to assess his fitness to drive. At the trial, the doctor gave evidence of the accused's unfitness to drive and the Court of Criminal Appeal quashed the conviction on the grounds that the trial judge should have exercised his discretion to exclude the doctor's evidence. In *R v Sang*[33] Lords Diplock, Fraser, and Scarman regarded the decision as based on the maxim *nemo tenetur se ipsum prodere* ('no man is to be compelled to incriminate himself') and analogous,

[28] See also *Niemietz v Germany* (1992) 16 EHRR 97; *Halford v UK* (1997) 24 EHRR 523; and *Imerman v Tchenguiz* [2011] 1 All ER 555, CA.
[29] [1980] AC 402, HL.
[30] See per Lord Goddard CJ in *Kuruma, Son of Kaniu v R* [1955] AC 197, PC at 203–4 (evidence obtained 'by a trick'); per Lord Parker CJ in *Callis v Gunn* [1964] 1 QB 495, DC at 505 (evidence obtained 'oppressively, by false representations, by a trick, by threats, by bribes, anything of that sort'); and per Lord Widgery CJ in *Jeffrey v Black* [1978] QB 490, DC at 497–8 (exceptional cases where 'not only have the police officers entered without authority, but they have been guilty of trickery, or they have misled someone, or they have been oppressive, or they have been unfair, or in other respects they have behaved in a manner which is morally reprehensible'). See also per Lord Hodson in *King v R* [1969] 1 AC 304, PC at 319.
[31] See per Lord McDermott CJ in *R v Murphy* [1965] NI 138, C-MAC, a case decided before the rejection of entrapment as a defence. See also *R v Foulder, Foulkes and Johns* [1973] Crim LR 45; *R v Burnett and Lee* [1973] Crim LR 748; and *R v Ameer and Lucas* [1977] Crim LR 104, CA.
[32] [1963] 1 WLR 637.
[33] [1980] AC 402.

therefore, to cases in which an accused is unfairly induced to confess to, or make a damaging admission in respect of, an offence.[34]

In *R v Sang* the House of Lords held that the judicial discretion to exclude admissible evidence does not extend to excluding evidence of a crime on the grounds that it was instigated by an agent provocateur, because if it did it would amount to a procedural device whereby the judge could avoid the substantive law under which it is clearly established that there is no defence of entrapment.[35] The primary importance of *R v Sang*, however, is the obiter answer given to the certified point of law of general importance, namely 'Does a trial judge have a discretion to refuse to allow evidence, being evidence other than evidence of an admission, to be given in any circumstances in which such evidence is relevant and of more than minimal probative value?' On that wider issue, the House was of the unanimous opinion that: (i) a trial judge always has a discretion to exclude prosecution evidence where its prejudicial effect outweighs its probative value;[36] but (ii) since the court is not concerned with how evidence sought to be adduced by the prosecution has been obtained, but with how it is used by the prosecution at the trial, a judge has no discretion to refuse to admit admissible evidence on the grounds that it was obtained by improper or unfair means except in the case of admissions, confessions, and evidence obtained from the accused after the commission of the offence. Although the judgment in this respect was obiter, Lord Roskill declared later that it would be a retrograde step to enlarge the narrow limits of, or to engraft an exception on, the discretion to exclude as defined in *R v Sang*.[37] Unfortunately, however, the scope of the discretion defined, despite their Lordships' apparent unanimity, is far from clear, particularly insofar as it extends to 'evidence obtained from the accused after the commission of the offence'. For Lord Diplock, that phrase seems to refer to evidence tantamount to a self-incriminating admission obtained from the accused by means which would justify a judge in excluding an actual confession which had the like self-incriminating effect[38] and there is no discretion to exclude evidence discovered as the result of an illegal search.[39] For Lord Salmon, the decision whether to exclude being dependent upon the 'infinitely variable' facts and circumstances of each particular case, the category of cases in which evidence could be rejected on the grounds that it would make a trial unfair was not closed and never could be closed except by statute.[40] Lord Fraser appears to have understood the phrase as referring to evidence and documents obtained from an accused or from premises occupied by him, but also said that their Lordships' decision would leave judges with a discretion to be exercised in accordance with their individual views of what is unfair, oppressive, or morally

[34] At 435, 449, and 455 respectively. Cf *R v McDonald* [1991] Crim LR 122, CA, a decision under the Police and Criminal Evidence Act 1984, s 78: it is not unfair for a psychiatrist to give evidence of an admission made by the accused on a non-medical issue in the course of a psychiatric examination. *R v McDonald* was followed in *R v Gayle* [1994] Crim LR 679, CA and, in the case of confessions to probation officers, *R v Elleray* [2003] 2 Cr App R 165, CA.

[35] See *R v McEvilly; R v Lee* (1973) 60 Cr App R 150, CA; and *R v Mealey; R v Sheridan* (1974) 60 Cr App R 59, CA. However, as to the discretion to exclude under the Police and Criminal Evidence Act 1984, s 78, see *R v Looseley* [2001] 1 WLR 2060, considered in this chapter under **Discretion, Criminal cases: section 78 of the Police and Criminal Evidence Act 1984, The reliability principle.**

[36] See Ch 2, under **Judicial discretion, Exclusionary discretion, Criminal cases.**

[37] *Morris v Beardmore* [1981] AC 446, HL at 469.

[38] See also *R v Payne* [1963] 1 WLR 637, CCA at n 32.

[39] *R v Sang* [1980] AC 402 at 436. See also *R v Adams* [1980] QB 575, CA at n 50.

[40] *R v Sang* [1980] AC 402 at 445. See also per Lord Fraser at 450.

reprehensible.[41] For Lord Scarman, it referred exclusively to the obtaining of evidence from the *accused*.[42]

The subsequent case law has done little to clarify the meaning of the phrase 'evidence obtained from the accused after the commission of the offence' but has put a major gloss on *R v Sang* to the effect that the discretion should not be exercised if those who obtained such evidence unlawfully did so on the basis of a bona fide mistake as to their powers. In *R v Trump*[43] the Court of Appeal, while acknowledging that the phrase was not fully considered by the House, treated it as referring to cases analogous to improperly obtained admissions. The accused was convicted of driving while unfit through drink. Following an unlawful arrest, a specimen of blood was obtained without the accused's consent within the meaning of s 7 of the Road Traffic Act 1972. It was held that the giving of blood by the accused was very close to an oral admission by him that he had drunk to excess, and was therefore subject to the discretion, but that the judge would have erred if he had excluded the evidence because, although the sample was given as a result of a threat, the police officer in question was acting in good faith and the evidence could not undermine the fairness of the trial. On a similar charge in *Fox v Chief Constable of Gwent*[44] the House of Lords held that evidence of a breath specimen obtained by officers acting in good faith and in accordance with the statutory procedure was not inadmissible merely because the accused had been unlawfully arrested. Lord Fraser said:[45]

> Of course, if the appellant had been lured to the police station by some trick or deception, or if the police officers had behaved oppressively towards the appellant, the justices' jurisdiction to exclude otherwise admissible evidence recognized in *R v Sang* might have come into play. But there is nothing of that sort suggested here. The police officers did no more than make a bona fide mistake as to their powers.[46]

In *R v Khan (Sultan)*[47] it was held that evidence of an incriminating conversation obtained by means of a secret electronic surveillance device did not fall within the category of admissions, confessions, and other evidence obtained from the accused after the commission of the offence, on the basis that the accused had not been 'induced' to make the recorded admissions.

In *R v Apicella*[48] the accused was convicted on three counts of rape. Each of the victims had contracted an unusual strain of gonorrhoea. The accused, whilst held on remand, was suspected by the prison doctor to be suffering from gonorrhoea. The doctor, for solely therapeutic reasons, called in a consultant who took a sample of body fluid in order to enable diagnosis. The consultant assumed that the accused was consenting. In fact, he submitted because he had been told by a prison officer that he had no choice. The sample showed that the accused was suffering from the same strain of gonorrhoea as the victims, and the prosecution called evidence to that effect. The Court of Appeal flatly rejected a submission that the evidence was

---

[41] *R v Sang* [1980] AC 402 at 450.

[42] *R v Sang* [1980] AC 402 at 456.

[43] (1979) 70 Cr App R 300, CA at 302.

[44] [1985] 3 All ER 392, HL.

[45] At 397.

[46] Applied in *Gull v Scarborough* [1987] RTR 261n. See also *DPP v Wilson* [1991] RTR 284; and *Public Prosecution Service of Northern Ireland v Elliott* [2013] 2 Cr App R 180, SC (fingerprints taken using an electronic device that had not been officially approved) (see Ch 22).

[47] [1997] AC 558, HL.

[48] (1985) 82 Cr App R 295, CA.

the physical equivalent of an oral confession.[49] It was held that use of the evidence was not unfair and the judge correct in the exercise of his discretion not to exclude it.[50]

Criminal cases: section 78 of the Police and Criminal Evidence Act 1984

Section 78 of the 1984 Act provides as follows:

(1) In any proceedings the court may refuse to allow evidence on which the prosecution proposes to rely to be given if it appears to the court that, having regard to all the circumstances, including the circumstances in which the evidence was obtained, the admission of the evidence would have such an adverse effect on the fairness of the proceedings that the court ought not to admit it.

(2) Nothing in this section shall prejudice any rule of law requiring a court to exclude evidence.

The effect of s 78(2) is that if an item of evidence is inadmissible by virtue of any of the exclusionary rules of evidence, it *must* be excluded. As to the discretionary power to exclude under s 78(1), the question of exclusion may be raised by any accused against whom the evidence is to be used or by the court on its own motion.[51] However, if the accused is represented by an apparently competent advocate, who does not raise the issue, perhaps for tactical reasons, the judge is under no duty to exercise the discretion of his own motion, even in the case of a flagrant abuse of police power, although he may make a pertinent enquiry of the advocate in the jury's absence.[52] Section 78(1) refers to evidence on which the prosecution *proposes* to rely. Thus in *R v Harwood*[53] it was doubted whether s 78(1) empowers a judge to exclude evidence, after it has been adduced, in the absence of any submission to exclude before it was adduced. At trials on indictment, if there is a dispute as to the circumstances in which the evidence was obtained, it would seem to be necessary to hold a trial within a trial.[54] Thus if the accused disputes that he was cautioned, it is the duty of the judge to hold a *voir dire* and make a finding on the issue.[55] However, concerning the admissibility of identification evidence, it has been held that although there may be rare occasions when it will be desirable to hold a *voir dire*, in general the judge should decide on the basis of the depositions, statements, and submissions of counsel.[56] It is not clear under s 78(1) where the burden of proof lies.[57] If there is a dispute as to the circumstances in which the evidence was obtained, it is submitted that, in principle, there should be an evidential burden on the accused in relation to his version of events, on the discharge of which there should be a legal burden on the prosecution to disprove the

---

[49] No reference was made to *R v Trump* (1979) 70 Cr App R 300 (see at n 43).

[50] See also *R v Adams* [1980] QB 575, CA, where it was held that a judge should not exercise the discretion to exclude as evidence articles obtained by means of an unlawful entry, search, and seizure: 'There is no material suggesting that the error of the police as to the continuing validity of the warrant…was oppressive in the sense that the adjective is used in *R v Sang*.' According to Lord Diplock in *R v Sang*, evidence discovered as the result of an illegal search is not even subject to the discretion to exclude.

[51] *Re Saifi* [2001] 4 All ER 168, DC at [52].

[52] *R v Raphaie* [1996] Crim LR 812, CA.

[53] [1989] Crim LR 285, CA.

[54] Concerning proceedings before magistrates, see Ch 2, under **The functions of the judge and jury**.

[55] *R v Manji* [1990] Crim LR 512, CA.

[56] *R v Beveridge* [1987] Crim LR 401, CA (identification parade evidence); and *R v Martin and Nicholls* [1994] Crim LR 218, CA (evidence of informal identification). Cf *R v Flemming* (1987) 86 Cr App R 32, CA. Concerning confessions, see also *R v Keenan* [1990] 2 QB 54, CA (see Ch 13).

[57] Acknowledged, *per curiam*, in *R v Anderson* [1993] Crim LR 447, CA.

accused's version beyond reasonable doubt.[58] However, it was said in *Re Saifi*,[59] in the context of extradition proceedings, that the words of s 78 provide no support for such a contention, and that the absence from s 78 of words suggesting that facts are to be established or proved to any particular standard is deliberate, leaving the matter open and untrammelled by rigid evidential considerations.

Scope

Concerning the scope of s 78(1), it applies to *any* evidence on which the prosecution propose to rely, whether tendered by the prosecution or (presumably) a co-accused. Thus it may be used to attempt to exclude, inter alia, the following types of otherwise admissible evidence: hearsay evidence, including depositions and documentary records[60] and admissions and confessions;[61] evidence of opinion, including identification evidence;[62] and evidence of an intoximeter reading.[63] Insofar as s 78(1) may be used to exclude evidence obtained by improper or unfair means, it is *not* confined, as is the common law power described in *R v Sang*, to admissions, confessions, and evidence obtained from the accused after the commission of the offence—it extends to any evidence on which the prosecution propose to rely, whenever it was obtained and whether it was obtained from the accused, his premises, or any other source.[64]

'...having regard to all the circumstances...'

In deciding whether or not to exercise the discretion, s 78(1) directs the court to have regard to all the circumstances, including those in which the evidence was obtained. In particular, the court may be invited to take into account any illegality, impropriety, or unfairness by means of which the evidence was obtained, including conduct in breach of the European Convention on Human Rights, or any abuse by the police of their powers under the 1984 Act, and the Codes of Practice issued pursuant to that Act, including those relating to stop and search (Code A), the search of premises and the seizure of property (Code B), detention, treatment, and questioning (Code C), identification (Code D), and audio recording of interviews (Code E).[65] When breaches of an earlier Code are considered, the provisions of the current version may well be relevant to the question of unfairness under s 78, because they reflect current thinking as to what is fair.[66]

---

[58] See generally Ch 4.

[59] [2001] 4 All ER 168, DC at [50]–[61].

[60] *R v O'Loughlin* [1988] 3 All ER 431, CCC.

[61] *R v Mason* [1988] 1 WLR 139, CA.

[62] *R v Nagah* (1990) 92 Cr App R 344, CA. See also *R v Deenik* [1992] Crim LR 578, CA (voice identification).

[63] *McGrath v Field* [1987] RTR 349, DC.

[64] The dictum of Watkins LJ in *R v Mason* [1987] 3 All ER 481 at 484, that 's 78...does no more than restate the power which judges had at common law before the 1984 Act was passed', is best regarded as having been made *per incuriam*.

[65] Even where the evidence in question was obtained by someone other than a police officer (or a person charged with the duty of investigating offences or charging offenders—see the 1984 Act, s 67(9) (see Ch 13)), the principles underlying Code C may be of assistance in considering the discretion to exclude under s 78(1): *R v Smith* (1994) 99 Cr App R 233, CA. Regard may also be had to the guidance set out in Home Office, *Achieving Best Evidence in Criminal Proceedings: Guidance for Vulnerable or Intimidated Witnesses, Including Children* (2007): see *R v Dunphy* (1993) 98 Cr App R 393, CA, a decision on the precursor to the current ABE guidance. See also Keenan et al, 'Interviewing Allegedly Abused Children' [1999] Crim LR 863.

[66] *R v Ward* (1993) 98 Cr App R 337, CA at 340.

'... the fairness of the proceedings...'

Section 78 can only be exercised if in all the circumstances admission of the evidence would have an adverse effect on the fairness of the 'proceedings'. The first use of the word 'proceedings' in s 78(1) suggests that it means 'court proceedings' rather than both the investigative and trial process. Section 78(3), since repealed, which referred to 'proceedings before a magistrates' court' supports such an interpretation.

As to 'fairness', trial judges, as we have seen, already have a duty to ensure that the accused receives a fair trial, in the exercise of which they may exclude any evidence the prejudicial effect of which outweighs its probative value. Section 78(1), however, goes beyond this. Thus although the fact that evidence was obtained improperly or unfairly will not by itself automatically have such an adverse effect on the fairness of the proceedings that the court should not admit it, it is implicit in the wording of the subsection that the circumstances in which the evidence was obtained *may* have such an adverse effect.[67]

It is, of course, impossible to catalogue, precisely or at all, the kinds of impropriety which will be treated as having an adverse effect on the fairness of the proceedings. As we shall see, a breach of the 1984 Act or of the Codes does not mean that any statement made by an accused after such breach will necessarily be excluded—every case has to be determined on its own particular facts.[68] Equally, the fact that evidence has been obtained by conduct which may be typified as 'oppressive' will not automatically result in exclusion, because oppressive conduct, depending on its degree and actual or possible effect, may or may not affect the fairness of admitting particular evidence.[69]

A judge's exercise of her discretion under the subsection can be impugned if it is perverse according to *Wednesbury* principles,[70] ie a decision to which no reasonable trial judge could have come, in which case the Court of Appeal will exercise its own discretion.[71] The Court of Appeal will also interfere if the trial judge exercised his discretion on a wrong basis, eg by adverting to an out-of-date version of a relevant Code of Practice.[72] Circumstances vary infinitely, and for this reason it has been said that it is undesirable to attempt any general guidance on the way in which the discretion should be exercised.[73] However, some such guidance is available from the reported decisions. They show, with a reasonable degree of clarity, that the purpose of s 78(1) is to give effect to the reliability principle.

The reliability principle

Section 78 has spawned much appellate authority and most of it indicates that the section should be taken to have been designed primarily to give effect to the reliability principle.[74]

---

[67] Per Woolf LJ in *Matto v Crown Court at Wolverhampton* [1987] RTR 337.

[68] Per Lord Lane CJ in *R v Parris* (1988) 89 Cr App R 68, CA at 72. See also per Hodgson J in *R v Keenan* [1990] 2 QB 54 at 69.

[69] *R v Chalkley and Jeffries* [1998] 2 All ER 155, CA at 177–8.

[70] *Associated Provincial Picture Houses Ltd v Wednesbury Corpn* [1948] 1 KB 223.

[71] *R v O'Leary* (1988) 87 Cr App R 387 at 391, CA; *R v Christou* [1992] QB 979, CA; *R v Dures* [1997] 2 Cr App R 247, CA; and *R v Khan* [1997] Crim LR 508, CA. See also Tucker J, *per curiam*, in *R v Grannell* (1989) 90 Cr App R 149, CA: the citation of decisions of judges or recorders of the Crown Court, not being High Court judges, is of no assistance to the Court of Appeal in deciding whether a judge has exercised his discretion properly.

[72] See *R v Miller* [1998] Crim LR 209, CA.

[73] Per Hodgson J in *R v Samuel* [1988] QB 615, CA.

[74] For the disparate views of *trial judges* as to how s 78 should be exercised, see Hunter, 'Judicial Discretion: Section 78 in Practice' [1994] Crim LR 558.

The prevailing view is summarized well by Lord Nicholls in *R v Looseley; Attorney General's Reference (No 3 of 2000)*[75] who said that the phrase 'fairness of the proceedings' is 'directed primarily at matters going to fairness in the actual conduct of the trial; for instance the reliability of the evidence and the defendant's ability to test its reliability'.[76] Thus in *R v Cooke*,[77] a rape case, it was said, obiter, that where a sample of hair is not taken in accordance with the relevant statutory provisions but obtained by an assault, and is then used to prepare a DNA profile implicating the accused, the evidence will be admitted on the basis that the means used to obtain the evidence have done nothing to cast doubt on its reliability and strength.[78]

On its wording, however, s 78 does not indicate that it is underpinned by the reliability principle, and for that reason, most probably, some of the authorities, especially the earlier authorities, seem to have been decided in reliance on the disciplinary principle or the rights-based principle.[79] It will be useful, therefore, to consider some of these decisions before turning to the various types of illegality and impropriety that have fallen to be considered under s 78.

The disciplinary principle

There are rare cases in which it has been held that *reliable* evidence could or should have been excluded where the police acted mala fide, deliberately flouting the law or wilfully abusing their powers. An example is *Matto v Crown Court at Wolverhampton*.[80] In that case the accused was convicted of driving with excess alcohol. Police officers, when requesting a specimen of breath on the accused's property, had realized that they were acting illegally. The specimen was positive. The accused was arrested and later provided another positive specimen of breath at the police station. Allowing the appeal, it was held that the officers, having acted mala fide and oppressively, the circumstances were such that if the Crown Court had directed itself properly it could have exercised its discretion to exclude the evidence under s 78.

Another example is *R v Nathaniel*.[81] In that case a DNA profile taken from the appellant's blood in relation to charges of raping A and B, of which he was acquitted, was not destroyed in accordance with s 64 of the 1984 Act, but formed the main prosecution evidence on a charge of raping C. It was held that the evidence should have been excluded. The accused was misled, in consenting to give the blood sample, by statements and promises which were not honoured. He was told that it was required for the purposes of the case involving A and B; that it would be destroyed if he was prosecuted in relation to A and B and acquitted; and that if he refused without good cause to give the sample, the jury, in any proceedings against him for the rape of A and B, could draw inferences from his refusal.[82] Similarly, in *R v*

---

[75] [2001] 1 WLR 2060, HL.

[76] Lord Hutton, in *Attorney General's Reference (No 3 of 1999)* [2001] 1 All ER 577, HL at 590, was of the obiter view that in cases involving the commission of a very grave crime, the interests of the victim and the public must be considered, as well as the interests of the accused. However, balancing exercises of this kind have found little favour in subsequent authorities, except in the context of police undercover operations, considered in this chapter under **Discretion, Criminal cases: section 78 of the Police and Criminal Evidence Act 1984, Entrapment and undercover operations.**

[77] [1995] 1 Cr App R 318, CA.

[78] See also *Attorney General's Reference (No 3 of 1999)* [2001] 1 All ER 577, HL, another rape case in which there was no question as to the reliability of the DNA evidence, the admissibility of which was in dispute.

[79] See Ormerod and Birch, 'The Evolution of the Discretionary Exclusion of Evidence' [2004] Crim LR 767 at 779.

[80] [1987] RTR 337.

[81] [1995] 2 Cr App R 565, CA.

[82] See now the 1984 Act, s 64(3B).

Alladice,[83] in which, despite improper denial of the right of access to a solicitor under s 58 of the 1984 Act, it was held that a confession should not be excluded, it was also held that if the police had acted in bad faith, the court would have had little difficulty in ruling any confession inadmissible. The Court of Appeal has also deplored police ignorance of the provisions of the Codes[84] and lamented deliberate, cynical, and flagrant breaches of such provisions.[85]

However, despite these decisions and dicta, it seems clear that although deliberate or wilful misconduct on the part of the police may make exclusion more likely, it should not by itself be used as the basis for exclusion. Thus it has been said that the court cannot exclude simply as a mark of its disapproval of the way in which evidence was obtained[86] or simply in order to punish the police for failure to observe the Codes of Practice.[87] Watkins LJ put the matter very clearly in *R v Mason*:[88] the *effect* of excluding relevant evidence which has been obtained improperly or unfairly may be to discourage the police from obtaining evidence in such a way, but a decision to exclude under s 78 should not be taken *in order to* discipline or punish the police. However, evidence should be excluded where deliberate misconduct has rendered evidence unreliable, as *R v Mason* itself illustrates. A confession had been made, after the police had practised a deceit on the accused and his solicitor by alleging that they had fingerprint evidence which they did not in fact have. It was held that the trial judge should have excluded the evidence under s 78.[89] It does not follow from *R v Mason*, of course, that s 78 can be used only in the case of deliberate misconduct: if the reliability of the evidence has been impaired by misconduct, the discretion may be exercised on this basis whether the misconduct was wilful or merely ignorant.

The rights-based principle

There are very rare instances of exclusion under s 78 *simply* on the basis of a substantial breach of a suspect's rights, ie where the breach has had no effect on the reliability of the evidence obtained.[90] The Court of Appeal has also used language that might suggest that s 78 is underpinned by the rights-based principle, for example its description of the right to legal advice under s 58 of the 1984 Act as 'one of the most important and fundamental rights of a citizen'[91] and references to 'significant and substantial breaches' of Code C.[92] This language is apt to mislead: it is very clear from the authorities that ultimately what matters is not how important or significant any particular provision is thought to be, but the effect, if any, of its breach on the fairness of the trial. This is illustrated well by cases involving breaches of s 58 of the 1984 Act.

[83] (1988) 87 Cr App R 380, CA, considered more fully in this chapter under **Discretion, Criminal cases: section 78 of the Police and Criminal Evidence Act 1984, The rights-based principle**.

[84] See per Hodgson J in *R v Keenan* [1989] 3 All ER 598, CA at 601.

[85] See per Lord Lane CJ in *R v Canale* [1990] 2 All ER 187, CA at 190 and 192.

[86] Per Auld LJ in *R v Chalkley and Jeffries* [1998] 2 All ER 155, CA at 178–80.

[87] Per Lord Lane CJ in *R v Delaney* (1988) 88 Cr App R 338, CA at 341.

[88] [1988] 1 WLR 139, CA.

[89] See also *R v Alladice* (1988) 87 Cr App R 380, CA at n 94 and *R v Canale* [1990] Crim LR 329, CA at n 114; and cf *R v Christou* [1992] QB 979, CA at n 169.

[90] See *DPP v Goodwin* [1991] RTR 303, in the case of evidence of a positive breath specimen obtained following an unlawful arrest.

[91] Per Hodgson J in *R v Samuel* [1988] 2 All ER 135, CA. Cf *Brennan v UK* (2002) 34 EHRR 18, ECHR (the right to consult with a lawyer *in private* is part of the basic requirements of a fair trial and follows from Art 6(3)(c) of the European Convention on Human Rights) and *Salduz v Turkey* (2008) 49 EHRR 421, ECHR (it is of fundamental importance to provide access to a lawyer where the person in custody is a minor).

[92] *R v Keenan* [1990] 2 QB 54, CA.

It has been held that significant and substantial breaches of s 58 (or the provisions of Code C) will, prima facie, have an adverse effect on the fairness of the proceedings.[93] Breach of the section, however, is no guarantee of the exclusion of any statement made thereafter. In *R v Alladice*,[94] for example, it was held that if the trial judge had considered s 78, he would not have been obliged to exclude the confession, because the circumstances showed that the accused was well able to cope with the interviews, understood the cautions that he had been given, at times exercising his right to silence, and was aware of his rights, so that, had the solicitor been present, his advice would have added nothing to the knowledge of his rights which the accused already had.[95] In *R v Parris*,[96] on the other hand, another case involving breach of s 58, it was held that evidence of a confession should have been excluded because, had a solicitor been present, the accused would probably have accepted his advice to remain silent. Furthermore, the solicitor could have given evidence on whether the police had fabricated the confession; alternatively, his presence would have discouraged any such fabrication.[97]

Breaches of Code B (search of premises)

The reliability principle serves to explain the admission in evidence of the fruits of an improper search in *R v Stewart*,[98] where, following an entry involving a number of breaches of Code B, the accused was found in possession of apparatus to divert the gas and electricity supplies so as to bypass the meters. The outcome was the same in *R v Sanghera*[99] where, a search having been conducted in breach of the Code without written consent, there was no issue as to the reliability of the evidence as to what had been discovered. However, it should be otherwise if the means used to obtain the evidence could have affected its quality, for example a case in which the accused, following a search of his premises during which he was improperly kept out of the way, claims that the property found was 'planted'.[100] Equally, although officers are entitled to delay taking a suspect to a police station in order that a search may be conducted with his assistance, if they abuse that entitlement to ask questions, beyond those necessary to the search, on matters which properly ought to be asked under the rules of Code C applying at a police station, the answers may be excluded on the grounds of unfairness.[101]

Breaches of Code C (detention, treatment, and questioning)

It is clear that the outcome, in the case of breaches of Code C, as in all cases, depends upon the precise facts. In *R v Pall*[102] it was said that the absence of a caution was bound to be significant

[93] Per Saville J in *R v Walsh* (1989) 91 Cr App R 161, CA at 163. However, in the case of drink-driving offences, the public interest requires that the obtaining of specimens should not be delayed to any significant extent to enable a suspect to take legal advice: *Kennedy v DPP* [2003] Crim LR 120, DC. See also *Campbell v DPP* [2003] Crim LR 118, DC; *Kirkup v DPP* [2004] Crim LR 230, DC; and *Whitley v DPP* [2003] EWHC 2512 (Admin). Similarly, in the case of juveniles, there is no reason to delay the obtaining of specimens in order for an 'appropriate adult' to be present: *DPP v Evans* [2003] Crim LR 338, DC.

[94] (1988) 87 Cr App R 380, CA.

[95] See also, to similar effect, *R v Dunford* (1990) 91 Cr App R 150, CA.

[96] (1988) 89 Cr App R 68, CA. See also *R v Walsh* (1989) 91 Cr App R 161.

[97] This argument was not employed in *R v Alladice* (1988) 87 Cr App R 380, CA, where fabrication was also alleged.

[98] [1995] Crim LR 500, CA. See also *R v McCarthy* [1996] Crim LR 818, CA.

[99] [2001] 1 Cr App R 299, CA.

[100] But cf *R v Wright* [1994] Crim LR 55, CA, and see also *R v Khan* [1997] Crim LR 508, CA.

[101] *R v Khan* [1993] Crim LR 54, CA, applied in *R v Raphaie* [1996] Crim LR 812, CA.

[102] (1991) 156 JP 424, CA.

in most circumstances, and in *R v Nelson and Rose*[103] it was held that a failure to caution should have led to the exclusion of the whole of an interview. However, in *R v Hoyte*[104] a confession was admitted, despite a failure to caution, on the basis that the police had acted in good faith and in the particular circumstances there could have been no unfairness.[105] Similarly in *R v Gill*[106] it was held that lies told during an Inland Revenue investigation of tax fraud were admissible, despite a failure to caution. Clarke LJ said that the principal purpose of the caution was to ensure, so far as possible, that interviewees do not make admissions unless they wish to do so and are aware of the consequences, and not to prevent interviewees from telling lies. Although lies may be excluded where there has been a failure to caution, each case depends on its own facts. On the facts, the Revenue had not acted in bad faith and the appellants were aware that criminal proceedings were in prospect and must have known that they were not obliged to answer the questions.[107] In *R v Aspinal*[108] the accused, a schizophrenic, was interviewed, about 13 hours after his arrest, without an 'appropriate adult', in breach of what is now para 11.15 of Code C, and without a solicitor. It was held that an accused of this kind may not be able to judge for himself what is in his best interests, which may put him at a considerable disadvantage, not least because the record of the interview may not seem unreliable to a jury. However, in appropriate circumstances the confession of a mentally disordered accused may be properly admitted notwithstanding that it was made in breach of para 11.15.[109]

In *R v Konscol*[110] the trial judge admitted evidence of an interview with K, containing lies, conducted by a Belgian customs officer. There was no dispute that K had said what was recorded, and that the interview was conducted fairly according to Belgian law, but K was neither cautioned nor advised that he could have a lawyer present. The Court of Appeal dismissed the appeal and—unhelpfully—declined to lay down guidelines as to when a court should admit a statement made overseas according to rules which did not coincide with the provisions of the 1984 Act.[111] The obvious guideline, it is submitted, is that however fair, according to foreign law, the means by which the evidence was obtained, the outcome should be determined by reference to the effect of those means on the fairness of the domestic criminal proceedings.

In *R v Keenan*[112] records of an interview with the accused were compiled in plain breach of Code C: the record was not made during the course of the interview; the reason for not completing it at that time was not recorded in the officer's pocket book; and the accused was not given the opportunity to read it and to sign it as correct or to indicate the respects in which he considered it inaccurate. The accused's defence, unknown to the trial judge at the time when the submission on admissibility was made, was that the interview had been fabricated. The judge,

[103] [1998] 2 Cr App R 399, CA.

[104] [1994] Crim LR 215, CA.

[105] See also *R v Ibrahim* [2008] 2 Cr App R 311, concerning the application of s 78 to 'safety interviews' under the Terrorism Act 2008, Sch 8, where it was said that much will turn on the nature of the warning or caution given, if any.

[106] [2004] 1 WLR 49, CA.

[107] See also *R v Senior* [2004] 3 All ER 9, CA, applied in *R v Rehman* [2007] Crim LR 101, CA (questioning by customs officers to establish ownership of a suspicious baggage, prior to administering a caution) and *R v Devani* [2008] 1 Cr App R 65 (the questioning of a suspect, who was a solicitor, without a caution, but in the presence of her principal).

[108] [1999] Crim LR 741, CA.

[109] See *R v Law-Thompson* [1997] Crim LR 674, CA.

[110] [1993] Crim LR 950.

[111] See also *R v Quinn* [1990] Crim LR 581, CA and *R v McNab* [2002] Crim LR 129, CA.

[112] [1990] 2 QB 54, CA.

ruling that any unfairness to the accused could be cured by the accused going into the witness box and giving his version of the interview, admitted the evidence. On appeal, it was held that the relevant provisions of Code C are designed to make it difficult for detained persons to make unfounded allegations against the police which might otherwise appear credible and to provide safeguards against the police inaccurately recording or inventing the words used in questioning a detained person. Where there have been significant and substantial breaches of the 'verballing' provisions, evidence so obtained should be excluded, because if the other evidence in the case is strong, then it may make no difference to the eventual result if the evidence in question is excluded, and if the other evidence is weak or non-existent, that is just the situation where the protection of the rules is most needed. It was wrong to assume that any unfairness could be cured by the accused going into the witness box: if he intended not to testify if the evidence was excluded, then its admission unfairly robbed him of his right to remain silent; if the defence case was to be (as it turned out to be) that the evidence was concocted, then its admission forced the accused to give evidence and also, by attacking the police, to put his character in issue; and if the defence was to be that the interview was inaccurately recorded, it placed the accused at a substantial disadvantage because he had been given no contemporaneous opportunity to correct any inaccuracies. For these reasons, the conviction was quashed.[113]

In *R v Canale*[114] the way in which records of two interviews with the accused were obtained involved breaches very similar to those which occurred in *R v Keenan*. In this case, however, at two subsequent and contemporaneously recorded interviews, the accused repeated admissions allegedly made in the first two interviews. On the *voir dire* and in evidence the accused admitted that he had made the admissions but said that they were untrue and that the police had induced him to make them by a trick. The Court of Appeal held that by reason of the flagrant and cynical breaches of the Code, the judge was deprived of the very evidence which would have enabled him to reach a more certain conclusion on the question of admissibility and, had he ruled in favour of admission, the jury would have been deprived of the evidence necessary to decide the truth of the accused's denial of the offence. The initial breaches affected the whole series of alleged admissions, all of which should have been excluded.[115]

Breaches of Code D (identification)

Many of the reported decisions under s 78 have involved breaches of Code D (identification). Under para 3.12 of Code D, whenever (i) a witness has identified or purported to identify a suspect; or (ii) there is a witness available who expresses an ability to identify the suspect, or there is a reasonable chance of the witness being able to do so, and the suspect disputes the identification, an identification procedure shall be held, ie a video identification, an identification parade, or a group identification. The exception is where an identification procedure is not practicable or it would serve no useful purpose, for example when it is not disputed that the suspect is already well known to the witness.[116] Breach of para 3.12 will not

---

[113] See also *R v Williams* [2012] EWCA Crim 264.

[114] [1990] 2 All ER 187, CA.

[115] See also *R v Absolam* (1988) 88 Cr App R 332, CA, and *R v Sparks* [1991] Crim LR 128, CA; and cf *R v Langiert* [1991] Crim LR 777, CA (failure to record the reason for not making a contemporaneous record), and *R v Rajakuruna* [1991] Crim LR 458, CA (failure to inform a person not under arrest that he is not obliged to remain with the officer).

[116] For the issues that arise where a suspect admits his presence at the scene of the offence, but denies committing the offence, see Roberts, 'Questions of "Who was there?" and "Who did what?": The Application of Code D in Cases of Dispute as to Participation but not Presence' [2003] Crim LR 709.

necessarily result in the exclusion of the other evidence of identification, of which there may be an abundance.[117] The critical issue is the impact of the breach on the fairness of the trial.[118] Thus in *R v Samms*,[119] where it was not shown that it was impracticable to hold a parade (or group identification),[120] it was held that it would be unfair to admit the evidence of identification of the suspect by confrontation because the confrontation that occurred partook of the dangers sought to be prevented by a parade (or group identification).[121] It will be unfair to make use of identification evidence obtained by a video identification procedure which uses images of persons bearing an insufficient resemblance to the accused.[122] It will also be unfair to use the CCTV recognition evidence of an officer where there has been a wholesale breach of Code D, involving another officer's improper indication as to the suspect's identity and a failure to keep a proper record of the recognition.[123] On the other hand, in *R v Grannell*[124] it was held that no unfairness arose from the failure, in breach of what is now para 3.17 of the Code, to explain to the suspect prior to an identification procedure such matters as the purpose of the identification and the procedures for holding it; and in *R v Ryan*[125] it was held that a clear breach of what is now para 3.11 of the Code—an officer involved with the investigation of the case took part in the identification procedures—had caused no prejudice to the accused.[126]

Where a breach of Code D has been established but the judge has rejected an application to exclude the evidence in question, he should explain to the jury that there has been a breach and how it has arisen and invite them to consider the possible effects of the breach. For example, in the case of an improper failure to hold an identification parade, the jury should ordinarily be told that a parade enables a suspect to put the reliability of the identification to the test, that he has lost the benefit of that safeguard, and that they should take account of that fact in their assessment of the whole case, giving it such weight as they think fair. However,

---

[117] See *R v McEvoy* [1997] Crim LR 887, CA, a decision under an earlier version of para 3.12.

[118] This remains the case where the identification is not strictly governed by Code D at all (see *R v Hickin* [1996] Crim LR 584, CA) or where the evidence of identification has come into existence abroad as a result of arrangements made by a foreign police force (see *R v Quinn* [1990] Crim LR 581, CA).

[119] [1991] Crim LR 197, CC.

[120] See also *R v Johnson* [1996] Crim LR 504, CA (confrontation by video).

[121] See now para 3.23, Code D. See also *R v Martin and Nicholls* [1994] Crim LR 218, CA (evidence of informal identification by young witnesses a very long time after the offence and in unsatisfactory conditions outside the court while the accused and witnesses were awaiting allocation of the case to a court). Cf *R v Tiplady* [1995] Crim LR 651, CA (a group identification in the foyer of a magistrates' court where T had been bailed to attend). It was held that the venue was not inappropriate and *Martin and Nicholls* was distinguished on the basis that whereas in that case there were striking limitations on the choice open to the identifying witnesses (the accused wore 'funky dreads'), in *Tiplady* at any one time between 20 and 30 people had been present, most of them in T's age group. Cf also *R v Quinn* [1990] Crim LR 581, CA: evidence of an informal identification as a result of a chance meeting would be admissible. See also *R v Oscar* [1991] Crim LR 778, CA, and *R v Rogers* [1993] Crim LR 386, CA.

[122] See *R v Marcus* [2005] Crim LR 384, CA. See also *R v Preddie* [2011] EWCA Crim 312 (improper street identification that rendered valueless a later video identification procedure).

[123] See *R v Deakin* [2012] EWCA Crim 2637 and paras 3.35 and 3.36 of Code D.

[124] (1989) 90 Cr App R 149, CA.

[125] [1992] Crim LR 187, CA. See also *R v Jones (Terence)* [1992] Crim LR 365, CA, and *R v Khan* [1997] Crim LR 584, CA; and cf *R v Gall* (1989) 90 Cr App R 64, CA, and *R v Finley* [1993] Crim LR 50, CA.

[126] See also, *sed quaere, Marsh v DPP* [2007] Crim LR 163 (failure, in breach of para 3.1(b), to make a record of a witness's description of a suspect *before* participation in any identification procedure), and *R v Cole* [2013] EWCA Crim 1149.

failure to direct the jury about a breach of Code D will not necessarily infringe an accused's right to a fair trial or render a conviction unsafe.[127]

Covert recording and filming

In *R v Bailey*[128] two co-accused, having exercised their right to silence when interviewed, were charged and placed in the same bugged cell by officers who, in order to lull them into a false sense of security, pretended that they had been forced to put them in the same cell by an uncooperative custody officer. Evidence of incriminating conversations obtained by this subterfuge was held to be admissible. In *R v King*[129] evidence of incriminating conversations was obtained when the accused, after their arrest, were put in a police vehicle fitted with recording equipment. The evidence was held to be admissible: the officers did not engage the accused in conversation or trick them into speaking and although the recording took place before interview under caution, that placed the accused at no greater disadvantage than if they had been covertly recorded after such an interview.

In *R v Khan (Sultan)*[130] the House of Lords held that the fact that evidence has been obtained in circumstances which amount to a breach of Art 8 of the European Convention on Human Rights (the right to respect for private life, home, and correspondence) may be relevant to exercise of the s 78 power, but the significance of the breach turns on its effect on the fairness of the proceedings. In that case, the police had made a recording of an incriminating conversation relating to the importation of heroin, by means of an electronic surveillance device attached to a house without the knowledge or consent of the owner or occupier. It was held that the judge had been entitled to conclude that the circumstances in which the evidence had been obtained, even if they constituted a breach of Art 8, were not such as to require exclusion of the evidence.[131] The European Court of Human Rights subsequently held that although the recording was obtained in breach of Art 8, its use at the trial did not conflict with the right to a fair hearing under Art 6, because there was no risk of the recording being unreliable, the accused had the opportunity to challenge its admissibility, and if its admission would have given rise to substantive unfairness, the domestic court could have excluded it under s 78.[132] The European Court has reached similar conclusions in relation to evidence obtained in breach of Art 8 by the unlawful installation of a listening device in the accused's home[133] and, in *PG and JH v United Kingdom*,[134] by the unlawful use of covert listening devices in police cells.[135] In *PG and JH v United Kingdom*, where the recordings did not contain any incriminating statements, but were used at trial as a control to identify the voices of the accused on other tapes, it was held that they could be regarded as akin to

---

[127] See *R v Forbes* [2001] 2 WLR 1, HL, applied in *R v Gojra* [2010] EWCA Crim 1939.

[128] [1993] 3 All ER 513, CA.

[129] [2012] EWCA Crim 805.

[130] [1997] AC 558.

[131] See also *R v Plunkett* [2013] 2 Cr App R 10, CA (covert recordings authorized under the Regulation of Investigatory Powers Act 2000).

[132] *Khan v United Kingdom* (2001) 31 EHRR 1016.

[133] *Chalkley v United Kingdom* [2003] Crim LR 51.

[134] [2002] Crim LR 308.

[135] See also *R v Mason* [2002] 2 Cr App R 628, CA; and *R v Button* [2005] Crim LR 571, where the 'startling proposition' that the court is bound to exclude any evidence obtained in breach of Art 8 because otherwise it would be acting unlawfully was rejected on the basis that any breach of Art 8 is subsumed by the Art 6 duty to ensure a fair trial.

blood, hair, or other physical or objective specimens used in forensic analysis and to which the privilege against self-incrimination does not apply. In that case the European Court also reiterated that:

> Whilst Article 6 guarantees the right to a fair hearing, it does not lay down any rules on the admissibility of evidence as such, which is therefore primarily a matter for regulation under national law...It is not the role of the court to determine, as a matter of principle whether particular types of evidence, for example unlawfully obtained evidence—may be admissible or, indeed, whether the applicant was guilty or not. The question which must be answered is whether the proceedings as a whole, including the way in which the evidence was obtained, were fair.[136]

The European Court has followed the same approach in relation to covert filming. In *Perry v United Kingdom*,[137] the applicant having failed to attend identification parades, the police, infringing official guidelines, filmed him covertly for the purposes of a video identification of which neither he nor his solicitor was aware. It was held that the application was manifestly ill-founded on the grounds that the use of evidence obtained without a proper legal basis or through unlawful means will not generally contravene Art 6(1) so long as proper procedural safeguards are in place and the source of the material is not tainted.[138]

In *R v P*[139] it was argued that although telephone intercept evidence was properly obtained in accordance with the Convention and the law of a country overseas, its use in an English trial was contrary to Art 6 and the policy of the English law. Rejecting this argument, the House of Lords held that the fair use of intercept evidence at a trial is not a breach of Art 6, that even if it was unlawfully obtained, the criterion of fairness in Art 6 is the criterion to be applied by the judge under s 78, and that there is no principle of exclusion of intercept evidence independently of the statutory provisions.[140] The House has also held that where intercept evidence is inadmissible pursuant to statutory provisions, there is no rule prohibiting the use of the intercepts at police interviews and, subject to s 78, such use will not render the interview evidence inadmissible, although the interview transcript will need to be edited to remove any direct or indirect references to the intercept.[141]

Entrapment and undercover operations

R v Looseley and *Attorney General's Reference (No 3 of 2000)*[142] are the leading authorities on the circumstances in which criminal proceedings should be stayed, or evidence excluded, on the grounds of entrapment.[143] Hearing both appeals together, the House of Lords held as follows:

---

[136] For a fuller examination of approaches to exclusion of evidence obtained in breach of Art 8, see Ormerod, 'ECHR and the Exclusion of Evidence: Trial Remedies for Article 8 Breaches' [2003] Crim LR 61. See also Mahoney, 'Abolition of New Zealand's Prima Facie Exclusionary Rule' [2003] Crim LR 607.

[137] [2003] Crim LR 281.

[138] See also *R v Loveridge* [2001] 2 Cr App R 591, CA, where the accused were covertly filmed in court, which was both unlawful and in breach of Art 8, to enable comparison with pictures of the crime as recorded on a CCTV film; *R v Marriner* [2002] EWCA Crim 2855, where the accused were covertly recorded on video and tape by undercover journalists; and *R v Rosenberg* [2006] Crim LR 540, CA, where the accused and the police were aware of surveillance by the accused's neighbour that had been neither initiated nor encouraged by the police.

[139] [2002] 1 AC 46, HL.

[140] See the Regulation of Investigatory Powers Act 2000.

[141] *R v Sargent* [2003] 1 AC 347, HL.

[142] [2001] 1 WLR 2060, HL.

[143] See Ashworth, 'Redrawing the Boundaries of Entrapment' [2002] Crim LR 161.

1. Entrapment is not a substantive defence, but where an accused can show entrapment the court may stay the proceedings as an abuse of the court's process or it may exclude evidence under s 78.

2. As a matter of principle, a stay of the proceedings rather than exclusion of evidence should normally be regarded as the appropriate response. A prosecution founded on entrapment would be an abuse of the court's process. Police conduct which brings about state-created crime is unacceptable and improper and to prosecute in such circumstances would be an affront to the public conscience.[144]

3. In deciding whether conduct amounts to state-created crime, the existence or absence of a predisposition on the part of the accused to commit the crime is not the criterion by which the acceptability of police conduct is to be decided, because it does not make acceptable what would otherwise be unacceptable conduct on the part of the police or negative misuse of state power.[145]

4. A useful guide is to consider whether the police did no more than present the accused with an unexceptional opportunity to commit a crime. The yardstick for these purposes is, in general, whether the police conduct preceding the commission of the offence was no more than might have been expected from others in the circumstances. 'The State can justify the use of entrapment techniques to induce the commission of an offence only when the inducement is consistent with the ordinary temptations and stratagems that are likely to be encountered in the course of criminal activity...But once the State goes beyond the ordinary, it is likely to increase the incidence of crime by artificial means.'[146] Of its nature, the technique of providing an opportunity to commit a crime is intrusive. The greater the degree of intrusiveness, the more closely will the courts scrutinize the reason for using it.

5. Usually, a most important factor, but not necessarily decisive, will be whether an officer can be said to have caused the commission of the offence, rather than merely providing an opportunity for the accused to commit it with an officer rather than in secrecy with someone else. A good example of the latter situation is furnished by *Nottingham City Council v Amin*[147] where a taxi driver who was not licensed to ply for hire in a particular district, and was flagged down by plain-clothes officers in that district, took them to their stated destination. Lord Bingham CJ said:[148]

> it has been regarded as unobjectionable if a law enforcement officer gives a defendant an opportunity to break the law, of which the defendant freely takes advantage, in circumstances where it appears that the defendant would have behaved in the same way if the opportunity had been offered by anyone else,

---

[144] The possibility of a stay on the basis of entrapment by non-state agents, eg journalists, seems to be remote: see *Re Saluja* [2007] 2 All ER 905, QBD at [81].

[145] Cf *R v Moon* [2004] All ER (D) 167 (Nov), CA, where the absence of predisposition on the part of M to deal with or supply heroin was regarded as a critical factor in concluding that a test purchase by an undercover officer, who claimed that she was suffering from heroin withdrawal symptoms, was an abuse of process.

[146] Per McHugh J in *Ridgeway v The Queen* (1995) 184 CLR 19 at 92.

[147] [2000] 1 WLR 1071, DC. See also *East Riding of Yorkshire Council v Dearlove* [2012] EWHC 278, DC.

[148] At 1076–7.

by which the Lord Chief Justice meant, in that case, that the officers behaved like ordinary members of the public in flagging the taxi down. They did not, for example, wave £50 notes or pretend to be in distress. The test of whether a police officer acted like an ordinary member of the public works well and is likely to be decisive in many cases of regulatory offences committed with ordinary members of the public, such as selling liquor without a licence, but ordinary members of the public do not become involved in large-scale drug dealing, conspiracy to rob, or hiring assassins. The appropriate standards of behaviour in such cases are more problematic; and even in the case of offences committed with ordinary members of the public, other factors may require a purely causal test to be modified.

6. The causal question cannot be answered by a mechanical application of a distinction between 'active' and 'passive' conduct on the part of the undercover policeman. For example, drug dealers can be expected to show some wariness about dealing with a stranger and therefore some protective colour in dress or manner as well as a certain degree of persistence may be necessary.[149] Equally, undercover officers who infiltrate conspiracies to murder, rob, or commit terrorist offences could hardly remain concealed unless they showed some enthusiasm for the enterprise. A good deal of active behaviour may therefore be acceptable without crossing the boundary between causing the offence to be committed and providing an opportunity for the accused to commit it.

7. Ultimately the overall consideration is always whether the conduct of the police was so seriously improper as to bring the administration of justice into disrepute. Other formulations substantially to the same effect are: a prosecution which would affront the public conscience[150] or conviction and punishment which would be deeply offensive to ordinary notions of fairness.[151] In applying these formulations, the court has regard to all the circumstances of the case. One cannot isolate any single factor or devise any formula that will always produce the correct answer. There are a cluster of relevant factors but their relevant weight and importance depends on the particular facts of the case. The following are of particular relevance.

(a) The nature of the offence. The use of proactive techniques is more appropriate in the case of some offences, for example dealing in unlawful substances, offences with no immediate victim, such as bribery, offences which victims are reluctant to report, and conspiracies. The secrecy and difficulty of detection, and the manner in which the criminal activity is carried on, are relevant considerations. However, the fact that the offence is a serious one is not in itself a sufficient ground for the police to ignore the provisions of the Undercover Operations Code of Practice (issued jointly by all UK police authorities and HM Customs and Excise in response to the Human Rights Act 1998) or for the courts to condone their actions by allowing the prosecution to proceed.[152]

---

[149] See, eg, *R v Jones* [2010] 2 Cr App R 69, a case of incitement to produce cannabis, and *R v Moore* [2013] EWCA Crim 85.

[150] Per Lord Steyn in *R v Latif* [1996] 1 WLR 104, HL at 112.

[151] Per Lord Bingham in *Nottingham City Council v Amin* [2000] 1 WLR 1071, DC at 1076.

[152] For an example of an undercover officer going far beyond his authority, see *R v Barkshire* [2011] EWCA Crim 1885.

(b) The reason for the particular police operation and supervision. As to the former, the police must act in good faith. Having reasonable grounds for suspicion is one way good faith may be established. It is not normally considered a legitimate use of police power to provide people not suspected of any criminal activity with the opportunity to commit crimes.[153] However, having grounds for suspicion of a particular individual is not always essential. The police may, in the course of a bona fide investigation into suspected criminality, provide an opportunity for the commission of an offence which is taken by someone to whom no suspicion previously attached, as in *Williams v DPP*.[154] This can happen when a human or inanimate decoy is used in the course of the detection of crime which has been prevalent in a particular place. Sometimes, random testing may be the only way of policing a particular trading activity. As to supervision, to allow officers or controlled informers to undertake entrapment activities unsupervised carries great danger, not only that they will try to improve their performances in court, but of oppression, extortion, and corruption. The need for reasonable suspicion and proper supervision are both stressed in the Undercover Operations Code of Practice.

(c) The nature and extent of police participation in the crime. The greater the inducement held out by the police, and the more forceful or persistent their overtures, the more readily may a court conclude that they overstepped the boundary.[155] In assessing the weight to be attached to the police inducement, regard is to be had to the accused's circumstances, including his vulnerability. It will not normally be regarded as objectionable for the police to behave as would an ordinary customer of a trade, whether lawful or unlawful, being carried on by the accused.

(d) The accused's criminal record. This is unlikely to be relevant unless it can be linked to other factors grounding reasonable suspicion that he is engaged in criminal activity.

8. A decision on whether to stay the proceedings is distinct from a decision on the fairness of admitting evidence.[156] Different tests are applicable to these two decisions. If an application under s 78 is in substance a belated application for a stay, it should be treated as such and decided according to the principles appropriate to the grant of a stay. If the court is not satisfied that a stay should be granted, the question under s 78 is not whether the proceedings should have been brought but, as Potter LJ held in *R v Shannon*:[157]

> It is whether the fairness of the proceedings will be adversely affected by admitting the evidence of the agent provocateur or evidence which is available as the result of his action or activities. So, for instance, if there is good reason to question the credibility of evidence given by an agent provocateur, or which casts doubt on the reliability of other evidence procured by

---

[153] See, eg, *Ramanauskas v Lithuania* [2008] Crim LR 639, where an officer acted on mere rumours about a prosecutor's openness to bribery.

[154] [1993] 3 All ER 365. See at n 167.

[155] See also *R v M* [2011] EWCA Crim 648 at [18]: in the absence of persuasion or pressure or the offer of a significant inducement, it will not generally amount to an abuse of process for an officer to so insinuate himself into the confidence of the accused as to offer him an opportunity to commit a crime.

[156] Citing *R v Chalkley* [1998] 2 Cr App R 79, CA at 105.

[157] [2001] 1 WLR 51, CA at 68.

or resulting from his actions, and that question is not susceptible of being properly or fairly resolved in the course of the proceedings from available, admissible and 'untainted' evidence, then the judge may readily conclude that such evidence should be excluded.

9. Neither s 78 nor the power to stay proceedings has been modified by Article 6 of the European Convention on Human Rights and the jurisprudence of the European Court of Human Rights. There is no appreciable difference between the requirements of Art 6, or the Strasbourg jurisprudence on Art 6, and the English law. Nor is there anything in *Teixeira de Castro v Portugal*[158] which suggests any difference from the current English approach to entrapment.

In *R v Smurthwaite and Gill*[159] the Court of Appeal considered the application of s 78(1) to evidence obtained as a result of police undercover operations. It was held that the relevant factors include:

1. whether the undercover officer was acting as an agent provocateur, ie enticing the accused to commit an offence he would not otherwise have committed;

2. the nature of any entrapment;

3. whether the evidence consists of admissions to a completed offence or relates to the actual commission of an offence;

4. how active or passive the officer's role was in obtaining the evidence;

5. whether there is an unassailable record of what occurred or whether it is strongly corroborated; and

6. whether the officer abused his role to ask questions which ought properly to have been asked as a police officer and in accordance with the Codes.[160]

Both *Smurthwaite* and *Gill* were trials for soliciting to murder. In each case the person solicited was an undercover police officer posing as a contract killer and the prosecution case depended upon secret tape recordings of meetings held between the undercover officer and the accused. In S's case, the Court of Appeal was not persuaded that the officer was an agent provocateur. There was an element of entrapment and a trick. However, the tapes recorded not admissions about some previous offence but the actual offence being committed; they showed that S made the running and that the officer had taken a minimal role in the planning and had used no persuasion towards S; they were an accurate and unchallenged record; and the officer had not abused his role to ask questions which ought properly to have been asked as a police officer. In these circumstances, the judge's decision not to exclude the evidence was upheld. The outcome was the same in G's case: the facts were very similar and although the first meeting between G and the officer was not recorded and there was a stark conflict of evidence as to what was said at that meeting, the existence of a total record was only one factor, and both the contents of the subsequent taped conversations and

---

[158] (1998) 28 EHRR 101.

[159] [1994] 1 All ER 898, CA.

[160] The same factors also apply in the case of evidence obtained by undercover journalists acting on their own initiative and not on police instructions: *R v Shannon* [2001] 1 WLR 51, CA and *Shannon v UK* [2005] Crim LR 133, ECHR. See also Hofmeyr, 'The Problem of Private Entrapment' [2006] Crim LR 319. As to the sixth factor, see also *R v Christou* [1992] QB 979, CA, and *R v Bryce* [1992] 4 All ER 567, CA.

statements made by G in her formal police interviews supported the officer's account of the first meeting.[161]

R v Governor of Pentonville Prison, ex p Chinoy[162] concerned the setting up of a bank account to facilitate the laundering of money alleged to be the proceeds of drug trafficking. The Divisional Court held that the fact of entrapment was one of the circumstances which should be taken into account when carrying out the balancing exercise under s 78(1), but concluded that the circumstances did not require the exclusion of the evidence. It was held that the detection and proof of certain types of criminal activity may necessitate the employment of underhand and even unlawful means. On the facts, although the evidence was obtained by means which were criminal in France and, according to French law, in breach of the European Convention on Human Rights, there was no breach of English law and the means employed by the undercover agents were appropriate to the situation they were investigating and did not require the exclusion of the evidence they obtained. In *R v Latif*[163] S was convicted of being knowingly concerned in the importation of drugs which had been brought into the country by an undercover customs officer. Although S had been lured into England by the deceit of an informer, and both he and the undercover officer had possibly committed the offence of possessing heroin in Pakistan, the House of Lords upheld the judge's refusal to either stay the proceedings or exclude the informer's evidence under s 78.[164]

An application under s 78 will not succeed where a police officer gives an accused an opportunity to break the law, of which the accused freely takes advantage, in circumstances in which the accused would have behaved in the same way if the opportunity had been offered by anyone else. An example is *DPP v Marshall*,[165] where, on a charge of selling alcohol without a licence, evidence was received of purchases made by plain clothes officers. The same approach was adopted in *Ealing London Borough v Woolworths plc*,[166] in which it was held that, on a charge under s 11(1) of the Video Recordings Act 1984, justices were in error in excluding evidence that a boy aged 11, acting under instructions of officers of the Trading Standards Department, had entered the store and purchased an 18-category video film. In *Williams v DPP*,[167] the trick, based on the expectation that someone might act dishonestly, was to leave in a busy street an insecure van containing an apparently valuable load, a stratagem which, it was held, left the accused free whether to succumb or not.

It seems that the police cannot circumvent s 78(1) by using, as agents provocateurs, informants who will not be called as witnesses. Thus if an informant, C, acting on police instructions rather than on his own initiative, incites or entraps an accused, D, into committing an offence (the supply of drugs, say) and D is then approached by E, an undercover police officer, in whose presence the offence is committed (D supplies E with drugs), this may form the basis of a submission to exclude E's evidence under s 78(1) notwithstanding that E, by reference to the relevant factors as set out in *R v Smurthwaite and Gill*, behaved throughout with perfect propriety.[168]

---

[161] Cf *Re Proulx* [2001] 1 All ER 57, DC.

[162] [1992] 1 All ER 317.

[163] [1996] 1 WLR 104, HL.

[164] See also *R v Pattemore* [1994] Crim LR 836, CA, and *R v Morley* [1994] Crim LR 919, CA.

[165] [1988] 3 All ER 683, DC.

[166] [1995] Crim LR 58, DC.

[167] [1993] 3 All ER 365, DC.

[168] See *R v Smith (Brian)* [1995] Crim LR 658, CA, and cf *R v Mann* [1995] Crim LR 647, CA.

Undercover operations after commission of an offence

In *R v Christou*[169] the police set up a shop staffed by two undercover police officers who purported to be willing to buy stolen jewellery. Transactions in the shop were recorded, the object being to recover stolen property and obtain evidence against thieves or receivers. The accused, charged as a result of the operation, unsuccessfully sought to exclude all the evidence obtained thereby. It was argued that the evidence was obtained by a trick designed to deprive visitors to the shop of their privilege against self-incrimination and that a caution should have been administered. The Court of Appeal, distinguishing *R v Payne*[170] and *R v Mason*,[171] held that the accused had voluntarily applied themselves to the trick (in the sense that what they did in the shop was exactly what they intended to do) and this had resulted in no unfairness.[172] Concerning the absence of a caution, the court acknowledged that the officers had grounds to suspect the accused of an offence, but held that Code C was not intended to apply in the present context. The Code was intended to protect suspects who are vulnerable to abuse or pressure from officers or who may believe themselves to be so. Where a suspect, even if not in detention, is being questioned by an officer, acting as such, for the purpose of obtaining evidence, the officer and the suspect are not on equal terms: the officer is perceived to be in a position of authority and the suspect may be intimidated or undermined. On the facts, however, the accused were not questioned by officers acting as such, conversation was on equal terms, and there was no question of pressure or intimidation.

In *Christou* the court held that it *would* be wrong for the police to adopt an undercover pose or disguise to enable them to ask questions about an offence uninhibited by the Code and with the effect of circumventing it, and it would then be open to a judge to exclude under s 78. On the facts, however, the questions and comments of the officers were, for the most part, simply those necessary to conduct the bartering and to maintain their cover, and not questions about the offence. Thus, although officers had asked questions about the origin of the goods, they had formed a part of their undercover pose as receivers: receivers need such information to prevent them from re-selling goods in the area from which they were stolen.[173] In *R v Bryce*,[174] on the other hand, in which an undercover officer, posing as a potential buyer of a car, asked B how recently the car had been stolen, it was held that evidence of the answers should have been excluded. The questions were not necessary to the maintenance of the undercover pose. They went directly to the issue of guilty knowledge, they were hotly disputed, and there had been no caution and no contemporary record.

In a number of cases, the trickery or subterfuge has involved the use of an accomplice. In *R v Cadette*[175] B, arrested as a suspected drugs courier, was asked by customs officers to telephone C, in accordance with an arrangement previously made between B and C, but to pretend that she had not been arrested and to try to persuade C to come to the airport. Evidence of their conversation, which was recorded, was held to have been properly admitted. The

---

[169] [1992] QB 979, CA.

[170] [1963] 1 WLR 637, CCA.

[171] [1988] 1 WLR 139, CA.

[172] Similar reasoning was applied in *R v Maclean* [1993] Crim LR 687, CA, and *R v Cadette* [1995] Crim LR 229, CA, considered at n 175. See also *R v Deenik* [1992] Crim LR 578, CA (police evidence of voice identification, D not having been warned that an officer was listening).

[173] See also *R v Lin* [1995] Crim LR 817, CA.

[174] [1992] 4 All ER 567, CA.

[175] [1995] Crim LR 229, CA.

court observed that, in practical terms, there comes a point when officers move from following up available lines of inquiry to obtain evidence against others involved to a stage where they seek in effect to deprive a suspect of the protection afforded by the 1984 Act and the Codes, but held that the officers had not crossed the line. The provisions of the 1984 Act did not apply; there was a reliable record of the conversation; and the ruse, of itself, did not give rise to unfairness for the purposes of s 78.[176]

The line was crossed, however, in *Allan v United Kingdom.*[177] A, suspected of murder, was interviewed by officers on several occasions but, acting on legal advice, consistently refused to answer questions. H, an experienced informer, who had undergone coaching by police informers, was fitted with recording devices and placed in A's cell for the specific purpose of questioning him to obtain information about the murder. At the trial H gave evidence, which proved to be decisive, that A had admitted his presence at the scene of the murder, but this conversation had not been recorded on tape. A was convicted. The European Court of Human Rights was satisfied that using statements obtained in a manner which effectively undermines a suspect's right to make a meaningful choice whether to speak to the authorities or to remain silent infringes procedural rights inherent in Art 6. The court acknowledged that whether the right to silence is undermined to such an extent as to invoke Art 6 will depend upon the circumstances of the case, but, distinguishing *Khan v United Kingdom*, was satisfied that evidence of the conversation had been obtained without sufficient regard to fair trial guarantees:

> the admissions allegedly made by the applicant to H…were not spontaneous and unprompted statements volunteered by the applicant, but were induced by the persistent questioning of H who, at the instance of the police, channeled their conversations into discussions of the murder in circumstances which can be regarded as the functional equivalent of interrogation, without any of the safeguards which would attach to a formal police interview, including the attendance of a solicitor and the issuing of the usual caution.[178]

The conviction was subsequently quashed by the Court of Appeal[179] on the basis that H was a 'police stooge' carrying out the equivalent of interrogation after A had exercised a right of silence, impinging on that right and the privilege against self-incrimination.

ADDITIONAL READING

Ashworth, 'Redrawing the Boundaries of Entrapment' [2002] Crim LR 161.

Choo and Nash, 'Improperly obtained evidence in the Commonwealth: lessons for England and Wales?' (2007) 11 E&P 75.

Hock Lai Ho, 'State entrapment' (2011) 31 Legal Studies 71.

Home Office, *Achieving Best Evidence in Criminal Proceedings: Guidance for Vulnerable or Intimidated Witnesses, Including Children* (2007) <www.homeoffice.gov.uk>.

Hunter, 'Judicial Discretion: Section 78 in Practice' [1994] Crim LR 558.

Keenan et al, 'Interviewing Allegedly Abused Children' [1999] Crim LR 863.

Mahoney, 'Abolition of New Zealand's Prima Facie Exclusionary Rule' [2003] Crim LR 607.

---

[176] See also *R v Jelen; R v Katz* (1989) 90 Cr App R 456, CA and *R v Edwards* [1997] Crim LR 348, CA.

[177] (2002) 36 EHRR 143.

[178] At para 52. Cf *Bykof v Russia* [2010] Crim LR 413, ECHR.

[179] *R v Allan* [2005] Crim LR 716, CA.

Mirfield, *Silence, Confessions and Improperly Obtained Evidence* (Oxford, 1997) Chs 2, 6, and 12.

Ormerod, 'ECHR and the Exclusion of Evidence: Trial Remedies for Article 8 Breaches' [2003] Crim LR 61.

Ormerod and Birch, 'The Evolution of the Discretionary Exclusion of Evidence' [2004] Crim LR 767.

Rasiah, '*A v Secretary of State for the Home Department (No 2)*: Occupying the Moral High Ground?' (2006) 69 MLR 995.

Roberts, 'Questions of "Who was there?" and "Who did what?": The Application of Code D in Cases of Dispute as to Participation but not Presence' [2003] Crim LR 709.

Zuckerman, *The Principles of Criminal Evidence* (Oxford, 1989) Ch 16.

The burden and standard of proof

4

Key issues

- Where facts are in issue in either a civil or criminal trial, which party should have an obligation to prove those facts, and why?

- Where a party in a criminal trial has an obligation to prove facts, why should a judge, before allowing the party to attempt to prove the facts to a jury, first require the party to adduce sufficient evidence to found a prima facie case?

- How persuasive must the evidence of facts adduced by a party be before those facts can be regarded as having been legally proved (a) where the party is prosecuting; (b) where the party is the accused and is relying on those facts in his defence; and (c) where the party is a party in a civil trial?

- Should an accused have an obligation to prove facts in his defence?

The burden of proof

Standing alone, the expression 'burden of proof' is self-explanatory: it is the obligation to prove. There are two principal kinds of burden, the legal burden and the evidential burden. The legal burden is a burden of proof. However, as we shall see, it is confusing and misleading to speak of the evidential burden as a burden of proof, first because when borne by a defendant it may be discharged by evidence other than the evidence adduced by the defence and therefore may not in substance be a burden at all,[1] and second because it can be discharged by the production of evidence that falls short of proof.[2]

The content of the first half of this chapter is largely concerned with the rules governing which party bears the legal and evidential burdens on which facts in issue. The practical importance of these rules is fourfold. They can, of course, determine the eventual outcome of proceedings. Additionally they determine which party has the right to begin adducing evidence in court; in what circumstances a defendant, at the end of the case for the prosecution, or claimant, may make a successful submission of no case to answer; and how the trial judge should direct the jury. However, easy as it is to outline the nature and importance of this subject, detailed analysis is made difficult by problems of classification and terminology. It will be convenient, then, to begin by defining and distinguishing the legal, evidential, and other burdens before considering in detail which burden is borne by each of the parties on the various facts in issue in any given case.

The legal burden

This burden has been referred to as 'the burden of proof' or 'probative burden'[3] and as 'the ultimate burden'. Another label, 'the burden of proof on the pleadings',[4] is used to show that this burden is sometimes indicated by the pleadings. Two further phrases, 'the risk of non-persuasion'[5] and 'the persuasive burden', are used to show that a party bearing the burden on a particular fact in issue will lose on that issue if he fails to discharge the burden. Most of these labels are, to some extent, misleading, and in the ensuing text this burden will be referred to simply as 'the legal burden'.

The legal burden may be defined as the obligation imposed on a party by a rule of law to prove a fact in issue. Whether a party has discharged this burden and proved a fact in issue is decided only once, by the tribunal of fact, at the end of the case when both parties have called all their evidence. The standard of proof required to discharge the legal burden depends upon whether the proceedings are criminal or civil. In the former the standard required of the prosecution is proof which makes the tribunal of fact 'sure'; in the latter the standard required is proof 'on the balance of probabilities'. A party who fails to discharge a legal burden borne by him to the required standard of proof will lose on the issue in question.

The legal burden relates to particular facts in issue.[6] Most cases, of course, involve more than one issue and the legal burden of proof in relation to these issues may be distributed

---

[1] See *Bullard v R* [1957] AC 635, PC, at n 108, and per Pill LJ in *L v DPP* [2003] QB 137, DC at [23].

[2] Per Lord Devlin in *Jayasena v R* [1970] AC 618, PC at 624.

[3] See *DPP v Morgan* [1976] AC 182, HL.

[4] Phipson, *Law of Evidence* (17th edn, London, 2010) ch 6 para 6–02.

[5] Wigmore, *A Treatise on the Anglo-American System of Evidence* (3rd edn, Boston, 1940) ch IX, paras 248–9.

[6] A question of construction is a question of *law* in respect of which no burden lies on either side; but if a party relies on surrounding circumstances as an aid to construction, then the onus is on him to prove them: see per Nourse LJ, construing a conveyance in *Scott v Martin* [1987] 2 All ER 813, CA at 817.

between the parties to the action. We shall see, for example, that in a criminal case where insanity is raised as a defence, the legal burden in relation to that issue is borne by the defendant, whereas the prosecution may well bear the legal burden on all the other facts in issue. In civil proceedings, an example would be a negligence action in which the defendant alleges contributory negligence: the claimant bears the legal burden on the issue of negligence, the defendant on contributory negligence. The obligation on a party to prove a fact in issue may oblige that party to negative or disprove a particular fact. In criminal proceedings, for example, the prosecution bear the legal burden of proving lack of consent on a charge of rape.[7]

In civil cases, a judge may find it impossible to make a finding one way or the other on a fact in issue, so that it will then fall to be decided by reference to which party bears the legal burden on the issue. The principles governing this situation were summarized in *Stephens v Cannon*:[8] the situation has to be exceptional but can arise in relation to any issue; and the court is only entitled to have such resort to the legal burden if it cannot reasonably make a finding, in which case it should tell the parties that it has striven to make a finding and explain why it cannot do so, except in those few cases where such matters can readily be inferred from the circumstances.

Which party bears the legal burden of proof in relation to any given fact in issue is determined by the rules of substantive law discussed in this chapter. Judges sometimes refer to the 'shifting' of a burden of proof from one party to his opponent. The phrase is apt to mislead. The only sense in which the legal burden may be said to shift is on the operation of a rebuttable presumption of law. Rebuttable presumptions of law are considered in detail in Chapter 22, but it is convenient, at this stage, briefly to consider their operation. Where such a presumption applies, once a primary fact is proved or admitted, in the absence of further evidence another fact must be presumed. The quantity and quality of evidence required to rebut the presumed fact is determined by the substantive law in relation to the presumption in question. The party relying on the presumption bears the burden of proving the primary fact. Once he has adduced sufficient evidence on that fact, in the case of a 'persuasive' presumption his adversary will bear the legal burden of disproving the presumed fact. The burden may be said to have shifted. However, when judges refer to a shifting of the burden in circumstances other than on the operation of rebuttable presumptions of law, they mean that the burden may, at any given moment in the course of the trial, *appear* to have been satisfied by the party on whom it lies by virtue of the evidence adduced by that party. Insofar as this places a burden on that party's opponent, the opponent bears a 'tactical' burden. The legal burden has not shifted because, as has been noted, whether the legal burden has been discharged by a party is only determined once and that is at the end of the trial when *all* the evidence has been adduced.[9] The tactical burden is discussed more fully in contrast with the evidential burden.

[7] The operation of the legal burden in rape cases has been affected by the creation of presumptions of lack of consent under the Sexual Offences Act 2003 where certain circumstances or acts are proved by the prosecution. The presumptions are mostly 'evidential' presumptions, but in rare cases a 'conclusive' presumption may arise. Presumptions are touched on shortly in this chapter and dealt with more fully in Ch 22.

[8] [2005] CP Rep 31, CA.

[9] See per Sir Christopher Staughton in *Re W* [2001] 4 All ER 88, CA at 93–4. See also per Mustill LJ in *Brady (Inspector of Taxes) v Group Lotus Car Companies plc* [1987] 3 All ER 1050, CA at 1059.

The evidential burden

This burden is also referred to as 'the burden of adducing evidence' and 'the duty of passing the judge'. It may be defined as the obligation on a party to adduce sufficient evidence of a fact to justify a finding on that fact in favour of the party so obliged. In other words, it obliges a party to adduce sufficient evidence for the issue to go before the tribunal of fact. It is confusing and misleading, therefore, to call the evidential burden a burden of *proof*: it can be discharged by the production of evidence that falls short of proof.[10] Whether a party has discharged the burden is decided only once in the course of a trial, and by the judge as opposed to the tribunal of fact. The burden is discharged when there is sufficient evidence to justify, as a possibility, a favourable finding by the tribunal of fact. Thus in a criminal trial in which the prosecution bear the evidential burden on a particular issue, they must adduce sufficient evidence to prevent the judge from withdrawing that issue from the jury. If the prosecution discharge the evidential burden, it does not necessarily mean that they will succeed on the issue in question. The accused will not necessarily lose on that issue, even if he adduces no evidence in rebuttal, although if he takes that course that is a clear risk he runs. If the prosecution also bear the legal burden on the same issue, and fail to discharge the evidential burden, they necessarily fail on that issue since the judge refuses to let the issue go before the jury. However, it does not follow that a discharge of the evidential burden necessarily results in a discharge of the legal burden; the issue in question goes before the jury, who may or may not find in favour of the prosecution on that issue.

Like the legal burden, the evidential burden relates to particular facts in issue. The evidential burden in relation to the various issues in a given case may be distributed between the parties to the action. Normally, a party bearing the legal burden in relation to a particular fact at the commencement of the proceedings also bears an evidential burden in relation to the same fact. However, this is not invariably so. Thus although, as we shall see, the prosecution bear the legal burden of negativing most common law and certain statutory defences (including the defences of self-defence, duress, and non-insane automatism), such a defence will not be put before the jury unless the accused has discharged the evidential burden in that regard. Equally, and to complicate matters further, the evidential burden borne by the accused in these circumstances may be discharged by *any* evidence in the case, whether given by the accused, a co-accused, or the prosecution, and in this sense the so-called evidential burden is not a burden on the accused at all.[11] If the evidential burden is discharged, whether by defence or prosecution evidence, the prosecution will then bear the legal burden of disproving the defence in question, but if there is no evidence to support the defence, then the judge is entitled to withdraw it from the jury.[12]

As in the case of the legal burden, judges sometimes refer to the 'shifting' of the evidential burden. The evidential burden may sensibly be said to shift on the operation of a rebuttable presumption of law of the 'evidential' variety.[13] However, the phrase has also been employed

[10] Per Lord Devlin in *Jayasena v R* [1970] AC 618 PC at 624.

[11] Per Pill LJ in *L v DPP* [2003] QB 137, DC at [23].

[12] *R v Pommell* [1995] 2 Cr App R 607, CA, where it was also held that although normally a judge will not have to decide whether to leave a particular defence to the jury until the conclusion of the evidence, in rare cases where the nature of the evidence to be called is clear, it may be appropriate, in order to save time and costs, for the judge to indicate at an early stage what his ruling is likely to be.

[13] Where a party relying on an 'evidential' presumption has adduced sufficient evidence on the primary or basic fact, his adversary will bear an evidential burden to adduce some evidence to rebut the presumed fact. See further Ch 22.

in other circumstances. Where a party discharges an evidential burden borne by him in relation to a particular fact, his adversary will be under an obligation, referred to as the provisional or tactical burden, to adduce counter-evidence in order to convince the tribunal of fact in his favour. If he chooses not to adduce such counter-evidence, he runs the risk of a finding on that issue in favour of the other party. It is in these circumstances, also, that judges refer to a shifting of the evidential burden.[14] This conjures up a vision of the trial as a ball-game, with the evidential burden as the ball, which is continuously bounced to and fro between the contenders. This is misleading because although examination followed by cross-examination of witnesses often results in swings of fortune for and then against a party, normally in a trial, whether civil or criminal, one party first adduces all of his evidence before his adversary then adduces his. But there is a more important sense in which the phrase misleads. The evidential burden only needs to be considered by the court on two occasions, first at the beginning of a trial, to determine which party starts, and second when, during the trial, the judge determines whether sufficient evidence has been adduced to leave an issue before the tribunal of fact. If the judge decides at the latter stage that insufficient evidence has been adduced, the issue will be withdrawn from the tribunal of fact and further consideration of the evidential burden is irrelevant. But further consideration of the evidential burden is equally irrelevant when the judge allows the issue to go before the tribunal of fact. It is certainly possible to say, at this stage, that the evidential burden has shifted to the opponent and that he, by adducing counter-evidence, may cause the evidential burden to shift back to the first party, and so on, but such observations are of no legal significance. So far as the court is concerned, the evidential burden requires no further consideration; the only burden remaining at this stage is the legal burden.[15]

The incidence of the legal burden

Which party bears the legal burden is determined by the rules of substantive law set out in precedents and statutes. Speaking generally, the determination of where the legal burden falls is a matter of common sense. If certain facts are essential to the claim of, for example, the claimant in civil proceedings or the prosecution in criminal proceedings, that party must prove them. A useful starting-point—although, as we shall see, a far from reliable guide—is the maxim 'he who asserts must prove' (*ei incumbit probatio qui dicit, non qui negat*). In *Wakelin v London and South Western Rly Co*[16] a widow brought an action in negligence under the Fatal Accidents Act 1846. The only available evidence was that her husband had been found dead near a level crossing at the side of a railway line. Lord Halsbury LC held that the widow bore the burden of proving that her husband's death had been caused by the defendants' negligence; if she could not discharge that burden, she failed. Even assuming that the husband had been knocked down by a train while on the crossing, the evidence adduced was as capable of leading to the conclusion that the husband had been negligent as it was of showing the defendants' negligence and, accordingly, the defendants' negligence was not proved.[17]

A detailed examination of the incidence of the legal burden of proof requires that criminal and civil cases be considered separately.

---

[14] See, eg, per Lord Goddard CJ in *R v Matheson* [1958] 1 WLR 474, CCA at 478. See also *Rickards and Rickards v Kerrier District Council* (1987) 151 JP 625, DC.

[15] See *Sutton v Sadler* (1857) 3 CBNS 87 (see Ch 22).

[16] (1886) 12 App Cas 41, HL.

[17] Cf *Jones v Great Western Rly Co* (1930) 144 LT 194, HL.

Criminal cases

Speaking generally, the legal burden of proving any fact essential to the prosecution case rests upon the prosecution and remains with the prosecution throughout the trial. Negative as well as positive allegations may be essential to the case for the prosecution. Thus the prosecution bear the legal burden of proving absence of consent on a charge of rape or assault.[18] Generally, therefore, the accused bears no legal burden in respect of the essential ingredients of an offence, whether positive or negative and whether or not he denies any or all of them. In *Woolmington v DPP*[19] the accused, charged with the murder of his wife, gave evidence that he had shot her accidentally. The trial judge directed the jury that once it was proved that the accused had shot his wife, he bore the burden of disproving malice aforethought. The House of Lords held this to be a misdirection and Lord Sankey LC said, in a now famous passage:[20]

> Throughout the web of the English criminal law one golden thread is always to be seen, that it is the duty of the prosecution to prove the prisoner's guilt subject to what I have already said as to the defence of insanity and subject also to any statutory exception…No matter what the charge or where the trial, the principle that the prosecution must prove the guilt of the prisoner is part of the common law of England and no attempt to whittle it down can be entertained…It is not the law of England to say, as was said in the summing up in the present case: 'if the Crown satisfy you that this woman died at the prisoner's hands then he has to show that there are circumstances to be found in the evidence which has been given from the witness-box in this case which alleviate the crime so that it is only manslaughter or which excuse the homicide altogether by showing it was a pure accident…'

The rule enunciated by Lord Sankey is subject to three categories of exception: (i) where the accused raises the defence of insanity; (ii) where a statute expressly places the legal burden on the defence, and (iii) where a statute impliedly places the legal burden on the defence. The statutory exceptions are often referred to as reverse onus provisions. Since the coming into force of the Human Rights Act 1998, any such provision is open to challenge on the basis of its incompatibility with the presumption of innocence guaranteed by Art 6(2) of the European Convention on Human Rights. This aspect of the topic receives separate treatment, below.

Insanity

Where an accused raises insanity as a defence, he bears the legal burden of proving it.[21] The justification is based on the difficulty of disproving false claims of insanity, given that the accused may not cooperate with an investigation of his state of mind.[22] Where an accused is charged with murder and raises the issue of either insanity or diminished responsibility, the prosecution, pursuant to s 6 of the Criminal Procedure (Insanity) Act 1964, is allowed to adduce evidence to prove the other of those issues. In this event, the prosecution bear the legal burden of proving the other issue on which they have adduced evidence.[23] If an accused

---

[18] *R v Horn* (1912) 7 Cr App R 200; *R v Donovan* [1934] 2 KB 498. But see also the Sexual Offences Act 2003, ss 75 and 76.

[19] [1935] AC 462, HL.

[20] [1935] AC 462 at 481–2.

[21] *M'Naghten's Case* (1843) 10 Cl&Fin 200, HL.

[22] For a critique of the justification, see Ashworth, 'Four threats to the presumption of innocence' (2006) 10 E&P 241 at 263–5.

[23] The standard to be met by the prosecution in these circumstances is proof beyond reasonable doubt: *R v Grant* [1960] Crim LR 424.

is alleged to be under a disability rendering him unfit to plead and stand trial, the issue may be raised, under s 4 of the 1964 Act, by *either* the prosecution *or* the defence. If the issue is raised by the prosecution, they must prove it and satisfy the jury beyond reasonable doubt;[24] if the issue is raised by the defence, they must prove it, but only on a balance of probabilities, the lower standard of proof.[25]

Express statutory exceptions

A number of statutes expressly place on the accused the legal burden of proving specified issues. The legal burden of proof in relation to all issues other than those so specified remains on the prosecution. For example, s 2(2) of the Homicide Act 1957 places upon the accused the legal burden of establishing the statutory defence of diminished responsibility on a charge of murder.[26] Section 2(2) does not contravene Art 6 of the European Convention on Human Rights.[27] Other examples are considered under the heading of *Reverse onus provisions and the Human Rights Act 1998.*

Implied statutory exceptions: section 101 of the Magistrates' Courts Act 1980

Section 101 of the Magistrates' Courts Act 1980, formerly s 81 of the Magistrates' Courts Act 1952, provides as follows:

> Where the defendant to an information or complaint relies for his defence on any exception, exemption, proviso, excuse or qualification, whether or not it accompanies the description of the offence or matter of complaint in the enactment creating the offence or on which the complaint is founded, the burden of proving the exception, exemption, proviso, excuse or qualification shall be on him; and this notwithstanding that the information or complaint contains an allegation negativing the exception, exemption, proviso, excuse or qualification.

Section 81 applies to summary trials but at common law similar principles applied to trials on indictment and it was held by the Court of Appeal in *R v Edwards,*[28] and confirmed by the House of Lords in *R v Hunt,*[29] that the section sets out the common law rule in statutory form. If this were not so, then in the case of an offence triable either way, the incidence of the burden of proof could vary—but for no good reason—according to whether the accused is tried summarily or on indictment.

Implied statutory exceptions within s 101 of the Magistrates' Courts Act 1980 are capable of derogating from Art 6 of the European Convention;[30] and the cases in which, by virtue of s 101 or the common law principles on which it is based,[31] particular statutory provisions have been construed to impose a legal burden on the accused, must now be read subject to the

---

[24] *R v Robertson* [1968] 1 WLR 1767, CA.

[25] *R v Podola* [1960] 1 QB 325, CCA.

[26] Section 2(2) not only dictates which party shoulders the burden of proof once the issue is raised, but also leaves it to the defence to decide whether the issue should be raised at all; if, therefore, the defence does not raise the issue but there is evidence of diminished responsibility, the trial judge is not bound to direct the jury to consider the matter but, at most, should in the absence of the jury draw the matter to the attention of the defence so that they may decide whether they wish the issue to be considered by the jury: per Lord Lane CJ, obiter, in *R v Campbell* (1986) 84 Cr App R 255, CA.

[27] See *R v Lambert; R v Ali; and R v Jordan* [2001] 2 WLR 211, CA.

[28] [1975] QB 27.

[29] [1987] AC 352, HL.

[30] See per Clarke LJ in *R (Grundy & Co Excavations Ltd) v Halton Division Magistrates' Court* (2003) 167 JP 387, DC at [61].

[31] See, in this chapter, under **The burden of proof, The incidence of the legal burden, Criminal cases, Examples of statutory provisions to which section 101 applies.**

Human Rights Act 1998 and the cases in which reverse onus provisions have been challenged on the basis of incompatibility with Art 6.[32]

Examples of statutory provisions to which section 101 applies
Section 101 applies to statutory provisions which define a criminal offence and use words such as 'unless', 'provided that', 'except', or 'other than', to set out an exception, proviso, etc which amounts to a defence. The definition of an offence, and the exception or proviso to it, are not always readily distinguishable. However, before considering the kind of statutory provision capable of giving rise to difficulty, two reasonably straightforward examples of the kind of provision to which s 101 applies may be given: (i) s 87(1) of the Road Traffic Act 1988, which provides that it is an offence for a person to drive a vehicle on a road otherwise than in accordance with a licence;[33] and (ii) s 161(1) of the Highways Act 1980, which provides that if a person, without lawful authority or excuse, deposits anything whatsoever on a highway in consequence of which a user of the highway is injured or endangered, that person shall be guilty of an offence. In *Gatland v Metropolitan Police Comr*[34] Lord Parker CJ held that although it was for the prosecution to prove that a thing had been deposited on the highway and that in consequence thereof a user of the highway had been injured or endangered, it was for the accused to raise and prove lawful authority or excuse pursuant to s 81 of the Magistrates' Courts Act 1952.[35]

Provisions giving rise to difficulty
The point has been made that in some statutory provisions the definition of an offence and the exception or proviso to it are not always readily distinguishable. Concerning the application of section 101, these kinds of provisions are capable of giving rise to difficulty. In *Westminster City Council v Croyalgrange Ltd*,[36] by contrast with *Gatland*, no reliance could be placed on what is now s 101 of the Magistrates' Courts Act 1980. A company which had let premises to a person who used them as a sex establishment without a licence was charged under Sch 3, para 20(1)(a) to the Local Government (Miscellaneous Provisions) Act 1982, whereby a person who knowingly causes or permits the use of premises contrary to Sch 3, para 6 commits an offence. Paragraph 6 provides that no persons shall use any premises as a sex establishment except under and in accordance with a licence. The House of Lords held that s 101 was inapplicable because the exception in question qualified the prohibition created by para 6 and not the offence created by para 20(1)(a). The prosecution bore the burden of proving, inter alia, that the directors of the company knew that no licence had been obtained by the tenant.[37]

---

[32] See, in this chapter, under **The burden of proof, The incidence of the legal burden, Criminal cases, Reverse onus provisions and the Human Rights Act 1998**.

[33] On being charged with this offence, it is for an accused to prove that he satisfies the proviso of holding a current driving licence. See *John v Humphreys* [1955] 1 WLR 325, DC. See also *Leeds City Council v Azam* (1988) 153 JP 157, DC: it is for the accused to prove that he is *exempted* from the need for a licence for the operation of a private hire vehicle under the Local Government (Miscellaneous Provisions) Act 1976, s 75.

[34] [1968] 2 QB 279, a decision under the Highways Act 1959, s 140(1), re-enacted in the Magistrates' Courts Act 1980, s 161(1).

[35] Cf Offences Against the Person Act 1861, s 16: a person who without lawful excuse makes to another a threat, intending that the other would fear it would be carried out, to kill that other or a third person shall be guilty of an offence. In *R v Cousins* [1982] QB 526, CA, it was held that on a charge under s 16, the onus is on the prosecution to prove absence of lawful excuse for making the threat.

[36] (1986) 83 Cr App R 155, HL.

[37] See also, construing the Environmental Protection Act 1990, s 33(1)(a), *Environment Agency v ME Foley Contractors Ltd* [2002] 1 WLR 1754, DC.

Nimmo v Alexander Cowan & Sons Ltd[38] was another case giving rise to difficulty. This was a Scottish case brought by an injured workman under s 29(1) of the Factories Act 1961, which provides that 'every place at which any person has at any time to work...shall, so far as is reasonably practicable, be made and kept safe for any person working therein'. The workman alleged that his place of work was not kept safe but did not aver that it was reasonably practicable to make it safe. Section 155(1) of the 1961 Act makes a breach of s 29(1) a summary offence and although the case in question was a civil one, the House of Lords referred to the Scottish equivalent of s 81 of the Magistrates' Courts Act 1952 and Lord Pearson made it clear that the incidence of the burden of proof would be the same whether the proceedings were civil or criminal.[39] The House held, Lords Reid and Wilberforce dissenting, that there was no burden on the plaintiff employee to prove that it was reasonably practicable to keep the premises safe; the defendant employers bore the burden of proving that it was *not* reasonably practicable to keep the premises safe. In reaching this decision, the majority was of the opinion that where, on the face of the statute, it is unclear on whom the burden should lie, a court, in order to determine Parliament's intention, may go beyond the mere form of the enactment and look to other, policy, considerations such as the mischief at which the Act was aimed and the ease or difficulty that the respective parties would encounter in discharging the burden. Given that the defendant was better able to discharge the legal burden than the plaintiff, the construction of the majority, it is submitted, best achieved the object of the enactment in question, namely to provide a safe place of work.

Implied statutory exceptions: trials on indictment

On its wording, s 101 applies to summary trials. Concerning trials on indictment, the leading authorities are *R v Edwards*[40] and *R v Hunt*.[41] In *R v Edwards* the accused was convicted on indictment of selling intoxicating liquor without holding a justices' licence authorizing such sale contrary to s 160(1)(a) of the Licensing Act 1964. Edwards appealed, one of his grounds being that the prosecution had not called any evidence to prove that he did not hold a licence. It was submitted, on his behalf, that at common law the burden of proving an exception, exemption, proviso, excuse, or qualification fell on the defence only when the facts constituting it were peculiarly within the defendant's own knowledge[42] and that in the instant case they were not. The clerk to the licensing justices for any district is statutorily bound to keep a register of local licences and accordingly the police had access to a public source of knowledge. The Court of Appeal held that the legal burden of proving that the accused was the holder of a justices' licence rested on the defence and not the prosecution. After an extensive review of the authorities, Lawton LJ continued:[43]

> In our judgment this line of authority establishes that over the centuries the common law, as a
> result of experience and the need to ensure that justice is done both to the community and to
> the defendants, has evolved an exception to the fundamental rule of our common law that the

---

[38] [1968] AC 107, HL.

[39] [1968] AC 107, HL at 134. Although Lord Reid dissented, his opinion on this point, at [115], was the same.

[40] [1975] QB 27, CA.

[41] [1987] AC 352, HL.

[42] See *R v Turner* (1816) 5 M&S 206 at 211, followed in *R v Oliver* [1944] KB 68 (dealing in sugar without a licence) and *John v Humphreys* [1955] 1 WLR 325, DC (driving without a licence). See also *R v Ewens* [1967] 1 QB 322, CCA (possessing drugs without a prescription).

[43] [1975] QB 27 at 39–40.

prosecution must prove every element of the offence charged. This exception…is limited to offences arising under enactments which prohibit the doing of an act save in specified circumstances or by persons of specified classes or with specified qualifications or with the licence or permission of specified authorities. Whenever the prosecution seeks to rely on this exception, the court must construe the enactment under which the charge is laid. If the true construction is that the enactment prohibits the doing of acts, subject to provisos, exemptions and the like, then the prosecution can rely upon the exception.

In our judgment its application does not depend upon either the fact, or the presumption, that the defendant has peculiar knowledge enabling him to prove the positive of any negative averment.

In *R v Hunt*[44] the accused was charged with the unlawful possession of morphine contrary to s 5 of the Misuse of Drugs Act 1971. Under the Misuse of Drugs Regulations 1973, it is provided that s 5 shall not have effect in relation to, inter alia, any preparation of morphine containing not more than 0.2 per cent of morphine. At the trial the defence submitted that there was no case to answer because the prosecution had adduced no evidence as to the proportion of morphine in the powder which had been found in Hunt's possession. The judge rejected the submission and Hunt changed his plea to guilty. His appeal to the Court of Appeal was dismissed, but on a further appeal to the House of Lords, two arguments were raised: (i) *R v Edwards* was wrongly decided; and (ii) on the true construction of the provisions in question, the prosecution bore the burden of proving that the facts fell outside the 'exception' contained in the Misuse of Drugs Regulations 1973. The prosecution submitted that *R v Edwards* did apply and the burden was on the accused to show that the facts fell within the 'exception'.

The House of Lords allowed the appeal. The reasoning was as follows:

1. When, in *Woolmington v DPP*,[45] Lord Sankey used the phrase 'any statutory exception', he was not referring *only* to statutory exceptions in which Parliament has placed the burden of proof on the accused expressly. A statute can place the legal burden of proof on an accused either expressly or by implication, ie on its true construction.[46]

2. Where a statute places the legal burden on the accused by implication, that burden is on the accused whether the case be tried summarily or on indictment; s 101 of the Magistrates' Courts Act 1980 reflects and applies to summary trials the rule relating to the incidence of the burden of proof evolved by judges on trials on indictment.

3. *R v Edwards* was decided correctly subject to one qualification: on occasions, albeit rarely, a statute will be construed as imposing the legal burden on the accused although it is outside the ambit of the formula given by Lawton LJ. The present case did not come within the formula, which was 'limited to offences arising under enactments which prohibit the doing of an act save in specified circumstances or by persons of specified classes or with specified qualifications or with the licence or permission of specified authorities'. The formula, although 'a helpful approach'[47] and 'an excellent guide to construction',[48] was not intended to be and is not exclusive in its effect.

---

[44] [1987] AC 352, HL.
[45] [1935] AC 462, HL.
[46] See per Lords Griffiths and Ackner [1987] AC 352 at [6]–[7] and [15] respectively.
[47] Per Lord Ackner at [19].
[48] Per Lord Griffiths at [11].

4. Ultimately, each case must turn on the construction of the particular legislation. If the linguistic construction of a statute does not clearly indicate on whom the burden should lie, the court, in construing it, is not confined to the form of wording of the provision but, as in *Nimmo v Alexander Cowan & Sons Ltd*,[49] may have regard to matters of policy including practical considerations and in particular the ease or otherwise that the respective parties would encounter if required to discharge the burden.[50] Parliament, however, can never lightly be taken to have imposed the duty on an accused to prove his innocence in a criminal case and the courts should be very slow to draw any such inference from the language of a statute.[51]

5. Policy, in the present case, pointed to the legal burden being on the prosecution. This would not be an undue burden because in most cases the substance in question would have been analysed before a prosecution was brought and therefore there would be no difficulty in producing evidence to show that it did contain a certain percentage of morphine. If the burden was on the accused, however, he would have real practical difficulties because the substance is usually seized by the police and he has no statutory entitlement to a proportion of it. Moreover, the substance may already have been analysed by the police and destroyed in the process.

6. The question of construction being one of obviously real difficulty and offences involving the misuse of hard drugs being among the most serious of offences, any ambiguity should be resolved in favour of the accused.

In its 11th report, the Criminal Law Revision Committee was strongly of the opinion that both on principle and for the sake of clarity and convenience in practice, burdens on the defence should be evidential only.[52] In *R v Hunt*, Lord Griffiths thought that such a fundamental change was a matter for Parliament and not a decision for the House of Lords.[53]

Reverse onus provisions and the Human Rights Act 1998

Since the coming into force of the Human Rights Act 1998, any reverse onus provision is open to challenge on the basis of its incompatibility with Art 6(2) of the European Convention on Human Rights, under which 'Everyone charged with a criminal offence shall be presumed innocent until proved guilty according to law'.[54] Clearly, a reverse onus provision will not inevitably give rise to a finding of incompatibility,[55] but if a provision does unjustifiably infringe Art 6(2), the further issue will arise whether it should be read down, in accordance with the obligation under s 3 of the Human Rights Act 1998, so as to impose an evidential and not a legal burden on the accused.

---

[49] [1968] AC 107, HL.

[50] On this basis it is possible to explain cases formerly difficult to reconcile with *R v Edwards* such as *R v Putland and Sorrell* [1946] 1 All ER 85, CCA, *R v Cousins* [1982] QB 526, CA, above, *R v Curgerwen* (1865) LR 1 CCR 1, and *R v Audley* [1907] 1 KB 383.

[51] Per Lord Griffiths [1987] 1 All ER 1 at 11.

[52] Subject to two minor exceptions: see Cmnd 4991, paras 140–1.

[53] [1987] 1 All ER 1 at 12.

[54] Article 6(2) does not apply to confiscation proceedings pursuant to the Drugs Trafficking Act 1994, Pt I, since the defendant has already been proved guilty of the offences to which the proceedings relate. See *R v Briggs-Price* [2009] 1 AC 1026, HL. However, civil proceedings which are penal in nature and could expose a party to prosecution may engage Art 6(2). See *Watkins v Woolas* [2010] EWHC 2702, QB.

[55] Per Lord Hope in *R v Lambert* [2002] 2 AC 545, HL, at [87].

The underlying rationale of the presumption of innocence in both domestic law and the Convention is that it is repugnant to ordinary notions of fairness for a prosecutor to accuse an accused of a crime and for the accused then to be required to disprove the accusation on pain of conviction and punishment if he fails to do so.[56] Under domestic law, as will be apparent from the foregoing text, Parliament does not regard the presumption as an absolute or unqualified right. Equally, the Art 6(2) right is neither absolute nor unqualified. In reaching a decision on the question of incompatibility, the test is whether the modification or limitation of the Art 6(2) right pursues a legitimate aim and whether it satisfies the principle of proportionality: a balance has to be struck between the general interest of the community and the protection of the fundamental rights of the individual.[57] In *Attorney General's Reference (No 4 of 2002)*[58] Lord Bingham considered the scope of the presumption under the Convention. After an extensive review of the jurisprudence of the European Court, including the leading authority of *Salabiaku v France*,[59] his Lordship summarized the relevant principles to be derived from the Strasbourg case law:

> The overriding concern is that a trial should be fair, and the presumption of innocence is a fundamental right directed to that end. The Convention does not outlaw presumptions of fact or law[60] but requires that these should be kept within reasonable limits and should not be arbitrary. It is open to states to define the constituent elements of a criminal offence, excluding the requirement of *mens rea*. But the substance and effect of any presumption adverse to a defendant must be examined, and must be reasonable. Relevant to any judgment on reasonableness or proportionality will be the opportunity given to the defendant to rebut the presumption, maintenance of the rights of the defence, flexibility in application of the presumption, retention by the court of a power to assess the evidence, the importance of what is at stake and the difficulty which a prosecutor may face in the absence of a presumption. Security concerns do not absolve member states from their duty to observe basic standards of fairness. The justifiability of any infringement of the presumption of innocence cannot be resolved by any rule of thumb, but on examination of all the facts and circumstances of the particular provision as applied in the particular case.

It is convenient at this point to consider some of the leading authorities on reverse onus provisions.

R v Lambert

In *R v Lambert*,[61] L, found in possession of a duffle bag containing two kilograms of cocaine, was convicted of possession of cocaine with intent to supply, contrary to s 5(3) of the Misuse of Drugs Act 1971. L had relied upon s 28 of the 1971 Act, asserting that he did not believe or suspect or have reason to suspect that the bag contained cocaine or any controlled drug. The trial judge had directed the jury that in order to establish possession of a controlled drug, the Crown need only prove that L had the bag in his possession and that it contained a controlled drug. Thereafter the burden was on L to bring himself within s 28 and 'to prove', on a balance of probabilities, that he did not know that the bag contained a controlled drug. The House of Lords held, by majority, that since the trial had taken place before the coming into force of

[56] Per Lord Bingham in *Attorney General's Reference (No 4 of 2002)* [2005] 1 AC 264, HL at [9].
[57] Per Lord Hope in *R v Lambert* [2002] 2 AC 545, HL at [88].
[58] [2005] 1 AC 264, HL at [21].
[59] (1988) 13 EHRR 379, ECHR.
[60] See Ch 22.
[61] [2002] 2 AC 545, HL.

the Human Rights Act 1998, L was not entitled to rely on an alleged breach of his rights under the European Convention. However, the House was of the view (Lord Hutton dissenting) that s 28 is not compatible with Art 6(2) and, under s 3 of the 1998 Act, may be read as imposing no more than an evidential burden on the accused.

Lord Steyn approached the question of compatibility by applying a three-stage test:

1. whether there has been a legislative interference with the presumption in Art 6(2);

2. if so, whether there is an objective justification for such interference; and

3. if so, whether the interference is proportionate, ie no greater than is necessary.

As to the first stage, it was held that, taking account of the fact that under s 28 an accused will be denying moral blameworthiness and that the maximum penalty for the offence is life imprisonment, knowledge of the existence and control of the contents of the container is the gravamen of the offence, and therefore s 28 derogates from the presumption of innocence. Lord Steyn also reached this conclusion on broader grounds. His Lordship noted that the distinction between constituent elements of the crime and defensive issues will sometimes be unprincipled and arbitrary: a true constituent element may not be within the definition of the crime but cast as a defensive issue and conversely a definition of the crime may be so formulated as to include all possible defences within it. It is necessary, therefore, to concentrate not on technicalities and niceties of language, but on matters of substance. A defence may be so closely linked with *mens rea* and moral blameworthiness that it will derogate from the presumption of innocence to place the burden of proving that defence on the accused. Accordingly, the issues under s 28, even if regarded as a pure defence, bore directly on the moral blameworthiness of the accused and therefore derogated from the presumption of innocence.

As to the second stage, Lord Steyn was satisfied that there is an objective justification for the legislative interference with the presumption of innocence, namely that sophisticated drug smugglers, dealers, and couriers typically secrete drugs in some container, thereby enabling the person in possession of the container to say that he was unaware of the contents. Such a defence is commonplace and poses real difficulties for the police and prosecuting authorities.

As to the third stage, it was held that the burden is on the state to show that the legislative means adopted were no greater than necessary. The principle of proportionality required the House to consider whether there was a pressing necessity to impose a legal rather than an evidential burden. The obligation to show that only a reverse legal burden can overcome the difficulties of the prosecution in drugs cases is strong. In a case of possession of controlled drugs with intent to supply, although the prosecution must establish that controlled drugs were in the possession of the accused and that he knew that the package contained something, under s 28 the accused must prove on a balance of probabilities that he did not know that the package contained controlled drugs. If the jury is not satisfied of this on a balance of probabilities, or considers that the accused's version is as likely to be true as not, they must convict him. Thus a guilty verdict may be returned in respect of an offence punishable by life imprisonment even though the jury may consider that it is reasonably possible that the accused has been duped. Consequently, s 28 was a disproportionate reaction to perceived difficulties facing the prosecution in drugs cases. A new realism had significantly reduced the scope of the problems faced by the prosecution. First, possession of the container presumptively suggests, in the absence of exculpatory evidence, that the possessor knew of its contents. Second, s 34 of the Criminal Justice and Public Order Act 1994, enabling a judge to comment on an accused's failure to mention facts when questioned or charged, has strengthened the position of the prosecution.[62] Third, where a 'mixed statement', ie an out-of-court statement made by the accused which is partly inculpatory and partly exculpatory, is introduced in evidence, and the accused elects not to testify, the judge may point out to the jury that the incriminating parts are likely to be true whereas the excuses do not have the same weight, and may also comment on the election of the accused not to testify.[63] For these reasons, Lord Steyn concluded that s 28 was incompatible with Art 6(2). It was further held that under s 3 of the Human Rights Act 1998, where s 28(2) and (3) require the accused to 'prove' the matters specified, the word can be read to mean 'give sufficient evidence', thereby placing only an evidential burden on the accused.

L v DPP

L v DPP[64] involved a charge of being in possession of a lock-knife in a public place contrary to s 139 of the Criminal Justice Act 1988, and the related defence under s 139(4), which provides that it shall be a defence for an accused to prove that he had good reason or lawful authority for having the knife with him in a public place. Distinguishing *Lambert*, the court held that, striking a fair balance, s 139(4) does not conflict with Art 6 of the Convention.[65] Six reasons were given. (1) Unlike s 28 of the Misuse of Drugs Act 1971, under s 139 of the Criminal Justice Act 1988 it is for the prosecution to prove that the accused knowingly had the offending article in his possession. (2) There is a strong public interest in bladed articles not being carried in public without good reason. Parliament is entitled, without infringing the Convention, to deter the carrying of bladed or sharply pointed articles in public to the extent of placing the burden of proving a good reason on the carrier. (3) The accused is proving something within his own knowledge. (4) The accused is entitled under Art 6 to expect the court to scrutinize the evidence with a view to deciding if a good reason exists, whether he gives evidence or not. (5) Although there will be cases in which the tribunal of fact may attach significance to where the burden of proof rests, in the great majority of cases it needs to make a value judgment as to whether, upon all the evidence, the reason is a good one, without the decision depending on whether it has to be proved that there is a good reason. (6) In striking the balance, some, albeit limited, weight should be given to the much more restricted power of sentence for an offence under s 139 than for an offence under s 5 of the Misuse of Drugs Act 1971.

R v Drummond

R v Drummond[66] concerned the so-called 'hip flask' defence in s 15 of the Road Traffic Offenders Act 1988, under which it is for the accused to prove that he consumed alcohol after the offence but before providing a specimen.[67] It was held, *Lambert* again distinguished, that driving while

---

[62] See Ch 14.

[63] See *R v Duncan* (1981) 73 Cr App R 359, Ch 6.

[64] [2003] QB 137, DC.

[65] See also *R v Mathews* [2004] QB 690, CA: the court, agreeing with and adopting the reasoning in *L v DPP*, held that neither s 139(4) nor s 139(5) of the Criminal Justice Act 1988 was incompatible with Art 6.

[66] [2002] 2 Cr App R 352, CA.

[67] Section 15 applies to trials only. Accordingly, the reverse burden will not apply where an accused pleads guilty but raises the issue in order to mitigate sentence. In these circumstances, the issue will be determined in a *Newton* hearing where the burden is on the prosecution and the standard of proof is the criminal standard. See *Goldsmith v DPP* (2010) 174 JP 84, DC.

over the limit and causing death by driving while over the limit are both social evils which Parliament sought to minimize by the legislation and that the legislative interference with the presumption of innocence was not only justified, but no greater than was necessary. Four reasons were given. (1) Conviction follows after a scientific test which is intended to be as exact as possible. (2) In most cases the test is exact or, to the extent that it is less than exact, the inexactness works in favour of the accused. (3) It is the accused himself who, by drinking after the event, defeats the aim of the legislature by doing something which makes the scientific test potentially unreliable. In many, perhaps most cases, the accused will have taken the alcohol after the event for the precise purpose of defeating the scientific test. (4) The relevant scientific evidence to set against the result ascertained from the specimen of breath or blood, including the amount which the accused drank after the offence, is all within the knowledge or means of access of the accused.

R v S and R v Johnstone

In *R v S*[68] the Court of Appeal considered s 92(5) of the Trade Marks Act 1994, which provides that it is a defence for a person charged with the unauthorized use of a registered trade mark to show that he believed on reasonable grounds that the use of the sign was not an infringement of the registered trade mark. It was held that s 92(5) imposed a legal burden on the accused and was compatible with Art 6(2).

The same issue arose, but did not call for decision, in *R v Johnstone*.[69] The House of Lords, approving *R v S*, was of the same, albeit obiter, view. Lord Nicholls, in a speech endorsed by Lords Hope, Hutton, and Rodger, said:[70]

> for a reverse burden of proof to be acceptable there must be a compelling reason why it is fair and reasonable to deny the accused person the protection normally guaranteed to everyone by the presumption of innocence...A sound starting point is to remember that if an accused is required to prove a fact on the balance of probability to avoid conviction, this permits a conviction in spite of the fact-finding tribunal having a reasonable doubt as to the guilt of the accused...This consequence of a reverse burden of proof should colour one's approach when evaluating the reasons why it is said that, in the absence of a persuasive burden on the accused, the public interest will be prejudiced to an extent which justifies placing a persuasive burden on the accused. The more serious the punishment which may flow from conviction, the more compelling must be the reasons. The extent and nature of the factual matters required to be proved by the accused, and their importance relative to the matters required to be proved by the prosecution, have to be taken into account. So also does the extent to which the burden on the accused relates to facts which, if they exist, are readily provable by him as matters within his own knowledge or to which he already has access. In evaluating these factors the court's role is one of review. Parliament, not the court, is charged with the primary responsibility for deciding, as a matter of policy, what should be the constituent elements of a criminal offence...The court will reach a different conclusion from the legislature only when...it is apparent the legislature has attached insufficient importance to the fundamental right of an individual to be presumed innocent until proved guilty.

As to s 92(5), Lord Nicholls had regard to the fact that counterfeiting is a serious problem with adverse economic effects on genuine trade and adverse effects on consumers in terms of quality of goods and, sometimes, on the health or safety of consumers. Further, the s 92(5)

---

[68] [2003] 1 Cr App R 602, CA.
[69] [2003] 1 WLR 1736, HL.
[70] [2003] 1 WLR 1736, HL at [49]–[51].

defence relates to facts within the accused's own knowledge. Two other factors were said to constitute compelling reasons why s 92(5) should place a legal burden on the accused. First, those who trade in brand products are aware of the need to be on guard against counterfeit goods. Second, by and large it is to be expected that those who supply traders with counterfeit goods, if traceable at all by outside investigators, are unlikely to be cooperative, so if the prosecution are required to prove that traders acted dishonestly, fewer investigations will be undertaken and there will be fewer prosecutions.

DPP v Barker

The concept of facts within the accused's own knowledge is separate from the concept of ease of proof, but in some cases both will point in the same direction. *DPP v Barker*[71] concerned s 37(3) of the Road Traffic Act 1988, whereby a disqualified driver may hold a provisional licence and drive in accordance with its conditions. In support of the conclusion that it was proportionate for the accused to bear the burden under the subsection, it was said that, as to being the holder of a provisional licence, the burden could easily be discharged by producing the licence and, as to the conditions of the licence, in some cases, in the absence of any information from the accused as to the identity of a passenger, it would be impossible for the prosecution to establish his identity and that he was the holder of a licence and therefore qualified to be supervising the accused.[72]

DPP v Wright

In *DPP v Wright*,[73] by contrast, it was held that it was disproportionate to impose a legal burden on an accused who sought to rely on an exemption under s 1 of the Hunting Act 2004, considering the knowledge of facts required and the difficulty involved. The section makes it an offence for a person to hunt a wild mammal with a dog unless the hunting is exempt under s 2, being within a category of hunting specified in Sch 1 to the Act. The court noted the 'diverse and massive potential content' of the categories in Sch 1, which made it difficult for an accused to know within which category his hunting might come. Further, if the burden was a legal one, an accused would have to prove the substantial (and difficult) issues in the case once the prosecution had proved the prima facie (and easy) fact that he had been in pursuit of a mammal with a dog. Accordingly, the exemption was read down to impose an evidential burden only. Imposition of a legal burden would have been '...an oppressive, disproportionate, unfair and, in particular, an unnecessary intrusion upon the presumption of innocence in article 6'.[74]

---

[71] (2004) 168 JP 617, DC; [2006] Crim LR 140, DC.

[72] See also *R v Makuwa* [2006] 1 WLR 2755, CA: the prosecution will find it difficult, if not impossible, to prove, for the purposes of the defence set out in the Immigration and Asylum Act 1999, s 31(1), that the accused's life or freedom was *not* threatened overseas and that he had *not* presented himself to the UK authorities without delay. These are matters on which the accused is likely to be as well, if not better, informed than the prosecution. See also *R v Clarke* [2008] EWCA Crim 893.

[73] [2010] QB 224, DC.

[74] At [85]. See also *R v Charles* [2010] 1 WLR 644, CA: where an accused is charged with breaching an anti-social behaviour order (ASBO) the burden of proving a reasonable excuse under the Crime and Disorder Act 1998, s 1(10) is evidential only. The legal burden of proving lack of reasonable excuse lies with the prosecution. Parliament could not have intended to place a legal burden of proof on the accused as it had not specified the terms in which ASBOs would be made which, if breached, would be an offence and, also, it would have contemplated that conduct prohibited by an ASBO would often not be a breach of the criminal law. Similarly, see *R v Evans* [2005] 1 WLR 1435, CA, concerning breach of a restraining order under the Protection from Harassment Act 1997.

Attorney General's Reference (No 1 of 2004)

In *Attorney General's Reference (No 1 of 2004)*[75] a five-judge Court of Appeal heard five conjoined appeals concerning different reverse onus provisions. In the third appeal the court considered s 1(2) of the Protection from Eviction Act 1977, whereby a person is guilty of an offence if he unlawfully deprives the residential occupier of any premises of his occupation of the premises 'unless he proves that he believed, and had reasonable cause to believe, that the residential occupier had ceased to reside in the premises'. The court gave three reasons to justify this reverse burden: that the essence of the offence is unlawful deprivation of occupation, the defence only being available to the accused who can bring himself within a narrow exception; the circumstances relied upon by the accused are peculiarly within his own knowledge;[76] the public interest in deterring landlords from ejecting tenants unlawfully.

The fourth appeal concerned s 4 of the Homicide Act 1957. Under s 4(1), it is manslaughter and not murder for a person acting in pursuance of a suicide pact between himself and another to kill the other. Under s 4(2), 'Where it is shown that a person charged with the murder of another killed the other, it shall be for the defence to prove that the person charged was acting in pursuance of a suicide pact between him and the other.' This reverse burden was justified on the basis that it provides protection for society from murder disguised as a suicide pact killing and that the defence only arises once the prosecution have proved murder and the facts necessary to establish the defence lie within the accused's knowledge.

In the fifth appeal, the court considered s 51 of the Criminal Justice and Public Order Act 1994. Under s 51(1):

A person commits an offence if
    (a) he does an act which intimidates, or is intended to intimidate another person;
    (b) he does the act knowing or believing that the victim is assisting in the investigation of an offence or is a witness or potential witness or a juror or a potential juror in proceedings for an offence; and
    (c) he does it intending thereby to cause the investigation or the course of justice to be obstructed, perverted or interfered with.

Under s 51(7), if the matters in s 51(1)(a) and (b) are proved, the accused shall be presumed to have done the act with the intention required by s 51(1)(c) unless the contrary is proved. This reverse burden was justified on the basis that although it related to an ingredient of the offence rather than a special defence, witness and jury intimidation, which continues to increase, is a very serious threat to the proper administration of criminal justice, and in balancing the potential detriment to the accused against the mischief which Parliament is seeking to eradicate, the balance comes down firmly in favour of the prosecution.

In *Attorney General's Reference (No 1 of 2004)*, Lord Woolf CJ noted the significant difference in emphasis between the approaches of Lord Steyn in *R v Lambert* and Lord Nicholls in *R v Johnstone*, and noted in particular the likelihood that 'few provisions will be left as imposing

---

[75] [2004] 1 WLR 2111, CA.

[76] See also the first appeal concerning the Bankruptcy Act 1986, ss 352 and 353(1): facts relating to the defence were within the accused's knowledge and the imposition of a legal burden did not breach Art 6. By contrast, see the second appeal: the very wide ambit of the Bankruptcy Act 1986, s 357 made the defence difficult to prove and to impose a legal burden would be a breach of Art 6. See also *R (Griffin) v Richmond Magistrates' Court* [2008] 1 WLR 1525, DC: the defence under s 208(4)(a) of the Insolvency Act 1986 imposes a legal burden on the accused.

a legal burden on Lord Steyn's approach'.[77] It was held that until clarification of a further decision of the House of Lords, lower courts, if in doubt as to the outcome of a challenge to a reverse burden, should follow the approach of Lord Nicholls.

In *Attorney General's Reference (No 4 of 2002)*,[78] however, the House of Lords held that both *R v Lambert* and *R v Johnstone*, unless or until revised or supplemented, should be regarded as the primary domestic authorities on reverse burdens; that nothing said in *R v Johnstone* suggested an intention to depart from or modify *R v Lambert*, which should not be treated as superseded or implicitly overruled; and that the differences in emphasis were explicable by the difference in the subject matter of the two cases.[79] Lord Bingham said that the task of the court is never to decide whether a reverse burden should be imposed on a defendant, but always to assess whether a burden enacted by Parliament unjustifiably infringes the presumption of innocence.[80]

Attorney General's Reference (No 4 of 2002)

Attorney General's Reference (No 4 of 2002)[81] considered two reverse onus provisions in two conjoined appeals. The first appeal concerned s 5(2) of the Road Traffic Act 1988. Under s 5(2) it is a defence for a person charged with an offence of being in charge of a motor vehicle on a road or other public place after consuming excess alcohol, to prove that at the time he is alleged to have committed the offence, the circumstances were such that there was no likelihood of his driving the vehicle whilst the proportion of alcohol in his breath, blood, or urine remained likely to exceed the prescribed limit. It was held that even on the assumption that s 5(2) infringes the presumption of innocence, it was directed to the legitimate object of preventing death, injury, and damage caused by unfit drivers and met the tests of acceptability identified in the Strasbourg jurisprudence. It was not objectionable to criminalize conduct in these circumstances without requiring the prosecutor to prove criminal intent. The accused has a full opportunity to show that there was no likelihood of his driving, a matter so closely conditioned by his own knowledge at the time as to make it much more appropriate for him to prove the absence of a likelihood of his driving on the balance of probabilities than for the prosecutor to prove such a likelihood beyond reasonable doubt. The imposition of a legal burden therefore did not go beyond what was necessary.[82]

Regulatory offences

According to the authorities, the imposition of a legal burden on the accused is likely to be more acceptable in the case of offences which are concerned to regulate the conduct of

[77] [2004] 1 WLR 2111, CA at [38].

[78] [2003] 3 WLR 1153, HL.

[79] [2003] 3 WLR 1153, HL. See per Lord Bingham at [30] and [32]. Lords Steyn and Phillips agreed with the speech of Lord Bingham and Lords Rodger and Carswell appear to endorse these parts of Lord Bingham's speech.

[80] Lord Bingham also questioned Lord Woolf's assumption that Parliament would not have made an exception without good reason. Such an assumption, it was held, may lead the court to give too much weight to the enactment under review and too little to the presumption of innocence and the obligation imposed on it by s 3 (at [30] and [32]).

[81] [2003] 3 WLR 1153, HL.

[82] By contrast, see the second appeal which concerned the Terrorism Act 2000, s 11(1) and (2): the defence contained in s 11(2) imposed an evidential burden only as the imposition of a legal burden would have been an unjustifiable infringement of the presumption of innocence. See also, generally, Dennis, 'Reverse Onuses and the Presumption of Innocence: In Search of Principle' [2005] Crim LR 901.

particular action taken in the public interest and which are not regarded as 'truly criminal'. In *R v Lambert*,[83] Lord Clyde said:

> The requirement to have a licence in order to carry on certain types of activity is an obvious example. The promotion of health and safety and the avoidance of pollution are among the purposes to be served by such controls. These kinds of cases may properly be seen as not truly criminal. Many may be relatively trivial and only involve a monetary penalty. Many may carry with them no real social disgrace or infamy.[84]

R v Davies[85] concerned s 40 of the Health and Safety at Work Act 1974, which requires the accused to prove that 'it was not reasonably practicable to do more than was in fact done' to satisfy his health and safety duties. It was held that s 40 is not incompatible with the Convention, but justified, necessary, and proportionate.[86] In reaching this conclusion, the court relied upon the regulatory nature of the 1974 Act and the 'convincing and extremely helpful' analysis of Cory J in the Canadian Supreme Court in *R v Wholesale Travel Group*.[87] Cory J expressed the rationale for the distinction between truly criminal and regulatory offences as follows:

> Regulatory legislation involves the shift of emphasis from the protection of individual interests and the deterrence and punishment of acts involving moral fault to the protection of public and societal interests. While criminal offences are usually designed to condemn and punish past, inherently wrongful conduct, regulatory measures are generally directed to the prevention of future harm through the enforcement of minimum standards of conduct and care.
>
> It follows that regulatory offences and crimes embody different concepts of fault. Since regulatory offences are directed primarily not to conduct itself but to the consequences of conduct, conviction of a regulatory offence may be thought to import a significantly lesser degree of culpability than conviction of a true crime. The concept of fault in regulatory offences is based upon a reasonable care standard and, as such, does not imply moral blameworthiness in the same manner as criminal fault. Conviction for breach of a regulatory offence suggests nothing more than that the defendant has failed to meet a prescribed standard of care.

Justifying the distinction by what he called the licensing argument and the vulnerability justification, he continued:

> while in the criminal context the essential question to be determined is whether the accused has made the choice to act in the manner alleged in the indictment, the regulated defendant is by virtue of the licensing argument, assumed to have made the choice to engage in the regulated activity. Those who choose to participate in regulated activities have…placed themselves in a responsible relationship to the public…and must accept the consequences of that responsibility…Regulatory legislation…plays a legitimate and vital role in protecting those who are most vulnerable and least able to protect themselves.

In *R (Grundy & Co Excavations Ltd) v Halton Division Magistrates' Court*,[88] it was held that the offence of tree felling without a licence contrary to s 17 of the Forestry Act 1967 was a case

---

[83] [2002] 2 AC 545, HL at [154].
[84] See *R v S* [2003] 1 Cr App R 602, CA at [48], where this dictum was applied.
[85] [2003] ICR 586, CA.
[86] See also *R v Chargot Ltd (trading as Contract Services) and others* [2009] 1 WLR 1, HL, where the reverse burden under s 40 was not rendered *disproportionate* by the fact that penalties had been increased under the Health and Safety (Offences) Act 2008, s 1(1) and (2) and Sch 1.
[87] (1991) 3 SCR 154.
[88] (2003) 167 JP 387.

of the kind which Lord Clyde had in mind in *R v Lambert* and which Cory J had in mind in *R v Wholesale Travel Group*: it was a classic regulatory offence, designed to protect the nation's trees, involving only a monetary penalty and carrying no real social disgrace or infamy and no real moral stigma or obloquy.

To some, including the authors of this work, it remains repugnant in principle, especially in the case of imprisonable offences, that jurors or magistrates should be under a legal duty to convict if left in doubt as to whether the accused has established his defence, or are of the view that his version of events is as likely to be true as not. In some cases, as we have seen, the courts will rule that the reverse onus provision in question is incompatible with Art 6 and can be read down so as to impose only an evidential burden. However, Parliament has decided not to legislate that all burdens borne by the accused should be evidential only. In previous editions of this work, reference has been made to the views of one distinguished commentator who pointed out that if Parliament did not intervene and therefore the question of compatibility fell to be determined in respect of each reverse onus provision, there would be a long period of uncertainty and much expensive and wasteful litigation, with inconsistent results, because courts would have differing views.[89] That prediction is proving to be all too accurate, and the scale of the problem remains vast because some 40 per cent of the offences triable in the Crown Court impose a legal burden on the accused to prove at least one element of the offence or statutory defence.[90]

For a number of reasons, the various criteria that have been developed to determine compatibility compound the problems of uncertainty and inconsistency. Some courts are clearly adopting a 'pick 'n' mix' approach to the criteria; there is no guidance as to the weight to be attached to such important and potentially competing criteria as the seriousness of the potential punishment, the ease of proof, and whether a matter is within the knowledge of the accused; the criterion of deference, albeit limited, to the considered opinion of Parliament is of dubious validity given the very nature of the obligation under s 3 of the Human Rights Act 1998; and the distinction between 'truly criminal' and regulatory offences is inherently tenuous, not least because views are bound to differ as to which particular regulatory offences involve moral fault. In these circumstances, in many cases it will be as easy to draw a rational conclusion of compatibility as incompatibility.[91] As another commentator has put it, in the absence of broader principles for applying the relevant factors, decisions will continue to resemble a 'forensic lottery'.[92]

Civil cases

The general rule, in civil cases, is that he who asserts must prove. Certain issues are 'essential' to the case of a party to civil proceedings in the sense that they must be proved by him if he is to succeed in the action. The legal burden of proof will generally lie on the party asserting the affirmative of such an issue. For example, in an action for negligence, the claimant bears the

---

[89] See Professor Sir John Smith's commentary on *R v DPP, ex p Kebilene* [1999] Crim LR 994.

[90] See Ashworth and Blake 'The Presumption of Innocence in English Criminal Law' [1996] Crim LR 306. There is also a legal burden on the defendant in confiscation proceedings in the Crown Court; see *Grayson v United Kingdom* (2009) 48 EHRR 30.

[91] For a good example, see *R v Keogh* [2007] 2 Cr App R 112, where the Court of Appeal read down the Official Secrets Act 1989, ss 2(3) and 3(4) on the basis that the reverse burden was not a necessary element in the operation of ss 2 and 3, it being 'practicable' to require the prosecution to prove that the accused knew, or had reasonable cause to believe, that the information disclosed related to such matters as defence and that its disclosure would be damaging.

[92] Dennis, 'Reverse Onuses and the Presumption of Innocence: In Search of Principle' [2005] Crim LR 901 at 927. See also Ashworth, 'Four threats to the presumption of innocence' (2006) 10 E&P 241.

legal burden of proving duty of care, breach of such duty, and loss suffered in consequence. The legal burden of proving a defence which goes beyond a simple denial of the claimant's assertions, such as *volenti non fit injuria* or contributory negligence, lies on the defendant. The burden of proving a failure to mitigate is also borne by the defendant.[93] Similarly, the legal burden of proving a contract, its breach, and consequential loss lies on the claimant; and the legal burden of proving a defence which goes beyond a simple denial of the claimant's assertions, such as discharge by agreement or by frustration, lies on the defendant.

In *BHP Billiton Petroleum Ltd v Dalmine SpA*[94] it was held that, although in most civil proceedings the statements of case are likely to be a good guide to the incidence of the legal burden of proof, they cannot be definitive, because a party cannot, by poor pleading, take upon himself a burden which the law does not impose on him, or free himself from a burden which the law does impose on him. Thus a party cannot escape a legal burden borne by him on a particular issue essential to his case by drafting his claim or defence, in relation to the issue, by way of a negative allegation. In *Soward v Leggatt*[95] the plaintiff, a landlord, alleged that his tenant 'did not repair' a certain house. The defendant replied that he 'did well and sufficiently repair' the house. Lord Abinger CB, observing that the plaintiff might have pleaded that the defendant 'let the house become dilapidated', held that it was not the form of the issue which required consideration, but its substance and effect. Accordingly, it was for the plaintiff to prove the defendant's breach of covenant.[96]

The incidence of the legal burden of proof in civil cases can often be discovered from the precedents concerned with the issue of substantive law in question. In the absence of such a precedent, however, the courts are prepared to decide not on the basis of any general principles but more as a matter of policy given the particular rule of substantive law in question.[97] In *Joseph Constantine Steamship Line Ltd v Imperial Smelting Corpn Ltd*[98] a ship on charter was destroyed by an explosion the cause of which was unclear. The charterers claimed damages from the owners for failure to load. The owners' defence was frustration. The charterers argued that the owners could not rely upon frustration unless they proved that the explosion was not caused by fault on their part. The owners replied that they could rely upon frustration unless the charterers showed that the explosion was caused by their fault, that is fault on the part of the owners. The House of Lords held that in order to defeat the defence of frustration, the burden of proof was upon the charterers to prove fault on the part of the owners. Accordingly, the cause of the explosion being unclear, the appeal of the owners was allowed. It is possible to justify this outcome on the basis that it is more difficult to prove absence of fault than it is to prove fault. This justification, however, should not be regarded as an inflexible *rule*: in bailment

---

[93] *Geest plc v Lansiquot* [2002] 1 WLR 3111, PC, disapproving *Selvanayagam v University of the West Indies* [1983] 1 WLR 585, PC.

[94] [2003] BLR 271, CA at [28].

[95] (1836) 7 C&P 613.

[96] See also *Arbrath v North Eastern Rly Co* (1883) 11 QBD 440, CA, concerning an action for malicious prosecution in which the plaintiff bore the burden of proving both that the defendant had instituted proceedings and that he had done so without reasonable and probable cause. This was because, according to Bowen LJ, the assertion of a 'negative' was an essential part of the plaintiff's case. The case was affirmed on appeal ((1886) 11 App Cas 247, HL) and applied in *Reynolds v Metropolitan Police Comr* (1984) 80 Cr App R 125, CA (procuring the grant of a search warrant falsely, maliciously, and *without reasonable and probable cause*).

[97] See Stone (1944) 60 LQR 262.

[98] [1942] AC 154, HL.

cases, for example, the bailor having proved bailment, the bailee has the onus of proving that the goods were lost or damaged without fault on his part.[99] Similarly, in an action for conversion, the burden is on the bailee to prove that he dealt with the goods in good faith and without notice.[100] Thus the cases have been decided as a matter of policy on their own merits.[101]

In civil cases, as in criminal cases, the incidence of the legal burden of proof may be determined by statute. For example, whereas it is for the former employee claiming unfair dismissal to prove that he was dismissed, it is for the employer to show the reason for the dismissal and that it constitutes one of the grounds set out in the statute on which a dismissal is capable of being fair. If the employer fails to show such a reason, the dismissal is automatically unfair.[102] Equally, the parties themselves may expressly agree upon the incidence of the burden of proof.[103] The parties may do this, for example, in the case of written contracts, but in the absence of express agreement the matter becomes one of construction for the court. In *Munro, Brice & Co v War Risks Association*[104] an insurance policy covered a ship subject to an exemption in respect of loss by capture or in consequence of hostilities. The ship in question had disappeared for reasons unknown and a claim was made. The question for the court was whether the plaintiffs had to prove that the ship was not lost by reason of enemy action. The court found for the plaintiff on the basis that the defendants bore the burden of proving that the facts fell within the exception and this they had clearly failed to do.[105] However, where a claimant in these circumstances relies upon a proviso to an exemption clause, the burden of proving that the facts fall within the proviso may well be on him. In *The Glendarroch*[106] the plaintiffs brought an action in negligence for non-delivery of goods, the goods in question having been lost when the boat carrying them sank. Under the bill of lading, there was a clause exempting the defendants in respect of loss or damage caused by perils of the sea provided that the defendants were not negligent. It was held that the plaintiffs bore the burden of proving the contract and non-delivery; that if the defendants relied upon the exemption clause, it was for them to prove that the facts fell within it, ie that loss was caused by a peril of the sea; but that if the plaintiffs then relied upon the proviso to the exemption clause, it was for them to prove that the facts fell within the proviso, ie that loss was caused by the negligence of the defendants.

The incidence of the evidential burden

As a general rule in both civil and criminal proceedings, a party bearing the legal burden on a particular issue will also bear the evidential burden on that issue. This rule has given rise

[99] *Coldman v Hill* [1919] 1 KB 443, CA; cf *Levison v Patent Steam Carpet Cleaning Ltd* [1978] QB 69, CA.

[100] *Marcq v Christie Manson and Woods Ltd* [2002] 4 All ER 1005, QBD.

[101] In some civil cases exposition of the law is rendered difficult by a judicial failure to make clear which burden, legal or evidential, is in contemplation. One example is where rape is pleaded as a defence to adultery. It is unclear whether the legal burden is on the petitioner to prove that the intercourse was consensual or on the defendant to prove that it was non-consensual. In *Redpath v Redpath and Milligan* [1950] 1 All ER 600, CA the judgment of Bucknill LJ suggests the former, that of Vaisey J the latter, although neither distinguished between the legal and evidential burden.

[102] See Employment Rights Act 1996, s 98. A further example is the Consumer Credit Act 1974, s 171(7): if a debtor alleges that a credit bargain is extortionate (within the meaning of ss 137 and 138), it is for the creditor to prove to the contrary.

[103] See, eg, *Levy v Assicurazioni Generali* [1940] AC 791, PC and *Fred Chappell Ltd v National Car Parks Ltd* (1987) The Times, 22 May, QBD.

[104] [1918] 2 KB 78.

[105] Cf *Hurst v Evans* [1917] 1 KB 352.

[106] [1894] P 226, CA.

to little difficulty or case law in civil proceedings. As in criminal cases, the incidence of the evidential burden in civil cases may be affected by the operation of a presumption, a matter considered in detail in Chapter 22.[107] In criminal cases, where, as we have seen, the prosecution generally bear the legal burden of proving those facts essential to the Crown case, the prosecution normally also bear the evidential burden in relation to those facts. Similarly, where the defence bear the legal burden of proving insanity (as required at common law) or some other issue (pursuant to an express or implied statutory exception), the defence also bear the evidential burden on such issues.

In the case of all common law defences except insanity, the evidential burden is on the defence and, once discharged, the legal burden of disproving the defence is then on the prosecution.[108] However, the evidential burden may be discharged by *any* evidence in the case, whether adduced or elicited by the defence, a co-accused, or the prosecution;[109] and where there is sufficiently cogent evidence of such a defence, then the judge must leave it to the jury, even if it has not been mentioned by the defence[110] or has been expressly disclaimed by them[111] (or they have conveyed to the judge their opinion that he should not leave it to the jury)[112] and notwithstanding that it may be inconsistent with the accused's defence.[113]

The above principles apply to the common law defences of self-defence,[114] duress,[115] non-insane automatism,[116] and drunkenness.[117] However, the common law defence of

[107] See, eg, the Bills of Exchange Act 1882, s 30(2): 'Every holder of a bill is prima facie deemed to be a holder in due course; but if in an action on a bill it is admitted or proved that the acceptance, issue, or subsequent negotiation of the bill is affected with fraud, duress, or force and fear, or illegality, the burden of proof is shifted, unless and until the holder proves that subsequent to the alleged fraud or illegality, value has in good faith been given for the bill.' The effect of this provision is that if a party sues on a bill of exchange he only bears the evidential burden on the issue whether he gave value for the bill in good faith if the defendant has adduced prima facie evidence that the acceptance, issue, etc of the bill is affected with fraud, duress, etc. See *Talbot v Von Boris* [1911] 1 KB 854, CA at 866.

[108] This is also the case in relation to a variety of statutory defences. See, eg, the Criminal Law Act 1967, s 3(1) (reasonable force in the prevention of crime, etc) and *R v Cameron* [1973] Crim LR 520, CA and *R v Khan* [1995] Crim LR 78, CA. See also the Sexual Offences Act 2003, s 75, the Terrorism Act 2000, s 118(2), and the Coroners and Justice Act 2009, s 54(5).

[109] *Bullard v R* [1957] AC 635, PC.

[110] *Palmer v R* [1971] AC 814, PC at 823. See also *R v Hopper* [1915] 2 KB 431; *R v Cascoe* [1970] 2 All ER 833, CA; *R v Bonnick* (1977) 66 Cr App R 266, CA; *R v Johnson* [1989] 2 All ER 839, CA; and *DPP (Jamaica) v Bailey* [1995] 1 Cr App R 257, PC.

[111] *R v Kachikwu* (1968) 52 Cr App R 538, CA at 543.

[112] *R v Burgess and McLean* [1995] Crim LR 425, CA and *R v Dhillon* [1997] 2 Cr App R 104, CA. But see also *R v Groark* [1999] Crim LR 669, CA at n 117.

[113] See *R v Newell* [1989] Crim LR 906 and generally Doran, 'Alternative Defences: the "invisible burden" on the trial judge' [1991] Crim LR 878.

[114] *R v Lobell* [1957] 1 QB 547, CCA and *Chan Kau v R* [1955] AC 206, PC. See also the Criminal Justice and Immigration Act 2008, s 76(7), concerning evidence of reasonable force where self-defence is raised.

[115] *R v Gill* [1963] 1 WLR 841, CCA. See also *R v Bone* [1968] 1 WLR 983, CA.

[116] *Bratty v A-G for Northern Ireland* [1963] AC 386, HL. See also *R v Stripp* (1978) 69 Cr App R 318, CA at 321 and *R v Pullen* [1991] Crim LR 457, CA. The situation is different in the case of insanity, because that defence places a burden of proof on the accused, although in rare and exceptional cases the judge may of his own volition raise the issue and leave it to the jury: see *R v Thomas (Sharon)* [1995] Crim LR 314, CA.

[117] See *Kennedy v HM Advocate* 1944 JC 171 and *R v Foote* [1964] Crim LR 405. However, in *R v Groark* [1999] Crim LR 669, CA, it was held that if, in a case of wounding with intent, there is evidence of drunkenness which might give rise to the issue whether the accused had the specific intent, but the defence is that the accused knew what was happening and acted in self-defence, if the defence object to a direction on drunkenness in relation to intent, such a direction need not be given.

provocation, to which these principles also applied,[118] has been replaced by a statutory defence of loss of self-control. Under s 54(5) of the Coroners and Justice Act 2009, if sufficient evidence is adduced to raise an issue with respect to the statutory defence, the jury must assume that the defence is satisfied unless the prosecution prove beyond reasonable doubt that it is not.[119] Section 54(6) provides that sufficient evidence is adduced to raise an issue with respect to the defence if evidence is adduced on which, in the opinion of the trial judge, a jury, properly directed, could reasonably conclude that the defence might apply. Whether there is sufficient evidence of loss of self-control to permit the defence to go to the jury is now a question of law to be resolved by the judge.[120]

In *R v Cox*,[121] it was held, concerning the old defence of provocation, that where there was evidence of provocation and the defence did not rely upon it at trial, it was most unsatisfactory that the judge's failure to direct the jury on it could then found an appeal against conviction. Therefore if it appeared to counsel for either side that there was evidence of provocation, it was their duty to point it out to the judge before he summed up.[122] It is submitted that this duty extends to other current common law and statutory defences in respect of which the accused bears the evidential but not the legal burden and as regards the new defence of loss of self-control which replaces provocation, the duty will be to point out evidence which is capable of being 'sufficient' within the meaning of s 54(6) of the 2009 Act.

Where the defence of non-insane automatism is raised by an accused, the judge must decide two questions before it can be left to the jury: whether there is a proper evidential foundation for it and whether the evidence shows the case to be one of insane or non-insane automatism. If the judge rules it to be a case of insanity, the jury must then decide whether the accused is guilty or not guilty by reason of insanity.[123] It was held by the Court of Appeal in *R v Burns*[124] that where the issues of both insanity and non-insane automatism arise in the same case, the judge should direct the jury that while the accused bears the legal burden of proving insanity, he bears only the evidential burden in relation to non-insane automatism.

The law relating to the above defences is reasonably well settled and clear. It is less clear, however, whether the defence bears the evidential burden in relation to a defence which amounts to nothing more than a denial of the prosecution case and therefore raises no new issue. On one view, an accused should not bear an evidential burden in relation to a defence of, say, alibi or accident, because the onus is already on the prosecution to prove, in the one

---

[118] *Mancini v DPP* [1942] AC 1, HL and *R v Cascoe* [1970] 2 All ER 83, CA. See also *R v Rossiter* [1994] 2 All ER 752, CA and *R v Cambridge* [1994] 2 All ER 760, CA.

[119] The phrase 'beyond reasonable doubt' must now be avoided in any direction to the jury on the criminal standard of proof to be met by the prosecution (see *R v Majid* [2009] EWCA Crim 2563, CA, and generally under **The standard of proof, Criminal cases**). Notwithstanding the use of the phrase in the Coroners and Justice Act 2009, s 54(5), it is submitted that the jury will be directed that they must assume the defence is satisfied unless the prosecution make them 'sure' that it is not.

[120] See the Explanatory Notes to the Coroners and Justice Act 2009, para 340. As to when a judge was required to leave the old defence of provocation to the jury, see *R v Acott* [1977] 1 WLR 306, HL. See also *R v Kromer* [2002] All ER (D) 420 (May), CA, *R v Miao* (2003) The Times, 26 Nov, CA, and *R v Serrano* [2007] Crim LR 569, CA.

[121] [1995] 2 Cr App R 513, CA.

[122] It was also held that where there was sufficient evidence of provocation but the judge failed to leave the issue before the jury, the Court of Appeal could nonetheless conclude that the conviction was safe: see *R v Van Dongen* [2005] 2 Cr App R 632, CA.

[123] *R v Burgess* (1991) 93 Cr App R 41, CA.

[124] (1973) 58 Cr App R 364; cf *Bratty v A-G for Northern Ireland* [1963] AC 386 at 402–3.

case, that the accused was present at the scene of the crime and, in the other, that he had the requisite *mens rea*.[125] There are obiter dicta, however, to the effect that the evidential burden, in the case of both of these defences, is on the accused.[126] Moreover, in *R v Bennett*[127] it was held that the accused bore the evidential burden in relation to impossibility on a charge of conspiracy to contravene the provisions of the Misuse of Drugs Act 1971[128] and in *Bratty v A-G for Northern Ireland*, as we have seen, the accused was held to bear the evidential burden on non-insane automatism.

Where the evidential burden alone, in relation to a particular defence, is borne by the accused, the judge, if he decides that insufficient evidence has been adduced on the matter, will direct the jury that the issue must be taken as proved against the accused. If the accused has adduced sufficient evidence, the judge will direct the jury that the prosecution bears the legal burden of negativing the defence in question and must satisfy them beyond reasonable doubt on the matter. However, where the legal burden is borne by the accused, the jury should be directed that it is for the defence to satisfy them on a balance of probabilities and that if they are not so satisfied the issue must be taken as proved against the accused.[129] Accordingly, the judge may direct the jury that if they cannot decide on the evidence whether the defence case is more probable than not, they should find against the accused.

The right to begin

The right to begin adducing evidence is determined by the incidence of the evidential burden. As a general rule, the claimant has the right to begin adducing evidence in civil proceedings and the prosecution in criminal proceedings. In civil cases, the claimant has the right to adduce his evidence first unless the defendant bears the evidential burden on every issue.[130] In *Mercer v Whall*[131] an attorney's clerk brought an action for unliquidated damages for wrongful dismissal. The defendant admitted the dismissal but pleaded justification on the basis of the plaintiff's misconduct. It was held that the plaintiff was entitled to begin because he bore the evidential burden in relation to damages. The defendant would have had the right to begin if the claim had been for a liquidated sum because the only fact in issue would then have been the question of misconduct on which the defendant bore the evidential burden. In criminal cases where there is a plea of not guilty, the prosecution will normally have the right

---

[125] See Professor Glanville Williams (1977) 127 NLJ at 157–8 and generally per Lord Hailsham LC in *R v Howe* [1987] 1 All ER 771, HL at 781 ff.

[126] *R v Johnson* [1961] 3 All ER 969, CCA (alibi); *Bratty v A-G for Northern Ireland* [1963] AC 386, HL per Lord Kilmuir LC at 405 (accident). There is no dispute, however, that if the defence do adduce evidence in support of an alibi, the prosecution bear the legal burden of disproof (*R v Helliwell* [1995] Crim LR 79, CA and *R v Fergus* (1993) 98 Cr App R 313, CA) and ideally the judge should give a specific direction on the burden of proof in relation to the alibi (*R v Anderson* [1991] Crim LR 361, CA and *R v Johnson* [1995] Crim LR 242, CA). See also *R v Mussell* [1995] Crim LR 887, CA: a specific direction is needed if the nature of the alibi is that the accused was at a specific place elsewhere, raising the question why he did not call witnesses in support, but not if the evidence amounts to little more than a denial that he committed the crime.

[127] (1978) 68 Cr App R 168, CA.

[128] However, it was further held that if the prosecution have in their possession evidence which might show that at the time when the agreement was made the carrying out of the agreement would have been impossible, it is the duty of the prosecution either to call the evidence or to make it available to the defence.

[129] See *R v Evans-Jones, R v Jenkins* (1923) 87 JP 115, and *R v Carr-Briant* [1943] KB 607.

[130] See *Pontifex v Jolly* (1839) 9 C&P 202 and *Re Parry's Estate, Parry v Fraser* [1977] 1 All ER 309.

[131] (1845) 14 LJ QB 267.

to adduce their evidence first. The reason appears to be that they will almost always bear an evidential burden on at least one issue. However, this may not be the case where the accused has made formal admissions pursuant to s 10 of the Criminal Justice Act 1967 or agreed to a statement of facts admitted in evidence pursuant to s 9 of the same Act. Where the accused pleads *autrefois acquit* or *convict* and there is a dispute of fact requiring evidence, the accused has the right to begin.

The standard of proof

The legal burden

Whether a party to civil or criminal proceedings has discharged a legal burden borne by him in relation to a particular issue is, as we have seen, decided by the tribunal of fact at the end of the case. To discharge the burden and succeed on that issue the evidence adduced by that party must, in the opinion of the tribunal of fact, be more cogent or convincing than that adduced by his opponent. How much more cogent or convincing the evidence is required to be is determined by rules of law relating to the standard of proof. If the evidence adduced by a party is sufficiently cogent or convincing to meet the appropriate standard of proof, the legal burden will be discharged and facts in issue will be legally proved and taken to have happened. In *Re B (Children) (Sexual Abuse)*,[132] Lord Hoffmann explained this process in the following way:[133]

> If a legal rule requires a fact to be proved (a 'fact in issue'), a judge or jury must decide whether or not it happened. There is no room for a finding that it might have happened. The law operates a binary system in which the only values are 0 and 1. The fact either happened or it did not. If the tribunal is left in doubt, the doubt is resolved by a rule that one party or the other carries the burden of proof. If the party who bears the burden of proof fails to discharge it, a value of 0 is returned and the fact is treated as not having happened. If he does discharge it, a value of 1 is returned and the fact is treated as having happened.

The standard of proof required to discharge a legal burden depends upon whether the proceedings are criminal or civil, the standard being higher in the former than in the latter. In criminal proceedings, the standard required of the prosecution before the jury can find the accused guilty was previously expressed as proof beyond reasonable doubt.[134] However, the standard is now expressed as proof which makes the jury sure. In civil proceedings, the standard of proof required to be met by either party seeking to discharge a legal burden is proof on a balance of probabilities.

The notion of a third and intermediate standard of proof lying between the standards required in criminal and civil cases has not found favour in the courts.[135]

The standard of proof in Criminal cases

The rules prescribing the standard of proof are a matter of law for the judge. Whether the evidence adduced meets the standard is a question for the jury as tribunal of fact. In criminal

---

[132] [2009] 1 AC 11.

[133] *Re B (Children) (Sexual Abuse)* [2009] 1 AC 11 at [2].

[134] See *Ferguson v R* [1979] 1 WLR 94, where Lord Scarman stated that, 'The time honoured formula is that the jury must be satisfied beyond reasonable doubt'. The phrase was also approved by the House of Lords in *Woolmington v DPP* [1935] AC 462 and *Mancini v DPP* [1942] AC 1.

[135] See, eg, per Lord Tucker in *Dingwall v J Wharton (Shipping) Ltd* [1961] 2 Lloyd's Rep 213, HL at 216.

trials, therefore, the judge must direct the jury on the standard of proof that the prosecution are required to meet.[136] As has been noted, the criminal standard of proof is now expressed as proof which makes the jury sure and judges must no longer direct juries by reference to proof beyond a reasonable doubt. This is because directions which refer to proof beyond a reasonable doubt have great potential to confuse juries. Particular difficulties have arisen where judges attempt to define and explain the concept of proof beyond a reasonable doubt, sometimes by combining it with the concept of being 'sure' and by drawing distinctions with the concept of being 'certain'.[137] In *R v Majid*[138] the Court of Appeal, by way of clarification, made the following points concerning the direction to be given.

1. Judges are advised by the Judicial Studies Board, as they have been for many years, to direct the jury that before they can return a verdict of guilty, they must be sure that the defendant is guilty.[139]

2. When giving the direction, judges should avoid drawing distinctions between 'sure' and 'certain' as such a distinction is difficult for anyone to articulate clearly and helpfully.[140]

3. Where the jury raise an issue with the judge about what possibilities could justifiably leave them 'unsure', it would be appropriate for the judge to direct them simply that they should exclude fanciful possibilities and act only on realistic ones.[141]

In respect of point (1) above, the longstanding advice given to judges by the Judicial Studies Board is contained in the Crown Court Bench Book. That advice is simply that the prosecution prove their case if the jury, having considered all the relevant evidence, are sure that the

---

[136] See Ch 2 under **The functions of the judge and jury**, **The summing-up**. The same standard, ie the same standard as for the prosecution, also has to be met: (i) by a judge determining the facts for the purpose of sentence, the accused having pleaded guilty and having put forward a version of the facts which differs significantly from the prosecution's version (*R v McGrath and Casey* (1983) 5 Cr App R (S) 460 and *R v Ahmed* (1984) 6 Cr App R (S) 391), although in respect of extraneous facts put forward in mitigation the burden is on the accused and the standard is the civil standard—see *R v Guppy* [1995] 16 Cr App R (S) 25; (ii) by a judge determining whether exceptional circumstances exist to justify departing from the requirement to impose a statutory minimum sentence under the Firearms Act 1968, s 51(A) (*R v Lashari* [2011] 1 Cr App R (S) 72, CA and also *R v Boetang* [2011] EWCA Crim 861); (iii) by a jury in a coroner's court considering a verdict of unlawful killing (including cases where an issue of insanity is raised) or suicide (*R v West London Coroner, ex p Gray* [1987] 2 All ER 129, DC, *R v Wolverhampton Coroner, ex p McCurbin* [1990] 2 All ER 759, CA, and *R v HM Coroner for District of Avon, ex p O'Connor* [2009] EWHC 854, DC); (iv) where in confiscation proceedings pursuant to the Drugs Trafficking Act 1994, Pt I, the prosecution asks the judge to consider whether a convicted person has benefited from an offence with which he had not been charged (*R v Briggs-Price* [2009] 1 AC 1026, HL); and (v) by a Solicitors Disciplinary Tribunal investigating what is tantamount to a criminal offence: *Re a Solicitor* [1991] NLJR 1447, DC. See also reg 10 of the Disciplinary Tribunals Regulations 1993, Annexe N, Code of Conduct of the Bar of England and Wales and *Campbell v Hamlet* [2005] 3 All ER 1116, PC.
[137] See *R v Yap Chuan Ching* (1976) 63 Cr App R 7, CA, where the jury sought clarification of a direction which combined the concepts of 'proof beyond reasonable doubt' and 'sure'. In *R v Ferguson* [1979] 1 WLR 94 at 99, Lord Scarman suggested a direction which conflated the concepts: 'It is generally sufficient and safe to direct the jury that they must be satisfied beyond a reasonable doubt so that they feel sure of the defendant's guilt.' In *R v Stephens* [2002] EWCA Crim 1529, an unhelpful distinction was drawn between being sure of guilt and being certain of guilt. See also the trial judge's direction in *R v Majid* [2009] EWCA Crim 2563, CA, quoted by Moses LJ at [14]. For earlier definitions and explanations of the concept of reasonable doubt, see *Miller v Minister of Pensions* [1947] 2 All ER 372 at 373–4, *R v Summers* (1952) 36 Cr App R 14, *R v Hepworth and Fearnley* [1955] 2 QB 600, CCA, and *R v Kritz* [1950] 1 KB 82, CCA.
[138] [2009] EWCA Crim 2563.
[139] Per Moses LJ, *R v Majid* [2009] EWCA Crim 2563, CA at [11].
[140] *R v Majid* [2009] EWCA Crim 2563, CA at [16]. See also *R v Stephens* [2002] EWCA Crim 1529 at [14]–[15].
[141] At [12]. See also *Miller v Minister of Pensions* [1947] 2 All ER 372 at 373–4.

accused is guilty.[142] Further explanation is described as 'unwise'.[143] If the jury are not sure then they must find the accused not guilty.

Where the accused bears the legal burden

In criminal cases, the legal burden is, as we have seen, generally borne by the prosecution. Where the legal burden on a particular issue is borne by the accused, it is discharged by the defence satisfying the jury on a balance of probabilities.[144] So, where the defence bear the legal burden of proving insanity[145] or diminished responsibility,[146] the burden is discharged by satisfying the jury on a balance of probabilities.[147]

The standard of proof in Civil cases

In civil trials, the standard of proof required to be met by either party seeking to discharge the legal burden of proof is on a balance of probabilities.[148] The same standard should also be used in reaching a decision on a submission of no case to answer when the defendant has elected not to adduce any evidence.[149] In *Miller v Minister of Pensions*[150] Denning J described as well settled the degree of cogency required to discharge the legal burden in a civil case. He continued:[151]

> It must carry a reasonable degree of probability, but not so high as is required in a criminal case. If the evidence is such that the tribunal can say: 'we think it more probable than not', the burden is discharged, but if the probabilities are equal it is not.

To the general rule on the standard of proof in civil proceedings are a number of clearly defined exceptions. First, the appropriate standard in committal proceedings for civil contempt of court is the criminal standard, proof beyond reasonable doubt.[152] Second, the criminal standard may also be required in civil proceedings pursuant to statute.[153] Third, it has been

---

[142] Crown Court Bench Book 2010, 16. Where the jury are told in clear terms that they should return a verdict of guilty only if they are sure, failure to tell them that they should return a *not guilty* verdict if they are *not* sure will not necessarily render a conviction unsafe: see *R v Blackford* [2009] EWCA Crim 1684. Where the phrase 'beyond reasonable doubt' has been used during a trial, for example by counsel in their speeches, the jury should be simply directed that it means the same as being sure: see *R v Adey*, unreported (97/5306/W2).

[143] Crown Court Bench Book 2010, 16.

[144] See *R v Carr-Briant* [1943] KB 607, CCA. In particular see at 612.

[145] *Sodeman v R* [1936] 2 All ER 1138, PC at 1140.

[146] *R v Dunbar* [1958] 1 QB 1.

[147] See the Crown Court Bench Book, 2010, 16: 'The defendant proves the matter in issue if the jury conclude, having considered all the relevant evidence, that the matter asserted is more probable (or more likely) than not.'

[148] The same standard is not necessarily appropriate for interim applications. For example, an application for summary judgment is decided not by application of the normal standard of proof but by application of the test whether the respondent has a case with a real prospect of success: *Royal Brompton Hospital NHS Trust v Hammond* [2001] BLR 297, CA.

[149] *Miller v Cawley* (2002) The Times, 6 Sept, CA.

[150] [1947] 2 All ER 372.

[151] [1947] 2 All ER 372 at 374.

[152] *Re Bramblevale Ltd* [1970] Ch 128, CA; *Dean v Dean* [1987] 1 FLR 517, CA; see also *Re A (A Child) (Abduction: Contempt)* [2009] 1 FLR 1, CA and *Re LW (Children) (Enforcement and Committal: Contact)* [2011] 1 FCR 78, CA. Where contempt is proved, the contemnor bears the burden of proving that he has purged his contempt and the civil standard applies (see *JSC BTA Bank v Solodchenko* [2010] EWHC 2843, (Ch)). Proceedings to bind over for breach of the peace are probably criminal proceedings, but even if properly classified as civil proceedings, call for proof to the criminal standard, because failure to comply with an order to enter into a recognisance may result in imprisonment: *Percy v DPP* [1995] 3 All ER 124, DC.

[153] See *Judd v Minister of Pensions and National Insurance* [1966] 2 QB 580. See also *Watkins v Wollas* [2010] EWHC 2702, QB.

held that an exacting civil standard of proof, which for all practical purposes is indistinguishable from the criminal standard of proof, applies to the following civil proceedings: applications for sex offender orders (in relation to the condition, set out in s 2(1)(a) of the Crime and Disorder Act 1998, that the person against whom the order is sought is a 'sex offender');[154] applications for Sexual Offences Prevention Orders (in relation to the conditions set out in s 104 of the Sexual Offences Act 2003, including that the person is a qualifying offender and his behaviour is such that the order is necessary to protect the public from serious sexual harm);[155] applications for football banning orders under s 14B of the Football Spectators Act 1989;[156] and applications for anti-social behaviour orders (in relation to the condition, set out in s 1(1)(a) of the Crime and Disorder Act 1998, that the person against whom the order is sought has acted 'in an anti-social manner').[157] As to the last case, it has been held that magistrates, to make their task more straightforward, should always apply the *criminal* standard.[158]

There are only two standards of proof, the civil and the criminal standard. There is no intermediate standard. Nor is the civil standard to be broken down into sub-categories designed to produce one or more intermediate standards. However, although there is a single civil standard, it is flexible in its *application*. In particular, the more serious the allegation or the more serious the consequences if the allegation is proved, the stronger must be the evidence before a court will find the allegation proved on the balance of probabilities.[159] Thus although there are indications in some of the authorities that the flexibility of the standard lies in an adjustment of the degree of probability required for an allegation to be proved,[160] the flexibility does not lie in any such adjustment but in the strength or quality of the evidence required for the allegation to be proved on the balance of probabilities.[161] 'The more serious the allegation the more cogent is the evidence required to overcome the unlikelihood of what is alleged and thus to prove it.'[162] As Morris LJ remarked in *Hornal v Neuberger Products Ltd*, 'the very elements of gravity become a part of the whole range of circumstances which have to be weighed in the scale when deciding as to the balance of probabilities'.[163]

Some authorities clearly focus on the seriousness of the allegation rather than the seriousness of the consequences if the allegation is proved, on the reasoning that the more serious the allegation the less likely it is that the event occurred, and that the inherent probability or improbability of an event is itself a matter to be taken into account.[164] However, this

[154] *B v Chief Constable of Avon and Somerset Constabulary* [2001] 1 WLR 340, DC.

[155] See *R (Chief Constable of Cleveland Police) v H* (2010) 174 JP 132, DC.

[156] *Gough v Chief Constable of the Derbyshire Constabulary* [2002] QB 1213, CA.

[157] *R (McCann) v Crown Court at Manchester* [2003] 1 AC 787, HL.

[158] *R (McCann) v Crown Court at Manchester* [2003] 1 AC 787, HL.

[159] See *R (D) v Life Sentence Review Commissioners* (Northern Ireland) [2008] 1 WLR 1499, HL, where it was held that although the civil standard of proof was unvarying, it was flexible in its application. For a conceptual framework for understanding the civil standard of proof, see Redmayne, 'Standards of Proof in Civil Litigation' (1999) 62 MLR 167.

[160] See, eg, per Denning LJ in *Bater v Bater* [1951] P 35 at 37 and in *Hornal v Neuberger Products Ltd* [1957] 1 QB 247.

[161] Per Richards LJ, after an extensive review of the authorities, in *R (on the application of N) v Mental Health Review Tribunal* [2006] QB 468, CA at [60]–[62].

[162] Per Ungoed-Thomas J in *Re Dellow's Will Trusts* [1964] 1 WLR 451, Ch D.

[163] [1957] 1 QB 247, CA at 266. These words of Morris LJ were approved and adopted by the House of Lords in *Khawaja v Secretary of State for the Home Department* [1983] 1 All ER 765 in relation to the detention pending deportation of persons alleged to be illegal immigrants: see per Lord Scarman at 783–4.

[164] See *Re H (Minors) (Sexual Abuse: Standard of Proof)* [1996] AC 563, followed in *Secretary of State for the Home Department v Rehman* [2003] 1 AC 153.

rationalization will take due account of the seriousness of the consequences if an allegation is proved, because in general the seriousness of an allegation is a function of the seriousness of its consequences. Nonetheless, there will be cases where proof of an allegation may have serious consequences even though it cannot be said that the matter alleged is inherently improbable, and in such cases the more serious the consequences, the stronger the evidence required to prove the matter on the balance of probabilities.[165]

Issues calling for flexibility in the application of the civil standard defy comprehensive classification, but will be explored by reference to (i) allegations of crime in civil proceedings; (ii) matrimonial causes; and (iii) a miscellany of different cases.

Allegations of crime in civil proceedings
Prior to the decision of the Court of Appeal in *Hornal v Neuberger Products Ltd*,[166] it was unclear, on the authorities, what standard of proof was appropriate in civil cases in which a party made an allegation of criminal conduct. One line of authorities supported the view that the standard was as high as that required of the prosecution in a criminal case.[167] Other authorities took the view that the appropriate standard was the normal civil standard on a balance of probabilities.[168] In *Hornal v Neuberger Products Ltd* the plaintiff claimed damages for breach of warranty or alternatively for fraud. The defendant company had sold a lathe to the plaintiff. The plaintiff alleged that one of the company directors had represented that the lathe had been 'Soag reconditioned'. If the director did so represent, there was clearly a fraudulent misrepresentation because he knew that the machine had not been reconditioned. The question became whether the representation had been made or not. Dismissing the claim for damages for breach of warranty on the grounds that the parties did not intend the director's statement to have contractual effect, the trial judge said that he was satisfied on a balance of probabilities, but not beyond reasonable doubt, that the statement was made and accordingly awarded damages for fraud. On appeal, the Court of Appeal held that on an allegation of a crime in civil proceedings the standard of proof is on a balance of probabilities.

One of the reasons for the decision was put clearly by Denning LJ:[169] 'I think it would bring the law into contempt if a judge were to say on the issue of warranty he finds the statement was made, and that on the issue of fraud he finds it was not made.' In support of his conclusion that the civil standard applied, his Lordship referred to the views which he had expressed in *Bater v Bater*[170] where he said that civil cases must be proved by a preponderance of probability, but there may be degrees of probability within that standard. However, as we have seen, it is now recognized that the flexibility of the civil standard does not lie in an adjustment of the degree of probability but in the strength of the evidence required for serious allegations to be proved.

Against the background of conflicting authorities preceding it, *Hornal v Neuberger Products Ltd* would appear to have settled this area of the law in favour of the normal civil standard.

[165] Per Richards LJ in *R (on the application of N) v Mental Health Review Tribunal* [2006] QB 468, CA at [64].
[166] [1957] 1 QB 247.
[167] See, eg, *Issais v Marine Insurance Co Ltd* (1923) 15 Ll L Rep 186, CA (allegations of arson on the part of the assured in an action on an insurance policy).
[168] See, eg, *Hurst v Evans* [1917] 1 KB 352, KBD (an allegation of theft on the part of the servant of the assured in an action on an insurance policy).
[169] [1957] 1 QB 247 at 258.
[170] [1951] P 35 at 37, CA.

It was applied in *Re Dellow's Will Trusts*,[171] civil proceedings in which the issue was whether a wife feloniously killed her husband. As Ungoed-Thomas J pertinently observed: 'There can hardly be a graver issue than that.' It was also applied in *Post Office v Estuary Radio Ltd*,[172] where an allegation of a criminal offence under the Wireless Telegraphy Act 1949 was made on an application for an injunction under the same Act.[173] Similarly, in *Re B (Children) (Care Proceedings: Standard of Proof)*,[174] the House of Lords held that the normal civil standard applied where allegations of sexual crimes against children were made in care proceedings, notwithstanding that such allegations were grave.[175]

Matrimonial causes

The authorities remain in conflict as to the standard of proof appropriate to matrimonial causes, earlier decisions requiring the criminal standard of beyond reasonable doubt, more recent cases favouring the ordinary civil standard on a balance of probabilities. In *Ginesi v Ginesi*,[176] where it was held that adultery must be proved to the criminal standard, the Court of Appeal relied upon the fact that adultery was regarded by the ecclesiastical courts as a quasi-criminal offence.[177] In *Preston-Jones v Preston-Jones*,[178] a husband petitioned for divorce on the ground of adultery and proved that his wife had given birth to a normal child 360 days after the last opportunity he could have had for intercourse with her. The House of Lords held that adultery had been proved beyond reasonable doubt, Lord MacDermott stressing the gravity and public importance of the issues involved: 'The jurisdiction in divorce involves the status of the parties and the public interest requires that the marriage bond shall not be set aside lightly or without strict inquiry.'[179] Because the result of a finding of adultery would have been in effect to render the child illegitimate, this decision may be regarded as little more than an application of the law, as it then stood,[180] that the presumption of legitimacy could only be rebutted by proof beyond reasonable doubt.[181]

When the question of the appropriate standard in matrimonial causes next fell to be considered by the House of Lords, in *Blyth v Blyth*,[182] the tide had begun to turn. A husband petitioning for divorce on the ground of adultery sought to negative the presumption of condonation which arose from his sexual intercourse with his wife on a date subsequent to the

---

[171] [1964] 1 WLR 451, Ch D.

[172] [1967] 1 WLR 1396, CA.

[173] See also *Piermay Shipping Co SA and Brandt's Ltd v Chester, The Michael* [1979] 1 Lloyd's Rep 55 (an allegation of deliberately scuttling a ship); *Khawaja v Secretary of State for the Home Department* [1983] 1 All ER 765, HL (detention pending deportation of persons alleged to be illegal immigrants), distinguished in *Ali v Secretary of State for the Home Department* [1988] Imm AR 274, CA; and *Parks v Clout* [2003] EWCA Civ 893 (an allegation of obtaining letters of administration by fraud).

[174] [2009] 1 AC 11, HL.

[175] Followed in *Re D (Children)* [2009] 2 FLR 668, CA. See also *Smithkline Beecham plc v Avery* [2011] Bus LR D 40 which, drawing on *Re B* [2009] 1 AC 11, HL at [59]–[61], determined that a single civil standard applied in a claim for an injunction to restrain harassment under the Protection From Harassment Act 1994, s 1(1)(A).

[176] [1948] P 179, CA.

[177] See also *Bater v Bater* [1951] P 35, CA. However, cf *Briginshaw v Briginshaw* (1938) 60 CLR 336, a decision of the High Court of Australia favouring proof to the civil standard.

[178] [1951] AC 391.

[179] See also *Galler v Galler* [1954] P 252.

[180] See now Family Law Reform Act 1969, s 26, but see also *Serio v Serio* (1983) 13 Fam Law 255, CA (see n 204).

[181] See particularly the speech of Lord Simonds. See also *F v F* [1968] P 506.

[182] [1966] AC 643.

adultery. The question arose as to the standard of proof required to negative condonation. The majority of the House, comprising Lords Pearson, Denning, and Pearce, held that proof was required on a balance of probabilities. Lord Pearson was of the view that the requirement of proof beyond reasonable doubt was confined to the grounds of divorce and did not extend to the bars to divorce. Lord Denning, however, held that both the grounds for and the bars to divorce may be proved on a preponderance of probability. His Lordship disapproved *Ginesi v Ginesi*, preferring *Wright v Wright*,[183] a decision of the High Court of Australia in the same year, and relied upon his own dicta in *Bater v Bater*[184] and the decision in *Hornal v Neuberger Products Ltd*.[185]

In the light of the various dicta in *Preston-Jones v Preston-Jones*[186] and *Blyth v Blyth*,[187] it was not surprising to find the Court of Appeal in the ensuing case of *Bastable v Bastable and Sanders*[188] openly expressing the difficulties of determining what standard of proof should be applied in relation to proof of adultery.[189] Wilmer LJ adopted the dicta of Lord Denning in *Bater v Bater*, which were approved in *Hornal v Neuberger Products Ltd*, that the court requires a degree of probability proportionate to the subject matter. Accordingly, he was satisfied that the commission of adultery is a serious matrimonial offence and held that a high standard of proof is required.

Bastable v Bastable, it is submitted, is a decision which accords with the spirit of the then un-enacted Divorce Reform Act 1969,[190] which abolished the old grounds for divorce, largely based on the concept of the matrimonial offence, replacing them with one ground, that the marriage has irretrievably broken down established if the petitioner 'satisfies' the court of one of five facts. The fact that the ecclesiastical courts regarded adultery as a quasi-criminal offence is, under the present philosophy of divorce law, not a convincing reason for the application of the criminal standard of proof, especially now that the civil standard of proof is held to be appropriate in civil cases in which allegations of crime are made.[191] The matter may be one of statutory construction under the current legislation. The same word 'satisfied' was used in the legislation prior to the Divorce Reform Act 1969 under which the above decisions were decided. However, it is inconceivable that the criminal standard would ever be re-imposed by way of statutory construction or because of the importance of divorce to the parties and to the state.

Miscellaneous

On various different issues arising in civil cases it has been suggested either (a) that the appropriate standard is higher than the ordinary civil standard (sometimes as high as the criminal

---

[183] (1948) 77 CLR 191.

[184] [1951] P 35, CA at 37.

[185] [1957] 1 QB 247.

[186] [1951] AC 391.

[187] [1966] AC 643.

[188] [1968] 1 WLR 1684, CA.

[189] See per Willmer LJ [1968] WLR 1684, CA at 1685.

[190] See now the Matrimonial Causes Act 1973.

[191] See, for example, the views expressed in *Raydon and Jackson on Divorce and Family Matters* (18th edn, London, 2005) ch 9 para 9.13: '...It is wrong...to say that adultery must be proved with the same strictness that is required in a criminal case. As far as the standard of proof is concerned, adultery, like any other fact with which irretrievable breakdown of marriage is concerned, may be proved by a preponderance of probability.'

standard) or, in any event, (b) that the more improbable the event being alleged, the stronger the evidence required to prove it (on a balance of probabilities). The following examples may be given.

1. A party desiring to prove an intention to change domicile must do so 'clearly and unequivocally'.[192]

2. There is a strong common law presumption that a marriage ceremony celebrated between persons who intended it to constitute a valid marriage is formally valid. Evidence in rebuttal is required to be 'strong, distinct, and satisfactory'[193] or 'evidence which satisfied beyond reasonable doubt that there was no valid marriage'.[194]

3. A party claiming rectification is required to prove his case by 'strong irrefragable evidence'.[195]

4. In cases involving the care of children, the standard is the ordinary civil standard but it had been held that the more serious or improbable an allegation of abuse, the stronger the evidence required to prove both the abuse[196] and the identity of the abuser.[197] Following *Re B (Children) (Sexual Abuse: Standard of Proof)*,[198] it is now settled law that the standard is the simple balance of probabilities[199] and that the seriousness and probability of an allegation are simply factors to be taken into account when determining where the truth lies.[200] In *Re B*, Baroness Hale observed that there is no 'logical or necessary connection' between the seriousness of an allegation and the probability that what is alleged occurred, as a serious allegation can be more or less probable according to other evidence.[201] Her Ladyship observed:[202]

> It may be unlikely that any person looking after a baby would take him by the wrist and swing him against a wall, causing multiple fractures and other injuries. But once the evidence is clear that that is indeed what has happened to the child, it ceases to be improbable. Some-one looking after the child at the relevant time must have done it. The inherent improbability of the event has no relevance to deciding who that was. The simple balance of probabilities test should be applied.

[192] *Moorhouse v Lord* (1863) 10 HL Cas 272 at 236. See also *Fuld's Estate (No 3)* [1968] P 675 at 685.

[193] *Piers v Piers* (1849) 2 HL Cas 331 at 389.

[194] *Mahadervan v Mahadervan* [1964] P 233 at 246.

[195] *Countess of Shelburne v Earl of Inchiquin* (1784) 1 Bro CC 338 at 341. See also *Earl v Hector Whaling Ltd* [1961] 1 Lloyd's Rep 459, CA.

[196] See *Re H (minors) (sexual abuse: standard of proof)* [1996] AC 563, HL and *Re U (a Child) (Serious Injury: Standard of Proof)* [2005] Fam 134, CA. See also Smith, 'Sexual Abuse: Standard of Proof' [1994] *Fam Law* 626 and Spencer, 'Evidence in child abuse cases—too high a price for too high a standard?' (1994) 6 JCL 160.

[197] *Re G (A Child) (Non-accidental Injury: Standard of Proof)* [2001] 1 FCR 97, CA. See also *Re M (Children)* [2008] EWCA Civ 1216.

[198] [2009] 1 AC 61, HL.

[199] See *Re S-B (Children) (Care Proceedings: Standard of Proof)* [2010] 1 AC 278, SC, per Baroness Hale at 692.

[200] Per Lord Hoffmann at [70]–[73]. There is no necessary connection between seriousness and probability, as a serious allegation can be more or less probable according to other evidence. It could be rare for a person to harm a child he is looking after, but it ceases to be improbable if other evidence shows that the child sustained injuries at a time when being looked after. See also Phipson, *Law of Evidence* (17th edn, London, 2012) ch 6 para 6–02.

[201] [2009] 1 AC 61, HL at [72].

[202] [2009] 1 AC 61, HL at [73].

5. The standard required to make a finding of paternity is a heavy one, commensurate with the gravity of the issue, and although not as heavy as in criminal proceedings, more than the ordinary civil standard of balance of probabilities.[203]

6. For a court to approve medical treatment for an incompetent mentally ill patient without infringing Art 3 of the European Convention on Human Rights, it must be 'convincingly shown' that the proposed treatment is medically necessary, a standard that may be met notwithstanding that there is a responsible body of opinion against the proposed treatment.[204]

7. Cogent evidence is in practice required to satisfy a mental health review tribunal, on the balance of probabilities, that the conditions for continuing detention under ss 72 and 73 of the Mental Health Act 1983 have been met.[205]

8. The gravity of civil recovery proceedings under Pt V of the Proceeds of Crime Act 2002 is 'very great indeed' and evidence that the property sought to be recovered is or represents property obtained through unlawful conduct must satisfy the court to a standard that is commensurate with the gravity of the case.[206]

9. Where a risk of sexual harm order is made under s 123(4) of the Sexual Offences Act 2003, the consequences of a breach of the order are very serious and can have a significant impact on someone who may never have been convicted of a child sex offence. Accordingly, on an application for a risk of sexual harm order on grounds that the defendant has done an act specified in s 123(3) and that the order is necessary to protect a child, the standard of proof must be the same as for an offence. Even though the Act is silent on the standard of proof and there are a range of cases that are civil, the standard of proof to be applied is the criminal standard.[207]

The evidential burden

Whether a party to civil or criminal proceedings has discharged an evidential burden borne by him in relation to a particular issue is, as we have seen, decided by the judge as opposed to the tribunal of fact. This may account for the dearth of authority on the standard required to discharge the evidential burden. In criminal cases, the standard required to discharge the evidential burden depends upon whether it is borne by the prosecution or defence. We have seen that in criminal trials either party bearing an evidential burden must adduce sufficient evidence to prevent the judge from withdrawing the issue in question from the jury, and this is done when there is sufficient evidence to justify as a possibility a favourable finding by the tribunal of fact. Where the evidential burden is borne by the prosecution, it is discharged by the

---

[203] *W v K* [1988] Fam Law 64. See also *Serio v Serio* (1983) 13 Fam Law 255, divorce proceedings in which the paternity of the wife's son was in dispute. The Court of Appeal held that notwithstanding the Family Law Reform Act 1969, s 26, the standard on an issue of paternity is slightly higher than the balance of probabilities.

[204] *R (N) v Dr M* [2003] 1 WLR 562, CA.

[205] *R (on the application of N) v Mental Health Review Tribunal* [2006] QB 468, CA.

[206] Per Tugendhat J in *The Assets Recovery Agency v Virtosu* [2009] 1 WLR 2808 at [18]. See also the Proceeds of Crime Act 2002, s 241(3). See also *Gale v Serious Organised Crime Agency* [2011] 1 WLR 2760, SC: although such proceedings involve proof of unlawful conduct, they do not involve the bringing of criminal charges and do not engage Art 6(2) of the European Convention on Human Rights. Accordingly, there is no entitlement to the presumption of innocence and it is correct to apply the civil and not the criminal standard.

[207] *Commissioner of Police of the Metropolis v Ebanks* (2012) 176 JP 751, DC.

adduction of 'such evidence as, if believed and if left uncontradicted and unexplained, could be accepted by the jury as proof'.[208] This means that the prosecution must adduce sufficient evidence to justify as a possibility a finding by the tribunal of fact that the legal burden on the same issue has been discharged, discharge of the legal burden, of course, requiring proof beyond reasonable doubt. However, where the evidential burden is borne by the accused, it is discharged by the adduction of such evidence as 'might leave a jury in reasonable doubt'.[209] This standard applies only where the defence bear the evidential but not the legal burden on a particular issue, as when the defence is one of self-defence or duress. Where the defence bear both the legal and evidential burden in relation to an issue, as when the defence is one of insanity or diminished responsibility, the evidential burden is discharged by the adduction of such evidence as *might* satisfy the jury of the probability of that which the accused is called upon to establish.[210] In civil cases, whichever party bears the evidential burden on a particular issue, it is discharged by the adduction of sufficient evidence to justify as a possibility a finding by the tribunal of fact that the legal burden on the same issue has been discharged, discharge of the legal burden, of course, requiring proof on a balance of probabilities.

The burden and standard of proof in a trial within a trial

Preliminary facts are those facts which must be proved as a condition precedent to the admissibility of certain items of evidence. It is for the judge alone, if necessary in a trial within a trial, to determine whether preliminary facts have been proved. The burden of proving such facts is borne by the party who alleges their existence and who seeks to admit the evidence in question.[211] On the question whether a witness is competent to give evidence in criminal proceedings, it is for the party calling the witness to satisfy the court on a balance of probabilities that the witness is competent.[212] Where the prosecution bear the burden of proving preliminary facts, the standard of proof required to discharge the burden is proof beyond reasonable doubt.[213] It would seem to follow that where the burden under discussion is borne by the defendant in criminal proceedings, or by either party to civil proceedings, the appropriate standard is proof on a balance of probabilities.[214] In *R v Ewing*[215] the Court of

---

[208] Per Lord Devlin in *Jayasena v R* [1970] AC 618 at 624.

[209] Per Lord Morris in *Bratty v A-G for Northern Ireland* [1963] AC 386, HL at 419.

[210] See per Humphreys J in *R v Carr-Briant* [1943] KB 607 at 612.

[211] See, at common law, *R v Jenkins* (1869) LR 1 CCR 187 (a dying declaration) and *R v Thompson* [1893] 2 QB 12 (a confession). As to the former, see now the Criminal Justice Act 2003, s 116. As to the latter, see now the Police and Criminal Evidence Act 1984, s 76(2). See generally Pattenden, 'Authenticating "Things" in English Law: Principles for Adducing Tangible Evidence in Common Law Jury Trials' (2008) 12 E&P 273, especially at 281 and, further, Pattenden, 'The Proof Rules of Pre-verdict Judicial Fact-Finding in Criminal Trials by Jury' [2009] 125 LQR 79. For an example of a preliminary issue in civil proceedings, see *Morris v Davies* [2011] EWHC 1773 (Ch) (domicile of the deceased in the administration of an estate).

[212] Youth Justice and Criminal Evidence Act 1999, s 54(2).

[213] See *R v Sartori* [1961] Crim LR 397 in relation to confessions, *R v Jenkins* (1869) LR 1 CCR 187 in relation to dying declarations, and generally *R v Ewing* [1983] 3 WLR 1, CA. By contrast, in Australia, New Zealand and Canada, the civil standard has been held to apply: see *Wendo v R* (1963) 109 CLR 559; *R v Donohoe* [1963] SRNSW 38; *Police v Anderson* [1972] NZLR 233; and *R v Lee* (1953) 104 CCC 400.

[214] See, in the case of a defence application under the Criminal Justice Act 1988, s 23, *R v Mattey and Queeley* [1995] 2 Cr App R 409, CA.

[215] [1983] 3 WLR 1, CA.

Appeal considered what standard of proof was appropriate to the question whether samples of handwriting, allegedly written by the accused, were 'genuine' for the purposes of s 8 of the Criminal Procedure Act 1865. That section provides as follows:

> Comparison of a disputed writing with any writing proved to the satisfaction of the judge to be genuine shall be permitted to be made by witnesses; and such writings, and the evidence of witnesses respecting the same, may be submitted to the court and jury as evidence of the genuineness or otherwise of the writing in dispute.

In the earlier decision of *R v Angeli*,[216] the Court of Appeal, on the basis that the 1865 Act applied to the criminal courts a provision which had already been in operation in the civil courts, held that the standard of proof under the section, whether applied in criminal or civil proceedings, was the civil one, on the balance of probabilities. In *R v Ewing* the Court of Appeal, unable to agree with this reasoning, and of the view that *R v Angeli* was decided *per incuriam*, held that, since s 8 did not deal with the standard of proof required to satisfy the judge, the matter was governed by common law. O'Connor LJ said:[217] 'It follows that when the section is applied in civil cases, the civil standard of proof is used, and when it is applied in criminal cases, the criminal standard should be used.'

There are cases similar to, but quite distinct from, those discussed in which the judge, before allowing particular issues to go before the jury, must be satisfied of certain matters by prima facie evidence. For example, if the prosecution seek to admit a confession allegedly made by the accused, the defence case being that the confession was never made, the judge must be satisfied by prima facie evidence that the accused did make the confession.[218] Likewise, if the prosecution seek to adduce an audio recording in evidence, the judge must be satisfied that the prosecution have made out a prima facie case of originality and genuineness by evidence which defines and describes the provenance and history of the recording up to the moment of its production in court.[219] In *R v Robson, R v Harris*[220] it was held that in these circumstances the judge is required to be satisfied to the civil standard, on a balance of probabilities, because application of the higher criminal standard of proof would amount to a usurpation by the judge of the function of the jury. If the judge satisfies himself that the evidence is competent to be considered by the jury and should not be withdrawn from them, the very same issues of originality and genuineness may then fall to be considered by them. The standard of proof is then the criminal standard. It has been convincingly argued, however, that a better approach, also involving no usurpation of the function of the jury, would be for the judge to decide the issue in exactly the same way as he is required to decide whether an evidential burden has been discharged.[221] In other words, the judge should not be required to be satisfied on a balance of probabilities; the test should be whether the party seeking to put the evidence before

---

[216] [1978] 3 All ER 950.

[217] [1983] QB 1039, CA at 1047.

[218] See, further, *Ajodha v The State* [1981] 2 All ER 193, PC (see Ch 13).

[219] See *R v Rampling* [1987] Crim LR 823, CA for general guidance given by the Court of Appeal upon the use in trials of tape recordings and transcripts of police interviews. See also *R v Emmerson* (1990) 92 Cr App R 284, CA; *R v Riaz* (1991) 94 Cr App R 339, CA; and *R v Tonge* [1993] Crim LR 876, CA (all in Ch 5); the Code of Practice on Audio Recording of Interviews with Suspects, Code E; para IV.43 of the Practice Direction; and Baldwin and Bedward, 'Summarising Tape Recordings of Police Interviews' [1991] Crim LR 671.

[220] Cf *R v Stevenson* [1971] 1 WLR 1.

[221] *Cross & Tapper on Evidence* (12th edn, London, 2010) 184.

the jury has adduced sufficient evidence on the facts in issue to justify, as a possibility, a finding by the jury on those facts in that party's favour.

ADDITIONAL READING

Ashworth, 'Four threats to the presumption of innocence' (2006) 10 E&P 241.

Ashworth and Blake, 'The Presumption of Innocence in English Criminal Law' [1996] Crim LR 306.

Boyle, 'Reasonable doubt in credibility contests: sexual assault and sexual equality' (2009) 13 E&P 269.

Dennis, 'Reverse Onuses and the Presumption of Innocence: In Search of Principle' [2005] Crim LR 901.

Harmer, 'The Presumption of Innocence and Reverse Burdens: A Balancing Act' (2007) 66(1) CLJ 142.

Mirfield, 'How Many Standards of Proof Are There?' (2009) 125 LQR 31.

Roberts and Zuckerman, *Criminal Evidence* (Oxford, 2010) Ch 8.

Witnesses

5

Key issues

- Which types of witness should be eligible to give evidence and which ineligible?

- Which types of witness, if eligible to give evidence, should the court have the power to compel to give evidence?

- When and why should witnesses be allowed to give evidence through a live television link?

- When and why should parties to litigation be allowed to call additional evidence after the close of their case?

- In civil proceedings, what are the advantages of (a) exchanging witness statements prior to trial; and (b) allowing a statement to stand as a witness's evidence-in-chief?

- When and why should witnesses in criminal proceedings be allowed to give their evidence-in-chief by video recording?

- What measures can be taken to minimize the ordeal and trauma experienced by children and other vulnerable or intimidated witnesses when giving evidence in criminal cases?

- When and why should witnesses be allowed to preserve their anonymity?

- Why is witness training or coaching prohibited, but witness familiarization allowed?

Competence and compellability

A witness is said to be competent if he may be called to give evidence and compellable if, being competent, he may be compelled by the court to do so.[1] A compellable witness who chooses to ignore a witness summons is in contempt of court and faces the penalty of imprisonment.[2] The same applies in the case of a compellable witness who attends court but refuses to testify, although such a witness may be entitled, on grounds of public policy or privilege, to refuse to answer some or all of the questions put to him.[3]

No party has any property in the evidence of a witness. Even if there is a contract between a party and a witness under which the latter binds himself not to give evidence to the court on a matter on which the judge can compel him to give evidence, it is contrary to public policy and unenforceable. Thus an expert witness is compellable if, having inadvertently advised both parties, he is loath to appear on behalf of one of them.[4] However, once a witness in criminal proceedings has given evidence for the prosecution, he cannot be called to give evidence for the defence;[5] and an expert witness may not be called by one party if his opinion is based on privileged information, such as communications with the other party, and cannot be divorced from it.[6]

The general rule

At common law, the law of competence and compellability is governed by a general rule with two limbs. The first limb is that anyone is a competent witness in any proceedings. Many former categories of exception to the first limb have been swept away, over the centuries, by judicial and statutory reform.[7] The first limb has now been put on a statutory footing in criminal cases. Section 53(1) of the Youth Justice and Criminal Evidence Act 1999 (the 1999 Act) provides that: 'At every stage in criminal proceedings all persons are (whatever their age) competent to give evidence.' The only remaining exceptions to the first limb of the general rule relate to the accused as a witness for the prosecution, children, and persons with a disorder or disability of the mind.

The second limb of the general rule is that all competent witnesses are compellable. The only remaining exceptions to the second limb relate to the accused, his or her spouse or civil partner, heads of sovereign states, diplomats, and, in certain circumstances, bankers.[8]

[1] In civil cases, a witness summons may be issued by the court: see CPR r 34.2–34.6. In trials on indictment, the attendance of witnesses may also be secured by means of a witness summons: see Criminal Procedure (Attendance of Witnesses) Act 1965. For the position in magistrates' courts, see s 97 of the Magistrates' Courts Act 1980.

[2] See *R v Yusuf* [2003] 2 Cr App R 488, CA.

[3] See Chs 19 and 20.

[4] *Harmony Shipping Co SA v Saudi Europe Line Ltd* [1979] 1 WLR 1380, CA. See further Ch 18.

[5] *R v Kelly* (1985) The Times, 27 July, CA.

[6] *R v Davies* (2002) 166 JP 243, CA. See also *R v R* [1994] 4 All ER 260, CA (see Ch 20).

[7] For details, see earlier editions of this work.

[8] The leave of the wardship court is not required to call a ward to give evidence at a criminal trial: *Re K (minors)* [1988] 1 All ER 214, Fam D; and *Re R (minors)* [1991] 2 All ER 193, CA. Concerning interviews with wards by the prosecution or police, see para 5 of the *Consolidated Criminal Practice Direction*; and *Re R, Re G (minors)* [1990] 2 All ER 633, Fam D. As to interviews with wards by those representing the accused, see *Re R (minors)* [1991] 2 All ER 193, CA.

The accused

For the prosecution

Under s 53 of the 1999 Act, the accused, whether charged solely or jointly, is not competent as a witness for the prosecution. Section 53 provides as follows:

(1) At every stage in criminal proceedings all persons are (whatever their age) competent to give evidence.

(2) Subsection (1) has effect subject to subsections (3) and (4).

(3) A person is not competent to give evidence in criminal proceedings if it appears to the court that he is not a person who is able to—

    (a) understand questions put to him as a witness, and

    (b) give answers to them which can be understood.

(4) A person charged in criminal proceedings is not competent to give evidence in the proceedings for the prosecution (whether he is the only person, or is one of two or more persons, charged in the proceedings).

(5) In subsection (4) the reference to a person charged in criminal proceedings does not include a person who is not, or is no longer, liable to be convicted of any offence in the proceedings (whether as a result of pleading guilty or for any other reason).

Thus if the prosecution wish to call a co-accused to give evidence for them, they may only do so if, in effect, he has ceased to be a co-accused. This may happen, as s 53(5) indicates, as a result of pleading guilty, even if, in his evidence, he suggests that he was not a participant in the offence, unless the plea is set aside.[9] It may also happen in three other ways: the co-accused may be acquitted, for example where no evidence is offered against him or he makes a successful submission of no case to answer at the close of the prosecution case; an application to sever the indictment may succeed so that he is not tried with the other accused; or the Attorney General may enter a *nolle prosequi*, thereby putting an end to the proceedings against him. In any of these circumstances a former co-accused becomes both a competent and compellable witness for the prosecution.[10]

For himself

The accused is a competent but not compellable witness for the defence in all criminal proceedings. As to competence, the authority is now to be found in s 53(1) of the 1999 Act. As to compellability, s 1(1) of the Criminal Evidence Act 1898 provides that: 'A person charged in criminal proceedings shall not be called as a witness in the proceedings except upon his own application.'

The phrase in s 53(1), 'at every stage in criminal proceedings', is most likely to be construed in the same way as was the phrase 'at every stage of the proceedings' in the original unamended version of s 1 of the Criminal Evidence Act 1898, so as to allow the accused to give evidence on the *voir dire*[11] and, after conviction, in mitigation of sentence,[12] as well as during the trial proper. If the accused elects to give evidence, he may of course be cross-examined

---

[9] *R v McEwan* [2011] EWCA Crim 1026.

[10] An accomplice who is not an accused in the proceedings in question but against whom proceedings are pending should only be called by the prosecution if they have undertaken to discontinue the proceedings against him: *R v Pipe* (1966) 51 Cr App R 17, CA. However, this is a rule of practice only and a matter within the discretion of the judge: *R v Turner* (1975) 61 Cr App R 67, CA.

[11] *R v Cowell* [1940] 2 KB 49.

[12] *R v Wheeler* [1917] 1 KB 283.

by the prosecution and, even if he has not given evidence against a co-accused, by any co-accused.[13] Indeed, having elected to give evidence, then subject to s 1(2) and (4) of the Criminal Evidence Act 1898, and s 101 of the Criminal Justice Act 2003 (the 2003 Act),[14] he will be treated like any other witness and his evidence will be evidence for all the purposes of the case. Thus the evidence of an accused in his own defence may be used against a co-accused whether such evidence was given in chief[15] or elicited in cross-examination. In *R v Paul*[16] an accused had confined his evidence-in-chief to an admission of his own guilt. A cross-examination of him, which had elicited evidence undermining the defence of a co-accused, was held by the Court of Criminal Appeal to have been properly permitted.[17]

Section 1(2) of the Criminal Evidence Act 1898 removes from the accused who testifies the privilege against self-incrimination in respect of any offence with which he is charged. It provides that 'Subject to section 101 of the 2003 Act (admissibility of evidence of defendant's bad character), a person charged in criminal proceedings who is called as a witness in the proceedings may be asked any question in cross-examination notwithstanding that it would tend to criminate him as to any offence with which he is charged in the proceedings.'[18] Section 101 of the 2003 Act sets out the only circumstances in which evidence of the bad character of the accused is admissible.[19] Section 1(4) of the Criminal Evidence Act 1898 provides that 'every person charged in criminal proceedings who is called as a witness in the proceedings shall, unless otherwise ordered by the court, give his evidence from the witness box or other place from which the other witnesses give their evidence'. The court may 'order otherwise' if the accused is too infirm to walk to the witness box or too violent to be controlled there.[20] Subject to exceptional circumstances of this kind, the proviso does not confer a discretion to direct where evidence should be given from, and it is improper to offer the accused a choice as to whether he wishes to give his evidence from the dock or witness box.[21] If an accused elects not to give evidence, it should be the invariable practice of counsel to record the decision and to cause the accused to sign the record, giving a clear indication that he has by his own will decided not to testify bearing in mind the advice, if any, given to him by his counsel.[22]

For a co-accused

It will be clear from s 53(1) of the 1999 Act and s 1(1) of the 1898 Act that an accused is a competent but not compellable witness for a co-accused. A person who has ceased to be an accused is both competent and compellable for a co-accused. This may happen where he has pleaded guilty,[23] where he has been acquitted (for example where no evidence has been offered against him, or he has made a successful submission of no case to answer at the close

---

[13] *R v Hilton* [1972] 1 QB 421, CA.

[14] Described at nn 18–20.

[15] See *R v Rudd* (1948) 32 Cr App R 138; cf *R v Meredith* (1943) 29 Cr App R 40.

[16] [1920] 2 KB 183.

[17] But see *Young v HM Advocate* 1932 JC 63, where the view was expressed that in these circumstances the judge should exercise his discretion to prevent such cross-examination.

[18] See also Ch 20, under **The privilege against self-incrimination**.

[19] See further Ch 17, under **Evidence of the bad character of the defendant**.

[20] *R v Symonds* (1924) 18 Cr App R 100 at 101.

[21] *R v Farnham Justices, ex p Gibson* [1991] Crim LR 642, DC.

[22] *R v Bevan* (1993) 98 Cr App R 354, CA.

[23] *R v Boal* [1965] 1 QB 402 at 414.

of the prosecution case),[24] or where an application to sever the indictment has succeeded so that he is not tried with the other accused.[25]

The spouse or civil partner of an accused

For the prosecution

In its 11th Report, the Criminal Law Revision Committee considered to what extent the spouse of the accused should be competent and compellable for the prosecution.[26] Concerning competence, the Committee concluded that the wife should be competent for the prosecution in all cases: 'If she is willing to give evidence, we think that the law would be showing excessive concern for the preservation of marital harmony if it were to say that she must not do so.'[27] This view was given effect by s 80(1) of the Police and Criminal Evidence Act 1984 (the 1984 Act). Section 80(1) was repealed: the spouse or civil partner of an accused is now competent for the prosecution under s 53(1) of the 1999 Act whereby, as we have seen, subject to s 53(3), in criminal proceedings all persons are competent to give evidence. As we have also seen, s 53(1) is also subject to s 53(4), whereby a person charged in criminal proceedings is not competent to give evidence in the proceedings for the prosecution, whether he is the only person, or one of two or more, charged in the proceedings. Thus if a husband and wife are co-accused, whether charged jointly with the same offence or charged with different offences, neither is competent to give evidence for the prosecution. As s 53(5) indicates, the spouse may only become competent for the prosecution if he or she ceases to be a co-accused. This may happen if the spouse pleads guilty or is acquitted (because no evidence is offered against the spouse or the spouse makes a successful submission of no case to answer), or if one of the spouses makes a successful application to sever the indictment. Section 53(4) and (5) apply in relation to a civil partner of an accused in the same way as they apply to a spouse of an accused.

Concerning compellability, the Criminal Law Revision Committee was in favour of maintaining the common law rule, as it then stood, of compellability in the case of offences involving personal violence by the accused against his or her spouse. The reasons included the public interest in the punishment of those committing crimes of violence and the fact that compellability would make it easier for the accused's spouse to counter the effect of possible intimidation by the accused and persuade him or her to give evidence.[28] It was also proposed to make the spouse compellable in the case of offences of a violent or sexual nature against children under the age of 16 belonging to the same household as the accused. Subsequent to the Committee's Report and prior to the 1984 Act, a majority of the House of Lords in *Hoskyn v Metropolitan Police Comr*[29] held that where an accused is charged with an offence of violence against his or her spouse, that spouse is competent but *not compellable* for the prosecution. The majority of their Lordships were reluctant to compel a wife to testify against her husband on a charge of violence, however trivial, and regardless of the consequences to herself, her family, and her marriage. Lord Edmund Davies, the sole dissentient, regarded as extremely

---

[24] *R v Conti* (1973) 58 Cr App R 387, CA.
[25] *R v Richardson* (1967) 51 Cr App R 381.
[26] Criminal Law Revision Committee, 11th Report, *Evidence (General)*, Cmnd 4991 (1972), para 147.
[27] Criminal Law Revision Committee, 11th Report, para 148.
[28] Criminal Law Revision Committee, 11th Report, para 149.
[29] [1979] AC 474, HL.

unlikely prosecutions based on trivial violence and was of the opinion that cases of serious physical violence by one spouse against the other were too grave to depend upon the willingness of the injured spouse to testify and 'ought not to be regarded as having no importance extending beyond the domestic hearth'. Against this background of differing and strongly held opinion, Parliament not only adopted but extended the proposals of the Criminal Law Revision Committee. The relevant subsections of s 80 of the 1984 Act, as since amended, provide as follows:

> (2A) In any proceedings the spouse or civil partner of a person charged in the proceedings shall, subject to subsection (4) below, be compellable
> - (a) to give evidence on behalf of any other person charged in the proceedings but only in respect of any specified offence with which that other person is charged; or
> - (b) to give evidence for the prosecution but only in respect of any specified offence with which any person is charged in the proceedings.
> (3) In relation to the spouse or civil partner of a person charged in any proceedings, an offence is a specified offence for the purposes of subsection (2A) above if
> - (a) it involves an assault on, or injury or a threat of injury to, the spouse or civil partner or a person who was at the material time under the age of 16;[30]
> - (b) it is a sexual offence alleged to have been committed in respect of a person who was at the material time under that age; or
> - (c) it consists of attempting or conspiring to commit, or of aiding, abetting, counselling, procuring or inciting the commission of, an offence falling within paragraph (a) or (b) above.[31]
> (4) No person who is charged in any proceedings shall be compellable by virtue of subsection (2) or (2A) above to give evidence in the proceedings.
> (4A) References in this section to a person charged in any proceedings do not include a person who is not, or is no longer, liable to be convicted of any offence in the proceedings (whether as a result of pleading guilty or for any other reason).

These subsections apply 'in any proceedings', a phrase which encompasses criminal proceedings brought by one spouse against the other. Thus in the unlikely event of such proceedings being pursued by a spouse who declines to give evidence, then he or she may nonetheless be compellable in accordance with s 80(2A) and (3).

It is submitted that the words 'wife' and 'husband' refer to a married person whose marriage, wherever it was celebrated, would be recognized by English law,[32] but not cohabitees (whether heterosexual or same-sex couples). In *Van Der Heijden v The Netherlands*[33] the Grand Chamber of the European Court of Human Rights held, by majority, that to compel a cohabitee with two children from a relationship of 18 years' standing, to give evidence against her partner, would interfere with her right to respect for family life under Art 8 of the Convention, but would be 'necessary...for the prevention of...crime' under Art 8(2).[34] Concerning the word

---

[30] Where the age of any person at any time is material for the purposes of s 80(3), his age at the material time shall 'be deemed to be or to have been that which appears to the court to be or to have been his age at that time': s 80(6).

[31] The reference to incitement has effect as a reference to (or to conduct amounting to) the offences of encouraging or assisting crime under the Serious Crime Act 2007, Pt 2 (the 2007 Act, s 63(1) and Sch 6 para 9).

[32] See, at common law, *R v Khan* (1987) 84 Cr App R 44, CA and *R v Yacoob* (1981) 72 Cr App R 313, CA.

[33] [2012] ECHR 588.

[34] See also *R v Pearce* [2002] 1 WLR 1553, CA, construing s 80 prior to its amendment by the 1999 Act.

'involves', in the phrase 'involves an assault on, or injury or a threat of an injury to', it was held in *R v A(B)*[35] that it means that the offence must have as one of its ingredients, or must encompass the real possibility of, 'an assault...' etc and therefore does not cover cases where there is no such legal requirement but the way in which the offence was committed did in fact involve, or is alleged to have involved, 'an assault...' etc. In that case, the accused said to his wife that he was going to burn their house down with the children in it and was charged under s 2(a) of the Criminal Damage Act 1971 with making a threat to another, intending the other to fear it would be carried out, to destroy or damage any property. It was held that s 2(a) was directed at property and did not have as an ingredient, or encompass the real possibility of, 'an assault...' etc, and therefore the wife was not compellable to give evidence against him. In s (3)(b), 'sexual offence' means an offence under the Protection of Children Act 1978 or Pt 1 of the Sexual Offences Act 2003.[36]

In *R v A(B)*, the Court of Appeal also noted three anomalies to which s 80(2A) and (3) give rise. First, as already noted, the restriction on compellability only applies to spouses and civil partners and does not extend to cohabitees, even if they have been living together for a considerable period of time. Second, the judge has the discretion to admit a hearsay statement of a spouse or civil partner, even if not compellable, under s 114(2) of the Criminal Justice Act 2003.[37] Third, the accused may be charged with two or more offences in respect of only one of which the spouse or civil partner is compellable. It seems from the wording of s (2A)(b) that the spouse or civil partner is compellable to give evidence for the prosecution on the one offence, but not the other or others, even where such a distinction is artificial because the evidence is relevant to the other or others. Let us suppose, for example, that in the course of a neighbourhood dispute that develops into a fracas, A assaults both B and B's 15-year-old son. It seems that A's wife would only be compellable to give evidence in relation to the assault on B's son, but her evidence would be likely to be relevant to both offences charged. Presumably, in such a case, A could apply for separate trials for each of the offences, or might apply to exclude the evidence of his wife relying upon s 78(1) of the 1984 Act or the common law discretion to exclude in order to ensure a fair trial. It may be doubted, however, that either application would have much prospect of success.[38]

These are not the only anomalies to which s 80 gives rise. Non-compellability is borne of concern for the preservation of marital harmony, but it operates regardless of the state of the marriage or civil partnership, gives protection for only the spouse or civil partner, but not other family members (whose compulsion could easily disrupt the harmony of the relationship), and, in the case of offences against children, including children of the family, draws an arbitrary distinction between those under and over the age of 16. By reason of these and other anomalies, it has been convincingly argued that, in principle, spousal non-compellability cannot be justified and should be abolished.[39]

There is no requirement, before interviewing a spouse who is competent but not compellable for the prosecution in relation to the crime of which her husband is suspected, to tell her

---

[35] [2012] 2 Cr App R 467, CA.

[36] Section 80(7).

[37] See *R v L* [2009] 1 WLR 626, CA, considered in Ch 10.

[38] See Creighton, 'Spouse Competence and Compellability' [1990] Crim LR 34.

[39] Hoyano, 'Commentary' [2003] Crim LR 170. For the counter-argument in favour of retention and modification, see Brabyn, 'A criminal defendant's spouse as a prosecution witness' [2011] Crim LR 613.

that she is not compellable.[40] An accused's spouse who is called as a competent but not compellable witness for the prosecution but proves adverse for the purposes of s 3 of the Criminal Procedure Act 1865,[41] may be treated as a hostile witness in the normal way. This was established prior to the 1984 Act in *R v Pitt*,[42] an authority which may be assumed to remain good law. The Court of Appeal held that the choice of a wife whether or not to give evidence, being a competent but not compellable witness for the prosecution, is not lost because she makes a witness statement or gives evidence at the committal proceedings. She retains the right of refusal up to the point when she takes the oath in the witness box, and waiver of her right of refusal is effective only if made with full knowledge of her right to refuse. However, if she knowingly waives her right of refusal, she becomes an ordinary witness and, having started her evidence, must complete it, unable to retreat behind the barrier of non-compellability. Accordingly, if the nature of her evidence warrants it, an application may be made to treat her as a hostile witness. For these reasons, the Court of Appeal thought it desirable that the judge should explain to the wife, in the absence of the jury and before she takes the oath, that she has the right to give evidence but that if she chooses to do so she may be treated like any other witness. In appropriate circumstances the Court of Appeal may upset a verdict if it feels that injustice may have occurred because a wife gave evidence without appreciating that she had a right to refuse to do so.

For the accused

The Criminal Law Revision Committee had no doubt that the accused's spouse should be made competent and compellable for the accused in all cases,[43] a recommendation implemented by the 1984 Act. The spouse or civil partner of an accused is now competent to give evidence on behalf of the accused under s 53(1) of the 1999 Act, and this remains the case even if he or she is also charged in the same proceedings. As to compellability, s 80(2) provides as follows:

> (2) In any proceedings the spouse or civil partner of a person charged in the proceedings shall, subject to subsection (4) below, be compellable to give evidence on behalf of that person.

The only exception to s 80(2) is in cases in which the spouses or civil partners are both charged in the same proceedings.[44]

For a co-accused

Under the Criminal Evidence Act 1898, the accused's spouse was, with the consent of the accused, competent as a witness for any other person jointly charged with the accused,[45] but not compellable. The Criminal Law Revision Committee recommended that the spouse of an accused should be competent to give evidence on behalf of any co-accused whether or not the accused consents. This proposal was given effect by s 80(1) of the 1984 Act, which was repealed by the 1999 Act. The spouse or civil partner of an accused is now competent to give evidence on behalf of any person jointly charged with the accused by virtue of s 53(1) of the

---

[40] *R v L (R)* [2008] 2 Cr App R 243, CA.
[41] See Ch 6.
[42] [1982] 3 All ER 63.
[43] Criminal Law Revision Committee, 11th Report, para 153.
[44] Section 80(4).
[45] Section 1 and proviso (c) thereto.

1999 Act, and this is the case even if the spouse or civil partner is also charged in the same proceedings.

The more difficult question related to compellability on behalf of a co-accused. The interests of justice would seem to require that the co-accused should be able to compel the spouse if he or she is able to give relevant evidence in his defence. On the other hand, if the spouse is compelled to testify in such circumstances, the prosecution, in cross-examination of him or her, may well elicit evidence incriminating the accused, a result which is inconsistent with the general rule that the prosecution may not compel a spouse to testify for them. Given these competing interests of the accused and the co-accused, the Committee proposed that the spouse should be compellable on behalf of a co-accused in any case where he or she would be compellable on behalf of the prosecution.[46] The substance of these proposals has been enacted in s 80(2A) and (3) of the 1984 Act, which, as amended, provide that in any proceedings the spouse or civil partner of the accused shall be compellable to give evidence on behalf of any other person charged in the proceedings, but only in respect of any specified offence with which that other person is charged.[47] The only exception is in cases in which the spouse or civil partner is charged in the same proceedings.[48] Where co-accused A and B are charged with two or more offences in respect of only one of which the spouse or civil partner of B is compellable to give evidence on behalf of A, then it seems from the wording of s 80(2A)(a) that the spouse or civil partner of B is compellable to give evidence on behalf of A on that offence even if that evidence is also relevant to the other offence(s).

Former spouses

In criminal proceedings, a former spouse or civil partner of an accused is competent under s 53(1) of the 1999 Act. Such a person is also compellable. Section 80(5) and (5A) of the 1984 Act provide as follows:

(5) In any proceedings a person who has been but is no longer married to the accused shall be compellable to give evidence as if that person and the accused had never been married.

(5A) In any proceedings a person who has been but is no longer the civil partner of the accused shall be compellable to give evidence as if that person and the accused had never been civil partners.

The effect of these provisions is to render former spouses (or civil partners), after their marriage (or civil partnership) has been dissolved, both competent and compellable to give evidence for either the defence or the prosecution, whether the evidence relates to events which occurred before, during, or after the terminated marriage (or civil partnership).[49] In s 80(5) of the 1984 Act the phrase 'in any proceedings' means any proceedings which took place after s 80(5) came into effect on 1 January 1986, and therefore an ex-spouse is competent and compellable to give evidence in such proceedings about any relevant matter whether it took place before or after that date.[50] The phrase 'is no longer married' is apt to apply where the spouses have been divorced and where their marriage, being voidable, has been annulled. If

[46] Criminal Law Revision Committee, 11th Report, para 155.

[47] The offences are set out in s 80(3), (see, in this chapter, under **Competence and compellability, The spouse or civil partner of an accused, For the prosecution**).

[48] Section 80(4), (see, in this chapter, under **Competence and compellability, The spouse or civil partner of an accused, For the prosecution**).

[49] See *R v Mathias* [1989] Crim LR 64, CC.

[50] *R v Cruttenden* [1991] 3 All ER 242, CA.

there is evidence to show that a marriage was void *ab initio*, a legally valid marriage never having existed, the parties to such a union are, in accordance with the general rules, both competent and compellable throughout. Spouses who are judicially separated, although often treated in law as the equivalent of divorced spouses, cannot be said to be 'no longer married' for the purposes of s 80(5). Likewise, the subsection has no application to spouses who are not cohabiting, whether without any arrangement or agreement, or pursuant to a separation agreement, non-cohabitation order, or informal arrangement. The Criminal Law Revision Committee considered whether to provide that judicially separated or non-cohabiting spouses should be treated for the purposes of competence and compellability as if they were unmarried. It is difficult to disagree with their conclusions against such a provision:[51]

> if there is little prospect that they will become reconciled, the spouse in question is likely to be willing to give evidence; and if there is a prospect of reconciliation, it may be better to avoid the risk of spoiling this prospect by compelling the spouse to give evidence when he or she would not have been compellable in the ordinary case.

Children and persons with a disorder or disability of the mind—criminal cases

The test for competence

The competence of all witnesses to give evidence in criminal proceedings is governed by s 53(1)–(3) of the 1999 Act, which provides as follows:

(1) At every stage in criminal proceedings all persons are (whatever their age) competent to give evidence.

(2) Subsection (1) has effect subject to subsections (3) and (4).[52]

(3) A person is not competent to give evidence in criminal proceedings if it appears to the court that he is not a person who is able to—

   (a) understand questions put to him as a witness, and

   (b) give answers to them which can be understood.

In *R v MacPherson*[53] it was held that the words 'put to him as a witness' in s 53(3)(a) mean the equivalent of 'being asked of him in court' and therefore an infant who can only communicate in baby language with its mother will not ordinarily be competent but a child who can speak and understand basic English with strangers will be competent. The court in that case, rejecting a submission to the effect that a judge must decide whether a child appreciates the difference between truth and falsehood, also held that there is no requirement that the child be aware of his witness status and that questions of credibility and reliability are not relevant to competence but go to the weight of the evidence and thus may be considered on a submission of no case to answer. Equally, a child who has no recollection of an event may be a perfectly competent witness.[54] In *R v Barker*[55] it was held that: in each case under s 53, the question is witness and trial specific; there are no presumptions; the witness does not need to understand the special importance of telling the truth in court; the issue is whether the witness can answer the questions, although not necessarily every single question, put to him by

[51] Criminal Law Revision Committee, 11th Report para 156.
[52] As to s 53(4), see, in this chapter, under **Competence and compellability, The accused, For the prosecution**.
[53] [2006] 1 Cr App R 459, CA.
[54] *DPP v R* [2007] All ER (D) 176 (Jul).
[55] [2010] EWCA Crim 4.

both sides,[56] and also provide understandable answers to them; and s 53 requires not the exercise of a discretion, but the making of a judgment on whether the witness fulfils the statutory criteria—it is not open to the judge to impose additional criteria based on former approaches to the evidence of children. However, it is submitted that where it is clear that a proposed witness, although satisfying the statutory criteria, is unable to distinguish truth from fiction or fact from fantasy, his evidence should be excluded under s 78 of the 1984 Act.[57]

In the case of young children, obviously, the younger the child the more likely it is that he or she will be incapable of satisfying the test in s 53(3), and care clearly needs to be taken if the question of competence arises. However, a court cannot properly decide that a child is incapable of satisfying the test simply on the basis that he or she is of or below a certain age.[58] This accords with the views of Lord Lane CJ in *R v Z*,[59] disapproving *R v Wallwork*.[60] In the latter case, Lord Goddard CJ said that it was most undesirable to call a child as young as five years old, a dictum approved in *R v Wright, R v Ormerod*.[61] However, in *R v Z* Lord Lane CJ was of the opinion that the decision in *R v Wallwork* had been overtaken by events. Part of Lord Goddard's concern related to the presence of the child in court, a problem largely cured by the introduction of video links.[62] Furthermore, the repeal of the proviso to s 38(1) of the Children and Young Persons Act 1933, whereby an accused was not liable to be convicted on the uncorroborated unsworn evidence of a child, indicated 'a change of attitude by Parliament, reflecting in its turn a change of attitude by the public in general to the acceptability of the evidence of young children'.

In *R v Sed*,[63] which concerned the competence of an 81-year-old woman who suffered from Alzheimer's disease, it was said that, depending on the length and nature of the questioning and the complexity of the subject matter, s 53 may not always require 100 per cent, or near 100 per cent, mutual understanding between the questioner and the questioned and that the judge should also make allowance for the fact that the witness's performance and command of detail may vary according to the importance to him of the subject matter, how recent it was, and any strong feelings that it may have engendered.[64]

The procedure

The question whether a witness is competent to give evidence in criminal proceedings may be raised either by a party to the proceedings or by the court of its own motion, but either way must be determined by the court in accordance with s 54 of the 1999 Act.[65] It is clear from this that a judge is only bound to investigate a witness's competence if he has, or is given, any reason to doubt it. Under s 54(2), the burden is on the party calling the witness to satisfy the

---

[56] See, eg, *R v IA* [2013] EWCA Crim 1308.

[57] Cf *R v D* (1995) The Times, 15 Nov, CA.

[58] *R v MacPherson* [2006] 1 Cr App R 459, CA and *R v Powell* [2006] 1 Cr App R 468, CA.

[59] [1990] 2 All ER 971, CA at 974.

[60] (1958) 42 Cr App R 153.

[61] (1987) 90 Cr App R 91, CA.

[62] See the 1999 Act, s 24 and other 'special measures directions', in this chapter, under **Witnesses in criminal cases**.

[63] [2005] 1 Cr App R 55, CA at [45].

[64] The weight to be attached to the evidence given by a mentally handicapped person is for the jury: *R v Hill* (1851) 2 Den CC 254. A person suffering from a mental illness may be a reliable witness in relation to matters not affected by the condition: see *R v Barratt and Sheehan* [1996] Crim LR 495, CA (fixed belief paranoia). See also *R (B) v DPP* [2009] EWHC 106 (Admin).

[65] Section 54(1).

court, on a balance of probabilities, that the witness is competent. In determining whether the witness is competent, the court must treat the witness as having the benefit of any special measures directions under s 19 of the 1999 Act[66] which the court has given or proposes to give in relation to the witness.[67] Under s 54(4), any proceedings for the determination of the question shall take place in the absence of the jury (if there is one); under s 54(5), expert evidence may be received on the question (which is always likely to be required in the case of the mentally handicapped);[68] and under s 54(6), any questioning of the witness, where the court considers that necessary, shall be conducted by the court in the presence of the parties.

The issue of a child's competence should be decided before he or she is sworn, usually as a preliminary issue at the start of the trial when the judge should watch any videotaped interview of the child[69] and/or ask the child appropriate questions.[70] Where an *Achieving Best Evidence* ('ABE') interview[71] indicates competence, a competence hearing may serve only to cause delay, increase expense, and put unnecessary strain on the witness.[72] Any questioning thought to be necessary under s 54(6), it is submitted, is best conducted in the spirit suggested in *R v Hampshire*:[73] 'it should be a matter of the judge's perception of the child's understanding demonstrated in the course of ordinary discourse'.

A decision that a child is competent should be kept under review and may need to be reconsidered when his or her evidence is complete. Thus although at the start of a trial a videotaped interview may indicate competence, a ruling to that effect should be reversed if the child is unable to understand questions or give answers which can be understood, which may be the result of a lapse of time and lack of memory.[74] There is a risk that the child will not have an accurate recollection of the events, and a further risk that if shown the video before or during the trial, may recollect only what was said on the video and be incapable of distinguishing that from the events themselves. Effective cross-examination, in such circumstances, would be virtually impossible.[75] However, it does not follow from this that in cases involving very young children, delay on its own automatically requires the court to prevent or stop the evidence of the child from being considered by the jury.[76] Furthermore, it has been doubted that a child's evidence should be excluded where she no longer has a reliably independent memory of the events—it is not infrequent for witnesses to have no such memory and to be able to say no more than that their statement is accurate.[77]

[66] See, in this chapter, under **Witnesses in criminal cases.**

[67] Section 54(3). See also *R v F (JR)* [2013] 2 Cr App R 13, CA at [25]: the competency test is not failed because the forensic techniques of the advocate or the processes of the court have to be adapted to enable the witness to give his best evidence.

[68] In *R v Barratt and Sheehan* [1996] Crim LR 495, CA it was held that the proper course is to adduce expert medical evidence so that it is not normally necessary to call the witness said to suffer from mental illness.

[69] See the 1999 Act, s 27, in this chapter, under **Witnesses in criminal cases.**

[70] *R v MacPherson* [2006] 1 Cr App R 459, CA.

[71] See Home Office, *Achieving Best Evidence in Criminal Proceedings: Guidance for Vulnerable or Intimidated Witnesses, including Children* (3rd edn, 2011) <www.homeoffice.gov.uk>.

[72] *R v F* [2013] EWCA Crim 424 at [39].

[73] [1995] 2 All ER 1019, CA.

[74] *R v Powell* [2006] 1 Cr App R 468, CA, applied in *R v Malicki* [2009] EWCA Crim 365.

[75] *R v Malicki* [2009] EWCA Crim 365.

[76] *R v Barker* [2010] EWCA Crim 4.

[77] *R v R* [2010] EWCA Crim 2469.

Evidence on oath or unsworn

A witness who is competent to give evidence in criminal proceedings may be sworn for the purpose of giving his evidence on oath, or may give his evidence unsworn. Section 55(1)–(4) of the 1999 Act provides as follows:

(1) Any question whether a witness in criminal proceedings may be sworn for the purpose of giving evidence on oath, whether raised—
    (a) by a party to the proceedings, or
    (b) by the court of its own motion,
    shall be determined by the court in accordance with this section.

(2) The witness may not be sworn for that purpose unless—
    (a) he has attained the age of 14, and
    (b) he has a sufficient appreciation of the solemnity of the occasion and of the particular responsibility to tell the truth which is involved in taking an oath.

(3) The witness shall, if he is able to give intelligible testimony, be presumed to have a sufficient appreciation of those matters if no evidence tending to show the contrary is adduced (by any party).

(4) If any such evidence is adduced, it is for the party seeking to have the witness sworn to satisfy the court that, on a balance of probabilities, the witness has attained the age of 14 and has a sufficient appreciation of the matters mentioned in subsection (2)(b).

For the purposes of s 55(3), a person is able to give intelligible testimony if he is able to (a) understand questions put to him as a witness; and (b) give answers to them which can be understood.[78] This test is the same as that for testing competence in s 53(3). Thus a witness aged 14 or over who is competent as a witness must be presumed to satisfy the test set out in s 55(2)(b), provided that there is no evidence tending to show the contrary. Under s 55(5), any proceedings for the determination of the question whether a witness may be sworn for the purpose of giving his evidence on oath shall take place in the absence of the jury (if there is one); under s 55(6), expert evidence may be received on the question; and, under s 55(7), any questioning of the witness, where the court considers that necessary, shall be conducted by the court in the presence of the parties.

Sections 56(1)–(4) of the 1999 Act provide as follows:

(1) Subsections (2) and (3) apply to a person (of any age) who—
    (a) is competent to give evidence in criminal proceedings, but
    (b) (by virtue of s 55(2)) is not permitted to be sworn for the purpose of giving evidence on oath in such proceedings.

(2) The evidence in criminal proceedings of a person to whom this subsection applies shall be given unsworn.

(3) A deposition of unsworn evidence given by a person to whom this subsection applies may be taken for the purpose of criminal proceedings as if that evidence had been given on oath.

(4) A court in criminal proceedings shall accordingly receive in evidence any evidence given unsworn in pursuance of subsection (2) or (3).

Under the mandatory terms of s 56(2), the evidence of any child under the age of 14 who is competent to testify must be given unsworn; and the same applies to anyone who has attained that age and is competent to testify if (a) evidence is adduced that he does not have a sufficient appreciation of the solemnity of the occasion and of the particular responsibility

---

[78] Section 55(8).

to tell the truth which is involved in taking an oath; and (b) the party seeking to have him sworn fails to satisfy the court, on a balance of probabilities, that he has such an appreciation.

It is an offence for a person giving unsworn evidence in pursuance of s 56(2) and (3) wilfully to give false evidence in such circumstances that, had the evidence been given on oath, he would have been guilty of perjury;[79] but the mere fact that a child under the age of 10 cannot be prosecuted is not a reason to prevent him from giving unsworn evidence.[80]

Civil cases

Children

At common law, a child who did not understand the nature of an oath was not competent to testify and could not be called as a witness.[81] Section 96 of the Children Act 1989 now provides that:

(1) Subsection (2) applies where a child who is called as a witness in any civil proceedings does not, in the opinion of the court, understand the nature of an oath.
(2) The child's evidence may be heard by the court if, in its opinion—
    (a) he understands that it is his duty to speak the truth; and
    (b) he has sufficient understanding to justify his evidence being heard.

A child, for these purposes, is a person under the age of 18.[82] In deciding, under s 96(1), whether or not a child understands the nature of an oath, it is submitted that the court should be guided by the common law authorities which governed in criminal as well as civil cases prior to parliamentary intervention. The issue is for the court to decide and the judge should put preliminary questions in order to form an opinion.[83] Whether a child warrants such examination is a matter of discretion for the judge. There is no fixed age above which a child should be treated as competent and below which a child should be examined. In *R v Khan*,[84] however, it was held that although much depends on the type of child before the court, as a general working rule, inquiry is necessary in the case of a child under the age of 14. Originally, the competence of children to give sworn evidence depended on 'the sense and reason they entertain of the danger and impiety of falsehood'.[85] On this basis, judges would ask questions designed to discover whether the child was aware of the divine sanction of the oath, such as 'Do you have religious instruction at school?' and 'Do you know what I mean by God?' It was questioning of this kind that led the Court of Appeal in *R v Hayes*[86] to adopt a secular approach. Acknowledging that in the present state of society the divine sanction of the oath is probably not generally recognized amongst the adult population, it was held that the important consideration is:[87]

whether the child has a sufficient appreciation of the solemnity of the occasion and the added responsibility to tell the truth, which is involved in taking an oath, over and above the duty to tell the truth which is an ordinary duty of normal social conduct.

[79] The 1999 Act, s 57.
[80] See *R v N* (1992) 95 Cr App R 256, CA.
[81] *Baker v Rabetts* (1954) 118 JPN 303.
[82] Children Act 1989, s 105.
[83] *R v Surgenor* (1940) 27 Cr App R 175.
[84] (1981) 73 Cr App R 190, CA. But see also *Bains v DPP* [1992] Crim LR 795, DC.
[85] *R v Brasier* (1779) 1 Leach 199.
[86] [1977] 1 WLR 234.
[87] [1977] 1 WLR 234 at 237.

The court, in *R v Hayes*, also appears to have been of the view that 'the watershed dividing children who are normally considered old enough to take the oath and children normally considered too young to take the oath, probably falls between the ages of eight and ten'.

If, in civil proceedings, a child fails on the secular test in *R v Hayes*, his or her evidence may be given unsworn if, in the opinion of the court, the conditions in s 96(2)(a) and (b) are satisfied. It would appear that 'the duty to speak the truth' under s 96(2)(a) should be taken to mean the duty to tell the truth which is an ordinary duty of normal social conduct.

Special factors bear on the question whether a child should give evidence in family proceedings. Video recordings of ABE interviews,[88] if available, are routinely used in care proceedings and it has been rare for children to be called for examination or cross-examination. However, there is no longer a presumption against a child giving evidence in such proceedings; in deciding whether a particular child should be called, the court must weigh two considerations, the advantages that doing so may bring to the determination of the truth and the damage it may do to the welfare of the child or any other child, and should have regard to a range of factors, including the quality of any ABE interview, the nature of any challenge to the child's evidence, the age and maturity of the child, the length of time since the events in question, and whether the child is willing to give evidence.[89]

Persons with a disorder or disability of the mind

In civil proceedings, in deciding on the competence of a person with a disorder or disability of the mind, it is submitted that the courts should be guided by the common law authorities which governed in criminal as well as civil cases prior to parliamentary intervention. In *R v Hill*[90] a patient of a lunatic asylum, labouring under a delusion that he had a number of spirits about him which were continually talking to him, but with a clear understanding of the obligation of the oath, was held competent to give evidence for the Crown on a charge of manslaughter.[91] Three principles were established in the case:

1. If in the opinion of the judge a proposed witness, by reason of impaired intellect, does not understand the nature and sanction of an oath, he is incompetent to testify.

2. A person of impaired intellect who does understand the nature of an oath may give evidence and it will be left to the jury to attach such weight to his testimony as they see fit.

3. If his evidence is so tainted with insanity as to be unworthy of credit, the jury may properly disregard it.

Since *R v Hill* there has been one important development: the test to be applied by the judge should be the secular one adopted in *R v Hayes*, namely whether the proposed witness has a sufficient appreciation of the seriousness of the occasion and a realization that taking the oath involves something more than the duty to tell the truth in ordinary day-to-day life.[92]

[88] See, in this chapter, under **Witnesses in criminal cases, Special measures directions for vulnerable and intimidated witnesses.**

[89] *Re W (Children) (Family Proceedings: Evidence)* [2010] UK SC 12. See also, in relation to the matters to be taken into account, Working Party of the Family Justice Council, *Guidelines in relation to children giving evidence in family proceedings* (2011) and *Re X (a child)(evidence)* [2011] EWHC 3401 (Fam).

[90] (1851) 2 Den 254.

[91] Lord Campbell CJ was doubtless sobered by his observation that any rule to the contrary would have excluded the evidence of Socrates 'for he believed that he had a spirit always prompting him'.

[92] *R v Bellamy* (1985) 82 Cr App R 222, CA.

Resolution of the question calls for appropriate expert medical evidence: it will not normally be necessary to call the witness said to be suffering from mental illness.[93]

A witness unable to understand the nature of the oath, his intellect being temporarily impaired by reason of drink or drugs, may become competent after an adjournment of suitable length.

The sovereign and diplomats

The Sovereign and heads of other sovereign states are competent but not compellable to give evidence. A number of statutes provide for varying degrees of immunity from compellability in the case of diplomats, consular officials, and certain officers of prescribed international organizations.[94]

Bankers

We shall see in Chapter 9 that, pursuant to the Bankers' Books Evidence Act 1879, copies of entries in bankers' books are, subject to certain safeguards, admissible as evidence of their contents. To protect bank personnel from the unnecessary inconvenience of either providing the originals of such books or appearing as witnesses, s 6 of the Act provides that:

> A banker or official of a bank shall not, in any legal proceedings to which the bank is not a party, be compellable to produce any banker's book the contents of which can be proved under this Act, or to appear as a witness to prove the matters, transactions, and accounts therein recorded, unless by order of a judge made for special cause.

Oaths and affirmations

Sworn evidence is evidence given by a witness who has either taken an oath or made an affirmation. The general rule in both civil and criminal proceedings is that the evidence of any witness should be sworn.[95] The exceptions in the case of certain children and those with a disorder or disability of the mind have already been considered. There are two other minor exceptions at common law. A witness called only to produce a document may give unsworn evidence provided that the identity of the document is either not disputed or can be established by another witness.[96] Counsel acting for one of two parties who have reached a compromise may give unsworn evidence of its terms.[97] Where a video recording of an interview with a child is admitted in evidence, and the child is at that stage aged 14 or over, the oath should be administered before the start of the cross-examination.[98] However, under s 56(5) of the 1999 Act, where a witness who is competent to give evidence in criminal proceedings has given evidence in such proceedings unsworn, no conviction, verdict, or finding in those

---

[93] *R v Barratt and Sheehan* [1996] Crim LR 495, CA.

[94] See the Diplomatic Privileges Act 1964, Consular Relations Act 1968, International Organisations Act 1968, and State Immunity Act 1978.

[95] In civil claims which have been allocated to the small claims track, the court need not take evidence on oath: CPR r 27.8(4).

[96] *Perry v Gibson* (1834) 1 Ad&El 48.

[97] *Hickman v Berens* [1895] 2 Ch 638, CA.

[98] *R v Simmonds* [1996] Crim LR 816, CA, a decision under the Criminal Justice Act 1988, s 32A. See now the 1999 Act, s 27, in this chapter, under **Witnesses in criminal cases.**

proceedings shall be taken to be unsafe, for the purposes of the grounds of appeal set out in ss 2(1), 13(1), or 16(1) of the Criminal Appeal Act 1968, by reason only that the witness was in fact a person falling within s 55(2) of the 1999 Act[99] and accordingly should have given his evidence on oath.

The modern law of oaths and affirmations is governed by the Oaths Act 1978. Section 1(1) provides for the manner of administration of the oath in the case of Christians and Jews. Unless a person about to take the oath in this form and manner objects thereto, or is physically incapable of so taking the oath, it will be administered without inquiry on the part of the judge.[100] It is therefore incumbent on those of other religious beliefs or those who wish to affirm, to object to the taking of such an oath.[101] In the case of those of other religious beliefs, s 1(3) provides that the oath shall be administered 'in any lawful manner'. Such witnesses usually take the oath upon such holy book as is appropriate to their religious belief. Section 3 of the Oaths Act 1978 expressly permits a witness to be sworn with uplifted hand in the form and manner in which an oath is usually administered in Scotland. Whether an oath is administered in a 'lawful manner' under s 1(3) does not depend on the intricacies of the particular religion which is adhered to by the witness but on whether the oath is one which appears to the court to be binding on the conscience of the witness and, if so, whether it is an oath which the witness himself considers to be binding on his conscience. Both conditions were satisfied in *R v Kemble*,[102] in which a Muslim had taken the oath using the New Testament, whereas under the strict tenets of Islam, no oath taken by a Muslim is valid unless taken on a copy of the Koran in Arabic.

Any person who objects to the taking of an oath shall be permitted instead, the choice being his, to make a solemn affirmation.[103] An affirmation is of the same force and effect as an oath.[104] It is improper, in cross-examination of a Muslim, to ask questions designed to challenge whether he regards himself as bound to tell the truth by virtue of the fact that he affirmed and did not swear on the Koran.[105] However, if there is a real risk that the jury will attach less weight to the evidence of a witness of a particular faith because he has affirmed, rather than taken the oath on the relevant holy book, then the judge has a discretion to allow the witness to be questioned, in a sensitive manner, as to why he did not take the oath on the particular holy book.[106]

Occasionally, a court may find itself unequipped to administer an oath in the manner appropriate to a person's particular religious belief. Accordingly, it is provided that a person may be permitted, and indeed required, to affirm where 'it is not reasonably practicable without inconvenience or delay to administer an oath in the manner appropriate to his religious belief'.[107]

---

[99] See, in this chapter, under **Competence and compellability, Children and persons with a disorder or disability of the mind—criminal cases.**

[100] Oaths Act 1978, s 1(2).

[101] For the arguments against the continued use of religious oaths, see Criminal Law Revision Committee, 11th Report, paras 279–81 and Lord Justice Auld's *Review of the Criminal Courts of England and Wales* (HMSO, 2001) 598–600.

[102] [1990] 3 All ER 116, CA.

[103] Oaths Act 1978, s 5(1). See *R v Bellamy* (1985) 82 Cr App R 222, CA.

[104] Oaths Act 1978, s 5(4).

[105] *R v Majid* [2009] EWCA Crim 2563.

[106] See *R v Mehrban* [2002] 1 Cr App R 561, CA, where one of the accused, a Muslim, had affirmed because 'unclean', not having been able to wash himself in the appropriate way before swearing.

[107] Oaths Act 1978, s 5(2) and (3).

A person who has taken a duly administered oath could with relative ease subsequently allege that it was of no binding effect because at the time of taking it he had no religious belief. Section 4(2) avoids this possibility by providing that the fact that a person had, at the time of taking the oath, no religious belief 'shall not for any purpose affect the validity of the oath'.

A witness who, having taken an oath or made an affirmation, wilfully makes a statement material to the proceedings in question which he knows to be false or does not believe to be true, commits perjury and may be prosecuted accordingly.[108]

Live links

Civil proceedings

In civil proceedings, Civil Procedure Rules (CPR) r 32.3 provides that the court may allow a witness to give evidence 'through a video link or by other means'.[109] No defined limit or set of circumstances should be placed upon discretionary exercise of this power to permit video link evidence, which is not confined to cases of 'pressing need', as when a witness is too ill to attend in person. Relevant factors include whether failure to attend is an abuse or contemptuous or designed to obtain a collateral advantage, as well as considerations of cost, time, and inconvenience. The court should also have regard to Art 6 of the European Convention on Human Rights and the need to see that the parties are on an equal footing.[110] In *Polanski v Condé Nast Publications Ltd*[111] the House of Lords held, by a majority, that although special cases may arise, as a general rule a claimant's unwillingness to come to the UK because he is a fugitive from justice is a valid reason, and can be a sufficient reason, for making a video conferencing order, because such a person, despite his status, is entitled to invoke the assistance of the court and its procedures in protection of his civil rights.

Criminal proceedings

In criminal cases, there are three sets of rules governing the use that may be made of live links. First, s 32 of the Criminal Justice Act 1988, which provides that, in trials on indictment[112] or proceedings in youth courts,[113] a person other than the accused who is outside the United Kingdom may, with the leave of the court, give evidence through a live television link.[114] Second, under s 24 of the 1999 Act, a special measures direction may provide for a child or other vulnerable witness to give evidence by a live television link. Section 24 is considered,

[108] See the Perjury Act 1911, s 1, and the Oaths Act 1978, s 5(4), at n 104.

[109] See also CPR Practice Direction (PD) 32, Annex 3, *Videoconferencing Guidance*, and *Black v Pastouna* [2005] EWCA Civ 1389.

[110] *Rowland v Bock* [2002] 4 All ER 370, QBD.

[111] [2005] 1 All ER 945, HL.

[112] Or an appeal to the Court of Appeal (Criminal Division) or the hearing of a reference of a case to the Court of Appeal under the Criminal Appeal Act 1995, s 9.

[113] Or appeals to the Crown Court arising out of such proceedings or hearings of references under the Criminal Appeal Act 1995, s 11 so arising.

[114] A statement made on oath by such a witness shall be treated for the purposes of the Perjury Act 1911, s 1, as having been made in the proceedings in which it is given in evidence: s 32(3). See also *R v Forsyth* [1997] 2 Cr App R 299, CA. There is no provision for hearing the evidence of a witness abroad by telephone in a trial in the United Kingdom: *R v Diane* [2010] 2 Cr App R 1, CA.

together with other special measures directions, separately, in text at n 213. Third, under Pt 8 of the Criminal Justice Act 2003 (ss 51–56), general provision is made for the use of live links in criminal cases.[115] There is no common law power to permit evidence to be given by live link: the statutory regime provides exclusively for the circumstances in which live link evidence may be used in the course of a criminal trial.[116]

Part 8 of the 2003 Act has been introduced without any indication as to the relationship between its general provisions and the provisions in the 1999 Act, except to state that Pt 8 is without prejudice to 'any power of a court…to give directions…in relation to any witness'.[117] Under s 51(1)–(3) of the 2003 Act, a court may, on the application of a party, or of its own motion, direct that a witness, other than the accused, give evidence through a live link in the following criminal proceedings: a summary trial, an appeal to the Crown Court arising out of such a trial, a trial on indictment, and an appeal to the criminal division of the Court of Appeal.[118] A 'live link' means a live television link or other arrangement by which a witness, while at a place in the United Kingdom which is outside the building where the proceedings are being held, is able both to see and hear a person at the place where the proceedings are being held and to be seen and heard by the accused, the judge, the justices, and the jury (if there is one), the legal representatives, and any interpreter or other person appointed by the court to assist the witness.[119] Rules of court may make provision as to the procedure to be followed in connection with an application for a direction to give evidence through a live link and as to the arrangements or safeguards to be put in place in connection with the operation of the link.[120] Under s 51(4)(a), a direction may not be given unless the court is satisfied that it is in the interests of the efficient or effective administration of justice. Under s 51(6), in deciding whether to give a direction, the court must consider all the circumstances. Section 51(7) provides that:

(7) Those circumstances include in particular—
   (a) the availability of the witness,
   (b) the need for the witness to attend in person,
   (c) the importance of the witness's evidence to the proceedings,
   (d) the views of the witness,
   (e) the suitability of the facilities at the place where the witness would give evidence through a live link,
   (f) whether a direction might tend to inhibit any party to the proceedings from effectively testing the witness's evidence.

If the court refuses an application for a direction, it must state its reasons in open court and, if it is a magistrates' court, must cause them to be entered in the register of its proceedings.

---

[115] See also the Crime (International Cooperation) Act 2003.

[116] *R (S) v Waltham Forest Youth Court* [2004] 2 Cr App R 335, DC at [86]–[89].

[117] The Criminal Justice Act 2003, s 56(5)(a).

[118] Also the hearing of a reference under the Criminal Appeal Act 1995, s 9 or s 11, a hearing before a magistrates' court or the Crown Court which is held after the accused has entered a plea of guilty, and a hearing before the Court of Appeal under the 2003 Act, s 80 (application for retrial following acquittal): s 51(2).

[119] Section 56(2) and (3). For these purposes, the extent (if any) to which a person is unable to see or hear by reason of any impairment of eyesight or hearing is to be disregarded: s 56(4).

[120] Section 55.

Where a direction has been given, the witness may not give evidence otherwise than through the link,[121] and therefore will also be subject to cross-examination and any re-examination through the link, but the court may rescind a direction if there has been a material change of circumstances since the direction was given.[122] Where the evidence is given through a live link, the court retains the power to exclude evidence at its discretion (whether by preventing questions from being put or otherwise),[123] and the judge may give the jury such direction as he thinks necessary to ensure that the jury gives the same weight to the evidence as if it had been given by the witness in the courtroom.[124]

The time at which evidence should be adduced

In both civil and criminal proceedings, as a general rule of practice rather than law, a party should adduce all the evidence on which he intends to rely before the close of his case.[125] However, in a civil case, the claimant, after the close of the trial but before the judgment has been handed down, may introduce in evidence a document which ought to have been disclosed by the defendant and which the claimant could not have obtained by other means.[126]

Prosecution evidence

If, in a criminal case, evidence becomes available to the prosecution for the first time *after* the close of its case, the question of its admissibility should be referred to and decided by the judge.[127] The evidence may be admitted, even if not strictly of a rebutting character, but the court should take care, in the exercise of its discretion, in case injustice is done to the accused, and should consider whether to grant the defence an adjournment.[128]

Although, in criminal cases, the general rule applies not only to the adducing of evidence, but also to matters to be put in cross-examination of an accused,[129] it is confined to evidence probative of his guilt, rather than evidence going only to his credit.[130] If evidence capable of forming part of the affirmative case for the prosecution case did not form part of the evidence on which the accused was committed for trial, the practice is to give notice of the additional evidence to the defence before it is tendered.[131] The fact that the accused might then trim his evidence is not a reason for withholding the material until he gives evidence, because an accused needs to know in advance the case against him if he is to have a proper opportunity of answering that case to the best of his ability. He is also entitled to such knowledge when deciding whether to testify. It is better in the interests of justice that an accused is not induced, by thinking it is safe to do so, to exaggerate, embroider, or lie. To do so might be to ambush the accused.[132]

[121] Section 52(2).
[122] Section 52(5) and (6).
[123] Section 56(5)(b).
[124] Section 54.
[125] *R v Rice* (1963) 47 Cr App R 79, CCA.
[126] *Stocznia Gdanska SA v Latvian Shipping Co* (2000) LTL 19/10/2000, QBD.
[127] *R v Kane* (1977) 65 Cr App R 270, CA.
[128] *R v Doran* (1972) 56 Cr App R 429, CA and *R v Patel* [1992] Crim LR 739, CA; cf *R v Pilcher* (1974) 60 Cr App R 1, CA.
[129] *R v Kane* (1977) 65 Cr App R 270, CA.
[130] *R v Halford* (1978) 67 Cr App R 318, CA.
[131] *R v Kane* (1977) 65 Cr App R 270, CA.
[132] *R v Phillipson* (1989) 91 Cr App R 226, CA. See also *R v Sansom* [1991] 2 QB 130, CA.

To the general rule of practice there are two exceptions and a 'wider discretion' to be exercised outside the two exceptions sparingly. As to the first exception, evidence is allowed in rebuttal of matters arising *ex improviso*, which no human ingenuity could have foreseen.[133] Under this exception, it is for the judge, in his discretion, to determine whether the relevance of the evidence could *reasonably* have been anticipated.[134] If the prosecution can reasonably foresee that the evidence is relevant to their case, it must be adduced as a part of that case and not to remedy defects in that case after it has been closed.[135] In *R v Milliken*,[136] the accused, when giving evidence, for the first time accused officers of a conspiracy to fabricate evidence. Evidence in rebuttal was allowed, because it only became relevant when the accused gave evidence. Equally, the prosecution may rely on this exception where the evidence in question was not, at the outset, *clearly* relevant, but only marginally, minimally, or doubtfully relevant[137] or constituted fanciful and unreal statements such as allegations which were obviously ridiculous and untrue.[138]

Under the second exception, the judge has a discretion to admit evidence which has not been adduced by reason of inadvertence or oversight. Although this exception is usually said to apply only in the case of evidence of a formal or uncontentious nature,[139] the cases show that the evidence may relate to a matter of substance.[140]

In *R v Francis*[141] the prosecution established where a man was standing at a group identification, but failed to call evidence that the man in that position was the accused. After the close of their case, the prosecution were allowed to adduce such evidence. It was held that although the failure was not a mere technicality, but an essential if minor link in the chain of identification evidence, the discretion of the judge to admit evidence after the close of the prosecution case is not confined to the two well-established exceptions: there is a wider discretion, but it should only be exercised outside the two exceptions on the rarest of occasions. In *R v Munnery*[142] it was held that this last proposition could be expanded to include the words 'especially when the evidence is tendered after the case for the defendant has begun'. An example of evidence being admitted even at this late stage is *James v South Glamorgan County Council*.[143] In that case, in which the defence had not made a submission of no case to answer, the prosecution, after the accused had given his evidence-in-chief, were allowed to re-open their case to call their main

---

[133] *R v Frost* (1839) 4 State Tr NS 85. The exception may be used by the prosecution to adduce evidence in rebuttal of not only defence *evidence*, but also matters unsupported by evidence but arising by implication from the defence closing speech: *R v O'Hadhmaill* [1996] Crim LR 509, CA.

[134] *R v Scott* (1984) 79 Cr App R 49, CA.

[135] *R v Day* (1940) 27 Cr App R 168.

[136] (1969) 53 Cr App R 330, CA.

[137] *R v Levy* (1966) 50 Cr App R 198.

[138] *R v Hutchinson* (1985) 82 Cr App R 51, CA.

[139] For example, failure to prove that leave of the Director of Public Prosecutions to bring proceedings has been obtained (*R v Waller* [1910] 1 KB 364, CCA, applied in *Price v Humphries* [1958] 2 All ER 725, DC) or failure to prove a statutory instrument by production of a Stationery Office copy (*Palastanga v Solman* [1962] Crim LR 334 and *Hammond v Wilkinson* [2001] Crim LR 323). See also *R v McKenna* (1956) 40 Cr App R 65.

[140] See, eg, *Piggott v Sims* [1973] RTR 15 (an analyst's certificate); *Matthews v Morris* [1981] Crim LR 495 (a statement by the owner of the property allegedly stolen); and *Middleton v Rowlett* [1954] 1 WLR 831 and *Smith v DPP* [2008] EWHC 771 (Admin) (evidence of identification).

[141] [1991] 1 All ER 225, CA.

[142] (1990) 94 Cr App R 164, CA.

[143] (1994) 99 Cr App R 321, DC. See also (applying *R v Francis*) *R v Jackson* [1996] 2 Cr App R 420, CA.

witness, whose evidence was important, if not essential to their case, the witness having arrived late by reason of transport difficulties and genuine confusion about the location of the court house. *Jolly v DPP*,[144] a decision relating to a summary trial, also supports a wider discretionary approach to admissibility. It was held that it was 'beyond argument' that there was a general discretion to permit the prosecution to call evidence after the close of their case, which, in a magistrates' court, extended up to the time when the bench retired. The court would look carefully at the interests of justice overall and in particular the risk of prejudice to the accused, as when the defence would have been conducted differently had the evidence been adduced as part of the prosecution case. Thus the discretion would be exercised sparingly, but it was doubted whether it assisted to speak in terms of 'exceptional circumstances'.[145]

In appropriate circumstances, rather than have the prosecution re-open their case, a judge may, in the interests of justice, admit evidence himself. In *R v Bowles*[146] it was held that a judge was justified in calling certain evidence to provide an answer to a question raised by the jury during the defence case: the defence had not closed their case, and the evidence, which was non-controversial and did not contradict that of the accused, helped the jury resolve an issue on the basis of known facts, rather than speculation. In the exercise of his discretion, the judge may also recall or permit the recall of a witness at any stage in the proceedings before the end of his summing-up.[147]

Defence evidence

A judge may permit an accused to be recalled to deal with matters which arose after he gave evidence if he could not reasonably have anticipated them and it appears to be in the interests of justice.[148] A judge may, as a matter of discretion and in the interests of justice, allow an accused to be recalled to clarify some feature of his evidence or to address a possible source of misunderstanding or to be given the opportunity to answer new allegations by a co-accused not put to him under cross-examination. However, it is difficult to imagine a situation in which an accused should be allowed to be recalled to advance a new account of facts contradicting his earlier evidence, which would normally constitute an abuse of process.[149]

Evidence after the retirement of the magistrates or jury

In the magistrates' court, evidence may be called even after the magistrates have retired, provided that there are special circumstances, as when the defence seek to ambush the prosecution by raising an issue for the first time in their closing speech.[150] In the Crown Court, once the jury have retired to consider their verdict on the conclusion of the summing-up, no further evidence may be admitted, whether by the calling or recalling of witnesses,[151] and

---

[144] [2000] Crim LR 471, DC.

[145] See also *Cook v DPP* [2001] Crim LR 321, DC.

[146] [1992] Crim LR 726, CA. See also *R v Aitken* (1991) 94 Cr App R 85, CA.

[147] *R v Sullivan* [1923] 1 KB 47; *R v McKenna* (1956) 40 Cr App R 65. The witness may be cross-examined on new evidence given: *R v Watson* (1834) 6 C&P 653.

[148] *R v Cook* [2005] EWCA Crim 2011 at [28].

[149] *R v Ikram* [2008] 2 Cr App R 347, CA.

[150] *Malcolm v DPP* [2007] 2 Cr App R 1, DC.

[151] *R v Owen* (1952) 36 Cr App R 16. In *R v Flynn* (1957) 42 Cr App R 15, evidence in rebuttal was called immediately before the summing-up. In *R v Sanderson* (1953) 37 Cr App R 32, fresh evidence was called after the summing-up but before the jury retired. The Criminal Law Revision Committee proposed that evidence be allowed to be given at any time prior to verdict: see 11th Report, Cmnd 4991 (1972), paras 213–16.

the jury must not be given any additional matter or material to assist them,[152] either at their own request, or in error.[153] However, this principle has been relaxed in the case of additional evidence put before the jury at the request of the accused because it assists his case.[154]

When the jury retire, an exhibit may be taken into the jury room for inspection. Where a silent film or video has been shown in court and the jury, after retirement, ask to see it again, they may do so, but it is better that they do so in open court.[155] Concerning tapes, if nothing turns on tone of voice, it will usually suffice for the jury to have a transcript, much of which should be summarized, but where tone of voice is all-important, then, subject to editing out inadmissible material, the jury should have the original tape.[156] If the tape is not played during the trial, the jury may listen to it after retirement, but if there is a risk that they may hear inadmissible material, the tape should be played in open court.[157] If the prosecution do not rely on parts of a tape, the jury may only hear it as edited.[158] However, if the tape, of which there is an agreed transcript, has already been played in court and does not contain inadmissible material, the judge has a discretion to permit the jury to play it in their retiring room.[159] In the case of a video recording used as a child's evidence pursuant to s 27 of the 1999 Act, if the jury, after they have retired, wish to be reminded of *what* the witness said, the judge should remind them from the transcript or his own notes; but if they wish to be reminded of how the words were spoken, the judge may in his discretion allow the video, or relevant part, to be replayed, provided that the replay takes place in court.[160] Either way, the judge should warn the jury that by reason of hearing the evidence again they should guard against the risk of giving it disproportionate weight and bear well in mind the other evidence in the case, and the judge should remind the jury, from his notes, of the cross-examination and re-examination of the witness.[161]

A jury request for equipment, such as weighing scales, to enable them to carry out unsupervised scientific experiments with exhibits, should not be met.[162]

[152] *R v Davis* (1975) 62 Cr App R 194. See also *R v Crees* [1996] Crim LR 830, CA, where the jury were improperly given a ruler which they wished to use as if it were a knife, for the purposes of a re-enactment.

[153] See *R v Gilder* [1997] Crim LR 668, CA.

[154] See *R v Hallam* [2007] EWCA Crim 1495 and *R v Khan* [2008] EWCA Crim 1112; and cf *R v Cadman* [2008] EWCA Crim 1418.

[155] *R v Imran* [1997] Crim LR 754, CA.

[156] *R v Emmerson* (1990) 92 Cr App R 284, CA.

[157] *R v Riaz* (1991) 94 Cr App R 339, CA.

[158] See *R v Hagan* [1997] 1 Cr App R 464, CA.

[159] *R v Tonge* [1993] Crim LR 876, CA.

[160] In normal circumstances it is inappropriate for the video to be replayed unless there has been a specific request to that effect from the jury: *R v M* [1996] 2 Cr App R 56, CA.

[161] See, in the case of a reminder from the transcript, *R v McQuiston* [1998] 1 Cr App R 139, CA and *R v Morris* [1998] Crim LR 416, CA; and see, in the case of a replay, *R v Rawlings* [1995] 1 All ER 580, CA, applied in *R v M* [1996] 2 Cr App R 56, CA, *R v B* [1996] Crim LR 499, CA, and *R v W* [2011] EWCA Crim 1142. The principles, however, do not lay down an inflexible practice to be followed to the letter in every case: *R v Horley* [1999] Crim LR 488, CA. See, eg, *R v Saunders* [1995] 2 Cr App R 313, CA.

[162] *R v Stewart, R v Sappleton* (1989) 89 Cr App R 273, CA; cf *R v Wright* [1993] Crim LR 607, CA. A magnifying glass, a ruler, or a tape-measure do not normally raise the possibility of such an experiment: *R v Maggs* (1990) 91 Cr App R 243, CA.

Witnesses in civil cases

The witnesses to be called

Prior to the Civil Procedure Rules, a party to civil proceedings was under no obligation to call particular witnesses, could call such witnesses to support his case as he saw fit, and could call them in the order of his choice.[163] As to the judge, he had no right to call witnesses against the will of the parties,[164] except in cases of civil contempt,[165] but did have the power to recall a witness called by a party.[166] CPR r 32.1(1) now provides that the court may control the evidence by giving directions as to the nature of the evidence which it requires to decide the issues on which it requires evidence, and the way in which the evidence is to be placed before the court; and under r 32.1(2) the court may use its power under the rule to exclude evidence that would otherwise be admissible. In exercising these powers, the judge must seek to give effect to the 'overriding objective' of the rules, which is to enable the court 'to deal with cases justly'.[167] It seems that CPR r 32.1(1) does not empower the court to dictate to a litigant what evidence he should tender. Thus a party who has disclosed a witness statement in accordance with pre-trial directions cannot be ordered by the court to call the witness, although he should notify the other parties of his decision and whether he proposes to put the statement in as hearsay.[168] In appropriate circumstances, however, the judge may take the view that, in order to give effect to the overriding objective, he should give directions under CPR r 32.1(1) as to the order in which witnesses should give their evidence, and as to those witnesses who are not required to decide the issues and whose evidence, therefore, although admissible, should not be heard.

Witness statements

The rules for the exchange of witness statements in civil cases have been designed to promote the fair disposal of proceedings and to save costs: they identify the real issues, encourage the parties to make appropriate admissions of fact, promote fair settlements, remove the element of surprise as to the witnesses each party intends to call, and give to the cross-examining party the advantage of knowing in advance what each witness will say in his examination-in-chief.

A witness statement is a written statement signed by a person which contains the evidence which that person would be allowed to give orally.[169] Under CPR r 32.4(2), the court will order a party to serve on the other parties any witness statement of the oral evidence which the party serving the statement intends to rely on in relation to any issues of fact to be decided at the trial; and under r 32.4(3) the court may give directions as to the order in which the statements are to be served.[170] The court will give directions for the service of witness statements when it allocates a case to the fast track[171] or multi-track.[172] Normally, the court will direct the

---

[163] *Briscoe v Briscoe* [1966] 1 All ER 465; but cf *Bayer v Clarkson Puckle Overseas Ltd* [1989] NLJR 256.

[164] *Re Enoch and Zaretzky, Bock & Co's Arbitration* [1910] 1 KB 327, CA.

[165] *Yianni v Yianni* [1966] 1 WLR 120.

[166] *Fallon v Calvert* [1960] 2 QB 201, CA.

[167] See further Ch 2, under **Judicial discretion, Exclusionary discretion, Civil cases**.

[168] *Society of Lloyd's v Jaffray* (2000) The Times, 3 Aug, QBD.

[169] Rule 32.4(1). The statement, therefore, should not contain material which is irrelevant or otherwise inadmissible.

[170] Although CPR Pt 32 (except r 32.1) does not apply to claims which have been allocated to the small claims track (r 27.2(1)), in the case of many such claims directions for the exchange of witness statements will be given nonetheless: see r 27.4 and PD 27.

[171] Rule 28.2, r 28.3 and PD 28.

[172] Rule 29.2 and PD 29.

simultaneous exchange of statements,[173] but sequential exchange may be appropriate where one party will not know fully or precisely the case he has to answer until he has had sight of his opponent's witness statements. If a party fails to serve witness statements, any other party may apply for an order to enforce compliance or for a sanction to be imposed,[174] and, ultimately, the court has the power to strike out the claim or defence.[175]

A witness statement should be dated.[176] It must, if practicable, be in the intended witness's own words and should be expressed in the first person.[177] It must also indicate which of the statements in it are made from the witness's own knowledge and which are matters of information or belief.[178] The statement is the equivalent of the oral evidence which the witness would, if called, give in evidence, and must include a statement of truth by the intended witness, ie a signed statement that he believes the facts in it are true.[179] If it is not verified by a statement of truth, then the court may direct that it shall not be admissible as evidence.[180] Equally, if it does not comply with CPR Pt 32 or PD 32 in relation to its form, the court may refuse to admit it as evidence.[181]

CPR r 32.5 provides as follows:

(1) If—
   (a) a party has served a witness statement; and
   (b) he wishes to rely at trial on the evidence of the witness who made the statement,
   he must call the witness to give oral evidence unless the court orders otherwise or he puts the statement in as hearsay evidence.
(2) Where a witness is called to give oral evidence under paragraph (1), his witness statement shall stand as his evidence in chief unless the court orders otherwise.
(3) A witness giving oral evidence at trial may with the permission of the court—
   (a) amplify his witness statement; and
   (b) give evidence in relation to new matters which have arisen since the witness statement was served on the other parties.
(4) The court will give permission under paragraph (3) only if it considers that there is good reason not to confine the evidence of the witness to the contents of his witness statement.
(5) If a party who has served a witness statement does not—
   (a) call the witness to give evidence at trial; or
   (b) put the witness statement in as hearsay evidence,
   any other party may put the witness statement in as hearsay evidence.

As to CPR r 32.5(2), it is likely that the court, in deciding whether to order that the statement should not stand as the witness's evidence-in-chief, will have regard to such matters as the

---

[173] PD 28, para 3.9 and PD 29, para 4.10.

[174] See PD 28, para 5.1 and PD 29, para 7.1.

[175] See CPR r 3.4.

[176] Rule 32.8 and PD 32, para 17.2.

[177] Rule 32.8 and PD 32, para 18.1.

[178] Rule 32.8 and PD 32, para 18.2.

[179] PD 32, para 20.1 and r 22.1(6). Proceedings for contempt of court may be brought against a person making a false statement in a document verified by a statement of truth without an honest belief in its truth: r 32.14. It is part of the duty of solicitors to ensure, so far as it is within their power, that statements are taken either by themselves or, if that is not practicable, by somebody who can be relied upon to exercise the same standard as should apply when statements are taken by solicitors: *Aquarius Financial Enterprises Inc v Certain Underwriters at Lloyd's* (2001) NLJ 694, QBD.

[180] Rule 22.3.

[181] PD 32, para 25.1.

extent to which his evidence is likely to be controversial and to go to the heart of the dispute, and the extent to which his credibility will be in issue.[182] An order may well be appropriate if it is alleged that the witness is not merely mistaken, but deliberately lying.[183] As to r 32.5(4), the pertinent factors would seem to be the relevance of the evidence to the issues, any prejudice likely to be caused to the party against whom the evidence is to be used and, in the case of r 32.5(3)(a), the reason why the witness statement did not include the additional material.

Under r 32.9, provision is made for a party who is unable to obtain a witness statement to apply for permission to serve a witness summary instead. Rule 32.9 covers cases where a party knows the name and address of a particular witness, but the witness is reluctant or unwilling to give evidence or, having indicated his willingness to give evidence, changes his mind. A typical example is the employee who is loath to give evidence, on behalf of an ex-employee, against his employer.[184] Rule 32.9 provides as follows:

(1) A party who—
    (a) is required to serve a witness statement for use at trial; but
    (b) is unable to obtain one,
    may apply, without notice, for permission to serve a witness summary instead.
(2) A witness summary is a summary of—
    (a) the evidence, if known, which would otherwise be included in a witness statement; or
    (b) if the evidence is not known, the matters about which the party serving the witness summary proposes to question the witness.
(3) Unless the court orders otherwise, a witness summary must include the name and address of the intended witness.
(4) Unless the court orders otherwise, a witness summary must be served within the period in which a witness statement would have had to be served.
(5) Where a party serves a witness summary, so far as practicable, rules 32.4 (requirement to serve witness statements for use at trial), 32.5(3) (amplifying witness statements), and 32.8 (form of witness statement) shall apply to the summary.

Under r 32.10, if a witness statement or witness summary is not served in respect of an intended witness within the time specified by the court, then the witness may not be called to give oral evidence unless the court gives permission. In deciding whether to give permission, the relevant factors would appear to be the length of delay, whether there is a good reason for failure to serve the statement or it is a result of incompetence on the part of the legal advisers, the relevance of the evidence, including the risk of injustice to the party seeking to call the witness if permission is not given, and any prejudice likely to be caused to his opponent if permission is given.

Witnesses in criminal cases

Under r 3.3 of the Criminal Procedure Rules 2013,[185] each party to criminal proceedings must (a) actively assist the court in fulfilling its duty to further the overriding objective (that

---

[182] See *Mercer v Chief Constable of the Lancashire Constabulary* [1991] 2 All ER 504, CA, a decision under an earlier version of the rules.

[183] *JN Dairies Ltd v Johal Dairies Ltd* [2010] EWCA Civ 348 at [44].

[184] See further Ch 6, under **Unfavourable and hostile witnesses**.

[185] SI 2013/1554.

criminal cases be dealt with justly) by actively managing the case, without or if necessary with a direction; and (b) apply for a direction if needed to further the overriding objective. Under r 3.9, which applies to the parties' preparation for trial, each party, in fulfilling his duty under r 3.3, must, inter alia, take every reasonable step to make sure his witnesses will attend when they are needed; and under r 3.10, in order to manage the trial, the court may require a party to identify (a) which witnesses he wants to give evidence in person; (b) the order in which he wants those witnesses to give their evidence; (c) whether he requires an order compelling the attendance of a witness; and (d) what arrangements are desirable to facilitate the giving of evidence by a witness.

The witnesses to be called

In criminal proceedings, the choice as to which witnesses are called rests primarily with the parties. However, a trial judge is entitled to invite either party to consider putting further evidence before the jury as part of the duty to ensure a fair trial for both sides.[186] A judge also has the right to call a witness not called by either the prosecution or defence, and without the consent of either party if, in his opinion, this course is necessary in the interests of justice.[187] Justices have the same right in summary proceedings.[188] This right may be exercised by the judge even after the close of the case for the defence, but only where a matter has arisen *ex improviso*.[189]

The prosecution are under an obligation to call certain witnesses and to have others available at court to be called by the defence. In the case of trials on indictment, the principles were set out in *R v Russell-Jones*:[190]

1. Generally speaking the prosecution must bring to court all the witnesses 'named on the back of the indictment', a phrase reflecting the old practice, nowadays meaning those whose statements have been served as witnesses on whom the prosecution intend to rely, if the defence want those witnesses to attend.[191]

2. The prosecution have a discretion to call, or to tender for cross-examination by the defence, any witness they require to attend, but the discretion is not unfettered.

3. The discretion must be exercised in the interests of justice so as to promote a fair trial.

4. The prosecution should normally call or offer to call all the witnesses who can give direct evidence of the primary facts of the case, even if there are inconsistencies between one

---

[186] Per Hooper LJ in *R v Malcolm* [2011] EWCA Crim 2069 at [83].

[187] *R v Chapman* (1838) 8 C&P 558 and *R v Holden* (1838) 8 C&P 606; cf *R v McDowell* [1984] Crim LR 486, CA. The power may be exercised, eg, where the prosecution exercise improperly their discretion not to call a witness (considered in this chapter at nn 192–194): per Lord Parker CJ in *R v Oliva* [1965] 1 WLR 1028 at 1035–6. However, the power should rarely be exercised: *R v Grafton* (1993) 96 Cr App R 156, CA. If it is, an adjournment may be necessary to enable one of the parties to call evidence in rebuttal: see *R v Coleman* (1987) The Times, 21 Nov, CA.

[188] *R v Wellingborough Magistrates' Court, ex p François* (1994) 158 JP 813 and *R v Haringey Justices, ex p DPP* [1996] 2 Cr App R 119, DC.

[189] See *R v Cleghorn* [1967] 2 QB 584, CA; cf *R v Tregear* [1967] 2 QB 574, CA.

[190] [1995] 3 All ER 239, CA. See also *R v Brown and Brown* [1997] 1 Cr App R 112, CA. Similar principles apply to summary proceedings: see *R v Haringey Justices, ex p DPP* [1996] 2 Cr App R 119, DC.

[191] The prosecution are under no duty to call the makers of statements which have never formed part of the prosecution case because inconsistent with it and which have been served on the defence as unused material: *R v Richardson* (1993) 98 Cr App R 174, CA.

witness and another, unless for good reason, in any instance, the prosecutor regards the witness's evidence as unworthy of belief.[192] In *R v Oliva*,[193] for example, it was held that the prosecution were not obliged to call the victim of an offence who gave evidence at the committal proceedings first implicating and then exonerating the accused. The witness had proved himself unworthy of belief and, if called by the prosecution, would have confused the jury.[194] However, if the prosecution are of the view that part of a witness's evidence is capable of belief, even though they do not rely on other parts of his evidence, they are entitled to exercise their discretion to call him, since it would be contrary to the interests of justice to deprive the jury of that part of his evidence which could be of assistance to them.[195]

5. It is for the prosecution to decide which witnesses can give direct evidence of the primary facts.

6. The prosecutor is also the primary judge of whether or not a witness to the material events is unworthy of belief.

7. A prosecutor properly exercising his discretion will not be obliged to proffer a witness merely in order to give the defence material with which to attack the credit of other witnesses on whom the Crown relies.

The order of witnesses

Although in criminal proceedings the parties are generally free to call their witnesses in the order of their choice, at common law the defence was required to call the accused before any of his witnesses: 'He ought to give his evidence before he has heard the evidence and cross-examination of any witness he is going to call.'[196] In *R v Smith*[197] the Court of Appeal approved this rule, subject to 'rare exceptions such as when a formal witness, or a witness about whom there is no controversy, is interposed before the accused person with the consent of the court in the special circumstances then prevailing'. The Criminal Law Revision Committee favoured retention of the rule but was of the opinion that the court should be given a discretion, wider than that stated in *R v Smith*, to call other witnesses before the accused.[198] Section 79 of the 1984 Act, implementing this recommendation, provides that:

> If at the trial of any person for an offence—
> (a) the defence intends to call two or more witnesses to the facts of the case; and
> (b) those witnesses include the accused,
> the accused shall be called before the other witness or witnesses unless the court in its discretion otherwise directs.

[192] Reading out the material parts of the statement of a witness may discharge the duty on the prosecution: see *R v Armstrong* [1995] Crim LR 831, CA.

[193] [1965] 1 WLR 1028. Cf *R v Witts and Witts* [1991] Crim LR 562, CA.

[194] See also *R v Nugent* [1977] 3 All ER 662 and *R v Balmforth* [1992] Crim LR 825, CA.

[195] *R v Cairns* [2003] 1 Cr App R 662, CA.

[196] Per Lord Alverstone CJ in *R v Morrison* (1911) 6 Cr App R 159 at 165.

[197] (1968) 52 Cr App R 224.

[198] Criminal Law Revision Committee, para 107. The Committee gave as an example a witness who is to speak of some event which occurred before the events about which the accused is to give evidence.

Evidence-in-chief by video recording

In his *Review of the Criminal Courts of England and Wales*[199] Lord Justice Auld recommended that, further to the use of video-recorded evidence-in-chief for vulnerable witnesses,[200] video-recorded evidence should also be admissible for the witnesses of all serious crimes. The Government, in adopting this proposal, recognized the two key advantages of allowing the video recording to replace the witness's evidence-in-chief, namely the fact that the witness's recollection of the events in question is likely to have been better at the time of the recording, and the reduction in levels of stress when giving evidence on oath. The danger that the witness may, in the recording, make statements elicited in answer to leading questions, was not thought to be serious given that it would be 'completely evident' whether the witness had been led. Under s 137 of the 2003 Act, therefore, where a video recording of a witness's account of events has been made at a time when the events were fresh in his memory, the court may direct that the recording be admitted as his evidence-in-chief if it appears to the court that his recollection of events is likely to have been significantly better at the time of the recording than it will be when he gives oral evidence and it is in the interests of justice for the recording to be admitted, having regard in particular to certain prescribed matters. Under s 137(2), which effectively side-steps the hearsay rule, the statements in the recorded account are not treated as out-of-court statements admissible as evidence of the matters stated, but shall be treated as if made by the witness in his evidence if, or to the extent that, in his oral evidence he asserts the truth of them. Section 137, which has yet to be brought into force, provides as follows:

(1) This section applies where—
    (a) a person is called as a witness in proceedings for an offence triable only on indictment, or for a prescribed offence triable either way,
    (b) the person claims to have witnessed (whether visually or in any other way)—
        (i) events alleged by the prosecution to include conduct constituting the offence or part of the offence, or
        (ii) events closely connected with such events,
    (c) he has previously given an account of the events in question (whether in response to questions asked or otherwise),
    (d) the account was given at a time when those events were fresh in the person's memory (or would have been, assuming the truth of the claim mentioned in paragraph (b)),
    (e) a video recording was made of the account,
    (f) the court has made a direction that the recording should be admitted as evidence in chief of the witness, and the direction has not been rescinded, and
    (g) the recording is played in the proceedings in accordance with the direction.
(2) If, or to the extent that, the witness in his oral evidence in the proceedings asserts the truth of the statements made by him in the recorded account, they shall be treated as if made by him in that evidence.
(3) A direction under subsection (1)(f)—
    (a) may not be made in relation to a recorded account given by the defendant;
    (b) may be made only if it appears to the court that—

---

[199] (HMSO, 2001) 555.
[200] See, in this chapter, under **Witnesses in criminal cases, Special measures directions for vulnerable and intimidated witnesses.**

(i) the witness's recollection of the events in question is likely to have been significantly better when he gave the recorded account than it will be when he gives oral evidence in the proceedings, and

(ii) it is in the interests of justice for the recording to be admitted, having regard in particular to the matters mentioned in subsection (4).

(4) Those matters are—

(a) the interval between the time of the events in question and the time when the recorded account was made;

(b) any other factors that might affect the reliability of what the witness said in that account;

(c) the quality of the recording;

(d) any views of the witness as to whether his evidence in chief should be given orally or by means of the recording.

(5) For the purposes of subsection (2) it does not matter if the statements in the recorded account were not made on oath.

(6) In this section 'prescribed' means of a description specified in an order made by the Secretary of State.

Nothing in s 137 affects the admissibility of any video recording which would be admissible apart from the section.[201]

Section 138(2) and (3) of the 2003 Act provide as follows:

(2) The reference in subsection (1)(f) of section 137 to the admission of a recording includes a reference to the admission of part of the recording; and references in that section and this one to the video recording or to the witness's recorded account shall, where appropriate, be read accordingly.

(3) In considering whether any part of a recording should not be admitted under section 137, the court must consider—

(a) whether admitting that part would carry a risk of prejudice to the defendant, and

(b) if so, whether the interests of justice nevertheless require it to be admitted in view of the desirability of showing the whole, or substantially the whole, of the recorded interview.

Special measures directions for vulnerable and intimidated witnesses

Sections 16–33 of the 1999 Act introduced a range of 'special measures' which were proposed in *Speaking Up for Justice*[202] and are designed to minimize the ordeal and trauma experienced by certain types of vulnerable and intimidated witnesses when giving evidence in criminal cases.[203] The provisions in the 1999 Act have been amended by the Coroners and Justice Act

---

[201] Section 138(5).

[202] (Home Office, 1998).

[203] See also *Report of the Advisory Group on Video-Recorded Evidence* (Home Office, 1989) (the 'Pigot Report'), Law Commission Consultation Paper No 130, *Mentally Incapacitated and Other Vulnerable Adults: Public Law Protection*, and generally Birch, 'A Better Deal for Vulnerable Witnesses?' [2000] Crim LR 223 and Hoyano, 'Variations on a Theme by Pigot: Special Measures Directions for Child Witnesses' [2000] Crim LR 250 and 'Striking a Balance between the Rights of Defendants and Vulnerable Witnesses: Will Special Measures Directions Contravene Guarantees of a Fair Trial?' [2001] Crim LR 948. There are no equivalent statutory special measures available in civil cases, but in the case of children in family proceedings, consideration should be given to the use of intermediaries, live link, screens, and other special measures (presumably in exercise of the courts' inherent jurisdiction): see Working Party of the Family Justice Council, *Guidelines in relation to children giving evidence in family proceedings* (2011) para 14 (a), (b), and (c).

2009.[204] The provisions are sensible modifications to orthodox trial procedures designed to meet the real needs of children and other vulnerable witnesses and most applications for special measures succeed.[205] However, there are five failings. (1) The new statutory scheme is needlessly complex, in parts almost impenetrable. (2) It is unduly inflexible and makes somewhat arbitrary distinctions between, (a) sexual offences (together with offences involving the use of firearms, knives, and other weapons), and (b) all other types of serious offence. (3) The accused is excluded from the statutory scheme, except in the case of live link and examination through an intermediary, and in those two cases the eligibility criteria for the accused are different from those that apply to other witnesses, and some of the differences are difficult to justify.[206] (4) The provision relating to the video recording of cross-examination and re-examination has simply not been brought into force.[207] (5) More could be achieved, both in improving the processes for the identification of vulnerable and intimidated witnesses[208] and by the introduction of specific new measures such as improved assessment of individual need, the mandatory visual recording of initial interviews, and the curtailment of inappropriate questioning and cross-examination tactics.[209]

The judge may give a direction providing for the following special measures to apply to evidence given by vulnerable and intimidated witnesses: screening the witness; giving evidence by live link; giving evidence in private; the removal of wigs and gowns; admitting a video recording of an interview of the witness as the evidence-in-chief of the witness; video recording the cross-examination and re-examination of the witness and admitting such a recording as the evidence of the witness under cross-examination and on re-examination;[210] the examination of the witness through an intermediary; and the provision of appropriate aids to communication with the witness.

Special measures are only available to 'eligible witnesses', namely (i) witnesses other than the accused eligible for assistance on grounds of age or incapacity, for whom all the above special measures are available, and (ii) witnesses other than the accused eligible for assistance on grounds of fear or distress about testifying, for whom all but the last two of the above special measures are available.[211] It will be convenient to consider in more detail the nature of the special measures available and the above types of witness eligible for assistance before turning to consider the circumstances in which a special measures direction may or must be given. Finally, consideration will be given to the special position of the accused.

---

[204] For analysis of the amendments, see Hoyano, 'Special Measures Directions Take Two: Entrenching Unequal Access to Justice?' [2010] Crim LR 345.

[205] See Roberts et al, 'Monitoring success, accounting for failure: The outcome of prosecutors' applications for special measures directions under the Youth Justice and Criminal Evidence Act 1999' (2005) 9 E&P 269.

[206] See generally McEwan, 'Vulnerable Defendants and the Fairness of Trials' [2013] Crim LR 100.

[207] See generally Cooper, 'Pigot Unfulfilled: Video-recorded Cross-examination under section 28 of the Youth Justice and Criminal Evidence Act 1999' [2005] Crim LR 456.

[208] See Burton et al, 'Implementing Special Measures for Vulnerable and Intimidated Witnesses: The Problem of Identification' [2006] Crim LR 229.

[209] See Burton et al, 'Vulnerable and intimidated witnesses and the adversarial process in England and Wales' (2007) 11 E&P 1; but see also, in relation to the examination and cross-examination of vulnerable witnesses, under **Young witnesses**, Ch 6 and **Cross-examination**, **Young and vulnerable witnesses**, Ch 7.

[210] This special measure has yet to be introduced.

[211] See s 18(1).

Special measures directions

Screens

Under s 23(1) of the 1999 Act, a special measures direction may provide for the witness while giving evidence or being sworn in court to be prevented by means of a screen or other arrangement from seeing the accused. However, the screen must not prevent the witness from being able to see, and to be seen by, the judge or justices, the jury (if there is one), legal representatives acting in the case, and any interpreter or other person appointed to assist the witness.[212]

Live link

Under s 24 of the 1999 Act, a special measures direction may provide for the witness to give evidence by a live television link or other arrangement whereby the witness, while absent from the courtroom, is able to see and hear a person there and to be seen and heard by the judge or justices, the jury (if there is one), the legal representatives in the case, and any interpreter or other person appointed to assist the witness. Such a direction may also provide for a specified person to accompany the witness while giving evidence by live link.[213] Where a direction has been given providing for the witness to give evidence by live link, the court may later give permission for the witness to give evidence in some other way, if it appears to be in the interests of justice to do so.[214]

Evidence in private

Under s 25 of the 1999 Act, a special measures direction may provide for the exclusion from the court, during the giving of the witness's evidence, of persons of any description specified in the direction other than the accused, legal representatives acting in the case, or any interpreter or other person appointed to assist the witness.[215] However, such a direction may only be given where the proceedings relate to a sexual offence[216] or it appears to the court that there are reasonable grounds for believing that any person other than the accused has sought, or will seek, to intimidate the witness in connection with testifying in the proceedings.[217]

Removal of wigs and gowns

Under s 26 of the 1999 Act, provision may be made for the wearing of wigs and gowns to be dispensed with during the giving of the witness's evidence.

Video-recorded evidence-in-chief

Sections 27(1)–(3) of the 1999 Act provide as follows:

(1) A special measures direction may provide for a video recording of an interview of the witness to be admitted as evidence in chief of the witness.
(2) A special measures direction may, however, not provide for a video-recording, or part of such a recording, to be admitted under this section if the court is of the opinion, having regard to

---

[212] Section 23(2). See also, prior to the enactment of s 23, Home Office Circular 61/1990, *Use of Screens in Magistrates' Courts*; and *R v X, Y and Z* (1989) 91 Cr App R 36, CA; *R v Watford Magistrates' Court, ex p Lenman* [1993] Crim LR 388, DC; *R v Cooper and Schaub* [1994] Crim LR 531, CA; and *R v Foster* [1995] Crim LR 333, CA.

[213] Section 24(1A).

[214] Section 24(3).

[215] Where the persons specified are representatives of the media, the direction shall be expressed not to apply to one named person nominated by one or more news gathering or reporting organizations: s 25(3).

[216] 'Sexual offence' is defined in the 1999 Act, s 62 as any offence under the Sexual Offences Act 2003, Pt 1 or any relevant superseded offence.

[217] Section 25(4).

all the circumstances of the case, that in the interests of justice the recording, or that part of it, should not be so admitted.

(3) In considering, for the purposes of subsection (2) whether any part of a recording should not be admitted under this section, the court must consider whether any prejudice to the accused which might result from that part being so admitted is outweighed by the desirability of showing the whole, or substantially the whole, of the recorded interview.

Section 27(2) allows the court to direct that any part of the recording be excluded, in which case the party admitting the video must then edit it accordingly.[218] The effect of s 27(3) is not to extend the common law rules as to the admissibility of evidence so as to lead to the admission of otherwise inadmissible evidence, for example inadmissible evidence of bad character. Such evidence will normally be edited out. Section 27(3) is designed to cover unusual cases in which the evidence of the witness cannot be given in a way that is coherent and understandable to the listener without the inclusion of the inadmissible material.[219] In such cases, it is submitted, the judge will need to give a direction to the jury—which, in the circumstances, is likely to be difficult for them to comprehend—that the offending material is not evidence of the matters stated.

Where a recording (or part of it) is admitted, then: (a) the witness must be called by the party tendering it in evidence, unless either (i) a special measures direction provides for the witness's evidence on cross-examination to be given in any recording admissible under s 28 of the 1999 Act, or (ii) the parties in the proceedings have agreed that there is no need for the witness to be available for cross-examination; and (b) the witness may not without the permission of the court give evidence-in-chief otherwise than by means of the recording (or part of it) as to any matter which, in the opinion of the court, is dealt with in the witness's recorded testimony (or part of it).[220] The court may give such permission if it appears to the court to be in the interests of justice to do so either (a) on an application by a party to the proceedings; or (b) of its own motion.[221] Where a special measures direction provides for a recording (or part of it) to be admitted under s 27, the court may nevertheless subsequently make a direction to the contrary if it appears to the court that (i) the witness will not be available for cross-examination (whether conducted in the ordinary way or in accordance with a special measures direction) and the parties have not agreed that there is no need for the witness to be so available, or (ii) any rules of court requiring disclosure of the circumstances in which the recording (or part of it) was made have not been complied with to the satisfaction of the court.[222] Nothing in s 27 affects the admissibility of any video recording which would be admissible apart from the section.[223]

[218] See para 40 of the *Consolidated Criminal Practice Direction*, which also governs the procedure for production and proof of the recording. The parties themselves may agree on the editing of an ABE interview (considered at nn 224–225) and such an agreement should be adhered to, unless there is very good reason to depart from it: *R v M(A)* [2013] 1 Cr App R 245, CA.

[219] *R (on the application of the Crown Prosecution Service Harrow) v Brentford Youth Court* [2004] Crim LR 159 (DC).

[220] Section 27(5) and (6).

[221] Section 27(7). The court may, in giving permission, direct that the evidence in question be given by the witness by means of a live link: s 27(9). If such a direction is given, the court may also provide for a specified person to accompany the witness while the witness is giving evidence by live link: s 27(9A).

[222] Section 27(4) and (6).

[223] Section 27(11).

Video-recorded interviews with child witnesses should be conducted in accordance with the guidance given in *Achieving Best Evidence: Guidance on interviewing victims and witnesses and guidance on using special measures*,[224] a non-statutory code which deals with such matters as leading questions, previous statements, and the bad character of the accused. The guidance should be regarded as expert advice as to what will normally be the best practice to adopt in seeking to ensure that a child's evidence is reliable, and if it is not observed there are grounds for a judge or jury to consider with particular care whether the child is reliable.[225] In *R v K*[226] it was held that, in deciding whether to exclude evidence obtained in breach of the Guidance, the starting point is the statutory wording and the strong presumption in favour of the use of special measures, and the test is 'Could a reasonable jury properly directed be sure that the witness has given a credible and accurate account notwithstanding the breaches?' The prime consideration is reliability, which will normally be assessed by reference to the interview itself, the conditions under which it was held, the age of the child, and the nature and extent of the breaches. There may be cases in which other evidence in the case demonstrates that the breaches did not undermine the credibility or accuracy of the interview, but references to other evidence should be undertaken with considerable caution.

In order to reach a decision under s 27(2), the judge, in most—if not all—cases, must watch the video recording. In the case of interviews with some child witnesses, the court will need to decide upon the competence of the child.[227] If, on viewing the recording, the judge considers that the child is not competent to give evidence, the evidence should not be admitted; but if he concludes that the child is competent, there is no need to investigate the child's competence again at the trial before the playing of the recording. Nonetheless, he still has the power to exclude the evidence if, in the course of it, he forms the view that the child is, after all, not competent.[228]

In *R v Popescu*[229] it was held that: where a video recording has been admitted, any transcript of it should only be given to the jury for good reason,[230] in which case the judge should warn the jury to take care to examine the video as it was shown, not least because of the demeanour of the witness;[231] the transcript should generally be withdrawn from the jury after the video has been shown, but might be retained during cross-examination, in exceptional circumstances, in which case the reason for retention should be explained to the jury; if retained during cross-examination, the transcript should generally be withdrawn from the jury at the conclusion of the witness's evidence, but might be retained when the jury retire, in exceptional circumstances, which would usually only be present if the defence want the jury to have the transcript and the judge is satisfied that there is a good reason for the jury to retire with it.[232]

---

[224] Now in its 3rd edition (Home Office, 2011).

[225] *R v Dunphy* (1993) 98 Cr App R 393 at 395, CA, a decision under an earlier version of the Guidance.

[226] [2006] 2 Cr App R 175, CA.

[227] In deciding, the court shall treat the witness as having the benefit of any directions under the 1999 Act, s 19 which the court has given, or proposes to give, in relation to the witness: the 1999 Act, s 54(3).

[228] See *R v Hampshire* [1995] 2 All ER 1019, CA, a decision under the Criminal Justice Act 1988, s 32A.

[229] [2011] Crim LR 227, CA.

[230] As when, eg, a child suffers from a speech disorder, poor articulation, or a strong accent.

[231] There is a risk of disproportionate weight being given to the transcript: see *R v Welstead* [1996] 1 Cr App R 59, CA.

[232] It is not a good reason, for these purposes, that the jury, on retirement, have with them a transcript of the accused's interview: *R v Sardar* [2012] EWCA Crim 134.

Video-recorded cross-examination or re-examination

Under s 28(1) of the 1999 Act, which has not been brought into force, where a special measures direction provides for a video recording to be admitted as evidence-in-chief of the witness under s 27, the direction may also provide for any cross-examination and any re-examination of the witness to be recorded by means of a video recording and for such a recording, so far as it relates to any such cross-examination or re-examination, to be admitted as evidence of the witness under cross-examination or re-examination. Under s 28(2), such a recording must be made in the presence of such persons as rules of court or the direction may provide, and in the absence of the accused, but in circumstances in which (a) the judge or justices (or both) and legal representatives acting in the proceedings are able to see and hear the examination of the witness and to communicate with those in whose presence the recording is being made; and (b) the accused is able to see and hear any such examination and to communicate with any legal representative acting for him.[233] Where a special measures direction provides for a recording to be admitted under s 28, the court may nevertheless subsequently make a direction to the contrary if any requirement of s 28(2) or rules of court or the direction itself has not been complied with to the satisfaction of the court.[234] Where in pursuance of s 28(1) a recording has been made, the witness may not be subsequently cross-examined or re-examined in respect of any evidence given by the witness (whether or not in any recording admissible under s 27 or s 28) unless the court gives a further special measures direction,[235] but such a further direction may only be given if it appears to the court (a) that the proposed cross-examination is sought by a party to the proceedings as a result of that party having become aware, since the time when the original recording was made, of a matter which that party could not with reasonable diligence have ascertained by then; or (b) that for any other reason it is in the interests of justice to give the further direction.[236]

Examination of witness through intermediary

Under s 29 of the 1999 Act, a special measures direction may provide for any examination of the witness (however and wherever conducted) to be conducted through an interpreter or other intermediary approved by the court. The function of the intermediary is to communicate to the witness questions put to the witness, to communicate to the person asking such questions the answers given by the witness in reply, and to explain such questions or answers so far as necessary to enable them to be understood.[237] Any examination under s 29 must take place in the presence of such persons as the Criminal Procedure Rules or the direction may provide, but in circumstances in which (a) the judge or justices (or both) and legal representatives acting in the proceedings are able to see and hear the examination of the witness and to communicate with the intermediary; and (b) the jury, if there is one, are able to see and

---

[233] Section 28 has no application in relation to any cross-examination of the witness by the accused in person: s 28(7).

[234] Section 28(4).

[235] Section 28(5).

[236] Section 28(6).

[237] Section 29(2). As to the extent to which s 29 will assist eligible witnesses to give their best evidence or promote more empathic communication during cross-examination, see Ellison, 'The Mosaic Art?: cross-examination and the vulnerable witness' (2001) 21 Legal Studies 353 and 'Cross-examination and the Intermediary: Bridging the Language Divide?' [2002] Crim LR 114. For examples of the use of intermediaries in the case of the profoundly disabled, see *R v Watts* [2010] EWCA Crim 1824.

hear the examination of the witness (except in the case of a video-recorded examination).[238] A special measures direction may provide for a recording of an interview, conducted through an intermediary, to be admitted under s 27, provided that the intermediary has been approved by the court before the direction is given.[239]

Aids to communication
Under s 30 of the 1999 Act, a special measures direction may provide for the witness, while giving evidence (whether in court or otherwise), to be provided with such device as the court considers appropriate with a view to enabling questions or answers to be communicated to or by the witness despite any disability or disorder or other impairment which the witness has or suffers from.

The witnesses eligible for assistance
Witnesses eligible for assistance on grounds of age or incapacity
Sections 16(1) and (2) of the 1999 Act provide as follows:

> (1) …a witness in criminal proceedings (other than the accused) is eligible for assistance by virtue of this section—
>   (a) if under the age of 18 at the time of the hearing; or
>   (b) if the court considers that the quality of the evidence given by the witness is likely to be diminished by reason of any circumstances falling within subsection (2).
> (2) The circumstances falling within this subsection are—
>   (a) that the witness—
>   (i) suffers from mental disorder within the meaning of the Mental Health Act 1983; or
>   (ii) otherwise has a significant impairment of intelligence and social functioning;
>   (b) that the witness has a physical disability or is suffering from a physical disorder.

In s 16(1)(a), 'the time of the hearing', in relation to a witness, means the time when it falls to the court to decide whether to make a special measures direction.[240] In deciding whether a witness has a physical disability or is suffering from a physical disorder, the court must consider any views expressed by the witness.[241] References to the quality of a witness's evidence, in s 16 and in other sections relating to special measures directions, are to its quality in terms of completeness, coherence, and accuracy; and for this purpose 'coherence' refers to a witness's ability in giving evidence to give answers which address the questions put to the witness and can be understood both individually and collectively.[242]

Witnesses eligible for assistance on grounds of fear or distress about testifying
Under s 17(1) of the 1999 Act, a witness other than the accused is eligible for assistance if the court is satisfied that the quality of evidence given by the witness is likely to be diminished by reason of fear or distress on the part of the witness in connection with testifying in the proceedings. In deciding whether a witness falls within s 17(1), the court must take into account, in particular: (a) the nature and alleged circumstances of the offence to which the proceedings relate; (b) the age of the witness; (c) such of the following matters as appear to the court to

---

[238] Section 29(3).
[239] Section 29(6).
[240] Section 16(3).
[241] Section 16(4).
[242] Section 16(5).

be relevant, namely (i) the social and cultural background and ethnic origins of the witness, (ii) the domestic and employment circumstances of the witness, and (iii) any religious beliefs or political opinions of the witness; and (d) any behaviour towards the witness on the part of the accused, members of the family or associates of the accused, or any other person who is likely to be an accused or a witness in the proceedings.[243] In deciding, the court must also consider any views expressed by the witness.[244] A complainant in respect of a sexual offence[245] or one of a number of other specified offences (including offences of murder, manslaughter, and offences against the person involving the use of a firearm or knife and other weapons and firearms offences) who is a witness in proceedings relating to that offence, or to that offence and any other offences, is automatically eligible for assistance unless he or she has informed the court of his or her wish not to be so eligible.[246]

The circumstances in which special measures directions are given
General
A party to the proceedings may make an application for the court to give a special measures direction or the court of its own motion may raise the issue whether such a direction should be given.[247] Section 19(2) provides as follows:

> (2) Where the court decides that the witness is eligible for assistance by virtue of section 16 or 17, the court must then—
>
> (a) determine whether any of the special measures available in relation to the witness (or any combination of them), would, in its opinion, be likely to improve the quality of evidence given by the witness; and
>
> (b) if so—
>
> (i) determine which of those measures (or combination of them) would, in its opinion, be likely to maximise so far as practicable the quality of such evidence; and
>
> (ii) give a direction under this section providing for the measure or measures so determined to apply to evidence given by the witness.

In deciding whether any special measure or measures would or would not be likely to improve, or to maximize so far as practicable, the quality of evidence given by the witness, the court must consider all the circumstances of the case, including in particular any views expressed by the witness and whether the measure or measures might tend to inhibit such evidence being effectively tested by a party to the proceedings.[248] In the case of rape complainants, there is some research evidence to suggest that a video recording is always 'likely to improve the quality of evidence given by the witness'.[249] If a court decides under s 19 to direct that a video recording should be admitted as the evidence-in-chief of a witness, the speculative possibility that the witness, if he were to give live evidence-in-chief instead, might say something

---

[243] Section 17(2).

[244] Section 17(3).

[245] See s 62 at n 216.

[246] Section 17(4).

[247] Section 19(1).

[248] Section 19(3).

[249] In a study comparing the content of video-recorded police interviews with the live evidence-in-chief of the same adult rape complainants, over two-thirds of the details that were central to establishing whether the crime had occurred were later omitted from live evidence: see Westera and Milne, 'Losing Two Thirds of the Story: A Comparison of the Video-Recorded Police Interview and Live Evidence of Rape Complainants' [2013] Crim LR 290.

different from what was said in the recording and therefore become open to cross-examination on any such difference, is not, in itself, an adequate reason for refusing to allow the playing of the interview.[250]

Under s 20(1), as a general rule a special measures direction has binding effect from the time it is made until the proceedings for the purposes of which it is made are either determined or abandoned in relation to the accused or (if there is more than one) in relation to each of them. The court may discharge or vary a special measures direction if it appears to the court to be in the interests of justice to do so.[251] The court must state in open court its reasons for giving or varying, or refusing an application for, a special measures direction.[252]

Child witnesses

Section 21 of the 1999 Act makes special provision in the case of child witnesses. In the case of witnesses under the age of 18, in effect it creates a presumption in favour of a special measures direction in accordance with s 27 (video-recorded evidence to be admitted as evidence-in-chief) and, in the case of any evidence given by such witnesses which is not given by means of a video recording, in accordance with s 24 (evidence by live link). Section 21 provides as follows:

(1) For the purposes of this section—
    (a) a witness in criminal proceedings is a 'child witness' if he is an eligible witness by reason of section 16(1)(a) (whether or not he is an eligible witness by reason of any other provision of sections 16 or 17);
    .... and
    (c) a 'relevant recording', in relation to a child witness, is a video recording of an interview of the witness made with a view to its admission as evidence in chief of the witness.

(2) Where the court, in making a determination for the purposes of section 19(2), determines that a witness in criminal proceedings is a child witness, the court must—
    (a) first have regard to subsections (3) to (4C) below; and
    (b) then have regard to section 19(2);
    and for the purposes of section 19(2), as it then applies to the witness, any special measures required to be applied in relation to him by virtue of this section shall be treated as if they were measures determined by the court, pursuant to section 19(2)(a) and (b)(i), to be ones that (whether on their own or with any other special measures) would be likely to maximise, so far as practicable, the quality of his evidence.

(3) The primary rule in the case of a child witness is that the court must give a special measures direction in relation to the witness which complies with the following requirements—
    (a) it must provide for any relevant recording to be admitted under section 27 (video recorded evidence in chief); and
    (b) it must provide for any evidence given by the witness in the proceedings which is not given by means of a video recording (whether in chief or otherwise) to be given by means of a live link in accordance with section 24.

(4) The primary rule is subject to the following limitations—
    (a) ...
    (b) the requirement contained in subsection (3)(a)... has effect subject to subsection 27(2);

---

[250] *R v Davies* [2011] EWCA Crim 1177.
[251] Section 20(2).
[252] Section 20(5).

(ba) if the witness informs the court of the witness's wish that the rule should not apply or should apply only in part, the rule does not apply to the extent that the court is satisfied that not complying with the rule would not diminish the quality of the witness's evidence; and

(c) the rule does not apply to the extent that the court is satisfied that compliance with it would not be likely to maximise the quality of the witness's evidence so far as practicable (whether because the application to that evidence of one or more other special measures available in relation to the witness would have the result or for any other reason).

(4A) Where as a consequence of all or part of the primary rule being disapplied under subsection (4)(ba) a witness's evidence or any part of it would fall to be given as testimony in court, the court must give a special measures direction making such provision as is described in section 23 for the evidence or that part of it.

(4B) The requirement in subsection (4A) is subject to the following limitations—

(a) if the witness informs the court of the witness's wish that the rule should not apply, the requirement does not apply to the extent that the court is satisfied that not complying with it would not diminish the quality of the witness's evidence; and

(b) the requirement does not apply to the extent that the court is satisfied that making such a provision would not be likely to maximize the quality of the witness's evidence so far as practicable (whether because the application to that evidence of one or more other special measures available in relation to the witness would have that result or for any other reason).

(4C) In making a decision under subsection 4(ba) or (4B)(a), the court must take into account the following factors (and any others it considers relevant)—

(a) the age and maturity of the witness;

(b) the ability of the witness to understand the consequences of giving evidence otherwise than in accordance with the requirements in subsection (3) or (as the case may be) in accordance with the requirements in subsection (4A);

(c) the relationship (if any) between the witness and the accused;

(d) the witness's social and cultural background and ethnic origins;

(e) the nature and alleged circumstances of the offence to which the proceedings relate.

(8) Where a special measures direction is given in relation to a child witness who is an eligible witness by reason only of section 16(1)(a), then—

(a) subject to subsection (9) below, and

(b) except where the witness has already begun to give evidence in the proceedings, the direction shall cease to have effect at the time when the witness attains the age of 18.

(9) Where a special measures direction is given in relation to a child witness who is an eligible witness by reason only of section 16(1)(a) and

(a) the direction provides—

(i) for any relevant recording to be admitted under section 27 as evidence in chief of the witness, or

(ii) for the special measure available under section 28 to apply in relation to the witness, and

(b) if it provides for that special measure to so apply, the witness is still under the age of 18 when the video recording is made for the purposes of section 28,

then, so far as it provides as mentioned in paragraph (a)(i) or (ii) above, the direction shall continue to have effect in accordance with section 20(1) even though the witness subsequently attains that age.[253]

---

[253] Section 21(2)–(4) and (4C), so far as relating to the giving of a direction complying with the requirement in s 21(3)(a), also apply to witnesses who were over the age of 18 at the time of the hearing, but who were under that age when a relevant recording was made: see s 22.

In *R (D) v Camberwell Green Youth Court*,[254] an appeal in relation to s 21 of the 1999 Act prior to its amendment by the Coroners and Justice Act 2009, the House of Lords held that there is nothing in the special measures provisions inconsistent with the principles set out by the European Court of Human Rights in *Kostovski v Netherlands*.[255] All the evidence is produced at the trial in the presence of the accused, some of it in pre-recorded form and some of it by contemporaneous television transmission. The accused can see and hear it all and has every opportunity to challenge and question the witnesses against him at the trial itself. A face-to-face confrontation is missing, but the Convention does not guarantee a right to such a confrontation. The court also has the opportunity to scrutinize the video-recorded interview at the outset and exclude all or part of it. Furthermore, at the trial it has the fallback position of allowing the witness to give evidence in the courtroom or to expand upon the video recording if the interests of justice require this.

Complainants in respect of sexual offences

Section 22A of the 1999 Act makes special provision for complainants in respect of sexual offences. It provides as follows:

(1) This section applies where in criminal proceedings relating to a sexual offence (or to a sexual offence and other offences) the complainant in respect of that offence is a witness in the proceedings.

(2) This section does not apply if the place of trial is a magistrates' court.

(3) This section does not apply if the complainant is an eligible witness by reason of section 16(1)(a) (whether or not the complainant is an eligible witness by reason of any other provision of section 16 or 17).

(4) If a party to the proceedings makes an application under section 19(1)(a) for a special measures direction in relation to the complainant, the party may request that the direction provide for any relevant recording to be admitted under section 27 (video recorded evidence in chief).

(5) Subsection (6) applies if—
   (a) a party to the proceedings makes a request under subsection (4) with respect to the complainant, and
   (b) the court determines for the purposes of section 19(2) that the complainant is eligible for assistance by virtue of section 16(1)(b) or 17.

(6) The court must—
   (a) first have regard to subsections (7) to (9); and
   (b) then have regard to section 19(2)
   and for the purpose of section 19(2), as it then applies to the complainant, any special measure required to be applied in relation to the complainant by virtue of this section is to be treated as if it were a measure determined by the court, pursuant to section 19(2)(a) and (b)(i), to be one that (whether on its own or with any other special measures) would be likely to maximize, so far as practicable, the quality of the complainant's evidence.

(7) The court must give a special measures direction in relation to the complainant that provides for any relevant recording to be admitted under section 27.

(8) The requirement in subsection (7) has effect subject to section 27(2).

(9) The requirement in subsection (7) does not apply to the extent that the court is satisfied that compliance with it would not be likely to maximize the quality of the complainant's evidence so far as practicable (whether because the application to that evidence of one or more other special measures available in relation to the complainant would have that result or for any other reason).

---

[254] [2005] 1 All ER 999, HL.
[255] (1990) 12 EHRR 434 at 447–8.

(10) In this section 'relevant recording', in relation to a complainant, is a video recording of an interview of the complainant made with a view to its admission as the evidence in chief of the complainant.

The status of video-recorded evidence, etc
Section 31(1)–(4) of the 1999 Act provide as follows:

(1) Subsections (2) to (4) apply to a statement[256] made by a witness in criminal proceedings which, in accordance with a special measures direction, is not made by the witness in direct oral testimony in court but forms part of the witness's evidence in those proceedings.[257]
(2) The statement shall be treated as if made by the witness in direct oral testimony in court; and accordingly—
   (a) it is admissible evidence of any fact of which such testimony from the witness would be admissible;
   (b) it is not capable of corroborating any other evidence given by the witness.
(3) Subsection (2) applies to a statement admitted under sections 27 or 28 which is not made by the witness on oath even though it would have been required to be made on oath if made by the witness in direct oral testimony in court.
(4) In estimating the weight (if any) to be attached to the statement, the court must have regard to all the circumstances from which an inference can reasonably be drawn (as to the accuracy of the statement or otherwise).

Section 32 of the 1999 Act provides that where, on a trial on indictment with a jury, evidence has been given in accordance with a special measures direction, the judge must give the jury such warning (if any) as the judge considers necessary to ensure that the fact that the direction was given in relation to the witness does not prejudice the accused. In the case of the use of screens, for example, it may suffice to say that they must not allow their use by witnesses to prejudice them in any way against the accused.[258]

The accused
The availability of special measures for the accused is of particular importance given that, under Art 6 of the European Convention on Human Rights, an accused has the right to effective participation in his trial. Such participation includes the right to be present and to hear and follow the proceedings.[259] In the case of a child accused, he must be dealt with in a manner that takes full account of his age, level of maturity, and intellectual and emotional capacities, and steps must be taken to promote his ability to understand and participate in the proceedings and to reduce as far as possible his feelings of intimidation and inhibition.[260]

Live link
Under s 33A of the 1999 Act, inserted by s 47 of the Police and Justice Act 2007, a court may permit an accused to give his oral evidence through a live link if the conditions in either s 33A(4) or s 33A(5) are met and it is in the interests of justice to do so.[261] The conditions in

---

[256] 'Statement' includes any representation of fact, whether made in words or otherwise: s 31(8).

[257] ie statements given in evidence by live television link or recorded in a video recording admitted as evidence: see *R (S) v Waltham Forest Youth Court* [2004] 2 Cr App R 335 at [76].

[258] See *R v Brown* [2004] Crim LR 1034, CA.

[259] *Stanford v UK* [1994] ECHR 16757/90 at para 26.

[260] *T v UK* (1999) 7 BHRC 659 at para 84 and 85. See further *SC v UK* (2004) 17 BHRC 607, ECHR.

[261] Section 33A(2).

s 33A(4), which apply to an accused aged under 18, are that (a) his ability to participate effectively as a witness giving oral evidence in court is compromised by his level of intellectual ability or social functioning; and (b) use of a live link would enable him to participate more effectively.[262] The conditions in s 33A(5), which apply where the accused has attained the age of 18, are that (a) he suffers from a mental disorder (within the meaning of the Mental Health Act 1983) or otherwise has a significant impairment of intelligence and social function; (b) he is for that reason unable to participate effectively as a witness giving oral evidence in court; and (c) use of a live link would enable him to participate more effectively.[263]

In *R (S) v Waltham Forest Youth Court*,[264] a decision prior to the amendment of the 1999 Act, it was held that since Parliament had sought to provide exclusively for the circumstances in which a live link might be used in a criminal trial, there was no residual common law power to allow an accused to give evidence by live link. This approach was followed in *R v Ukpabio*,[265] a decision after the amendment but prior to its coming into force, but doubted by the House of Lords in *R (D) v Camberwell Green Youth Court*,[266] where it was held that the court had wide and flexible inherent powers to ensure that the accused is not at a substantial disadvantage compared with the prosecution and receives a fair trial, including a fair opportunity of giving the best evidence he can.[267] Baroness Hale was of the view that in exceptional circumstances special measures designed to shield a vulnerable or intimidated witness can apply in the case of the accused, giving as a possible example the use of live link by a younger child accused too scared to give evidence in the presence of her co-accused.

Examination of accused through intermediary.

Under s 33BA of the 1999 Act, inserted by s 104 of the Coroners and Justice Act 2009, but not yet in force, a court may, on the application of the accused, direct that any examination of the accused be conducted through an intermediary.[268] Such a direction may be given if the conditions in either s 33BA(5) or s 33BA(6) are met and it is necessary in order to ensure that the accused receives a fair trial.[269] The conditions in s 33BA(5) (for an accused aged under 18) and s 33BA(6) (for an accused who has attained that age) are essentially the same as those that apply in respect of live link for an accused, as set out in s 33A(4) and (5) respectively.[270] The function of an intermediary for an accused is the same as for any other witness.[271] Any examination under s 33BA must take place in the presence of such persons as the Criminal Procedure Rules or the direction may provide and in circumstances in which (a) the judge or justices (or both) and legal representatives acting in the proceedings are able to see and hear the examination of the accused and to communicate with the intermediary (b) the jury, if there is one, are able

---

[262] Section 33A(4).

[263] Section 33A(5).

[264] [2004] 2 Cr App R 335, DC.

[265] [2008] 1 Cr App R 101, CA.

[266] [2005] 1 All ER 999.

[267] For example, the court can allow an accused with learning and communication difficulties to have the equivalent of an interpreter to assist with communication, and his written statement can be read to the jury so that they know what he wants to say: see *R v H* [2003] EWCA Crim 1208.

[268] See generally, Cooper and Wurtzel, 'A Day Late and a Dollar Short: In Search of an Intermediary Scheme for Vulnerable Defendants in England and Wales' [2013] Crim LR 4.

[269] Section 33BA(2).

[270] See at nn 262 and 263.

[271] See s 33BA(4) and s 29(2), above.

to see and hear the examination of the accused and (c) where there are two or more accused, each of the other accused is able to see and hear the examination of the accused.[272]

Until s 33BA is brought into force, the courts may use their inherent jurisdiction to direct that an accused be assisted by an intermediary;[273] there is a right, which may in certain circumstances amount to a duty, to appoint a registered intermediary to assist the accused to follow the proceedings and give evidence if, without assistance, he would not be able to have a fair trial.[274] Where a judge directs that an intermediary should be made available, but every step to identify an available intermediary has been unsuccessful, the judge should make an informed assessment whether the absence of an intermediary would make the trial unfair or whether the specific communication problems could be dealt with by procedural modifications to the ordinary trial process, such as the use of simply phrased questions, short periods of evidence, and breaks to allow counsel to summarize the evidence and to take further instructions.[275]

Other special measures

In the case of a witness who is not an eligible witness under the statutory scheme, the scheme has no effect on the powers of the court in the exercise of its inherent jurisdiction,[276] eg the powers to provide for the use of screens or the removal of wigs and gowns. Judges are expected to deal with specific communication problems faced by an accused (or other witness) as part and parcel of their ordinary control of the judicial process, when necessary adapting the processes to ensure that a particular individual is not disadvantaged as a result of personal difficulties, whatever form they may take; the overall responsibility of the judge for the fairness of the trial has not been altered by the availability of the statutory special measures.[277]

Witness anonymity

In some cases, witnesses will be in genuine and justified fear of serious consequences should their true identity become known. If such witnesses do not give evidence, criminals may walk free and the innocent may be convicted. To ensure the safety of such witnesses and induce them to give evidence, various measures can be taken, including the use of a pseudonym, the withholding from the defence of any particulars which might identify them, the banning of any questions in cross-examination of the witnesses which might enable any of them to be identified, and the giving of evidence behind screens.[278] The obvious danger, however, is the potential or actual disadvantage to the accused, which has been likened to taking blind shots at a hidden target,[279] and the concomitant risk of an unfair trial. In *R v Davis*[280] the House of Lords held that the use of such measures, in the circumstances of the case, hampered the conduct of the defence in a

---

[272] Section 33BA(7).

[273] See *R(C) v Sevenoaks Youth Court* [2010] 1 All ER 375 and *R v H* [2003] EWCA Crim 1208.

[274] *R(AS) v Great Yarmouth Youth Court* [2011] EWHC 2059 (Admin), where, without the assistance of an intermediary, the court would not necessarily have realized that the accused, who suffered from ADHD but was able to communicate his evidence to the court, was put in difficulty by complex questions and might react by not answering a question because concentrating on a previous question.

[275] *R v Cox* [2012] 2 Cr App R 63, CA.

[276] Section 19(6).

[277] *R v Cox* [2012] 2 Cr App R 63, CA at [29].

[278] The alternative or supplementary measure of secret relocation of witnesses and their families, which has found favour in the US, is costly and effectively penalizes the witness for doing his civic duty, as well as his family.

[279] *R v Davis* [2008] 3 All ER 461, per Lord Bingham at [32].

[280] [2008] 3 All ER 461, per Lord Bingham at [32].

manner and to an extent which was unlawful and rendered the trial unfair. Their Lordships were in agreement that it was a long-established principle of the English common law that subject to certain exceptions and statutory qualifications, the accused should be confronted by his accusers in order that he may cross-examine them and challenge their evidence. Article 6(3)(d) of the European Convention, guaranteeing the accused the right to examine or have examined witnesses against him, had not added anything of significance to English law. The Strasbourg case law has established that no conviction should be based solely or to a decisive extent upon the statements or testimony of anonymous witnesses, because it results from a trial which cannot be regarded as fair. However, their Lordships did not doubt that the problem of witness intimidation was real and prevalent and might well call for urgent attention by Parliament.

The parliamentary response was swift and decisive, not least because the decision in *R v Davis* was bound to lead to the collapse of numerous trials, including a number of murder trials, in which applications had been or were being made for witness anonymity orders. The Criminal Evidence (Witness Anonymity) Act 2008 abolished the common law rules and provided for the making of witness anonymity orders in relation to witnesses in criminal proceedings. The 2008 Act had a 'sunset clause', and expired, but the Coroners and Justice Act 2009 re-enacted the provisions of the 2008 Act, subject to relatively minor amendment.[281]

The relevant provisions of the 2009 Act may be summarized as follows.[282] A witness, for the purposes of an anonymity order, is any person called or proposed to be called, to give evidence at the trial or hearing.[283] The measures that can be taken under a witness anonymity order are (a) the withholding, and removal from materials disclosed to any party to the proceedings, of the witness's name and other identifying details; (b) use of a pseudonym; (c) not permitting the witness to be asked questions that might lead to his identification; (d) screening the witness, but not to the extent that the witness cannot be seen by the judge or jury; or (e) subjecting the witness's voice to modulation, but not to the extent that his natural voice cannot be heard by the judge or jury.[284] Application for an order may be made by the prosecution or defence; where it is made by the prosecution, they must inform the court of the identity of the witness, but are not required to disclose either identity or information that may lead to identification to any other party to the proceedings or his lawyers; and where it is made by the defence, they must inform the court and the prosecutor of the identity of the witness, but are not required to disclose either identity or information that might lead to identification to any other accused or his lawyers.[285] Every party must be given the opportunity to be heard on an application for an order, except that the court may hear one or more parties in the absence of an accused and his lawyers if it appears to the court appropriate to do so.[286]

Under s 88 of the Act, the court may only make an order if satisfied that Conditions A to C are met. Condition A is that the proposed order is necessary (a) in order to protect the safety

---

[281] The 2009 Act also provides for investigation anonymity orders (ss 74–85), ie orders prohibiting the disclosure of information identifying an individual as having aided an investigation into an offence of murder or manslaughter caused by a firearm or knife. The circumstances in which such orders can be made are tightly circumscribed.

[282] See also the Attorney General's guidelines on the prosecutor's role in applications for witness anonymity orders, rr 29.18–29.22, Criminal Procedure Rules 2013, SI 2013/1554 and para 1.15 of the *Consolidated Criminal Practice Direction*. For a detailed analysis of the provisions of the 2009 Act, see Ormerod et al, 'Coroners and Justice Act 2009: the "Witness Anonymity" and "Investigation Anonymity" Provisions' [2010] Crim LR 368.

[283] Section 97.

[284] Section 86.

[285] Section 87(1)–(3).

[286] Section 87(6) and (7).

of the witness or another or to prevent any serious damage to property (and in deciding the question of necessity in this respect, the court must have regard in particular to any reasonable fear on the part of the witness that, if identified, he or another would suffer death or injury or there would be serious damage to property); or (b) in order to prevent real harm to the public interest. Condition A will not be met if the witness's identity is already known to the accused, because an anonymity order cannot reasonably serve to protect the witness and is therefore not necessary for that purpose.[287] Condition B is that, having regard to all the circumstances, the effect of the proposed order would be consistent with the accused receiving a fair trial. Condition C is that the importance of the witness's testimony is such that in the interests of justice the witness ought to testify and (a) the witness would not testify if the proposed order were not made or (b) there would be real harm to the public interest if the witness were to testify without the proposed order being made. When deciding whether Conditions A to C are met, the court must have regard to the considerations set out in s 89(2) and such other matters as the court considers relevant. The considerations in s 89(2) are:

(a) the general right of an accused to know the identity of a witness;

(b) the extent to which the credibility of the witness would be a relevant factor when assessing the weight of his evidence;

(c) whether the evidence given by the witness might be the sole or decisive evidence implicating the accused;

(d) whether the witness's evidence could be properly tested (on grounds of credibility or otherwise) without his identity being disclosed;

(e) whether there is any reason to believe that the witness (i) has a tendency to be dishonest, or (ii) has any motive to be dishonest in the circumstances of the case, having regard in particular to any previous convictions and to any relationship between him and the accused or any of his associates; and

(f) whether it would be reasonably practicable to protect the witness by any means other than by making a witness anonymity order specifying the measures under consideration by the court.

Under s 90 of the Act, in jury trials the judge must give the jury such warning as he considers appropriate to ensure that the fact that the order was made does not prejudice the accused.

R v Mayers[288] provided detailed guidance on the meaning and application of the provisions of the Criminal Evidence (Witness Anonymity) Act 2008. It is submitted that the guidance remains valid despite the amendments made by the 2009 Act. In the summary of the guidance that follows, for convenience reference has been made to the relevant statutory provisions of the 2009 Act.

1. Save in the exceptional circumstances permitted by the Act, the ancient principle that the accused is entitled to know the identity of the witnesses who incriminate him is maintained.

2. The Act seeks to address the provisions of the European Convention and the relevant jurisprudence of the European Court by seeking to preserve the delicate balance between

---

[287] *R v Willett* [2011] EWCA Crim 2710.
[288] [2009] 1 WLR 1915, CA.

the rights of the accused, including his entitlement to a fair trial and public hearing, and to examine or have the witnesses who inculpate him properly examined (Art 6) and the witness's right to life (Art 2) and physical security (Art 3) and the right to respect for his private life (Art 8).

3. Bearing in mind other provisions such as special measures under the 1999 Act[289] and the admissibility of evidence under s 116 of the 2003 Act where a witness is unavailable,[290] an anonymity order should be regarded as a special measure of last practicable resort.

4. The principles which govern the use of special counsel for public interest immunity purposes[291] should be adapted when the use of such counsel arises in the context of witness anonymity, when the issue will be whether sufficient and complete investigation and consequential disclosure have taken place. A detailed investigation into the background of each potential anonymous witness will almost inevitably be required.

5. The judge should normally reflect both at the close of the prosecution and when the defence evidence is concluded, whether properly directed and in the light of the evidence as a whole, the case can safely be left to the jury.

6. The s 90 warning must be sufficient to ensure that the jury do not make any assumptions adverse to the accused or favourable to the witness and, in particular, do not draw an inference of guilt against the accused.

7. None of the s 89(2) considerations outweighs any of the others, none is conclusive on the question whether the individual accused will receive a fair trial, and none precludes the possibility of an order.

8. Section 89(2)(a) restates the common law principle that the accused is normally entitled to know the identity of any witness who gives incriminating evidence against him and s 89(2)(f) confirms that an order represents the last resort.

9. Concerning the considerations in s 89(2)(b)(d) and (e), the process of investigation and disclosure is crucial. The three considerations are distinct but linked and are likely to require an overall view of the potential impact of the witness on the trial. Thus, for example, there may be no reason to doubt the integrity or motive or credibility of a witness; the issue may be his accuracy, which may be fully tested without disclosure of his identity.

10. Concerning the consideration in s 89(2)(c), which addresses the jurisprudence of the European Court, the fact that a witness provides the sole or decisive evidence against the accused is not conclusive whether conditions A, B, and C are met, but does directly impinge on the question whether condition B may be met. Whether the evidence is sole or decisive raises two separate questions, but if the evidence is both sole and decisive condition B may be harder to meet. The court should examine whether the evidence is supported extraneously. The more facts independent of the witness which tend to support him (and which may derive from the conduct of the accused himself), the safer it is to admit anonymous evidence.[292] Where there are a number of anonymous

---

[289] See, in this chapter, under **Witnesses in criminal cases, Special measures directions for vulnerable and intimidated witnesses**.

[290] See Ch 10.

[291] See Ch 19.

witnesses who incriminate the accused, whether there is a link between them, and if so its nature, should be investigated, addressing any question of possible improper collusion or cross-contamination. Suspicion is less likely to be engendered about the integrity of witnesses who immediately or virtually immediately are identified or identify themselves, before a sufficient opportunity to engineer a sophisticated conspiracy, than witnesses who turn up late and 'out of the blue'.

11. Condition C should probably be addressed first. The order should not be made where the oral testimony of the witness is not potentially important or where the proposed anonymous evidence could be addressed by admissions or agreed facts or, subject to proper editing, is capable of being read. In relation to Condition C(a), it must be clear that, notwithstanding the powers invested in the court in relation to contempt, the witness 'would not testify' without the order: it is insufficient that the witness might prefer not to testify or would be reluctant or unhappy at the prospect. However, the court may conclude that the witness would not testify if the circumstances of the offence justify the inference.

12. Condition A does not require the risk to the safety to the witness to be attributable to the action of the accused personally: the threat may come from any source. Under Condition A, the order must be necessary, which goes well beyond what may be described as desirable or convenient. A specific problem arises in relation to police witnesses, especially those working undercover, for there are often sound operational reasons for maintaining anonymity; the court would normally be entitled to follow the unequivocal assertion by an undercover officer that without an order he would not be prepared to testify. The witnesses may well be known to the accused by a false identity, and the accused may be able to advance criticisms of their evidence or conduct without being disadvantaged by ignorance of their true identities. Condition A covers a potentially very wide group, ranging from undercover officers working in areas of terrorism to test purchase officers. It is worth identifying the public interest which is involved in the deployment of these witnesses. At the most dangerous level, extreme measures might be taken to discover the identity of undercover officers who have penetrated criminal associations, not merely out of revenge, but to prevent their use as witnesses and compromise or damage sensitive covert techniques or to discourage them or others from continuing with their activities (all of which serve a valuable public interest).

13. Condition B appears to be focused on the *accused* receiving a fair trial, even when it is the accused seeking the anonymity order. Condition B is fact-specific. In the vast majority of cases, all of the s 89(2) considerations will require attention.

14. The Act is silent about the use of anonymous *hearsay* evidence, or evidence in the form of a statement by an unidentified witness. Such evidence is not admissible under either s 114 or s 116 of the 2003 Act.[293]

Witness anonymity orders may be a 'last resort' to be used sparingly, but they are unlikely to be rare. As the Court of Appeal observed in *R v Powar*:[294] '...the calling of anonymous witnesses

[292] Cf Lord Phillips in *R v Horncastle* [2010] 2 WLR 47, SC at [50]: the extent of the disadvantage for the accused will depend on the facts of the particular case.
[293] See Ch 10.

must not become a routine event in the prosecution of serious crime but we reject the submission that witness anonymity orders should be confined to cases of terrorism or gangland killings. The intimidation of witnesses has become an ugly feature of contemporary life'.

Witness training and witness familiarization

The Court of Appeal in *R v Momodou*[295] has made it clear that in criminal proceedings, witness training or coaching is prohibited, but witness familiarization is permitted. The following reasons were given for the ban on training or coaching. It reduces the possibility that one witness may tailor his evidence in the light of what anyone else has said. Even if the training takes place one-to-one with someone completely remote from the facts of the case, the witness may come, even unconsciously, to appreciate which aspects of his evidence are not quite consistent with what others are saying or not quite what is required of him. An honest witness may alter the emphasis of his evidence. A dishonest witness will very rapidly calculate how his evidence may be 'improved'. Where a witness is jointly trained with other witnesses to the same events, the dangers dramatically increase: recollections change, memories are contaminated, and witnesses bring their respective accounts into what they believe to be better alignment with others. They may even collude deliberately.

The ban on witness training or coaching, however, does not preclude pre-trial arrangements, usually in the form of a visit to the court, to familiarize witnesses with the court layout, the likely sequence of events, and a balanced appraisal of the different responsibilities of the various participants. Such arrangements are welcomed because witnesses should not be disadvantaged by ignorance of the process nor, when they come to give evidence, be taken by surprise at the way it works.[296] None of this involves discussions about proposed evidence. Equally, the ban does not prohibit the out-of-court training of expert and similar witnesses in, for example, the technique of giving comprehensive evidence of a specialist kind to a jury, both in examination-in-chief and in cross-examination, and developing the ability to resist the inevitable pressure of going further in evidence than matters covered by the witness's specific expertise. However, such training should not be arranged in the context of, nor be related to, any forthcoming trial.

It was also held in *R v Momodou* that where arrangements are to be made for familiarization in the case of prosecution witnesses by outside agencies, the Crown Prosecution Service (CPS) should be informed in advance and the proposals should be reduced into writing so that they can be amended if they breach the permitted limits. If the defence engage in the process, it is wise to seek counsel's advice in advance, and in any event the trial judge and the CPS should be informed of any familiarization process organized using outside agencies. The familiarization process itself should normally be supervised or conducted by a solicitor or barrister, but no one involved should have any personal knowledge of the matters in issue, none of the material should bear any similarity whatever to the issues in the trial, nothing in it should play on or trigger the witness's recollection of events, and if discussion of the trial begins, it must be stopped. Records should be maintained of all those present and the identity of those

---

[294] [2009] EWCA Crim 594.

[295] [2005] 2 All ER 571, CA.

[296] For the potential positive effects of written guidance about the nature of cross-examination, including enhanced witness accuracy, see Ellison and Wheatcroft, '"Could You Ask Me That in a Different Way Please?" Exploring the Impact of Courtroom Questioning and Witness Familiarisation on Adult Witness Accuracy' [2010] Crim LR 823.

responsible for the process. All documents used in the process should be retained and handed to the CPS or, in the case of defence witnesses, should be produced to the court.

ADDITIONAL READING

Birch, 'A Better Deal for Vulnerable Witnesses?' [2000] Crim LR 223.

Burton et al, 'Implementing Special Measures for Vulnerable and Intimidated Witnesses: The Problem of Identification' [2006] Crim LR 229.

Burton et al, 'Vulnerable and intimidated witnesses and the adversarial process in England and Wales' (2007) 11 E&P 1.

Creighton, 'Spouse Competence and Compellability' [1990] Crim LR 34.

Ellison, 'The Mosaic Art?: Cross-examination and the vulnerable witness' (2001) 21 Legal Studies 353.

Ellison, 'Cross-examination and the Intermediary: Bridging the Language Divide?' [2002] Crim LR 114.

Ellison and Wheatcroft, ' "Could You Ask Me That in a Different Way Please?" Exploring the Impact of Courtroom Questioning and Witness Familiarisation on Adult Witness Accuracy' [2010] Crim LR 823.

Hoyano, 'Variations on a Theme by Pigot: Special Measures Directions for Child Witnesses' [2000] Crim LR 250.

Hoyano, 'Striking a Balance between the Rights of Defendants and Vulnerable Witnesses: Will Special Measures Directions Contravene Guarantees of a Fair Trial?' [2001] Crim LR 948.

Hoyano, 'The Child Witness Review: Much Ado about Too Little' [2007] Crim LR 849.

Law Commission Consultation Paper No 130, *Mentally Incapacitated and Other Vulnerable Adults: Public Law Protection* (1993).

McEwan, 'Vulnerable Defendants and the Fairness of Trials' [2013] Crim LR 100.

Ormerod et al, 'Coroners and Justice Act 2009: the "Witness Anonymity" and "Investigation Anonymity" Provisions' [2010] Crim LR 368.

Plotnikoff and Woolfson, 'Making Best Use of the Intermediary Special Measure at Trial' [2008] Crim LR 91.

Report of the Advisory Group on Video-Recorded Evidence (the *Pigot Report*) (Home Office, 1989).

Report of the Advocacy Training Council, Raising the bar: the handling of vulnerable witnesses, victims and defendants in court (2011).

Spencer and Flin, *The Evidence of Children* (2nd edn, London, 1993).

Examination-in-chief $\quad$ 6

Key issues

- What restrictions should be placed on the manner in which evidence is elicited from witnesses in their evidence-in-chief?

- Should a party calling a witness be permitted to ask questions which suggest the answer sought?

- In what circumstances should a witness be permitted to refresh his memory from a record containing his earlier recollection of an event about which he is called to give evidence?

- What is the evidential status of a document used by a witness to refresh his memory?

- When and why should a party calling a witness be permitted to adduce evidence of a statement made by him on a previous occasion consistent with his testimony at trial?

- What steps should be open to a party calling a witness if the witness fails to come up to proof or gives evidence supporting another party?

- What steps should be open to a party calling a witness if the witness shows no desire to tell the truth?

The general rule, in both civil and criminal trials, is that any fact which needs to be proved by the evidence of witnesses is to be proved by their oral evidence, given in public.[1] The questioning of witnesses, which generally falls into three stages known as examination-in-chief, cross-examination, and re-examination, is central to the English adversary system of justice. The first stage, examination-in-chief, is the questioning of a witness by the party calling him. In examination-in-chief, the party calling a witness, or counsel on his behalf, will seek to elicit evidence which supports his version of the facts in issue.[2] This chapter concerns the rules governing the manner in which this may be done.

Young witnesses

With a view to enabling young witnesses to give their 'best evidence', the *Judicial College Bench Checklist: Young Witness Cases*[3] lists the various matters to be considered in this respect at the first hearing in a magistrates' court or the preliminary or plea and case management hearing in the Crown Court. They include: the provision of information about the child's development, health, and concentration span; whether the child is unlikely to recognize a problematic question or say that he or she has not understood; time estimates; and the need to schedule a 'ground rules' discussion about questioning, which is recommended in the case of any young witness and required where use is made of an intermediary.[4] The *Checklist* also sets out the directions that may be given at a 'ground rules' discussion to the advocates appearing for both sides. They include the following: adapt questions to the child's developmental stage; ask short, simple questions (one idea at a time); follow a logical sequence; speak slowly and allow enough time for questions to be processed; and use a body diagram rather than ask a child to demonstrate intimate touching on his or her body. The *Checklist* also refers to the more detailed guidance provided by Plotnikoff and Woolfson in *Measuring Up? Evaluating implementation of Government commitments to young witnesses in criminal proceedings*, Annexes A and B,[5] which includes, for example, the need to avoid negatives and restricted choice questions, and to recognize that children, even adolescents, cannot be relied upon to say that they have not understood a question.

Similar guidelines have been drawn up by the Family Justice Council in relation to children giving evidence in family proceedings.[6]

---

[1] However, in civil cases this is subject to any provision to the contrary, whether in the Civil Procedure Rules (CPR) or elsewhere, or to any order of the court: CPR r 32.2. A civil court, in exercise of its power under r 32.1 to control evidence, may direct that in order to decide a particular issue, it only requires evidence in written form.

[2] Excessive questioning of a witness by the judge may improperly interfere with the opportunity which counsel should be given to present the witness's evidence in the most impressive way he or she can devise: see *R v Gunning* (1994) 98 Cr App R 303, CA.

[3] Accessible at <www.judiciary.gov.uk/publications-and-reports/guidance/2012/jc-bench-checklist-young-wit-cases>.

[4] As to when intermediaries should be used, see under **Witnesses in criminal cases, Special measures directions for vulnerable and intimidated witnesses**, Ch 5.

[5] Accessible at <www.nspcc.org.uk/Inform/research/Findings/measuring_up_wda66048.html>.

[6] Accessible at <www.judiciary.gov.uk/NR/rdonlyres/C4F34729-B530-485F-90E3-987202297B02/0FJC Guidelines in relation children giving evide in family procs Dec2011.pdf>.

Leading questions

A party calling a witness and seeking to elicit evidence supporting his case often faces a witness who, although favourable, is not particularly forthcoming. The party calling him may be tempted to suggest to him what he wants him to say. In both examination-in-chief and re-examination, however, the general rule is that a witness may not be asked leading questions.[7] Evidence elicited by leading questions is not inadmissible but the weight to be attached to it may be reduced.[8] Leading questions are usually those so framed as to suggest the answer sought. Thus it would be a leading question if counsel for the prosecution, seeking to establish an assault, were to ask the victim, 'Did X hit you in the face with his fist?' The proper course would be to ask, 'Did X do anything to you?' and, if the witness then gives evidence of having been hit, to ask the questions 'Where did X hit you?' and 'How did X hit you?' Questions are also leading if so framed as to assume the existence of facts yet to be established. If evidence has yet to be given of the assault, it would be improper, for example, to ask, 'What were you doing immediately before X hit you?' The examples given are reasonably straightforward, but in practice the avoidance of leading questions often requires considerable skill and experience. An over-strict adherence to the rule against leading questions would render examination-in-chief extremely difficult. The question 'Did X do anything to you?', even if it does not suggest that X hit the witness, suggests that X did something, whereas in fact he might have been asleep at the relevant time. 'And what happened next?' is a solution often resorted to. However, the judge, and counsel for the other side, will not always demand strict adherence to the rule, and for good reason: ' "leading" is a relative, not an absolute term'.[9]

To the general prohibition on leading questions there are frequently recurring 'exceptions'. A witness may be asked leading questions on formal and introductory matters, such as his name, address, and occupation. Leading questions are also permissible on facts which are not in dispute, and counsel for the other side may well indicate, in the case of any witness, those matters on which he has no objection to such questions being put. Leading questions may also be put to a witness called by a party who has been granted leave to treat him as hostile.[10]

Leading questions may be put in cross-examination.[11]

Refreshing the memory

Witnesses often experience difficulty in recollecting the events to which their evidence relates, especially when the events took place a long time ago. In consequence, common law rules have evolved to allow a witness to refresh his memory from a document made or verified by him at an earlier time. The common law rules have been supplemented and, to a large extent, superseded by, statutory provisions. However, the scope for use of the memory-refreshing rules has diminished by reason of the growth in the categories of

---

[7] For critical analysis of the rationale, scope, and complexity of the rule, see Keane and Fortson, 'Leading Questions: A Critical Analysis' [2011] Crim LR 280.

[8] *Moor v Moor* [1954] 1 WLR 927, CA.

[9] Best, *Law of Evidence* (12th edn, London, 1922) 562.

[10] See, in this chapter, under **Unfavourable and hostile witnesses, Hostile witnesses**.

[11] *Parkin v Moon* (1836) 7 C&P 408.

admissible hearsay[12] and the introduction of rules permitting a witness statement to stand as a witness's evidence-in-chief.[13]

Refreshing the memory in court

The rules

At common law, a witness in either civil or criminal proceedings, in the course of giving his evidence, may refer to a document, such as a diary, log-book, or account-book, in order to refresh his memory. The conditions are that the document (i) was made or verified by him either contemporaneously with the events in question or so shortly thereafter that the facts were still fresh in his memory; (ii) is, in prescribed cases, the original; and (iii) is produced for inspection by either the court or the opposite party.

In criminal proceedings, this common law rule has not been repealed, but has in effect been replaced, and relaxed, by s 139(1) of the Criminal Justice Act 2003 (the 2003 Act). Section 139(1) substitutes for the requirement of contemporaneity, or that the facts were still fresh in the memory, two different conditions. The first is that the witness testifies that the document records his recollection at the time when he made it. The second is that his recollection is likely to have been significantly better at that time than at the time of his oral evidence. The common law rule has also been supplemented by s 139(2), which provides for the refreshing of memory from a transcript of a sound recording, a provision designed to avoid the practical difficulties that would otherwise be encountered in refreshing the memory from the sound recording itself. Section 139 is in the following terms:

(1) A person giving oral evidence in criminal proceedings about any matter may, at any stage in the course of doing so, refresh his memory of it from a document made or verified by him at an earlier time if—

 (a) he states in his oral evidence that the document records his recollection of the matter at that earlier time, and

 (b) his recollection of the matter is likely to have been significantly better at that time than it is at the time of his oral evidence.

(2) Where—

 (a) a person giving oral evidence in criminal proceedings about any matter has previously given an oral account, of which a sound recording was made, and he states in that evidence that the account represented his recollection of the matter at that time,

 (b) his recollection of the matter is likely to have been significantly better at the time of the previous account than it is at the time of his oral evidence, and

 (c) a transcript has been made of the sound recording,

 he may at any stage in the course of giving his evidence, refresh his memory of the matter from that transcript.

An application for a witness to refresh his memory will normally be made by the party calling the witness, but it is a proper function of the judge, where the interests of justice so demand, to suggest that a witness, including in a criminal case, a witness for the prosecution, refresh

---

[12] In civil proceedings, see the Civil Evidence Act 1995, s 6(2)(a) (the previous documentary statement of a witness) (Ch 11). In criminal proceedings, see the Criminal Justice Act 2003, s 117 (trade, business, and professional records) and that Act, s 114(1)(d) (hearsay admissible in the interests of justice) (Ch 10).

[13] See CPR r 32.5 (witness statements) (Ch 5). See also, in criminal proceedings, the Criminal Justice Act 2003, s 137 (video recordings), which has yet to be brought into force (Ch 5).

his memory.[14] Both s 139(1) and s 139(2) refer to 'a person giving oral evidence', ie any person giving oral evidence, including, as at common law, the accused.[15] Both subsections also permit the witness to refresh his memory 'at any stage' in the course of giving his evidence. Thus, as at common law, although a witness will normally refresh his memory in examination-in-chief, there is nothing wrong in principle in allowing him to do so during re-examination.[16]

Whether the condition in s 139(1)(b) is met is ultimately a decision for the judge, whatever the witness's view of the matter;[17] but the judge has a residual discretion to refuse an application under s 139 even if the statutory conditions are met.

Present recollection revived and past recollection recorded

The common law rule on refreshing memory applies in the case of both 'present recollection revived' and 'past recollection recorded'.[18] 'Present recollection revived' is a phrase used to describe the genuine refreshing of memory on sight of the document. In the case of 'present recollection revived', both at common law and under s 139, it is the oral testimony of the witness whose memory has been refreshed, and not the document, which constitutes the evidence in the case. 'Past recollection recorded' refers to the situation in which the witness, although he has no current recollection of the events, his memory being a perfect blank, is prepared to testify as to the accuracy of the contents of the document. Thus in *Maugham v Hubbard*[19] a witness, called to prove that he had received a sum of money, looked at an unstamped acknowledgment signed by himself and thereupon gave evidence that he had no doubt that he had received the money although he had no recollection of having done so. It was held that the witness's oral evidence sufficed to establish receipt of the money, the written acknowledgment not being evidence in the case because it was unstamped.[20] It has always been inaccurate to describe the witness in such a case as having 'refreshed his memory'.[21] The term is equally inapposite in the case of the police officer who, with no recollection of the relevant events, simply reads from his notes. However, at common law, cases of 'past recollection recorded' are treated in the same way as cases of 'present recollection recorded' in that the oral evidence of the witness, and not the document, constitutes the evidence in the case.[22] In principle, it would be better to regard such out-of-court documentary statements as a variety of admissible hearsay, which is the case, in criminal proceedings, under s 120 of the 2003 Act. Under s 120, a previous statement of a witness, which may be a statement made orally or a statement made in a document,[23] is admissible as evidence of any matter stated, provided that the witness testifies that to the best of his belief he made the statement and it states the truth, and that he does not remember the matters and cannot reasonably be expected to do so. Section 120(1), (4) and (6) of the 2003 Act provide as follows:

---

[14] *R v Tyagi* (1986) The Times, 21 July, CA.

[15] See *R v Britton* [1987] 1 WLR 539, CA.

[16] *R v Harman* (1984) 148 JP 289, CA and *R v Sutton* (1991) 94 Cr App R 70, CA.

[17] *R v Mangena* [2009] EWCA Crim 2535. The judge's decision should be upheld unless obviously wrong, unreasonable, or perverse: *R v McAfee* [2006] EWCA Crim 2914.

[18] See Wigmore, *Evidence in Trials at Common Law*, vol 3 (rev Chadbourn) (Boston, 1970) ch 28.

[19] (1828) 8 B&C 14.

[20] See also *R v Simmonds* [1969] 1 QB 685 CA.

[21] See per Hayes J in *Lord Talbot de Malahide v Cusack* (1864) 17 ICLR 213 at 220.

[22] See *Maugham v Hubbard* (1828) 8 B&C 14, but see also *R v Sekhon* (1987) 85 Cr App R 19 CA (considered at n 44, n 45 and n 47) and *R v Virgo* (1978) 67 Cr App R 323, CA.

[23] *R v Chinn* [2012] 2 Cr App R 39, CA.

(1) This section applies where a person (the witness) is called to give evidence in criminal proceedings.

. . .

(4) A previous statement by the witness is admissible as evidence of any matter stated of which oral evidence by him would be admissible, if—

   (a) any of the following three conditions is satisfied, and

   (b) while giving evidence the witness indicates that to the best of his belief he made the statement, and to the best of his belief it states the truth.

. . .

(6) The second condition is that the statement was made by the witness when the matters stated were fresh in his memory but he does not remember them, and cannot reasonably be expected to remember them, well enough to give oral evidence of them in the proceedings.

Section 120(4) only applies in the case of a statement *made* by the witness, and has no application, therefore, in the case of a statement *verified* by him.

The following principles relating to s 120(4) and (6) derive from *R v Chinn*.[24]

1. The subsections are not limited to statements about 'routine' matters.

2. If any matter in s 120(6) is disputed, the judge must decide the issue.

3. If there is a dispute about whether the witness cannot reasonably be expected to remember the matters stated well enough to give oral evidence of them, the judge must decide the matter objectively, taking into account all relevant factors, including, for example, the characteristics of the witness and the nature and circumstances of the incident and what has happened to the witness thereafter.

4. When a witness gives evidence that satisfies the condition in s 120(6), but this is disputed, then in the absence of the jury he can be asked why he does not recall the matters and may be cross-examined on the issue.

5. Arguments about discretionary exclusion under s 78 of the Police and Criminal Evidence Act 1984 should also be addressed at this stage.

6. If the previous statement is ruled admissible, the judge should explain to the jury, when he sums up, that they may consider it because the witness could not reasonably be expected to remember the matters well enough to give oral evidence of them.

7. The judge should also direct the jury to consider the reliability of the witness's earlier recollection and emphasise that it is for them to decide what weight to give to the evidence.

The conditions

A document

At common law a document includes a tape recording,[25] but in criminal proceedings, for the purposes of s 139(1) of the 2003 Act, it means anything in which information of any description is recorded, but not including any recordings of sounds or moving images.[26]

Made or verified

Both at common law and under s 139(1) of the 2003 Act, a witness may refresh his memory either from a document made by himself or by another, provided that, if made by another,

[24] *R v Chinn* [2012] 2 Cr App R 39, CA.

[25] *R v Bailey* [2001] EWCA Crim 733.

[26] The 2003 Act, s 140.

the witness verified the document, ie checked the contents of the document, while the events were still fresh in his memory, and satisfied himself as to their accuracy.[27] For example, in *Anderson v Whalley*[28] it was held that entries in a ship's log-book made by the mate and verified by the captain about a week later could be used to refresh the memory of the latter. It is submitted that under s 139(1), as at common law, verification can be either visual or aural. In *R v Kelsey*,[29] H, a witness called for the prosecution, was allowed to refresh his memory as to the registration number of a car from a note which he had dictated to a police officer. The officer had read his note back aloud and H had confirmed that it was correct. Although H had seen the officer making the note, he had not read it himself. The officer gave evidence that the note used in court was the one that the witness saw him make. The Court of Appeal held that verification could be either visual or aural, the important matter being that the witness satisfies himself, while the matters are fresh in his mind, (i) that a record has been made; and (ii) that it is accurate. However, where a witness dictates a note to another, hears it read back, and confirms its accuracy without reading it himself, another witness must be called to prove that the note used in court is the one that was dictated and read back. The officer in the instant case had given evidence to that effect.[30]

Contemporaneity

At common law, but not under s 139 of the 2003 Act, the document, whether made or verified by the witness, 'must have been written either at the time of the transaction or so shortly afterwards that the facts were fresh in his memory'.[31] Commenting on this definition, the Court of Appeal has observed that it provides 'a measure of elasticity and should not be taken to confine witnesses to an over-short period'.[32] The question is a matter of fact and degree;[33] the permitted gap between the date of the statement and that of the events to which it relates cannot be fixed with precision. The precedents are therefore of very limited value.[34]

Originals and copies

There is no requirement, either at common law or under s 139(1) of the 2003 Act, that the memory-refreshing document be the first or only document made or verified by the witness recording his recollection of the matters in question. A witness, therefore, may refresh his memory from a document which is based on original notes or a tape recording made by him. In *A-G's Reference (No 3 of 1979)*[35] the Court of Appeal held that a police officer could refresh his memory from notes compiled, at a time when the facts were still fresh in his memory, from earlier brief jottings of an interview. In *R v Cheng*[36] the Court of Appeal held that a police officer was entitled to rely on a statement which was a partial but not exact copy of earlier notes from which it was prepared (and which were not available at the trial) on the grounds

---

[27] See *Burrough v Martin* (1809) 2 Camp 112 and *R v Langton* (1876) 2 QBD 296, CCR.

[28] (1852) 3 Car&Kir 54. See also *R v Sekhon* (1986) 85 Cr App R 19, CA and cf *R v Eleftheriou* [1993] Crim LR 947, CA.

[29] (1982) 74 Cr App R 213.

[30] Cf *R v Mills* [1962] 1 WLR 1152, CCA at 1156, per Winn J, obiter. The officer's note, in *R v Kelsey*, would now be admissible as evidence of the matters stated under the 2003 Act, s 117 (business and other documents): see Ch 10.

[31] See *Phipson on Evidence* (11th edn, London, 1970) 634, para 1528.

[32] *R v Richardson* [1971] 2 QB 484.

[33] *R v Simmonds* [1969] 1 QB 685, CA.

[34] *R v Woodcock* [1963] Crim LR 273, CCA (three-month gap treated as too long); *R v Graham* [1973] Crim LR 628, CA (one-month gap regarded as doubtful); *R v Fotheringham* [1975] Crim LR 710, CA (21-day gap accepted).

[35] (1979) 69 Cr App R 411.

[36] (1976) 63 Cr App R 20.

that the statement 'substantially' reproduced the notes. Similarly, in *R v Mills*[37] a police officer, who had heard and made a tape recording of a conversation between two accused, was allowed to refer to his notes written up with the assistance of that tape recording, which was not itself put in evidence. A witness may also refresh his memory from a copy of his original document, provided that the court is satisfied that the copy is accurate or substantially reproduces the contents of the original.[38] In *R v Chisnell*[39] an officer was allowed to use a statement made nine months after an interview and compiled on the basis of a contemporaneous note, the court being satisfied that the note, which had been lost, had been accurately transcribed into the statement. However, in cases of 'past recollection recorded' in which the original has *not* been lost or destroyed, then there is old authority that the original document must be used.[40]

Production of the document

A document used to refresh memory in court must be produced for inspection by the opposite party who may wish to cross-examine the witness on its contents.[41] At the request of the opposite party, the document may also be shown to the jury, if this is necessary to their determination of a point in issue in the case. In *R v Bass*[42] the only evidence against the appellant was a confession allegedly made to two police officers. They read identical accounts of the interview with the appellant but denied that they had been prepared in collaboration. The trial judge refused a defence application that the jury be allowed to examine the notebooks. The Court of Criminal Appeal, allowing the appeal, held that the jury, by an inspection of the notebooks, might have been assisted in their evaluation of the credibility and accuracy of the officers.[43] Similarly, in cases in which the witness's evidence is long and involved, it may be convenient for the jury to use the document as an aide-memoire as to that evidence, but care should be exercised in adopting this course in cases where the evidence is bitterly contested, because of the danger that the jury will improperly regard the document as constituting evidence in the case.[44]

Cross-examination on the document

In the majority of cases, the fact that there is cross-examination on the basis of a document used to refresh memory in court will neither entitle the jury to inspect the document nor make

---

[37] [1962] 1 WLR 1152, CCA.
[38] *Topham v McGregor* (1844) 1 Car&Kir 320.
[39] [1992] Crim LR 507, CA.
[40] *Doe d Church and Phillips v Perkins* (1790) 3 Term Rep 749.
[41] *Beech v Jones* (1848) 5 CB 696.
[42] [1953] 1 QB 680, CCA; cf *R v Fenlon* (1980) 71 Cr App R 307, CA.
[43] The court also made it clear that it is not improper for two or more police officers to refresh their memories from notes in the making of which they have collaborated. See also *R (Saunders) v Independent Police Complaint Commission* [2009] 1 All ER 379 in which the Divisional Court, while acknowledging the risks of innocent contamination and deliberate collusion, asserted that the pooling of recollections could also improve the accuracy of an officer's notes. Moreover, a prohibition on the practice would have serious operational disadvantages. However, as a general rule discussions between witnesses as to the evidence they will give should not take place: *R v Skinner* (1993) 99 Cr App R 212, CA. If a discussion may have led to fabrication, it may be unsafe to leave any of the evidence to the jury. In other cases it may suffice to direct the jury on the implications of such conduct in relation to the reliability of the evidence. See *R v Arif* (1993) The Times, 17 June, CA.
[44] Per Woolf LJ in *R v Sekhon* (1986) 85 Cr App R 19, CA at 23: the document may also be put before the jury where it is difficult for them to follow the *cross-examination* of the witness who has refreshed his memory without having the document before them. But cf *R v Dillon* (1983) 85 Cr App R 29, CA.

it evidence in the case.[45] Cross-examining counsel may inspect the document without thereby making it evidence and may cross-examine on it without thereby making it evidence, provided that his cross-examination goes no further than the parts which were used by the witness to refresh his memory. However, cross-examination on new matters deriving from other parts of the document entitles the party calling the witness to put the document in evidence and to let the tribunal of fact see the document upon which such cross-examination is based.[46] Two other situations have been identified in which the document may be admitted in evidence.[47] First, where the nature of the cross-examination involves a suggestion that the witness has subsequently fabricated his evidence, which will usually involve the allegation that the record is concocted, the document is then admissible to rebut this suggestion and, if the document assists as to this, to show whether or not it has the appearance of being a contemporaneous record which has not subsequently been altered.[48] Second, where the document is inconsistent with the evidence, the document is then admissible as evidence of this inconsistency.

Where, as a result of cross-examination, a memory-refreshing document is admitted in evidence, it is admitted as evidence of any matter stated. Under s 1 of the Civil Evidence Act 1995 (the 1995 Act), in civil proceedings evidence shall not be excluded on the ground that it is hearsay. Section 6(4) and (5) of the 1995 Act provide as follows:

> (4) Nothing in this Act affects any of the rules of law as to the circumstances in which, where a person called as a witness in civil proceedings is cross-examined on a document used by him to refresh his memory, that document may be made evidence in the proceedings.
> (5) Nothing in this section shall be construed as preventing a statement of any description referred to above from being admissible by virtue of s 1 as evidence of the matters stated.

Although s 6(5) refers to 'a statement of any description referred to above' and s 6(4) makes no reference to a 'statement' as such, it seems reasonably clear that the parliamentary intention was to perpetuate the rule formerly stated with clarity in s 3(2) of the Civil Evidence Act 1968, ie that where a memory-refreshing document is made evidence in civil proceedings, any statement made in the document is admissible as evidence of any matter stated therein. As to criminal proceedings, s 120(1) and (3) of the 2003 Act provide as follows:

> (1) This section applies where a person (the witness) is called to give evidence in criminal proceedings.
> ...
> (3) A statement made by the witness in a document—
>   (a) which is used by him to refresh his memory while giving evidence,
>   (b) on which he is cross-examined, and
>   (c) which as a consequence is received in evidence in the proceedings,
>   is admissible as evidence of any matter stated of which oral evidence by him would be admissible.

Section 120(1) and (3) provide not for the circumstances in which a documentary statement may be received in evidence, but merely for the evidential status of a document where it is received in evidence.[49]

---

[45] Per Woolf LJ in *R v Sekhon* (1986) 85 Cr App R 19, CA at 22.

[46] *Gregory v Tavernor* (1833) 6 C&P 280; *Senat v Senat* [1965] P 172 P, D and Admlty per Sir Jocelyn Simon P at 177; and *R v Britton* [1987] 1 WLR 539, CA.

[47] *R v Sekhon* (1986) 85 Cr App R 19, CA at 22–3.

[48] Cf *R v Fenlon* (1980) 71 Cr App R 307, CA and *R v Dillon* (1983) 85 Cr App R 29, CA.

[49] *R v Pashmfouroush* [2006] EWCA Crim 2330.

In *R v Chinn*,[50] the Court of Appeal, construing s 120(3) of the 2003 Act, held that: the word 'which' refers back to 'a document'; s 120(3)(a) contemplates use of the document by the witness to refresh his memory while giving evidence in chief; his evidence about the facts of which he has refreshed his memory is admissible oral evidence; the 'statement' in the document used to refresh memory also becomes evidence of the matters stated; and if the witness fails to refresh his memory, the situation is covered not by s 120(3) but by ss 120(4) and 120(6).[51]

Section 120 does not apply in the case of a statement *verified* by a witness which, as a result of cross-examination, is admitted in evidence. In criminal proceedings, therefore, such a statement is not admitted as evidence of any of the matters stated in it, but as evidence of the witness's consistency or inconsistency, going only to his credit.

Use of exhibited document by jury

If, in a trial before a judge and jury, a statement made in a document is admitted in evidence under s 120, and the document or a copy of it is produced as an exhibit, the exhibit must not accompany the jury when they retire to consider their verdict unless the court considers it appropriate or all the parties to the proceedings agree that it should accompany the jury.[52]

Refreshing the memory out of court

It is a common practice, in both civil and criminal proceedings, for witnesses, before going into the witness box, to look at and refresh their memories from their own previous statements. Such a statement may have been made by a witness for some personal reason, may constitute a 'proof of evidence' made at the request of the solicitor for the party calling him or, in the case of a prosecution witness, may be a signed statement which he made to the police.[53] Whatever form it takes, however, it would appear that the conditions on which a witness may refresh his memory while giving evidence do not apply to the witness who refreshes his memory outside the witness box.[54] In *R v Richardson*[55] the Court of Appeal approved the following two observations of the Supreme Court of Hong Kong in *Lau Pak Ngam v R*:[56]

1. Testimony in the witness box becomes more a test of memory than of truthfulness if witnesses are deprived of the opportunity of checking their recollection beforehand by reference to statements or notes made at a time closer to the events in question.

2. Refusal of access to statements would tend to create difficulties for honest witnesses but be likely to do little to hamper dishonest witnesses.

[50] [2012] 2 Cr App R 39, CA.

[51] See, in this chapter, under **Refreshing the memory, Refreshing the memory in court, The rules**.

[52] The Criminal Justice Act 2003, s 122.

[53] A circular issued in April 1969, with the approval of the Lord Chief Justice and the judges of the Queen's Bench Division, recognized that prosecution witnesses are normally entitled, if they so request, to copies of any statements taken from them by the police.

[54] Yet see *R v Thomas* [1994] Crim LR 745, CA, where, for reasons that are not disclosed, it was held to be undesirable for a child aged 8 to be shown her signed police statement. See also *Owen v Edwards* (1983) 77 Cr App R 191, DC, at n 66.

[55] [1971] 2 QB 484.

[56] [1966] Crim LR 443.

However, it was also observed in *R v Richardson* that it would obviously be wrong for several witnesses to be handed statements in circumstances enabling one to compare with another what each had said. Equally, as a general rule, discussions between witnesses, particularly just before going into court to give evidence, should not take place, and statements or proofs should not be read to witnesses in each other's presence.[57] It is incumbent on prosecuting authorities and judges to ensure that witnesses are informed that they should not discuss cases in which they are involved.[58]

In *R v Da Silva*[59] it was held that it is open to the judge, in the exercise of his discretion and in the interests of justice, to permit a witness who has begun to give his evidence, to withdraw and refresh his memory from a statement made near to the time of the events in question, even if not 'contemporaneous', provided he is satisfied that: (i) the witness indicates that he cannot now recall the details of the events because of the lapse of time; (ii) he made a statement much nearer the time of the event,[60] the contents of which represented his recollection at the time he made it; (iii) he has not read the statement before giving evidence; and (iv) he wishes to read the statement before he continues to give evidence. It does not matter whether the witness withdraws from the witness box to read his statement or reads it in the witness box, but if the former course is adopted, no communication must be had with the witness other than to see that he can read the statement in peace. If either course is adopted, the statement must be removed from him when he continues to give his evidence and he should not be permitted to refer to it again. However, in criminal proceedings, the witness may be permitted to make further use of the document to refresh his memory in the witness box, provided that the conditions of s 139 of the 2003 Act are met.[61]

In *R v South Ribble Magistrates' Court, ex p Cochrane*[62] it was held that *R v Da Silva* does not lay down as a matter of law that all four conditions to which it refers must be satisfied, because the court has a 'real discretion', ie a choice free of binding criteria, whether to permit a witness to refresh his memory from a non-contemporaneous statement. In that case it was held that a witness who had read his statement before giving evidence, but who had not taken it in properly, and therefore did not satisfy condition (iii), had been properly permitted to refresh his memory. The discretion is a broad fact-sensitive discretion to be exercised in the interests of fairness and justice.[63]

The fact that a witness has refreshed his memory out of court and before entering the witness box may be relevant to the weight which can properly be attached to his evidence, so that in a criminal case injustice may be caused to the accused if the matter is not brought to the attention of the jury. For this reason, the Court of Appeal in *R v Westwell*[64] held that the prosecution, if aware that statements have been seen by their witnesses, should inform the defence. Informing the defence, however, is 'desirable but not essential' and 'if for any reason this is

---

[57] *R v Skinner* (1993) 99 Cr App R 212, CA at 216.

[58] *R v Shaw* [2002] EWCA Crim 3004.

[59] [1990] 1 WLR 31, CA.

[60] In *R v Da Silva* itself, the statement was made one month after the events to which it related.

[61] See, in this chapter, under **Refreshing the memory**, **Refreshing the memory in court**, **The rules**.

[62] [1996] 2 Cr App R 544, DC.

[63] *R v Gordon* [2002] EWCA Crim 412, where a witness who was dyslexic and unable to read the statement himself, adopted it after it had been read out to him by counsel in the absence of the jury.

[64] [1976] 2 All ER 812. See also *Worley v Bentley* [1976] 2 All ER 449, DC.

not done, the omission cannot of itself be a ground for acquittal'.[65] *R v Westwell* left undecided the question whether a party may call for, inspect, and cross-examine on a document which a witness called by the opposite party has used to refresh his memory outside court but has not used while giving evidence. The issue arose in *Owen v Edwards*.[66] A policeman, outside the courtroom and before giving evidence for the prosecution, refreshed his memory from a notebook which he did not use in the witness box. The Divisional Court held that defence counsel was entitled not only to inspect the notebook but also to cross-examine the witness upon relevant matters contained in it. It was further held that although defence counsel may cross-examine upon the material in the notebook from which the witness has refreshed his memory without the notebook being made evidence in the case, if he cross-examines on material in the notebook which has not been referred to by the witness, he runs the risk of the notebook being put in evidence. As we have seen, in civil cases, the document will be admitted as evidence of the matters stated. The same applies in criminal cases, but only in the case of statements made, as opposed to verified, by the witness. The weight to be attached to the documentary evidence will obviously vary according to the precise circumstances, but a note made a long time after the events in question may be viewed by the tribunal of fact with considerable caution, if not suspicion.

Previous consistent or self-serving statements

The general rule

There is a general common law rule that a witness may not be asked in examination-in-chief about former oral or written statements made by him and consistent with his evidence in the proceedings. Evidence of the earlier statement may not be given either by the witness who made it or by any other witness. The reason usually given for the rule is the danger of manufactured evidence.[67] A resourceful witness, minded to deceive the court, could with ease deliberately repeat his version of the facts to a number of people prior to trial with a view to showing consistency with the story he tells in the witness box, thereby bolstering his credibility.[68]

The rule also applies to re-examination. Thus the credibility of a witness may not be bolstered by evidence of a previous consistent statement merely because his testimony has been impeached in cross-examination.[69] This remains the case 'even if the impeachment takes the form of showing a contradiction or inconsistency between the evidence given at the trial and something said by the witness on a former occasion'.[70] However, the court does have a residual

---

[65] See also, *sed quaere*, *R v H* [1992] Crim LR 516, CA: child victims of sexual offences should only refresh their memory out of court with the *consent* of the defence.

[66] (1983) 77 Cr App R 191.

[67] See, eg, per Humphreys J in *R v Roberts* [1942] 1 All ER 187, CCA at 191.

[68] See also *Fennell v Jerome Property Maintenance Ltd* (1986) The Times, 26 Nov, QBD: as a matter of principle, evidence produced by the administration of some mechanical, chemical, or hypnotic truth test on a witness is inadmissible to show the veracity (or otherwise) of that witness. See further *R v McKay* [1967] NZLR 139, NZCA: a psychiatrist is not permitted to give evidence of statements made by the accused while under the influence of a truth drug and consistent with his (the accused's) evidence.

[69] *R v Coll* (1889) 25 LR Ir 522.

[70] Per Holmes J (1889) 25 LR Ir 522 at 541. See also *R v Weekes* [1988] Crim LR 244, CA; *R v Beattie* (1989) 89 Cr App R 302, CA per Lord Lane CJ at 306–7; and *R v P (GR)* [1998] Crim LR 663, CA. Contrast, *sed quaere*, *Ahmed v Brumfitt* (1967) 112 Sol Jo 32, CA.

discretion to permit re-examination to show consistency by reference to a previous statement to ensure that the jury is not positively misled by the cross-examination as to the existence of some fact or the terms of an earlier statement.[71]

The rule is distinct from the common law rule against hearsay, whereby an out-of-court statement is inadmissible as evidence of the facts stated. A previous consistent or self-serving statement of a witness is excluded as evidence of his consistency. The distinction may be illustrated by the following two cases. In *Corke v Corke and Cook*[72] a husband petitioned for divorce on the ground of adultery. Late one night he had accused his wife of having recently committed adultery with a lodger. The Court of Appeal held that the wife, who denied adultery, had been improperly permitted to give evidence that some 10 minutes after the husband's accusation she had telephoned her doctor and asked him to examine her and the lodger with a view to showing that there had been no recent sexual intercourse. In *R v Roberts*[73] the accused was convicted of the murder of a girl by shooting her. His defence was that the gun went off accidentally while he was trying to make up a quarrel with the girl. Evidence that two days after the event the accused had told his father that his defence would be accident was held by the Court of Criminal Appeal to have been properly excluded. In both of these cases the evidence in question was hearsay and inadmissible as evidence of the facts stated, that is to show in the one case that there was no sexual intercourse and in the other that the gun went off accidentally. But it was also inadmissible, by reason of the rule against previous consistent statements, to bolster the credibility of the witnesses in question by demonstrating their consistency.

Where a previous statement of a witness is admitted as hearsay, ie as evidence of the matters stated, it will also be received as evidence of consistency. Thus a decision such as *Corke v Corke and Cook* might be decided differently today, because in civil proceedings the previous statements of a witness may be admitted, with the leave of the court, both as evidence of the matters stated, and also, therefore, as evidence of consistency, under s 6(2) of the Civil Evidence Act 1995.[74] Similarly, if a previous statement of a witness is admitted in criminal proceedings as evidence of the matters stated, under s 114(1)(c) of the 2003 Act, ie where all parties agree to it being admissible, or under s 114(1)(d) of that Act, ie where the court is satisfied that it is in the interests of justice for it to be admissible, then it will also be received as evidence of consistency.

To the rule against previous consistent statements, there are a number of common law exceptions. The statutory categories of admissible hearsay now embrace almost all of the varieties of statement admissible by way of the common law exceptions to the rule against previous consistent statements, in some cases expanding their scope. The justification for separate treatment of the common law exceptions stems from the facts that: (a) the overlap is not total (wholly exculpatory statements made on accusation, for example, are not admissible as evidence of the matters asserted); (b) Parliament has elected not to repeal any of the common law exceptions; and (c) in some cases (statements admissible to rebut allegations of recent fabrication and statements in documents used to refresh the memory and received in evidence), Parliament, rather than give the common law exception a statutory formulation,

[71] *R v Ali* [2004] 1 Cr App R 501, CA.
[72] [1958] P 93.
[73] [1942] 1 All ER 187.
[74] See Ch 11.

has chosen to identify it as a category of hearsay by simply referring to the circumstances in which the statement may be admitted at common law.

The common law exceptions

Complaints in sexual cases

If, in the case of sexual offences, the complainant made a voluntary complaint shortly after the alleged offence, the person to whom the complaint was made may give evidence of the particulars of that complaint in order to show the consistency of that conduct with the complainant's evidence and, in cases in which consent is in issue, as evidence inconsistent with such consent. Section 120(7) of the 2003 Act has extended the principle to cover a previous statement by a person against whom *any* offence has been committed, provided that it is an offence to which the proceedings relate, that the statement consists of a complaint about conduct which would, if proved, constitute the offence, and the complainant, in giving evidence, indicates that to the best of his belief, he made the statement and it states the truth. A statement received under s 120(7) is admissible as evidence of the matters stated and, provided that the evidence is given by the person to whom the complaint was made,[75] also goes to the consistency of the witness. Section 120(7), which is considered in Chapter 10, is much wider than the common law exception. The common law exception, therefore, is likely to be invoked only rarely and falls to be considered in outline only.

The common law exception applies to written, as well as oral, complaints, and even extends to a written note given to a friend by mistake.[76] Where the exception applies, it is essential to direct the jury that the complaint is not evidence of the facts complained of, and cannot be independent confirmation of the complainant's evidence since it does not come from a source independent of her, but may assist in assessing her veracity.[77]

In *White v R*[78] it was held that if the person to whom the complaint was made does not give evidence, the complainant's own evidence that she made a complaint cannot assist in either proving her consistency or negativing consent because, without independent confirmation, her own evidence that she complained takes the jury nowhere in deciding whether she is worthy of belief.

Sexual offences

The common law exception applies only in the case of sexual offences, but is not restricted to sexual offences where absence of consent is among the facts in issue.[79] Nor is the exception confined to sexual offences against females,[80] as was once thought.[81]

The fact and the particulars of the complaint

There is a two-stage test for the jury to follow, first to decide whether the recent complaint was in fact made and, if so, second to decide whether it is consistent with the complainant's evidence.[82] In *R v Lillyman*,[83] it was held that the person to whom the complaint was made

[75] See *White v R* [1999] 1 Cr App R 153, PC.

[76] *R v B* [1997] Crim LR 220, CA.

[77] *R v Islam* [1999] 1 Cr App R 22, CA, applied in *R v NK* [1999] Crim LR 980, CA.

[78] [1999] 1 Cr App R 153, PC.

[79] *R v Osborne* [1905] 1 KB 551, CCR.

[80] *R v Camelleri* [1922] 2 KB 122, CCA. See also *R v Wannell* (1924) 17 Cr App R 53, CCA.

[81] *R v Christie* [1914] AC 545, HL.

[82] *R v Hartley* [2003] EWCA Crim 3027.

[83] [1896] 2 QB 167, CCR.

can give detailed evidence as to what the complainant said, rather than simply evidence of the bare fact that the complaint was made, in order that the jurors can judge for themselves whether the complaint in question is consistent with the complainant's evidence.

Consistency is a question of degree. In *R v S*[84] it was held that evidence of a recent complaint will be admissible where it is sufficiently consistent that it can, depending on the view of the evidence taken by the jury, support or enhance the credibility of the complainant. Whether the complaint is sufficiently consistent must depend on the facts.[85] It is not necessary that the complaint discloses the ingredients of the offence, but it is usually necessary that it discloses evidence of material and relevant unlawful sexual conduct on the part of the accused which can support the complainant's credibility.

Voluntariness

It is a condition of the admissibility of a complaint in a sexual case that it should have been made voluntarily, and not in reply to questions of a suggestive, leading, or intimidating character.[86]

The time of complaint

A complaint is only admissible in evidence under the exception if 'it was made at the first opportunity after the offence which reasonably offered itself'[87] and was 'recent'.[88] Whether a complaint was made as soon as was reasonably practicable after the occurrence of the offence is a question of fact and degree.[89] The answer will depend on the circumstances, including the character of the complainant and the relationship between the complainant and the person to whom she might have complained but did not do so. Victims often need time before they can bring themselves to tell what has happened, and whereas some will find it impossible to complain to anyone other than a parent or member of their family, others may feel it impossible to tell their parents or members of their family.[90] As to 'recency', in *R v Birks*[91] it was held, albeit reluctantly, that a complaint made at the earliest two months after the alleged offences, was inadmissible, notwithstanding that the complaint was made spontaneously and that the accused had allegedly threatened her by saying that if she told her mother she would be put in a home.

Admissibility to show consistency

At common law, the complaint is not evidence of the facts complained of and may be used only as evidence of the consistency of the complaint with the testimony of the complainant and, in cases where consent is in issue, as evidence inconsistent with consent. Thus if the terms of the complaint are not ostensibly consistent with the terms of the complainant's testimony, the introduction of the complaint has no purpose.[92] Likewise, in cases where the

---

[84] [2004] 1 WLR 2940, CA.

[85] There may be sufficient consistency even if the complaint is, in parts, inconsistent with the evidence of the complainant: see *R v S* [2004] 1 WLR 2940, CA.

[86] *R v Osbourne* [1905] 1 KB 551, CCR at 556.

[87] Per Ridley J in *R v Osbourne* [1905] 1 KB 551, CCR at 561. See also *R v Cummings* [1948] 1 All ER 551, CCA. However, the fact that the complaint was not the first to be made is not, per se, sufficient to exclude it: *R v Wilbourne* (1917) 12 Cr App R 280, CCA.

[88] *R v Birks* [2003] 2 Cr App R 122, CA.

[89] A complaint made one week after the offence was admitted in *R v Hedges* (1910) 3 Cr App R 262, CCA.

[90] *R v Valentine* [1996] 2 Cr App R 213, CA.

[91] [2003] 2 Cr App R 122, CA.

[92] *R v Wright* and *R v Ormerod* (1987) 90 Cr App R 91, CA.

complainant does not testify, there being no evidence with which the complaint may be consistent, the particulars of the complaint are inadmissible.[93]

Statements admissible to rebut allegations of recent fabrication

If, in cross-examination, it is suggested to a witness that her account of some incident or set of facts is a recent invention or fabrication, evidence of prior statements made by her to the same effect is admissible to support her credit.[94] Such prior statements will normally be put to the witness in re-examination. In *R v Oyesiku*[95] the accused was convicted of assaulting a police officer. In cross-examination, it was put to the accused's wife, who had given evidence that the police officer was the aggressor, that her evidence had been recently fabricated. The Court of Appeal held that the trial judge had improperly refused to admit evidence of a previous statement consistent with her testimony and made by her to a solicitor after her husband's arrest but before she had seen him. Karminski LJ, giving the judgment of the court, accepted as a correct statement of the law the judgment of Dixon CJ in *Nominal Defendant v Clement*,[96] from which the following propositions derive. The exception is brought into play where it is suggested in cross-examination that the witness's account 'is a late invention or has been recently reconstructed, even though not with conscious dishonesty'. The prior statement is admissible 'if it was made by the witness contemporaneously with the event or at a time sufficiently early to be inconsistent with the suggestion that his account is a late invention or reconstruction'. The judge, in determining whether the exception has been brought into play, should exercise care to assure himself of the following three matters: (i) 'that the account given by the witness in his testimony is attacked on the ground of recent invention or reconstruction or that a foundation for such an attack has been laid'; (ii) 'that the contents of the statement are in fact to the like effect as his account given in his evidence'; and (iii) 'that having regard to the time and circumstances in which it was made, it (the statement) rationally tends to answer the attack'.

'Recent' in this context should not be confined within a temporal straitjacket but is an 'elastic' description designed to assist in the identification of circumstances in which a previous consistent statement should be admitted where there is a rational and cogent basis on which it could assist the tribunal of fact in determining where the truth lies.[97] *R v MH*[98] furnishes a good illustration. MH alleged that his son had been coached by his mother to give false evidence against him to prevent him from seeing his children. He asserted that she was also motivated by the financial dispute between them following their separation. It was held that evidence of the son's complaints to the mother prior to the breakdown of the marriage was admissible in rebuttal, but not evidence of complaints made at a time when MH was not permitted to see his children and when he and his wife were in financial dispute.

In both civil and criminal proceedings, the previous consistent statement is now admissible both to negative the suggestion of invention or reconstruction and thereby confirm the

---

[93] See, eg, *R v Wallwork* (1958) 42 Cr App R 153, CCA.

[94] Evidence of a complaint in a sexual case may be admissible on this basis notwithstanding that it was not made at the first reasonably practicable opportunity (see, in this chapter, under **Previous consistent or self-serving statements, The common law exceptions, Complaints in sexual cases, The time of complaint**): *R v Tyndale* [1999] Crim LR 320, CA.

[95] (1971) 56 Cr App R 240. See also *R v Benjamin* (1913) 8 Cr App R 146, CCA; *Flanagan v Fahy* [1918] 2 IR 361, Ir KBD; and *Fox v General Medical Council* [1960] 1 WLR 1017, PC.

[96] (1961) 104 CLR 476, High Court of Australia. The extracts given in the text are at 479.

[97] *R v Athwal* [2009] 1 WLR 2430, CA at [58].

[98] [2012] EWCA Crim 2725.

witness's credit, and as evidence of the matters stated. Under s 1 of the Civil Evidence Act 1995, in civil proceedings evidence shall not be excluded on the ground that it is hearsay. Section 6(2) and (5) of the 1995 Act provide as follows:

(2) A party who has called or intends to call a person as a witness in civil proceedings may not in those proceedings adduce evidence of a previous statement made by that person, except—...
(b) for the purposes of rebutting a suggestion that his evidence has been fabricated.
...
(5) Nothing in this section shall be construed as preventing a statement of any description referred to above from being admissible by virtue of section 1 as evidence of the matters stated.

In criminal proceedings, s 120(1) and (2) of the 2003 Act provide as follows:

(1) This section applies where a person (the witness) is called to give evidence in criminal proceedings.
(2) If a previous statement by the witness is admitted as evidence to rebut a suggestion that his oral evidence has been fabricated, that statement is admissible as evidence of any matter stated of which oral evidence by the witness would be admissible.

Sections 120(1) and (2) do not provide for the circumstances in which a previous statement by a witness may be received in evidence, but merely regulate the use to which such evidence, once admitted, may be put.[99] It follows that although s 120(2) omits reference to the recency of the fabrication, this omission does not mean, as one commentator has suggested,[100] that it is no longer a requirement for admissibility.

Statements made on accusation
Exculpatory statements
Provided that the conditions of admissibility are satisfied, and subject to the exclusionary discretion of the court, an admission made by an accused is admissible, by way of exception to the general rule against hearsay, as evidence of the facts contained in it.[101] There is also, however, a well-established practice on the part of the prosecution, which has been approved by the Court of Appeal,[102] 'to admit in evidence all unwritten and most written statements made by an accused person to the police whether they contain admissions or whether they contain denials of guilt'. If such statements are wholly exculpatory, they are not admitted as evidence of the facts stated. In *R v Storey*,[103] the police having found a large quantity of cannabis in the accused's flat, she explained that it belonged to a man who had brought it there against her will. The Court of Appeal held that this statement was not evidence of the facts contained in it, but admissible 'because of its vital relevance as showing the reaction of the accused when first taxed with the incriminating facts'.[104] It does not follow from these words, however, that the only statements admissible as evidence of reaction are those which the accused made on the first encounter with his accusers. In *R v Pearce*[105] the Court of Appeal

[99] *R v T* [2008] EWCA Crim 484. See also *R v Athwal* [2009] 1 WLR 2430, CA.
[100] Ormerod, '*R v Athwal*' (case comment) [2009] Crim LR 726. See also Pattenden, '*R v Athwal*' (case comment) (2009) 13 E&P 342.
[101] See Ch 13.
[102] *R v Pearce* (1979) 69 Cr App R 365, CA at 368 and 370.
[103] (1968) 52 Cr App R 334.
[104] See per Widgery LJ in *R v Storey* (1968) 52 Cr App R 334 at 337.
[105] (1979) 69 Cr App R 365 at 369.

decided that statements subsequently made are also admissible, although 'the longer the time that has elapsed after the first encounter the less the weight which will be attached to the denial', a matter on which the judge may direct the jury. Thus, in that case it was held that a judge had improperly excluded self-serving statements made by the accused to the police after his arrest, which took place two days after he was first taxed by his employer's security officer with incriminating facts.

However, this principle cannot be relied upon to admit a statement which adds nothing to evidence of reaction which has already been admitted. In *R v Tooke*[106] the accused made an exculpatory statement shortly after the time of the offence. Some 40 minutes later, he went to the police station and made a spontaneous exculpatory witness statement. The first statement was admitted, but the defence were not permitted to cross-examine a constable to prove the statement made at the station. The fact that it was a witness statement and not a statement in answer to a charge made no difference, because the same test applied. It was inadmissible because it added nothing to the evidence of reaction already before the jury.

Impromptu exculpatory statements made on accusation are admissible as evidence of consistency in the case of an accused who testifies. However, in a case where the accused gives no evidence, there is no duty on the judge to remind the jury of voluntary statements made by the accused to the police exonerating himself.[107] Moreover, the accused will not be permitted to take unfair advantage of the rule:

> Although in practice most statements are given in evidence even when they are largely self-serving, there may be a rare occasion when an accused produces a carefully prepared written statement to the police, with a view to it being made a part of the prosecution evidence. The trial judge would probably exclude such a statement as inadmissible.[108]

'Mixed' statements

A careful distinction needs to be drawn between a purely exculpatory statement and a 'mixed' statement, ie a statement containing both inculpatory and exculpatory parts, such as 'I killed X. If I had not done so, X would certainly have killed me there and then.'[109] When the prosecution admits in evidence a statement relied upon as an admission, the whole statement, including qualifications, explanations, and other exculpatory parts of it favourable to the accused, becomes admissible. Any other course would be unfair and misleading.[110] The jury must decide whether the statement viewed as a whole constitutes an admission. As to the question whether the judge should then direct the jury (a) that the statement is not evidence of the facts contained in it except insofar as it constitutes an admission (the 'purist' approach); or (b) that the whole statement is evidence of the truth of the facts it contains (the 'common sense' approach), in *R v Duncan*[111] the Court of Appeal came down firmly in favour of the latter approach. Lord Lane CJ, in a dictum which has subsequently been applied

---

[106] (1989) 90 Cr App R 417, CA.

[107] *R v Barbery* (1975) 62 Cr App R 248, CA. Cf *R v Donaldson* (1977) 64 Cr App R 59, CA at 69.

[108] *R v Pearce* (1979) 69 Cr App R 365, CA at 370. See, eg, *R v Newsome* (1980) 71 Cr App R 325, CA. Such a statement remains inadmissible notwithstanding that access to the solicitor is delayed by the police in exercise of their right to do so under the Police and Criminal Evidence Act 1984, s 58: *R v Hutton* (1988) The Times, 27 Oct, CA.

[109] See per Lord Lane CJ in *R v Duncan* (1981) 73 Cr App R 359, CA at 364.

[110] *R v Pearce* (1979) 69 Cr App R 365, CA at 369–70.

[111] (1981) 73 Cr App R 359.

by the Court of Appeal (*R v Hamand*[112]) and unanimously endorsed by the House of Lords (*R v Sharp*[113]), said:[114]

> Where a 'mixed' statement is under consideration by the jury in a case where the defendant has not given evidence, it seems to us that the simplest, and, therefore, the method most likely to produce a just result, is for the jury to be told that the whole statement, both the incriminating parts and the excuses or explanations, must be considered by them in deciding where the truth lies. It is, to say the least, not helpful to try to explain to the jury that the exculpatory parts of the statement are something less than evidence of the facts they state. Equally, where appropriate, as it usually will be, the judge may, and should, point out that the incriminatory parts are likely to be true (otherwise why say them?) whereas the excuses do not have the same weight.

The requirement to give such a direction on weight, it is submitted, is to introduce a new and different source of potential confusion for the jury. In *R v Rojas*[115] the Supreme Court of Canada refused to adopt the direction on the ground that in most circumstances expounding the rationale for an evidentiary rule may only serve to confuse the jury unnecessarily or risk encroaching unduly upon their role as fact finders. Such observations may be better left to the advocacy of counsel.

The principle established in *R v Duncan* applies whether the 'mixed' statement is a written statement or a record of questions and answers at an interview.[116] In the case of a suspect who asserts his innocence, his answers in interview will almost always contain *some* admissions of relevant fact, but statements will only be treated as 'mixed' for the purposes of the principle if they contain an admission of fact which is 'significant' in relation to an issue in the case, ie capable of adding some degree of weight to the prosecution case on an issue which is relevant to guilt.[117] The admission in interview of an ingredient of the offence will often constitute a significant admission.[118] However, there is no requirement that any act admitted be unlawful per se.[119] Whether a mixed statement is 'significant' in relation to an issue in the case can only be determined by reference to what happens at trial and, therefore, can only be finally resolved at the close of the evidence. In particular, the greater the reliance the prosecution place on the inculpatory parts of the statement at trial, the more likely it is that the jury should be told that the exculpatory parts are also evidence in the case.[120]

It remains unclear whether the principle applies if the statement is not relied on by the prosecution. On one view, the self-serving parts of the statement are only admissible for their truth if the prosecution elect to rely on the statement as containing an admission.[121] However, it is submitted that there are compelling reasons against any such additional requirement. As Butterfield J pointed out in *Western v DPP*,[122] whether a statement is mixed or not should not depend on the accident of what other evidence is available to the prosecution; and in cases

---

[112] (1985) 82 Cr App R 65, CA.
[113] [1988] 1 WLR 7. See also *R v Aziz* [1995] AC 41, HL.
[114] (1981) 73 Cr App R 359 at 365.
[115] [2008] SCC 56; [2009] Crim LR 130.
[116] *R v Polin* [1991] Crim LR 293, CA.
[117] *R v Garrod* [1997] Crim LR 445, CA. See also *R v Papworth* [2008] 1 Cr App R 439, CA.
[118] *R v Papworth* [2008] 1 Cr App R 439, CA.
[119] *R v McCleary* [1994] Crim LR 121, CA.
[120] *R v Papworth* [2008] 1 Cr App R 439, CA.
[121] See per Lord Steyn in *R v Aziz* [1995] AC 41, HL at 50.
[122] [1997] 1 Cr App R 474, DC at 484–5.

in which the statement is *not* relied on by the prosecution, the view advanced would mean reviving the unintelligible direction, repudiated in *R v Duncan*, to the effect that although the admission is evidence of the facts stated, the self-serving parts of the statement are only evidence of reaction.[123]

The common law rule relating to the admissibility of mixed statements as evidence of the matters stated is among the common law rules preserved by s 118 of the 2003 Act.[124]

Statements made on discovery of incriminating articles

In cases of handling and theft, if it is shown that the accused was found in possession of recently stolen goods, but failed to give a credible innocent explanation, the jury *may* infer guilty knowledge or belief and return a finding of guilt.[125] Any explanation which is given by the accused is admissible, if the accused testifies to the same effect, as evidence of consistency.[126]

Previous identification

Where, in criminal proceedings, a witness gives evidence identifying the accused as the person who committed the offence charged, evidence of a previous identification of the accused by that witness may be given, either by the witness himself or by any other person who witnessed the previous identification,[127] for example a police officer who conducted a formal identification procedure such as a video identification or an identification parade, as evidence of consistency.[128] Section 120(5) of the 2003 Act, when read in conjunction with section 120(1) and (4) of the 2003 Act, has extended the principle to cover a previous statement of a witness which identifies *or describes* a person, *object or place*, provided that the witness, while giving evidence, indicates that to the best of his belief, he made the statement and it states the truth. A statement received under s 120(5) is admitted as evidence of any matter stated, and will also be evidence of the witness's consistency. Section 120(5) is considered in Chapter 10. The text which follows relates to the common law principle.

In *R v Christie*[129] the accused was convicted of indecent assault on a boy. The boy gave unsworn evidence in which he described the assault, and identified the accused, but made no reference to any previous identification. The House of Lords, by a majority of five to two, held that both the boy's mother and a constable had been properly allowed to give evidence that shortly after the alleged act they saw the boy approach the accused, touch his sleeve, and identify him by saying, 'That is the man'. Evidence of the previous identification was admissible as evidence of the witness's consistency, 'to show that the witness was able to identify at the time' and 'to exclude the idea that the identification of the prisoner in the dock was an

---

[123] See generally Birch, 'The Sharp End of the Wedge: Use of Mixed Statements by the Defence' [1997] Crim LR 416.

[124] Section 118(1)5.

[125] See Ch 22, under **Presumptions, Definitions and classification, Presumptions of fact, The presumption of guilty knowledge**.

[126] See *R v Abraham* (1848) 3 Cox CC 430. For further authorities and discussion, see Gooderson 'Previous Consistent Statements' (1968) CLJ 64 at 70-73.

[127] For the difficulties which arise where the witness fails to identify the accused in court, having previously identified him outside court, see *R v Osbourne* and *R v Virtue* [1973] QB 678, CA and *R v Burke and Kelly* (1847) 2 Cox CC 295.

[128] The detailed rules governing the proper conduct of formal identification procedures, which are contained in the Code of Practice issued by the Home Secretary pursuant to the Police and Criminal Evidence Act 1984, s 66 are beyond the scope of this book. Failure on the part of the police to observe the provisions may be taken into account by the court when deciding whether to exclude identification evidence and by the jury when assessing the weight of such evidence (see Ch 3).

[129] [1914] AC 545.

afterthought or mistake'.[130] Evidence that a witness previously identified the accused from a photograph is also admissible for these purposes provided that the photograph does not come from police files or, if it does, cannot be identified as such.[131] Thus, evidence of identification from a photograph which forms part of an album of police photographs[132] or which shows the accused wearing prison clothes[133] should be excluded, unless the jury have been or will be made aware of the accused's record for some other good reason.[134] The accused should not be prejudiced by the jury being informed or allowed to suspect that he has previous convictions.[135]

The admissibility of evidence of previous identification of the accused has been justified on the ground that:

> In cases where there has been a considerable lapse of time between the offence and the trial, and where there might be a danger of the witness's recollection of the prisoner's features having become dimmed, no doubt it strengthens the value of the evidence if it can be shown that in the meantime, soon after the commission of the offence, the witness saw and recognized the prisoner.[136]

Dock identifications

The evidence of a witness who identifies the accused for the first time in court is properly treated with considerable suspicion. There are no safeguards of the kind offered by a formal identification procedure. There is the obvious danger stemming from delay. There is also the real risk of prejudice, because a witness, asked if he sees the person who committed the offence in court, might all too readily point to the person standing in the dock, overriding any doubts in his mind, especially in cases where he gave a description to the police, by the thought: 'Surely the police would not have brought the wrong person to court?'[137] For these reasons, it is undesirable to invite a witness to make a 'dock identification', that is to identify the accused for the first time in court;[138] the normal and proper practice should be to hold a formal identification procedure;[139] and the usual practice, in cases where there has been a

---

[130] Per Viscount Haldane LC in *R v Christie* [1914] AC 545 at 551.

[131] Such a photograph may also be used to show that between commission of the offence and arrest, the accused had strikingly changed his appearance and thereby thwarted an attempt by the identifying witness to pick him out of an identification parade: *R v Byrne and Trump* [1987] Crim LR 689, CA.

[132] *R v Wainwright* (1925) 19 Cr App R 52, CCA.

[133] *R v Dwyer* and *R v Ferguson* [1925] 2 KB 799, CCA. See also *R v Varley* (1914) 10 Cr App R 125, CCA.

[134] See, eg, *R v Allen* [1996] Crim LR 426, CA.

[135] But see also *R v Governor of Pentonville Prison, ex p Voets* [1986] 1 WLR 470, QBD: such photographs are admissible in law and their exclusion discretionary. The police should not show photographs, including that of a suspect, to potential witnesses where the suspect is already under arrest: *R v Haslam* (1925) 19 Cr App R 59, CCA. Such witnesses should not be shown photographs of an accused whom they will be asked to identify in court: *R v Dwyer* and *R v Ferguson* [1925] 2 KB 799, CCA. However, the police, if in doubt as to the identity of a criminal, may show photographs to potential witnesses in order to discover who the offender is: *R v Palmer* (1914) 10 Cr App R 77, CCA. See also *R v Crabtree* [1992] Crim LR 65, CA: it is permissible for officers to identify the accused from photographs taken as part of a surveillance operation and shown to them before the offence was committed. As to the rules to be observed when a witness is shown photographs for identification purposes, see paras 3.3 and 3.28 of, and Annex E to, Code D, the Code of Practice on Identification issued pursuant to the Police and Criminal Evidence Act 1984, s 66.

[136] Per Ferguson J in *R v Fannon* (1922) 22 SRNSW 427 at 430.

[137] See generally *Holland v Her Majesty's Advocate* [2005] HRLR 25, PC at [47].

[138] *R v Cartwright* (1914) 10 Cr App R 219, CCA.

[139] *Neilly v R* [2012] 2 Cr App R 248, PC at [31].

prior out-of-court identification, is to elicit evidence on this *before* asking a question such as, 'Is that person in court today?'

The making of a dock identification is not, by its very nature, incompatible with the right to a fair trial in Art 6(1) of the European Convention on Human Rights, but may be incompatible depending on all the circumstances of the case.[140] In *Tido v R*,[141] the Privy Council held that although a dock identification is not inadmissible per se, and that admission of such evidence is not to be regarded as permissible in only the most exceptional circumstances, a trial judge should always consider whether admission might imperil the fair trial of the accused. The judge should consider all the relevant circumstances, including any reason for not holding a formal identification procedure.[142] A dock identification may be justified if the suspect has refused to take part in a formal identification procedure,[143] but as was observed in *Tido v R*,[144] given the variety of formal identification procedures available in England and Wales, even if the accused is unwilling to participate, dock identifications are rare. A dock identification is justified if the identifying witness claims to recognize the suspect as a person he already knows well.[145] However, a formal identification procedure is necessary when the witness has seen the suspect only once, or on a few occasions, before.[146]

In *Tido v R*,[147] it was also held that where there has been a dock identification, the jury should always be given a careful direction as to the danger of relying on it and also a particular warning of the disadvantages to the accused of having been denied a formal identification procedure, including the possibility of an inconclusive result which the defence could have used to cast doubt on the accuracy of a subsequent identification. The jury should also be reminded of the obvious danger that an accused in the dock might automatically be assumed by even a well-intentioned witness to be the person who had committed the crime. Where a dock identification is made but not solicited by the prosecution, it is insufficient for the judge merely to direct the jury that such an identification is abnormal and unfair—they should probably be told to disregard it altogether.[148]

Although it has been held that it would be wrong to apply one approach to dock identifications for minor offences and another for more serious offences,[149] in *Barnes v Chief Constable of Durham*,[150] the Divisional Court held that dock identifications were customary in magistrates' courts, in relation to driving offences at least, and that if, in every case where the defendant did not distinctly admit driving there had to be a formal identification procedure, the whole process of justice in a magistrates' court would be severely impaired. This approach was followed in *Karia v DPP*,[151] a case of speeding and failing to produce insurance and other documents, where the court rejected a submission that *Barnes v Chief Constable of Durham*

[140] *Holland v Her Majesty's Advocate* [2005] HRLR 25, PC. See also *Young v Trinidad and Tobago* [2008] UKPC 27.

[141] [2011] 2 Cr App R 336, PC.

[142] *Neilly v R* [2012] 2 Cr App R 248, PC at [32].

[143] *R v John* [1973] Crim LR 113, CA.

[144] [2011] 2 Cr App R 336, PC at [22].

[145] See para 3.12(ii) of Code D and *R v France* [2012] UKPC 28.

[146] *R v Fergus* [1992] Crim LR 363, CA.

[147] [2011] 2 Cr App R 336, PC.

[148] *R v Thomas* [1994] Crim LR 128, CA.

[149] See *North Yorkshire Trading Standards Dept v Williams* (1994) 159 JP 383, DC.

[150] [1997] 2 Cr App R 505, DC.

[151] (2002) 166 JP 753, QBD.

could be distinguished on the basis that in that case the defendant had been arrested and interviewed, whereas Karia was summonsed and had had no opportunity to explain that he was not the driver.

Statements admissible as part of the res gestae

The common law principle of *res gestae*, which is considered in Chapter 12, renders admissible all those events and statements which may be said to constitute a part of a transaction which is in issue. For example, in *R v Fowkes*[152] the accused, charged with murder, was commonly known, in the circumstances somewhat unfortunately it may be thought, as 'the butcher'. The son of the deceased gave evidence that he was sitting in a room with his father and a police officer, that a face appeared at the window through which a shot was fired, and that he thought the face was that of the accused. Both the son and the police officer, who had not seen the face, were allowed to give evidence that the son, on seeing the face, had shouted, 'There's Butcher'. A statement forming part of the *res gestae* is admissible at common law as evidence of the matters stated and also as evidence of consistency insofar as it confirms testimony given by the witness to the same effect. In criminal proceedings the common law rules in this regard have been preserved by the 2003 Act.[153] In civil proceedings, a previous statement forming part of the *res gestae* may only be adduced with the leave of the court.[154]

Statements in documents used to refresh the memory and received in evidence

As we have seen earlier in this chapter, where a party, or counsel on his behalf, cross-examines a witness on a document used by him to refresh his memory, and goes beyond the parts relied upon by the witness, the document may be received in evidence. As we have also seen, in civil proceedings, statements in the document are admitted as evidence of the matters stated; and the same applies in criminal proceedings, provided that the statement was made, as opposed to verified, by the witness. Where such statements are received in evidence, they may also go to the consistency of the witness.

Unfavourable and hostile witnesses

The rule against a party impeaching the credit of his own witness

A party seeking to elicit evidence in support of his version of the facts in issue may call a witness who, in the witness box, fails to come up to proof or gives evidence in support of the other party's version of the facts in issue. A party thus disappointed, in order to remedy the situation, may understandably wish to change course and attack the credibility of the witness. The general rule at common law, however, is that a party is not permitted to impeach the credit of a witness he calls: the party may neither question the witness about, nor call evidence concerning, his bad character,[155] convictions, prior inconsistent statements, or bias. In short, if the witness gives adverse evidence, the party may not turn round and cross-examine him as if he were a witness for the opposite party: 'It would be repugnant to principle, and likely to lead to abuse, to enable

---

[152] (1856) The Times, 8 Mar, Assizes.

[153] Section 118(1)4.

[154] See the Civil Evidence Act 1995, s 6(2)(a) (see Ch 11).

[155] It appears that a party is permitted to adduce evidence of the witness's bad character where the evidence is relevant to an issue in the case but does not discredit him or his credibility in relation to the discrete issue on which he gives evidence: *R v Ross* [2008] Crim LR 306, CA.

a party, having called a witness on the basis that he is at least in general going to tell the truth, to question him or call other evidence designed to show that he is a liar.'[156]

Unfavourable witnesses

An unfavourable witness may be defined as a witness who, although he displays no hostile animus to the party calling him, fails to come up to proof or gives evidence unfavourable to the case of that party. At common law, a party is not permitted to impeach the credit of an unfavourable witness by any of the means outlined in the preceding paragraph but may call other witnesses to give evidence of those matters in relation to which the unfavourable witness failed to come up to proof. Thus in *Ewer v Ambrose*,[157] the defendant having called a witness to prove a partnership and the witness having testified to the contrary, it was held that while the defendant could not adduce general evidence to show that the witness was not to be believed on his oath, he was entitled to contradict him by calling other witnesses. If the rule were otherwise, undue importance would attach to the order in which witnesses are called. As Littledale J observed, 'if a party had four witnesses upon whom he relied to prove his case, it would be very hard that, by calling first the one who happened to disprove it, he should be deprived of the testimony of the other three'.

Hostile witnesses

A hostile witness is a witness who, in the opinion of the judge, shows no desire to tell the truth at the instance of the party calling him, to whom he displays a hostile animus.[158] In a civil case, it seems that a party may call a person even if he has shown signs that he is likely to be a hostile witness by refusing to make a statement.[159] In a criminal case, it appears that if a person refuses to assist the prosecution or court, or claims to be no longer able to remember anything, the judge has a discretion to hold a *voir dire* in order to decide whether to prevent him from being called.[160] However, it has also been held that the prosecution may call a person who has shown signs that he is likely to be a hostile witness, for example by retracting a statement, or making a second statement, prior to the trial.[161] In *R v Mazekelua*[162] the prosecution called a person who had shown every sign that he would be a hostile witness, had him treated as a hostile witness, and cross-examined him on the contents of a video recording of an interview that the judge had earlier ruled should not stand as his evidence-in-chief because it was not in the interests of justice for that to happen.[163] It has also been held that where an accused calls a witness to give evidence against a co-accused, he may, if appropriate, apply to have him treated as hostile notwithstanding that he was expected to resile from what he said previously, and the previous inconsistent statement, if

[156] Criminal Law Revision Committee, 11th Report, Cmnd 4991 (1972), para 162.

[157] (1825) 3 B&C 746. See also *Bradley v Ricardo* (1831) 8 Bing 57; cf Hamilton J in *Sumner and Leivesley v John Brown & Co* (1909) 25 TLR 745, Assizes.

[158] See Stephen, *Digest of the Law of Evidence* (12th edn, London, 1948) Art 147.

[159] See CPR r 32.9, whereby a party unable to obtain a witness statement may seek permission to serve a witness summary instead (see Ch 5).

[160] *R v Honeyghon and Sayles* [1999] Crim LR 221, CA. See also *R v Dat* [1998] Crim LR 488, CA.

[161] See *R v Mann* (1972) 56 Cr App R 750, CA; *R v Vibert* (21 Oct 1974, unreported), CA; and *R v Dat* [1998] Crim LR 488, CA.

[162] [2011] EWCA Crim 1458.

[163] See Youth Justice and Criminal Evidence Act 1999, s 27 (see Ch 5).

proved, will be evidence of the truth of its contents under s 119 of the Criminal Justice Act 2003.[164]

Although the question whether a witness is hostile is for the judge alone, the evidence and demeanour of the potentially hostile witness should usually be tested in the presence of the jury.[165] It is only in very exceptional cases that a *voir dire* should be held to decide whether or not a witness who has yet to be called might prove to be hostile.[166] Equally, once a witness has started to give his evidence, a *voir dire* before a decision on whether to treat him as hostile is only appropriate in exceptional circumstances, because the jury may see the witness apparently giving evidence in one frame of mind and then see a complete turn-around after events which have taken place in their absence.[167]

At common law a judge may allow cross-examination of a hostile witness by the party calling him.[168] An application to treat a witness as hostile may be made at any time during the witness's evidence, even at the late stage of re-examination.[169] The judge has a discretion whether to grant leave to cross-examine and his decision will seldom be challenged successfully on appeal.[170] In deciding whether a witness is not merely unfavourable but should be treated as hostile, the judge may take into account the attitude and demeanour displayed by the witness, his willingness to cooperate, and the extent to which any prior statement made by him is inconsistent with his testimony. If a hostile witness gives evidence contrary to an earlier statement, or fails to give the evidence expected, the party calling him and the trial judge should first consider inviting him to refresh his memory from material which it is legitimate to use for that purpose, and should not immediately proceed to treat him as hostile, unless he displays such an excessive degree of hostility that that is the only appropriate course.[171] In *R v Fraser* and *R v Warren*[172] Lord Goddard CJ went so far as to state, and it is perhaps best regarded as an over-statement, that if the prosecution have in their possession a previous statement 'in flat contradiction' of the witness's testimony, they are *entitled* to cross-examine and should apply for leave to do so.

If a witness is treated as hostile, the party calling him may ask leading questions[173] but may neither cross-examine him on his previous misconduct or convictions, nor adduce evidence to show that he is not to be believed on oath. At common law, it was doubtful whether the party could prove prior statements made by the witness and inconsistent with his testimony, a matter which is now governed by s 3 of the Criminal Procedure Act 1865.[174] Section 3 provides that:

---

[164] *R v Osborne* [2010] EWCA Crim 1981. Cf, in the case of a prosecution witness, *R v Dat* [1998] Crim LR 488, CA: the prosecution should limit the damage which might occur as a result of wide-ranging cross-examination on the previous statement. Section 119 of the 2003 Act is considered at nn 183–7.

[165] *R v Darby* [1989] Crim LR 817, CA. Cf *R v Jones* [1998] Crim LR 579, CA.

[166] *R v Olumegbon* [2004] EWCA Crim 2337.

[167] *R v Khan* [2003] Crim LR 428, CA.

[168] It appears that the party calling the witness retains the right to *re-examine* him on any new matters arising out of cross-examination by the other party to the action: *R v Wong* [1986] Crim LR 683 (Crown Court).

[169] *R v Powell* [1985] Crim LR 592, CA.

[170] *Rice v Howard* (1886) 16 QBD 681 and *Price v Manning* (1889) 42 Ch D 372, CA.

[171] *R v Maw* [1994] Crim LR 841, CA.

[172] (1956) 40 Cr App R 160, CCA.

[173] *R v Thompson* (1976) 64 Cr App R 96, CA.

[174] Section 3 applies to both civil and criminal proceedings. In civil proceedings the prior statement of any witness may with the leave of the court be admitted as evidence of the facts contained in it: see the Civil Evidence Act 1995, s 6(2)(a) (see Ch 11). The evidential status of a prior inconsistent statement of a hostile witness in civil proceedings is governed by the 1995 Act, s 6(3): see at n 182.

A party producing a witness shall not be allowed to impeach his credit by general evidence of bad character, but he may, in case the witness shall, in the opinion of the judge, prove adverse, contradict him by other evidence, or, by leave of the judge, prove that he has made at other times a statement inconsistent with his present testimony; but before such last mentioned proof can be given the circumstances of the supposed statement, sufficient to designate the particular occasion, must be mentioned to the witness, and he must be asked whether or not he has made such statement.

Section 3 was not drafted with felicity.[175] In *Greenough v Eccles*[176] it was held that the word 'adverse' in the section means 'hostile' and not 'unfavourable'. Bearing this in mind, the section may be analysed in terms of three rules governing a party's entitlement to discredit his own witness. The first is that he is not entitled to impeach the witness's credit by general evidence of his bad character. In other words, he may neither cross-examine the witness on his previous misconduct or convictions nor adduce evidence of a general nature to show that the witness is not to be believed on oath. This rule applies to both unfavourable and hostile witnesses and amounts to no more than a statutory restatement of the common law. The second rule, that the party may contradict the witness by other evidence, applies under the statute only to hostile witnesses. The section suggests that this rule does not apply to unfavourable witnesses, but in *Greenough v Eccles*, Williams and Willes JJ held that the section has not affected the rule at common law that a party may contradict an unfavourable witness by calling other witnesses.[177] The third rule, that the party may prove that the witness made at other times a statement inconsistent with his present testimony, applies only in the case of hostile witnesses.[178] In this connection, it remains to note that section 3 has not removed the common law right of the judge, in his discretion, to allow cross-examination when a witness proves hostile. In *R v Thompson*[179] the accused was convicted of indecent assault and incest. His daughter, who had given a statement to the police implicating him, was called into the witness box but stood mute of malice, refusing to give evidence. The judge gave leave to treat her as a hostile witness, and she was then asked leading questions and her former statement was put to her. On appeal, it was argued that since the girl had given no 'testimony', the case did not fall within s 3. Dismissing the appeal, Lord Parker CJ held it unnecessary to decide whether s 3 applied, since there was authority at common law for what the judge had done.[180]

If a hostile witness, on being cross-examined on a previous inconsistent statement, adopts and confirms the contents (or part of them), then what he says becomes part of his evidence and, subject to the assessment of his credibility by the tribunal of fact, it is capable of being accepted.[181] However, even if the witness does not admit the truth of the previous statement, it is admissible in both civil and criminal proceedings as evidence of the matters stated. Under

---

[175] 'Section 3 of the 1865 Act certainly requires thorough revision': Criminal Law Revision Committee, 11th Report, Cmnd 4991 (1972), para 161. See also cl 11 of the draft Bill.

[176] (1859) 5 CBNS 786, a decision on the construction of the Common Law Procedure (Amendment) Act 1856, s 22, which was repealed but re-enacted by the 1865 Act, s 3.

[177] See *Ewer v Ambrose* (1825) 3 B&C 746, at n 157.

[178] Acceptance by the witness that he made some parts of the statement and signed it may constitute proof for these purposes: see *R v Baldwin* [1986] Crim LR 681, CA.

[179] (1976) 64 Cr App R 96, CA.

[180] Reliance was placed upon *Clarke v Saffery* (1824) Ry&M 126 and *Bastin v Carew* (1824) Ry&M 127. It remains unclear whether if, in circumstances such as those in *R v Thompson*, the witness denies making the previous statement, it can be proved at common law.

[181] *R v Maw* [1994] Crim LR 841, CA. See also *R v Gibbons* [2009] Crim LR 197, CA.

s 1 of the 1995 Act, in civil proceedings evidence shall not be excluded on the ground that it is hearsay. Section 6(3) and (5) of the 1995 Act provide as follows:

(3) Where in the case of civil proceedings sections 3, 4 or 5 of the Criminal Procedure Act 1865 applies, which make provision as to—
   (a) how far a witness may be discredited by the party producing him,...this Act does not authorise the adducing of evidence of a previous inconsistent or contradictory statement otherwise than in accordance with those sections.
   ...
(5) Nothing in this section shall be construed as preventing a statement of any description referred to above from being admissible by virtue of section 1 as evidence of the matters stated.

As to criminal proceedings, s 119 of the 2003 Act provides as follows:

(1) If in criminal proceedings a person gives oral evidence and—
   (a) he admits making a previous inconsistent statement,[182] or
   (b) a previous inconsistent statement made by him is proved by virtue of section 3, 4 or 5 of the Criminal Procedure Act 1865 (c. 18),
   the statement is admissible as evidence of any matter stated of which oral evidence by him would be admissible.

In both civil and criminal cases, therefore, the tribunal of fact may accept as the truth of the matter the previous statement of a witness who has been declared hostile. However, s 119 does not apply to a witness who, once sworn, stands mute of malice because the provision only applies where a witness 'gives oral evidence'.[183]

Section 119 of the 2003 Act, by allowing previous inconsistent statements to be admitted for the truth of the matter stated, has changed the landscape of the criminal trial. Protection for defendants is contained in the court's powers to exclude evidence,[184] to direct an acquittal or discharge the jury where the evidence provided by the statement is unconvincing,[185] and to give appropriate directions to the jury.[186]

As to how the judge should direct a jury in relation to a witness's evidence and any prior statement that is admitted in evidence, in *R v Golder*,[187] which was decided prior to the 2003 Act, Lord Parker CJ said: 'When a witness is shown to have made previous statements inconsistent with the evidence given by that witness at the trial, the jury should...be directed that the evidence given at the trial should be regarded as unreliable.' The statement has since been cited with approval[188] but it may be doubted whether it was ever intended to be regarded as a rigid formula or precise form of words to be recited to juries in every case. It has since been said that it is not always necessary or appropriate, as an inflexible rule, to

---

[182] The effect of the 2003 Act, s 119(1)(a) is to make a prior statement admissible for the truth of the matter stated where a witness admits having made the prior statement without an application having been made to treat him as hostile. See *R v Joyce* [2005] EWCA Crim 1785.

[183] However, in such circumstances it would be open to the court to admit the statement as evidence of the truth of the matter stated under the 2003 Act, s 114(1)(d) (see Ch 10).

[184] See, eg, *R v Coates* [2008] 1 Cr App R 52, CA.

[185] The Criminal Justice Act 2003, s 125.

[186] See *R v Joyce* [2005] EWCA Crim 1798 and *R v Bennett* [2008] EWCA Crim 248.

[187] [1960] 1 WLR 1169, CCA at 1172–3. See also *R v Nyberg* (1922) 17 Cr App R 59, CCA and *R v Harris* (1928) 20 Cr App R 144, CCA.

[188] See *R v Oliva* [1965] 1 WLR 1028, CCA at 1036–7.

direct the jury that the evidence of the witness should be treated as unreliable.[189] In some cases, the evidence given by the witness may be regarded as reliable notwithstanding his prior inconsistent statement—for example when the witness is able to give a convincing explanation of the inconsistency. In *R v Joyce*,[190] which was decided under the 2003 Act, it was held that the jury may accept what the witness said either on the previous occasion or when giving evidence. As to the strength of the direction on the weight to be attached to the witness's evidence or previous statement, it is submitted that it should vary according to the particular circumstances of the case in question. The jury should not be directed that a previous statement is just as much evidence as the witness's testimony in court because the jury may take the direction to mean that they are obliged to give both the same evidential weight.[191] However, it is necessary for the jury to consider whether a hostile witness should be treated as creditworthy at all. The judge should give a clear warning about the dangers of a witness who has contradicted himself. It is insufficient to tell the jury to approach the evidence with great caution and reservation. Before the jury may rely on either the witness's evidence or prior statement as evidence of truth supporting the prosecution case, they must be sure that it is true.[192] However, where it is exculpatory of the accused, it is sufficient if the jury are persuaded that it may be true.[193] Where a witness is declared hostile but subsequently reverts to his original account, the trial judge is still obliged to warn the jury to approach his evidence with caution, the precise nature of the direction depending on the particular circumstances of the case.[194]

Under s 122 of the 2003 Act, if in a jury trial a statement made in a document is admitted under s 119 and produced as an exhibit, it must not accompany the jury when they retire to consider their verdict unless the court considers it appropriate or all parties agree that it should accompany them. The reason for the general rule in s 122 is the risk that the jury, by having the document in front of them, will place disproportionate weight on its contents as compared with the oral evidence. Normally, in the absence of some special feature of the document, it is sufficient for the judge to give a reminder in the summing-up of the contents of the statement and anything said by the witness about the document and the circumstances in which it was made. In cases where it is appropriate for the jury to take the document with them, the judge should not only give the general direction about a hostile witness, but also impress upon the jury the reason why they are being given the document and the importance of not attaching disproportionate weight to it simply because they have it before them.[195]

---

[189] *Driscoll v R* (1977) 137 CLR 517, High Court of Australia, a view supported by *R v Pestano* [1981] Crim LR 397, CA; *Alves v DPP* [1992] 4 All ER 787, HL; and *R v Goodway* [1993] 4 All ER 894, CA at 899. See also *R v Billingham* [2009] 2 Cr App R 341, CA. See also *Himanshu @ Chintu v State of NCT of Delhi* 2011 STPL (Web) 6 SC, 4 Jan 2011, Supreme Court of India: the fact that a prosecution witness is hostile does not prevent the prosecution from relying on his evidence to the extent that it supports their case.

[190] [2005] EWCA Crim 1785 at [29]–[30].

[191] *R v Billingham* [2009] 2 Cr App R 341, CA.

[192] See, eg, *R v Parvez* [2010] EWCA Crim 3229: where it is alleged that an earlier statement was retracted through fear, the proper direction is whether the jury are sure that the statement is true and was retracted through fear, in which case, subject to caution, they may act on it.

[193] *R v Billingham* [2009] 2 Cr App R 341, CA; see also *R v Maw* [1994] Crim LR 841, CA.

[194] *R v Greene* (2009) The Times, 28 Oct.

[195] *R v Hulme* [2007] 1 Cr App R 334, CA.

ADDITIONAL READING

Birch, 'The Sharp End of the Wedge: Use of Mixed Statements by the Defence' [1997] Crim LR 416.

Keane and Fortson, 'Leading Questions: A Critical Analysis' [2011] Crim LR 280.

Lewis, 'Delayed complaints in childhood sexual abuse prosecutions—a comparative evaluation of admissibility determinations and judicial warnings' (2006) 10 E&P 104.

Cross-examination and re-examination

7

Key issues

- When and why should a party to litigation be entitled to cross-examine a witness?

- Should an accused himself always be entitled to cross-examine a witness? If not, when should such cross-examination be prohibited?

- What is the object of cross-examination?

- What restrictions should be placed on the form of questioning in cross-examination?

- What are the consequences for a party to litigation who fails to cross-examine a witness?

- When and why is a party to litigation permitted to prove that a witness called by another party has made a prior inconsistent statement?

- In proceedings for sexual offences, when and why should questions or evidence concerning the previous sexual experiences of the complainant be allowed?

- If a witness denies a matter under cross-examination, when and why should the cross-examining party be permitted to call evidence in rebuttal?

- What is the object of re-examination?

Cross-examination

Cross-examination is the questioning of a witness, immediately after his examination-in-chief, by the legal representative of the opponent of the party calling him, or by the opposing party in person, and by the legal representative of any other party to the proceedings or by any other party in person.[1] Thus if an accused elects to testify, he will be open to cross-examination not only by the prosecution but also by a co-accused; and the co-accused is entitled to cross-examine him whether he has given evidence unfavourable to the co-accused or has merely given evidence in his own defence.[2] The order of cross-examination where two or more are jointly indicted and separately represented is the order in which their names appear on the indictment.[3]

Liability to cross-examination

The general rule is that all witnesses are liable to be cross-examined. If a witness dies before cross-examination, his evidence-in-chief is admissible, though little weight may attach to it.[4] If a prosecution witness, during cross-examination, becomes incapable through illness of giving further evidence, the judge may allow the trial to continue on the basis of the evidence already given, subject to an appropriate direction to the jury to acquit if they feel that the truncated cross-examination prevented them from judging fairly the witness's credibility.[5]

To the general rule that all witnesses are liable to cross-examination, there are three minor exceptions in the case of: (i) a witness who is not sworn, being called merely to produce a document;[6] (ii) a witness called by mistake, because he is unable to speak as to the matters supposed to be within his knowledge, where the mistake is discovered before the examination-in-chief has begun but after the witness has been sworn;[7] and (iii) a witness called by the judge, in which case neither party is entitled to cross-examine him without the leave of the judge, although such leave should be given if the evidence is adverse to either party.[8]

---

[1] Concerning the extent to which the judge may intervene, see *R v Sharp* [1994] QB 261, CA, *R v Roncoli* [1998] Crim LR 584, CA, and *R v Zarezadeh* [2011] EWCA Crim 271. Interventions which may raise an eyebrow do not necessarily result in an unfair trial: *R v Denton* [2007] All ER (D) 492 (Apr), [2007] EWCA Crim 1111. However, interventions carry the risk of depriving the judge of the advantage of calm and dispassionate observation and lengthy interrogation may so hamper his ability properly to evaluate and weigh the evidence as to impair his judgment and render the trial unfair: *Southwark London Borough Council v Kofi-Adu* [2006] HLR 33, CA.

[2] *R v Hilton* [1972] 1 QB 421, CA.

[3] *R v Barber* (1844) 1 Car&Kir 434; *R v Richards* (1844) 1 Cox CC 62.

[4] *R v Doolin* (1882) 1 Jebb CC 123, IR.

[5] *R v Stretton* and *R v McCallion* (1986) 86 Cr App R 7, CA. See also *R v Wyatt* [1990] Crim LR 343, CA. However, if the only direct evidence on one important part of the prosecution case is given by a witness who, at the end of his examination-in-chief, is unable to give further evidence, it is at least doubtful whether any direction to the jury, however strongly expressed, can overcome the powerful prejudice of his evidence going wholly untested by cross-examination: see *R v Lawless* (1993) 98 Cr App R 342, CA.

[6] *Summers v Moseley* (1834) 2 Cr&M 477. Nor may such a witness be cross-examined if he was sworn unnecessarily: *Rush v Smith* (1834) 1 Cr M&R 94.

[7] However, if counsel seeks to withdraw a witness who can give relevant evidence because he might also reveal other inconvenient matters, the witness is liable to cross-examination: *Wood v Mackinson* (1840) 2 Mood&R 273.

[8] *Coulson v Disborough* [1894] 2 QB 316, CA; *R v Cliburn* (1898) 62 JP 232, CCC. See also *R v Tregear* [1967] 2 QB 574, CA at 580.

Cross-examination by accused in person

Cross-examination may be conducted by a legal representative or by a party in person. In criminal cases, as a general rule, an unrepresented accused is entitled to cross-examine in person any witness called by the prosecution. However, there are common law restrictions on this rule, as well as statutory exceptions to it. As to the former, the judge is not obliged to give an unrepresented accused his head to ask whatever questions, at whatever length, he wishes;[9] and although he should not descend into the arena on behalf of the accused, it is generally desirable for the judge to ask such questions as he sees fit to test the reliability and accuracy of the witness.[10] Sections 34–39 of the Youth Justice and Criminal Evidence Act 1999 (the 1999 Act) protect three categories of witness from cross-examination by an accused in person.[11] Under s 34, no person charged with a sexual offence[12] may cross-examine in person the complainant, either in connection with the offence, or in connection with any other offence (of whatever nature) with which that person is charged in the proceedings. Under s 35, no person charged with one of a number of specified offences[13] may cross-examine in person a 'protected witness', either in connection with the offence, or in connection with any other offence (of whatever nature) with which that person is charged in the proceedings. A 'protected witness' is a witness[14] who (a) is the complainant or is alleged to have been a witness to the commission of the offence; and (b) either is a child or falls to be cross-examined after giving evidence-in-chief (i) by means of a video recording made for the purposes of s 27 of the 1999 Act (video-recorded evidence admitted as evidence-in-chief)[15] at a time when the witness was a child, or (ii) in any other way at any such time.[16]

Section 36 gives the court a general power, in a case where neither s 34 nor s 35 operates, to give a direction prohibiting the accused from cross-examining a witness in person.[17] Under s 36(2), such a direction may be given if it appears to the court that (a) 'the quality of evidence[18] given by the witness on cross-examination—(i) is likely to be diminished if

---

[9] *R v Brown* [1998] 2 Cr App R 364, CA.

[10] *R v De Oliveira* [1997] Crim LR 600, CA.

[11] As to the need for similar statutory protection in civil cases, see per Wood J in *H v L and R, Re* [2007] 2 FLR 162, Fam D.

[12] A 'sexual offence' is defined in s 62 as any offence under the Sexual Offences Act 2003, Pt 1 or any relevant superseded offence. 'Relevant superseded offence' means rape or burglary with intent to rape, an offence under any of ss 2–12 and 14–17 of the Sexual Offences Act 1956, an offence under the Mental Health Act 1959, s 128, an offence under the Indecency with Children Act 1960, s 1 (indecent conduct towards child under 14), and an offence under the Criminal Law Act 1977, s 54 (incitement of child under 16 to commit incest).

[13] The offences are any offence under any of ss 33–36 of the Sexual Offences Act 1956, the Protection of Children Act 1978, the Sexual Offences Act 2003, Pt 1, any of ss 1–32 of the Sexual Offences Act 1956, the Indecency with Children Act 1960, the Sexual Offences Act 1967, or the Criminal Law Act 1977, s 54 (s 35(3)(a)); and kidnapping, false imprisonment, or an offence under the Child Abduction Act 1984, s 1 or s 2, any offence under the Children and Young Persons Act 1933, s 1, and any offence (not already listed) which involves an assault on, or injury, or a threat of injury to, any person (s 35(3)(b), (c), and (d)).

[14] A 'witness' includes a witness who is a co-accused: s 35(5) and *R (S) v Waltham Forest Youth Court* [2004] 2 Cr App R 335, DC at [27].

[15] See Ch 5.

[16] Section 35(2). Child means, where the offence falls within s 35(3)(a), a person under the age of 18; or, where the offence falls within s 35(3)(b), (c), or (d), a person under the age of 14. See n 13.

[17] A 'witness', for these purposes, does not include a co-accused: s 36(4)(a).

[18] 'The quality of evidence' is to be construed in accordance with s 16(5) (s 36(4)(b)): see Ch 5, under **Witnesses in criminal cases, Special measures directions for vulnerable and intimidated witnesses.**

the cross-examination...is conducted by the accused in person, and (ii) would be likely to be improved if a direction were given...' and (b) it would not be contrary to the interests of justice.[19] Where an accused is prevented from cross-examining a witness in person under s 34, s 35, or s 36, the court must invite the accused to arrange for a legal representative to act for him for the purpose of the cross-examination, and if the invitation is not taken up, must consider whether it is necessary in the interests of justice for the witness to be cross-examined by a legal representative, chosen and appointed by the court, to represent the interests of the accused.[20]

The permitted form of questioning in cross-examination

The permitted form of questioning in cross-examination is most conveniently considered by reference to the objects of cross-examination. These are twofold. The cross-examiner will seek (i) to elicit evidence which supports his version of the facts in issue; and (ii) to cast doubt upon the witness's evidence. Before giving further consideration to these objects, it will be useful to note three general matters. First, there are special restrictions on the cross-examination of young and vulnerable witnesses and also of complainants in proceedings for sexual offences. These restrictions are considered later in this chapter. Second, a witness under cross-examination may be asked leading questions. Such questions may be asked even if he appears to be more favourable to the cross-examiner than to the party who called him, and whether the questions are directed to either the first or second of the two objects of cross-examination.[21] Third, all cross-examination is subject to an important general constraint which applies whether the questions to be put to the witness go to the matters in issue or to credit only. This is the discretion of the judge to prevent any questions which in his opinion are unnecessary, improper, or oppressive. Cross-examination, a powerful weapon entrusted to counsel, should be conducted with restraint and with a measure of courtesy and consideration to the witness.[22] Thus counsel will be restrained from embarking on lengthy cross-examination on matters that are not really in issue[23] and from framing his questions in such a way as to invite argument rather than elicit evidence on the facts in issue.[24] In criminal cases, entitlement to a fair trial is not inconsistent with proper judicial control over the use of time as part of the judge's responsibility to manage the trial.[25] It should not become a routine feature of trial management to impose time limits for cross-examination (or examination-in-chief), but if counsel indulges in prolix and repetitious questioning, judges are obliged to impose reasonable time limits; counsel has a duty to put his client's case fearlessly but also to avoid wasting time.[26] In civil proceedings, CPR r 32.1(3) bluntly provides that: 'The court may limit cross-examination.' When

---

[19] As to the matters to be taken into account, in deciding whether s 36(2)(a) applies, see s 36(3).

[20] Section 38(1)–(5). As to warning the jury to prevent prejudice to the accused, see s 39.

[21] *Parkin v Moon* (1836) 7 C&P 408.

[22] See per Sankey LC in *Mechanical & General Inventions Co Ltd v Austin* [1935] AC 346, HL at 360. See also the Code of Conduct of the Bar of England and Wales at para 708 and para 5.10, Written Standards for the Conduct of Professional Work.

[23] *R v Kalia* [1975] Crim LR 181, CA and *Mechanical & General Inventions Co Ltd v Austin* [1935] AC 346, HL at 359.

[24] See per Lord Hewart CJ in *R v Baldwin* (1925) 18 Cr App R 175, CCA. Thus counsel should not put to a witness what somebody else has said or is expected to say (at 178–9). Nor should the judge put such questions: *R v Wilson* [1991] Crim LR 838, CA.

[25] *R v Chaaban* [2003] Crim LR 658, CA and the Criminal Procedure Rules 2013, SI 2013/1554, paras 1.1(2)(e), 3.2(2)(e), and 3.2(3).

[26] *R v B* [2006] Crim LR 54, CA. See also para 6(v) (Controlling prolix cross-examination), Protocol for the control and management of heavy fraud and other complex criminal cases [2005] 2 All ER 429.

exercising this power, the judge must seek to give effect to the 'overriding objective',[27] which is to enable the court 'to deal with cases justly',[28] and in deciding how long cross-examination should last in the interests of justice, for both parties and the witness, the judge may take into account any medical condition which the witness may have.[29]

Cross-examination as to matters in issue

The questions of the cross-examiner are not restricted to matters proved in examination-in-chief but may relate to any fact in issue or relevant to a fact in issue. This does not mean that evidence which is otherwise inadmissible can become admissible by being put to a witness in cross-examination: the ordinary rules relating to the inadmissibility of certain types of evidence operate to prevent such evidence from being elicited in cross-examination as well as in examination-in-chief. Thus an accused cannot be cross-examined upon inadmissible confessions inconsistent with his testimony.[30] Similarly, a party is unable to admit an inadmissible hearsay statement contained in a document by handing it to a witness under cross-examination and requiring him to read it aloud. Counsel may, of course, properly produce the document to the witness and ask him if he accepts the contents as true,[31] and, if the witness does, the contents of the document become evidence in the case. However, if the witness does not accept the contents as true, it would be improper for counsel to request the witness to read aloud from the document, the contents of which remain inadmissible hearsay.[32]

The principle that an accused cannot be cross-examined by the *prosecution* in such a way as to reveal that he made a confession which has been ruled inadmissible also obtains in favour of any co-accused of the maker of such a confession.[33] However, where an accused has made a confession which has been ruled inadmissible but which is relevant to the defence of a co-accused, then if the accused gives evidence which is inconsistent with his statement, he may be cross-examined on it by the *co-accused*, provided that the judge directs the jury not to treat it as evidence of its maker's guilt.[34]

Cross-examination as to credit

Concerning the second object of cross-examination, at common law there is a wide variety of ways in which the cross-examining party may seek to cast doubt upon the witness's evidence-in-chief and to show that the witness ought not to be believed on his oath. He may cross-examine him about omissions or inconsistencies in previous statements, if either will affect

---

[27] CPR r 1.2.

[28] CPR r 1.1(1). See further Ch 2, under **Judicial discretion, Exclusionary discretion, Civil cases.**

[29] *Three Rivers District Council v Bank of England* [2005] CP Rep 46, CA.

[30] *R v Treacy* [1944] 2 All ER 229, CCA. See also *R v Thomson* [1912] 3 KB 19, CCA and *R v Windass* (1988) 89 Cr App R 258, CA (inadmissible hearsay); *Re P* [1989] Crim LR 897, CA (inadmissible complaint in a sexual case); and *R v Gray* [1998] Crim LR 570, CA (interview with a co-accused inadmissible as against the accused). In civil proceedings, see *Beare v Garrod* (1915) 85 LJKB 717, CA and *Sharp v Loddington Ironstone Co Ltd* (1924) 132 LT 229, CA.

[31] He should not, however, describe the nature or contents of the document to the court: see *R v Yousry* (1914) 11 Cr App R 13, CCA.

[32] *R v Gillespie* and *R v Simpson* (1967) 51 Cr App R 172, CA, applied in *R v Cooper* (1985) 82 Cr App R 74, CA; and *R v Cross* (1990) 91 Cr App R 115, CA.

[33] Per Winn J in *R v Rice* [1963] 1 QB 857, CCA at 868–9.

[34] *R v Rowson* [1986] QB 174, CA, followed in *Lui-Mei Lin v R* [1989] AC 288, PC and *R v Corelli* [2001] Crim LR 913, CA. See also *R v O'Boyle* (1990) 92 Cr App R 202, CA. The co-accused may also cross-examine prosecution witnesses on the confession if to do so will affect the cogency of the prosecution evidence against him: *R v Beckford* (1991) 94 Cr App R 43, CA. See also *R v Myers* [1998] AC 124, HL (Ch 13).

his likely standing with the tribunal of fact;[35] he may question him about his means of knowledge of the facts to which he has testified; he may challenge the quality of his memory[36] and his powers of perception; he may ask him about his unreliability by reason of any physical or mental disability; and he may ask him to explain any delay in reporting the offence[37] as well as any omissions, mistakes, or inconsistencies in his evidence insofar as they militate against his veracity or plausibility. As to omissions, eg, where an accused is charged with a sexual offence and asserts fabrication on the part of the complainant, he may be cross-examined as to what facts are known to him that might explain why the complainant would make a false accusation against him.[38] Questions about omissions or inconsistencies in previous statements, often relating to matters of less than central importance, are the stock-in-trade of cross-examination with a view to discrediting a witness by implying his unreliability or untruthfulness. However, as to omissions, research shows that, in the case of stressful events, central details are more likely to be remembered than peripheral details; equally, as to inconsistency, research shows that variability of memory is the norm, and can be exacerbated both by the impact of trauma, such as that experienced by victims of sexual assaults and, in the case of children, by under-developed communication skills.[39]

The cross-examining party may also ask questions about the witness's bad character and previous misconduct, including questions about previous convictions and questions with a view to showing his prejudice or bias. However, s 99 of the Criminal Justice Act 2003 (the 2003 Act) abolishes the common law rules governing the admissibility of evidence of 'bad character' in criminal proceedings and the intention appears to be to abolish not only the rules as to the introduction of such evidence, but also the rules governing cross-examination about conduct that comes within the statutory definition of 'bad character' in s 98 of the 2003 Act. The effect is that in criminal cases such cross-examination is only permitted if it comes within one of a number of specified categories of admissibility set out in s 100 (non-defendant's bad character) or s 101 (defendant's bad character). Evidence of bad character, for the purposes of these provisions, is evidence of, or a disposition towards, misconduct, other than evidence which 'has to do' with the alleged facts of the offence charged or evidence of misconduct in connection with the investigation or prosecution of that offence. Section 108 of the 2003 Act imposes an additional restriction in relation to offences committed by the accused when a child. Finally, under s 41 of the Youth Justice and Criminal Evidence Act 1999, in the case of

---

[35] He may do so even if evidence of the making of the statement would not be allowed because it is not 'relative to the subject matter of the indictment or proceeding' for the purposes of the Criminal Procedure Act 1865, s 4: *R v Funderburk* [1990] 1 WLR 587, CA. Section 4 of the 1865 Act is considered, in this chapter, under **Cross-examination, Previous inconsistent statements, Section 4 of the 1865 Act**.

[36] For a consideration of issues relating to memory as they arise in legal proceedings, see The British Psychological Society Memory and the Law Working Party, *Guidelines on Memory and the Law: Recommendations from the Scientific Study of Human Memory* (British Psychological Society, 2008).

[37] In *R v D* [2009] Crim LR 591, CA, it was recognized that the trauma of serious sexual assault may cause feelings of shame and guilt which might inhibit a person from making a complaint. The judge is therefore entitled to direct the jury as to how to approach the complainant's evidence so as to prevent them from coming to an unjustified conclusion as to her credibility, but he must be careful to do so in a measured and balanced way.

[38] *R v B* [2003] 1 WLR 2809, CA, preferring *R v T* [1998] 2 NZLR 257 (New Zealand Court of Appeal) to *R v Palmer* (1998) 193 CLR 1 (Australian High Court).

[39] See Ellison, 'Closing the credibility gap; The prosecutorial use of expert witness testimony in sexual assault cases' (2006) 9 E&P 239 at 241–8, which cross-refers to much of the psychological and other research literature.

sexual offences, except with the leave of the court, no question may be asked in cross-examination about any sexual behaviour of the complainant.[40]

Hobbs v Tinling[41] and *R v Sweet-Escott*[42] set out the general principles as to the propriety of cross-examining a witness as to his credit. They apply fully in civil proceedings but in criminal proceedings apply only insofar as the cross-examination relates to conduct which falls short of the statutory definition of 'bad character' in s 98 of the 2003 Act. In *Hobbs v Tinling*, Sankey LJ held that the court, in the exercise of its discretion to disallow questions as to credit in cross-examination, should have regard to the following considerations:

1. Such questions are proper if they are of such a nature that the truth of the imputation conveyed by them would seriously affect the opinion of the court as to the credibility of the witness on the matter to which he testifies.

2. Such questions are improper if the imputation which they convey relates to matters so remote in time, or of such a character, that the truth of the imputation would not affect, or would affect in a slight degree, the opinion of the court as to the credibility of the witness on the matter to which he testifies.

3. Such questions are improper if there is a great disproportion between the importance of the imputation made against the witness's character and the importance of his evidence.

In *R v Sweet-Escott* Lawton J posed the question: 'How far back is it permissible for advocates when cross-examining as to credit to delve into a man's past and to drag up such dirt as they can find there?' It was held that:

> Since the purpose of cross-examination as to credit is to show that the witness ought not to be believed on oath, the matters about which he is questioned must relate to his likely standing after cross-examination with the tribunal which is trying him or listening to his evidence.[43]

The effect of a party's failure to cross-examine

A party may decide that there is no need to cross-examine at all, especially if the witness in question has proved to be unfavourable or even hostile to the party calling him. A party's failure to cross-examine, however, has important consequences. It amounts to a tacit acceptance of the witness's evidence-in-chief. A party who has failed to cross-examine a witness upon a particular matter in respect of which it is proposed to contradict his evidence-in-chief or impeach his credit by calling other witnesses, will not be permitted to invite the jury or tribunal of fact to disbelieve the witness's evidence on that matter.[44] A cross-examiner who wishes to suggest to the jury that the witness is not speaking the truth on a particular matter must lay a proper foundation by putting that matter to the witness so that he has an opportunity of giving any explanation which is open to him.[45] The rule, however, is not absolute

---

[40] The restrictions in the 2003 Act are considered in Ch 17. The restriction in the 1999 Act, s 41 is considered, in this chapter, under **Cross-examination, Complainants in proceedings for sexual offences, The restriction**.

[41] [1929] 2 KB 1 at 51, CA.

[42] (1971) 55 Cr App R 316, Assizes.

[43] (1971) 55 Cr App R 316, Assizes at 320.

[44] Evidence to contradict a witness which was not put to the witness in cross-examination may still be admitted, provided that the witness is recalled and cross-examination of him reopened in order to put the new evidence to him: *R v Cannan* [1998] Crim LR 284, CA.

[45] *Browne v Dunn* (1893) 6 R 67, HL. See also *R v Hart* (1932) 23 Cr App R 202, CCA; *R v Bircham* [1972] Crim LR 430, CA; and *R v Fenlon* (1980) 71 Cr App R 307, CA.

or inflexible. Thus if it is proposed to invite the jury to disbelieve a witness on a matter, it is not always necessary to put to him explicitly that he is lying, provided that the overall tenor of the cross-examination is designed to show that his account is incapable of belief.[46] In other cases, the story told by a witness may be so incredible that the matter upon which he is to be impeached is manifest, and in such circumstances it is unnecessary to waste time in putting questions to him upon it.[47] The most effective cross-examination in such a situation would be, in the words of Lord Morris, 'to ask him to leave the box'. The rule has also been held to be unsuitable in the case of proceedings in magistrates' courts.[48] It could be argued[49] that the rule should not apply in any criminal case, because there is no obligation on the accused to put his case by adducing evidence, but there is no authority to that effect. It could also be argued that the rule requires modification in the case of the cross-examination of a young child, because of the real possibility that the child will assent to what is suggested to please or to bring the questioning to an end, or a speedier end, making it very difficult to tell whether he is truly changing his account or just taking the line of least resistance. In the case of such assent on the part of a child appearing for the prosecution, it has been said that it may lead to a successful submission of no case to answer, where the evidence, taken at its highest, is such that no jury could safely be sure of guilt, but not where the jury can conclude, particularly in the light of other evidence, that the child was not agreeing in any meaningful way.[50]

Cross-examination on documents

In civil proceedings, where a witness is called to give evidence at trial, he may be cross-examined on his witness statement,[51] whether or not the statement or any part of it was referred to during his evidence-in-chief.[52] Cross-examining counsel may also put to an opposing witness a statement taken on behalf of the cross-examiner's own client, but may not, it seems, cross-examine a witness called by an opposing party by reference to a statement of another witness who may or may not be called in the future by that opposing party or by someone other than the party on whose behalf the cross-examination is being conducted.[53]

The law relating to the cross-examination of a witness upon a previous statement made by him relative to the subject matter of the indictment or proceeding and inconsistent with his testimony is governed by ss 4 and 5 of the Criminal Procedure Act 1865 (the 1865 Act).[54] The common law and statutory rules on the cross-examination of a witness upon a document used by him to refresh his memory are considered in Chapter 6.

So far as other documents are concerned, there is an obscure common law rule that, where a party calls for and inspects a document in the possession of another party, that other party may require him to put it in evidence.[55] It is submitted that the rule is obsolete in both

---

[46] *R v Lovelock* [1997] Crim LR 821, CA.

[47] *Browne v Dunn* (1893) 6 R 67, HL.

[48] *O'Connell v Adams* [1973] Crim LR 313, DC. See also *Wilkinson v DPP* [2003] EWHC 865 (Admin).

[49] As in *R v Livistis* [2004] NSWCCA 287.

[50] *R v W* [2010] EWCA Crim 126.

[51] See Ch 5.

[52] CPR r 32.11.

[53] *Fairfield-Mabey Ltd v Shell UK Ltd* [1989] 1 All ER 576, QBD, a decision on an earlier version of the rules.

[54] Sections 4 and 5 are considered, in this chapter, under **Cross-examination**, **Previous inconsistent statements**, **Section 4 of the 1865 Act** and **Section 5 of the 1865 Act**.

[55] *Stroud v Stroud* [1963] 1 WLR 1080, P, D and Admlty, relying on *Calvert v Flower* (1836) 7 C&P 386.

civil proceedings, given the combined effect of the law on disclosure and the provisions of the Civil Evidence Act 1995, and criminal proceedings, given the hearsay provisions of the Criminal Justice Act 2003, and should be abolished.[56]

Previous inconsistent statements

If it is put to a witness, in cross-examination, that he has made a previous oral or written statement inconsistent with his testimony, and the witness admits that he has made such a statement, no further proof of the making of the statement is needed or permitted.[57] However, if the witness denies making the statement, or does not distinctly admit that he made it, and the statement is 'relative to the subject matter of the indictment', then it may be proved against him. The proof of such a statement in both civil and criminal proceedings is governed by ss 4 and 5 of the 1865 Act. Section 5 applies only to written statements, whereas s 4 applies to both oral and written statements.[58]

Section 4 of the 1865 Act

Section 4 provides that:

> If a witness, upon cross-examination as to a former statement made by him relative to the subject matter of the indictment or proceeding, and inconsistent with his present testimony, does not distinctly admit that he has made such a statement, proof may be given that he did in fact make it; but before such proof can be given, the circumstances of the supposed statement, sufficient to designate the particular occasion, must be mentioned to the witness, and he must be asked whether or not he has made such statement.

This section assumes, correctly, the existence of a common law right to cross-examine a witness about a former inconsistent statement. It is not confined to previous statements made on oath.[59] The section refers to a witness who 'does not distinctly admit' his previous statement and accordingly applies not only to a witness who clearly denies the statement but also to a witness who, neither denying nor admitting the statement, is equivocal, asserts that he has no recollection of it, or refuses to answer.

Whether a statement is 'relative to the subject matter of the indictment or proceeding' is a matter within the discretion of the judge.[60] In *R v Funderburk*[61] F was charged with counts of sexual intercourse with a girl of 13. She gave evidence of a number of acts of intercourse with F, and her evidence of the first act clearly described the loss of her virginity. The defence claimed that she was lying and in order to explain how a girl of her age, if lying, could have given such detailed and varied accounts of the acts of intercourse, wished to show that she was sexually experienced and had either transposed to F experiences with others or fantasized about experiences with F. They wished (a) to put to her that she had told a Miss P that, before the first incident complained of, she had had sexual intercourse with two men; and, if she denied making this previous inconsistent statement, (b) to call P to prove the conversation. As to (a), it was held that

---

[56] See further Criminal Law Revision Committee, 11th Report, Cmnd 4991 (1972), para 223 and cl 29 of the draft Bill.

[57] *R v P (GR)* [1998] Crim LR 663, CA.

[58] *R v Derby Magistrates' Court, ex p B* [1996] AC 487, HL, per Lord Taylor CJ at 498.

[59] *R v Hart* (1957) 42 Cr App R 47, CCA; *R v O'Neill* [1969] Crim LR 260, CA.

[60] See per Veale J in *R v Bashir and Manzur* [1969] 1 WLR 1303, Assizes at 1306.

[61] [1990] 1 WLR 587, CA. Cf, *sed quaere, R v Gibson* [1993] Crim LR 453, CA.

the proper test for cross-examination as to credit was not the test set out in the 1865 Act, but that suggested by Lawton LJ in *R v Sweet-Escott*,[62] and that the cross-examination should have been allowed because the jury might then have wished to reappraise the girl's evidence about the loss of her virginity. As to (b), it was held that the conversation, if denied, could have been proved, because the previous statement did not merely go to credit but was also 'relative to the subject matter of the indictment': where the disputed issue is a sexual one between two persons in private, the difference between questions going to credit and questions going to the issue is reduced to vanishing point.[63] This principle, as we shall see, is not confined to sexual cases.[64]

Section 5 of the 1865 Act

Unlike s 4, s 5 applies only to previous written statements. It provides that:

> A witness may be cross-examined as to previous statements made by him in writing or reduced into writing relative to the subject-matter of the indictment or proceeding, without such writing being shown to him; but if it is intended to contradict such witness by the writing, his attention must, before such contradictory proof can be given, be called to those parts of the writing which are to be used for the purpose of so contradicting him; provided always, that it shall be competent for the judge, at any time during the trial, to require the production of the writing for his inspection, and he may thereupon make such use of it for the purposes of the trial as he may think fit.

Section 5 expressly permits the cross-examination of a witness about a previous statement contained in a document without that document being shown to him, but because the judge, pursuant to s 5, may require production of the document and make such use of it as he may think fit, the cross-examining party must have the document with him even if he does not intend to contradict the witness with it.[65] If that party wishes to contradict the witness, he should, without reading the contents of the document aloud, hand it to the witness, direct his attention to the relevant part of its contents, ask him to read that part of the document to himself and then inquire whether he still wishes to stand by the evidence which he has given. If the witness adopts the previous statement, it becomes part of his evidence, which has therefore changed, and to that extent his credibility will have been impeached. If the witness adheres to his original evidence, there is no obligation on the cross-examining party to put the document in evidence, a course which he may well wish to avoid if the discrepancy is minor or the document, taken as a whole, tends to confirm rather than contradict the witness.[66] The cross-examining party, therefore, may simply accept the answer given and move on to some other matter. However, if the cross-examining party does wish to contradict the witness, he must then prove the document and put it in evidence.[67] After reading aloud the relevant parts of the previous statement, or inviting the witness to do so, the cross-examining party will put it to the witness that the truth of the matter is contained in the earlier statement as opposed to his evidence. Once the document has been put in evidence, the tribunal of fact may inspect it in its entirety,

---

[62] (1971) 55 Cr App R 316, CA (see nn 42 and 43).

[63] See also *R v Nagrecha* [1997] 2 Cr App R 401, CA; and cf *R v Neale* [1998] Crim LR 737, CA.

[64] See, in this chapter, under **Cross-examination, Finality of answers to collateral questions**.

[65] *R v Anderson* (1930) 21 Cr App R 178, CCA.

[66] For an example of a case where the admission of a prior inconsistent statement must have been, at best, a mixed blessing, see *R v Askew* [1981] Crim LR 398, CA, where defence counsel cross-examined the victim of an alleged rape on a statement made to the police in which she had incriminated the appellant. But see *R v Beattie* (1989) 89 Cr App R 302, CA (see n 68).

[67] Per Channell B in *R v Riley* (1866) 4 F&F 964; *R v Wright* (1866) 4 F&F 967.

looking at those passages, if any, which are consistent, as well as those which are inconsistent with the evidence given by the witness. However, although the *whole* document may be put before the jury, because under s 5 the judge may 'make such use of it for the purposes of the trial as he may think fit', he has a discretion to permit the jury to see only those parts on which the cross-examination was based, and not other parts relating to other unconnected matters.[68]

Admissibility as evidence of the matter stated

Where a prior inconsistent statement has been put in evidence under s 4 or s 5 of the 1865 Act, in both civil and criminal proceedings it is admissible not merely as evidence of inconsistency going to credit, but also as evidence of the matters stated. Under s 1 of the Civil Evidence Act 1995, in civil proceedings evidence shall not be excluded on the ground that it is hearsay. Section 6(3) and (5) of the 1995 Act provide as follows:

> (3) Where in the case of civil proceedings section…4 or 5 of the Criminal Procedure Act 1865 applies, which make provision as to—
>
> …
>
> (b) the proof of contradictory statements made by a witness, and
> (c) cross-examination as to previous statements made in writing,
> this Act does not authorise the adducing of evidence of a previous inconsistent or contradictory statement otherwise than in accordance with those sections.…
>
> (5) Nothing in this section shall be construed as preventing a statement of any description referred to above from being admissible by virtue of s 1 as evidence of the matters stated.

As to criminal proceedings, s 119(1) of the Criminal Justice Act 2003, which is considered further in Chapter 10, provides as follows:

> (1) If in criminal proceedings, a person gives oral evidence and—
> (a) he admits making a previous inconsistent statement, or
> (b) a previous inconsistent statement made by him is proved by virtue of section 3, 4 or 5 of the Criminal Procedure Act 1865,
> the statement is admissible as evidence of any matter stated of which oral evidence by him would be admissible.

In both civil and criminal cases, therefore, the tribunal of fact will have to decide whether the truth is to be found in what the witness said on oath, in what he said in the previous statement but denied on oath, or is to be found elsewhere because neither version can be accepted as the truth of the matter.[69] By allowing a previous inconsistent statement to be put before the tribunal of fact for the truth of the matter stated, s 119 of the 2003 Act has introduced a significant change to criminal proceedings which can operate unfairly to the prejudice of the accused. Protection is contained in the court's powers to exclude evidence,[70] to direct an acquittal, or discharge the jury where the evidence provided by the statement is unconvincing,[71] and to give appropriate directions to the jury.[72]

---

[68] *R v Beattie* (1989) 89 Cr App R 302, CA.

[69] In criminal proceedings, before the jury may rely on either the witness's evidence or prior statement as evidence of truth supporting the prosecution case, they must be sure that it is true. Where it is exculpatory of the defendant, it is sufficient if the jury are persuaded that it *may* be true: *R v Billingham* [2009] 2 Cr App R 341, CA.

[70] See, eg, *R v Coates* [2008] 1 Cr App R 52, CA.

[71] The 2003 Act, s125.

[72] See *R v Joyce* [2005] EWCA Crim 1798 and *R v Bennett* [2008] EWCA Crim 248.

Young and vulnerable witnesses

Children and vulnerable witnesses, including people with learning disabilities or disabilities of the mind, older adults, victims of sexual assaults and those who have experienced a traumatic event, have particular needs when appearing as witnesses. Furthermore, traditional cross-examination techniques can confuse such witnesses, reducing their ability to understand the questions and the accuracy of their answers.[73] There have been a number of relatively recent developments by way of belated recognition of these matters.

In 2013, the Lord Chief Justice announced that only judges specially trained by the Judicial College will be used for cases involving 'significantly vulnerable' witnesses or serious sex cases likely to last more than ten days.[74]

Concerning children, the *Judicial College Bench Checklist: Young Witness Cases*[75] seeks to ensure that young witnesses give their 'best evidence' and lists the various matters to be addressed at the first hearing in a magistrates' court or the preliminary or plea and case management hearing in the Crown Court.[76] Included in the list are the directions that may be given to the advocates appearing for both sides at a 'ground rules' discussion. Many of the directions relate to both examination-in-chief and cross-examination and are considered in Chapter 6. The list includes the following three additional directions, which relate to cross-examination.

1. Avoid types of question which may produce unreliable answers. 'Tag' questions are particularly complex. A 'tag' question is a positive or negative statement followed by a question inviting acceptance that the statement is true, such as 'He was kind to you, wasn't he?' and 'He didn't touch you, did he?' The question should be put more directly, eg 'Did Jim touch you?' and, if the answer is 'Yes', 'How did Jim touch you?' (using Jim's name and not the pronoun 'he').

2. Avoid allegations of misconduct without reasonable grounds. Being accused of lying, particularly if repeated, may cause a child to give inaccurate answers or to agree simply to bring questioning to an end.

3. In putting the defence case to younger children, inform the jury of the evidence believed to undermine credibility, which does not necessarily need to be covered in detail in cross-examination.

Concerning the third direction, the Checklist refers to *R v Barker*,[77] where Lord Judge CJ said that: '...the advocate may have to forego much of the kind of contemporary cross-examination which consists of no more than comments on matters which will be before the jury in any event from different sources...Comment on the evidence, including comment on evidence which may bear adversely on the credibility of the child, should be addressed after the child has finished giving evidence'.[78]

---

[73] On the need for new systems for the training and accreditation of advocates in this respect, see Keane, 'Cross-examination of vulnerable witnesses—towards a blueprint for re-professionalisation' (2012) 16 E&P 153.

[74] See (2013) NLJ 16 August, p 5.

[75] Accessible at <www.judiciary.gov.uk/publications-and-reports/guidance/2012/jc-bench-checklist-young-wit-cases>.

[76] For similar provision in family proceedings, see Family Justice Council, *Guidelines in relation to children giving evidence in family proceedings*, accessible at <www.judiciary.gov.uk/NR/rdonlyres/C4F34729-B530-485F-9 0E3-987202297B02/0/FJC Guidelines in relation children giving evid in family procs Dec2011.pdf>.

[77] [2012] EWCA Crim 4.

[78] Which has been taken to mean, in the case of important inconsistencies at any rate, immediately after the child has given evidence: *R v Wills* [2012] 1 Cr App R 2 at [39].

The Checklist also refers to the further and more detailed guidance provided by Plotnikoff and Woolfson in *Measuring Up? Evaluating implementation of Government commitments to young witnesses in criminal proceedings, Annexes A and B*.[79] That guidance states that prefatory phrases such as 'I suggest to you that...' and 'Isn't it a fact that...' are wholly inappropriate for children, because when an adult in a powerful position formally suggests that something is a fact, it becomes extremely difficult for children—even those aged 11 and 12—to know how to disagree if necessary. The guidance also says that tag questions of all kinds should be avoided, because they are one of the most powerfully suggestive forms of speech and children often answer 'Yes' to a negative 'tag' question because it indicates cooperation and is often perceived to be the answer that the adult wants.[80]

The Checklist also recommends judicial monitoring of the questioning of young witnesses with a view to ensuring that the tenor, tone, language, and duration of the questioning is developmentally appropriate to the particular child, preventing questioning that lacks relevance or is repetitive, oppressive, or intimidating, and identifying possible difficulties in understanding and asking the advocate to re-phrase.

In *R v Wills*,[81] a number of observations were made that appear to have been intended to apply in respect of both children and vulnerable witnesses: limitations on cross-examination must be clearly defined and one way of achieving this, as suggested in the report of the Advocacy Training Council (ATC), *Raising the Bar: The handling of vulnerable witnesses, victims and defendants in court*[82] is for a protocol to be drafted for use by advocates and the trial judge concerning the matters set out in para 15 of Pt 5 of the report; where appropriate, the judge, in fairness to the accused, should explain the limitations to the jury and the reasons for them; there is a duty on the judge to ensure that limitations on cross-examination are complied with; and if counsel fails to comply, it is important that the judge immediately gives a relevant direction to the jury, both for their benefit and for that of any co-accused. Paragraph 15 of Pt 5 of the ATC report sets out a list of topics that the protocol may cover, including such matters as how questions should be formulated, what pauses may be required between questions, whether questions should be written down and given to the witness in addition to being put orally, and how the jury should be directed about the witness.

In the case of a child or vulnerable witness, counsel cross-examining may be properly prevented from challenging the evidence of the witness in the traditional way, including putting his party's case, but only in appropriate circumstances and subject to an appropriate direction to the jury. In *R v E*,[83] E was convicted of cruelty to C, aged 5 at the time of the offence and 6½ by the time of the trial, by punching her in the stomach. E denied causing C's injuries. C's *Achieving Best Evidence* interview, in which she said that she had been punched, was admitted in evidence. However, there was also evidence from C that she had fallen out of bed and had been thrown to the floor by another girl. She also said that she never fell out of bed and denied the incident involving the other girl. There was evidence from E that he had been told by a neighbour that C had fallen down some steps. Two medical experts were called in

[79] Accessible at <www.nspcc.org.uk/Inform/research/Findings/measuring_up_wda66048.html>.

[80] Additional guidance on how to question vulnerable witnesses and how to conduct a 'ground rules' hearing are to be found on *The Advocate's Gateway* website (<www.theadvocatesgateway.org>) and in the Criminal Bar Association's film, *A Question of Practice*, accessible at <www.criminalbar.com>.

[81] [2012] 1 Cr App R 16 at [36]–[39].

[82] Accessible at <www.advocacytrainingcouncil.org/images/word/raising%20the%20bar.pdf>.

[83] [2011] EWCA Crim 3028.

support of the prosecution case as to the likely cause of the injuries. The trial judge directed counsel for E that, in cross-examination of C, he should not put the defence case to her, nor challenge her about it. The jury were told about this direction and the reason for it. They were also directed 'to make proper fair allowances for the difficulties faced by the defence in asking questions'. On appeal it was submitted that the trial became, and had the appearance of being, one-sided, because defence counsel could not put the essentials of his case nor explore inconsistencies, credibility, and reliability, for example by putting to C that she had lied to those who had questioned her. The appeal was dismissed. The jury were fully aware of E's case and knew from cross-examination of both C and the expert witnesses that the defence were exploring alternative causes for C's injuries. The judge had explained to the jury his decision on the limitations on cross-examination and asked them to make proper and fair allowances for the difficulties faced by the defence. The right to a fair trial had not been compromised by preventing defence counsel from putting to C that E had not punched her in the stomach, a confrontation that would have confused her. In any event, the Crown were far from wholly reliant on C's evidence, having strong supporting evidence from the experts and evidence that when C became poorly, she was in E's care.[84]

Complainants in proceedings for sexual offences

The rationale

In cases of rape and other sexual offences, whether, and to what extent, evidence may be adduced, or the complainant cross-examined, by or on behalf of the accused, about her or his sexual experience with the accused or any other person, is now governed by ss 41–43 of the Youth Justice and Criminal Evidence Act 1999. These provisions, which restrict the use that the accused can make of evidence of the complainant's sexual history, reflect a recognition that it is bad for society if victims of sexual crimes do not complain, for fear that they will be harassed unfairly at trial by questions about their previous sexual experiences, because in consequence the guilty may escape justice. The intention underlying the provisions is also to counter what in the Canadian jurisprudence has been described as the twin myths that unchaste women are more likely to consent to intercourse and in any event are less worthy of belief.[85] Lord Steyn, in the leading case of *R v A (No 2)*, said:[86]

> Such generalized, stereotyped and unfounded prejudices ought to have no place in our legal system. But even in the very recent past such defensive strategies were habitually employed. It resulted in an absurdly low conviction rate in rape cases. It also inflicted unacceptable humiliation on complainants in rape cases.

Prior to the 1999 Act, a distinction was drawn between evidence of previous sexual experiences with the accused, which was admissible as rendering it more likely that the complainant consented on the occasion under investigation, and evidence of previous sexual experiences with others, which, under s 2 of the Sexual Offences (Amendment) Act 1976, now repealed, was only admissible if the judge was satisfied that it would be unfair to the accused to refuse its

---

[84] As to the correctness of the decision and how use could have been made of evidential human rights norms developed under Art 6.1 and 6.3(d) of the European Convention on Human Rights, see Keane, 'Towards a Principled Approach to the Cross-examination of Vulnerable Witnesses' [2012] Crim LR 407.

[85] See per McLachlin J in *R v Seaboyer* [1991] 2 SCR 577 (Supreme Court of Canada) at 604 and per Lords Steyn and Hutton in *R v A (No 2)* [2002] 1 AC 45, HL at [27] and [147] respectively.

[86] [2002] 1 AC 45, HL at [27].

admission. No such distinction exists under the 1999 Act, but a number of new and difficult distinctions have been introduced and have given rise to lively academic debate.[87] However, the impact of the provisions of the Act on the use of sexual history evidence appears to have been limited and the conviction rate for rape continued to fall after their implementation; there is certainly scope for strengthening the legislation.[88]

The restriction

Section 41(1) of the 1999 Act provides as follows:

(1) If at a trial a person is charged with a sexual offence, then, except with the leave of the court—
   (a) no evidence may be adduced, and
   (b) no question may be asked in cross-examination, by or on behalf of any accused at the trial, about any sexual behaviour of the complainant.

Section 41 applies to a number of other proceedings, as it applies to a trial, including any hearing held, between conviction and sentencing, for the purposes of deciding matters relevant to the court's decision as to how the accused is to be dealt with, and the hearing of an appeal; and references in s 41 to a person charged with an offence accordingly include a person convicted of an offence.[89] Under s 62, a 'sexual offence', for the purposes of s 41, means any offence under Pt 1 of the Sexual Offences Act 2003[90] or any 'relevant superseded offence'.[91] 'Sexual behaviour' is defined in s 42(1)(c), which provides as follows:

(c) 'sexual behaviour' means any sexual behaviour or other sexual experience, whether or not involving any accused or other person, but excluding (except in s 41(3)(c)(i) and (5)(a)) anything alleged to have taken place as part of the event which is the subject matter of the charge against the accused.

Such a definition, it is submitted, covers not only physical advances of a sexual nature, but also verbal advances.[92] The definition covers the viewing of pornography, sexually charged internet messaging and answering questions in a sexually explicit quiz.[93] It also covers sexual behaviour or sexual experience even if it does not involve any other person, for example the use of a vibrator, which could be relevant as evidence of the possible cause of the ruptured state of a complainant's hymen.[94] Whether behaviour or experience is 'sexual' cannot depend upon the perception of the complainant, because that would result in many vulnerable people, including children and those with learning difficulties, losing the protection of s 41.[95]

---

[87] For relevant articles, see under **Additional Reading** at the end of this chapter.

[88] For an evaluation of the impact of s 41 and recommendations for improvement, see the study commissioned by the Home Office, Kelly et al, *Section 41: an evaluation of new legislation limiting sexual history evidence in rape trials*, Home Office Online Report 20/06. Cf Wolchover and Heaton-Armstrong, 'Debunking rape myths' (2008) 158 NLJ 117.

[89] Section 42(3).

[90] See also s 42(1)(d) and (2).

[91] See n 12.

[92] See *R v Hinds* [1979] Crim LR 111 (Crown Court) and *R v Viola* [1982] 1 WLR 1138, CA, both decided under the Sexual Offences (Amendment) Act 1976.

[93] *R v Ben-Rejab* [2012] 1 Cr App R 35, CA.

[94] Cf *R v Barnes* [1994] Crim LR 691, CA.

[95] *R v E* [2005] Crim LR 227, CA.

In *R v B*[96] it was held that there is no difference in substance between questions of a female complainant about her suggested sexual habits or promiscuity or frequency of casual sexual engagement and questions of a male complainant about his suggested homosexuality and casual homosexual encounters. In each case the questions are predicated on the proposition that previous consent is evidence of present consent and fall squarely within the restriction in s 41(1).

False statements or failure to complain

In *R v T*[97] it was held that, normally, questions or evidence about the complainant's past false statements about sexual assaults, or about a failure to complain about the assault which is the subject matter of the charge at the time when she complained about sexual assaults by others, are not 'about' any sexual behaviour of the complainant, because they relate not to her sexual behaviour but to her past statements or her past failure to complain, and the purpose of the 1999 Act was not to exclude such evidence. However, it was also held, *per curiam*, that if the defence wish to put questions about previous false complaints, they should seek a ruling from the judge that s 41 does not exclude them. It would be improper to put such questions as a device to smuggle in evidence about the complainant's past sexual behaviour. In any such case, the defence must have a proper evidential basis for asserting that the previous statement was both made and untrue. Without such a basis, the questions are not about lies but about sexual behaviour within the meaning of s 41(1).[98] Concerning falsity, in *R v M*[99] it was held that a 'proper evidential basis' is less than a strong factual foundation for concluding that the previous complaint was false, but must comprise some material from which that conclusion can properly be reached. Similarly, it has been held that the defence must be able to point to material that is capable of supporting, and not which must inevitably support, the inference of falsity.[100] However, in *R v D*[101] it was held, confusingly, that the earlier authorities are not to be taken as authorizing the use of a trial to investigate the truth or falsity of a previous allegation merely because there is some material which could be used to try and persuade a jury that it was in fact false. Where there is evidence of a complaint, a 'proper evidential basis' for falsity may, depending on the circumstances, derive from the complainant's subsequent failure to cooperate with the police,[102] but presumably not where there is evidence to establish reasons for non-cooperation other than fabrication, such as fear of the criminal process itself. The mere fact that the police decided that there was insufficient evidence to prosecute does not provide a 'proper evidential basis' for falsity;[103] and the decision of the Crown Prosecution Service not to prosecute is irrelevant—it is for the court to decide whether there is a 'proper evidential basis'.[104] Where there is a 'proper evidential basis', there is an additional hurdle: leave is required under s 100(1) of the 2003 Act,[105] because questioning about previous

---

[96] [2007] Crim LR 910, CA.

[97] [2002] 1 WLR 632, CA.

[98] Applied in *R v E* [2005] Crim LR 227, CA.

[99] [2009] EWCA Crim 618; see also *R v Garaxo* [2005] Crim LR 883, CA.

[100] *R v E* [2009] EWCA Crim 2668. The number of previous allegations, by itself, will not entitle the defence to explore the possibility of their falsity: *R v A* [2012] EWCA Crim 1273.

[101] [2009] EWCA Crim 2137.

[102] *R v V* [2006] EWCA Crim 1901 and *R v Garaxo* [2005] Crim LR 883, CA.

[103] *R v D* [2009] EWCA Crim 2137.

[104] *Davarifar v R* [2009] EWCA Crim 2294.

[105] See Ch 17.

false complaints would relate to the bad character of the complainant.[106] However, leave may not be required if the complaint was not a deliberate lie but, for example, the product of alcoholism and personality problems and so is not 'reprehensible behaviour' and therefore not misconduct as defined in s 98 of the 2003 Act.[107]

The principle established in *R v T* has no application where an accused seeks to adduce evidence of the fact that a statement was made by the complainant about her previous sexual experience simply to show that the statement was made, rather than that it was false, as when it is argued that it is relevant to a defence of belief in consent: such evidence falls within s 41(1).[108] Nor does the principle apply to evidence or questions about the complainant's false denials concerning her previous sexual experiences because the falsity of the denial can only be exposed if the complainant's sexual behaviour is established.[109]

Evidence adduced by the prosecution
Section 41 only applies to evidence to be adduced or questions to be put 'by or on behalf of any accused at the trial'. In appropriate circumstances, therefore, evidence of the complainant's sexual behaviour may be adduced by the prosecution, as in *R v Soroya*,[110] where the evidence was relevant to the issue of consent because it showed that the complainant had *falsely* told the accused that she was a virgin in the hope that this might cause him to desist from the assault on her. The court rejected the argument that because such evidence cannot be introduced by the defence, its admission infringes the principle of equality of arms between the defence and prosecution in breach of the right to a fair trial under Art 6 of the European Convention on Human Rights, observing that, where appropriate, s 78 of the Police and Criminal Evidence Act 1984 can be deployed.

When the restriction may be lifted
Under s 41(2) of the 1999 Act, the court may not give leave in relation to any evidence or question unless satisfied that (a) the evidence or question is of the kind specified in s 41(3) or (5) and (b) a refusal of leave might render unsafe a conclusion of the jury or court on any 'relevant issues in the case', ie any issue falling to be proved by the prosecution or defence in the trial of the accused.[111] Subsection (3) covers evidence or questions relating to a relevant issue in the case and draws an important distinction between cases in which that issue is not an 'issue of consent' and cases in which it is. An 'issue of consent', for these purposes, means any issue whether the complainant in fact consented to the conduct constituting the offence with which the accused is charged (and accordingly does not include any issue as to the belief of the accused that the complainant so consented).[112] Subsection (5) covers evidence or questions to rebut or explain evidence adduced by the prosecution about any sexual behaviour of the complainant.

Section 41(2) to (8) provide as follows:

(2) The court may give leave in relation to any evidence or question only on an application made by or on behalf of an accused, and may not give such leave unless it is satisfied—

---

[106] *R v V* [2006] EWCA Crim 1901.
[107] *Davarifar v R* [2009] EWCA Crim 2294.
[108] *R v W* [2005] Crim LR 965, CA.
[109] *R v Winter* [2008] Crim LR 971, CA.
[110] [2007] Crim LR 181, CA.
[111] Section 42(1)(a).
[112] Section 42(1)(b).

(a) that subsection (3) or (5) applies; and

(b) that a refusal of leave might have the result of rendering unsafe a conclusion of the jury or (as the case may be) the court on any relevant issue in the case.

(3) This subsection applies if the evidence or question relates to a relevant issue in the case and either—

(a) that issue is not an issue of consent; or

(b) it is an issue of consent and the sexual behaviour of the complainant to which the evidence or question relates is alleged to have taken place at or about the same time as the event which is the subject matter of the charge against the accused; or

(c) it is an issue of consent and the sexual behaviour of the complainant to which the evidence or question relates is alleged to have been, in any respect, so similar—

(i) to any sexual behaviour of the complainant which (according to evidence adduced or to be adduced by or on behalf of the accused) took place as part of the event which is the subject matter of the charge against the accused, or

(ii) to any other sexual behaviour of the complainant which (according to such evidence) took place at or about the same time as that event,

that the similarity cannot reasonably be explained as a coincidence.

(4) For the purposes of subsection (3) no evidence or question shall be regarded as relating to a relevant issue in the case if it appears to the court to be reasonable to assume that the purpose (or main purpose) for which it would be adduced or asked is to establish or elicit material for impugning the credibility of the complainant as a witness.

(5) This subsection applies if the evidence or question—

(a) relates to any evidence adduced by the prosecution about any sexual behaviour of the complainant; and

(b) in the opinion of the court, would go no further than is necessary to enable the evidence adduced by the prosecution to be rebutted or explained by or on behalf of the accused.

(6) For the purposes of subsections (3) and (5) the evidence or question must relate to a specific instance (or specific instances) of alleged sexual behaviour on the part of the complainant (and accordingly nothing in those subsections is capable of applying in relation to the evidence or question to the extent that it does not so relate).

(7) Where this section applies in relation to a trial by virtue of the fact that one or more of a number of persons charged in the proceedings is or are charged with a sexual offence—

(a) it shall cease to apply in relation to the trial if the prosecutor decides not to proceed with the case against that person or those persons in respect of that charge; but

(b) it shall not cease to do so in the event of that person or those persons pleading guilty to, or being convicted of, that charge.

(8) Nothing in this section authorizes any evidence to be adduced or any question to be asked which cannot be adduced or asked apart from this section.

The test in section 41(2)(b)

Before leave can be granted, the test in s 41(2)(b) must always be met. It would seem that 'a refusal of leave might have the result of rendering unsafe a conclusion of the jury...on any relevant issue' (which typically, in a rape case, will be the issue of consent or mistaken belief in consent), where to disallow the evidence or question would prevent the jury (or court) from hearing (taking into account) something which might cause them to change their minds on that issue. This hurdle, therefore, is not particularly high: the court need only be satisfied that a refusal of leave *might* have the consequence specified, not that such a consequence is probable. The last point is of particular significance where s 41(3)(a) applies, ie where the evidence or question relates to a relevant issue in the case other than whether the complainant in fact consented, because in such cases s 41(2)(b) is the *only* condition to be met.

Exercise of judgment, not discretion

The operation of s 41 involves, not the exercise of judicial discretion, but making a judgment whether to admit evidence said by the defence to be relevant. The judge has no discretion to exclude evidence admissible under s 41 and therefore cannot exclude it, for example, on the basis that it has been raised without advance notice, which goes to weight, not admissibility.[113] Equally, although a judge must ensure that a complainant is not unnecessarily humiliated or cross-examined with inappropriate aggression, and is treated with proper courtesy, this does not permit him, by way of general discretion, to exclude evidence admissible under s 41 merely because it comes in a stark, uncompromising form.[114]

Section 41(3)(a)—an issue other than consent

The following examples may be given of issues falling within s 41(3)(a): (i) the defence of reasonable belief in consent; (ii) that the complainant was biased against the accused or had a motive to fabricate the evidence; (iii) that there is an alternative explanation for the physical conditions on which the Crown relies to establish that intercourse took place; and (iv) especially in the case of young complainants, that the detail of their account must have come from some other sexual activity before or after the event which provides an explanation for their knowledge of that activity.[115]

As to (i), in *R v Barton*[116] it was stressed that, when considering the effect of the complainant's past sexual behaviour on the accused's belief in consent, whereas evidence of his belief that the complainant was consenting to intercourse is relevant, evidence of his belief that the complainant would consent if advances were made is irrelevant. Although *R v Barton* was a decision under s 2 of the Sexual Offences (Amendment) Act 1976 relating to a defence of *mistaken* belief in consent, the distinction was subsequently approved by the Court of Appeal in *R v Winter*[117] in relation to a decision under s 41 of the 1999 Act relating to a defence of *reasonable* belief in consent under the Sexual Offences Act 2003.

As to (ii), in *R v T*,[118] evidence of a photograph allegedly sent to the accused around Valentine's day, and showing the complainant scantily dressed, went to a relevant issue other than consent, the defence case being that the complainant was interested in him, he was not interested in her, and the motive for her false allegation was her affront at his lack of interest.[119]

An issue of consent

Subsections (3)(b) and (c) were designed to reverse the decision in *R v Riley*:[120] in a rape case where consent is in issue, leave will not be granted in relation to evidence or questions about sexual behaviour of the complainant simply because the behaviour in question is previous voluntary sexual intercourse with the accused. In many cases, however, the jury will be likely to infer such behaviour by virtue of the other evidence in the case, as when evidence is introduced that the accused and the complainant are married or have cohabited for a period of time, and in this situation, it is submitted, the judge, rather than simply ignore the likelihood

---

[113] *R v T* [2012] EWCA Crim 2358.

[114] *R v F* [2005] 1 WLR 2848, CA (videotapes of the complainant stripping and masturbating).

[115] See per Lord Hope in *R v A (No 2)* [2002] 1 AC 45 at [79]. As to (i), Lord Hope referred to the defence of 'honest' belief in consent, but see now the Sexual Offences Act 2003, ss 1(1)(c) and 75–77.

[116] (1986) 85 Cr App R 5, CA.

[117] [2008] Crim LR 971, CA.

[118] [2012] EWCA Crim 2358.

[119] See also *R v F* [2005] 1 WLR 2848, and cf *R v Mokrecovas* [2002] 1 Cr App R 226, CA.

[120] (1887) 18 QBD 481, CCR.

of such an inference being drawn, should direct the jury that any such inference can have no bearing on the issues to be decided.

Section 41(3)(b)—behaviour at or about the same time

To come within s41(3)(b), the evidence or question must relate to sexual behaviour alleged to have taken place at or about the same time as the event which is the subject matter of the charge, other than anything alleged to have taken place as part of that event.[121] The distinction between sexual behaviour which took place at the same time as the event, and sexual behaviour which took place as part of the event, is not readily apparent. The meaning of 'the event which is the subject matter of the charge' is also unclear, but seems designed to embrace more than 'the conduct constituting the offence'.[122] The phrase 'at or about the same time as the event', although it provides a degree of elasticity, is a narrow temporal restriction and prima facie prohibits questions both as to a continuous period of cohabitation or sexual activity, and as to individual events more than a very limited period before or after the 'event', generally no more than 24 hours before or after the offence.[123] Section 41(3)(b) could cover behaviour such as any sexual advances made by the complainant towards the accused or other men shortly before or after 'the event' and other behaviour relevant to the issue of consent. An example would be an allegation that the complainant invited the accused to have sexual intercourse with her earlier in the evening.[124]

Subsection 41(3)(c)—similar behaviour

Subsection (3)(c) covers the sexual behaviour of the complainant with the accused (or another man) on another occasion, provided that it is sufficiently similar in nature to her behaviour during, or shortly before or after, the event which is the subject matter of the charge. It was included in the Act in response to the *Romeo and Juliet* scenario advanced by Baroness Mallalieu.[125] She envisaged a complainant in a rape case who says that the accused climbed up on to her balcony and into her bedroom, but who, on occasions both before and after the alleged rape—but not 'at or about the same time as the event' under s 41(3)(b)—invited men to re-enact the *Romeo and Juliet* balcony scene prior to consensual sexual intercourse. An example, provided by Lord Steyn in *R v A (No 2)*,[126] is, in a rape case in which the accused says that after consensual intercourse the complainant tried to blackmail him by alleging rape, evidence of a previous occasion when she similarly tried to blackmail him.[127] Such evidence is introduced under s 41(3)(c) not so much to show that history has been repeated as to indicate

---

[121] Section 42(1)(c).

[122] A phrase also used in s 42(1): see s 42(1)(b).

[123] *R v A (No 2)* [2002] 1 AC 45, per Lords Slynn, Steyn, and Hope at [9], [40], and [82] respectively. But see also per Lord Clyde at [132], who was of the view that it is undesirable to prescribe any test in terms of days or hours, while accepting that it may be difficult to extend the period to 'several days'.

[124] *R v A (No 2)* [2002] 1 AC 45 per Lord Steyn at [40]. Cf the example furnished by *R v Mukadi* [2004] Crim LR 373, CA, which is hard to justify.

[125] House of Lords Committee Stage, Hansard, 1 Feb 1999, col 45.

[126] [2002] 1 AC 45 at [42].

[127] See also *R v T* [2004] 2 Cr App R 32, CA, where the alleged rape took place in a climbing frame in a park and there was evidence that three to four weeks earlier the accused and the complainant had had consensual intercourse in the same climbing frame and had adopted the same positions (both standing and the complainant facing away from the accused); and cf *R v MM* [2011] EWCA Crim 1291, where the similarity test was not met. In *R v Harris* [2010] Crim LR 54 the Court of Appeal stated that *R v T* was an easy case, the similarity being so clear that it was not disputed. The court indicated that in more difficult cases it would not interfere where the judge adopted a view on similarity which was open to him within the margin of judgment open to a decision maker.

a state of mind on the part of the complainant which is potentially highly relevant to her state of mind on the occasion in question.[128] A comparison can be made between the wording of s 41(3)(c) and the concept of similar fact evidence as formulated by Lord Salmon in *DPP v Boardman*:[129] 'The similarity would have to be so unique or striking that common sense makes it inexplicable on the basis of coincidence.' However, as Lord Clyde said in *R v A (No 2)*[130] the phrase 'striking similarity' is not used in s 41(3)(c)—the standard is something short of a striking similarity. Elaborating on this, Lord Clyde said:[131]

> It is only a similarity that is required, not an identity. Moreover the words 'in any respect' deserve to be stressed. On one view any single factor of similarity might suffice to attract the application of the provision, provided that it is not a matter of coincidence. That the behaviour was with the same person, the defendant, must be at least a relevant consideration. But if the identity of the defendant was alone sufficient as the non-coincidental factor that would seem to open the way in almost every case for a complete inquiry into the whole of the complainant's sexual behaviour with the defendant at least in the recent past, and that can hardly have been the intention of the provision. What must be found is a similarity in some other or additional respect. Further the similarity must be such as cannot reasonably be explained as coincidence. To my mind that does not necessitate that the similarity has to be in some rare or bizarre conduct.

However, in *R v A (No 2)* the House of Lords also recognized that as a matter of common sense a prior sexual relationship between the accused and the complainant may, depending on the circumstances, be relevant to the issue of consent, as a species of prospectant evidence which, although it cannot prove consent on the occasion in question, may throw light on the complainant's state of mind.[132] Recognizing further that s 41 is therefore prima facie capable of preventing an accused from putting forward relevant evidence which may be critical to his defence, whether one of consent or belief in consent, the House was of the unanimous view that it is possible under s 3 of the Human Rights Act 1998 to read s 41 of the 1999 Act, and in particular s 41(3)(c), as subject to the implied provision that evidence or questioning which is required to ensure a fair trial under Art 6 of the European Convention on Human Rights should not be treated as inadmissible. The result is that sometimes logically relevant evidence of sexual experience between a complainant and an accused may be admitted under section 41(3)(c). Lord Steyn said:[133] 'section 3 of the 1998 Act requires the court to subordinate the niceties of the language of section 41(3)(c) of the 1999 Act, and in particular the touchstone of coincidence, to broader considerations of relevance judged by logical and commonsense criteria of time and circumstances'. Members of the House were agreed as to the effect of its decision, namely that:

> under s 41(3)(c) of the 1999 Act, construed where necessary by applying the interpretative obligation under s 3 of the 1998 Act, and due regard always being paid to the importance of seeking to protect the complainant from indignity and from humiliating questions, the test of admissibility is whether the evidence (and questioning in relation to it) is nevertheless so relevant to the issue of consent that to exclude it would endanger the fairness of the trial under art 6 of the Convention. If this test is satisfied, the evidence should not be excluded.[134]

---

[128] Per Lord Clyde in *R v A (No 2)* at [133].

[129] [1975] AC 421, HL at 462.

[130] [2002] 1 AC 45 at [133].

[131] [2002] 1 AC 45 at [135].

[132] [2002] 1 AC 45 per Lord Steyn at [31].

[133] [2002] 1 AC 45 at [45].

[134] [2002] 1 AC 45 per Lord Steyn at [46].

Thus where there has been a recent close and affectionate relationship between the complainant and the accused, it is probable that the evidence will be relevant and admissible, not to prove consent, but to show the complainant's specific mindset towards the accused, namely her affection for him. But where, as in *R v A (No 2)* itself, there have only been some isolated acts of intercourse, even if fairly recently, without the background of an affectionate relationship, it is probable that the evidence will not be relevant. It is not possible to state with precision where the line is to be drawn—it will depend on the facts of the individual case as assessed by the trial judge.[135] *R v A (No 2)* was applied in *R v R*[136] where it was held that permission should have been given to the defence to cross-examine the complainant about both a previous consensual sexual relationship with the accused and consensual sexual intercourse with the accused occurring some 11 months after the alleged offence.[137]

It is very much more difficult to show relevance to the issue of consent in the case of evidence of the complainant's sexual behaviour with men other than the accused than in the case of evidence of sexual behaviour with the accused himself.[138] In *R v White*,[139] W denied rape and said that the complainant had asked him for money which he had refused to give her, and that after consensual intercourse he had woken up to find her with his wallet. It was held that the judge had properly refused an application to cross-examine the complainant on her previous and ongoing activities as a prostitute. A prostitute was as entitled as any other person to say 'no' to sex and the fact that the complainant was a prostitute did not mean that she was more ready than any other to say 'yes'. The bare fact that the complainant was a prostitute was therefore irrelevant to the issue of consent. There had to be something about the specific circumstances that satisfied the test in s 41(3)(c). *R v A (No 2)*, it was held, could be distinguished, since it did not concern the introduction of evidence of sexual behaviour with men other than the accused, and it would take a very special case to admit such evidence in circumstances where it could not be admitted by an ordinary reading of s 41.

Section 41(4)—where the purpose is to impugn credibility

Section 41(4) operates where 'the purpose' or the 'main purpose' for adducing the evidence or asking the question is to impugn the credibility of the complainant. *R v Sunny Islam*[140] illustrates its application. On a charge of rape, the defence being consent, it was held that the defence had been properly prevented from questioning the complainant about her flirtatious behaviour towards other men in a bar a few hours before the alleged offence, in order to suggest that she was 'up for sex'. The Court of Appeal upheld the ruling of the trial judge that the questions did not pass the test under s 41(2) and fell foul of s 41(4), having as their main purpose impugning the credibility of the complainant by reason of her unchaste behaviour. In *R v Martin*,[141] on the other hand, a case of indecent assault involving enforced oral sex, in which M alleged that the complainant had fabricated her evidence because he had rejected

---

[135] [2002] 1 AC 45 per Lord Hutton at [152].

[136] [2003] EWCA Crim 2754.

[137] Cf *R v S* [2010] EWCA Crim 1579 where, the jury being aware of a previous consensual sexual relationship, evidence of the fact that the last act of intercourse had taken place nine days before the alleged rape was of no relevance to the issue of consent.

[138] See per Lord Clyde at [125]–[127].

[139] [2004] EWCA Crim 946.

[140] [2012] EWCA Crim 3106.

[141] [2004] 2 Cr App R 354, CA.

her advances, it was held that the defence should have been allowed to question her about his allegation that two days earlier she had not merely pestered him for sex, but performed an act of oral sex upon him, after which he had rejected her. It was held that although one purpose of the questioning was to impugn the credibility of the complainant, it also went to the accused's credibility and strengthened the defence case of fabrication, because the jury might have interpreted a rejection after the performance of oral sex as more hurtful than rejection after mere verbal advances.

Following *R v Martin*, it has been properly observed that merely because evidence may impugn the complainant's credibility, it does not follow that the purpose or main purpose for deploying it is to do so.[142] However, the application of s 41(4) is, it is submitted, bound to give rise to real difficulties in the many cases where, as we have seen, the difference between questions going to credit and those going to the issue is reduced to vanishing point.[143] As Lord Hutton observed in *R v A (No 2)*, in the context of the issue of consent:[144] 'Issues of consent and issues of credibility may well run so close to each other as almost to coincide. A very sharp knife may be required to separate what may be admitted from what may not'.

Section 41(5)—evidence in rebuttal or explanation
Section 41(4) applies only for the purposes of s 41(3) and not for the purposes of s 41(5), which concerns evidence, or a question, in rebuttal or explanation of evidence adduced by the prosecution about *any* sexual behaviour of the complainant, including anything alleged to have taken place as part of the event which is the subject matter of the charge.[145] Thus, in *R v F*[146] where the complainant gave evidence that she had been raped by her mother's partner, that she had subsequently become pregnant but had not been sexually active with anyone else at the time, the Court of Appeal held that the accused ought to have been permitted to ask questions about the complainant's medical notes which recorded that to her doctor she had attributed her pregnancy to a 'condom accident' with her boyfriend and that subsequently she had been prescribed oral contraceptives. However, in *R v Winter*,[147] where the complainant, who claimed that she had been raped by the accused, sought to give evidence that at the time of the alleged offence she was in a happy long-term relationship with her partner, the statement was held not to be so misleading that evidence of an affair with another man was admissible in rebuttal.

'Evidence adduced by the prosecution' refers to evidence placed before the jury by prosecution witnesses in the course of their evidence-in-chief and by other witnesses in the course of cross-examination by prosecuting counsel and, where it is necessary to ensure a fair trial, may also include something said by a prosecution witness in cross-examination about the complainant's sexual behaviour which was not deliberately elicited by defence counsel and is potentially damaging to the accused's case.[148] Section 41(5) only allows the defence to rebut *evidence* adduced by the prosecution about the sexual behaviour of the complainant, and not,

[142] Per Judge LJ in *R v F* [2005] 1 WLR 2848, CA at [27].
[143] See *R v Funderburk* [1990] 1 WLR 587, CA (see n 61).
[144] [2002] 1 AC 45, HL at [138].
[145] See s 42(1)(c).
[146] [2008] EWCA Crim 2859.
[147] [2008] Crim LR 971, CA.
[148] *R v Hamadi* [2008] Crim LR 635, CA.

it seems, inferences about her sexual behaviour that may reasonably be drawn from evidence adduced by the prosecution.

Section 41(6)—specific instances of behaviour

Section 41(6) would rule out, for example, evidence or questions revealing the complainant to be, for example, a prostitute or of a promiscuous nature. Nor will the requirements of s 41(6) be met, in the case of a prostitute, by the information contained in a list of previous convictions for prostitution.[149] However, in some cases, of course, evidence or questions relating to specific instances may well allow the jury to infer that the complainant was a prostitute or promiscuous, as would happen, for example, if evidence were to be introduced that she had, on a number of previous occasions, agreed to sleep with men for money.

The procedure on applications under section 41

Where the defence wish to make use of s 41, they must apply in writing pre-trial, identifying the issue to which the sexual behaviour is relevant and the exception to the general prohibition on which they rely and giving particulars of the evidence they want to introduce or the questions they want to ask; and a party who wishes to make representations about such an application must also do so in writing.[150] An application for leave under s 41 shall be heard in private and in the absence of the complainant.[151] After the court has reached its decision, it must state in open court, but in the absence of the jury (if there is one), its reasons for giving or refusing leave and, if it gives leave, the extent to which evidence may be adduced or questions asked in pursuance of the leave.[152]

Finality of answers to collateral questions

The rule

A party eliciting from a witness under cross-examination evidence unfavourable to his case, may understandably seek to adduce evidence in rebuttal. To allow that party to adduce such evidence without restriction, however, would lead to a multiplicity of issues, some of which might be of minimal relevance to the facts in issue in the case, and thereby prolong the trial unnecessarily. As a general rule, therefore, the answers given by a witness under cross-examination to questions concerning collateral matters, that is, matters which are irrelevant to the issues in the proceedings, must be treated as final. Finality for these purposes does not mean that the tribunal of fact is obliged to accept the answers as true, but simply that the cross-examining party is not permitted to call further evidence with a view to contradicting the witness.

Whether a question is collateral is not always easy to decide. According to the often cited test formulated by Pollock CB in *A-G v Hitchcock*,[153] if the witness's answer is a matter on which the cross-examining party would be allowed to introduce evidence-in-chief, because of its connection with the issues in the case, then the matter is not collateral and may be

[149] *R v White* [2004] EWCA Crim 946.
[150] See Pt 36 of the Criminal Procedure Rules 2013, SI 2013/1554.
[151] Section 43(1).
[152] Section 43(2). A magistrates' court must also cause such matters to be entered in the register of its proceedings: s 43(2).
[153] (1847) 1 Exch 91 at 99.

rebutted.[154] Relevance, however, is a question of degree, the answer to which may turn on whether the matter which the cross-examining party seeks to prove is a single fact which is easy of proof or a broad issue which will require the jury to embark on a difficult and complex task.[155] Questions which go merely to the credit of the witness are clearly collateral. However, where the disputed issue is a sexual one between two persons in private, the difference between questions going to credit and questions going to the issue is reduced to vanishing point because sexual intercourse, whether or not consensual, most often takes place in private and leaves few visible traces of having occurred, so that the evidence is often effectively limited to that of the parties, and much is likely to depend upon the balance of credibility between them.[156] This principle, however, is not confined to cases involving sexual intercourse.[157]

Whether cross-examination goes merely to credit or can be said to be relevant to the issue in the proceedings is clearly a question of some difficulty. The nicety of the distinction is apparent in the authorities, some of which are difficult to reconcile. In *R v Burke*[158] an Irish witness who gave evidence through an interpreter and was cross-examined about his knowledge of English, denied that he was able to speak the language. The witness's ability to speak English being irrelevant to any matter directly in issue in the proceedings, it was held that evidence in rebuttal was inadmissible. In *A-G v Hitchcock*[159] a maltster was charged with the use of a cistern in breach of certain statutory requirements. A prosecution witness, who gave evidence that the cistern had been used, was asked in cross-examination whether he had not said to one Cook that the Excise officers offered him £20 to give evidence that the cistern had been used. The witness denied this allegation and it was held that counsel for the defence was not permitted to call Cook to give evidence in rebuttal of what the witness had said. Pollock CB said:[160]

> it is totally irrelevant to the matter in issue, that some person should have thought fit to offer a bribe to the witness to give an untrue account of a transaction, and it is of no importance whatever, if that bribe was not accepted.

Some of the criminal authorities as to the application of the rule, such as *R v Edwards*,[161] must be treated with caution insofar as they involved questioning the witness about his previous misconduct or disposition towards such misconduct. As previously noted, in criminal proceedings, the asking of questions about a witness's bad character is governed by ss 100 and 101 of the 2003 Act, which are considered in Chapter 17.

The exceptions

To the general rule on the finality of answers to collateral questions there are three exceptions, although it may be that the categories of exception are not closed.[162]

---

[154] The test seems to be circular, but its utility may lie in the fact that the answer is an instinctive one, based on the sense of fair play of the prosecutor and the court rather than any philosophic or analytic process: per Henry J in *R v Funderburk* [1990] 1 WLR 587, CA at 598. But see also per Evans LJ in *R v Neale* [1998] Crim LR 737, CA: the decision is ultimately a matter of common sense and logic.

[155] *R v S* [1992] Crim LR 307, CA.

[156] Per Henry J in *R v Funderburk* [1990] 1 WLR 587, CA at 597, citing *Cross on Evidence* (6th edn, London, 1985) 295.

[157] See *R v Nagrecha* [1997] 2 Cr App R 401, CA, a case of indecent assault, and *R v David R* [1999] Crim LR 909, CA.

[158] (1858) 8 Cox CC 44.

[159] (1847) 1 Exch 91; cf *R v Phillips* (1936) 26 Cr App R 17, CCA, at n 180.

[160] (1847) 1 Exch 91 at 101.

[161] [1991] 1 WLR 207, CA. See also *R v Clancy* [1997] Crim LR 290, CA and *R v Irish* [1995] Crim LR 145, CA.

[162] *R v Funderburk* [1990] 1 WLR 587, CA, per Henry J at 599.

Previous convictions

Under s 6 of the Criminal Procedure Act 1865:

> If, upon a witness being lawfully questioned as to whether he has been convicted of any felony or misdemeanour, he either denies or does not admit the fact, or refuses to answer, it shall be lawful for the cross-examining party to prove such conviction.[163]

Section 6 applies to both civil and criminal proceedings. In criminal proceedings, a witness will only be 'lawfully questioned' as to his previous convictions where the questions are lawful having regard to the relevant provisions of the 2003 Act, namely s 100 in the case of the previous convictions of a non-defendant and s 101 in the case of the previous convictions of the defendant. In civil proceedings, cross-examination of any witness about 'spent' convictions is prohibited by s 4(1) of the Rehabilitation of Offenders Act 1974, unless the judge is satisfied that it is not possible for justice to be done except by admitting the convictions.[164] This section does not apply in criminal proceedings, but under a Practice Direction issued by the Lord Chief Justice in 1975 no reference should be made to a spent conviction if that 'can reasonably be avoided'.[165] However, according to *R v Corelli*,[166] the Practice Direction does not operate to remove an unfettered statutory entitlement of a co-accused to cross-examine another co-accused on his previous convictions.[167] Subject to *R v Corelli*, the effect of the Practice Direction is to give the judge a wide discretion with the exercise of which the Court of Appeal will be loath to interfere. Thus in *R v Lawrence*,[168] where the trial judge refused the defence permission to question the victim of a wounding in detail on his 20 previous spent convictions, most of which were for offences of dishonesty, but did allow questions on four more recent offences, the Court of Appeal held that although it might have exercised the discretion differently and permitted cross-examination on one of the spent convictions, which involved perverting the course of justice, the judge had not erred in principle. In *R v Evans*,[169] on the other hand, a case of wounding with intent, the defence being self-defence, it was held that the judge should have allowed cross-examination of the victim on her previous but spent convictions for dishonesty and violence because, evidentially speaking, there was a head-on collision between the accused and the victim.

There is authority to suggest that, in civil proceedings, subject to s 4(1) of the Rehabilitation of Offenders Act 1974, s 6 permits a witness to be cross-examined about his convictions irrespective of their relevance to his credibility or the issues in the case.[170] It seems clear, however, that cross-examination about a witness's previous convictions is subject to the general

---

[163] However, if the witness accepts the conviction but claims his innocence, the cross-examining party may be prevented from adducing evidence in rebuttal: see *R v Irish* [1995] Crim LR 145, CA.

[164] Section 7(3). Evidence of the conviction may be admitted under s 7(3) not only if relevant to an issue in the case, but also if relevant merely to the credit of the witness, but the judge should weigh its relevance and its prejudicial effect and only admit it if satisfied that otherwise the parties would not have a fair trial or the witness's credit could not be fairly assessed: *Thomas v Metropolitan Police Comr* [1997] QB 13, CA.

[165] See now *the Consolidated Criminal Practice Direction*, para 6. See also the Criminal Justice Act 2003, s 108 (see Ch 17).

[166] [2001] Crim LR 913, CA.

[167] The statutory entitlement in the case arose under the Criminal Evidence Act 1898, s 1(3)(iii). See now the Criminal Justice Act 2003, s 101(1)(e) (see Ch 17).

[168] [1995] Crim LR 815, CA.

[169] [1992] Crim LR 125, CA.

[170] *Clifford v Clifford* [1961] 1 WLR 1274 P, D and Admlty at 1276.

power of the judge to restrain unnecessary, irrelevant, or unduly oppressive questions in cross-examination.[171] In civil proceedings, a judge may use the general exclusionary discretion under CPR r 32[172] to limit cross-examination on previous convictions to the convictions for offences of dishonesty, although where sitting with a jury should be more hesitant in exercising the discretion.[173]

In criminal proceedings, s 101(1)(g) of the 2003 Act operates as a powerful disincentive to the use of s 6 by defence counsel in cross-examination of prosecution witnesses. We shall see in Chapter 17 that, under s 101(1)(g), the accused, by making an attack on another person's character, thereby renders admissible evidence of his own bad character.

Bias

'It has always been permissible to call evidence to contradict a witness's denial of bias or partiality towards one of the parties and to show that he is prejudicial so far as the case being tried is concerned.'[174] Thus where a female servant of the claimant is called as his witness and denies in cross-examination that she is his kept mistress, the defendant may call evidence to contradict her.[175] Under s 99 of the 2003 Act, this common law principle has been abolished in criminal proceedings to the extent that it allows the introduction of evidence of the witness's bad character, ie evidence of, or of a disposition towards, misconduct on his part. However, much evidence of bias is likely to remain admissible at common law, because outside the statutory definition of evidence of bad character in s 98 of the 2003 Act, which excludes 'evidence of, or of a disposition towards misconduct... which has to do with the alleged facts of the offence with which the defendant is charged, or is evidence of misconduct in connection with the investigation or prosecution of that offence'. Alternatively, to the extent that the evidence is not admissible on that basis, it is likely to be admitted under s 100(1)(b) of the 2003 Act, ie as evidence of the bad character of a person other than the defendant which has substantial probative value in relation to a matter which is in issue in the proceedings and of substantial importance in the context of the case as a whole.[176] Thus the *outcome* in each of the following examples of the common law doctrine is likely to remain the same.

In *R v Shaw*[177] it was held that the accused may call evidence to contradict a prosecution witness who, in cross-examination, denies having threatened to be revenged on the accused following a quarrel with him. In *R v Mendy*,[178] during a trial for assault, and while a detective was giving evidence, a man in the public gallery was observed to be taking notes. The man was seen to leave the court and hold a conversation, apparently concerning the detective's evidence, with the accused's husband, who, as a prospective witness, had been kept out of court in accordance with the normal practice. The husband subsequently gave evidence and under cross-examination denied that he had spoken to the man in question. The Court of Appeal held that the trial judge had properly allowed evidence to be given in rebuttal. The jury were entitled to know that, in order to deceive them and help the accused, the witness was prepared to cheat.

---

[171] See, eg, per Lawton J in *R v Sweet-Escott* (1971) 55 Cr App R 316, Assizes.

[172] See Ch 2.

[173] *Watson v Chief Constable of Cleveland Police* [2001] EWCA Civ 1547.

[174] Per Geoffrey Lane LJ in *R v Mendy* (1976) 64 Cr App R 4, CA at 6.

[175] *Thomas v David* (1836) 7 C&P 350.

[176] Sections 99 and 100 of the 2003 Act are considered in Ch 17.

[177] (1888) 16 Cox CC 503, Assizes.

[178] (1976) 64 Cr App R 4.

The line dividing questions put to a witness in cross-examination concerning facts tending to show prejudice or bias, and those concerning collateral facts on which the witness's answers must be treated as final, is often a very fine one. Although in *A-G v Hitchcock*,[179] as we have seen, it was held that the witness's denial of an alleged statement by him that he had been *offered* a bribe, being a collateral matter, could not be contradicted, the court acknowledged that where a witness denies *acceptance* of a bribe to testify, a matter tending to show his partiality, evidence in rebuttal is admissible. *R v Phillips*[180] also falls to be contrasted with the actual decision in *A-G v Hitchcock*. The accused was charged with incest. His defence was that the principal prosecution witnesses, his two daughters, had been 'schooled' by their mother into giving false evidence. In cross-examination, the girls denied that their testimony was no more than a repetition of what their mother had told them to say. The girls also denied that on separate occasions each of them had admitted to another person that their evidence in previous criminal proceedings against their father for indecent assault had been false. The trial judge refused to allow defence counsel to call two women to whom these admissions were alleged to have been made. The Court of Criminal Appeal, quashing the conviction, held that this evidence was admissible on the grounds that the questions were directed not to the credibility of the two girls but went to the very foundation of the accused's defence.

In *R v Busby*[181] police officers were cross-examined on the basis that they had made up statements attributed to the accused and indicative of his guilt, and had threatened W, a potential witness for the defence, to stop him giving evidence. The allegations were denied. The trial judge ruled that W, who was subsequently called for the defence, could not give evidence that he had been threatened by the officers, because this would go solely to their credit. The Court of Appeal, allowing the appeal against conviction, held that the judge had erred: W's evidence was relevant to an issue which had to be tried, in that, if true it showed that the police were prepared to go to improper lengths in order to secure a conviction, and this would have supported the accused's case that the statements attributed to him had been fabricated. In *R v Funderburk*[182] *R v Busby* was treated as having created a new exception to the rule against finality, but in *R v Edwards*[183] it was held that the facts came within the exception of bias and that if the case could not be explained on that basis, it was inconsistent with the general rule itself.

Evidence of physical or mental disability affecting reliability
The credibility of a witness may be impeached by expert medical evidence which shows that he suffers from some physical or mental disability that affects the reliability of his evidence.[184]

If a witness purported to give evidence of something which he believed that he had seen at a distance of 50 yards, it must surely be possible to call the evidence of an oculist to the effect that the witness could not possibly see anything at a greater distance than 20 yards, or the evidence of a surgeon who had removed a cataract from which the witness was suffering at the material time and which would have prevented him from seeing what he thought he saw. So, too, must it

[179] (1847) 1 Exch 91.
[180] (1936) 26 Cr App R 17.
[181] (1981) 75 Cr App R, CA.
[182] [1990] 1 WLR 587, CA at 591.
[183] [1991] 1 WLR 207, CA at 215.
[184] For a critique of the use of psychiatric evidence in rape trials, see Ellison, 'The use and abuse of psychiatric evidence in rape trials' [2009] 13 E&P 28.

be allowable to call medical evidence of mental illness which makes a witness incapable of giving reliable evidence, whether through the existence of delusions or otherwise.

These examples were given by Lord Pearce in *Toohey v Metropolitan Police Comr.*[185] Toohey was convicted with others of an assault with intent to rob. The defence was that the alleged victim had been drinking and that while they were trying to help him by taking him home, he became hysterical and accused them of the offence charged. The trial judge held that, although a doctor called for the defence could give evidence that when he examined the victim he was hysterical and smelt of alcohol, he could not give evidence that in his opinion drink could exacerbate hysteria and that the alleged victim was more prone to hysteria than a normal person. The Court of Criminal Appeal dismissed the appeal, but the House of Lords, quashing the convictions, held that the doctor's evidence had been improperly excluded. Lord Pearce, in a speech with which the other members of the House concurred, held that the evidence was admissible not only because of its relevance to the facts in issue, regardless of whether or not it affected the credibility of the alleged victim as a witness, but also to show that the evidence of the alleged victim was unreliable.

> Medical evidence is admissible to show that a witness suffers from some disease or defect or abnormality of mind that affects the reliability of his evidence. Such evidence is not confined to a general opinion of the unreliability of the witness but may give all the matters necessary to show, not only the foundation of and reasons for the diagnosis, but also the extent to which the credibility of the witness is affected.[186]

Expert opinion evidence is admissible in relation to matters requiring special knowledge or expertise, not matters within the ordinary experience and knowledge of the tribunal of fact. Thus expert medical evidence on the reliability of a witness will only be admissible if the disability from which the witness suffers is a proper subject of such evidence. As Lord Pearce observed in *Toohey v Metropolitan Police Comr:*[187]

> Human evidence...is subject to many cross-currents such as partiality, prejudice, self-interest and above all, imagination and inaccuracy. Those are matters with which the jury, helped by cross-examination and common sense, must do their best. But when a witness through physical (in which I include mental) disease or abnormality is not capable of giving a true or reliable account to the jury, it must surely be allowable for medical science to reveal this vital hidden fact to them.

In *R v MacKenney*[188] the accused were convicted of murder. At their trial, they had alleged that the chief prosecution witness had fabricated his evidence and wished to call a psychologist by whom the witness had refused to be examined. The psychologist had watched the witness give his evidence and as a result had formed the opinion that he was a psychopath who was likely to be lying and whose mental state was such that his demeanour and behaviour when giving evidence would not convey the usual indications to the jury as to when he was lying. The evidence of the psychologist was ruled inadmissible. The convictions were upheld on appeal. On referral to the Court of Appeal by the Criminal Cases Review Commission, there was fresh evidence from a psychiatrist. He, too, had not examined the

---

[185] [1965] AC 595 at 608. See also *R v Eades* [1972] Crim LR 99, Assizes.
[186] [1965] AC 595 at 609.
[187] [1965] AC 595 at 608.
[188] [2004] 2 Cr App R 32, CA.

witness. His opinion was very similar to that of the psychologist who had attended the trial. It was held that the evidence of the psychologist would today be admissible and that the absence of an examination by the expert went to the weight to be attached to his opinion, not its admissibility. Deciding the reference on the fresh evidence, the conviction was quashed.

In *R v Robinson*[189] it was held that although a party, A, cannot call a witness of fact, W, and then, without more, call a psychologist or psychiatrist to give reasons why the jury should regard W as reliable, if the other party, B, proposes to call an expert to say that W should be regarded as unreliable due to some mental abnormality outside the jury's experience, then A may call an expert in rebuttal or even, anticipating B's expert, as part of his own case. Where B does not call an expert, but puts a case in cross-examination that W is unreliable by reason of mental abnormality, this may also be open to rebuttal by expert evidence, although much may depend on the nature of the abnormality and of the cross-examination. If such expert evidence is admitted, it must be restricted to the specific challenge, and should not extend to 'oath-helping'. Thus on the facts of that case, since B had not called evidence impugning W's reliability and had not put a specific case in cross-examination that W was peculiarly suggestible or liable to fantasize as a result of her mental impairment, expert evidence to suggest the opposite was inadmissible.

R v Robinson was distinguished in *R v S*,[190] where it was held that the judge had not erred in allowing an expert to make a general observation that it would be unlikely for an autistic person, as the victim was, to have invented such an account as that given by her, leaving it to the jury to decide whether the victim was capable of belief. In *R v Eden*[191] where, on charges of numerous sexual offences against the complainant over a period of six years, E denied the offences and claimed that the complainant was simply lying, it was held that evidence of a psychologist that the complainant had symptoms which could be consistent with extensive child abuse or some other repeated prolonged trauma did not fall to be excluded as 'oath-helping' but was admissible as evidence of a psychological injury consistent with the complainant's allegations and relevant to the issue of where the truth lay.

The rule against 'oath-helping' will not necessarily prevent a non-expert from giving evidence as to the good character of a witness from which his likely reliability may be inferred. In *R v Tobin*,[192] a case of indecent assault on a girl, the defence claimed that the sexual activity had been initiated by the girl. The accused gave evidence that he was a married man with no previous convictions for sexual offences and called five character witnesses. The girl's mother was allowed to give evidence that she had never had problems with her daughter, who had done well at school, got on well with her siblings, was very polite and quiet, and had been brought up to respect people. It was held that the evidence did go to boost the claimant's credibility, but since full evidence had been given about the accused's character, the court's sense of fair play was not offended by admission of the evidence as to the complainant's character.

[189] [1994] 3 All ER 346, CA. See also *R v Beard* [1998] Crim LR 585, CA.
[190] [2006] EWCA Crim 2389.
[191] [2011] EWCA Crim 1690.
[192] [2003] Crim LR 408, CA.

Re-examination

A witness who has been cross-examined may be re-examined by the party who called him.[193] The object of re-examination is, in broad terms, to repair such damage as has been done by the cross-examining party insofar as he has elicited evidence from the witness supporting his version of the facts in issue and cast doubt upon the witness's evidence-in-chief.

The cardinal rule of re-examination is that it must be confined to such matters as arose out of the cross-examination.[194] Thus although the witness may be asked to clarify or explain any matters, including evidence of new facts, which arose in cross-examination, questions on other matters may only be asked with the leave of the judge. In *Prince v Samo*[195] Lord Denman CJ held that where a witness under cross-examination has given evidence of part of a conversation, evidence may not be given in re-examination about everything that was said in that conversation, but only about so much of it as is in some way connected with the evidence given in cross-examination. For example, the witness may be re-examined about things said which qualify or explain the statement on which he was cross-examined, but not about things said on other distinct and unrelated matters.

Evidence which was not admissible in examination-in-chief may become admissible in re-examination as a result of the nature of the cross-examination. Thus although in criminal proceedings an earlier statement of a witness which is consistent with his testimony on a particular matter is generally inadmissible in chief, it will become admissible in re-examination if, in cross-examination, it is suggested to him that his evidence on that matter is a recent fabrication.[196] It remains to note that leading questions may be asked in re-examination to the same limited extent as in examination-in-chief.

ADDITIONAL READING

Birch, 'Rethinking Sexual History Evidence: Proposals for Fairer Trials' [2002] Crim LR 531.

Birch, 'Untangling Sexual History Evidence: A Rejoinder to Professor Temkin' [2003] Crim LR 370.

Cohen, 'Errors of Recall and Credibility: Can omissions and discrepancies in successive statements reasonably be said to undermine credibility of testimony?' (2001) 96(I) Med Leg J 25–34.

Horvath and Brown, eds, *Rape: Challenging contemporary thinking* (Portland, 2009).

Keane, 'Cross-examination of vulnerable witnesses—towards a blueprint for re-professionalisation' (2012) 16 E&P 175.

Keane, 'Towards a Principled Approach to the Cross-examination of Vulnerable Witnesses' [2012] Crim LR 407.

Kibble, 'The Sexual History Provisions: Charting a course between inflexible legislative rules and wholly untrammelled judicial discretion?' [2000] Crim LR 274.

Kibble, 'Judicial Perspectives on the Operation of s 41 and the Relevance and Admissibility of Prior Sexual History Evidence: Four Scenarios' [2005] Crim LR 190.

Office for Criminal Justice Reform, 'Convicting Rapists and Protecting Victims—Justice for Victims of Rape' <www.homeoffice.gov.uk>.

---

[193] Even a hostile witness, apparently, may be re-examined by the party who called him (on any new matters which arose out of cross-examination by the other party to the action): *R v Wong* [1986] Crim LR 683 (Crown Court).

[194] The rule applies in the case of a witness whose name was 'on the back of the indictment' and who was called by the prosecution merely to allow the defence to cross-examine him: *R v Beezley* (1830) 4 C&P 220.

[195] (1838) 7 Ad&El 627. See also *Queen Caroline's Case* (1820) 2 Brod&Bing 284.

[196] See, eg, *R v Oyesiku* (1971) 56 Cr App R 240, CA (see Ch 6).

Redmayne, 'Myths, relationships and coincidences: The new problems of sexual history' (2003) 7 E&P 75.

Spencer and Lamb, eds, *Children and Cross-examination, Time to change the rules?* (Oxford, 2012).

Temkin, 'Sexual History Evidence—Beware the Backlash' [2003] Crim LR 217.

Temkin and Krahé, *Sexual Assault and the Justice Gap: A Question of Attitude* (Oxford, 2008).

Ward, 'Usurping the role of the jury? Expert evidence and witness credibility in English criminal trials' (2009) 13 E&P 83.

Corroboration and care warnings

8

Key issues

- Where a witness in a criminal trial gives evidence against the accused, why might it be desirable to have additional independent evidence by way of confirmation or support?

- Where a witness gives evidence that he saw or heard the accused committing a crime, why should his testimony be treated with caution?

- What should a judge do in order to meet the need for such caution?

- Where a potential witness to a crime states that he can identify the perpetrator by his distinctive voice, should the police be required to conduct a 'voice identification procedure', ie a procedure whereby the witness is called on to pick out the voice of the perpetrator from among the voices of other innocent parties who might sound like him?

- Where a party in a criminal trial wishes to ask the jury to compare the accused's voice or a recording of the accused's voice with a recording of the voice of the perpetrator of a crime, should such a comparison only be made with expert guidance?

- Where a witness who is mentally handicapped confesses that he has committed a crime (a) why should evidence of his confession be treated with care; and (b) what should a judge do to ensure that the confession is treated with care?

'Any risk of the conviction of an innocent person is lessened if conviction is based upon the testimony of more than one acceptable witness.'[1] In civil, as well as criminal, cases it would not be unreasonable to expect a general rule requiring a party, who seeks to prove certain facts by the testimony of a single witness, to adduce additional independent evidence, by way of confirmation or support, so that the tribunal of fact is double-sure before it makes a particular finding, or gives judgment, in that party's favour. Although this is the case in most civil law jurisdictions, there is no general rule to this effect in English law. Thus in a criminal trial, provided that the jury are sure of the guilt of the accused, a conviction may be based on the testimony of a single prosecution witness who swears that he saw the accused commit the crime in question, and this remains the case even if part or all of his evidence is contradicted by the testimony of one or more witnesses called by the defence.[2] A party is, of course, free to adduce evidence which corroborates or supports the other evidence that he has tendered,[3] and to the extent that this would strengthen an otherwise weak case, as a matter of common sense he would be well advised to do so. As a general rule, however, there is no requirement (a) that evidence be corroborated; and (b) that the tribunal of fact be warned of the danger of acting on uncorroborated evidence.

This chapter is concerned with the exceptions to the general rule. There are three categories of exception. The first is where corroboration (probably in a technical sense) is required as a matter of law. In cases falling within this category, the ambit of which is clearly defined, comprising as it does four cases governed by statute (speeding, perjury, treason, and attempts to commit such offences), a conviction cannot be based on uncorroborated evidence and, if it is, will be reversed on appeal. Thus in the absence of such corroboration, the judge should direct an acquittal. Depending on the statute in question, the corroboration may be required to take a particular form, such as the evidence of another witness, or may be permitted to take any form, whether testimony, real evidence, or documentary evidence.

In the second category, which comprises a miscellany of different cases, neither corroboration in a technical sense nor supportive evidence is required as a matter of law, but in appropriate circumstances the tribunal of fact should be warned to exercise caution before acting on the evidence of certain types of witness, if unsupported. The witnesses in question include: (i) accomplices giving evidence for the prosecution; (ii) complainants in sexual cases; (iii) other witnesses whose evidence may be tainted by an improper motive; (iv) children; and (v) anonymous witnesses. Whether a warning is given at all is a matter of judicial discretion dependent on the circumstances of the case, and therefore failure to give a warning will not necessarily furnish a good ground of appeal. Where a warning is given, the strength of the warning and the extent to which the judge should elaborate upon it, for example by referring to the potentially supportive material, also depends upon the particular circumstances of the case.

The third category comprises five cases in which corroboration in a technical sense is not required as a matter of law, and there is no obligation to warn the tribunal of fact of the danger of acting on the evidence in question *simply* by reason of the fact that it is uncorroborated or

---

[1] Per Lord Morris in *DPP v Hester* [1973] AC 296, HL at 315.

[2] However, a conviction in such circumstances may be set aside where it is unsafe: see *R v Cooper* [1969] 1 QB 267, CA at 271. In civil cases, a new trial may be ordered where the verdict of the jury is against the weight of the evidence: see per Lord Selborne in *Metropolitan Rly Co v Wright* (1886) 11 App Cas 152, HL at 153.

[3] Subject to the inherent power of the court to prevent the admission of superfluous evidence.

unsupported, but there is a special need for caution which has led to requirements analogous to, but distinct from, those relating to the first two categories. The five cases are confessions by mentally handicapped persons, identification evidence, lip-reading evidence, cases of Sudden Infant Death Syndrome (colloquially 'cot deaths'), and unconvincing hearsay. The last of these cases is governed by s 125 of the Criminal Justice Act 2003, which requires a judge to direct an acquittal or discharge the jury if satisfied that the case against the accused is based wholly or partly on a hearsay statement and the evidence provided by the statement is so unconvincing that the accused's conviction would be unsafe. Section 125 is considered in Chapter 10.[4]

Corroboration required by statute

At common law a trial judge was required as a matter of law to warn the jury of the danger of acting on certain types of evidence if uncorroborated. Corroboration, for these purposes, bore a technical meaning. Corroboration, where required by statute, probably bears the same technical meaning. This appears to have been the view of Lord Reading CJ in *R v Baskerville*.[5] Moreover, corroboration in the technical sense *is* required in the case of the statutory provision relating to perjury;[6] and although, as we shall see, neither the perjury provision nor the provisions relating to speeding and treason expressly require 'corroboration', s 2(2)(g) of the Criminal Attempts Act 1981 has been drafted on the assumption that that is exactly what they require. It is necessary to consider first, therefore, the meaning of corroboration in the technical sense.

To be capable of amounting to corroboration in the technical sense, evidence must be (i) relevant, (ii) admissible, (iii) credible, (iv) independent, and (v) evidence which implicates the accused in the way that the specific statute requires. The first two requirements[7] apply to evidence generally and need no further explanation in the present context. As to the third requirement: 'Corroboration can only be afforded...by a witness who is otherwise to be believed. If a witness's testimony falls of its own inanition, the question of his...being capable of giving corroboration does not arise.'[8] Under the fourth requirement, independence, the evidence must emanate from a source other than the witness who is to be corroborated.[9] The fifth requirement, implication, is best explored by reference to the statutory provisions themselves. Before turning to them, it remains to note the respective functions of the judge and jury.[10] Where a judge does give a direction to the jury on corroboration, he must explain what it is. No particular form of words is necessary and there is no need even to use the word 'corroboration' provided that the requirements of credibility, independence, and implication are made clear.[11] The judge should also indicate what evidence is (and is not) capable of being

---

[4] See Ch 10, under **Admissibility of hearsay under the Criminal Justice Act 2003, Other safeguards, Stopping the case where the evidence is unconvincing.**

[5] [1916] 2 KB 658 at 667.

[6] See para 3.9, Law Commission Working Paper No 115 (1990), citing *R v Hamid* (1979) 69 Cr App R 324.

[7] See per Scarman LJ in *R v Scarrott* [1978] QB 1016, CA at 1021.

[8] Per Lord Hailsham in *DPP v Kilbourne* [1973] AC 729 at 746. See also per Lord Morris in *DPP v Hester* [1973] AC 296 at 315 ('Corroborative evidence will only fill its role if it itself is completely credible') and *R v Thomas* (1985) 81 Cr App R 331, CA.

[9] See, eg, *R v Whitehead* [1929] 1 KB 99, CCA.

[10] It is submitted that the authorities that follow, which mainly related to common law corroboration requirements, also apply where corroboration is required by statute.

[11] See *R v Fallon* [1993] Crim LR 591, CA.

corroboration.[12] Having directed the jury as to what evidence is capable in law of amounting to corroboration, the judge should explain that it falls to them, as the tribunal of fact, to decide whether the evidence does in fact constitute corroboration.[13]

Speeding

The opinion evidence of non-experts is generally inadmissible.[14] One of the exceptions to this rule is opinion evidence relating to speed. Section 89(2) of the Road Traffic Regulation Act 1984, in recognition of the danger of such evidence being inaccurate, provides that a person charged with an offence of driving a motor vehicle on a road at an excessive speed 'shall not be liable to be convicted solely on the evidence of one witness to the effect that in the opinion of the witness the person prosecuted was driving the vehicle at a speed exceeding a specified limit'. The opinion evidence of two or more people that a vehicle was exceeding the speed limit is sufficient to justify a conviction under this provision provided that their evidence relates to the speed of the vehicle at the same place and time.[15] The provision only applies to evidence of mere opinion and not to evidence of fact.[16] Speedometers and other similar devices[17] will be presumed, in the absence of evidence to the contrary, to have been working properly at the material time and to be capable of providing evidence of fact.

In *Crossland v DPP*[18] Bingham LJ said: 'It is plain…that the subsection is intended to prevent the conviction of a defendant on evidence given by a single witness of his unsupported visual impression of a defendant's speed.' An expert in accident reconstruction testified that he had inspected the scene of a road traffic accident, including skid marks and damage to the defendant's car, carried out speed and braking tests on the car, and calculated that its speed had been not less than 41 mph. It was held that this was not just the opinion evidence of one witness: the expert had also described the objectively determined phenomena on which his opinion was based.

Perjury

The rationale for the requirement of corroboration in relation to offences of perjury is not entirely clear. Historically, perjury was first punished in the Star Chamber, which usually required a second witness. Prior to the statutory provisions, the requirement at common law was held to be justified 'else there is only oath against oath'.[19] This argument did not seem strong to the Criminal Law Revision Committee 'as there may be more than oath against oath

---

[12] *R v Charles* (1976) 68 Cr App R 334n; *R v Cullinane* [1984] Crim LR 420, CA; and *R v Webber* [1987] Crim LR 412, CA. If the judge fails to do so, this is unlikely to result in a successful appeal if there was in fact ample corroboration and the Court of Appeal is in no doubt that if a proper direction had been given, the jury would still have convicted: see *R v McInnes* (1989) 90 Cr App R 99, CA.

[13] *R v Tragen* [1956] Crim LR 332; *R v McInnes* (1989) 90 Cr App R 99, CA.

[14] See Ch 18.

[15] *Brighty v Pearson* [1938] 4 All ER 127.

[16] See *Nicholas v Penny* [1950] 2 KB 466 where it was held that magistrates could convict on the evidence of a police officer who had checked his speedometer and driven at an even distance behind the accused's car. However, see *Iaciofano v DPP* [2011] RTR 15, DC. See also *Connell v The Crown Prosecution Service* (2011) 175 JP 151, DC.

[17] See *Collinson v Mabbott* (1984) The Times, 10 Oct, DC (corroboration by radar gun); and *Burton v Gilbert* [1984] RTR 162, DC (corroboration by radar speed meter).

[18] [1988] 3 All ER 712 at 714.

[19] *R v Muscot* (1713) 10 Mod Rep 192.

when the falsity of the accused's evidence is corroborated although not by a second witness'. Furthermore, 'there are many cases where corroboration is not required but the decision depends on the choice between two pieces of sworn evidence'. However, a majority of the Committee felt that to make a prosecution for perjury too easy might discourage persons from giving evidence and create the danger of a successful party to litigation, his evidence having been preferred, seeking to have his adversary, or his adversary's witnesses, prosecuted for perjury.[20]

Section 13 of the Perjury Act 1911 provides that:

> A person shall not be liable to be convicted of any offence against this Act, or of any other offence declared by any other Act to be perjury or subornation of perjury, or to be punishable as perjury or subornation of perjury, solely upon the evidence of one witness as to the falsity of any statement alleged to be false.

The judge is therefore required to direct the jury that, before a conviction of perjury can be recorded, there must be evidence before them, which they accept, of more than one witness, ie either evidence of at least one other witness or some other supporting evidence, by way of confession or otherwise, which is independent of the evidence given by the witness[21] and which supplements it.[22]

The section requires corroboration not only in relation to the offence of perjury in judicial proceedings, but also in relation to the many other offences under the Perjury Act of making false statements, on oath, in statutory declarations or otherwise, but not in judicial proceedings.[23] The corroboration need relate only to the *falsity* of the statement in question. Thus, if the accused admits that the statement was untrue, the prosecution need call no evidence to prove this fact and s 13 does not apply.[24] Nor does the section apply to certain allegations of perjury contrary to s 1(1) of the 1911 Act, which provides that if any person lawfully sworn as a witness wilfully makes a statement material in the proceedings which he knows to be false *or does not believe to be true*, he shall be guilty of an offence.[25]

Treason

Section 1 of the Treason Act 1795 requires corroboration in the form of evidence given by a second witness. It provides that a person charged with the offence of treason by compassing the death or restraint of the Queen or her heirs shall not be convicted except on 'the oaths of two lawful and credible witnesses'. The Criminal Law Revision Committee recommended the repeal of this provision.[26]

---

[20] Criminal Law Revision Committee, 11th Report, Cmnd 4991 (1972), paras 178 and 190.

[21] See *R v Cooper* [2010] 1 WLR 2390, CA: business documents compiled by the witness himself, who is the single source of the document, will not qualify as corroboration for the purposes of s 13 of the Act.

[22] See *R v Hamid* (1979) 69 Cr App R 324, CA and *R v Carroll* (1993) 99 Cr App R 381, CA. Failure to direct the jury in accordance with s 13 may afford grounds for a successful appeal: see *R v Rider* (1986) 83 Cr App R 207, CA.

[23] The Criminal Law Revision Committee and the Law Commission (para 45, Published Working Paper No 33, *Perjury and Kindred Offences*) saw no need to preserve the latter requirement.

[24] *R v Rider* (1986) 83 Cr App R 207, CA.

[25] *R v Rider* (1986) 83 Cr App R 207, CA. Section 13 will not apply because the truth or falsehood of the statement forms no part of the prosecution case. Note that the requirements of s 13 will be satisfied by two witnesses hearing the accused admit the falsity of the statement on the same occasion: *R v Peach* [1990] 2 All ER 966, CA. See also *R v Threlfall* (1914) 10 Cr App R 112: a letter suborning another to commit perjury in relation to the same matter in respect of which the false statement was made may constitute corroboration.

[26] Criminal Law Revision Committee, 11th Report, Cmnd 4991 (1972), para 195.

Attempts

Under s 2(2)(g) of the 1981 Act, any provision whereby a person may not be convicted on the uncorroborated evidence of one witness (including any provision requiring the evidence of not less than two credible witnesses) shall have effect with respect to an offence under s 1 of the Act of attempting to commit an offence as it has effect with respect to the offence attempted.

Care warnings

Accomplices testifying for the prosecution and complainants in sexual cases

The background

Prior to the Criminal Justice and Public Order Act 1994 there existed at common law a category of exception to the general rule under which, although corroboration (in the technical sense) was not required as a matter of law, the tribunal of fact had to be warned, as a matter of law, of the danger of acting on evidence if not corroborated (in the technical sense). This obligatory warning was required in respect of the evidence of (a) accomplices testifying on behalf of the prosecution; and (b) complainants in sexual cases.[27] As to the former, accomplices were defined as: (i) parties to the offence in question; (ii) handlers of stolen goods, in the case of thieves from whom they receive, on the trial of the latter for theft; and (iii) parties to another offence committed by the accused in respect of which evidence is admitted under the similar fact evidence doctrine.[28] Whether a particular witness was an accomplice was a question usually answered by the witness himself, by confessing to participation, by pleading guilty to it, or by being convicted of it. If not answered by the witness himself, the question whether he was in fact an accomplice was for the jury (provided that there was evidence on which a reasonable jury could have concluded that the witness was an accomplice).[29] As to complainants in sexual cases, the warning was required in respect of the victims, whether male or female,[30] of sexual offences.[31]

There were only two exceptions to the requirement that a warning be given: first, where an accomplice gave evidence, on behalf of the prosecution, which was mainly favourable to the accused and more harm would have been done to the accused by giving the warning than by not giving it;[32] second, in sexual cases in which identification was in issue, but not the commission of the offence itself.[33] Subject to these exceptions, failure to give the warning

---

[27] The need for such a warning was not confined to criminal proceedings: see *Mattouk v Massad* [1943] AC 588.

[28] *Davies v DPP* [1954] AC 378, HL. An accomplice, for these purposes, also included a thief from whom a handler has received goods, on the trial of the latter for receiving (*R v Vernon* [1962] Crim LR 35) but not an agent provocateur (*R v Mullins* (1848) 3 Cox CC 526), a child victim of a sexual offence (*R v Pitts* (1912) 8 Cr App R 126), or a woman upon whose immoral earnings the accused was charged with having lived (per Lord Reading CJ in *R v King* (1914) 10 Cr App R 117, CCA) unless, on the facts, there was evidence of aiding and abetting the accused, eg evidence of collecting money on behalf of the accused from other prostitutes (as in *R v Stewart* (1986) 83 Cr App R 327, CA).

[29] *Davies v DPP* [1954] AC 378.

[30] *R v Burgess* (1956) 40 Cr App R 144, CCA.

[31] The rule did not apply to other kinds of offence, even if their commission was allegedly accompanied by some form of sexual activity on the part of the accused: *R v Simmons* [1987] Crim LR 630, CA.

[32] See *R v Royce-Bentley* [1974] 1 WLR 535, CA.

[33] See *R v Chance* [1988] 3 All ER 225, CA.

furnished a good ground of appeal. The warning to be given to the jury (the 'full' warning) comprised four parts:

1. The warning itself, ie that it was dangerous to convict on the uncorroborated evidence of the 'suspect' witness but that if they, the jury, were satisfied of the truth of such evidence, they might nonetheless convict.
2. An explanation of the meaning of corroboration in the technical sense.
3. An indication of what evidence was (and was not) capable in law of amounting to corroboration.
4. An explanation that it fell to the jury, as the tribunal of fact, to decide whether that evidence did in fact constitute corroboration.

By reason of s 32 of the 1994 Act, full warnings are no longer required. In order to understand the effect of s 32, it is important to consider first both the justification for the rules requiring a full warning and the reasons for their abolition. The justification given for the requirement of a warning in the case of an accomplice giving evidence for the prosecution was that such a witness may have a purpose of his own to serve: he may give false evidence against the accused out of spite, to exaggerate or even invent the accused's role in the crime, or with a view to minimizing the extent of his own culpability. Concerning sexual offences (as in procuration cases), the requirement of a warning stemmed from an assumption that such a charge is easy to make but difficult to refute. There is also 'the danger that the complainant may have made a false accusation owing to sexual neurosis, jealousy, fantasy, spite or a girl's refusal to admit that she consented to an act of which she is now ashamed'.[34] Such a danger may be hidden, yet the nature of the evidence may well make jurors sympathetic to the complainant and so prejudice them against the accused.

The reasons in favour of the abolition of mandatory corroboration warnings were compelling.[35] The first and most serious objection was that the rules applied on a class basis, ie irrespective of the circumstances of the particular case and the credibility of the particular witness. Thus even if there was no danger of the 'suspect' witness giving false evidence, the judge still had to give the warning. Second, since many sexual offences are committed in circumstances in which corroboration is difficult if not impossible to obtain, the requirement was capable of resulting in the acquittal of the guilty. In cases involving the sexual abuse of children, the mandatory warning simply compounded the difficulty of securing a conviction.[36] Third, the full warning had become extremely complex, not least because of the technical rules on what constituted corroboration, and this often led to successful appeals. Fourth, there was an element of self-contradiction in directing jurors that it was 'dangerous' to convict on uncorroborated evidence and then proceeding to direct them that they could nonetheless do so. Finally, there was some evidence to suggest that where

---

[34] Criminal Law Revision Committee, 11th Report, Cmnd 4991 (1972), para 186.

[35] See generally Criminal Law Revision Committee, 11th Report, Cmnd 4991 (1972), paras 183–6; Law Commission Working Paper No 115 (1990); Law Commission Report No 202, Cm 1620 (1991); and Royal Commission on Criminal Justice, Cm 2263 (1993), ch 8. Although note the Canadian case of *R v Khela* 2009 SCC 4, in which views to the contrary were expressed. For comment on this case, see Pattenden, 'Case Commentaries' (2009) 13 E&P 243.

[36] See *Report of the Advisory Group on Video Evidence* (Home Office, 1989) para 5.17.

a warning was given, far from operating as a safeguard for the accused, the jury were more likely to convict.[37]

Section 32 of the Criminal Justice and Public Order Act 1994

Section 32 of the 1994 Act provides as follows:

1. Any requirement whereby at a trial on indictment it is obligatory for the court to give the jury a warning about convicting the accused on the uncorroborated evidence of a person merely because that person is—
   (a) an alleged accomplice of the accused, or
   (b) where the offence charged is a sexual offence, the person in respect of whom it is alleged to have been committed,
   is hereby abrogated....
2. Any requirement that—
   (a) is applicable at the summary trial of a person for an offence, and
   (b) corresponds to the requirement mentioned in subsection (1) above...
   is hereby abrogated.

Thus in cases involving the evidence of an alleged accomplice or of a complainant in a sexual case, s 32 has simply abrogated any requirement whereby it was *obligatory* for the tribunal of fact to be given a full warning—the judge still has a discretion to give some form of warning whenever he considers it necessary to do so. The leading authority on s 32 is *R v Makanjuola*,[38] in which Lord Taylor CJ summarized the relevant principles:[39]

1. Section 32(1) abrogates the requirement to give a corroboration direction in respect of an alleged accomplice or a complainant of a sexual offence simply because a witness falls into one of those categories.
2. It is a matter for the judge's discretion what, if any, warning he considers appropriate in respect of such a witness, as indeed in respect of any other witness in whatever type of case. Whether he chooses to give a warning and in what terms will depend on the circumstances of the case, the issues raised, and the content and quality of the witness's evidence.
3. In some cases, it may be appropriate for the judge to warn the jury to exercise caution before acting upon the unsupported evidence of a witness. This will not be so simply because the witness is a complainant of a sexual offence nor will it necessarily be so because a witness is alleged to be an accomplice. There will need to be an evidential basis for suggesting that the evidence of the witness may be unreliable. An evidential basis does not include mere suggestions by cross-examining counsel.
4. If any question arises as to whether the judge should give a special warning in respect of a witness, it is desirable that the question be resolved by discussion with counsel in the absence of the jury before final speeches. (The judge will often consider that no special warning is required at all. Where, however, the witness has been shown to be unreliable, he or she may consider it necessary to urge caution.[40] In a more extreme case, if the witness is shown to have lied, to have made previous false complaints, or to bear the defendant some grudge, a stronger warning may be thought appropriate and the judge may suggest it

---

[37] See Law Commission Working Paper No 115 paras 2.9 and 2.18 and *Vetrovec v R* (1982) 136 DLR (3d) 89 at 95.

[38] [1995] 3 All ER 730, CA.

[39] [1995] 3 All ER 730 at 733. See also Lewis, 'A Comparative Examination of Corroboration and Care Warnings in Prosecutions of Sexual Offences' [2006] Crim LR 889.

[40] eg when a complainant's evidence is internally inconsistent or there are previous inconsistent statements: see *R v Walker* [1996] Crim LR 742, CA.

would be wise to look for some supporting material before acting on the impugned witness's evidence.[41] We stress that these observations are merely illustrative of some, not all, of the factors which judges may take into account in measuring where a witness stands in the scale of reliability...).[42]

5. Where the judge does decide to give some warning in respect of a witness, it will be appropriate to do so as part of the judge's review of the evidence and his comments as to how the jury should evaluate it rather than a set-piece legal direction.

6. Where some warning is required, it will be for the judge to decide the strength and terms of the warning. It does not have to be invested with the whole florid regime of the old corroboration rules.

7. It follows that we emphatically disagree with the tentative submission [that if a judge does give a warning, he should give a full warning and should tell the jury what corroboration is in the technical sense and identify the evidence capable of being corroborative]. Attempts to re-impose the straitjacket of the old corroboration rules are strongly to be deprecated.

8. Finally, this court will be disinclined to interfere with a judge's exercise of his discretion save in a case where that exercise is unreasonable in the *Wednesbury* sense.[43]

'*Supporting material*'

Following *R v Makanjuola*, if there is an evidential basis for suggesting that the witness may be unreliable, and the trial judge therefore decides to direct the jury that it would be wise to look for some 'supporting material', the judge is no longer required to identify for the jury what evidence is and is not capable of being corroboration in the technical sense. However, once such a direction is given, it has been held that it is then incumbent on the judge to identify any 'independent supporting evidence'.[44] It seems reasonably clear that such evidence may be furnished by the accused himself, as when evidence is given of an out-of-court confession or the accused makes a damaging admission in the course of giving his evidence.[45] It seems equally clear that it may be furnished by (i) the accused's lies, whether told in or out of court; (ii) his silence; (iii) his refusal to consent to the taking of samples; or (iv) his misconduct. It will be convenient to consider, briefly, these examples before turning to some items of evidence which, arguably, cannot constitute 'supporting material'.

Lies by the accused may amount to 'supporting material' depending on the nature of the lie and the nature of the other evidence in the case. It is submitted that the criteria for determining whether a lie constitutes 'supporting material' are the same as those previously employed for determining whether a lie amounted to corroboration in the technical sense. Those criteria, applicable to lies whether told in or out of court, were established in *R v Lucas*:[46]

---

[41] Delay in complaining will not, by itself, require either the 'stronger direction' or the urging of 'caution': see *R v R* [1996] Crim LR 815, CA and *R v Fallis* [2004] EWCA Crim 923.

[42] The bracketed material is set out in an earlier part of the judgment (at 732).

[43] See *Associated Provincial Picture Houses Ltd v Wednesbury Corpn* [1948] 1 KB 223. This is a heavy burden for an appellant to discharge: see *R v R* [1996] Crim LR 815, CA.

[44] *R v B (MT)* [2000] Crim LR 181, CA.

[45] See *R v Dossi* (1918) 13 Cr App R 158, CCA: on a charge of indecently assaulting a girl, an admission by the accused, in court, that he had innocently fondled her, is some corroboration of her evidence.

[46] [1981] QB 720, CA at 724.

To be capable of amounting to corroboration the lie...must first of all be deliberate.[47] Secondly it must relate to a material issue. Thirdly the motive for the lie must be a realisation of guilt and a fear of the truth. The jury should in appropriate cases be reminded that people sometimes lie, for example, in an attempt to bolster up a just cause, or out of shame or out of a wish to conceal disgraceful behaviour from their family. Fourthly the statement must clearly be shown to be a lie by evidence other than that of the [witness] who is to be corroborated, that is to say by admission or by evidence from an independent witness.

Thus where an accused, charged with a sexual offence, tells the police that on the evening in question he did not leave his house, but subsequently admits that this statement was false, his lie may be used to support the evidence of the victim that the offence had taken place near to the accused's home,[48] because 'a false statement...may give to a proved opportunity a different complexion from what it would have borne had no such false statement been made'.[49] R v Lucas itself concerned the fourth criterion. The appeal was allowed because the jury had been invited to prefer the evidence of an accomplice to that of the accused and then to use their disbelief of the accused as corroboration of the accomplice. The direction was erroneous because the 'lie' told by the accused was not shown to be a lie by evidence other than that of the accomplice who was to be corroborated.[50]

Where a person is accused of a crime, by a person speaking to him on even terms, in circumstances such that it would be natural for him to reply, evidence of his silence may be admitted, at common law, to show that he admits the truth of the charge made[51] and may constitute 'supporting material'.[52] Such material, it is submitted, may also be derived from inferences properly drawn from (i) the accused's failure to mention facts when questioned by a constable or on being charged with an offence; (ii) his silence at trial; (iii) his failure or refusal to account for objects, substances, marks, or presence at a particular place;[53] or (iv) his refusal to consent to the taking of 'intimate samples'.[54] Supporting material may also take the form of evidence of the accused's misconduct on some other occasion admitted under the similar fact evidence doctrine as evidence relevant to the question of guilt on the charge before the court.[55]

Whether a given item of evidence is capable of amounting to 'supporting material' is not always as easy as the above examples might suggest. For example, in a case of rape in which the complainant is shown to have made previous false complaints and a warning is properly given, should any of the following items be treated as 'supporting material', and in any event, how should the judge direct the jury in their regard: (i) evidence of recent complaint;[56] (ii) evidence of the distressed condition of the complainant; and (iii) medical evidence showing that someone had had intercourse with the complainant at a time consistent with her

---

[47] A lie being an *intentional* false statement, the meaning of the first requirement is obscure.

[48] See *Credland v Knowler* (1951) 35 Cr App R 48, DC. For an example of a lie told in court, see *Corfield v Hodgson* [1966] 2 All ER 205.

[49] Per Lord Dunedin in *Dawson v McKenzie* (1908) 45 SLR 473.

[50] See also per Lord MacDermott in *Tumahole Bereng v R* [1949] AC 253 at 270.

[51] See *R v Mitchell* (1892) 17 Cox CC 503; *R v Chandler* [1976] 3 All ER 105, CA; *Parkes v R* [1976] 1 WLR 1251; and generally Ch 13.

[52] See *R v Cramp* (1880) 14 Cox CC 390, a decision on corroboration in the technical sense.

[53] See Criminal Justice and Public Order Act 1994, ss 34–7 (see Ch 14).

[54] See *R v (Robert William) Smith* (1985) 81 Cr App R 286, CA and Police and Criminal Evidence Act 1984, s 62(10) (Ch 14).

[55] See Ch 17.

[56] See the Criminal Justice Act 2003, s 120.

evidence? There are compelling reasons to suggest that each of these items, by itself, should not be treated as 'supporting material' and the judge should direct the jury accordingly. As to a recent complaint, the trial judge should, at the least, explain to the jury that the evidence emanates from the complainant herself.[57] As to evidence of distress, the same point could be made, but such a direction would be inappropriate if, for example, the distress was witnessed shortly after the offence, the complainant was unaware that she was being observed, and there is nothing to suggest that she put on an act and simulated distress.[58] However, in appropriate cases the jury should be alerted to the risk that distress may have been feigned.[59] Concerning medical evidence of intercourse, the trial judge might sensibly direct the jury that it does not, by itself, show that intercourse took place without consent or that the accused was a party to it.[60] It is to be hoped that commonsensical guidance and helpful directions of this kind will not be regarded as 'attempts to re-impose the straitjacket of the old corroboration rules'. It would be a pity if the baby of common sense were to be thrown out with the corroboration bath water.

Sexual cases in which identification is in issue

There is nothing to suggest that the principles established in *R v Makanjuola* should not apply to sexual cases in which identification is in issue. If the identity of the offender is in issue, but the fact that someone committed the offence is not in issue, either because formally admitted by the accused or, if not formally admitted, because there has been no suggestion by the defence that there is any doubt as to the commission of the offence, it will normally suffice to direct the jury, in accordance with *R v Turnbull*,[61] about the need for caution before convicting on identification evidence; a further warning about the complainant's evidence as to the *offence* is only required where there is an evidential basis for suggesting that her evidence in that regard is unreliable.[62]

---

[57] Such evidence was not corroboration in the technical sense because not independent of the witness requiring to be corroborated: see *R v Whitehead* [1929] 1 KB 99, CCA.

[58] Evidence of distress *could* amount to corroboration in the technical sense, but juries had to be warned that except in special circumstances little weight should be given to it: see per Lord Parker CJ in *R v Knight* [1966] 1 WLR 230 at 233. For examples, see *R v Redpath* (1962) 46 Cr App R 319, CCA; *R v Chauhan* (1981) 73 Cr App R 232, CA; and *R v Dowley* [1983] Crim LR 168, CA.

[59] *R v Romeo* [2004] 1 Cr App R 417, CA. Conversely, an issue that has not uncommonly arisen in sexual cases has been a complainant's apparent lack of distress, inferred from such things as delay in reporting and demeanour after the offence and in the witness box. Where such an issue does arise, a careful direction should be given to the jury that the trauma of a serious sexual assault means that there is no one classic response. See *R v D* [2008] EWCA Crim 2557 and Neil Kibble's 'Commentary' [2009] Crim LR 591.

[60] For these reasons, such evidence was not corroboration in the technical sense: *James v R* (1970) 55 Cr App R 299, PC. However, if there was *also* evidence that the accused alone had been with the complainant at the relevant time, and evidence that her underclothing was torn and that she had injuries to her private parts, the combined effect of all the evidence was capable of amounting to corroboration: see per Lord Lane CJ in *R v Hills* (1987) 86 Cr App R 26, CA at 31. Where the only issue is consent, it would seem that evidence of injuries is, by itself, capable of supporting the complainant's assertion of lack of consent. However, where two or more accused are charged with successive acts of rape, the question whether the material can support the complainant's case against more than one of them will turn on the particular circumstances of the case: see *R v Pountney* [1989] Crim LR 216, CA and *R v Franklin* [1989] Crim LR 499, CA, decisions on corroboration in the technical sense. See also *R v Ensor* [1989] 1 WLR 497, CA.

[61] [1977] QB 224, CA (see, in this chapter, under **Identification cases, Visual identification by witnesses, n 119**).

[62] Cf *R v Chance* [1988] 3 All ER 225, CA, regarding corroboration in the technical sense.

Other witnesses whose evidence may be tainted by an improper motive

There are a number of common law authorities to the effect that the jury should be warned to exercise caution before acting on the evidence of a witness who may have a purpose of his own to serve. These authorities are considered in the paragraphs that follow. Some of the authorities preceding *R v Makanjuola* suggested that in some circumstances, at any rate, the warning was obligatory. It is now clear, from the decision in *R v Muncaster*,[63] that all such authorities need to be looked at afresh in the light of *R v Makanjuola*. It was held that the guidance in *R v Makanjuola* must be read as applying generally to all cases in which a witness may be suspect because he falls into a certain category.

An accomplice who is a co-accused may incriminate another co-accused when giving evidence in his own defence. Because, in these circumstances, an accomplice may be regarded as having some purpose of his own to serve, it has been held that it is desirable, but only as a matter of practice, to warn the jury of the danger of acting on his unsupported evidence, and that every case must be looked at in the light of its own facts.[64] In *R v Cheema*,[65] following a full review of the authorities, Lord Taylor CJ said:

> although a warning in suitable terms as to the danger of a co-defendant having an axe to grind is desirable, there is no rule of law or practice requiring a full corroboration direction...what is required when one defendant implicates another in evidence is simply to warn the jury of what may very often be obvious—namely that the defendant witness may have a purpose of his own to serve.[66]

Following *R v Makanjuola*, it is clear that whether a warning is given, and if so, its strength, remain matters of judicial discretion dependent on the circumstances of the case.[67] In *R v Jones*[68] it was held that in the case of cut-throat defences, including mirror-image cut-throat defences, a warning should normally be considered and given and, if given, should at least warn the jury to examine the evidence of each accused with care because each has or may have an interest of his own to serve.[69] There is a particular need for some such warning where, as in *R v Jones* itself, one of the accused has refused to answer questions in interview and is therefore able, if he wishes, to tailor his defence to the facts in evidence. It was further held that, subject to what justice demands on the particular facts of each case, in many or most cases a judge might consider four points to put to the jury: (1) to consider the case for and against each accused separately; (2) to decide the case on all the evidence, including the evidence of each co-accused; (3) when considering the evidence of each co-accused, to bear in mind that he may have an interest to serve or 'an axe to grind'; and

[63] [1999] Crim LR 409, CA.

[64] *R v Prater* [1960] 2 QB 464, CCA at 466. See also *R v Knowlden* (1983) 77 Cr App R 94, CA; *R v Stannard* [1964] 1 All ER 34 at 40, per Winn J; and *R v Whitaker* (1976) 63 Cr App R 193, CA at 197, per Lord Widgery. However, if the evidence incriminates the accused in one material respect but otherwise exonerates him, there is no need for a warning (which could operate to the *disadvantage* of the accused): see *R v Perman* [1995] Crim LR 736, CA.

[65] [1994] 1 All ER 639, CA at 647–9.

[66] See also *R v Sargent* [1993] Crim LR 713, CA: the defendant witness may well have a 'row of his own to hoe'.

[67] *R v Muncaster* [1999] Crim LR 409, CA.

[68] [2004] 1 Cr App R 60, CA.

[69] Contrast *R v Burrows* [2000] Crim LR 48, CA, where, according to *R v Jones*, the court was heavily influenced by the particular facts.

(4) to assess the evidence of co-defendants in the same way as the evidence of any other witness in the case.[70]

There are no special conditions of admissibility for cell confessions, and no requirement that they be corroborated.[71] However, in *Pringle v R*[72] it was held that a judge must always be alert to the possibility that the evidence of one prisoner against another is tainted by an improper motive, especially where a prisoner who has yet to face trial gives evidence that the other prisoner has confessed to the crime for which he is being held in custody. The indications that the evidence may be tainted by an improper motive must be found in the evidence—described as 'not an exacting test'—and the surrounding circumstances may justify the inference that his evidence is so tainted. This approach was followed in *Benedetto v R*,[73] where the Privy Council observed that the prisoners giving the evidence will almost always have strong reasons of self-interest for seeking to ingratiate themselves with those who may be in a position to reward them for volunteering the evidence, and that the accused is always at a disadvantage because he has none of the usual protections against the inaccurate recording or invention of words when interviewed by the police, and if the informer has a bad character, it may be difficult for him to obtain information needed to expose it fully. However, a much more flexible approach was adopted in *R v Stone*,[74] where the Court of Appeal held as follows.

1. Not every case involving a cell confession requires the detailed directions discussed in *Pringle v R* and *Benedetto v R*. Such cases prompt the most careful consideration by the trial judge, but that consideration is not trammelled by fixed rules; the trial judge is best placed to decide the strength of any warning and any accompanying analysis.

2. In the case of a 'standard two-line confession', there would generally be a need to point out that such confessions are often easy to concoct and difficult to disprove and that experience has shown that prisoners may have many motives to lie. Further, if the informant has a significant criminal record or history of lying, this should usually be pointed out, explaining why it gives rise to a need for great care.

3. However, a summing-up should be tailored to the circumstances of the particular case. Where an alleged confession would not be easy to invent, it would be absurd to give a direction on the ease of concoction. Similarly, where the defence deliberately do not cross-examine the complainant about the motive of hope of obtaining advantage, there is no requirement to tell the jury that the informant being a prisoner, there might, intrinsically, have been such a motive.

4. There will be cases where the prisoner has witnessed the acts constituting the offence in which it will be appropriate to treat him as an ordinary witness about whose evidence nothing out of the usual needs to be said.

---

[70] *R v Jones* was followed in *R v Petkar* [2004] 1 Cr App R 270, CA. However, in *Petkar*, Rix LJ voiced two concerns about *Jones* worth noting: first, the warning could devalue the evidence of both co-accused in the eyes of the jury and second, point (3) in *Jones* did not appear to lie easily with point (4).

[71] For an analysis of the issues, see Jeremy Dein, 'Non Tape Recorded Cell Confession Evidence—On Trial' [2002] Crim LR 630.

[72] [2003] UKPC 9.

[73] [2003] 1 WLR 1545, PC.

[74] [2005] Crim LR 569, CA. See *R v Cundell* [2009] EWCA Crim 2072, where, notwithstanding the more flexible approach in *Stone*, the judge should have given a warning in respect of the evidence of two prisoners awaiting sentence and one prisoner who hoped to be moved to an open and more local prison.

5. Indications that the prison informant's evidence may be tainted by an improper motive have to be found in the evidence.

In *R v Beck*[75] it was argued that an accomplice warning should be given in cases where a witness has a substantial interest of his own for giving false evidence even though there is no material to suggest any involvement by the witness in the crime. Although rejecting the argument, Ackner LJ said that the court did not wish to detract from 'the obligation on a judge to advise a jury to proceed with caution where there is material to suggest that a witness's evidence may be tainted by an improper motive', continuing, 'and the strength of that advice must vary according to the facts of the case'.[76] Thus a warning may be given where there is evidence to suggest that a witness is acting out of spite or malevolence, has a financial or other personal interest in the outcome of the proceedings, or is otherwise biased or partial.[77] Where a witness, awaiting sentence, gives evidence for the prosecution in another case in circumstances in which he knows that at the very least by doing so he stands a chance of having his sentence reduced, it has been held that the potential fallibility of his evidence should be put squarely before the jury.[78] In *R v Asghar*[79] a group of men became involved in a fight in which someone was fatally stabbed. A was charged with murder. Three others from the group pleaded guilty to affray and gave evidence for the prosecution against A. It was held that the judge should have exercised his discretion to direct the jury on the danger of convicting A on the evidence of the other three without some independent supporting evidence because: (i) the defence case was that the three had put their heads together with others to fabricate a story incriminating A in order to protect one of their number; (ii) this suggested the motive for their alleged lies was directly linked with the murder charge and did not arise from some unconnected cause; and (iii) the three were not on trial with A and not at risk, their position being akin to those of accomplices in the strict sense.[80] Equally, where a witness, having entered into an agreement to assist the authorities under s 73 of the Serious Organized Crime and Police Act 2005, gives evidence in return for a reduced sentence, a warning is called for to address the obvious risk that he is serving his own ends and not those of justice. In *R v Daniels*,[81] it was held that a carefully worded warning is the proper way to address this risk since, given the overwhelming public interest that major criminals should be convicted, there could be no objection to the admissibility of such evidence purely because the witness had 'self-interestedly done a deal or entered into a ... Faustian pact'.[82]

[75] [1982] 1 WLR 461, CA.

[76] [1982] 1 WLR 461 at 469. See also *R v Witts and Witts* [1991] Crim LR 562, CA.

[77] A warning is unnecessary, however, if it would do more harm than good, as when it is obvious to the jury, from the circumstances of the case, that a witness is suspect: *R v Lovell* [1990] Crim LR 111, CA.

[78] *Chan Wai-Keung v R* [1995] 2 All ER 438, PC.

[79] [1995] 1 Cr App R 223, CA.

[80] Although the final reason is no longer compelling (see, in this chapter, under **Care warnings, Accomplices testifying for the prosecution and complainants in sexual cases, Section 32 of the Criminal Justice and Public Order Act 1994**), it is submitted that in such a case the need for some form of warning remains. See, further, the judgment of Lord Reading CJ in *R v King* (1914) 10 Cr App R 117; and cf *R v Hanton* (1985) The Times, 14 Feb, CA; and *R v Evans* [1965] 2 QB 295.

[81] [2011] 1 Cr App R 18, CA. See also *R v Blackburn* [2008] 2 Cr App R (S) 5. See also *Krishna v Trinidad & Tobago* [2011] UKPC 18, PC: a witness does not cease to be an accomplice on the basis that he has agreed to and does give evidence for the authorities as a prosecution witness.

[82] Per Richards LJ at [40], quoting from a ruling of Langstaff J in the trial of the appellants.

R v Spencer, R v Smails[83] may be regarded as a further example. In that case, nursing staff at a secure hospital were charged with ill-treating patients convicted of crimes and suffering from mental disorders. The prosecution case consisted of the evidence of patients who were characterized as being mentally unbalanced, of bad character, anti-authoritarian, and prone to lie or exaggerate and who could have had old scores to settle. The House of Lords held that where the only evidence for the prosecution is that of a witness who, by reason of his particular mental condition and criminal connection, fulfils criteria analogous to those which (formerly) justified a full corroboration warning (accomplices testifying for the prosecution and complainants in sexual cases), the judge should warn the jury that it is dangerous to convict on his uncorroborated evidence, but such a warning need not amount to the full warning.[84] Thus while it may often be convenient to use the words 'danger' or 'dangerous', the use of such words is not essential to an adequate warning, so long as the jury are made fully aware of the dangers of convicting on such evidence, and the extent to which the judge should refer to the corroborative material, if any exists, depends on the facts of each case.[85] It may be doubted whether 'corroborative material', for these purposes, was ever intended to mean corroboration in the strict sense; and it is submitted that, notwithstanding the analogy drawn with cases which (formerly) justified a full corroboration warning (which, in the light of s 32 of the 1994 Act, would suggest that a warning is no longer obligatory), a warning of the kind indicated in *R v Spencer, R v Smails* should still be given in respect of witnesses sharing the same unfortunate characteristics as the witnesses in that case. Following *R v Makanjuola*, however, it is clear that where a warning is given, its terms will depend on the precise circumstances of the particular case.[86]

Children

Under the proviso to s 38(1) of the Children and Young Persons Act 1933, where the unsworn evidence of a child was given on behalf of the prosecution, the accused was not liable to be convicted unless that evidence was corroborated by some other material evidence implicating him; and at common law, the sworn evidence of a child required a corroboration warning as a matter of law.[87] Section 38(1) has been repealed[88] and s 34(2) of the Criminal Justice Act 1988[89] provides that: 'Any requirement whereby at a trial on indictment it is obligatory for the court to give the jury a warning about convicting the accused on the uncorroborated evidence of a child is abrogated.' The rationale underlying the proviso to s 38(1) and the common law rule was the danger that the evidence of a child, especially if unsworn, but even if sworn, may be unreliable by reason of childish imagination, suggestibility, or fallibility of memory. These dangers remain, and although in *R v Pryce*[90] it was held that a direction to treat the evidence of a six-year-old girl with caution was not required, because this would amount to a re-introduction of the abrogated rule, it is clear, following *R v Makanjuola*, that judges do

---

[83] [1986] 2 All ER 928, HL.

[84] Overruling, in this respect, *R v Bagshaw* [1984] 1 All ER 971, CA.

[85] See also, in this chapter, concerning confessions made by the mentally handicapped, *R v Bailey* [1995] Crim LR 723, CA and Police and Criminal Evidence Act 1984, s 77, under **Confessions by the mentally handicapped**.

[86] See *R v Causley* [1999] Crim LR 572, CA.

[87] See, eg, *R v Cleal* [1942] 1 All ER 203, CCA.

[88] Criminal Justice Act 1991, s 101(2) and Sch 13.

[89] As amended by Criminal Justice and Public Order Act 1994, s 32(2).

[90] [1991] Crim LR 379, CA.

retain a discretionary power to give such a direction, but whether such a direction should be given, and if so, its precise terms, are matters dependent on the circumstances of the case.[91] In the case of children, the relevant factors include the age and intelligence of the child, whether the evidence is given on oath, and, if the evidence is unsworn, how well the child in question understands the duty of speaking the truth. In *R v Pryce* itself, the Court of Appeal thought that it was sufficient for the trial judge to have told the jury to take into account the fact that the witness was a child. In other cases, a stronger direction will be called for.

Anonymous witnesses

In criminal cases witnesses may give evidence anonymously under the Coroners and Justice Act 2009,[92] provided certain express pre-conditions are satisfied.[93] Previously, at common law, the Court of Appeal had held in *R v Davis*[94] that where the prosecution rely on the evidence of anonymous witnesses, the judge 'would probably' suggest that the jury should consider whether there is any independent, supporting evidence tending to confirm their credibility and the incriminating evidence that they have given. Under s 90 of the Act, the judge is required to give the jury a 'judicial warning' to ensure that an accused is not prejudiced by the fact that a witness has given evidence anonymously.[95] According to the Crown Court Bench Book, the judicial warning, common to all directions, should include a warning that anonymity is not to be taken as any reflection on the accused or his case and, if necessary, an additional warning on how, if at all, the accused has been disadvantaged in the conduct of his case.[96] It is submitted that the warning should also invite the jury to consider the existence or absence of independent supporting evidence confirming the credibility of the anonymous witness and the evidence given.

Matrimonial cases

Where a matrimonial 'offence' is alleged, whether in proceedings in the High Court or in a summary court, the gravity of the consequences of proof of such an allegation and the risk of a miscarriage of justice in acting on the uncorroborated evidence of a spouse have led the courts to acknowledge the desirability of corroboration. Corroboration is sought as a matter of practice rather than as a matter of law. Thus the court may act on the uncorroborated evidence

---

[91] See *R v L* [1999] Crim LR 489, CA. As to the reliability of children's evidence generally, see the forceful observations of Lord Judge LCJ in *R v B* [2010] EWCA Crim 4, CA. His Lordship stated that: '... Many accreted suspicions and misunderstandings about children and their capacity to understand the nature and purpose of an oath and to give truthful and accurate evidence at a trial have been swept away...'. (at [33]). He further stated: 'We emphasise that in our collective experience the age of a witness is not determinative on his or her ability to give truthful and accurate evidence...' (at [40]). See also 'Commentary *R v B*' [2011] Crim LR 23. See also Spencer, 'Children's Evidence: the Barker case, and the case for Pigot' [2010] Arch Rev 3, 5–8.

[92] The 2009 Act replaced the Criminal Evidence (Witness Anonymity) Act 2008.

[93] See Ch 5, under **Witnesses in criminal cases, Witness anonymity**.

[94] [2006] 4 All ER 648, CA, per Sir Igor Judge, P, at [61]. The decision was overturned by the House of Lords (see *R v Davis* [2008] 1 AC 1128, HL). See also *R v Myers and others* [2009] 2 All ER 145, 1 Cr App R 30.

[95] According to the Explanatory Notes of the 2009 Act at [475], s 90 is based on the Youth Justice and Criminal Evidence Act 1999, s 32 which provides for jury warnings in cases where special measures have been enacted for vulnerable witnesses. See Ch 5, under **Witnesses in criminal cases, Special measures directions for vulnerable and intimidated witnesses, Special measures directions, The status of video-recorded evidence, etc.**

[96] For example, whether the accused has been deprived of making enquiries about the background and reputation of the witness which might have provided a basis for testing his evidence and reliability. See the Crown Court Bench Book, at 100–102.

of a spouse if in no doubt where the truth lies.[97] However, in cases where sexual misconduct is alleged, or the evidence of adultery is that of a willing participant,[98] the appellate court will intervene unless the trial court expressly warned itself of the danger of acting on uncorroborated evidence.[99]

Section 4 of the Affiliation Proceedings Act 1957 provides that in affiliation proceedings the court shall not adjudge the defendant to be the putative father of the child, in a case where evidence is given by the mother, unless her evidence is corroborated in some material particular. Despite the abolition of affiliation proceedings by s 17 of the Family Law Reform Act 1987, the question of paternity will continue to arise in family and other proceedings. What corroboration requirement, if any, remains? The justification for the corroboration requirement in s 4, which was the comparative ease with which a false allegation as to paternity could be made, and the difficulty of rebutting it, is no longer convincing. Section 20 of the Family Law Reform Act 1969 provides that, in any civil proceedings in which the parentage of any person falls to be determined, the court may direct the genetic paternity testing of that person, the mother of that person, and any party alleged to be the father of that person. Presumably, although there is no longer any requirement for corroboration, or even a warning, it is likely that the courts will be aware of the need for caution, if only in those cases in which, no direction having been given under s 20, the mother adduces no material in support of her allegation.

Claims against the estate of a deceased person

Where a claim is advanced by a person against the estate of a deceased person, it is natural to look for corroboration in support of the claimant's evidence, but there is no rule of law which prevents the court from acting on the claimant's uncorroborated evidence, if it is convincing.[100]

Confessions by the mentally handicapped

In *R v MacKenzie*[101] Lord Taylor CJ, applying the guidance given in *R v Galbraith*[102] to cases involving confessions by the mentally handicapped, held that where (i) the prosecution case depends wholly on confessions; (ii) the defendant suffers from a significant degree of mental handicap; and (iii) the confessions are unconvincing to a point where a jury properly directed could not properly convict on them, then the judge, assuming he has not excluded the confessions earlier, should withdraw the case from the jury. It was held that confessions may be unconvincing, for example because they lack the incriminating details to be expected of a guilty and willing confessor, because they are inconsistent with other evidence, or because they are otherwise inherently improbable. In a case which is not withdrawn from the jury, the fact that the confession was made by a mentally handicapped person may be taken into account by the judge not only for the purpose of deciding whether it should be excluded as a matter of law (under s 76 of the Police and Criminal Evidence Act 1984 (the 1984 Act)), but

---

[97] See *Curtis v Curtis* (1905) 21 TLR 676.

[98] See *Galler v Galler* [1954] P 252, CA and *Fairman v Fairman* [1949] P 341.

[99] However, see also *Joseph v Joseph* [1915] P 122 and *Alli v Alli* [1965] 3 All ER 480.

[100] *Re Hodgson, Beckett v Ramsdale* (1885) 31 Ch D 177, CA; *Re Cummins* [1972] Ch 62, CA.

[101] [1993] 1 WLR 453, CA.

[102] [1981] 2 All ER 1060 (see Ch 2).

also in deciding whether to exercise his discretion to exclude (under s 82(3) or s 78(1) of that Act).[103] Thus in *R v Moss*[104] it was held that confessions made by an accused on the borderline of mental handicap, in the absence of a solicitor or any other independent person, in the course of nine interviews held over nine days, should have been excluded under s 76(2)(b).

Where the confession of a mentally handicapped person *is* admitted in evidence, s 77 of the 1984 Act imposes on the court a duty, in certain circumstances, to warn the tribunal of fact of the dangers of convicting such a person in reliance on his confession. It provides that:

1. Without prejudice to the general duty of the court at a trial on indictment with a jury to direct the jury on any matter on which it appears to the court appropriate to do so, where at such a trial—
    (a) the case against the accused depends wholly or substantially on a confession by him; and
    (b) the court is satisfied—
        (i) that he is mentally handicapped; and
        (ii) that the confession was not made in the presence of an independent person,
    the court shall warn the jury that there is a special need for caution before convicting the accused in reliance on the confession, and shall explain that the need arises because of the circumstances mentioned in paragraphs (a) and (b) above.
2. In any case where at the summary trial of a person for an offence it appears to the court that a warning under subsection (1) above would be required if the trial were on indictment with a jury, the court shall treat the case as one in which there is a special need for caution before convicting the accused on his confession.[105]

Concerning the 'general duty' referred to in s 77(1), in *R v Bailey*[106] it was held that in cases where the accused is significantly mentally handicapped and the prosecution would not have a case in the absence of the accused's confessions, the judge should give a full and proper statement of the accused's case against the confessions being accepted by the jury as true and accurate, which should include not only the points made on the accused's behalf, but also any points which appear to the judge to be appropriate. The matters which in *that* case should have been put before the jury[107] included: (i) that the experience of the courts has shown that people with significant mental handicap do make false confessions for a variety of reasons; (ii) the various possible reasons for the accused having made false confessions; and (iii) that without the confessions, there was no case against the accused.

Concerning s 77(1)(a), the word 'substantially' should not be given a restricted meaning: s 77 is not confined to cases where either the whole or 'most of the case' depends on the confession.[108] In deciding whether a case depends 'substantially' on the confession, the test to be applied is whether the case for the Crown is substantially less strong without the confession, a test which may not be satisfied if there is other prosecution evidence such as identification evidence and evidence of another confession which was made in the presence of an independent adult.[109]

Although para (a) of s 77(1), unlike para (b), does not expressly state that it is for the court to be satisfied of the circumstances mentioned therein, it seems clear that the need for a

---

[103] See generally Ch 13.

[104] (1990) 91 Cr App R 371, CA. See also *R v Cox* [1991] Crim LR 276, CA and *R v Wood* [1994] Crim LR 222, CA.

[105] Section 2A makes the warning under s 77(1) a requirement in trials on indictment without a jury.

[106] [1995] Crim LR 723, CA.

[107] The court held that nothing in its judgment was to be taken as of general application.

[108] *R v Bailey* [1995] Crim LR 723, CA.

[109] See *R v Campbell* [1995] 1 Cr App R 522, CA.

direction to the jury can only arise where the *judge* is satisfied as to the circumstances mentioned in para (a) as well as para (b),[110] since the judge, when a warning is given, must explain that the need for caution arises because of the circumstances mentioned in both paragraphs. Accordingly, the judge should not direct the jury that a special need for caution *may* arise if *they* are satisfied of the circumstances mentioned in the paragraphs, but that there is a special need for caution which has arisen because the case against the accused *does* depend wholly or substantially on a confession, the accused is mentally handicapped, and the confession *was not* made in the presence of an independent person.

In *R v Campbell*[111] it was held that, as to the 'warning', the judge does not have to follow any specific form of words, but would be wise to use the phrase 'special need for caution', and as to the 'explanation', the judge should explain that persons who are mentally disordered or mentally handicapped may, without wishing to do so, provide information which is unreliable, misleading, or self-incriminating. The explanation should be tailored to the particular evidence in the case, for example evidence that the accused is particularly suggestible or prone to acquiesce, comply, or give in to pressure. The judge should then explain that the function of the appropriate adult is designed to minimize the risk of the accused giving unreliable information by seeing that the interview is conducted properly and fairly and facilitating, if need be, communication between the police and the suspect.

A person is mentally handicapped if 'he is in a state of arrested or incomplete development of mind which includes significant impairment of intelligence and social functioning'.[112] An 'independent person' is defined negatively as not including a police officer or a person employed for, or engaged on, 'police purposes'[113] and could include, for example, a relative or friend of the accused or his solicitor.[114] Should a dispute arise on the issue whether the accused is mentally handicapped (or whether his confession was made in the presence of an independent person), evidence, if necessary expert medical evidence, may be adduced to enable the judge to come to a decision. In these circumstances, the section is silent as to the incidence of the burden of proof. Presumably, the onus is on the defence to prove the circumstances mentioned in s 77(1)(b) on a balance of probabilities, rather than on the prosecution to prove their non-existence beyond reasonable doubt.

The number of cases in which a s 77 warning will be required is likely to be very small. The possibilities of withdrawing the case from the jury or excluding the confession under ss 76, 78, or 82(3) have already been mentioned. It should also be noted that, under Code C, a person who is mentally handicapped must not be interviewed in the absence of an 'appropriate adult' (a concept which in large measure overlaps with that of an 'independent person' for the purposes of s 77)[115] unless an officer of the rank of superintendent or above considers that delay would be likely (a) to lead to (i) interference with or harm to evidence, or (ii) interference with

[110] However, concerning para (b), see also, *sed quaere, R v Lamont* [1989] Crim LR 813, CA: the judge should have directed the jury to exercise the caution called for if *they* accepted the evidence of mental handicap.

[111] [1995] 1 Cr App R 522, CA.

[112] Section 77(3).

[113] Section 77(3). For the meaning of 'Police purposes' see the Police Act 1964, s 64.

[114] Although the definition of an 'independent person' suggests that s 77 only applies in the case of questioning by police officers, in *R v Bailey* [1995] Crim LR 723, CA it was held that a s 77 warning should have been given in respect of a confession made to a member of the public.

[115] It is defined to include, inter alia, a relative, guardian, or other person responsible for his care or custody: see para 1.7(b), Code C. See also *R v Lewis* [1996] Crim LR 260, CA.

or physical harm to other people, or (iii) serious loss of or damage to property; (b) to lead to the alerting of other people suspected of having committed an offence but not yet arrested for it; or (c) to hinder the recovery of property obtained in consequence of the commission of an offence.[116] Thus it seems that s 77 is confined to cases in which the confession was made either in an interview conducted in breach of the Code or in an 'urgent interview'.[117] In the rare cases in which s 77 does apply, however, failure to warn the jury as required is grounds for a successful appeal.[118]

Identification cases

Visual identification by witnesses

In *R v Turnbull*[119] Lord Widgery CJ, giving the judgment of the Court of Appeal, laid down important guidelines relating to evidence of allegedly mistaken visual identification of the accused.[120] Mistaken identification of the accused, especially in cases of visual identification, may be regarded as the greatest cause of wrong convictions.[121] The guidelines in *R v Turnbull* were designed to lessen this danger. The Court of Appeal attempted to follow the recommendations in the Report of the Committee on Evidence of Identification in Criminal Cases chaired by Lord Devlin.[122] The Committee had recommended the enactment of a general rule precluding a conviction in any case in which the prosecution relies wholly or mainly on evidence of visual identification by one or more witnesses, but the guidelines fall considerably short of the Committee's proposals.

Failure to follow the guidelines is likely to result in a conviction being quashed if, on all the evidence, the verdict is unsafe.[123] It will be otherwise, however, if the Court of Appeal is convinced that had the jury been directed correctly, they would nevertheless have come to the same conclusion.[124] Privy Council authority is to the same effect, so that in 'exceptional circumstances' a conviction based on unsupported identification evidence might be upheld even though a *Turnbull* direction was not given.[125] In *Freemantle v R*[126] the trial judge failed to give a *Turnbull* direction. The identification, which was by way of recognition evidence, was

---

[116] Paras 11.15 and 11.18 and Annex E, Code C.

[117] See per Taylor LJ in *R v Moss* (1990) 91 Cr App R 371, CA at 377.

[118] See *R v Lamont* [1989] Crim LR 813, CA: such a direction was not a matter of prudence, but an essential part of a fair summing-up. However, also see *R v Qayyum* [2007] Crim LR 160, CA, where it was held that giving a formal warning would have made no difference to the jury's approach.

[119] [1977] QB 224.

[120] Other aspects of visual identification evidence are considered elsewhere: the exclusion of such evidence, if obtained in breach of Code D, under the Police and Criminal Evidence Act 1984, s 78 (Ch 3); the admissibility of evidence of previous identification, and dock identifications (Ch 6); identification by samples (Ch 14); identification by photographs, films, photofits, and sketches (Ch 9); and expert evidence on identification by voice (Ch 18). As to the importance of pre-trial procedures relating to identification evidence, see Roberts, 'The problem of mistaken identity: Some observations on process' (2004) 8 E&P 100.

[121] See Criminal Law Revision Committee, 11th Report, Cmnd 4991 (1972), para 196.

[122] Cmnd 338 (1976).

[123] *R v Kane* (1977) 65 Cr App R 270, CA. See also *R v Tyson* [1985] Crim LR 48, CA.

[124] *R v Hunjan* (1978) 68 Cr App R 99, CA, where the conviction was in fact quashed; and cf *R v Clifton* [1986] Crim LR 399, CA, where the prosecution case was exceptionally strong.

[125] See *Reid v R* (1989) 90 Cr App R 121 at 130, PC and also the judgment of Lord Griffiths, in *Scott v R* [1989] 2 All ER 305, PC, at 314–15. However, see also Lord Ackner in *Reid v R* (1989) 90 Cr App R 121 at 130.

[126] [1994] 3 All ER 225, PC.

of exceptionally good quality: both identification witnesses had more than a fleeting glance at the accused and one of them said to the accused that he recognized him, to which the accused had replied in a way which appeared to acknowledge that he had been correctly identified. The Board was of the opinion that 'exceptional circumstances' include the fact that the evidence of identification is of exceptionally good quality and accordingly held that application of a proviso similar in its terms to s 2(1) of the Criminal Appeal Act 1968 was justified.

It is advisable, in every case in which a *Turnbull* direction may be required, for there to be a discussion between the judge and counsel, prior to the closing speeches and the summing-up, as to how identification issues will be addressed.[127]

The *Turnbull* guidelines are extensive. It will be convenient to consider separately seven extracts from the judgment of the Court of Appeal, together with subsequent developments in relation to each.

The special need for caution

Whenever the case against an accused depends wholly or substantially on the correctness of one or more identifications of the accused which the defence alleges to be mistaken, the judge should warn the jury of the special need for caution before convicting the accused in reliance on the correctness of the identification or identifications. In addition he should instruct them as to the reason for the need for such a warning and should make some reference to the possibility that a mistaken witness can be a convincing one and that a number of such witnesses can all be mistaken. Provided that this is done in clear terms, the judge need not use any particular form of words.

Although Lord Widgery CJ himself said that *Turnbull*'s case 'is intended primarily to deal with the ghastly risk run in cases of fleeting encounters...',[128] the warning should be given even if the opportunities for observation were good and the identifying witness is convinced that he has correctly identified the accused.[129] A warning must also be given notwithstanding that the identifying witness has picked out the accused at a formal identification procedure such as a video identification procedure.[130] It is of the utmost importance to give a warning where the sole evidence of identification is contained in the deposition of a deceased witness and the identification may have been based on a fleeting glance.[131]

Identification of persons with the accused

Where identification is in issue and there is strong prosecution evidence that the accused was with some other person at the relevant time, then the evidence identifying that other, unless unchallenged by the defence, should normally be the subject of a *Turnbull* direction.[132]

---

[127] *R v Stanton* (2004) The Times, 28 Apr, [2004] EWCA Crim 490.

[128] *R v Oakwell* (1978) 66 Cr App R 174 at 178.

[129] *R v Tyson* [1985] Crim LR 48, CA.

[130] Per Lord Griffiths in *Scott v R* [1989] 2 All ER 305, PC, at 314. Where the witness picks out a volunteer, there is no obligation to give a 'reverse *Turnbull* direction', ie that the witness may be honest but mistaken in identifying the volunteer, because the purpose of the *Turnbull* direction is to lessen the danger of a wrongful conviction, not a wrongful acquittal: see *R v Trew* [1996] Crim LR 441, CA. For the special issues that arise where there has been a qualified identification, see *R v George* [2003] Crim LR 282, CA and Roberts, 'The perils and possibilities of qualified identification: *R v George*' (2003) 7 E&P 130.

[131] *Scott v R* [1989] 2 All ER 305 at 314–15.

[132] *R v Bath* [1990] Crim LR 716, CA. Note that a *Turnbull* direction is not required in relation to the identification of cars: *R v Browning* (1991) 94 Cr App R 109, CA.

Where the issue is not identification but what the accused did

According to *R v Slater*,[133] where there is no issue as to the presence of the accused at or near the scene of the offence, but the issue is as to what he was doing, whether a *Turnbull* direction is necessary will depend on the circumstances of the case. It was held that it will be necessary where, on the evidence, the possibility exists that the identifying witness may have mistaken one person for another, for example because of similarities in face, build, or clothing between two or more people present,[134] but where there is no possibility of such a mistake, there is no need to give a *Turnbull* direction. On the facts, the accused was six foot six inches tall and there was no evidence to suggest that anyone else present was remotely similar in height. It was therefore held that there was no basis for any mistake: the issue in the case was not identi-fication, but what the accused did, and accordingly a *Turnbull* direction was not required. The court observed that in some cases, where presence is admitted but conduct disputed, it would be contrary to common sense to require a *Turnbull* direction, as when a black man and a white man are present and the complainant says that it was the white man.[135]

Where the evidence is a description rather than identification

It has also been said that a full direction is not required if none of the identifying witnesses purports to identify the accused, their evidence merely serving to provide a description which is not inconsistent with the appearance of the accused and forming only one part, albeit a very important part, of all the evidence, because such a case does not depend wholly or sub-stantially upon the correctness of their evidence.[136] In *R v Constantinou*,[137] where none of the witnesses purported to identify the accused but merely gave descriptions which might have been consistent with his appearance, and a photofit was admitted which also might have been consistent with his appearance, it was held that no *Turnbull* warning was required in respect of the photofit. This decision, it is submitted, is in need of review.

Where the truthfulness of the identifying witness is in issue

In a case where identification is in issue but the defence is that the identifying witness is lying, rather than mistaken, a *Turnbull* direction may not be required. In *R v Courtnell*[138] the defence was one of alibi and it was alleged that the purported identification, by someone who had known the accused for a week, was a fabrication. It was held that the trial judge had properly withdrawn the issue of mistaken identity from the jury: the sole issue was the veracity of the identifying witness and therefore a *Turnbull* direction would only have confused the jury.[139]

The terms of the direction

As to the terms of the direction, *R v Turnbull* is not a statute and does not require an incan-tation of a formula or set form of words: provided that the judge complies with the sense and spirit of the guidance given, he has a broad discretion to express himself in his own

---

[133] [1995] 1 Cr App R 584, CA.

[134] See, eg, *R v Thornton* [1995] 1 Cr App R 578, CA, where the appellant and others were similarly dressed.

[135] See also *R v Conibeer* [2002] EWCA Crim 2059 and cf *R v O'Leary* [2002] EWCA Crim 2055, CA.

[136] *R v Browning* (1991) 94 Cr App R 109. Cf *R v Andrews* [1993] Crim LR 590, CA.

[137] (1989) 91 Cr App R 74, CA.

[138] [1990] Crim LR 115, CA.

[139] See also, applying *R v Courtnell*, *R v Cape* [1996] 1 Cr App R 191, CA and *R v Beckles and Montague* [1999] Crim LR 148, CA; and *R v Ryder* [1994] 2 All ER 859, CA, *Capron v R* [2006] UKPC 34, and *R v Giga* [2007] Crim LR 571, CA, cases of recognition. But see further *Beckford v R* (1993) 97 Cr App R 409, PC, applied in *Shand v R* [1996] 1 All ER 511, PC, at n 156.

way.[140] Thus as to the reason for the warning, failure to use the word 'convincing' ('a mistaken witness can be a convincing one') need not be fatal to the summing-up.[141] Indeed, even prefacing the warning with advice to guard against 'allowing an oversophisticated approach to evidence relating to identification to become...a "mugger's charter"' was not fatal in *R v Shervington*[142] because, in the round, the judge did set out the direction sufficiently. Nonetheless, to depart from the standard form of the direction was 'singularly unwise' and the use of the words 'mugger's charter' was plainly inappropriate.[143] In relation to the general risk of mistaken identification, it is insufficient merely to say that 'even an honest witness may be mistaken': the judge should explain that evidence of visual identification is a category of evidence which experience has shown to be particularly vulnerable to error, in particular by honest and impressive witnesses, and that this has been known to result in wrong convictions.[144] There is a requirement to make clear that the need for special caution is rooted in the court's actual experience of miscarriages of justice.[145]

The circumstances of the identification and specific weaknesses in the identification evidence

The judge should direct the jury to examine closely the circumstances in which the identification by each witness came to be made.[146] How long did the witness have the accused under observation? At what distance? In what light? Was the observation impeded in any way, as for example by passing traffic or a press of people? Had the witness ever seen the accused before? How often? If only occasionally, had he any special reason for remembering the accused? How long a time elapsed between the original observation and the subsequent identification to the police? Was there any material discrepancy between the description of the accused given to the police by the witness when first seen by them and his actual appearance? If in any case the prosecution have reason to believe that there is such a material discrepancy, they should supply the accused or his legal advisers with particulars of the description the police were first given.[147] In all cases, if the accused asks to be given particulars of such descriptions, the prosecution should supply them. Finally, he should remind the jury of any specific weaknesses which had appeared in the identification evidence.

---

[140] Per Lord Steyn in *Mills v R* [1995] 3 All ER 865, PC at 872.

[141] See *Rose v R* [1995] Crim LR 939, PC. See also *France v The Queen* [2012] UKPC 28 at [18]. See also *R v Alexander* [2013] 1 Cr App R 26, CA at [38]–[39].

[142] [2008] Crim LR 581, CA.

[143] *R v Shervington* [2008] Crim LR 581, CA at [25] and [28].

[144] Per Lord Ackner in *Reid v R* (1989) 90 Cr App R 121 at 134–5.

[145] *R v Nash* [2005] Crim LR 232, CA. However, it has also been held that failure to refer to past miscarriages of justice is not fatal: *R v Tyler* [1993] Crim LR 60, CA. Indeed, in jurisdictions in which there is no history of well-publicized miscarriages of justice, eg Jamaica, such a reference would be unnecessary and unhelpful: *Amore v R* (1994) 99 Cr App R 279, PC.

[146] See also *R v Cole* [2013] EWCA Crim 1149 at [72]: it would be a misdirection to direct the jury in such a way as to suggest that evidence of an identification '...could or should be compartmentalised and the decision about its accuracy made without reference to extraneous circumstantial evidence which supported or undermined confidence in its reliability.'

[147] See Code D. See also *R v Cole* [2013] EWCA Crim 1149, where, in clear breach of Code D, a record of the witness's first description of the accused was not provided to the accused or his legal advisers before the accused's participation in an identification parade. See also Ch 3 and, in this chapter, under **Identification cases, Visual identification by witnesses, The circumstances of the identification and specific weaknesses in the identification evidence, Breaches of Code D.**

Simply paying lip service to the guidelines, without reference to the particular circumstances relevant to the accuracy of the identification will not suffice.[148] Nor is it sufficient for the judge simply to invite the jury to take into account what counsel for the defence has said about 'specific weaknesses': the judge must fairly and properly summarize for the jury any such weaknesses which can arguably be said to have been exposed in the evidence.[149] However, provided that the judge does identify all the specific weaknesses, there is no obligation to do so in a particular way, for example by bringing them together and listing them, rather than by dealing with them in context when reviewing the evidence in the case.[150] Equally, in the case of minor discrepancies between what the identifying witnesses have said, it is a matter for the judge's discretion whether simply to refer to them in his review of the evidence, or to categorize them specifically as potential weaknesses.[151]

The same rules apply to police officers as to other identifying witnesses, but sometimes an officer pays particular attention to the identity of a person, even in a fleeting glance type case. Where this issue arises, the judge should specifically direct the jury as to the likelihood of the officer being correct, when a 'mere casual observer' might not be, because an officer has a greater appreciation of the importance of identification, is trained, and is less likely to be affected by the excitement of the situation.[152]

Breaches of Code D

Where evidence of a formal identification procedure at which the accused was identified is central to the prosecution case but the judge, notwithstanding breaches of Code D, properly decides not to exercise his discretion under s 78 of the Police and Criminal Evidence Act 1984 to exclude it, then in his summing-up he should make specific references to the breaches and leave it to the jury to consider what their approach should be in the light of them.[153] However, the jury should be told that a failure to hold an identification procedure in breach of Code D is a breach of a positive obligation; to merely tell the jury that holding a procedure would have been 'desirable' is not sufficient.[154]

Recognition

Recognition may be more reliable than identification of a stranger; but even when the witness is purporting to recognize someone whom he knows, the jury should be reminded that mistakes in recognition of close relatives and friends are sometimes made.

Many people experience seeing someone in the street whom they know, only to discover that they are wrong. The expression 'I could have sworn it was you' indicates the sort of

---

[148] *R v Graham* [1994] Crim LR 212, CA, applied in *R v Allen* [1995] Crim LR 643, CA, where the trial judge took no steps to remove the possible prejudice resulting from an improper refusal to hold an identification parade. See also *R v I* [2007] 2 Cr App R 316, CA. Cf *R v Doldur* [2000] Crim LR 178, CA.

[149] *R v Fergus* (1993) 98 Cr App R 313, CA.

[150] *R v Mussell* [1995] Crim LR 887, CA; *R v Barnes* [1995] 2 Cr App R 491, CA; and *R v Qadir* [1998] Crim LR 828, CA. Cf *R v Pattinson* [1996] 1 Cr App R 51, CA.

[151] *R v Barnes* [1995] 2 Cr App R 491 at 500, CA.

[152] *R v Ramsden* [1991] Crim LR 295, CA; *R v Tyler* [1993] Crim LR 60, CA. Cf per Lord Ackner in *Reid v R* (1989) 90 Cr App R 121 at 137: 'experience has undoubtedly shown that police identification can be just as unreliable [as that of an ordinary member of the public].'

[153] *R v Quinn* [1995] 1 Cr App R 480, CA. See also *R v Preddie* [2011] EWCA Crim 312, where the judge should have exercised his discretion to exclude. See also Ch 3.

[154] *R v Gojra* [2010] EWCA Crim 1939.

warning which a judge should give, because that is exactly what a witness does—he swears that it was the person he thinks it was. In the field of recognition, there are degrees of danger, but perhaps less where the parties have known each other for many years or where there is no doubt that the person identified was at the scene at the time. Even here, it is at least advisable to alert the jury to the possibility of honest mistake and to the dangers, and the reasons why such dangers exist.[155]

In *Beckford v R*[156] the Privy Council held as follows. (1) A general warning on *Turnbull* lines *must* normally be given in recognition cases and failure to do so will nearly always *by itself* suffice to invalidate a conviction substantially based on identification evidence. (2) Such a warning should be given even if the sole or main thrust of the defence is directed to the issue of the identifying witness's credibility, ie whether his evidence is true or false as distinct from accurate or mistaken. The first question for the jury is whether the witness is honest, and if the answer to that question is Yes, the next question is whether he could be mistaken. (3) This 'strong general rule' is subject to only very rare exceptions:

> If, for example, the witness's identification evidence is that the accused was his workmate whom he has known for 20 years and that he was conversing with him for half an hour face to face in the same room and the witness is sane and sober, then, if credibility is the issue, it will be the only issue.[157]

However, in *Capron v R*[158] the Privy Council deprecated the use of phrases such as 'wholly exceptional' or 'very rare' to describe the situations in which the court can dispense with a *Turnbull* direction on the basis that the sole or main issue is the credibility of the identification witness or witnesses; what matters, it was said, is the nature of the identification evidence in each case. In *R v Giga*,[159] the Court of Appeal, affirming this approach, held that each case must turn on its own facts.

The 'strong general rule' referred to in *Beckford* means that in most cases where evidence of recognition is adduced, failure to warn the jury about its inherent dangers will be fatal to a conviction. In *R v Ali*,[160] a case involving a 'steaming robbery' whereby a train passenger was surrounded by a group and robbed, the accused was identified as a participant by the passenger. In addition to the evidence of identification given by the passenger, a police officer gave evidence that he recognized the accused from a CCTV 'still image' of a group of males on the platform of the station where the train had stopped. Although the judge provided a *Turnbull* warning in respect of the evidence of the passenger's identification, none was provided in respect of the evidence of the police officer's recognition. In quashing the conviction, the Court of Appeal observed that even with recognition, the risk of mistaken identification remains and a direction is required which brings home fully to the jury that an identifying witness can make a mistake when purporting to recognize someone he knows.[161] In this case, not

[155] *R v Bentley* (1991) 99 Cr App R 342, CA; *R v Bowden* [1993] Crim LR 379, CA. Cf *R v Curry* [1983] Crim LR 737 and *R v Oakwell* (1978) 66 Cr App R 174, CA.

[156] (1993) 97 Cr App R 409, PC.

[157] (1993) 97 Cr App R 409 at 415, applied in *Shand v R* [1996] 1 All ER 511, PC. Cf *R v Courtnell* [1990] Crim LR 115, CA and *R v Ryder* [1994] 2 All ER 859, CA, (see n 138 and n 139 repectively).

[158] [2006] UKPC 34.

[159] [2007] Crim LR 571, CA.

[160] [2009] Crim LR 40, CA.

[161] *R v Ali* [2009] Crim LR 40, CA at [35].

only had the judge failed to warn the jury, but he had directed them in such a way as to suggest that the correctness of the police officer's recognition could be treated as an established fact.

Recognition by police officers

It will be apparent from the facts in *Ali* that there is no general rule excluding evidence of recognition by police officers including recognition evidence based on viewing images recorded by a security camera, even though the jury may then infer that the accused has previously been in trouble with the police. This is because the fact of the officers' knowledge is of critical significance to the quality of the identification, and to exclude the evidence would unfairly advantage those with criminal records.[162] However, where police officers purport to recognize a suspect by viewing images recorded by a security camera, Code D is now directly applicable.

Recognition by film, photographs or other images

Code D contains the pre-trial procedure applicable to recognition by showing films, photographs, or other images.[163] Under the Code, a detailed record must be kept of the circumstances in which the recognition took place so that the accused is able to test its reliability.[164] Breach of the Code will not automatically result in exclusion of the recognition evidence. The courts will consider the seriousness of the breach[165] and whether there is other evidence sufficient to enable the reliability of the recognition to be tested.[166]

Identification evidence of good quality

When the quality [of the identification evidence] is good, as for example when the identification is made after a long period of observation, or in satisfactory conditions by a relative, a neighbour, a close friend, a workmate, and the like, the jury can safely be left to assess the value of the identifying evidence even though there is not other evidence to support it: provided always, however, that an adequate warning has been given about the special need for caution.

Where the quality of the identification evidence is such that the jury can be safely left to assess its value, even though there is no other evidence to support it, then the judge is fully entitled, if so minded, to direct the jury that an identification by one witness can constitute

---

[162] See *R v Crabtree* [1992] Crim LR 65, CA and *R v Caldwell* (1993) 99 Cr App R 73, CA; and cf *R v Fowden and White* [1982] Crim LR 588, CA. The defence then face difficulties in challenging the extent of the officers' knowledge of the accused. In *R v Caldwell* the Court of Appeal thought the difficulty was 'manageable', approving the sensitive ruling of the trial judge that the officers should not refer to any convictions or criminal associations of the accused, their families, etc.

[163] See the Police and Criminal Evidence Act 1984, Code D, 2011. Paragraphs D3.34–D3.37 supersede guidance given in *R v Smith* [2009] 1 Cr App R 521. See also Roberts, 'Commentary' [2009] Crim LR 437.

[164] Code D para D3.36.

[165] See *R v D* (2013) 177 J P 158, CA, where the evidence should have been excluded in the light of a 'wholesale breach of Code D' which was 'lamentable'. The court was particularly concerned by 'highly suggestive' comments made by a police officer to the witness (another police officer), namely that she believed the accused appeared in the CCTV footage which the witness was about to view.

[166] See *R v Moss* [2011] EWCA Crim 252, where an off-duty police officer had gone to a police station to check his emails and on passing by a computer screen recognized the suspect in an image from CCTV footage of a burglary. Although there had been a breach of Code D, it was held that the defence could test the reliability of the recognition because of evidence that the officer had reported it to his superior at the time and made a note in his notebook when he returned to work a week later. See also *R v Selwyn* [2012] EWCA Crim 2968 and *R v Singh* [2013] EWCA Crim 669.

support for the identification by another, *provided* that he warns them in clear terms that even a number of honest witnesses can all be mistaken.[167]

Identification evidence of poor quality

When, in the judgment of the trial judge, the quality of the identifying evidence is poor, as for example when it depends solely on a fleeting glance or on a longer observation made in difficult conditions, the situation is very different. The judge should then withdraw the case from the jury and direct an acquittal unless there is other evidence which goes to support the correctness of the identification. This may be corroboration in the sense that lawyers use that word; but it need not be so if its effect is to make the jury sure that there has been no mistaken identification.

Under this guideline, a case is withdrawn from the jury not because the judge considers that the witness is lying, but because the evidence, even if taken to be honest, has a base which is so slender that it is unreliable and therefore insufficient to found a conviction. The jury are protected from acting upon the type of evidence which, even if believed, experience has shown to be a possible source of injustice.[168]

Even in the absence of a submission, the judge is under a duty to invite submissions when, in his view, the identification evidence is poor and unsupported.[169] Moreover, *R v Turnbull* plainly contemplates that the position must be assessed not only at the end of the prosecution case, but also at the close of the defence case.[170] In exceptional cases, a ruling can be made even before the close of the prosecution case, on the depositions, but apparently in any event a *voir dire* should not be held.[171] A judge should not direct a jury that he would have withdrawn the case from them on a submission of no case to answer, had he thought that there was insufficient identification evidence, because the jury may mistakenly take this to mean that the evidence is sufficiently strong for them to convict.[172]

Supporting evidence

The trial judge should identify to the jury the evidence which he adjudges is capable of supporting the evidence of identification. If there is any evidence, or there are circumstances, which the jury might think was supporting, when the evidence or circumstances did not have this quality, the judge should say so. A jury, for example, might think that support could be found in the fact that the accused had not given evidence before them. An accused's absence from the witness box cannot provide evidence of anything and the judge should tell the jury so.[173] But he would be entitled to tell them that, when assessing the quality of the identification evidence, they could take into consideration the fact that it was uncontradicted by any evidence coming from the accused himself.

---

[167] Per Lord Lane CJ in *R v Weeder* (1980) 71 Cr App R 228, CA at 231. In *R v Breslin* (1984) 80 Cr App R 226, CA it was held that this direction (and warning) should be given in all identification cases to which it applies.

[168] Per Lord Mustill in *Daley v R* [1993] 4 All ER 86, PC, at 94.

[169] *R v Fergus* (1994) 98 Cr App R 313, CA.

[170] *R v Fergus* (1994) 98 Cr App R 313, CA, citing *R v Turnbull* [1977] QB 224 at 228–9.

[171] See *R v Flemming* (1987) 86 Cr App R 32, CA and cf *R v Beveridge* [1987] Crim LR 401, CA.

[172] *R v Smith and Doe* (1986) 85 Cr App R 197, CA. See also *R v Akaidere* [1990] Crim LR 808, CA: a judge should not direct the jury that the identification evidence is so poor that he would have stopped the case if it had stood alone.

[173] Failure to give such a direction will found a successful appeal. This remains the case, where the failure may have led the jury to believe that the accused's absence from the witness box was supportive, even if the quality of the identification evidence was good and there was evidence supportive of it: *R v Forbes* [1992] Crim LR 593, CA. But see now Criminal Justice and Public Order Act 1994, s 35 (see Ch 14).

It is essential for the judge to make clear to the jury that although he has adjudged that certain evidence is capable of supporting the evidence of identification, it is for them to decide, if they accept it, whether it does in fact support the evidence of identification.[174] The support may be provided by evidence of the accused's association with other suspects who have been identified[175] or by evidence that the identifying witness correctly identified another suspect seen with the accused at the relevant time.[176]

In a case of purported recognition in circumstances such that, had it been a case of identification by a stranger, the quality of the evidence would have been poor, the fact that it was a recognition may itself form part of the evidence in support.[177] However, it is doubtful that purported recognition of a suspect by a police officer would be supporting evidence for another witness's identification where the officer was not an expert and his recognition was based on viewing recorded images in which the suspect's face was partially hidden.[178] Further, it has been held that the physical appearance of an accused, however singular, and however closely it corresponds with the evidence of a witness describing the criminal, cannot amount without more to corroboration of that evidence because it does not establish the reliability of the witness's evidence that the criminal had such an appearance.[179]

It is for the jury to decide whether evidence is in fact supportive of the identification, and although there may be cases where in the light of the evidence that has unfolded the jury should be directed not to convict on the identification evidence alone, there is no general requirement to give such a direction.[180]

False alibis

Care should be taken by the judge when directing the jury about the support for an identification which may be derived from the fact that they have rejected an alibi. False alibis may be put forward for many reasons: an accused, for example, who has only his own truthful evidence to rely on may stupidly fabricate an alibi and get lying witnesses to support it out of fear that his own evidence will not be enough. Further, alibi witnesses can make genuine mistakes about dates and occasions just as any other witnesses can. Only when the jury are satisfied that the sole reason for the fabrication was to deceive them and there is no other explanation for its being put forward can fabrication provide any support for identification evidence. The jury should be reminded that proving the accused has told lies about where he was at the material time does not by itself prove that he was where the identifying witness says he was.

---

[174] *R v Akaidere* [1990] Crim LR 808, CA.

[175] *R v Penny* (1991) 94 Cr App R 345, CA.

[176] *R v Castle* [1989] Crim LR 567, CA and *R v Jones (Terence)* [1992] Crim LR 365, CA. See also *R v Brown* [1991] Crim LR 368, CA. See also *R v Hussain* [2004] EWCA Crim 1064.

[177] *R v Turnbull* [1977] QB 224. See also *R v Ryan* [1990] Crim LR 50, CA: it is rare for the court to feel concern about the rightness of a conviction based on evidence of recognition.

[178] See *R v Ali* [2009] Crim LR 40, CA. However, see also *R v Clare, R v Peach* [1995] 2 Cr App R 333, CA: an officer could acquire special knowledge which the court did not possess obtained by, for example, spending a long time analysing material from the crime scene.

[179] *R v Willoughby* (1988) 88 Cr App R 91, CA. However, see *R v McInnes* (1989) 90 Cr App R 99, CA, where a kidnapping victim's detailed knowledge of the inside of the alleged kidnapper's car was independent corroboration. See also *R v Nagy* [1990] Crim LR 187, CA.

[180] *R v Ley* [2007] 1 Cr App R 25, CA.

Such a direction should be given even if the prosecution have not relied on the collapse of the alibi as part of the material supporting their case.[181]

Visual identification by social networking sites

An identification is not invalidated because it is based on a witness's informal viewing of images contained on internet social networking sites such as Facebook.[182] However, the judge will need to carefully direct the jury on the circumstances of the identification and specific factors which could affect its reliability, including: (i) whether the witness obtained in advance the name of the person he identified; (ii) whether the witness read information about the person he identified, for example in 'personal profiles' or comments left on web pages; and (iii) whether other persons were present (or in contact) who prompted the witness;[183] and (iv) the nature and quality of the images viewed.

Concerning pre-trial procedure, Code D is not directly applicable and only limited guidance has been provided by the courts. In *R v Alexander*,[184] which involved an identification by Facebook, it was the subject of much concern that the prosecution had failed to provide the defence with the accused's Facebook entry or the Facebook pages looked at by the identifying witness and his sister (who had been present during the identification) and that no notes or statements had been taken by the police during initial discussions with the witness and his sister. The Court of Appeal held that it is incumbent on the police to obtain, in as much detail as possible, evidence about the circumstances of the identification. This should include the images that were looked at and a statement from the witness, so that the jury are able to properly assess how the identification occurred[185] and the defence are able to test its reliability. However, the court declined to set out what processes should be adopted in the future, taking the view that this was a matter for consideration by relevant statutory and professional bodies 'so that *short* and *simple* guidance can be given in short order, so that what happened in this case does not recur'.[186] It remains to be seen what, if any, guidance is issued in the future.

Visual identification by the jury

In a case in which the jurors themselves are asked to 'identify' the accused, whom they have seen in court, from a photograph or video recording of the offender committing the offence,[187] they should be warned of the risk of mistaken identity and of the need to exercise particular

---

[181] See *R v Duncan* (1992) The Times, 24 July, CA and *R v Pemberton* (1993) 99 Cr App R 228, CA.

[182] See *R v Alexander* [2013] 1 Cr App R 26, CA at [25].

[183] Another issue arising is the effect on a subsequent formal identification. In *R v McCullough* [2011] EWCA Crim 1413 at [13], an informal 'Facebook identification' was held to have been capable of having a substantial effect on the *weight* of a subsequent formal identification rather than its admissibility.

[184] [2013] 1 Cr App R 26, CA at [25].

[185] *R v Alexander* [2013] 1 Cr App R 26, CA at [22].

[186] *R v Alexander* [2013] 1 Cr App R 26, CA at [23].

[187] In *Attorney General's Reference (No 2 of 2002)* [2003] 1 Cr App R 21, CA, the Court of Appeal suggested circumstances where the jury might make an identification this way. These included where the image was clear enough to make a comparison with the accused, where the accused was recognized in the image by someone who knew him sufficiently well, or where the accused has been identified in the image by an expert in facial mapping or with some other relevant expertise. See also *R v Ali* [2009] Crim LR 40, CA, where images were not clear enough to permit a meaningful comparison and the judge had in any case failed to give the full and careful direction required when he invited the jury to 'use your own eyes' (at [40]–[41]).

care in any identification which they make. One factor which they must take into account is whether the appearance of the accused has changed since the visual recording was made, but a full *Turnbull* direction is inappropriate because the process of identifying a person from a photograph is a commonplace and everyday event and some things are obvious from the photograph itself. For example, the jury do not need to be told that the photograph is of good quality or poor, nor whether the person is shown in close-up or was distant from the camera, or was alone or part of a crowd.[188] However, an accused who has elected not to testify is under no obligation to meet a jury request that he stand up and turn around, in order that they may be given a better view of him.[189]

Voice identification

Unlike visual identification, in the case of aural or voice identification, little judicial thought has been given to the danger of mistakes being made or to the safeguards necessary to lessen the danger. Moreover Code D all but ignores the subject and simply states that the Code does not preclude the police from making use of aural identification procedures, such as a 'voice identification parade', where they judge that appropriate.[190] Such a parade was held in *R v Hersey*,[191] where 11 volunteers and the accused, H, read out a passage of text from an unrelated interview with H. This was listened to by the 'earwitness' who had heard considerable speech by two masked robbers during the robbery of his shop. On a *voir dire* an expert gave evidence that 12 voices was too many, that almost all of the volunteers' voices were of a pitch higher than that of H, and only H had read the passage in a way which made sense. He also gave evidence of the effect of stress on pitch. The trial judge decided not to exclude the identification evidence under s 78 of the 1984 Act, and ruled that the evidence of the expert was not admissible before the jury. The Court of Appeal held that evidence of the parade had been properly admitted and that the jurors did not require the assistance of the expert, who had dealt with matters which were within their own experience and competence.[192] It was also held that a warning based on the guidelines in *Turnbull* should be given, but tailored for the purposes of voice identification and recognition.

Subsequently, in *R v Roberts*,[193] the Court of Appeal acknowledged that according to the expert research that has been done, voice identification is more difficult than visual identification, especially in the case of a stranger, and therefore should attract an even more stringent warning than that given in the case of visual identification. It is also clear that where a tape recording, including a covert tape recording, of a voice alleged to be that of the accused is admitted in evidence, the opinion evidence of an expert in phonetics is admissible on the question whether the voice matches that of the accused. Indeed, in *R v Chenia*[194] it was held

---

[188] *R v Blenkinsop* [1995] 1 Cr App R 7, CA, approving *R v Downey* [1995] 1 Cr App R 547, CA. Cf *R v Dodson and Williams* (1984) 79 Cr App R 220, CA; see also *Taylor v Chief Constable of Cheshire* [1987] 1 All ER 225, DC (see Ch 10). Research, however, shows that there are dangers: see Bruce, 'Fleeting Images of Shade' (1998) *The Psychologist* 331 and Henderson et al, 'Matching the Faces of Robbers Captured on Video' (2001) 15 *Applied Cognitive Psychology* 445.

[189] *R v McNamara* [1996] Crim LR 750, CA.

[190] Para 1.2. See also para 18, Annex B, where a witness at a visual identification parade wishes to hear any parade member speak.

[191] [1998] Crim LR 281, CA.

[192] See *R v Turner* [1975] QB 834, CA (see Ch 18).

[193] [2000] Crim LR 183, CA.

[194] [2004] 1 All ER 543, CA at [106] and [107]. See also *R v O'Doherty* [2003] 1 Cr App R 77 (see Ch 18).

that without such expert assistance the jury should not be asked to compare what they hear on a recording with either what they hear on another recording or the voice of the accused when giving evidence. However, this must now be considered in the light of *R v Flynn*,[195] where the Court of Appeal concluded that, apart from *Chenia*, there was no other authority for the proposition that juries could only make such a comparison with expert assistance. Accordingly, it was held that it was wrong to direct the jury not to make their own comparison between the voices heard on a covert recording and the voices of the accused when they gave evidence where, during the trial, recognition evidence identifying the accused had been given by police officers as 'lay listeners'. Such a comparison *was* permissible provided the jury had received guidance from *either* experts or lay listeners. Nonetheless, the court stated that the increasing use of police officers to conduct 'lay listener' identifications of voice recordings was to be treated with 'great care and caution'.[196]

In *Flynn*, the Court of Appeal gave the following guidance concerning factors that should be taken into account by a judge when assessing evidence of voice recognition and, in particular, the ability of a lay listener to correctly identify voices.[197]

1. Identification by voice recognition is more difficult than visual identification.

2. Identification by voice is likely to be more reliable when carried out by experts using acoustic, spectrographic, and auditory techniques than lay listener identification.

3. A number of factors are relevant when considering the reliability of lay listener identification:

    (i)   the quality of the recording of the disputed voices;
    (ii) the time which has elapsed between the listener hearing the known voice and the disputed voice;
    (iii) the general ability of the lay individual listener to identify voices (this will vary from individual to individual);
    (iv) the nature and duration of the speech which the listener seeks to identify; and
    (v)   the degree of familiarity of the listener with the known voice.

Other guidance is to be found in the Crown Court Bench Book.[198] In cases of voice identification an explicit modified *Turnbull* direction is required and such a direction is likely to involve comment where there has been a failure to hold a 'voice comparison exercise'. Judicial comment is also likely to be made where expert evidence is adduced which is based solely on auditory phonetic analysis rather than quantitative acoustic analysis, the former being unable to distinguish between the vocal mechanisms of voices. However, in addition to those factors already mentioned, it is submitted that detailed guidance is also required on factors such as the effect of words being shouted[199] and the effect of stress or of an attempt to disguise a voice.[200]

---

[195] [2008] 2 Cr App R 20 at [56].

[196] *R v Flynn* [2008] 2 Cr App R 20 at [63].

[197] [2008] 2 Cr App R 20 at [16]. See also *R v Tamiz* [2010] EWCA Crim 2638 in which *Flynn* was distinguished.

[198] See The Crown Court Bench Book 2010, 132–6.

[199] See *R v Hussain* [2010] EWCA Crim 1327, CA: the evidence of voice recognition by hearing a small number of words shouted was on the borderline of admissibility.

[200] See generally Bull and Clifford, 'Earwitness Testimony' in Heaton-Armstrong et al (eds), *Analysing Witness Testimony* (London, 1999) ch 13.

Pre-trial procedure

As to the pre-trial procedure, it has been made clear since *R v Hersey* that there is no duty to hold a voice identification procedure under Code D, which relates only to visual identification, and that the matter is properly dealt with by a suitably adapted *Turnbull* warning.[201] However, there is an obvious need for a pre-trial procedure and not one crudely modelled on the procedures used in the case of visual identification, because that would be to duck important issues of the kind raised by the expert in *R v Hersey*, for example questions relating to the number of voices that should be heard, the nature of the text that should be used, and the method by which the police should select those whose voices, so far as possible, resemble that of the accused.[202] In *R v Flynn*[203] the Court of Appeal provided the following 'minimal safeguards' in respect of pre-trial procedure for 'lay listener' voice identification:

1. The evidence-gathering procedure should be properly recorded, in particular the amount of time spent in contact with the accused should be recorded as it is highly relevant to the issue of the officer's familiarity with the accused when identifying his voice.

2. The date and time spent by the police officer compiling a transcript of a covert recording must be noted and annotated with the officer's views as to who is speaking on the recording.

3. Before attempting to make a voice identification the police officer should not be supplied with a copy of a transcript bearing another officer's annotations of who he believes is speaking.

4. A voice identification should be carried out by someone other than an officer involved in investigating the case because of the risk that the identification might be influenced by knowledge already gained in the course of the investigation.

Valuable though these safeguards are, much more is needed in terms of pre-trial procedure.[204] Given that well over a decade has passed since the Court of Appeal acknowledged in *Roberts*[205] that voice identification was more difficult than visual identification, it is troubling to the authors of this work that, at the time of writing, not even minimal safeguards of the kind suggested in *Flynn*,[206] appear in Code D.

Lip-reading evidence

An expert lip-reader who has viewed a video or CCTV recording of a person talking may give expert opinion evidence as to what was said, notwithstanding that such evidence is always, to some extent, unreliable, because not all words can be identified by vision alone, single-syllable words with little context are very difficult to interpret, and even when the words are presented

---

[201] *R v Gummerson and Steadman* [1999] Crim LR 680, CA. See also *Phipps v DPP* [2012] UKPC 24. But see *R v Putland* [2010] EWCA Crim 459: a conviction was not unsafe where evidence of voice and visual identification was adduced and the judge gave a standard *Turnbull* warning with no specific reference to the risks of identification by voice.

[202] See Ormerod, 'Sounds Familiar?—Voice Identification Evidence' [2001] Crim LR 595.

[203] [2008] 2 Cr App R 20 at [53].

[204] See Warburton and Lewis, 'Opinion evidence; admissibility of ad hoc expert voice recognition evidence: *R v Flynn*' (2009) 13 E&P 50.

[205] *R v Roberts* [2000] Crim LR 183, CA.

[206] (2009) 13 E&P 50.

in clearly spoken sentences, the best lip-readers can only achieve up to 80 per cent correctness. In *R v Luttrell*[207] the Court of Appeal considered two issues: when such evidence should be excluded; and, where such evidence is admitted, the nature of the special warning that the judge must give to the jury. As to the former, Rose LJ said:[208]

> The decision in each case is likely to be highly fact sensitive. For example, a video may be of such poor quality or the view of the speaker's face so poor that no reliable interpretation is possible. There may also be cases where the interpreting witness is not sufficiently skilled. A judge may properly take into account: whether consistency with extrinsic facts confirms or inconsistency casts doubt on the reliability of an interpretation; whether information provided to the lip reader might have coloured the reading; and whether the probative effect of the evidence depends on the interpretation of a single word or phrase or on the whole thrust of the conversation. In the light of such considerations, (which are not intended to be exhaustive) a judge may well rule on the *voir dire* that any lip-reading evidence proffered should not be admitted before the jury.

The court was in no doubt that where the evidence is admitted, it requires a warning from the judge as to its limitations and the concomitant risk of error, not least because the expert may fall significantly short of complete accuracy. Rose LJ said:[209]

> As with any 'special warning', its precise terms will be fact-dependent, but in most, if not all cases, the judge should spell out to the jury the risk of mistakes as to the words that the lip reader believes were spoken; the reasons why the witness may be mistaken; and the way in which a convincing, authoritative and truthful witness may yet be a mistaken witness. Furthermore, the judge should deal with the particular strengths and weaknesses of the material in the instant case, carefully setting out the evidence, together with the criticisms that can properly be made of it because of other evidence. The jury should be reminded that the quality of the evidence will be affected by such matters as the lighting at the scene, the angle of the view in relation to those speaking, the distances involved, whether anything interfered with the observation, familiarity on the part of the lip-reader with the language spoken, the extent of the use of single syllable words, any awareness on the part of the expert witness of the context of the speech and whether the probative value of the evidence depends on isolated words or phrases or the general impact of long passages of conversation.

However, the court was also of the view that there was no reason in principle why lip-reading evidence adduced by the prosecution should not establish a prima facie case, although in reaching this conclusion the court may have been influenced by its own—and, it is submitted, questionable—observation that it is highly unlikely that lip-reading evidence will ever stand alone.

Sudden infant death syndrome

Infant deaths are attributed to Sudden Infant Death Syndrome (SIDS), known colloquially as 'cot deaths', where the immediate cause of death is apnoea, loss of breath or cessation of breathing occurring naturally, the underlying cause or causes being as yet unknown. Infant deaths cannot be attributed to SIDS, therefore, if they are clinically explicable or consequent on demonstrable trauma.

---

[207] [2004] 2 Cr App R 520, CA. For case comment, see *Rees and Roberts* [2004] Crim LR 939.
[208] [2004] 2 Cr App R 520, CA at [38].
[209] [2004] 2 Cr App R 520, CA at [44].

In *R v Cannings*[210] the appellant had been convicted of the murder of two of her four children, J who had died six weeks after his birth and M who had died 18 weeks after his birth. Her eldest child, G, had died 13 weeks after her birth. The Crown's case, for which there was no direct evidence, was that the accused had smothered all three of the children and that the deaths of J and M formed part of an overall 'pattern'. Their case depended on expert evidence that the conclusion of smothering could be drawn from the extreme rarity of three separate infant deaths in the same family. The appellant's case was that the deaths were attributable to SIDS and at the appeal she relied on fresh expert evidence to the effect that infant deaths occurring in the same family can and do occur naturally, even when unexplained. Allowing the appeal, it was held that where three infant deaths have occurred in the same family, each apparently unexplained, and for each of which there is no evidence extraneous to the expert evidence that harm was or must have been inflicted—for example, indications or admissions of violence or a pattern of ill-treatment—the proper approach is to start with the fact that three unexplained deaths in the same family are indeed rare, but to proceed on the basis that if there is nothing to explain them, in our current state of knowledge they remain unexplained and, despite the known fact that some parents do smother their infant children, possible natural deaths. Whether there are one, two, or even three deaths, the exclusion of currently known natural causes of infant death does not establish that the death or deaths resulted from the deliberate infliction of harm. If, on examination of all the evidence, every possible cause has been excluded, the cause remains unknown. It was further held that, for the time being, where a full investigation into two or more sudden unexplained infant deaths in the same family is followed by a serious disagreement between reputable experts about the cause of death, and a body of such expert opinion concludes that natural causes, whether explained or not, cannot be excluded as a reasonable (and not a fanciful) possibility, a prosecution for murder should not be started or continued unless there is additional cogent evidence, extraneous to the expert evidence tending to support the conclusion that one of the infants was deliberately harmed, such as indications or admissions of violence or a pattern of ill-treatment.

The impact of the decision in *R v Cannings* in care proceedings was considered in *In re U (a Child) (Serious Injury: Standard of Proof)*.[211] It was held that although *R v Cannings* had provided a useful warning to judges in care proceedings against ill-considered conclusions or conclusions resting on insufficient evidence, a local authority should not refrain from proceedings or discontinue proceedings in any case where there is a substantial disagreement among the medical experts. However, there were considerations emphasized by the judgment in *R v Cannings* that were of direct application in care proceedings: (i) the cause of an injury or episode that cannot be explained scientifically remains equivocal; (ii) recurrence is not of itself probative; (iii) particular caution is necessary where medical experts disagree, with one opinion declining to exclude a reasonable possibility of natural cause; (iv) the court has to be on its guard against the over-dogmatic expert, an expert whose reputation or amour propre is at stake or one who has developed a scientific prejudice; and (v) it should never be forgotten that today's medical certainty may be discarded by the next generation of experts or that scientific research will throw light into corners that are, at present, dark.

---

[210] [2004] 1 WLR 2607, CA.
[211] [2005] Fam 134, CA.

ADDITIONAL READING

Bruce, 'Fleeting Images of Shade' [1988] *The Psychologist* 331.

Bull and Clifford, 'Earwitness Testimony' in Heaton-Armstrong et al (eds), *Analysing Witness Testimony* (London, 1999), ch 13.

Costigan, 'Identification from CCTV: The Risk of Injustice' [2007] Crim LR 591.

Cutler and Penrod, *Mistaken Identification—The Eyewitness, Psychology and the Law* (Cambridge, 1995).

Dein, 'Non Tape Recorded Cell Confession Evidence—On Trial' [2002] Crim LR 630.

Henderson et al., 'Matching the Faces of Robbers Captured on Video' (2001) 15 *Applied Cognitive Psychology* 445.

Lewis, 'A Comparative Examination of Corroboration and Caution Warnings in Prosecutions of Sexual Offences' [2006] Crim LR 889.

O'Floinn and Ormerod, 'Social Networking Material as Criminal Evidence' [2012] Crim LR 486 at 499–501.

Ormerod, 'Sounds Familiar?—Voice Identification Evidence' [2001] Crim LR 595.

Ormerod, 'Sounding Out Expert Voice Identification' [2002] Crim LR 771.

Report to the Secretary of State for the Home Department of the Departmental Committee on Evidence of Identification in Criminal Cases (HMSO, 1976).

Warburton and Lewis, 'Opinion evidence; admissibility of ad hoc expert voice recognition evidence: *R v Flynn*' (2009) 13 E&P 50.

Documentary and real evidence

9

Key issues

- Where a party to litigation wishes to adduce in evidence a statement contained in a document, (a) should it be open to proof by production of a copy of the document and, if so, (b) in what circumstances and subject to what safeguards?

- Where a party to litigation wishes to admit a document in evidence, (a) should he be required to establish that it was written, signed, or attested by the person by whom it purports to be written, signed, or attested and, if so, (b) how should these matters be established?

- When should material objects be admissible in evidence and why do they need to be accompanied by oral testimony?

- When, and subject to what safeguards, should a court inspect a place or object out of court?

Documentary evidence

Statements contained in documents, like oral statements, are subject to the general rules of evidence on admissibility which are considered throughout this book.[1] This chapter concerns two additional requirements relating to the proof of documents on the contents of which a party seeks to rely. The first relates to proof of the contents, the essential question being whether the party relying on the document must produce primary evidence, for example the original, as opposed to secondary evidence, for example a copy of the original. The second relates to proof of the fact that the document was properly executed.[2]

In *R v Daye*[3] Darling J defined a document as 'any written thing capable of being evidence', whether the writing is on paper, parchment, stone, marble, or metal. Nowadays, the word should bear an even wider meaning: today's equivalent of paper is often a disc, memory stick, tape, or film and conveys information by symbols, diagrams, and pictures as well as by words and numbers. It is clear from the modern authorities, however, that the definition of a document varies according to the nature of the proceedings and the particular context in question. Concerning proof of a document in criminal proceedings, the word has been narrowly defined. In *Kajala v Noble*[4] Ackner LJ, referring to the rule that if an original document is available in a party's hands, that party must produce it and cannot give secondary evidence by producing a copy, concluded: 'the old rule is limited and confined to written documents in the strict sense of the term, and has no relevance to tapes or films'.[5]

In civil proceedings, by contrast, 'document', for the purposes of the rules on the disclosure and inspection of documents, means 'anything in which information of any description is recorded',[6] a definition wide enough to cover not only documents in writing, but also maps, plans, graphs, drawings, discs, audio tapes, soundtracks, photographs, negatives, videotapes, and films. The same definition is used in relation to documents, including computer-produced documents, containing hearsay statements admissible under the Civil Evidence Act 1995 (the 1995 Act) or the Criminal Justice Act 2003 (the 2003 Act).[7]

Proof of contents

General statutory provisions

Proof of the contents of a document on which a party seeks to rely is now largely governed, in criminal cases, by s 133 of the 2003 Act and s 71 of the Police and Criminal Evidence Act 1984,[8] and in civil cases by ss 8 and 9 of the 1995 Act. Section 133 of the 2003 Act provides that:

---

[1] Principal among these, in criminal cases, is the rule against hearsay. See Chs 10–12.

[2] A third issue, relating to the admissibility of extrinsic evidence for the purpose of explaining, contradicting, varying, or adding to the terms of a document, is beyond the scope of this work.

[3] [1908] 2 KB 333 at 340.

[4] (1982) 75 Cr App R 149, CA.

[5] (1982) 75 Cr App R 149 at 152. As an authority on the *proof of contents* in a criminal case, this decision should now be read subject to the Criminal Justice Act 2003, s 133: see, in this chapter, under **Documentary evidence, Proof of contents, General statutory provisions**.

[6] CPR r 31.4.

[7] The 1995 Act, s 13 and the 2003 Act, s 134(1).

[8] In the case of tape recordings and transcripts of police interviews sought to be introduced in criminal proceedings, see also the Code of Practice on Tape Recording of Interviews with Suspects (Code E) and para 43, the *Consolidated Criminal Practice Direction*.

Where a statement in a document is admissible as evidence in criminal proceedings, the statement may be proved by producing either—

(a) the document, or

(b) (whether or not the document exists) a copy of the document or of the material part of it, authenticated in whatever way the court may approve.[9]

Under s 71 of the Police and Criminal Evidence Act 1984, in any criminal proceedings the contents of a document may (whether or not the document is still in existence) be proved by the production of an enlargement of a microfilm copy of that document or the material part of it, authenticated in such manner as the court may approve.

Section 8 of the 1995 Act is cast in terms similar to those of s 133 of the 2003 Act. Under s 9(1) and (2) of the 1995 Act, a document which is certified as forming part of the records of a business or public authority may be received in evidence in civil proceedings without further proof; and under s 9(3) of that Act, the *absence* of an entry in the records of a business or public authority may be proved by the affidavit of an officer of the business or authority.[10]

Section 133 of the 2003 Act and s 8 of the 1995 Act appear to be of general application, ie to apply to *any* statement contained in a document, and thus not confined to hearsay statements in documents admissible under the 2003 Act or the 1995 Act. Likewise, s 9 of the 1995 Act appears to apply to *any* document forming part of the records of a business or public authority and not merely documents containing hearsay statements admissible under the 1995 Act. On this reading, these provisions have reversed completely the general rule at common law that a party seeking to rely on the contents of a document must adduce primary evidence (usually the original). Pending a definitive ruling to that effect, the general common law rule,[11] may continue to apply in the case of non-hearsay, a conclusion that has been described as 'absurd'.[12] In any event, s 133 of the 2003 Act is permissive as to the means of proof and therefore cannot be taken to have overridden (i) the common law rule that where secondary evidence of the contents of a private document is admissible, it may take the form of *oral* evidence (use of which is not sanctioned by s 133);[13] (ii) a number of statutory provisions, mainly relating to public documents, which provide for proof of their contents by copies which are required to take a particular form, such as an examined copy (ie a copy proved by oral evidence to correspond with the original) or a certified copy (ie a copy certified to be accurate by an official who has custody of the original); or (iii) the Bankers' Books Evidence Act 1879, whereby provision is made for the admission of copies of entries in a banker's book, but only subject to the fulfilment of certain conditions, one of which is that some person proves that he has examined the copy with the original and that it is correct.[14] The same may be said, concerning civil cases, of ss 8 and 9 of the 1995 Act. Section 14 of that Act provides that nothing in the Act affects (i) the proof of documents by means other than those specified in ss 8 or 9;[15] or

[9] For the meaning of the words 'statement', 'document', and 'copy', see s 115(2) and s 134(1) of the 2003 Act (see Ch 10).

[10] See further Ch 11.

[11] Considered, in this chapter, under **Documentary evidence, Proof of contents, The general rule at common law—primary evidence**.

[12] R Pattenden, 'Authenticating "things" in English law: principles for adducing tangible evidence in common law jury trials' (2008) 12 E&P 273 at 294.

[13] *R v Nazeer* [1998] Crim LR 750, CA.

[14] All three matters are considered, in this chapter, under **Documentary evidence, Proof of contents, The exceptions—secondary evidence, Public documents**, and **Bankers' books**.

[15] Section 14(2).

(ii) the operation of certain statutory provisions governing the means of proving certain public and official documents.[16]

The general rule at common law—primary evidence

The general rule is that a party seeking to rely upon the contents of a document must adduce primary evidence of those contents. The rule, often regarded as the only remaining instance of the 'best evidence rule',[17] under which a party must produce the best evidence that the nature of the case will allow, may be justified as a means of reducing the risks of fraud, mistake, and inaccuracy which might result from proof by either production of a copy of a document or oral evidence of its contents.

There are three recognized categories of primary evidence of the contents of a document: the original, copies of enrolled documents, and admissions made by parties. The best kind of primary evidence is the original document in question. Although the original is usually identifiable with ease, some cases do occasion difficulty. Where documents are produced in duplicate, each of them may constitute an original. Thus the duplicates of a deed which have been executed by all parties are all originals.[18] A copy of a document, however, whether produced by carbon, duplicator, or photocopying machine, is not original unless signed or otherwise duly executed. In the case of telegrams, the original, if tendered against the receiver, is the message he received; the original, if tendered against the sender, is the message that was handed in or recorded at the Post Office.[19] A counterpart lease executed by the lessee alone is the original if tendered against him, whereas the other part is the original if tendered against the lessor.[20] Where a private document is required to be enrolled, that is officially filed in either a court or some other public office, a copy issued by the court or office in question is treated as an original. Thus where executors obtain a grant of probate, the probate copy of the will is treated as primary evidence of the contents of the will.[21] Where a party to litigation has made an informal admission concerning the contents of a document, his admission constitutes primary evidence of the contents and is admissible in evidence against him.[22]

The general rule applies in any case where a party seeks to rely upon the actual contents of a document.[23] However, in cases where it is unnecessary to place reliance upon the contents of a document because the fact or matter in issue, even if recorded in a document, can be proved by other evidence, the general rule has no application. Thus, whereas production of a lease is necessary in order to prove the length of a tenancy[24] or the amount of rent due thereunder,[25] proof

---

[16] Section 14(3). It is unclear, however, why only some of the many statutory provisions governing the proof of various types of document have been specified. Those referred to in s 14(3) include the Documentary Evidence Act 1868, s 2 and the Documentary Evidence Act 1882, s 2 (see under **Documentary evidence, Proof of contents, The exceptions—secondary evidence, Public documents**, in this chapter); the Evidence (Colonial Statutes) Act 1907, s 1 (see Ch 18); and the Evidence (Foreign, Dominion and Colonial Documents) Act 1933, s 1 (see Chs 2 and 12).

[17] In fact it pre-dates the best evidence rule.

[18] *Forbes v Samuel* [1913] 3 KB 706.

[19] *R v Regan* (1887) 16 Cox CC 203.

[20] *Doe d West v Davis* (1806) 7 East 363.

[21] If a question arises concerning construction of the will, however, the court may examine the original: see *Re Battie-Wrightson, Cecil v Battie-Wrightson* [1920] 2 Ch 330.

[22] *Slatterie v Pooley* (1840) 6 M&W 664. But see now Civil Evidence Act 1995, s 7(1) (see Ch 11).

[23] *MacDonnell v Evans* (1852) 11 CB 930.

[24] *Twyman v Knowles* (1853) 13 CB 222.

[25] *Augustien v Challis* (1847) 1 Exch 279.

of the existence or fact of a tenancy, albeit created by a lease, may be proved by other evidence. In *R v Holy Trinity, Hull (Inhabitants)*,[26] the fact of a tenancy, created by a lease which defined its terms, could be proved without production of that lease; oral evidence, such as evidence on the payment of the rent, sufficed.[27] Likewise, the rule has no application where reference is made to a document merely for the purpose of establishing the bare fact of its existence. In *R v Elworthy*[28] the accused, a solicitor, was charged with perjury. It was alleged that he had falsely sworn that there was no draft of a certain statutory declaration which he had prepared. It was held that although secondary evidence of the contents of the draft and of certain alterations made in it was inadmissible, the prosecution could properly adduce oral evidence that such a draft existed and was in the possession of the accused.[29] Nor does the general rule apply when the contents of a document are referred to merely in order to identify it. Thus it has been said that 'in an action of trover for a promissory note, the contents of the promissory note may be stated verbally by a witness'.[30]

Although both the general rule and the common law exceptions to it are well established, in *Springsteen v Flute International Ltd*[31] the Court of Appeal favoured a more generalized discretionary approach to admissibility. It held as follows. (1) The best evidence rule, long on its deathbed, had finally expired. (2) In every case where a party seeks to adduce secondary evidence of the contents of a document, it is a matter for the court to decide, in the light of all the circumstances of the case, what, if any, weight to attach to the evidence. (3) Where such a party can readily adduce the document, it may be expected that, absent some special circumstances, the court will decline to admit the secondary evidence on the ground that it is worthless. (4) At the other extreme, where such a party genuinely cannot produce the document, it may be expected that, absent some special circumstances, the court will admit the secondary evidence and attach such weight to it as it considers appropriate. (5) In cases falling between these two extremes, it is for the court to make a judgment as to whether in all the circumstances any weight should be attached to the secondary evidence.[32]

The exceptions—secondary evidence

Public documents, which constitute one of the exceptions to the general rule, are considered later in this chapter.[33] In the case of private documents, secondary evidence of their contents, where admissible, may take the form of a copy, a copy of a copy,[34] or oral evidence. Where a copy is produced, proof is required that it is a true copy of the original and in the same terms.[35]

Where secondary evidence is admissible, there is a general rule that 'there are no degrees of secondary evidence'.[36] Thus although less weight may attach to inferior forms of secondary

---

[26] (1827) 7 B&C 611.

[27] See also *Alderson v Clay* (1816) 1 Stark 405 (proof of the fact of a partnership).

[28] (1867) LR 1 CCR 103.

[29] The Crown had not given notice to the accused to produce the original. Had they done so, secondary evidence of the contents of the draft would have been admissible (see, in this chapter, under **Documentary evidence, Proof of contents, The exceptions—secondary evidence**).

[30] Per Martin B in *Boyle v Wiseman* (1855) 11 Exch 360 at 367, citing *Whitehead v Scott* (1830) 1 Mood&R 2.

[31] [2001] EMLR 654, CA.

[32] See also *Post Office Counters Ltd v Mahida* [2003] EWCA Civ 1583, (2003) The Times, 31 Oct (see Ch 2).

[33] See under **Documentary evidence, Proof of contents, The exceptions—secondary evidence, Public documents**.

[34] *Lafone v Griffin* (1909) 25 TLR 308; *R v Collins* (1960) 44 Cr App R 170. Contrast *Everingham v Roundell* (1838) 2 Mood&R 138.

[35] *R v Collins* (1960) 44 Cr App R 170; cf *R v Wayte* (1982) 76 Cr App R 110, CA.

[36] Per Lord Abinger CB in *Doe d Gilbert v Ross* (1840) 7 M&W 102.

evidence, there is no obligation to tender the 'best' copy, rather than an inferior copy or a copy of a copy, and oral evidence of the contents is admissible even if a copy or some other more satisfactory type of secondary evidence is available. To this general rule there is a variety of exceptions. The contents of a will admitted to probate may not be proved by oral evidence if the original or probate copy exists. Judicial documents and bankers' books[37] are generally proved not by oral evidence but by office copies and examined copies respectively. Finally, many public documents may be proved by oral evidence only if examined, certified, or other copies are unavailable.[38]

Hearsay statements admissible by statute
Where the contents of a document are admissible hearsay under the 2003 Act, they may be proved in accordance with s 133 of that Act and s 71 of the Police and Criminal Evidence Act 1984; and where the contents of a document are admissible hearsay under the 1995 Act, they may be proved in accordance with ss 8 and 9 of that Act.[39]

Failure to produce after notice
A party seeking to rely upon a document may prove its contents by secondary evidence if the original is in the possession or control of another party to the proceedings who, having been served with a notice to produce it, has failed to do so. The purpose of serving such a notice is not to notify the other party that reliance will be placed on a document so that he can prepare evidence to explain or confirm it, but merely to give him sufficient opportunity to produce it if he wishes or, if he does not, to enable the first party to adduce secondary evidence. Thus it has been held that where the original is in court, secondary evidence is admissible even where a party fails to comply with a notice to produce served during the course of the trial.[40]

It is assumed that the foregoing principles remain good law notwithstanding that the Civil Procedure Rules make no provision for formal service of a notice to produce.[41]

A notice to produce has never *compelled* production of a document. A party to civil proceedings, who wishes to rely at the trial on the original of a document, should serve a witness summons requiring a witness to produce the document to the court.[42]

A stranger's lawful refusal to produce
Secondary evidence of the contents of a document may be given when the original is in the possession of a stranger to the litigation who, having been served with a *subpoena duces tecum* (now known as a witness summons requiring a witness to produce a document),[43] has lawfully refused to produce it, for example by reason of a claim to privilege[44] or diplomatic immunity[45] or because he is outside the jurisdiction and therefore cannot be compelled to produce it.[46]

---

[37] See, in this chapter, under **Documentary evidence, Proof of contents, The exceptions—secondary evidence, Bankers' books**.

[38] See, in this chapter, under **Documentary evidence, Proof of contents, The exceptions—secondary evidence, Public documents**.

[39] See, in this chapter, under **Documentary evidence, Proof of contents, General statutory provisions**. and see Chs 10 and 11.

[40] *Dwyer v Collins* (1852) 21 LJ Ex 225.

[41] See, formerly, RSC Ord 24, r 10.

[42] See CPR r 34.2.

[43] See CPR r 34.2.

[44] *Mills v Oddy* (1834) 6 C&P 728.

[45] *R v Nowaz* [1976] 3 All ER 5, CA.

[46] *Kilgour v Owen* (1889) 88 LT Jo 7.

However, if the stranger, in unlawful disobedience of the summons, refuses to produce the original, secondary evidence is inadmissible because he is bound to produce it and is punishable for contempt if he refuses to do so.[47] The effect of these rules is to cast a duty upon the party seeking to rely upon the document to compel the stranger to produce the original, thereby eliminating the risk of unreliable secondary evidence being admitted in consequence of their collusion.

Lost documents

Secondary evidence of the contents of a document is admissible on proof that the original has been destroyed or cannot be found after due search. The quality of evidence required to show the loss or destruction varies according to the nature and value of the document in question. In *Brewster v Sewell*[48] the plaintiff was unable to produce a policy of insurance against loss by fire on which a claim had been paid. Subsequent to the fire, which had occurred some years before the proceedings, a fresh policy had been issued. Evidence was given of a thorough but unsuccessful search for the earlier policy. It was held that, in the circumstances, the original policy had become 'mere waste paper' and that sufficient evidence of due search had been given to allow proof of its contents by secondary evidence. Bayley J said:[49]

> The presumption of law is that a man will keep all those papers which are valuable to himself, and which may, with any degree of probability, be of any future use to him. The presumption on the contrary is that a man will not keep those papers which have entirely discharged their duty, and which are never likely to be required for any purpose whatever.

Production of original impossible

Secondary evidence is admissible where production of the original is either physically impossible, for example because it is an inscription upon a tombstone or wall,[50] or legally impossible, for example because the document in question is a notice which is required by statute to be constantly affixed at a factory or workshop.[51]

Public documents

At common law, secondary evidence of the contents of a wide variety of public documents is admissible on the grounds that production of the originals would entail a high degree of public inconvenience.[52] Under the modern law, there is a large number of statutes which also provide for the proof of public documents by secondary evidence. Secondary evidence for these purposes is usually required to take the form of an examined, authenticated, certified, office, Queen's Printer's, or Stationery Office copy. Under s 7 of the Evidence Act 1851, for example, the contents of all proclamations, treaties, and other acts of state of any foreign state or of any British colony, and all judgments, decrees, orders, and other judicial proceedings of any court of justice in any foreign state or in any British colony may be proved by an examined copy, which is a copy proved by oral evidence to correspond with the original, or

---

[47] *R v Llanfaethly (Inhabitants)* (1853) 2 E&B 940.

[48] (1820) 3 B&Ald 296. See also *R v Wayte* (1982) 76 Cr App R 110, CA.

[49] (1820) 3 B&Ald 296 at 300.

[50] Per Alderson B in *Mortimer v M'Callan* (1840) 6 M&W 58. See also, *sed quaere, R v Hunt* (1820) 3 B&Ald 566 (inscriptions on flags or banners).

[51] *Owner v Bee Hive Spinning Co Ltd* [1914] 1 KB 105, DC. See also *Alivon v Furnival* (1834) 1 Cr M&R 277 (document in custody of foreign court).

[52] See, eg, *Mortimer v M'Callan* (1840) 6 M&W 58 (books of the Bank of England).

by copies authenticated with the seal of the foreign state, British colony, or foreign or colonial court, as the case may be.[53] Certified copies are copies certified to be accurate by an official who has custody of the original.[54] They are employed to prove byelaws and records kept in the Public Record Office.[55] They are also used to prove a birth or death,[56] an adoption,[57] and a marriage[58] or civil partnership.[59] Under s 14 of the Evidence Act 1851, certified or examined copies may be used to prove the contents of any document provided that it is of such a public nature that it is admissible in evidence on production from proper custody and no other statute provides for proof of its contents by means of a copy. Office copies, which are prepared by officials who have custody of original judicial documents and are authenticated with the seal of the court, may be used to prove judgments, orders, and other judicial documents. Queen's Printer's copies are used to prove private Acts of Parliament and journals of either House of Parliament,[60] royal proclamations, orders, and statutory instruments.[61]

Bankers' books

In both civil and criminal proceedings, it is often necessary to adduce evidence of the contents of bankers' books. In order to avoid the inconvenience that production of the originals would entail, the Bankers' Books Evidence Act 1879 (the 1879 Act) provides for the admission of copies. Section 3, an exception to the rule against hearsay, reads as follows:

> Subject to the provisions of this Act, a copy of an entry in a banker's book shall in all legal proceedings be received as prima facie evidence of such entry, and of the matters, transactions, and accounts therein recorded.

'Banker' is defined as a 'deposit-taker' or the National Savings Bank.[62] 'Bankers' books' were originally defined to include 'ledgers', 'day books', 'cash books', and 'account books'. The

---

[53] In the case of a foreign conviction, it remains necessary to establish that the examined copy relates to the person said to have been convicted, which may be achieved by the admission of any relevant evidence, including, eg, fingerprint evidence: *R v Mauricia* [2002] 2 Cr App R 377, CA.

[54] Where a statute provides for proof of a document by a certified, sealed, or stamped copy, the copy, provided it purports to be signed, sealed, or stamped, is admissible without any proof of the sign, seal or stamp, as the case may be: Evidence Act 1845, s 1.

[55] Local Government Act 1972, s 238 (the clerk to the local authority) and Public Records Act 1958, s 9 (the Keeper of Public Records).

[56] Births and Deaths Registration Act 1953, s 34.

[57] Adoption and Children Act 2002, s 77(4).

[58] Marriage Act 1949, s 65(3).

[59] Civil Partnership (Registration Provisions) Regulations 2005, SI 2005/3176, regs 13(4) and 14(4).

[60] Evidence Act 1845, s 3 and Documentary Evidence Act 1882, s 2. Stationery Office copies may also be used. The Interpretation Act 1978, s 3 provides that: 'Every Act is a public Act to be judicially noticed as such, unless the contrary is expressly provided by the Act.' This section applies to all Acts passed after 1850. At common law, judicial notice is taken of earlier enactments, if public: see Ch 22.

[61] Evidence Act 1845, s 3 and Documentary Evidence Act 1868, s 2. Such documents may also be proved by a copy of the Gazette containing them or by a copy certified to be true by the appropriate official. They may also be proved by a photocopy from a commercial publication, provided that there is no suggestion of any inaccuracy in the version before the court: *R v Koon Cheung Tang* [1995] Crim LR 813, CA. An 'order' under the 1868 Act, s 2 covers any executive act of government performed by the bringing into existence of a public document for the purpose of giving effect to an Act of Parliament: *R v Clarke* [1969] 2 QB 91 at 97. See also *West Midlands Probation Board v French* [2008] EWHC 2631 (a licence issued by the governor of a prison on behalf of the Secretary of State for the Home Office).

[62] Section 9(1). A 'deposit taker' will normally be someone with permission under the Financial Services and Markets Act 2000, Pt 4 to accept deposits: see s 9(1A)–(1C).

definition has since been extended to include 'other records used in the ordinary business of the bank, whether those records are in written form or are kept on microfilm, magnetic tape, or any other form of mechanical or electronic data retrieval mechanism'.[63] 'Other records used in the ordinary business of the bank' has to be read *eiusdem generis* with 'ledgers, day books, cash books', and 'account books', which are the means by which banks record day-to-day financial transactions, and therefore do not cover bank records of conversations between its employees and customers or others, or internal memoranda.[64] Paid cheques and paying-in slips retained by a bank after the conclusion of a banking transaction to which they relate have been held not to be bankers' books on the same basis or on the grounds that even if bundles of such documents can be treated as 'records used in the ordinary business of the bank', the addition of an individual cheque or paying-in slip cannot be regarded as making an 'entry' in those records.[65] The same reasoning may be used to justify the decision, reached prior to the extension of the definition of 'bankers' books', that copies of letters written by a bank and contained in a file of its correspondence do not constitute bankers' books.[66]

A copy is only admissible under s 3 of the 1879 Act if: (i) a partner or officer of the bank proves, by oral evidence or affidavit, that the book was at the time of the making of the entry one of the ordinary books of the bank, the entry was made in the usual and ordinary course of business, and the book is in the custody or control of the bank;[67] and (ii) some person proves, by oral evidence or affidavit, that he has examined the copy with the original and that it is correct.[68] Section 7 provides for any party to legal proceedings to apply to a court[69] or judge for an order to be at liberty to inspect and take copies of entries in bankers' books for the purposes of those proceedings. The order may be made without summoning the bank or any other party and shall be served on the bank three clear days before it is to be obeyed, unless the court or judge otherwise directs.[70] An order may be made under s 7 to inspect the account of a person who is not a party to the proceedings, even if that person is not compellable as a witness,[71] but in criminal cases such an order should be made only in exceptional circumstances and where the private interest in keeping a bank account confidential is outweighed by the public interest in assisting a prosecution.[72]

---

[63] Section 9(2).

[64] *Re Howglen Ltd* [2001] 1 All ER 376, Ch D.

[65] *Williams v Williams* [1987] 3 All ER 257, CA. In civil proceedings, if such documents relate to the bank account of the other party to the action, an order for disclosure may be made and the bank, as agent holding the documents on that party's behalf, may then be required to disclose them. In other cases, the party seeking disclosure of specific documents may be able to make use of CPR r 31.17, which provides for disclosure by a person who is not a party to the proceedings, or CPR r 34.2, which empowers the court to issue a witness summons requiring a witness to produce documents to the court.

[66] *R v Dadson* (1983) 77 Cr App R 91, CA. See also *Barker v Wilson* [1980] 1 WLR 884, DC.

[67] Section 4.

[68] Section 5.

[69] Justices constitute a court for these purposes: *R v Kinghorn* [1908] 2 KB 949.

[70] Although the Act allows an application to be made without notice, there is much to be said for notice being given: per Widgery LJ in *R v Marlborough Street Magistrates' Court, ex p Simpson* (1980) 70 Cr App R 291, DC at 294. In the case of an application in respect of accounts of a person who is not a party to the proceedings, the order either should not be made until the account owner has been informed and given an opportunity to be heard or should be made in the form of an order nisi, allowing a period for the person affected to show cause why the order should not take effect: per Oliver LJ in *R v Grossman* (1981) 73 Cr App R 302, CA at 309.

[71] *R v Andover Justices, ex p Rhodes* [1980] Crim LR 644, DC.

[72] *R v Grossman* (1981) 73 Cr App R 302 at 307, CA.

In civil proceedings, an application under s 7 to inspect entries in the bank account of a third party will only be granted if (i) the court is satisfied that the account is in fact the account of the other party to the action or an account with which he is so much concerned that items in it would be evidence against him; and (ii) the applicant shows very strong grounds for suspicion, almost amounting to certainty, that there are items in the account which would be material evidence against the other party.[73] A foreign bank which is not a party to the proceedings, even if it carries on business within the jurisdiction, should not, save in exceptional circumstances, be ordered to produce documents which are outside the jurisdiction and concern business transacted outside the jurisdiction, because an order under the 1879 Act is an exercise of sovereign authority to assist in the administration of justice, and foreign banks owe their customers a duty of confidence regulated by the law of the country where the documents are kept.[74] Although in criminal proceedings an order will not be refused on the grounds that it incriminates the party against whom it is made,[75] it is a serious interference with the liberty of the subject and the court should satisfy itself that the application is more than a mere fishing expedition by considering whether the prosecution has other evidence to support the charge.[76] In *R v Nottingham City Justices, ex p Lynn*[77] an order made by justices against an accused charged with drug smuggling, for the inspection of accounts over a three-year period, was reduced by the Divisional Court to cover a period of six months, there being insufficient evidence to link the accused with offences during most of the three years.

An order under s 7 is not a necessary pre-condition of producing evidence under s 3; an order enables bankers' books to be inspected and copied despite the duty of confidentiality owed by banker to customer and is clearly unnecessary if the customer waives the right to confidentiality and the bank agrees to the inspection and copying.[78]

Proof of due execution

The general rule, in both civil and criminal proceedings, is that a document will only be admitted in evidence on proof of due execution. An exception exists in the case of public documents covered by statutes of the kind previously referred to in this chapter,[79] most of which not only provide for the proof of contents by secondary evidence, but also exempt from proof of due execution. In the case of a private document, proof of due execution may be admitted or presumed, but otherwise usually involves proof of handwriting or a signature

---

[73] *South Staffordshire Tramways Co v Ebbsmith* [1895] 2 QB 669, CA (a pre-trial application) and *D B Deniz Nakliyati TAS v Yugopetrol* [1992] 1 All ER 205, CA (an application against a judgment debtor).

[74] *MacKinnon v Donaldson Lufkin and Jenrette Securities Corpn* [1986] 1 All ER 653, Ch D, applying *R v Grossman* (1981) 73 Cr App R 302, CA (a decision acknowledged to have been given *per incuriam*, the proceedings in the case being criminal and the Court of Appeal, therefore, having no jurisdiction). However, a party seeking to obtain documents from a foreign bank in these circumstances may apply to a master under CPR r 34.13 for the issue of letters of request to the courts of the country in question specifying the documents to be produced, or may apply directly to a court in that country under the relevant local provisions, having first obtained the permission of the English court on an application with notice.

[75] In civil proceedings the Act may not be used to compel disclosure of incriminating material: see *Waterhouse v Barker* [1924] 2 KB 759, CA and *Re Bankers' Books Evidence Act 1879, R v Bono* (1913) 29 TLR 635.

[76] *Williams v Summerfield* [1972] 2 QB 512, DC.

[77] [1984] Crim LR 554.

[78] *Wheatley v Commissioner of Police of the British Virgin Islands* [2006] 1 WLR 1683, PC, a decision under the equivalent statutory provisions of the British Virgin Islands.

[79] See under **Documentary evidence, Proof of contents, The exceptions—secondary evidence, Public documents.**

and, sometimes, proof of attestation. In some cases, documents are required to be stamped for the purposes of stamp duty. Each of these matters now falls to be considered further.

Proof of handwriting

Proof of the due execution of a private document usually involves showing that it was written or signed by the person by whom it purports to have been written or signed. For these purposes, direct oral evidence that the signatory signed in a particular name may be given by the signatory himself or by any other person who witnessed the execution of the document. Proof may also be effected by admissible hearsay assertions to the same effect; or by the opinion evidence of someone who, although not a witness to the execution of the document, is acquainted with the handwriting of the person in question.[80] It is clear, however, that the weight to be attached to such opinion evidence will vary according to the circumstances in question.

A final method of proving handwriting or a signature is by comparison of the document in question with another document which is proved or admitted to have been written by the person in question. Section 8 of the Criminal Procedure Act 1865 provides that:

> Comparison of a disputed writing with any writing proved to the satisfaction of the judge to be genuine shall be permitted to be made by witnesses;[81] and such writings, and the evidence of witnesses respecting the same, may be submitted to the court and jury as evidence of the genuineness or otherwise of the writing in dispute.

The section applies to both civil and criminal proceedings but whereas in the former the court must be satisfied as to the genuineness of the specimen handwriting only on a balance of probabilities, proof beyond reasonable doubt is the appropriate standard for the prosecution in criminal cases.[82] The tribunal of fact, in comparing the disputed and specimen handwriting, may be assisted by the evidence of someone who, although not an expert, is familiar with the handwriting in question[83] or by the opinion evidence of an expert in handwriting, whether his skill has been acquired professionally or otherwise.[84] As a general rule in criminal cases, the jury should not be left to draw their own unaided conclusion from a comparison without the assistance of an expert.[85] However, where an expert is called, it is his function to point out similarities or differences between the documents, leaving it to the tribunal of fact to draw their own conclusion.[86] In cases where the documents are placed before the jury as exhibits or for some proper purpose other than that of making a comparison and an expert is not called, the jury should be warned very carefully not to make a comparison.[87]

Any of the above forms of proof of handwriting may be used in the case of a document which, although not required by law to be attested, was in fact attested. Section 7 of the Criminal Procedure Act 1865 provides that such a document may be proved 'as if there had been no attesting witness thereto'.

---

[80] *Doe d Mudd v Suckermore* (1837) 5 Ad&El 703 at 705.

[81] A witness who has not seen the original 'disputed writing' (because, eg, it is lost) may use a photocopy of it to make the comparison: *Lockheed-Arabia Corpn v Owen* [1993] 3 All ER 641, CA.

[82] *R v Ewing* [1983] 2 All ER 645, CA (see Ch 4).

[83] *Fitzwalter Peerage Claim* (1844) 10 Cl&Fin 193, HL.

[84] *R v Silverlock* [1894] 2 QB 766.

[85] *R v Tilley* [1961] 1 WLR 1309, CCA; *R v Harden* [1963] 1 QB 8, CCA.

[86] *Wakeford v Bishop of Lincoln* (1921) 90 LJPC 174.

[87] *R v O'Sullivan* [1969] 1 WLR 497, CA.

Proof of attestation

Proof of due execution sometimes requires evidence of attestation. It will be convenient to consider first the proof of wills and other testamentary documents. Except where probate is sought in common form, in order to prove the due execution of a will, one of the attesting witnesses, if available, must be called. Witnesses to the execution of a will are treated as the court's witnesses and may be cross-examined by the party seeking to prove due execution.[88] If the witness denies the execution[89] or refuses to give evidence,[90] other evidence becomes admissible. If all of the attesting witnesses are dead, insane, beyond the jurisdiction, or untraceable, secondary evidence of attestation by proof of the handwriting of one of the attesting witnesses is required. If, despite every effort to do so, it is impossible to prove the handwriting of one of the attesting witnesses, other evidence of due execution is admissible, for example that of a non-attesting witness to the execution.[91]

Although at one time it was necessary in the case of any document required by law to be attested to call one of the attesting witnesses (unless they were all unavailable), s 3 of the Evidence Act 1938 provides that, except in the case of a will or other testamentary document, any document required by law to be attested 'may, instead of being proved by an attesting witness, be proved in the manner in which it might be proved if no attesting witness were alive', ie by evidence of the handwriting of an attesting witness or, if this is unobtainable, by other evidence.

Admissions and presumptions

In practice, due execution is frequently admitted or presumed, thereby rendering proof of handwriting and attestation unnecessary. Due execution may be formally admitted both in civil proceedings and, under s 10 of the Criminal Justice Act 1967, in criminal proceedings. Under CPR r 32.19(1), a party shall be deemed to admit the authenticity of a document disclosed to him under Pt 31 of the Rules (disclosure and inspection of documents) unless he serves notice that he wishes the document to be proved at trial. Proof of due execution is also unnecessary when the document in question is in the possession of an opponent who refuses to comply with a notice to produce it.[92]

A document which is more than 20 years old[93] and comes from proper custody is presumed to have been duly executed. Although proper custody, for these purposes, does not mean that the document should be found in 'the best and most proper place of deposit', if the document is found in some other place, the court must be satisfied that such custody was 'reasonable and natural' in the circumstances of the case. This was the view of Tindal CJ in *Meath (Bishop) v Marquis of Winchester*,[94] who accordingly held that certain documents relating to a bishopric had been produced from proper custody despite having been found among the papers of a deceased bishop rather than in the custody of his successor, which was the best place of deposit.

---

[88] *Oakes v Uzzell* [1932] P 19.

[89] *Bowman v Hodgson* (1867) LR 1 P&D 362.

[90] *Re Oven's Goods* (1892) 29 LR Ir 451.

[91] *Clarke v Clarke* (1879) 5 LR Ir 47.

[92] *Cooke v Tanswell* (1818) 8 Taunt 450.

[93] At common law, the period was 30 years. The period of 20 years was substituted by the Evidence Act 1938, s 4.

[94] (1836) 3 Bing NC 183, HL; cf *Doe d Lord Arundel v Fowler* (1850) 14 QB 700.

There are four other presumptions relating to documents. They are: (i) that a document was made on the date which it bears;[95] (ii) that an alteration or erasure in a deed was made before execution, in a will after execution (on the grounds that a deed, but not a will, would be invalidated if presumed to have been altered after execution);[96] and (iii) that a deed was duly sealed.[97]

Stamped documents

Certain documents are required to be stamped for the purposes of stamp duty. Although in criminal proceedings such a document is admissible if unstamped, in civil proceedings a document requiring a stamp shall not be given in evidence unless it is duly stamped in accordance with the law in force at the time when it was first executed or, the court having objected to the omission or insufficiency of the stamp, and the document being one which may be legally stamped after its execution, payment is made of the amount of unpaid duty, together with any penalty payable on stamping, and a further sum of one pound.[98] The parties cannot waive these rules.[99] If a document requiring a stamp cannot be found or is not produced after notice to do so, it is presumed to have been duly stamped. However, if there is evidence to show that the document was not duly stamped, it is presumed, in the absence of evidence to the contrary, that this remained the case.[100]

Real evidence

Real evidence usually takes the form of some material object examined by the tribunal of fact as a means of proof. This and other varieties of real evidence are considered separately as follows.

Material objects

Where the existence, condition, or value of some material object is in issue or relevant to an issue, it may be produced for inspection by the tribunal of fact. Thus where a purchaser alleges that certain goods do not answer the vendor's description, the goods in question may be produced to the judge so that he may act on his own perception. Likewise, a jury may inspect a knife alleged to have been used in the commission of a murder. Material objects, however, call for accompanying testimony. Thus in the examples given, the goods would require to be identified and the knife, as an item of evidence, would be of no value in the absence not only of some testimony connecting it with the accused, for example evidence that it was found in his possession, but also of expert testimony that it was capable of causing the injuries sustained by the victim.[101]

---

[95] *Anderson v Weston* (1840) 6 Bing NC 296.

[96] Per Lord Campbell CJ in *Doe d Tatum v Catomore* (1851) 16 QB 745. An alteration in a will is only valid and effective if executed in like manner as is required for the execution of the will: Wills Act 1837, s 21.

[97] *Sed quaere*: see *Re Sandilands* (1871) LR 6 CP 411.

[98] Stamp Act 1891, s 14.

[99] *Bowker v Williamson* (1889) 5 TLR 382.

[100] *Closmadeuc v Carrel* (1856) 18 CB 36.

[101] In some cases, the tribunal of fact may not draw its own unaided conclusion without the assistance of an expert witness: *R v Tilley* [1961] 1 WLR 1309 (comparison of handwriting). See, in this chapter, under **Documentary evidence, Proof of due execution, Proof of handwriting**. See also *Anderson v R* [1972] AC 100, PC.

There is no rule of law that unless a material object is produced, or its non-production excused, oral evidence respecting it is inadmissible. Thus in *Hocking v Ahlquist Bros Ltd*,[102] the issue concerning the method by which certain garments had been made, it was held that although the garments were not produced at the trial, the evidence of witnesses who had seen them and could speak to their condition was not inadmissible. However, non-production of the object in question may go to the weight of the oral evidence adduced[103] and give rise to an inference adverse to the party failing to produce. Thus, in *Armory v Delamirie*[104] an action in trover against a goldsmith who failed to produce certain stones which he had removed from a jewel found by a chimney sweeper's boy, Pratt CJ directed the jury to assess damages on the basis that the stones were of the first water.

The appearance of persons and animals

Real evidence may take the form of a person's physical appearance. Thus it may be relevant, for identification or some other purpose, to have regard to a person's physical characteristics such as his height or colour of eyes or the fact that he is left-handed or bears some scar or other distinguishing feature. His accent, as opposed to the actual words he utters, also constitutes real evidence. Personal injuries may be examined on a question of causation or quantum of damages. Although in many cases little weight should be attached to it, the facial resemblance of a child to its alleged father and mother may be relevant to the issue of legitimacy.[105] For the purposes of contempt of court, a person's misconduct in court may constitute real evidence. Real evidence may also take the form of an animal, as in *Line v Taylor*,[106] where a dog of allegedly vicious disposition was brought into court and examined by the jury.

The demeanour of witnesses

The way in which a witness gives his evidence is often just as important as what he actually says. While some witnesses may appear to be forthright and frank, others may present themselves as hesitant, equivocal, or even hostile. Whatever form it takes, the demeanour and attitude of a witness in the course of giving his evidence is real evidence which is relevant to his credit and the weight to be attached to the evidence he gives.[107]

Lip-reading and facial mapping

Where an expert lip-reader, after viewing a CCTV recording of a person talking, gives opinion evidence as to what that person said, he is providing expert assistance to the jury in their interpretation of a species of real evidence.[108] Expert opinion evidence of facial mapping may be regarded in the same way.[109]

---

[102] [1944] KB 120. See also *R v Uxbridge Justices, ex p Sofaer* (1986) 85 Cr App R 367.

[103] Per Lord Coleridge CJ in *R v Francis* (1874) LR 2 CCR 128 at 133.

[104] (1722) 1 Stra 505.

[105] *C v C* [1972] 3 All ER 577; cf *Slingsby v A-G* (1916) 33 TLR 120, HL at 122–3.

[106] (1862) 3 F&F 731.

[107] For a critical analysis of demeanour as a test of credibility, see Ekman, *Telling Lies* (3rd edn, New York, 2002) and Marcus Stone, 'Instant Lie Detection? Demeanour and Credibility in Criminal Trials' [1991] Crim LR 821.

[108] *R v Luttrell* [2004] 2 Cr App R 520, CA at [37].

[109] *R v Clarke* [1995] 2 Cr App R 425 at 429.

Documents

A document may be tendered in evidence for a variety of purposes. If it is produced by a party relying upon the statements it contains, whether that party is relying upon them as evidence of their truth, by way of exception to the hearsay rule, or simply as original evidence, for example to show that they were made,[110] it constitutes documentary evidence and is subject to the rules considered in this chapter.[111] However, if the document is tendered in evidence as a material object, regardless of the words contained in it, for instance to show the bare fact of its existence, the substance of which it is made (eg whether parchment or paper), or the condition that it is in (eg whether crumpled or torn), it constitutes real evidence.[112]

Tape recordings, films, and photographs

Tape recordings, films, and photographs are, as we have seen,[113] sometimes treated as documentary evidence. By playing over a tape recording in court, a statement recorded on it may be admitted as evidence of the truth of its contents, by way of exception to the hearsay rule,[114] or as original evidence, for example merely to show that it was made. To the extent, however, that the recording also reveals the way in which the person in question spoke, his accent, accentuation, tone, intonation, etc, it is real evidence.[115]

In *The Statue of Liberty*,[116] an action concerning a collision between two ships, the plaintiff sought to admit in evidence a cinematograph film of radar echoes recorded by a shore radar station. The defendants argued that the evidence, having been produced mechanically and without human intervention, was inadmissible hearsay. Rejecting this submission, Sir Jocelyn Simon P said:[117]

> If tape-recordings are admissible, it seems that a photograph of radar reception is equally admissible— or indeed, any other type of photograph. It would be an absurd distinction that a photograph should be admissible if the camera were operated manually by a photographer, but not if it were operated by a trip or clock mechanism. Similarly, if evidence of weather conditions were relevant, the law would affront commonsense if it were to say that those could be proved by a person who looked at a barometer from time to time, but not by producing a barograph record. So, too, with other types of dial recording. Again, cards from clocking-in-and-out machines are frequently admitted in accident cases.[118]

---

[110] See Ch 10.

[111] But this is not the case if the contents are referred to merely for the purpose of identifying the document: see under **Documentary evidence, Proof of contents, The general rule at common law—primary evidence**.

[112] But see *R v Rice* [1963] 1 QB 857, CCA (see Ch 10).

[113] Under **Documentary evidence**, in this chapter.

[114] As in *R v Senat; R v Sin* (1968) 52 Cr App R 282, CA, where tape recordings of incriminating telephone conversations were held to have been properly admitted. See also *R v Maqsud Ali* [1966] 1 QB 688, CCA at 701: provided the jury are guided by what they hear, there is no objection to a properly proved transcript being put before them. As to tape recordings and transcripts of police interviews sought to be adduced in criminal proceedings, see also *R v Rampling* [1987] Crim LR 823, CA, the Code of Practice on Tape Recording of Interviews with Suspects (Code E) and para 43, the *Consolidated Criminal Practice Direction*.

[115] See, eg, *R v Emmerson* (1990) 92 Cr App R 284, CA (tone of voice). Before it is played over to the jury, the judge must satisfy himself that there is a prima facie case that it is both original and authentic: see *R v Stevenson* [1971] 1 WLR 1 and *R v Robson; R v Harris* [1972] 1 WLR 651 (see Ch 4).

[116] [1968] 1 WLR 739.

[117] [1968] 1 WLR 739 at 740.

[118] Cf *R v Wood* (1982) 76 Cr App R 23, CA: a computer printout is an item of real evidence and not hearsay if the computer in question is used as a calculator, a tool which does not contribute its own knowledge but merely does calculations which can be performed manually (see Ch 10).

It is tempting, on the basis of these words of Sir Jocelyn Simon P, to conclude that photographs and films, the relevance of which can be established by the testimony of someone with personal knowledge of the circumstances in which they were taken or made, are admissible as items of real evidence and can never give rise to problems of a hearsay nature. If the evidence of a witness to certain events is admissible, it may be reasoned, then photographs or films recording those same events should be no less admissible. Thus in *R v Dodson; R v Williams*[119] the Court of Appeal entertained no doubt that photographs taken by security cameras installed at a building society office at which an armed robbery was attempted, were admissible in evidence, being relevant to the issues of both whether an offence was committed and, if so, who committed it.[120] As to the latter issue, the jury were entitled to compare the photographic images with the accused sitting in the dock; and that the jury can do this will not prevent the calling of a witness who was not present at the scene of the crime, but who knows the person shown in the photograph, video, or film, to give evidence as to his identity.[121] It is clear, however, that a photograph or film is as capable of containing an out-of-court statement as a tape or a document made of paper. Both the 1995 Act and the 2003 Act operate on this assumption by catering for the admissibility of a statement contained in a 'document', which is defined as 'anything in which information of any description is recorded',[122] a definition wide enough to cover not only audio tapes, but also photographs, videotapes, and films. Indeed, the film in *The Statue of Liberty*, which may be regarded as having constituted a statement as to the paths taken by the two ships, would now be admissible for the truth of its contents under the 1995 Act. In cases falling outside these statutory provisions, however, it would seem that a photograph or film, even if it contains, or can itself be treated as the equivalent of, an out-of-court statement, will, if relevant, be admitted as an item of real evidence rather than excluded as hearsay. Indeed, in *R v Cook*[123] Watkins LJ went so far as to state that the photograph, together with the sketch and the photofit, are in a class of evidence of their own to which neither the rule against hearsay nor the rule against previous consistent or self-serving statements applies.

For the purposes of disclosure in civil proceedings, a video, film, or recording is a document within the extended meaning contained in CPR r 31.4 and therefore a party proposing to use it is subject to all the rules as to disclosure and inspection of documents contained in CPR r 31. Equally, if it is disclosed in accordance with r 31, the other party will be deemed to admit its authenticity unless notice is served that he wishes it to be proved at trial.[124] If he does serve such notice, the first party will be obliged to serve a witness statement by the person who took the video, film, or recording in order to prove its authenticity. If authenticity

---

[119] (1984) 79 Cr App R 220, CA.

[120] See also *Kajala v Noble* (1982) 75 Cr App R 149, CA, *R v Thomas* [1986] Crim LR 682, and *Taylor v Chief Constable of Cheshire* [1987] 1 All ER 225, DC (Ch 10).

[121] See *R v Fowden and White* [1982] Crim LR 588, CA, *R v Grimer* [1982] Crim LR 674, CA, and *Attorney General's Reference (No 2 of 2002)* [2003] 1 Cr App R 21, CA. See also *R v Clare and Peach* [1995] 2 Cr App R 333, CA, where a witness who did *not* know the people shown in a video recording, but had spent time analysing the photographic images, thereby acquiring special knowledge that the jury lacked, was permitted to identify them as the same people shown in a film and still photographs of the accused; and *R v Clarke* [1995] 2 Cr App R 425, CA, where the witness was an expert in facial identification who, using the technique of video superimposition, had compared photographs of a bank robber taken by an automatic camera with police identification photographs of the accused.

[122] The 1995 Act, s 13 and the 2003 Act, s 134(1).

[123] [1987] 1 All ER 1049, CA at 1054. See also, in the case of photofits, *R v Constantinou* (1989) 91 Cr App R 74, CA.

[124] See CPR r 32.19(1).

is not challenged, in the absence of any ruling by the court to the contrary, it is available for use by the first party, which includes using it in cross-examination of the other party and his witnesses.[125]

Views and demonstrations

A view is an inspection out of court of the *locus in quo* or of some object which it is inconvenient or impossible to bring to court.[126] There is some dispute whether out-of-court demonstrations or re-enactments are properly to be regarded as real evidence or as the equivalent of testimonial evidence. If the latter, it is arguable that the demonstrator should take the oath and thereby offer himself for cross-examination. On balance, the authorities would appear to favour the former view. In *Buckingham v Daily News Ltd*,[127] a negligence action concerning a machine, the judge inspected the machine and watched the plaintiff demonstrate what he had done. Judgment was given for the defendants. On appeal, it was argued that the judge had acted improperly by substituting his own opinion, based on the impression which he had gained at the view, for the plaintiff's oral evidence. Rejecting this argument, the Court of Appeal held that what the judge had seen was as much a part of the evidence as if the machine had been brought into the well of the court and the plaintiff had there demonstrated what took place.[128]

It is critical, before a court embarks upon a view, that there is clarity about precisely what is to happen, who is to stand where, what, if any, objects should be placed where, and who will do what. These matters should not be decided at the scene of the view, which should be conducted without discussion.[129] As a general rule, a view should be attended by the judge, the tribunal of fact, the parties, and counsel. In civil proceedings, each of the parties must be given the opportunity of being present at a view and a failure to do so may result in a retrial.[130] In a summary trial, as a general rule a view by magistrates of the scene of the alleged offence should take place before the conclusion of the evidence and in the presence of the parties or their representatives so as to afford them an opportunity of commenting on any feature of the locality which has altered since the time of the incident or any feature not previously noticed by the parties which impresses the magistrates.[131] The presence of the accused at a view is important because he may be able to point out some important matter of which his legal adviser is ignorant or about which the magistrates are making a mistake.[132] In a criminal trial by jury, the judge should always be present at a view, whether or not any witness is present

[125] *Rall v Hume* [2001] 3 All ER 248, CA at [16].
[126] See, eg, *London General Omnibus Co Ltd v Lavell* [1901] 1 Ch 135, CA (an omnibus).
[127] [1956] 2 QB 534, CA.
[128] The court approved, in this respect, the views of Denning LJ in *Goold v Evans & Co* [1951] 2 TLR 1189, CA. But cf per Hodson LJ in the same case at 1191–2 and per Barwick CJ in *Railway Comr v Murphy* (1967) 41 ALJR 77, HC of A at 78.
[129] *M v DPP* [2009] EWHC 752 (Admin).
[130] *Goold v Evans & Co* [1951] 2 TLR 1189, CA. But see per Widgery LJ in *Salsbury v Woodland* [1970] 1 QB 324, CA at 343–4: although a judge attending a demonstration at which the events in question are reconstructed or simulated should be accompanied by representatives of both parties, he may visit the *locus in quo* in order to see that which has previously been represented to him in court by plan and photograph on his own and without reference to the parties at all.
[131] *Parry v Boyle* (1986) 83 Cr App R 310, DC.
[132] *R v Ely Justices, ex p Burgess* [1992] Crim LR 888, DC.

for the purposes of a demonstration,[133] in order to control the proceedings. In particular, she should take precautions to prevent any witnesses who are present from communicating, except by way of demonstration, with the jury.[134] Because the jury should remain together at all times when evidence is being received, it is improper for one juror to attend a view and report back to the others what he observed.[135]

ADDITIONAL READING

Ekman, *Telling Lies* (3rd edn, New York, 2002).

Hollander, *Documentary Evidence* (10th edn, London, 2009).

Porter, 'A new theoretical framework regarding the application and reliability of photographic evidence' (2011) 15 E&P 26.

Stone, 'Instant Lie Detection? Demeanour and Credibility in Criminal Trials' [1991] Crim LR 821.

---

[133] *R v Hunter* [1985] 2 All ER 173, CA. Cf *Tameshwar v R* [1957] AC 476, PC. See also *R v Turay* [2007] EWCA Crim 2821, where there was no disadvantage to the defence.

[134] *R v Martin* (1872) LR 1 CCR 378; *Karamat v R* [1956] AC 256, PC.

[135] *R v Gurney* [1976] Crim LR 567, CA.

Hearsay in criminal cases

10

Key issues

- If a statement is made out of court and tendered as evidence of the facts asserted (hearsay), when and why should it be excluded or admitted in criminal proceedings?

- If a statement is made out of court but is not tendered as evidence of the facts asserted, when and why should it be admitted in criminal proceedings?

- Should the definition of hearsay evidence encompass:

  - assertions that may be inferred from a person's out-of-court statement;

  - out-of-court statements tendered as evidence of the non-existence of a fact; and

  - statements produced by computers or other machines?

- To what extent is the admission of hearsay evidence compatible with Article 6 of the European Convention on Human Rights?

- Where hearsay evidence is admissible, what safeguards may be needed to address risks of unfair prejudice?

Background and rationale

This chapter covers the meaning of hearsay in criminal proceedings. It also deals with all but one of the categories of hearsay admissible by statute in such proceedings. The exceptional category, confessions, merits the discrete treatment given to it in Chapter 13. It is also convenient to consider separately the subsisting common law rules governing the admissibility of hearsay evidence in criminal proceedings. They are considered in Chapter 12.

Under the common law rule against hearsay, any assertion, other than one made by a person while giving oral evidence in the proceedings, was inadmissible if tendered as evidence of the facts asserted.[1] The rule operated to prevent counsel from eliciting such evidence from any witness, whether in examination-in-chief or cross-examination[2] and applied to assertions in documents as well as oral assertions. The rule is perhaps best explained by way of example. Suppose that A, who witnessed an act of dangerous driving, some weeks later said to B that the car in question was blue and at that time also made a written note to the same effect. B reported to C what A had said to him. If A is subsequently called as a witness in proceedings concerned with the incident in question, he may of course make a statement from the witness box in the course of giving his evidence to the effect that the colour of the car he saw was blue. However, evidence may not be given by A, B, or C, for the purpose of establishing the colour of the car, of the oral statement made by A out of court. Likewise, the written statement made by A is inadmissible for that purpose. This is a simple example, but the common law rule against hearsay was highly complex, technical, difficult to describe with accuracy, and of unclear scope.

The common law rule was subject to a variety of common law and statutory exceptions, and these too were often complex and technical in nature, some of them ill-considered and subject to frequent amendment. For example, the Criminal Evidence Act 1965, designed to admit hearsay in trade and business records, was passed as an interim measure, but few could have foreseen that the broader provisions set out in ss 68–72 of the Police and Criminal Evidence Act 1984 (the 1984 Act) relating to documentary hearsay by which it was replaced, would in turn be replaced only four years later by ss 23–28 of the Criminal Justice Act 1988 (the 1988 Act), provisions which unfortunately contained serious drafting errors and which have now been repealed.[3] In criminal cases, the meaning of hearsay and the circumstances in which it is admissible, are now governed by Chapter 2 of Pt 11 of the Criminal Justice Act 2003 (the 2003 Act).

A number of reasons have been advanced to justify the rule against hearsay, including the danger of manufactured evidence and, in the case of oral hearsay, especially multiple oral hearsay (X testifies as to what Y told him Z had said, for example), the danger of inaccuracy or mistake by reason of repetition. The principal rationale of the common law rule was summarized by Lord Bridge in *R v Blastland*:[4]

---

[1] Per Lord Havers in *R v Sharp* [1988] 1 WLR 7, HL and per Lords Ackner and Oliver in *R v Kearley* [1992] 2 AC 228, HL at 255 and 259 respectively. The rule also extended to out-of-court statements of otherwise admissible *opinion* (see Ch 18).

[2] For the application of the rule in cross-examination, see *R v Thomson* [1912] 3 KB 19, CCA (see Ch 7).

[3] Criminal Justice Act 2003, s 136.

[4] [1986] AC 41, HL at 53 and 54.

Hearsay evidence is not excluded because it has no logically probative value...The rationale of excluding it as inadmissible, rooted as it is in the system of trial by jury, is a recognition of the great difficulty, even more acute for a juror than for a trained judicial mind, of assessing what, if any, weight can properly be given to a statement by a person whom the jury have not seen or heard and who has not been subject to any test of reliability by cross-examination...The danger against which this fundamental rule provides a safeguard is that untested hearsay evidence will be treated as having a probative force which it does not deserve.

On the other hand, evidence of virtually unquestionable reliability has been excluded under the rule; cross-examination has been said to be arguably the poorest technique employed in the common law courts to elicit accurate testimony;[5] and there are dangers in deciding veracity on the basis of demeanour.[6] That the danger to which Lord Bridge referred can be overstated was recognized in the Report of the Royal Commission of Criminal Justice.[7] A reference to the Law Commission led to a consultation paper[8] and a final report.[9] The Commission, rejecting a range of other options, favoured retention of the rule but proposed a statutory formulation of both the rule and some of the exceptions to it, an expansion of the exceptions, and a 'safety valve' discretion to admit sufficiently reliable hearsay evidence not covered by any of the exceptions.[10] Subsequently, the Auld Report[11] recommended an alternative approach, that hearsay should be admissible if the original source or 'best evidence' is not available. This approach would have placed much greater trust in the fact finders to give hearsay evidence the weight it deserves. 'Many are of the view that both [judges and magistrates] are already more competent than we give them credit for assessing the weight of the evidence, including hearsay evidence.'[12] Greater trust in the fact finders would also have followed if the Government had accepted the plea, made during the passage of the 2003 Act through the House of Lords, for a simple rule giving judges a wide discretionary power. Lord Ackner referred to a paper, written by Lord Chief Justice Woolf and supported by all the judges of the criminal division of the Court of Appeal, in which he said:[13]

If we have got to the stage where it is considered that it is safe to allow juries to hear hearsay evidence, then we must be accepting that they can be trusted to use that evidence in accordance with the directions of the judge. Instead of the detailed and complex provisions which are contained in Chapter 2, what is needed is a simple rule putting the judge in charge of what evidence is admissible and giving him the responsibility of ensuring that the jury use the evidence in an appropriate manner.

---

[5] Australian Law Reform Commission Research Paper No 8 (1982), *Manner of Giving Evidence* ch 10, para 5. See also Law Commission Consultation Paper No 138 (1995), *Evidence in Criminal Proceedings: The Hearsay Rule and Related Topics* paras 6.49 and 6.62.

[6] See Law Commission Consultation Paper No 138 paras 6.22 and 6.27.

[7] Cm 2263 (1993).

[8] Consultation Paper No 138 (see n 5).

[9] Law Com No 245, *Evidence in Criminal Proceedings: Hearsay and Related Topics*, Cm 3670 (1997).

[10] For a critique of the Report, see Tapper, 'Hearsay in Criminal Cases: An Overview of Law Commission Report No 245' [1997] Crim LR 771.

[11] *Review of the Criminal Courts of England and Wales* (2001).

[12] *Review of the Criminal Courts of England and Wales* (2001), para 98, ch 11.

[13] *Hansard* HL vol 654 cols 752–3 (4 Nov 2003).

The Government rejected both this plea and the approach favoured by Lord Justice Auld. The provisions relating to hearsay in Chapter 2 of Pt 11 of the 2003 Act are, in very large measure, based on the proposals of the Law Commission.[14]

Admissibility of hearsay under the Criminal Justice Act 2003

General

The statutory scheme

The only heads under which hearsay is admissible in criminal proceedings are set out in s 114(1) of the 2003 Act. Section 114(1), which is subject to discretionary powers to exclude hearsay,[15] provides as follows:

(1) In criminal proceedings[16] a statement not made in oral evidence in the proceedings is admissible as evidence of any matter stated if, but only if—

    (a) any provision of this Chapter or any other statutory provision makes it admissible,

    (b) any rule of law preserved by s 118 makes it admissible,

    (c) all parties to the proceedings agree to it being admissible, or

    (d) the court is satisfied that it is in the interests of justice for it to be admissible.

Concerning the first part of s 114(1)(a), the categories of hearsay rendered admissible under the provisions of Chapter 2 of Pt 11 of the 2003 Act are (i) statements made by persons who are not available as witnesses; (ii) statements in business and other documents; (iii) certain inconsistent and other previous statements of witnesses; (iv) statements on which an expert will in evidence base an opinion; and, by virtue of s 128(1) of the 2003 Act, (v) confessions admissible on behalf of a co-accused.[17] Concerning the second part of s 114(1)(a), whereby hearsay may be admitted by virtue of 'any other statutory provision', 'statutory provision' means any provision contained in, or in an instrument made under, the 2003 Act or any other Act, including any Act passed after the 2003 Act.[18] These statutory provisions are considered in this chapter, except those relating to confessions, which are considered in Chapter 13.[19]

As to s 114(1)(b), the rules of law preserved by s 118 are most, but not all, of the common law rules providing for the admissibility of various categories of hearsay. With the exception of the rules preserved by s 118, the common law rules governing the admissibility of hearsay evidence in criminal proceedings are abolished.[20] The statute abolishes the common law rule as well as the exceptions which it does not preserve.[21] Some of the rules preserved by

---

[14] For a critique of the statutory framework, see Birch, 'Criminal Justice Act 2003 (4) Hearsay: Same Old Story, Same Old Song?' [2004] Crim LR 556.

[15] See s 126, considered under **Admissibility of hearsay under the Criminal Justice Act 2003, Other safeguards, Discretion to exclude** in this chapter.

[16] 'Criminal proceedings' means criminal proceedings in relation to which the strict rules of evidence apply: s 134(1). These include proceedings under the Criminal Procedure (Insanity) Act 1964, s 4A: *R v Chal* [2008] 1 Cr App R 18, CA.

[17] Section 128(2) provides that, subject to s 128(1), nothing in Ch 2 of Pt 11 makes a confession by an accused admissible if it would not be admissible under the Police and Criminal Evidence Act 1984, s 76.

[18] The 2003 Act, s 134(1).

[19] These statutory provisions are considered in this chapter under **Written statements under section 9 of the Criminal Justice Act 1967** and **Depositions of vulnerable children and young persons under section 43 of the Children and Young Persons Act 1933**.

[20] The 2003 Act, s 118(1)2.

[21] *R v Singh* [2006] 1 WLR 1564, CA.

s 118—statements in public documents, works of reference, evidence of age, evidence of reputation, and statements forming part of the *res gestae*—are considered in Chapter 12 (Hearsay admissible at common law). It is convenient to consider the remainder of the preserved rules in other parts of this work: mixed statements in Chapter 6 (Examination-in-chief); confessions, admissions by agents, and statements made by a party to a common enterprise in Chapter 13 (Confessions); and the rule whereby an expert may draw on the body of expertise relevant to his field in Chapter 18 (Opinion evidence).

Section 114(1)(c) permits hearsay to be admissible where the prosecution, the accused, and any co-accused agree to it being admissible.[22] Finally, s 114(1)(d) provides for the admissibility of hearsay which it would be in the interests of justice to admit, ie hearsay admissible by exercise of the inclusionary discretion.

Under s 114(3):

> Nothing in this Chapter affects the exclusion of evidence of a statement on grounds other than the fact that it is a statement not made in oral evidence in the proceedings.

Thus if hearsay evidence falls to be excluded because it is irrelevant or inadmissible on grounds of public policy, privilege or because of any other exclusionary rule of evidence, it will still fall to be excluded notwithstanding that it is otherwise admissible hearsay.

Article 6 of the European Convention on Human Rights

Article 6 of the European Convention on Human Rights provides:

> (1) In the determination…of any criminal charge against him, everyone is entitled to a fair and public hearing…
>
> (3) Everyone charged with a criminal offence has the following minimum rights:
>
>   …
>
>   (d) to have examined witnesses against him and to obtain the attendance and examination of witnesses on his behalf under the same conditions as witnesses against him.

The leading authority on the relationship between Art 6 and the hearsay provisions of the 2003 Act is *Al-Khawaja and Tahery v UK*.[23] In *Al-Khawaja and Tahery*, a 17-judge Grand Chamber of the European Court of Human Rights conducted a thorough review of Strasbourg jurisprudence and the national law of the United Kingdom relating to the admissibility of hearsay evidence, and the following principles were stated.[24]

1. The guarantees in para (3)(d) of Art 6 are specific aspects of the right to a fair hearing set forth in Art 6(1) which must be taken into account in any assessment of the fairness of proceedings. The primary concern is to evaluate the overall fairness of criminal proceedings and in making this assessment the proceedings as a whole will be considered so that regard is had for the rights of the defence and the interests of the public and victims that crime is properly prosecuted.[25]

---

[22] However, the leave of the judge may be required to ensure that potential public interest immunity issues are properly considered. See *R v DJ* [2010] 2 Cr App R 2, CA (social security files relating to a person other than the accused).

[23] (2012) 54 EHRR 23.

[24] See also the principles stated in *R v Horncastle* [2009] 2 Cr App R 15, CA and *R v Horncastle* [2010] 2 AC 373, SC. See also *R v Ibrahim* [2012] 2 Cr App R 32 at [85]–[87].

[25] *Al-Khawaja and Tahery v UK* (2012) 54 EHRR 23 at [118].

Although the propositions are addressed to the Crown Courts, in respect of proposition (2), 'a domestic court' includes the Court of Appeal and the obligation is to follow *Horncastle*, other than in wholly exceptional circumstances.[53]

Article 6 and the hearsay statements of an available witness

Section 114 is not restricted to the admission of a hearsay statement the maker of which is not available for cross-examination. Where hearsay evidence takes the form of a statement made by a person who is also called to give evidence at trial, for example, because it is admitted under s 119 or s 120,[54] and is therefore available for questioning, it is submitted that there can be no question of its admission being in breach of Art 6(3)(d).[55]

The statements to which Article 6 applies

In none of the decided cases has the expression 'witness' been extended beyond persons who have provided statements to the authorities as part of the prosecutorial process, and so it is doubtful whether the admission of statements less formal than a witness statement, deposition, or business documents would infringe the rights of the accused under Art 6(3)(d). The jurisprudence on Art 6(3)(d) is therefore of principal relevance where the prosecution seek to admit hearsay evidence under s 116 or s 114(1)(d).[56]

The meaning of hearsay in the Criminal Justice Act 2003

As we have seen from s 114(1), hearsay is 'a statement not made in oral evidence in the proceedings…admissible as evidence of any matter stated'. This formulation covers not only 'out-of-court' statements as such, but also statements made in previous criminal or civil proceedings. 'Oral evidence', for the purposes of s 114(1) and other provisions relating to hearsay in the 2003 Act, includes evidence which, by reason of any disability, disorder, or other impairment, a person called as a witness gives in writing or by signs or by way of any device.[57]

'A statement'

'A statement', for the purposes of the provisions relating to hearsay in the 2003 Act, is 'any representation of fact or opinion made by a person by whatever means; and it includes a representation made in a sketch, photofit, or other pictorial form'.[58] This is a very wide definition. It covers a statement of opinion, provided that it is admissible opinion of course,[59] as well as a statement of fact.[60] The statement may have been made unsworn or on oath by any person, whether or not a person called as a witness in the proceedings in question. The representation, however, must have been made by a person—statements in computer-generated

---

[53] *R v Ibrahim* [2012] 2 Cr App R 32, CA at [87].

[54] See under **Admissibility of hearsay under the Criminal Justice Act 2003, Previous inconsistent statements of witnesses** and **Admissibility of hearsay under the Criminal Justice Act 2003, Other previous statements of witnesses** in this chapter.

[55] See, eg, *R v Xhabri* [2006] 1 Cr App R 26, CA at [44].

[56] See, eg, *R v L* [2009] 1 WLR 626, CA.

[57] The 2003 Act, s 134(1).

[58] The 2003 Act, s 115(2).

[59] See the 2003 Act, s 114(3) under **Admissibility of hearsay under the Criminal Justice Act 2003, General, The statutory scheme** in this chapter.

[60] See also the Criminal Justice Act 1988, s 30, considered, in this chapter, under **Expert reports**.

documents are not covered. The admissibility of computer-generated documents is considered separately.[61]

The phrase 'any representation…by whatever means' clearly covers statements made orally as well as statements made in writing, whether by hand, or by means of a typewriter, word processor, computer, or other similar device. A common law example of oral hearsay, which continues to be hearsay under the 2003 Act, is *R v Rothwell*,[62] a case of supplying heroin. The prosecution sought to rely on evidence that the accused was seen on several occasions passing small packages to various people, coupled with the evidence of a drugs squad officer that the recipients were known to him as heroin users. It was held that, insofar as the officer's evidence was based on statements made to him by others, for example the alleged recipients, then the evidence would be inadmissible hearsay; but that it would not be hearsay insofar as it was based on the recipients' convictions for possession of heroin[63] or, for example, the officer's personal observation of needle marks on the recipients' forearms or his personal knowledge of the recipients being in possession of heroin or receiving treatment for heroin addiction. *Patel v Comptroller of Customs*[64] provides an example of written hearsay. The appellant was convicted of making a false declaration in an import entry form concerning certain bags of seed, having declared that the country of origin of the seed was India. Evidence was admitted that the bags of seed bore the words 'Produce of Morocco'. The Privy Council held that the evidence was inadmissible hearsay and advised that the conviction be quashed.[65]

The phrase 'any representation…by whatever means' is also wide enough to embrace statements made by conduct or signs and gestures, and statements made partly orally and partly by conduct or signs and gestures. A common law example of the last is *R v Gibson*,[66] a trial for malicious wounding in which the prosecutor gave evidence that after he had been hit by a stone, a woman, pointing to the door of a house, had said, 'The person who threw the stone went in there.' The occupant of the house was convicted. The conviction was quashed on the ground that evidence of the woman's statement was inadmissible.[67] *Chandrasekera v R*[68] provides an example of a hearsay statement made solely by signs or gestures. The appellant was charged with murder. At the trial evidence was admitted that the victim, whose throat had been cut, had made certain signs, the apparent effect of which was to indicate the accused. Asked whether it was the appellant who had cut her throat, she replied by nodding her head. Lord Roche was of the opinion that the case resembled that of a dumb person able to converse by means of finger alphabet, and held that the woman had effectively stated that the accused

[61] Under **Admissibility of hearsay under the Criminal Justice Act 2003, The meaning of hearsay in the Criminal Justice Act 2003, Statements produced by computers and mechanical and other devices** in this chapter.

[62] (1994) 99 Cr App R 388, CA.

[63] Admissible under the Police and Criminal Evidence Act 1984, s 74 (see Ch 2).

[64] [1966] AC 356, PC.

[65] See also *R v Sealby* [1965] 1 All ER 701 (Crown Court) and *R v Brown* [1991] Crim LR 835, CA (evidence of a name on an appliance inadmissible to establish its ownership); and cf *R v Rice* [1963] 1 QB 857 under **Admissibility of hearsay under the Criminal Justice Act 2003, The meaning of hearsay in the Criminal Justice Act 2003, The statement as evidence relevant to some other fact in issue, The statement as evidence of an association between the accused and a document** in this chapter.

[66] (1887) LR 18 QBD 537, CCR.

[67] The Court for Crown Cases Reserved gave no express reason as to why the evidence was inadmissible, but the decision has been cited subsequently in cases expressly concerned with the rule against hearsay: see, eg, *R v Saunders* [1899] 1 QB 490, CCR.

[68] [1937] AC 220, PC.

had cut her neck. The hearsay statement was nevertheless admissible under an exception contained in the Ceylon Evidence Ordinance 1895 and would now be admissible under s 116(1) and (2)(a) of the 2003 Act (a statement made by a person since deceased).[69]

The inclusion, within the definition of 'a statement', of 'a representation made in a sketch, photofit or other pictorial form' reflects a principled approach which was lacking in some of the common law authorities.[70] Photographs and films are excluded from the definition and continue to be admissible, at common law, as a variety of real evidence, if relevant to the issues, including the important issues of whether an offence was committed and who committed it.[71]

Original evidence

Under s 114(1) of the 2003 Act, hearsay is a statement not made in oral evidence in the proceedings 'admissible as evidence of any matter stated'. Hearsay falls to be distinguished from original evidence, which may be defined as a statement not made in oral evidence in the proceedings which is admissible for any relevant purpose other than that of establishing any matter stated. This is a difficult distinction, but is important, because whereas hearsay is admissible only under the heads set out in s 114(1), original evidence is admissible provided only that it is sufficiently relevant. Examples of original evidence may be classified according to whether they are admitted (i) simply to show that the statement was made, because that is a fact in issue in the proceedings; or (ii) because of their relevance to some other fact in issue in the proceedings.

The making of the statement as a fact in issue

If the making of a certain statement is itself a fact in issue in the proceedings, that statement, even if inadmissible as evidence of any matter stated, may be admitted as evidence of the fact that it was made.[72] For instance, on a charge of making a threat to kill, the victim may give evidence of the fact that the accused said to her, 'I am going to kill you.'[73] *R v Chapman*[74] provides an instructive example. Following a road traffic accident, the accused was taken to a hospital where a breath test was administered. He was subsequently convicted of driving a motor vehicle with excess alcohol. Section 2(2)(b) of the Road Safety Act 1967 provided that a hospital patient shall not be required to provide a specimen of breath if the medical practitioner in charge of his case 'objects' on the grounds that it would be prejudicial to the proper care or treatment of the patient. At the trial, a police officer gave evidence that the doctor in question had not objected to the provision of a specimen. Rejecting the argument that this evidence was inadmissible, the Court of Appeal held that the evidence had been properly adduced to establish that the doctor had made no objection.

---

[69] Where a police officer employs an interpreter to question a suspect whose language he does not understand: see *R v Attard* (1958) 43 Cr App R 90 and the consequent Home Office circular to the police on the use of interpreters.

[70] See *R v Cook* [1987] QB 417, CA, *R v Constantinou* (1989) 91 Cr App R 74, CA, and *R v Percy Smith* [1976] Crim LR 511, CA.

[71] See, eg, *R v Dodson and R v Williams* (1984) 79 Cr App R 220, CA (photographs), considered in Ch 9. See also *R v Roberts* [1998] Crim LR 682, CA.

[72] But see *West Midlands Probation Board v French* [2009] 1 WLR 1715, concerning proceedings for breach of a licence issued to a serving prisoner on his release from imprisonment, in which the Divisional Court held that the licence was hearsay. It is submitted that this decision is incorrect as the licence was adduced not as evidence *of* the matters stated but simply as evidence that the matters *were* stated in the licence and the accused had breached them. For further criticism of this decision see Ormerod, 'Commentary' [2009] Crim LR 283.

[73] In *R v Rizwan Mawji* (2003) LTL 16/10/2003, CA, where such a threat was contained in an e-mail sent from the accused's e-mail address, it was held that whether the jury accepted the e-mail as genuine was a matter manifestly for them.

[74] [1969] 2 QB 436, CA.

The statement as evidence relevant to some other fact in issue

A statement may also be admissible as a fact relevant to a fact in issue in the proceedings notwithstanding that it is inadmissible as evidence of any matter stated. Examples that may be given are many and various, such as a statement which is relevant to the state of mind of the person who makes it, or of the person who hears or reads it. These and other instructive examples will now be considered.

The statement as evidence relevant to the state of mind of the person who makes it

In some cases the statement is admitted as evidence of the state of mind of its maker. Thus a man's assertion in 2013 that he is Napoleon, Emperor of France, may be tendered for the purpose of showing his insanity. In *Ratten v R*,[75] Ratten was convicted of the murder of his wife by shooting her. His defence was that a gun went off accidentally while he was cleaning it. The evidence established that the shooting, from which the wife had died almost immediately, took place between 1.12 pm and about 1.20 pm. A telephonist from the local exchange gave evidence that at 1.15 pm she had received a telephone call from Ratten's house made by a sobbing woman who in an hysterical voice had said, 'Get me the police please.' The Privy Council held that there was no hearsay element in this evidence, which was relevant (i) in order to show that, contrary to the evidence of Ratten, who denied that any telephone call had been made by his wife, a call had been made; and (ii) as possibly showing that the wife was in a state of emotion or fear at an existing or impending emergency, which was capable of rebutting Ratten's defence that the shooting was accidental.[76] *Ratten* was held to be clearly distinguishable in *R v Blastland*.[77] In that case, the House of Lords held that the accused, convicted of buggery and murder, had been properly prevented from adducing evidence of statements made by a third party indicating *his* knowledge of the murder before the body was found, because the only issue was whether the accused had committed the crimes and what was relevant to that issue was not the third party's knowledge but how he had acquired it; since he could have done so in a number of different ways, there was no rational basis on which the jury could infer that he, rather than the accused, was the murderer.[78]

The statement as evidence relevant to the state of mind of the person who hears or reads it

In some cases, the statement is admitted as evidence of the state of mind of the person who heard or read it, ie to show what the person who heard or read it, knew, thought, or believed. If A is charged with the murder of B, evidence of a statement by C to A that B was having an adulterous relationship with A's spouse, even if not admissible as evidence of the adulterous relationship, has an obvious relevance on the question of A's motive. In *Subramaniam v Public Prosecutor*[79] the accused was convicted of being in unlawful possession of ammunition. His

---

[75] [1972] AC 378.

[76] See also *R v Gilfoyle* [1996] 3 All ER 883, CA (suicide notes admissible as evidence of a woman's suicidal frame of mind and further statements made by her which showed that when she wrote the notes she had no intention of taking her own life) and *R v Gregson* [2003] 2 Cr App R 521 (evidence that G had expressed concerns about how to dispose of a quantity of ecstasy tablets he had purchased admissible in relation to his intent to supply, the defence case being that he believed he was acquiring a much smaller amount).

[77] [1986] AC 41.

[78] An out-of-court statement made by the *accused* and disclosing his possession of certain knowledge which tends to incriminate him may be admitted, by way of statutory exception to the hearsay rule, as a confession: see Police and Criminal Evidence Act 1984, s 76 and Ch 13.

[79] [1956] 1 WLR 965. See also *R v Willis* [1960] 1 WLR 55, CCA and *R v Madden* [1986] Crim LR 804, CA.

defence was that he had been threatened by terrorists and had acted under duress. Evidence of what the terrorists had said was excluded by the trial judge as inadmissible hearsay. Quashing the conviction, the Privy Council held that the trial judge had erred. Statements could have been made by the terrorists which, even if not admissible as evidence of any matter stated, might reasonably have induced in the accused, if he believed them, an apprehension of instant death if he failed to conform to their wishes. The statements were accordingly admissible as potentially cogent evidence of duress.[80]

The statement as evidence of the fact that it is false

A statement may be admitted as original evidence where it is tendered for the purpose of allowing the tribunal of fact to conclude that its contents are false and to draw inferences from the falsity of those contents. In *A-G v Good*[81] the demonstrably false statement of a debtor's wife that her husband was not at home was admissible for the purpose of showing her husband's intention to defraud his creditors. If an unreasonable time had intervened between the demand for entrance and the opening of the door, that would have been a fact relevant to the issue, and the untrue statement of the wife was relevant in the same way. In *Mawaz Khan v R*[82] the appellants were convicted of murder. At the trial the prosecution had relied upon the fact that each of them had in his statement to the police sought to set up a joint alibi, many of the details of which were demonstrated to be false by other evidence. The Privy Council held that the trial judge had properly directed the jury that although a statement made by one of the accused in the absence of another was not evidence against the other, they were entitled to compare the statements of the two accused and, if they concluded that they were false, to draw the inference that the accused had cooperated after the alleged crime and jointly concocted the story out of a sense of guilt.[83]

The statement as evidence of the fact that an offer was made

In *Woodhouse v Hall*[84] the manageress of a sauna and massage parlour was charged with acting in the management of a brothel. Plain-clothes police officers, who had entered the premises as customers, alleged that they had been offered masturbation by the manageress and other women employed there. At the trial, the justices held that the police officers' evidence of the offers made to them was inadmissible hearsay. The information was dismissed. On the prosecutor's appeal by way of case stated, Donaldson LJ held that the evidence had been wrongly excluded: 'There is no question of the hearsay rule arising at all. The relevant issue was did these ladies make these offers?'[85] The very fact that such offers had been made was relevant to the central fact in issue, namely whether the premises were being used as a sauna and massage parlour or a brothel. As Lord Ackner pointed out in *R v Kearley*,[86] 'in order to establish that the premises are being used as a brothel it is sufficient to prove that at the premises more than one

---

[80] See also *R v Davis* [1998] Crim LR 659, CA (evidence of a solicitor's advice to the accused may be admissible for the purpose of establishing the accused's reason for not answering questions in interview).

[81] (1825) M'Cle&Yo 286.

[82] [1967] 1 AC 454.

[83] See also *R v Binham* [1991] Crim LR 774, CA, where evidence of B's previous statements in support of his alibi defence, together with evidence as to their falsity, was admissible as original evidence.

[84] (1981) 72 Cr App R 39, DC.

[85] *Woodhouse v Hall* (1981) 72 Cr App R 39, DC at 42. Cf, *sed quaere, R v Lawal* [1994] Crim LR 746, CA.

[86] [1992] 2 AC 228, HL at 257.

woman *offers* herself as a participant in physical acts of indecency for the sexual gratification of men'.[87]

The statement as evidence of an association between the accused and a document

A statement may be admitted as original evidence capable of establishing an association between the accused and a document which contains the statement. From the association, inferences may be drawn such as, in *Lydon*,[88] the accused's presence where the document was found or, as in *Rice*,[89] the accused's use of the document.

In *R v Lydon*, the appellant, whose first name was Sean, was convicted of robbery. His defence was one of alibi. A gun and two pieces of rolled paper were found near the scene of the robbery. On the pieces of paper someone had written 'Sean rules' and 'Sean rules 85'. Ink of similar appearance and composition to that on the paper was found on the gun barrel. The Court of Appeal held that evidence relating to the pieces of paper had been properly admitted as circumstantial evidence: if the jury were satisfied that the gun was used in the robbery and that the pieces of paper were linked to the gun, the references to Sean could be a fact which would fit in with the appellant having committed the offence.[90] In addition, the references were not hearsay because they involved no assertion as to the truth of the contents of the pieces of paper—they were not tendered to show that Sean ruled anything.

In *R v Rice* the accused were convicted of conspiracy. Part of the prosecution case involved proving that two accused, Rice and Hoather, had taken a certain flight to Manchester. A used airline ticket, bearing the name of Rice and of another accused, Moore, was admitted in evidence against Rice. The Court of Criminal Appeal held that although the ticket was inadmissible hearsay if tendered for the purposes of speaking its contents, ie to show that the booking was effected by Rice or even by any man of that name, it had been properly admitted. Winn J said:[91]

> The relevance of that ticket in logic and its legal admissibility as a piece of real evidence both stem from the same root, viz., the balance of probability recognized by common sense and common knowledge that an air ticket which has been used on a flight and which has a name upon it has more likely than not been used by a man of that name or by one of two men whose names are upon it.

Implied assertions

At common law a question which gave rise to considerable difficulty was whether the hearsay rule applied to implied assertions, an area of evidence law which has been characterized as a legalistic backwater which is 'the home of sophistry and the graveyard of common sense'.[92] An

---

[87] See *Kelly v Purvis* [1983] QB 663, DC.

[88] (1987) 85 Cr App R 221, CA.

[89] [1963] 1 QB 857, CCA.

[90] See also *R v McIntosh* [1992] Crim LR 651, CA (calculations as to the purchase and sale prices of 12 oz of an unnamed commodity, not in M's handwriting but found concealed in the chimney of a house where he had been living, admissible as circumstantial evidence tending to connect him with drug-related offences); *Roberts v DPP* [1994] Crim LR 926, DC (documents found at R's offices and home, including repair and gas bills and other accounts relating to certain premises, admissible as circumstantial evidence linking R with those premises, on charges of assisting in the management of a brothel and running a massage parlour without a licence); *R v Horne* [1992] Crim LR 304, CA; and cf *R v Chrysostomou* [2010] EWCA Crim 1403 (text messages requesting drugs showed a relationship of drugs supply between the accused and the sender).

[91] [1963] 1 QB 857 at 871.

[92] Birch, 'Criminal Justice Act 2003 (4) Hearsay: Same Old Story, Same Old Song?' [2004] Crim LR 556 at 564.

implied assertion is an assertion, whether made orally, in writing, or by conduct, from which it is possible to infer a particular matter. To take a simple example, if Harry, walking down the street, and not using a mobile telephone, says, 'Hello, Bill', it is possible to infer that Bill was in Harry's presence. The common law authorities treated as hearsay implied assertions made orally or in writing (or by a combination of an oral or written statement and conduct). Some examples follow.

Oral assertions

In *Teper v R*,[93] the accused was convicted of arson of a shop belonging to his wife. His defence was alibi. In order to establish his presence near the shop, a policeman gave evidence that, some 25 minutes after the fire had begun, an unidentified woman bystander shouted to a motorist resembling the accused, 'Your place burning and you going away from the fire.' The Privy Council, quashing the conviction, held that this assertion which, by implication, established Teper's presence, was inadmissible hearsay.[94] Another example of oral assertions treated as hearsay at common law is provided by *R v Kearley*.[95] This decision, which s 115(3) of the 2003 Act aimed to overturn, is considered under **Admissibility of hearsay under the Criminal Justice Act 2003, General, Matters stated in statements** in this chapter.

Written assertions

Wright v Doe d Tatham,[96] was a civil case which concerned, inter alia, the mental competence of a testator. It was held that the trial judge had properly disallowed the production in evidence of a number of letters written to the testator by certain of his acquaintances in terms from which it could legitimately be inferred that they regarded him as sane. As evidence of the truth of the implied assertion that the testator was sane, they constituted inadmissible hearsay.[97]

Assertions by conduct

Concerning implied assertions by conduct alone, there are few common law authorities. In *Chandrasekera v R*,[98] as we have seen,[99] the signs used by the victim to identify her assailant were treated as hearsay, and s 115(3) operates to preserve the decision. The victim, by nodding her head, was in effect making a statement that the accused had cut her throat; her only purpose in doing so was to cause others to believe that the accused had cut her throat. In *Manchester Brewery Co Ltd v Coombs*,[100] a case concerning an alleged breach by a brewer to supply a publican with good beer, it was held, obiter, that evidence would be admissible that

---

[93] [1952] AC 480, PC.

[94] It was also held that the statement did not form part of the *res gestae* (see Ch 12).

[95] [1992] 2 AC 28, HL.

[96] (1837) 7 Ad&El 313, Ex Ch.

[97] See also *R v Rice* (1963) 1 QB 857, CCA considered under **Admissibility of hearsay under the Criminal Justice Act 2003, The meaning of hearsay in the Criminal Justice Act 2003, Original evidence** in this chapter, and also *R v Van Verden* (1973) 57 Cr App R 818, CA, which concerned an implied assertion in an application for a credit card used to obtain property by deception. By contrast with *Rice* where the tickets were admissible circumstantial evidence, the application form in *Van Verden* was held to have been inadmissible hearsay. Note *R v Lydon* (1987) 85 Cr App R 21, CA (also considered under **Admissibility of hearsay under the Criminal Justice Act 2003, The meaning of hearsay in the Criminal Justice Act 2003, Original evidence**) where the Court of Appeal held that no assertions had been made by what was written.

[98] [1937] AC 220, PC.

[99] Under **Admissibility of hearsay under the Criminal Justice Act 2003, The meaning of hearsay in the Criminal Justice Act 2003, 'A statement'** in this chapter.

[100] (1901) 82 LT 347, Ch D at 34.

certain customers ordered the beer, tasted it, did not finish it, and then either left it or threw it away.[101]

Matters stated in statements

Under the statutory formulation of hearsay, as we have seen, s 114(1) refers to a statement not made in oral evidence in the proceedings which is admissible as evidence of any 'matter stated'. Under s 115(3):

> (3) A matter stated is one to which this Chapter applies if (and only if) the purpose, or one of the purposes, of the person making the statement appears to the court to have been—
> (a) to cause another person to believe the matter, or
> (b) to cause another person to act or a machine to operate on the basis that the matter is as stated.

The effect of s 115(3) is to narrow the ambit of s 114 so that it applies to render hearsay admissible as evidence of any matter stated under one of the heads set out in s 114(1) if and only if the purpose, or one of the purposes, of the person making the statement, was of the kind described in either s 115(3)(a) or s 115(3)(b). Under s 115(3)(a), the purpose, or one of the purposes, in making the statement is to cause another to believe the matter, ie to accept that matter as true, whereas under s 115(3)(b) the purpose, or one of the purposes, in making the statement, is simply to cause another to act on the basis that the matter is as stated, ie to act on the basis that the matter is true (or to cause a machine to operate on the basis that the matter is as stated). There appears to be a considerable overlap between the two subsections, in that if the purpose is to cause another to act on the basis that a certain matter is as it has been stated, then whether or not that is the truth of the matter, the purpose, in many situations, will also be to cause the other to believe the matter. Section 115(3)(b) will apply, but not s 115(3)(a), where the purpose is to cause another to do no more than to act on the basis that the matter is as stated, and not to cause the other to believe the matter, perhaps because, for example, the maker of the statement is aware that the matter is not as stated or is unsure as to the truth of the matter.

The Explanatory Notes to the 2003 Act state that the purpose of s 115(3) is 'to overturn the ruling in R v Kearley[102] that "implied assertions" are covered by the hearsay rule and therefore prima facie inadmissible'. In Kearley, the police found drugs in K's flat, but not in sufficient quantities to raise the inference that he was a dealer. The police remained there for several hours and intercepted ten telephone calls in which callers asked to speak to K and asked for drugs. Seven other people arrived at the flat, some with money, also asking for K and asking to be supplied with drugs, when K was either absent or not within earshot. At K's trial for possession with intent to supply, the officers who had intercepted the calls or received the visitors gave evidence of the conversations. The House of Lords, by a majority of three to two, allowed the appeal against conviction. It was held: (i) that evidence of requests made by the callers and visitors was irrelevant because it could only be evidence of the state of mind or belief of those making the requests, which was not a relevant issue at the trial, the issue being whether K intended to supply drugs; and (ii) applying Wright v Doe d Tatham,[103] that insofar as the evidence was relevant to the issue of K's intent to supply, ie as an implied assertion that K

[101] See also Wright v Doe d Tatham (1837) 7 Ad&El 313, Ex Ch. Parke B expressed the obiter view that, on a question of the seaworthiness of a vessel, evidence of the conduct of a deceased captain who, after examining every part of the vessel, embarked in it with his family, would constitute hearsay.
[102] [1992] 2 AC 228, HL.
[103] (1837) 7 Ad&El 313, Ex Ch, and approving R v Harry (1987) 86 Cr App R 105, CA.

was a supplier, it was inadmissible hearsay, and it made no difference that there were a large number of such requests all made at the same place on the same day. The decision is open to criticism on the basis that the evidence could have been admitted as circumstantial evidence, ie evidence from which K's intent to supply could be inferred.[104] Nonetheless, the effect of the decision was to classify implied assertions as hearsay and render them prima facie inadmissible.

The stated purpose of s 115(3)—to overturn the ruling in *Kearley*—is misleading because s 115(3) will operate to exclude from the ambit of s 114 some express as well as implied assertions. For example, if an express assertion is made by a person who is talking to himself and unaware that he is being overheard, or is contained in a memorandum or diary which is kept for purely personal purposes,[105] then plainly it is not among the purposes of the maker of the statement to cause another to believe the matter stated. Such statements are therefore not covered by, or subject to, s 114 of the 2003 Act. They would now be admissible, provided that they are relevant, and, if tendered by the prosecution, subject to the discretionary powers of exclusion. At first blush, it might be thought that s 115(3) might exclude from the ambit of s 114 an express assertion made with the purpose of causing another to *disbelieve* the matter stated, as when the maker says, for example, 'Of course X was present...and pigs were flying!' However, such a statement would surely be treated as a statement made with the purpose of causing another to believe that X was absent.

Implied assertions and the interpretation of 'statements' and 'matters stated'

In *R v Singh*,[106] it was baldly stated that 'when sections 114 and 118 are read together they...create...a new rule against hearsay which does not extend to implied assertions'.[107] *Singh* was approved in *R v Twist*,[108] which is now the leading authority on determining whether a statement qualifies as hearsay for the purposes of ss 114 and 115(3). In *Twist*, it was held that, by virtue of the 2003 Act, it was no longer necessary to examine statements to see whether they contained implied assertions. Hughes LJ stated:[109]

> What is undoubted is that the Act abolishes the common law of hearsay except where it is expressly preserved; this court so held in *Singh*...

His Lordship went on to observe:[110]

> The Act does not use the expression 'assertion'. Instead it speaks of a 'statement' and the 'matter stated' in it. This seems likely to have been because its framers wished to avoid the complex philosophical arguments which beset the common law, as explained in *DPP v Kearley* [1992] 2 AC 28, as to when an utterance contains an implied assertion...
>
> ...
>
> It is therefore helpful, as it seems to us, that the Act avoids the use of the expression 'assertion' altogether, and with it the difficult concept of the 'implied assertion'.

---

[104] See *R v Singh* [2006] 1 WLR 1564, CA per Rose LJ at [14]. See also *R v K* (2008) 172 JP 538, CA in which an inquiry about the availability and price of specific drugs made by a person during a telephone call to the defendant was held to have been correctly admitted as evidence from which it could properly be inferred that the defendant was a person concerned in the supply of drugs.

[105] See, eg, *R v N* (2007) 171 JP 158, CA. By contrast, see *R v Horsnell* [2012] EWCA Crim 227, where a diary was hearsay because it was kept for the purpose of assisting in possible future divorce proceedings.

[106] [2006] 1 WLR 1564, CA.

[107] [2006] 1 WLR 1564, CA at [14].

[108] [2011] 2 Cr App R 17, CA.

[109] [2011] 2 Cr App R 17, CA at [3].

[110] [2011] 2 Cr App R 17, CA at [8]–[9].

In *Twist*, the Court of Appeal considered four appeals concerning the admissibility of text messages and stated an approach to be taken when analysing whether a statement is hearsay under the 2003 Act. It is instructive to first cite the approach and to then consider how the approach was applied to the facts in each of the four appeals.[111]

> Generally...it is likely to be helpful to approach the question whether the hearsay rules apply in this way:
>   i)   identify what relevant fact (matter) it is sought to prove;
>   ii) ask whether there is a statement of that matter in the communication. If no, then no question of hearsay arises (whatever other matters may be contained in the communication);
>   iii) if yes, ask whether it was one of the purposes (not necessarily the only or dominant purpose) of the maker of the communication that the recipient, or any other person, should believe that matter or act upon it as true? If yes, it is hearsay. If no, it is not
> ....As we have sought to explain, it no longer matters whether a statement is analysed as containing an implicit (or 'implied') assertion if the speaker's purpose does not include getting anyone else to accept it as true.[112]

In the first appeal, *Twist*, the appellant had been convicted of possession of heroin with intent to supply. At his trial, evidence was admitted of 24 text messages received on two mobile phones over five days, which were mostly requests for drugs. Following its stated approach, the first step for the Court to take was to identify the matter sought to be proved. This was obviously that the accused supplied drugs. Taking the second step, the Court held that because the messages did not contain any statement that the accused supplied drugs (they were simply requests for drugs) they were not caught by the hearsay provisions. They were therefore admissible as relevant to show a relationship of 'buyer and seller' between the accused and the senders.

In the second appeal, *Boothman*, the appellant had been convicted of possession of cannabis and cocaine with intent to supply and at his trial evidence was adduced of over 100 text messages sent to and by him. A number of the messages were orders for drugs, some of which expressly referred to the number of 'lines' (of cocaine) obtained from a recent supply. The appellant had objected to their admissibility on the grounds that they were hearsay because the references to 'lines' were, according to the appellant, express representations of cocaine dealing relied on as true by the prosecution. It was held that the messages were not hearsay because, as with the first appeal, taking the second step in the approach, there was no statement in the messages of the matter which the Crown sought to prove, namely that the accused was a supplier of drugs.

In the third appeal, *Tomlinson and Kelly*, the two appellants had been convicted of robbing two girls at gunpoint. Evidence was admitted of a text message sent to one appellant on the morning of the robbery requesting a gun. The message read, 'Need dat gun today so can sell it and give you lot da tenner back. Does faws still want it?' It was held that although in this appeal the text message may have contained a statement that the appellants were in possession of a gun as the girls had said (the second step in the approach), the messages were not hearsay. Applying s 115(3) and taking the third step, the purpose of the sender was not to

---

[111] [2011] 2 Cr App R 17, CA at [17].
[112] [2011] 2 Cr App R 17, CA at [19].

cause the recipient to believe that he was in possession of a gun: this knowledge was assumed on the part of the sender.[113]

In the final appeal, *L*, the appellant had been convicted of the rape of his girlfriend when they were both 15. During his trial, evidence was admitted of text messages sent by him to his girlfriend, which had included confessions and apologies for the rape. Although the messages contained statements of the matter the prosecution sought to prove (the first and second steps in the approach), they were not hearsay because, at the third step, the purpose of the accused in sending them was to admit to what he had done and apologize, not to cause the complainant to believe she had been raped, something which they both already knew.

Twist received strong approval in *R v Mateza*,[114] with the Court of Appeal in that case stating that it could not in any way improve upon the analysis provided in *Twist* and commending it to the courts of the future.[115] However, the analysis is problematic. Notwithstanding some ambiguity in the third appeal, the analysis seems to suggest that a statement requires an express representation before the hearsay provisions apply. This, it is submitted, would run counter to what was intended by the framers of the Act, which was that s 115(3) should allow for some statements to be classified as hearsay even if the statement contained no express representation.[116] It would surely be correct to treat as hearsay a statement with an implied representation where it appeared that the purpose of the maker was to cause someone else to believe that what was impliedly represented was true, or to act on it as if it was true.[117] The risks associated with such a statement are no less real because the representation is implied.

Risks of implied assertion evidence

There can be little doubt that s 115(3) will operate to render admissible much evidence that was previously excluded as hearsay. Underlying this development of the law was the opinion that 'as a class, implied assertions are more reliable than assertions made for the purpose of communicating information'.[118] There are two compelling reasons, however, why such evidence will often need to be treated with caution. The first stems from the fact that it is often possible to draw different inferences from the same conduct and, depending on the precise circumstances, this will reduce the weight to be attached to the evidence. For example, in *Manchester Brewery Co Ltd v Coombs*,[119] the customers who rejected the beer could all have been French and unfamiliar with the taste of English beer. Second, there will be the risk, in some cases, of error or malicious concoction, the degree of risk varying according to the precise circumstances. For example, in *R v Kearley*, it was most unlikely that, without more, 17 callers

---

[113] See also *R v Elliot* (2011) 175 JP 39, CA. Letters containing gang symbols and references to gang membership sent to the accused in prison were properly admitted to show that he was a gang member. The letters were not hearsay since the authors did not have the purpose of causing the accused to believe that he himself was a member of the gang or to act on the basis that this was true. Gang membership was as assumed by the authors and the symbols and references were simply an expression of gang solidarity.

[114] [2011] EWCA Crim 2587.

[115] [2011] EWCA Crim 2587 at [21]–[22].

[116] See also under **Admissibility of hearsay under the Criminal Justice Act 2003, The meaning of hearsay in the Criminal Justice Act 2003**.

[117] For example, in *Teper v R* [1952] AC 480, PC. For further analysis of *Twist*, see Ormerod, 'Commentary' [2011] Crim LR 793.

[118] See Law Com No 245 *Evidence in Criminal Proceedings: Hearsay and Related Topics*, Cm 3670 (1997).

[119] See under **Admissibility of hearsay under the Criminal Justice Act 2003, The meaning of hearsay in the Criminal Justice Act 2003, Implied assertions**.

were all mistaken or all set out with the deliberate intention of deceiving the police into believing that the accused was a dealer, but if there had been only one or two callers, there would have been at least some risk of mistake or malice.[120]

Negative hearsay

Under the 2003 Act, as at common law, an oral out-of-court statement will amount to hearsay whether it is tendered as evidence of the existence or non-existence of a fact. Thus if the presence of A at a certain place on a certain date is in issue, evidence by B as to what he heard C say on the matter is hearsay, whether C said that he saw or did not see A on the occasion in question. At common law, however, the hearsay rule did not operate to prevent proof of the non-existence of a fact by a combination of (i) evidence of the absence of a recording of the fact in a written record; and (ii) testimony of an appropriate person to the effect that having regard to the method of compilation and custody of the record, one would have expected the fact, had it existed, to have been recorded. In *R v Patel*[121] the accused was charged, inter alia, with assisting the illegal entry of one Ashraf into the UK. In order to prove that Ashraf was an illegal immigrant, the prosecution called Mr Stone, an immigration officer at Manchester airport, who gave evidence that Ashraf's name was not in certain Home Office records of persons entitled to a certificate of registration in the UK and that at the material time Ashraf was therefore an illegal entrant. The Court of Appeal held that evidence relating to the Home Office records was inadmissible hearsay. However, Bristow J said:[122]

> an officer responsible for their compilation and custody should have been called to give evidence that the method of compilation and custody is such that if Ashraf's name is not there, he must be an illegal entrant. It is not suggested that Mr Stone is such an officer.

This dictum was applied in *R v Shone*.[123] The appellant was convicted of receiving three vehicle springs which bore numbers which enabled them to be identified as having been dispatched by the manufacturers to L Ltd. Their arrival at L Ltd was recorded on stock record cards. The prosecution called two employees of L Ltd responsible for these records, who gave evidence that the cards were marked to indicate when the spare parts were sold or used and that the cards in respect of the three springs bore no such marks. On appeal, it was argued that the absence of a mark on the cards amounted to an inadmissible hearsay statement that the springs had been neither sold nor used by L Ltd. The Court of Appeal held that the evidence of the employees in explaining the significance of the absence of the marks was not hearsay evidence but direct evidence from which the jury were entitled to draw the inference that all three springs were stolen.

It is submitted that evidence of the kind admitted in *R v Shone* remains admissible as direct evidence and is not covered by the 2003 Act simply because no statement has been made for the purposes of s 114.[124] However, according to the Explanatory Notes to the 2003 Act,[125] the situation is governed by s 115(3):[126]

---

[120] [1992] 2 AC 228, HL, see per Lord Griffiths, one of the minority, at 349 and 353.

[121] [1981] 3 All ER 94. Cf *R v Muir* (1983) 79 Cr App R 153, CA.

[122] [1981] 3 All ER 94 at 96.

[123] (1982) 76 Cr App R 72.

[124] See *DPP v Leigh* [2010] EWHC 3450, DC: constabulary records admitted to prove the failure of the registered keeper of a vehicle to respond to a request to name a driver were not 'statements' within the meaning of s 115(2) (see at [12]). Nor, according to the Divisional Court, were they caught by s 115(3) (at [14]).

[125] The 2003 Act, Explanatory Notes, para 401. See also *DPP v Leigh* [2010] EWHC 3450, DC at [14].

[126] See, in this chapter, under **Admissibility of hearsay under the Criminal Justice Act 2003, The meaning of hearsay in the Criminal Justice Act 2003, Implied assertions.**

(b) the person who made the statement (the relevant person) is identified to the court's satisfaction, and

(c) any of the five conditions mentioned in subsection (2) is satisfied.

(2) The conditions are—

(a) that the relevant person is dead;

(b) that the relevant person is unfit to be a witness because of his bodily or mental condition;

(c) that the relevant person is outside the United Kingdom and it is not reasonably practicable to secure his attendance;

(d) that the relevant person cannot be found although such steps as it is reasonably practicable to take to find him have been taken;

(e) that through fear the relevant person does not give (or does not continue to give) oral evidence in the proceedings, either at all or in connection with the subject matter of the statement, and the court gives leave for the statement to be given in evidence.

(3) For the purposes of subsection (2)(e) 'fear' is to be widely construed and (for example) includes fear of the death or injury of another person or of financial loss.

. . .

(5) A condition set out in any paragraph of subsection (2) which is in fact satisfied is to be treated as not satisfied if it is shown that the circumstances described in that paragraph are caused—

(a) by the person in support of whose case it is sought to give the statement in evidence, or

(b) by a person acting on his behalf,

in order to prevent the relevant person giving oral evidence in the proceedings (whether at all or in connection with the subject matter of the statement).

Concerning the opening words of s 116(1), 'criminal proceedings', 'statement', and 'matter stated' bear the same meaning as in s 114 of the Act and call for no additional comment in the present context. The purpose of s 116(1)(a) is to prevent s 116 from being used to admit evidence which, if the maker of the statement were to be called as a witness, would be inadmissible because, for example, he has no personal knowledge of the facts,[150] or the evidence constitutes expert opinion evidence which the maker is not qualified to give, or the evidence is simply irrelevant to the facts in issue.

Section 116 applies to both oral and written statements. Having regard to the requirements of s 116(1)(a), (b), and (c), it is plainly very important, in the case of statements made in writing, to identify correctly the person who made the statement (the 'relevant person'), and for this purpose valuable guidance is provided by the decisions reached under s 23 of the 1988 Act. If A makes an oral statement within the hearing of B, who writes down what A says, and A reads and signs the document, then clearly A is the relevant person. Similarly, if A dictates the statement to B and checks that what B has written down is an accurate record of what he said (by reading it or having it read back to him) then, even without his signature, A is the relevant person.[151] It would be otherwise, however, if B made a written record of A's oral statement which was not agreed to or approved or accepted by A because in these circumstances A has made an oral statement, not a statement in a document.[152] B has made a statement in a document, but his statement would not be admissible under s 116 because the condition in s 116(1)(a) cannot be met—oral evidence by B would not be admissible of the matter stated because B has no direct or personal knowledge of those matters.

---

[150] See *R v JP* [1999] Crim LR 401, CA, a decision under the Criminal Justice Act 1988, s 23.

[151] *R v McGillivray* (1992) 97 Cr App R 232, CA.

[152] Cf *Re D (a minor)* [1986] 2 FLR 189 Fam D.

Section 116(1)(b) reflects the view that the risk of unreliability in the case of hearsay statements made by unidentified individuals is high and ensures that where a statement is admitted, the opposing party is in a position to impugn the credibility of the maker of the statement.[153]

The reasons for not calling the maker of the statement to give evidence

Section 116(2)(a) to (e) of the 2003 Act have been cast in words similar, but not identical, to those employed in s 23(2)(a), (b), and (c) of the Criminal Justice Act 1988 and, subject to the significant alterations to some of the wording, the decisions interpreting the earlier provisions provide very useful guidance as to the way in which the provisions of the 2003 Act are likely to be construed.

Relevant person unfit to be a witness because of his bodily or mental condition

Unlike its statutory precursor, which referred to a person who was 'unfit to attend as a witness', s 116(2)(b) refers to a person who is 'unfit to be a witness'. However, it is submitted that subs (2)(b) is likely to cover a person physically unable to get to court 'to be a witness' as well as a person able to attend court but unfit to give evidence, such as a witness who, by reason of his mental condition, is unable to recall the events in question.[154] Ordinarily, a witness who is not competent to give evidence because of lack of mental capacity will also be 'unfit to be a witness because of his...mental condition' for the purposes of s 116(2)(b).[155]

Relevant person outside the United Kingdom and it is not reasonably practicable to secure his attendance

The requirement in s 116(2)(c) is likely to be treated, as before, as a requirement of a strictly territorial nature and therefore will not be satisfied if the person who made the statement is a consul or embassy official in the UK.[156] The word 'attendance' was treated as capable of including the giving of evidence through a live television link from outside the United Kingdom under s 32 of the 1988 Act, but not examination of a witness on commission by a court in his country of residence.[157]

The question whether it is reasonably practicable to secure the attendance of the maker of the statement should be examined not at the time when the trial opens, but against the whole background to the case. Thus in *R v Bray*[158] an argument that it was not reasonably practicable to secure the attendance of a person, because it was only when the trial started that it was realized that he was overseas, was rejected by the Court of Appeal: since the person had been overseas for some seven months before the trial began, it had not been shown that it was not reasonably practicable to secure his attendance at the trial. In *R v C*[159] it was held that what is reasonably practicable in s 116(2)(c) should be judged on the basis of the steps taken or not taken by the party seeking to ensure the attendance of the witness. This accords with the

---

[153] See under **Admissibility of hearsay under the Criminal Justice Act 2003, Other safeguards, Credibility,** in this chapter.

[154] See *R v Setz-Dempsey* (1994) 98 Cr App R 23, CA.

[155] *DPP v R* [2007] All ER 176, [2007] EWHC 1842. However, see also s 123(1), considered under **Admissibility of hearsay under the Criminal Justice Act 2003, Other safeguards, Capability,** in this chapter.

[156] *R v Jiminez-Paez* (1994) 98 Cr App R 239, CA.

[157] *R v Radak* [1999] 1 Cr App R 187, CA.

[158] (1988) 88 Cr App R 354, CA. This was a decision under the Police and Criminal Evidence Act 1984, s 68(2)(a)(ii), the identical statutory precursor to the Criminal Justice Act 1988, s 23(2)(b).

[159] [2006] Crim LR 637, CA.

If the evidence is tendered by the prosecution, its *admission* could result in unfairness to the accused; if it is tendered by an accused, its *exclusion* could result in unfairness to the accused but its *admission* could result in unfairness to a co-accused, in which case it seems that the court should conduct a balancing exercise which may result in the exclusion of the evidence on the basis that the damage done to the co-accused outweighs the benefit to the accused.[191] However, such an outcome would hardly be 'in the interests of justice' in a case in which, had the accused been tried separately, the evidence would have been of such benefit to him that it would have been admitted.[192]

In considering the risk of unfairness to the accused, particular regard must be had to the possible difficulty of controverting—under the 2003 Act, 'challenging'—the statement in the absence of its maker. The judge, in coming to a conclusion, should not embark on a detailed comparison between what might have happened if the maker of the statement had given oral evidence and had been cross-examined, and what might happen if his statement is admitted without him attending.[193] In *R v Cole*[194] it was held that the judge, in considering whether it was likely to be possible to controvert the statement, had properly taken into account not only the availability of prosecution witnesses for cross-examination, but also the availability of the accused or other witnesses to give evidence for the defence. Thus although the court cannot require to be told whether the accused intends to give evidence or to call witnesses, it is not required to assess the possibility of controverting the statement on the basis that the accused will not give evidence or call witnesses.[195] In *R v Gokal*[196] it was submitted that the statutory provisions should be so construed as to exclude, as a means of controverting the statement, the possibility of the accused himself giving evidence in rebuttal, having regard to the right to silence and the entitlement to a fair hearing under Art 6 of the European Convention on Human Rights. The Court of Appeal rejected the submission and approved *R v Cole*.[197] Noting that the possibilities for controverting the statement are wide, and include putting in issue the credibility of the maker of the statement,[198] the court held that although admission of the statement may make it more difficult for the accused to exercise his right of silence, the right is not abrogated. It was also held, after consideration of judgments of the European Commission and European Court of Human Rights, that, since the whole basis of the exercise of the discretion is to assess the interests of justice by reference to the risk of unfairness to the accused, 'our procedures appear to us to accord fully with our treaty obligations'.

In considering the risk of unfairness, it may also be relevant to consider whether the party against whom the statement is tendered had any opportunity of interviewing or making inquiries of the maker of the statement, but in any event this is another relevant circumstance (see now s 116(4)(d)).[199] 'Other relevant circumstances', for the purposes of s 116(4)(d), are also

[191] As in *R v Gregory and Mott* [1995] Crim LR 507, CA, a decision under the Criminal Justice Act 1988, s 25(2)(d).

[192] *R v Duffy* [1999] QB 919, CA.

[193] *R v Radak* [1999] 1 Cr App R 187, CA.

[194] [1990] 1 WLR 866, CA.

[195] See also *R v Price* [1991] Crim LR 707, CA (notes of a conversation between the accused and another were properly admitted even though the only way in which P could controvert the statement was by giving evidence himself, which he could not be required to do). See also *R v Samuel* [1992] Crim LR 189, CA and *R v Moore* [1992] Crim LR 882, CA.

[196] *R v Gokal* [1997] 2 Cr App R 266.

[197] [1990] 1 WLR 866, CA.

[198] See under **Admissibility of hearsay under the Criminal Justice Act 2003, Other safeguards** in this chapter.

[199] *R v Patel* (1992) 97 Cr App R 294, CA.

likely to include the circumstances in which the statement was made, including any attempts made to get the maker to make the statement in the way most favourable to the party seeking to rely upon it, the fact that the maker of the statement made prior inconsistent statements, whether oral or written,[200] and other facts or matters affecting his credibility. Thus, as to the last, although it may be in the interests of justice to admit the statement of a person even if he is of bad character, particularly when that bad character can readily be demonstrated, it should be excluded where he is so dishonest that the absence of an opportunity for the jury to assess him as a witness, to observe his demeanour and the manner in which he gives his evidence, would result in potential unfairness.[201] In *R v D*[202] the victim of an attempted rape was an 81-year-old woman whose police interview was recorded on video, at a time when she would have been competent as a witness. However, by the time of the preparatory hearing she was not mentally fit enough to give live evidence. The judge granted the prosecution leave to admit the video under ss 23 and 26 of the 1988 Act, taking the view that since he had concluded that it was in the interests of justice to admit the video, having balanced the interests of justice as between victim and defendant, then it was unlikely that there would be a breach of Art 6. On appeal it was held that the judge had adopted the right approach. Prima facie, the complainant had a right to have her complaint put before a jury, and the accused's rights would be protected because he could call medical evidence to challenge the complainant's capacity to remember, understand, and say what happened. Furthermore, if it was in the interests of justice to admit the video, it was unlikely to be unfair under s 78 of the Police and Criminal Evidence Act 1984.

As we have already noted,[203] as a *general rule*, Art 6(1) and (3)(d) require an accused to be given a proper and adequate opportunity to challenge and question witnesses. However, the right set out in Art 6(3)(d) is not absolute but can be qualified provided that there is adherence to the overriding principle that a criminal trial must be fair to the accused and his rights respected. In *R v Sellick*[204] it was held that while the provisions in the 2003 Act should not be abused, where the court can be *sure* that an identified witness has been kept away by the accused and provided that (a) the quality of the evidence is compelling; (b) firm steps are taken to draw the jury's attention to aspects of the witness's credibility; and (c) a clear direction is given to the jury to exercise caution, there will be no breach of Art 6; the accused himself has denied himself the opportunity of examining the witness.[205]

Business and other documents

Section 117 of the 2003 Act, which provides for the admissibility of hearsay statements contained in business and other documents, is modelled on s 24 of the 1988 Act, which it replaces,

---

[200] *R v Sweeting and Thomas* [1999] Crim LR 75, CA, in which it was also held that if the statement is admitted, the logical course is to admit the inconsistent statement. See now under the 2003 Act, s 124(2)(c), considered under **Admissibility of hearsay under the Criminal Justice Act 2003, Other safeguards, Credibility**, in this chapter.

[201] See *R v Lockley* [1995] 2 Cr App R 554, CA, a decision under the Criminal Justice Act 1988, s 25, where the maker of the statement had demonstrated and indeed boasted about his remarkable ability to deceive.

[202] [2003] QB 90, CA.

[203] See text at n 23, under **Admissibility of hearsay under the Criminal Justice Act 2003, General, Article 6 of the European Convention on Human Rights** in this chapter.

[204] [2005] 1 WLR 3257, CA.

[205] Approving *R v M (KJ)* [2003] 2 Cr App R 322, CA. See also *Al-Khawaja and Tahery v UK* (2012) 54 EHRR 23 at [122]–[124]. See also under **Admissibility of hearsay under the Criminal Justice Act 2003, General, Article 6 and the European Convention on Human Rights** in this chapter.

s 116(2)(d).[225] Additionally, it is clear from the authorities that the section cannot be used to admit anonymous hearsay evidence either from a known witness whose identity the prosecution seeks to withhold from the accused[226] or from a witness whose identity is not known at all.[227] More generally, s 114(1)(d) should obviously not be used if, having regard to Art 6 of the European Convention on Human Rights, this would result in an unfair trial.[228]

The Court of Appeal will only interfere with a decision of a trial judge under s 114(1)(d) if it was outwith the range of reasonable decisions, because the trial judge is best placed to assess accurately the fairness of admitting evidence in the context of the trial as a whole.[229]

Factors which must be considered

In deciding whether to exercise the power contained in s 114(1), the trial judge must have regard to the non-exhaustive list of factors set out in s 114(2).[230] Section 114(2) provides as follows:

(2) In deciding whether a statement not made in oral evidence should be admitted under subsection (1)(d), the court must have regard to the following factors (and to any others it considers relevant)—

    (a) how much probative value the statement has (assuming it to be true) in relation to a matter in issue in the proceedings, or how valuable it is for the understanding of other evidence in the case;

    (b) what other evidence has been, or can be, given on the matter or evidence mentioned in paragraph (a);

    (c) how important the matter or evidence mentioned in paragraph (a) is in the context of the case as a whole;

    (d) the circumstances in which the statement was made;

    (e) how reliable the maker of the statement appears to be;

    (f) how reliable the evidence of the making of the statement appears to be;

    (g) whether oral evidence of the matter stated can be given and, if not, why it cannot;

    (h) the amount of difficulty involved in challenging the statement;

    (i) the extent to which that difficulty would be likely to prejudice the party facing it.

[225] *R v T (D)* (2009) 173 JP 425, CA. Similarly, see *R v Burton* [2011] EWCA Crim 1990, an exceptional case where the Court of Appeal held that the trial judge had been justified in admitting under s 114(1)(d) statements made by a reluctant but available child witness with whom the adult accused was alleged to have had sexual activity.

[226] *R v Mayers* [2009] 1 WLR 195, CA at [109] and [113]; *R v Horncastle* [2010] 2 AC 373, SC at [48]; and *R v Fox* [2010] EWCA Crim 1280 at [12]. See also *R v Davies* [2008] 1 AC 1128, HL at [20].

[227] *R v Ford* [2010] EWCA Crim 2250. However, see Ormerod, 'Commentary' [2011] Crim LR 475. The prohibition against admitting anonymous hearsay under s 114(1)(d) is questionable, not least because the Law Commission intended that anonymous hearsay should be capable of being admitted under the section (see Law Com No 245, *Evidence in Criminal Proceedings: Hearsay and Related Topics*, Cm 3670 (1997), para 8.143) and the section itself does not contain an express prohibition. Furthermore the prohibition sits uncomfortably with s 117 of the Act, which provides scope for the admission of anonymous hearsay contained in documents. See also Ormerod, 'Commentary' [2011] Crim LR 793: in *R v Twist* [2011] 2 Cr App R 17 at [22], Hughes LJ hinted that there could be scope for admitting hearsay evidence from an unknown source in some cases. However, the Court did not hear full argument on the question of whether anonymous hearsay could ever be admissible under s 114(1)(d) and made no decision on it.

[228] See under **Admissibility of hearsay under the Criminal Justice Act 2003, General, Article 6 of the European Convention on Human Rights**.

[229] *R v Musone* [2007] 1 WLR 2467, CA at [20]. See also *R v Finch* [2007] 1 WLR 1645 at [23] and *R v Freeman* [2010] EWCA Crim 1997, CA at [25].

[230] The Court of Appeal will be more willing to interfere with a judge's decision under s 114(1)(d) where a judge fails to take into account, or fails to show that he has taken into account, the factors set out in s 114(2): *R v Z* [2009] 1 Cr App R 34, CA. See also *R v CT* (2011) 175 JP 462, CA where the judge failed, in particular, to take account of the factors in s 114(2)(c) and (g).

Although directly applicable to s 114(1)(d), in *R v Riat*[231] these factors were commended as useful aides-memoire when considering the admissibility of hearsay evidence under any other hearsay provision or its exclusion under s 78 of the Police and Criminal Evidence Act 1984.[232]

In respect of s 114(2)(a), evidence of considerable importance that would undermine the defence and point powerfully to a conviction makes the other factors even more significant, and in particular s 114(2)(g).[233] The Court of Appeal has stressed that s 114(2)(g) refers to the inability of a witness to give evidence rather than their reluctance to do so and it will be rare that potentially prejudicial evidence will be admitted under s 114(1)(d) where a witness is available, although reluctant, and the reluctance is not due to fear.[234] The correct approach to s 114(2)(h) is to focus on the difficulty in assessing the veracity of the declarant's statement and not the difficulties of challenging the witness who reports the statement,[235] which ought to be taken into account under s 114(2)(f).

In *R v Taylor*[236] two prosecution witnesses named T as a participant in an attack, having been told his name by someone else. The trial judge admitted this evidence under s 114(1)(d), although he was unable to reach a conclusion on a number of the factors set out in s 114(2), such as the circumstances in which the informant's statement was made, his reliability, and whether he could give oral evidence. The Court of Appeal held that s 114(2) requires an exercise of judgment in the light of the factors identified and does not require an investigation, resulting in some cases in the hearing of evidence, in order that the judge may reach a conclusion established by reference to each or any of the factors. On that basis, it was held that the judge's approach could not be challenged. The decision is somewhat surprising. As one commentator has submitted:[237]

> Surely the judge should engage in some degree of investigation and, in cases where the hearsay evidence is of great importance, this might involve receiving evidence. As to the outcome, and the value of the case as a precedent in that respect, it is important to note that the court seems to have been heavily influenced by the 'considerable body of evidence' against T apart from the naming of him by the two witnesses.[238]

The Law Commission gave three examples of how its 'safety valve' might be used. The first two examples, based on the facts of *Sparks v R*[239] and *R v Thomas*[240] are not entirely convincing.[241] The third example was based on the facts of *R v Cooper*.[242] Charged with assault, the accused was not allowed to introduce a hearsay statement made by a third party, of similar appearance to the accused, to a friend of his, that he had committed the assault. Subsequent authorities

---

[231] [2013] 1 WLR 2592, CA.

[232] [2013] 1 WLR 2592, CA at [22]

[233] *R v Z* [2009] 1 Cr App R 34, CA at [24].

[234] *R v Z* [2009], 1 Cr App R 34, CA at [24]. See also *R v Y* [2008] 1 WLR 1683 at [60] and *R v Khan* [2009] EWCA Crim 86 at [15]. See also *R v Freeman* [2010] EWCA Crim 1997 at [31] and [33], *R v ED* (2010) 174 JP 289, CA, and *R v CT* (2011) 175 JP 462, CA. See also *R v Burton* (2011) 175 JP 385, CA, where the statement of a reluctant child witness was properly admitted under s 114(1)(d). Her statement was not decisive evidence and it had been open to the accused to call her if he truly believed she would support his defence that he had not engaged in sexual activity with her.

[235] *R v Marsh* [2008] All ER (D) 338 (Jul), [2008] EWCA Crim 816, at [19].

[236] [2006] 2 Cr App R 222, CA.

[237] Ormerod, '*R v Taylor*' (case comment) [2006] Crim LR 640.

[238] See also *Maher v DPP* (2006) 170 JP 441, DC, considered below in the context of multiple hearsay.

[239] [1964] AC 964, PC.

[240] [1994] Crim LR 745, CA.

[241] For a critique, see the sixth edition of this work at 314.

[242] [1969] 1 QB 267, CA.

confirmed that an out-of-court confession, by a third party, to the offence with which the accused is charged, is inadmissible,[243] decisions which have been justified on the grounds that, since it is for the legislature, not the judiciary, to create new exceptions to the hearsay rule,[244] to hold otherwise 'would be to create a very significant and, many might think, a dangerous new exception'.[245] The obvious danger is the ease with which a third party confession may be manufactured or fabricated coupled with the fact that such a confession, by itself, could lead the jury to be 'unsure'. However, each case will now involve the court in a complex balancing exercise, having regard to the factors set out in s 114(2) in the context of the particular facts of the case. It is not without significance, for instance, that in the example given by the Law Commission, the third party was of similar appearance to the accused. *R v Finch*[246] concerned a confession by D2, who pleaded guilty, exonerating D1, D2 being 'reluctant' to give evidence for reasons that were not compelling. The trial judge concluded that the interests of justice did not call for the evidence to be admitted on behalf of D1. Although it was plainly of substantial probative value and without it there was only the evidence of D1 himself, and therefore it was of considerable importance in the context of the case as a whole, oral evidence could be given by D2. D2's reliability was open to question if he was not prepared to support in the witness box what he had said to the police, and there would be difficulties for the prosecution in challenging his statement in his absence. The principal factor was that D2 was compellable, and therefore could have been called and subjected to cross-examination.[247] The Court of Appeal upheld the decision, observing that s 114(2) calls for the exercise of judgment by the trial judge with which it should only interfere if it was exercised on wrong principles or if the conclusion reached was outside the band of legitimate decisions available.[248]

Examples of appropriate use

While each case turns upon its own facts the following are illustrative of circumstances in which the Court of Appeal has approved the use of s 114(1)(d) to admit otherwise inadmissible hearsay evidence. A wife having made a witness statement undermining her husband's defence to a charge of raping his daughter, having subsequently retracted it and, not being compellable by virtue of s 80 of the Police and Criminal Evidence Act 1984, having refused to testify, the prosecution were permitted to adduce the statement.[249] Where the victim of an attempted murder, and a crucial witness for the prosecution, sustained horrific injuries during the offence, as a result of which he was incapable of giving evidence other than through an intermediary, the transcript of his evidence at the first trial was admissible at a retrial.[250]

---

[243] *R v Turner* (1975) 61 Cr App R 67, CA. See also *R v Callan* (1994) 98 Cr App R 467, CA. As to the admissibility, for an accused, of a confession made by a *co-accused*, see the Police and Criminal Evidence Act 1984, s 76A (see Ch 13).

[244] See *Myers v DPP* [1965] AC 1001, HL.

[245] Per Lord Bridge in *R v Blastland* [1986] AC 41, HL, at 53. Contrast *Chambers v Mississippi* 410 US 295 (1973) (US Sup Court): excluding confessions of a third party deprives the accused of a fair trial.

[246] [2007] 1 WLR 1645, CA.

[247] See also *R v Marsh* [2008] EWCA Crim 1816, in which it was stated per Hughes LJ at [25] that there ought to be a pause before admitting hearsay evidence when the declarant is available to be seen by the jury and his stance in relation to the assertion which it is sought to prove can be discovered.

[248] See also *R v Seton* (2010) 174 JP 241, CA at [24] and *R v Z* [2009] 1 Cr App R 34, CA at [25].

[249] *R v L* [2009] 1 WLR 626, CA. See also *R v Horsnell* [2012] EWCA Crim 277: the fact that a witness is not compellable and, further, may have been advised that he or she was not compellable at the time of making the statement are very important factors to be borne in mind when making a decision as to the statement's admissibility under s 114(1)(d).

[250] *R v Sadiq* (2009) 173 JP 471, CA.

Where an accused charged with murder made admissions to his girlfriend, the prosecution were permitted to adduce the confession at the trial of the accomplice as evidence of his involvement in the offence.[251] Where an accused refused to agree the circumstances of a conviction admissible under the provisions of the 2003 Act relating to the admission of evidence of bad character, the prosecution were permitted to adduce a summary of the content of his police interviews and the evidence he gave at the trial for that offence.[252] Where a serving prisoner made telephone calls to his family from prison denying involvement in a murder for which the accused sought to blame him, and expressed outrage, recordings of the calls made by the prison authorities were admissible in circumstances where the prisoner made it clear that he would not give evidence or make a statement to the police.[253]

Previous inconsistent statements of witnesses

Under s 3 of the Criminal Procedure Act 1865 (the 1865 Act), a party calling a witness who proves to be hostile may, by leave of the judge, prove that he has made at other times a statement inconsistent with his testimony.[254] Under s 4 of the 1865 Act, if a witness, upon cross-examination as to a previous inconsistent statement, does not distinctly admit that he made such a statement, proof may be given by the cross-examining party that he did in fact make it. Proof of the statement is governed by both s 4 and s 5 of the 1865 Act, s 4 applying to both oral and written statements, and s 5 applying to written statements only.[255] If the hostile witness, or the witness under cross-examination, adopts the contents of the previous statement, then they become part of his evidence and will be evidence of the matter stated. However, as the law stood prior to the coming into force of s 119(1) of the 2003 Act, if, in criminal cases, the witness did not admit to making the statement and it was proved that he did in fact make it, the statement was not introduced as evidence of the matter stated, but went merely to his credit. Under s 119(1), the statement is admitted as evidence of any matter stated of which oral evidence by the witness would be admissible. The reasoning of the Law Commission was that if the tribunal of fact is trusted to decide that the witness lacks credibility and his testimony should be disregarded, they should also be free to accept the previous statement as reliable.[256] Section 119(1) provides as follows:

> (1) If in criminal proceedings, a person gives oral evidence and—
>   (a) he admits making a previous inconsistent statement, or
>   (b) a previous inconsistent statement made by him is proved by virtue of section 3, 4 or 5 of the Criminal Procedure Act 1865,
>   the statement is admissible as evidence of any matter stated of which oral evidence by him would be admissible.

---

[251] *R v Y* [2008] 1 WLR 1683, CA. See also *R v McLean* [2008] 1 Cr App R 156, *R v Ibrahim* [2009] 1 WLR 578, CA and *R v B* [2008] All ER 108, [2008] EWCA Crim 365.

[252] *R v Steen* [2008] 2 Cr App R 380, CA.

[253] *R v Seton* (2010) 174 JP 241, CA. It has been submitted that the evidence was admitted too readily in this case. The Court of Appeal may have applied the section more liberally than it might otherwise have done because the accused laid blame on the witness at a late stage, possibly for tactical reasons. See Blackstone's Criminal Practice 2013, 2665.

[254] See Ch 6, under **Unfavourable and hostile witnesses**.

[255] See Ch 7, under **Cross-examination, Previous inconsistent statements**.

[256] Law Com No 245 (1997), para. 10.89.

Section 119(1) has the merit of removing from the tribunal of fact, in this particular context, the difficult concept of a previous statement being admitted not as evidence of the matters stated but as evidence to undermine the credibility of its maker as a witness in the case. It is a radical change in the law and is a powerful tool in relation to hostile witnesses.[257] Section 119(1) is subject to the discretionary powers to exclude evidence on which the prosecution propose to rely; and, in jury trials in which the case against the accused is based wholly or partly on such a statement, the court has the power under s 125 of the Act to direct the jury to acquit if the evidence provided by the statement is so unconvincing that the conviction of the accused would be unsafe.[258] In cases where the statement is left before the jury, and the witness maintains that it is untrue, a careful direction is called for.[259]

Other previous statements of witnesses

At common law, the general rule against previous consistent statements prevents a witness from being asked in examination-in-chief about a former out-of-court statement made by him and consistent with his testimony. Under the rule, such a statement is excluded as evidence of consistency and is also inadmissible hearsay, except to the extent that it is admissible under the 2003 Act.[260] As with other types of hearsay, there is the usual danger of manufactured evidence, and to allow a witness to give evidence of a previous statement which is consistent with his testimony is to encourage the reception of superfluous evidence. On the other hand, one of the main justifications of the hearsay rule, the impossibility of cross-examining the maker of the statement, does not apply. Furthermore, an out-of-court statement made shortly after the events to which it relates, and while those events are fresh in the memory, is likely to be more reliable than testimony at a trial which takes place some months or years later. Under s 120 of the 2003 Act, a provision of compromise, the previous statements of a witness only become admissible as evidence of the matters stated in five situations, four of which are plainly based upon, and in some cases expanded versions of, the rather technical common law exceptions to the rule against previous consistent or self-serving statements. It provides as follows.

(1) This section applies where a person (the witness) is called to give evidence in criminal proceedings.
(2) If a previous statement by the witness is admitted as evidence to rebut a suggestion that his oral evidence has been fabricated, that statement is admissible as evidence of any matter stated of which oral evidence by the witness would be admissible.
(3) A statement made by the witness in a document—
　(a) which is used by him to refresh his memory while giving evidence,
　(b) on which he is cross-examined, and
　(c) which as a consequence is received in evidence in the proceedings,
　is admissible as evidence of any matter stated of which oral evidence by him would be admissible.
(4) A previous statement by the witness is admissible as evidence of any matter stated of which oral evidence by him would be admissible, if

---

[257] See Ch 6 under **Unfavourable and hostile witnesses.**

[258] See under **Admissibility of hearsay under the Criminal Justice Act 2003, Other safeguards, Stopping the case where the evidence is unconvincing,** in this chapter.

[259] See *R v Joyce* [2005] All ER 309, [2005] EWCA Crim 1785; and *R v Billingham* (2009) 2 Cr App R 20 at [63]. See the Crown Court Bench Book 2010, 221–2.

[260] See Ch 6.

(a) any of the following three conditions is satisfied, and

(b) while giving evidence the witness indicates that to the best of his belief he made the statement, and that to the best of his belief it states the truth.

(5) The first condition is that the statement identifies or describes a person, object or place.

(6) The second condition is that the statement was made by the witness when the matters stated
were fresh in his memory but he does not remember them, and cannot reasonably be expected
to remember them, well enough to give oral evidence of them in the proceedings.

(7) The third condition is that—

(a) the witness claims to be a person against whom an offence has been committed,

(b) the offence is one to which the proceedings relate,

(c) the statement consists of a complaint made by the witness (whether to a person in authority
or not) about conduct which would, if proved, constitute the offence or part of the offence,

(d) ...[261]

(e) the complaint was not made as a result of a threat or promise, and

(f) before the statement is adduced the witness gives oral evidence in connection with its
subject matter.

(8) For the purposes of subsection (7) the fact that the complaint was elicited (for example, by a
leading question) is irrelevant unless a threat or a promise was involved.

Statements in rebuttal of allegations of fabrication

Under s 120(2), a previous oral or written statement of a witness is admissible as evidence of
any matter stated of which oral evidence by him would be admissible 'if...admitted as evidence to rebut a suggestion that his oral evidence has been fabricated', ie if admitted under
the exception to the rule against previous consistent statements which arises when, in cross-
examination of the witness, it is suggested to him that the account given by him in his testimony is a recent invention or fabrication.[262]

Although such a statement may assist the jury in their assessment of the witness's reliability, it
is not independent evidence. In *R v A*[263] it was held that where such evidence is admitted under
s 120, it is incumbent on the judge to give a specific direction to the jury that the evidence is
not independent of the complainant and the direction that was recommended by Laws LJ in *R
v AA*[264] should be routinely given. As to the direction recommended in *R v AA*, Laws LJ stated:[265]

> In our judgment, in order to reflect (a) the substantive change to the law effected by section 120
> and (b) the circumstance that a previous consistent statement (whether in a sexual case or other-
> wise) comes from the same person as later makes the accusation in the witness box, juries should
> be directed that such a previous consistent statement or recent complaint is, if the jury accepts it
> was given or made and the conditions specified in section 120 are fulfilled, evidence of the truth
> of what was stated: but in deciding what weight such a statement should bear, the jury should
> have in mind the fact it comes from the same person who now makes the complaint in the wit-
> ness box and not from some independent source.

Statements in documents used to refresh the memory

Section 120(3), which mirrors an exception to the rule against previous consistent statements,
applies where the witness is cross-examined on a memory-refreshing document and, as a

---

[261] Repealed by the Coroners and Justice Act 2009, s 112.

[262] See further Ch 6, under **Previous consistent or self-serving statements**.

[263] (2011) 175 JP 437, CA.

[264] [2007] EWCA Crim 1779.

[265] [2007] EWCA Crim 1779 at [17].

(3) For the purposes of this section a person has the required capability if he is capable of—
    (a) understanding questions put to him about the matters stated, and
    (b) giving answers to such questions which can be understood.
(4) Where by reason of this section there is an issue as to whether a person had the required capability when he made a statement—
    (a) proceedings held for the determination of the issue must take place in the absence of the jury (if there is one);
    (b) in determining the issue the court may receive expert evidence and evidence from any person to whom the statement in question was made;
    (c) the burden of proof on the issue lies on the party seeking to adduce the statement, and the standard of proof is the balance of probabilities.

Credibility

The general purpose of s 124 of the 2003 Act is to enable the parties to attack or support the credibility of the maker of a hearsay statement who is not called as a witness as if he had been so called. In the case of a statement in a document admitted under s 117 (business and other documents), the person who supplied or received the information contained in the statement, or who created or received the document, if not called as a witness, is also to be treated as 'the maker of the statement' for the purposes of the section. Section 124 provides as follows:

(1) This section applies if in criminal proceedings—
    (a) a statement not made in oral evidence in the proceedings is admitted as evidence of a matter stated, and
    (b) the maker of the statement does not give oral evidence in connection with the subject matter of the statement.
(2) In such a case—
    (a) any evidence which (if he had given such evidence) would have been admissible as relevant to his credibility as a witness is so admissible in the proceedings;
    (b) evidence may with the court's leave be given of any matter which (if he had given such evidence) could have been put to him in cross-examination as relevant to his credibility as a witness but of which evidence could not have been adduced by the cross-examining party;
    (c) evidence tending to prove that he made (at whatever time) any other statement inconsistent with the statement admitted as evidence is admissible for the purpose of showing that he contradicted himself.
(3) If as a result of evidence admitted under this section an allegation is made against the maker of a statement, the court may permit a party to lead additional evidence of such description as the court may specify for the purposes of denying or answering the allegation.
(4) In the case of a statement in a document which is admitted as evidence under section 117 each person who, in order for the statement to be admissible, must have supplied or received the information concerned or created or received the document or part concerned is to be treated as the maker of the statement for the purposes of subsections (1) to (3) above.

Section 124(2)(a), (b), and (c) are largely concerned with situations which, if the maker had been called as a witness, would have been governed by the rule of finality of answers on collateral issues, by the exceptions to that rule,[282] or by s 100 of the 2003 Act (non-defendant's bad character).[283] Under the rule of finality, the answers given by a witness under cross-examination to questions concerning collateral matters, including questions which go merely to the

[282] See Ch 7.
[283] See Ch 17.

credit of the witness, must be treated as final in the sense that the cross-examining party is not permitted to call further evidence with a view to contradicting the witness. Section 124(2)(a) allows evidence attacking the credibility of the maker to be given where such evidence, had he been called as a witness, would have been admissible either under an *exception* to the rule of finality or, with the leave of the court, under s 100 of the 2003 Act. Accordingly, for example, evidence admissible under sub-paragraph (a) may include evidence that the maker is unfit to be believed because of some physical or mental disability,[284] one of the exceptions to the rule against finality, or, with the leave of the court under s 100 of the 2003 Act, evidence that he has been convicted of an offence.[285] The sub-paragraph may also be used to admit evidence to support the credibility of the maker. At common law a witness's previous consistent statement is exceptionally admissible in order to rebut a suggestion that his evidence has been fabricated.[286] Thus if the party against whom the hearsay statement is admitted suggests that it was fabricated by the maker, evidence to show that before making the statement in question he made a statement, whether written or oral, consistent with it, would be admissible to support his credibility under sub-paragraph (a).

Section 124(2)(b) applies to situations which, if the maker had been called as a witness, would have been governed by the *rule* of finality of answers on collateral issues, that is situations in which, if the maker had been cross-examined about a matter in order to attack his credibility as a witness but had denied the matter put, evidence in rebuttal would *not* have been admissible. Under sub-paragraph (b), evidence of the matter which could have been put to the maker in cross-examination, had he been called as a witness, for example the fact that whereas he is giving his evidence through an interpreter he is able to speak English,[287] may be adduced with the leave of the court. The reasoning underlying this provision, and the statutory precursors to it on which it is closely modelled, is that since, if the maker of the statement had given evidence, he might have admitted the matter put, or his denial might not have been believed, the party against whom the hearsay statement is given in evidence might be put at an unfair disadvantage because unable to cross-examine the maker of the statement. In deciding whether to grant leave, it would seem that the judge should balance the risk of such unfairness against the fact that to allow evidence to the discredit of the absent maker to be given without restriction, might be unfair to him and might lead to an undue prolongation of the trial.[288]

Section 124(2)(c) allows evidence tending to prove that the maker of the hearsay statement made another statement inconsistent with it to be admitted for the purpose of showing that he contradicted himself. The inconsistent statement may have been made orally or in writing and either before or after the hearsay statement. Under s 119(2) of the Act, if evidence of an

---

[284] *Toohey v Metropolitan Police Comr* [1965] AC 595, HL.

[285] See also s 6 of the Criminal Procedure Act 1865 (see Ch 7). See also *R v Riat* [2013] 1 WLR 2592, CA at [18]: in respect of evidence affecting the credibility of an absent witness for the prosecution, the judge is entitled to expect that very full enquiries have been made (over and above simply checking for convictions on the Police National Computer) and that all relevant material has been disclosed. In respect of an absent defence witness, the judge is entitled to expect that the defendant has supplied sufficient information to enable proper checks to be made. Further, both counsel and the judge must keep the necessity for disclosure of material affecting credibility in mind throughout the trial.

[286] See Ch 7.

[287] See *R v Burke* (1858) 8 Cox CC 44 (see Ch 7).

[288] See generally Criminal Law Revision Committee, 11th Report, *Evidence*, Cmnd 4991 (1972), para 263.

inconsistent statement by any person is given under s 124(2)(c), the statement is admissible as evidence of any matter stated in it of which oral evidence by that person would be admissible.

Under s 124(3), where as a result of evidence admitted under s 124(2), an allegation is made against the maker of the statement, the court may permit additional specified evidence to be adduced in rebuttal.

Stopping the case where the evidence is unconvincing

In *R v Galbraith*[289] it was held that a submission of no case to answer should fail where the Crown's case is such that its strength or weakness depends on the view to be taken of a witness's reliability, or other matters which are, generally speaking, within the jury's province, and where on one view of the facts there is evidence on which a jury could properly conclude that the accused is guilty. The Law Commission was of the view that a derogation from *R v Galbraith* could be justified in the case of hearsay evidence on the same basis as in identification cases. In identification cases, 'the case is withdrawn from the jury not because the judge considers that the witness is lying, but because the evidence even if taken to be honest has a base which is so slender that it is unreliable and therefore not sufficient to found a conviction'.[290] Similarly, in the case of hearsay, 'even though the (absent) declarant may be honest, his or her evidence, being hearsay, may be so poor that a conviction would be unsafe'.[291] Section 125 of the 2003 Act, based on cl 14 of the Law Commission's draft bill, provides as follows:

(1) If on a defendant's trial before a judge and jury for an offence the court is satisfied at any time after the close of the case for the prosecution that—

    (a) the case against the defendant is based wholly or partly on a statement not made in oral evidence in the proceedings, and

    (b) the evidence provided by the statement is so unconvincing that, considering its importance to the case against the defendant, his conviction of the offence would be unsafe,

the court must either direct the jury to acquit the defendant of the offence or, if it considers that there ought to be a retrial, discharge the jury.

(2) Where—

    (a) a jury is directed under subsection (1) to acquit a defendant of an offence, and

    (b) the circumstances are such that, apart from this subsection, the defendant could if acquitted of that offence be found guilty of another offence,

the defendant may not be found guilty of that other offence if the court is satisfied as mentioned in subsection (1) in respect of it.

While the judge may exercise the power under s 125 at 'any time after the close of the case for the prosecution' he ordinarily ought not do so until the close of all the evidence.[292] The same duty to direct an acquittal or discharge the jury also applies in cases in which a jury is required to determine under the Criminal Procedure (Insanity) Act 1964 whether the accused did the act or made the omission charged.[293] Section 125 is without prejudice to any other power a court may have to direct an acquittal or discharge a jury.[294]

---

[289] [1981] 1 WLR 1039, CA (see Ch 2).

[290] See per Lord Mustill in *Daley v R* [1994] 1 AC 117, PC at 129 (see Ch 8).

[291] Law Com No 245, Cm 3670 (1997). See also *R v Riat* [2013] 1 WLR 2592 at [28]: the test in s 125 is different from that in *R v Galbraith* and will involve, 'looking at…[the] strengths and weaknesses [of the hearsay evidence], at the tools available to the jury for testing it, and at its importance to the case as a whole'.

[292] *R v Horncastle* [2009] 2 Cr App R 15, CA at [74]. See also *R v Riat* [2013] 1 WLR 2592 at [29].

[293] Section 125(3).

[294] Section 125(4).

Discretion to exclude

Section 126 of the Act provides as follows:

(1) In criminal proceedings the court may refuse to admit a statement as evidence of a matter stated if—

    (a) the statement was made otherwise than in oral evidence in the proceedings, and

    (b) the court is satisfied that the case for excluding the statement, taking account of the danger that to admit it would result in undue waste of time, substantially outweighs the case for admitting it, taking account of the value of the evidence.

(2) Nothing in this Chapter prejudices—

    (a) any power of a court to exclude evidence under section 78 of the Police and Criminal Evidence Act 1984 (exclusion of unfair evidence), or

    (b) any other power of a court to exclude evidence at its discretion (whether from preventing questions from being put or otherwise).

As we have seen, there is a discretion to admit hearsay under s 114(1)(d) if it is 'in the interests of justice'. The same phrase is used in two other provisions: under s 116(4), leave may be given to admit the hearsay statement of someone who does not give oral evidence through fear only if the court considers that the statement ought to be admitted in the interests of justice; and under s 121(1)(c), which relates to multiple hearsay, a hearsay statement is not admissible to prove the fact that an earlier hearsay statement was made unless the interests of justice require it to be admissible for that purpose. Although strictly speaking, where a court has admitted a hearsay statement under s 114(1)(d), s 116(4), or s 121(1)(c), it may proceed to consider use of one of its three discretionary powers of exclusion, this is likely to be a pointless exercise given that it is of the opinion that it is in the interests of justice to admit the evidence. Furthermore, in the case of s 114(1)(d) and s 116(4), the court, in considering whether it is in the interests of justice, shall have regard, in addition to the matters listed in s 114(2)(a)–(i) and s 116(4)(a)–(c), to any other relevant factors or circumstances, which could, of course, include any of the factors or circumstances relevant to the exercise of any of the discretionary powers to exclude.[295] It is for reasons of this kind, presumably, that it has been observed that the test in s 78 of the 1984 Act is unlikely to produce a different result from that of 'the interests of justice' in ss 114(1)(d) and 116(4).[296]

In *R v Riat* it was stated that whatever section is applied when considering the admissibility of hearsay evidence, a careful assessment will be involved of (i) the importance of the evidence to the case; (ii) the risks of unreliability; and (iii) whether the reliability of the absent witness can safely be tested. In relation to (ii) and (iii), a court is not required to look for independent, complete confirmation of the reliability of the evidence.[297] What is required is that the evidence is shown to be *potentially* safely reliable.[298] In *R v Tahery*[299] the appellant was convicted of wounding with intent during a fight involving some members of the Iranian and Kurdish communities. The prosecution case relied on the statement of a witness, who was absent through fear, that the appellant had stabbed a member of the Iranian community (the appellant himself was a member of that community). It was held that objective factors pointed to

---

[295] See *R v Riat* [2013] 1 WLR 2592, CA at [22].

[296] See, in the case of s 114(1)(d), *R v Cole* [2008] 1 Cr App R 81, CA; and, in the case of s 116(4), *R v D* [2002] 2 Cr App R 601, CA.

[297] *R v Riat* [2013] 1 WLR 2592, CA at [25]. See also *R v Pedersen* [2013] EWCA Crim 464.

[298] *R v Ibrahim* [2012] Cr App R 32, CA at [107]. See also *R v Riat* [2013] 1 WLR 2592, CA at [33].

[299] [2013] EWCA Crim 1053.

the unreliability of the statement, including the witness's animosity toward the appellant, a contradictory initial statement to the police, and a lack of evidence to support the account that the appellant used the knife. Furthermore, because the Iranian community was close-knit, the appellant was unable to call evidence to rebut the statement. Consequently, the jury did not have any means to safely assess the reliability of the evidence and given its importance in the case (it was the only evidence, apart from evidence of the person stabbed), it ought not to have been admitted.

Section 126(1), which has been described as a 'general' discretion to exclude,[300] creates a discretionary power to exclude otherwise admissible hearsay, whether tendered by the prosecution or defence.[301] Under the balancing exercise described in s 126(1)(b), regard must be had, on the one hand, to the case for exclusion, taking account not of the danger of waste of time—the risk of *some* waste of time is plainly acceptable—but of the danger of *undue* waste of time. This has to be weighed against the case for admission of the evidence, taking account of its 'value', a word which appears to embrace not only its probative value, or its value in understanding other evidence in the case, but also its value in the sense of its reliability or weight. It is only if the court is satisfied that the case for exclusion *substantially* outweighs the case for admission, that the discretion should be exercised. This is likely to occur, for example, where the hearsay statement is of minimal probative value and wholly or to a very large extent superfluous, because other evidence has been or will be given on the matters stated.

Section 126(2) preserves the two pre-existing powers of the court to exclude otherwise admissible hearsay. The first is the power in s 78 of the Police and Criminal Evidence Act 1984 under which evidence on which the prosecution proposes to rely may be excluded where in all the circumstances, including those in which the evidence was obtained, it would have such an adverse effect on the fairness of the proceedings that the court ought not to admit it. The second is the common law power to exclude prosecution evidence on the basis that its prejudicial effect outweighs its probative value.

Under Art 6(1) of the European Convention on Human Rights, the accused is entitled to a fair hearing and under Art 6(3)(d) the accused has the right to examine or have examined witnesses against him. As we have seen, it is not necessarily incompatible with Art 6(1) and (3)(d) for depositions or witness statements to be read, even if there has been no opportunity to question the witness at any stage of the proceedings as long as there is a legitimate justification for the admission of the witness statement and, where appropriate, sufficient counterbalancing measures, the adequacy of which is to be determined by the fairness of the trial as a whole.

In *R v Cole*[302] Lord Phillips CJ stated that once one moves away from the proposition that there is an absolute rule that evidence of a statement cannot be adduced in evidence unless the defendant has an opportunity to examine the maker, there can only be one governing criterion, namely whether the admission of the evidence is compatible with a fair trial and it is that question alone with which Art 6 is concerned. Factors that are likely to be of concern to the court are set out in s 114(2) of the Act.[303]

---

[300] *R v C* [2006] Crim LR 637, CA.

[301] See *R v Riat* [2013] 1 WLR 2592, CA at [23].

[302] [2008] 1 Cr App R 81, CA at [20]–[21].

[303] See s 114(2), under **Admissibility of hearsay under the Criminal Justice Act 2003, Admissibility in the interests of justice**, in this chapter.

Rules of court

Under s 132 of the Act, rules of court may be made providing for the procedural conditions to be followed by a party proposing to tender a hearsay statement in evidence. The rules may require such a party to serve on the other party or parties notice and particulars of the evidence[304] and may provide that the evidence is admissible if a notice has been served but there has been no service of a counter-notice objecting to the admission of the evidence.[305] The rules applicable in magistrates' courts and Crown Courts are set out in Pt 34 of the Criminal Procedure Rules 2013.[306] If a party proposing to tender evidence fails to comply with a prescribed requirement, the evidence is not admissible except with the court's leave.[307] Where the defendant seeks to adduce hearsay evidence but fails to comply, leave should be granted where any unfairness to the prosecution or co-accused may be cured, for example by an adjournment, and where the interests of justice otherwise require the evidence to be admitted, but not where to admit the evidence would cause incurable unfairness.[308] Where leave is given the court or jury may draw such inferences from a failure to comply with a prescribed requirement as appear proper.[309] However, a person is not to be convicted of an offence solely on the basis of such an inference.[310]

The direction to the jury

A trial judge should give the jury a careful direction on the correct approach to hearsay. The following guidance was given in *Grant v The State*.[311] The jury should be told that a hearsay statement has not been verified on oath nor its author tested by cross-examination. The judge should point out the potential risk of relying on a statement by someone whom the jury have not been able to assess and should invite them to scrutinize the evidence with particular care. It is proper to direct the jury to give the statement such weight as they think fit. Finally, it is desirable to direct them to consider the statement in the context of the other evidence, drawing attention to any discrepancies between the statement and the oral evidence of other witnesses.[312]

Questions of proof

Proof of conditions of admissibility

It is submitted that many of the principles established in the cases concerning proof of the conditions of admissibility contained in ss 23 and 24 of the Criminal Justice Act 1988 (and other repealed statutory precursors to the hearsay provisions of the 2003 Act) remain valid. Thus where it is sought to admit a hearsay statement under s 116 (or to comply with the requirement of s 117(5)(a)), because the maker of the statement is unable to give oral evidence for one of the reasons set out in s 116(2), the court should make a finding of fact, based on

---

[304] Section 132(3).

[305] Section 132(4).

[306] Criminal Procedure Rules 2013, SI 2013/1554.

[307] Section 132(5).

[308] *R v Musone* [2007] 1 WLR 2467, CA at [37]. See also *Marine Fisheries Agency v Inter Fish Limited* [2009] EWHC 753, DC, where no unfairness was caused to the defence.

[309] Section 132(5).

[310] Section 132(7).

[311] [2006] 2 WLR 835, PC.

[312] See the Crown Court Bench Book 2010, Ch 14.

admissible evidence, that such a reason exists.[313] If necessary, the matter should be decided on a *voir dire*,[314] at which the party against whom the evidence is tendered is entitled to cross-examine witnesses relied on to establish the necessary facts.[315] The *voir dire* is of particular importance in cases covered by s 116(2)(e), ie where the maker of the statement does not give oral evidence through fear: it is highly desirable that any investigation of his reasons should be conducted in the absence of the jury and that some innocuous form of words should be used to explain his absence to the jury[316] and prevent the jury from speculating that the accused may be responsible for the absence.[317] However, there is no requirement that the judge should test statements of fear through video link or tape recording, particularly as to the reasons for the fear; courts should not test the basis of fear by calling witnesses before them, since that may create the very situation which s 116(2)(e) was designed to avoid.[318] As to the standard of proof, the prosecution must satisfy the court beyond reasonable doubt,[319] the defence on a balance of probabilities.[320] Evidence to establish one of the reasons may take the form of either direct testimony or admissible hearsay (including a statement itself admissible under the statutory provisions)[321] but cannot be furnished by the contents of the very statement sought to be introduced, because prima facie they are inadmissible hearsay.[322] In order to establish that the maker of a statement does not give oral evidence through fear, reliance may be placed on his sworn evidence,[323] his demeanour[324] (which may be particularly important if he does not state his fear explicitly),[325] and medical evidence.[326] Alternatively, use may be made of his out-of-court written statement of fear,[327] whether or not contained in the very statement sought to be admitted, on the basis that it constitutes original evidence admissible to prove state of mind[328] or, if it is treated as hearsay, is admissible under the *res gestae* principle which covers statements concerning the maker's contemporaneous state of mind.[329] This principle is among the common law categories of admissibility preserved by s 118 of the 2003 Act.

[313] See *R v T (D)* (2009) 173 JP 425, CA, a decision under s 116(2)(d), in which the court stated that given the importance of the right to confrontation, it is impermissible to proceed with an application under s 116(2)(d) informally; if the facts cannot be agreed, evidence must be called and the judge must make findings of fact.

[314] See *R v Minors; R v Harper* [1989] 1 WLR 441, CA.

[315] See *R v Wood and Fitzsimmons* [1998] Crim LR 213, CA.

[316] See *R v Jennings* [1995] Crim LR 810, CA.

[317] See *R v Wood and Fitzsimmons* [1998] Crim LR 213, CA. If the jury ask why the maker has not been called to give evidence, the judge should simply say that he cannot answer the question: *R v Churchill* [1993] Crim LR 285, CA.

[318] *R v Davies* [2007] 2 All ER 1070, CA.

[319] See *R (Meredith) v Harwich Magistrates' Court* (2007) 171 JP 249, DC, a decision under the Criminal Justice Act 2003, s 116(2)(b) (unfit to be a witness because of bodily or mental condition). See also, *R v Lyons* [2010] EWCA Crim 2029 at [9].

[320] See *R v Mattey, R v Queeley* [1995] 2 Cr App R 409.

[321] See *R v Castillo* [1996] 1 Cr App R 438, CA.

[322] See *R v Case* [1991] Crim LR 192, CA and *R v Mattey, R v Queeley* [1995] 2 Cr App R 409.

[323] Although in *R v Greer* [1998] Crim LR 572, CA reliance was placed on unsworn evidence, technically he should be sworn: see *R v Jennings* [1995] Crim LR 572, CA.

[324] See *R v Waters* [1997] Crim LR 823, CA.

[325] See *R v Ashford Magistrates' Court, ex p Hilden* [1993] QB 555, DC.

[326] See *R v Waters* [1997] Crim LR 823, CA.

[327] See *R v Rutherford* [1998] Crim LR 490, CA.

[328] See *R v Fairfax* [1995] Crim LR 949, CA, relying on *R v Blastland* [1986] AC 41, HL.

[329] See *R v Fairfax* [1995] Crim LR 949 (citing *Neill v North Antrim Magistrates' Court* [1992] 1 WLR 1220, HL: see per Lord Mustill, obiter at 1228) and *R v Wood and Fitzsimmons* [1998] Crim LR 213, CA. But see also *R v Belmarsh Magistrates' Court, ex p Gilligan* [1998] 1 Cr App R 14, DC: neither possible means of admissibility was even mentioned, and Astill J pointed out that in *R v Fairfax* there had been a great deal of oral evidence of fear.

According to *R v Foxley*[330] evidence of the requirements contained in s 24(1) of the 1988 Act, which were broadly similar to the requirements set out in s 117(2)(a) and (b) of the 2003 Act, was often desirable, but not always essential. In that case the trial judge was entitled to infer from the documents themselves and from the method or route by which they had been produced before the court that the requirements were satisfied. The purpose of s 24 was to enable the document to speak for itself, a purpose that would be defeated if oral evidence were to be required in every case from the creator or keeper of the document or the supplier of the information it contained.[331]

Proof of a statement contained in a document

Section 133 of the 2003 Act provides that:

> Where a statement in a document is admissible as evidence in criminal proceedings, the statement may be proved by producing either—
>
> (a) the document, or
>
> (b) (whether or not the document exists) a copy of the document or of the material part of it, authenticated in whatever way the court may approve.

The word 'document' means anything in which information of any description is recorded,[332] a definition wide enough to include, for example, audio tapes, films, and videotapes. 'Copy', in relation to a document, means anything on to which information recorded in the document has been copied, by whatever means, and whether directly or indirectly,[333] a definition which would cover, among other things, a transcript of an audio tape as well as reproductions or still reproductions of the images embodied in films and videotapes, whether enlarged or not. 'Producing' would seem to refer not to counsel handing the document to the court, but to a witness who is qualified to do so in accordance with the rules of evidence producing the document and saying what it is.[334] The reference to authentication appears to relate to the authentication of a copy of a document as a true copy of the original, and not to proof of the original.[335] Section 133 is considered further under **Documentary evidence** in Chapter 9.

Evidence by video recording

In the case of offences triable only on indictment and prescribed offences triable either way, where a person, other than the accused, is called as a witness, having witnessed the events constituting the offence or part of it, or events closely connected with it, and having previously given a video-recorded account of those events at a time when they were fresh in his memory, s 137 of the 2003 Act permits the court to direct that the recording be admitted as his evidence-in-chief. Section 137 is considered in Chapter 5.

---

[330] [1995] 2 Cr App R 523, CA.

[331] See also, applying *R v Foxley, R v Ilyas and Knight* [1996] Crim LR 810, CA.

[332] Section 134(1).

[333] Section 134(1).

[334] As under the Civil Evidence Act 1968, s 6(1) (see now the Civil Evidence Act 1995, s 8): per Staughton LJ in *Ventouris v Mountain (No 2)* [1992] 1 WLR 887, CA (see Ch 11).

[335] Cf *Ventouris v Mountain (No 2)* [1992] 1 WLR 887, CA (see Ch 11).

3. A party intending to rely on hearsay should be under a duty to give notice of that fact where this is reasonable and appropriate, according to the particular circumstances of the case. Although failure to give notice should not render the evidence inadmissible, it may detract from the weight that will be placed on it or lead to the imposition of costs sanctions.

4. There should be power for a party to call a witness for cross-examination on his hearsay statement.

5. Courts should be given guidelines to assist them in assessing the weight of hearsay evidence.

6. For business and other records there should be no additional safeguards, beyond those applicable to all other hearsay statements, and the procedure for proving such records should be simplified.

All of these recommendations were put into effect by the Civil Evidence Act 1995 (the 1995 Act).

Before considering the detail of the Act, it is important to note that it contains no special conditions of admissibility or other specific safeguards in the case of statements in computer-produced documents. The 1968 Act contained elaborate precautions in this regard, including requirements to prove that the document was produced in the normal course of business and in an uninterrupted course of activity. Requirements of this kind reflected a fundamental mistrust and fear of the potential for error and mechanical failure. However, as the Law Commission observed, since 1968 technology has developed to an extent where computers and computer-generated documents are relied on in every area of business. It also thought that it was at least questionable whether the requirements of the Civil Evidence Act 1968 provided any real safeguard in relation to the reliability of the hardware or software concerned, and noted that in any event they provided no protection against the inaccurate inputting of data. The Commission recognized that, as confidence in the inherent reliability of computers had grown, so had concern over the potential for misuse, through the capacity to hack, corrupt, or alter information in a manner which is undetectable, but could see no reason for maintaining a different regime for the admission of computer-generated documents. It considered that the potential for misuse was best dealt with by concentrating upon the weight to be attached to such evidence, rather than by the reformulation of complex and inflexible rules of admissibility.[5]

Admissibility of hearsay under the Civil Evidence Act 1995

Abolition of the rule against hearsay

Section 1 of the 1995 Act provides as follows:

(1) In civil proceedings evidence shall not be excluded on the ground that it is hearsay.
(2) In this Act—
   (a) 'hearsay' means a statement made otherwise than by a person while giving oral evidence[6] in the proceedings which is tendered as evidence of the matters stated; and
   (b) references to hearsay include hearsay of whatever degree.

---

[5] See generally Law Com No 216, Cm 2321 (1993), paras 3.14–3.21 and 4.43.

[6] 'Oral evidence' includes evidence which, by reason of a defect of speech or hearing, a person called as a witness gives in writing or by signs: s 13.

'In civil proceedings'

The phrase 'civil proceedings' is defined by s 11 as 'civil proceedings, before any tribunal, in relation to which the strict rules of evidence apply, whether as a matter of law or by agreement of the parties'. Thus the Act applies to civil proceedings in any of the ordinary courts of law and in both tribunals and arbitrations in which the strict rules of evidence are applied, but not to the wardship jurisdiction of the High Court[7] or Coroners' Courts. The strict rules of evidence do not apply to all civil proceedings in magistrates' courts. For example, the Act does not apply to magistrates when considering whether there is reasonable cause to suspend a private hire vehicle licence under the Local Government (Miscellaneous Provisions) Act 1976.[8] In *Savings and Investment Bank Ltd v Gasco Investments (Netherlands) BV (No 2)*,[9] a decision under the equivalent provision of the Civil Evidence Act 1968, it was held that an application to commit for contempt founded on the breach of an order made in civil proceedings was itself a civil proceeding, notwithstanding the criminal standard of proof appropriate to such an application[10] and its possible penal consequences.

'Shall not be excluded'

Under s 1(1) of the 1995 Act, 'evidence shall not be excluded on the ground that it is hearsay'. The subsection needs to be considered alongside s 14(1) of the Act, which provides that:

> Nothing in this Act affects the exclusion of evidence on grounds other than that it is hearsay.
> This applies whether the evidence falls to be excluded in pursuance of any enactment or rule of law, for failure to comply with rules of court or an order of the court, or otherwise.

Thus hearsay cannot be excluded because it is hearsay but will only be admissible if it does not fall to be excluded on some ground other than that it is hearsay. For example, hearsay opinion evidence which is inadmissible under the Civil Evidence Act 1972[11] falls to be excluded in pursuance of an enactment; hearsay which is irrelevant or inadmissible on grounds of public policy or privilege falls to be excluded in pursuance of a rule of law; and the hearsay opinion of an expert may fall to be excluded if a party fails to comply with r 35.13 of the Civil Procedure Rules (CPR), ie if he fails to disclose the expert's report.

'Hearsay'

The purpose of the statutory definition of hearsay in s 1(2) is to identify the type of evidence which would have formerly been excluded by virtue of the common law rule against hearsay, ie first-hand, second-hand, or multiple hearsay, and to which the safeguards and supplementary provisions of the Act apply. However, there is likely to continue to be reference to the common law authorities in cases in which the boundary of the definition is unclear.[12] Section 13 provides that 'statement' means 'any representation of fact or opinion, however made'.

[7] See *Official Solicitor to the Supreme Court v K* [1965] AC 201, HL. Proceedings in the Court of Protection fall within the definition of 'civil proceedings' under the 1995 Act, s 11: *Enfield London Borough Council v SA* [2010] 1 FLR 1836. However, confiscation proceedings under the Proceeds of Crime Act 2002 do not: *R v Clipston* [2011] 2 Cr App R (S) 101 at [46]–[50].
[8] *Westminster City Council v Zestfair Ltd* (1989) 88 LGR 288, DC; *Leeds City Council v Hussain* [2003] RTR 13, DC.
[9] [1988] 2 WLR 1212, CA.
[10] See Ch 4.
[11] See Ch 18.
[12] Law Com No 216, Cm 2321 (1993), para 4.6.

Thus the Act covers a statement of opinion, provided that it is admissible under the 1972 Act, as well as a statement of fact, whether the statement was made orally, in writing (whether hand-written, type-written, or produced by computer), or by conduct. It may be doubted, however, whether a written statement in an affidavit is covered by the Act.[13]

Original evidence

Under s 1(2)(a), hearsay is defined as a statement made otherwise than by a person while giving oral evidence in the proceedings which is 'tendered as evidence of the matter stated' and falls to be distinguished from original evidence, ie a statement made otherwise than by a person while giving oral evidence in the proceedings which is tendered for any relevant purpose other than that of establishing any matter stated. The distinction between hearsay and original evidence is important because whereas hearsay is only admissible subject to the conditions and safeguards set out in the 1995 Act, original evidence, if sufficiently relevant, is admissible without more. In some cases, original evidence is introduced simply to show that the statement in question was made, because that is among the facts in issue in the case. Thus in defamation proceedings in which it is in issue whether the allegedly defamatory statement was made, a witness may give evidence of the making of the statement, including its terms. So-called 'operative words' provide a further illustration. The utterance of such words binds the speaker under the substantive law because a reasonable person, on hearing them, would believe that the speaker intended to be bound. Thus if the parties dispute whether a contract was entered into, evidence of the terms of the contractual offer are admissible because under the law of contract the words spoken are of legal effect if a reasonable person in the position of the offeree would have believed that the offeror intended to be bound. Likewise, words of gift accompanying a transfer of property may be admitted as original evidence. In other types of case, original evidence is introduced because the statement in question is relevant to a fact in issue, typically the state of mind of the person who heard or read it, to show what he knew, thought or believed. Thus P may tender evidence of a certain alleged misrepresentation made to him by Q for the purpose of showing that he was thereby misled. If X brings an action against Y for malicious prosecution, then Y, in order to show the reasonableness of his conduct in the prosecution of X, may tender evidence of a statement made to him by Z that X had committed a criminal offence.[14] Almost all of the reported examples of original evidence have arisen in criminal cases and the topic is considered more fully in Chapter 10.[15]

Implied assertions

An implied assertion is an assertion, whether made orally, in writing, or by conduct, from which it is possible to infer a particular matter. For example, in *Wright v Doe d Tatham*,[16] one of the issues being the mental competence of a testator, it was held that the trial judge had properly excluded a number of letters written to the testator by certain of his acquaintances in terms from which it could legitimately be inferred that they regarded him as sane. As evidence of the truth of the implied assertion that the testator was sane, they constituted inadmissible hearsay. As to implied assertions by conduct, Parke B was of the obiter opinion that on the question of

---

[13] In *Rover International Ltd v Cannon Film Sales Ltd (No 2)* [1987] 1 WLR 1597, Ch D at 1603 Harman J doubted whether affidavits were 'documents' for the purposes of the 1968 Act.

[14] See *Perkins v Vaughan* (1842) 4 Man&G 988.

[15] See in Ch 10 under **Admissibility of hearsay under the Criminal Justice Act 2003, The meaning of hearsay in the Criminal Justice Act 2003, Original evidence.**

[16] (1837) 7 Ad&El 313, Ex Ch.

the seaworthiness of a vessel, evidence of the conduct of a deceased captain in examining every part of the vessel and then embarking on it with his family would also amount to hearsay. On the other hand, in *Manchester Brewery Co Ltd v Coombs*,[17] which concerned an alleged breach by a brewer to supply good beer, it was held, obiter, that evidence could be given that customers ordered the beer, tasted it, did not finish it, and then either left it or threw it away. Further examples are considered in Chapter 10.[18] In *criminal* proceedings, the courts avoid analysing hearsay by reference to the concept of implied assertions, focussing instead on whether there has been a statement of the matter sought to be proved and whether one of the purposes of the maker of the statement was to cause another to believe what was stated or act upon it as true.[19] There have been no equivalent developments in civil proceedings and it is unclear whether, for the purposes of the 1995 Act, a 'statement' covers an implied assertion. In the case of conduct, the Law Commission took the view that the question whether assertive or non-assertive conduct should come within the statutory definition of hearsay was 'a matter for judicial consideration and development'.[20] However, it seems that such consideration and development is also called for in the case of implied assertions made orally or in writing.

Evidence admissible apart from section 1

Section 1(3) and (4) of the 1995 Act provide as follows:

> (3) Nothing in this Act affects the admissibility of evidence admissible apart from this section.
> (4) The provisions of sections 2 to 6 (safeguards and supplementary provisions relating to hearsay evidence) do not apply in relation to hearsay evidence admissible apart from this section, notwithstanding that it may also be admissible by virtue of this section.

Various statutory provisions, apart from s 1 of the 1995 Act, provide for the admissibility of particular types of hearsay and the purpose of s 1(3) is to preserve their effect. An example is the Births and Deaths Registration Act 1953, s 34 of which provides for the admissibility of a certified copy of an entry in the register of births as evidence of the facts contained in it. Similarly, the same section provides for the proof of death, where there is evidence identifying the person named in the certificate with the person in question, by reliance on a death certificate.[21] Other important statutory provisions include the orders made under s 96 of the Children Act 1989,[22] whereby in civil proceedings[23] before the High Court or a county court, in family proceedings in a magistrates' court,[24] and in proceedings under the Child Support Act 1991, evidence given in connection with the upbringing, maintenance, or welfare of a child shall be admissible notwithstanding any rule of law relating to hearsay.[25]

---

[17] (1901) 82 LT 347, Ch D at 349.

[18] See in Ch 10 under **The admissibility of hearsay under the Criminal Justice Act 2003, The meaning of hearsay in the Criminal Justice Act 2003, Implied assertions**.

[19] The Criminal Justice Act 2003, s 115(3) and *R v Twist* [2011] 2 Cr App R 17, CA. See Ch 10.

[20] Law Com No 216, Cm 2321 (1993), para 4.35.

[21] See also the Bankers' Books Evidence Act 1879 (see Ch 9), the Marriage Act 1949, s 65(3) (see Ch 12). See also the Solicitors Act 1974, s 18.

[22] See The Children (Admissibility of Hearsay Evidence) Order 1993, SI 1993/621.

[23] 'Civil proceedings' has the same meaning as it has under the 1995 Act (by virtue of s 11): see the 1989 Act, s 96(7).

[24] The order extends not only to all the proceedings defined as 'family proceedings' by the 1989 Act, s 8(2), but also to other proceedings which are part of the magistrates' courts' family proceedings jurisdiction by virtue of the 1989 Act, s 92(2): *R v Oxfordshire County Council* [1992] 3 WLR 88 Fam D.

[25] The party seeking to adduce the evidence must show that it has a substantial connection with the upbringing, etc of the child.

Article 6(1) of the European Convention on Human Rights

In *Clingham v Kensington and Chelsea London Borough Council*[26] the Divisional Court held that there was nothing in the Human Rights Act 1998, nor in the jurisprudence of the European Court of Human Rights, which led to the automatic exclusion of hearsay evidence in civil proceedings, and that there was no requirement to give the 1995 Act any meaning which it did not naturally bear. The court also held that the admission of hearsay evidence, without the possibility of cross-examination, does not automatically result in an unfair trial under Art 6(1) of the Convention.[27]

Conditions of admissibility

Competence

As previously noted, hearsay admissible under s 1 of the 1995 Act must be evidence which is otherwise admissible. However, s 1 does not make clear whether hearsay may be admitted if the maker of the statement would not have been competent to give evidence at the time he made it. It is also unclear whether his statement, if admissible, may be proved by the statement of another who, at the time when he made his statement, would not have been competent as a witness. For example, if A makes an oral statement within the hearing of B, and A would have been competent to give evidence at that time, may A's statement be proved by B's written record as to what he said, the record having been made at a time when B would not have been competent? Section 5(1) of the Act renders explicit the competence requirements. It provides as follows:

> Hearsay evidence shall not be admitted in civil proceedings if or to the extent that it is shown to consist of, or to be proved by means of, a statement made by a person who at the time he made the statement was not competent as a witness.
>
> For this purpose 'not competent as a witness' means suffering from such mental or physical infirmity, or lack of understanding, as would render a person incompetent as a witness in civil proceedings; but a child shall be treated as competent as a witness if he satisfies the requirements of section 96(2)(a) and (b) of the Children Act 1989 (conditions for reception of unsworn evidence of child).[28]

The burden of proof, under s 5(1), is borne by the party seeking to exclude the evidence.[29]

The requirement of leave

Section 1 of the 1995 Act, if unqualified, would permit a party to adduce, as evidence of the matters stated, the previous out-of-court statement of a person called as a witness. The Law Commission took the view that, in the case of previous consistent statements, a leave requirement was necessary in order to prevent the pointless proliferation of superfluous evidence,

---

[26] (2001) 165 JP 322, DC.

[27] See also *R (McCann) v Crown Court at Manchester* [2003] 1 AC 787, HL at [35]. Equally, it does not automatically follow that it would be unfair to admit hearsay evidence in civil proceedings which would not be admissible in criminal proceedings, under the Criminal Justice Act 2003, s 114(1)(d) or s 116: *R (Bonhoeffer) v General Medical Council* [2011] EWHC 1585, DC at [39].

[28] See Ch 5. However, r 95(d) of the Court of Protection Rules 2007 gives the Court of Protection the power to admit hearsay evidence otherwise inadmissible under s 5.

[29] *JC v CC* [2001] EWCA Civ 1625.

which would needlessly prolong trials and increase costs.[30] Section 6 of the Act provides as follows:

(1) Subject as follows, the provisions of this Act as to hearsay evidence in civil proceedings apply equally (but with any necessary modifications) in relation to a previous statement made by a person called as a witness in the proceedings.

(2) A party who has called or intends to call a person as a witness in civil proceedings may not in those proceedings adduce evidence of a previous statement made by that person, except—

(a) with the leave of the court, or

(b) for the purpose of rebutting a suggestion that his evidence has been fabricated.[31]

This shall not be construed as preventing a witness statement (that is, a written statement of oral evidence which a party to the proceedings intends to lead) from being adopted by a witness in giving evidence or treated as his evidence.[32]

Leave is required under s 6(2)(a) whether the previous statement is a previous *consistent* statement or relates to matters other than those dealt with in the testimony of the witness, but the concluding words of s 6(2) make it clear that it is not intended that a witness statement which stands as a witness's evidence-in-chief under CPR r 32.5(2) should be regarded as a 'previous statement' for the purposes of the provision.

At common law, previous statements of a witness were generally excluded both as evidence of the truth of the facts they contained and as evidence of consistency.[33] The questions naturally arise as to what considerations the court should take into account in deciding whether to grant leave, and whether leave should be granted only exceptionally. As to the former, it is submitted that, in deciding whether to grant leave, the judge should consider the importance of the previous statement in relation to the facts in issue, the reliability and weight of the statement, including all the circumstances in which it was made, and whether admission would be unjust to the other parties to the proceedings. As to the latter, it is submitted that leave should be granted not only where the witness is incapable of giving direct evidence on the matter in question because, for example, he has no recollection of the matter (in which case, the statement would not be a previous *consistent* statement), but also where, although he is capable of giving direct evidence of the matter, it is of questionable reliability or unintelligible by reason of partial loss of memory, lapse of time, age, or illness. Such an approach would accord with the spirit of *Morris v Stratford-on-Avon RDC*,[34] a decision under the equivalent leave requirement in the Civil Evidence Act 1968.[35] That was an action against the council for damages for the alleged negligence of one of their employees. The trial began some five years after the cause of action arose and the

---

[30] See Law Com No 216, Cm 2321 (1993), para 4.30.

[31] Section 6(2)(b) is considered in Ch 6, under **Previous consistent or self-serving statements**.

[32] Pursuant to s 6(3), the Act does not authorize the adducing of evidence of previous *inconsistent* statements otherwise than in accordance with the Criminal Procedure Act 1865, ss 3, 4, and 5; and, pursuant to s 6(4), the Act does not affect the common law rules whereby a memory-refreshing document may be rendered admissible as a result of cross-examination. Section 6(3) is considered in Ch 6 (under **Unfavourable and hostile witnesses, Hostile witnesses**) and Ch 7 (under **Cross-examination, Previous inconsistent statements**); and s 6(4) is considered in Ch 6 (under **Refreshing the memory**).

[33] The exceptions, in effect preserved by the 1995 Act, s 6(2)(b) and (4), relate to statements admissible to rebut allegations of recent fabrication (see n 31 in this chapter) and memory-refreshing documents rendered admissible as a result of cross-examination (see n 32 in this chapter).

[34] [1973] 1 WLR 1059.

[35] Section 2(2).

employee gave confused and inconsistent evidence. After his examination-in-chief, counsel for the defendants was granted leave to admit in chief a written statement made by the employee and given to the defendants' insurers some nine months after the accident. The Court of Appeal held that the trial judge had not erred in allowing the evidence to be admitted.

Where leave is given, there is no restriction in s 6 as to when the previous statement may be given in evidence. Thus according to the circumstances, the statement may be given in evidence before or during the witness's examination-in-chief (which would seem appropriate if likely to improve the intelligibility of his evidence), rather than at the conclusion of his examination-in-chief. Equally, there is no restriction as to *who* may prove the statement: the court may allow evidence of the making of the previous statement to be given by someone other than its maker.

Safeguards

The requirement to give advance notice

The notice provisions of the 1995 Act are simpler and more flexible than those in operation under the Civil Evidence Act 1968. The objectives of the earlier provisions were that all issues arising out of the adduction of hearsay evidence should be dealt with pre-trial and that there should be no surprises at trial. The Law Commission endorsed these objectives but believed that they could be met by a notice provision which (i) requires a party to give notice of the fact that he or she proposes to adduce hearsay; and (ii) puts the onus on the receiving party to demand such particulars as he requires in order to be able to make a proper assessment of the weight and cogency of the hearsay in question and to be in a position to respond adequately to it. The Commission also appreciated that circumstances can arise in litigation rendering compliance with a notice requirement impracticable. For example, some hearings need to be arranged urgently and in other cases advance notification may carry a real risk of danger to the witness or some other person. For reasons of this kind, it recommended that allowance should be made for the possibility that, in some circumstances, it would be unreasonable and impracticable to give any notice at all. With a view to further maximizing flexibility, it also recommended that the notice provisions should be subject to rules of court to allow them to be disapplied in respect of certain classes of proceedings if, as experience is gained, that is felt to be appropriate; and that the parties should also be free to agree to exclude the notice provisions.[36] Reflecting these recommendations, s 2 of the Act provides as follows:

(1) [37]A party proposing to adduce hearsay evidence in civil proceedings shall, subject to the following provisions of this section, give to the other party or parties to the proceedings—
  (a) such notice (if any) of that fact, and
  (b) on request, such particulars of or relating to the evidence,
  as is reasonable and practicable in the circumstances for the purpose of enabling him or them to deal with any matters arising from its being hearsay.

(2) Provision may be made by rules of court—
  (a) specifying classes of proceedings or evidence in relation to which subsection (1) does not apply, and
  (b) as to the manner in which (including the time within which) the duties imposed by that subsection are to be complied with in the cases where it does apply.

[36] See generally Law Com No 216, Cm 2321 (1993), paras 4.9 and 4.10.

[37] By virtue of r 61.8 of the Criminal Procedure Rules 2013, the Civil Evidence Act 1995, s 2(1), does not apply to evidence in restraint of trade proceedings and receivership proceedings.

(3) Subsection (1) may also be excluded by agreement of the parties; and compliance with the duty to give notice may in any case be waived by the person to whom notice is required to be given.

The relevant rules of court are CPR r 33.2 and 33.3.[38]

33.2 Notice of intention to rely on hearsay evidence

(1) Where a party intends to rely on hearsay evidence at trial and either—
   (a) that evidence is to be given by a witness giving oral evidence; or
   (b) that evidence is contained in a witness statement of a person who is not being called to give oral evidence;
   that party complies with section 2(1)(a) of the Civil Evidence Act 1995 by serving a witness statement on the other parties in accordance with the court's order.[39]

(2) Where paragraph (1)(b) applies, the party intending to rely on the hearsay evidence must, when he serves the witness statement—
   (a) inform the other parties that the witness is not being called to give oral evidence; and
   (b) give the reason why the witness will not be called.

(3) In all other cases where a party intends to rely on hearsay evidence at trial, that party complies with section 2(1)(a) of the Civil Evidence Act 1995 by serving a notice on the other parties which—
   (a) identifies the hearsay evidence;
   (b) states that the party serving the notice proposes to rely on the hearsay evidence at trial; and
   (c) gives the reason why the witness will not be called.

(4) The party proposing to rely on the hearsay evidence must—
   (a) serve the notice no later than the latest date for serving witness statements; and
   (b) if the hearsay evidence is to be in a document, supply a copy to any party who requests him to do so.

33.3 Circumstances in which notice of intention to rely on hearsay evidence is not required

Section 2.1 of the Civil Evidence Act 1995 (duty to give notice of intention to rely on hearsay evidence) does not apply—
   (a) to evidence at hearings other than trials;
   (aa) to an affidavit or witness statement which is to be used at trial but which does not contain hearsay evidence;
   (b) to a statement which a party to a probate action wishes to put in evidence and which is alleged to have been made by the person whose estate is the subject of the proceedings; or
   (c) where the requirement is excluded by a practice direction.

Section 2(4) of the 1995 Act provides as follows:
   (4) A failure to comply with subsection (1), or with rules under subsection (2)(b), does not affect the admissibility of the evidence but may be taken into account by the court—
     (a) in considering the exercise of its powers with respect to the course of proceedings and costs, and
     (b) as a matter adversely affecting the weight to be given to the evidence in accordance with section 4.

---

[38] CPR r 33 does not apply to claims which have been allocated to the small claims track: CPR r 27.2.
[39] See Ch 5.

This subsection reflects the view of the Law Commission that if a party does not give notice, where it would have been reasonable and practicable in all the circumstances for him to have done so, the court should *not* be allowed to refuse to admit evidence.[40] Instead, under s 2(4)(a) of the 1995 Act, the court, in exercise of its inherent powers to control the conduct of the proceedings, may grant an adjournment (to compel a party to perfect an inadequate notice or to allow the recipient time to deal with the effect of late notification) and/or may impose a costs sanction; and under s 2(4)(b), the court may take the non-compliance as a matter reducing the weight to be attached to the evidence.[41]

The power to call witnesses for cross-examination

Where a party adduces hearsay evidence of a statement but does not call the maker of the statement as a witness, and the other party to the proceedings wishes to challenge the statement, it is an obvious safeguard to allow the other party to call the maker with a view to cross-examining him as to both the accuracy of the statement and his credibility as a witness. The other party is allowed to do so under s 3 of the 1995 Act, but only with the leave of the court. Section 3 provides that:

> Rules of court may provide that where a party to civil proceedings adduces hearsay evidence of a statement made by a person and does not call that person as a witness, any other party to the proceedings may, with the leave of the court, call that person as a witness and cross-examine him on the statement as if he had been called by the first-mentioned party and as if the hearsay statement were his evidence in chief.

The relevant rule is CPR r 33.4, which provides as follows:

(1) Where a party—
   (a) proposes to rely on hearsay evidence; and
   (b) does not propose to call the person who made the original statement to give oral evidence,
   the court may, on the application of any other party, permit that party to call the maker of the statement to be cross-examined on the contents of the statement.
(2) An application for permission to cross-examine under this rule must be made not more than 14 days after the day on which a notice of intention to rely on the hearsay evidence was served on the applicant.

If the court considers that the maker of the statement, even if overseas, should attend and be cross-examined at court in person, but the party proposing to rely on the evidence refuses to obey the order of the court, then the consequence will ordinarily be that the party will not be entitled to rely upon the evidence. In such a case, the court has ample powers to exclude the statement under CPR r 32.1.[42]

Rule 33.4 normally applies when a party, having served a witness statement, proposes to rely upon it as hearsay and does not propose to call its maker as a witness. It also applies when, in the event, such a party does not put the statement in as hearsay evidence or call the

---

[40] The Commission was of the view that such a sanction could have the effect of simply reintroducing the rule against hearsay.

[41] See *TSB (Scotland) plc v James Mills (Montrose) Ltd (in receivership)* 1992 SLT 519, a decision under the Civil Evidence (Scotland) Act 1988: in certain circumstances the courts may declare the evidence wholly unreliable, in effect according it no weight.

[42] *Polanski v Condé Nast Publications Ltd* [2004] 1 WLR 387, CA at [22]–[23] and [62]. As to CPR r 32.1, see Ch 2.

witness to give evidence at the trial, and the other party, in reliance upon CPR r 32.5(5)(b),[43] then puts the statement in as hearsay evidence. In these circumstances, the first party may apply to the court for permission to call the maker of the statement to be cross-examined on its contents.[44]

Weighing hearsay evidence

The statutory guidelines on weighing hearsay evidence do not impose any new obligation on the courts but simply indicate the more important factors which a court should bear in mind when it performs its usual function of weighing the evidence before it. The Law Commission recommended such guidelines for two reasons. First, having abolished the exclusionary rule, it wished to place extra emphasis on the need for courts to be vigilant in testing the reliability of such evidence. Secondly, it thought that it was important to deter the parties from abusing abolition of the rule, for example by deliberately failing to give notice or by giving late and inadequate notice,[45] by relying on hearsay evidence in preference to calling a dubious witness to give direct evidence of a fact,[46] or by attempting to conceal an essential witness in a case by amassing hearsay statements on a point.[47] Section 4 of the 1995 Act provides that:

(1) In estimating the weight (if any) to be given to hearsay evidence in civil proceedings the court shall have regard to any circumstances from which any inference can reasonably be drawn as to the reliability or otherwise of the evidence.

(2) Regard may be had, in particular, to the following—

    (a) whether it would have been reasonable and practicable for the party by whom the evidence was adduced to have produced the maker of the original statement as a witness;

    (b) whether the original statement was made contemporaneously with the occurrence or existence of the matters stated;

    (c) whether the evidence involves multiple hearsay;

    (d) whether any person involved had any motive to conceal or misrepresent matters;

    (e) whether the original statement was an edited account, or was made in collaboration with another or for a particular purpose;

    (f) whether the circumstances in which the evidence is adduced as hearsay are such as to suggest an attempt to prevent proper evaluation of its weight.

The phrase 'the original statement', which is used in s 4(2)(a), (b), and (e), is defined as 'the underlying statement (if any) by—(a) in the case of evidence of fact, a person having personal knowledge of that fact, or (b) in the case of evidence of opinion, the person whose opinion it is'.[48]

Section 4(2) will be of particular importance in cases in which hearsay carries inherent dangers, making it difficult for the judge to assess the truth in the absence of the original maker of the statement, as when a defendant to a claim for a possession or anti-social behaviour order is faced in court with serious complaints made by anonymous or absent witnesses about matters that took place, if at all, many months earlier.[49]

---

[43] See Ch 5, under **Witnesses in civil cases, Witness statements**.

[44] *Douglas v Hello! Ltd* [2003] CP Rep 42, CA.

[45] See the 1995 Act, s 4(2)(f).

[46] See the 1995 Act, s 4(2)(a).

[47] See Law Com No 216, Cm 2321 (1993), para 4.19.

[48] Section 13.

[49] *Moat Housing Group South Ltd v Harris* [2006] QB 606, CA, applied in *R (Cleary) v Highbury Corner Magistrates' Court* [2007] 1 WLR 1272, DC.

Concerning s 4(2)(a), it seems that if it would have been reasonable and practicable for the party by whom the evidence was adduced to have produced the maker of the original statement as a witness, an inference as to unreliability may be drawn, a very strong inference indeed if, had the maker been called as a witness, the court would not have granted leave under s 6(2) to adduce evidence of the statement. It also seems that such inferences may be drawn whether or not the maker is called for cross-examination by any other party to the proceedings under s 3, although it may be that such inferences are less likely to be drawn where the other party or parties have *not* applied for leave to call and cross-examine the maker under that section.

As to s 4(2)(d), the obscure phrase 'any person involved' may be taken to include (i) the maker of the 'original statement'; (ii) the 'receiver' of the statement, ie the person who claims to have heard or otherwise perceived the statement and/or to have recorded it in a document; and (iii) in the case of multiple hearsay, ie in cases in which the information contained in the original statement is not supplied to the 'receiver' directly, any intermediaries through whom it was supplied indirectly.

Under s 4(2)(e), whether the 'original statement' was made 'for a particular purpose' (and more importantly, if it was, what that purpose was) has an obvious bearing on its likely reliability. To take an extreme example, the express purpose of the 'original statement' may have been to mislead or deceive. On the other hand, the fact that the 'original statement' was made under an important statutory or other duty may well give rise to a strong inference as to the truth of its contents.

Impeaching credibility

Section 5(2) of the 1995 Act provides that:

> Where in civil proceedings hearsay evidence is adduced and the maker of the original statement, or of any statement relied upon to prove another statement, is not called as a witness—
> (a) evidence which if he had been so called would be admissible for the purpose of attacking or supporting his credibility as a witness is admissible for that purpose in the proceedings; and
> (b) evidence tending to prove that, whether before or after he made the statement, he made any other statement inconsistent with it is admissible for the purpose of showing that he had contradicted himself.
> Provided that evidence may not be given of any matter of which, if he had been called as a witness and had denied that matter in cross-examination, evidence could not have been adduced by the cross-examining party.

The general purpose of s 5(2) is to ensure that evidence relating to the credibility of certain persons not called as witnesses is as admissible as if those persons had been called as witnesses. The persons in question are (i) 'the maker of the original statement' and (ii) 'the maker...of any statement relied upon to prove another statement'. As to the former, it seems that where the maker of the 'original statement', although not called, is available as a witness, evidence is admissible for the purpose of attacking credibility notwithstanding that the party adducing it has elected not to call and cross-examine him (with the leave of the court) under s 3. As to the latter, the meaning of 'another statement' is not clear, but presumably will be taken to mean not 'a statement other than the original statement' but 'either the original statement or any other statement'. Let us suppose that A makes an oral statement (the 'original statement') within the hearing of B; B tells C what A said; C makes a written record of his conversation with B; A, B, and C are all unavailable to give evidence; and C's written record is used to prove A's oral statement. In these circumstances, evidence relating to the credibility of A and C is clearly admissible and, it is submitted, evidence relating to the credibility of B should also be admissible.

Concerning s 5(2)(a), evidence admissible for the purpose of attacking credibility would include evidence of bias or previous convictions. Concerning s 5(2)(b), it seems that whereas in civil proceedings a prior inconsistent statement of a *witness* is not only admissible to attack his credibility but, by virtue of s 6(3) and (5) of the 1995 Act, is also admissible as evidence of any matter stated therein, a prior inconsistent statement introduced under s 5(2)(b) goes to consistency only.[50] The proviso to s 5(2) ensures that the rule on finality of answers on collateral issues[51] operates to restrict the evidence admissible under s 5(2) in the same way as it applies in relation to *witnesses*.

Where a party, in reliance on s 5(2), intends to attack the credibility of the maker of the original statement, he must give notice of his intention to do so, to the party who proposes to give the hearsay statement in evidence, not more than 14 days after the day on which a notice of intention to rely on the hearsay evidence was served on him.[52]

Proof of statements contained in documents

The provisions of the 1995 Act governing the proof of statements contained in documents draw a distinction between (i) documents generally; and (ii) documents which are shown to form part of the records of a business or public authority.[53]

Documents generally

Section 8 of the 1995 Act provides that:

(1) Where a statement contained in a document is admissible as evidence in civil proceedings, it may be proved—
   (a) by the production of that document, or
   (b) whether or not that document is still in existence, by the production of a copy of that document or of the material part of it, authenticated in such manner as the court may approve.
(2) It is immaterial for this purpose how many removes there are between a copy and the original.

A 'document' for these purposes means 'anything in which information of any description is recorded',[54] a definition covering documents in any form and therefore wide enough to include maps, plans, graphs, drawings, photographs, discs, audio tapes, videotapes, films, microfilms, negatives, and computer-generated printouts. A 'copy', in relation to a document, means 'anything onto which information recorded in the document has been copied, by whatever means and whether directly or indirectly',[55] a definition wide enough to cover, inter

---

[50] Although the Law Commission thought it important to preserve the position under the 1968 Act in this regard, cf the 1968 Act, s 7(5).

[51] See Ch 7.

[52] CPR r 33.5.

[53] See also Ch 9, under **Documentary evidence**.

[54] The 1995 Act, s 13.

[55] The 1995 Act, s 13.

alia, a transcript of an audio tape as well as reproductions or still reproductions of the images embodied in films and videotapes, etc, whether enlarged or not.

Concerning s 8(1)(a), 'production' refers not to counsel handing the document to the court, but to a witness who is qualified to do so in accordance with the rules of evidence producing the document and saying what it is.[56] However, although such direct oral evidence is preferable and will carry greater weight, it would seem that the document may also be proved by another hearsay statement admissible under the 1995 Act. Thus, where a statement has been deliberately tape-recorded but its maker is unavailable to produce the tape and give direct evidence that it is the tape he made, it seems that his out-of-court statements to the same effect could be used to prove the tape.[57]

The reference to 'authentication' at the end of s 8(1) appears to relate to the authentication of copies of a document as true copies of the original, and not to proof of the original.[58]

Section 8(2) makes clear that copies of copies may be received in evidence (subject to authentication in such manner as the court may approve).

Records of a business or public authority

Although at one time records of a business or public authority were kept manually and responsibility could often be attributed to an individual record keeper, nowadays record keeping within an organization has been largely taken over by technology and there is often unlikely to be a witness who can give direct evidence of all or any aspects of the compilation of the records kept. For these reasons, the Law Commission recommended that documents certified as forming part of the records of a business or public authority should be capable of being received in evidence without further proof.[59] Section 9 of the 1995 Act provides that:

(1) A document which is shown to form part of the records of a business or public authority may be received in evidence in civil proceedings without further proof.
(2) A document shall be taken to form part of the records of a business or public authority if there is produced to the court a certificate to that effect signed by an officer of the business or authority to which the records belong.
   For this purpose—
   (a) a document purporting to be a certificate signed by an officer of a business or public authority shall be deemed to have been duly given by such an officer and signed by him; and
   (b) a certificate shall be treated as signed by a person if it purports to bear a facsimile of his signature.

The precise scope of s 9(1) is unclear because the word 'records', said to mean 'records in whatever form',[60] is not otherwise defined. Hopefully, the word will not be construed as narrowly as it was under the Civil Evidence Act 1968, where it was taken to mean 'records which a historian would regard as original or primary sources, that is documents which either give effect to a transaction itself or which contain a contemporaneous register of

---

[56] Per Staughton LJ in *Ventouris v Mountain (No 2)* [1992] 1 WLR 887, CA at 901, a decision under the 1968 Act, s 6(1).
[57] *Ventouris v Mountain (No 2)* [1992] 1 WLR 887, CA.
[58] *Ventouris v Mountain (No 2)* [1992] 1 WLR 887, CA.
[59] See Law Com No 216, Cm 2321 (1993), paras 3.12 and 4.39.
[60] Section 9(4).

information supplied by those with direct knowledge of the facts'. Accordingly, copies of documents consisting of summaries of the results of research into a drug and articles and letters about the drug published in medical journals were held not to be records, but merely a digest or analysis of records.[61] On this test, it was said, a bill of lading or cargo manifest,[62] a tithe map,[63] or a transcript of criminal proceedings[64] would rank as a record, but not a file of correspondence[65] or an anonymous document setting out a summary of legal proceedings taken or contemplated against a company.[66] In *Savings and Investment Bank Ltd v Gasco Investments (Netherlands) BV*[67] it was held that a report of inspectors appointed by the Secretary of State for Trade on the affairs and ownership of a company was not a record: it fell short of a compilation of the information supplied because it contained only a selection of that information, and went beyond such a compilation because it also contained the opinions of the inspectors.[68]

Under s 9(4), 'business' includes 'any activity regularly carried on over a period of time, whether for profit or not, by any body (whether corporate or not) or by an individual'; and 'public authority' includes 'any public or statutory undertaking, any government department and any person holding office under Her Majesty'. The wide definition of 'business' reflects the Law Commission's view that it is the quality of regularity that lends a business record its reliability, not the existence of a profit motive or the judicial nature of the person carrying on the activity. A business defined in this way may not have 'officers' in the strict sense of that word and, accordingly, under s 9(4), 'officer' includes 'any person occupying a responsible position in relation to the relevant activities of the business or public authority or in relation to its records'.

Unless the court orders otherwise, a document which may be received in evidence under s 9(1) shall not be receivable at trial unless the party intending to put it in evidence has given notice of his intention to the other parties; and where he intends to use the evidence as evidence of any fact, then he must give notice not later than the latest date for serving witness statements.[69] Where a party has given such notice, he must also give every other party an opportunity to inspect the document and to agree to its admission without further proof.[70]

The Law Commission considered that the absence of an entry in a record should be capable of being formally proved, despite the fact that proving a negative (and drawing inferences from it) is rarely possible by reference to any human source.[71] The most appropriate method of doing this was thought to be by way of affidavit. Section 9(3) provides that:

---

[61] *H v Schering Chemicals Ltd* [1983] 1 WLR 143, QBD.

[62] See *R v Jones; R v Sullivan* [1978] 1 WLR 195, CA, a decision under the Criminal Evidence Act 1965 (see Ch 10).

[63] See *Knight v David* [1971] 1 WLR 1671, Ch D.

[64] See *Taylor v Taylor* [1970] 1 WLR 1148, CA.

[65] See *R v Tirado* (1974) 59 Cr App R 80, CA, a decision under the Criminal Evidence Act 1965. Cf *R v Olisa* [1990] Crim LR 721, CA: for the purposes of the Police and Criminal Evidence Act 1984, s 68, three application forms completed by a customer of a bank did 'form part of a record' compiled by the bank officials.

[66] See *Re Koscot Interplanetary (UK) Ltd, Re Koscot AG* [1972] 3 All ER 829.

[67] [1984] 1 WLR 271, Ch D.

[68] See also *Re D (a minor)* [1986] 2 FLR 189, Fam D: notes of an interview between a solicitor and his client fell short of being a complete record of what was said. They were treated as a selective and necessarily subjective aide memoire.

[69] CPR r 33.6(2), (3), and (4).

[70] CPR r 33.6(8).

[71] See *R v Patel* (1981) 73 Cr App R 117, CA; *R v Shone* (1983) 76 Cr App R 72, CA; and generally Ch 10, under **The admissibility of hearsay under the Criminal Justice Act 2003, The meaning of hearsay in the Criminal Justice Act 2003, Negative hearsay.**

> The absence of an entry in the records of a business or public authority may be proved in civil proceedings by affidavit of an officer of the business or authority to which the records belong.

Presumably, the contents of the affidavit constitute hearsay and are therefore subject to the usual safeguards relating to notice, power to call for cross-examination, and weight.

The Law Commission recognized that, although business and other records have long been treated as belonging to a class of evidence which can be regarded as likely to be reliable, there are bound to be exceptions, and it therefore recommended a specific discretion, allowing courts to disapply the certification provisions.[72] Section 9(5) provides that:

> The court may, having regard to the circumstances of the case, direct that all or any of the above provisions of this section do not apply in relation to a particular document or record, or description of documents or records.

Evidence formerly admissible at common law

General

Section 9 of the Civil Evidence Act 1968 preserved and gave statutory force to a number of common law exceptions to the hearsay rule (informal admissions, published works dealing with matters of a public nature, and public documents and records) without purporting to amend the law in relation to those exceptions. Subject to one important difference, this state of affairs is perpetuated by the 1995 Act. The important difference relates to informal admissions. The Law Commission considered that there was no longer any need to preserve this common law exception and recommended that the general provisions of the Act, including the notice and weight provisions, should apply to informal admissions as they apply to other hearsay statements.[73] Section 7(1) of the 1995 Act gives statutory effect to this recommendation and is considered further under **Informal admissions**. Concerning published works dealing with matters of a public nature, and public documents and records, however, the Commission recommended preserving the relevant common law rules because: (a) some of the statutory provisions which it believed should not be affected by its proposals presuppose the existence of the common law rules about public registers;[74] (b) it was not the policy of the Commission to add the procedural burden of the notice procedure where no such burden already existed; and (c) it would be rare for the weight to be attached to such evidence to be a matter for debate.[75] Section 7(2) gives statutory effect to this recommendation. The common law rules effectively preserved by the 1995 Act are considered in Chapter 12.

Informal admissions

Under s 7(1) of the 1995 Act, 'the common law rule effectively preserved by section 9(1) and (2)(a) of the Civil Evidence Act 1968 (admissibility of admissions adverse to a party) is superseded by the provisions of this Act'. As already noted,[76] the purpose of the subsection is to give

---

[72] Law Com No 216, Cm 2321 (1993), para 4.42.

[73] Law Com No 216, Cm 2321 (1993), paras 4.32 and 4.33.

[74] Evidence (Foreign, Dominion and Colonial Documents) Act 1933, s 1 (see Chs 2 and 12) and the Oaths and Evidence (Overseas Authorities and Countries) Act 1963, s 5.

[75] Law Com No 216, Cm 2321 (1993), para 4.33.

[76] Under **Evidence formerly admissible at common law**, **General**, in this chapter.

effect to the Law Commission's recommendation that the general provisions of the Act should apply to informal admissions.[77]

The application of section 1 of the 1995 Act (admissibility)

At common law an informal admission was a statement by a party to the proceedings (or someone in privity with him) made other than while testifying in those proceedings and adverse to his case. Any such statement is now covered by s 1(1) of the Act and, by reason of the wide statutory definition of statement ('any representation of fact or opinion, however made'), an admission may be admitted whether made orally, in writing, or by conduct, demeanour, or even silence. Thus, as at common law, a person may make an oral admission when talking either to another[78] or to himself.[79] Similarly, in the case of written admissions, the admission may be contained in a communication, such as a letter, or in a diary or other private memorandum.[80] A common law example of an admission by conduct is *Moriarty v London, Chatham and Dover Rly Co*,[81] where evidence of the plaintiff's conduct in suborning witnesses was admitted as an admission by him of the weakness and falsity of his claim. Where an out-of-court accusation is made against a party, his answer, whether given by words or conduct, may constitute an admission insofar as it amounts to an acknowledgment of the truth of the whole or part of the accusation made. Presumably, even silence, by way of reply, will amount to a 'statement' where the accusation is made in circumstances such that it would be reasonable to expect some explanation or denial. At common law, in *Wiedemann v Walpole*[82] Lord Esher MR said that, in the case of a letter written upon a matter of business, the court could take notice of the ordinary course adopted by men of business to answer letters the contents of which they do not intend to admit, so that a failure to reply to such a letter could be taken as some evidence of the truth of the statements contained in it, but that a man could not reasonably be expected to reply to a letter charging him with some offence or impropriety because 'it is the ordinary and wise practice of mankind not to answer such letters'.[83]

The application of section 4 of the Act (weight)

Section 4 of the 1995 Act applies to informal admissions as it applies to other hearsay statements. However, there are a number of special considerations which are relevant to the weighing of admissions. Some of these are of a general character, but there are also two specific considerations: whether the admission relates to facts of which its maker had no personal knowledge, and whether the admission was vicarious, ie made by someone in privity with a party to legal proceedings.

General considerations

The weight to be attached to an informal admission depends upon its precise contents, the circumstances in which it was made (for example whether it was made as a result of some threat or inducement), and any contradictory or other evidence adduced by its maker at the trial with a view to explaining it away. In some cases, the tribunal of fact will need to consider carefully whether the statement is, in fact, adverse to the case of its maker, and for this purpose

---

[77] Section 3, however, could hardly apply to an informal admission made by a party to legal proceedings (as opposed to someone in privity with him): it would involve that party calling and cross-examining himself!

[78] See *Rumping v DPP* [1964] AC 814, HL (the maker's wife).

[79] See per Alderson B in *R v Simons* (1834) 6 C&P 540.

[80] See *Bruce v Garden* (1869) 18 WR 384.

[81] (1870) LR 5 QB 314. See also *Alderson v Clay* (1816) 1 Stark 405.

[82] [1891] 2 QB 534, CA.

[83] Cf *Bessela v Stern* (1877) 2 CPD 265, CA.

regard should be had to the whole statement, including any passages favourable to its maker which qualify, explain, or even nullify so much of the statement as is relied upon as an admission. Although it may be that less weight may be attached to the favourable or self-serving parts of the statement,[84] it is clear that under the 1995 Act they are as much evidence of the facts they state as the passages relied upon as constituting an admission.[85]

Personal knowledge

An informal admission may be admitted under the 1995 Act notwithstanding that it relates to facts of which its maker has no personal knowledge[86] or amounts to no more than an expression of opinion or belief.[87] The weight to be attached to such evidence will vary according to the circumstances. For example, an admission by a party as to his age, although obviously based on hearsay, concerns a matter as to which it is reasonable to expect that he has been accurately informed.[88] On the other hand, in *Comptroller of Customs v Western Lectric Co Ltd*,[89] the Privy Council was of the view that an admission concerning the countries of origin of certain imported goods, made in reliance on the fact that the goods bore marks and labels indicating that they came from those countries, was evidentially worthless.[90]

Vicarious admissions

The rationale of the common law exception was the presumed unlikelihood of a person speaking falsely against his own interest, a rationale reflected in the rule that an informal admission could only be received in evidence if it was made directly (ie by a party to the legal proceedings) or vicariously (ie by someone in privity with a party). 'Privity' in this context usually denoted some common or successive interest in the subject matter of the litigation or some other relationship between the party and the privy, for example that of principal and agent, whereby the latter had actual or imputed authority to speak on behalf of the former. Under the 1995 Act, an out-of-court statement adverse to the case of a party may be received in evidence whether made by that party or by *anyone else*. However, the weight to be attached to an admission made by someone who, at common law, would have been in privity with a party is generally likely to be greater than an admission made by anyone else.

Those in privity included: (i) a predecessor in title of a party to proceedings (provided that the admission concerned title to the property in question and was made at a time when he had an interest in the property);[91] (ii) a partner (an admission or representation made by any partner concerning the partnership affairs and in the ordinary course of its business being evidence against the firm);[92] (iii) referees;[93] and (iv) agents. At common law, an admission by an

---

[84] See *Smith v Blandy* (1825) Ry&M 257.

[85] See *Harrison v Turner* (1847) 10 QB 482.

[86] Under s 1(2)(b), 'references to hearsay include hearsay of whatever degree'.

[87] Under s 13, a 'statement' is defined to include 'any representation of opinion'.

[88] See, at common law, *R v Turner* [1910] 1 KB 346, CCA and *Lustre Hosiery Ltd v York* (1936) 54 CLR 134, High Court of Australia.

[89] [1966] AC 367.

[90] [1966] AC 367 per Lord Hodson at 371.

[91] *Woolway v Rowe* (1834) 1 Ad&El 114. See also *Smith v Smith* (1836) 3 Bing NC 29.

[92] See the Partnership Act 1890, s 15, giving statutory force to a common law principle to the same effect. See also *Jaggers v Binnings* (1815) 1 Stark 64 and *Wood v Braddick* (1808) 1 Taunt 104.

[93] *Williams v Innes* (1808) 1 Camp 364, KB, where Lord Ellenborough CJ said (at 365): 'If a man refers another upon any particular business to a third person, he is bound by what this third person says or does concerning it, as much as if that had been said or done by himself.'

agent could only be received against his principal if (a) it was made at a time when the agency existed (a matter which, apparently, could be inferred from the statements and conduct of the alleged agent himself);[94] (b) the communication in which it was made was authorized, whether expressly or by implication, by the principal;[95] and (c) it was made in the course of a communication with some third party as opposed to the principal himself.[96] Under the 1995 Act, failure to establish these three matters will not affect admissibility, but is likely to affect adversely the weight to be attached to the 'admission'.

The weight to be attached to an 'admission' made by someone who at common law would not have been in privity with a party is generally likely to be less than an admission made by that party himself or someone who would have been in privity with him. At common law there was no privity between (i) spouses, merely by virtue of their relationship of husband and wife; (ii) a parent and a child, merely by virtue of that relationship;[97] (iii) co-parties, ie co-plaintiffs or co-defendants (or, in divorce proceedings, a respondent and a co-respondent);[98] or (iv) a witness and the party calling him.[99]

Ogden tables

Section 10 of the 1995 Act provides that:

> The actuarial tables (together with explanatory notes) for use in personal injury and fatal accident cases issued from time to time by the Government Actuary's Department are admissible in evidence for the purpose of assessing, in an action for personal injury, the sum to be awarded as general damages for future pecuniary loss.

ADDITIONAL READING

Law Commission, *The Hearsay Rule in Civil Proceedings*, Cm 2321 (Law Com No 216, London, 1993).

---

[94] See, *sed quaere, Edwards v Brookes (Milk) Ltd* [1963] 1 WLR 795, QBD.

[95] *Wagstaff v Wilson* (1832) 4 B&Ad 339; *G (A) v G (T)* [1970] 2 QB 643, CA; and *Johnson v Lindsay* (1889) 53 JP 599, DC. See also *Burr v Ware RDC* [1939] 2 All ER 688, CA and cf *Beer v W H Clench (1930) Ltd* [1936] 1 All ER 449, DC.

[96] See *Re Devala Provident Gold Mining Co* (1883) 22 Ch D 593, and cf *The Solway* (1885) 10 PD 137, P, D and Admlty.

[97] *G (A) v G (T)* [1970] 2 QB 643, CA.

[98] *Morton v Morton, Daly and McNaught* [1937] P 151, P, D and Admlty and *Myatt v Myatt and Parker* [1962] 1 WLR 570, P, D and Admlty.

[99] See *British Thomson-Houston Co Ltd v British Insulated and Helsby Cables Ltd* [1924] 2 Ch 160, CA and cf *Richards v Morgan* (1863) 4 B&S 641.

Hearsay admissible at common law

12

Key issues

- If a statement is made out of court and tendered as evidence of the facts asserted (hearsay), why should it be admissible when:
  - it was made in a public document, eg a public register;
  - it was made in a work of reference dealing with a matter of a public nature, eg histories and maps;
  - it was made by a person who, at the time, was emotionally overpowered by an event, eg a victim of a serious assault; or
  - it relates to the contemporaneous physical sensation or mental state of its maker?

Under the common law rule against hearsay, any assertion, other than one made by a person while giving oral evidence in the proceedings, was inadmissible if tendered as evidence of the facts asserted. As we have seen in Chapters 10 and 11, the circumstances in which hearsay is admissible in criminal proceedings are now governed by Chapter 2 of Pt 11 of the Criminal Justice Act 2003 (the 2003 Act), and in civil proceedings hearsay is admissible subject to compliance with the conditions of admissibility set out in the Civil Evidence Act 1995 (the 1995 Act). The categories of hearsay considered in this chapter—statements in public documents, works of reference, evidence of age, evidence of reputation, and statements forming part of the *res gestae*—share two common features: all of them were established at common law as exceptions to the rule against hearsay and all of them have been preserved by statute. All of the cases considered, apart from evidence of age and *res gestae* statements, have been expressly preserved and given statutory force in both criminal proceedings (by s 118(1) of the 2003 Act) and civil proceedings (by s 7(2) and (3) of the 1995 Act). The categories relating to evidence of age and statements forming part of the *res gestae* have been preserved in criminal but not civil proceedings. However, evidence formerly admissible in these cases at common law will now be admissible in civil proceedings under the general provisions of the 1995 Act.

It is convenient to consider the common law rules separately, here, under the rubric of hearsay admissible at common law, because neither s 118 of the 2003 Act nor s 7 of the 1995 Act purports to amend the rules to which they have given statutory force. Section 7(4) of the 1995 Act provides that the words in which a rule of law mentioned in the s is described 'are intended only to identify the rule and shall not be construed as altering it in any way'; and although there is no express equivalent in s 118 of the 2003 Act, it is plain that it too is designed to identify rules of law rather than alter them. Furthermore, where evidence is admissible under one of the preserved rules, it is not subject to other statutory conditions of admissibility and safeguards. However, the common law exceptions have been narrowly construed, and much evidence failing to meet all of the common law conditions of admissibility may well be admissible in civil proceedings under the general provisions of the 1995 Act (subject to compliance with the statutory conditions) and in criminal proceedings under statutory provisions of a general nature such as ss 116 and 117 of the 2003 Act (cases where a witness is unavailable and business and other documents).

Statements in public documents

Section 7(2)(b) and (c) of the 1995 Act preserve any rule of law whereby in civil proceedings—

(b) public documents (for example, public registers, and returns made under public authority with respect to matters of public interest) are admissible as evidence of the facts stated in them, or
(c) records (for example, the records of certain courts, treaties, Crown grants, pardons and commissions) are admissible as evidence of facts stated in them.

Section 118(1)1(b) and (c) of the 2003 Act preserve the same rules in criminal proceedings.

General

At common law, statements made in most public documents are admissible in both civil and criminal cases as evidence of the matters stated.[1] The admissibility of such evidence may be

---

[1] Concerning proof of the contents of a public document upon which a party seeks to rely, see Ch 9.

plans generally offered for sale to the public, even if not prepared by someone acting under a public duty, concerning facts of geographical notoriety.[44]

Evidence of age

Section 118(1)1(d) of the 2003 Act preserves the following rule of law in criminal proceedings:

> (d) evidence relating to a person's age or date or place of birth may be given by a person without personal knowledge of the matter.

Since the date of a person's birth is contained in his or her birth certificate, the normal way of proving a person's age is to produce a certified copy of an entry in the register of births, which is admissible under s 34 of the Births and Deaths Registration Act 1953 as evidence of the matters stated, accompanied by some evidence to identify the person whose age is in question with the person named in the certificate. At common law, accompanying evidence of identification may be given by a person without personal knowledge of the matter, such as the evidence of a grandmother who, although present at the birth of her grandchild, was not present at the registration.[45] Similarly, the courts have acted on evidence as to age given by the person whose age is in question[46] or by another who has made enquiries as to his or her age.[47]

Evidence of reputation

Section 7(3)(a) and (b) of the 1995 Act provide as follows:

> The common law rules . . . whereby in civil proceedings
> (a) evidence of a person's reputation is admissible for the purpose of establishing his good or bad character, or
> (b) evidence of reputation or family tradition is admissible—
>> (i) for the purpose of proving or disproving pedigree or the existence of a marriage,[48] or
>> (ii) for the purpose of proving or disproving the existence of any public or general right or of identifying any person or thing,
>> shall continue to have effect in so far as they authorise the court to treat such evidence as proving or disproving that matter.
> Where any such rule applies, reputation or family tradition shall be treated for the purposes of this Act as a fact and not as a statement or multiplicity of statements about the matter in question.

As to the concluding part of s 7(3), it is born of a recognition that evidence of reputation or family tradition, if tendered to establish the facts reputed or the facts according to family tradition, is necessarily composed of a multiplicity of hearsay statements and therefore, if treated as such in civil proceedings, would render impossible application of the notice and weighing provisions of the 1995 Act.[49] The effect of treating such evidence as evidence of fact,

---

[44] See *R v Orton* (1873) and *R v Jameson* (1896) *Stephen's Digest of the Law of Evidence* (10th edn) 48.

[45] *R v Weaver* (1873) LR 2 CCR 85. See also *Wilton & Co v Phillips* (1903) 19 TLR 390, KBD.

[46] *Re Bulley's Settlement* [1886] WN 80, Ch D.

[47] *R v Bellis* (1911) 6 Cr App R 283, CCA; *R (Y) v The London Borough of Hillingdon* [2011] EWHC 1477 (Admin).

[48] The rule preserved by s 7(3)(b)(i) for the purpose of proof or disproof of the existence of a marriage applies in an equivalent way for the purpose of proof or disproof of the existence of a civil partnership: see the Civil Partnership Act 2004, s 84(5).

[49] Law Commission, *The Hearsay Rule in Civil Proceedings*, Report No 216, Cm 2321 (1993), para 4.34.

in contrast, is that the party proposing to adduce the evidence will not be expected to give to the other party to the proceedings particulars of the person who had personal knowledge of the matter in question and of all the intermediaries through whom the information was conveyed to the declarant;[50] and the court, in assessing the weight of the evidence, will not be expected to have regard to a factor such as whether the person with personal knowledge made the 'original statement' contemporaneously with the occurrence or existence of the matters stated.[51]

Section 118(1)2 and 3 of the 2003 Act preserve, in criminal proceedings, the same rules as those identified in s 7(3)(a) and (b) of the 1995 Act. They also make clear that the rules are preserved in criminal proceedings only insofar as they allow the court to treat such evidence as proving the matter concerned. Thus if the matter concerned should not be open to proof of any kind, because that would be to introduce, for example, inadmissible evidence of bad character, then plainly the matter cannot be proved under any of the preserved common law rules.

Evidence of reputation for the purpose of establishing good or bad character requires no further explanation. The other preserved common law rules are technical and complex and are, perhaps, best considered under two headings, declarations as to pedigree and declarations as to public and general rights.

Declarations as to pedigree

At common law, a declaration concerning pedigree is admissible, after its maker's death, as evidence of the truth of its contents. This exception to the hearsay rule has been justified on the grounds that such declarations are often the only evidence that can be obtained concerning facts which may have occurred many years before the trial.[52] Matters of pedigree concern the relationship by blood or marriage between persons and therefore include, for example, the fact and date of births, marriages, and deaths, legitimacy, celibacy, failure of issue, and intestacy. Pedigree declarations may be oral, for example, declarations by deceased parents that one of their children, whose legitimacy is in issue, was born before their marriage; in writing, for example an entry in a family Bible, an inscription on a tombstone or a pedigree hung up in the family home; or by conduct, as when parents always treat one child as illegitimate and introduce and treat another child as the heir of the family.[53] There are three conditions of admissibility. First, the declaration is only admissible in proceedings in which a question of pedigree is directly in issue.[54] Second, the declaration must have been made by a blood relation or the spouse of a blood relation as opposed to, for example, relations in law,[55] domestic servants, or intimate acquaintances.[56] There is no requirement, however, of personal knowledge on the part of the declarant as to the facts stated, which may amount to no more than family tradition or reputation handed down from one generation to another.[57] Third,

---

[50] See the 1995 Act, s 2 (see Ch 11).

[51] See the 1995 Act, s 4 (see Ch 11).

[52] See per Best CJ in *Johnston v Lawson* (1824) 2 Bing 86 at 89 and generally per Lord Mansfield CJ in the *Berkeley Peerage Case* (1811) 4 Camp 401, HL.

[53] Per Lord Mansfield CJ in *Goodright d Stevens v Moss* (1777) 2 Cowp 591. See also *Vowles v Young* (1806) 13 Ves 140 (engravings upon rings).

[54] *Haines v Guthrie* (1884) 13 QBD 818, CA.

[55] *Shrewsbury Peerage Case* (1858) 7 HL Cas 1.

[56] *Johnson v Lawson* (1824) 2 Bing 86.

[57] *Davies v Lowndes* (1843) 6 Man&G 471; *Doe d Banning v Griffin* (1812) 15 East 293.

the declaration must have been made *ante litem motam*, that is before any controversy arose upon the matter in question.[58] The controversy may create bias in the minds of members of the family rendering their declarations unreliable. However, provided that the declaration was made *ante litem motam*, the fact that the declarant had an interest in establishing the relationship in question would appear to go only to weight and not admissibility.[59]

Declarations as to public and general rights

At common law, an oral or written statement concerning the reputed existence of a public or general right is admissible, after its maker's death, as evidence of the existence of that right. The primary justification for the admissibility of such evidence is the fact that other evidence, especially in the case of ancient rights, is usually unavailable. The declaration must concern a public or general and not a private right,[60] unless the private right coincides with a public right. Thus when a question arises as to the boundary of a private estate that is conterminous with a hamlet, evidence of reputation concerning the boundary of the latter is admissible to prove the boundary of the former.[61] Public rights are those common to the public at large, such as rights to use paths,[62] highways,[63] ferries,[64] or landing-places on the banks of a river.[65] General rights are those common to a section of the public or a considerable class of persons, such as the inhabitants of a parish or the tenants of a manor.[66] In the case of a public right, it seems that any person is competent to make a declaration as to its reputed existence, because it concerns everyone, and the fact that the declarant has no knowledge of the subject goes only to weight, not admissibility. A declaration as to general rights, however, is only admissible if it was made by a person with some connection with or knowledge of the matter in question.[67] There are two further conditions of admissibility and these apply whether the declaration concerns public or general rights. First, as in the case of declarations as to pedigree, the declaration must have been made *ante litem motam*.[68] Second, the declaration must concern the reputed existence of the right in question and not particular facts tending to support or negative the existence of that right.[69]

---

[58] *Berkeley Peerage Case* (1811) 4 Camp 401, HL; *Shedden v A-G* (1860) 2 Sw&Tr 170; and *Butler v Mountgarret* (1859) 7 HL Cas 633.

[59] *Doe d Tilman v Tarver* (1824) Ry&M 141; *Doe d Jenkins v Davies* (1847) 10 QB 314. But see *Plant v Taylor* (1861) 7 H&N 211.

[60] *Lonsdale v Heaton* (1830) 1 You 58.

[61] *Thomas v Jenkins* (1837) 6 Ad&El 525. See also *Stoney v Eastbourne RDC* [1927] 1 Ch 367, CA.

[62] See *Radcliffe v Marsden UDC* (1908) 72 JP 475 Ch D.

[63] See *R v Bliss* (1837) 7 Ad&El 550. See now Highways Act 1980, s 32.

[64] *Pim v Curell* (1840) 6 M&W 234.

[65] *Drinkwater v Porter* (1835) 7 C&P 181.

[66] *Nicholls v Parker* (1805) 14 East 331. However, numerous private rights of common of the several tenants of a manor do not amount to one public right: see *Earl of Dunraven v Llewellyn* (1850) 15 QB 791. See also *White v Taylor* [1969] 1 Ch 150, Ch D (individual rights of pasturage for sheep).

[67] See *Berkeley Peerage Case* (1811) 4 Camp 401, HL; *Rogers v Wood* (1831) 2 B&Ad 245; and *Crease v Barrett* (1835) 1 Cr M&R 919.

[68] *Berkeley Peerage Case* (1811) 4 Camp 401, HL. See also *Moseley v Davies* (1822) 11 Price 162.

[69] *Mercer v Denne* [1905] 2 Ch 538, CA. See also *R v Bliss* (1837) 7 Ad&El 550.

Statements forming part of the *res gestae*

'*Res gestae*', it has been said, is 'a phrase adopted to provide a respectable legal cloak for a variety of cases to which no formula of precision can be applied'.[70] The words themselves simply mean a transaction. Under the inclusionary common law doctrine of *res gestae*, a fact or a statement of fact or opinion which is so closely associated in time, place, and circumstances with some act, event, or state of affairs which is in issue that it can be said to form a part of the same transaction as the act or event in issue, is itself admissible in evidence. The justification given for the reception of such evidence is the light that it sheds upon the act or event in issue: in its absence, the transaction in question may not be fully or truly understood and may even appear to be meaningless, inexplicable, or unintelligible. Despite judicial dicta to the contrary,[71] it is clear from the authorities that such statements have been received by way of exception to the common law rule against hearsay as evidence of the matters asserted. The multiplicity of cases in which hearsay statements have been received under the doctrine were usefully subdivided, by the late Sir Rupert Cross, into the following categories: (i) statements by participants in or observers of events or, as they would more accurately be described in the light of subsequent developments, statements by persons emotionally overpowered by an event; (ii) statements accompanying the maker's performance of an act; (iii) statements relating to a physical sensation; and (iv) statements relating to a mental state. The same categorization has been used in the 2003 Act to identify the common law rules preserved and put on a statutory footing.

In *R v Callender*[72] the Court of Appeal said that *res gestae* is a single principle and that a statement can only be admitted under the *res gestae* exception to the hearsay rule if the trial judge is satisfied that there is no real possibility of concoction or distortion. This dictum, it is submitted, has been made *per incuriam*. The requirement referred to only applies to *res gestae* statements in the first of the categories set out above.

Statements by persons emotionally overpowered by an event

Section 118(1)4(a) of the 2003 Act preserves the following rule of law in criminal proceedings:

> Any rule of law under which in criminal proceedings a statement is admissible as evidence of any matter stated if—
>> (a) the statement was made by a person so emotionally overpowered by an event that the possibility of concoction or distortion can be disregarded.

Statements made concerning an event in issue in circumstances of such spontaneity or involvement in the event that the possibility of concoction, distortion, or error can be disregarded, are admissible as evidence of the truth of their contents. One of the earliest illustrations of the principle is to be found in *Thompson v Trevanion*,[73] where 'what the wife said immediate upon the hurt received and before that she had time to devise or contrive anything for her own advantage' was held to be admissible in evidence. In *R v Foster*,[74] on a charge of

---

[70] Per Lord Tomlin in *Homes v Newman* [1931] 2 Ch 112, Ch D at 120.

[71] See, eg, per Lord Atkinson in *R v Christie* [1914] AC 545, HL at 553 and per Dixon J in *Adelaide Chemical and Fertilizer Co Ltd v Carlyle* (1940) 64 CLR 514 (High Court of Australia) at 531.

[72] [1998] Crim LR 337, CA.

[73] (1693) Skin 402.

[74] (1834) 6 C&P 325 (Central Criminal Court).

manslaughter by reckless driving, a statement made by the deceased immediately after he had been run down was admitted to show the cause of the accident.[75]

To the extent that some of the earlier cases were decided without regard to the likelihood of concoction, distortion, or error, but merely on the basis of whether the statement was spontaneous in the sense that it could be regarded as part of the event in question, they must be treated with considerable caution. Thus it has been said that *R v Bedingfield*,[76] one of the most famous cases on the subject, 'is more useful as a focus for discussion than for the decision on the facts'.[77] Bedingfield was charged with the murder of a woman. The deceased, her throat cut, came out of a room where she had been with the accused and immediately exclaimed, 'Oh dear, Aunt, see what Bedingfield has done to me!' Cockburn CJ held that although statements made while the act is being done, such as 'Don't, Harry!' are admissible, the victim's statement could not be received in evidence because 'it was something stated by her after it was all over, whatever it was, and after the act was completed'. Commenting upon this decision in *Ratten v R*,[78] Lord Wilberforce said: 'though in a historical sense the emergence of the victim could be described as a different "*res*" from the cutting of the throat, there could hardly be a case where the words uttered carried more clearly the mark of spontaneity and intense involvement.' It follows, of course, that *R v Bedingfield* would be decided differently today.[79]

In *Ratten v R*, Ratten was convicted of the murder of his wife by shooting her. His defence was that a gun went off accidentally while he was cleaning it. An appeal to the Privy Council concerned the admissibility of the evidence of a telephonist that around the time of the shooting she had received a call from Ratten's house made by a sobbing woman who in a hysterical voice had said, 'Get me the police please'. It was held that the evidence was not hearsay and was properly admitted because of its relevance to the issues.[80] However, it was also held that had the statement contained an element of hearsay (i.e. if the words used by the wife amounted to an implied assertion of truth that she was being attacked by her husband) it would have been admissible as part of the *res gestae*. Not only was there a close association in place and time between the statement and the shooting, but also the way in which the statement came to be made, in a call for the police, and the tone of voice used, showed intrinsically that the statement was being forced from the wife by an overwhelming pressure of contemporary events.[81]

In *Ratten v R*, Lord Wilberforce, delivering the reasons of the Board, said:[82]

> the test should be not the uncertain one whether the making of the statement was in some sense part of the event or transaction. This may often be difficult to establish: such external matters as the time which elapses between the events and the speaking of the words (or vice versa), and differences in location being relevant factors but not, taken by themselves, decisive criteria. As regards statements made after the event it must be for the judge, by preliminary ruling, to satisfy himself that the statement was so clearly made in circumstances of spontaneity or involvement

---

[75] See also *Davies v Fortior Ltd* [1952] 1 All ER 1359, QBD where the statement in question would now be admissible under the Civil Evidence Act 1995.

[76] (1879) 14 Cox CC 341, Assizes; cf *R v Fowkes* (1856) The Times, 8 Mar (see Ch 6).

[77] Per Lord Wilberforce in *Ratten v R* [1972] AC 378, PC at 390.

[78] [1972] AC 378, PC.

[79] Per Lord Ackner in *R v Andrews* [1987] AC 281, HL.

[80] See Ch 10.

[81] By contrast, see *R v Newport* [1998] Crim LR 581, CA: evidence of the contents of a telephone call made by the victim of a murder to her friend 20 minutes before she was stabbed had been improperly admitted because the call was not a spontaneous and unconsidered reaction to an immediately impending emergency.

[82] [1972] AC 378, PC at 389.

in the event that the possibility of concoction can be disregarded. Conversely, if he considers that the statement was made by way of narrative of a detached prior event so that the speaker was so disengaged from it as to be able to construct or adapt his account, he should exclude it. And the same must in principle be true of statements made before the event. The test should be not the uncertain one, whether the making of the statement should be regarded as part of the event or transaction. This may often be difficult to show. But if the drama, leading up to the climax, has commenced and assumed such intensity and pressure that the utterance can safely be regarded as a true reflection of what was unrolling or actually happening, it ought to be received.

This test was applied by the Court of Appeal in *R v Nye, R v Loan*,[83] and *R v Turnbull*,[84] and affirmed, by the House of Lords, in *R v Andrews*.[85] In *R v Nye, R v Loan*, Loan was convicted of 'road rage' assault. Following a collision between two cars, Loan, the passenger from one of the cars, assaulted Lucas, the driver of the other, by punching him in the face. Shaken, Lucas sat in his car waiting for the effect of the assault to subside. The police arrived shortly afterwards and Lucas made a statement in the police station only a few yards away in which he identified Loan, as opposed to the driver of the other car, as his assailant. The Court of Appeal added what was described as a gloss to the test in *Ratten*, namely 'was there any real possibility of error?'[86] The court was satisfied that there had been no opportunity for concoction and no chance of error and held that Lucas' statement had been properly admitted under the *res gestae* principle as a spontaneous identification. Lawton LJ said:[87]

> Was there an opportunity for concoction? The interval of time was very short indeed. During part of that interval Mr Lucas was sitting down in his car trying to overcome the effects of the blows which had been struck. Commonsense and experience of life tells us that in that interval he would not be thinking of concocting a case against anybody.

Similarly in *R v Andrews*, the House of Lords held that the statement of the victim purporting to identify the person who had stabbed him was properly admitted under the *res gestae* doctrine. The statement was made to police officers who had arrived within minutes and was admissible even though a police officer inaccurately recorded the name spoken ('Donovan' instead of 'Donald') and the victim had been drinking to excess and had a motive to fabricate because he bore malice against the accused. Lord Ackner summarized the relevant principles to be applied as follows:[88]

(1) The primary question which the judge must ask himself is: can the possibility of concoction or distortion be disregarded?

---

[83] (1977) 66 Cr App R 252, CA.

[84] (1984) 80 Cr App R 104, CA. Statements by the victim which purported to identify the person who had stabbed him were admissible under the *res gestae* principle as stated in *Ratten*. Having been stabbed, the victim staggered to a public house 100 yards away where he had made the statements in response to being asked who had stabbed him, and repeated the statements in an ambulance which had arrived three minutes later. The evidence was admitted despite the victim having been drinking heavily and speaking with a strong Scottish accent. See also *R v Saunders* [2012] EWCA Crim 1185.

[85] [1987] AC 281, HL.

[86] But see further, *R v Andrews* [1987] AC 281, HL under **Statements forming part of the *res gestae*, Statements by persons emotionally overpowered by an event, Res gestae statements by an available witness.**

[87] (1977) 66 Cr App R 252 at 256.

[88] [1987] AC 281 at 300–1. See also *R v Carnall* [1995] Crim LR 944, CA. Applying *Andrews*, the statement of a victim of stabbing in which he identified his attacker was admissible under the *res gestae* principle despite the fact that the victim had crawled for an hour before finding help and the statement was only made in response to questions. It was held that, although the victim had been dishonest in the past, his thoughts would have been so dominated by what had happened that they would not have been affected by reasoning after the event or by fabrication.

(2) To answer that question the judge must first consider the circumstances in which the particular statement was made, in order to satisfy himself that the event was so unusual or startling or dramatic as to dominate the thoughts of the victim, so that his utterance was an instinctive reaction to that event, thus giving no real opportunity for reasoned reflection. In such a situation the judge would be entitled to conclude that the involvement or pressure of the event would exclude the possibility of concoction or distortion, providing that the statement was made in conditions of approximate but not exact contemporaneity.

(3) In order for the statement to be sufficiently 'spontaneous' it must be so closely associated with the event which has excited the statement that it can fairly be stated that the mind of the declarant was still dominated by the event. Thus the judge must be satisfied that the event which provided the trigger mechanism for the statement was still operative. The fact that the statement was made in answer to a question is but one factor to consider under this heading.

(4) Quite apart from the time factor, there may be special features in the case, which relate to the possibility of concoction or distortion. In the instant appeal the defence relied on evidence to support the contention that the deceased had a motive of his own to fabricate or concoct, namely a malice...The judge must be satisfied that the circumstances were such that, having regard to the special feature of malice, there was no possibility of any concoction or distortion to the advantage of the maker or the disadvantage of the accused.

(5) As to the possibility of error in the facts narrated in the statement, if only the ordinary fallibility of human recollection is relied on, this goes to the weight to be attached to and not to the admissibility of the statement and is therefore a matter for the jury. However, here again there may be special features that may give rise to the possibility of error. In the instant case there was evidence that the deceased had drunk to excess...Another example would be where the identification was made in circumstances of particular difficulty or where the declarant suffered from defective eyesight. In such circumstances the trial judge must consider whether he can exclude the possibility of error.

Res gestae statements by an available witness

In *R v Andrews* Lord Ackner said that while he accepted that the doctrine admits hearsay statements not only where the declarant is dead or otherwise not available but also when he is called as a witness, he would strongly deprecate any attempt in criminal prosecutions to use the doctrine as a device to avoid calling the maker of the statement, when available.[89] However, it is clear from *Attorney General's Reference (No 1 of 2003)*[90] that this dictum is not to be treated as an extra bar, in law, to admissibility. W was charged with a serious assault on his mother. The prosecution proposed to call witnesses to give evidence that they found Mrs W lying by the steps of her house greatly distressed and had implicated her son, saying, among other things, 'He's gone bonkers. He threw me downstairs and set me on fire. Phone the police and the ambulance.' The prosecution did not intend to call the mother because they believed that she would give untruthful evidence and exculpate her son. She had declined to make a witness statement but had made a deposition in which she said that she was not

---

[89] [1987] AC 281, HL at 302. This dictum was applied in *Tobi v Nicholas* [1987] Crim LR 774, DC. See also *Edwards and Osakwe v DPP* [1992] Crim LR 576, DC: the dictum does not prevent the admission of a *res gestae* statement of a person who is served with a witness summons but fails to attend trial.

[90] [2003] 2 Cr App R 453, CA.

prepared to attend court to give evidence against her son. The judge held that the evidence of the witnesses was inadmissible. As a result, the prosecution offered no evidence and not guilty verdicts were entered. The Court of Appeal held that once evidence is within the *res gestae* exception it is admissible and there is no rider, in law, that it is not to be admitted if better evidence is available or because the maker of the statement is available to give evidence. However, the judge should entertain an application to exclude the evidence under s 78 of the Police and Criminal Evidence Act 1984 (the 1984 Act). If the purpose of the Crown was to adduce *res gestae* evidence without any opportunity for the defence to cross-examine the maker of the statement, the court might well conclude that the evidence would have such an adverse effect on the fairness of the proceedings that it ought to be excluded. As a general principle, the Crown should not be permitted to rely on such part of a victim's evidence as they considered reliable, without being prepared to tender the victim to the defence, so that the defence can challenge that part of the victim's evidence on which the Crown seeks to rely and elicit that part of her evidence on which the defence might seek to rely. Applying these principles to the facts of the case, the Court of Appeal concluded that it had effectively come to the same conclusion as the judge, the difference being that whereas the judge had erroneously added an extra legal bar to admissibility, their Lordships would have excluded the evidence under s 78 of the 1984 Act.

Res gestae statements by an accused

The *res gestae* doctrine applies whether the statement was made by the victim of the offence, a bystander, or even, in appropriate circumstances, the accused himself. In *R v Glover*[91] a man assaulted J and was forcibly restrained. In anger, he then uttered the words, 'I am David Glover...', followed by a threat to shoot J and his family. Despite the possibility that the assailant was not Glover but deliberately pretending to be him, the words were held to be admissible on the basis that the opportunity for concoction or distortion was so unlikely that it could be disregarded.

Proof

Concerning the nature of the proof required to establish that a statement was made in such conditions of involvement or pressure that the possibility of concoction or error can be ruled out, it would appear that although the trial judge may refer to the contents of the statement itself, the necessary connection between the statement and the event cannot be shown *solely* by reference to those contents because 'otherwise the statement would be lifting itself into the area of admissibility'.[92]

Directions to the jury

Concerning the summing-up, in *R v Andrews* it was held that the judge should make it clear to the jury that it is for them to decide what was said and that they should be sure that the witnesses were not mistaken in what they believed to have been said. The jury should also be satisfied that the declarant did not concoct or distort and, if there is material to raise the issue, that he was not activated by malice or ill-will. Further, the jury's attention should be drawn to any special features that bear on the possibility of mistake. In some cases judges may think

---

[91] [1991] Crim LR 48, CA.

[92] Per Lord Wilberforce in *Ratten v R* [1972] AC 378, PC at 391. See also *R v Taylor* 1961 (3) SA 614.

it appropriate to alert the jury to the need for extra caution because the evidence cannot be tested by cross-examination, but failure to do so, by itself, will not amount to a misdirection.[93]

Statements accompanying the maker's performance of an act

Section 118(1)4(b) of the 2003 Act preserves the following rule of law in criminal proceedings:

> Any rule of law under which in criminal proceedings a statement is admissible as evidence of any matter stated if—
>
> (b) ...the statement accompanied an act which can properly be evaluated as evidence only if considered in conjunction with the statement.

Statements explaining an act in issue or relevant to an issue made by a person contemporaneously with his performance of that act are admissible as evidence of the truth of their contents. The best person to explain the significance of an act is often the person who performed it and the requirement of contemporaneity affords some guarantee of reliability. Typical examples are a bankrupt's statement as to his intention in going or remaining abroad[94] and, on a question of domicile, a statement of a person who has lived abroad as to whether he intends to live there permanently or only temporarily.[95] There are three conditions of admissibility. First, the statement must explain or otherwise relate to the act in question. In *R v Bliss*,[96] a deceased's declaration to the owner of adjoining land that he was planting a willow to mark the boundary of his estate was not connected with the act performed and was in any case irrelevant to the issue in the case, namely whether a certain road was public or private. Second, the statement must be more or less contemporaneous with the act performed. In the case of continuing acts, it suffices if the statement was made during their continuance, albeit some considerable time after their commencement. Thus in *Rawson v Haigh*,[97] where the question was whether a debtor had gone overseas with the intention of avoiding his creditors, letters indicating such an intention written subsequent to the act of departure were held to be admissible on the grounds that departing the realm is a continuing act and the letters were written during its continuance. Third, the statement must be made by the person performing the act and not, for example, by someone witnessing it. In *Howe v Malkin*,[98] an action for trespass, evidence of a statement concerning the position of a boundary made by the plaintiff's father while certain work was being carried out on the land by builders was excluded. Grove J said:

> no act was shown to have been done by the plaintiff's father at the time of making the alleged statement, so that the declaration was by one person, and the accompanying act by another. That does not appear to me to come within the rule.

Under this head of *res gestae*, the statement is usually admissible to explain the declarant's reasons for, or intention in, performing some independent physical act. However, in *R v cCay*,[99]

---

[93] *R v Carnall* [1995] Crim LR 944, CA.

[94] *Rawson v Haigh* (1824) 2 Bing 99; *Rouch v Great Western Rly Co* (1841) 1 QB 51.

[95] *Bryce v Bryce* [1933] P 83. See also *Scappaticci v A-G* [1955] P 47, P, D and Admlty (declarations concerning domicile of choice).

[96] (1837) 7 Ad&El 550.

[97] (1824) 2 Bing 99. See also *Homes v Newman* [1931] 2 Ch 112, Ch D.

[98] (1878) 40 LT 196, DC.

[99] [1990] 1 WLR 645, CA.

in which a witness was unable to remember the number of the man he had picked out at an identification parade carried out from behind a two-way mirror, an officer who had been present was allowed to give evidence that the witness had said 'It is number eight'. The physical activity of looking at the suspect, and the intellectual activity of recognizing him, were together sufficient to amount to a relevant act in respect of which the accompanying words were admissible. In *R v Lynch*[100] the Court of Appeal confirmed that, despite earlier authority which assumed that words of identification were not covered by the *res gestae* exception,[101] the interpretation of the doctrine in *R v McCay* accurately reflected the exception. However, the court noted that the concept of words spoken being part and parcel of an act implies a very limited scope and so a description of the role played by a suspect during an alleged offence is not admissible under the exception.

Statements relating to a physical sensation or a mental state

Section 118(1)4(c) of the 2003 Act preserves the following rule of law in criminal proceedings:

> Any rule of law under which in criminal proceedings a statement is admissible as evidence of any matter stated if—
>
> (c) ...the statement relates to a physical sensation or a mental state (such as intention or emotion).

Statements relating to a physical sensation

Statements of contemporaneous physical sensation experienced by a person are admissible as evidence of the existence of that sensation, if it is in issue or is relevant, but not as evidence of its possible causes. Thus a statement made by an ill workman to the effect that his illness was caused by an accident during employment and is causing him certain bodily or mental pain is admissible to prove the sensation of pain but not the cause of the illness.[102] *Aveson v Lord Kinnaird*[103] is an early example concerning the truth or falsity of a statement, made when a policy of life insurance was taken out by a husband in respect of his wife, that she was in a good state of health. It was held that statements of bodily symptoms made by her when lying in bed, apparently ill, were admissible to show her bad state of health at the time when the policy was effected. The authorities indicate that the exception is not confined to statements of sensation experienced at the actual moment when the maker is speaking, the requirement of contemporaneity being a question of degree.[104]

Statements relating to a mental state

Statements made by a person concerning his contemporaneous state of mind or emotion are admissible as evidence of the existence of his state of mind or emotion at that time, if it is in

---

[100] [2008] 1 Cr App R 338, CA.

[101] Even if there had been pointing or touching of the suspect: see, eg, *R v Christie* [1914] AC 545, HL, in which a child touched the sleeve of the accused and said, 'That is the man'; and *R v Gibson* (1887) 18 QBD 537, in which a woman pointed to the door of a house and said 'The person who threw the stone went in there'.

[102] *Gilbey v Great Western Rly Co* (1910) 102 LT 202, CA. See also *R v Johnson* (1847) 2 Car&Kir 354; *R v Conde* (1867) 10 Cox CC 547; *R v Gloster* (1888) 16 Cox CC 471; and cf *R v Black* (1922) 16 Cr App R 118, CCA.

[103] (1805) 6 East 188.

[104] See per Salter J, *arguendo*, in *R v Black* (1922) 16 Cr App R 118, CCA at 119; *Aveson v Lord Kinnaird* (1805) 6 East 188; and cf per Charles J in *R v Gloster* (1888) 16 Cox CC 471 (Central Criminal Court).

issue or is relevant, but not as evidence of any other fact or matter stated. Thus where a bankrupt makes a payment which is alleged to be a fraudulent preference, evidence of a statement by him that he knew he was insolvent is admissible to prove his knowledge of that fact at the time when the payment was made, but not to prove the insolvency.[105] Statements may be admitted under this head to prove such diverse matters as political opinion,[106] marital affection,[107] fear,[108] and dislike of a child.[109] It seems reasonably clear that a statement made by a person as to his intention is also admissible under this exception as evidence of the existence of such intention at the time when the statement was made.[110] The admissibility of such a statement, however, gives rise to two further questions: first, whether it can support an inference that the intention also existed at a date prior or subsequent to the date on which the statement was made and, second, in the case of a statement of intention to do a certain act, whether it is admissible to prove that such an act was done. Concerning the first question, the authorities support an affirmative answer[111] except in the case of a party's self-serving statements of intention, which, it has been said, cannot support an inference that the speaker's intention also existed at some later (or earlier) time than the date on which the statement was made, because 'otherwise it would be easy for a man to lay grounds for escaping the consequences of his wrongful acts by making such declarations'.[112] Concerning the second question, the authorities conflict.[113] In *R v Moghal*,[114] M was charged with aiding and abetting his mistress, S, to commit murder. S had already been tried separately and acquitted and M's defence was that S had committed the offence and that he was no more than a terrified spectator. The Court of Appeal expressed the opinion that a tape-recorded statement by S made some six months before the murder to the effect that she intended to kill the victim would have been admissible on the accused's behalf.[115] By contrast, in *R v Wainwright*,[116] Cockburn CJ ruled that evidence of a statement made by the victim of a murder on leaving her lodgings that she was going to the accused's premises was inadmissible because 'it was only a statement of intention which might or might not have been carried out'.

[105] *Thomas v Connell* (1838) 4 M&W 267.

[106] *R v Tooke* (1794) 25 State Tr 344.

[107] *Trelawney v Coleman* (1817) 1 B&Ald 90; *Willis v Bernard* (1832) 8 Bing 376.

[108] *R v Vincent, Frost and Edwards* (1840) 9 C&P 275; *R v Gandfield* (1846) 2 Cox CC 43; and *Neill v North Antrim Magistrates' Court* [1992] 1 WLR 1220 HL at 1228–9.

[109] *R v Hagan* (1873) 12 Cox CC 357. See also per Mahon J in *Customglass Boats Ltd v Salthouse Bros Ltd* [1976] 1 NZLR 36 (New Zealand Supreme Court).

[110] See per Mellish LJ in *Sugden v Lord St Leonards* (1876) 1 PD 154 CA at 251.

[111] See per Cozens-Hardy MR in *Re Fletcher, Reading v Fletcher* [1917] 1 Ch 339, CA at 342 (proof of earlier intention) and per Lord Ellenborough in *Robson v Kemp* (1802) 4 Esp 233 (proof of subsequent intention).

[112] Per Crampton J in *R v Petcherini* (1855) 7 Cox CC 79. See also *R v Callender* [1998] Crim LR 337, CA.

[113] For a consideration of this aspect of the doctrine of *res gestae* (and what it means to 'preserve' a disputed rule of common law) see Munday, 'Legislation that would "preserve" the common law: the case of the declaration of intention' [2008] LQR 46.

[114] (1977) 65 Cr App R 56, CA. See also *R v Buckley* (1873) 13 Cox CC 293, Assizes.

[115] It has been doubted, however, whether the evidence was of any relevance to the issue, namely whether M was a willing accomplice or an unwilling spectator: per Lord Bridge in *R v Blastland* [1986] AC 41, HL at 59–60.

[116] (1875) 13 Cox CC 171 (Central Criminal Court). See also *R v Pook* (1871) 13 Cox CC 172, *R v Thomson* [1912] 3 KB, CCA, and the much discussed decision of the United States Supreme Court in *Mutual Life Insurance Co v Hillman* 145 US 285 (1892).

Admissions by agents

Section 118(1)6(a) preserves the following rule of law in criminal proceedings:

> Any rule of law under which in criminal proceedings—
> an admission made by an agent of a defendant is admissible against the defendant as evidence of any matter stated...

In respect of how the rule may apply in criminal proceedings, in *R v Turner*,[117] Lawton LJ set out three principles:[118] (i) an authorized agent may make an admission on behalf of his principal; (ii) a party seeking to rely on an admission must prove the agent was so authorized; and (iii) a court is entitled to assume that what is said in court by a barrister on his client's behalf is said with his client's authority. As to the third principle, it extends to written admissions made by an advocate on his client's behalf at pre-trial proceedings. Such admissions are capable of being made in forms issued under the Criminal Procedure Rules for the purposes of case management.[119] In the magistrates' court for example, trial preparation forms provide for the making of admissions or the acknowledgment of matters that are not in issue. Relevant admissions made in those sections of the form will be admissible, but statements made elsewhere on the form will not be admissible provided the advocate follows the letter and spirit of the Criminal Procedure Rules.[120] In the Crown Court however, a different disclosure and case management regime applies in pre-trial proceedings and to ensure that the administration of justice is not hampered, the courts should ordinarily exclude under s 78 of the Police and Criminal Evidence Act 1984 admissions made in plea and case management forms, provided the advocate follows the letter and spirit of the Criminal Procedure Rules.[121]

ADDITIONAL READING

Munday, 'Legislation that would "preserve" the common law: the case of the declaration of intention' [2008] LQR 46.

---

[117] (1975) 61 Cr App R 67, CA.

[118] (1975) 61 Cr App R 67, CA at [82].

[119] See *R (Firth) v Epping Magistrates' Court* [2011] Cr App R 32, DC.

[120] *R (Firth) v Epping Magistrates' Court* [2011] Cr App R 32, DC. See also *R v Newell* [2012] 1 WLR 3142, CA at [35].

[121] *R v Newell* [2012] 1 WLR 3142, CA.

Confessions

13

Key issues

- Why should a confession made by an accused be admissible in evidence to prove what he admitted?

- Having regard to the ways in which a confession made by an accused may be obtained, when should the prosecution be prevented from relying upon a confession?

- When should a confession made by an accused be admissible for a co-accused?

- Should the trial judge have discretion to exclude a confession, even if it is admissible in law, and if so, on what basis (a) where the prosecution rely on the confession; (b) where a co-accused relies upon the confession?

- When a confession is given in evidence by the prosecution and implicates both its maker and a co-accused, when, if at all, should it be used against the co-accused?

- In what circumstances may a statement made in the presence of the accused be treated as a confession made by him?

- If a confession is inadmissible, should it prevent the admissibility in evidence of incriminating facts discovered in consequence of the confession (as when, for example, a confession to theft includes a statement that the stolen goods are in the accused's home, where they are subsequently found)?

Admissibility

The background

The Police and Criminal Evidence Act 1984 (the 1984 Act) brought about major changes in the law relating to the admissibility of confessions. It will be useful, however, before examining the statutory provisions, to summarize briefly the position at common law. At common law an informal admission (ie an out-of-court statement made by an accused against his interest), was admissible by way of exception to the hearsay rule, as evidence of the truth of its contents, on the basis that what a person says against himself is likely to be true. An informal admission made by an accused person prior to his trial to a person in authority was known as a confession, an expression which included not only a full admission of guilt but also any incriminating statement.[1] A person in authority, generally speaking, was anyone who had authority or control over the accused or over the proceedings or the prosecution against him.[2] In most cases, the person in authority was the police officer investigating the case or interrogating the accused. A confession could not be given in evidence by the prosecution unless shown by them to be a voluntary statement in the sense that it was not obtained from the accused by fear of prejudice or hope of advantage exercised or held out by a person in authority[3] or by oppression.[4] If the admissibility of the confession was in dispute, the issue fell to be determined by the trial judge on a *voir dire* in the absence of the jury. The prosecution bore the legal burden of proving beyond reasonable doubt that the confession was voluntary.[5] If the prosecution failed to discharge this burden, the confession was inadmissible. However, even if satisfied beyond reasonable doubt that it was made voluntarily, the trial judge could exclude it, in the exercise of his discretion, on the grounds that (i) its prejudicial effect outweighed its probative value; (ii) it was obtained by improper or unfair means;[6] or (iii) it was obtained in breach of the Judges' Rules.[7]

Confessions defined

Confessions are now admissible, on behalf of the prosecution, under s 76(1) of the 1984 Act and, on behalf of a co-accused, under s 76A(1) of the 1984 Act. As to the meaning of 'confession' under the Act, section 82(1) adopts the inclusive definition of the word recommended by the Criminal Law Revision Committee.[8] It provides that:

> In this . . . . Act—
>
>   'confession' includes any statement wholly or partly adverse to the person who made it, whether made to a person in authority or not and whether made in words or otherwise;

---

[1] See per Lord Reid in *Customs and Excise Comrs v Harz and Power* [1967] 1 AC 760 at 817–18.

[2] Per Viscount Dilhorne in *Deokinanan v R* [1969] 1 AC 20, PC at 33.

[3] Per Lord Sumner in *Ibrahim v R* [1914] AC 599, PC at 609. In *DPP v Ping Lin* [1976] AC 574 at 597, Lord Hailsham said that he thought Lord Sumner had really said, not 'exercised', but 'excited'.

[4] Per Lord Parker CJ in *Callis v Gunn* [1964] 1 QB 495, DC at 501 and per Edmund Davies LJ in *R v Prager* [1972] 1 WLR 260, CA at 266.

[5] *R v Thompson* [1893] 2 QB 12, CCR.

[6] See *R v Sang* [1980] AC 402, HL.

[7] Per Lord Goddard CJ in *R v May* (1952) 36 Cr App R 91 at 93 and per Edmund Davies LJ in *R v Prager* [1972] 1 WLR 260, CA at 265–6.

[8] *Evidence (General)*, 11th Report, Cmnd 4991 (1972), paras 58 and 66.

Section 82(1) is wide enough to cover a plea of guilty. Thus if an accused pleads guilty but is subsequently granted leave to vacate the plea, the guilty plea, together with the basis of the plea, may be admitted in evidence at his trial as a confession statement.[9] In suitable cases, for example where the evidence is admissible on behalf of the prosecution under s 76(1) of the 1984 Act and the accused, at the time of entering the guilty plea was unrepresented or mis-understood the nature of the charge, it seems that the judge, as at common law, can exclude the evidence in the exercise of his discretion;[10] but if the evidence is admissible on behalf of a co-accused under s 76A(1) of the Act, there is no residual discretion to exclude it in the interests of a fair trial.[11]

Section 82(1) covers 'mixed' statements, that is statements which are both inculpatory and exculpatory in nature.[12] However, in *R v Hasan*,[13] the House of Lords, approving *R v Sat-Bhambra*,[14] held that the subsection does not cover a statement intended by its maker to be wholly exculpatory or neutral, and which appears to be so on its face, but which becomes damaging to him at the trial because, for example, its contents can then be shown to be evasive or false or inconsistent with the maker's evidence on oath. It was further held, distinguishing *Saunders v United Kingdom*[15] that s 76(1) (and s 82(1)) were compatible with Art 6 of the European Convention on Human Rights given the unrestricted capability of s 78 to avoid injustice by excluding any evidence obtained by unfairness, including wholly exculpatory or neutral statements obtained by oppression. However, the effect is that it will be for the accused to convince the judge that the evidence was so obtained and not for the prosecution, on a *voir dire*, to disprove the matter beyond reasonable doubt. This approach is in contrast to that adopted in the United States[16] and Canada.[17]

Section 82(1) abolishes the rule at common law that a threat or inducement only operates to exclude a resulting confession if it was made or held out by 'a person in authority'. A confession, for the purposes of the Act, can be made to anyone. The assumption is that the risk of an inducement resulting in an untrue confession is similar whether or not the inducement comes from a person in authority.[18]

The phrase 'whether made in words or otherwise' means that a confession can be made orally, in writing or by conduct. The Criminal Law Revision Committee gave as an example of conduct, the accused nodding his head in reply to an accusation.[19] Presumably, as at common law, the accused may also accept the accusation of another, so as to make all or part of it a confession statement of his own, by other conduct, by his demeanour, or even by his silence at the time when the accusation was made. It will be convenient to consider this topic and the

---

[9] *R v Johnson* [2007] EWCA Crim 1651.

[10] *R v Rimmer* [1972] 1 WLR 268, CA. See also *R v Hetherington* [1972] Crim LR 703, CA and, generally, under **The discretion to exclude** in this chapter.

[11] *R v Johnson* [2007] EWCA Crim 1651.

[12] See per Lord Steyn in *R v Aziz* [1995] 3 All ER 149, HL at 155; *R v Sharp* [1988] 1 All ER 65, HL (see Ch 6).

[13] [2005] 2 AC 467, HL.

[14] (1988) 88 Cr App R 55, CA.

[15] (1997) 2 BHRC 358.

[16] See per Chief Justice Warren in *Miranda v Arizona* (1975) 384 US 436, US Supreme Court, at 477.

[17] See *Piché v R* (1970) 11 DLR (3d) 709, Supreme Court of Canada. See further Munday, 'Adverse Denial and Purposive Confession' [2003] Crim LR 850.

[18] See per Viscount Dilhorne in *Deokinanan v R* [1969] 1 AC 20, PC at 33. See also Criminal Law Revision Committee, 11th Report, Cmnd 4991 (1972), para 58.

[19] 11th Report, Cmnd 4991 (1972) Annex 2 at 214.

common law authorities in that regard separately.[20] A confession can also be made otherwise than in words by a re-enactment by the accused of the crime committed. In *Li Shu-ling v R*[21] the accused, two days after he had confessed to murder by strangulation, agreed to re-enact the crime. He was reminded that he was still under caution and told that he was not obliged to re-enact the crime. The Privy Council held that a video recording made of the re-enactment, accompanied by a running commentary by the accused explaining his movements, had properly been admitted in evidence as a confession. By way of safeguard, it was held that: the video film should be made reasonably soon after the oral confession; the accused should be warned that he need not take part and, if he agrees to take part, should do so voluntarily; and the video recording should be shown to the accused as soon as practicable after it has been completed so that he has an opportunity to make and have recorded any comments he wishes to make about the film. It was also acknowledged that there are some crimes which it would be wholly inappropriate to attempt to re-enact on video, such as a killing committed in the course of an affray involving many people.

The conditions of admissibility

Section 76 of the 1984 Act provides that:

(1) In any proceedings[22] a confession made by an accused person may be given in evidence against him in so far as it is relevant to any matter in issue in the proceedings and is not excluded by the court in pursuance of this section.

(2) If, in any proceedings where the prosecution proposes to give in evidence a confession made by an accused person, it is represented to the court that the confession was or may have been obtained—

(a) by oppression of the person who made it; or

(b) in consequence of anything said or done which was likely, in the circumstances existing at the time, to render unreliable any confession which might be made by him in consequence thereof,

the court shall not allow the confession to be given in evidence against him except in so far as the prosecution proves to the court beyond reasonable doubt that the confession (notwithstanding that it may be true) was not obtained as aforesaid.

(3) In any proceedings where the prosecution proposes to give in evidence a confession made by an accused person, the court may of its own motion require the prosecution, as a condition of allowing it to do so, to prove that the confession was not obtained as mentioned in subsection (2) above.

Section 76(1) only applies to a confession 'made by an accused'. Thus where there is no dispute that a confession was made, but the identity of the maker is disputed, the prosecution must prove that the maker was the accused, although it seems that this may be inferred if the confession contains information about the accused which, even if known by others, is best known by the accused himself.[23]

---

[20] See, in this chapter, under **Statements made in the presence of the accused**.

[21] [1988] 3 All ER 138, PC.

[22] 'Proceedings' means criminal proceedings, including proceedings in the UK or elsewhere before a court-martial or the Courts-Martial Appeal Court, and proceedings before a Standing Civilian Court: s 82(1).

[23] Such as his date of birth and address: see *R v Ward* [2001] Crim LR 316, CA. See also *Mawdesley v Chief Constable of the Cheshire Constabulary* [2004] 1 WLR 1035, Admin Court (an unsigned form containing information as to the identity of the driver of a car).

It has been held that a confession can only be given in evidence, pursuant to s 76(1), by the prosecution.[24] However, an accused's confession, if it could have been but was not introduced by the prosecution, may be introduced by a co-accused, being admissible at common law as an admission by a party against his interest,[25] provided that it is relevant to the defence of the co-accused or undermines the prosecution case against him and was not obtained in the circumstances referred to in s 76(2) of the 1984 Act.[26] The matter is now governed by statute. Under s 76A of the 1984 Act, confessions may be given in evidence for a co-accused, and the conditions of admissibility are the same as those which apply in the case of confessions adduced on behalf of the prosecution, except that the co-accused need only prove that the confession was not obtained by oppression or 'in consequence of anything said or done' on the balance of probabilities. Section 76A provides as follows:

(1) In any proceedings a confession made by an accused person may be given in evidence for another person charged in the same proceedings (a co-accused) in so far as it is relevant to any matter in issue in the proceedings and is not excluded by the court in pursuance of this section.

(2) If, in any proceedings where a co-accused proposes to give in evidence a confession made by an accused person, it is represented to the court that the confession was or may have been obtained—

(a) by oppression of the person who made it; or

(b) in consequence of anything said or done which was likely, in the circumstances existing at the time, to render unreliable any confession which might be made by him in consequence thereof,

the court shall not allow the confession to be given in evidence for the co-accused except in so far as it is proved to the court on the balance of probabilities that the confession (notwithstanding that it may be true) was not so obtained.

(3) Before allowing a confession made by an accused person to be given in evidence for a co-accused in any proceedings, the court may of its own motion require the fact that the confession was not obtained as mentioned in subsection (2) above to be proved in the proceedings on the balance of probabilities.

The purpose of s 76A is to ensure that where a co-accused proposes to rely upon a confession made by an accused, the accused has a protection against unfairness similar to that which he has when the prosecution propose to rely upon a confession. If a confession is admissible against the accused and undermines the defence of a co-accused, but in law is inadmissible against the co-accused, the prejudice to the co-accused is thought to be cured by a clear direction to the jury that the confession is no evidence against him and s 76A cannot be used to challenge its admissibility.[27]

Section 76A only operates in the case of co-accused. Thus a confession made by D1 cannot be given in evidence under s 76A for D2 if D1 pleads guilty, because D1 will then cease to be an accused and D2 will then no longer be 'charged in the same proceedings' as D1.[28] On the same reasoning, it is submitted, s 76A has no application where D1 is acquitted (either because

[24] *R v Beckford; R v Daley* [1991] Crim LR 833, CA.

[25] *R v Campbell and Williams* [1993] Crim LR 448, CA.

[26] *R v Myers* [1998] AC 124, HL.

[27] *R v Ibrahim* [2008] 2 Cr App R 311, CA.

[28] *R v Finch* [2007] 1 Cr App R 439, CA.

no evidence is offered against him or he makes a successful submission of no case to answer) or he makes a successful application to sever the indictment. In such circumstances, however, D1's confession may be admissible, depending on the circumstances, under s 114(1)(d) of the Criminal Justice Act 2003.[29]

More controversial is the question whether the s 82(1) definition of a confession will be applied strictly in the context of s 76A so as to cover only that part of a statement adverse to its maker or will extend to those parts of the statement going beyond the confession and serving the interests of a co-accused.[30] Plainly, not everything said at the same time as a confession will fall within the definition, but it is submitted that it would be artificial, misleading, and unfair to adopt a strict approach to statements such as 'I did it *alone*' or 'I did it, *not D2*' and that there is a strong case for going beyond this and using s 76A to admit anything that could fairly be said to form a part of D1's confession which is relevant to D2's defence or undermines the prosecution case against him.

A confession admitted in evidence under s 76 or s 76A is admitted as evidence of the matters stated. At common law, an admissible confession was sufficient to warrant a conviction even in the absence of other evidence implicating the accused.[31] However, where a conviction was based on a confession which was equivocal or otherwise of poor quality, it could be quashed on appeal.[32] Similar principles should operate, it is submitted, in the case of confessions admitted under s 76 and s 76A.[33]

Under s 76(2) (or s 76A(2)), an accused (co-accused) may raise the question of admissibility merely by representing to the court, without adducing any evidence in support of such a representation, that the confession was or may have been obtained by the methods described in that subsection.[34] However, even if the accused (co-accused) has not raised the question, the court of its own motion may require the prosecution (co-accused) to prove that the confession was not obtained by the methods described, in exercise of the power conferred on it by s 76(3) (s 76A(3)). In either event, the question will then be determined in the absence of the jury on a *voir dire* at which the prosecution (co-accused) will bear the burden of proving beyond reasonable doubt (on a balance of probabilities) that the conditions of admissibility have been satisfied. If this burden is not discharged, the court has no *inclusionary* discretion, but *shall not* allow the confession to be given in evidence, even if satisfied that its contents are true.

Although the 1984 Act and the Codes of Practice issued thereunder contain a wide variety of provisions regulating, inter alia, the arrest, detention, treatment, and questioning of suspects, the fact that a confession was obtained in breach of the Act or Codes will not necessarily mean that it was obtained by the methods described in s 76(2) (and s 76A(2)).[35] However, evidence of non-compliance with the Act or Codes, either alone or together with other evidence, may

[29] See Ch 10.

[30] The question was raised, but not answered, in *R v Finch* [2007] 1 Cr App R 439, CA.

[31] See *R v Sullivan* (1887) 16 Cox CC 347 and *R v Mallinson* [1977] Crim LR 161, CA and contrast per Cave J in *R v Thompson* [1893] 2 QB 12.

[32] See *R v Barker* (1915) 11 Cr App R 191; *R v Schofield* (1917) 12 Cr App R 191; and *R v Pattinson* (1973) 58 Cr App R 417, CA.

[33] See also, in the case of confessions by mentally handicapped persons, s 77 (see Ch 8).

[34] However, a representation by counsel would normally be based on a proof of evidence or other document, such as a record of interview: see *R v Dhorajiwala* [2010] 2 Cr App R 161 at [23].

[35] Some of the more important provisions of the Act and Codes are considered in this chapter, under **The discretion to exclude**.

show that the confession was obtained by such methods or, failing that, in a case in which the *prosecution* propose to adduce evidence of the confession, ie under s 76, may nonetheless result in the confession being excluded by the court in the exercise of its discretion. Under s 67(11) of the Act, the Codes are admissible in evidence and if any provision of the Codes appears to the court to be relevant to any question arising in the proceedings, it shall be taken into account in determining that question.

Oppression

General

Under s 76(2)(a) (and s 76A(2)), a confession, in order to be admissible, must not have been obtained by oppression. Broadly speaking, this reflects the views of both the Criminal Law Revision Committee[36] and the Royal Commission on Criminal Procedure[37] that a confession obtained by oppression of a suspect should be automatically excluded in view of society's abhorrence of the use of such methods during interrogation. Before considering the meaning of 'oppression', three matters of a general nature may be noted. First, a confession obtained by oppression will be excluded whether or not it is unreliable and notwithstanding that it may be true. Second, the confession must not have been 'obtained by' oppression. Thus a confession will not be excluded where the accused confessed *before* he was subjected to some form of oppression. Equally, there will be no causal link between an interview not complying with the 1984 Act and a subsequent confession freely and voluntarily made.[38] Third, although the statute refers to oppression 'of the person who made' the confession, ie the accused, in appropriate circumstances the oppression of another could also amount to oppression of the accused (or constitute conduct likely to render unreliable any confession which might be made by him).

The meaning of oppression

Concerning the meaning of oppression, although, as we shall see, it is an exercise of only limited value, it is convenient to examine first the way in which the word was defined at common law. Prior to the 1984 Act, oppression was taken to mean 'something which tends to sap and has sapped that free will which must exist before a confession is voluntary'[39] or, in the context of interrogation, 'questioning which by its nature, duration or other attendant circumstances (including the fact of custody) excites hopes (such as the hope of release) or fears, or so affects the mind of the suspect that his will crumbles and he speaks when otherwise he would have stayed silent'.[40] Whether or not there was oppression in any particular case involved a consideration of a wide variety of factors, including the length of time of any period of questioning, whether the accused had been given proper refreshment, and the characteristics of the accused in question.

Section 76(8) (and s 76A(7)) defines 'oppression' as including 'torture, inhuman or degrading treatment, and the use or threat of violence (whether or not amounting to torture)'. The phrase

---

[36] 11th Report, Cmnd 4991 (1972), para 60.

[37] Cmnd 8092 (1981), para 4.132. The Commission proposed exclusion on this ground only if the confession was obtained from the suspect by torture, violence, the threat of violence, or inhuman or degrading treatment.

[38] *R v Parker* [1995] Crim LR 233, CA.

[39] Per Sachs J in *R v Priestley* (1965) 51 Cr App R 1n at 1–2; applied in *R v Prager* [1972] 1 WLR 260, CA.

[40] Lord MacDermott in an address to the Bentham Club (1968) 21 CLP 10.

'torture or inhuman or degrading treatment' derives from Art 3 of the European Convention on Human Rights and it is submitted that the English courts should be guided by the decisions of the European Court of Human Rights and the European Commission of Human Rights. In the *Greek Case*,[41] for example, the Commission defined 'degrading treatment' as that which grossly humiliates a person before others or drives a person to act against his will or conscience. Concerning the meaning of 'torture', assistance may also be derived from the way in which the offence of torture is defined in s 134 of the Criminal Justice Act 1988.[42] The inclusive nature of the definition in s 76(8) plainly indicates that the varieties of oppression it contains do not constitute a comprehensive list.

There was no reference to s 76(8) in *R v Fulling*,[43] the first case to come before the Court of Appeal on the meaning of oppression for the purposes of the 1984 Act. F was convicted of obtaining property by deception. After her arrest she was taken into custody and interviewed twice on that day and once on the following day. Despite persistent questioning, she exercised her right to remain silent, but after a break in the interview on the second day, she made a confession. According to her evidence on the *voir dire*, she made the confession because during the break in that interview one of the officers told her that for the last three years her lover had been having an affair with another woman who was presently in the cell next to hers. F said that these revelations so distressed her that she could not stand being in the cells any longer and thought that by making a statement she would be released. The police denied that they had made the revelations suggested. The defence submitted that the confession was or may have been obtained by oppression. The judge ruled that, even on the assumption that F's version of events was the true one, there was no oppression because oppression meant something above and beyond that which is inherently oppressive in police custody and must import some oppression actively applied in an improper manner by the police.

The Court of Appeal upheld this ruling and dismissed the appeal. It was held, applying the principles set out in *Bank of England v Vagliano Bros*,[44] that since the 1984 Act was a codifying Act, rather than a consolidating Act or an Act declaratory of the common law, the court should give to the words used in it their natural meaning, uninfluenced by any considerations derived from the previous state of the law. Accordingly, the word 'oppression' was given its ordinary dictionary definition, namely, 'exercise of authority or power in a burdensome, harsh, or wrongful manner;[45] unjust or cruel treatment of subjects, inferiors, etc; the imposition of unreasonable or unjust burdens'. Lord Lane CJ pointed out that, according to one of

---

[41] (1969) 12 Yearbook 1, EComHR at 186. See also *Ireland v United Kingdom* (1978) 2 EHRR 25, para 167 (torture and inhuman treatment) and *Campbell and Cosans v United Kingdom* (1982) 4 EHRR 293. Assistance may also be derived from the decisions under the Northern Ireland (Emergency Provisions) Act 1978, s 8(2). See also the definition of 'torture' contained in Art 1 of the Draft United Nations Convention against Torture and Other Cruel, Inhuman or Degrading Treatment or Punishment.

[42] The intentional infliction by act or omission of severe physical or mental pain or suffering by (a) a public official, or a person acting in an official capacity, in the performance or purported performance of his official duties; or (b) by some other person at the instigation or with the consent or acquiescence of a public official, or person acting in an official capacity, performing or purporting to perform his official duties when he instigates the commission of the offence or consents to or acquiesces in it.

[43] [1987] 2 All ER 65, CA.

[44] [1891] AC 107, HL at 144–5.

[45] The word 'wrongful' should be understood in the context of the rest of the definition, particularly the words which precede and follow it, otherwise any breach of the Code, which might be said to be 'wrongful', could be said to amount to oppression, which clearly is not so: *R v Parker* [1995] Crim LR 233, CA.

the quotations given in the *Oxford English Dictionary*, 'There is not a word in our language which expresses more detestable wickedness than *oppression*.' His Lordship found it hard to envisage any circumstances in which oppression thus defined would not entail some impropriety on the part of the interrogator. It was held that although s 76(2)(b) is wide enough to cover some of the circumstances which were embraced by the 'artificially wide' definition of oppression at common law, and although a confession may be excluded, under s 76(2)(b), where there is no suspicion of impropriety, the remarks alleged to have been made by the officer were not likely to have made unreliable any confession which the appellant might have made.

The decision in *R v Fulling*[46] calls for comment in a number of respects. First, the first two parts of the definition of oppression given would appear to apply only in the case of someone vested with some authority, power, or control over the accused, someone akin to a person who, at common law, would have been regarded as a 'person in authority'. Second, concerning impropriety, the decision, although not explicit on the point, suggests strongly that it must be deliberate or intentional. This would accord with the former decision at common law in *R v Miller*,[47] in which it was held that, although it could amount to oppression if questions, addressed to a suspect suffering from paranoid schizophrenia, were skilfully and deliberately asked with the intention of triggering off hallucinations and flights of fancy, the mere fact that questions put to such a suspect did produce such a disordered state of mind would not, by itself, be indicative of oppression. Third, however, although oppression normally requires deliberate impropriety, not all deliberate impropriety amounts to oppression. Sometimes it will be a question of degree. Thus if an interrogator is rude and discourteous, raising his voice and using bad language, this does not constitute oppression;[48] but bullying and hectoring by officers adopting a highly hostile and intimidatory approach will amount to oppression,[49] as will a deliberate mis-statement of the evidence in order to pressurize the suspect.[50] Trickery, per se, will not necessarily constitute oppression. Thus it does not amount to oppression to make a covert tape recording of an incriminating conversation between two suspects sharing a police cell.[51]

Fourth, it seems clear that, as at common law, regard should be had to the personal characteristics of the accused, which may be of critical relevance in deciding not only whether the confession was *obtained* by oppression, but also whether particular conduct was 'burdensome', 'harsh', or 'cruel'. Thus account may be taken of the fact that the suspect is, for example, intelligent, sophisticated, and an experienced professional person,[52] or a person of below normal

---

[46] [1987] 2 All ER 65, CA.

[47] [1986] 3 All ER 119, CA.

[48] *R v Emmerson* (1990) 92 Cr App R 284, CA. See also *R v Heaton* [1993] Crim LR 593, CA.

[49] *R v Paris* (1992) 97 Cr App R 99, CA, where the accused, who was of limited intelligence, had denied his involvement over 300 times! But see also *R v L* [1994] Crim LR 839, CA, a decision under s 76(2)(b), in which although similar methods were employed, *R v Paris* was distinguished on the grounds, inter alia, that L was of normal intelligence and the length of the interviews not excessive.

[50] *R v Beales* [1991] Crim LR 118, CC.

[51] *R v Parker* [1995] Crim LR 233, CA.

[52] *R v Seelig* [1991] 4 All ER 429, CA at 439, where it was held not to be oppressive for Department of Trade and Industry inspectors conducting an investigation of a company's affairs, to question such a person, notwithstanding that (a) in conformity with normal practice, no caution was given; and (b) refusal to answer such questions could have resulted in committal for contempt under the Companies Act 1985, s 436. It was also held that the confession made did not fall to be excluded under s 76(2)(b) or s 78.

intelligence on the borderline of mental handicap.[53] The will of a particular suspect may be so affected by oppression in an interview that a confession made in a subsequent but properly conducted interview should be excluded.[54]

A final matter concerns the relevance of the common law authorities to s 76(2)(b). Paragraph (b) is considered wide enough to cover only *some* of the circumstances embraced by the common law definition of oppression. The facts of *R v Fulling*[55] itself are instructive in this regard because, although at common law a strong argument could have been advanced to the effect that in all the circumstances of the case what the officer said, assuming that he did in fact say it, had sapped the free will of the accused or so affected her mind that her will crumbled and she spoke when otherwise she would have remained silent, the court was satisfied that, for the purposes of s 76(2)(b), what was said was not likely, in the circumstances, to have rendered unreliable any confession which she might have made in consequence.

Unreliability

The background

Section 76(2)(b) in large measure reflects the recommendations of the Criminal Law Revision Committee.[56] In order to appreciate the significance of the reliability test, it will be useful to summarize the Committee's reasons for changing the rules at common law. At common law, as we have seen, the fundamental condition of the admissibility of a confession was that it should have been made voluntarily. Two reasons have been given for that rule: the first, the reliability principle, is that an involuntary confession may not be reliable because an accused subjected to threats, inducements, or oppression may make a false confession; the second, the disciplinary principle, is that the police must be discouraged from using improper methods to obtain a confession by being prevented from using the confession for the purposes of obtaining a conviction. A majority of the Committee were in favour of accepting the mixture of these two principles as the basis of the law. However, although they were also in favour of preserving the law in general, they proposed a relaxation of the strict rule that any threat or inducement, however mild or slight, should render inadmissible any resulting confession.[57] Accordingly, cases of oppression apart, they recommended that a confession should only be rendered inadmissible if made as a result of a threat or inducement of a kind likely to produce an unreliable confession.

The test

Unreliability

The word 'unreliable' is the keynote to s 76(2)(b) (and s 76A(2)(b)). It is not defined in the Act, but means 'cannot be relied upon as being the truth'.[58] Section 76(2)(b), by its express incorporation of the reliability principle, offers less scope for exclusion than existed at common law. However, it offers greater scope for exclusion than would have been the case under cl 2(2)

---

[53] *R v Paris* (1992) 97 Cr App R 99, CA.

[54] See *R v Ismail* (1990) 92 Cr App R 92, CA and cf *Y v DPP* [1991] Crim LR 917, DC.

[55] [1987] 2 All ER 65, CA.

[56] 11th Report, Cmnd 4991 (1972), paras 53–69. The Government rejected the proposals relating to confessions made by The Royal Commission on Criminal Procedure, Cmnd 8092 (1981).

[57] See *R v Northam* (1967) 52 Cr App R 97 and *R v Zaveckas* (1970) 54 Cr App R 202.

[58] Per Stuart-Smith LJ in *R v Crampton* (1990) 92 Cr App R 369 at 372, CA.

(b) of the draft bill annexed to the 11th Report of the Criminal Law Revision Committee because although it closely resembles the clause, it is different in one significant respect: the phrase 'anything said or done' has been substituted for 'any threat or inducement'.[59]

In reaching a decision under s 76(2)(b), a trial judge must examine all the relevant circumstances of the interrogation, both before and after what was 'said' or 'done', and take into account the nature and effect of what was said or done, the seriousness of the offence in question and, if necessary, the terms of the confession, which may throw light on the facts concerning the interrogation.[60] The test of reliability is hypothetical: it applies not to the confession made by the accused, but to 'any confession which might be made by him'.[61] However, as Mance LJ said in *Re Proulx*, the test cannot be satisfied by postulating some entirely different confession:[62]

> The word 'any' must...be understood as indicating 'any such', or 'such a', confession as the applicant made. The abstract element involved also reflects the fact that the test is not whether the actual confession was untruthful or inaccurate. It is whether whatever was said or done was, in the circumstances existing as at the time of the confession, *likely* to have rendered such a confession unreliable, whether or not it may be seen subsequently (with hindsight and in the light of all the material available at trial) that it did or did not actually do so.

'Anything said or done'

The phrase 'anything said or done' has been given a wide interpretation. It includes omissions to say, or do, certain things.[63] It is not restricted to things said or done by persons in authority. However, advice properly given to the accused by his solicitor will not normally provide a basis for excluding a subsequent confession, even when, as it sometimes ought to be, it is robust and, for example, points to the advantages which may derive from an acceptance of guilt or the corresponding disadvantages of a 'no comment' interview, but it may do so in the case of a particularly vulnerable accused.[64] In *R v Roberts*,[65] a confession made after a shop manager's statement that, if R confessed, the police would not be called, was held to be inadmissible under s 76(2)(b), and the fact that, when the police were then called, R did not retract his confession, could not render it reliable.[66]

The phrase 'anything said or done' requires something external to the accused which was likely to have some influence on him. Thus a confession cannot be excluded on the basis that it may have been obtained in consequence of anything said or done by the accused himself which was likely to render unreliable any confession which he might have made in

---

[59] See *R v Harvey* [1988] Crim LR 241, CC in this chapter, under **Admissibility, Unreliability, The test, The characteristics of the accused**.

[60] 11th Report, Cmnd 4991 (1972) para 65.

[61] *R v Barry* (1991) 95 Cr App R 384, CA. The test is objective, but all the circumstances should be taken into account, including those affecting the accused, including his desires etc: ibid.

[62] [2001] 1 All ER 57, DC at [46]. But see also *R v Cox* [1991] Crim LR 276, CA, *R v Crampton* (1990) 92 Cr App R 369, CA at 372, and *R v Kenny* [1994] Crim LR 284, CA.

[63] See, eg, *R v Doolan* [1988] Crim LR 747, CA: failure to caution, to keep a proper record of the interview, and to show that record to the suspect.

[64] *R v Wahab* [2003] 1 Cr App R 232, CA at [42].

[65] [2011] EWCA Crim 2974.

[66] Cf *R v Sherif* [2008] EWCA Crim 2653 where, notwithstanding a deliberate and improper decision not to arrest and caution a suspect, his confession was admitted on the basis of subsequent and properly conducted interviews in which he adopted what he had said in his first interview.

consequence thereof. An example is *R v Wahab*,[67] where W instructed his solicitor to approach the police to see if members of his family might be released from custody if he admitted his guilt. In *R v Goldenberg*[68] the suspect, a heroin addict, while in police custody, requested an interview. The admissions he made were alleged by the defence to be an attempt by him to obtain bail and to be released in order to feed his addiction. It was held that the case fell outside s 76(2)(b). In *R v Crampton*[69] a heroin addict made admissions at interviews in the police station after he had been undergoing withdrawal symptoms. It was sought to distinguish *R v Goldenberg* on the grounds that the interviews held were not at the request of the accused, but conducted by the police at their own convenience. The Court of Appeal, however, doubted whether the mere holding of an interview, at a time when the suspect is undergoing withdrawal symptoms, is something 'done' under s 76(2), the wording of which seemed to postulate some 'words spoken' or 'acts done'.

Causation

Section 76(2)(b) imposes on the prosecution the burden of proving that the confession was not obtained 'in consequence' of anything said or done. This reflects the position at common law. In *DPP v Ping Lin*[70] the accused, suspected of a drugs offence, attempted to make a deal with the police whereby they would release him and in return he would disclose the name of his supplier. When told that this could not be done, he admitted that he had been dealing in heroin but made two more attempts to effect some sort of bargain. An officer then said: 'If you show the judge that you have helped the police to trace bigger drug people, I am sure he will bear it in mind when he sentences you.' Subsequently, the accused disclosed the name of his supplier. The House of Lords held that the accused's statements were voluntary because there was no question of any threat or inducement being held out to him *before* he confessed. The accused may have hoped to obtain immunity or lenience, but that hope was entirely self-generated. In *R v Weeks*,[71] a decision under s 76(2)(b), the trial judge was satisfied that a confession was not obtained in consequence of what was said or done on the basis of the evidence and demeanour of the accused on the *voir dire*—he came across as a very astute young man who had previous experience of being interviewed at a police station.[72]

In *R v Rennie*,[73] a common law authority, the accused was convicted of conspiracy to obtain a pecuniary advantage by deception. The co-accused, his sister, had pleaded guilty to obtaining a pecuniary advantage by deception and a charge of conspiring with her brother was allowed to lie on the file. After his arrest, the accused at first denied any part in the offence but when a detective sergeant revealed the strength of the evidence known to him and asked, 'This was a joint operation by your family to defraud the bank, wasn't it?', the accused replied, 'No, don't bring the rest of the family into this, I admit it was my fault'. On the *voir dire*, the detective sergeant denied that he had told the accused that he would involve other members of his family but admitted that the accused was frightened of this happening. He said, 'I think he made the

---

[67] [2003] 1 Cr App R 232, CA at [42].
[68] (1988) 88 Cr App R 285, CA.
[69] (1990) 92 Cr App R 369, CA.
[70] [1976] AC 574, HL.
[71] [1995] Crim LR 52, CA.
[72] See also *R v Tyrer* (1989) 90 Cr App R 446, CA at 449.
[73] [1982] 1 WLR 64, CA.

confession in the hope that I would terminate my inquiries into members of his family'. The judge ruled that the evidence was admissible. The Court of Appeal, observing that the evidence as to the motives of the accused should not have been admitted, because the drawing of inferences was a matter for the judge and not witnesses, nonetheless acted on the assumption that the accused confessed because he hoped that inquiries would cease into the part played by his family, and posed the following question:[74]

> How is this principle[75] to be applied where a prisoner, when deciding to confess, not only realizes the strength of the evidence known to the police and the hopelessness of escaping conviction but is conscious at the same time of the fact that it may well be advantageous to him or...to someone close to him, if he confesses? How, in particular, is the judge to approach the question when these different thoughts may all, to some extent at least, have been prompted by something said by the police officer questioning him?

The answer, it was held, was not to be found from any refined analysis of the concept of causation. The judge should approach the question much as would jurors if it were for them, understanding the principle and the spirit behind it and applying common sense. Dismissing the appeal, Lord Lane CJ said:[76]

> Very few confessions are inspired solely by remorse. Often the motives of an accused are mixed and include a hope that an early admission may lead to an earlier release or a lighter sentence. If it were the law that the mere presence of such a motive, even if prompted by something said or done by a person in authority, led inexorably to the exclusion of a confession, nearly every confession would be rendered inadmissible. This is not the law. In some cases the hope may be self-generated. If so, it is irrelevant, even if it provides the dominant motive for making the confession. In such a case the confession will not have been obtained by anything said or done by a person in authority. More commonly the presence of such a hope will, in part at least, owe its origin to something said or done by such a person. There can be few prisoners who are being firmly but fairly questioned in a police station to whom it does not occur that they might be able to bring both their interrogation and their detention to an earlier end by confession.

This dictum was approved and applied in *R v Crampton*,[77] a decision under s 76(2)(b): the mere fact that the accused had been undergoing withdrawal symptoms and may have had a motive for making a confession did not mean that the confession was necessarily unreliable.

The question of causation poses particular problems when a confession made at an improperly conducted interview is repeated at a subsequent but properly conducted interview. In *R v McGovern*[78] it was held that a confession made in an interview in consequence of an improper denial of access to a solicitor was likely to be unreliable and should have been excluded. It was also held that a confession made in a properly conducted second interview on the following day was also inadmissible because the first interview tainted the second and the very fact that the suspect had already made a confession was likely to have had an effect on her in the second interview.[79]

---

[74] [1982] 1 WLR 64 at 70.

[75] ie the common law principle of voluntariness.

[76] [1982] 1 WLR 64 at 69.

[77] (1990) 92 Cr App R 369, CA. See also *R v Wahab* [2003] 1 Cr App R 232, CA at [44]–[45].

[78] (1990) 92 Cr App R 228, CA.

[79] See also *R v Blake* [1991] Crim LR 119, CC; and cf *R v Ismail* (1990) 92 Cr App R 92, CA.

The characteristics of the accused

The physical condition and mental characteristics of the accused are a part of the 'circumstances existing at the time' for the purposes of s 76(2)(b). Thus, in *R v Everett*[80] it was held that these circumstances obviously included the mental condition of a 42-year-old with a mental age of 8, and the material consideration was not what the police thought about his mental condition, but the nature of that condition itself. Similarly, in *R v McGovern*[81] it was held that the particular vulnerability and physical condition of the suspect at the time of her interview—she was borderline mentally subnormal, six months pregnant, and in a highly emotional state—formed the background for the submission that her confession should be excluded. However, the mental characteristics which may have a bearing on the question of reliability are not confined to cases of 'mental impairment' or 'impairment of intelligence or social functioning': any mental or personality abnormalities may be of relevance.[82]

The judge must consider the likely effect of what was 'said or done' on the mind of the particular accused. In some cases the things said or done may be unjustified, improper, illegal, or in breach of the 1984 Act or Codes of Practice yet not of a kind likely to render unreliable any confession which might be made by an accused who, for the sake of argument, is an experienced professional criminal with a tough character or who is otherwise capable of coping with even a vigorous interrogation.[83] In *R v Alladice*,[84] for example, it was held that although the accused, who was charged with robbery of £29,000 in cash, had been refused access to a solicitor in contravention of s 58 of the 1984 Act,[85] which was relevant to the question of whether to exclude his confession under s 76(2)(b), it was not only doubtful whether the confession had been obtained as a result of the refusal of access, but in all the circumstances there was no reason to believe that that refusal was likely to render unreliable any confession which the accused might have made. The circumstances showed that the police had acted with propriety, apart from the breach of s 58, and that the accused was well able to cope with the interviews, understood the cautions that he had been given, at times exercising his right to silence, and was aware of his rights so that, had the solicitor been present, his advice would have added nothing to the knowledge of his rights which the accused already had.[86] On the other hand, it is easy to imagine cases where, although it would be impossible to criticize the propriety of what was 'said or done', any confession which might be made by the accused would be likely to be unreliable in all the circumstances because the accused is, for example, of previous good character and highly suggestible, easily intimidated, of very low intelligence, or mentally handicapped.[87] In *R v Harvey*[88] the accused, a woman of low intelligence suffering from a psychopathic disorder, was charged with murder. Her confession was excluded under

---

[80] [1988] Crim LR 826, CA.

[81] (1990) 92 Cr App R 228, CA.

[82] *R v Walker* [1998] Crim LR 211, CA.

[83] In *R v Gowan* [1982] Crim LR 821, CA, O'Connor LJ, although not sanctioning improper or unfair questioning on the part of the police, said: 'serious and experienced professional criminals…must, and do, expect that their interrogation by trained and experienced police officers will be vigorous'.

[84] (1988) 87 Cr App R 380, CA.

[85] See, in this chapter, under **The discretion to exclude, The right to have someone informed and the right of access to a lawyer**.

[86] For these reasons it was also held that the confession should not be excluded under s 78 (see Ch 3).

[87] See generally Gudjohnsson, *The Psychology of Interrogations, Confessions and Testimony* (London, 1992). In the case of confessions by mentally handicapped persons, see also the 1984 Act, s 77 (see Ch 8).

[88] [1988] Crim LR 241, CC.

s 76(2)(b) on the grounds that it may have been obtained as a result of hearing a confession made by her lover. There was psychiatric evidence that her state of mind at the relevant time could have been such that, on hearing her lover's confession, she confessed to protect the lover in a child-like attempt to try to take the blame. There was no threat or inducement; there was no impropriety or illegality; what was said (done) was not said (done) by a person in authority; the crucial factor, in deciding whether what was said was likely to render unreliable any confession which she might have made, was her own state of mind.[89]

In some cases, of course, the confession will be excluded on the basis of *both* unjustified police behaviour *and* the personal nature and characteristics of the accused, as in *R v Delaney*,[90] where the police failed to make a contemporaneous note of a one-and-a-half-hour interview with the accused, who was educationally subnormal, of low IQ, and poorly equipped to cope with sustained interrogation.[91]

Breach of provisions governing procedural fairness
It is clear from cases such as *R v Fulling*[92] and *R v Harvey*[93] that a confession may be excluded under s 76(2)(b) if there is not even a suspicion of impropriety. Equally, as we have seen, confessions obtained as a result of even serious breaches of the provisions of the 1984 Act and the Codes of Practice will not necessarily result in exclusion. Nonetheless, exclusion in many of the reported cases has been based wholly or mainly on such breaches, including the following: failure to caution, to keep a proper record of the interview or to show it to the suspect;[94] an offer of bail and numerous breaches of Code C, including a failure to keep a proper record of the interviews held;[95] questioning before allowing access to a solicitor, failure to record the admissions immediately and failure to show the note of the interview to the suspect;[96] asking a question after the suspect has been charged which is not for the purpose of clearing up an ambiguity;[97] and conducting an interview with a juvenile without an 'appropriate adult',[98] the adult present having a low IQ, being virtually illiterate, and probably incapable of appreciating the gravity of the juvenile's situation[99] or being a person with whom the juvenile has no empathy (her estranged father whom she did not wish to attend).[100]

Section 105 of the Taxes Management Act 1970

Concerning the admissibility of confessions in any criminal proceedings against a person for any form of fraudulent conduct in relation to tax, s 76 of the 1984 Act must be read in conjunction with s 105 of the Taxes Management Act 1970, which operates in such proceedings

[89] See also *R v Sat-Bhambra* (1988) 88 Cr App R 55, CA, where evidence of a confession was excluded on the basis that the accused may have been affected at the time by valium given to him by the police doctor to calm his nerves.
[90] (1988) 88 Cr App R 338, CA.
[91] See also *R v Waters* [1989] Crim LR 62, CA and *R v Moss* (1990) 91 Cr App R 371, CA.
[92] [1987] 2 All ER 65, CA in this chapter, at n 43.
[93] [1988] Crim LR 241, CC in this chapter, at n 88.
[94] See paras 10, 11.7, and 11.11, Code C and *R v Doolan* [1988] Crim LR 747, CA.
[95] *R v Barry* (1991) 95 Cr App R 384, CA.
[96] See the 1984 Act, s 58(4), paras 11.7 and 11.11, Code C, and *R v Chung* (1990) 92 Cr App R 314, CA.
[97] See para 16.5, Code C and *R v Waters* [1989] Crim LR 62, CA.
[98] See para 11.15, Code C.
[99] See *R v Morse* [1991] Crim LR 195.
[100] See *DPP v Blake* (1989) 89 Cr App R 179, DC, now reflected in Note 1B to Code C; and cf *R v Jefferson* [1994] 1 All ER 270, CA. See generally Hodgson, 'Vulnerable Suspects and the Appropriate Adult' [1997] Crim LR 785.

to prevent the exclusion of statements made or documents produced in so-called 'Hansard interviews', ie interviews at which the accused is informed of the practice of HM Revenue & Customs to take into account the cooperation of the taxpayer in deciding whether to bring any prosecution for fraud.[101] Section 105(1) is in the following terms:

> Statements made or documents produced by or on behalf of a person shall not be inadmissible ... by reason only that it has been drawn to his attention that—
> (a) pecuniary settlements may be accepted instead of a penalty being determined, or proceedings being instituted, in relation to any tax,
> (b) though no undertaking can be given as to whether or not the Board will accept such a settlement in the case of any particular person, it is the practice of the Board to be influenced by the fact that a person has made a full confession of any fraudulent conduct to which he has been a party and has given full facilities for investigation,
> and that he was or may have been induced thereby to make the statements or produce the documents.

Section 105 does not prevent reliance upon s 78 of the 1984 Act where the interview has been conducted in breach of Code C, but it is relevant to exercise of the discretion under s 78 that Parliament expected statements made at Hansard interviews to be admissible in evidence.[102]

The discretion to exclude

If the prosecution fails to discharge the burden of proving that a confession was not obtained by the methods described in s 76(2), the court, as we have seen, shall not allow the confession to be given in evidence and has no discretion to admit it, even if satisfied that it is true. It does not follow from this, however, that the confession *must* be admitted if the prosecution succeeds in proving that the confession was not obtained by those methods: s 76(1) provides that a confession *may* be given in evidence if not excluded under the section. In such cases the trial judge may exclude the confession in the exercise of her common law discretion or under s 78(1). Although these two discretionary powers overlap to a considerable extent, s 78(1) has in very large measure superseded the common law power.

Section 82(3) of the Police and Criminal Evidence Act 1984

Section 82(3) provides that:

> Nothing in this Part of this Act (ss 73–82) shall prejudice any power of a court to exclude evidence (whether by preventing questions from being put or otherwise) at its discretion.

The effect of this subsection is, in the present context, to preserve any discretion to exclude an otherwise admissible confession that the court possessed at common law prior to the 1984 Act. At common law, a trial judge, even if satisfied that a confession was made voluntarily, could exclude it as a matter of discretion on a number of different albeit overlapping grounds. Two of the grounds were made clear by the House of Lords in *R v Sang*.[103] First, as a part of

---

[101] Section 105 also applies to any proceedings for the recovery of any tax due from him and any proceedings for a penalty: s 105(2).

[102] *R v Gill* [2004] 1 WLR 49, CA at [45].

[103] [1980] AC 402.

his function at a criminal trial to ensure that the accused receives a fair trial, the judge has a discretion to refuse to admit evidence where, in his opinion, its prejudicial effect outweighs its probative value. Second, the judge has a discretion to exclude an otherwise admissible confession obtained by improper or unfair means. A third ground was that the confession was obtained in contravention of the Judges' Rules[104] or the statutory provisions governing the detention and treatment of suspects.

The discretion, in so far as it may be exercised on the first ground, was of particular use in the case of confessions made by accused suffering from mental disability.[105] Thus it was held that the discretion could be exercised in the case of a confession that came from an irrational mind or was the product of delusions and hallucinations,[106] or was made by an accused with the mental age and comprehension level of a young child.[107] However, confessions in cases of this kind and in analogous cases in which a confession was obtained when the accused was under the influence of drugs,[108] would now fall to be excluded as a matter of law under s 76(2)(b).

Most of the reported cases in which the common law discretion was exercised on either the second or the third ground were cases involving some breach of the Judges' Rules. However, a voluntary confession could be admitted notwithstanding a breach of the rules.[109] In the exercise of the discretion (which was rarely reversed on appeal) the trial judge could examine, in addition to the breaches alleged, all the circumstances of the case, including in particular the probative value of the confession and the nature and seriousness of the offence charged.

The Judges' Rules, and many of the old statutory provisions governing the detention and treatment of suspects, have now been replaced by a wide variety of provisions contained in the 1984 Act and the Codes of Practice which have been issued pursuant to the Act. Before turning to consider the exclusion of confessions under s 78(1) of the 1984 Act, it will be convenient, therefore, to examine some general and particular provisions of the Codes of Practice and the 1984 Act.

The Codes of Practice

The matters covered

Codes A to F relate to the following matters—A: the exercise by police officers of statutory powers of stop and search; B: the searching of premises by police officers and the seizure of property found by police officers on persons or premises; C: the detention, treatment, and questioning of persons by police officers; D: the identification of persons by police officers; E: the audio recording of interviews with suspects;[110] and F: the visual recording with sound of interviews with suspects.

---

[104] The Judges' Rules were rules of practice, not law, originally drawn up by the judges of the King's Bench Division in 1912 for the guidance of the police, and designed to regulate the interrogation and treatment of suspects.

[105] On confessions by mentally handicapped persons, see also the 1984 Act, s 77 (see Ch 8).

[106] *R v Miller* [1986] 3 All ER 119, CA.

[107] *R v Stewart* (1972) 56 Cr App R 272, CCC. See also per Lord Widgery CJ in *R v Isequilla* [1975] 1 WLR 716, CA.

[108] *R v Davis* [1979] Crim LR 167, CC.

[109] *R v Prager* [1972] 1 WLR 260.

[110] The Code on Tape Recording applies to interviews held at police stations of persons suspected of committing indictable offences (except certain terrorism offences). See also para 43, the *Consolidated Criminal Practice Direction*, which deals with such matters as the practice to be followed for: (a) amending a transcript of an interview (or editing a tape) by agreement; (b) notification of intention to play a tape in court; (c) notification of objection to production

Persons governed by the Codes

The Codes do not apply only to police officers: under s 67(9) of the 1984 Act they also apply to other persons 'charged with the duty of investigating offences or charging offenders'.[111] This phrase covers those charged with a legal duty of the kind in question, whether imposed by statute or by the common law or by contract.[112] It covers Customs and Excise officers,[113] but is not restricted to government officials and others acting under statutory powers.[114] Whether a person satisfies the test is a question of fact in each case[115] or, more accurately, a question of mixed law and fact, involving an examination of the statute, contract, or other authority under which a person carries out his functions, as well as a consideration of his actual work.[116] Thus the test will not necessarily be satisfied by line managers conducting disciplinary interviews,[117] Department of Trade inspectors investigating a company's affairs,[118] or by those supervising a bank on behalf of the Bank of England under the Banking Act 1987,[119] but may be satisfied by commercial investigators such as company investigators,[120] store detectives,[121] and investigators employed by the Federation against Copyright Theft.[122] The test is met by officers of the Special Compliance Office, HM Revenue & Customs' investigation branch charged with investigating serious tax fraud, because such fraud inevitably involves the commission of an offence or offences.[123]

The right to a caution

Paragraphs 10 and 16 of Code C, the Code of Practice for the Detention, Treatment and Questioning of Persons by Police Officers, provide as follows:

> 10.1 A person whom there are grounds to suspect of an offence must be cautioned before any questions about an offence, or further questions if the answers provide the grounds for suspicion, are put to them if either the accused's answers or silence (ie failure or refusal

---

of a tape; and (d) proof of a tape. Concerning video-recorded interviews with children (see Ch 5), departure from the 'Achieving Best Evidence' guidance on interviewing may be treated as the equivalent of a breach of one of the Codes of Practice. Account has also been taken of a failure to conform to the recommendations contained in the report of Butler Sloss LJ, the *Inquiry into Child Abuse in Cleveland*, Cm 412 (1987): see *R v H* [1992] Crim LR 516, CA. See also *R v Dunphy* (1993) 98 Cr App R 393, CA.

[111] The principles of fairness enshrined in Code C may have an even wider application: see *R v Smith* (1993) 99 Cr App R 233, CA (see Ch 3).

[112] *Joy v Federation against Copyright Theft Ltd* [1993] Crim LR 588, DC.

[113] *R v Sanusi* [1992] Crim LR 43, CA.

[114] *R v Bayliss* (1993) 98 Cr App R 235, CA at 237–8.

[115] Per Watkins LJ in *R v Seelig* [1991] 4 All ER 429, CA at 439.

[116] Per Neill LJ in *R v Bayliss* (1993) 98 Cr App R 235 at 238–9 and in *R v Smith* (1993) 99 Cr App R 233, CA.

[117] *R v Welcher* [2007] Crim LR 804, CA.

[118] See *R v Seelig* [1991] 4 All ER 429, CA.

[119] See *R v Smith* (1993) 99 Cr App R 233, CA.

[120] *R v Twaites; R v Brown* (1990) 92 Cr App R 106, CA.

[121] *R v Bayliss* (1993) 98 Cr App R 235, CA.

[122] *Joy v Federation against Copyright Theft Ltd* [1993] Crim LR 588, DC. In the case of an investigation by the Director of the Serious Fraud Office into a suspected offence involving serious or complex fraud, the general provisions of Code C yield to the inquisitorial regime established by the Criminal Justice Act 1987: see *R v Director of Serious Fraud Office, ex p Smith* [1992] 3 All ER 456, HL.

[123] *R v Gill* [2004] 1 WLR 49, CA.

to answer or answer satisfactorily) may be given in evidence to a court in a prosecution. A person need not be cautioned if questions are for other necessary purposes, e.g.:

    (a) solely to establish their identity or ownership of any vehicle;

    (b) to obtain information in accordance with any relevant statutory requirement[124]...;

    (c) in furtherance of the proper and effective conduct of a search, e.g. to determine the need to search in the exercise of powers of stop and search or to seek cooperation while carrying out a search;

    (d) to seek verification of a written record as in paragraph 11.13;[125] or

    ...

10.4 A person who is arrested, or further arrested, must also be cautioned unless:

    (a) it is impracticable to do so by reason of their condition or behaviour at the time;

    (b) they have already been cautioned immediately prior to arrest as in paragraph 10.1.

10.5 The caution which must be given on:

    (a) arrest;

    (b) all other occasions before a person is charged or informed that they may be prosecuted, (see section 16),

should, unless the restriction on drawing adverse inferences from silence applies, (see Annex C), be in the following terms:

'You do not have to say anything. But it may harm your defence if you do not mention when questioned something which you later rely on in Court. Anything you do say may be given in evidence.'

...

10.7 Minor deviations from the words of any caution given in accordance with this Code do not constitute a breach of this Code, provided the sense of the relevant caution is preserved...

10.8 After any break in questioning under caution, the person being questioned must be made aware they remain under caution. If there is any doubt the relevant caution should be given again in full when the interview resumes...

...

16.1 When the officer in charge of the investigation reasonably believes that there is sufficient evidence to provide a realistic prospect of...conviction for the offence...they shall without delay, and subject to the following qualification, inform the custody officer who will be responsible for considering whether the detainee should be charged...When a person is detained in respect of more than one offence it is permissible to delay informing the custody officer until the above conditions are satisfied in respect of all the offences...

...

16.2 When a detainee is charged with or informed they may be prosecuted for an offence, [see Note 16B], they shall, unless the restriction on drawing adverse inferences from silence applies, (see Annex C), be cautioned as follows:

'You do not have to say anything. But it may harm your defence if you do not mention now something which you later rely on in court. Anything you do say may be given in evidence.'[126]

---

[124] For example, under the Road Traffic Act 1988.

[125] Para 11.13 relates to records of comments made by a suspect outside the context of an interview.

[126] Where a person wishes to make a written statement under caution, he shall first be asked to write out and sign: 'I make this statement of my own free will. I understand that I do not have to say anything but that it may harm my defence if I do not mention when questioned something which I later rely on in court. This statement may be given in evidence': see para 2, Annex D, Code C. See also *R v Pall* (1991) 156 JP 424, CA and cf *R v Hoyte* [1994] Crim LR 215, CA.

Although para 10.1 does not include a requirement that the grounds to suspect be reasonable, this is implicit, because the grounds must be assessed objectively.[127]

In *R v Shah*[128] it was held that a mere hunch or sixth sense, or the simple fact that the questioner is suspicious, will not suffice to bring para 10.1 into play; para 10.1 sets out an objective test in that there must be grounds for suspicion before the need to caution arises and although they may well fall short of evidence supportive of a prima facie case of guilt, they must exist and be such as to lead both to a suspicion that an offence has been committed and that the person being questioned has committed it.[129] In *R v Hunt*,[130] where officers saw H in someone else's garden putting a flick-knife in his pocket, searched him, and found the knife, it was held that at that stage the officers had ample evidence on which to suspect the commission of an offence and should have cautioned him. The answers to the questions then put, without a caution, should have been excluded under s 78. However, if a person is cautioned in respect of one offence and minutes later the police have grounds to suspect another offence, it seems that there is no requirement to caution again, under either para 10.1 or para 10.8, before putting questions about the other offence.[131]

A caution is not required under para 10.1, in respect of a person whom there are grounds to suspect of an offence, if questions are not put to him regarding his involvement or suspected involvement in that offence, but for other purposes. However, if the questions are put for two purposes, partly regarding his involvement or suspected involvement in an offence, and partly for other purposes, then a caution should be given.[132]

Paragraph 10.1 and other requirements of the Code were not intended to apply to a conversation between a suspect and officers who adopt an undercover pose or disguise, because there can be no question of pressure or intimidation by the officers as persons actually in authority or believed to be so. However, it is wrong for officers to adopt such a pose or disguise to ask questions about an offence uninhibited by the provisions of the Code and with the effect of circumventing it, and if they do so, the questions and answers may be excluded under s 78.[133]

Paragraph 16.2 of the Code is designed to apply to that stage in the course of an interrogation when there is sufficient evidence to prosecute and for the prosecution to succeed. At that time, and subject to exceptions, questioning should cease.[134] Some of the words and phrases used in para 16.2 are the same as those used in its precursor, r III of the Judges' Rules

---

[127] *R v James* [1996] Crim LR 650, CA. *R v James* and other authorities in the ensuing text and footnotes in this chapter are decisions on an earlier version of Code C.

[128] [1994] Crim LR 125, CA.

[129] See also, and cf *R v Nelson and Rose* [1998] 2 Cr App R 399, CA.

[130] [1992] Crim LR 582, CA. Cf *R v Purcell* [1992] Crim LR 806, CA.

[131] *R v Oni* [1992] Crim LR 183, CA.

[132] *R v Nelson and Rose* [1998] 2 Cr App R 399, CA.

[133] See *R v Christou* [1992] QB 979, CA (see Ch 3).

[134] See para 16.5, Code C and *R v Bailey* [1993] 3 All ER 513, CA. Where a suspect is charged by the police and then required by the Serious Fraud Office to attend for an interview, the Director is not required to caution him, because the Criminal Justice Act 1987 showed a parliamentary intention to establish an inquisitorial regime in relation to serious or complex fraud in which the Director could obtain by compulsion answers which might be self-incriminating. Under s 2(13), a person who without reasonable excuse fails to answer questions or provide relevant information is liable to imprisonment, a fine, or both. But see also s 2(8): subject to minor exceptions, statements made by the suspect cannot be used in evidence against him.

and are likely to be interpreted in the same way. For the purposes of r III, it was held that the word 'charged' means formally charged;[135] that when a person is told 'you will be charged' it is the same as saying that a charge has in fact already been preferred;[136] and that the phrase 'informed that he may be prosecuted' covers a case where, during interrogation of a suspect who has not been arrested, the time comes when the police contemplate that a summons may be issued against him.[137]

The right to have someone informed and the right of access to a lawyer

A detailed analysis of the relevant provisions of the 1984 Act and the various Codes of Practice is well beyond the scope of this work. However, two provisions of particular significance in the present context, ss 56 and 58, do merit close consideration. They relate to the right to have someone informed when arrested and what has been called 'one of the most important and fundamental rights of a citizen',[138] namely the right of access to legal advice.[139] Section 56(1) provides that:

> Where a person has been arrested and is being held in custody in a police station or other premises, he shall be entitled, if he so requests, to have one friend or relative or other person who is known to him or who is likely to take an interest in his welfare told, as soon as is practicable except to the extent that delay is permitted by this section, that he has been arrested and is being detained there.[140]

Section 58 provides that:

(1) A person arrested and held in custody in a police station or other premises shall be entitled, if he so requests, to consult a solicitor privately at any time.
(2) Subject to subsection (3) below, a request under subsection (1) above and the time at which it was made shall be recorded in the custody record.
(3) Such a request need not be recorded in the custody record of a person who makes it at a time while he is at a court after being charged with an offence.
(4) If a person makes such a request, he must be permitted to consult a solicitor as soon as is practicable except to the extent that delay is permitted by this section.[141]

The intention behind the opening words of both s 56(1) and s 58(1) is to limit the application of the sections to a person whose detention in custody has been authorized, ie an arrested person taken to a police station in respect of whom the custody officer is satisfied that the statutory conditions for detention are made out. Thus a person arrested while committing

---

[135] *R v Brackenbury* [1965] 1 WLR 1475n.

[136] *Conway v Hotten* [1976] 2 All ER 213, DC.

[137] *R v Collier; R v Stenning* [1965] 1 WLR 1470, CCA.

[138] Per Hodgson J in *R v Samuel* [1988] 2 All ER 135, CA at 147.

[139] See also paras 5 and 6, Code C.

[140] The rights conferred are exercisable whenever the person detained is transferred from one place to another: s 56(8).

[141] Section 58 does not entitle a person, suspected of committing an offence of driving when unfit through drink or drugs or driving after consuming excess alcohol, to consult a solicitor *before* supplying a specimen for analysis: *DPP v Billington* [1988] 1 All ER 435, DC. Procedures undertaken under the Road Traffic Act 1988, s 7 (ie questions and answers leading to the giving of a specimen) do not constitute interviewing for the purposes of Code C: see *DPP v D; DPP v Rous* (1992) 94 Cr App R 185, DC and para 11.1A, Code C.

burglary is *in custody* on premises, but is not *held* in custody, and is therefore outside the terms of ss 56 and 58.[142] However, in *Ambrose v Harris*,[143] the Supreme Court held that under Art 6(1) and (3)(c) of the European Convention on Human Rights, the right to legal advice may arise when, even if a suspect has not been formally arrested or taken into custody, there has been a significant curtailment of his freedom of action, as in one of the cases before the court, where a suspect was detained, handcuffed, and questioned during a police search.[144]

A 'solicitor', for the purposes of s 58, means a solicitor who holds a current practising certificate and an accredited or probationary representative included on the register of representatives maintained by the Legal Services Commission.[145]

Many of the subsections of ss 56 and 58 are cast in identical or very similar terms. In any case the person in custody must be permitted to exercise the rights conferred within 36 hours from the 'relevant time',[146] which is usually either the time at which the person arrives at the police station or the time 24 hours after the time of arrest, whichever is the earlier.[147] Delay is only permitted if four conditions are met. The first is that the person detained is in police detention for an indictable offence. The second is that the delay is authorized by an officer of at least the rank of inspector or superintendent.[148] The third condition is that the person in detention has not yet been charged with an offence, that is any offence, whether or not the one in respect of which he was originally arrested.[149] The fourth condition, contained in ss 56(5) and 58(8), is that the officer must have:

> reasonable grounds for believing that telling the named person of the arrest (exercise of the right … [to consult a solicitor] at the time when the person detained desires to exercise it) (a) will lead to interference with or harm to evidence connected with an indictable offence or interference with or physical injury to other persons or (b) will lead to the alerting of other persons

---

[142] *R v Kerawalla* [1991] Crim LR 451, CA.

[143] [2011] 1 WLR 2435.

[144] Although s 58(1) does not apply to a person in custody after being remanded by a magistrates' court, such a person has a common law right to be permitted on request to consult a solicitor as soon as is reasonably practicable: *R v Chief Constable of South Wales, ex p Merrick* [1994] Crim LR 852, DC.

[145] Para 6.12, Code C. If a solicitor wishes to send a non-accredited or probationary representative to provide advice on his behalf, that person shall be admitted to the police station for this purpose unless an officer of the rank of inspector or above considers that such a visit will hinder the investigation of crime and directs otherwise: para 6.12A, Code C. In exercising his discretion, the officer should take into account in particular whether the identity and status of the representative have been satisfactorily established; whether he is of suitable character to provide legal advice (a person with a criminal record is unlikely to be suitable unless the conviction was for a minor offence and not recent); and any other matters in any written letter of authorization provided by the solicitor on whose behalf he is attending: para 6.13, Code C. The discretion cannot be used to make a blanket direction that a representative should not be admitted to any police station in a particular area, and although senior officers may give general advice, the responsibility rests with the officer concerned with the investigation in question as to whether that particular investigation will be hindered: *R (Thompson) v Chief Constable of the Northumberland Constabulary* [2001] 1 WLR 1342, CA.

[146] Sections 56(3) and 58(5).

[147] Section 41(2).

[148] Sections 56(2)(b) and 58(6)(b) respectively. The authorization may be oral, in which case it shall be confirmed in writing as soon as possible: ss 56(4) and 58(7). The authorization under s 58(6)(b) may also be given by an officer of the rank of chief inspector if he has been authorized to do so by an officer of at least the rank of chief superintendent: s 107(1). The holder of an acting rank may be treated for the purpose of these provisions as the holder of the substantive rank: *R v Alladice* (1988) 87 Cr App R 380, CA.

[149] Para A1, Annex B, Code C and *R v Samuel* [1988] 2 All ER 135, CA.

suspected of having committed such an offence but not yet arrested for it or (c) will hinder the recovery of any property obtained as a result of such an offence.[150]

If a delay is authorized, the detainee shall be told the reason for it, which shall be noted on his custody record.[151] Once the reason for authorizing delay ceases to subsist, there may be no further delay in permitting the exercise of the rights conferred.[152] This may occur, for example, if the police succeed in recovering the property obtained as a result of an indictable offence or arrest the other persons suspected of having committed such an offence.[153]

The occasions for properly authorizing delay under s 58(8) will be infrequent[154] and the task of satisfying a court that reasonable grounds existed at the time when the decision was made will prove formidable.[155] In *R v Samuel* Hodgson J said:[156]

> a court which has to decide whether denial of access to a solicitor was lawful has to ask itself two questions: 'Did the officer believe?', a subjective test; and 'Were there reasonable grounds for that belief?', an objective test.
>
> What it is the officer must satisfy the court that he believed is this: that (1) allowing consultation with a solicitor (2) will (3) lead to or hinder one or more of the things set out in paragraphs (a) to (c) of s 58(8). The use of the word 'will' is clearly of great importance. There were available to the draftsman many words or phrases by which he could have described differing nuances as to the officer's state of mind, for example 'might', 'could', 'there was a risk', 'there was a substantial risk' etc. The choice of 'will' must have been deliberately restrictive.
>
> Of course, anyone who says that he believes that something will happen, unless he is speaking of one of the immutable laws of nature, accepts the possibility that it will not happen, but the use of the word 'will' in conjunction with belief implies in the believer a belief that it will very probably happen.

Furthermore, it was held that the circumstances in which delay may be authorized necessarily involve conduct, on the part of the solicitor, which is either deliberate and criminal or inadvertent. As to the former, the number of times that a police officer could genuinely believe that a solicitor, an officer of the court, would commit a criminal offence would be rare, and in any event the grounds put forward to justify the delay would have to have reference to a specific solicitor and could never be advanced in relation to solicitors generally. As to inadvertent conduct, solicitors were intelligent, professional people whereas persons detained were frequently not very clever; the expectation that one of the events in paras (a) to (c) would be brought about by such conduct contemplated a degree of intelligence and sophistication

---

[150] It is not an adequate ground for the authorization of delay under s 58(8) that access to a solicitor might 'prejudice inquiries' or result in advice to the suspect to remain silent (*R v McIvor* [1987] Crim LR 409, CC) or to refuse to answer any more questions (*R v Samuel* [1988] 2 All ER 135, CA). See also para A4, Annex B, Code C. Sections 56(5) and 58(8) are expressed to be subject to ss 56(5A) and 58(8A) respectively. These latter subsections provide that an officer may also authorize delay where he has reasonable grounds for believing that—(a) the person detained for the indictable offence has benefited from his criminal conduct; and (b) the recovery of the value of the property constituting the benefit will be hindered by telling the named person of the arrest (the exercise of the right to consult a solicitor).

[151] Sections 56(6) and 58(9). These duties shall be performed as soon as is practicable: ss 56(7) and 58(10).

[152] Sections 56(9) and 58(11).

[153] As in *R v (Eric) Smith* [1987] Crim LR 579, CC.

[154] Per Lord Lane CJ in *R v Alladice* (1988) 87 Cr App R 380, CA.

[155] Per Hodgson J in *R v Samuel* [1988] 2 All ER 135, CA at 144.

[156] [1988] 2 All ER 135 at 143.

in persons detained and perhaps a naivety and lack of common sense in solicitors which was of doubtful occurrence; and the grounds put forward would have to have reference to the specific person detained, the archetype being a sophisticated criminal who was known or suspected to be a member of a gang of criminals.

The facts of *R v Samuel* revealed that the solicitor in question was highly respected, very experienced, and unlikely to be hoodwinked by the suspect, who was 24 years old. Accordingly, it was held that there could have been no reasonable grounds for the belief that s 58(8) required.[157] Similarly, in *R v Alladice*,[158] a case of robbery in which access had been denied on the grounds that one of the suspects was still at large, none of the proceeds of the robbery had been recovered, and a gun which had been used in the crime had not been located, Lord Lane CJ, giving the reserved judgment of the Court of Appeal, held that although their Lordships did not share the scepticism expressed in *R v Samuel* as to solicitors being used as unwitting channels of communication, there had been a breach of s 58 because the suspect still at large had already been alerted by events, there was no reason to believe that access to a solicitor would impede recovery of the stolen money or gun, there was no suggestion that the solicitor requested would involve himself in any dishonesty or malpractice, and the suspect could not be classed as a sophisticated criminal.

Section 78(1) of the Police and Criminal Evidence Act 1984

General

Section 78(1) provides that:

> In any proceedings the court may refuse to allow evidence on which the prosecution proposes to rely to be given if it appears to the court that, having regard to all the circumstances, including the circumstances in which the evidence was obtained, the admission of the evidence would have such an adverse effect on the fairness of the proceedings that the court ought not to admit it.

Many of the most important cases on s 78(1) have concerned confessions, to which the subsection clearly applies,[159] and some of these have already been considered, as part of the general consideration of the subsection, in Chapters 2 and 3. Section 78 operates without prejudice to the common law discretion to exclude[160] but, as already noted, has in very large measure superseded the common law power.

A confession may be excluded under s 78(1) in the absence of any breaches of the 1984 Act or Codes of Practice. Thus if an interview is held with a suspect who does not appear to have hearing difficulties, but it is subsequently established that his hearing was so impaired that it would be unfair for his answers to be admitted in evidence, the answers will be excluded under s 78(1).[161] However, the chief importance of s 78(1), in relation to confessions, lies in its potential for the exclusion of confessions obtained illegally or improperly. As we saw in Chapter 3, although breaches of the Act or Codes will not necessarily result in exclusion, it is

---

[157] Cf *Re Walters* [1987] Crim LR 577, DC, an application for habeas corpus following extradition proceedings, where it was held that there were reasonable grounds for believing that the applicant would use the solicitor as an innocent agent to get a message out and thereby alert other suspects.

[158] (1988) 87 Cr App R 380, CA. See also *R v Parris* (1988) 89 Cr App R 68, CA.

[159] *R v Mason* [1988] 1 WLR 139, CA.

[160] *R v O'Leary* (1988) 87 Cr App R 387, CA and *Matto v Crown Court at Wolverhampton* [1987] RTR 337, DC.

[161] See *R v Clarke* [1989] Crim LR 892, CA and para 13.5, Code C.

implicit in the wording of the subsection that the circumstances in which the evidence was obtained may have such an adverse effect that it should be excluded.[162] As we also saw, the purpose of the subsection is to give effect to the reliability principle, and therefore although *mala fides* or deliberate misconduct may render exclusion more likely, the determinative factor is the extent to which the defendant has been denied the right of a fair trial by reason of breaches of the provisions governing procedural fairness.[163]

The procedure for exclusion

Before considering some examples of such breaches, it will be convenient to consider first the procedure to be adopted when the defence seeks to exclude a confession obtained in such circumstances. In *R v Keenan*[164] Hodgson J identified three different situations: (a) breaches of a code may be apparent from the custody record (as when an order has been made by an officer of insufficient rank) or the witness statements; (b) there may be a prima facie breach which, if objection is taken, must be justified by evidence adduced by the prosecution (eg an order refusing access to a solicitor can only be justified by compelling evidence from the senior officer who made the order); and (c) there may be breaches which can probably only be established by the evidence of the accused himself (eg cases involving persons at risk, such as the mentally handicapped).[165] The procedure appropriate in each case may vary. In (a), it may be that all that is necessary is an admission by the police, followed by argument. However, the prosecution will not often be content to take this course in cases where they wish to show how or why the breaches occurred and to submit that the evidence should be adduced despite the breaches. In (b), the prosecution clearly have to call evidence to justify the order made and the defence may wish to call evidence from, eg, the solicitor to whom access was sought, or the accused himself. Cases under (c) are likely to be rare. It is unlikely that, in (a) and (b), the accused will be called. If the proper procedures have, on the face of the record, been observed, the contentions of the accused, for example that a properly recorded interview is inaccurate, would be unlikely to succeed. But if the breaches are obvious, the trial judge has no means of knowing what will ensue after he has made his ruling. If he excludes, the accused may exercise his right not to testify. To admit the evidence of the interview may therefore effectively deprive the accused of a right he otherwise had. And if the evidence is admitted, the accused may then give evidence that the interview never took place, or that it did take place but the questions and answers were fabricated or inaccurately recorded, or that it did take place and the record is accurate. Although it seems unjust that evidence should be excluded under s 78 when, if all the facts and the defence response were known, it would be clear that the evidence should not be excluded under the section, the difficulty cannot be avoided: the decision has to be made at a stage when the judge does not know the full facts. In *R v Dunford*,[166] a case involving denial of access to a solicitor, it was held that the trial judge was entitled (i) to take account of the accused's previous convictions; and (ii) to look at the contents of the record of the interview, including the terms of the confession, in order to help him to decide whether the presence of a solicitor might have made it less likely that the accused would confess. However, it was also

[162] Per Woolf LJ in *Matto v Crown Court at Wolverhampton* [1987] RTR 337, DC.
[163] See *R v Alladice* (1988) 87 Cr App R 380, CA and *R v Walsh* (1989) 91 Cr App R 161, CA at 163.
[164] [1989] 3 All ER 598, CA at 604–5, 606, and 608.
[165] See paras 11.15 and 11.17–11.20, Code C.
[166] (1990) 91 Cr App R 150, CA.

said that it may not be right to refer to or rely on the record where evidence has been adduced on the *voir dire* and there is a root and branch challenge to its contents.

Denial of access to a solicitor

Denial of access to a solicitor contrary to s 58 of the 1984 Act will, prima facie, have an adverse effect on the fairness of the proceedings.[167] In *Salduz v Turkey*[168] the Grand Chamber of the European Court of Human Rights held that early access to a lawyer is part of the procedural safeguards stemming from the privilege against self-incrimination and stressed the fundamental importance of providing access to a lawyer where the person in custody is a child. In *R v Samuel*[169] Hodgson J held that had the trial judge decided, as he should have done, that the accused had been improperly denied 'one of the most important and fundamental rights of a citizen', he might well have concluded that the refusal of access and consequent unlawful interview compelled him to find that admission of the confession would have had an adverse effect on the fairness of the proceedings. Similarly, where, in breach of Code C,[170] an arrested person is not properly informed, both orally and in writing, of his right to consult a solicitor, this may well result in exclusion, especially in the case of a foreigner with no previous convictions who is unfamiliar with the rights of a suspect at interview,[171] and such breaches will not necessarily be cured if he is later asked whether he agrees to be interviewed without a solicitor, and replies in the affirmative.[172] However, breach of s 58 or the accompanying provisions of the Code is no guarantee of exclusion.[173] Thus where a suspect is kept incommunicado, contrary to s 58, but after interview says that the absence of a solicitor made no difference and, following a belated granting of access to a solicitor, signs the notes of the interview, the evidence is admissible.[174] Similarly, if a suspect, who has agreed to be interviewed without a solicitor present, changes his mind, and the police improperly continue to interview him without allowing him to receive legal advice,[175] although this is a serious inroad into his rights, admissions subsequently made are admissible if the solicitor would have added nothing to his knowledge of his rights.[176]

In *R v Kirk*[177] it was held that where the police, having arrested a suspect in respect of one offence, propose to question him in respect of another more serious offence, they must first either charge him with the more serious offence, as envisaged by s 37 of the 1984 Act, or ensure that he is aware of the true nature of the investigation: that is the thrust and purport of para 10.1 of Code C. The accused can then give proper weight to the nature of the investigation when deciding whether or not to exercise his right to obtain free legal advice under the Code and when deciding how to respond to the questions which the police propose to ask.

[167] Per Saville J in *R v Walsh* (1989) 91 Cr App R 161, CA at 163. See also *R v Parris* (1988) 89 Cr App R 68, CA (see Ch 3).
[168] [2010] Crim LR 419, ECHR.
[169] [1988] 2 All ER 135, CA.
[170] See paras 3.1, 3.2, and 3.5.
[171] *R v Sanusi* [1992] Crim LR 43, CA.
[172] *R v Beycan* [1990] Crim LR 185, CA.
[173] See *R v Alladice* (1988) 87 Cr App R 380, CA and *R v Dunford* (1990) 91 Cr App R 150, CA (see Ch 3). See Hodgson, 'Tipping the Scales of Justice' [1992] Crim LR 854.
[174] *R v Findlay; R v Francis* [1992] Crim LR 372, CA.
[175] See para 6.6, Code C.
[176] *R v Oliphant* [1992] Crim LR 40, CA. See also *R v Anderson* [1993] Crim LR 447, CA.
[177] [1999] 4 All ER 698, CA.

The Act and the Codes, it was held, proceed on the assumption that a suspect in custody will know why he is there and, when being interviewed, will know at least in general terms the level of offence in respect of which he is suspected; and if he does not know, and as a result does not seek legal advice and gives critical answers which he might not otherwise have given, the evidence should normally be excluded under s 78, because its admission will have a seriously adverse effect on the fairness of the proceedings.

Breach of the 'verballing' provisions

In *R v Keenan*[178] it was held that if there have been serious and substantial breaches of the 'verballing' provisions of the Code (whereby, for example, an accurate contemporaneous record of an interview should be made), evidence so obtained should be excluded.[179] Thus confessions have been excluded on the basis of the following breaches: interviewing a juvenile in the absence of an 'appropriate adult';[180] interviewing a suspect before he has arrived at the police station and been informed of his right to free legal advice;[181] failure to tell a suspect that he is not under arrest coupled with failure to make a contemporaneous record of an interview;[182] failure to caution and to make such a record;[183] failure to give the suspect the opportunity to read and sign it as correct or to indicate the respects in which he considers it inaccurate;[184] failure to record a statement made other than in English in the language used and failure to give the opportunity to read a record and check its accuracy;[185] in a case in which the accused denied making a confession allegedly made *after* a taped interview with him, failure to give the suspect such an opportunity;[186] and undue pressure, by threatening

---

[178] [1989] 3 All ER 598, CA (see Ch 3).

[179] Under para 11.1A, Code C, an interview is the questioning of a person regarding his involvement or suspected involvement in a criminal offence or offences which, under para 10.1, Code C, must be carried out under caution. Whether there is an interview primarily turns on the nature of the questioning, rather than the number of questions or their length. Thus if an officer asks a single question directly relating to the crime, his motive being to clarify an ambiguity in a comment made by the suspect on arrest, that question and the answer to it may constitute an interview, although the officer's motive may be very relevant to the question of exclusion under s 78: *R v Ward* (1993) 98 Cr App R 337, CA. If an accused, under arrest, voluntarily offers to provide information and officers, without asking any questions, accede to that request and make a record of that information, that is not an interview, but nothing said at such a meeting can be produced in evidence at any subsequent trial: *R v Menard* [1995] 1 Cr App R 306, CA.

[180] *R v Weekes* (1993) 97 Cr App R 222, CA (para 11.15, Code C).

[181] *R v Cox* (1992) 96 Cr App R 464, CA (para 11.1; also paras 3.1, 3.2, and 10.1).

[182] *R v Joseph* [1993] Crim LR 206, CA (paras 10.2 and 11.7, Code C). Cf *Watson v DPP* [2003] All ER (D) 132 (Jun), DC.

[183] See *R v Sparks* [1991] Crim LR 128, CA (paras 10.1 and 11.7, Code C) and *R v Bryce* [1992] 4 All ER 567, CA (paras 10.8 and 11.7, Code C). See also *R v Okafor* [1994] 3 All ER 741, CA, where there was *also* a failure to remind of the right to legal advice (para 11.2, Code C).

[184] See *R v Foster* [1987] Crim LR 821, CC (para 11.11, Code C) and *R v Weerdesteyn* [1995] 1 Cr App R 405, CA, where there was also a failure to caution. Cf *R v Courtney* [1995] Crim LR 63, CA, where failure to give the suspect an opportunity to read and sign a record of comments outside the context of an interview (in breach of para 11.13, Code C) was treated as 'insubstantial'. See also *R v Park* (1993) 99 Cr App R 270, CA: if answers to exploratory questions give rise in due course to a well-founded suspicion that an offence has been committed, what has started out as an inquiry may have become an interview and if it does, the requirements of the Code must be followed in relation to both the earlier and later questioning. Thus, although a contemporaneous note is no longer possible, a record should be made as soon as practicable of the earlier questions and answers, the reason for the absence of a contemporaneous note should be recorded, and the suspect should be given the opportunity to check the record.

[185] *R v Coelho* [2008] EWCA Crim 627 (paras 13.4 and 11.13, Code C).

[186] *R v Scott* [1991] Crim LR 56, CA, where it was held that by admitting the confession, the judge effectively compelled the accused to give evidence. Cf *R v Matthews, R v Dennison,* and *R v Voss* (1989) 91 Cr App R 43, CA.

a number of charges, instead of only two, if the suspect continued to deny the charge.[187] However, relatively trivial breaches, such as a failure to record the reason why an interview record was not completed in the course of an interview,[188] or such a breach coupled with a failure to record the time when an interview record was made,[189] have not resulted in exclusion. Moreover, even serious breaches of the 'verballing' provisions may be 'cured' by the presence of a solicitor or his clerk. In *R v Dunn*[190] D denied making a confession, allegedly made *after* his interview, during the signing of the interview notes, and in the presence of his solicitor's clerk. The 'conversation' in which the confession was made was not recorded contemporaneously and no note of it was shown to D. It was held that, despite these serious breaches, the evidence was admissible because the clerk was present to protect D's interests: she could have intervened to prevent the accused from answering, her presence would have inhibited the police from fabricating the conversation, and, if they were to fabricate, it would not simply be a question of their evidence against that of D, because she would also be able to give evidence for the accused.

The effect of breaches of Code C on subsequent interviews

If a confession is excluded under s 78 by reason of a breach of the Code, a confession made in a subsequent, but properly conducted interview *may* be tainted by the earlier breach and therefore also fall to be excluded under s 78. The question of exclusion is a matter of fact and degree which is likely to depend on whether the breaches leading to the exclusion of the first interview were of a fundamental and continuing nature and, if so, if the arrangements for the subsequent interview gave the accused a sufficient opportunity to exercise an informed and independent choice as to whether he should repeat or retract what he said in the first interview or say nothing.[191] In *R v Canale*,[192] where the first two interviews were not contemporaneously recorded and no record was shown to the accused for verification, it was held that these breaches had affected subsequent admissions which therefore should have been excluded under s 78. However, in *R v Gillard and Barrett*[193] it was held that breaches of the Code, similar to those in *R v Canale*, in earlier interviews had not tainted confessions made in subsequent but properly conducted interviews. *R v Canale* was distinguished on the basis that in that case there was a nexus between the earlier and later interviews: the accused claimed that he had been induced by promises to make the admissions in the first interview and these promises may have continued to affect answers in the later interviews. The length of time separating the interviews is clearly relevant,[194] but the critical factor, it seems, is whether there is any

---

[187] *R v Howden-Simpson* [1991] Crim LR 49, CA (para 11.5, Code C). See also *R v De Silva* [2003] 2 Cr App R 74, CA, where the confessions were made, after being cautioned, in telephone calls to other suspects which the police had induced the accused to make by the promise of a reduced sentence, if convicted.

[188] See *R v White* [1991] Crim LR 779, CA and para 11.10, Code C.

[189] See *R v Findlay; R v Francis* [1992] Crim LR 372, CA and para 11.9, Code C.

[190] (1990) 91 Cr App R 237, CA. See also Roberts, 'Questioning the Suspect' [1993] Crim LR 368 and Baldwin, 'Legal Advice at the Police Station' [1993] Crim LR 371.

[191] *R v Neil* [1994] Crim LR 441, CA, applied in *R v Nelson and Rose* [1998] 2 Cr App R 399, CA.

[192] [1990] 2 All ER 187, CA (see Ch 3). See also *R v Blake* [1991] Crim LR 119, CC.

[193] (1990) 92 Cr App R 61, CA.

[194] See *R v Conway* [1994] Crim LR 838, CA, where account was taken of the fact that only 20 minutes separated the interviews.

suggestion of oppression, inducement, stress, or pressure in the earlier interview which might continue to exert a malign influence during the later interview.[195]

Interviews with persons not governed by the Codes

As already noted in this chapter,[196] the Codes only apply to police officers and others charged with the duty of investigating offences or charging offenders. However, where a confession has been made in the course of an interview with some other person, eg a doctor or psychiatrist, the court, in deciding whether to exercise the s 78 discretion, is entitled to take into account the fact that the accused did not have the benefit of the safeguards provided by the Codes. In *R v Elleray*[197] it was held that, given the need for frankness in the exchanges between a probation officer and an offender, the prosecution should only rely upon a confession made to a probation officer if it is in the public interest to do so, but where they do rely on such a confession, the court, in deciding whether to exclude it under s 78, is entitled to take into account not only the need for frankness, but also the reliability of the record of what was said, that the offender was not cautioned, and that he did not have the benefit of legal representation. On the facts of the case, the confessions, which were of rape, were held to have been properly admitted.[198]

The *voir dire*

When a *voir dire* is necessary

If either (i) the prosecution rely on oral statements and the defence case is simply that the interview never took place or that the incriminating statements were never made; or (ii) the prosecution rely on written statements and the defence case is that they are forgeries, no question of admissibility falls for the judge's decision. The issue of fact whether or not the statement was made by the accused is for the jury. However, if the accused denies authorship of a written statement and claims that he signed it involuntarily, or claims that his signature to what in fact was a confession statement was obtained by the fraudulent misrepresentation that he was signing a document of an entirely different character, he puts in issue the admissibility of the statement on which the judge must rule and, if the judge admits the statement, all issues of fact as to the circumstances of the making and signing of the statement should then be left for the jury to consider and evaluate.[199]

Subject to the foregoing, if the prosecution propose to admit evidence of a confession, the defence have two options. They may represent[200] to the court that the confession was or may have been obtained by the methods set out in s 76(2) (or in any event should be excluded by the judge in the exercise of his discretion) and the question of admissibility must then be

---

[195] See per Taylor LJ in *Y v DPP* [1991] Crim LR 917, DC. See also *R v Glaves* [1993] Crim LR 685, CA; *R v Wood* [1994] Crim LR 222, CA; and generally Mirfield, 'Successive Confessions and the Poisonous Tree' [1996] Crim LR 554.

[196] Under **The discretion to exclude, The Codes of Practice, Persons governed by the Codes.**

[197] [2003] 2 Cr App R 165, CA.

[198] See also *R v McDonald* [1991] Crim LR 122, CA (see Ch 3).

[199] Per Lord Bridge in *Ajodha v The State* [1981] 2 All ER 193, PC at 201–2, applied in *R v Flemming* (1987) 86 Cr App R 32, CA.

[200] A suggestion, in cross-examination, that a confession was obtained improperly does not amount to a representation for the purposes of s 76(2): per Russell LJ, expressly confining his rulings to summary trials, in *R v Liverpool Juvenile Court, ex p R* [1987] 2 All ER 668, DC at 673.

determined on the *voir dire*.[201] Alternatively, the defence may choose not to dispute the admissibility of the confession, in which case, assuming that the court does not exercise its own powers under s 76(3) to require the prosecution to prove that the confession was not obtained by the methods set out in s 76(2), the confession may be given in evidence.[202] At common law, prior to the 1984 Act, there was a third option, namely to allow the jury to hear the evidence of the confession and subsequently, when all the evidence had been heard, to submit to the judge that, if he doubted the admissibility of the statement, he should direct the jury to disregard it.[203] However, this option has not survived the 1984 Act: on its wording, s 76 only permits the question of legal admissibility to be raised where the prosecution 'propose…' to give a confession in evidence. Similarly, s 78 refers to evidence on which the prosecution 'propose…' to rely. Accordingly, it has been said that if an accused wishes to exclude a confession under s 76, the time to make such a submission is before the confession is put in evidence and not afterwards.[204] This would also appear to be the time at which a submission based on s 78 should be made.[205]

The procedure

In cases in which defence counsel intends to make a submission that a confession should be excluded, his intention will be conveyed to prosecuting counsel at the Plea and Case Management Hearing or immediately before the trial commences, so that the confession is not referred to in the presence of the jury, whether in the prosecution opening speech or otherwise.[206] The prosecution will adduce their evidence in the normal way but at that point in time when the confession would otherwise be admitted, counsel will intimate to the court that a point of law has arisen which falls to be determined in the absence of the jury.[207] The defence have no right to insist on the presence of the jury at the *voir dire*: the judge, after listening to the views of the defence, has the final word on whether the jury should remain in court.[208] At the *voir dire*, the prosecution will bear the burden of proving beyond reasonable doubt that the confession was not obtained by the methods described in s 76(2). Witnesses, in the usual case police officers, will be called to give evidence of the confession and the circumstances in which it was made and will be open to cross-examination by defence counsel.

---

[201] Concerning summary trials, see Ch 2, under **The functions of the judge and jury, The *voir dire*, or trial within a trial**.

[202] However, any resulting conviction may be quashed if the prosecution failed to disclose material which would have provided the defence with an informed opportunity to seek a *voir dire*: *R v Langley* [2001] Crim LR 651, CA.

[203] See per Lord Bridge in *Ajodha v The State* [1981] 2 All ER 193 at 202–3.

[204] See *R v Sat-Bhambra* (1988) 88 Cr App R 55, CA at n 230. See also *R v Davis* [1990] Crim LR 860, CA and *Alagaratnam v R* [2011] Crim LR 232, CA. For the position in summary trials, see *R v Liverpool Juvenile Court, ex p R* [1987] 2 All ER 668, DC (see Ch 2).

[205] But see, in the case of summary trials, per Russell LJ in *R v Liverpool Juvenile Court, ex p R* [1987] 2 All ER 668, DC (see Ch 2).

[206] *R v Cole* (1941) 165 LT 125. In the trial of an unrepresented accused, it may be prudent, if the judge has any reason to suppose that the admissibility of a statement proposed to be put in evidence by the prosecution is likely to be in issue, to explain to the accused his rights in the matter before the trial begins: per Lord Bridge in *Ajodha v The State* [1981] 2 All ER 193, PC at 203.

[207] Occasionally it is convenient to determine admissibility immediately after the jury have been empanelled, as when the evidence of the confession is so important to the prosecution case that without reference to it they cannot even open their case: see *R v Hammond* [1941] 3 All ER 318.

[208] *R v Hendry* (1988) 153 JP 166, CA, applied in *R v Davis* [1990] Crim LR 860, CA.

The accused may then give evidence and call any witnesses who can support his version of events. The defence witnesses will also be open to cross-examination. The judge may also take into account any relevant evidence already given in the main trial, because the issue of admissibility cannot be tried in total isolation from the whole background of the case.[209] After speeches from counsel, the judge gives his ruling. If the confession is excluded, then nothing more should be heard of it.[210] If the confession is admitted, it may be put in evidence before the jury. Either way, however, in modern English practice the judge's decision is never revealed to the jury.[211]

Wong Kam-Ming v R

The case of *Wong Kam-Ming v R*[212] gave rise to three important questions concerning the *voir dire*. They were: (i) during cross-examination of an accused on the *voir dire*, whether questions may be put as to the truth of the confession; (ii) whether the prosecution are permitted, on the resumption of the trial proper, to adduce evidence of what the accused said on the *voir dire*; and (iii) whether the prosecution are permitted, in the trial proper, to cross-examine the accused about what he said on the *voir dire*. The accused was charged with murder at a massage parlour. The only evidence against him was a signed confession in which he admitted that he was present at the parlour at the relevant time, had a knife in his hand, and 'chopped' someone. The admissibility of the confession was challenged on the ground that it was not made voluntarily. Under cross-examination on the *voir dire*, the accused was asked questions about the contents of the confession statement which were directed at establishing their truth. In answer, the accused admitted that he was present at the parlour and involved in the incident in question. The trial judge ruled that the signed confession was inadmissible. Before the jury, the judge allowed the prosecution to establish the accused's presence at the parlour by calling the shorthand writers to produce extracts from the transcript of the cross-examination on the *voir dire*. After the accused had given his evidence-in-chief before the jury, the prosecution were also permitted to cross-examine him on inconsistencies between that evidence and his evidence on the *voir dire* as recorded in the shorthand transcript. The accused was convicted and the Court of Appeal of Hong Kong dismissed his appeal. The Privy Council allowed the appeal on three grounds. First, it was held by a majority that the accused had been improperly cross-examined on the *voir dire* as to the truth of his confession statement because the sole issue on the *voir dire* was whether the statement had been made involuntarily, an issue to which its truth or falsity was irrelevant.[213] Second, it was held that the prosecution had been improperly permitted to adduce before the jury evidence of the answers given by the accused on the *voir dire*. In the opinion of their Lordships, such evidence should not be adduced, regardless of whether the confession is excluded or admitted, because a clear distinction should be maintained between the issue of voluntariness, which is

---

[209] *R v Tyrer* (1989) 90 Cr App R 446, CA.

[210] *R v Treacy* [1944] 2 All ER 229, CCA. But see also *R v Rowson* [1985] 2 All ER 539, CA (see Ch 7); and s 76A, under **Admissibility, The conditions of admissibility** in this chapter.

[211] Per Lord Steyn in *Mitchell v R* [1998] 2 Cr App R 35, PC at 42.

[212] [1980] AC 247.

[213] Lord Hailsham, dissenting, was of the opinion that in many cases the truth or falsity of the alleged confession could be relevant to the question at issue on the *voir dire* or to the credibility of either the defence or prosecution witnesses. See also *R v Hammond* [1941] 3 All ER 318, CCA, which, in the view of the majority in *Wong Kam-Ming v R*, was wrongly decided.

alone relevant to the *voir dire*, and the issue of guilt, which falls to be decided in the main trial.[214] Third, it was held that the prosecution had been improperly permitted to cross-examine the accused on inconsistencies between his evidence before the jury and his statements on the *voir dire* because such a course is only permitted where the *voir dire* results in the admission of the confession and the accused gives evidence before the jury on some matter other than the voluntariness of the confession, which is no longer in issue, and in so doing gives answers which are inconsistent with his testimony on the *voir dire*.[215]

What is the status of the decision in *Wong Kam-Ming v R* in the light of the Police and Criminal Evidence Act 1984? Concerning the first part of the decision, the law remains the same under the Act. The truth of the confession is as irrelevant to the issue of 'oppression' or 'unreliability' as it was to the issue of 'voluntariness'. Section 76(2), it will be recalled, requires the prosecution to prove that the confession, 'notwithstanding that it may be true', was not obtained by the methods it describes.[216] The second and third parts of the decision, insofar as they prohibit the prosecution from leading evidence on or cross-examining the accused about what he said on the *voir dire*, continue to represent the law under the Act but only, it would appear, in relation to statements made by the accused on the *voir dire* which are not 'adverse' to him. Section 82(1) defines a confession to include *any* statement wholly or partly adverse to the person who made it. Thus if, on the *voir dire*, the accused makes an inculpatory statement relevant to his guilt on the offence charged, which can hardly be said to have been obtained by oppression or in circumstances such as to render unreliable any confession which he might have made, then regardless of whether the extrajudicial confession is excluded or admitted, the statement may be given in evidence by the prosecution under s 76(1) and the accused may be cross-examined on any inconsistencies between that statement and the evidence he gives before the jury.[217] If this is correct, it presents the accused with an unenviable choice. An accused seeking to challenge the admissibility of a confession may be obliged to testify on the *voir dire* if his challenge is to have any chance of succeeding. If he elects to contest admissibility, then to the extent that evidence given by him on the *voir dire* is admissible in evidence at the trial, he is in effect deprived of the right to choose not to give evidence before the jury. If he elects to preserve that right, however, he deprives himself of the right to challenge the admissibility of the confession.[218] An accused deprived of his rights in this manner, it has been said, would not receive a fair trial.[219] The solution, it is submitted, is for the judge to exercise his discretion under s 78 of the 1984 Act to exclude the statements made by the accused on the

---

[214] See also *R v Brophy* [1982] AC 476, HL, discussed in text at n 220.

[215] Cf the Criminal Procedure Act 1865, s 4, which provides that 'if a witness, upon cross-examination as to a former statement made by him…does not distinctly admit that he has made such statement, proof may be given that he did in fact make it': see Ch 7. Section 13 of the Hong Kong Evidence Ordinance is to the same effect. Lord Edmund Davies said at 259: 'But these statutory provisions have no relevance if the earlier statements cannot be put in evidence.'

[216] *Wong Kam-Ming v R* is strong persuasive authority that the accused should not be cross-examined as to the truth of his confession on the *voir dire: R v Davis* [1990] Crim LR 860, CA.

[217] See Mirfield, 'The Future of the Law of Confessions' [1984] Crim LR 63 at 74.

[218] See generally per Lord Hailsham in *Wong Kam-Ming v R* [1980] AC 247 at 261 and per Lord Fraser in *R v Brophy* [1982] AC 476 at 481. For views different to those expressed, see Murphy [1979] Crim LR 364 and Pattenden (1983) 32 ICLQ 812.

[219] Per Lord Fraser in *R v Brophy* [1982] AC 476 at 482.

voir dire on the grounds that they would have such an adverse effect on the fairness of the proceedings that the court ought not to admit them.

The issue of discretion, in this context, arose in *R v Brophy*.[220] The accused was tried by a judge sitting without a jury under the Northern Ireland (Emergency Provisions) Act 1978 on an indictment containing 49 counts including counts of murder, causing explosions, and belonging to a proscribed organization, namely the IRA (count 49). The only evidence connecting him with the crimes was a number of oral and written statements made to the police. The accused challenged the admissibility of the statements on the grounds that they had been obtained by torture and inhuman or degrading treatment. The trial judge, after a *voir dire*, excluded evidence of the statements. The accused, in his evidence-in-chief on the *voir dire*, said that he had been a member of the IRA during most of the period charged in count 49. When the trial resumed, the prosecution called the shorthand writer to prove the statements of the accused as to his membership of the IRA. The accused was acquitted of the first 48 counts, which were unsupported by any evidence, but convicted on count 49. The Court of Appeal in Northern Ireland allowed the appeal and the appeal to the House of Lords was dismissed. It was held that the accused's membership of the IRA was relevant to the issue on the *voir dire* because the police would probably have known this and therefore would not only have been more hostile to him but also would have expected him to have received instruction on how to avoid succumbing to the normal techniques of interrogation not involving physical ill-treatment. It was further held that, in any event, the evidence-in-chief given by an accused on the *voir dire* should be treated as relevant, unless clearly and obviously irrelevant, with the accused being given the benefit of any reasonable doubt.[221] The House concluded that the relevance of the evidence in question to the issue at the *voir dire* having been established, the consequence was that it was inadmissible in the substantive trial. In answer to a submission by counsel for the prosecution that if the evidence on the *voir dire* were admissible in the trial proper, the accused would be adequately safeguarded if the judge had a discretion to exclude any such evidence which would prejudice him unfairly, Lord Fraser said:[222]

> The right of the accused to give evidence at the *voir dire* without affecting his right to remain silent at the substantive trial is in my opinion absolute and is not to be made conditional on an exercise of judicial discretion.

Now that the actual decision in this case would appear to have been reversed by the 1984 Act, it is submitted that evidence given on the *voir dire* should be excluded from the trial proper by exercise of the discretion under s 78.[223]

The trial

Once the trial judge has ruled that a confession is admissible, the weight to be attached to it, which depends upon its content and all the circumstances in which it was obtained, is

---

[220] [1982] AC 476.

[221] However, if the accused goes out of his way to boast of having committed the crimes charged or uses the witness box as a platform for a political speech, such evidence will almost certainly be irrelevant to the issue at the *voir dire*: per Lord Fraser [1982] AC 476 at 481.

[222] [1982] AC 476 at 483.

[223] However, concerning Lord Fraser's reference to the 'right to remain silent at the substantive trial', see now the Criminal Justice and Public Order Act 1994, s 35 (see Ch 14) and generally Mirfield, 'Two Side-Effects of Sections 34 to 37 of the Criminal Justice and Public Order Act 1994' [1995] Crim LR 612.

entirely a question of fact for the jury.[224] On the resumption of the trial proper, therefore, the defence is fully entitled to adduce evidence and cross-examine prosecution witnesses with a view to impeaching the credibility of the person to whom the confession was allegedly made and showing, for example, that the confession was fabricated, in whole or in part, or made in circumstances different from those alleged by the prosecution. Although, as we have seen, the truth of the confession is irrelevant on the *voir dire*, it is a crucial issue for the jury to consider.[225] The judge, pursuant to s 67(11) of the 1984 Act, may refer the jury to any relevant breaches of the Codes.[226] Moreover, the House of Lords in *R v Mushtaq*,[227] disapproving *Chan Wei Keung v R*,[228] held by a majority that where the judge has ruled that a confession was not obtained by oppression nor in consequence of anything said or done which was likely to render unreliable any confession, but there is some evidence before the jury that the confession may have been so obtained, and they conclude that the alleged confession was or may have been so obtained, they must disregard it. If the jury reach such a conclusion, to permit them to rely upon the confession would be to fly in the face of the policy considerations said to underlie s 76(2), namely that the rejection of an improperly obtained confession is dependent not only upon possible unreliability, but also upon the principle that a man cannot be compelled to incriminate himself and upon the importance that attaches in a civilized society to proper behaviour by the police towards those in their custody. The judge should therefore direct the jury that unless they are satisfied beyond reasonable doubt that the confession was not obtained by the means set out in s 76(2)(a) and (b), they should disregard it.[229] Furthermore, permission to rely upon the confession in these circumstances would also be an invitation to the jury to act in a way that was incompatible with the accused's right against self-incrimination under Art 6(1) of the European Convention on Human Rights.

The trial judge, once he has determined that a confession is admissible under s 76 of the 1984 Act, has no power, at some later stage in the trial, to reconsider its admissibility as a matter of *law*. In *R v Sat-Bhambra*[230] a confession was ruled to be admissible after a trial within a trial in which a doctor had given expert evidence to the effect that the accused, who suffered from a mild form of diabetes, could have been affected by hypoglycaemia at the time of his interrogation. When the doctor was called in the trial proper, his evidence on the issue came out more in favour of the accused. The trial judge, however, declined to reconsider his decision on admissibility on the grounds that he was precluded from so doing by the terms of s 76. The Court of Appeal held that the trial judge had acted properly. Section 76 refers to a confession which the prosecution 'proposes to give in evidence' and which the court 'shall not allow...to be given in evidence' and therefore, once the judge has ruled that a confession is admissible, section 76 ceases to have effect. Section 78, which, similarly, refers to evidence on which the prosecution 'proposes to rely', also ceases to have effect.[231] The judge, however,

---

[224] Per Lord Parker CJ in *R v Burgess* [1968] 2 QB 112, CA at 117–18. But see the 1984 Act, s 77 (see Ch 8).

[225] *R v Murray* (1950) 34 Cr App R 203 at 207.

[226] See *R v Kenny* [1992] Crim LR 800, CA.

[227] [2005] 1 WLR 1513, HL.

[228] [1967] 2 AC 160, PC.

[229] *R v Pham* [2008] All ER (D) 96 (Dec), CA.

[230] (1988) 88 Cr App R 55, CA.

[231] Cf per Russell LJ in *R v Liverpool Juvenile Court, ex p R* [1987] 2 All ER 668 at 672–3, dealing with similar issues in relation to summary trials (see Ch 2).

is not powerless: if, in the light of the evidence given in the trial proper, he concludes that his previous decision on admissibility has been invalidated, he may, in the exercise of his discretion to exclude under s 82(3), direct the jury to disregard the confession.[232] Alternatively, and depending on the circumstances of the case, he may either point out to the jury the evidence which affects the weight of the confession and leave the matter in their hands or, if he thinks that the matter is not capable of remedy by any form of direction, discharge the jury from giving a verdict. The same options, presumably, would be open to a judge when a confession is put in evidence and the accused *then* gives evidence to the effect that it was obtained by one of the methods described in section 76(2).[233]

Confessions implicating co-accused

If an accused goes into the witness box and gives evidence implicating a co-accused, then what he says becomes evidence for all purposes of the case and accordingly may be used by the jury as evidence against the co-accused.[234] However, subject to three exceptions,[235] where a confession is given in evidence by the prosecution and implicates both its maker and a co-accused, it is no evidence against the co-accused because a confession is admissible as evidence of the truth of its contents only as against its maker. In these circumstances, therefore, the judge is duty bound to impress upon the jury that the confession cannot be used against the co-accused.[236] It may be doubted, however, whether such a direction, even if clear and emphatic, can ever fully remove the prejudice likely to be caused to the co-accused.[237] In one case it was said that it would require mental gymnastics of Olympic standards for the jury to approach their task without prejudice.[238] One obvious solution is to order separate trials for the accused, but although the Court of Appeal in *R v Lake*[239] recognized that exceptionally this can be done, it nevertheless upheld a trial judge's refusal to order a separate trial. Another solution is to edit the confession, for example by replacing the names of any co-accused with letters of the alphabet or expressions such as 'another person' or 'someone'.[240] Alternatively, counsel for the prosecution may agree not to read those parts of a confession statement which implicate a co-accused but have no real bearing on the case against its author. However, if the reference to the co-accused is exculpatory of the maker of the statement, he is entitled to have

---

[232] Section 82(3) is the source of the power, but the judge is likely to re-apply the s 78 criteria in the light of the new evidence: see *R v Hassan* [1995] Crim LR 404, CA.

[233] It may also be assumed that the judge has a discretion, in this situation, to require the relevant prosecution witnesses to be recalled for further cross-examination: see per Lord Bridge in *Ajodha v The State* [1981] 2 All ER 193, PC at 202–3.

[234] See per Humphreys J in *R v Rudd* (1948) 32 Cr App R 138.

[235] Discussed in the text at nn 243–259.

[236] *R v Gunewardene* [1951] 2 KB 600, CCA. See also *R v Blake* [1993] Crim LR 133, CA and per Lord Steyn in *Lobban v R* [1995] 2 All ER 602, PC at 613.

[237] See, eg, *R v Williams; R v Davis* (1992) 95 Cr App R 1, CA. See also Thornton, 'The Prejudiced Defendant: Unfairness Suffered by a Defendant in a Joint Trial' [2003] Crim LR 433.

[238] *R v Silcott* [1987] Crim LR 765, CC.

[239] (1976) 64 Cr App R 172.

[240] As suggested in *R v Silcott* [1987] Crim LR 765, CC. See also *R v Rogers and Tarran* [1971] Crim LR 413 and *R v Mathias* [1989] Crim LR 64, CC. However, insofar as *R v Silcott* and *R v Mathias* suggest that a judge has a discretionary power at the request of one accused to exclude evidence tending to support the defence of another, they do not correctly reflect the law: per Lord Steyn in *Lobban v R* [1995] 2 All ER 602, PC at 613 (see Ch 2).

the statement read out in its entirety. As Lord Goddard CJ observed in *R v Gunewardene*,[241] in a passage approved by the Privy Council in *Lobban v R*:[242]

> It not infrequently happens that a prisoner, in making a statement, though admitting his guilt up to a certain extent, puts greater blame upon the co-prisoner, or is asserting that certain of his actions were really innocent and it was the conduct of the co-prisoner that gave them a sinister appearance or led to the belief that the prisoner making the statement was implicated in the crime. In such a case that prisoner would have a right to have the whole statement read and could complain if the prosecution picked out certain passages and left out others…

In three exceptional situations, a confession may be admitted not only as evidence against its maker but also as evidence against a co-accused. The first exception was established in *R v Hayter*,[243] where the House of Lords held, by a majority, that in a joint trial of two or more accused for a joint offence, a jury are entitled to consider first the case in respect of accused A which is solely based on his own out-of-court admissions, and then to use their findings of A's guilt as a fact to be used evidentially in respect of co-accused B, and further that where proof of A's guilt is necessary for there to be a case to answer against B, there will be a case to answer against him notwithstanding that the only evidence of A's guilt is his own out-of-court admissions. A's confession, however, can only be admitted against B on two conditions: first, that the jury are sufficiently sure of its truthfulness to decide that on that basis alone they can safely convict A; and second, that the jury are expressly directed that when deciding the case against B they must disregard entirely anything said out of court by A which might otherwise be thought to incriminate B. In reaching this conclusion, the majority were heavily influenced by the policy considerations underlying s 74 of the 1984 Act, whereby the fact that someone other than the accused has been convicted of an offence is admissible to prove, where to do so is relevant to an issue in the proceedings, that that person committed the offence.[244] If there had been separate trials and A had been convicted, evidence of the conviction would have been admissible under s 74 of the 1984 Act in a subsequent trial of B. *R v Hayter* was distinguished in *Persad v State of Trinidad and Tobago*[245] where (i) the co-accused was *not* jointly liable for the offence; and (ii) it *was* sought to rely on A's statement insofar as it incriminated B.

The second exception is where the co-accused by his words or conduct accepts the truth of the statement so as to make all or part of it a confession statement of his own.[246]

The third exception, which is perhaps best understood in terms of implied agency, applies in the case of conspiracy: statements (or acts) of one conspirator which the jury are satisfied were said (or done) in the execution or furtherance of the common design are admissible in evidence against another conspirator, even though he was not present at the time, to prove the nature and scope of the conspiracy, provided that there is some independent evidence to show the existence of the conspiracy and that the other conspirator was a party to it.[247] Thus in

---

[241] [1951] 2 KB 600 at 610–11.

[242] [1995] 2 All ER 602 at 612 (see Ch 2).

[243] [2005] 1 WLR 605, HL.

[244] See Ch 21.

[245] [2008] 1 Cr App R 140, PC.

[246] See generally, in this chapter, under **Statements made in the presence of the accused**.

[247] *R v Shellard* (1840) 9 C&P 277, *R v Meany* (1867) 10 Cox CC 506, *R v Walters, R v Tovey* (1979) 69 Cr App R 115, and *R v Jenkins* [2003] Crim LR 107, CA. However, if there are two conspiracies, what A does in pursuance of the first is not admissible against B in respect of his involvement in the second: *R v Gray* [1995] 2 Cr App R 100, CA at 131. For a comparative examination of this exception to the hearsay rule, including an evaluation of its possible rationale, see Spencer, 'The common enterprise exception to the hearsay rule' (2007) 11 E&P 106.

R v Blake and Tye,[248] where the accused were charged with conspiracy to pass goods through the Custom House without paying duty, it was held that whereas a false entry by T in a counterfoil of a cheque, by which he received his share of the proceeds of the crime, was not admissible against B because it was not made in pursuance of the conspiracy, but simply as a matter of record and convenience, another false entry by T in a day book could be used in evidence against B since it was made in the execution or furtherance of their common design. *R v Blake and Tye* was applied in *R v Devonport*,[249] in which the prosecution were allowed to rely on a document, dictated by one accused, which showed the proposed division of the proceeds of the conspiracy among all five accused.[250]

It does not matter in what order the evidence of the statements (or acts) of the conspirator and the 'independent evidence' is adduced.[251] Evidence of the statements (or acts) may be admitted conditionally, ie conditional upon some other evidence of the common design being adduced; if it transpires that there is no other evidence of common design, then the statements (or acts) should be excluded.[252] The decision whether there is sufficient 'independent evidence' is for the judge alone,[253] but any consequential risk that the jury may see the 'independent evidence' as unconvincing and yet act upon the statement or act of the one conspirator in the absence of the other, may be avoided by directing the jury about any shortcomings in the evidence of the statement or act, including, if it be the case, the absence of any opportunity to cross-examine the maker of the statement or act and the absence of corroborative evidence.[254]

The following elaborations on the principle derive from *R v Platten*.[255] (1) The exception does not cover narrative, after the conclusion of the conspiracy, describing past events. (2) It covers statements made during a conspiracy and as part of the natural process of making the arrangements to carry it out, which are admissible not just as to the nature and extent of the conspiracy, but also as to the participation in it of persons absent when the statements were made. (3) Such statements can be admitted against all the conspirators even if made by one conspirator to a non-conspirator. (4) Statements about a conspirator having 'second thoughts' would be made in furtherance of the common design, because it is typical of a conspiracy for one conspirator to have doubts and to be persuaded by his co-conspirators to forget them. (5) Statements made before a conspirator was alleged to have joined the agreement can only be evidence of the origin of the conspiracy, not evidence of his part in it.

The principle does apply when, although a conspiracy is not charged, two or more people are engaged in a common enterprise: the acts and declarations of one in pursuance of the common purpose are admissible against another.[256] This extension of the principle applies to the

[248] (1844) 6 QB 126.
[249] [1996] 1 Cr App R 221, CA.
[250] See also *R v Ilyas and Knight* [1996] Crim LR 810, CA.
[251] *R v Governor of Pentonville Prison, ex p Osman* [1989] 3 All ER 701, QBD at 731.
[252] *R v Donat* (1985) 82 Cr App R 173, CA.
[253] *R v Barham* [1997] 2 Cr App R 119, CA and *R v King* [2012] EWCA Crim 805, where it was said that it is also for the judge alone to decide whether the statement (or act) was said (done) in furtherance of the conspiracy.
[254] *R v King* [2012] EWCA Crim 805, citing *Ahern v R* [1988] ALR 162, High Court of Australia.
[255] [2006] Crim LR 920, CA.
[256] See, eg, *R v Jones* [1997] 2 Cr App R 119, CA.

commission of a substantive offence or series of offences by two or more people acting in concert, but is limited to evidence which shows the involvement of each accused in the commission of the offence or offences.[257] However, it does not apply to cases where individual defendants are charged with a number of separate substantive offences and the terms of a common enterprise are not proved or are ill-defined.[258] The rule is that the acts and declarations of one, in furtherance of a sufficiently defined common design, are admissible to prove a substantive offence committed by another alone, but in pursuance of the same common design.[259]

The foregoing common law exceptions have been preserved by statute. Section 118(1) of the Criminal Justice Act 2003 preserves: '5 Any rule of law relating to the admissibility of confessions... in criminal proceedings' and '7 Any rule of law under which in criminal proceedings a statement made by a party to a common enterprise is admissible against another party to the enterprise as evidence of any matter stated'.

Editing

Where a confession is given in evidence, the whole statement, including qualifications, explanations, or other exculpatory parts of it should be admitted so that the jury can fairly decide whether the statement, viewed as a whole, incriminates the accused.[260] However, where a confession statement contains inadmissible matter prejudicial to the accused, such as a reference to his previous convictions or bad character, it should be edited so as to eliminate the offending material.[261] Counsel may confer on the matter and, if necessary, the judge can take his part in ensuring that the statement is edited properly and to the right degree.[262] Although the rule is one of practice rather than law, a failure to edit may result in a conviction on indictment being quashed.[263] If the confession and the offending material are so interwoven as to be inseparable, or the removal of the latter would seriously alter the sense and meaning of the former so that they stand or fall together, the judge may, in the exercise of his discretion, exclude the entire statement on the grounds that its prejudicial effect outweighs its probative value.[264]

Statements made in the presence of the accused

Under s 82(1) of the 1984 Act, a confession, as we have seen, includes any statement adverse to the person who made it 'whether made in words or otherwise'. It would seem, therefore,

---

[257] *R v Gray* [1995] 2 Cr App R 100, CA. See also *Tripodi v R* (1961) 104 CLR 1, HC of A.

[258] *R v Murray* [1997] 2 Cr App R 136, CA, per Otton LJ at 148.

[259] *R v Williams* [2002] EWCA Crim 2208, approving *R v Murray* [1997] 2 Cr App R 136, CA, per Otton LJ at 148.

[260] *R v Pearce* (1979) 69 Cr App R 365 at 369–70. How the judge should properly direct the jury in relation to a statement containing both inculpatory and exculpatory parts is considered in Ch 6, under **Previous consistent or self-serving statements**.

[261] When a suspect is interviewed about more offences than are eventually made the subject of charges, a fresh statement should be prepared and signed omitting all questions and answers about the uncharged offences unless either they might appropriately be taken into consideration or evidence about them is admissible on the charges preferred (eg as similar fact evidence). It may, however, be desirable to replace the omitted questions and answers with a phrase such as: 'After referring to some other matters, I then said...', so as to make it clear that part of the interview has been omitted: see para 24.4(b), the *Consolidated Criminal Practice Direction*.

[262] *R v Weaver* [1968] 1 QB 353, CA.

[263] *R v Knight; R v Thompson* (1946) 31 Cr App R 52; *Turner v Underwood* [1948] 2 KB 284, DC.

[264] See discussion of s 82(3), under **The discretion to exclude, Section 82(3) of the Police and Criminal Evidence Act 1984**, in this chapter.

that under the Act, as at common law, the accused may accept the accusation of another so as to make it wholly or in part a confession statement of his own, not only by his words but also, in appropriate circumstances, by his conduct, demeanour, or even silence. An alternative basis for the same conclusion is the inclusive nature of the statutory definition. Either way, if this construction is correct, it would enable the accused, in appropriate circumstances, to make a representation under s 76(2) (or s 76A(2)) and thereby oblige the prosecution (or co-accused) to prove that such a confession was not obtained by the methods described in s 76(2) (or s 76A(2)). If such a confession is admitted under s 76 (or s 76A), the common law authorities will provide guidance to the judge as to how she should direct the jury; and the common law principle of conditional admissibility will still apply (so that, in appropriate circumstances, the judge may direct the jury to disregard the evidence). The common law rules relating to statements made in the presence of the accused, which now fall to be considered in more detail, have been preserved by s 118 of the Criminal Justice Act 2003. Section 118 preserves '5 Any rule of law relating to the admissibility of confessions...in criminal proceedings'.[265]

In *R v Norton*[266] the accused was convicted of having sexual intercourse with a girl under 13. Evidence was admitted of a statement made by the girl and directed at the accused, in which she identified him as the offender, and of his replies. The conviction was quashed on the grounds that there was no evidence that the accused had accepted the truth of the statement. Pickford J, giving the judgment of the Court of Criminal Appeal, made a number of important observations which may be summarized in terms of four propositions:

1. Statements made in the presence of the accused upon an occasion on which he might reasonably be expected to make some observation, explanation or denial are admissible in evidence if the judge is satisfied that there is evidence fit to be submitted to the jury that the accused by his answer to them, whether given by word or conduct, including silence, acknowledged the truth of the whole or part of them.

2. Although if there is no such evidence fit to be left to the jury, the contents of the statements should be excluded, they may be given in evidence even when they were denied by the accused as it is possible that a denial may be given under such circumstances and in such a manner as to constitute evidence from which an acknowledgment may be inferred.[267]

3. If the statements are admitted, the question whether the accused's answer, by words or conduct, did or did not in fact amount to an acknowledgment of them should be left to the jury.

4. The judge should direct the jury that if they conclude that the accused acknowledged the truth of the whole or any part of the statement, they may take the statement or part of it into consideration as evidence, but that without such an acknowledgment they should disregard the statement altogether.[268]

---

[265] As to inferences that may be drawn pursuant to *statute* from an accused's silence on being questioned under caution by a constable or on being charged, see the Criminal Justice and Public Order Act 1994, ss 34, 36, 37, and 38 (see Ch 14).

[266] [1910] 2 KB 496.

[267] The denial may also give rise to such an inference if inconsistent with statements subsequently made by him or inconsistent with his defence at the trial, as when he denies an assault but at his trial pleads self-defence: see per Lord Moulton in *R v Christie* [1914] AC 545 at 560. See further *R v Z* [2003] 1 WLR 1489, CA.

[268] Cf *R v Black* (1922) 16 Cr App R 118.

In *R v Christie*[269] the accused was convicted of indecent assault on a boy, who gave unsworn evidence. The boy's mother and a constable gave evidence to the effect that shortly after the alleged act, the boy approached the accused, identified him by saying, 'That is the man', and described the assault. They also gave evidence that the accused then said, 'I am innocent'. The Court of Criminal Appeal quashed the conviction on the grounds that, the accused having denied the truth of the boy's statement, the evidence of the mother and constable had been improperly admitted.[270] The House approved the approach taken in *R v Norton* but regarded the principles enunciated by Pickford J as valuable rules of guidance rather than strict rules of law.

When a person is accused of a crime in circumstances such that it would be reasonable to expect some explanation or denial from him, whether the accused's silence can give rise to an inference that he accepted the truth of the charge would appear to depend upon whether it was made by a police officer or some other person in authority or charged with the investigation of the crime as opposed to some other person with whom the accused can be said to have been 'on even terms'. In *Hall v R*[271] the question arose whether the silence of the accused *before* being cautioned could give rise to an inference that he accepted the truth of an accusation made by or through a police officer. The accused was convicted of unlawful possession of drugs which were found in premises occupied by him and two co-accused. A police officer told the accused that one of the co-accused had said that the drugs belonged to him, that is the accused. The accused, who at that stage had not been cautioned, remained silent. All of the accused were convicted. The Privy Council advised that the accused's conviction be quashed. Lord Diplock, delivering the judgment of the Board, said:[272]

> It is a clear and widely known principle of the common law in Jamaica, as in England, that a person is entitled to refrain from answering a question put to him for the purpose of discovering whether he has committed a criminal offence. *A fortiori* he is under no obligation to comment when he is informed that someone else has accused him of an offence. It may be that in very exceptional circumstances an inference may be drawn from a failure to give an explanation or a disclaimer, but in their Lordships' view silence alone on being informed by a police officer that someone else has made an accusation against him cannot give rise to an inference that the person to whom this information is communicated accepts the truth of the accusation...
>
> The caution merely serves to remind the accused of a right which he already possesses at common law. The fact that in a particular case he has not been reminded of it is no ground for inferring that his silence was not in exercise of that right, but was an acknowledgment of the truth of the accusation.

Where there are two suspects and one of them answers a question put by an officer to both of them by telling a lie, similar principles apply to the issue whether the other of them, by his silence, adopted the answer of the first.[273]

In *Parkes v R*[274] the appellant was convicted of murder. At the trial, the victim's mother gave evidence that, having found her daughter injured, she went to the appellant and accused him

---

[269] [1914] AC 545.
[270] The House of Lords affirmed the order quashing the conviction on a different ground.
[271] [1971] 1 WLR 298.
[272] [1971] 1 WLR 298 at 301.
[273] *R v Collins* [2003] 2 Cr App R 199, CA.
[274] [1976] 1 WLR 1251, PC.

twice of stabbing her daughter. The appellant said nothing and, when the mother threatened to detain him while the police were sent for, drew a knife and attempted to stab her. On these facts the Privy Council applied the following dictum of Cave J in *R v Mitchell*:[275]

> Undoubtedly, when persons are speaking on even terms, and a charge is made, and the person charged says nothing, and expresses no indignation, and does nothing to repel the charge, that is some evidence to show that he admits the charge to be true.

Accordingly, it was held that the trial judge had not erred in instructing the jury that the appellant's reactions to the accusations, including his silence, were matters from which they could, if they saw fit, infer that he had accepted the truth of the accusation.[276] *Hall v R* was distinguished on the grounds that, in that case, the person by whom the accusation was communicated was a police officer and there was no evidence of the accused's reaction other than his silence.

It seems that the accuser and the accused may be regarded as being on even terms notwithstanding that the police have brought them together and are present when the accusation is made. In *R v Horne*,[277] shortly after an assault, the police took the accused to the scene of the crime and sat him down opposite the victim. It was held that the accused's silent reaction to an accusation then made by the victim, but unprompted by the officers present, was capable of amounting to an acceptance of the accusation made.

The dictum of Cave J in *R v Mitchell* was also applied in *R v Chandler*.[278] The accused was convicted of conspiracy to defraud, the only evidence against him being an interview with a detective sergeant in the presence of his solicitor when, both *before* and *after* being cautioned, he answered some questions and remained silent or refused to answer others. The jury were directed that it was for them to decide whether the accused had remained silent before the caution in exercise of his common law right or because he thought that had he answered he might have incriminated himself. The Court of Appeal, satisfied that the accused and the detective sergeant were speaking on equal terms, since the former had his solicitor present to advise him and, if needed, subsequently to testify as to what had been said, held that some comment on the accused's lack of frankness before he was cautioned was justified. The conviction was quashed, however, on the grounds that the trial judge had short-circuited the proper intellectual process, which involved directing the jury to determine, first, whether the accused's silence amounted to an acceptance by him of what was said and, second, if satisfied that he did accept what was said, whether guilt could reasonably be inferred from what he had accepted. The importance of the decision lies in the reservations expressed about the dicta of Lord Diplock in *R v Hall*. Lawton LJ was of the opinion that they seemed to conflict with *R v Christie* and the earlier authorities and said:[279]

> The law has long accepted that an accused person is not bound to incriminate himself; but it does not follow that a failure to answer an accusation or question when an answer could reasonably be expected may not provide some evidence in support of an accusation. Whether it does will depend on the circumstances.

---

[275] (1892) 17 Cox CC 503 at 508.
[276] For a further example, see *R v Coll* [2005] EWCA Crim 3675.
[277] [1990] Crim LR 188, CA.
[278] [1976] 1 WLR 585.
[279] [1976] 1 WLR 585 at 589.

In a later passage, his Lordship said:[280]

> We do not accept that a police officer always has an advantage over someone he is questioning…A young detective questioning a local dignitary in the course of an inquiry into alleged local government corruption may be very much at a disadvantage. This kind of situation is to be contrasted with that of a tearful housewife accused of shoplifting or of a parent being questioned about the suspected wrongdoing of his son.

It remains to be seen, however, whether this flexible approach will prevail over Lord Diplock's view that silence alone, on being accused by or through a police officer, cannot give rise to an inference that the accused accepts the truth of the accusation made.

Facts discovered in consequence of inadmissible confessions

At common law, the fact that a confession was inadmissible did not affect the admissibility of any incriminating facts discovered in consequence of that confession. In *R v Warickshall*[281] a woman was charged with receiving stolen property. In consequence of a confession made by her, the property was found concealed in her bed at her lodgings. The confession was excluded on the grounds that it had been obtained by promises of favour. Counsel for the defence argued that evidence of the fact of finding the stolen property in her custody should also be excluded since it was obtained in consequence of the inadmissible evidence. Rejecting this argument, it was said:

> Confessions are received in evidence, or rejected as inadmissible, under a consideration whether they are or are not entitled to credit…This principle respecting confessions has no application whatever as to the admission or rejection of facts, whether the knowledge of them be obtained in consequence of an extorted confession, or whether it arises from any other source; for a fact, if it exists at all, must exist invariably in the same manner, whether the confession from which it is derived be in other respects true or false.[282]

The Criminal Law Revision Committee was in no doubt that this rule should be preserved on the grounds that to prevent the police from using any 'leads' obtained from an inadmissible confession would interfere unduly with justice and the detection of crime.[283] The rule is preserved by s 76(4) and by s 76A(4) of the 1984 Act, both of which provide that:

> The fact that a confession is wholly or partly excluded in pursuance of this section shall not affect the admissibility in evidence—
> (a) of any facts discovered as a result of the confession;…

These subsections appear to be compatible with the rights guaranteed by Art 6 of the European Convention on Human Rights, especially given the court's discretionary power to exclude facts discovered as a result of inadmissible confessions under s 78(1) of the 1984 Act.[284]

---

[280] [1976] 1 WLR 585 at 590.

[281] (1783) 1 Leach 263.

[282] See also, in relation to evidence of facts discovered as a result of an illegal search, *Kuruma v R* [1955] AC 197 at 203–5 and *King v R* [1969] 1 AC 304.

[283] 11th Report, Cmnd 4991 (1972), para 68.

[284] See *Her Majesty's Advocate v P (Scotland)* [2011] UKSC 44.

and (iii) his failure or refusal to account for objects, substances, or marks (s 36) or his presence at a particular place (s 37).[10]

Failure to testify

Section 35 of the 1994 Act provides as follows:

(1) At the trial of any person for an offence, subsections (2) and (3) below apply unless—
  (a) the accused's guilt is not in issue; or
  (b) it appears to the court that the physical or mental condition of the accused makes it undesirable for him to give evidence;
  but subsection (2) below does not apply if, at the conclusion of the evidence for the prosecution, his legal representative informs the court that the accused will give evidence or, where he is unrepresented, the court ascertains from him that he will give evidence.

(2) Where this subsection applies, the court shall, at the conclusion of the evidence for the prosecution, satisfy itself (in the case of proceedings on indictment with a jury, in the presence of the jury) that the accused is aware that the stage has been reached at which evidence can be given for the defence and that he can, if he wishes, give evidence and that, if he chooses not to give evidence, or having been sworn, without good cause refuses to answer any question, it will be permissible for the court or jury to draw such inferences as appear proper from his failure to give evidence or his refusal, without good cause, to answer any question.

(3) Where this subsection applies, the court or jury, in determining whether the accused is guilty of the offence charged,[11] may draw such inferences as appear proper from the failure of the accused to give evidence or his refusal, without good cause, to answer any question.

(4) This section does not render the accused compellable to give evidence on his own behalf, and he shall accordingly not be guilty of contempt of court by reason of a failure to do so.

(5) For the purposes of this section a person who, having been sworn, refuses to answer any question shall be taken to do so without good cause unless—
  (a) he is entitled to refuse to answer the question by virtue of any enactment, whenever passed or made, or on the ground of privilege; or
  (b) the court in the exercise of its general discretion excuses him from answering it.

Although s 35 is expressly without prejudice to the accused's right not to testify on his own behalf (s 35(4)), under s 35(3) the court or jury may draw 'proper' inferences from his failure to testify or his refusal, without good cause, to answer any question. Section 35(5) creates a conclusive presumption: an accused who has been sworn and refuses to answer any question will be deemed to have so refused without good cause unless either (a) he is entitled to refuse by reason of an enactment[12] or on the ground of privilege (eg legal professional privilege);[13] or (b) the court excuses him from answering in the exercise of its general discretion.

Under s 38(3):

A person shall not...be convicted of an offence solely on an inference drawn from such a failure as is mentioned in section...35(3)...

---

[10] See generally Buckle, Street, and Brown, *The Right of Silence: The Impact of the Criminal Justice and Public Order Act 1994* (Home Office Research Study No 199, 2000) and Jackson, Wolfe, and Quinn, *Legislating Against Silence: The Northern Ireland Experience* (Northern Ireland Office, 2000). See also Jackson, 'Silence and Proof: extending the boundaries of criminal proceedings in the United Kingdom' (2001) 5 E&P 145.

[11] Or any other offence of which the accused could lawfully be convicted on that charge: s 38(2).

[12] See, eg, the Criminal Justice Act 2003, s 101 (see Ch 17).

[13] See Ch 20.

However, as we shall see, in *Condron v United Kingdom*[14] the European Court of Human Rights has held that it is incompatible with the right to silence to base a conviction solely *or mainly* on the accused's silence or refusal to answer questions or give evidence.

The 'physical or mental condition' exception

Concerning s 35(1)(b), where an accused charged with murder relies upon the defence of diminished responsibility, he will not necessarily fall within the 'mental condition' exception, but whether there is scope for the drawing of an inference from his silence will turn upon the circumstances of the case.[15] There must be an evidential basis for a defence application that s 35(1)(b) applies. If there is, the judge should decide the matter in a *voir dire*, but if there is not, it is not incumbent on him to order a *voir dire* of his own volition.[16] There must also be an evidential basis for the finding of the court under s 35(1)(b). 'Extreme difficulty in giving evidence', which is quite common among accused and other witnesses who give evidence in criminal trials, does not, in itself, make it 'undesirable' for the accused to give evidence.[17] In some cases, it may be 'undesirable' for the accused to give evidence because it would have a significantly adverse effect on his physical or mental state.[18] However, s 35(1)(b) is not confined to such cases;[19] 'undesirability' may stem from other matters, such as an accused's intellectual and cognitive deficits[20] or his inability to control himself or remember his evidence.[21] In deciding, the judge may take account of such additional factors as the accused's behaviour after the event, the significance of his evidence, and the extent to which any problems of communication or comprehension can be overcome by the use of an intermediary.[22] A finding of undesirability does not always need to be based on expert medical evidence, but such evidence will be necessary in some cases, as when it is said that the accused's depression makes it undesirable for him to give evidence.[23] However, expert evidence will not necessarily be determinative.[24] In *R v Friend*[25] it was said that the language of s 35(1)(b) was such as to give a wide discretion to the trial judge, whose decision can only be impugned if *Wednesbury* unreasonable.[26]

Warning the accused

Section 35(2) places a mandatory requirement on the court to satisfy itself of the matters set out therein and the court can only do this by asking either the accused or his representative.[27] By inference, counsel has to be asked in a situation where it is possible to take instructions

---

[14] (2001) 31 EHRR 1, ECHR.
[15] *R v Barry* [2011] 1 Cr App R 466, CA.
[16] *R v A* [1997] Crim LR 883, CA. See also *R v Anwoir* [2008] 4 All ER 582, CA.
[17] *R v Ensor* [2010] 1 Cr App R 255, CA at [27] and [35].
[18] *R v Ensor* [2010] 1 Cr App R 255, CA.
[19] *R v Dixon* [2013] 3 All ER 242, CA.
[20] *R v Friend (No 2)* [2004] EWCA Crim 2661.
[21] *R v Tabbakh* [2009] EWCA Crim 464.
[22] *R v Dixon* [2013] 3 All ER 242, CA.
[23] *R (DPP) v Kavanagh* [2006] Crim LR 370, DC, approved in *R v Tabbakh* [2009] EWCA Crim 464.
[24] See *R v Ullah* [2007] All ER (D) 156 (Mar) (psychiatric evidence of 'severe social phobia') and *R v Ensor* [2010] 1 Cr App R 255, CA.
[25] [1997] 1 WLR 1433, CA.
[26] *Associated Provincial Picture Houses Ltd v Wednesbury Corpn* [1948] 1 KB 223, CA.
[27] *R v Cowan* [1996] 1 Cr App R 1, CA at 9.

from the accused, which will not be possible where the accused has absconded.[28] Thus an adverse inference may be drawn in the case of an accused who attends court but fails to give evidence notwithstanding that no such inference may be drawn in respect of a co-accused who has absconded.[29]

Under s 35(1) the court is not required to satisfy itself of the matters specified in s 35(2) if, at the end of the prosecution case, the accused's representative informs the court that the accused will give evidence. According to para 44.2, the Consolidated Criminal Practice Direction, this should be done in the presence of the jury and, if the representative indicates that the accused will give evidence, the case should proceed in the usual way. Somewhat bizarrely, therefore, if a represented accused indicates that he will testify, there is no obligation on the *court* to ascertain whether he is aware of the potential consequence of refusing without good cause to answer any question. It has been held that if, in the event, such an accused does refuse to answer any question without good cause, the judge may then tell him, in an unoppressive way, of the potential consequences.[30] It is submitted that in these circumstances, such a warning should be mandatory.

The Practice Direction continues as follows:

44.3 If the court is not so informed, or if the court is informed that the accused does not intend to give evidence, the judge should in the presence of the jury inquire of the representative in these terms:
'Have you advised your client that the stage has now been reached at which he may give evidence and, if he chooses not to do so or, having been sworn, without good cause refuses to answer any question, the jury may draw such inferences as appear proper from his failure to do so?'

44.4 If the representative replies to the judge that the accused has been so advised, then the case shall proceed. If counsel replies that the accused has not been so advised, then the judge shall direct the representative to advise his client of the consequences set out in paragraph 44.3 and should adjourn briefly for this purpose before proceeding further.

44.5 If the accused is not represented, the judge shall at the conclusion of the evidence for the prosecution and in the presence of the jury say to the accused:
'You have heard the evidence against you. Now is the time for you to make your defence. You may give evidence on oath, and be cross-examined like any other witness. If you do not give evidence or, having been sworn, without good cause refuse to answer any question the jury may draw such inferences as appear proper. That means they may hold it against you. You may also call any witness or witnesses whom you have arranged to attend court. Afterwards you may also, if you wish, address the jury by arguing your case from the dock. But you cannot at that stage give evidence. Do you now intend to give evidence?'

R v Cowan

In *R v Cowan*[31] the Court of Appeal rejected as contrary to the plain words of s 35, a submission that the operation of s 35(3) should be confined to exceptional cases. In answer to the first argument in support of the submission, that the section constituted an infringement of the accused's right to silence, the court stressed that the 'right of silence' had not been abolished by the section, but expressly preserved by s 35(4). Second, it was argued that the section had

[28] *R v Gough* [2002] Cr App R 121, CA.
[29] *R v Hamidi* [2010] EWCA Crim 66, CA
[30] *R v Ackinclose* [1996] Crim LR 74, CA.
[31] [1995] 4 All ER 939.

watered down the burden of proof and in effect put a burden on the accused to testify in order to avoid conviction. Lord Taylor CJ held that this argument was misconceived because (i) the prosecution have to establish a prima facie case before any question of the accused testifying is raised;[32] (ii) the court or jury are prohibited from convicting solely because of an inference drawn from silence (s 38(3)); and (iii) the burden of proving guilt beyond reasonable doubt remains on the prosecution throughout. Thus although the effect of s 35 is that the court or jury may regard the inference drawn from silence as, in effect, a further evidential factor in support of the prosecution case, it cannot be the only factor to justify a conviction: the totality of the evidence must prove guilt beyond reasonable doubt.

A third argument in support of the submission was that an inference should only be drawn where there is no reasonable possibility of an innocent explanation for the accused's silence; that an inference should not be drawn where there are 'good reasons' for silence consistent with innocence, for example (a) where there is other defence evidence to contradict the prosecution case; (b) where an accused is nervous, inarticulate, or unlikely to perform well in the witness box; (c) where an accused is under duress or fear for his or another's safety; or (d) where—as in two of the cases before the court—an accused has attacked prosecution witnesses and decided not to give evidence because it would expose him to cross-examination on his previous convictions; and that counsel may properly advance such reasons without the need for evidence. This argument was also rejected. The court accepted that, apart from the mandatory exceptions in s 35(1), it is open to the court to decline to draw an adverse inference and for a judge to direct or advise a jury against drawing such an inference if the circumstances of the case justify such a course, but held that there needs to be either some evidential basis for declining to draw an adverse inference[33] or some exceptional factors in the case making that a fair course to take[34] —it is improper for defence counsel to give to the jury reasons for his client's silence at trial in the absence of evidence to support such reasons. The court stressed that the inferences permitted are only such 'as appear proper', a phrase intended to leave a broad discretion to a trial judge to decide in all the circumstances whether any proper inference is capable of being drawn by the jury. If not, he should tell them so; otherwise, it is for the jury to decide whether in fact an inference should properly be drawn.

The court also rejected the specific submission that an inference should not be drawn where an accused seeks to avoid cross-examination on his record. It was pointed out that to hold otherwise would lead to the bizarre result of an accused with previous convictions being in a more privileged position than an accused with a clean record. *R v Cowan* was endorsed, in this respect, in *R v Becouarn*,[35] where the House of Lords gave two reasons for rejecting a submission that in these circumstances the judge should at least give a direction along the lines that there may be various possible other reasons why the accused did not give evidence: first, that such a direction would either signal to the jurors that the accused *does* have previous convictions, or set them off on a trail of unfounded speculation about the existence of other imaginary reasons; and second, that although fear of allowing in his convictions may be an

---

[32] For an exception, see the Domestic Violence, Crime and Victims Act 2004, s 6.

[33] Presumably it is open to the judge to hear such evidence on a *voir dire*, a course that would seem to be particularly important in cases in which the reasons for silence can only be established, in effect, by the accused himself.

[34] In *R v Napper* [1996] Crim LR 591, CA, it was held that the fact that the police failed to interview the accused while the alleged frauds were reasonably fresh in his mind did not warrant the conclusion that an adverse inference should not be drawn.

[35] [2005] 1 WLR 2589, HL. See also *R v Taylor* [1999] Crim LR 77, CA.

element in a decision not to testify, reluctance to face cross-examination may be another and much more predominant element.

The direction to the jury

In *R v Cowan* the Court of Appeal considered the following matters to be essential to a proper direction to the jury on inferences from failure to testify.

1. The judge must direct the jury that the burden remains on the prosecution throughout and must direct them as to the required standard of proof.

2. The judge should make clear that the accused is entitled to remain silent: it is his right and his choice.

3. The jury must be told that an inference from failure to give evidence cannot on its own prove guilt (s 38(3)).[36]

4. The jury must be satisfied that the prosecution have established a case to answer before drawing any inferences from silence.[37] Although the judge must have thought that there was a case to answer, the jury may not believe the witnesses whose evidence the judge considered sufficient to raise a prima facie case. It must therefore be made clear that they must find that there is a case to answer on the prosecution evidence before drawing an adverse inference from silence.[38]

5. The jury should also be directed that if, despite any evidence relied upon to explain the accused's silence, or in the absence of such evidence, they conclude that the silence can only sensibly be attributed to his having no answer, or none that would stand up to cross-examination, they may draw an adverse inference.[39]

The court further held that it is not possible to anticipate all the circumstances in which a judge might think it right to direct or advise a jury against drawing an adverse inference. Noting that it would not be wise even to give examples, as each case must turn on its own facts, the court cited with approval the following dictum of Kelly LJ in *R v McLernon*:[40]

> the court has then a complete discretion as to whether inferences should be drawn or not. In these circumstances it is a matter for the court in any criminal case (1) to decide whether to draw inferences or not; and (2) if it decides to draw inferences what their nature, extent and degree of adversity, if any, may be. It would be improper and indeed quite unwise for any court to set out the bounds of either steps (1) or (2). Their application will depend on factors peculiar to the individual case...

---

[36] Cowan's appeal was allowed on the basis that the jury had not been directed in accordance with point (3) (and (5)).

[37] 'Inescapable logic' and fairness demand that this fourth 'essential' direction be given: see *R v Birchall* [1999] Crim LR 311, CA. See also *R v El-Hannachi* [1998] 2 Cr App R 226, CA. In both cases, failure to give the direction resulted in a successful appeal against conviction. But see further the Domestic Violence, Crime and Victims Act 2004, s 6.

[38] See further per Lord Slynn in *Murray v DPP* (1994) 99 Cr App R 396, HL, at n 45. Presumably, the jury will need specific guidance on the concept of 'a case to answer'. The task of deciding that matter, at the end of the trial, but on the basis of the prosecution evidence alone, would seem to be particularly onerous.

[39] Where there is no evidence to explain the accused's silence, it is not incumbent on a judge to embark on, or to invite the jury to embark on, possible speculative reasons consistent with innocence which might theoretically prompt an accused to remain silent: per Lord Taylor CJ, [1995] 4 All ER 939 at 949.

[40] [1992] NIJB 41, a decision on the equivalent provision in Art 4 of the Criminal Evidence (NI) Order 1988, SI 1988/1987 (NI 120).

Finally, the court in *R v Cowan* stressed that the Court of Appeal will not lightly interfere with a judge's exercise of discretion to direct or advise the jury as to the drawing of inferences from silence and as to the nature, extent, and degree of such inferences. As long as the judge gives the jury adequate directions of law of the kind indicated, and leaves the decision to them, the Court of Appeal will be slow to substitute its own view.

The circumstances in which inferences may be drawn

In some cases, failure to go into the witness box is unlikely to have any real bearing on the issues in the case, as when the facts are not in dispute and the only issue is whether they fall within the offence charged[41] and as when an accused charged with murder admits the assault on the victim but denies causation, an issue which is then resolved on the basis of the expert witnesses called.[42] It seems equally clear, however, that in other cases it may be perfectly proper to draw a strong adverse inference. Typically, such an inference is likely to be drawn where the uncontested or clearly established facts point so strongly to the guilt of the accused as to call for an explanation,[43] or where the defence case involves alleged facts which are at variance with the prosecution evidence or additional to it and exculpatory and must, if true, be within the accused's knowledge.[44]

The inferences that may be drawn

It does not follow from the last sentence that inferences may only be drawn in respect of specific facts: in appropriate circumstances, it may be proper to draw a general inference that by reason of his silence, the accused is guilty of the offence charged. In *Murray v DPP*,[45] a decision under the equivalent provision in the Criminal Evidence (NI) Order 1988,[46] M was convicted of attempted murder and possession of a firearm with intent to endanger life. There was evidence to link the accused with the attack, but he gave no evidence at the trial. The trial judge said that it seemed to him remarkable that the accused had not given evidence and that it was only common sense to infer 'that he is not prepared to assert his innocence on oath because that is not the case'. The House of Lords, upholding the conviction, held that having regard to the cumulative effect of all the circumstantial evidence against the accused, the trial judge was entitled as a matter of common sense to infer that there was no innocent explanation to the prima facie case that he was guilty. Lord Slynn said:[47]

> The accused cannot be compelled to give evidence but he must risk the consequences if he does not do so. Those consequences are not simply...that specific inferences may be drawn from specific facts. They include in a proper case the drawing of an inference that the accused is guilty...
>
> This does not mean that the court can conclude simply because the accused does not give evidence that he is guilty. In the first place the prosecutor must establish a prima facie case—a case for him to answer. In the second place in determining whether the accused is guilty the judge or jury can draw only 'such inferences from the refusal as appear proper'. As Lord Diplock said in *Haw Tua Tau v Public Prosecutor*:[48]

[41] *R v McManus* [2001] EWCA Crim 2455.

[42] See Wasik and Taylor, *Blackstone's Guide to the Criminal Justice and Public Order Act 1994* (London, 1995) 65.

[43] See, at common law, *R v Mutch* [1973] 1 All ER 178, CA. See also *R v Corrie* (1904) 20 TLR 365.

[44] See, at common law, *R v Martinez-Tobon* [1994] 2 All ER 90, CA; and in cases where the accused bears the burden of proof, *R v Bathurst* [1968] 2 QB 99 at 107, CA.

[45] (1994) 99 Cr App R 369.

[46] Art 4, SI 1988/1987 (NI 120).

[47] (1993) 99 Cr App R 369 at 405.

[48] [1982] AC 136 at 153.

'What inferences are proper to be drawn from an accused's refusal to give evidence depend upon the circumstances of the particular case, and is a question to be decided by applying ordinary common sense.'

There must thus be some basis derived from the circumstances which justify the inference.

If there is no prima facie case shown by the prosecution there is no case to answer. Equally, if parts of the prosecution case had so little evidential value that they called for no answer, a failure to deal with those specific matters cannot justify an inference of guilt.

On the other hand, if aspects of the evidence taken alone or in combination with other facts clearly call for an explanation which the accused ought to be in a position to give, if an explanation exists, then a failure to give any explanation may as a matter of common sense allow the drawing of an inference that there is no explanation and that the accused is guilty.[49]

Prosecution comment

Under proviso (b) to s 1 of the Criminal Evidence Act 1898, the failure of any person charged with an offence to give evidence was not to be made the subject of any comment by the prosecution. Section 1(b) was repealed by the 1994 Act. Comment is permissible. However, if the trial judge is minded to direct or advise a jury against drawing an adverse inference, it is submitted that it would be good practice for him to inform prosecuting counsel of this before closing speeches, so that counsel refrains from comment. Conversely, if the judge is minded to direct the jury that they may draw proper inferences, it is submitted that prosecuting counsel should adhere to the kind of comment suggested (for the judge) in *R v Cowan*.

Failure to mention facts when questioned or charged

Background

In its 11th Report, the Criminal Law Revision Committee proposed that where an accused fails to mention any fact relied on in his defence which he could reasonably have been expected to mention either (i) before he was charged on being questioned by the police; or (ii) on being charged, the court should be entitled to draw such inferences as appear proper, and the caution should be replaced by a notice explaining the potentially adverse effect of silence.[50] These proposals attracted widespread criticism at the time, but in 1976 were adopted in Singapore[51] and in 1988 were adopted in Northern Ireland.[52] There was also strong judicial comment in favour of their adoption in England and Wales. In *R v Alladice*[53] Lord Lane CJ, giving the reserved judgment of the Court of Appeal, observed that the effect of s 58 of the Police and Criminal Evidence Act 1984 (the 1984 Act)[54] was that in many cases a detainee who would otherwise have answered the questions of the police would be advised by his solicitor to remain silent and weeks later, at the trial, would not infrequently produce an explanation of,

---

[49] The drawing of adverse inferences from silence in *Murray v DPP* did not violate the European Convention on Human Rights: *Murray v United Kingdom* (1996) 22 EHRR 29, ECHR; but see also Munday, 'Inferences from Silence and European Human Rights Law' [1996] Crim LR 370.

[50] Paras 28–52 and cl 11 of the draft bill: 11th Report, Cmnd 4991 (1972).

[51] See Meng Heong Yeo, 'Diminishing the Right of Silence: The Singapore Experience' [1983] Crim LR 89 and Tan, 'Adverse Inferences and the Right to Silence: Re-examining the Singapore Experience' [1997] Crim LR 471.

[52] See SI 1988/1987 (NI 120) and Jackson, 'Curtailing the Right of Silence: Lessons from Northern Ireland' [1991] Crim LR 404.

[53] (1988) 87 Cr App R 380.

[54] See Ch 13.

or a defence to, the charge, the truthfulness of which the police would have had no chance to check. Thus despite the fact that the explanation or defence, if true, could have been disclosed at the outset, and despite the advantage which the accused had gained by those tactics, no comment could be made to the jury to that effect. The effect of s 58, it was said, was such that the balance of fairness between prosecution and defence could not be maintained unless proper comment was permitted on silence in such circumstances.

The report of the Working Group set up by the Home Secretary in 1988 expressed the view that failure to answer police questions, even before the accused is brought to the police station, should be admissible evidence against him to show that his defence is untrue and to undermine his credibility, and he should be warned of the possibility at the outset.[55] The majority recommendation of the Royal Commission on Criminal Justice, in contrast, was that no inferences should be drawn from silence at the police station, but that when the prosecution case has been disclosed, an accused should be required to disclose his case, at the risk of adverse comment by the judge on any new defence then disclosed or any departure from the defence previously disclosed.

Section 34 of the 1994 Act reflects the recommendations of the Criminal Law Revision Committee, and not those of the Royal Commission on Criminal Justice.[56] In *R v Hoare*[57] Auld LJ said: 'The whole basis of section 34, in its qualification of the otherwise general right of an accused to remain silent and require the prosecution to prove its case, is an assumption that an innocent defendant—as distinct from one who is entitled to require the prosecution to prove its case—would give an early explanation to demonstrate his innocence.'

Section 34 provides that:

(1) Where, in any proceedings against a person for an offence, evidence is given that the accused—
  (a) at any time before he was charged with the offence, on being questioned under caution by a constable trying to discover whether or by whom the offence had been committed, failed to mention any fact relied on in his defence in those proceedings; or
  (b) on being charged with the offence or officially informed that he might be prosecuted for it, failed to mention any such fact,
  being a fact which in the circumstances existing at the time the accused could reasonably have been expected to mention when so questioned, charged or informed, as the case may be, subsection (2) below applies.
(2) Where this subsection applies—
  (a) [repealed];
  (b) a judge, in deciding whether to grant an application made by the accused under paragraph 2 of Schedule 3 to the Crime and Disorder Act 1998;[58]
  (c) the court, in determining whether there is a case to answer; and
  (d) the court or jury, in determining whether the accused is guilty of the offence charged,[59]
  may draw such inferences from the failure as appear proper.

---

[55] See Zuckerman, 'Trial by Unfair Means—The Report of the Working Group on the Right of Silence' [1989] Crim LR 855. See also Greer, 'The Right of Silence: A Review of the Current Debate' (1990) 53 MLR 709.

[56] See generally Birch, 'Suffering in Silence: A Cost–Benefit Analysis of Section 34' [1999] Crim LR 769 and Leng, 'Silence pre-trial, reasonable expectations and the normative distortion of fact-finding' (2001) 5 E&P 240.

[57] [2005] 1 Cr App R 355, CA at [53].

[58] ie an application by an accused to dismiss the charge or any of the charges in respect of which he has been sent to the Crown Court (as an adult charged with an offence triable only on indictment) under the Crime and Disorder Act 1998, s 51.

[59] Or any other offence of which the accused could lawfully be convicted on that charge: s 38(2).

(2A) Where the accused was at an authorised place of detention[60] at the time of the failure, subsections (1) and (2) above do not apply if he had not been allowed an opportunity to consult a solicitor prior to being questioned, charged or informed as mentioned in subsection (1) above.

'On being questioned under caution... or on being charged'

Section 34(1)(a) only applies in the case of an accused 'on being questioned under caution'. Thus it has no application in the case of an accused who simply refuses to leave the police cell in which he is being detained in order to be interviewed by the police, but s 34(1)(b) will apply if such an accused, on being subsequently charged, fails to mention any fact relied on in his defence.[61] Paragraph 10.5 of Code C (the Code of Practice for the Detention, Treatment and Questioning of Persons by Police Officers) provides that the caution given before a person is charged or informed he may be prosecuted should be in the following terms:

> You do not have to say anything. But it may harm your defence if you do not mention when questioned something which you later rely on in court. Anything you do say may be given in evidence.

Paragraph 10.7 provides that:

> Minor deviations from the words of any caution given in accordance with this Code do not constitute a breach of this Code, provided the sense of the relevant caution is preserved.

Under Note 10D of the Code:

> If it appears a person does not understand the caution, the person giving it should explain it in their own words.

Under para 11.4 of the Code, where a 'significant silence' (a silence which might give rise to an inference under the 1994 Act) has occurred before the start of the interview at the police station, then at the start of the interview, the interviewer, after cautioning the suspect, shall put the earlier 'significant silence' to the suspect and ask him whether he confirms or denies it and if he wants to add anything.

Section 34 applies in relation to questioning not only by constables, but also 'by persons (other than constables) charged with the duty of investigating offences or charging offenders' and in s 34(1) 'officially informed' means informed by a constable or any such person.[62] Under s 67(9) of the 1984 Act, which also refers to 'persons charged with the duty of investigating offences or charging offenders', it has been held, somewhat unsatisfactorily, that whether a person satisfies the test is a question of fact in each case.[63]

Section 34(1)(a) applies to questioning under caution by a constable 'trying to discover whether or by whom the offence had been committed'. Where there is sufficient evidence for a suspect to be charged and the interview should be brought to an end,[64] but questioning continues and is met with silence from which adverse inferences may be drawn, evidence of

---

[60] 'Authorised place of detention' means a police station or other place prescribed by order made by the Secretary of State: s 38(2A).

[61] *R v Johnson* [2006] Crim LR 567, CA.

[62] Section 34(4).

[63] See *R v Seelig* [1991] 4 All ER 429, CA etc (see Ch 13).

[64] See paras 11.6 and 16.1 of Code C.

the silence may be excluded.[65] However, it has also been held that the sufficiency of evidence can normally only be judged after the suspect has been given an opportunity to volunteer an explanation, and that further questioning will not be in breach of the Code if the officer is still open-minded about the possibility of an explanation which might prevent the suspect from being charged,[66] in which case the officer will still be 'trying to discover whether or by whom the offence has been committed'.[67]

Section 34(1)(b) applies when the accused is 'charged with the offence or officially informed that he might be prosecuted for it', at which stage para 16.2 of Code C requires that the caution should be in the following terms:

> You do not have to say anything. But it may harm your defence if you do not mention now something which you later rely on in court. Anything you do say may be given in evidence.

Given this wording, there is no requirement—in order to rely on s 34(1)(b)—that an officer should go further and, for example, invite the detainee to give any explanation he may have for his conduct.[68]

An inference may be drawn from silence on being questioned under s 34(1)(a), or from silence on being charged under s 34(1)(b), or from both. Thus although in most cases it will add nothing to invite the jury to consider drawing an additional inference at the later stage, in some cases it may be possible to draw a stronger inference then, as when a suspect, after interview, is bailed to come back to the police station a week later, when he is charged, having had a long time to think back over the events. These principles derive from *R v Dervish*,[69] where it was held that if no inference can be drawn under s 34(1)(a)—the interviews in that case were inadmissible by reason of breaches of the Codes of Practice—then subject to any issue of unfairness, the trial judge may leave to the jury the possibility of drawing an inference under s 34(1)(b). However, the court added that the trial judge should not permit the jury to draw such an inference if to do so would nullify the safeguards of the 1984 Act and Codes, or if there was bad faith by the police deliberately breaching the safeguards with a view to falling back on s 34(1)(b).

'Failed to mention any fact relied on in his defence'

Where an accused, in interview after arrest, gives to the police a prepared statement and thereafter refuses to answer questions, he has not 'failed to mention' the facts set out in his statement. Thus in *R v Knight*,[70] where the prepared statement was wholly consistent with the defence evidence at trial, an adverse inference could not be drawn. The court held that the purpose of s 34(1)(a) was early disclosure of a suspect's account and not, separately and distinctly, the subjection of that account to the test of police cross-examination. However, as the court went on to stress, giving a prepared statement is not of itself an inevitable antidote to later adverse inferences because the statement may be incomplete in comparison with the accused's later account at trial. As was pointed out in *R v Turner*,[71] the submission of a prepared

---

[65] See *R v Pointer* [1997] Crim LR 676, CA and *R v Gayle* [1999] Crim LR 502, CA.

[66] *R v McGuinness* [1999] Crim LR 318, CA and *R v Ioannou* [1999] Crim LR 586, CA.

[67] *R v Odeyemi* [1999] Crim LR 828, CA. But see also s 37(7) of the 1984 Act and generally Cape, 'Detention Without Charge; What Does "Sufficient Evidence to Charge" Mean?' [1999] Crim LR 874.

[68] *R v Goodsir* [2006] EWCA Crim 852.

[69] [2002] 2 Cr App R 105, CA.

[70] [2004] 1 WLR 340, CA. See also *T v DPP* [2007] EWHC 7193 (Admin).

[71] [2004] 1 All ER 1025, CA.

statement is a dangerous course for an innocent person, who may subsequently discover at trial that something significant was omitted. In that case, it was held that the judge must identify any fact not mentioned in the prepared statement, which should be the subject of a specific direction. The court also noted that inconsistencies between the prepared statement and the accused's evidence do not necessarily amount to reliance on a fact not previously mentioned; and that where there are differences between the statement and the evidence given at trial, then depending on the precise circumstances, it may be better to direct the jury to consider the difference as constituting a previous lie,[72] rather than the foundation for a s 34 inference.

Inferences can only be drawn under s 34 where the accused has failed to mention 'any fact', as opposed to some speculative possibility, relied on in his defence. In *R v Nickolson*[73] N, charged with sexual offences against the complainant in his house, denied in interview that anything indecent had ever occurred, but said that he was in the habit of masturbating in the bathroom. Subsequently, seminal stains were found on the complainant's nightdress and, at the trial, when asked if he could provide an explanation, N suggested that the complainant could have entered the bathroom after he had masturbated there. It was held that s 34 did not apply because N had not asserted as a fact that the complainant had visited the bathroom, but had proffered it as an explanation, something more in the nature of a theory, a possibility, or speculation. Section 34 will apply, however, if such speculation is based on a fact and the accused could reasonably have been expected to mention both the speculation and the factual basis for it.[74]

It seems clear that an inference may be drawn under s 34 from an accused's failure to mention a fact not only when the fact is first disclosed at trial, but also when the accused, having initially failed to mention a fact on being questioned under caution, disclosed it at a later stage of police questioning or in a written statement to the police.[75] In any event, however, the fact that the accused failed to mention must be relied on in his defence. In *R v Moshaid*,[76] in which the accused did not give or call any evidence, it was held that s 34 did not bite. It does not follow, however, that the relevant fact may be established only by the accused or a defence witness: it may also be established by a prosecution witness, either in cross-examination or examination-in-chief.[77] Thus s 34 does apply where defence counsel puts or suggests the fact to a prosecution witness in cross-examination and the witness accepts it.[78] It can also apply even if the witness under cross-examination does not accept the fact put or suggested. In *R v Webber*[79] the House of Lords held that an accused relies on a fact in his defence when counsel, acting on his instructions, puts a specific and positive case to a prosecution witness, as opposed to asking questions intended to probe or test the prosecution case,[80] even if the witness rejects the case being put. Two reasons were given. First, although questions only become

---

[72] See *R v Lucas* [1981] QB 720, CA etc, Ch 2.

[73] [1999] Crim LR 61, CA.

[74] *R v B (MT)* [2000] Crim LR 181, CA.

[75] See *R v McLernon* (1990) Belfast CC, 20 Dec, a decision under Art 3 of the Criminal Evidence (NI) Order 1988, SI 1988/1987 (NI 120).

[76] [1998] Crim LR 420, CA.

[77] *R v Bowers* [1998] Crim LR 817, CA.

[78] See *R v McLernon* [1992] NIJB 41, CA.

[79] [2004] 1 WLR 404, HL.

[80] If the judge is in doubt whether counsel is testing the prosecution evidence or advancing a positive case, he should ask counsel in the absence of the jury: *R v Webber* [2004] 1 WLR 404, HL at [36].

evidence if accepted by the witness, where specific positive suggestions have been made, the jury may for whatever reason distrust the witness's evidence and ask themselves whether the version put for the accused may not be true. Second, since s 34(2)(c) permits the court to draw proper inferences when determining whether there is a case to answer, ie at a stage when the accused has had no opportunity to give or adduce evidence, it would be surprising if s 34(2)(c) were intended to apply only when, unusually, specific suggestions put to a prosecution witness are *accepted* by him. It was further held that where defence counsel adopts on behalf of his client in closing submissions evidence given by a co-accused, this may also amount to reliance on facts for the purposes of s 34.

In *R v Betts*[81] it was held that the bare admission at trial of a fact asserted by the prosecution cannot amount to reliance on a fact, but where explanation for the admitted fact is advanced by reliance on other facts, those facts may give rise to an inference if they were not mentioned on being questioned or charged. The court gave an example: if an accused admits for the first time at trial that a fingerprint was his and offers no explanation for it being found where it was, he relies on no fact, but it will be different if he also puts forward an explanation for the finding of the fingerprint. The most compelling reason for the conclusion of the court in relation to a bare admission was given by Lord Bingham in *R v Webber*:[82] rarely if ever can a s 34 direction be appropriate on failure to mention at interview an admittedly true fact, because the adverse inference to be drawn under the section is that the fact not mentioned by the accused at interview but relied on in his defence is likely to be *untrue*.

'A fact which...the accused could reasonably have been expected to mention'

The fact relied on must be 'a fact which in the circumstances existing at the time the accused could reasonably have been expected to mention when...questioned, charged, or informed, as the case may be'. If the accused gives evidence, his reason for not putting forward any fact relied on should be explored.[83] In deciding the matter, the jury will be very much concerned with the truth or otherwise of any explanation given by the accused for not mentioning the fact, because if they accept an exculpatory explanation as true, or possibly so, it will be obviously unfair to draw any adverse inference.[84]

In *R v Argent*[85] it was held that the expression 'in the circumstances' is not to be construed restrictively: account may be taken of such matters as time of day, the accused's age, experience, mental capacity, state of health, sobriety, tiredness, knowledge, personality, and legal advice. 'The accused', it was said, refers not to some hypothetical reasonable accused of ordinary phlegm and fortitude, but to the actual accused, with such qualities, apprehensions, knowledge, and advice as he is shown to have had at the time. Sometimes, therefore, the jury may conclude that it was reasonable for the accused not to have mentioned a fact because, for example, he was tired, ill, frightened, drunk, drugged, unable to understand what was going on, suspicious of the police, afraid that his answer would not be fairly recorded, worried at committing himself without legal advice, or acting on legal advice. In other cases, the jury

---

[81] [2001] 2 Cr App R 257, CA.

[82] [2004] 1 WLR 404, HL at [28].

[83] *T v DPP* [2007] EWHC 1793 (Admin).

[84] Per Lord Bingham in *R v Webber* [2004] 1 WLR 404, HL at [29].

[85] [1997] 2 Cr App R 27, CA.

may conclude that the accused could reasonably have been expected to mention the fact. In *R v Howell*[86] Laws LJ said:

> we do not consider the absence of a written statement from the complainant to be good reason for silence (if adequate oral disclosure of the complaint has been given), and it does not become good reason merely because a solicitor has so advised. Nor is the possibility that the complainant may not pursue his complaint good reason, nor a belief by the solicitor that the suspect will be charged in any event whatever he says. The kind of circumstance which may most likely justify silence will be such matters as the suspect's condition (ill-health, in particular mental disability; confusion; intoxication; shock, and so forth—of course we are not laying down an authoritative list), or his inability genuinely to recollect events without reference to documents which are not to hand, or communication with other persons who may be able to assist his recollection.

In deciding whether a fact is one that the accused could reasonably have been expected to mention, another relevant factor, it is submitted, is the importance of the fact to the defence in question, whether central to that defence or of only peripheral importance, because an accused cannot reasonably be expected to mention every fact, for example every last detail of an alibi as opposed to the key facts relating to where he was, when, and with whom (if anybody). The nature of the fact itself may also be highly relevant, especially if of a kind likely to embarrass the accused or compromise his personal or professional life, for example the fact, in support of an alibi, that at the time of the alleged offence he was not at the scene of the crime but elsewhere, in bed with a prostitute. It would be equally relevant, to take another example, if the fact in question were of a kind likely to create a danger of reprisals against the accused, his family, or friends. Account also needs to be taken of the accused's knowledge of the case against him, and his understanding of (a) the nature of the offence in question; and (b) the facts which might go to show his innocence of that offence. Account should also be taken of any important respect in which the accused may have been misled. In *R v M(I)*[87] when officers interviewed M about an offence, they incorrectly alleged that he had committed it on a date some three months after the date alleged by the complainant. M made no comment other than to deny having committed the offence on the date put to him. At the trial, M, in his defence, relied on a fact relating to the earlier date. It was held that this was not a fact which he could reasonably have been expected to mention when interviewed about an offence on the later date.

Establishing the failure to mention a fact
Section 34(3) of the 1994 Act provides that:

> Subject to any directions by the court, evidence tending to establish the failure may be given before or after evidence tending to establish the fact which the accused is alleged to have failed to mention.

In *R v Condron and Condron* the Court of Appeal, while stressing that no hard and fast procedure should be laid down, gave the following guidance:

> In the ordinary way…it would seem appropriate for prosecuting counsel to adduce evidence limited to the fact that after the appropriate caution the accused did not answer questions or made no comment. Unless the relevance of a particular point has been revealed in cross-examination,

[86] [2005] 1 Cr App R 1, CA at [24].
[87] [2012] 1 Cr App R 26, CA.

it would not seem appropriate to spend time at this stage going through the questions asked at interview.

If and when the accused gives evidence and mentions facts which, in the view of prosecuting counsel, he can reasonably have been expected to mention in interview, he can be asked why he did not mention them. The accused's attention will then no doubt be drawn to any relevant and pertinent questions asked at interview. The accused's explanation for his failure can then be tested in cross-examination. It will not generally be necessary to call evidence in rebuttal, unless there is a dispute as to the relevant contents of the interview.

Silence on legal advice

In *R v Condron and Condron*[88] the question arose whether an adverse inference can be drawn if the accused remained silent on legal advice. The accused, both heroin addicts, were convicted of offences relating to the supply of heroin. On their arrest, although a police doctor considered that they were fit for interview, a view of which they were aware, their solicitor considered that they were unfit to be interviewed because of their drug withdrawal symptoms. The solicitor therefore advised them not to answer questions, also advising them of the potential consequences, and making it plain that it was entirely their choice. At their trial, they gave detailed innocent explanations in relation to the prosecution evidence, which could have been given in answer to specific questions by the police in their interview. The Court of Appeal held that the trial judge had properly directed the jury that it was for them to decide whether any adverse inference should be drawn, but that it would have been *desirable* if he had given an additional direction to the effect that an adverse inference may be drawn if, despite any evidence relied on to explain the silence at interview, or in the absence of such evidence, they conclude that the silence can only sensibly be attributed to the accused having fabricated the evidence subsequently. However, when the case came before the European Court of Human Rights, it held that a direction along these lines is mandatory.[89] The Court held as follows: (1) The right to silence could not be considered as an absolute right and the fact that the issue was left to the jury could not of itself be considered incompatible with Art 6. (2) The right was at the heart of the notion of a fair procedure under Art 6 and particular caution was required before a domestic court could invoke an accused's silence against him. It was incompatible with the right to base a conviction solely or mainly on the accused's silence or refusal to answer questions, or give evidence, but where a situation called for an explanation from an accused, then his silence could be taken into account in assessing the persuasiveness of the evidence against him. (3) The judge had not reflected the balance between the right to silence and the circumstances in which an adverse inference could be drawn. The judge's direction was such that the jury may have drawn an adverse inference even if satisfied with the accused's explanation of the silence. As a matter of fairness, the jury should have been directed that if they were satisfied that the accused's silence at interview could not sensibly be attributed to their having no answer or none that would stand up to cross-examination, then they should not draw an adverse inference.

The direction of the kind suggested by the Court of Appeal in *R v Condron and Condron* does not have to be geared only to the inference of subsequent fabrication, but may deal with the different inference that the accused, by the time of the interview, had already invented a false

---

[88] [1997] 1 WLR 827, CA.

[89] *Condron v United Kingdom* (2001) 31 EHRR 1.

story, in whole or in part, but did not want to reveal it, because of the risk that the police might then be able to expose its falsity.[90]

In *R v Condron and Condron* it was also held that the bare assertion, by an accused, that he did not answer questions because he was advised by his solicitor not to do so, is unlikely to prevent an adverse inference from being drawn:[91] it is necessary, if the accused wishes to invite the court not to draw an adverse inference, to go further and give the basis or reason for the advice. However, as the court pointed out, whereas a 'bare assertion' will not amount to a waiver of the legal professional privilege that attaches to communications between an accused and his solicitor prior to a police interview,[92] once the basis or reason for the advice is stated, this will amount to a waiver entitling the prosecution to ask the accused or, if the solicitor is also called, the solicitor, whether there were any other reasons for the advice, and the nature of the advice given, so as to explore whether the advice may also have been given for tactical reasons. It is desirable, therefore, that the judge warn counsel or the accused that the privilege may be lost.[93] In *R v Bowden*[94] it was held that if the defence reveal the basis or reason for the solicitor's advice to the accused not to answer questions, this amounts to a waiver of privilege, whether the revelation is made by the accused or by the solicitor acting as his authorized agent, and whether it is made during pre-trial questioning, in evidence before the jury, or in evidence in a *voir dire* which is not repeated before the jury. If the defence do not reveal the basis or reason for the solicitor's advice, the judge should not, in the summing-up, comment as to what a competent solicitor would have advised, which would be speculation and, if incorrect, might in effect force the accused to waive his privilege and call the solicitor to give evidence.[95]

The courts have stressed that the jury are not concerned with the correctness of the solicitor's advice, nor with whether it complies with the Law Society's guidelines, but with the reasonableness of the accused's conduct in all the circumstances, including the giving of the advice.[96] Such conduct is likely to be regarded as reasonable in some cases, for example where there is evidence that the interviewing officer disclosed to the solicitor little or nothing of the nature of the case against the accused, so that the solicitor could not usefully advise the client, or where the nature of the offence or the material in the hands of the police is so complex, or relates to matters so long ago, that no sensible immediate response is feasible.[97] However, if an accused has stayed silent on legal advice and his silence is objectively unreasonable, it will not become reasonable merely because the solicitor's advice was ill-judged or bad,[98] which has

[90] See, eg, *R v Taylor* [1999] Crim LR 77, CA, where T, who had given the 'bare bones' of his alibi to his solicitor, failed to mention it in interview, only furnishing the details of it in his alibi notice.

[91] See, eg, *R v Roble* [1997] Crim LR 449, CA.

[92] See Ch 20.

[93] It was also said that an accused (or his solicitor) who gives evidence of what was said to the solicitor in response to a prosecution allegation of recent fabrication does not thereby waive privilege. The reason is that there is no way of dealing with the allegation other than by revealing what was said, whereas when an accused volunteers information about what was said, which may enable an allegation of fabrication to be made, that is the consequence of the voluntary provision: per Hooper LJ in *R v Loizou* [2006] EWCA Crim 1719 at [84].

[94] [1999] 4 All ER 43, CA.

[95] *R v Turner* [2013] 1 Cr App R 327, CA.

[96] See per Lord Bingham CJ in *R v Argent* [1997] 2 Cr App R 27, CA at 35–6 and per Rose LJ in *R v Roble* [1997] Crim LR 449, CA.

[97] Per Rose LJ in *R v Roble* [1997] Crim LR 449, CA.

[98] *R v Connolly and McCartney* (1992) Belfast CC, 5 June.

led one commentator to observe that, if that is the law, then it punishes the accused for the failings of his solicitor.[99]

In *R v Betts*,[100] applied in *R v Chenia*,[101] it was said that it is not the *quality* of the decision not to answer questions that matters, but the genuineness of the decision, whereas in *R v Howell*,[102] approved, obiter, in *R v Knight*,[103] the Court of Appeal rejected the notion that once it is shown that the advice, of whatever quality, has genuinely been relied on as the reason for silence, adverse comment is thereby disallowed. However, as was pointed out in *R v Hoare*,[104] there is no real inconsistency in the authorities, because it is plain from the judgment in *R v Betts* that even where an accused has genuinely relied on legal advice to remain silent, an adverse inference may still be drawn if the jury are sure that the true reason for silence is that he had no or no satisfactory explanation consistent with innocence to give. In other words, the jury must consider whether the accused relied on the legal advice to remain silent both genuinely and reasonably. In *R v Beckles*,[105] Lord Woolf CJ said:

> in a case where a solicitor's advice is relied upon by the defendant, the ultimate question for the jury remains under s 34 whether the facts relied on at trial were facts which the defendant could reasonably have been expected to mention at interview. If they were not, that is the end of the matter. If the jury consider that the defendant genuinely relied on the advice, that is not the end of the matter. It may still not have been reasonable of him to rely on the advice, or the advice may not have been the true explanation for his silence.
>
> In *R v Betts*...at [54] Kay LJ...says:
>
> 'A person, who is anxious not to answer questions because he has no or no adequate explanation to offer, gains no protection from his lawyer's advice because that advice is no more than a convenient way of disguising his true motivation for not mentioning facts.'
>
> If, in the last situation, it is possible to say that the defendant genuinely acted upon the advice, the fact that he did so because it suited his purpose may mean he was not acting reasonably in not mentioning the facts. His reasonableness in not mentioning the facts remains to be determined by the jury. If they conclude that he was acting unreasonably they can draw an adverse inference from the failure to mention the facts.

The legal test, therefore, now requires both genuine and reasonable reliance. However, it is submitted that to direct the jury in such terms is both potentially misleading and needlessly complex. Ultimately, what matters is the reasonableness of the accused in relying on the advice. A lack of genuine reliance is no more than an example—and there are many examples—of unreasonableness: if an accused has relied on the advice, but not genuinely, the reliance is a sham or pretence, and the accused will not have acted reasonably in following it.[106] It is submitted that it would be better to remove any reference to genuineness from the jury direction.

[99] See Pattenden, 'Inferences from Silence' [1995] Crim LR 602. See also *R v Kinsella* (1993) Belfast CC, Dec.
[100] [2001] 2 Cr App R 257, CA at [53].
[101] [2004] 1 All ER 543, CA. See also *R v Compton* [2002] EWCA Crim 2835.
[102] [2005] 1 Cr App R 1.
[103] [2004] 1 WLR 340, CA.
[104] [2005] 1 Cr App R 355, CA at [51].
[105] [2005] 1 All ER 705, CA at [46].
[106] See, to similar effect, Fitzpatrick, 'Commentary' [2005] Crim LR 562 and Cooper, 'Legal advice and pre-trial silence—unreasonable developments' (2006) 10 E&P 60. See also Malik, 'Silence on legal advice: Clarity but not justice?: R v Beckles' (2005) 9 E&P 211.

Circumstances in which a section 34 direction is not appropriate

A s 34 direction is not appropriate, as we have seen, where an accused fails to mention facts on which the prosecution rely and which he accepts as true, because the adverse inference to be drawn under the section is that a matter not mentioned is untrue.[107] Where a lie told by the accused is relied on by the prosecution, it is usually unhelpful to give the jury, in that regard, both a s 34 and a *Lucas* direction;[108] the judge should select and adapt the direction more appropriate to the facts and issues in the case.[109] If an accused gives an explanation for his failure to mention a fact and it is that explanation which is alleged to be the lie, it suffices to give a s 34 direction which incorporates the explanation. It is unnecessary, confusing, and unduly favourable to the defence to include, in the direction to the jury, the examples of innocent reasons for lying required by the *Lucas* direction.[110] Even if the conditions for drawing an inference set out in s 34 are satisfied, it does not necessarily follow that the section should be invoked. In *Brizzalari v R*[111] the Court of Appeal noted that the mischief at which s 34 was primarily aimed was the positive defence following a 'no comment' interview and/or the ambush defence. The court counselled against 'the further complicating of trials and summings-up by invoking this statute, unless the merits of the individual case require that it should be done'. Thus there may be no point in invoking the section, even if it applies, if the direction of the judge will be substantially the same whether or not the section is invoked, as in *R v Maguire*,[112] where M gave one account in interview and another, different, account at trial so that in any event the Crown case was that the evidence was untruthful and the judge would have directed the jury that it was for them to decide whether to draw an adverse inference.

Should an inference be drawn by the jury under s 34 if it can only logically be drawn by first concluding that the accused is guilty? In *R v Mountford*[113] the police entered W's flat and saw M drop from a window a package later found to contain heroin. On being interviewed, M made no comment. W pleaded guilty to permitting his premises to be used for the purposes of supplying heroin and, at M's trial on a charge of possession of heroin with intent to supply, gave evidence against him. M's evidence was that he was at the flat to buy heroin from W, who was the dealer, and that when the police had arrived, W had thrown him the heroin which he had dropped from the window. His reason for not volunteering this information on interview was that he did not know what W had said and did not want to get him into trouble. It was held that inferences could not be drawn under s 34 because the jury could only be sure that this explanation was true if they were to conclude that W was the dealer, not M, and conversely could only be sure that this explanation was false if they were to conclude that M was the dealer, and not W. This element of circularity, it was held, could only be resolved by a verdict founded in no way upon an inference under s 34, but on the other evidence in the case. The same conclusion was reached in *R v Gill*,[114] but it has since been held that *R v Mountford* was concerned with its own set of specific facts and was not intended to have a

[107] *R v Webber* [2004] 1 WLR 404, HL, per Lord Bingham at [28], applied in *R v Hackett* [2011] 2 Cr App R 35, CA.
[108] See Ch 2 under **The varieties of evidence, Circumstantial evidence, Examples, Lies**.
[109] *R v Rana* [2007] EWCA Crim 2261, CA at [10] and [11] and *R v Hackett* [2011] 2 Cr App R 35, CA at [13].
[110] *R v Hackett* [2011] 2 Cr App R 35, CA at [26]–[28].
[111] [2004] EWCA Crim 310.
[112] [2008] EWCA Crim 1028.
[113] [1999] Crim LR 575, CA.
[114] [2001] 1 Cr App R 160 (CA).

general application[115] and that it will only be in rare cases of the simplest and most straight-forward kind that the *Mountford* approach is appropriate.[116] In *R v Daly*[117] the Court of Appeal cast doubt on the decision in *R v Mountford* on the basis that although it accepted that the fact not mentioned was closely related to the issue in the case, it could find nothing in the statutory wording which requires that the s 34 issue be capable of resolution as a separate issue in the case. In *R v Gowland-Wynn*[118] the Court of Appeal went further, Lord Woolf CJ being of the view that although it may be that *R v Mountford* and *R v Gill* can be confined to their special facts, they had the effect of emasculating and defeating the very purpose of s 34, and should be consigned to oblivion and should not be followed. Similarly in *R v Webber*[119] the House of Lords, while not expressly overruling *R v Mountford*, expressed the view that s 34 did apply to the case.

The direction to the jury

In cases where a direction under s 34 is called for, then subject to the facts of the particular case, juries should be directed in accordance with the Judicial Studies Board specimen direction,[120] which was approved by the European Court of Human Rights in *Beckles v UK*[121] in the context of the accused's silence on legal advice. The trial judge must remind the jury of the words of the caution given to the accused.[122] The judge must also direct the jury to the effect that an adverse inference can only be drawn if, despite any evidence relied upon by the accused, they conclude that the silence can only sensibly be attributed to the accused having no answer or no answer that would stand up to questioning and investigation.[123] The alternative in the last sentence is worth stressing. Section 34 is not limited to cases of recent invention, ie where the jury may conclude that the facts were invented after the interview, but also covers cases where they may conclude that the accused had the facts in mind at the time of the interview but did not believe that they would stand up to scrutiny at that time.[124] The judge must clearly identify for the jury the inferences which they may properly draw.[125] Contrary to the ruling of the Court of Appeal in *R v Doldur*,[126] the trial judge must also make clear to the jury that they must be satisfied that the prosecution have established a case to answer before drawing any inference.[127] The jury should be told that, if an inference is drawn, they should not convict 'wholly or mainly on the strength of it'. The first of those alternatives, 'wholly', is a clear way of putting the need for the prosecution to be able to prove a case to answer, otherwise than by means of an inference drawn. The second alternative, 'mainly', buttresses that need.[128]

[115] *R v Hearne*, 4 May 2000, unreported, CA, followed in *R v Milford* [2001] Crim LR 330, CA.
[116] *R v Chenia* [2004] 1 All ER 543, CA at [34]–[35].
[117] [2002] 2 Cr App R 201.
[118] [2002] 1 Cr App R 569.
[119] [2004] 1 WLR 404, HL.
[120] *R v Chenia* [2004] 1 All ER 543, CA at [47].
[121] [2001] 31 EHRR 1.
[122] *R v Chenia* [2004] 1 All ER 543, CA at [49]–[51].
[123] See *Condron v UK* [2001] 31 EHRR 1 at para 61, *R v Betts* [2001] 2 Cr App R 257, CA, *R v Daly* [2002] 2 Cr App R 201, CA, and *R v Petkar* [2004] 1 Cr App R 270, CA.
[124] *R v Milford* [2001] Crim LR 330, CA. See also *R v Daniel* (1998) 2 Cr App R 373, CA at 382–3 and *R v Argent* [1997] 2 Cr App R 27, CA at 34 and 36.
[125] *R v Petkar* [2004] 1 Cr App R 270, CA at [51].
[126] [2000] Crim LR 178, CA.
[127] See *R v Milford* [2001] Crim LR 330, CA, *Beckles v UK* [2001] 31 EHRR 1, and *R v Chenia* [2004] 1 All ER 543, CA.
[128] *R v Petkar* [2004] 1 Cr App R 270, CA at [51], citing *Murray v UK* (1996) 22 EHRR 29 at 60, para 47.

The specimen direction emphasizes the desirability of any proposed direction being discussed with counsel before closing speeches and suggests that the discussion should start by a consideration whether any direction under s 34 should be given. In both respects, the specimen direction has been strongly endorsed by the Court of Appeal.[129] However, it does not necessarily follow from a failure to give a proper direction that there has been a breach of Art 6 of the Convention or that a conviction is unsafe. The Court of Appeal will have regard to the particular facts of the case. Factors which may count against the accused, depending on the precise nature of the misdirection or non-direction, may include the strength of the case to answer, the strength of the prosecution evidence, the fact that the accused declined to answer questions himself, rather than on legal advice, and the fact that a clear and accurate direction was given under s 35 of the 1994 Act.[130] Thus in a case involving legal advice to remain silent, failure to say anything about having to be sure that the accused remained silent not because of the legal advice, but because he had no answer to give, is likely to be fatal;[131] but failure to direct the jury to consider whether there was a case to answer will not render the trial unfair or the conviction unsafe where, on the facts, no jury could have concluded that there was no case to answer.[132] In *Adetoro v UK*[133] it was held that failure to direct the jury that adverse inferences could only be drawn if they specifically rejected the accused's explanation for silence did not render the trial unfair or the conviction unsafe, because the circumstantial evidence against the accused was overwhelming and the defence to the charge and the explanation for the silence were essentially the same, so that it was implausible that the jury would draw an adverse inference because satisfied with the explanation for silence and use that inference to reject the defence.

The trial judge, in directing the jury, must take care to identify the specific facts relied on at trial which were not mentioned on being questioned or charged:[134] s 34 does not apply simply because the accused made no comments at interview.[135] In *R v Argent*[136] it was made clear that under s 34 the following matters are all questions of fact for the jury: (i) whether there is some fact which the accused has relied on in his defence; (ii) whether the accused failed to mention it on being questioned or charged; and (iii) whether it is a fact which in the circumstances existing at the time he could reasonably have been expected to mention when questioned or charged. It was also held that the 'proper' inferences that the jurors are permitted to draw means such inferences as appear proper to them. However, although (i) and (ii) above are questions of fact for the jury, in *R v McGarry*[137] it was held that there will plainly be cases in which it is appropriate for the judge to decide as a matter of law whether there is any evidence on which a reasonable jury properly directed could conclude that either or both of those requirements has been satisfied. Thus if the prosecution accept that those requirements

---

[129] See *R v Chenia* [2004] 1 All ER 543 at [36] and *R v Beckles* [2005] 1 All ER 705, CA at [34].

[130] See *R v Chenia* [2004] 1 All ER 543 at [59]–[65].

[131] See *R v Bresa* [2006] Crim LR 179, CA.

[132] *R v Chenia* [2004] 1 All ER 543 at [53]–[55].

[133] [2010] ECHR 609.

[134] *R v Webber* [2004] 1 WLR 404, HL at [27] and *R v Chenia* [2004] 1 All ER 543 at [29] and [87]. A failure to do so, however, will not necessarily render a conviction unsafe: see *R v Chivers* [2011] EWCA Crim 1212.

[135] *R v Argent* [1997] 2 Cr App R 27, CA and *T v DPP* [2007] EWHC 1793 (Admin).

[136] [1997] 2 Cr App R 27, CA at 32.

[137] [1999] 1 Cr App R 377, CA at 382–3.

have not been satisfied, and the judge considers that this is a proper view, no question of inviting the jury to draw inferences from the failure of the accused to answer some of the questions put to him can arise. In *R v Argent* it was held that although the question whether the fact was one which the accused could reasonably have been expected to mention is an issue on which the judge should give appropriate directions, ordinarily the issue should be left to the jury to decide, and that only rarely should the judge direct that they should, or should not draw the appropriate inference. As to the latter direction, in *R v McGarry* it was held that where the jury are aware that the accused failed to answer questions and the judge rules that there is no evidence on which they can properly conclude that he failed to mention any fact relied on in his defence, then there should be a specific direction not to draw any adverse inference.[138] However, such a specific direction is plainly not called for where the accused gives a 'no comment' interview and gives no evidence at trial, thereby attracting a direction under s 35 of the 1994 Act, because in such a case it would be fanciful to suggest that an inference of the kind permitted by s 34 might be drawn by the jury in the absence of a direction not to do so.[139]

The inferences that may be drawn

Under s 34(2) the inferences that may be drawn are 'such inferences from the failure as appear proper'. The breadth of this phrase is such that it could be construed to permit a general inference that the accused is guilty of the offence charged, a construction supported, arguably, by s 38(3) of the Act. In fact, the logical inference to be drawn is narrower and more precise, that the facts relied on in the accused's defence are not true, on the basis that, if they were true, the accused could reasonably have been expected to have mentioned them in interview or on being charged, but did not do so because of the risk that the police might then have been able to expose their falsity or because he had yet to invent them, or all of them.

The extent to which an inference drawn under s 34 will assist the prosecution in establishing a case to answer, or in proving the guilt of the accused, will obviously turn on the nature of the fact relied on in the defence and its importance to that defence. However, s 38(3) and (4) of the 1994 Act provide that:

> (3) A person shall not have the proceedings against him transferred to the Crown Court for trial, have a case to answer or be convicted of an offence solely on an inference drawn from such a failure or refusal as is mentioned in section 34(2), 35(3), 36(2) or 37(2).
>
> (4) A judge shall not refuse to grant such an application as is mentioned in section 34(2)(b), 36(2)(b) and 37(2)(b) solely on an inference drawn from such a failure as is mentioned in section 34(2), 36(2) or 37(2).

These provisions, in relation to s 34(2), appear to be otiose. It is true that in cases of confession and avoidance, as when the accused admits an assault but raises a defence of self-defence, rejection of that defence may result in a finding of guilt. However, since the worst possible inference that can be drawn is that the fact relied upon in the defence is untrue, then, as the example given illustrates, such an inference could not *by itself* justify a conviction (or a decision that there is a case to answer). The purpose of s 38(3) in the present context seems to be twofold. First, it requires the judge to remind himself that he is not entitled to decide that there is a case

---

[138] But failure to give such a direction will not necessarily render a conviction unsafe: *R v Bowers* [1998] Crim LR 817, CA. See also *R v Bansal* [1999] Crim LR 484, CA.

[139] *R v La Rose* [2003] EWCA Crim 1471.

to answer solely on the basis that the relevant facts relied on by the accused in his defence are untrue. Second, it requires him to direct the jury that they are not entitled to convict solely—or, in the light of *Condron v United Kingdom*, mainly—on the basis that such facts are untrue.

Acceptance of the accusation of another by silence

Section 34(5) of the 1994 Act provides that:

This section does not—
(a) prejudice the admissibility in evidence of the silence or other reaction of the accused in the face of anything said in his presence relating to the conduct in respect of which he is charged, in so far as evidence thereof would be admissible apart from this section; or
(b) preclude the drawing of any inference from any such silence or other reaction of the accused which could properly be drawn apart from this section.

The effect of this subsection is to preserve the common law authorities whereby, in appropriate circumstances, the accused, by his conduct, demeanour, or silence, may be treated as having accepted the accusation of another so as to make it a confession statement of his own.[140]

Failure or refusal to account for objects, substances, marks, etc

Sections 36 and 37 of the 1994 Act, which are based on ss 18 and 19 of the Irish Criminal Justice Act 1984, fall to be considered together.

Section 36 of the 1994 Act provides that:

(1) Where—
(a) a person is arrested by a constable, and there is—
(i) on his person; or
(ii) in or on his clothing or footwear; or
(iii) otherwise in his possession; or
(iv) in any place[141] in which he is at the time of his arrest,
any object, substance or mark, or there is any mark on any such object; and
(b) that or another constable investigating the case reasonably believes that the presence of the object, substance or mark may be attributable to the participation of the person arrested in the commission of an offence specified by the constable;[142] and
(c) the constable informs the person arrested that he so believes, and requests him to account for the presence of the object, substance or mark; and
(d) the person fails or refuses to do so,
then if, in any proceedings against the person for the offence so specified, evidence of those matters is given, subsection (2) below applies.
(2) Where this subsection applies—
(a) [repealed];
(b) a judge, in deciding whether to grant an application made by the accused under paragraph 2 of Schedule 3 to the Crime and Disorder Act 1998;[143]

[140] See **Statements made in the presence of the accused** in Ch 13. See further Mirfield, 'Two Side-Effects of Sections 34 to 37 of the Criminal Justice and Public Order Act 1994' [1995] Crim LR 612, who argues that it may now be permissible to draw an inference that a suspect who has been cautioned but remains silent in the face of police accusations accepts the truth of the accusations.

[141] For the purposes of both s 36 and s 37 'place' includes any building or part of a building, any vehicle, vessel, aircraft or hovercraft, and any other place whatsoever: s 38(1).

[142] ie not necessarily the offence for which arrested. Cf s 37(1)(b).

[143] See n 58.

(c) the court, in determining whether there is a case to answer; and

(d) the court or jury, in determining whether the accused is guilty of the offence charged,[144] may draw such inferences from the failure or refusal as appear proper.

(3)   Subsections (1) and (2) above apply to the condition of clothing or footwear as they apply to a substance or mark thereon.

(4)   Subsections (1) and (2) above do not apply unless the accused was told in ordinary language by the constable when making the request mentioned in subsection (1)(c) above what the effect of this section would be if he failed or refused to comply with that request.

(4A) Where the accused was at an authorised place of detention[145] at the time of the failure or refusal, subsections (1) and (2) above do not apply if he had not been allowed an opportunity to consult a solicitor prior to the request being made.

(5)   This section applies in relation to officers of customs and excise as it applies in relation to constables.[146]

(6)   This section does not preclude the drawing of any inference from a failure or refusal of the accused to account for the presence of an object, substance or mark or from the condition of clothing or footwear which could properly be drawn apart from this section.

Section 37 of the 1994 Act provides that:

(1)   Where—

(a) a person arrested by a constable was found by him at a place at or about the time the offence for which he was arrested is alleged to have been committed; and

(b) that or another constable investigating the offence reasonably believes that the presence of the person at that place and at that time may be attributable to his participation in the commission of the offence; and

(c) the constable informs the person that he so believes, and requests him to account for that presence; and

(d) the person fails or refuses to do so,

then if, in any proceedings against the person for the offence, evidence of those matters is given, subsection (2) below applies.

(2)   [Identical, in its terms, to s 36(2).]

(3)   [Identical, in its terms, to s 36(4).]

(4)   [Identical, in its terms, to s 36(5).]

(3A) Where the accused was at an authorised place of detention[147] at the time of the failure or refusal, subsections (1) and (2) do not apply if he had not been allowed an opportunity to consult a solicitor prior to the request being made.

    . . .

(5)   This section does not preclude the drawing of any inference from a failure or refusal of the accused to account for his presence at a place which could properly be drawn apart from this section.

It has been held that, under s 36, the jury must be satisfied that the accused failed (or refused) to account for the object, substance, or mark; and that s 36(1)(b) does not require the constable to specify in precise terms the offence in question.[148]

---

[144] Or any other offence of which the accused could lawfully be convicted on that charge: s 38(2).

[145] See n 60.

[146] Arrest by others charged with the duty of investigating offences and charging offenders will not suffice.

[147] See n 60.

[148] *R v Compton* [2002] EWCA Crim 2835.

Sections 36 and 37 contain no proviso, analogous to that contained in s 34(1), whereby an inference may only be drawn if the accused could reasonably have been expected to account for the object, substance, etc at the time when questioned about it. Notwithstanding this omission, it is submitted that the trial judge should give a clear direction to the jury that, in deciding whether to draw an inference, and if so the strength of the inference to be drawn, they should take into account the nature and personal characteristics of the accused, including, as appropriate, his age, intelligence, language, and literacy and his physical, mental, and emotional state at the time when he was questioned. The nature and strength of any inference drawn under s 36 will also depend on the nature of the object, substance, etc, the extent to which evidence of its presence supports the prosecution case and the other circumstances of the case. For example, if the accused, on arrest for murder by stabbing, is found with a blood-stained knife in his pocket, his failure or refusal to account for its presence is likely to result in a highly damaging adverse inference. However, if the stabbing takes place in a very crowded pub and the blood-stained knife is found on the floor,[149] the accused's failure to account for its presence is unlikely, without more, to result in any adverse inference. Similar considerations apply to s 37.

The scope of both s 36 and s 37 has been fixed somewhat arbitrarily. For example, if a person, suspected of murder by stabbing, fails to explain why the jacket he is wearing on arrest is blood-stained, an adverse inference may be drawn under s 36. But if such a suspect, having abandoned his blood-stained jacket at the scene of the crime, where it is found by the police, is then arrested by them on his way home and fails to explain why his jacket is blood-stained (or even why he abandoned it), no statutory adverse inference may be drawn.

Inferences under s 36 and s 37 can only be drawn where evidence is given of the presence of the object, substance, etc, or of the presence of the accused, at a place at or about the time of the offence. Clearly, in some cases, that evidence, either taken alone or together with the adverse inference that can be drawn under the statutory provisions, will be sufficient to establish a case to answer or, indeed, to convict, as when a drug courier is arrested carrying a large package of heroin. Presumably, as in the case of s 34, the purpose of s 38(3)[150] in relation to s 36(2) and s 37(2), is simply to require the judge to direct the jury (or himself) that they are not entitled to convict (he is not entitled to decide that there is a case to answer) solely or, in the light of *Condron v United Kingdom*, mainly, on the basis of the inference drawn.

The discretion to exclude evidence of failure to mention facts

Section 38(6) provides that:

> Nothing in sections 34, 35, 36 or 37 prejudices any power of a court, in any proceedings, to exclude evidence (whether by preventing questions being put or otherwise) at its discretion.

In appropriate circumstances, therefore, the court could exclude evidence of the accused's failure to mention any fact on the basis of either s 78 of the 1984 Act or the common law discretion to exclude.[151] This might be appropriate, in relation to s 34, for example, in cases where it would be unfair to make use of the accused's silence by reason of breach of the

---

[149] See s 36(1)(a)(iv) at n 141.
[150] See in this chapter, under **Inferences from silence, Failure to mention facts when questioned or charged, The inferences that may be drawn.**
[151] See Ch 2.

provisions of the 1984 Act or the Codes, especially those relating to the caution, interrogation, and access to a solicitor (for example, failure to caution) or because the accused's silence was brought about by some other improper or unfair means (for example, threatening to beat up the accused unless he remains silent). Equally, in relation to s 36, there is obvious potential for discretionary exclusion where the evidence of the object, substance, etc was obtained illegally, improperly or unfairly.

In *R v Condron and Condron* it was held that if the defence objection is simply that the jury should not be invited to draw any adverse inference, it will seldom be appropriate to invite the judge to rule on this before the conclusion of all the evidence, because it will not be apparent until then what are the material facts that were not disclosed or the reason for non-disclosure. It was said that only in the most exceptional case could it be appropriate to make such a submission before the introduction of the evidence by the Crown, for example where the accused is of very low intelligence and understanding and has been advised by his solicitor to say nothing.

Inferences from refusal to consent to the taking of samples

In appropriate circumstances, an adverse inference may be drawn from a suspect's refusal, without good cause, to consent to the taking of 'intimate samples' from his body. Under s 65 of the 1984 Act, an intimate sample is defined as (a) a sample of blood, semen, or any other tissue fluid, urine, or pubic hair; (b) a dental impression; and (c) a swab taken from any part of a person's genitals (including pubic hair) or from a person's body orifice other than the mouth. Section 62 of the 1984 Act, detailed consideration of which is outside the scope of this work, sets out the various conditions to be met before an intimate sample can be taken from a person. One of the conditions is that appropriate consent is given.[152] Section 62(10) provides that:

> Where the appropriate consent to the taking of an intimate sample from a person was refused without good cause, in any proceedings against that person for an offence—
> (a) the court, in determining...
> (ii) whether there is a case to answer; and...
> (b) the court or jury, in determining whether that person is guilty of the offence charged, may draw such inferences from the refusal as appear proper.

Before a person is asked to provide an intimate sample, he must be warned that if he refuses without good cause, his refusal may harm his case if it comes to trial.[153] Whether consent was refused 'without good cause' is a question of fact. In appropriate circumstances, a person's bodily or mental condition may amount to good cause. However, whether a refusal out of embarrassment or on the grounds of some deeply held personal conviction is capable of constituting good cause is less clear.

There is no equivalent to s 62(10) in the case of 'non-intimate samples' because such samples may be taken without consent, subject to compliance with the conditions that have to

---

[152] See s 62(1)(b), (1A)(b), and (2A)(c). 'Appropriate consent' means, in relation to a person aged 17 or over, the consent of that person; in relation to a person aged 14 or over but under 17, the consent of that person and his parent or guardian; and in relation to a person aged under 14, the consent of his parent or guardian: s 65. The consent must be given in writing: s 62(4).
[153] Para 6.3 and Note 6D, Code D.

be met set out in s 63 of the 1984 Act.[154] Under s 65 of the 1984 Act, a non-intimate sample means: (a) a sample of hair other than pubic hair; (b) a sample taken from a nail or from under a nail; (c) a swab taken from any part of a person's body other than a part from which a swab taken would be an intimate sample; (d) saliva; and (e) a skin impression (which means any record (other than a fingerprint) which is a record (in any form and produced by any method) of the skin pattern and other physical characteristics or features of the whole or any part of a foot or any other part of a body).

Inferences from failure to provide advance disclosure of the defence case

Trials on indictment

Under the rules of primary prosecution disclosure in s 3 of the Criminal Procedure and Investigations Act 1996 (the 1996 Act), the prosecutor must disclose to the accused previously undisclosed material which might reasonably be considered capable of undermining the case for the prosecution against the accused or of assisting the case for the accused, or give the accused a written statement that there is no such material. Section 5(5) of the 1996 Act is to the effect that where a person is charged with an offence for which he is sent for trial to a Crown Court and the prosecutor complies or purports to comply with s 3, the accused must give a defence statement to the court and the prosecutor.[155] The defence statement must be served during a prescribed 'relevant period' (within 28 days of primary prosecution disclosure).[156] The contents of the defence statement are prescribed by s 6A, which provides as follows:

(1) …a defence statement is a written statement—
   (a) setting out the nature of the accused's defence, including any particular defences on which he intends to rely,
   (b) indicating the matters of fact on which he takes issue with the prosecution,
   (c) setting out, in the case of each such matter, why he takes issue with the prosecution,
   (ca) setting out particulars of the matters of fact on which he intends to rely for the purposes of his defence, and
   (d) indicating any point of law (including any point as to the admissibility of evidence or an abuse of process) which he wishes to take, and any authority on which he intends to rely for that purpose.
(2) A defence statement that discloses an alibi must give particulars of it, including—
   (a) the name, address and date of birth of any witness the accused believes is able to give evidence in support of the alibi, or as many of those details as are known to the accused when the statement is given;
   (b) any information in the accused's possession which might be of material assistance in identifying or finding any such witness in whose case any of the details mentioned in paragraph (a) are not known to the accused when the statement is given.

---

[154] The 1984 Act, s 61, makes similar provision for fingerprints of a person to be taken without his consent.

[155] Although there is no obligation on an accused to give a defence statement to a co-accused, if the prosecutor forms the view that a defence statement of one co-accused might reasonably be expected to assist the defence of another, it should be disclosed to the other on secondary prosecution disclosure: *R v Cairns* [2003] 1 Cr App R 38, CA.

[156] See s 5(C), s 12, and the Criminal Procedure and Investigations Act 1996 (Defence Disclosure Time Limits) Regulations 2011, SI 2011/209, reg 2.

(3) For the purposes of this section evidence in support of an alibi is evidence tending to show that by reason of the presence of the accused at a particular place or in a particular area at a particular time he was not, or was unlikely to have been, at the place where the offence is alleged to have been committed at the time of its alleged commission.

R v Rochford[157] established three important matters. First, it is not open to a lawyer to advise his client not to file a defence statement, because to file such a statement is a statutory obligation. Second, s 6A does not take away the fundamental rights of legal professional privilege and the privilege against self-incrimination; the accused is required to disclose what is going to happen at the trial, not his confidential discussions with his lawyer and he is not obliged to incriminate himself, if he does not want to.[158] Third, if an accused has no positive case to advance at trial, but pleads not guilty, the defence statement should say that the accused does not admit the offence, has no positive case to advance, and calls for the Crown to prove its case.[159]

As a matter of good practice a defence statement should be signed by the accused as an acknowledgment of its accuracy to obviate error and dispute that can arise, for example, where part of the defence statement is contrary to the original instructions given by the accused to his solicitors.[160]

The obligation under s 6A(2)(a) to give the name and address of an alibi witness is triggered by the accused's belief that the witness is able to give evidence in support of the alibi; it is not necessary that the witness can give such evidence and is willing to do so. Nor is the accused's belief in the witness's ability to give evidence dependent upon the witness giving a proof of evidence.[161]

Under s 6C, there is an obligation on the defence, during a prescribed 'relevant period', to give notification of intention to call defence witnesses. Section 6C(1) provides as follows:

(1) The accused must give to the court and the prosecutor a notice indicating whether he intends to call any persons (other than himself) as witnesses at his trial and, if so—
   (a) giving the name, address and date of birth of each such proposed witness, or as many of those details as are known to the accused when the notice is given;
   (b) providing any information in the accused's possession which might be of material assistance in identifying or finding any such proposed witness in whose case any of the details mentioned in paragraph (a) are not known to the accused when the notice is given.[162]

Under s 11(5) of the 1996 Act, where an accused fails to comply with the disclosure requirements of ss 5, 6A, or 6C, the court or any other party may make appropriate adverse comment and the court or jury, in deciding the question of guilt, may draw proper adverse inferences.[163] It is not open to the court to order compliance and then vest itself with the extra-statutory power to punish as a contempt of court disobedience to the order.[164] If it appears to the court

[157] [2011] 1 Cr App R 127, CA.
[158] [2011] 1 Cr App R 127, CA at [21].
[159] [2011] 1 Cr App R 127, CA at [24].
[160] *R v Wheeler* [2001] Crim LR 745, CA.
[161] *Joseph Hill & Co, In re* [2013] 2 Cr App R 218, CA.
[162] For the guidance that police officers must follow if they interview proposed witnesses whose details are disclosed, see the Code of Practice for Arranging and Conducting Interviews of Witnesses notified by the Accused.
[163] Failure to give notice of alibi witnesses does not render their evidence inadmissible: see *R (Tinnion) v Reading Crown Court* [2009] EWHC 2930 (Admin).
[164] *R v Rochford* [2011] 1 Cr App R 127, CA.

at a pre-trial hearing that an accused has failed to comply fully with s 5 or s 6C, so that there is a possibility of comment being made or inferences being drawn under s 11(5), he shall warn the accused accordingly.[165] Section 11 provides as follows:

(1) This section applies in the cases set out in subsections (2), (3), and (4).

(2) The first case is where section 5 applies and the accused—

    (a) fails to give an initial defence statement,

    (b) gives an initial defence statement but does so after the end of the . . . relevant period for section 5,

    . . .

    (e) sets out inconsistent defences in his defence statement, or

    (f) at his trial—

        (i) puts forward a defence which was not mentioned in his defence statement or is different from any defence set out in the statement,

        (ii) relies on a matter which in breach of the requirements imposed by or under section 6A, was not mentioned in his defence statement,

        (iii) adduces evidence in support of an alibi[166] without having given particulars of the alibi in his defence statement, or

        (iv) calls a witness to give evidence in support of an alibi without having complied with section 6A(2)(a) or (b) as regards the witness in his defence statement.

(3) The second case is . . .[167]

(4) The third case is where the accused—

    (a) gives a witness notice but does so after the end of . . . the relevant period for section 6C, or

    (b) at his trial calls a witness (other than himself) not included, or not adequately identified, in a witness notice.

(5) Where this section applies—

    (a) the court or any other party may make such comment as appears appropriate;

    (b) the court or jury may draw such inferences as appear proper in deciding whether the accused is guilty of the offence concerned.

(6) Where—

    (a) this section applies by virtue of subsection (2)(f)(ii) . . . , and

    (b) the matter which was not mentioned is a point of law (including any point as to the admissibility of evidence or an abuse of process) or an authority,

comment by another party under subsection 5(a) may be made only with the leave of the court.

(7) Where this section applies by virtue of subsection (4), comment by another party under subsection (5)(a) may be made only with the leave of the court.

(8) Where the accused puts forward a defence which is different from any defence set out in his defence statement, in doing anything under subsection (5) or in deciding whether to do anything under it the court shall have regard—

    (a) to the extent of the difference in the defences, and

    (b) to whether there is any justification for it.

(9) Where the accused calls a witness whom he has failed to include, or to identify adequately, in a witness notice,[168] in doing anything under subsection (5) or in deciding to do anything under it the court shall have regard to whether there is any justification for the failure.

(10) A person shall not be convicted of an offence solely on an inference drawn under subsection (5).

---

[165] Section 6E(2).

[166] A reference to 'evidence in support of an alibi' shall be construed in accordance with s 6A(3): s 11(12)(d).

[167] The second case relates to failure to disclose prior to summary trial: see in this chapter under **Inferences from failure to provide advance disclosure of the defence case, Summary trials**.

[168] 'Witness notice' means a notice given under s 6C: s 11(12)(e).

Under section 11(5)(b), proper inferences may be drawn only in deciding whether the accused is guilty of the offence charged, and not in deciding whether there is a case to answer.[169]

Three important matters were established in *R v Tibbs*.[170] First, s 11 does not disallow or require leave for cross-examination of an accused on differences between his defence at trial and his defence statement—it precludes comment or invitation to the jury to draw an inference from the differences unless the court gives leave. Second, the word 'defence' in s 11 is not restricted to its general legal description (eg 'self-defence' or 'mistaken identification'), but includes the facts and matters to be relied on in the defence, otherwise there would be little, if any, scope for comparing the extent of the difference in the defences under s 11(8)(a)—on the restrictive interpretation, the defence put forward would either be the same as or different from the defence in the defence statement. Third, failure to warn the jury in accordance with s 11(10) that they cannot convict solely from drawing an adverse inference will not necessarily result in a successful appeal against conviction. The issue will turn on the particular circumstances, including the strength of the prosecution case.

In some cases, the defence statement may be relied on by the Crown, or may be used by the jury, as a lie by the accused indicative of a consciousness of his guilt, in which case the jury will need to be directed in accordance with *R v Goodway*.[171]

Summary trials

Section 6 of the 1996 Act is to the effect that where a person is charged with an offence in respect of which the court proceeds to summary trial and the prosecutor complies or purports to comply with its duty to disclose unused material, then the accused *may* give a defence statement to the prosecutor, and, if he does so, must also give such a statement to the court, and must give the statement during a prescribed 'relevant period'. The magistrates' court may permit appropriate comment and draw proper inferences in the same circumstances as such comment may be permitted and such inferences may be drawn in a trial on indictment, ie late disclosure, inconsistent defences, etc, but with the obvious exception of failure to give a defence statement.[172] As in trials on indictment, in summary cases a person shall not be convicted of an offence solely on an inference drawn under s 11(5).[173]

Preparatory hearings

Under s 29 of the 1996 Act, a Crown Court judge may order a preparatory hearing where it appears to him that the indictment reveals a case of such complexity, a case of such seriousness, or a case whose trial is likely to be of such length that substantial benefits are likely to accrue from such a hearing.[174] Section 31(4) provides that at the preparatory hearing the judge may order the prosecutor to give the court and the accused a case statement of such matters as the facts of the case for the prosecution, the witnesses who will speak to them, and relevant exhibits. Under s 31(6), where the prosecutor has complied with such an order, the judge may order the accused to give the court and prosecutor written notice of any objections that he has

[169] Cf the 1994 Act, ss 34(2), 36(2), and 37(2).
[170] [2000] 2 Cr App R 309, CA.
[171] [1993] 4 All ER 894, CA (see Ch 2).
[172] Section 11(3).
[173] Section 11(10).
[174] Separate but similar provision is made for cases of serious or complex fraud—see the Criminal Justice Act 1987, ss 7, 9, and 10.

to the case statement. If he does so, he shall warn the accused of the possible consequences under s 34 of the Act of not complying with his order.[175]

Section 34 provides as follows:

(1) Any party may depart from the case he disclosed in pursuance of a requirement imposed under section 31.

(2) Where—

(a) a party departs from the case he disclosed in pursuance of a requirement imposed under section 31, or

(b) a party fails to comply with such a requirement,

the judge or, with the leave of the judge, any other party may make such comment as appears to the judge or the other party (as the case may be) to be appropriate and the jury or, in the case of a trial without a jury, the judge, may draw such inferences as appear proper.

(3) In doing anything under subsection (2) or in deciding whether to do anything under it the judge shall have regard—

(a) to the extent of the departure or failure, and

(b) to whether there is any justification for it.

(4) Except as provided by this section, in the case of a trial with a jury no part—

(a) of a statement given under section 31(6)(a), or

(b) of any other information relating to the case for the accused or, if there is more than one, the case for any of them, which was given in pursuance of a requirement imposed under section 31,

may be disclosed at a stage in the trial after the jury have been sworn without the consent of the accused concerned.

ADDITIONAL READING

Birch, 'Suffering in Silence: A Cost–Benefit Analysis of Section 34' [1999] Crim LR 769.

Buckle et al, *The Right of Silence: The Impact of the Criminal Justice and Public Order Act 1994* (Home Office Research Study No 199, 2000).

Cooper, 'Legal advice and pre-trial silence—unreasonable developments' (2006) 10 E&P 60.

Greer, 'The Right of Silence: A Review of the Current Debate' (1990) 53 MLR 709.

Jackson, 'Silence and Proof: Extending the boundaries of criminal proceedings in the United Kingdom' (2001) 5 E&P 145.

Jackson et al, *Legislating Against Silence: The Northern Ireland Experience* (Northern Ireland Office, 2000).

Leng, 'Silence pre-trial, reasonable expectations and the normative distortion of fact-finding' (2001) 5 E&P 240.

Meng Heong Yeo, 'Diminishing the Right of Silence: The Singapore Experience' [1983] Crim LR 89.

Mirfield, 'Two Side-Effects of Sections 34 to 37 of the Criminal Justice and Public Order Act 1994' [1995] Crim LR 612.

Munday, 'Inferences from Silence and European Human Rights Law' [1996] Crim LR 370.

Pattenden, 'Inferences from Silence' [1995] Crim LR 602.

Tan, 'Adverse Inferences and the Right to Silence: Re-examining the Singapore Experience' [1974] Crim LR 471.

Zuckerman, 'Trial by Unfair Means—The Report of the Working Group on the Right of Silence' [1989] Crim LR 855.

[175] Section 31(8).

Evidence of character: evidence of character in civil cases

15

Key issues

- Should evidence be admitted in civil proceedings to show the disposition of the claimant or defendant towards good conduct?

- When and why should evidence be admitted in civil proceedings to show the disposition of the defendant towards misconduct?

- Why might it be more acceptable in a civil case than in a criminal case to admit evidence of the disposition of a party towards misconduct?

This chapter, together with Chapters 16 and 17 of this book, considers the admissibility of evidence of character. The admissibility of character evidence is governed by a number of factors which it will be useful to summarize before considering the law in detail. Two obvious considerations are whether the proceedings are civil or criminal and whether the evidence relates to the character of a party or non-party. Additionally, it is necessary to consider the nature of the character evidence in question. It may relate to either good or bad character and, in either event, may constitute evidence of a person's actual disposition, that is his propensity to act, think, or feel in a given way, or evidence of his reputation, that is his *reputed* disposition or propensity to act, think, or feel in a given way. Thus the character of a person may be proved by evidence of general disposition, by evidence of specific examples of his conduct on other occasions (including, in the case of bad conduct, evidence of his previous convictions), or by evidence of his reputation among those to whom he is known. The final important consideration is the purpose for which the character evidence in question is sought to be adduced or elicited in cross-examination. There are three possibilities. First, it may be adduced because the character of a person is itself in issue in the proceedings. Second, it may be adduced because of its relevance to a fact in issue, that is because of its tendency to prove that a person did a certain act, whether he did that act being in issue in the proceedings. Third, evidence of the character of a party or witness may be adduced because of its relevance to his credibility.

Character in issue or relevant to a fact in issue

In civil proceedings, evidence of the character of a party or non-party is admissible if it is in issue or of relevance to a fact in issue. The law of defamation provides a number of examples. Thus on the question of liability in an action for defamation in which justification is pleaded, the claimant's character will obviously be in issue. If, for example, the defendant has alleged that the claimant is a thief, evidence of the claimant's convictions for theft may be admitted to justify the allegation.[1] Similarly, the claimant, in order to rebut a defence of fair comment, may adduce evidence of his good reputation at the time of publication of the allegedly defamatory material.[2] The character of a claimant in an action for defamation is also of direct relevance, if he succeeds, to the quantum of recoverable damages, the damage sustained being dependent on the estimation in which he was previously held.[3]

Evidence of the disposition of the parties towards good conduct

It is submitted that evidence of the disposition of the parties to civil proceedings towards good conduct on other occasions should be admitted if it meets the ordinary requirement of relevance. However, according to the few reported decisions on the topic, such evidence has been treated as irrelevant to the facts in issue and accordingly excluded.

[1] Section 13 of the Civil Evidence Act 1968 provides that in libel or slander actions in which the question whether a person committed a criminal offence is relevant to an issue in the action, proof of his conviction shall be conclusive evidence that he committed the offence: see Ch 21.

[2] See *Cornwell v Myskow* [1987] 2 All ER 504, CA.

[3] See *Gatley on Libel and Slander* (11th edn, London, 2010), paras 35.30–35.33

As to good conduct on the part of the defendant, in *A-G v Bowman*,[4] at the trial of an information for keeping false weights, a civil suit, Eyre CB held that the evidence of a witness to character called by the defendant was inadmissible because the proceedings were not criminal. Similarly in *A-G v Radloff*[5] the rule was justified on the basis that whereas there is a fair and just presumption that a person of good character would not commit a crime, no presumption fairly arises in most civil cases, from the good character of the defendant, that he did not commit the breach of contract or civil duty alleged against him.

As to the claimant, in *Hatton v Cooper*,[6] a case involving a collision between two cars in which there was an unusual dearth of relevant evidence, it was held that the trial judge, on the question of liability, had improperly relied on evidence from the claimant's employer that the claimant was an excellent driver, calm, assured, and composed, who never took risks. Jonathan Parker LJ said that in the context of this collision, the opinion of a third party as to the driving ability of either party was 'completely worthless'.

Evidence of the disposition of the parties towards bad conduct

In civil proceedings, evidence of the disposition of the defendant towards wrongdoing or the commission of a particular kind of civil wrong may be admissible if it is of sufficient relevance or probative value in relation to the facts in issue. Such evidence, which relates to particular acts of misconduct on other occasions, whether occurring before or after the occurrence of the facts in issue,[7] is designated 'similar fact evidence'.

Whereas in criminal proceedings the rules relating to the admissibility of similar fact evidence have reflected a paramount concern to safeguard the accused from the admission of unduly prejudicial evidence,[8] in civil proceedings, where trial is seldom by jury, the emphasis has been on probative value rather than prejudicial effect. To this extent, in civil cases, the principle of admissibility has tended to approximate to the ordinary test of relevance and accordingly similar fact evidence has been admitted more readily. In *Hales v Kerr*,[9] a negligence action in which the plaintiff alleged that he had contracted ringworm from a dirty razor used by the defendant, a hairdresser, evidence was admitted that two other customers shaved by the defendant had also contracted ringworm. In *Joy v Phillips, Mills & Co Ltd*[10] a claim was made for workmen's compensation by the father of a deceased stable boy. The boy was kicked by a horse and found nearby holding a halter. Evidence that the boy had previously teased horses with a halter was held to be admissible in rebuttal of the applicant's allegation that the accident had occurred in the course of the boy's employment. More recently, in *Jones v Greater Manchester Police Authority*,[11] civil proceedings for a sex offender order under s 2 of the Crime

---

[4] (1791) 2 Bos&P 532n.

[5] (1854) 10 Exch 84 at 97.

[6] [2001] RTR 544, CA.

[7] *Desmond v Bower* [2010] EMLR 5, CA.

[8] See the Criminal Justice Act 2003, s 101(3) and the Police and Criminal Evidence Act 1984 s 78.

[9] [1908] 2 KB 601.

[10] [1916] 1 KB 849. See also *Barrett v Long* (1851) 3 HL Cas 395; *Osborne v Chocqueel* [1896] 2 QB 109; and *Sattin v National Union Bank* (1978) 122 Sol Jo 367, CA.

[11] [2002] ACD 4, DC.

and Disorder Act 1998, it was held that evidence of propensity to commit sexual offences against young males was relevant and admissible because the purpose of the proceedings was to seek to predict the extent to which past events gave rise to reasonable cause for believing that an order was necessary to protect the public from serious harm; and that the admission of such evidence did not breach either Art 6 or Art 8 of the European Convention on Human Rights or render the proceedings unfair.

In *Mood Music Publishing Co Ltd v De Wolfe Publishing Ltd*,[12] similar fact evidence was admitted in an action for infringement of copyright. The defendants admitted the similarity between the musical work in which the plaintiffs owned the copyright and the work which they had produced, but alleged that the similarity was coincidental. Evidence was admitted to show that on other occasions the defendants had produced musical works bearing a close resemblance to musical works which were the subject of copyright. The Court of Appeal held that the evidence had been properly admitted to rebut the allegation of coincidence.

The leading authority is *O'Brien v Chief Constable of South Wales Police*.[13] The claimant had been convicted of murder. After serving 11 years in prison, his case had been referred to the Criminal Cases Review Commission and his appeal had been allowed. He then brought proceedings against the Chief Constable for misfeasance in public office and malicious prosecution, alleging that he had been 'framed' by a Detective Inspector L and a Detective Chief Superintendent C, who was said to have approved some aspects of the misconduct alleged against L. The House of Lords held that evidence had properly been admitted to show that L had behaved with similar impropriety on two other occasions and that C had done so on one other occasion. The House of Lords held that the test of admissibility in civil cases was different from that which applied in criminal cases. The test in criminal cases, propounded in *R v P*[14] and the Criminal Justice Act 2003, required an enhanced relevance or substantial probative value because, if the evidence was not cogent, the prejudice that it would cause to the accused might render the proceedings unfair. That test led to the exclusion of evidence which was relevant on the grounds that it was not sufficiently probative. (The test, as described, is as propounded in *R v P*, but is *not* as now set out in the Criminal Justice Act 2003.[15]) There was no warrant for the automatic application of such a test in a civil suit. To do so would be to introduce an inflexibility which was inappropriate and undesirable. Lord Phillips said:[16]

I would simply apply the test of relevance as the test of admissibility of similar fact evidence in a civil suit. Such evidence is admissible if it is potentially probative of an issue in the action. That is not to say that the policy considerations that have given rise to the complex rules…in sections 100 to 106 of the 2003 Act have no part to play in the conduct of civil litigation. They are policy considerations which the judge who has the management of the civil litigation will wish to keep well in mind. CPR r 1.2 requires the court to give effect to the overriding objective of dealing with cases justly. This includes dealing with the case in a way which is proportionate to what is involved in the case, and in a manner which is expeditious and fair. CPR r 1.4 requires the court actively to manage the case in order to further the overriding objective. CPR r 2.1 gives the court

[12] [1976] Ch 119; cf *EG Music v SF (Film) Distributors* [1978] FSR 121. See also *Berger v Raymond & Son Ltd* [1984] 1 WLR 625.

[13] [2005] 2 WLR 2038, HL.

[14] [1991] 3 All ER 337, HL.

[15] See Ch 17.

[16] *R v P* [1991] 3 All ER 337, HL at [53]–[56].

the power to control the evidence. This power expressly enables the court to exclude evidence that would otherwise be admissible and to limit cross-examination.

Similar fact evidence will not necessarily risk causing any unfair prejudice to the party against whom it is directed…It may, however, carry such a risk. Evidence of impropriety which reflects adversely on the character of a party may risk causing prejudice that is disproportionate to its relevance, particularly where the trial is taking place before a jury. In such a case the judge will be astute to see that the probative cogency of the evidence justifies this risk of prejudice in the interests of a fair trial.[17]

Equally, when considering whether to admit evidence, or permit cross-examination, on matters that are collateral to the central issues, the judge will have regard to the need for proportionality and expedition. He will consider whether the evidence in question is likely to be relatively uncontroversial, or whether its admission is likely to create side issues which will unbalance the trial and make it harder to see the wood from the trees.

Character relevant to credit

In civil proceedings, any person who gives evidence, whether or not a party to the proceedings, is liable to cross-examination as to his credibility as a witness.[18] However, as a general rule, the cross-examining party is not allowed to adduce evidence to contradict a witness's answer to a question concerning credit. The rule, and the exceptions to it, are considered in detail in Chapter 7.

ADDITIONAL READING

Munday, 'Case management, similar fact evidence in civil cases, and a divided law of evidence' (2006) 10 E&P 81.

---

[17] Experimental data suggest that judges are no better than jurors at excluding from their calculations prejudicial and inadmissible evidence. For a review, prompted by Lord Phillips' dicta, see Munday, 'Case management, similar fact evidence in civil cases, and a divided law of evidence' (2006) 10 E&P 81.

[18] See Ch 7, under **Cross-examination, The permitted form of questioning in cross-examination, Cross-examination as to credit**.

Evidence of character: evidence of the good character of the accused

16

Key issues

- Why, and to what extent should an accused be allowed to call evidence of his previous good character?

- Where an accused has previous convictions, in what circumstances might it be acceptable for a judge to tell a jury that they should treat the accused as a person of good character?

- Where an accused has no previous convictions, in what circumstances might it be acceptable for a judge to refuse to tell a jury that they should treat the accused as a person of good character?

This chapter concerns the circumstances in which, in criminal proceedings, evidence of the good character of the accused may be adduced because of its relevance either to a fact in issue or to his credibility.[1]

The evidence admissible

In criminal proceedings, the accused is allowed to adduce evidence of his good character. It may be proved either in chief, by the evidence of the accused himself or other defence witnesses, or in cross-examination of witnesses called for the prosecution. In *R v Rowton*[2] the accused, charged with indecent assault on a boy, called witnesses to his character. It was held that such evidence should be confined to evidence of the reputation of the accused amongst those to whom he is known and should not include evidence of specific creditable acts of the accused nor evidence of the witness's opinion of his disposition. Although this case was decided prior to the Criminal Evidence Act 1898, s 1 of which made the accused a competent witness for the defence in all criminal cases,[3] the rule would appear to apply even when the evidence of good character is given by the accused himself. Thus notwithstanding that in the normal case the accused would be much better qualified to give evidence of his disposition as revealed by specific acts of creditable conduct, as opposed to evidence of his reputation, strictly speaking he must confine himself to the latter. However, although *R v Rowton* has never been expressly overruled, nowadays it is not, in practice, strictly adhered to. In *R v Redgrave*,[4] a case of importuning for immoral purposes in which the Court of Appeal held that the accused was not entitled to produce documents and photographs to show that he had had relationships of a heterosexual nature, because this amounted to calling evidence of particular facts to show that he was of a disposition which made it unlikely that he would have committed the offence charged, the court also said that an accused, in such a case, was entitled to give evidence of a normal sexual relationship with his wife or girlfriend.

The common law rule under which in criminal proceedings evidence of a person's reputation is admissible for the purpose of proving his good (or bad) character has been preserved and put on a statutory basis by s 118(1) of the Criminal Justice Act 2003 (the 2003 Act).

The direction to the jury

The leading authority on how to direct the jury about evidence of the good character of the accused is *R v Vye*.[5] Prior to *R v Vye*, the law was unclear as to (a) whether a judge is under a duty to direct the jury about evidence of the good character of the accused; and (b) if so, whether he should direct them not only that the evidence is relevant to credibility (the first

---

[1] Other aspects of the subject are more conveniently considered in ch 6 under **Unfavourable and hostile witnesses, The rule against a party impeaching the credit of his own witness**, and in ch 7 under **Cross-examination as to credit** and **Cross-examination, Finality of answers to collateral questions**. In criminal cases, the character of a person who is neither a party nor a witness is rarely relevant to a fact in issue: for an example, see *R v Murray* [1994] Crim LR 927, CA.

[2] (1865) Le&Ca 520, CCR.

[3] See now the Youth Justice and Criminal Evidence Act 1999, s 53(1) (see Ch 5).

[4] (1981) 74 Cr App R 10, CA.

[5] [1993] 1 WLR 471.

limb of the direction) but also that it has a probative value in relation to the issue of guilt, in that a person of good character is less likely to have committed the offence (the second limb). Lord Chief Justice Taylor, giving the reserved judgment of the Court of Appeal, laid down the following three principles.

1. If the accused testifies, the judge should give a first limb direction. If the accused does not give evidence at trial but relies on pre-trial answers or statements, that is, exculpatory statements made to the police or others, the judge, who is entitled to make observations about the way the jury should approach such evidence in contrast to evidence given on oath, should give a first limb direction by directing the jury to have regard to the accused's good character when considering the credibility of those statements.[6] If the accused does not give evidence and has given no pre-trial answers or statements, no issue as to his credibility arises and a first limb direction is not required.

2. A second limb direction should be given, whether or not the accused has testified or made pre-trial answers or statements.[7] It is for the judge in each case to decide how he tailors the direction to the particular circumstances. He would probably wish to indicate, as is commonly done, that good character cannot amount to a defence.

3. Where an accused of good character is jointly tried with an accused of bad character, principles 1 and 2 still apply: the accused of good character is entitled to a full direction.[8] As to any direction concerning the accused of bad character, in some cases the judge may think it best to tell the jury that there has been no evidence about his character and they must not speculate or take the absence of such information as any evidence against him. In other cases, the judge may think it best to say nothing about the absence of such information. The course to be taken depends on the circumstances of the individual case, including how great an issue was made of character during the evidence and speeches.

In cases involving historic sexual abuse a full good character direction involves an additional component—sometimes referred to as a 'third limb'—to the effect that because so much time has passed between the alleged offences and the present time without the accused committing any offence, it is less likely that he committed the offences charged. In *R v GJB*[9] it was held that this third limb was in reality an adaptation of the normal second limb of a *Vye* direction, but is required in such cases because the accused's defence is frequently a straightforward denial and he may have little more than his good character to rely on.

The terms of the direction
Where good character directions are required in accordance with *R v Vye*, it is not necessary for judges to use any particular form of words, but they may be wise to avoid saying that the jury are 'entitled' to take the evidence into account, which suggests that the jury have a choice

---

[6] See also *R v Chapman* [1989] Crim LR 60, CA.

[7] Improper disclosure that the accused had previously been arrested for an offence of the same type as the offence charged will undermine a second limb direction and effectively deprive the accused of the good character direction: *Arthurton v R* [2004] 2 Cr App R 559, PC.

[8] It was held that the suggestion of Lord Lane CJ in *R v Gibson* (1991) 93 Cr App R 9, CA, that the judge may decide to say little if anything about the good character of the one accused, was not satisfactory and ought not to be followed. *R v Vye*, in this respect, was applied in *R v Houlden* (1993) 99 Cr App R 244, CA.

[9] [2011] EWCA Crim 867 at [19].

whether or not to take it into account for the purposes in question.[10] Similarly, judges should avoid saying, 'the defence ask you to consider the evidence' because this may leave the jury with the impression that the direction was no more than a reminder of a defence submission.[11] Further, it is a serious misdirection to tell the jury that they can put good character into the scales[12] or, in the case of the first limb, that good character 'might assist' them on the question of credibility.[13] Equally, character directions should not be given in the form of a question or rhetorical question (eg, 'Is it more likely that he is telling you the truth because he is a man of good character?'), but in the form of an affirmative statement,[14] as in the Crown Court Bench Book illustrative direction for the first limb ('First, the defendant has given evidence. His good character is a positive feature of the defendant which you should take into account when considering whether you accept what he told you').[15] In *R v Vye* it was held that if the judge gives both limbs of the direction, the Court of Appeal will be slow to criticize any qualifying remarks based on the facts of the individual case. Such remarks, however, must be justified.[16]

'Pre-trial answers or statements'

In *R v Aziz*[17] the House of Lords has made clear that the phrase 'pre-trial answers or statements', as used in the first principle in *R v Vye*, refers not to wholly exculpatory statements, but only to 'mixed' statements, ie statements containing inculpatory as well as exculpatory material which are, for that reason, tendered as evidence of the truth of the facts they contain.[18] Thus an accused who does not give evidence but relies on wholly exculpatory statements is not entitled to a first limb direction. It was further held in *R v Aziz* that an accused who is entitled to directions as to good character in accordance with *R v Vye* will not lose that entitlement by mounting an attack on a co-accused such as a cut-throat defence.[19]

The accused of 'bad character'

As to the third principle in *R v Vye*, relating to directions about the accused of 'bad character' with whom the accused of good character is jointly tried, that phrase appears to cover both

---

[10] *R v Miah* [1997] 2 Cr App R 12, CA. See also *R v Moustakim* [2008] EWCA Crim 3096: the use of the word 'perhaps' is a significant dilution of the direction required.

[11] *R v Gbajabiamila* [2011] EWCA Crim 734 at [18]. See also *R v Moustakim* [2008] EWCA Crim 3096, *R v MW* [2008] EWCA Crim 3091, and *R v Dillon* [2013] EWCA Crim 122.

[12] *R v Boyson* [1991] Crim LR 274, CA.

[13] *R v Gray* [2004] 2 Cr App R 498, CA. See also *R v Dillon* [2013] EWCA Crim 122 at [23]: what is required is a clear statement that the jury should take the accused's good character into account when deciding whether they believe his evidence and an oblique reference to 'assessing' the accused is insufficient.

[14] *R v Lloyd* [2000] 2 Cr App R 355, CA and *R v Scranage* [2001] EWCA Crim 1171.

[15] The Crown Court Bench Book 2010, 164.

[16] See *R v Fitton* [2001] EWCA Crim 215, CA where the judge misdirected the jury in a qualification to the standard directions to the effect that a doorman's good character was of less relevance and weight given that the offence he was alleged to have committed was spontaneous. See also *R v Handbridge* [1993] Crim LR 287, CA, where the judge was wrong and unfair to have directed the jury to ignore good character unless the rest of the evidence left them in doubt about guilt. See also *R v Dillon* [2013] EWCA Crim 122, where the judge, in relation to propensity, should not have made remarks that the accused had 'not been caught out in the past knocking a woman about' because the remarks implied that the accused might have committed offences but had not been caught.

[17] [1996] AC 41, HL.

[18] See *R v Duncan* (1981) 73 Cr App R 359, CA and *R v Sharp* [1988] 1 All ER 65, HL. A statement is only 'mixed' if it contains an admission of fact which is 'significant' in relation to an issue in the case: see *R v Garrod* [1997] Crim LR 445, CA and generally Ch 6. See also *R v Patel* [2010] EWCA Crim 976, CA.

[19] [1996] AC 41, HL at 52–53.

an accused in respect of whom there is no evidence of character, one way or the other, and an accused of bad character whose bad character is not revealed in evidence, but not an accused whose bad character is revealed in evidence.[20]

Failure to give a good character direction

A good character direction will be of some value in every case in which it should be given[21] and therefore, although a failure to give the direction will not necessarily render a conviction unsafe, with each case to be reviewed in the light of its own facts,[22] it will rarely be possible for an appellate court to say that such a failure could not have affected the outcome of the trial.[23] However, the good character of the accused must be distinctly raised, by defence evidence or in cross-examination of prosecution witnesses, and it is the duty of defence counsel to ensure that a direction is obtained; if the issue is not raised by the defence, the judge is under no duty to raise it himself.[24]

In *R v Campbell*,[25] an appeal concerning a direction relating to an accused's *bad* character, Lord Phillips CJ, in a passage which borders on suggesting that the common law rules relating to directions to the jury on the *good* character of the accused have been modified by the 2003 Act,[26] referred to both limbs of the good character direction and observed that although the second limb was no more than common sense that one might have expected a jury to be capable of applying without assistance, failure to give either limb of the direction automatically resulted in the quashing of a conviction. His Lordship described this as a 'lamentable state of affairs' and said: 'Failure to give a direction that is no more than assistance in applying common sense to the evidence should not automatically be treated as a ground of appeal, let alone a reason to allow an appeal'. It is submitted that these obiter remarks, made without any reference to the relevant jurisprudence, should not be used to reverse the earlier authorities that clearly indicate an entitlement to a second limb direction.[27]

The meaning of 'good character'

As to what 'good character' means for the purposes of the principles established in *R v Vye*, there is no simple answer.[28] For example, previous convictions will not necessarily prevent an accused from being treated as of previous good character, particularly if they are spent or convictions for minor offences which have no relevance to credibility and took place a long

---

[20] See *R v Cain* [1994] 2 All ER 398, CA, where the evidence relating to the character of three co-accused was different: there was evidence of positive good character of A, no evidence in relation to the character of B, and evidence of the previous convictions of C. Only A was covered by *Vye*.

[21] *R v Fulcher* [1995] 2 Cr App R 251, CA at 260.

[22] *Singh v The State* [2006] 1 WLR 146, PC.

[23] *R v Kamar* (1999) The Times, 14 May.

[24] *Thompson v The Queen* [1998] AC 811, affirmed in *Teeluck v The State* [2005] 2 Cr App R 378, PC. See also *Stewart v The Queen* [2011] UKPC 11, PC.

[25] [2007] 1 WLR 2798, CA at [20]–[23].

[26] See also *R v Doncaster* (2008) 172 JP 202 per Rix LJ at [42]: 'Although there is no…abolition of the common law rules as to good character, it is difficult to think that the new law (as to bad character) has no impact for the old law (as to good character).'

[27] See *R v Garnham* [2008] EWCA Crim 266 where it was held that the judge was wrong to withhold a modified good character direction in favour of a modified bad character direction.

[28] See generally Munday 'What Constitutes a Good Character?' [1997] Crim LR 247. See also Roberts, 'Commentary' [2010] Crim LR 232.

time ago.[29] In these circumstances, the judge has a discretion whether or not to give directions in accordance with *R v Vye*, and if so in what terms, but he should give directions in *unqualified* terms if the previous convictions can only be regarded as irrelevant or of no significance in relation to the offence charged.[30] In *R v M*[31] the accused was tried for assaulting and raping a child under 13 (his niece). He had two old previous convictions for criminal damage which were spent. It was held that the judge had erred in not giving the 'full direction' on good character which she herself had clearly decided the accused was entitled to. First, by simply telling the jury it was 'a factor that [they] should take into account', she had failed to make it sufficiently clear that his good character and his credibility were factors *in his favour*.[32] Second, and more strikingly, she failed to mention explicitly the fact that he had never shown any propensity to commit offences of a sexual nature.[33]

However, it does not follow from this that a direction will be given automatically to those whose bad character is not of sufficient probative value or relevance to be admitted against them, and still less should it be given to those whose bad character is excluded as a matter of discretion; a good character direction is appropriate in the case of those who the judge rules may be treated as if they are without known bad character at all.[34]

An unqualified direction will be appropriate where, although there is evidence of previous misconduct on the part of the accused, it is disputed, and its potential for distracting the jury from the main issues in the case outweighs any benefit to be had from a qualified direction.[35] By the same token, there will be cases where the accused is not of absolutely good character and the fact of the previous conviction or other character blemish is known to the jury, but where the only proper course is to give a qualified direction, which is likely to mean that careful consideration should be given to the distinction between the two limbs of credibility and propensity.[36] In *R v Gray*,[37] a murder trial in which the accused denied being present at the killing and volunteered that he had been convicted of driving with excess alcohol and

[29] See, eg, *R v Goss* [2005] Crim LR 61, CA (on a charge of possessing a firearm, a previous conviction for driving a motor vehicle without car insurance, in the absence of evidence to show that the accused had deliberately flouted road traffic law). See also *R v Hamer* [2011] 1 WLR 528, CA (a fixed penalty notice issued for disorder (PND) has been held to have no effect on an accused's entitlement to a full good character direction as, by virtue of the PND scheme, such a notice does not involve an admission of guilt nor is it proof that a crime has been committed). See further *R v Olu* [2011] 1 Cr App R 33, CA.

[30] *R v Durbin* [1995] 2 Cr App R 84, citing *R v Herrox* (5 Oct 1993, unreported), CA and *R v Heath* [1994] 13 LS Gaz R 34, CA. But cf *R v Nye* (1982) 75 Cr App R 247, CA, as understood by the Court of Appeal in *R v O'Shea* [1993] Crim LR 951: an accused with previous but spent convictions may not be put forward as being of good character without qualifications but may be referred to as of good character 'without relevant convictions' because although, so far as possible, the judge should exercise the discretion favourably towards the accused, the jury must not be misled or told lies.

[31] [2009] 2 Cr App R 3, CA. See also *R v Nye* (1982) 75 Cr App R 247, CA and *R v Lloyd* [2000] 2 Cr App R 355, CA.

[32] *R v M* [2009] 2 Cr App R 3, CA at [11].

[33] See also *R v GJB* [2011] EWCA Crim 867.

[34] Per Hughes LJ in *R v Lawson* [2007] 1 Cr App R 178, CA at [40].

[35] *R v Butler* [1999] Crim LR 835, CA.

[36] *R v Durbin* [1995] 2 Cr App R 84. See also *R v Aziz* [1996] AC 41, HL at 46–47; *R v Timson* [1993] Crim LR 58, CA; *R v H* [1994] Crim LR 205, CA; and *R v Mentor* [2005] Crim LR 472, CA; and cf *R v Hickmet* [1996] Crim LR 588, CA, where it was held that a direction would have had no significant effect and might have simply confused the jury. There are obvious difficulties in the way of a qualified direction, as when the accused admits that he has lied (credibility) or set out with a criminal intent (propensity): see *R v Burnham* [1995] Crim LR 491, CA.

[37] [2004] 2 Cr App R 498, CA.

without a licence or insurance, it was held that he was entitled to an ordinary first limb direction and a modified second limb direction.[38] In *R v Garnham*[39] the accused was charged with rape and volunteered evidence of his single previous conviction for assault occasioning actual bodily harm. Under cross-examination he conceded that in respect of the previous conviction, his defence of self-defence had been rejected by the jury. It was held that the judge had been wrong to withhold a modified good character direction on the basis that the accused had been disbelieved in his trial for assault and this showed a propensity to be untruthful. The judge had fallen into error in his approach and the appellant had been entitled to a modified good character direction, although the Court of Appeal did not indicate what form it should have taken.

Accused without previous convictions

An accused without previous convictions is not necessarily of good character, for he may have been dishonest or guilty of other criminal behaviour even if not convicted of any offence in that respect. In *R v Durbin*[40] the accused was charged with the unlawful importation of cannabis. When interviewed, he gave a false account of his movements on the Continent prior to his arrival in the UK; at the trial he admitted having misled two prosecution witnesses in relation to his dealings with his co-accused; and in both interview and evidence he admitted that in the course of the visit to the Continent which gave rise to the charge, he had knowingly engaged in smuggling computer parts across European frontiers in order to avoid customs duties. The Court of Appeal rejected the idea that in these circumstances it was a matter of discretion for the trial judge to decide what direction, if any, should be given: the accused was *entitled* to qualified *Vye* directions. It was held that where an accused is of previous good character then he is entitled to the good character direction (both limbs if his credibility is in issue, the second limb only if it is not), notwithstanding that he may have admitted telling lies in interview[41] and may have admitted other offences or disreputable conduct in relation to the subject matter of the charge, but the terms of the direction should be modified to take account of the circumstances of the case, including all facts known to the jury, either as regards credibility or propensity or both.[42]

R v Durbin was not brought to the attention of the House of Lords in *R v Aziz*.[43] In that case two of the accused, charged with conspiracy to cheat the public revenue of VAT, pleaded not guilty and relied on the fact that they had no previous convictions, but also gave evidence of previous misconduct, including evidence of making false mortgage applications, telling lies during interview, and not declaring full earnings for Inland Revenue purposes. Lord Steyn, acknowledging that this was an area in which generalizations are hazardous, and that a wide spectrum of cases must be kept in mind, held as follows:

1. A trial judge has a residual discretion to decline to give *Vye* directions in the case of an accused without previous convictions if he considers it an insult to common sense to give such directions. A judge should never be compelled to give meaningless or absurd

---

[38] Cf *R v Payton* [2006] Crim LR 997, CA.
[39] [2008] EWCA Crim 266.
[40] [1995] 2 Cr App R 84, CA.
[41] Citing *R v Kabariti* (1990) 92 Cr App R 362.
[42] See also *R v Zoppola-Barraza* [1994] Crim LR 833, CA. See also *R v Buzalek* [1991] Crim LR 115, CA.
[43] [1996] AC 41, HL.

directions. Cases occur where an accused with no previous convictions is shown beyond doubt to have been guilty of serious criminal behaviour similar to the offence charged. A judge is not compelled to go through the charade of giving *Vye* directions where the accused's claim to good character is spurious.

2. This discretionary power is narrowly circumscribed.

3. Prima facie the directions must be given. The judge will often be able to place a fair and balanced picture before the jury by giving *Vye* directions and then adding words of qualification concerning the proved or possible misconduct.

4. Whenever a judge proposes to give a direction not likely to be anticipated by counsel, he should invite submissions on his proposed directions.

On the facts, it was held that the two accused had not lost the right to *Vye* directions, but it would have been proper for the judge to have qualified them by reference to the admitted misconduct.

In respect of the principle stated in Lord Steyn's paragraph (1), it will apply to cases where the accused has no convictions, but evidence of 'misconduct' is admitted under the 'bad character' provisions of the Criminal Justice Act 2003. In such cases the jury are bound to receive a *bad* character direction and a judge is entitled to consider that a good character direction would be an insult to common sense.[44] However, it may be appropriate for the judge to modify the bad character direction by adding that the accused has no previous convictions and would have been entitled to a good character direction but for the evidence of his misconduct. The jury might then be told to consider which counted more with them—the absence of previous convictions or the evidence of the misconduct. If they considered the former counted more, they could take this into account in the accused's favour. If the latter counted more, then this could be taken into account against him.[45]

However, a further problem arises where evidence of an accused's misconduct is adduced which the accused disputes and, but for that evidence, he would be of good character. In such circumstances, the judge should, in addition to a *bad* character direction, direct the jury that if they accept that the accused did not commit the disputed misconduct they should treat him as a person of good character, and further direct them to approach his good character in accordance with the principles in *Vye*.[46]

Other problems arise when an accused pleads guilty to only some counts on the indictment. It is clear from *R v Teasdale*[47] that if an accused pleads guilty to an offence which is an alternative to that on which he is being tried, and the facts are such that, if he is convicted on the greater offence then the guilty plea on the lesser offence will have to be vacated, a good character direction should be given, tailored to take into account the guilty plea. However, in *R v Challenger*[48] it was held that in all other cases in which an accused pleads guilty to another

---

[44] See *R v Doncaster* (2008) JP 202, CA.

[45] *R v Doncaster* (2008) JP 202, CA at [43]. See also *R v Ferdhaus* [2010] EWCA Crim 220, CA.

[46] See *R v Olu* [2011] 1 Cr App R 33, CA, where the accused disputed admissions he had made in a caution, the caution having been adduced as evidence of bad character by the prosecution. See also the First Supplement to The Crown Court Bench Book, October 2011, 41, which provides 'an illustration of an attempt to configure...good and bad character directions in a way which assists the jury to approach...issues sequentially and correctly'.

[47] [1994] 99 Cr App R 80, CA.

[48] [1994] Crim LR 202, CA.

count on the indictment, he ceases to be a person of good character and the full character direction becomes inappropriate.[49]

ADDITIONAL READING

Crinion, 'Adducing the Good Character of Prosecution Witnesses' [2010] Crim LR 570.

Munday, 'What Constitutes a Good Character?' [1997] Crim LR 247.

[49] It was further held that it would be misleading to tell a jury that an accused was of good character where they had not been made aware of his guilty plea. However, if an accused gives evidence of his guilty plea then the judge may remind the jury about any argument made to the effect that, by virtue of his admission of guilt on one count, greater weight should be attached to his assertions of innocence on the remaining counts. Note also *R v Shepherd* [1995] Crim LR 153, CA, where formal admissions went some way towards informing the jury that S had pleaded guilty to other counts. It was held that if the defence had grasped the nettle and brought out in evidence that S, apart from the matters covered by the admissions, had no other convictions, then it might have been appropriate for the judge to have directed the jury that, apart from attaching such weight as they saw fit to the admissions, S was entitled to ask them to consider his case on the basis of previous good character.

Evidence of character: evidence of bad character in criminal cases ⑰

Key issues

- In a criminal trial, when and why should the prosecution or an accused be permitted to adduce evidence of the bad character of a witness or some other person?

- How might evidence of an accused's bad character prove (a) that he has committed the crime with which he is charged; and (b) that he should not be believed if he gives evidence that he did not commit the crime?

- Should evidence of an accused's bad character be admissible by the prosecution to show that he has a propensity to be untruthful?

- When and why should a co-accused be permitted to adduce evidence of an accused's bad character?

Introductory

The background to the Criminal Justice Act 2003

The admissibility of evidence of bad character in criminal cases is governed, almost exclusively, by Chapter 1 of Pt 11 of the Criminal Justice Act 2003 (the 2003 Act). However, it is necessary first to consider in outline the applicable rules before the scheme introduced by the 2003 Act, most of which have been repealed but some of which have survived.

Before the 2003 Act, there were both common law and statutory rules. Under s 3 of the Criminal Procedure Act 1865, which remains in force, a party is not entitled to impeach the credit of his own witness by general evidence of his bad character.[1] At common law a witness other than the accused could be *cross-examined* about his previous misconduct in order to impugn his credibility.[2] However, under the rule of finality of answers to collateral questions, answers given by the witness to questions on his previous misconduct, insofar as they could properly be regarded as questions on collateral matters, were final, in the sense that the cross-examining party could not call further evidence with a view to contradicting the witness. The exceptions to the rule, ie the cases in which evidence in rebuttal was admissible, included cases of denial of previous convictions, admissible under s 6 of the Criminal Procedure Act 1865, and, at common law, denial by the witness of his bias or his reputation for untruthfulness.

As to the accused, the law was, as it was put in an earlier edition of this work, 'complex, unprincipled and riddled with anomalies'. The general rule was exclusionary. The prosecution were not permitted either to adduce evidence of the accused's bad character, other than that relating directly to the offence charged, or to cross-examine witnesses for the defence with a view to eliciting such evidence. The rule prevented the prosecution from introducing evidence of previous convictions, previous misconduct, and disposition towards wrongdoing or misconduct, the principal rationale of the rule being that the prejudice created by such evidence outweighed any probative value it might have.

At common law, there were only two exceptions to the general rule: first, where the evidence in question was so-called 'similar fact evidence', including so-called 'background evidence', and second where the defence raised the issue of the accused's character. As to the former, similar fact evidence, which could be admitted by the prosecution or a co-accused, was evidence of the disposition of the accused towards wrongdoing or specific acts of misconduct on other occasions judged to be of sufficient probative force in relation to the facts in issue in the case to make it just to admit it notwithstanding its prejudicial effect. As to the latter, the prosecution were entitled to adduce evidence of the bad character of the accused in rebuttal of evidence of his good character adduced by the defence.

The most important statutory exception to the general rule was contained in s 1(3) of the Criminal Evidence Act 1898 (the 1898 Act). The first part of s 1(3) armed an accused with what was often referred to as a 'shield' against cross-examination about his bad character, and the latter part of the subsection set out certain situations in which the shield could be lost, including the following: (i) where the accused asserted his good character; (ii) where the nature or conduct of the defence was such as to involve imputations on the character of witnesses for the prosecution or the deceased victim of the alleged crime; and (iii) where the accused gave evidence against any other person charged in the same proceedings.

---

[1] See Ch 6.

[2] Subject to restrictions on cross-examination of complainants in proceedings for sexual offences: see the Youth Justice and Criminal Evidence Act 1999, ss 41–3: see Ch 7.

Reform

Chapter 1 of Pt 11 of the 2003 Act (ss 98–113) all but codifies the law governing the admissibility of evidence of bad character in criminal cases, abolishing the common law rules,[3] amending s 6 of the Criminal Procedure Act 1865[4] to ensure that cross-examination on a witness's previous convictions is governed by the new statutory rules, and repealing s 1(3) of the 1898 Act.[5] In general terms, the Government's approach to reform has been informed by Lord Justice Auld's *Review of the Criminal Courts of England and Wales*[6] and the Law Commission Report, *Evidence of Bad Character in Criminal Proceedings*.[7] There are, however, substantial differences between the proposals of both the Review and the Commission and the measures subsequently enacted.

The Review made no firm recommendations about character evidence but was highly critical of the law, as it then stood, and recommended that the law of criminal evidence should, in general, move away from technical rules of admissibility to trusting judicial and lay fact-finders to give relevant evidence the weight it deserves.[8] The Government's proposals were also said to be underpinned by the concept that the criminal justice system should be more trusting of fact-finders to assess relevant evidence. However, the Government did not opt for an approach based on the general admissibility of all evidence of bad character.

The Law Commission was also highly critical of the law as it then stood. Fundamental to the scheme recommended by the Commission was the idea that in any trial there is a central set of facts about which any party should be free to adduce relevant evidence, including evidence of bad character, without restraint. Such evidence 'has to do' with the offence charged or is evidence of misconduct connected with the investigation or prosecution of the offence. The Commission recommended that evidence of bad character falling outside this category should only be admissible with leave or if all parties agree to its admission or it is evidence of the accused's bad character and he wishes to adduce it. Witnesses and the accused were both to be protected against allegations of misconduct extraneous to the events which are the subject of the trial and which have only marginal relevance to the facts of the case.[9] Under the recommended scheme, and under the scheme as enacted, evidence is only admissible if it falls within one of a number of specified categories of admissibility, many of which replicate the cases in which evidence of bad character was admissible at common law. However, whereas the Law Commission recommended in effect an exclusionary rule subject to exceptions under which bad character evidence could be admitted with the leave of the court, overall the 2003 Act is designed to be more inclusionary,[10] and under its provisions evidence of the bad character of the accused falling within one of the categories of admissibility may be introduced without leave, subject, in some cases, to a discretion to exclude.

Unfortunately, the scheme contained in the 2003 Act, as we shall see, is not simple and is in parts unclear, some of the key provisions being open to widely differing interpretations.

---

[3] Section 99(1).

[4] Section 331 and para 79, Sch 36.

[5] Section 331 and para 80(b), Sch 36.

[6] HMSO, 2001.

[7] Law Com No 273, Cm 5257 (2001). For critiques of the Report, see Redmayne, 'The Law Commission's character convictions' (2002) 6 E&P 71 and Mirfield, 'Bad character and the Law Commission' (2002) 6 E&P 141.

[8] Para 78.

[9] See paras 1.12 and 1.13.

[10] See Hansard, HL, vol 654, col 739 (4 Nov 2003) and para 365 of the Home Office Explanatory Notes to the 2003 Act.

A former Lord Chief Justice described s 1 of the 1898 Act, with justification, as 'a nightmare of construction'.[11] The same may be said of some of the provisions of the 2003 Act, especially those governing admissibility of the bad character of the accused. It would not be unfair to describe them, to be colloquial, as something of a dog's breakfast.

Abolition of the common law rules

Section 99 of the 2003 provides as follows:

(1) The common law rules governing the admissibility of evidence of bad character in criminal proceedings[12] are abolished.

(2) Subsection (1) is subject to section 118(1) in so far as it preserves the rule under which in criminal proceedings a person's reputation is admissible for the purposes of proving his bad character.

Although s 99(1) refers only to the rules governing the admissibility of evidence of bad character and not to the common law rules governing cross-examination of a witness other than the accused about his bad character, it is submitted that the intention is to cover both. As to the questioning of witnesses on matters covered by the exceptions to the rule of finality of answers to collateral questions, the common law rules can certainly be said to 'govern' the admissibility of evidence of bad character, because the matters are put to the witness with a view to eliciting such evidence and, if the matters are denied, they can be proved. The common law rules permitting the questioning of witnesses on their bad character in relation to matters not covered by the exceptions to the rule of finality may also be said to 'govern' the admissibility of evidence of bad character in that they too are questions put with a view to eliciting such evidence and notwithstanding that if the witness denies the matters put, they cannot be proved.

It would seem that the general common law discretion to exclude prosecution evidence where its prejudicial effect outweighs its probative value[13] may continue to be exercised in respect of evidence of bad character. It is submitted that the phrase 'common law rules governing...admissibility' is not apt to cover a common law *discretion* to exclude.

'Bad character' defined

Under s 98 of the 2003 Act:

References in this Chapter to evidence of a person's 'bad character' are to evidence of, or of a disposition towards, misconduct on his part, other than evidence which—

(a) has to do with the alleged facts of the offence with which the defendant is charged, or

(b) is evidence of misconduct in connection with the investigation or prosecution of that offence.

The definition of bad character in s 98 applies in the case of both the accused and non-defendants and appears to cover misconduct occurring, or disposition towards misconduct existing, either before or after the offence with which the accused is charged. The

---

[11] Lord Lane CJ in *R v Anderson* [1988] QB 678 at 686.

[12] 'Criminal proceedings', for the purposes of the provisions of the 2003 Act relating to evidence of bad character, means criminal proceedings in relation to which the strict rules of evidence apply: s 112(1). The provisions cover proceedings concerning an accused's fitness to plead under the Criminal Procedure (Insanity) Act 1964, s 4A: *R v Creed* [2011] EWCA Crim 144.

[13] See Ch 2.

definition covers circumstantial as well as direct evidence of bad character, notwithstanding that when dealing with circumstantial evidence the question is begged whether the evidence goes to show misconduct until the inference is drawn.[14] 'Bad character' has been defined broadly by s 98, a definition that generally reflects the common law concept. The broad definition is designed to prevent evidence which, under the pre-existing law, would have been excluded, from falling outside the statutory scheme and thereby becoming admissible.[15] Although the definition does not include a person's reputation for misconduct, the common law rule under which a person's reputation is admissible for the purpose of proving his bad character, has been preserved by s 118(1)2.

Misconduct

'Misconduct', for the purposes of the definition, means 'the commission of an offence or other reprehensible behaviour',[16] 'offence' in its turn being defined to include a service offence.[17] Evidence of bad character under the Act therefore covers evidence of a person's misconduct whether or not unlawful; if unlawful, whether or not it resulted in a prosecution; and where it did result in a prosecution, whether within the jurisdiction or overseas, and whether it resulted in a conviction or an acquittal. As to acquittals, the definition in effect preserves the decision of the House of Lords in *R v Z*[18] that where evidence of misconduct on the part of the accused is relevant and otherwise admissible prosecution evidence, it does not fall to be excluded because it shows or tends to show that the accused was guilty of an offence of which he was previously acquitted. The definition also covers evidence of misconduct in respect of which a trial is pending, evidence of an accused's misconduct which relates to other charges on the indictment, and allegations that have never been tried, for example because of a stay for abuse of process,[19] but not arrest on suspicion followed by release without charge,[20] nor, it seems, an allegation made but later withdrawn.[21] Although the definition does not cover, by itself, evidence that someone has been suspected or informally charged with misconduct, evidence concerning such suspicions and accusations is generally irrelevant and therefore inadmissible on that basis.[22] Likewise, although the definition does not cover evidence of the bare fact that someone has been formally charged with an offence, such evidence is generally inadmissible because irrelevant, the fact that a man has been charged with an offence being

---

[14] *R v Wallace* [2008] 1 WLR 572, CA. Circumstantial evidence from three robberies and an attempted robbery charged as separate counts on the same indictment came *technically* within the definition in s 98 and so, strictly speaking, fell to be admitted as evidence of bad character which was cross-admissible from one count to another. A further question is begged whether a judge should give a jury a 'bad character' direction in respect of circumstantial evidence which falls within the definition of bad character. The Court of Appeal remarked that no bad character direction would be needed and indeed references to 'bad character' would not be necessary (at [44]). It may well be that, in spite of the deliberately broad definition in s 98, the bad character provisions were not intended to capture such a case (at [41]).

[15] See Hilary Benn MP, HC Committee, 23 Jan 2003, col 545.

[16] See Munday, 'What Constitutes "Other Reprehensible Behaviour" under the Bad Character Provisions of the Criminal Justice Act 2003?' [2005] Crim LR 24.

[17] Section 112(1).

[18] [2002] 2 AC 483, HL.

[19] *R v Edwards* [2006] 1 WLR 1524, CA at [78] and [81].

[20] *R v Weir* [2006] 1 WLR 1885, CA at [118].

[21] *R v Bovell* [2005] 2 Cr App R 27 at [21]. Although a *number* of 'strikingly similar' allegations, made and then withdrawn, could be covered: see *R v Ladds* [2009] EWCA Crim 1249.

[22] See *Stirland v DPP* [1944] AC 315, HL, a decision under the Criminal Evidence Act 1898.

no proof that he committed it and having no bearing on his credibility as a witness.[23] Nor does the definition cover the bare fact that someone has been convicted where that conviction has been quashed.[24]

The word 'reprehensible' carries with it some element of culpability or blameworthiness,[25] but whether conduct is 'reprehensible' is not determined by an exercise in moral judgment. So, in *R v Fox*[26] where the accused was charged with sexual offences against children, the keeping of a private notebook recording what Scott Baker LJ called 'dirty sexual thoughts' was judged, although with caution, not to be a disposition towards reprehensible behaviour. Whether particular lawful behaviour involves culpability or blameworthiness will depend on the particular circumstances and is a question on which views are likely to differ.[27] In *R v Weir*[28] the appellant M was convicted of indecently assaulting A. At the time of the offences, M was 39 and A was 13. It was held that evidence was admissible of an earlier sexual relationship with another girl B, who was 16, M then being 34. There was no feature of this lawful relationship to make it reprehensible, such as evidence of grooming. However, since evidence of the relationship was not 'evidence of bad character', and therefore the abolition of the common law rules governing the admissibility of 'evidence of bad character' by s 99(1) did not apply, it was admissible at common law as demonstrating a sexual interest in early- or mid-teenage girls much younger than M and therefore bore on the truth of his case of a truly supportive asexual interest in A.[29]

If evidence of bad character does fall within the statutory definition it can only be admitted in evidence if it satisfies the further conditions of admissibility in s 100 (non-defendant's bad character) or s 101 (defendant's bad character). Where the evidence to be adduced is evidence of the bad character of an accused who disputes the facts relied upon to establish his bad character, then a *voir dire* may also be required.[30]

[23] See *Maxwell v DPP* [1935] AC 309, HL, a decision under the 1898 Act. See also *R v Renda* [2006] 1 WLR 2984, CA at [46], on the different and, it is submitted, unconvincing reasoning that in the circumstances there was 'a bare allegation, itself wholly unproved'.

[24] See *R v Hussain* [2008] EWCA Crim 1117: evidence of an accused's quashed conviction for manslaughter was not evidence of bad character, it being no more than an unproven charge.

[25] *R v Renda* [2006] 1 WLR 2948, CA at [24], where the court held that the mere fact that the appellant was found unfit to plead some 18 months after an apparent incident of gratuitous violence did not, by itself, extinguish culpability at the time of the offence.

[26] [2009] EWCA Crim 653 at [30].

[27] Verbal aggression is not necessarily reprehensible: see *R v Osbourne* [2007] Crim LR 712, CA. Possession of rap lyrics personally altered to include a vague threat could be reprehensible when combined with possession of photographs of victims of a violent assault: see *R v Saleem* [2007] EWCA Crim 1923. It is doubtful that exaggeration to fellow pupils about being pushed by a teacher after everyday classroom misbehaviour is reprehensible: see *R v V* [2006] EWCA Crim 1901. It is not reprehensible to have recently taken a drugs overdose: see *R v Hall-Chung* (2007) 151 SJLB 1020, CA. Possession of 'self-portrait' photographs depicting the subject sleeping but holding a large knife across his chest were 'bad taste rather than bad character': see *R v Allen* [2009] EWCA Crim 2881 at [19]. It is not reprehensible behaviour for a married heterosexual man to indulge in the homosexual side of his nature with another consenting person above the age of consent: see *R v IJ* [2011] EWCA Crim 2734. It may well be reprehensible behaviour for an accused, in the absence of the jury, to make a remark from the dock to a pupil barrister, along the lines of, 'What are you looking at?' where the remark is alleged to have been made in an aggressive way: see *R v Mahil* [2013] EWCA Crim 673.

[28] [2006] 1 WLR 1885, CA.

[29] See also *R v P* (31 May 2012, unreported), CA. It was also held in *Weir* that a refusal, without reasons, to give a witness statement when a victim of crime, is not reprehensible behaviour. However, it is submitted that the evidential status of such behaviour could be affected by the motive of the victim, eg where the motive was to protect the criminal.

[30] See *R v Wright* [2000] Crim LR 851, CA, a decision under the Criminal Evidence Act 1898.

The admissibility of evidence of bad character 'to do with' the facts of the offence or in connection with its investigation or prosecution

Section 99(1) of the 2003 Act, as we have seen, abolishes the common law rules governing admissibility of evidence of bad character as defined by s 98. It follows, of course, that the common law rules continue to operate insofar as they permit evidence to be adduced which, looking to the wording of s 98(a) 'has to do with the alleged facts of the offence' or, looking to the wording of s 98(b) 'is evidence of misconduct in connection with the investigation or prosecution of that offence'.

Evidence 'to do with' the alleged facts of the offence

Section 98(a) covers such prosecution evidence, other than evidence of previous misconduct or evidence of disposition towards misconduct, as tends to show that the accused is guilty of the offence charged, such as evidence of witnesses to the crime and fingerprint evidence. Provided that there is some 'nexus in time',[31] it also covers misconduct other than the offence charged, for example an assault or criminal damage committed by the accused in the course of the burglary with which he is charged. Similarly, it may cover misconduct that was the subject of another count originally in the indictment but subsequently severed.[32] Section 98(a) can also cover misconduct on the part of someone other than the accused, for example evidence in support of a defence of self-defence that the victim was the aggressor. In *R v Machado*,[33] it was held that on a charge of robbery, evidence was admissible that the victim had offered to supply drugs to the appellant and that he had said that he had taken an ecstasy tablet. However, the court appears to have overlooked the basic requirement of relevance. That the victim had taken drugs may well have been relevant because there was a suggestion that rather than being pushed to the ground, he fell over, but his alleged offer to supply drugs had no obvious relevance to any of the issues in the case.

Evidence admissible by virtue of s 98(a) falls to be distinguished from so-called 'background evidence', which is evidence of bad character potentially admissible under s 101(1)(c), a distinction which is likely to be difficult to draw in some cases.[34] However, if s 98(a) applies, then the evidence is admissible without more ado,[35] subject of course to the requirement of relevance and the discretion to exclude.[36]

---

[31] *R v Tirnaveanu* [2007] 1 WLR 3049.

[32] *R v Edwards* [2006] 1 WLR 1524, CA at [23]. See also *R v Mullings* [2011] 2 Cr App R 2, CA.

[33] (2006) 170 JP 400.

[34] See, in this chapter, under **Evidence of the bad character of the defendant, Section 101(1)(c)—important explanatory evidence**.

[35] *R v Edwards* [2006] 1 WLR 1524, CA at [1](i). See also *R v Kalu* [2007] EWCA Crim 22. See also *R v Leonard* (2009) 173 JP 366, CA at [11]: text messages sent to the accused's mobile phone which were suggestive of drug-dealing had to do with the alleged facts of the offence of possession of controlled drugs with intent to supply and did not fall to be adduced as evidence of bad character (at [11]; however, the texts were deemed to be hearsay and inadmissible). By contrast, see *R v Chrysostomou* [2010] Crim LR 942, CA: text messages recovered from the accused's mobile phone suggestive of small scale drug-dealing were held to be evidence of bad character (but were not hearsay). See also Ch 10 under **Admissibility of hearsay under the Criminal Justice Act 2003, The meaning of hearsay in the Criminal Justice Act 2003, Implied assertions**.

[36] In cases of familial sexual abuse where evidence has been adduced alleging sexual abuse in relation to particular counts but the judge rules that there is no case to answer on those counts, the evidence no longer has to do with the facts of the offence with which the accused is charged and becomes evidence of bad character. See *R v B* [2010] EWCA Crim 1251 at [14].

Evidence in connection with the investigation or prosecution of the offence

Section 98(b) covers, for example: evidence that during the investigation the police obtained evidence unlawfully or unfairly, for instance by fabricating a confession or planting evidence on the accused or in his premises; evidence that during interview the accused told lies; and evidence that during the investigation or proceedings the prosecution or the accused had sought to intimidate potential witnesses. In *DPP v Agyemayang*,[37] the Divisional Court held that previous convictions which resulted in the accused being disqualified from driving were plainly evidence of misconduct in connection with the investigation and prosecution of the offence of driving whilst disqualified and were also, in the court's view, to do with the alleged facts of the offence (see s 98(a)).

The role of the trial judge and the Court of Appeal

Provided that a trial judge has not erred in principle, the Court of Appeal will be loath to interfere with a judge's ruling in relation to the admissibility of evidence of bad character, whether of the accused or of someone other than the accused, under the 2003 Act. In *R v Renda*,[38] Sir Igor Judge P said:

> The circumstances in which this court would interfere with the exercise of a judicial discretion are limited. The principles need no repetition.[39] However, we emphasise that the same general approach will be adopted when the court is being invited to interfere with what in reality is a fact-specific judgment...the trial judge's 'feel' for the case is usually the critical ingredient of the decision at first instance which this court lacks. Context therefore is vital...This legislation has now been in force for nearly a year. The principles have been considered by this court on a number of occasions. The responsibility for their application is not for this court but for the trial judge.

In previous editions of this text it was submitted that the last three sentences of this passage should not be taken to mean that as from the date of the decision in *Renda* there were unlikely to be new points of principle for the appellate courts to consider or, worse, that if there were, appellate courts might side-step them by deferring to the 'feel' of the trial judge in the context of the specific case. It should be apparent from those editions and the current edition of this text that the appellate courts have, in fact, continued to consider and refine points of principle at what could be fairly described as an 'industrial rate'.

Evidence of the bad character of a person other than the defendant

Section 100 of the Criminal Justice Act 2003

At common law a witness could be cross-examined about his previous misconduct with a view to impugning his credibility. He could be cross-examined, for example, about acts of dishonesty or immorality on his part, about lies he told or false allegations he made, about his drink or drug abuse, and so on. However, as we have already seen, insofar as the questions could properly be said to be on collateral matters and the witness denied them, evidence was

---

[37] (2009) 173 JP 487, DC.
[38] [2006] 1 WLR 2948, CA at [3].
[39] See Ch 2, under **Judicial discretion**.

admissible in rebuttal only exceptionally. The exceptions covered previous convictions, bias and general reputation for untruthfulness.

In *R v Edwards*[40] it was held that subject to the limits laid down in *Hobbs v Tinling*,[41] a witness could be cross-examined about any improper conduct of which he may have been guilty, for the purpose of testing his credit. The following three principles were established in *Hobbs v Tinling*.[42]

1. Questions as to credit in cross-examination are proper if of such a nature that the truth of the imputation conveyed by them would seriously affect the opinion of the court as to the credibility of the witness on the matters to which he testifies.

2. Such questions are improper if the imputation which they convey relates to matters so remote in time or of such a character that the truth of the imputation would not affect, or would affect in a slight degree, the opinion of the court as to the credibility of the witness on the matter to which he testifies.

3. Such questions are improper if there is a great disproportion between the importance of the imputation made against the witness's character and the importance of his evidence.

The Law Commission was of the view that further restraints were necessary. Three reasons were given: the power of evidence of bad character to distort the fact-finding process; the need to encourage witnesses to give evidence; and the need for courts 'to control gratuitous and offensive cross-examination of little or no purpose other than to intimidate or embarrass the witness or muddy the waters'.[43] Balancing these factors against the need not to prejudice a fair trial, the Commission recommended a test based on the degree of relevance of bad character evidence to the issues in the case. Evidence of only trivial relevance would be excluded. The views of the Commission are reflected in s 100 of the 2003 Act.

Section 100(1) provides as follows:

(1) In criminal proceedings evidence of the bad character of a person other than the defendant is admissible if and only if—
  (a) it is important explanatory evidence,
  (b) it has substantial probative value in relation to a matter which—
     (i) is a matter in issue in the proceedings, and
     (ii) is of substantial importance in the context of the case as a whole, or
  (c) all parties to the proceedings agree to the evidence being admissible.

Section 100 may be used by the prosecution, the accused, or any co-accused. The meaning of 'bad character' has already been considered. A 'person other than the defendant' may or may not be a witness in the case. Although, on its face, s 100 governs only the admissibility of evidence of bad character and does not, in terms, govern the asking of questions about bad character in cross-examination,[44] it is submitted that the intention is to cover both. This would be consistent with the interpretation of s 99(1) of the Act that it abolishes the

---

[40] [1991] 1 WLR 207.

[41] [1929] 2 KB 1, CA.

[42] [1929] 2 KB 1, CA at 51.

[43] Law Com No 273, Cm 5257 (2001), para 9.35. See also *R v Garratty* [2010] EWCA Crim 1156: the purpose of s 100 is to remove the right of a party to adduce misconduct which is old, irrelevant, or trivial in order to unfairly blacken the standing of a witness in the eyes of the jury, or permit unsubstantiated attacks on credit.

[44] Cf, in this regard, the Youth Justice and Criminal Evidence Act 1999, s 41.

common law rules relating not only to the admissibility of evidence of bad character but also to cross-examination of witnesses about bad character.[45]

Threshold conditions for admissibility

Important explanatory evidence

Section 100(2) provides as follows:

> (2) For the purposes of subsection (1)(a) evidence is important explanatory evidence if—
> > (a) without it, the court or jury would find it impossible or difficult properly to understand other evidence in the case, and
> > (b) its value for understanding the case as a whole is substantial.

Section 100(2) covers evidence of or a disposition towards misconduct on the part of someone other than the accused, without which the prosecution (or defence) account would be incomplete or incoherent.[46] Thus if the matter to which the evidence relates is largely comprehensible without the explanatory evidence, the evidence will be inadmissible. The wording of s 100(2)(a) is a slightly different formulation of the common law rule permitting the use of background evidence, notwithstanding that it reveals the bad character or criminal disposition of the accused, where it is part of a continual background or history which is relevant to the offence charged and without the totality of which the account placed before the jury would be incomplete or incomprehensible.[47] The first option, 'incomplete', is probably best ignored: in the nature of things the account will be incomplete. The Explanatory Notes to the Act provide an example of s 100(2)(a) arising in a case which involves the abuse by one person of another over a long period of time: 'For the jury to understand properly the victim's account of the offending and why they (sic) did not seek help from, for example, a parent or other guardian, it might be necessary for evidence to be given of a wider pattern of abuse involving that other person.'[48] Another example could be evidence which sheds light on a witness's motive for acting in a particular way. In *R v Miller*[49] the Court of Appeal held that bad character evidence exposing a witness's motive could constitute important explanatory evidence under s 100. However, the court also held such evidence should not be admitted to support merely speculative suggestions as this would be the very type of exercise which s 100 is designed to prevent.[50]

Explanatory evidence, to be admissible, must also satisfy s 100(1)(b), ie its value for understanding the case as a whole must be 'substantial', as opposed to minor or trivial.[51]

Evidence of substantial probative value

Under s 100(1)(b), evidence of the bad character of a person other than the accused is admissible if it has substantial probative value in relation to a matter which—(i) is a matter in issue in the proceedings; and (ii) is of substantial importance in the context of the case as a whole. The probative value must be 'substantial'—evidence of only minor probative force should not be

---

[45] See, in this chapter, under **Introductory, Abolition of the common law rules**.

[46] Law Com No 273, Cm 5257 (2001), para 9.13.

[47] Per Purchase LJ in *R v Pettman*, 2 May 1985, CA, unreported.

[48] Para 360. For an exploration of the dangers of using the Explanatory Notes as an aid to construction, see Munday, 'Bad Character Rules and Riddles: "Explanatory Notes" and True Meanings of s. 103(1) of the Criminal Justice Act 2003' [2005] Crim LR 337.

[49] [2010] 2 Cr App R 19.

[50] [2010] 2 Cr App R 19 at [19]–[20].

[51] Law Com No 273, Cm 5257 (2001), para 9.1.

admitted.[52] A 'matter in issue in the proceedings' means any matter in issue, whether an issue of disputed fact or an issue of credibility, and credibility as an issue for the purposes of s 100 is wider than a propensity to be untruthful.[53] In order to be admissible, however, the evidence must also be of substantial importance in the context of the case as a whole—evidence which goes only to some minor or trivial issue should not be admitted.

Section 100(3) sets out a non-exhaustive list of the factors to which the court must have regard in assessing the probative value of the evidence. It provides as follows:

(3) In assessing the probative value of evidence for the purposes of subsection (1)(b) the court must have regard to the following factors (and to any others it considers relevant)—
   (a) the nature and number of the events, or other things, to which the evidence relates;
   (b) when those events or things are alleged to have happened or existed;
   (c) where—
      (i) the evidence is evidence of a person's misconduct, and
      (ii) it is suggested that the evidence has probative value by reason of similarity between that misconduct and other alleged misconduct, the nature and extent of the similarities and dissimilarities between each of the alleged instances of misconduct;
   (d) where—
      (i) the evidence is evidence of a person's misconduct,
      (ii) it is suggested that that person is also responsible for the misconduct charged, and
      (iii) the identity of the person responsible for the misconduct charged is disputed, the extent to which the evidence shows or tends to show that the same person was responsible each time.

Nature and number of the events etc

As to s 100(3)(a), if, for example, a key witness has previous convictions or has been guilty of improper conduct in the past, the nature and number of the offences committed or of the incidents of misconduct will have an obvious bearing in deciding its probative value in relation to the issue of his credibility as a witness. A conviction for perjury will have a probative force normally lacking in a conviction for, say, a minor motoring offence. Similarly, evidence of previous false accusations may have a probative value not to be found in, say, evidence of cruelty to animals. However, previous convictions which do not involve either the making of false statements or the giving of false evidence are also capable of having substantial probative value in relation to the credibility of a witness.[54] Each case will turn on its own facts and the question will be whether a fair-minded tribunal would regard the convictions as having an impact on the worth of the witness's evidence.[55]

In *R v S*,[56] S, charged with indecent assault, was of good character. He claimed that the complainant, a prostitute, had agreed to sexual activities for £10 and that when, afterwards, he

---

[52] See, eg, *R v Braithwaite* [2010] EWCA Crim 1194 and *R v Warren* [2010] EWCA Crim 3267: unsupported allegations recorded against witnesses in police reports were inadmissible considering their evidential status (hearsay) and lack of probative value.

[53] *R v S* [2006] 2 Cr App R 437 at [7] and [10]. See also *R v Weir* [2006] 1 WLR 1885, CA at [73].

[54] *R v Stephenson* [2006] EWCA Crim 2325. This is also the case where an accused seeks to adduce the bad character of a co-accused under s 101(1)(e) (per Hughes LJ at [27]). See also *R v Ul-Haq* [2010] EWCA Crim 1683, where a witness's previous dishonesty offences were unrelated to the offence charged and too historical. The latter is a consideration under s 100(3)(b)—see, in this chapter, under **Evidence of the bad character of a person other than the accused, Threshold conditions for admissibility, Evidence of substantial probative value, When events or things are alleged to have happened, etc.**

[55] *R v Brewster* [2011] 1 WLR 601, CA.

[56] [2006] 2 Cr App R 437, CA.

refused her demand for more money, she threatened to accuse him of rape and tried to grab a gold chain he was wearing. It was held that S should have been allowed to cross-examine her on her convictions for going equipped for theft, handling, and burglary, because they showed a propensity to act dishonestly and possessed substantial probative value on the issues whether, in effect, she had demanded money with menaces and had tried to take S's property. By contrast, in *R v Garnham*[57] it was held that the accused, tried for rape, was properly prevented from cross-examining the complainant about any of her 65 previous convictions for theft. The judge had been correct in his conclusion that a propensity to be dishonest was not the same as a propensity to be untruthful and that, in the circumstances of the case, the complainant's previous convictions were not of substantial probative value in relation to her credibility.

However, it is difficult, without more, to justify the conclusion in *R v Renda*[58] that a defence witness's conviction for a violent offence was of substantial probative value in relation to the issue of his credibility, being 'particularly germane' to the question whether a robbery had occurred or been fabricated by the complainant. One possible explanation is that it was a conviction after a not guilty plea, which can operate to impugn credibility.[59] In *R v South*[60] the question of whether a witness's convictions were based on guilty or not guilty pleas was considered to be relevant when assessing the probative value of the convictions in relation to credibility.[61] In *South*, the accused's alibi witness had 53 convictions recorded between 1978 and 1996, including convictions for theft, burglary, handling stolen goods, forgery, obtaining property by deception, and using false instruments. The court held that the judge had been wrong to permit the prosecution to cross-examine on all of these convictions without first distinguishing which offences involved 'untruthfulness' and which of those 'untruthfulness offences' were the subject of guilty or not guilty pleas. A proper assessment of the probative value of the convictions to the credibility of the accused's alibi witness required such distinctions to be made.

When events or things are alleged to have happened, etc
As to s 100(3)(b), evidence of misconduct occurring many years ago is usually likely to have less probative value than more recent misconduct,[62] although plainly very serious misconduct in the past may have much greater probative value than recent but relatively minor misconduct. Misconduct capable of having substantial probative value includes misconduct after the commission of the offence charged in the proceedings. So, for example, where an accused seeks to blame another person who was previously a suspect but not charged, misconduct by that person after the offence could be probative of whether he rather than the accused committed the offence. In such a case, the more time that has elapsed since the offence, the less probative the misconduct is likely to be. This can be further affected by factors such as

[57] [2008] All ER 50, CA
[58] [2006] 1 WLR 2948, CA at [59].
[59] See *R v Renda* [2006] 1 WLR 2948, CA at [59], but in the case of another appellant, Razaq, at [73]. Although this may remain the position in respect of witnesses *other* than an accused, in respect of an accused, it is questionable whether a conviction after a not guilty plea can impugn credibility in the light of *R v Campbell* [2007] 1 WLR 2798 (considered in this chapter under **Evidence of the bad character of the defendant, Bad character evidence under section 101(1)(d) relevant to the guilt of the accused, Bad character evidence under section 101(1)(d) relevant to the credibility of the accused**).
[60] [2011] EWCA Crim 754.
[61] [2011] EWCA Crim 754 at [25].
[62] See *R v Ul-Haq* [2010] EWCA Crim 1683.

the person's age at the time of the offence and his age at the time of the trial. In *R v Ross*,[63] the Court of Appeal held that the trial judge was correct to exclude previous convictions of a former suspect, N, whom the accused sought to blame for the murder of an old lady in her home some 13 years previously. N's convictions included burglary, housebreaking, rape, and violence committed between two and nine years *after* the date of the murder. During the trial the jury had heard highly probative hearsay evidence implicating N and it was held that the convictions added little. Also, considering that N was 15 years old at the time of the murder, some of the convictions for violence committed as an adult could not be probative to show a propensity for using severe violence as a 15-year-old during a burglary.

Similarities between the misconduct and other alleged misconduct, etc.
Section 100(3)(c) relates to evidence of a person's misconduct, the probative value of which, in relation to a matter in issue in the proceedings, derives from its similarity to other misconduct on his part. Thus if the accused alleges that the case against him has been fabricated by a police officer who has threatened a potential witness for the defence—evidence of which would be admissible under s 98(b)—and there is evidence that in other cases the officer has also gone to improper lengths to secure a conviction, in assessing the probative value of the evidence the court should have regard to the nature and extent of the similarities, for example, whether in some of the cases he had also threatened potential defence witnesses.

Relevance of misconduct to identity, etc
Section 100(3)(d) relates to evidence, in cases in which the identity of the offender is in dispute, suggesting that a person other than the accused is responsible for the offence charged. Such evidence will often take the form of evidence of similar facts. For example, if the accused is charged with a sexual assault in a public park, the prosecution case being that the crime was committed by someone wearing eccentric clothes, and the defence being one of mistaken identity, and there is evidence that X, the resident of a house overlooking the park has previously committed sexual assaults in the park, then in assessing the probative value of the evidence, the court must have regard to the extent to which the evidence shows or tends to show that X was responsible for each of the offences, for example whether the evidence shows that X wore eccentric clothing or the same eccentric clothing on each occasion.

Satellite litigation
Where a person disputes evidence of misconduct sought to be adduced, the risk of 'satellite litigation' is a relevant consideration when assessing the probative value of the evidence.[64] The court should reflect on whether the disputed evidence would make it difficult for the jury to understand the remainder of the evidence in the case or diminish the jury's understanding of the case as a whole.[65]

Evidence admitted by agreement

Under s 100(1)(c) evidence of the bad character of a person other than the accused may be admitted by agreement of 'all parties to the proceedings', ie the prosecution, the accused, and

---

[63] [2009] EWCA Crim 1165. See [24].

[64] *See R v Dizaei* [2013] EWCA Crim 88. Evidence of an allegation against the witness that he had raped his girl-friend was inadmissible: the witness had bitterly contested the allegation and there was a risk that if the evidence was admitted two trials might be simultaneously in progress before the same jury.

[65] *R v Dizaei* [2013] EWCA Crim 88 at [31]–[38].

any co-accused. Under s 100(4), evidence may be admitted under s 100(1)(c) without the leave of the court.

The requirement of leave

Section 100(4) of the 2003 Act provides that 'Except where subsection (1)(c) applies, evidence of the bad character of a person other than the defendant must not be given without the leave of the court.' Thus evidence admissible under s 100(1)(a) or (b) must not be adduced without leave. Unfortunately, however, the subsection gives no guidance as to what factors, if any, should be taken into account in deciding whether or not to grant leave, over and above the factors set out in s 100(2) and (3). In *R v S*,[66] the Court of Appeal expressed the view that the leave requirement did not give the court any further discretion as regards the admissibility of bad character evidence under s 100.[67]

On one view, s 100(4) also applies to evidence of bad character of complainants admissible under s 41 of the Youth Justice and Criminal Evidence Act 1999. If that is so, then in this context also the purpose of the subsection is elusive, because it is unclear what factors, if any, should be taken into account in deciding whether or not to grant leave, over and above the matters that have to be taken into account in deciding whether to grant leave under s 41 itself. The further question arises as to what kinds of sexual behaviour on the part of the complainant should be treated as 'bad character' as defined in the 2003 Act. An alternative and preferable view, it is submitted, is that when evidence of bad character is admitted under s 41, there will of necessity be compliance with s 100(4) of the 2003 Act because of the leave requirement in s 41 itself.

Discretion to exclude

It is submitted that the general common law discretionary power to exclude evidence where its prejudicial effect outweighs its probative value may be exercised in respect of *prosecution* evidence of bad character admissible under s 100.[68] As to whether the general discretionary power to exclude prosecution evidence under s 78 of the Police and Criminal Evidence Act 1984[69] applies in the case of prosecution evidence of bad character otherwise admissible under the 2003 Act, the case law suggests an affirmative answer.[70] If so, then it will be open to the defence to submit that evidence admissible under s 100 of the 2003 Act upon which the prosecution propose to rely should be excluded where, having regard to all the circumstances, its admission would have such an adverse effect on the fairness of the proceedings that the court ought not to admit it.

Evidence of the bad character of the defendant

The background to section 101 of the Criminal Justice Act 2003

Before the coming into force of the 2003 Act, evidence of the bad character of the accused was admissible only exceptionally and a sharp distinction was drawn between evidence adduced

---

[66] [2009] EWCA Crim 2457.

[67] [2009] EWCA Crim 2457 at [62].

[68] See, in this chapter, under **Introductory, Abolition of the common law rules**.

[69] See Ch 2.

[70] See *R v Highton* [2005] 1 WLR 3472, CA; *R v Weir* [2006] 1 WLR 1885, CA; *R v Tirnaveanu* [2007] 1 WLR 3049, CA; and *R v O'Dowd* [2009] 2 Cr App R 280, CA.

because of its relevance to the issue of guilt, and evidence elicited in cross-examination of the accused and bearing upon his credibility as a witness. The approach under s 101 of the 2003 Act is radically different. It is not one of inadmissibility subject to exceptions, but of admissibility if certain criteria are met.[71] Section 101 sets out seven gateways through which evidence of the bad character of the accused can be admitted. Collectively, these grounds for admissibility are much wider than those which they have replaced. Under the section, (a) no distinction is drawn between evidence introduced as a part of the prosecution's case and evidence elicited in cross-examination of the accused; (b) evidence is admissible irrespective of whether the accused gives evidence; and (c) there are no explicit limitations on the purpose for which the evidence is adduced.

The provisions in the 2003 Act relating to evidence of the bad character of the accused provoked much controversy during their parliamentary passage, especially in the House of Lords, where some members voiced the opinion that s 101 undermined the presumption of innocence.[72] A major criticism of the statutory scheme is that although it is based on the proposals of the Law Commission, each of the safeguards contained in the Law Commission framework and designed to protect the accused from the introduction of prejudicial evidence has been either abandoned or diluted.[73] For example, under the Commission's proposals, in each of the four situations in which evidence of bad character of the accused was admissible, leave was required and in three of those situations there was a condition that the interests of justice required the evidence to be admissible, even taking account of its potentially prejudicial effect. Under s 101, however, leave is not required and instead of an 'interests of justice' condition, there is a discretionary power to exclude, but only on the application of the defence and only in respect of evidence admissible under two of the seven 'gateways'. The breadth of s 101, coupled with the absence of the much tighter restrictions on admissibility contained in the Law Commission's proposals, permit evidence of the accused's bad character to be admitted more readily than in the past. The effect, it is submitted, will be to oblige judges to make much greater use of their discretionary powers to exclude such evidence.

It does not follow however that the prosecution should routinely apply to admit evidence of the accused's bad character. In *R v Hanson*,[74] the first Court of Appeal decision on the new provisions, it was held that the starting point should be for judges and practitioners to bear in mind that Parliament's purpose was to assist in the evidence-based conviction of the guilty, without putting those who are not guilty at risk of conviction by prejudice, and that it was accordingly to be hoped that prosecution applications to adduce evidence of an accused's bad character will not be made routinely, simply because an accused has previous convictions,[75] but will be based on the particular circumstances of each case. It was held in that case that if a judge has directed himself correctly, the Court of Appeal will be very slow to interfere with a ruling as to admissibility[76] and will not interfere unless the judge's judgment as to the capacity

---

[71] *R v Weir* [2006] 1 WLR 1885, CA at [35].

[72] See, eg, Lord Alexander and Lord Kingsland, *Hansard*, HL, Vol 654, cols 729, 731, and 741 (4 Nov 2003).

[73] See generally Tapper, 'Criminal Justice Act 2003 (3) Evidence of Bad Character' [2004] Crim LR 533.

[74] [2005] 1 WLR 3169, CA.

[75] See *R v Eyidah* [2010] EWCA Crim 987, 'a simple case [where] the jury should not have been deluged with a mass of prejudicial material, a great deal of which had absolutely nothing to do with the case at all' (per Hooper LJ at [13]).

[76] Or as to the consequences of non-compliance with the regulations for giving notice of intention to rely on bad character evidence: *R v Malone* [2006] All ER 32, CA, *R v Spartley* [2007] All ER 233, CA, *R v Ramirez* [2009] EWCA Crim 1721, and *R v Ellis* [2010] EWCA Crim 1893.

of prior events to establish propensity is plainly wrong or discretion has been exercised unreasonably in a *Wednesbury* sense.[77] It was also held that if, following a ruling that evidence of bad character is admissible, an accused pleads guilty, it is highly unlikely that an appeal against conviction will be entertained.

Section 101 of the Criminal Justice Act 2003

Section 101 provides as follows:

(1) In criminal proceedings evidence of the defendant's[78] bad character is admissible if, but only if
   (a) all parties to the proceedings agree to the evidence being admissible,
   (b) the evidence is adduced by the defendant himself or is given in answer to a question asked by him in cross-examination and intended to elicit it,
   (c) it is important explanatory evidence,
   (d) it is relevant to an important matter in issue between the defendant and the prosecution,
   (e) it has substantial probative value in relation to an important matter in issue between the defendant and a co-defendant,[79]
   (f) it is evidence to correct a false impression given by the defendant, or
   (g) the defendant has made an attack on another person's character.

(2) Sections 102 to 106 contain provision supplementing subsection (1).

(3) The court must not admit evidence under subsection (1)(d) or (g) if, on an application by the defendant to exclude it, it appears to the court that the admission of the evidence would have such an adverse effect on the fairness of the proceedings that the court ought not to admit it.

(4) On an application to exclude evidence under subsection (3) the court must have regard, in particular, to the length of time between the matters to which that evidence relates and the matters which form the subject of the offence charged.

Although s 101(1) governs only the admissibility of evidence of bad character and does not explicitly deal with the asking of questions about bad character in cross-examination, the intention is to cover both. The phrase 'prosecution evidence' is defined to include evidence which a witness is to be invited to give (or has given) in cross-examination by the prosecution;[80] the 'only evidence' admissible under s 101(1)(e) includes evidence which a witness is invited to give (or has given) in cross-examination by the co-defendant;[81] and the rules of court require a party to serve notice on the defendant where it is proposed to cross-examine a witness with a view to eliciting evidence of the accused's bad character.[82]

There are seven 'gateways' under s 101(1) through which evidence of the bad character of the accused may be admitted. Section 101(1)(a) provides for the admissibility of such evidence by consent of the parties. Under s 101(1)(b) such evidence may be admitted at the election

---

[77] *Wednesbury Corpn v Ministry of Housing and Local Government* [1965] 1 WLR 261, CA. The position is the same when the Divisional Court is considering an appeal against a decision of a magistrates' court: *DPP v Chard* [2007] EWHC 90, DC.

[78] 'Defendant', in relation to criminal proceedings, means a person charged with an offence in those proceedings: s 112(1).

[79] 'Co-defendant', in relation to a defendant means a person charged with an offence in the same proceedings: s 112(1).

[80] Section 112(1).

[81] Section 104(2)(b).

[82] Section 111(2)(b). See The Criminal Procedure Rules 2013, SI 2013/1544, r 35.2.

of the accused, without the agreement of the other parties. Speaking generally, s 101(1)(c) is designed to admit evidence which would have been admissible at common law as so-called 'background evidence'. Section 101(1)(d) covers prosecution evidence relevant to an important matter, ie a matter of substantial importance in the context of the case as a whole, which is in issue between the prosecution and the defence. Subsections (1)(e), (f), and (g) broadly correspond to and widen pre-existing grounds of admissibility. Section 101(1)(e) relates to evidence formerly admissible on behalf of a co-accused either on the basis of its relevance to the guilt of the accused or, in cases where the nature or conduct of the defence of the accused undermines the defence of the co-accused, to attack the credibility of the accused; s 101(1) (f) relates to prosecution evidence formerly admissible to rebut evidence of good character adduced by an accused; and s 101(1)(g) is designed to admit prosecution evidence in cases where the accused has cast an imputation on the character of another.

Before considering further each of the 'gateways', it is convenient first to consider some issues of general importance relating to admissibility, use, leave, and discretionary exclusion.

Admissibility and use

Parties are well advised to reflect, at the time of the application to admit evidence of bad character, as to the use to which such evidence is likely to be put and be in a position to assist the judge in this regard.[83] Lord Woolf CJ made clear in *R v Highton*[84] that the use to which the evidence may be put depends upon the matters to which it is relevant rather than the gateway through which it was admitted. The reasoning that leads to the admission of evidence under s 101(1)(d) may also determine the matter to which the evidence is relevant or primarily relevant once admitted. This is because, as we shall see, that provision deals separately with the accused's propensity to commit offences of the kind with which he is charged (s 103(1)(a)) and his propensity to be untruthful (s 103(1)(b)). However, under other gateways, which make no reference to the use to which the bad character evidence may be put, for example under s 101(1)(g), where admissibility depends on the accused having made an attack on another person's character, the evidence may, depending on the particular facts, be relevant not only to credibility but also to propensity to commit offences of the kind charged.

The full implications of Lord Woolf's reasoning became explicit in *R v Campbell*.[85] In that case it was submitted that in directing the jury as to the relevance of bad character evidence, the judge should have regard only to the gateway through which the evidence was introduced, unless the evidence could have been introduced through an additional gateway, in which case the jury could be directed as to its additional relevance under that gateway. Lord Phillips CJ rejected the submission on the basis that to direct the jury to have regard to bad character evidence for some purposes and disregard its relevance in other respects 'would be to revert to the unsatisfactory practices that prevailed under the old law'. This was an explicit reference to the fact that under s 1(f) of the Criminal Evidence Act 1898 it was often the case that the judge was required to direct the jury that the previous conviction was relevant only to the accused's credibility, not guilt. As Lord Phillips CJ says, this was contrary to common sense where the previous convictions showed propensity to commit the type of offence with which the accused was charged. However, with respect it is no justification for his rejection

---

[83] *R v Edwards* [2006] 1 WLR 1524, CA at [1](ii).
[84] [2006] 1 Cr App R 125, CA.
[85] [2007] 1 WLR 2798, CA.

of the submission made because in such a case, under the 2003 Act, insofar as the evidence is relevant to propensity to commit the offence charged, it is admissible under s 101(1)(d), provided it meets the requirements of that gateway, in addition to any other gateway through which it is admissible and relevant to credit. The consequence of the view adopted by the Lord Chief Justice is that, for example, evidence of propensity to commit offences of the kind charged can now be admitted under s 101(1)(g) (making an attack on another person's character) even if it is not relevant to an important matter in issue between the prosecution and the defence (a requirement under s 101(1)(d), but not under s 101(1)(g)) or does not have substantial probative value in relation to an important matter in issue between the accused and a co-accused (a requirement under s 101(1)(e), but not under s 101(1)(g)). It seems most unlikely that this is what Parliament intended.[86]

The judge's summing-up

It will be clear, from the foregoing, that the judge must exercise care when summing up. She will need to warn the jury against placing undue reliance on previous convictions, which cannot by themselves prove guilt, and also explain why they have heard the evidence and the ways in which it is relevant to and may help their decision.[87] Where bad character evidence is admitted and thereafter 'the ground shifts', the judge may need to direct the jury that, given the course taken by the trial, the evidence is of little weight.[88] In appropriate circumstances, which may arise when evidence of previous convictions is adduced by the accused himself under s 101(1)(b), the judge may even be required to direct the jury that the evidence does not assist on either propensity or untruthfulness.[89]

   In *R v Campbell*, Lord Phillips CJ set out the following general principles governing the way in which juries should be directed about evidence admitted under s 101.

1. The changes introduced by the 2003 Act should be the occasion for simplifying the directions to juries in relation to evidence of the accused's bad character.[90]

2. Decisions in this field before the 2003 Act came into force are unhelpful and should not be cited.

3. The jury should be given assistance as to the relevance of bad character evidence that is tailored to the facts of the individual case.

4. Relevance can normally be deduced by the application of common sense. The summing-up that assists the jury with the relevance of bad character evidence will accord with common sense and assist them to avoid prejudice that is at odds with this.

5. Once evidence has been admitted through a gateway it is open to the jury to attach significance to it in any respect in which it is relevant. There is no rule to the effect that in directing the jury as to relevance, the judge shall have regard only to the gateway through which the evidence was introduced or any other gateway through which it could have been introduced.

---

[86] For further implications and a powerful critique of *R v Highton* [2005] 1 WLR 3472, CA, see Munday, 'The Purposes of Gateway (g): Yet Another Problematic of the Criminal Justice Act 2003' [2006] Crim LR 300.

[87] See per Rose LJ in *R v Edwards* [2006] 1 WLR 1524, CA at [3].

[88] *R v Edwards* [2006] 1 WLR 1524, CA at [1](iv).

[89] *R v Edwards* [2006] 1 WLR 1524, CA at [87]–[104].

[90] See the Crown Court Bench Book 2010, 175–90.

6. The extent of the significance to be attached to previous convictions is likely to depend upon a number of variables, including their number, their similarity to the offence charged, how recently they were incurred, and the nature of the defence.

7. In considering the inference to be drawn from bad character the courts have in the past distinguished propensity to offend and credibility. This distinction is usually unrealistic. If the jury learn that an accused has shown a propensity to commit criminal acts they may well also conclude that it is more likely that he is guilty and that he is less likely to be telling the truth when he says that he is not. It will be comparatively rare for the case of an accused who has pleaded not guilty not to involve some element that the prosecution suggest is untruthful.

8. Reciting the statutory wording of the gateway by which the evidence was admitted is unlikely to be helpful. The jury should be told in simple language and with reference, where appropriate, to the particular facts of the case, why the bad character may be relevant.

9. Where evidence of a crime or other blameworthy act on the part of the accused is adduced because it bears on a particular issue of fact and the evidence has no bearing on the accused's propensity to commit the offence charged,[91] this should be made plain to the jury.

10. It is highly desirable that the jury should be warned against attaching too much weight to bad character evidence, let alone concluding that he is guilty simply because of his bad character.[92]

Leave

As we have seen, s 100(4) of the 2003 Act expressly states that evidence of the bad character of a *non-defendant* 'must not be given without the leave of the court'. There is no equivalent in relation to evidence of the bad character of an *accused* admissible under s 101(1)(c) to (g). However, whether any of the requirements for admissibility in those sub-paragraphs has been met is a question of law for the judge to decide, in appropriate cases only after holding a *voir dire*, and it is submitted that given the potentially irremediable harm of the jury hearing evidence which is later ruled inadmissible, counsel for the prosecution or, as appropriate, the co-accused, before introducing the evidence, will need to satisfy the judge that the statutory requirements are met.

Discretion to exclude
Section 101(3)
Turning to the issue of discretionary exclusion, in the case of evidence meeting the requirements of s 101(1)(d) or (g), the court has the discretionary power to exclude it under s 101(3) on the basis of its adverse effect on the fairness of the proceedings. Provided that the judge, in exercising the discretion, has in mind the time factor in s 101(4), the Court of Appeal will not ordinarily interfere with his decision unless there has been some error in principle.[93] If the evidence is

[91] See, in this chapter, under **Evidence of the bad character of the defendant, Section 101(1)(d)-prosecution evidence relevant to an importanr matter in issue between the defendant and the prosecution, Important matters in issue**.

[92] As to the further principles enunciated in and relating to the 2003 Act, s 103(1)(b), see in this chapter, under **Evidence of the bad character of the defendant, Bad character evidence under section 101(1)(d) relevant to the guilt of the accused, Bad character evidence under section 101(1)(d) relevant to the credibility of the accused**.

[93] *R v Edwards* [2006] 1 WLR 1524, CA at [75]. See also *R v Malone* [2006] All ER 32, CA and *R v Spartley* [2007] All ER 233,CA.

inherently incredible, that is likely to be a strong factor against admitting it, but whilst the judge will have regard to the potential weight of the evidence, he should not usurp the jury's function of deciding what evidence is accepted and what rejected.[94] If the evidence is based on information received by a witness from unidentified third parties, by its nature it will be difficult for the accused to meet and therefore should be excluded.[95] It is not an error in principle to admit allegations of misconduct in respect of which the accused was told that he would not be prosecuted.[96]

Section 101(3) is brought into play 'on an application by the accused to exclude' the evidence, wording which seems to preclude the court from exercising the power under the subsection of its own motion. However, bearing in mind Art 6 of the European Convention on Human Rights, a judge should if necessary encourage an application to exclude if it appears that admission of the evidence may have such an adverse effect on the fairness of the proceedings that it ought not to admit it.[97] Where the trial judge has used s 101(3) to exclude evidence potentially admissible under s 101(1)(d), that will not prevent him later in the trial from admitting the evidence under s 101(1)(g), because the fairness of the proceedings and the impact on it of admitting the evidence has to be gauged at the time at which the application is made and by reference to the gateway under which admissibility is sought.[98]

The fact that s 101(3) does not apply to s 101(1)(a), (b), and (e) makes perfect sense. In the case of s 101(1)(a) and (b), there is no need for a discretion to exclude—the accused already has control over whether the evidence is admitted or not. As to s 101(1)(e), which relates to evidence admissible on behalf of a co-accused, the good reason for the absence of a discretionary power to exclude is that a co-accused should be free to adduce any evidence relevant to his case whether or not it prejudices any other accused. The principle was the same, before the coming into force of s 101, in the case of both 'similar fact evidence' tendered by a co-accused and cross-examination of an accused by a co-accused under the 1898 Act.[99]

Common law and section 78 of the Police and Criminal Evidence Act 1984

The fact that s 101(3) does not apply to s 101(1)(c) and (f) is difficult to justify and raises the question whether evidence otherwise admissible under those sub-paras can be excluded using common law discretionary power or s 78 of the Police and Criminal Evidence Act 1984.[100] As to the former, it is submitted that the general common law discretionary power to exclude prosecution evidence where its prejudicial effect outweighs its probative value may be exercised in respect of evidence of bad character admissible under s 101(1)(c) (if it is to be adduced by the prosecution) and s 101(1)(f) (under which only prosecution evidence is admissible).[101] As noted, when considering s 100 of the 2003 Act, it is unclear whether s 78 of the 1984 Act applies in the case of prosecution evidence of bad character otherwise admissible under the 2003 Act. Two

---

[94] *R v Edwards* [2006] 1 WLR 1524, CA at [82].

[95] *R v Weir* [2006] 1 WLR 1885, CA at [40].

[96] *R v Edwards* [2006] 1 WLR 1524, CA at [76]. See also *R v Nguyen* (2008) 2 Cr App 9, CA, where it was held that it was not unfair to admit evidence of previous assaults which the Crown Prosecution Service had decided not to prosecute.

[97] *R v Weir* [2006] 1 WLR 1885, CA.

[98] *R v Edwards* [2006] 1 WLR 1524, CA at [14].

[99] See *Lobban v R* [1995] 2 All ER 602, PC approving the description of this principle appearing in the 3rd edition of this book. However, in rare cases the evidence may now be excluded for failure to comply with the requirement to give notice: see *R v Musone* [2007] 1 WLR 2467, CA 517 in this chapter, under **General, Rules of court**.

[100] See Ch 2.

[101] See, in this chapter, under **Introductory, Abolition of the common law rules**.

strong arguments support the view that Parliament's intention was to exclude the operation of s 78. First, there is express provision in Chapter 2 of Pt 11 of the 2003 Act, concerning hearsay evidence, that nothing in that chapter prejudices any power of a court to exclude evidence under s 78.[102] Second, if s 78 does apply, s 101(3), the critical words of which mirror those to be found in s 78, is otiose.[103] On the other hand, s 78 is plainly a provision of general application, applying to any evidence on which the prosecution propose to rely, and, arguably, should not be taken to cease to apply to particular types of prosecution evidence without express provision to that effect. The balance of case law falls firmly in favour of this position. In *R v Highton*[104] Lord Woolf CJ expressed a preliminary view that reliance can be placed on s 78 and that judges might apply s 78, as appropriate, which would avoid any risk of injustice to the accused, and that to do so would be consistent with the result to which the court would come if it complied with obligations under s 3 of the Human Rights Act 1998 to construe ss 101 and 103 of the 2003 Act in accordance with the European Convention on Human Rights. Although it was observed in *R v D*[105] that the operation of s 78 to exclude evidence of an accused's bad character was 'possibly controversial', in *R v O'Dowd*,[106] it was held that s 78 should be considered where s 101(3) was not available. This is consistent with a number of other authorities.[107]

Section 101(1)(a)—evidence admitted by agreement of all the parties

Evidence of the accused's bad character may be admitted under s 101(1)(a) with the consent of all the parties, ie the prosecution, accused, and any co-accused, and without the leave of the court.[108]

Section 101(1)(b)—evidence admitted by the defendant himself

Section 101(1)(b) permits evidence of the accused's bad character to be admitted by the accused himself without the leave of the court. This option is of limited if any value in cases in which the prosecution have already adduced the evidence by virtue of one of the other sub-paras of s 101(1). However, where the evidence is not admissible as a part of the prosecution case, there are two situations in which the accused may sensibly elect to admit it himself. First, if it is evidence of comparatively minor misconduct, he may adduce it on the basis that otherwise the jurors, especially if they have gained some experience by serving in other cases, might

---

[102] Section 126(2).

[103] Although it has been said that a 'significant difference' is to be found in the mandatory opening words of s 101(3) and s 78 (per Kennedy LJ in *R v Weir* [2006] 1 WLR 1885, CA at [46]), this is a distinction without a difference, as under s 78 a court has no discretion once the condition is, in its view, satisfied (per Thomas LJ in *R v Tirnaveanu* [2007] 1 WLR 3049, CA at [28]).

[104] [2006] 1 Cr App R 125, CA.

[105] [2009] 2 Cr App R 17, CA at [36].

[106] [2009] 2 Cr App R 280, CA.

[107] *R v Weir* [2006] 1 WLR 1885; *R v Tirnaveanu* [2007] 1 WLR 3049. See also *R v B* [2008] EWCA Crim 1850 and *R v Fox* [2009] Crim LR 881. Where s 101(3) *is* available, the focus must be on that section and not s 78: see *R v Chrysostomou* [2010] EWCA Crim 1403 at [38]–[39], concerning admissibility under s 101(1)(g).

[108] See *R v Hussain* [2008] EWCA Crim 1117: both an accused and a co-accused, running cut-throat defences, had convictions for dishonesty admitted by agreement because, realistically, they were bound to have been admitted in the absence of agreement. See also *R v Kalu* [2007] EWCA Crim 22: evidence of a caution for excessive chastisement was admitted by agreement in a child cruelty case, presumably for the same reason. However, the court observed that a more correct analysis was that the caution may well have been to do with the facts of the offences charged. If so it was admissible on that basis rather than on the basis that it was evidence of bad character admissible by agreement (see [12]).

speculate that his character is worse than it is. Second, where he adduces evidence attacking another person's character and therefore brings into play s 101(1)(g), when it may be tactically wiser for him to be frank with the jury and give evidence of his bad character himself, rather than allow the prosecution to elicit evidence on the matter in cross-examination. This may be a sensible course of action where the previous convictions were all based on guilty pleas because however the judge directs the jury about the bad character evidence, there is obvious scope for the defence to say to the jury, in closing submissions, that the fact that the accused has for the first time pleaded not guilty indicates that his denial on oath ought to be believed.

Under s 101(1)(b), the evidence may be either adduced by the accused himself or given in answer to a question asked by the defence in cross-examination,[109] provided that the question was intended to elicit it. Thus if the witness under cross-examination volunteers the evidence of bad character, it is inadmissible and the judge will need to direct the jury to ignore it or, if no direction is capable of neutralizing the prejudice to the accused and there is therefore a real risk of injustice occurring, exercise his discretion to discharge the jury and order a re-trial.[110]

Section 101(1)(c)—important explanatory evidence

Under s 101(1)(c), which may be used by either the prosecution or a co-accused, evidence of the accused's bad character is admissible if it is 'important explanatory evidence'. Section 102 provides that:

For the purposes of section 101(1)(c) evidence is important explanatory evidence if—
  (a) without it, the court or jury would find it impossible or difficult properly to understand other evidence in the case, and
  (b) its value for understanding the case as a whole is substantial.

Section 101(c) is closely based on the recommendation of the Law Commission except that it lacks the safeguard contained in the Commission's draft clause that the court be satisfied either that the evidence carries no risk of prejudice to the accused or that the value of the evidence for understanding the case as a whole is such that, taking account of the risk of prejudice, the interests of justice nevertheless require it to be admissible.

This definition in s 102 is the same as that contained in s 100(2)(a), which applies in relation to evidence of a non-defendant's bad character. If the matter to which the proposed explanatory evidence relates is largely comprehensible without the evidence, the evidence will be inadmissible.[111] Explanatory evidence, to be admissible, must also satisfy s 102(b), ie its value for understanding the case as a whole must be 'substantial', as opposed to minor or trivial. In *R v Edwards*,[112] a case of robbery and possession of an imitation firearm, the statement of an identification witness that she was able to recognize the accused because she had bought heroin from him every other day for a year or so, was held to have been properly admitted as important explanatory evidence in relation to the basis of her identification. However, no convincing reason was given for rejecting the submission that, given the prejudice arising from the allegation of heroin dealing, the statement should have been edited so as to disclose the frequency of the encounters, but not the reason for them.

[109] See, eg, *R v Tollady* [2010] EWCA Crim 2614.
[110] See, in this chapter, under **Other provisions governing the admissibility of evidence of bad character, Evidence admitted through inadvertence**.
[111] See *R v L* (2012) 176 JP 231, CA and also *R v Sheikh* [2013] EWCA Crim 907.
[112] [2006] 1 WLR 1524, CA.

Overlap with propensity

In *R v D*[113] it was emphasized that the test for admissibility under s 101(1)(c) should be applied cautiously where it was also possible to argue that evidence showed propensity to commit offences. The accused was charged with murdering his common law wife whom he had accused of having an affair. Using s 101(1)(c), the prosecution adduced the evidence of a former girlfriend that some 20 years previously he had acted towards her with jealous aggression and made threats to kill. The Court of Appeal held that the evidence did not have a substantial value for understanding the case, and indeed could have undermined the jury's understanding of the accused's relationship with his wife and the events leading up to her death. The evidence was really evidence of propensity and it should not have been allowed to 'slide in' as explanatory evidence.[114] Furthermore, where evidence 'is admitted under gateway (c) [it] should not readily be used, once admitted, for a purpose such as propensity, for which additional safeguards on different tests have first to be met'.[115]

However, a difficult borderline exists between explanatory evidence and evidence of propensity and in some cases evidence may be properly admitted under s 101(1)(c) even though it is evidence which is strongly indicative of the accused's propensity. In *R v Ladds*[116] the accused stabbed her partner, F, and was convicted of wounding with intent. Her defence had been that F had inflicted the wounds on himself and, in support, she adduced evidence that F had attempted suicide in the past. The Court of Appeal held that evidence of previous 'strikingly similar' incidents where F had suffered injuries and reported that they had been inflicted by the accused was properly admissible as important explanatory evidence. It would have been 'positively misleading' for the jury not to have heard about these incidents considering the evidence adduced by F.[117]

Evidence revealing motive

Since s 101(1)(c) in effect gives statutory force to a doctrine established at common law,[118] it is submitted that the common law authorities will continue to provide valuable guidance, notwithstanding that they reveal an occasional tendency to admit evidence with a high risk of prejudice but providing comparatively limited assistance to the jury in understanding the other evidence in the case. The authorities show that the evidence often relates to other acts done or statements made by the accused revealing his desire to commit, or reason for committing, the offence charged.[119] Similarly in *R v Ball*[120] Lord Atkinson was of the view that in an ordinary prosecution for murder evidence is admissible of previous acts or words of the accused to show that he entertained feelings of enmity towards the deceased, and although

---

[113] [2009] 2 Cr App R 17, CA.

[114] *R v D* [2009] 2 Cr App R 17, CA per Hughes LJ at [34]. See also *R v Saint* [2010] EWCA Crim 1924 and *R v L* (2012) 176 JP 231, CA. See also the common law authority of *R v Dolan* [2003] 1 Cr App R 281, CA: 'background evidence' needed to be distinguished from so-called 'similar fact' evidence and should not be used for smuggling in such evidence which would be otherwise inadmissible. See also *R v M(T)* [2000] 1 WLR 421, CA.

[115] *R v D* [2009] 2 Cr App R 17, CA.

[116] [2009] EWCA Crim 1249.

[117] [2009] EWCA Crim 1249 at [12]–[15].

[118] Albeit that the formulation of s 101(1)(c) is slightly different to the common law test. See *R v Pettman*, 2 May 1985, CA, unreported.

[119] See, eg, *R v Bond* [1906] 2 KB 389. See also, in this chapter, under **Evidence of the bad character of a person other than the defendant, Threshold conditions for admissibility, Important explanatory evidence**.

[120] [1911] AC 47, HL at 68.

R v Ball was disapproved in *R v Berry*,[121] it was affirmed in *R v Williams*[122] and reaffirmed in *R v Phillips*.[123] In *R v Phillips*,[124] the accused denied being the murderer of his wife and evidence was admitted of the unhappy state of the marriage over a number of years.[125] However, although evidence may be admitted as explanatory evidence under s 101(1)(c) to expose an accused's motive for acting in a particular way, as with s 100(2), evidence will not be admitted where it is being used to construct speculative suggestions about the accused's motive.[126]

Proximity in time

Evidence will not be admitted under the principle if it relates to events so distant in time from the crime as to be of little if any probative value. For example, in *R v Phillips* it was held that it would have been quite wrong to have admitted the evidence of a stormy relationship eight years before the crime was committed, especially if thereafter it was a happy marriage.[127] Similarly in *R v Dolan*,[128] where the accused was charged with the murder of his baby son by shaking him forcefully, it was held to be irrelevant that in the past he had lost his temper and shown violence towards inanimate objects. The touchstones of the principle, said the court, were relevance and necessity.[129]

The judge's summing-up

Where background evidence is properly admitted, the jury will often need to be directed carefully as to the use to which the evidence may and may not be put. In *R v Sawoniuk*[130] the accused was convicted of the murder of Jews in Belarus in 1942. The Court of Appeal upheld the decision of the trial judge to admit evidence of his participation in a 'search and kill' operation against Jewish survivors of an earlier massacre. The evidence was relevant to the identification evidence in the case, but it was also held to be admissible as background evidence because, as Lord Bingham CJ put it, 'criminal charges cannot fairly be judged in a factual vacuum'.[131] The case pre-dated the 2003 Act and the court was concerned with whether the evidence was background evidence or similar fact evidence, and whether the trial judge had adequately directed the jury. The court noted that the evidence was not similar fact evidence and that the trial judge had adequately directed the jury not to follow what was then a forbidden line of reasoning, ie that by reason of his earlier actions the accused was more likely to have committed the offences with which he was charged. As to the direction to be given in respect of background evidence admitted under s 101(1)(c) of the 2003 Act, the Crown Court Bench Book provides that the jury will need to be

---

[121] (1986) Cr App R 7, CA.

[122] (1986) 84 Cr App R 299, CA.

[123] [2003] 2 Cr App R 528, CA per Dyson LJ at 534. See also *R v Campbell*, 20 Dec 1984, CA, unreported; *R v Giannette* [1996] Crim LR 722, CA; and *R v Williams* (1986) 84 Cr App R 299, CA. Cf also *R v Berry* (1986) 83 Cr App R 7, CA.

[124] [2003] 2 Cr App R 528, CA.

[125] See also *R v Asif* (1985) 82 Cr App R 123, CA, concerning the failure to comply with statutory VAT requirements. For further examples, see *R v Carrington* [1990] Crim LR 330, CA; *R v Sidhu* (1993) 98 Cr App R 59, CA; *R v Fulcher* [1995] 2 Cr App R 251, CA; and *R v Shaw* [2003] Crim LR 278. See also, *sed quaere*, *R v Underwood* [1999] Crim LR 227, CA.

[126] *R v Broome* [2012] EWCA Crim 2879.

[127] [2003] 2 Cr App R 528 at 536. See also *R v Butler* [1999] Crim LR 835, CA, where the events had taken place three years before the offence charged.

[128] [2003] 1 Cr App R 281, CA.

[129] *R v Dolan* [2003] 1 Cr App R 281, CA at 285–6.

[130] [2002] 2 Cr App R 220, CA.

[131] *R v Sawoniuk* [2002] 2 Cr App R 220, CA at 234.

۱ a warning on the relevance and limits of background evidence and be warned, in particu-
at such evidence alone cannot prove the guilt of an accused.[132]

... up with evidence which has to do with the alleged facts of the offence

The point has already been made that evidence of misconduct 'which has to do with the
alleged facts of the offence' and is admissible by virtue of s 98(a) will often be difficult to distinguish from background evidence admissible under s 101(1)(c). The overlap will typically
arise where the misconduct and the facts of the offence are part of one continuous transaction.
R v Ellis[133] is an old but good example. A shop assistant was charged with stealing six marked
shillings from a till. Evidence was given that on several occasions on the day in question he
was seen to take money from the till and that, on his arrest, he was found in possession of a
sum of money equal to that missing from the till and made up of the six marked shillings and
some other unmarked money. The evidence, insofar as it tended to show that the assistant
had stolen unmarked money as well as the marked money, was held to be admissible on the
grounds that it went to show the history of the till from the time when the marked money was
put into it up to the time when it was found in the possession of the accused. Bayley J said:

> Generally speaking it is not competent to a prosecutor to prove a man guilty of one felony, by prov-
> ing him guilty of another unconnected felony; but where several felonies are connected together, and
> form part of one entire transaction, then the one is evidence to show the character of the other.[134]

Since the test in s 101(1)(c) does not require the court to balance the value of the evidence
to be admitted against the prejudice to the accused, then when the *prosecution* seek to admit
evidence under the sub-paragraph, as will usually be the case, there is obvious scope for use
of the common law discretionary power to exclude, assuming, as submitted earlier, that that
power subsists in relation to prosecution evidence admissible under s 101.[135] The court should
exercise the discretion where the prejudicial effect of the evidence is out of all proportion to
its probative value, as when it relates to particularly serious misconduct on the part of the
accused and without it the jury would find it difficult, but perhaps not especially difficult,
properly to understand other evidence in the case.

Section 101(1)(d)—prosecution evidence relevant to an important matter in issue between the defendant and the prosecution

Under the carefully wrought proposals of the Law Commission, there were separate clauses
governing admissibility of evidence of the bad character of the accused going to the issue of
his guilt and admissibility of evidence of his bad character going to the issue of his credibility.[136] This distinction was born of a recognition that the two issues usually arise at different
stages of the trial and that the relevant factors for the purpose of deciding the admissibility of
each type of evidence are different. In relation to the issue of guilt, the Commission proposed,
that in order to be admissible, bad character evidence should be of substantial probative value
in relation to a matter of substantial importance and should carry no risk of prejudice to the
accused or, taking into account the risk of prejudice, its probative value justified its admission

---

[132] The Crown Court Bench Book 2010, 172–4.

[133] (1826) 6 B&C 145.

[134] See also *R v Rearden* (1864) 4 F&F 76.

[135] See, in this chapter, under **Evidence of the bad character of the defendant, Section 101 of the Criminal Justice Act 2003.**

[136] Law Com No 273, Cm 5257 (2001), Draft Bill, cl 8 and cl 9.

in the interests of justice. As to credibility, bad character evidence was only admissible where an attack had been made on another's truthfulness.

Section 101(1)(d) of the 2003 Act however, which reflects a markedly different and less sophisticated approach, provides a single 'gateway' for the admissibility of prosecution evidence going to the guilt of the accused as well as evidence going to his credibility. Under s 101(1)(d), prosecution evidence of the accused's bad character is admissible if 'it is relevant to an important matter in issue between the defendant and the prosecution'.[137] The test is one of simple relevance or probative value.[138] There is no requirement of enhanced relevance or 'substantial probative value' as there is under s 101(1)(e) and, in relation to the bad character of someone other than the accused, under s 100(1)(b). The evidence, however, must be relevant to an important matter in issue between the accused and the prosecution.

Important matters in issue

The matters in issue between the accused and the prosecution are, of course, the disputed facts and issues of credit or credibility. In a sense, all such matters in issue between the accused and the prosecution are important, but 'important matter' is defined in the Act as 'a matter of substantial importance in the context of the case as a whole',[139] a definition which, it is submitted, will only operate to exclude evidence relevant to matters in issue which are of minor or marginal significance. The overall effect of s 101(1)(d), therefore, is to permit the introduction of prosecution evidence of the bad character of the accused whenever it is relevant to any of the main matters in issue between the prosecution and the defence, and is not limited to propensity.[140] In many cases the main issue on which the evidence of bad character has a bearing will be the accused's defence. Accordingly, in a case of possession with intent to supply Class A drugs, for example, where the matter in issue is the accused's knowledge of the drugs, a previous conviction for importing such drugs could be relevant to rebut his defence.[141] Evidence of an accused's bad character might also be relevant to rebut a defence which the accused may not actually have raised, but which is fairly open to him. A defence which is fairly open to the accused, but not relied upon, could become an important matter in issue because a submission of no case to answer might succeed when evidence properly available to support the prosecution case might have been withheld.[142] Another example of an important matter

---

[137] Only prosecution evidence is admissible under s 101(1)(d): s 103(6).

[138] *R v Weir* [2006] 1 WLR 1885, CA at [36].

[139] Section 112(1).

[140] Nor, it is submitted, will there be a closed list of defined categories of relevance such as 'proof of identity', 'rebutting accident', or 'innocent association'. Such a notion was firmly rejected at common law, in respect of the relevance of 'similar fact' evidence. See *Harris v DPP* [1952] AC 694, HL at 705.

[141] *R v Colliard* [2008] EWCA Crim 1175. See also *R v Jordan* [2009] EWCA Crim 953: the accused's convictions for robbery and possession of a firearm were relevant to the issue of whether he knew about the presence of a gun in the car in which he was travelling or was an innocent passenger. See also common law authorities of how the principle may apply: *R v Willis* (29 Jan 1979, unreported), CA (the evidence of the drugs was relevant even though they were of a different kind); *R v Peters* [1995] 2 Cr App R 77, CA (where the drugs were too different to be relevant); and *R v Yalman* [1998] 2 Cr App R 269, CA. See also an old but good example of evidence admitted to prove the issue of the accused's presence: *R v Salisbury* (1831) 5 C&P 155. See also *R v Voke* (1823) Russ&Ry 531; *R v Cobden* (1862) 3 F&F 833; and *R v Rearden* (1864) 4 F&F 76.

[142] See *Harris v DPP* [1952] AC 694, HL. It is submitted that this common law principle continues to operate under the 2003 Act. For an example, in relation to a defence actually raised, see *R v Anderson* [1988] 2 All ER 549, CA; and for an example in relation to a defence which was fairly open to the accused (and in the event raised), see *R v Lunt* (1986) 85 Cr App R 241, CA.

in issue might be the accused's identity. So, in a case of dangerous driving, the accused's previous convictions for driving whilst disqualified could be relevant to the issue of whether a police officer has correctly recognized the accused driving dangerously.[143] The breadth of the provision means that prosecution applications to admit bad character evidence and defence applications to exclude under s 101(3) have become a regular feature of most trials.

Section 101(1)(d) is supplemented by s 103, which makes it clear that 'matters in issue' between the accused and the prosecution can include (a) the question whether the accused has a propensity to commit offences of the kind with which he is charged and (b) the question whether he has a propensity to be untruthful. For the purposes of exposition, it will be convenient to consider these two issues separately, albeit, in the case of the former, as part of the wider issue of bad character relevant to the guilt of the accused.

Bad character evidence under section 101(1)(d) relevant to the guilt of the accused

Evidence of propensity under section 103 of the Criminal Justice Act 2003

Section 103(1) and (2) of the 2003 Act provides as follows:

(1) For the purposes of section 101(1)(d) the matters in issue between the defendant and the prosecution include—
  (a) the question whether the defendant has a propensity to commit offences of the kind with which he is charged, except where his having such a propensity makes it no more likely that he is guilty of the offence;
  (b) the question whether the defendant has a propensity to be untruthful, except where it is not suggested that the defendant's case is untruthful in any respect.
(2) Where subsection (1)(a) applies, a defendant's propensity to commit offences of the kind with which he is charged may (without prejudice to any other way of doing so) be established by evidence that he has been convicted of—
  (a) an offence of the same description as the one with which he is charged, or
  (b) an offence of the same category as the one with which he is charged.
(3) Subsection (2) does not apply in the case of a particular defendant if the court is satisfied, by reason of the length of time since the conviction or for any other reason, that it would be unjust for it to apply in his case.
(4) For the purposes of subsection (2)—
  (a) two offences are of the same description as each other if the statement of the offences in a written charge or indictment would, in each case, be in the same terms;
  (b) two offences are of the same category as each other if they belong to the same category of offences prescribed for the purposes of this section by an order made by the Secretary of State.
(5) A category prescribed by an order under subsection 4(b) must consist of offences of the same type.
(6) Only prosecution evidence is admissible under s 101(1)(d)...

Offences of the same description or category

Under s 103(7)–(11) offences committed outside England and Wales may be admissible as offences of the same description or category if they would constitute offences of the same description and category had they been committed in England and Wales. The inclusionary nature of s 103(1) indicates that the matters in issue to which evidence of bad character may be relevant are not confined to those specified in the subsection.

---

[143] *R v Spittle* [2009] RTR 14, CA. See also *R v Eastlake* (2007) 151 SJLB 258, CA.

Propensity to commit offences of the kind charged

As to s 103(1)(a), it is conceptually confusing because propensity of the kind to which it refers has never before been treated as a matter in issue. In the past, propensity, or to be more accurate, admissible evidence of propensity, has been the means of establishing the matters in issue. Under the subsection, in any case in which the prosecution seek to rely upon s 101(1) (d) in relation to the issue of guilt, propensity will always be deemed to be a matter in issue, provided that it is of the kind referred to in the subsection. However, the prosecution will still need to establish that the propensity in question is an 'important' matter in issue, ie 'a matter of substantial importance in the context of the case as a whole'[144] because s 103 is not free-standing but operates 'for the purposes of s 101(1)(d)'. If the prosecution can establish such importance, then subject to s 101(3) and, it is submitted, the common law discretion to exclude on the basis of prejudicial effect outweighing probative value, the propensity may be established under s 103(2) by evidence of a relevant conviction or in 'any other way'. Insofar as s 103(2) permits proof by evidence of a conviction, it is submitted that it too is a deeming provision, in the sense that evidence of the conviction is to be treated as, in the words of s 101(1)(d), 'evidence of the defendant's bad character' that 'is relevant to an important matter in issue', ie the propensity.

The meaning of the exception within s 103(1)(a)—'except where his having such a propensity makes it no more likely that he is guilty of the offence'—is obscure, given that all too often evidence of propensity to commit offences of the kind charged will make it more probable that the accused committed the offence charged, albeit that in many cases it will have only limited or very limited probative force. The Explanatory Notes to the Act furnish only one illustration: where facts are undisputed and the question is whether the facts constitute the offence, 'for example, in a homicide case, whether the defendant's actions caused death'.[145]

Questions of proof

Section 103(2) provides that where the matter in issue is whether the accused has a propensity to commit offences of the kind with which he is charged, the propensity can be proved by evidence that he has been convicted of an offence of the kind referred to in either s 103(2)(a) or (b). This is subject to s 103(3), whereby evidence of the conviction should not be given if the court is satisfied that it would be unjust to do so 'by reason of the length of time since the conviction or for any other reason'. Bearing in mind that s 103 exists 'for the purposes of section 101(1)(d)', that any evidence admissible under s 101(1)(d) is subject to the discretionary power to exclude contained in s 101(3) and (4), and that those subsections contain a test for exclusion similar to, but obviously cast in different language from, the test in s 103(3), there appears to be a large degree of unnecessary overlap between those subsections and s 103(3).

The wording of s 103(2) indicates that in at least some cases proof of the mere fact of the conviction or convictions may be used to establish propensity. In other cases, however, the propensity will be established not simply by the fact of the conviction, but by evidence of the conduct which resulted in the conviction. In the latter type of case, the prosecution will doubtless use s 103(2) in conjunction with ss 74(3) and 75 of the Police and Criminal Evidence Act 1984.[146] Under s 74(3), as amended by the 2003 Act, where evidence of the fact that the accused has committed an offence is admissible and proof is given that he has been convicted

---

[144] Section 112(1).
[145] Para 371.
[146] See Ch 21. See, in the case of s 74(3), *R v O'Dowd* [2009] 2 Cr App R 280, CA at [71].

of the offence, there is a rebuttable presumption that he committed the offence.[147] Under s 75, where evidence of a conviction is admissible by virtue of s 74, then without prejudice to the admissibility of any other evidence for the purpose of identifying the facts on which the conviction was based, the contents of, inter alia, the information or indictment shall be admissible for that purpose. Where reliance is placed on specific facts relating to modus operandi beyond those contained in the information or indictment, and they are disputed, then they need to be established by calling a witness to give first-hand evidence or by adducing admissible hearsay evidence in that regard.[148] However, this runs the risk of 'satellite litigation' during a trial, which could distract from the real issues and unnecessarily lengthen proceedings.[149]

Section 103(2) permits propensity to be proved by evidence of a conviction of an offence falling within either s 103(2)(a) or (b). Subsection (2)(a) refers to an offence of the same description as the one with which the accused is charged. Section 103(4)(a) makes clear that an offence will only be 'of the same description' if the statement of the offence in a written charge or indictment would, in each case, be the same. Thus, as it says in the Explanatory Notes,[150] the test relates to the law broken rather than the circumstances of the offence. Section 103(2)(b) refers to an offence of the same category as the one with which the accused is charged. By reason of s 103(4)(b) and s 103(5), an offence will be 'of the same category' if it falls within a category consisting of offences of the same type drawn up by the Secretary of State in secondary legislation. Two categories have been drawn up, a 'Theft Category' and a 'Sexual Offences (persons under the age of 16) Category'.[151] The first includes offences of theft, robbery, burglary, handling stolen goods, etc. The second includes offences of rape of a person under the age of 16, assault by penetration of a person under the age of 16, sexual assault on a person under the age of 16, etc.[152]

The admissibility of evidence showing a propensity to offend

According to *R v Chopra*,[153] whereas at common law evidence of the accused's propensity to offend in the manner charged was prima facie inadmissible, under the 2003 Act it is prima facie admissible. In *R v Hanson*[154] the Court of Appeal laid down the following important principles relating to the admissibility of evidence of propensity under s 103.

1. Where propensity to commit the offence is relied upon by reference to s 101(1)(d) and s 103(1)(a), there are three questions to be considered: (i) whether the history of conviction(s) establishes a propensity to commit offences of the kind charged; (ii) whether that propensity makes it more likely that the accused committed the offence charged; and (iii) whether it is unjust to rely on the conviction(s) of the same description or category and, in any event, whether the proceedings will be unfair if they are admitted.

---

[147] See, in this chapter, under **General, The right of an accused to challenge evidence of a conviction**.

[148] *R v Humphris* (2005) 169 JP 441, CA and *R v Ainscough* [2006] Crim LR 635, CA.

[149] *R v O'Dowd* [2009] 2 Cr App R 280, CA at [71]. See *R v McKenzie* [2008] RTR 277, CA, where the Court of Appeal deprecated the admission of evidence relating to collateral matters which could add to the length and cost of a trial and complicate the issues the jury had to decide. See also *R v McAllister* (2009) 1 Cr App R 10, CA.

[150] Para 373.

[151] See Criminal Justice Act 2003 (Categories of Offences) Order 2004, SI 2004/3346.

[152] Both categories also include an offence of (a) aiding, abetting, counselling, procuring, or inciting the commission of an offence specified; or (b) attempting to commit an offence specified.

[153] [2007] 1 Cr App R 225, CA.

[154] [2005] 1 WLR 3169, CA.

2. In referring to offences of the same description or category, s 103(2) is not exhaustive of the types of misconduct which may be relied upon to show evidence of propensity to commit offences of the kind charged.[155] Nor, however, is it necessarily sufficient in order to show such propensity that a conviction is of the same description or type as that charged.

3. There is no minimum number of events necessary to demonstrate such a propensity. The fewer the number of convictions, the weaker the evidence of propensity is likely to be. A single previous conviction for an offence of the same description or category will often not show propensity,[156] but may do so where, for example, it shows a tendency to unusual behaviour, or where its circumstances demonstrate probative force in relation to the offence charged.[157]

4. Circumstances demonstrating probative force are not confined to those sharing striking similarity, but if the modus operandi has significant features shared by the offence charged, it may show propensity. When considering what is just under s 103(3), and the fairness of the proceedings under s 101(3), the judge may, along with other factors, take into consideration the degree of similarity between the previous conviction and the offence charged (albeit that they are both within the same description or prescribed category). This does not mean, however, that what used to be referred to as striking similarity must be shown before convictions become admissible.[158]

5. The judge may also take into consideration the respective gravity of the past and present offences.[159]

6. The judge must also consider the strength of the prosecution case. If there is no, or very little, other evidence against an accused, it is unlikely to be just to admit his previous convictions, whatever they are.

7. In principle, if there is a substantial gap between the dates of the commission of, and conviction for, earlier offence(s), the date of commission is, generally, to be regarded as being of more significance than the date of conviction when assessing admissibility. Old convictions with no special features shared with the offence charged are likely seriously to affect the fairness of proceedings adversely unless, despite their age, it can properly be said that they show a continuing propensity.[160]

---

[155] See *R v Johnson* [2009] 2 Cr App R 101, CA: conspiracy to burgle is not an offence of the same description or category as the substantive offence of burglary, but may be admissible as evidence of propensity.

[156] See *R v Bagot* [2010] EWCA Crim 1983.

[157] In *R v Turner* [2010] EWCA Crim 2300, a case of ruthless murder, a single 15-year-old conviction for an offence contrary to the Offences Against the Person Act 1861, s 18, was properly admitted because it revealed violence of greater than normal gravity and demonstrated a propensity to commit acts of ruthless violence on strangers.

[158] See *R v M* [2010] EWCA Crim 1578, CA, which applied the principles set out in paras (3) and (4).

[159] Sometimes, therefore, a ruling on admissibility should be deferred until all of the prosecution evidence has been adduced: *R v Gyima* [2007] Crim LR 890, CA. See also *R v Hewlett* [2008] EWCA Crim 270.

[160] See *R v Royston Jackson* [2011] EWCA Crim 1870: in a case of murder by strangulation the accused's previous conviction for murder was unsurprisingly admitted because, although it was 20 years old, it was also a murder by strangulation. Other common features included both victims being male, both murders beginning with a social meeting, both involving the use of a vehicle, and the victim's bodies being left in a remote location. See also *R v DS* [2010] EWCA Crim 1016: an extremely stale allegation of indecent assault was inadmissible; and *R v Bagot* [2010] EWCA Crim 1983: a single offence of vehicle taking when the accused was 14 did not show a propensity to steal cars at 18.

8. It will often be necessary, before determining admissibility, and even when considering offences of the same description or category, to examine each individual conviction rather than merely to look at the nature of the offence or at the accused's record as a whole.

9. The sentence passed will not normally be probative or admissible at the behest of the Crown.

10. Where past events are disputed, the judge must take care not to permit the trial unreasonably to be diverted into an investigation of matters not charged on the indictment.

11. The Crown needs to have decided, at the time of giving notice of the application, whether it proposes to rely simply on the fact of conviction or also upon the circumstances of it. It is to be expected that the relevant circumstances of previous convictions will, generally, be capable of agreement, and that, subject to the trial judge's ruling as to admissibility, they will be put before the jury by way of admission. Even where the circumstances are genuinely in dispute, it is to be expected that the minimum indisputable facts will thus be admitted. It will be very rare indeed for it to be necessary for the judge to hear evidence before ruling on admissibility under the Act.

12. In any case in which evidence of bad character is admitted to show propensity the judge in summing up should warn the jury clearly against placing undue reliance on previous convictions. Evidence of bad character cannot be used simply to bolster a weak case or to prejudice the minds of the jury against the defendant. A jury should be directed: (i) that they should not conclude that an accused is guilty or untruthful merely because he has previous convictions; (ii) that, although the convictions may show a propensity, this does not mean that he committed the offence charged or has been untruthful in the case; (iii) that whether they in fact show a propensity is for them to decide; (iv) that they must take into account what an accused has said about his previous convictions; and, (v) that, although they are entitled, if they find propensity is shown, to take this into account when determining guilt, propensity is only one relevant factor and they must assess its significance in the light of all the other evidence in the case.[161]

The number and age of convictions

The principles in paras (3) and (7) were refined and developed in *R v M*.[162] At the appellant's trial for possession of a firearm with intent to cause fear of violence the prosecution were permitted to adduce, under s 101(1)(d), evidence of a previous conviction for possession of a firearm without a certificate, which dated from some 20 years before. The Court of Appeal held that the evidence had been improperly admitted. Whilst there could be cases where the factual circumstances of a single previous conviction, even as long ago as 20 years, might be relevant to show an accused's propensity, the court observed that such cases would be rare and would involve the previous conviction exhibiting some very special and distinctive feature, such as a predilection for a highly unusual form of sexual activity,[163] or some arcane or highly specialized knowledge relevant to the offence charged. Where there were less distinctive features in common, some evidence of the propensity manifesting itself in the intervening

---

[161] For illustrative directions, see the Crown Court Bench Book 2010, 166–201.

[162] [2007] Crim LR 637, CA. See also *R v McKenzie* [2008] RTR 277, CA.

[163] A general sexual interest in children will suffice: see *R v B* [2011] EWCA Crim 1403.

period would be necessary in order to render the previous conviction admissible as evidence of a continuing propensity.

Misconduct after the offence charged

For the purposes of ss 101 and 103, evidence of propensity to offend may relate to events that occurred after the offence charged and not just to those that occurred before it. In some cases the events may occur a long time after the offence charged. In *R v B*,[164] for example, evidence of the accused's guilty pleas in 2010 to charges of making, possessing, and distributing child pornography between 2001 and 2007, was admissible as evidence of propensity in relation to offences of indecent assault against his stepdaughters between 1979 and 1982. The evidence showed sexual inclinations toward young girls of ages similar to the ages of his stepdaughters at the time of the assaults and, according to the court, as a matter of common sense it was unlikely that his interest in child pornography had sprung up in his later years and was wholly different from his inclinations between 1979 and 1982.

Misconduct other than convictions

Section 103(2) states that it is without prejudice to other ways of establishing an accused's propensity to commit offences of the kind with which he is charged. Thus propensity may be established by evidence of an offence other than an offence 'of the same description' or 'of the same category' within s 103(2); the purpose of that subsection is simply to make it easier to admit evidence of convictions of the kind to which it refers.[165] It may also be established by evidence of misconduct or disposition towards misconduct that did not result in a conviction, in which case it may be proved, subject to the rules of evidence generally, in the same way as any other relevant facts.[166] Concerning misconduct, there are three types of case. The first is where the misconduct did not result in a prosecution, including cases in which the accused was formally cautioned or previously asked to have offences taken into consideration.[167] The second is where the misconduct did result in a prosecution, but the outcome was an acquittal.[168] The third arises out of s 112(2) of the 2003 Act, which provides that:

(2) Where a defendant is charged with two or more offences in the same criminal proceedings, this Chapter (except section 101(3)) has effect as if each offence were charged in separate proceedings; and references to the offence with which the defendant is charged are to be read accordingly.

In *R v Chopra*[169] it was held that this subsection means that where an accused faces two or more counts on an indictment, the evidence which suggests that he committed count 2 is, so far as count 1 is concerned, bad character evidence and can be admitted in relation to count 1 if, but only if, it passes through one of the s 101 gateways; and that the same applies vice versa and however many counts there may be. A similar principle applies where no single

---

[164] [2011] EWCA Crim 1630. See also *R v Adenusi* [2006] Crim LR 929, CA. See also *R v Norris* [2013] EWCA Crim 712.

[165] *R v Weir* [2006] 1 WLR 1885, CA at [7].

[166] See *R v McKenzie* [2008] RTR 277, CA. In a case of dangerous driving the accused's girlfriend had properly been permitted to give evidence of an incident when she was the accused's passenger and he had driven aggressively and taken dangerous risks.

[167] *R v Weir* [2006] 1 WLR 1885, CA at [7].

[168] See *R v Z* [2002] 2 AC 483, HL, considered, in this chapter, under **Introductory, 'Bad character' defined**.

[169] [2007] 1 Cr App R 225, CA.

piece of evidence is enough to convict the accused of any of the offences charged, and the important matter in issue is not whether the accused had a propensity to commit offences or to be untruthful, but whether the circumstantial evidence linking him to the offences, when viewed as a whole, points to his guilt of each offence.[170]

It remains to stress that even in cases where the misconduct did result in a conviction, in some such cases, as already indicated, propensity can only be established by going beyond the fact of the conviction and introducing evidence of the misconduct which resulted in the conviction. Where, in such a case, the conviction was based on a guilty plea, it is submitted that under the Act, as at common law, it would not be unfair for the prosecution to prove the plea, together with confessions made by the accused in police interviews. Although this denies the accused the opportunity to cross-examine the victim or other witnesses to the offence of which he stands convicted, it is fairer to the accused to adduce only what he admitted rather than to call the victim or other witnesses, who may give additional prejudicial evidence.[171]

Misconduct which is disputed

As at common law,[172] if evidence of the accused's misconduct is admissible on the issue of his guilt, it is no bar to its admissibility that it is disputed and that the jury may, in the event, reject it. Thus although bad character evidence may take the form of conclusive or indisputable evidence, it may also take the form of unproved allegations, as when, as we have seen, propensity is advanced by way of multiple counts none of which has been proved, their proof being a question for the jury.[173] Equally, however, it is submitted that the evidence must be cogent enough to lead a reasonable jury to conclude, as a possibility, that the misconduct did in fact occur. In *Harris v DPP*,[174] a common law authority, the evidence was insufficiently cogent. H, a police constable, charged and tried on an indictment containing eight counts of larceny, was acquitted on the first seven but convicted on the eighth. The offences occurred in May, June, and July 1951 and the evidence showed that on each occasion someone had entered, by the same method, the same office in Bradford market and stolen only part of the money which could have been taken. On the first seven counts, the only evidence connecting H with the offences was that none of them had occurred when he was on leave and on each occasion he might have been on solitary duty in the vicinity of the market. Concerning the eighth count, H was on duty in the market at the relevant time and was found by detectives near the office shortly after the sounding of a burglar alarm. The stolen money was found hidden in a nearby bin. The House of Lords quashed the conviction because the judge had failed to warn the jury that the evidence on the first seven counts could not confirm the eighth charge. As Lord Morton observed, H was not proved to have been near the office or even in the market at the time when the first seven thefts occurred.[175]

In *R v Brima*[176] it was made clear that the task of the judge is not to determine whether misconduct does establish propensity, an issue for the jury, but whether it has the capacity to do

---

[170] *R v Wallace* [2008] 1 WLR 572, CA. See also *R v Freeman* [2009] 1 Cr App R 137, CA, where evidence relating to two or more counts in the same indictment was 'cross-admissible'.

[171] See *R v Bedford* (1990) 93 Cr App R 113, CA.

[172] See *R v Rance and Herron* (1975) 62 Cr App R 118, CA.

[173] *R v Chopra* [2007] 1 Cr App R 225, CA at [15].

[174] [1952] AC 694.

[175] Cf *R v Mansfield* (1977) 65 Cr App R 276, CA. See also *R v Lunt* (1986) 85 Cr App R 241, CA (similar fact evidence provided by an accomplice) and *R v Seaman* (1978) 67 Cr App R 234, CA.

[176] [2007] 1 Cr App R 316, CA.

element. The accused was convicted of counts of rape and incest. The victims were his two daughters. The trial judge found striking similarities between the various offences in (i) the extreme discipline exercised over the daughters; (ii) abortions carried out on each girl paid for by P; and (iii) the acquiescence of the mother in P's sexual attentions to the daughters. The Court of Appeal allowed the appeal on the grounds that the similarities did not go beyond what was described as 'the incestuous father's stock-in-trade'. Thus it held that, with the possible exception of (ii), the similarities did not relate to P's modus operandi and could not be described as unusual features rendering the account of one girl more credible because mirrored in the statement of the other. The House of Lords restored the conviction. Lord Mackay LC, with whom the rest of the House concurred, after extensive citations from *DPP v Boardman*, held that, from all that was said in that case, 'the essential feature of evidence which is to be admitted is that its probative force in support of the allegation that an accused person committed a crime is sufficiently great to make it just to admit the evidence, notwithstanding that it is prejudicial to the accused in tending to show that he was guilty of another crime'.[198]

Whether the evidence has sufficient probative value to outweigh its prejudicial effect must in each case be a question of degree. Insofar as some authorities had held that similar fact evidence is inadmissible in the absence of some feature of similarity going beyond 'the pederast's or the incestuous father's stock-in-trade',[199] they were overruled. Turning to the facts, it was held that certain circumstances, when taken together, gave a sufficient probative force to the evidence of each of the girls in relation to the incidents involving the other. Those circumstances included the prolonged course of conduct in relation to each girl, the force used against each girl, the general domination of the girls and of the wife, and P's involvement in the payment for the abortions.

R v P, in making clear that probative value may but need not be derived from 'unusual characteristics', necessarily lowered the standard for admissibility.[200] Section 101(1)(d) has lowered the standard even further in that the test has become one of mere relevance, provided only that the evidence of misconduct is relevant to a matter in issue that is 'important'. It follows that evidence formerly admissible as similar fact evidence will now be admissible as 'relevant' evidence under s 101(1)(d). It also follows that evidence which would not have satisfied the test in *R v P may* also be admissible under s 101(1)(d). However, since such evidence was excluded at common law if it had insufficient probative value to outweigh its prejudicial effect, in these circumstances there is obvious scope for a defence argument that the court should exclude the evidence, either in exercise of its common law discretion to exclude on this basis (assuming, as has been submitted, the discretion survives in this context)[201] or in reliance on s 101(3), ie on the basis that admission of the evidence would have such an adverse effect on the fairness of the proceedings that the court ought not to admit it.

The admissibility of bad character evidence to prove identity
Much care is needed before admitting evidence of bad character in order to prove the identity of the accused as the offender, not least because where reliance is placed on evidence of

[198] [1991] 2 AC 447 at 460.

[199] *R v Inder* (1977) 67 Cr App R 143; *R v Clarke* (1977) 67 Cr App R 398; *R v Tudor* (18 July 1988, unreported); and *R v Brooks* (1990) 92 Cr App R 36, CA.

[200] See, eg, *R v Roy* [1992] Crim LR 185, CA; *R v Simpson* (1993) 99 Cr App R 48, CA; and *R v Gurney* [1994] Crim LR 116, CA.

[201] See, in this chapter, under **Evidence of the bad character of the defendant, Section 101 of the Criminal Justice Act 2003, Discretion to exclude.**

similar facts, in many cases the evidence, without more, will usually only show that the same person committed both offences and not that that person is the accused. It is submitted that the following principles, established at common law, remain instructive for the purposes of s 101(1)(d).

1. According to the dictum of Lord Mackay LC in *R v P*,[202] as construed by Hooper J in *R v W (John)*,[203] identity can be established where the only evidence of any substance against the accused is similar fact evidence which affords something in the nature of a personal hallmark or signature or other very striking similarity. *R v Mullen*[204] shows that even if the hallmark is not peculiar to the accused it may still be admissible if of sufficient probative force. M pleaded not guilty to three burglaries in the north-east of England, but admitted three other burglaries in which the method of entry involved use of a blowtorch to crack glass. Only six offenders from the north or north-east of England were known to have used such a method. Evidence of the burglaries to which M had admitted was properly adduced.[205] However, where such evidence is adduced, it is submitted that it should be accompanied by a very clear warning to the jury that they need to be sure that the crime was committed by the accused and not by one of the others known to commit the crime in the same strikingly similar or unusual way.

2. Identity can also be established in the absence of evidence affording something in the nature of a personal hallmark or signature. In *R v W (John)*[206] W was convicted of false imprisonment of, and indecent assault on, C in Aldershot (counts 1 and 2) and of false imprisonment of S in Farnham two weeks later (count 3). The issue in both cases was identity, but the evidence revealed no signature or other special feature. W appealed on the basis that the trial judge had failed to make it clear that the evidence on counts 1 and 2 was not admissible on count 3 and vice versa. The Court of Appeal held that the evidence on the Aldershot counts and the Farnham count did not need to be strikingly similar or of the nature of a signature. The court identified the proper test in a case of this kind:[207] evidence tending to show that a defendant has committed an offence charged in count A may be used to reach a verdict on count B and vice versa, if the circumstances of both offences (as the jury would be entitled to find them) are such as to provide sufficient probative support for the conclusion that the defendant committed both offences, and it would therefore be fair for the evidence to be used in this way notwithstanding the prejudicial effect of so doing. On the facts of the case, this test was satisfied: most (but not all) of the descriptions of the attacker fitted the appellant; the descriptions of some of the attacker's clothes fitted the clothes that the appellant was known to be wearing; the appellant lived near both attacks, having moved from Aldershot to Farnham in the period between the time of the two attacks; the attacks took place within a short time of each other; and the attacks bore certain similarities.

---

[202] [1991] 2 AC 447, at 462.
[203] [1998] 2 Cr App R 289, CA.
[204] [1992] Crim LR 735, CA.
[205] See also *R v Ruiz* [1995] Crim LR 151, CA and *R v West* [1996] 2 Cr App R 374, and cf *R v Johnson* [1995] 2 Cr App R 41, CA.
[206] [1998] 2 Cr App R 289, CA.
[207] [1998] 2 Cr App R 289 at 303.

3. In similar fact cases in which identity is in issue, in directing the jury a careful distinction needs to be drawn between the similar fact evidence and the other evidence in the case. There are two different types of situation, one calling for a 'sequential approach' and the other for a 'cumulative approach'.[208]

   (i) The sequential approach is where, in deciding whether the accused committed offence A, the jury can have regard to evidence that he also committed offence B. This sequential approach involves proof not only of similarity, but also that the accused did in fact commit offence B. In *R v McGranaghan*[209] M was convicted of three separate aggravated burglaries of homes and rapes or indecent assaults on the women occupants. M denied having had anything to do with any of the offences. The appeal was allowed on the grounds that although, on the evidence at the time of the trial, the similarities in the features of the offences rendered the evidence on each admissible in relation to the others, the jury should have been directed to consider first whether, disregarding the similarity of the facts, the other evidence in the case was sufficient to make them sure that M committed at least one of the offences. Only if they were so sure, could they then use the similarity to prove that the accused committed the other offences. Glidewell LJ said:[210] 'The similar facts go to show that the same man committed both offences, not that the defendant was that man. There must be some evidence to make the jury sure that on at least one offence the defendant was that man.'[211]

   (ii) The cumulative approach applies where there is evidence, other than the evidence of visual identification, on the basis of which the jury can conclude that offences A and B were committed by the same man, but that evidence, by itself, falls short of proving that that man was the accused in either case. In this situation, once the jury are satisfied that the 'other' evidence shows both offences to have been committed by the same man, the identification evidence of the victims can be used cumulatively in deciding whether that man was the accused. In *R v Barnes*[212] the accused was convicted of three separate offences, indecent assaults on two females and the wounding of a third. Evidence was admitted of three other similar incidents. There was no dispute that the six incidents were sufficiently similar to be admitted in order to show that all of the offences were committed by the same man. It was held that the identification evidence of the three victims could be considered cumulatively in deciding whether that man was the accused.[213]

4. In respect of the cumulative approach, it may also be used where offences A and B bear the hallmark or signature of the same gang, of which the accused is alleged to be a member. The danger, however, is that membership of the gang may alter after the

---

[208] *R v Barnes* [1995] 2 Cr App R 491, CA, relying upon *R v Downey* [1995] 1 Cr App R 547, CA.

[209] [1995] 1 Cr App R 559n, CA.

[210] [1995] 1 Cr App R 559 at 572.

[211] See also *R v Rubin* [1995] Crim LR 332, CA. The principle is confined to cases in which identification is in issue: see *R v S* [1993] Crim LR 293, CA. It is probably also confined to cases in which the indictment contains two or more counts and it is the evidence on each which is potentially admissible, in relation to the other or others, as similar fact evidence. Thus it does not extend to a case in which there is also similar fact evidence relating to an offence of which the accused already stands convicted: see *R v Black* [1995] Crim LR 640, CA. See also *R v Mullen* [1992] Crim LR 735, CA.

[212] [1995] 2 Cr App R 491, CA.

[213] See also *R v Grant* [1996] 2 Cr App R 272, CA and *R v Wallace* [2008] 1 WLR 572, CA.

commission of the first offence, and there may be nothing in the hallmark or signature which identifies the accused as opposed to the gang. For reasons of this kind, in *R v Brown*[214] it was held that the issue for the jury, once they were satisfied that the same gang committed both offences, was whether the totality of the evidence established beyond reasonable doubt that the accused was a member of the gang and then whether he was a member of the gang on both occasions.[215]

Sexual cases

Common law developments were such that by the mid-1970s it was established that there were no special rules of admissibility for sexual offences or sexual offences against men, boys, or children of either sex. In sexual cases, therefore, the admissibility of 'similar fact' evidence was decided by applying the same principles as in any other type of case. It is submitted that the position is the same under the 2003 Act and that there are no special rules in sexual cases in which evidence of bad character is sought to be admitted on the basis of its relevance to the issue of guilt under s 101(1)(d).

Evidence of sexual disposition

In the case of evidence of sexual disposition, the threshold issue, under the Act, is whether it amounts to evidence of a disposition towards, 'misconduct'[216] which, it will be recalled, means 'the commission of an offence or other reprehensible behaviour'.[217] If there is evidence of the commission of a sexual offence of the kind with which the accused is charged, then the prosecution will rely upon s 103(1)(a) and, if it resulted in a conviction, s 103(2).[218] However, in the case of sexual disposition which has not involved the commission of any offence, a disposition towards, say, paedophilia, incest, or bestiality will be regarded as evidence of disposition towards 'reprehensible behaviour', but it seems most unlikely that a homosexual disposition, any more than a heterosexual disposition, could properly be so regarded.

The admissibility of evidence of homosexual or heterosexual disposition, therefore, is not governed by the Act and will simply turn on whether it is relevant and, if so, whether it should be excluded by virtue of the common law discretion to exclude where its prejudicial effect outweighs its probative value. Such evidence, it is submitted, will very often be irrelevant or unduly prejudicial, but obviously each case will turn on its own facts.[219] Thus if the accused, charged with a sexual offence against a man, were to assert his heterosexual disposition, then evidence of his homosexual disposition would be plainly relevant to the issue.[220] The common law authorities have provided examples of the approach taken by the courts to evidence of a

---

[214] [1997] Crim LR 502, CA.

[215] See also *R v Lee* [1996] Crim LR 825, CA.

[216] Section 98, see, in this chapter, under **Introductory**, **'Bad character' defined**.

[217] Section 112(1).

[218] See, in this chapter, under **Evidence of the bad character of the defendant**, **Bad character evidence under section 101(1)(d) relevant to the guilt of the accused**, **Evidence of propensity under section 103 of the Criminal Justice Act 2003**, **Questions of proof**.

[219] See, eg, *R v IJ* [2011] EWCA Crim 2734: it was not unduly prejudicial to admit evidence of homosexual disposition to rebut the accused's defence that his son and stepson had made up allegations that he had committed sexual offences against them. Evidence that he had embarked on a year-long homosexual affair while married was, on the particular facts of the case, relevant to the true nature of his family life and whether he was a victim of malicious allegations by his son and stepson.

[220] Since such evidence is not evidence of bad character, it would not be required to be admitted under s 101(1) (f) as 'prosecution evidence to correct a false impression given by the defendant': see *R v IJ* [2011] EWCA Crim 2734.

homosexual disposition. In *DPP v Boardman*[221] the House of Lords decisively rejected the suggestion that there is a special rule for sexual offences or sexual offences against men or boys. Views expressed in a previous decision of the House in *Thompson v R*,[222] that a homosexual disposition could be regarded as an 'abnormal propensity' and could be relevant to identifying the perpetrator of sexual offences against men or boys, were repudiated. In the words of Lord Wilberforce:[223] 'In matters of experience it is for the judge to keep close to current mores. What is striking in one age is normal in another: the perversions of yesterday may be the routine or the fashions of tomorrow.'

Evidence of homosexual disposition, however, has been admitted on account of its *particular* relevance in disproving a defence of innocent association. In *R v King*,[224] a decision reached prior to *DPP v Boardman*, the appellant was convicted of a number of sexual offences against boys. His defence, in relation to some of the incidents, was innocent association. He admitted that he had met two boys in a public lavatory and asked them to spend the night in his room and also that one had slept on the floor while the other had shared his bed, but he denied the offence charged. In cross-examination he confirmed that he was a homosexual. The Court of Appeal held that this evidence fell within the principle in *Thompson v R* and had been properly admitted.

R v King may be compared with *R v Horwood*,[225] where the appellant was convicted of attempted gross indecency with a boy. The boy's evidence was that they drove to a wood, got out to look for rabbits, that the offence took place, and that he then ran away and was chased by the appellant. The appellant admitted that he had driven the boy to a wood but said that he had got out of the car to urinate and had returned to find that the boy had vanished. During police interrogation, the appellant said that he used to be a homosexual but had been cured and now went out with girls. The Court of Appeal, quashing the conviction, held that the evidence of homosexual propensity had been improperly admitted. O'Connor LJ held that it was only in exceptional circumstances that such evidence could be admitted to rebut innocent association and that *R v King* was such a case because the evidence could properly be said to be relevant to an issue before the jury. It would appear that *R v King* was distinguished on the basis of the greater degree of admitted intimacy in that case. The nature of the admitted association in the instant case (taking a boy for a drive in a car in broad daylight) was contrasted with that in *R v King* (taking a boy home and getting into bed with him).[226]

Possession of incriminating articles

At common law, evidence of the possession of articles of the kind used in the commission of the offence charged, albeit not used in the commission of the offence charged, could be admitted in order to identify the accused as the offender. Evidence of the possession of such articles is likely to be treated as evidence of a disposition towards misconduct for the purposes of s 98 of the 2003 Act, or evidence of propensity to commit offences of the kind

[221] [1975] AC 421. But see *Reza v General Medical Council* [1991] 2 All ER 796, PC.

[222] [1918] AC 221, HL.

[223] [1975] AC 421 at 444.

[224] [1967] 2 QB 338, CA. In *Thompson v R*, it could be argued that the accused's homosexual disposition could have been admitted because of its *particular* relevance to the question of whether he had been mistakenly identified as the perpetrator of offences of gross indecency with boys in a public lavatory.

[225] [1970] 1 QB 133, CA.

[226] See also *R v King* (7 Apr 1982, unreported), CA. The appellant provided boys with inducements (games and bicycles) to come to his flat.

with which the accused is charged for the purposes of s 103(1)(a), and to be admitted under s 101(1)(d) because of its relevance in identifying the accused as the offender. For example, in *R v Reading*,[227] Reading, alleged to have hijacked a lorry, was convicted of robbery and taking a motor vehicle. The Court of Criminal Appeal held that evidence of his possession of articles, including a walkie-talkie radio set and a police-type uniform capable of being used in the type of robbery charged, albeit not proved to have been used in the commission of the offence charged, was admissible to rebut his defence of alibi and mistaken identity.[228]

Bad character evidence under section 101(1)(d) relevant to the credibility of the accused

Under s 101(1)(d), as we have seen, prosecution evidence of the accused's bad character is admissible if 'it is relevant to an important matter in issue between the defendant and the prosecution' and although the test is one of simple rather than enhanced relevance, the requirement of relevance to an 'important matter' is a requirement of relevance to a matter in issue 'of substantial importance in the context of the case as a whole'.[229] Insofar as s 101(1)(d) may be used to attack the credibility of the accused, it is supplemented by s 103(1)(b), which provides as follows:

> (1) For the purposes of section 101(1)(d) the matters in issue between the defendant and the prosecution include—
>
>   ...
>
>   (b) the question whether the defendant has a propensity to be untruthful, except where it is not suggested that the defendant's case is untruthful in any respect.

The effect of s 103(1)(b) is that in any case in which the prosecution seek to rely upon s 101(1)(d) to attack the credibility of the accused, his propensity to be untruthful will always be deemed to be a matter in issue, except in the very rare cases in which it is not suggested that his case is untruthful in any respect. The exception would apply, for example, when the defence do not dispute the facts established by the prosecution and the only question is whether the judge should stop the case on the basis that the prosecution evidence, taken at its highest, is such that the jury, properly directed, could not convict on it.[230] The meaning of 'defendant's case' is undefined and unclear, but it appears to refer to the defendant's case at trial, rather than what he said during police questioning or in his disclosed defence statement but which he does not rely on at trial, albeit that in many cases the prosecution case will be that the accused is not telling the truth about a particular matter at trial having regard to what he did or did not say to the police or in his defence statement. It is submitted that a plea of not guilty, by itself, cannot lead to the conclusion that the accused's case will be untruthful in some respect, because the plea simply puts the prosecution to proof.

The admissibility of evidence of untruthfulness

The scope for use of s 103(1)(b) appears to be very limited, having regard to the views of Lord Phillips CJ in *R v Campbell*.[231]

---

[227] [1966] 1 WLR 836, CCA.

[228] Cf *R v Taylor* (1923) 17 Cr App R 109. See also *R v Mustafa* (1976) 65 Cr App R 26, CA.

[229] Section 112(1).

[230] See *R v Galbraith* [1981] 1 WLR 1039, CA; see Ch 2.

[231] [2007] 1 WLR 2798, CA at [29]–[31].

It will be comparatively rare for the case of a defendant who has pleaded not guilty not to involve some element that the prosecution suggest is untruthful. It does not, however, follow that, whenever there is an issue as to whether the defendant's case is truthful evidence can be admitted to show that he has a propensity to be untruthful.

The question whether a defendant has a propensity for being untruthful will not normally be described as an important matter in issue between the defendant and the prosecution. A propensity for untruthfulness will not, of itself, go very far to establishing the commission of a criminal offence. To suggest that a propensity for untruthfulness makes it more likely that a defendant has lied to the jury is not likely to help them. If they apply common sense they will conclude that a defendant who has committed a criminal offence may well be prepared to lie about it, even if he has not shown a propensity for lying whereas a defendant who has not committed the offence charged will be likely to tell the truth, even if he has shown a propensity for telling lies. In short, whether or not a defendant is telling the truth to the jury is likely to depend simply on whether or not he committed the offence charged. The jury should focus on the latter question rather than on whether or not he has a propensity for telling lies.

For these reasons, the only circumstances in which there is likely to be an important issue as to whether a defendant has a propensity to tell lies is where telling lies is an element of the offence charged. Even then, the propensity to tell lies is only likely to be significant if the lying is in the context of committing criminal offences, in which case the evidence is likely to be admissible under section 103(1)(a).

This reasoning, it is respectfully submitted, is flawed. It may well be that whether or not an accused is telling the truth is likely to depend on whether or not he committed the offence, but it simply does not follow that a propensity for untruthfulness is unlikely to be an important matter in issue or that evidence of such propensity is unlikely to assist the jury. As to the former, in many cases there is a direct conflict between the evidence of the accused and that of the prosecution witnesses and the question is which side is lying as opposed to mistaken, which will be a matter of importance, if not the most important matter, in the context of the case as a whole. As to the latter, in such a case it is submitted that it will plainly assist the jury to know that the accused has a propensity for untruthfulness, especially if the prosecution witnesses do not, and that this is so whether or not telling lies is an element of the offence charged.[232]

Lord Phillips' reasoning is also difficult to reconcile with the fact that under s 101(1)(e) it has been readily recognized that evidence of propensity to untruthfulness is capable of having substantial probative value in relation to the credibility of the accused.[233] The reasoning narrows the ambit of s 101(1)(d) to such an extent that it will rarely be used to admit evidence other than evidence of propensity to commit offences of the kind charged.

According to the Explanatory Notes, s 103(1)(b) 'is intended to enable the admission of a limited range of evidence such as convictions for perjury or other offences involving deception (for example, obtaining property by deception) as opposed to the wider range of evidence that will be admissible where the defendant puts his character in issue by, for example, attacking the character of another person', ie under s 101(1)(g).[234] However, the range of evidence admissible under s 101(1)(d) is neither as clear nor as limited as the Notes suggest. As to the former, for example, interesting questions are likely to arise as to which offences, other than

---

[232] Similarly, where the sole issue in a case is whether an accused's defence of duress is truthful, evidence that he has made untruthful statements in the past to get himself out of trouble with the courts will plainly be of assistance to the jury: see *R v Belogun* [2008] EWCA Crim 2006.

[233] See *R v Lawson* [2007] 1 Cr App R 178, CA and *R v Jarvis* [2008] EWCA Crim 488, CA.

[234] Explanatory Notes to the 2003 Act, para 374.

'perjury or other offences involving deception' will also be characterized as offences showing 'a propensity to be untruthful'. In *R v Hanson*[235] it was held that propensity to untruthfulness is not the same as propensity to dishonesty. Thus offences of benefit fraud may show a propensity to be untruthful but offences of theft by shoplifting may show no more than propensity to dishonesty.[236] As to the limits on the range of evidence admissible under s 101(1)(d), it is not confined to evidence of convictions, but may relate to instances of untruthfulness which did not amount to criminal behaviour, or which did amount to criminal behaviour, but did not result, or by the time of the trial in question had not resulted, in a conviction. Equally, propensity to be untruthful may be established by reference to convictions for offences other than, and not necessarily similar to, 'perjury or other offences involving deception', where it is clear that the jury rejected the accused's version of events. An example would be previous convictions for sexual offences, the accused having run an unsuccessful defence of alibi in each case. In *R v Hanson*[237] it was held that previous convictions, whether for offences of dishonesty or otherwise, are only likely to be capable of showing a propensity to be untruthful where, in the present case, truthfulness is in issue and, in the earlier case, either there was a plea of not guilty and the accused gave an account (on arrest, in interview, or in evidence) which the jury must have disbelieved, or the way in which the offence was committed shows a propensity for untruthfulness, for example by the making of false representations.[238] It was also made clear that the court's observations as to the number of previous convictions in relation to s 103(1)(a)[239] apply equally in relation to s 103(1)(b).

Where evidence is admissible under s 101(1)(d) by virtue of s 103(1)(b), the court has a discretionary power to exclude it under s 101(3).[240] In cases where evidence is admissible only to go to truthfulness or credit, there is a danger that the jury may even subconsciously and despite careful direction be influenced by the evidence on the question of propensity and thus guilt, and for this reason it has been said that 'a cautious test of admissibility' should be applied, whether on examination of the test of relevance under s 101(1)(d) or, which seems more apposite, on application of the discretion under s 101(3).[241]

Section 101(1)(e)—evidence of substantial probative value in relation to an important issue between the defendant and a co-defendant

Section 101(1)(e), like section 101(1)(d), is a single gateway providing for the admissibility of evidence going to the guilt of the defendant as well as evidence going to his credit or propensity to be untruthful. It can only be used by a co-defendant. However, simply because an application to admit evidence of bad character is made by a co-defendant, the judge is not bound to admit

---

[235] [2005] 1 WLR 3169, CA.

[236] *R v Edwards* [2006] 1 WLR 1524, CA at [33]. See also *R v Garnham* [2008] EWCA Crim 266.

[237] [2005] 1 WLR 3169, CA.

[238] See *R v Gumbrell* [2009] EWCA Crim 550: evidence of past false representations by the accused as to his competence and qualifications as a builder was properly admitted to show a propensity to make false representations. See also *R v Ellis* [2010] EWCA Crim 163. See also *R v Foster* [2009] EWCA Crim 353 at [17] where the trial judge wrongly directed the jury that they could take previous robbery convictions into account in deciding the accused's truthfulness.

[239] See, in this chapter, under **Evidence of the bad character of the defendant**, **Bad character evidence under section 101(1)(d) relevant to the guilt of the accused**, **Evidence of propensity under section 103 of the Criminal Justice Act 2003**, **The admissibility of evidence showing a propensity to offend**.

[240] Or, it is submitted, under the common law discretion. See, in this chapter, under **Evidence of the bad character of the defendant**, **Section 101 of the Criminal Justice Act 2003**, **Discretion to exclude**.

[241] See per Hughes LJ in *R v Lawson* [2007] 1 Cr App R 178, CA at [33].

it; the gateway in s 101(1)(e) must be gone through.[242] Under s 101(1)(e), evidence of the defendant's bad character is admissible if 'it has substantial probative value in relation to an important matter in issue between the defendant and a co-defendant'. According to the Explanatory Notes, the requirement that the probative value of the evidence be 'substantial' will have the effect of excluding evidence of no more than marginal or trivial value.[243] An 'important matter' is 'a matter of substantial importance in the context of the case as a whole',[244] and not, according to the Explanatory Notes, a matter of 'marginal or trivial' importance in that context;[245] and because it is the context of the case as a whole that matters, in determining an application under s 101(1)(e), analysis with a fine-tooth comb is unlikely to be helpful.[246] In *R v Lawson*[247] it was said that 'the feel' of the trial judge will often be critical on the question whether evidence is capable of having substantial probative value under s 101(1)(e) and that the Court of Appeal is unlikely to interfere unless the judge was plainly wrong or *Wednesbury* unreasonable.[248]

Admissibility

Concerning the admissibility of an accused's bad character under s 101(1)(e), in *R v Phillips*[249] the following principles were laid down.

1. When considering the admissibility of an accused's bad character under s 101(1)(e), the section, together with s 112(1), requires separate consideration of two questions. First, does the evidence that the co-accused wishes to adduce have substantial probative value? Second, is the matter in respect of which the evidence is substantially probative, a matter of substantial importance in the context of the case as a whole?

2. Although there is an element of overlap in the two questions, it is necessary to address them in turn, especially where the character evidence is not the bare fact of a conviction, but is comprised of detailed allegations and where a number of factual issues arise between the accused and co-accused.

3. The second question requires the judge to make a fact-sensitive assessment of the importance of the issue between the accused and co-accused in the context of the case as a whole. This means that where there is already evidence before the jury that is probative of the same issue, the judge is entitled to consider whether further evidence (the character evidence) is of substantial probative value to the same issue.

4. 'Substantial probative value' means enhanced capability to prove or disprove a fact in issue and the threshold is not to be understated. The purpose of the enhancement is to ensure that the probative strength of the evidence removes the risk of unfair prejudice and it is important that when considering admissibility under s 101(1)(e), regard is had for the rigour of the statutory test of *substantial* probative value to a matter in issue between the accused and co-accused which is of *substantial* importance in the context of the case as a whole.[250]

---

[242] *R v Edwards* [2006] 1 WLR 1524, CA at [1](v).

[243] Explanatory Notes, para 375. Unproven and unsupported allegations against a co-accused recorded on a police computer lack substantial probative value for the purposes of s 101(1)(e). See *R v Turner* [2011] EWCA Crim 450.

[244] Section 112(1).

[245] Explanatory Notes, para 375.

[246] *R v Edwards* [2006] 1 WLR 1524, CA at [1](v).

[247] [2007] 1 Cr App R 178, CA.

[248] *Associated Provincial Picture Houses Ltd v Wednesbury Corpn* [1948] 1 KB 223, CA.

[249] [2012] 1 Cr App R 25, CA.

[250] See also *R v Apabhai* [2011] EWCA Crim 917.

Evidence is only admissible under s 101(1)(e) on behalf of the co-defendant. The prosecution cannot rely upon s 101(1)(e), nor can another co-defendant, unless the evidence is also of substantial probative value in relation to an important matter in issue between the defendant and that other co-defendant. Section 104(2) provides that:

(2) only evidence—
    (a) which is to be (or has been) adduced by the co-defendant, or
    (b) which a witness is to be invited to give (or has given) in cross-examination by the co-defendant,
  is admissible under section 101(1)(e).

Because evidence admissible under s 101(1)(e) is only admissible on behalf of a co-defendant, there is no discretionary power to exclude it.[251] As noted previously, a co-defendant should be free to adduce any evidence relevant to his case, whether or not it prejudices the defendant, a principle established at common law and which applied in relation both to evidence going to the guilt of the defendant and to cross-examination of the defendant in order to impugn his credibility.

It will be convenient to consider separately evidence admissible under s 101(1)(e) which is relevant to the guilt of the accused and which is relevant to his credibility.

Bad character evidence under section 101(1)(e) relevant to the guilt of the accused
Evidence of propensity

R v Edwards[252] illustrates how s 101(1)(e) may be used by a co-accused to introduce evidence of the bad character of the accused which is relevant to the issue of his guilt. In *Edwards*, a case of wounding, each of the accused told an entirely different story as to what had occurred and each said that he was not involved in the violence. It was held that the previous convictions for violence of D1 had substantial probative value on the issue between him and D2, evidence of D1's propensity to commit offences of violence being relevant to the issue of which of D1 and D2 was more likely to have been the assailant.

The leading authority at common law was the decision of the House of Lords in *R v Randall*.[253] In *Randall*, R and G were tried together on a charge of murder. Each raised a cut-throat defence, blaming the other for the infliction of the fatal injuries. Both thereby lost the protection of s 1 of the 1898 Act and were asked questions about their previous convictions and bad character. R had relatively minor convictions. G had a bad record, including convictions for burglary, when he had armed himself with a screwdriver. G also admitted that he had been involved in a robbery in which all the robbers had been armed with knives. The House of Lords held that in the particular circumstances of the case the evidence of G's propensity to use and threaten violence was relevant not only in relation to the truthfulness of his evidence, but also because the imbalance between that history and the antecedent history of R tended to show that the version of events put forward by R was more probable than that put forward by G. Lord Steyn said:[254]

> Postulate a joint trial involving two accused arising from an assault committed in a pub. Assume it to be clear that one of the two men committed the assault. The one man has a long list of

[251] *R v Assani* [2008] EWCA Crim 2563 at [10]; [2009] Crim LR 514, CA.
[252] [2006] 3 All ER 882, CA at [51]–[52].
[253] [2004] 1 WLR 56. See also Elliott, 'Cut Throat Tactics: the freedom of an accused to prejudice a co-accused' [1991] Crim LR 5.
[254] At [22].

previous convictions involving assaults in pubs. It shows him to be prone to fighting when he has consumed alcohol. The other man has an unblemished record. Relying on experience and common sense one may rhetorically ask why the propensity to violence of one man should not be deployed by the other man as part of his defence that he did not commit the assault. Surely such evidence is capable, depending on the jury's assessment of all the evidence, of making it more probable that the man with the violent disposition when he had consumed alcohol committed the assault. To rule that the jury may use the convictions in regard to his credibility but that convictions revealing his propensity to violence must otherwise be ignored is to ask the jury to put to one side their common sense and experience. It would be curious if the law compelled such an unrealistic result.

Later, Lord Steyn said:[255]

> For the avoidance of doubt I would further add that in my view where evidence of propensity of a co-accused is relevant to a fact in issue between the Crown and the other accused it is not necessary for a trial judge to direct the jury to ignore that evidence in considering the case against the co-accused. Justice does not require that such a direction be given. Moreover, such a direction would needlessly perplex juries.

This passage, however, is open to differing interpretations. *R v Randall* was followed in *R v Price*,[256] a murder trial where one accused, another, *or both*, had committed the offence. It was held that the propensity of D2 to be aggressive was relevant to the question whether, had only one person killed the deceased, that person was D1, and did not become irrelevant simply because, if the jury answered no to that question, they still had to decide whether D1 had been a party to the attack. It was further held that the evidence was relevant to determination of the Crown's case against D2 and could be taken into account by the jury against D2 'as they thought appropriate'.

R v Randall was distinguished in *R v B (C)*,[257] where there was no joint charge, no cut-throat defence, no attempt to support the credibility of D1 by reference to the evidence of D2's previous misconduct, and that evidence, therefore, had no relevance to D1's defence. As to Lord Steyn's dictum 'for the avoidance of doubt', the court was of the view that where D2's propensity becomes relevant as between D1 and the Crown, no distinction is to be attempted in viewing the position as between D2 and the Crown ('the Crown becomes the beneficiary'), but added that the jury should be warned to be cautious before using propensity as a guide to guilt. In *R v Mertens*,[258] on the other hand, it was held that the 'evidence of propensity' to which Lord Steyn had referred was evidence of disposition admissible on behalf of the Crown and that where the evidence of D2's misconduct is not admissible on that basis, although it can be relied upon by D1 in his case against the Crown with a view to showing that D2 was more likely to have committed the offence, it should be disregarded in considering the case against D2.[259] However, as Hooper LJ observed in *R v Robinson*,[260] if the evidence was, in any event, admissible at the behest of the Crown, then there was no need for Lord Steyn to address the issue.

---

[255] At [35].

[256] [2005] Crim LR 304. See also *R v Robinson* [2006] 1 Cr App R 480, CA.

[257] [2004] 2 Cr App R 570, CA.

[258] [2005] Crim LR 301, CA.

[259] See also *R v Murrell* [2005] Crim LR 869, CA: it is perfectly possible to describe the Crown's case against D2 without referring to the evidence admissible in support of D1, before making clear the relevance of that evidence.

[260] [2006] 1 Cr App R 480, CA at [71].

In *R v Miller*,[261] A, B, and C were charged with conspiracy to evade customs duties. B's
defence was that he was not concerned in the illegal acts but that C masqueraded as him
(B) and used his (B's) office for their commission. In furtherance of that defence, B's counsel
asked a prosecution witness whether C was not in prison during a period when no illegal
importations had occurred. Devlin J held that whereas in the case of the prosecution there
is a duty to exclude questions tending to show the previous commission of some crime if its
prejudicial effect outweighs its probative value, no such limitation applies to a question asked
by counsel for a co-accused, whose duty is to adduce any evidence relevant to his case whether
or not it prejudices any other accused. The evidence was relevant to B's case and accordingly was
admissible.[262] The dicta of Devlin J in *R v Miller* were affirmed in *R v Neale*,[263] a decision on the
other side of the line. N and B were charged with arson and manslaughter. Counsel for N sought
to adduce evidence, either by cross-examining prosecution witnesses or by calling evidence himself, that B had admitted that he had started fires by himself on four other occasions. The Court
of Appeal upheld the ruling of the trial judge that the evidence was inadmissible: it was evidence
only of B's propensity to commit wanton and unaided arson and contained nothing of relevance
to N's defence, which was that at the relevant time he was elsewhere and asleep in bed.[264] In *R v
Randall*[265] the House of Lords considered that *R v Neale* was a borderline decision and 'wondered'
how the case would have been decided if N had admitted that he was on the scene.

Propensity where the accused has put his own character in issue
Miller was also approved by the Privy Council in *R v Lowery*[266] where either the accused L or
K, or both, must have murdered a little girl. L emphasized his good character and said that his
fear of K meant that he could not prevent the murder. K said that he was under the influence
of drugs and was powerless to prevent L from killing. The Privy Council held that, because L
had put his character in issue by stating that he was not the sort of man to have committed
the offence, K was properly allowed to call evidence of a psychologist to the effect that L was
aggressive, lacked self-control, and was more likely to have committed the offence than K. In
R v Douglass[267] it was held that where a cut-throat defence is being run by two accused jointly
charged with an offence and evidence of the bad character of one of them is relevant to the
guilt or innocence of the other, the evidence is admissible whether they are alleged to have
committed the offence by way of joint enterprise or by separate but contributory means. D
and P were charged with causing death by reckless driving. The prosecution alleged that D had
been drinking and was trying to prevent P from overtaking and that P, in vying for position,
had collided with an oncoming car. P did not testify, but his counsel cross-examined P's girlfriend to elicit from her that P had never drunk alcohol in the two years that she had known
him. The clear purpose was to suggest that P, unlike D, was unlikely to have been affected by

[261] [1952] 2 All ER 667, Winchester Assizes.
[262] See also *R v Bracewell* (1978) 68 Cr App R 44 per Ormrod LJ at 50: 'The problem generally arises in connection
with evidence tendered by the Crown, so that marginal cases can be dealt with by the exercise of the discretion.
"When in doubt, exclude", is a good working rule in such cases. But where the evidence is tendered by a co-accused,
the test of relevance must be applied, and applied strictly...'.
[263] (1977) 65 Cr App R 304. See also *R v Campbell and Williams* [1993] Crim LR 448, CA and *R v Myers* [1997] 4 All
ER 314, HL (see Ch 13).
[264] See also *R v Nightingale* [1977] Crim LR 744 and *R v Knutton* (1992) 97 Cr App R 115, CA.
[265] [2004] 1 WLR 56, HL.
[266] [1974] AC 85, PC.
[267] (1989) 89 Cr App R 264, CA. Cf *R v Kennedy* [1992] Crim LR 37, CA.

alcohol so as to have driven badly. Applying *Lowery v R*, *R v Bracewell*, and *R v Miller*, it was held that where one accused adduces evidence of his own lack of propensity and this goes to the issue of a co-accused's guilt, the co-accused may call contradictory evidence. Accordingly, D should have been allowed to adduce evidence of P's previous convictions for motoring offences, including two drink-driving offences.

In both *Lowery v R* and *R v Douglass* the evidence was admitted against an accused who had put his character in issue.[268] However in *R v Randall* the House of Lords, while approving *Lowery v R*, was confident that 'there must be cases in which the propensity of one accused may be relied on by the other, irrespective of whether he has put his character in issue'.[269]

Bad character evidence under section 101(1)(e) relevant to the credibility of the accused

Insofar as s 101(1)(e) permits a co-accused to introduce evidence of the bad character of the accused which is relevant to his credibility, it is qualified by s 104(1), which provides as follows:

(1) Evidence which is relevant to the question whether the defendant has a propensity to be untruthful is admissible on that basis under section 101(1)(e) only if the nature or conduct of his defence is such as to undermine the co-defendant's defence.

One might have supposed that the phrase 'propensity to be untruthful' would bear the same restrictive meaning in s 104(1) as it is said to bear in s 103(1)(b)[270] and that generally it would be as unlikely to assist the jury as is thought to be the case under s 103(1)(b).[271] However, in *R v Lawson*[272] the court, while accepting that an offence of dishonesty will not necessarily be capable of establishing a propensity for untruthfulness, held that it did not follow that previous convictions not involving the making of false statements or the giving of false evidence are incapable of having substantial probative value in relation to the credibility of an accused. The court was also of the view that 'unreliability'—and it is possible that the court fell into error at this point by departing from the statutory wording of 'propensity to be untruthful'— was capable of being shown by conduct which did not involve an offence of untruthfulness, ranging from large-scale drug- or people-trafficking via housebreaking to criminal violence; but that whether in a particular case conduct is in fact capable of having the requisite probative value is for the trial judge to decide on all the facts. On the facts of the case before it, it was held that the trial judge was entitled to conclude that a previous conviction for wounding did have the requisite probative value in relation to the credibility of the accused who was charged with manslaughter. Unfortunately, however, no reasons are given—it was felt to be sufficient to defer to 'the feel of the trial judge'.[273]

---

[268] See also *R v Sullivan* (2003) The Times, 18 Mar and *R v Rafiq* [2005] Crim LR 963, CA.

[269] [2004] 1 WLR 56, per Lord Steyn at [29]. See also *R v Robinson* [2006] 1 Cr App R 480, CA.

[270] See *R v Hanson* [2005] 1 WLR 3169, CA, in this chapter, in text at n 235. Propensity to be untruthful is not restricted to evidence of past untruthfulness in the witness box: see *R v Jarvis* [2008] Crim LR 266, CA.

[271] See *R v Campbell* [2007] 1 WLR 2789, CA, in this chapter, under **Evidence of the bad character of the defendant, Bad character evidence under section 101(1)(d) relevant to the guilt of the accused, Bad character evidence under section 101(1)(d) relevant to the credibility of the accused, The admissibility of evidence of untruthfulness**.

[272] [2007] 1 Cr App R 178, CA.

[273] See also *R v Miah* [2011] Crim LR 662, CA, where, in a case of murder by arson, the Court of Appeal stated obiter that it was very difficult to see how one accused's previous conviction for robbery had substantial probative value in relation to his credibility, given his guilty plea. For an exploration of the difficulties of construction posed by s 104, see Munday, 'Cut-throat Defences and the "Propensity to be Untruthful" under s. 104 of the Criminal Justice Act 2003' [2005] Crim LR 624.

The words 'nature or conduct of his defence' in s 104(1) make clear that the defence of the co-accused may be undermined not only by the evidence of the accused or witnesses called on his behalf, but also in cross-examination of witnesses called by the prosecution or co-accused. The words 'nature or conduct' were also used in s 1(3)(ii) of the Criminal Evidence Act 1898, under which the accused could lose his shield and be cross-examined on his bad character when the nature or conduct of the defence was such as to involve imputations on the character of, among others, witnesses for the prosecution. For the purposes of s 1(3)(ii) of the 1898 Act it was held in *R v Jones*[274] that answers given by an accused under cross-examination were generally to be treated as part of the cross-examiner's case and therefore prima facie should not be taken into account, and that the shield should not be lost where the accused was trapped into making an imputation by the form of the question put.[275] On the other hand, it was held that the shield could be lost where the imputation was not necessary in answer to the question put[276] or was voluntary and gratuitous.[277] These principles, it is submitted, remain valid, in the context of s 104, in relation to cross-examination of the accused, whether at the hands of the prosecution or a co-accused.

Under s 1(3)(iii) of the 1898 Act an accused could lose his shield where he had 'given evidence against' a co-accused.[278] In the leading case of *Murdoch v Taylor*[279] the House of Lords held that 'evidence against' included evidence which either supported the prosecution's case in a material respect or 'undermined the defence' of a co-accused. *Murdoch v Taylor* and some of the subsequent decisions provide much valuable guidance as to the way in which s 104(1) is likely to be interpreted, both generally and in relation to the phrase 'to undermine the co-defendant's defence'.

In *Murdoch v Taylor* it was held that s 1(3)(iii) does not refer only to evidence given by one accused against another with hostile intent, that it is the effect of the evidence upon the minds of the jury which is material and not the state of mind of the person who gives it, and that the test to be applied is therefore objective and not subjective. The same may be said, it is submitted, in relation to s 104(1). However, s 104(1) of the 2003 Act is narrower in its scope than s 1(3)(iii) of the 1898 Act, as interpreted in *Murdoch v Taylor*, in that the former is not triggered by evidence which does no more than support the prosecution case. Thus although in many cases evidence which supports the prosecution case will also undermine the defence of the co-accused, if the evidence supports the prosecution case but does not undermine the defence of the co-accused, because for example he has not raised a defence, evidence of the accused's bad character will not be admissible to attack his credibility under s 101(1)(e).[280] Such evidence will also be inadmissible, it is submitted, where the accused gives evidence to the same effect as the prosecution on a factual matter on which there is no issue between the Crown and the co-accused, because such evidence will not undermine the defence of the co-accused.[281] However, it would seem that if a co-accused has only a scintilla or iota of a defence, as when his defence is almost completely

---

[274] (1909) 3 Cr App R 67, CCA.

[275] See also and cf *R v Britzman; R v Hall* [1983] 1 WLR 350, CA.

[276] *R v Jones* (1909) 3 Cr App R 67, CCA.

[277] *R v Courtney* [1995] Crim LR 63, CA.

[278] In *R v Miah* [2011] Crim LR 662, CA under the 2003 Act, the accused did not give evidence, and statements implicating the co-accused which were made by the accused in police interview and to medical experts (who interviewed the accused in relation to a defence of diminished responsibility) were not *evidence against* the co-accused.

[279] [1965] AC 574, HL.

[280] Cf *R v Adair* [1990] Crim LR 571, CA.

[281] Cf *R v Crawford* [1998] 1 Cr App R 338, CA.

undermined by his own testimony which, although he declines to change his plea, amounts to an admission of guilt, there is still the possibility of undermining it.[282]

The meaning of 'undermining' the defence

The meaning of undermining the defence of the co-accused gave rise to some difficulty in cases in which the accused appeared merely to have contradicted the evidence given by a co-accused or to have denied participation in a joint venture. In *R v Bruce*[283] it was held that evidence which undermined a co-accused's defence would only trigger s 1(3)(iii) if it made his acquittal less likely.[284] Eight accused were charged with robbery, one of whom, M, admitted that there had been a plan to commit robbery but said that he had not been a party to its execution. Another accused, B, testified that there had been no plan to rob. Counsel for M was then permitted to cross-examine B about his previous convictions. B, acquitted of robbery but convicted of theft, appealed. The Court of Appeal held that s 1(3)(iii) had not been triggered because although B had contradicted M, his evidence was more in M's favour than against him in that it provided him with a different and possibly better defence.[285] It remains to be seen whether s 104(1) of the 2003 Act will be interpreted in the same way.

It seems clear, however, from the decisions in *R v Davis*[286] and *R v Varley*,[287] that evidence which on its face amounts to no more than a denial of participation in a crime or which appears merely to contradict something said by a co-accused, may, in appropriate circumstances, undermine the defence of a co-accused. In *R v Davis*, D and O were jointly charged with the theft of certain items in circumstances such that the offence had been committed by either one or both of them. D, having denied the theft of one of the items, was cross-examined under s 1(3)(iii). He appealed on the ground that a mere denial did not amount to giving evidence against a co-accused. The Court of Appeal held that as only D, O, or both of them could have stolen the items in question, D's denial that he had done so necessarily meant that O had, and the appeal was dismissed.[288] In *R v Varley*, V and D were jointly charged with robbery. D's defence was that he did take part but was forced to do so by threats on his life by V. V gave evidence that he had not taken part in the robbery and that D's evidence was untrue. D's counsel was given leave to cross-examine V as to his previous convictions. V was convicted and appealed. Dismissing the appeal, it was held that a mere denial of participation in a joint venture is not of itself sufficient to trigger s 1(3)(iii)—for s 1(3)(iii) such denial 'must' lead to the conclusion that if the one accused did not participate then it must have been the other who did. It was further held that where one accused asserts a view of the joint venture which is directly contradicted by the other, such contradiction may be evidence against the co-accused. Applying these principles to the facts of the case, V's evidence was against D because it amounted to saying not only that D was telling lies, but also that D was a participant on his own and not acting under duress.

---

[282] *R v Mir* [1989] Crim LR 894, CA.

[283] [1975] 1 WLR 1252, CA. Cf *R v Hatton* (1976) 64 Cr App R 88, CA. A denied that there was a plan to steal scrap metal. H gave evidence that both he and A had been parties to a plan to steal but denied that either of them had acted dishonestly. It was held that H had given evidence against A.

[284] Per Stephenson LJ [1975] 1 WLR 1252 at 1259.

[285] The appeal was dismissed because of the overwhelming evidence of guilt. See also *R v Kirkpatrick* [1998] Crim LR 63, CA.

[286] [1975] 1 WLR 345, CA.

[287] [1982] 75 Cr App R 242, CA.

[288] Cf *R v Hendrick* [1992] Crim LR 427, CA.

In *R v Crawford*[289] the victim of a robbery alleged that she had been alone in the lavatories of a restaurant with three other women, all of whom had committed the offence. The three were the accused, C, her co-accused, A, and a third woman, L. C's evidence was to the effect that A and L were in the lavatories at the material time, but that she, C, was not. A's evidence, which was put to C during cross-examination, was that C and L had committed the robbery while she, A, was merely an innocent bystander. It was held that the trial judge had properly allowed A to cross-examine C on her previous convictions, because if the jury accepted C's evidence that only A and L were in the lavatories at the material time, that was very damaging to the credibility of A and made it much less likely that A was simply a passive bystander.[290] It was submitted on appeal that this outcome was in conflict with the proposition in *R v Varley* to the effect that, for s 1(3)(iii) to apply, a mere denial of participation in a joint venture 'must' lead to the conclusion that if the accused did not participate, then it must have been the co-accused who did: this was not a case where it was either C or A who had committed the offence, and if it was not C therefore it must have been A. Rejecting this submission, the Court of Appeal held that, insofar as the proposition from *R v Varley* had been cast in mandatory terms, it went too far: the word 'may' was more appropriate.

In *R v Edwards*[291] it was held, referring to *R v Varley*, that whether an accused's stance amounts to no more than a denial of participation or gives rise to an important matter in issue between a defendant and a co-defendant under s 101(1)(e) will inevitably turn on the facts of the individual case. It is submitted that in appropriate circumstances, evidence of a conviction admissible under s 101(1)(e) to impugn the credibility of the accused need not be confined to the fact of the previous conviction but may extend to the details of the offence. This would reflect the position in relation to s 1(3)(iii) of the 1898 Act.[292]

Section 101(1)(f)—prosecution evidence to correct a false impression given by the defendant

Under s 101(1)(f), prosecution evidence of the defendant's bad character is admissible if 'it is evidence to correct a false impression given by the defendant'.[293] Section 101(1)(f), together with s 105, by which it is supplemented, are based upon the recommendations of the Law Commission, but lack the Commission's important safeguards. These included a requirement of enhanced relevance, ie *substantial* probative value in correcting the false impression, a requirement to consider a number of detailed factors and, in the case of evidence of prejudicial effect, a requirement that admissibility be in the interests of justice.[294] Furthermore, although it is submitted that evidence admissible under s 101(1)(f) is subject to the common

---

[289] [1998] 1 Cr App R 338, CA.

[290] Cf *R v Kirkpatrick* [1998] Crim LR 63, CA.

[291] [2006] 1 WLR 1524 at [1](vi).

[292] See also *R v Reid* [1989] Crim LR 719, CA. Cf *R v McLeod* [1994] 1 WLR 1500, CA, in this chapter, under **Evidence of the bad character of the defendant, Section 101(1)(g)—prosecution evidence where the defendant has made an attack on another person's character, Similarities between the facts of previous offences and the offence charged**.

[293] See *R v Assani* [2008] All ER (D) 188 (Nov), CA which makes it clear that the gateways under s 101(1)(f) and (g) (see in this chapter under **Evidence of the bad character of the defendant, Section 101(1)(g)—prosecution evidence where the defendant has made an attack on another person's character**) are restricted to prosecution evidence and are not available to a co-accused.

[294] Law Com No 273, Cm 5257 (2001), Draft Bill, cl 10.

law discretion to exclude and s 78 of the Police and Criminal Evidence Act 1984, it is not subject to the exclusionary discretion in s 101(3).

Section 105 of the 2003 Act provides as follows:

(1) For the purposes of section 101(1)(f)—
   (a) the defendant gives a false impression if he is responsible for the making of an express or implied assertion which is apt to give the court or jury a false or misleading impression about the defendant;
   (b) evidence to correct such an impression is evidence which has probative value in correcting it.
(2) A defendant is treated as being responsible for the making of an assertion if—
   (a) the assertion is made by the defendant in the proceedings (whether or not in evidence given by him),
   (b) the assertion was made by the defendant—
      (i) on being questioned under caution, before charge, about the offence with which he is charged, or
      (ii) on being charged with the offence or officially informed that he might be prosecuted for it, and evidence of the assertion is given in the proceedings,
   (c) the assertion is made by a witness called by the defendant,
   (d) the assertion is made by any witness in cross-examination in response to a question asked by the defendant that is intended to elicit it, or is likely to do so, or
   (e) the assertion was made by any person out of court, and the defendant adduces evidence of it in the proceedings.
(3) A defendant who would otherwise be treated as responsible for the making of an assertion shall not be so treated if, or to the extent that, he withdraws it or disassociates himself from it.
(4) Where it appears to the court that a defendant, by means of his conduct (other than the giving of evidence) in the proceedings, is seeking to give the court or jury an impression about himself that is false or misleading, the court may if it appears just to do so treat the defendant as being responsible for the making of an assertion which is apt to give that impression.
(5) In subsection (4) 'conduct' includes appearance or dress.
(6) Evidence is admissible under section 101(1)(f) only if it goes no further than is necessary to correct the false impression.
(7) Only prosecution evidence is admissible under section 101(1)(f).

Whether the accused has given a false impression is obviously a question for the judge. That question and the question whether there is evidence which may properly serve to correct the false impression, are fact-specific.[295] It is submitted that the risk of prejudice, where corrective evidence is admitted only to be subsequently ruled inadmissible, is such that in many cases the question of admissibility will need to be the subject of a ruling by the judge in the absence of the jury. Indeed, where the accused denies that the impression conveyed is false and disputes the corrective evidence on which the prosecution seek to rely, it would seem that the judge could only properly decide the matter by holding a *voir dire*.

False impression by express or implied assertions, or assertions by conduct

A simple denial of the offence cannot be treated as either an express or implied false impression for the purposes of s 101(1)(f).[296] 'Express' false assertions, for the purposes of s 105(1)(a), would cover, for example, false assertions that the accused is of good character or a religious

---

[295] *R v Renda* [2006] 1 WLR 2948, CA at [19].
[296] *R v Weir* [2006] 1 WLR 1885, CA at [43].

man or a man who earns an honest living or who would never use violence. 'Implied' false assertions would cover false assertions relating to the accused's conduct or behaviour from which it can be implied that he is of good character or honest. *R v Samuel*,[297] a decision under s 1(3)(ii) of the 1898 Act, provides a good example. In that case, the accused, charged with larceny, gave evidence of previous occasions on which he had restored lost property to its owner and was held to have been properly cross-examined about his previous convictions for theft. Section 105(1)(a) is also apt to cover false assertions by the accused about his bad character. If, for example, the accused, charged with a sexual offence, falsely asserts that he has only one previous conviction, also for a sexual offence, then corrective evidence would be admissible that in fact he also has previous convictions for offences of dishonesty. *R v Spartley*[298] provides an example of where evidence, not of convictions but of misconduct, was admitted to correct a false impression. The accused was charged with conspiracy to import ecstasy and possession of cannabis with intent to supply. In his police interview he stated that he had never been involved in the supply of drugs. It was held that evidence from an interview with Dutch police some seven years earlier, in which he had admitted being a cannabis courier between Spain and Holland, was admissible under s 101(1)(f) to correct the false impression.

An example of a false or misleading impression conveyed by conduct, for the purposes of s 105(4) and (5), would be an accused who, not being a priest, appears in the proceedings wearing a clerical dog collar. However, an accused with many previous convictions for dishonesty does not make a false assertion as to his good character by simply taking the oath or reminding the jury of the oath that he has sworn on the Bible and, on that reasoning, nor will he do so by his conduct in holding and gesticulating with a Bible while in the witness box.[299]

Under s 105(4), the court will only treat the accused as being responsible for the making of an assertion by means of his conduct 'if it appears just to do so', a hurdle presumably designed to prevent overuse or abuse of the subsection. For example, many accused will dress up for their court appearance, wearing outfits which they would normally wear only on very special occasions. Section 105 should not cover, it is submitted, the case of the plumber or plasterer who appears in court in his best suit. It would be otherwise, however, if he were to sport a regimental tie or blazer, never having served in the army.

The evidence correcting a false impression

Evidence to correct the false impression must have probative value in correcting it,[300] but must go no further than is necessary to correct it.[301] Thus if the accused expressly asserts that he 'earns an honest living', the corrective evidence may include evidence of his previous convictions for crimes of dishonesty, but not evidence of his previous convictions for, say, assault or driving with excess alcohol. However, problems are likely to be encountered, in some cases, in identifying precisely what the false or misleading impression is. For example, if an accused is charged with inflicting grievous bodily harm in an 'off the ball' incident during the course of a rugby match, and gives evidence that he has no previous convictions, is evidence admissible to show his disciplinary record of violent play on the rugby field?[302] The same problem

[297] (1956) 40 Cr App R 8, CCA.
[298] [2007] 151 Sol Jo LB 670, CA.
[299] See *R v Robinson* [2001] Crim LR 478, CA, decided under the 1898 Act, s 1(3)(ii).
[300] Section 105(1)(b).
[301] Section 105(6).
[302] Applying the 1898 Act, s 1(3)(ii), the answer in *R v Marsh* [1994] Crim LR 52, CA was, 'Yes'.

exists in the case of implied assertions or assertions by conduct. The accused wearing a clerical collar presumably conveys the impression not only that he is a priest, but also that he behaves as a priest should, and therefore the corrective evidence should not be confined to evidence which goes to show that he is not a priest, or has been defrocked, but should extend to general evidence of his misconduct or disposition to misconduct.

Withdrawal or disassociation from an assertion

Under s 105(2)(d), an accused is treated as being responsible for the making of an assertion made by a witness cross-examined by (or, presumably, on behalf of) him, but only if the assertion was in response to a question intended to elicit it or which was likely to elicit it. Thus if the witness volunteers a false impression about the accused, the accused will not be treated as being responsible for the making of the volunteered assertion and evidence will be admissible to correct it. In contrast, under s 105(2)(c) an accused is treated as being responsible for the making of an assertion made by a witness called by him, and corrective evidence will be admissible in this situation where the witness volunteers a false impression as much as when he asserts it in answer to a question intended to elicit it or which was likely to elicit it. However, in this situation it seems that the accused can prevent the introduction of corrective evidence by disassociating himself from the assertion made by the witness, in reliance upon s 105(3). An accused who no longer stands by a false assertion made by him and introduced in evidence under s 105(2)(b) by the prosecution, would also be well advised to withdraw it.

In cases in which the accused himself makes, or adduces evidence of, a false assertion, s 105(3) also provides him with the opportunity to embark upon a damage limitation exercise. For example, if the accused makes, or adduces evidence of, a false assertion to the effect that he is of good character, but then withdraws or disassociates himself from the assertion, he will thereby prevent the admission of corrective evidence of, say, his previous convictions, but the jury will by then be aware that he is not of good character and also, in cases in which the assertion was made by him in giving his evidence, that he is not always a reliable witness. However, an accused must take the initiative if he wishes to rely on s 105(3); a concession extracted in cross-examination will not normally amount to a withdrawal or disassociation for the purposes of s 105(3).[303]

Corrective evidence as to guilt or credibility of the accused

Given the breadth of provision for the admissibility of evidence of disposition under s 101(1)(d), presumably such evidence will only rarely be admitted as corrective evidence under s 101(1)(f). Where such evidence is admitted under s 101(1)(f), however, it seems clear that it will go not only to the credibility of the accused but also to the likelihood of his guilt, and that the jury should be directed accordingly. It remains to be seen whether the position will be the same in the case of corrective evidence which involves misconduct, ie the commission of an offence or other reprehensible behaviour. However, it is submitted that there is much force in the argument that where an accused makes, or adduces evidence of, a false assertion as to his good character, he generally does so for the purpose of showing that it is unlikely that he committed the offence charged, and the corrective evidence is introduced to show the contrary, and not merely to attack his credibility.[304]

---

[303] *R v Renda* [2006] 1 WLR 2948, CA at [21].

[304] For dicta to this effect in relation to the 1898 Act, s 1(3)(ii), see per Viscount Sankey in *Maxwell v DPP* [1935] AC 309 at 319 and per Lord Goddard CJ in *R v Samuel* (1956) 40 Cr App R 8 at 12.

Discretionary exclusion

If, as has been submitted, prosecution evidence admissible under s 101 may be excluded in reliance upon the common law discretionary power to exclude prosecution evidence the prejudicial effect of which outweighs its probative value, there may well be only limited scope for the exercise of the discretion in relation to evidence admissible under s 101(1)(f) since the exclusion of such evidence may seriously mislead the jury.[305]

Section 101(1)(g)—prosecution evidence where the defendant has made an attack on another person's character

Under s 101(1)(g) of the 2003 Act, prosecution evidence of the accused's bad character is admissible if 'the defendant has made an attack on another person's character'. Where s 101(1)(g) is triggered, evidence of the accused's bad character is admissible even if he elects not to testify.[306] The purpose of the gateway was explained by Underhill J in *R v Lamaletie*:[307]

> The conception underlying [the] gateway…is that where a defendant has impugned the character of a prosecution witness the jury will be assisted in deciding who to believe by knowing the defendant's character.

Section 101(1)(g), as supplemented by s 106, is in some measure based on the recommendations of the Law Commission but, as in the case of s 101(1)(f), lacks the Commission's important safeguards, including the requirement of enhanced relevance, the requirement to consider a number of detailed factors and, in the case of evidence of prejudicial effect, the requirement that admissibility be in the interests of justice.[308] The provisions also depart from the recommendation that evidence should not be admissible under the gateway where the attack has to do with the alleged facts of the offence or is in connection with the investigation or prosecution of the offence, as when the accused blames another for the offence or asserts that another has invented the allegation against him.[309]

The evidence admissible

In terms of the evidence admissible under the gateway, the courts take the 'broad brush' approach.[310] Accordingly, convictions will be admitted which differ significantly from the offence charged, but which nonetheless enable the jury to know from what sort of person allegations against the witness came.[311] In *R v C*,[312] the Court of Appeal observed that where credibility is in issue, the authorities demonstrated that 'all the convictions of an accused

---

[305] See *R v Marsh* [1994] Crim LR 52, CA, in this chapter, under **Evidence of the bad character of the defendant, Section 101(1)(f)—prosecution evidence to correct a false impression given by the defendant, The evidence correcting a false impression**. See also *R v D* [2012] EWCA Crim 2163.

[306] At common law, if the accused did not give evidence but attacked witnesses for the prosecution, then, without more, evidence of the accused's bad character could not be introduced: *R v Butterwasser* [1948] 1 KB 4, CCA.

[307] (2008) 172 JP 249, CA at [15]. Lord Devlin's explanation in *R v Cook* [1959] 2 QB 340 at 347 of the same principle underlying the old law was cited with approval.

[308] Law Com No 273, Cm 5257 (2001), Draft Bill, cl 9.

[309] See Law Com No 273, Cm 5257 (2001), Draft Bill, cl 9(2).

[310] Spencer, *Evidence of Bad Character* (Oxford, 2009) para 4.138. See also *R v W* [2011] Crim 472.

[311] See *R v Singh* [2007] EWCA Crim 2140 at [10]. On a charge of robbery and assault, evidence of bad character relevant to credibility properly included the accused's convictions for violent disorder, assault on police officers, harassment, criminal damage, and driving with excess alcohol.

[312] (2011) 175 JP 281, CA.

could be potentially relevant under s 101(1)(g)' to help the jury assess his character, although, in the court's view, the factual details and circumstances of the convictions would not be required unless the issue was propensity to be untruthful.[313] In *C*, the accused was charged with sexual offences against his stepdaughters and gave evidence that they had colluded to make false allegations against him. Noting the fundamental nature of the accused's attack, the court held that the judge was justified in admitting convictions for vehicle theft, possession of an offensive weapon, robbery, and firearms, some of which dated from 20 years previously.

An attack on another person's character

Section 106 of the 2003 Act provides as follows:

(1) For the purposes of section 101(1)(g) a defendant makes an attack on another person's character if—

    (a) he adduces evidence attacking the other person's character,

    (b) he (or any legal representative appointed under section 38(4) of the Youth Justice and Criminal Evidence Act 1999 to cross-examine a witness in his interests) asks questions in cross-examination that are intended to elicit such evidence, or are likely to do so, or

    (c) evidence is given of an imputation about the other person made by the defendant—

        (i) on being questioned under caution, before charge, about the offence with which he is charged, or

        (ii) on being charged with the offence or officially informed that he might be prosecuted for it.

(2) In subsection (1) 'evidence attacking the other person's character' means evidence to the effect that the other person—

    (a) has committed an offence (whether a different offence from the one with which the defendant is charged or the same one), or

    (b) has behaved, or is disposed to behave, in a reprehensible way;

    and 'imputation about the other person' means an assertion to that effect.

(3) Only prosecution evidence is admissible under section 101(1)(g).

Under s 106, the circumstances in which a defendant makes an attack on another person's character are different from the circumstances under s 105 in which the accused is treated as being responsible for the making of a false assertion. Thus s 106 appears not to apply where an attack on another person's character is made by the accused while being cross-examined at the hands of either the prosecution or any co-accused. However, although matters are not spelt out in the way that they are in s 105, it seems reasonably clear that s 106(1)(a) covers an attack on another person's character when either made by a witness called by the accused or contained in a hearsay statement adduced by the accused. Evidence 'given' under s 106(1)(c) may be 'given' by the prosecution, provided that it is relevant to the issues in the case and otherwise admissible, as opposed to merely providing a basis for satisfying gateway (g);[314] and because s 106 contains no equivalent of s 105(3), this will trigger s 101(1)(g) even if the accused wishes to withdraw the out-of-court statement on which the prosecution rely or to disassociate himself from it.

The admissibility of the attacking evidence

The definition of 'evidence attacking the other person's character' in s 106(2) must be read together with s 100 of the Act. Under s 100, it will be recalled, except where all parties agree

---

[313] (2011) 175 JP 281, CA at [29]. See *R v Jenkins* (1945) 31 Cr App R, CA, and *Selvey v DPP* [1970] AC 304, HL, both cited by the court in *C*.

[314] *R v Nelson* [2007] Crim LR 709, CA. See also *R v Renda* [2006] 1 WLR 2948, CA at [29]–[38].

to the admissibility of evidence of the bad character of a person other than the accused, such evidence is only admissible with the leave of the court and such leave can only be granted if the evidence is either (a) important explanatory evidence; or (b) has substantial probative value in relation to a matter which is in issue in the proceedings and is of substantial importance in the context of the case as a whole. Thus evidence to attack another person's character which does not meet the requirements of s 100 will be inadmissible.

The person whose character has been attacked

It is clear from s 106 that 'another person' may or may not be a witness in the case. Thus an attack may be made on a victim who dies by reason of the crime, for example a victim of murder, manslaughter, or causing death by dangerous driving, a victim of an offence of violence who, by reason of the injuries sustained, is unable to be called as a witness, a victim who does not give evidence by reason of threats, interference, or intimidation, a person whose hearsay statement is in evidence in the proceedings, and so on. However, it is also reasonably clear that 'another person' must be an identified individual. The definition of 'evidence attacking the other person's character' in s 106(2) clearly envisages that the identity of that person is known.

Evidence which amounts to an attack

Section 106(2)(a) covers cases in which the evidence is to the effect that the person has committed either the very offence with which the accused is charged or some other offence. Section 106(2)(b), which refers to evidence to the effect that the other person has behaved or is disposed to behave in a reprehensible way, will typically cover evidence of misconduct on the part of the police or prosecution witnesses which amounted to 'imputations' for the purposes of s 1(3)(ii) of the 1898 Act. Examples included allegations that the prosecutor or a witness for the prosecution invented the crime alleged,[315] obtained a confession by bribes,[316] deliberately held the accused on remand in order to concoct evidence,[317] manufactured a confession statement,[318] completely fabricated part of his evidence,[319] or asked a relative to have a quiet word with the accused to get him to talk and admit the offence.[320] Looking at s 106(2) as a whole, there is no doubt that, subject to discretionary exclusion, evidence of the bad character of the accused is admissible under s 101(1)(g) notwithstanding that the attack on another person's character is a necessary or justifiable part of his defence.

In *R v Hanson*[321] it was held that pre-2003 Act authorities will continue to apply when assessing whether an attack has been made on another person's character under s 101(1)(g), to the extent that they are compatible with s 106.

The distinction between an attack and assertions of innocence or denials of guilt

Under s 1(3)(ii) of the 1898 Act, it was held that mere assertions of innocence by the accused, or his emphatic denials of guilt, did not result in a loss of the shield and were to be distinguished from attacks on the veracity of the prosecutor or a prosecution witness, which did

---

[315] *Selvey v DPP* [1970] AC 304, HL. See *R v Singh* [2007] EWCA Crim 2140.
[316] *R v Wright* (1910) 5 Cr App R 131.
[317] *R v Jones* (1923) 17 Cr App R 117.
[318] *R v Clark* [1955] 2 QB 469.
[319] *R v Levy* (1966) 50 Cr App R 238. See also *R v Dunkley* [1927] 1 KB 323, CCA.
[320] *R v Courtney* [1995] Crim LR 63, CA.
[321] [2005] 1 WLR 3169, CA.

have that result.[322] It is submitted that such a distinction remains valid for the purposes of s 101(1)(g). The distinction, however, is difficult and narrow, as is apparent in an early and classic example given by Lord Hewart CJ in *R v Jones*:[323]

> It was one thing for the appellant to deny that he had made the confession; but it is another thing to say that the whole thing was an elaborate and deliberate concoction on the part of the inspector.

The difficulty and narrowness lies in the fact that, in some cases, to deny that the confession was made necessarily means, by implication, that the police have fabricated evidence, and although s 106, unlike s 105, does not refer to implied as well as express assertions, it is submitted that an accused will trigger s 101(1)(g) where an attack on another person's character is made by necessary implication, rather than in terms. Under s 1(3)(ii) of the 1898 Act, it was said that 'each case falls to be determined upon the exact facts, the exact circumstances, the exact language used',[324] but some of the authorities were very difficult to reconcile.[325] In *R v Britzman; R v Hall*[326] the Court of Appeal set out guidelines. In that case, police officers gave evidence of admissions made by the appellant during a lengthy interview, of which there was a written record, and in the course of a shouting-match between Britzman and Hall in the cells. The appellant denied that the interview and the shouting-match had ever taken place and, in cross-examination of the officers, this was suggested to them by counsel for the appellant. The Court of Appeal, noting that it was not a case of a denial of a single answer and that there was no suggestion of mistake or misunderstanding, held that the nature and conduct of the defence did involve imputations on the character of the prosecution witnesses. To deny that the conversations took place at all necessarily meant by implication that the police officers had given false evidence which they had made up for the purposes of a conviction. It was held that a distinction could not be drawn between a defence so conducted as to make specific allegations of fabrication and one in which such allegations arose by way of necessary and reasonable implication.[327] It is submitted that some of the guidelines set out by Lawton LJ, giving the judgment of the court, are likely to remain valid for the purposes of s 101(1)(g). His Lordship said:

> the exercise of discretion in favour of defendants...should be used if there is nothing more than a denial, however emphatic or offensively made, of an act or even a short series of acts amounting to one incident or in what was said to have been a short interview...The position would be different however if there were a denial of evidence of a long period of detailed observation extending over hours and...where there were denials of long conversations...cross-examination should only be allowed if the judge is sure that there is no possibility of mistake, misunderstanding or confusion and that the jury will inevitably have to decide whether the prosecution witnesses have fabricated evidence. Defendants sometimes make wild allegations when giving evidence. Allowance should be made for the strain of being in the witness box and the exaggerated use of language which sometimes results from such strain or lack of education or mental stability.[328]

---

[322] See per Lord Goddard CJ in *R v Clark* [1955] 2 QB 469 at 478, applied in *R v St Louis and Fitzroy Case* (1984) 79 Cr App R 53, CA.

[323] (1923) 17 Cr App R 117 at 120.

[324] Per Lord Parker CJ in *R v Levy* (1966) 50 Cr App R 238 at 241.

[325] See, eg, *R v Rouse* [1904] 1 KB 184 and cf *R v Rappolt* (1911) 6 Cr App R, 156, CCA; and see *R v Tanner* (1977) 66 CR App R 56, CA and cf *R v Nelson* (1978) 68 Cr App R 12, CA.

[326] [1983] 1 WLR 350.

[327] See also *R v Owen* (1985) 83 Cr App R 100, CA.

[328] [1983] 1 WLR 350 at 355.

Discretionary exclusion

Evidence admissible under s 101(1)(g) is open to discretionary exclusion under s 101(3) if it appears to the court that the admission of the evidence would have such an adverse effect on the fairness of the proceedings that the court ought not to admit it.[329] Such evidence, it is submitted, is also open to exclusion in reliance upon the common law discretion to exclude prosecution evidence the prejudicial effect of which outweighs its probative value.[330]

The likely grounds for discretionary exclusion are now considered.

An attack on the character of a person who is not a witness or victim

To admit evidence of the accused's bad character under s 101(1)(g) by reason of an attack on the character of someone who is neither a witness nor a victim of the offence, will *normally* have such an adverse effect on the fairness of the proceedings that the court ought not to admit it; an exception would be, for example, where there is an attack on the witness victim that he conspired with the non-witness non-victim to fabricate the allegation, because the attack on the character of the non-witness may influence the jury in their view of the victim's evidence.[331]

Evidence of bad character irrelevant or disproportionate to the bad character in the attack

As noted earlier, evidence admissible under s 101(1)(g) may be relevant not only to credibility but also to propensity to commit offences of the kind charged.[332]

However, it is submitted that bad character evidence that has little or no bearing on the credibility of the accused or his defence and does not show his propensity to commit offences of the kind charged, even if admissible in law, should be excluded by the exercise of discretion. For example, in a case of fraud, a previous conviction for fraud may be relevant to both credibility and propensity, but evidence of the accused's disposition towards sexual misconduct or cruelty to animals could serve no purpose but prejudice.[333] Equally, it is submitted, there is scope for exercise of the discretion where the bad character of the accused is disproportionate to the bad character of the person whose character has been attacked. In *R v Burke*,[334] Ackner LJ, rehearsing the principles set out in *Selvey v DPP*[335] upon which the discretion to exclude was exercised under s 1(3)(ii) of the 1898 Act, said that in the ordinary and normal case the trial judge may feel that if the credit of the prosecutor or his witnesses has been attacked, it is only fair that the jury should have before them material on which they can form their judgment whether the accused is any more worthy of belief than those he has attacked. Earlier, however, he said:

> The trial judge must weigh the prejudicial effect of the questions against the damage done by the attack on the prosecution's witnesses, and must generally exercise his discretion so as to secure a trial that is fair both to the prosecution and the defence...

[329] See *R v Chrysostomou* [2010] Crim LR 942. See also *R v Woodhead* (2011) The Times, 30 March, CA: once the evidence is admitted it may be used for any relevant purpose.

[330] See, in this chapter, under **Evidence of the bad character of the defendant, Section 101 of the Criminal Justice Act 2003, Discretion to exclude**.

[331] *R v Nelson* [2007] Crim LR 709, CA.

[332] See, in this chapter, under **Evidence of the bad character of the defendant, Section 101 of the Criminal Justice Act 2003, Admissibility and use**.

[333] But see *R v Highton* [2006] 1 Cr App R 125, CA: the Court of Appeal could see no grounds to challenge the judge's refusal to exclude, under s 101(3), two drink-related driving offences, failure to provide a specimen, and driving with excess alcohol.

[334] (1985) 82 Cr App R 156, CA.

[335] [1970] AC 304, HL.

Cases must occur in which it would be unjust to admit evidence of a character gravely prejudicial to the accused, even though there may be some tenuous grounds for holding it technically admissible...

Attacks which are a necessary or justifiable part of the defence
It is clear that under s 101(3), impact on the fairness of the proceedings must be assessed by reference to matters other than what the motive or intention of the accused was in making an attack on another's character.[336] However, in some cases it will be obvious that the attack was necessary to enable him to establish his defence and although, as we have seen, this will not prevent the admissibility in law of his bad character, and although the discretion to exclude should not invariably or even generally be exercised in these circumstances, because that would amount to a qualification to s 101(1)(g) under the guise of discretion, it is submitted that the discretion should be exercised, as necessary, to prevent too severe an application of s 101(1)(g). As the House of Lords observed in *Selvey v DPP*,[337] (in relation to s 1(3)(ii) of the 1898 Act), the discretion is unfettered, its exercise being dependent on the circumstances of each case and the overriding duty of the judge to ensure a fair trial.

Similarities between the facts of previous offences and the offence charged
As previously noted, evidence of the accused's bad character is admissible under s 101(1)(g) because of the bearing it has on the credibility of the defence case and, it is submitted, a judge should direct the jury accordingly and, in cases in which the bad character is not also admissible as propensity evidence, should further direct the jury that the evidence does not show propensity to commit the offence charged. It does not follow from this that the exclusionary discretion should always be exercised to prevent cross-examination which would lead the jury to infer that the accused is guilty of the offence charged, as when the accused is cross-examined on previous offences of a type similar to that charged, but the nature of that offence and the extent to which it resembles the offence charged, are certainly relevant matters for the judge to take into account. In deciding whether and how to exercise the discretion in respect of evidence admissible under s 101(1)(g), valuable guidance is likely to be derived from the decisions reached in relation to exercise of the discretion to prevent cross-examination under s 1(3)(ii) of the 1898 Act.

In *R v McLeod*[338] M was convicted of an armed robbery which involved the use of a number of stolen cars. At interview he made a confession, but in evidence he said he had nothing to do with the robbery and that the police had created a false case against him and fabricated his confession. Anticipating cross-examination on previous convictions, his counsel asked M about them briefly during his examination-in-chief. In cross-examination on the previous convictions M was asked about: (i) a robbery, following a not guilty plea and a defence of alibi; (ii) another robbery in which the victim had been locked in an understairs cupboard; (iii) theft of a car involving a change of the plates to a false registration; and (iv) handling of a car with false registration plates. On appeal it was submitted that the questions should not have been asked. Stuart-Smith LJ, giving the judgment of the court, set out the following principles:

1. The primary purpose of cross-examination as to previous convictions and bad character of the accused is to show that he is not worthy of belief, not to show that he has a

[336] *R v Bovell* [2005] 2 Cr App R 401, CA at [32]. See also *R v Singh* [2007] EWCA Crim 2140, CA, where it was argued unsuccessfully that the accused's attack was not gratuitous.
[337] [1970] AC 304, HL.
[338] [1994] 1 WLR 1500, CA.

disposition to commit the type of offence with which he is charged.[339] But the mere fact that the offences are of a similar type to that charged or because of their number and type have the incidental effect of suggesting a tendency or disposition to commit the offence charged will not make them improper.[340]

2. It is undesirable that there should be prolonged or extensive cross-examination in relation to previous offences, because it will divert the jury from the principal issue in the case, the guilt of the accused on the instant offence, and not the details of earlier ones. Unless the earlier ones are admissible as similar fact evidence, prosecuting counsel should not seek to probe or emphasize similarities between the underlying facts of previous offences and the instant offence.[341]

3. Similarities of defences which have been rejected by juries on previous occasions, for example false alibis or the defence that the incriminating substance has been planted and whether or not the accused pleaded guilty or was disbelieved having given evidence on oath, may be a legitimate matter for questions. These matters do not show a propensity to commit the offence in question but are clearly relevant to credibility.

4. Underlying facts that show particularly bad character over and above the bare facts of the case are not necessarily to be excluded. However, the judge should be careful to balance the gravity of the attack on the prosecution with the degree of prejudice to the defence which will result from the disclosure of the facts in question. Details of sexual offences against children are likely to be regarded by the jury as particularly prejudicial to an accused and may well be the reason why in *R v Watts*[342] the court thought the questions impermissible.

Applying those principles to the facts, the appeal against conviction was dismissed. The questions were not unduly prolonged or extensive. Concerning the first offence, there was nothing wrong in asking about the plea and the rejected defence of alibi. As to the victim of the second offence being locked under the stairs, it merely showed that the offence was somewhat more ruthless than may normally be the case in a robbery where, by definition, violence or the threat of it, is used. As to the other two offences, it was fanciful to contend that the facts elicited were designed to show a propensity to commit armed robbery, merely because the use of stolen vehicles with false registration plates is the stock in trade of armed robbery.[343]

Discretionary exclusion of evidence described in section 106(1)(c)
In cases in which the prosecution seek to rely on evidence falling within s 106(2), ie evidence of an imputation made by the accused on being questioned under caution or on being charged with the offence,[344] then insofar as the accused can show that the evidence was obtained illegally, improperly, or unfairly, whether by virtue of breaches of the Codes of Practice or otherwise, there will be obvious scope for discretionary exclusion of the evidence, which in turn

---

[339] *R v Vickers* [1972] Crim LR 101, CA.

[340] See *R v Powell* [1986] 1 All ER 193, CA; *Selvey v DPP* [1970] AC 304, HL; and *R v Wheeler* [1995] Crim LR 312, CA. See also *R v Davison-Jenkins* [1997] Crim LR 816, CA.

[341] See, eg, the subsequent decision in *R v Davison-Jenkins* [1997] Crim LR 816, CA.

[342] (1983) 77 Cr App R 126.

[343] Cf *R v Barsoum* [1994] Crim LR 194, CA. Although note *R v Barratt* [2000] Crim LR 847, CA, where the accused should not have been cross-examined on an old spent conviction which had little impact on credibility.

[344] See *R v Ball*, the conjoined appeal in *R v Renda* [2006] 1 WLR 2948, CA, where the attack was made in a police interview. See also *R v Lamaletie* (2008) 172 JP 249, CA.

could prevent s 101(1)(g) from being triggered.[345] There may also be scope for discretionary exclusion of evidence of an imputation made by the accused on being questioned or charged where the accused wishes to withdraw or disassociate himself from the imputation at the trial. This may require more from the accused than simply not repeating it in evidence.[346]

Offences committed by defendant when a child

Section 108(2) and (3) of the 2003 Act, which replace s 16(2) and (3) of the Children and Young Persons Act 1963, provide as follows:

> (2) In proceedings for an offence committed or alleged to have been committed by the defendant when aged 21 or over, evidence of his conviction for an offence when under the age of 14 is not admissible unless—
> (a) both of the offences are triable only on indictment, and
> (b) the court is satisfied that the interests of justice require the evidence to be admissible.
> (3) Subsection (2) applies in addition to section 101.

Under s 108(2A) and (2B) offences committed by the defendant when a child include convictions for offences committed in any country outside England and Wales which would constitute offences triable only on indictment if committed in England and Wales.

General

Assumption of truth in the assessment of relevance or probative value

Section 109 of the 2003 Act, provides that a court, when considering the relevance or probative value of evidence of bad character under s 100 (non-defendant) or s 101 (defendant) in order to decide whether it is admissible, should operate on the assumption that the evidence is true,[347] but need not do so if no reasonable court or jury could reasonably find it to be true. Section 109 provides as follows:

> (1) Subject to subsection (2), a reference in this Chapter to the relevance or probative value of evidence is a reference to its relevance or probative value on the assumption that it is true.
> (2) In assessing the relevance or probative value of an item of evidence for any purpose of this Chapter, a court need not assume that the evidence is true if it appears, on the basis of any material before the court (including any evidence it decides to hear on the matter), that no court or jury could reasonably find it to be true.

Section 109 applies to s 101(1)(e) (the admission of evidence of a defendant's bad character by a co-defendant) and to s 101(1)(f) (evidence to correct a false impression given by the defendant). Its chief importance, however, is likely to be in relation to the assessment of the probative value of 'similar fact evidence' properly so called under s 101(1)(d) (evidence of the defendant's bad character relevant to an important matter in issue between the defendant and the prosecution) and under s 100(3)(c) and (d) (evidence of a non-defendant's bad character of substantial probative value). The probative value of similar fact evidence often arises out of the nexus between the spontaneous and independent accounts of two or more witnesses.

---

[345] See Ch 3.

[346] See *R v Ball* [1911] AC 47, HL.

[347] Section 109 does not bind the jury, but they cannot use evidence of bad character unless they are sure that it is true: see *R v Dizaei* [2013] EWCA Crim 88.

That probative value disappears, therefore, if there is also evidence to suggest that the witnesses have deliberately concocted false evidence by conspiracy or collaboration or, which is more common, the evidence of each of them has been innocently contaminated by knowledge of the account of the other, whether acquired directly, ie in discussion with the other,[348] or indirectly, from a third person,[349] or as a result of media publicity.[350] In *R v H*[351] the House of Lords considered whether evidence carrying a real risk of collusion or contamination should be excluded by the judge or should be left to the jury with an appropriate warning. *R v H* was a case of sexual offences against a daughter and a step-daughter between whom, the parties agreed, there existed a risk of collusion. It was held that save in very rare cases, the question of collusion goes not to the admissibility of similar fact evidence, but to its credibility, an issue for the jury, and that it would be wrong for the judge to decide whether there is a risk of collusion because he would inevitably be drawn into considering whether the evidence is untrue and hence whether there is a real possibility that the accused is innocent, the very question which the jury have to decide. The following principles derive from the judgments given.

1. Normally, where there is an application to exclude similar fact evidence carrying a risk of collusion or contamination, the judge should approach the question of admissibility on the basis that the similar facts alleged are true.

2. In very exceptional cases, evidence of collusion or contamination may be taken into account and in such cases the judge would be compelled to hold a *voir dire*.

3. If the evidence is admitted and it becomes apparent that no reasonable jury could accept it as free from collusion, the judge should direct the jury that it cannot be used for any purpose adverse to the defence.

4. Where this is not so, but the question of collusion has been raised, the judge must draw the importance of collusion to the attention of the jury and direct them that if they are not satisfied that the evidence can be relied upon as free from collusion, they cannot rely upon it for any purpose adverse to the defence.

Although s 109 is clearly based on the common law rules it replaces, there are two significant differences. First, as we have seen, it is much wider in its ambit in that it applies for the purpose of assessing the relevance or probative value of the bad character of the non-defendant as well as the defendant. Second, there is nothing to suggest that s 109(2) should be invoked only exceptionally. However, s 109(2), as drafted, is a somewhat curious provision in that where it appears to the court on the basis of the material before it, including any evidence given in a *voir dire*, that no court or jury could find the facts in question to be true, then the court 'need not assume' that those facts are true. It is submitted that the unstated but more obvious action that the court needs to take, once it has concluded that no court or jury could find the facts in question to be true, is to exclude the evidence. Whether or not the courts adopt such a robust approach, and also different approaches depending upon whether the evidence is relied upon by the defence or the prosecution, it is submitted that the third and fourth principles derived from *R v H* as set out above remain good law.

[348] See *R v W* [1994] 1 WLR 800, CA.
[349] See *R v Ananthanarayanan* [1994] 1 WLR 788, CA.
[350] See per Lord Wilberforce in *DPP v Boardman* [1975] AC 421, HL at 444 and per Stuart-Smith LJ in *R v Bedford* (1990) 93 Cr App R 113, CA at 116.
[351] [1995] 2 AC 596, HL.

Stopping the case where evidence contaminated

Under s 107 of the 2003 Act, which applies only to trials before a judge and jury, if evidence of the bad character of the accused has been admitted under any of paragraphs (c) to (g) of s 101(1), and the court is satisfied, at any time after the close of the prosecution case, that the evidence is so contaminated that the accused's conviction of the offence would be unsafe, the court must either direct the jury to acquit or, if there ought to be a retrial, discharge the jury. Section 107 of the 2003 Act provides as follows:

(1) If on a defendant's trial before a judge and jury for an offence—
    (a) evidence of his bad character has been admitted under any of paragraphs (c) to (g) of section 101(1), and
    (b) the court is satisfied at any time after the close of the case for the prosecution that—
        (i) the evidence is contaminated, and
        (ii) the contamination is such that, considering the importance of the evidence to the case against the defendant, his conviction of the offence would be unsafe,
    the court must either direct the jury to acquit the defendant of the offence or, if it considers that there ought to be a retrial, discharge the jury.
(2) Where—
    (a) a jury is directed under subsection (1) to acquit a defendant of an offence, and
    (b) the circumstances are such that, apart from this subsection, the defendant could if acquitted of that offence be found guilty of another offence,
    the defendant may not be found guilty of that other offence if the court is satisfied as mentioned in subsection (1)(b) in respect of it.
    ...[352]
(4) This section does not prejudice any other power a court may have to direct a jury to acquit a person of an offence or to discharge a jury.
(5) For the purposes of this section a person's evidence is contaminated where—
    (a) as a result of an agreement or understanding between the person and one or more others, or
    (b) as a result of the person being aware of anything alleged by one or more others whose evidence may be, or has been, given in the proceedings,
    the evidence is false or misleading in any respect, or is different from what it would otherwise have been.

Section 107(5)(a) covers cases of conspiracy and collaboration, whereas s 107(5)(b) seems designed to cover cases of innocent contamination and has been cast in sufficiently wide terms, it is submitted, to cover cases in which a person became aware of the allegation of another not only directly, but also indirectly, through some third person or as a result of media coverage.

It appears that s 107 may be brought into play either on an application by the accused or by the court of its own motion. However, according to the Explanatory Notes to the Act, the test in s 107(1)(b)(ii) is designed to be a high test so that if the judge were to consider that a jury direction along the lines described in *R v H*[353] would be sufficient to deal with any potential

---

[352] Section 107(3) is cast in terms similar to s 107(1) and is to the same effect, but applies not to a trial but to a jury determination under the Criminal Procedure (Insanity) Act 1964, s 4A(2), whether a person charged on indictment did the act or made the omission charged.

[353] [1995] 2 AC 596, HL. See also, in this chapter, principles (3) and (4), under **General, Assumption of truth in the assessment of relevance or probative value.**

difficulties, then the question of the safety of the conviction would not arise and the case should not be withdrawn.[354]

The following propositions relating to s 107 derive from *R v C*:[355]

1. Contamination may result from deliberate collusion, or the exercise of improper pressure, but equally may arise innocently or through inadvertence.

2. Contamination issues extend to evidence of bad character in the broad sense, as well as to unequivocal evidence of bad character arising from unchallenged evidence of previous convictions.

3. Whether the evidence of a witness is false or misleading or different from what it would have been if it had not been contaminated, requires the judge to form his own assessment, or judgment, of matters traditionally regarded as questions of fact for the jury.

4. The effect of s 107 is to reduce the risk of a conviction based on over-reliance on evidence of previous misconduct: the dangers inherent in contamination may be obscured by the evidence of bad character.

5. If the judge is satisfied of the matters in s 107(1)(b), then what follows is not a matter of discretion.

6. An order for retrial would not normally be susceptible to a subsequent application based on an asserted abuse of process.

In *R v C* there was a two-count indictment, the first alleging sexual assault on one child, V1, and the second alleging sexual assault on another child, V2, and the prosecution evidence on count 1 was admissible evidence of bad character relevant to the issue of guilt on count 2. In such circumstances, it is submitted, if the court is satisfied that by reason of the contamination of V1's evidence, there should be an acquittal on count 2, then the court may also be compelled, depending on the circumstances, to direct an acquittal on count 1.[356] However, the question of whether evidence has been contaminated is highly fact sensitive. Unless there is a clear misdirection or a clear failure to consider material evidence, appellate courts will not overturn a decision of the trial judge, who is considered to be in the best position to make the assessment required by s 107.[357]

Court's duty to give reasons for rulings

Section 110 of the 2003 Act gives effect to the Law Commission's proposal that there should be a duty on the court to give reasons for its rulings. The section applies not only to rulings on whether an item of evidence is evidence of bad character, but also to rulings on admissibility under s 100 (non-defendant's bad character), s 101 (defendant's bad character), and s 107 (stopping the case where the evidence is 'contaminated'). Section 110 provides as follows:

> (1) Where the court makes a relevant ruling—
> (a) it must state in open court (but in the absence of the jury, if there is one) its reasons for the ruling;

---

[354] Explanatory Notes, paras 384 and 385.
[355] [2006] 1 WLR 2994, CA.
[356] See Richardson, 'Commentary' [2006] Crim LR 1060.
[357] *R v K* [2008] EWCA Crim 3177. See also *R v Lamb* [2007] EWCA Crim 1766.

(b) if it is a magistrates' court, it must cause the ruling and the reasons for it to be entered in the register of the court's proceedings.

(2) In this section 'relevant ruling' means—

(a) a ruling on whether an item of evidence is evidence of a person's bad character;

(b) a ruling on whether an item of such evidence is admissible under section 100 or 101 (including a ruling on an application under section 101(3));[358]

(c) a ruling under section 107.

Despite the mandatory nature of s 110(1), it seems likely that a failure to give reasons for a relevant ruling is, by itself, unlikely to render a conviction unsafe: the appellate court is likely to concentrate on whether the ruling itself was wrong.

Rules of court

Under s 111(1) of the 2003 Act, rules of court may make such provision as appear to be necessary or expedient for the purposes of the Act. Under s 111(2) of the 2003 Act:

(2) The rules may, and, where the party in question is the prosecution, must, contain provisions requiring a party who—

(a) proposes to adduce evidence of a defendant's bad character, or

(b) proposes to cross-examine a witness with a view to eliciting such evidence,

to serve on the defendant such notice, and such particulars of or relating to the evidence, as may be prescribed.

The rules applicable in magistrates' courts and Crown Courts are set out in rule 35 of the Criminal Procedure Rules 2013.[359] Under rule 35, where a party wants to introduce evidence of an accused's bad character, there is a requirement to give notice, whether that party is the prosecution or a co-accused.[360] Where notice has not been given, the judge has a discretion to permit notice to be given orally or in a different form to that prescribed and has power to shorten the time limit or to extend it after it has expired.[361] The time limits must be observed, but there is no requirement that an extension should only be granted in exceptional circumstances. The court should take account of the overriding objective, the reason for failure to comply, when relevant inquiries were initiated, why they were not completed in time, and whether the accused's position has been prejudiced.[362] The judge can shorten the time limit to any degree and thus dispense with the notice requirement altogether.[363] When dealing with late applications to admit evidence of bad character, key considerations include whether the target of the application would simply be unable to deal with it and whether there was a risk of 'satellite litigation'.[364] Where a co-accused proposes to adduce bad character evidence, he

---

[358] Under s 101(3), the court has a discretionary power to exclude evidence otherwise admissible under either s 101(1)(d) or s 101(1)(g).

[359] SI 2013/1544.

[360] Rule 35.4. Where the basis of an application to admit evidence of bad character changes from the basis stated in the notice, it is submitted that the application should be carefully re-thought and amended notice given. For an example of how things can go wrong when this is not done, see *R v Bullen* [2008] 2 Cr App R 75, CA.

[361] Rule 35.6.

[362] *R (Robinson) v Sutton Coldfield Magistrates' Court* [2006] 2 Cr App R 13, DC.

[363] *R v Lawson* [2007] 1 Cr App R 178, CA at [18].

[364] *R v Jarvis* [2008] EWCA Crim 488.

should always alert counsel for the other accused to his intentions, even in a case where notice has not or could not be given.[365]

Failure to give notice

There is no provision in The Criminal Procedure Rules 2013 r 35 to the effect that where a party fails to give notice, evidence is only admissible with leave, but in *R v Musone*[366] the Court of Appeal, relying on the overriding objective in r 1.1, including its recognition of the right to a fair trial under Art 6 of the European Convention on Human Rights, held that the court does have power to exclude the evidence. The court emphasized that it would be rare to exclude evidence of substantial probative value on this basis, and acknowledged that the judge should also consider the possibility of discharging the jury, but held that in some cases exclusion will be the only way of ensuring fairness, as in the case before it, where an accused, relying on s 101(1)(e), had deliberately sought to ambush a co-accused by giving him no opportunity of dealing properly with the allegation made. In *R v Mahil*[367] the Court of Appeal stated that a very high degree of necessity is required before a jury is discharged, but if such a necessity arises then the jury will be discharged regardless of the stage the trial has reached.[368]

The right of an accused to challenge evidence of a conviction

Where an accused seeks to challenge evidence of his bad character, the risk of 'satellite litigation' arises. Where such a risk arises, the courts will have regard for the overriding objective in determining whether and to what extent the accused may challenge the evidence. However, where the evidence is in the form of a conviction adduced by the prosecution under s 74(3) of the Police and Criminal Evidence Act 1984,[369] the overriding objective does not nullify the accused's right to attempt to rebut the presumption in the section that he committed the offence to which the conviction relates. Regardless of the risk of satellite litigation, to deny an accused the opportunity to adduce admissible evidence showing that he did not commit the offence would be likely to render a trial unfair.[370]

Inaccurate evidence of convictions

A trial may be rendered unfair if the jury are presented with inaccurate evidence of an accused's convictions. First, such evidence may project the accused's past offending in such a way as to make it appear worse than it is. Second, where the accused denies its accuracy before the jury, the jury might reasonably conclude that the evidence is correct and by denying it, the accused's evidence is not creditworthy. It is imperative then that the judge is supplied with meticulously accurate information when considering the admissibility of the accused's convictions and that during the trial the jury are not misinformed in any way which could suggest that the convictions are worse and more serious than they in fact are.[371]

---

[365] *R v Jarvis* [2008] EWCA Crim 488 at [41].

[366] [2007] 1 WLR 2467, CA. See also *R v Ramirez* [2009] EWCA Crim 1721.

[367] [2013] EWCA Crim 673 at [113]–[125].

[368] [2013] EWCA Crim 673 at [120].

[369] See also Ch 21.

[370] *R v C* [2011] 1 WLR 1942, CA. The right extends to challenging admissions made in cautions, and notice requirements apply to such challenges: *R v Olu* [2011] 1 Cr App R 33, CA.

[371] *R v M* [2012] EWCA Crim 1588 at [15].

Evidence admitted through inadvertence

At common law the general rule was that the prosecution were not permitted either to adduce evidence of the accused's bad character or to cross-examine witnesses for the defence with a view to eliciting such evidence, the rationale of the rule being the risk of the tribunal of fact becoming biased against an accused. The importance that English law attached to the rule was such that in cases where none of the exceptions to it applied but the bad character of the accused was inadvertently revealed to the jury, whether by a witness or counsel, the judge could exercise his discretion to discharge the whole jury from giving a verdict and order a retrial.[372] It is submitted that the principles established at common law to deal with the problem of disclosure of the accused's bad character by inadvertence will continue to provide valuable guidance. Thus, as at common law, much may depend on how explicit the reference to bad character was, the extent to which, if at all, the defence was to blame, and whether a direction to the jury is capable of neutralizing the prejudice to the accused.[373] Another factor which may be taken into consideration is whether bad character which is revealed would have been admissible had the prosecution or a co-accused made an application to admit it.[374] The question for the judge is likely to remain whether there is a real danger of injustice occurring because the jury, having heard the prejudicial matter, may be biased.[375] Thus in appropriate circumstances, as when the effect on the jury appears to be minimal, the trial may properly continue.[376] The starting point is not that the jury should be discharged; nor is there a sliding scale whereby the burden on an accused seeking a discharge increases according to the weight or length of the case or the stage it has reached when the point arises for determination.[377]

Other provisions governing the admissibility of evidence of bad character

In addition to the provisions of the 2003 Act, various other provisions have a bearing on the admissibility or exclusion of evidence of bad character. Thus, as to admissibility, there are a number of statutory provisions whereby the conviction of, or sentence for, one offence is an essential ingredient of another. For example, under s 103 of the Road Traffic Act 1988, it is an offence to obtain a licence or drive a vehicle on a road 'while disqualified for holding or

---

[372] See, eg, *R v Tyrer* (1988) The Times, 13 Oct, CA. See generally Munday, 'Irregular Disclosure of Evidence of Bad Character' [1990] Crim LR 92.

[373] *R v Weaver* [1968] 1 QB 353, CA. See also *R v Gopal* (12 July 2013, unreported), CA: a full good character direction, which included references to positive evidence from the accused's character witnesses, was sufficient to remedy prejudice caused when the complainant unexpectedly commented that the accused was a violent person. See also *R v Mihal* [2013] EWCA Crim 673 at [113]–[125]. Counsel for the prosecution made a misjudgment in choosing to adduce, without notice, evidence of an allegedly aggressive remark by the accused in order to suggest that the accused had falsely portrayed himself as a mild-mannered person. Prejudice to the accused was neutralized by an emphatic direction to the jury to ignore the remark and what had been said about it, and by a generous full good character direction.

[374] See *R v Rabheru* [2013] EWCA Crim 137.

[375] *R v Docherty* [1999] 1 Cr App R 274, CA.

[376] See *R v Coughlan* and *R v Young* (1976) 63 Cr App R 33, CA and *R v Sutton* (1969) 53 Cr App R 504, CA. See also *R v Wilson* [2008] 2 Cr App R 39, CA where there was minimal prejudice from the risk of the jury having seen the accused's name on a Crown Court list for another unspecified matter pending.

[377] *R v Lawson* [2007] 1 Cr App R 277, CA at [65]. However, procedural and evidential problems may arise in summary proceedings where magistrates perform the combined role of tribunal of law and fact. See Wasik, 'Magistrates: Knowledge of Previous Convictions' [1996] Crim LR 851, where the cases are reviewed.

obtaining a licence'. Similarly under s 21 of the Firearms Act 1968, 'a person who has been sentenced to imprisonment for a term of three years or more' shall not at any time have a firearm or ammunition in his possession.[378] Evidence of conviction or sentence for the purposes of such statutes is probably best categorized as evidence 'which has to do with the alleged facts of the offence with which the defendant is charged' within s 98(b) of the 2003 Act.[379] As to the exclusion of evidence of bad character, nothing in the scheme under the 2003 Act affects the exclusion of evidence under either (a) the rule in s 3 of the Criminal Procedure Act 1865,[380] which prevents a party from impeaching the credit of his own witness by general evidence of bad character; or (b) s 41 of the Youth Justice and Criminal Evidence Act 1999,[381] which restricts evidence or questions about the complainant's sexual history in proceedings for sexual offences.[382]

In this final section of this chapter consideration is given to three other provisions. The first two, s 27(3) of the Theft Act 1968 and s 1(2) of the Official Secrets Act 1911, provide for the admissibility of the accused's disposition towards certain kinds of wrongdoing. The third, para I.6 of the Practice Direction, provides for the exclusion of spent convictions.

Section 27(3) of the Theft Act 1968

It will be seen in Chapter 22 that where an accused is found in possession of recently stolen goods, an explanation is called for which, if not forthcoming, will entitle the jury to presume guilty knowledge or belief on a charge of receiving stolen goods. The task of the prosecution in proving guilty knowledge or belief is further assisted by s 27(3), which provides that:

Where a person is being proceeded against for handling stolen goods (but not for any offence other than handling stolen goods), then at any stage of the proceedings, if evidence has been given of his having or arranging to have in his possession the goods the subject of the charge, or of his undertaking or assisting in, or arranging to undertake or assist in, their retention, removal, disposal or realisation, the following evidence shall be admissible for the purpose of proving that he knew or believed the goods to be stolen goods:
(a) evidence that he has had in his possession, or has undertaken or assisted in the retention, removal, disposal or realisation of, stolen goods from any theft taking place not earlier than twelve months before the offence charged; and
(b) (provided that seven days' notice in writing has been given to him of the intention to prove the conviction) evidence that he has within the five years preceding the date of the offence charged been convicted of theft or of handling stolen goods.

Where evidence is introduced under s 27(3)(a), strict regard must be had to its terms: it was not designed to allow evidence to be given of what is in effect another offence of handling committed before the offence charged and does not permit the introduction of details of the transaction as a result of which the earlier property came into the possession of the

---

[378] Previous convictions may also be admitted, after a verdict of guilty, if directly relevant to the question of sentence and, unless the accused denies them, formal proof is not required. Evidence of a conviction, if disputed, is also admissible where the accused pleads *autrefois convict* to prevent the prosecution proceeding against him in respect of an offence of which he has already been convicted.

[379] See, in this chapter, under **Introductory, The admissibility of evidence of bad character 'to do with' the facts of the offence or in connection with its investigation or prosecution**.

[380] See Ch 6.

[381] See Ch 7.

[382] The 2003 Act, s 112(3).

accused.[383] However, under s 27(3)(a), providing a description of the stolen goods appears to be unavoidable.[384] Subsection 3(b) has to be read with s 73 of the Police and Criminal Evidence Act 1984, whereby the fact of a conviction may be proved by producing a certificate of conviction giving 'the substance and effect (omitting the formal parts) of the indictment and of the conviction',[385] wording which renders admissible not only the fact, date, and place of the conviction, but also a description of the stolen goods.[386] In cases in which there are a number of counts of handling on some of which the accused denies possession, the judge should warn the jury that evidence admitted under s 27(3) is relevant only to those counts in which guilty knowledge is involved and not those in which possession is the only or primary issue.[387]

It is no answer to an application to admit evidence under s 27(3)(b) to say that the previous convictions are for theft or handling of a different kind or have no bearing on a specific prosecution argument based on a system or modus operandi, because the very purpose of the subsection is to admit evidence of the general disposition of the accused to be dishonest.[388] Nevertheless, it is well established that the judge does have a discretion to exclude evidence admissible under s 27(3) where it would only be of minimal assistance to the jury or its prejudicial effect would outweigh its probative value.[389] In *R v Hacker*,[390] a trial for handling the bodyshell of an Escort RS Turbo motor car, in which the accused denied that the goods had been stolen and also denied guilty knowledge or belief, it was held that the judge was entitled, in his discretion, to admit evidence of a previous conviction of receiving a Ford RS Turbo motor car, evidence said to be highly relevant to the issue of knowledge.

Section 1(2) of the Official Secrets Act 1911

Under s 1(1) of the Official Secrets Act 1911, it is an offence to commit various acts of espionage 'for any purpose prejudicial to the safety or interests of the State'. Evidence of disposition to commit such acts is admissible under s 1(2), which provides that:

(2) On a prosecution under this section, it shall not be necessary to show that the accused person was guilty of any particular act tending to show a purpose prejudicial to the safety or interests of the State, and notwithstanding that no such act is proved against him, he may be convicted if, from the circumstances of the case, or his conduct, or his known character as proved, it appears that his purpose was a purpose prejudicial to the safety or interests of the State...

Paragraph I.6 of the Consolidated Practice Direction

The Rehabilitation of Offenders Act 1974 provides that in civil proceedings no evidence shall be admissible to prove that a 'rehabilitated' person has committed, been charged with,

---

[383] *R v Bradley* (1979) 70 Cr App R 200, applied in *R v Wood* [1987] 1 WLR 779, CA. Possession of the earlier property may be proved by evidence of an admission made by the accused under caution, in a written statement to the police, provided that the statement is edited so as to disclose only the bare fact of such possession.

[384] *R v Fowler* (1987) 86 Cr App R 219 at 226, CA.

[385] See Ch 2.

[386] *R v Hacker* [1995] 1 All ER 45, HL.

[387] *R v Wilkins* [1975] 2 All ER 734, CA.

[388] *R v Perry* [1984] Crim LR 680, CA.

[389] See *R v List* [1965] 3 All ER 710; *R v Herron* [1967] 1 QB 107 (decided under the Larceny Act 1916, s 43(1), re-enacted, with some modification, in s 27(3)); *R v Knott* [1973] Crim LR 36, CA; and *R v Perry* [1984] Crim LR 680, CA. See also *R v Rasini* (1986) The Times, 20 Mar, CA.

[390] [1995] 1 All ER 45, HL.

prosecuted for, convicted of, or sentenced for any offence which was the subject of a 'spent' conviction[391] unless the judge is satisfied that in the circumstances justice cannot be done in the case except by admitting such evidence.[392] The Act does not apply to criminal proceedings[393] but under para I.6.4 of the Consolidated Practice Direction in criminal proceedings, 'both court and advocates should give effect to the general intention of Parliament by never referring to a spent conviction when such reference can reasonably be avoided'. Paragraph I.6.6 provides that 'No one should refer in open court to a spent conviction without the authority of the judge, which authority should not be given unless the interests of justice so require.' A conviction becomes 'spent' on the expiry of a 'rehabilitation period', which runs from the date of conviction, varies according to the sentence imposed and is reduced by half for persons under 18 years old at the date of conviction.[394] Certain sentences are excluded from rehabilitation under the Act and these include imprisonment for life or for a term exceeding 30 months and a sentence of detention during Her Majesty's pleasure.[395]

ADDITIONAL READING

Elliott, 'Cut Throat Tactics: the Freedom of an Accused to Prejudice a Co-accused' [1991] Crim LR 5.

Fortson and Ormrod, 'Bad Character Evidence and Cross-Admissibility' [2009] Crim LR 313.

Goudkamp, 'Bad Character' (2008) 12 E&P 116.

Law Commission, *Evidence of Bad Character in Criminal Proceedings*, Cm 5257 (Law Com No 273, London, 2001).

Lloyd-Bostock, 'The Effects on Juries of Hearing that the Defendant has a Previous Conviction' [2000] Crim LR 734.

Mirfield, 'Bad character and the Law Commission' (2002) 6 E&P 141.

Mirfield, 'Character and Credibility' [2009] Crim LR 135.

Munday, 'Irregular Disclosure of Evidence of Bad Character' [1990] Crim LR 92.

Munday, 'Cut-throat Defences and the "Propensity to be Untruthful" under s.104 of the Criminal Justice Act 2003' [2005] Crim LR 624.

Munday, 'The Purposes of Gateway (g): Yet Another Problematic of the Criminal Justice Act 2003' [2006] Crim LR 300.

Redmayne, 'The Law Commission's character convictions' (2002) 6 E&P 71.

Redmayne, 'Recognising Propensity' [2011] Crim LR 117.

Tapper, 'Criminal Justice Act 2003 (3) Evidence of Bad Character' [2004] Crim LR 533.

Wasik, 'Magistrates: Knowledge of Previous Convictions' [1996] Crim LR 851.

---

[391] Section 4(1)(a).

[392] Section 7(3). See also *Thomas v Metropolitan Police Comr* [1997] 1 All ER 747, CA. As to the procedure to be adopted by licensing justices in deciding whether to admit the spent convictions of the person applying for the licence, see *Adamson v Waveney District Council* [1997] 2 All ER 898, DC.

[393] Section 7(2)(a).

[394] See Tables A and B under s 5(2).

[395] Section 5(1). As to how a jury should be directed on the character of an accused with previous but spent convictions, see Ch 16.

Opinion evidence

Key issues

- When and why should experts be allowed to give expert opinion evidence on facts in issue?

- When and why should non-experts be allowed to give non-expert opinion evidence on facts in issue?

- What are the dangers of allowing experts to give expert opinion evidence?

- What safeguards can be used against such dangers?

- What duties to the court should an expert witness have?

- If two or more parties to litigation wish to submit expert evidence on an issue, when should the court direct that the evidence on the issue be given by a single joint expert?

- Why should the parties disclose their expert opinion evidence before the trial?

The general rule and the two exceptions

As a general rule, opinion evidence is inadmissible: a witness may only speak of facts which he personally perceived, not of inferences drawn from those facts. To this general rule there are two exceptions: (i) an appropriately qualified expert may state his opinion on a matter calling for the expertise which he possesses; and (ii) a non-expert witness may state his opinion on a matter not calling for any particular expertise as a way of conveying the facts which he personally perceived. There are two main reasons for the general rule. First, it has been said that, whereas any fact that a witness can prove is relevant, his opinion is not.[1] The opinion of a non-expert has no probative value in relation to a subject calling for expertise and is usually insufficiently relevant to a subject not calling for any particular expertise. Second, the general rule prevents witnesses from usurping the role of the tribunal of fact. The tribunal of fact, although free to reject any opinions proffered, might be tempted simply to accept those opinions rather than draw its own inferences from the facts of the case.

The first exception assumes that a distinction can easily be drawn between a person who gives evidence of expert opinion as opposed to evidence of fact, but that is not always so.[2] The exception stems from an acknowledgment that in some cases the tribunal of fact, in the absence of opinion evidence, may be unable properly to reach a conclusion. Expert opinion evidence is admitted because the drawing of certain inferences calls for an expertise which the tribunal of fact simply does not possess. This rationale is essentially flawed: if the tribunal of fact lacks the relevant expertise, it will often be unlikely to be able to evaluate the cogency or reliability of the expert evidence.[3] In any event, and as already noted, there is a danger that the tribunal of fact may blindly defer to the opinion given. The danger is particularly acute in the case of opinions expressed by expert witnesses, whose dogmatic views, on subjects in respect of which scientific knowledge may be limited or incomplete, may occasion miscarriages of justice. Following the successful appeal in the 'cot death' case of *R v Cannings*,[4] the Attorney General announced a review of 258 convictions relating to homicide or infanticide of a baby under two years old by a parent, and a similar review in civil cases was ordered by the Children's Minister. The risks of miscarriage of justice are increased by the current absence of any scheme of compulsory accreditation or registration for expert witnesses and any scheme of mandatory practical training for judges and practitioners in understanding expert evidence and in assessing its likely reliability.[5]

If objection is taken to the admissibility of expert opinion evidence, it is for the party tendering it to establish its admissibility under the first exception.[6]

The second non-expert exception stems from a recognition that the fundamental assumption upon which the general rule is based, that it is possible to distinguish between fact and opinion, is false.[7] The words of a witness testifying as to perceived facts are always coloured,

---

[1] Per Goddard LJ in *Hollington v Hewthorn & Co Ltd* [1943] KB 587 at 595, CA.

[2] The distinction is of considerable procedural significance, especially in civil cases, where expert witnesses are subject to strict case management compared to witnesses of fact: see Dwyer, 'The effect of the fact/opinion distinction on CPR r.35.2: *Kirkman v Euro Oxide Corporation; Gall v Chief Constable of the West Midlands*' (2008) 12 E&P 141. See also *Multiplex Construction (UK) Ltd v Cleveland Bridge UK Ltd* [2008] All ER (D) 04 (Oct), TCC.

[3] See Roberts and Zuckerman, *Criminal Evidence* (Oxford, 2004) 294–5.

[4] [2004] 1 WLR 2607, CA (see Ch 8).

[5] For an analysis of the need for forensic science training, and specific recommendations, see the House of Commons Science and Technology Committee, *Forensic Science on Trial*, HC 96-I 2005.

[6] *R v Atkins* [2010] 1 Cr App R 17, CA at [9], approved in *R v Reed* [2010] 1 Cr App R 310, CA at [113].

[7] 'In a sense all testimony to matter of fact is opinion evidence; ie it is a conclusion formed from phenomena and mental impressions': Thayer, *A Preliminary Treatise on Evidence at the Common Law* (Boston, 1898) 524.

to some extent, by his opinion as to what he perceived. The separation of an inference or value judgment from the facts on which it is based is often extremely difficult and sometimes impossible. In criminal proceedings, for example, a witness may identify the accused as the culprit, saying, 'He is the man I saw'. It is evidence of opinion, not fact. The witness means: 'He so resembles the man I saw that I am prepared to say that they are one and the same.' He could confine himself to a description of the man he saw and leave it to the jury to decide whether the description fits the accused. In cases of this kind, the opinion expressed conveys the facts perceived. The witness, in such cases, is allowed to give his evidence in his own way which is often, although not invariably, the most natural and comprehensible way in which to convey to the tribunal of fact the facts as he perceived them.

Expert opinion evidence

Matters calling for expertise

Examples

The opinion evidence of an expert is only admissible on a matter calling for expertise.[8] The field of expertise is large and ever-expanding. It embraces subjects as diverse as accident investigation and driver behaviour,[9] the age of a person,[10] ballistics, battered women's syndrome,[11] blood tests, breath tests, blood-alcohol levels and back-calculations thereof,[12] earprint identification,[13] facial mapping[14] or facial identification by video superimposition,[15] fingerprint identification,[16] voice identification,[17] DNA or genetic fingerprinting,[18] indented impressions left on one document

---

[8] This section of the chapter concerns expert *evidence*. Civil actions without a jury in the High Court may be tried by a judge sitting with assessors. The function of assessors, who are principally used in the Admiralty Court in cases concerning collisions between vessels, is to assist the judge on matters of fact calling for specialized knowledge: see the Senior Courts Act 1981, s 70, the County Courts Act 1984, s 63, and the Civil Procedure Rules (CPR) r 35.15.

[9] See *R v Dudley* [2004] All ER (D) 374 (Nov).

[10] *R (I) v Secretary of State for the Home Department* [2005] EWHC 1025 (Admin) and *N (a child) (residence order), Re* [2006] EWHC 1189 (Fam).

[11] See *R v Hobson* [1998] 1 Cr App R 31, CA.

[12] ie calculation of the amount of alcohol eliminated in the period between driving and providing a specimen in order to show that a person's alcohol level was above the prescribed limit at the time of driving. See *Gumbley v Cunningham* [1989] 1 All ER 5, HL.

[13] *R v Dallagher* [2003] 1 Cr App R 195, C; *R v Kempster (No 2)* [2008] 2 Cr App R 256, CA.

[14] *R v Stockwell* (1993) 97 Cr App R 260, CA; *R v Mitchell* [2005] All ER (D) 182 (Mar).

[15] *R v Clarke* [1995] 2 Cr App R 425, CA.

[16] See generally *R v Smith* [2011] 2 Cr App R 174, CA and Cole and Roberts, 'Certainty, Individualisation and the Subjective Nature of Expert Fingerprint Evidence' [2012] Crim LR 824.

[17] *R v Robb* (1991) 93 Cr App R 161, CA.

[18] For a basic description of the method by which DNA profiling is carried out, see *R v Gordon* [1995] 1 Cr App R 290, CA at 293–4. The technique may be used not only to identify criminal suspects but also to decide questions of pedigree. In evaluating DNA evidence, use should not be made of Bayes Theorem, or any similar statistical method of analysis, because it plunges the jury into inappropriate and unnecessary realms of theory and complexity: *R v Adams* [1996] 2 Cr App R 467, CA. As to the procedure to be adopted when DNA evidence is introduced, see *R v Doheny and Adams* [1997] 1 Cr App R 369, CA. See also Redmayne, 'The DNA Database: Civil Liberty and Evidentiary Issues' [1995] Crim LR 437, 'Sittin' in the Dock with the Bayes' (2001) NLJ 201 and The Forensic Science Regulator, *The Interpretation of DNA Evidence (including low-template DNA)* (2012). For the controversy about the use of Low Copy Number DNA analysis, following the concerns expressed in *R v Hoey* [2007] NICC 49, see *R v Reed* [2010] 1 Cr App R 310, CA, *R v Broughton* [2010] EWCA Crim 549, CA, *R v C* [2011] 3 All ER 509, CA, Jamieson, 'LCN DNA analysis and opinion on transfer: *R v Reed and Reed*' (2011) 15 E&P 161, and Naughton and Tan, 'The need for caution in the use of DNA evidence to avoid convicting the innocent' (2011) 15 E&P 245.

as a result of writing on another,[19] insanity, lip-reading,[20] physical signs of child sexual abuse,[21] 'shaken baby syndrome',[22] Sudden Infant Death Syndrome (SIDS),[23] terrorism,[24] the genuineness of works of art, and the state of public opinion.[25] Frequently recurring examples of matters upon which expert evidence is admissible include medical, scientific, architectural, engineering, and technological issues and questions relating to standards of professional competence, market values, customary terms of contracts, and the existence of professional and trade practices. Handwriting may be proved either by a non-expert familiar with the handwriting in question[26] or by a qualified expert, but an expert should be called in criminal cases tried by jury when, pursuant to s 8 of the Criminal Procedure Act 1865, disputed handwriting is compared with a specimen sample of handwriting proved to the satisfaction of the court to be genuine.[27] Expert opinion is admissible on questions of a literary or artistic nature, for example in relation to the defence of 'public good' under s 4 of the Obscene Publications Act 1959.

Points of foreign law

A final example, calling for special attention, is a point of foreign law, which, as we have seen in Chapter 2, is a question of fact to be decided on the evidence by the judge. Foreign law is usually proved by the evidence, including opinion evidence, of an expert[28] who may refer to foreign statutes, decisions, and textbooks.[29] If the evidence of the experts conflicts, the judge is bound to look at the sources of knowledge from which the experts have drawn, in order to decide between the conflicting testimony.[30] However, he is not at liberty to conduct his own

---

[19] The impressions may be detected by the use of Electrostatic Detection Apparatus (ESDA). ESDA has been useful not only in dating documents and determining the origin of anonymous communications, but also in showing whether pages were written in sequence and whether there were subsequent additions to the contents: see *R v Wellington* [1991] Crim LR 543, CA and generally Giles, 'Good Impressions' (1991) NLJ 605.

[20] *R v Luttrell* [2004] 2 Cr App R 520, CA.

[21] *R v S* [2012] EWCA Crim 1433.

[22] *R v Henderson* [2010] 2 Cr App R 185, CA.

[23] See *R v Cannings* [2004] 1 WLR 2607, CA (see Ch 8).

[24] *R v Ahmed* [2011] EWCA Crim 184.

[25] eg on the issue of reputation in passing-off actions. See *Sodastream Ltd v Thorn Cascade Co Ltd* [1982] RPC 459 and *Lego Systems A/S v Lego M Lemelstrich Ltd* [1983] FSR 155. Cf *Reckitt & Colman Products v Borden Inc (No 2)* [1987] FSR 407.

[26] *Doe d Mudd v Suckermore* (1837) 5 Ad&El 703.

[27] *R v Harden* [1963] 1 QB 8, CCA: see generally Ch 9.

[28] An exception exists in the case of the construction of provisions of foreign legislation admitted in evidence under the Evidence (Colonial Statutes) Act 1907: see the authorities cited in *Jasiewicz v Jasiewicz* [1962] 1 WLR 1426. Under the 1907 Act, s 1, copies of Acts, ordinances, and statutes passed by the legislature of any part of Her Majesty's dominions exclusive of the UK and of orders, regulations, and other instruments issued or made under the authority of any such Act, ordinance, or statute, if purporting to be printed by the government printer of the possession shall be received in evidence by all courts in the UK without proof that copies were so printed. See also the Colonial Laws Validity Act 1865, s 6. The British Law Ascertainment Act 1859 permits English courts to state a case on a point of foreign law for the opinion of a superior court in another part of Her Majesty's dominions. The opinion pronounced is admissible in evidence on the point of foreign law in question. See also the Foreign Law Ascertainment Act 1861.

[29] It may also be proved by the witness statement of an expert (if admissible) or by a statement of agreed facts pursuant to the Criminal Justice Act 1967, s 10: *R v Ofori (No 2)* (1993) 99 Cr App R 223, CA.

[30] Per Lord Langdale MR in *Nelson (Earl) v Lord Bridport* (1845) 8 Beav 527 at 537 and per Scarman J in *Re Fuld's Estate (No 3), Hartley v Fuld* [1968] P 675 at 700–3.

research into those sources and to rely on material not adduced in evidence in order to reject the expert evidence.[31]

At common law, the consequence of treating foreign law as a question of fact is that where there has been an English decision on a particular point of foreign law and the same point subsequently arises again, it must be decided afresh on new expert evidence.[32] This remains the position where a point of foreign law arises in English criminal proceedings. The position in civil proceedings, however, has now been altered by s 4 of the Civil Evidence Act 1972. Section 4(2)(a) provides that a previous determination by an English court of superior status, whether civil or criminal, on a point of foreign law shall, if reported in citable form,[33] be admissible in evidence in civil proceedings. Section 4(2)(b) provides that except where there are two or more previous determinations which are in conflict, the foreign law on the point in question shall be taken to be as previously determined unless the contrary is proved. S 4(2)(b) raises a presumption that the earlier decision is correct. However, the court which has to consider the question for a second time decides for itself what weight to attach to the previous decision and, although it is desirable to reach consistent conclusions, the subsection is not to be construed as laying down a general rule that the presumption can only be displaced by particularly cogent evidence.[34]

Matters within the experience and knowledge of the tribunal of fact

In *R v Turner*[35] it was held that where the triers of fact can form their own opinion without the assistance of an expert, the matter in question being within their own experience and knowledge, the opinion evidence of an expert is inadmissible because unnecessary.[36] This test has been applied time and again, but with scant recognition, in the authorities which now fall to be considered, that views may legitimately differ as to whether a particular matter is within the experience and knowledge of jurors and that, even if it is not, expert evidence may be unnecessary because the matter could be dealt with better by an educative judicial direction, as in, for example, cases of allegedly mistaken identification.[37]

Leave should not be granted to call a professor of psychology or other medical evidence to demonstrate the likely deterioration of the memory of an ordinary witness.[38] On the other hand, although a witness's ability to remember events will ordinarily be well within the experience of jurors, in rare cases in which a witness gives evidence of an event said to have occurred during 'the period of childhood amnesia', which extends to the age of about seven, and the evidence is very detailed and contains a number of details that are extraneous to the central feature of the event, an appropriately qualified expert may give evidence that it should be treated with caution and may be unreliable because recall of events during that period

[31] Per Lord Chelmsford in *Duchess Di Sora v Phillipps* (1863) 10 HL Cas 624 at 640 and per Purchas LJ in *Bumper Development Corpn Ltd v Metropolitan Police Comr* [1991] 4 All ER 638, CA at 643–6. See also *Harley v Smith* [2010] EWCA Civ 78.

[32] *M'Cormick v Garnett* (1854) 23 LJ Ch 777.

[33] ie where the report, if the question had been as to the law of England and Wales, could have been cited as an authority in legal proceedings in England and Wales: s 4(5).

[34] *Phoenix Marine Inc v China Ocean Shipping Co* [1999] 1 Lloyd's Rep 682, QBD.

[35] [1975] QB 834, per Lawton LJ at 841.

[36] The position is now the same in family proceedings—expert evidence will only be admissible if 'necessary': see Family Procedure Rules 2010, SI 2010/2955, r 25.1 and *Re H-L (a child)* [2013] EWCA Civ 655.

[37] See Ch 8.

[38] *R v Browning* [1995] Crim LR 227, CA.

will be fragmented, disjointed, and idiosyncratic rather than a detailed narrative account.[39] Similarly, although expert opinion evidence is likely to be inadmissible in relation to the dangers of visual identification evidence,[40] it is submitted that it may properly be admitted on such matters as the accuracy of estimates of age and the relative accuracy of sequential and simultaneous identification procedures.[41] Expert evidence may be admitted as to the dangers of evidence produced by hypnotherapy, not to express an opinion on the witness's truthfulness, but to criticize the techniques of the hypnotherapist and express an opinion about the danger that *if* the witness's recollection was falsely engendered, the witness would regard it as genuine memory.[42]

Expert evidence is inadmissible on the question whether an unidentified person shown in a photograph is under the age of 16.[43] It is also inadmissible on a trial for posting packets containing indecent articles, on the ordinary meaning of the words 'indecent or obscene'.[44] Similarly, in the ordinary case, the issue of obscenity in prosecutions under the Obscene Publications Act 1959 falls to be tried without the assistance of expert evidence.[45] *DPP v A & B C Chewing Gum Ltd*[46] was not an 'ordinary case', but 'a very special case'[47] which should be regarded as 'highly exceptional and confined to its own circumstances'.[48] The accused was charged with publishing for gain obscene battle cards which were sold together with packets of bubble gum. The Divisional Court held that the magistrates had improperly refused to admit the evidence of experts in child psychiatry concerning the likely effect of the cards on children.

Mental states

The distinction between matters calling for expertise and matters within the experience and knowledge of the jury is also illustrated by cases concerning a person's mental state. As we

---

[39] *R v H (JR) (Childhood Amnesia)* [2006] 1 Cr App R 195, CA. However, the correctness of the decision has been doubted, having regard to criticisms of the methodology of the expert: *R v Anderson* [2012] EWCA Crim 1785. In any event, the ambit of the decision should not be widened and care should be taken in the case of a narrative which has become 'polished' simply as a part of the process of the police questioning a witness and then drafting his statement: *R v S; R v W* [2007] 2 All ER 974, CA.

[40] See *Gage v HM Advocate* [2011] HCAJC 40 and Roberts, 'Expert evidence on the reliability of eyewitness identification—some observations on the justifications for exclusion: *Gage v HM Advocate*' (2012) 16 E&P 93.

[41] See *R v Forbes* [2009] ACTSC 1, considered by Roberts, 'Eyewitness identification and expert insight: *R v Forbes*' (2010) 14 E&P 57. A jury may also be assisted by a non-expert who is 'sufficiently expert ad hoc' (see *R v Howe* [1982] 1 NZLR 618 at 627) as in *R v Clare and Peach* [1995] 2 Cr App R 333, CA, where an officer who had viewed a video about 40 times, examining it in slow motion, gave evidence as to whether those shown were the accused. Ironically, research suggests that the accuracy of identification is not significantly enhanced by repeated replay: Bruce et al, 'Face Recognition in Poor Quality Video Evidence from Security Surveillance' (1999) 10 *Psychological Science* 243. See also Munday, 'Videotape Evidence and the Advent of the Expert Ad Hoc' (1995) 159 JP 547.

[42] *R v Clark* [2006] EWCA Crim 231. As to the dangers of admitting evidence of recovered memory, see Ring, 'Due process and the admission of expert evidence on recovered memory in historic child sexual abuse cases: lessons from America' [2012] 16 E&P 66.

[43] *R v Land* [1998] 1 Cr App R 301, CA.

[44] *R v Stamford* [1972] 2 QB 391.

[45] *R v Anderson* [1972] 1 QB 304 per Lord Widgery CJ at 313. Cf *R v Skirving; R v Grossman* [1985] 2 All ER 705, where the jury needed expert evidence on the characteristics of cocaine and the different effects of the various methods of ingesting the drug on the user and abuser in order to decide whether a book had a tendency to deprave and corrupt.

[46] [1968] 1 QB 159.

[47] Per Ashworth J in *R v Stamford* [1972] 2 QB 391, CA at 397.

[48] Per Lord Widgery CJ in *R v Anderson* [1972] 1 QB 304 at 313. See also the doubts expressed about the case by Lord Dilhorne in *DPP v Jordan* [1977] AC 699, HL at 722.

shall see, many of the decisions reflect the view that expertise is only called for in the case of a person suffering from a mental illness, a view which, it is submitted, is unnecessarily inflexible. As Farquharson LJ observed in *R v Strudwick*:[49]

> The law is in a state of development in this area. There may well be other mental conditions about which a jury might require expert assistance in order to understand and evaluate their effect on the issues in a case.

Expert psychiatric evidence is a practical necessity in order to establish insanity[50] or diminished responsibility.[51] In *R v Smith*[52] the accused was convicted of murder by stabbing. His defence was automatism while asleep. The Court of Appeal held that psychiatric evidence adduced by the prosecution as to whether the evidence of the accused was consistent with his defence had been properly admitted, the type of automatism in question not being within the realm of the ordinary juror's experience. Concerning the defence of duress by threats, expert medical evidence is admissible for the purposes of the subjective (but not the objective) test, provided that the mental condition or abnormality in question is relevant and its effects are outside the knowledge and experience of laymen.[53] However, according to *R v Walker*[54] psychiatric evidence may be admissible to show that an accused was suffering from some mental illness, mental impairment, or recognized psychiatric condition, provided persons generally suffering from such a condition might be more susceptible to pressure and threats, and thus to assist the jury in deciding whether a reasonable person suffering from such a condition might have been impelled to act as the accused did, but evidence is not admissible that an accused who was not suffering from such an illness, impairment, or condition was especially timid, suggestible, or vulnerable to pressure and threats. Concerning the defence of loss of self-control under s 54 of the Coroners and Justice Act 2009, it is submitted that psychiatric evidence will generally be inadmissible but, by analogy with the authorities relating to duress, may be admitted to show that an accused was suffering from some disorder or disability of the mind affecting his degree of tolerance and self-restraint.

Except where the accused comes into the class of mental defective or is afflicted by some medical condition affecting his mental state, expert medical or psychiatric evidence is not admissible on the question of *mens rea*.[55] In *R v Masih*,[56] in which the appellant, who was convicted of rape, suffered from no psychiatric illness but had an intelligence quotient of only 72, just above the level of subnormality, it was held that on the question of whether he knew that the complainant was not consenting or was reckless as to whether she consented or not,

---

[49] (1993) 99 Cr App R 326, CA at 332.

[50] See the Criminal Procedure (Insanity and Unfitness to Plead) Act 1991, s 1(1), in this chapter, under **Expert opinion evidence, Expert witnesses, Expertise**.

[51] See *R v Byrne* [1960] 2 QB 396 at 402, applied in *R v Dix* (1981) 74 Cr App R 306, CA. See also *R v Chan-Fook* [1994] 2 All ER 552, CA, applied in *R v Morris* [1998] 1 Cr App R 386, CA: where psychiatric injury is relied on as the basis for a charge of assault occasioning actual bodily harm and is not admitted by the defence, the Crown should call expert evidence.

[52] [1979] 1 WLR 1445, CA.

[53] *R v Hegarty* [1994] Crim LR 353, CA. See also *R v Horne* [1994] Crim LR 584, CA; and cf *R v Hurst* [1995] 1 Cr App R 82, CA.

[54] [2003] All ER (D) 64 (Jun).

[55] *R v Chard* (1971) 56 Cr App R 268, CA. See also *R v Reynolds* [1989] Crim LR 220, CA, *R v Wood* [1990] Crim LR 264, CA and, in the case of adolescents, *R v Coles* [1995] 1 Cr App R 157, CA.

[56] [1986] Crim LR 395, CA.

expert psychiatric evidence about his state of mind, intelligence, and ability to appreciate the situation had been properly excluded.[57] The Court of Appeal held that, generally speaking, if an accused comes into the class of mental defective, with an IQ of 69 or below, then insofar as that defectiveness is relevant to an issue, expert evidence may be admitted, provided that it is confined to an assessment of the accused's IQ and an explanation of any relevant abnormal characteristics, to enlighten the jury on a matter that is abnormal and *ex hypothesi* outside their experience; but where an accused is within the scale of normality, albeit at the lower end, as the appellant was, expert evidence should generally be excluded.[58]

In *R v Toner*,[59] a case of attempted murder in which a doctor gave evidence that T may have been suffering from a minor hypoglycaemic state, it was held that the defence should have been permitted to cross-examine him as to whether the effect of such an attack could have negatived T's special intent to kill and to cause serious bodily harm. The Court of Appeal could see no distinction between such medical evidence and medical evidence as to the effect of a drug on intent: both matters were outside the ordinary experience of jurors. Similarly in *R v Huckerby*[60] it was held that evidence that the accused was suffering from post-traumatic stress disorder, a recognized mental condition with which the jury would not be expected to be familiar, was admissible because relevant to an essential issue bearing upon his guilt or innocence, namely whether it caused him to panic and cooperate with criminals in circumstances where he would otherwise not have done so.

Credibility

Expert evidence is generally inadmissible on the issue of a witness's credibility.[61] In *Re S (a child) (adoption: psychological evidence)*,[62] an appeal against a care order, the judge at first instance had relied on the results of a personality questionnaire, including a 'Lie-Scale' measuring the mother's willingness to distort her responses in order to create a good impression. Allowing the appeal, it was held that the results of personality or psychometric tests should only rarely have any place in such cases because it is for judges to decide questions of credibility.

Impact of sexual offences on victims

In its consultation paper *Convicting Rapists and Protecting Victims—Justice for Victims of Rape* (2006), the Government proposed that prosecutors should be able to present general expert evidence about the psychological impact of sexual offences upon victims. This impact is not necessarily within the understanding of the average juror and expert evidence is capable of dispelling popular myths and misconceptions and explaining behaviour which might

---

[57] See also *R v Hall* (1987) 86 Cr App R 159, CA and *R v Henry* [2006] 1 Cr App R 118, CA and contrast *Schultz v R* [1982] WAR 171 (Supreme Court of Western Australia). In *R v Lupien* (1970) 9 DLR (3d) 1 (Supreme Court of Canada) it was held that psychiatric evidence is admissible to show a person's lack of capacity to form intent.

[58] However, as Hodgson J stated in *R v Silcott* [1987] Crim LR 765 (see [1988] Crim LR 293): 'To draw a strict line at 69/70 does seem somewhat artificial.' For a critical analysis of the notion that there is a clear line dividing normality and subnormality, see Mackay, 'Excluding Expert Evidence: a tale of ordinary folk and common experience' [1991] Crim LR 800.

[59] (1991) 93 Cr App R 382, CA.

[60] [2004] EWCA Crim 3251.

[61] See *R v Henry* [2006] 1 Cr App R 118, CA (the accused), *R v C* [2012] EWCA Crim 1478 (a complainant in a sexual case) and *R v Joyce* [2005] NTS 21 (a prosecution witness) and cf *R v S* [2006] EWCA Crim 2389 (see Ch 7). See also *R v Robinson* [1994] 3 All ER 346, CA and, in the case of children, *G v DPP* [1997] 2 All ER 755, CA at 759–60. But see also, in this chapter, *Re M and R (minors)* [1996] 4 All ER 239, CA, under **Expert opinion evidence, Expert witnesses, Evidence on ultimate issues**.

[62] [2004] EWCA Civ 1029.

body of knowledge or experience which is sufficiently organized or recognized to be accepted as a reliable body of knowledge or experience, a special acquaintance with which by the witness would render his opinion of assistance to the court'.[106] However, English law, with notable exceptions, shows a general reluctance to apply any such condition of admissibility, which is curious given the obvious dangers, especially in criminal trials, of allowing the tribunal of fact to rely on 'expert' testimony of questionable reliability.[107] In *R v I*,[108] for example, it was held that expert opinion evidence should have been admitted notwithstanding that it rested on a hypothesis that could have been tested to ensure its reliability, but was not.

R v Gilfoyle,[109] one of the exceptions, was a murder trial in which the only other possible explanation for the death was suicide. The Court of Appeal refused to hear the fresh evidence of a psychologist who had carried out a 'psychological autopsy' of the deceased. One of the reasons given for this conclusion was that the expert had identified no criteria by reference to which the court could test the quality of his opinions: there was no database comparing real and questionable suicides and there was no substantial body of academic writing approving his methodology. Another reason was the Canadian and United States authority pointing against the admission of such evidence. The court was of the view that the English approach accorded with the guiding principle in the United States, as stated in *Frye v United States*,[110] and to the effect that expert evidence based on novel or developing scientific techniques that are not generally accepted by the scientific community should be excluded. In fact, the test in *Frye* is no longer the guiding principle in the United States. In *Daubert v Merrell Dow Pharmaceuticals*[111] the Supreme Court held that in federal courts the test had been superseded by r 702 of the Federal Rules of Evidence 1975; that the courts must ensure the reliability, as well as the relevance, of scientific evidence before admitting it; and that reliability is to be determined having regard to a number of factors, including whether the technique can be and has been tested, whether it has been the subject of publication and peer review, its error rate, and whether it is generally accepted.

In *R v Dallagher*,[112] where identity was in issue, evidence was received from two experts who had examined earprints. The expertise of earprint comparison is in its relative infancy, and after the trial it emerged that other forensic scientists had misgivings about the extent to which earprint evidence alone can, in the present state of knowledge, safely be used to identify a suspect. It was held that the expert evidence had been properly admitted, but the appeal was allowed and a retrial ordered on the basis that the fresh evidence, if given at trial, might reasonably have affected the approach of the jury to the identification evidence of the

---

[106] Extraneous information may also affect the reliability of an expert's opinion, as when expert fingerprint examiners are told, eg, that the suspect has an alibi or has confessed: see Dror and Cole, 'The vision in "blind justice": Expert perception, judgment and visual cognition in forensic pattern recognition' (2012) 17(2) *Psychonomic Bulletin & Review* 161 and Dror and Rosenthal, 'Meta-analytically Quantifying the Reliability and Biasability of Forensic Experts' (2008) 53(4) *J Forensic Sci* 900.

[107] See generally Redmayne, *Expert Evidence and Criminal Justice* (Oxford, 2001) ch 5, O'Brian Jr, 'Court scrutiny of expert evidence: Recent decisions highlight the tensions' (2003) 7 E&P 172 and the report of the House of Commons Science and Technology Committee, *Forensic Science on Trial*, HC 96–1 2005, which recommends the establishment of a Forensic Science Advisory Council to develop a gate-keeping test for expert evidence.

[108] [2012] EWCA Crim 1288.

[109] [2001] 2 Cr App R 57, CA.

[110] 293 F 1013 (DC Cir, 1923).

[111] 509 US 579 (1993).

[112] [2003] 1 Cr App R 195, CA.

experts and thus affected their decision to convict.[113] In reaching its decision that the expert evidence had been properly admitted, the court appeared to accept that the English approach is analogous to that to be found in r 702 of the Federal Rules of Evidence and also referred to *Daubert*.[114] However, it had no regard to the factors listed in that case, none of which, if considered, would have supported the case for admission. Instead, it simply approved a passage from *Cross and Tapper on Evidence*[115] which, after a reference to the *Frye* approach, states:

> The better, and now more widely accepted, view is that so long as a field is sufficiently well-established to pass the ordinary tests of relevance and reliability, then no enhanced test for admissibility should be applied, but the weight of the evidence should be established by the same adversarial forensic techniques applicable elsewhere.

The same passage was also approved in *R v Luttrell*[116] where the court, while accepting that the reliability of expert evidence can be relevant to the issue of admissibility, rejected the argument that lip-reading evidence as to what was said by someone talking on a CCTV recording should not be admitted unless it could be seen to be reliable because the methods used were sufficiently explained to be tested in cross-examination and so to be verifiable or falsifiable. The passage was further approved in *R v Reed*[117] in which expert evidence as to the possible ways in which DNA may have been transferred was held to be admissible: the underlying scientific knowledge on such transferability was thought to be sufficiently reliable but 'plainly incomplete'. In *R v Atkins*[118] it was held that an expert in facial mapping could express a view as to the extent to which his findings supported identification of the accused notwithstanding the absence of a statistical database by which such a view could be given a numerical value, provided that it was made crystal clear to the jury that such a view was an expression of subjective opinion. *R v Atkins* was followed in *R v Dlugosz*,[119] where experts were permitted to give evaluative evidence on low-template DNA derived from mixed samples in the absence of statistical evidence of the relevant DNA match probability. Similarly, in *R v T*,[120] where it was held, in relation to footwear mark comparison evidence, that there are no sufficiently reliable data for an expert to express an opinion based on the use of a mathematical probability formula, the court was nonetheless of the view that an expert may give an evaluative opinion that a shoe could have made a mark based on class characteristics resulting from manufacture and identifying characteristics such as damage to the sole.[121]

The dangers of this relaxed approach are highlighted by the decisions in *R v Robb*[122] and *R v O'Doherty*.[123] In *R v Robb* a lecturer in phonetics was held to be well qualified by his academic training and practical experience to express an opinion as to the identity of a voice, notwithstanding that his auditory technique, which was to pay close attention to voice quality, pitch,

---

[113] See also *R v Kempster (No 2)* [2008] 2 Cr App R 256, CA.

[114] 509 US 579 (1993).

[115] (9th edn, London, 1999) 523.

[116] [2004] 2 Cr App R 520, CA.

[117] [2010] 1 Cr App R 310, CA at [111] and [119].

[118] [2010] 1 Cr App R 117, CA.

[119] [2013] 1 Cr App R 425, CA.

[120] [2011] 1 Cr App R 85, CA.

[121] For critical analysis, see Redmayne et al, 'Forensic Science Evidence in Question' [2011] Crim LR 347 and Morrison, 'The likelihood-ratio framework and forensic evidence in court: a response to *R v T*' (2012) 16 E&P 1.

[122] (1991) 93 Cr App R 161, CA.

[123] [2003] 1 Cr App R 77, CA (NI).

expertise lies in their knowledge and evaluation of unpublished material. The only proviso is that they should refer to such material in their evidence so that the cogency and probative value of their conclusions can be tested and evaluated by reference to it.[160]

R v Abadom was applied in *R v Hodges*,[161] a case of conspiracy to supply heroin, in which a very experienced drugs officer gave evidence partially derived from what he had been told by others, including other officers, informants, and drug users, as to the usual method of supplying heroin, its purchase price in a particular place at the time, and what weight was more than would have been for personal use alone. The relevant primary facts were the observations of the activities of the accused, the finding of 14 grams of heroin in the possession of one of them, and the finding of other drugs paraphernalia in his house. The court distinguished *R v Edwards*.[162] In that case, the issue was whether the accused intended to supply the ecstasy tablets found in his possession or whether they were for personal consumption. Witnesses for both the prosecution and defence, neither of whom had any medical or toxicological qualification, were not allowed to give evidence, based on what they had been told by drugs users, rather than any academic materials, as to the personal consumption rates of ecstasy tablet users, and the impact of use in terms of developing tolerance or suffering serious harm. The evidence was held to have been properly excluded on the basis that the witnesses lacked the appropriate expertise to exempt their opinions from the rule against hearsay.[163]

The common law doctrine under discussion has been preserved, in criminal proceedings, by statute. Section 118(1)8 of the Criminal Justice Act 2003 preserves 'Any rule of law under which in criminal proceedings an expert witness may draw on the body of expertise relevant to his field'.

Evidence on ultimate issues

Historically, the courts have striven to prevent any witness from expressing his opinion on an ultimate issue, that is one of the very issues which the court has to determine.[164] The justification of the rule is that insofar as such evidence might unduly influence the tribunal of fact, it prevents witnesses from usurping the function of the court: witnesses are called to testify, not to decide the case. The rule is open to criticism on a number of levels.[165] The objection of undue influence makes no allowance for cases in which the tribunal of fact is a professional judge rather than a jury, overlooks the frequency of conflicts in expert testimony, and is largely incompatible with the very justification for admitting expert evidence, that the drawing of inferences from the facts in question calls for an expertise which the tribunal of fact does not possess. However, in practice the rule is often of no more than semantic effect: the expert is allowed to express his opinion provided that the diction employed is not noticeably the same as that which will be used when the matter is subsequently considered by the

---

[160] Cf *R v Bradshaw* (1985) 82 Cr App R 79, CA (in text at n 154), where it was held that if the doctors' opinions had been based entirely upon the 'hearsay' statements of the accused as to his past symptoms and the accused had elected not to testify and thus not provided any direct evidence as to such symptoms, the judge would have been justified in telling the jury that the defence case was based upon a flimsy or non-existent foundation.

[161] [2003] 2 Cr App R 247, CA.

[162] [2001] EWCA Crim 2185.

[163] Cf *R v Ibrahima* [2005] Crim LR 887, CA at n 84.

[164] See *Haynes v Doman* [1899] 2 Ch 13, CA.

[165] See generally the 17th Report of the Law Reform Committee, *Evidence of Opinion and Expert Evidence*, Cmnd 4889 (1970), paras 266–71; 11th Report, Criminal Law Revision Committee, Cmnd 4991 (1972); and Jackson, 'The Ultimate Issue Rule: One Rule Too Many' [1984] Crim LR 75.

court![166] In civil proceedings the rule has been abolished. Section 3(1) of the Civil Evidence Act 1972 provides that:

> Subject to any rules of court made in pursuance of this Act, where a person is called as a witness in any civil proceedings, his opinion on any relevant matter on which he is qualified to give expert evidence shall be admissible in evidence.

Section 3(3) reads:

> In this section 'relevant matter' includes an issue in the proceedings in question.

In family law cases involving suspected child abuse, expert evidence may relate to the presence and interpretation of physical, mental, behavioural, and emotional signs, but often necessarily includes a view as to the likely veracity of the child. In this context, in *Re M and R (minors)*,[167] it was held that it is 'plainly right' that 'issue' in s 3(3) *can* include an issue of credibility and that when dealing with children the court needs 'all the help it can get'.[168] In the normal case, as we have seen, expert evidence of credibility will be inadmissible because unnecessary, being a matter on which the tribunal of fact can form its own opinion unaided.

Technically, the ultimate issue rule still operates in criminal proceedings, but in relation to expert witnesses is in practice ignored.[169] In *R v Hookway*,[170] for example, it was recognized that expert evidence of 'facial mapping' is sufficient, by itself, to establish the identity of the accused; in *R v Mason*,[171] as we have seen, a surgeon was asked for his opinion whether a person died in consequence of his wounds and whether they could have been self-inflicted;[172] and in *R v Holmes*[173] the Court of Criminal Appeal held that it was not improper to cross-examine a doctor called by the accused in a murder trial about whether the accused's conduct after the offence indicated that he knew the nature of the act and that it was contrary to the law of the land, both issues, of course, being central to the defence of insanity within the M'Naghten rules.[174] In *DPP v A & B C Chewing Gum Ltd*[175] Lord Parker CJ, although of the opinion that in a prosecution under the Obscene Publications Act 1959 it would be wrong to ask an expert directly whether a publication tended to deprave and corrupt, later observed that more and more inroads had been made into the rule against opinion evidence on ultimate issues:[176]

---

[166] See, eg, *Rich v Pierpont* (1862) 3 F&F 35 and per Lord Parker CJ in *DPP v A & B C Chewing Gum Ltd* [1968] 1 QB 159 at 164.

[167] [1996] 4 All ER 239, CA.

[168] [1996] 4 All ER 239 at 249.

[169] In its 11th Report, the Criminal Law Revision Committee was of the opinion that the rule probably no longer existed: Cmnd 4991 (1972), para 268. See also per Lord Taylor CJ in *R v Stockwell* (1993) 97 Cr App R 260 at 265: the rule has become 'a matter of form rather than substance'. Cf, *sed quaere, R v Jeffries* [1997] Crim LR 819, CA.

[170] [1999] Crim LR 750, CA.

[171] (1911) 7 Cr App R 67, CCA.

[172] See also *R v Smith* [1979] 1 WLR 1445, CA at n 52; and *R v Silcott* [1987] Crim LR 765, CC, where the educational subnormality of one accused was described by the experts as 'very likely' and 'significantly likely' to render 'unreliable' a confession allegedly made by him. See the Police and Criminal Evidence Act 1984, s 76(2)(b) (see Ch 13).

[173] [1953] 1 WLR 686. Cf *R v Wright* (1821) Russ&Ry 456.

[174] See also *R v Udenze* [2001] EWCA Crim 1381 (in a rape case, expert evidence as to the effects of alcohol on the complainant's ability to give informed consent); and *R v Hodges* [2003] 2 Cr App R 247, at n 161 (in a case of supplying drugs, expert evidence that the amount found was more than would have been for personal use alone).

[175] [1968] 1 QB 159.

[176] [1968] 1 QB 159 at 164.

Those who practise in the criminal courts see every day cases of experts being called on the question of diminished responsibility, and although technically the final question 'Do you think he was suffering from diminished responsibility?' is strictly inadmissible, it is allowed time and time again without any objection.

Weight

In cases in which expert opinion evidence is properly adduced, the weight to be attached to it is a matter entirely for the tribunal of fact. The duty of experts, it has been said, 'is to furnish the judge or jury with the necessary scientific criteria for testing the accuracy of their conclusions, so as to enable the judge or jury to form their own independent judgment by the application of these criteria to the facts proved in evidence'.[177] Thus, in the civil context, although lay evidence should not be preferred to expert evidence without good reason,[178] it has been held that there is no principle of law preventing a judge from preferring the evidence of lay claimants whom he finds to be honest over the evidence of a jointly instructed expert with whose evidence he can find no fault.[179] Similarly, on the question whether or not a will was forged, a court may prefer the evidence of non-expert attesting witnesses to that of a handwriting expert.[180] Equally, in the criminal context, it has been held that it is incumbent on magistrates to approach expert evidence critically, even if no expert is called on the other side and to be willing to reject it if it leaves questions unanswered.[181] In Crown Court cases in which expert opinion evidence is given on an ultimate issue, the judge should make clear to the jury that they are not bound by the opinion, and that the issue is for them to decide.[182] The same applies where the evidence does not relate to an ultimate issue, but there is no inflexible requirement that the warning take any particular form.[183] It is a misdirection to tell the jury that expert evidence should be accepted if uncontradicted[184] or in the absence of reasons for rejecting it.[185] However, it has also been held to be wrong to direct a jury that they may disregard expert opinion evidence when the only evidence adduced dictates one answer.[186] In an attempt to reconcile the authorities, in R v Sanders,[187] a case concerning the defence of diminished responsibility, it was held that if there are no other circumstances to consider, unequivocal, uncontradicted medical evidence favourable to an accused should be accepted by a jury and they should be so directed; but where

[177] Per Lord President Cooper in *Davie v Edinburgh Magistrates* 1953 SC 34 Court of Session at 40. Thus concerning voice identification, the jury, in forming their own judgment on the opinions of the experts, are entitled to know the features of the voice to which they paid attention (*R v Robb* (1991) 93 Cr App R 161 at 166) and to hear the tapes which they analysed (*R v Bentum* (1989) 153 JP 538, CA).

[178] See *Re B (a minor)* [2000] 1 WLR 790, CA.

[179] *Armstrong v First York Ltd* (2005) The Times, 19 Jan. See also *Stevens v Simons* [1988] CLY 1161, CA.

[180] *Fuller v Strum* (2000) *The Times* 14 Feb 2001.

[181] *DPP v Wynne* (2001) *The Independent* 19 Feb, DC.

[182] Per Lord Taylor CJ in *R v Stockwell* (1993) 97 Cr App R 260.

[183] *R v Fitzpatrick* [1999] Crim LR 832, CA.

[184] *Davie v Edinburgh Magistrates* 1953 SC 34 at 40.

[185] Per Diplock LJ in *R v Lanfear* [1968] 2 QB 77, CA.

[186] *Anderson v R* [1972] AC 100, PC. See also *R v Matheson* [1958] 1 WLR 474, CCA: in a murder trial, if there are no facts or circumstances to displace or throw a doubt on unchallenged medical evidence of diminished responsibility, a verdict of guilty will not be in accordance with the evidence; and *R v Bailey* (1977) 66 Cr App R 31n, CCA: although juries are not bound to accept such expert medical evidence, they must act on it, and if there is nothing before them to cast doubt on it, cannot reject it. But see also *Walton v R* [1978] AC 788, PC, followed in *R v Kiszko* (1978) 68 Cr App R 62, CA.

[187] (1991) 93 Cr App R 245, CA.

there are other circumstances to consider (including, presumably, the nature of the killing, the conduct of the accused before, at the time of, and after it, and any history of mental abnormality), then the medical evidence, though unequivocal and uncontradicted, must be assessed in the light of those circumstances.[188]

On a trial of fitness to plead, unless the unfitness is clear, the court should rigorously examine the psychiatric evidence before reaching its conclusion.[189]

If there is conflicting expert evidence, the tribunal of fact is obviously forced to make a choice. For these purposes, no less than when deciding whether to accept the evidence of even a single expert witness, the tribunal of fact may take into account an expert's qualifications and how they were acquired, his credibility, the degree of reliability of his opinion, and the extent to which, if at all, his evidence-in-chief was based on assumed facts which do not accord with those ultimately established.

An opinion will not necessarily be more persuasive simply because it is shared by two experts.[190]

In *R v Henderson*[191] it was held that in cases concerning 'shaken baby syndrome' in which the prosecution is able by calling experts to identify a non-accidental injury and the defence can identify no alternative cause, it does not automatically follow that the prosecution has proved its case, because the evidence may be insufficient to exclude, beyond reasonable doubt, an unknown cause. The jury should be reminded of any realistic possibility of an unknown cause and directed that, unless the evidence leads them to exclude it, they cannot convict; and they should also be reminded that special caution is needed where expert evidence is fundamental to the prosecution.[192] The court also gave the following general guidance on the content of the summing-up in cases in which the evidence to prove guilt consists only of expert evidence. There must be a logically justifiable basis for accepting or rejecting the evidence. The issues should be identified and, one by one, the evidence which goes to the resolution of each should be identified. The guidance given in *R v Harris*[193] is of assistance not only to judges, practitioners, and experts, but also juries. The jury should be asked to judge, if the issue arises, whether the expert has assumed the role of an advocate, influenced by the side calling him, or whether he has gone outside his area of expertise. The jury should examine the basis of the opinion. Can the expert point to a recognized, peer-reviewed source of the opinion? Is his clinical experience up to date and equal to the experience of others whose evidence he seeks to contradict? Finally, the judge should identify those reasons which would justify accepting or rejecting any conflicting expert opinion.

The capacity of jurors to apply the *Henderson* directions and accept or reject expert evidence, especially in complex cases, is open to debate. As commentators have observed, there is an urgent need for empirical research to gauge jury comprehension of expert evidence and for consideration of reforms aimed at increasing juror engagement and understanding, such as guidance on note-taking and greater use of technological aids.[194]

---

[188] However only in very exceptional cases will it be justifiable for a judge to withdraw a charge of murder from the jury at the close of the case: see *R v Khan* [2010] 1 Cr App R 74, CA.

[189] *R v Walls* [2011] 2 Cr App R 61, CA.

[190] *R v Meachen* [2009] EWCA Crim 1701.

[191] [2010] 2 Cr App R 185, CA.

[192] What matters is the essence of the direction, not its precise terms: *R v Arshad* [2012] EWCA Crim 18.

[193] [2006] 1 Cr App R 55, CA, considered at n 141.

[194] Cohen and Heffernan, 'Juror Comprehension of Expert Evidence: A Reform Agenda' [2010] Crim LR 195.

(3) An expert's answers to questions put in accordance with paragraph (1) shall be treated as part of the expert's report.

(4) Where—

(a) a party has put a written question to an expert instructed by another party; and

(b) the expert does not answer that question,

the court may make one or both of the following orders in relation to the party who instructed the expert—

(i) that the party may not rely on the evidence of that expert; or

(ii) that the party may not recover the fees and expenses of that expert from any other party.

Rule 35.6(2)(c) allows a party, with the permission of the court or other party, to ask about matters not covered in the expert's report, provided that they are within his expertise, and thereby renders the expert akin to a court expert.[213] The fact that experts can be required to answer written questions normally means that there is no need for a single joint expert's evidence to be amplified or tested by cross-examination of the expert. The court has a discretion to permit such amplification or cross-examination, but this should be restricted as far as possible.[214] If, exceptionally, the expert is to be subject to cross-examination, then he should know in advance what topics are to be covered, and where fresh material is to be adduced for his consideration, this should be done in advance of the hearing.[215]

The contents of the expert's report

An expert's report must comply with the requirements set out in Practice Direction 35,[216] which provides that a report must give details of the expert's qualifications; give details of any literature or other material relied on; set out the substance of all facts and instructions given to him which are material to the opinions expressed or upon which those opinions are based; make clear which facts in the report are within his own knowledge; say who carried out any examination, measurement, test, or experiment which he has used for the report, give the qualifications of that person, and say whether or not it was carried out under his supervision; where there is a range of opinion on the matters dealt with in the report, summarise it and give reasons for his own opinion; contain a summary of his conclusions; if he is not able to give his opinion without qualification, state the qualification; and state that he understands his duty to the court and has complied with that duty.[217] His report must also be verified by a statement of truth.[218] Under r 35.10(2), at the end of the expert's report there must be a statement that he understands his duty to the court and has complied with it. Rule 35.10(3) and (4) provide as follows:

(3) The expert's report must state the substance of all material instructions, whether written or oral, on the basis of which the report was written.

(4) The instructions referred to in paragraph (3) shall not be privileged against disclosure but the court will not, in relation to those instructions—

(a) order disclosure of any specific document; or

---

[213] *Mutch v Allen* [2001] CPLR 200, CA.

[214] *Peet v Mid Kent Healthcare Trust* [2002] 1 WLR 210, CA at [28].

[215] *Popek v National Westminster Bank plc* [2002] EWCA Civ 42.

[216] CPR r 35.10(1).

[217] PD 35, para 3.2.

[218] PD 35, para 3.3.

(b) permit any questioning in court, other than by the party who instructed the expert, unless it is satisfied that there are reasonable grounds to consider the statement of instructions given under paragraph (3) to be inaccurate or incomplete.

Paragraph 5 of PD 35 states that cross-examination of the expert on the contents of his instructions will not be allowed unless the court permits it (or unless the party who gave the instructions consents to it). Paragraph 5 also states that if the court is satisfied that there are 'reasonable grounds' under r 35.10(4)(b), then it will allow the cross-examination where it appears to be in the interests of justice to do so.

The intention behind r 35.10(4) is to encourage the setting out fully of material instructions and facts, including, for example, witness statements provided to the experts and the previous report of another expert. However, the obligation under r 35.10(3) is not to set out all the information and material supplied to the expert, but to disclose the 'substance of all material instructions'. Ordinarily the expert is to be trusted to comply with r 35.10(3), and under r 35.10(4) the party on the other side may not as a matter of course call for disclosure: there must be some concrete fact giving rise to the 'reasonable grounds' to which r 35.10(4) refers.[219]

The requirements of PD 35 are intended to focus the mind of the expert on his responsibilities in order that litigation may progress in accordance with the overriding principles in CPR Pt 1. If an expert demonstrates that he has no conception of those requirements, as when he fails to include in his report statements that he understands his duty to the court and has complied with it, and statements setting out the substance of all material instructions, then he may properly be debarred from acting as an expert witness in the case.[220] Moreover, in appropriate circumstances, the court may make a costs order against an expert who, by his evidence, has caused significant expense to be incurred, and has done so in flagrant and reckless disregard of his duties to the court.[221]

Discussions between experts

Rule 35.12 is another provision designed to save court time and reduce costs. It allows the court, at any stage, in cases in which the parties have been permitted to use competing experts, to direct a 'without prejudice'[222] discussion between the experts for the purpose of requiring them to identify the issues in the proceedings and, where possible, to reach agreement on an issue. The court may specify the issues which the experts must discuss. It may also direct that following the discussion the experts must prepare a statement for the court showing the issues on which they agreed and the issues on which they disagreed with a summary of their reasons for disagreeing. Such a statement is not an admission and does not bind the parties, but is not privileged, even if made with an eye to assisting a mediation which, in the event, is unsuccessful.[223] However, the content of the *discussion* between the experts shall not be referred to at the trial unless the parties agree; and where the experts do agree on an issue, their agreement will not bind the parties unless they expressly agree to be bound by it.

If a party is dissatisfied with the revised opinion of his own expert following a discussion between experts, permission to call a further expert should only be granted where there is good

---

[219] *Lucas v Barking, Havering and Redbridge Hospitals NHS Trust* [2003] 4 All ER 720, CA.
[220] *Stevens v Gullis* [2000] 1 All ER 527, CA.
[221] *Phillips v Symes* [2005] 4 All ER 519 (Ch).
[222] See Ch 20.
[223] *Aird v Prime Meridian Ltd* (2007) The Times, 14 Feb.

of the accused should satisfy themselves that any such report or criticism is disclosed. Failure to do so by either side will only cast suspicion upon the cogency of the opinion.

Non-expert opinion evidence

A non-expert witness, as we have seen, may give opinion evidence on matters in relation to which it is impossible or virtually impossible to separate his inferences from the perceived facts on which those inferences are based. In these circumstances, the witness is permitted to express his opinion as a compendious means of conveying to the court the facts he perceived. The admissibility of non-expert opinion evidence is largely a question of degree and the matters open to proof by such evidence defy comprehensive classification. Examples include the identification of persons,[247] voices,[248] objects[249] and handwriting,[250] speed,[251] temperature, weather, and the passing of time. A non-expert may describe the condition of objects, using adjectives such as 'good', 'new', 'worn', and 'old'. Similarly, non-expert opinion evidence is admissible as to the value of objects. In *R v Beckett*,[252] a non-expert expressed the opinion that a plate-glass window was worth more than five pounds. However, although the point was not canvassed in the case, it seems clear that non-expert opinion evidence of value is only admissible in respect of commonplace objects, of which a plate-glass window is perhaps best regarded as a borderline example, as opposed to works of art, antiques, and other objects the valuation of which obviously calls for specialized skill or knowledge. A non-expert may also give opinion evidence of a person's age,[253] health, bodily or emotional state, or reaction to an event or set of circumstances. Although a person's sanity is a matter calling for expertise, it would appear that a close acquaintance may express his opinion as a convenient way of conveying the results of his observations of that person's behaviour.[254] A similar distinction was drawn in *R v Davies*.[255] It was held that on a charge of driving when unfit through drink, whereas the fitness of the accused to drive is a matter calling for expert evidence, a non-expert may properly give his general impression as to whether the accused had 'taken drink', provided that he describes the facts upon which his impression was based. Similarly, and subject to the same proviso, a non-expert may give his opinion as to whether an accused was 'drunk'.[256] In *R v Hill*[257] it was held that scientific evidence is not always required to identify a prohibited drug, but police officers' descriptions of a drug must be sufficient to justify the inference that it is the drug alleged.

---

[247] *R v Tolson* (1864) 4 F&F 103.

[248] *R v Robb* (1991) 93 Cr App R 161, CA; *R v Deenik* [1992] Crim LR 578, CA. The key to the admissibility of lay listener evidence is the degree of familiarity of the witness with the voice. If the prosecution call police officers to give such evidence, it should be treated with caution and it is desirable that an expert give an opinion on its veracity: *R v Flynn* [2008] 2 Cr App R 266 at 281, considered in Ch 8.

[249] *Lucas v Williams & Sons* [1892] 2 QB 113 (a picture); *Fryer v Gathercole* (1849) 13 Jur 542 (a pamphlet).

[250] *Doe d Mudd v Suckermore* (1837) 5 Ad&El 703: see Ch 9.

[251] The Road Traffic Regulation Act 1984, s 89(2) : see Ch 8.

[252] (1913) 8 Cr App R 204.

[253] *R v Cox* [1898] 1 QB 179.

[254] Per Parke B in *Wright v Doe d Tatham* (1838) 4 Bing NC 489 at 543–4. But in criminal cases, expert psychiatric evidence is necessary in order to establish insanity: the Criminal Procedure (Insanity and Unfitness to Plead) Act 1991, s 1(1), considered at n 74.

[255] [1962] 1 WLR 1111, C-MAC.

[256] *R v Tagg* [2002] 1 Cr App R 22, CA.

[257] (1992) 96 Cr App R 456, CA.

At common law, as we have seen, the courts were opposed to any witness expressing his opinion on an ultimate issue, that is one of the very issues which the judge or jury have to decide. In civil proceedings the rule has been abolished. Section 3(2) of the Civil Evidence Act 1972 declares that:

> where a person is called as a witness in any civil proceedings, a statement of opinion by him on any relevant matter on which he is not qualified to give expert evidence, if made as a way of conveying relevant facts personally perceived by him, is admissible as evidence of what he perceived.

Section 3(3) reads:

> In this section 'relevant matter' includes an issue in the proceedings in question.

Concerning non-expert opinion evidence in criminal proceedings, the rule may subsist.[258] In *R v Davies*[259] Lord Parker CJ held that although a witness could properly state the impression he formed as to whether the accused driver had taken drink, his opinion as to whether as a result of that drink he was fit or unfit to drive a car was inadmissible, being 'the very matter which the court itself has to determine'.[260] However, the rule is easily evaded by a careful use of words, and sometimes it is simply ignored. In *R v Beckett*,[261] it will be recalled, a witness valued a window at more than five pounds, yet that was exactly the issue to be determined by the court.

ADDITIONAL READING

Bogan and Roberts, *Identification, Investigation, Trial and Scientific Evidence* (London, 2011).

Cohen and Heffernan, 'Juror Comprehension of Expert Evidence: A Reform Agenda' [2010] Crim LR 195.

Cossins, 'Expert witness evidence in sexual assault trials: questions, answers and law reform in Australia and England' (2013) 17 E&P 74.

Edmond and Roberts, 'The Law Commission's Report on Expert Evidence in Criminal Proceedings' [2011] Crim LR 844.

Ellison, 'Closing the credibility gap: The prosecutorial use of expert witness testimony in sexual assault cases' (2005) 9 E&P 239.

Hartshorne and Miola, 'Expert evidence: difficulties and solutions in prosecutions for infant harm' (2010) (30)2 Legal Studies 279.

Jackson, 'The Ultimate Issue Rule: One Rule Too Many' [1984] Crim LR 75.

Law Commission, *Expert Evidence in Criminal Proceedings in England and Wales*, Law Com No 325 (2011).

Lewis, 'Expert evidence of delay in complaint in childhood sexual abuse prosecutions' (2006) 10 E&P 157.

O'Brian Jr, 'Court scrutiny of expert evidence: Recent decisions highlight the tensions' (2003) 7 E&P 172.

Redmayne, *Expert Evidence and Criminal Justice* (Oxford, 2001).

Roberts, 'Drawing on Expertise: Legal Decision-making and the Reception of Expert Evidence' [2008] Crim LR 443.

Roberts, 'Rejecting General Acceptance, Confounding the Gate-keeper: the Law Commission and Expert Evidence' [2009] Crim LR 551.

Ward, 'Expert Evidence and the Law Commission: Implementation without Legislation?' [2013] Crim LR 561.

[258] But see 11th Report, Criminal Law Revision Committee, Cmnd 4991 (1972), para 270. The Committee, recommending the enactment for criminal proceedings of provisions similar to those contained in the 1972 Act, s 3, said: 'we have no doubt that this is the present law, but it seems desirable for the statute to be explicit'.

[259] [1962] 1 WLR 1111, C-MAC. See also *Sherrard v Jacob* [1965] NI 151, NICA.

[260] In Eire, the witness has been allowed to express an opinion on both matters: see *A-G (Rudely) v James Kenny* (1960) 94 ILTR 185.

[261] (1913) 8 Cr App R 204, CCA.

recently that the English courts have given any consideration to the applicability to criminal proceedings of the general doctrine of public interest immunity. The question appears to have arisen for the first time in *R v Governor of Brixton Prison, ex p Osman*.[20] Noting that the seminal cases make no reference to criminal proceedings, Mann LJ held that the civil principles do apply in criminal cases, but involve a different balancing exercise: although the judge should balance the public interest in non-disclosure against the interests of justice in the particular case, the weight to be attached to the interests of justice in a criminal case touching and concerning liberty, and very occasionally life, is plainly very great indeed.[21] In *R v Keane*[22] Lord Taylor CJ held that when the court is seised of the material, the judge should balance the weight of the public interest in non-disclosure against the importance of the documents to the issues of interest to the defence, present and potential, so far as they have been disclosed to him or he can foresee them. However, as we shall see, the House of Lords has since made clear in *R v H*[23] that the golden rule is full prosecution disclosure and that although some derogation from the golden rule can be justified, it should always be to the minimum necessary to protect the public interest and it should never imperil the overall fairness of the trial. It was also held that if it does imperil the overall fairness of the trial, then fuller disclosure should be ordered even if this leads or may lead the prosecution to discontinue the proceedings so as to avoid having to make disclosure. Furthermore, the judge's initial ruling is not necessarily final. He is under a continuous duty to keep his initial decision under review—issues may emerge at a later stage so that the public interest in non-disclosure may be eclipsed by the defendant's need for access.[24] In deciding whether or not to order disclosure, the judge is not confined to admissible evidence but may take into account hearsay material.[25]

In *R v Ward*[26] it was held that the decision as to what should be withheld from disclosure is for the court, not the prosecution, the police, the DPP, or counsel.[27] A prosecution decision to withhold relevant evidence without notifying the judge would be a violation of Art 6 of the European Convention on Human Rights.[28] The prosecution cannot be judge in their own cause and if they are not prepared to let the court decide, the prosecution will have to be abandoned. However, in exceptional cases, the Crown Prosecution Service may voluntarily disclose to the defence documents in a class covered by public interest immunity without referring the matter to the court for a ruling, subject to the safeguard of first seeking the written approval of the Treasury Solicitor.[29]

The rule in *R v Ward*[30] that it is for the *court* to decide what material should be withheld is now reflected in the statutory rules relating to pre-trial disclosure in Pt 1 of the Criminal Procedure and Investigations Act 1996. Section 21(2) preserves the common law rules as to whether disclosure is in the public interest.

---

[20] [1992] 1 All ER 108, QBD.

[21] Approved in *R v Keane* [1994] 2 All ER 478, CA.

[22] [1994] 2 All ER 478, CA.

[23] [2004] 2 AC 134, HL.

[24] *R v H* [2004] 2 AC 134, HL at [36]. See also *R v Bower* [1994] Crim LR 281, CA; *R v Brown (Winston)* [1994] 1 WLR 1599, CA; and ss 14 and 15 of the Criminal Procedure and Investigations Act 1996.

[25] *R v Law* (1996) The Times, 15 Aug.

[26] [1993] 1 WLR 619, CA.

[27] See also, in the case of a co-accused, *R v Adams* [1997] Crim LR 292, CA.

[28] *Rowe and Davis v UK* (2000) 30 EHRR 1. See also *Dowsett v UK* [2003] Crim LR 890.

[29] See *R v Horseferry Road Magistrates, ex p Bennett (No 2)* [1994] 1 All ER 289, DC.

[30] [1993] 1 WLR 619, CA.

The scope of exclusion on grounds of public policy

General

Conway v Rimmer paved the way for a generalization of the principles of public policy, which has led to a widening of the heads of public interest which the courts will recognize. Thus it is now clear that documents, to be protected, need not relate to the workings of central government at all: the public also has an interest in the effective working of non-governmental bodies and agencies performing public functions such as local authorities,[31] the Gaming Board,[32] the National Society for the Prevention of Cruelty to Children (NSPCC),[33] and the Law Society.[34] It is tempting to generalize the principles completely and to say that evidence will be excluded whenever a public interest in its non-disclosure is asserted which outweighs the importance of receiving the evidence in the particular case. This was an argument put forward in *D v NSPCC*[35] in answer to the proposition that public interest immunity is restricted to the effective functioning of departments or organs of central government. Both propositions were rejected by the House of Lords in favour of the middle view that although 'the categories of the public interest are not closed and must alter from time to time whether by restriction or extension as social conditions and social legislation develop',[36] nevertheless the court can proceed only by analogy with interests which have previously been recognized by the authorities.[37]

In that case, the NSPCC, a body established by royal charter and given statutory power, along with the police and local authorities, to bring care proceedings, sought to honour a promise given to an informant that his identity would not be revealed. The plaintiff claimed damages for the injury to her health caused by the negligence of the NSPCC in pursuing the allegations of the informant that she had maltreated her child, allegations which proved groundless. The House of Lords upheld the NSPCC's application to withhold from discovery documents disclosing the identity of the informant. Their Lordships held that the value of the NSPCC's work was indicated by statutory recognition of its function, by evidence that informants were more willing to approach the NSPCC than the police or local authorities, and by other statutory and common law authority acknowledging the importance of providing for the welfare of children. Relying on the analogy of judicial refusal to compel disclosure of sources of police information, they held that in both situations the public interest in the uninhibited flow of information justified the refusal to order disclosure since otherwise the sources of information would be expected to dry up.[38] Although the actual result of the case

---

[31] See, eg, *Re D (Infants)* [1970] 1 WLR 599, CA and *Gaskin v Liverpool City Council* [1980] 1 WLR 1549, CA (childcare records).

[32] *R v Lewes Justices, ex p Home Secretary* [1973] AC 388, HL, see, in this chapter, under **The scope of exclusion on grounds of public policy, The proper functioning of the public service, Examples**.

[33] *D v NSPCC* [1978] AC 171, HL (name of informant who prompted NSPCC inquiry).

[34] *Buckley v Law Society (No 2)* [1984] 1 WLR 1101, Ch D (names of informants whose complaints led to the Law Society's inquiry into a solicitor's conduct). See also *Medway v Doublelock Ltd* [1978] 1 WLR 710: an affidavit of means supplied in divorce proceedings can be withheld in subsequent litigation on grounds of public policy.

[35] [1978] AC 171, HL. See per Lord Diplock at 219–20 where the arguments are summarized.

[36] Per Lord Hailsham at 230.

[37] Per Lord Simon at 240, Lord Diplock at 219, and Lord Hailsham (with whom Lord Kilbrandon agreed) at 226.

[38] Cf *R v Bournemouth Justices, ex p Grey* [1987] 1 FLR 36, DC: it was difficult to envisage a father being dissuaded from admitting parentage to an adoption society on the basis of his knowledge that a later denial of such parentage might result in the earlier admission being used against him.

was no doubt desirable, the reasoning by which that result was achieved is open to criticism. In particular, reliance on the constraint of precedent seems an unsatisfactory means of containing the undesirable effect of an overgeneralized principle. If the constraint is applied, it must result in arbitrary distinctions. The relevance of statutory recognition must also be questioned: activities conducted without statutory provision or regulation can also be of great public importance.

It is convenient to consider the cases in which a claim to public interest immunity has been made under the heads of 'National security, diplomatic relations and international comity', 'Information for the detection of crime', 'Judicial disclosures', 'The proper functioning of the public service', and 'Confidential relationships'. In considering these cases, it needs to be remembered that there are always four variables capable of affecting the outcome, namely: (i) the importance of the public function in question; (ii) the extent to which disclosure would prejudice the effective exercise of that function; (iii) the importance of the material in question to the just determination of the litigation; and (iv) the public importance of that litigation.

National security, diplomatic relations, and international comity

Evidence will almost certainly be excluded in the interests of national security, good diplomatic relations, and international comity. *Duncan v Cammell Laird & Co Ltd*, as we have seen, furnishes an example in relation to national security. In *Asiatic Petroleum Co Ltd v Anglo-Persian Oil Co Ltd*[39] the Court of Appeal upheld a decision not to produce a letter containing information concerning the Government's plans in respect of its campaign in Persia during the First World War. Other examples under this head include a report of a military court of inquiry concerning the conduct of an officer,[40] communications between the governor of a colony and the colonial secretary,[41] and communications between the commander-in-chief of forces overseas and the Government[42] and diplomatic despatches.[43]

Concerning national security, it now seems that a ministerial certificate will be conclusive. In *Balfour v Foreign and Commonwealth Office*[44] B, dismissed from his post as Vice-Consul in Dubai, complained to an industrial tribunal of unfair dismissal and sought disclosure of documents in the possession of the Foreign Office. Immunity was claimed on the grounds that disclosure of material in the documents relating to the security and intelligence services would be contrary to the public interest. Both the Foreign Secretary and Home Secretary signed certificates particularizing the nature and content of the material attracting immunity and the reasons for the claim. The Court of Appeal upheld the decision to refuse disclosure. It was held that although there must always be vigilance by the courts to ensure that public interest immunity of whatever kind is raised only in appropriate circumstances and with appropriate particularity, once there is an actual or potential risk to national security demonstrated by an appropriate certificate, the court should not exercise its right to inspect. In reaching its decision, the court approved and applied the dictum of Lord Diplock in *Council of Civil Service*

---

[39] [1916] 1 KB 822, CA.
[40] *Home v Bentinck* (1820) 2 Brod&Bing 130; *Beatson v Skene* (1860) 5 H&N 838.
[41] *Hennessy v Wright* (1888) 21 QBD 509.
[42] *Chatterton v Secretary of State for India in Council* [1895] 2 QB 189, CA.
[43] *M Isaacs & Sons Ltd v Cook* [1925] 2 KB 391.
[44] [1994] 2 All ER 588, CA.

Unions v Minister for the Civil Service[45] (when dealing with the question of national security in a completely different context):

> National security is the responsibility of the executive government; what action is needed to protect its interests is...a matter on which those on whom the responsibility rests, and not the courts of justice, must have the last word. It is par excellence a non-justiciable question. The judicial process is totally inept to deal with the sort of problems which it involves.

It is also in the public interest of the United Kingdom that the contents of confidential documents addressed to, or emanating from, foreign sovereign states, or concerning the interests of such states in relation to international territorial disputes between them, should not be ordered by the courts of this country to be disclosed by a private litigant without the consent of the states in question, because to order disclosure in such cases may be against the public interest in the maintenance of international comity and an English court should not be seen to be forcing the disclosure of such documents for the ostensible purpose of pronouncing, albeit indirectly, on the merits of such a dispute, the resolution of which is a question of politics.[46] The comity of nations also justifies an English court, in the exercise of its discretion, in refusing to authorize the issue of letters of request inviting the courts of a friendly foreign state to use their powers to assist in the obtaining of evidence, from witnesses resident in that or another friendly state, in order to show that the motives of the government of the friendly foreign state, in promulgating a particular law, were such that the law is unenforceable in the United Kingdom.[47]

Information for the detection of crime

Police informers

If a witness called at trial is a police informer in relation to the crime charged, the court should be told and, unless there is a very strong countervailing interest not to do so, his status should be revealed.[48] However, it is in the public interest to protect the identity of informers, not only for their own safety, but also to ensure that the supply of information about criminal activities does not dry up. Accordingly, there is a rule, established since at least the late eighteenth century, that a witness in civil or criminal proceedings may not be asked to disclose the name of a police informer.[49] Likewise, no order for disclosure will be made which will have that effect. Even if the party entitled to object does not invoke the rule, the judge is nonetheless obliged to apply it.[50] However, the rule will be overridden where, in a criminal trial, strict enforcement would be likely to cause a miscarriage of justice, ie where the accused can show good reason

---

[45] [1985] AC 374, HL at 412.

[46] See per Brightman and Donaldson LJJ in *Buttes Gas & Oil Co v Hammer (No 3)* [1981] QB 223, CA.

[47] *Settebello Ltd v Banco Totta and Acores* [1985] 2 All ER 1025, CA. See also *Fayed v Al-Tajir* [1987] 2 All ER 396 per Mustill and Kerr LJJ, CA at 480 and 410 respectively: international comity requires that an inter-departmental memorandum prepared and circulated in the London embassy of a friendly foreign state should not be admitted as the foundation of an action for libel.

[48] *R v Patel* [2002] Crim LR 304.

[49] *R v Hardy* (1794) 24 State Tr 199. In principle, the rule should prevent disclosure of not only the name of the informer but also any information that will enable him to be identified: see *R v Omar* 2007 ONCA 117. See also s 17 of the Regulation of Investigatory Powers Act 2000, which renders inadmissible telephone-tap evidence, if lawfully obtained. See Mirfield, 'Regulation of Investigatory Powers Act 2000 (2): Evidential Aspects' [2001] Crim LR 91.

[50] See per Lord Esher MR in *Marks v Beyfus* (1890) 25 QBD 494, CA at 500 and per Mann J in *R v Rankine* [1986] 2 All ER 566, CA at 569.

to expect that disclosure of the name of the informant will assist him in establishing his innocence.[51] The decision on disclosure is for the judge and therefore if the prosecution are of the view that there should be disclosure, they should refer the matter to the court, which must reach its own decision.[52]

In *Marks v Beyfus*[53] the plaintiff claimed damages for malicious prosecution. In the course of the trial, he asked the Director of Public Prosecutions (DPP) to name his informants, but the judge disallowed the question. This ruling was upheld by the Court of Appeal on the ground 'that this was a public prosecution, ordered by the Government (or by an official equivalent to the Government) for what was considered to be a public object, and that therefore the information ought not, on grounds of public policy, to be disclosed'.[54] Lord Esher said:[55]

> I do not say it is a rule which can never be departed from; if upon the trial of a prisoner the judge should be of opinion that the disclosure of the name of the informant is necessary or right in order to show the prisoner's innocence, then one public policy is in conflict with another public policy, and that which says that an innocent man is not to be condemned when his innocence can be proved is the policy that must prevail. But, except in that case, this rule of public policy is not a matter of discretion; it is a rule of law...

Although it has been suggested that the possibility of a miscarriage of justice *dictates* disclosure,[56] it seems that a balancing exercise should be performed, even though, if the disputed material may prove the accused's innocence or avoid a miscarriage of justice, the balance will come down resoundingly in favour of disclosure.[57] Nonetheless, it has been held that judges need to scrutinize applications for disclosure of details about informants with very great care. They should be astute to see that assertions of a need to know such details (because essential to the running of a defence) are justified. In some cases, the informant is an informant and no more; in others he may have participated in the events constituting, surrounding, or following the crime. Even when the informant has participated, the judge will need to consider whether his role so impinges on an issue of interest to the defence, present or potential, as to make disclosure necessary.[58]

In *R v Agar*[59] the prosecution case was that A, on arrival at the house of X, found police officers present and, when he ran off, threw away a packet containing drugs. A alleged that the police had entered into an arrangement with X, an informer, to ask him to go to X's house and that the drugs allegedly found had been planted by the police. It was held that although an accused cannot discover the identity of an informer by pretending that something is part of his case when in truth it adds nothing to it, and although it *may* be that a defence which is manifestly frivolous and doomed to failure must be sacrificed to the general rule protecting informers, on the facts the defence should have been permitted to elicit that X had told the police that A would be coming to his house (which would have identified him as an

---

[51] Per Lawton LJ in *R v Hennessey* (1978) 68 Cr App R 419, CA at 426. See also *R v Hallett* [1986] Crim LR 462, CA.

[52] *R(WV) v Crown Prosecution Service* [2011] EWHC 2480 (Admin).

[53] (1890) 25 QBD 494, CA.

[54] Per Lord Esher MR at 496–7. It would seem that bodies authorized by statute to bring prosecutions may claim the immunity, but not an individual prosecuting in a private capacity.

[55] (1890) 25 QBD 494, CA at 498.

[56] Per Mann LJ in *R v Governor of Brixton Prison, ex p Osman* [1992] 1 All ER 108 at 118.

[57] Per Lord Taylor CJ in *R v Keane* [1994] 2 All ER 478, CA at 484.

[58] Per Lord Taylor CJ in *R v Turner* [1995] 3 All ER 432, CA.

[59] [1990] 2 All ER 442, CA.

informer)—such evidence was necessary to enable A to put forward his defence that he had been set up by X and the police acting in concert.[60]

Owners or occupiers of premises used for police surveillance

In *R v Rankine*[61] it was held that the rule is not confined to the identification of police informers but also prevents the identification of premises used for police surveillance and the owners and occupiers of such premises. However, if the accused alleges that disclosure of the identification of such premises is necessary in order to establish his innocence, the prosecution must provide a sufficient evidential base to enable the trial judge properly to determine whether to afford the protection sought. In *R v Johnson*[62] the Court of Appeal held that the minimal evidential requirements for these purposes are twofold. First, the officer in charge of the observations, who normally should be of at least the rank of sergeant, should give evidence that he visited the premises to be used and ascertained the attitude of the occupiers to the use to be made of the premises and the possible disclosure thereafter of the use made and of facts which could lead to the identification of both premises and occupiers. He may additionally inform the court of any difficulties encountered in the particular locality in obtaining assistance from the public. Second, an officer of at least the rank of chief inspector should give evidence that immediately before the trial he visited the premises and ascertained whether the occupiers were still the same and, whether they were or not, what their attitude was to the possible disclosure of the use made of the premises and of facts which could lead to the identification of both premises and occupiers.[63]

Johnson was convicted of supplying drugs. The police alleged that he had been seen selling the drugs in a particular street by officers situated in buildings in the locality. The prosecution argued that the evidence which their witnesses should be compelled to give should not go further than revealing that all the observation points were within a given maximum distance from the scene of the offence. Defence counsel submitted that this would enable officers to cover up inconsistencies in their evidence and gravely embarrass him in his efforts to test in cross-examination precisely what they could see from their various locations having regard to the layout of the street and the objects in it, including trees. In the jury's absence, the police gave evidence as to the difficulty of obtaining assistance from the public for observation purposes and revealed that the occupiers, all of whom were also occupiers at the material time, did not wish their names and addresses to be disclosed because they feared for their safety. The judge ruled that the officers should not reveal the location of the premises used. The appeal was dismissed: although the conduct of the defence was to some extent affected by this restraint, it had led to no injustice.[64]

In *R v Brown, R v Daley*[65] the Court of Appeal emphasized that the extension of the exclusionary rule established in *R v Rankine* was based on the protection of the owner or occupier

---

[60] Applied in *R v Langford* [1990] Crim LR 653, CC. See also *R v Vaillencourt* [1993] Crim LR 311, CA and *R v Reilly* [1994] Crim LR 279, CA. Cf *R v Slowcombe* [1991] Crim LR 198, CA, where the identity of the informer would have contributed little or nothing to the defence being run, and *R v Menza and Marshalleck* [1998] Crim LR 58, CA.

[61] [1986] 2 All ER 566, CA.

[62] [1989] 1 All ER 121, CA.

[63] There is no requirement of a threat of violence before protection can be afforded to the occupier—it suffices if he is in fear of harassment: *Blake v DPP* (1992) 97 Cr App R 169, DC.

[64] *R v Johnson* was applied in *R v Hewitt; R v Davis* (1991) 95 Cr App R 81, CA. See also *R v Grimes* [1994] Crim LR 213, CA.

[65] (1987) 87 Cr App R 52, CA.

disclosure is 'necessary'.[112] However, if a party seeks disclosure on an interim application, the court should be careful not to order disclosure unless the evidence before it establishes that the inference of necessity is unlikely to be displaced when all the evidence is produced and tested at trial.[113] Section 10 requires actual necessity to be established: expediency, however great, is not enough.[114]

Disclosure necessary in the interests of justice

Concerning 'justice', in the interest of which disclosure may be necessary, Lord Diplock, in *Secretary of State for Defence v Guardian Newspapers Ltd*, said that the word is used in the sense of the administration of justice in the course of legal proceedings in a court of law or tribunal.[115] This approach was adopted in *Maxwell v Pressdram Ltd*,[116] where it was held to be essential to identify and define the issue in the legal proceedings. Similarly, in *Handmade Films (Productions) Ltd v Express Newspapers*[117] it was held that although a claim for discovery based on the *Norwich Pharmacal* principle may come within 'the interests of justice', the claimant must show that he needs the name of the unknown wrongdoer because he intends to sue him—it is insufficient that an action *may* be brought.

Lord Diplock's definition, however, was rejected as too narrow in the leading domestic authority, *X Ltd v Morgan-Grampian Ltd*.[118] The plaintiffs, X Ltd, two private companies, prepared a business plan in order to negotiate a bank loan to raise additional working capital. A copy of the plan was stolen. The next day, an unidentified source gave G, a journalist, information about the planned loan. G decided to write an article about X Ltd. X Ltd obtained an injunction against the defendant publishers, M-G Ltd, restraining publication of information derived from the plan, and applied under s 10 for an order disclosing the name of the source, their intention being to bring proceedings against him for recovery of the plan, an injunction to prevent further publication, and damages. The House of Lords held that, by reason of the *Norwich Pharmacal* principles, the court had jurisdiction to order M-G Ltd to disclose G's notes and that although the information obtained from the source had not been 'contained in a publication', the information having been received for the purposes of publication, it should be subject to s 10, since the purpose underlying the statutory protection of sources is as much applicable before as after publication.

The following propositions derive from the judgment of Lord Bridge.

1. Where a judge asks himself the question, 'Can I be satisfied that disclosure of the source of *this* information is necessary to serve *this* interest?' he has to engage in a balancing exercise.

2. He starts with three assumptions: that the protection of sources is itself a matter of high public importance; that nothing less than necessity will suffice to override it; and that the

---

[112] Per Lords Diplock and Scarman at 607 and 618 respectively.

[113] Per Lord Scarman at 618. See also *Handmade Films (Productions) Ltd v Express Newspapers* [1986] FSR 463, Ch D.

[114] Per Lord Diplock at 607, applied in *Handmade Films (Productions) Ltd v Express Newspapers* [1986] FSR 463, Ch D. Cf per Lord Griffiths in *Re an inquiry under the Company Securities (Insider Dealing) Act 1985* [1988] 1 All ER 203 HL at 208–9: 'I doubt if it is possible to go further than to say that "necessary" has a meaning that lies somewhere between "indispensable" on the one hand and "useful" or "expedient" on the other, and to leave it to the judge to decide towards which end of the scale of meaning he will place it on the facts of any particular case.'

[115] [1984] 3 All ER 601 at 607.

[116] [1987] 1 All ER 656, CA at 665.

[117] [1986] FSR 463, Ch D.

[118] [1990] 2 All ER 1, HL.

necessity can only arise out of concern for another matter of high public importance, one of the four interests listed in s 10.

3. The question whether disclosure is necessary 'in the interests of justice' gives rise to a difficult problem of weighing one public interest against another. Lord Diplock's definition of justice was too narrow: it is 'in the interests of justice' that persons should be enabled to exercise important legal rights and to protect themselves from serious legal wrongs, whether or not resort to legal proceedings in a court of law is necessary to obtain those objectives. Thus if an employer is suffering grave damage from the activities of an unidentified disloyal employee, it is in the interests of justice that he should be able to identify him to end his contract of employment, notwithstanding that no legal proceedings may be necessary to do so.

4. It is only if the judge is satisfied that disclosure in the interests of justice is of such preponderating importance as to override the statutory privilege that the threshold of necessity will be reached.

5. This is a question of fact, but calls for the exercise of discriminating and sometimes difficult value judgments, to which many factors will be relevant on both sides of the scale. In favour of disclosure there will be a wide spectrum within which the particular case must be located. For example, if the party seeking disclosure shows that his very livelihood depends on it, the case will be near one end of the spectrum, but if what he seeks to protect is a minor interest in property, the case will be at or near the other end. On the other side, there is also a wide spectrum. One important factor is the nature of the information: the greater the legitimate public interest in it, the greater the importance of protecting the source. Another significant factor is the manner in which the information was obtained by the source: the importance of protecting the source will be enhanced if the information was obtained legitimately, but will be diminished if obtained illegally, unless counterbalanced by a clear public interest in publication, as when the source acts in order to expose iniquity.

Applying those principles to the facts, it was held that disclosure of G's notes was necessary in the interests of justice. The publication of X Ltd's plan during their refinancing negotiations would involve a threat of severe damage to their business, and consequently to the livelihood of their employees, which could only be defused by identification of the source, either as the thief or as the means of identifying the thief, which would then allow X Ltd to bring proceedings to recover the plan. Furthermore, the source was involved in a gross breach of confidentiality which was not counterbalanced by any legitimate interest in publication of the information.

In *Ashworth Hospital Authority v MGM Ltd*[119] it was said that the wider interpretation of the 'interests of justice' in *X Ltd v Morgan-Grampian Ltd* accords more happily with the scheme of Art 10 than the interpretation of Lord Diplock in *Secretary of State for Defence v Guardian Newspapers Ltd*. Confirming that 'interests of justice' in s 10 means interests that are justiciable, it was also observed that it is difficult to envisage any such interest that would not fall within one or more of the Art 10 'legitimate aims'.

[119] [2002] 1 WLR 2033, HL. The text derives from the judgment of Lord Phillips in the Court of Appeal ([2001] 1 WLR 515), which was expressly endorsed by the House of Lords.

against the interest of the proper administration of justice in disclosure. Knox J, while acknowledging that it was a matter of degree in any particular case, said that if the cat had got all four legs out of the bag, there was little point in holding on to its tail.

In *R v Governor of Brixton Prison, ex p Osman*[142] certain documents protected by public interest immunity had been disclosed in a previous application for habeas corpus, although they had not been read in open court. It was held that prior disclosure of a document is a matter to be taken into account in the balance: if there has been publication to the whole world, then the public interest in non-disclosure must collapse. On the facts, however, the small degree of publication that had occurred could not upset the balance, which came down heavily in favour of immunity.

Similar considerations presumably apply in relation to secondary evidence. Obviously, the submarine plans in *Duncan v Cammell Laird & Co Ltd*[143] could not be proved by any means; in *R v Lewes Justices, ex p Home Secretary*[144] a copy of the allegedly libellous letter had somehow been obtained by the person to whom it referred, but because public interest immunity applied he was not able to prove that letter by any means. However, if information is freely available to the public, the fact that that information also forms the subject matter of a protected communication will surely not prevent proof of the information from the public sources. In each case, it is submitted, the question should be whether, on the particular facts, the public interest really does require non-disclosure; if there has been limited disclosure, immunity may still be justified, especially if the disclosure was wrongful.

Disclosure, production, and inspection

Disclosure involves two stages, disclosure of the existence of a document and production of that document for inspection. Before any question of public interest immunity can be raised, the document has to be one which should be disclosed within the rules normally applicable in civil litigation.[145] Under CPR r 31.6, standard disclosure requires a party to disclose only (a) the documents on which he relies; (b) the documents which adversely affect his own case, adversely affect another party's case, or support another party's case; and (c) the documents he is required to disclose by a relevant practice direction. If the party seeking disclosure falls at this hurdle, the question of public interest immunity will simply not arise.[146] Moreover, the court, in deciding whether to dispense with or limit standard disclosure, or whether to make an order for specific disclosure or specific inspection under r 31.12, must seek to give effect to the 'overriding objective' of enabling it to deal with the case justly, which includes saving expense and ensuring that it is dealt with expeditiously and fairly, etc.[147] If the party seeking disclosure falls at these hurdles, again the question of immunity will simply not arise.[148]

---

[142] [1992] 1 All ER 108 at 118.

[143] [1942] AC 624, HL.

[144] [1973] AC 388, HL.

[145] Per Wood J in *Evans v Chief Constable of Surrey* [1989] 2 All ER 594, QBD at 597–8, citing Lord Scarman in *Burmah Oil Co Ltd v Bank of England* [1980] AC 1090 at 1141 and Lord Edmund-Davies in *Air Canada v Secretary of State for Trade (No 2)* [1983] 2 AC 394 at 441.

[146] See *Evans v Chief Constable of Surrey* [1989] 2 All ER 594, a decision under the Rules of the Supreme Court, now replaced by the Civil Procedure Rules.

[147] See Ch 2, under **Judicial discretion, Exclusionary discretion, Civil cases**.

[148] See per Lord Woolf in *R v Chief Constable of the West Midlands Police, ex p Wiley* [1994] 3 All ER 420, HL at 430 and per Sir Thomas Bingham MR in *Taylor v Anderton* [1995] 2 All ER 420, CA at 432–5, all decisions under the Rules of the Supreme Court.

If these hurdles are surmounted, but public interest immunity is claimed, the judge will have to ask first whether the head of public interest on which reliance is placed is at least 'analogous' to those which have already been recognized by authority. He will also have to assess the strength of the objector's reasons for saying that disclosure will prejudice that public interest. If a prima facie claim to immunity is thus made out, the person seeking disclosure must establish that the public interest in the administration of justice in the case 'tips the scales decisively in his favour'.[149] In some cases, it will be obvious from the description of the documents and the nature of the litigation that the claim to immunity is either groundless or unanswerable. In other cases a more detailed assessment of the content of the documents is needed. In *Conway v Rimmer*[150] Lord Reid said:

> If [the judge] decides that on balance the documents probably ought to be produced, I think that it would generally be best that he should see them before ordering production and if he thinks that the Minister's reasons are not clearly expressed he will have to see the documents before ordering inspection.

Various objections to judicial inspection have been put forward. In *Duncan v Cammell Laird & Co Ltd*[151] the House of Lords regarded it as a wrongful communication between the judge and one party to the exclusion of the other. This reasoning was firmly rejected in *Conway v Rimmer*, but it remains true that a party may be aggrieved that the judge has seen material to which he has been denied access.[152] Other considerations were put forward by Lord Wilberforce in *Burmah Oil Co v Bank of England*,[153] namely (i) that judges should not lightly undertake to question a responsible minister's assessment of the weight of the public interest in non-disclosure; and (ii) that inspection can be a very time-consuming activity which has to be conducted without the assistance of fully informed argument. Such considerations led Lord Wilberforce to uphold the claim to immunity without inspecting the documents. However, the other members of the House of Lords held that inspection was justified once it was shown that it was likely that the documents would contain material substantially useful to the party seeking discovery. On the facts, this test was satisfied, but after inspection disclosure was refused because it was not found to be 'necessary either for disposing fairly of the cause or matter or for saving costs'.

In *Air Canada v Secretary of State for Trade*[154] it was accepted that the ministerial documents probably did contain material which was relevant to the issues in the case, but without inspection it was impossible to know which side that material would favour. Lord Fraser was of the opinion that a court should not embark upon a private inspection of documents unless persuaded that such an inspection is likely to satisfy it that it ought to take the further step of ordering the documents to be produced publicly. On this basis, Lord Fraser, together with Lords Wilberforce and Edmund-Davies, held that the court should only inspect if the party seeking disclosure has shown 'that the documents are very likely to contain material which would give substantial support to his contention on an issue which arises in the case and that,

---

[149] Per Lord Edmund-Davies in *Burmah Oil Co Ltd v Bank of England* [1980] AC 1090 at 1127, citing Lord Cross in *Alfred Crompton Amusement Machines Ltd v Customs and Excise Comrs (No 2)* [1974] AC 405 at 434.
[150] [1968] AC 910 at 953.
[151] [1942] AC 624 per Viscount Simon LC at 640–1.
[152] Per Lord Denning MR in *Neilson v Laugharne* [1981] QB 736 at 748–9.
[153] [1980] AC 1090 at 1117.
[154] [1983] 2 AC 394.

(and any legal representative of the party) is excluded,[177] but who is not responsible to that party.[178]

The circumstances in which a declaration may be made under s 6(1) are governed by s 6(3)–(6).

(3) The court may make such a declaration if it considers that the following two conditions are met.

(4) The first condition is that—

    (a) a party to the proceedings would be required to disclose sensitive material in the course of the proceedings to another person (whether or not another party to the proceedings), or

    (b) a party to the proceedings would be required to make such a disclosure were it not for one or more of the following—

        (i)   the possibility of a claim for public interest immunity in relation to the material,

        (ii) the fact that there would be no requirement to disclose if the party chose not to rely on the material,

        (iii) section 17(1) of the Regulation of Investigatory Powers Act 2000 (exclusion for intercept material),

        (iv) any other enactment that would prevent the party from disclosing the material but would not do so if the proceedings were proceedings in relation to which there was a declaration under this section.

(5) The second condition is that it is in the interests of the fair and effective administration of justice in the proceedings to make a declaration.

(6) The two conditions are met if the court considers that they are met in relation to any material that would be required to be disclosed in the course of the proceedings (and an application under subsection (2)(a) need not be based on all of the material that might meet the conditions or on material that the applicant would be required to disclose).

In the case of an application by the Secretary of State, there is an additional hurdle set out in s 6(7).

(7) The court must not consider an application by the Secretary of State under subsection 2(a) unless it is satisfied that the Secretary of State has, before making the application, considered whether to make, or advise another person to make, a claim for public interest immunity in relation to the material on which the application is based.

Under s 7 of the Act, where a court has made a declaration under s 6, it must keep the declaration under review and may at any time, including the stage at which it has examined the relevant material, revoke it if it considers that 'the declaration is no longer in the interests of the fair and effective administration of justice in the proceedings'.

It is clear, from the deliberate use of the word 'may' in both s 6(3) and s 7, that whether a declaration is made and, if so, whether it should be revoked, are matters for the judge to decide in the exercise of his discretion. However, Parliament has also deliberately not required the court, in deciding these matters, to conduct a balancing exercise under which the public interest in the fair and open administration of justice should be weighed against the public interest in favour of a closed material procedure. It remains to be seen, therefore, how the courts will interpret the phrase 'the interests of the fair and effective administration of justice in the proceedings', for the purposes of s 6(3) and s 7, given that it appears that they will not

---

[177] Section 9(1) and s 8(1).
[178] Section 9(4).

be entitled to use the kind of reasoning adopted by the House of Lords in *Al Rawi v Security Service*.

Criminal cases

General

Under para 20 of the *Attorney General's Guidelines: Disclosure of Information in Criminal Proceedings*, before making an application to the court to withhold material in the public interest, a prosecutor should aim to disclose as much material as he properly can, by giving the defence redacted or edited copies or summaries. Under para 21 of the *Guidelines*, prior to or at the hearing the court must be provided with full and accurate information. The Court of Appeal has stressed that where an *ex parte* hearing is held, it is imperative in all cases that the Crown is scrupulously accurate in the information provided.[179] Where a trial judge or the Court of Appeal learns that prosecution witnesses, in the course of a public interest immunity hearing, lied in their evidence, the prosecution are likely to be tainted beyond redemption, however strong the evidence against the accused otherwise was.[180] Paragraph 21 of the *Guidelines* also provides that the prosecution advocate must examine all material which is the subject matter of the application and make any necessary enquiries of the investigator.[181]

The procedure to be adopted where the prosecution apply for immunity from disclosure is set out in Pt 22 of the Criminal Procedure Rules 2013[182] which, generally speaking, reflect the following principles laid down by Lord Taylor CJ in *R v Davis*.[183] Whenever possible, which will be in most cases, the prosecution must notify the defence of the application, indicating the category of material in question, so that the defence have the opportunity of making representations to the court. If to disclose even the category would be to reveal too much, the prosecution should notify the defence that an *ex parte* application will be made. In highly exceptional circumstances where to reveal even the fact of an *ex parte* application would be to reveal too much, an *ex parte* application may be made without notice. However if, in any case, the judge takes the view that the defence should be aware of the category of material and should have the opportunity of making representations, or at any rate should have notice of the application, he may so order.

The *ex parte* procedure is contrary to the general principles of open justice in criminal trials and should only be adopted on the application of the Crown for the specific purpose of enabling the court to test a claim that immunity or sensitivity justifies non-disclosure.[184] Thus, a *defence* application, such as an application for details of an informer to be disclosed, should not be heard *ex parte*.[185] An *ex parte* application on the part of the prosecution will not necessarily amount to a violation of Art 6 of the European Convention on Human Rights, whether the application is made at the trial[186] or in the Court of Appeal,[187] but unfairness caused at the

---

[179] *R v Jackson* [2000] Crim LR 377, CA.

[180] *R v Early* [2003] 1 Cr App R 288, CA.

[181] See also *R v Menga* [1998] Crim LR 58, CA.

[182] SI 2013/1554.

[183] [1993] 1 WLR 613, CA.

[184] *R v Keane* [1994] 2 All ER 478 at 483. See also *R v Smith* [1998] 2 Cr App R 1, CA.

[185] *R v Turner* [1995] 3 All ER 432, CA; *R v Tattenhove* [1996] 1 Cr App R 408, CA.

[186] *Jasper v UK* (2000) 30 EHRR 441. See also *Atlan v UK* [2002] 34 EHRR 833 and *R v Lawrence* [2002] Crim LR 584, CA.

[187] *R v Botmeh* [2002] 1 WLR 531, CA.

trial by an improper failure to disclose material to the judge will not necessarily be remedied by an *ex parte* examination of the material by the Court of Appeal.[188]

Judicial use of information immune from disclosure

It is wrong and contrary to Art 6(1) for a judge to make use of information immune from disclosure to the defence in reaching a decision on the admissibility of evidence. In *Edwards v UK*[189] the applicant was charged with a drugs offence following an undercover operation. On an *ex parte* application to withhold material, the judge ruled against disclosure. On a subsequent unsuccessful defence application under s 78 of the Police and Criminal Evidence Act 1984 to exclude the evidence of the only undercover officer to be called by the prosecution, on the basis of entrapment, the judge ruled that he had seen nothing in the course of the *ex parte* application that would have assisted the defence in their application under s 78. The European Court, finding a violation of Art 6(1), held that since the public interest immunity evidence may have related to facts connected with the s 78 application, the defence were not able fully to argue the case on entrapment. However certain the trial judge was that the evidence did not assist the defence, this overlooked the possibility that the defence could have countered the evidence or shown it to be mistaken or otherwise unreliable. The denial of that opportunity on an issue so fundamental to the trial was a failure to comply with the requirements to provide adversarial proceedings and equality of arms and to incorporate adequate safeguards to protect the interests of the accused.[190]

Edwards v UK was distinguished in *R v May*[191] where the judge, in confiscation proceedings under the Criminal Justice Act 1988, stated that he had ignored anything attracting immunity that had been revealed to him in earlier *ex parte* public interest immunity proceedings. The Court of Appeal rejected a submission, made in reliance on *Edwards v UK*, that since the judge may have been influenced by the material he had seen, however much he had tried to put it out of his mind, he should have recused himself or at least appointed special counsel.[192] *Edwards v UK* was distinguished on the grounds that the Strasbourg court had proceeded on the basis that the trial judge *had* taken into account the material that the accused had been denied an opportunity to counter. It was held that if a judge is of the view that despite his best efforts he is unlikely to be able to ignore the undisclosed material, to the detriment of the accused, then he should consider the appointment of special counsel, but that in many cases the judge can be relied upon to put such material out of his mind.

Special counsel

Special counsel are independent counsel appointed to represent the interests of the accused, to whom material may be disclosed that must not be disclosed to the accused and who have been approved to act as special counsel by the Attorney General. In *Edwards v UK*, the court referred to the recommendation, in Sir Robin Auld's *Review of the Criminal Courts of England and Wales*,[193] that special counsel be introduced in those cases at first instance and on appeal where the court considers prosecution applications for immunity

---

[188] *Rowe and Davis v UK* (2000) 30 EHRR 1. See also *Atlan v UK* [2002] 34 EHRR 833.

[189] (2003) 15 BHRC 189.

[190] See also *R v H* [2004] 2 AC 134, HL, overruling *R v Smith* [2001] 1 WLR 1031; and *R v Ali* [2008] EWCA Crim 146.

[191] [2005] 1 WLR 2902, CA.

[192] See, in this chapter, under **Procedural issues**, **Criminal cases**, **Special counsel**.

[193] HMSO, 2001, paras 193–7.

from disclosure in the absence of the defence.[194] In *R v H*[195] it was argued that it is a violation of Art 6 for a trial judge to rule on a claim to immunity, in the absence of adversarial argument on behalf of the accused, where the material in question is or may be relevant to a disputed issue of fact which the judge has to decide in order to rule on an application which will effectively determine the outcome of the proceedings. It was also argued that the *Edwards v UK* principle applies whenever the defence relies on entrapment as a basis for staying the case as an abuse of process or excluding prosecution evidence. The House of Lords held that to adopt such an approach would be to put the judge in a straitjacket. Lord Bingham laid down the following governing principles. The golden rule is full disclosure to the defence of any material held by the prosecution which weakens its case or strengthens that of the defence. In circumstances where such material cannot be disclosed, fully or at all, without the risk of serious prejudice to an important public interest, some derogation from the rule can be justified, but should always be to the minimum necessary to protect the public interest, and should never imperil the overall fairness of the trial. If prosecution claims for public interest immunity were operated with scrupulous attention to these principles, and with continuing regard to the proper interests of the accused, there should be no violation of Art 6. The appointment of special counsel raises ethical problems, since the lawyer cannot disclose to his client the material which is the basis of the application and cannot take full instructions from him, as well as practical problems of delay, expense, and continuing review.[196] None of these problems should deter the court from appointing an approved advocate as special counsel where it is necessary, in the interests of justice, to secure protection of an accused's right to a fair trial. However, such appointments would be exceptional and should not be ordered unless and until the trial judge is satisfied that no other course will adequately meet the overriding requirement of fairness to the accused.

In *R v Austin*,[197] the Court of Appeal stressed that the dicta in *R v H* about the use of special counsel related to the issues of disclosure and admissibility and expressly declined to reach a conclusion on the separate question whether special counsel can be appointed at first instance to assist a judge, on the substantive issue of abuse of process, in reaching his decision by reference to material not seen by the defence. A distinction was also drawn between use of special counsel at first instance and on appeal. It is essential that the Court of Appeal can view material which is undisclosed to an appellant, the prime consideration of the court being the safety of the conviction, and although in many cases the Court of Appeal will be able to reach a view without the need for special counsel, in some cases it may be in the interests of justice for special counsel to be appointed.[198]

Magistrates' courts

Where a magistrates' court, whether made up of a stipendiary magistrate or lay justices, hears an application for non-disclosure on the grounds of public interest immunity and rules that the material in question is inadmissible, ordinarily it should proceed to hear the case itself, because of the court's duty of continuing review, and should exercise its discretion to order the

---

[194] See also *Jasper v UK* (2000) 30 EHRR 441.
[195] [2004] 2 AC 134, HL.
[196] [2004] 2 AC 134, HL per Lord Bingham at [22].
[197] [2013] EWCA Crim 1028.
[198] [2013] EWCA Crim 1028, citing *R v Chisholm* [2010] EWCA Crim 258 at [46].

case to be tried by a different bench only in exceptional circumstances, as when material was introduced at the non-disclosure hearing which was prejudicial and irrelevant to the question of admissibility.[199] Magistrates, in deciding an application for non-disclosure, should apply the same principles that apply in proceedings on indictment, but where it is known that a contested issue as to the disclosure of sensitive material is likely to arise, and the magistrates have discretion to send the case to the Crown Court for trial, they would be well advised to commit.[200] For this reason, the occasions on which it will be appropriate to appoint special counsel in the magistrates' court will be even rarer than in the Crown Court.[201]

ADDITIONAL READING

HM Government Response to the Joint Committee of Human Rights Fourth Report of Session 2012–13: Legislative Scrutiny: Justice and Security Bill, Cm 8533 (2013).

Joint Committee on Human Rights, *Report on Counter-Terrorism Policy and Human Rights (16th Report): Annual Renewal of Control Orders Legislation 2010*, HL Paper 64/HC 395 (2010).

Joint Committee on Human Rights, *Legislative Scrutiny: Justice and Security Bill*, HL Paper 59, HC 370 (2012).

Joint Committee on Human Rights, *Legislative Scrutiny: Justice and Security Bill (Second Report)*, HL Paper 128, HC 1014 (2013).

Mirfield, 'Regulation of Investigatory Powers Act 2000 (2): Evidential Aspects' [2001] Crim LR 91.

[199] *R v Stipendiary Magistrate for Norfolk, ex p Taylor* [1998] Crim LR 276, DC. See also *R v Bromley Magistrates' Court, ex p Smith* [1995] 4 All ER 146 (and cf *R v South Worcestershire Magistrates, ex p Lilley* [1995] 4 All ER 186, DC); *R (DPP) v Acton Youth Court* [2001] 1 WLR 1828; *R v H* [2004] 2 AC 134, HL at [43]–[44]; and s 14 of the Criminal Procedure and Investigations Act 1996. See also Bisgrove, 'Judges as Tribunal of Fact: To What Extent do the Provisions for a Defendant to be Tried on Indictment by a Judge sitting without a Jury Conflict With the Defendant's Right to a Fair Trial Where Issues of PII are Present?' [2010] Crim LR 702.

[200] See generally *R v Bromley Magistrates' Court, ex p Smith* [1995] 4 All ER 146, DC, distinguishing *R v DPP, ex p Warby* [1994] Crim LR 281, DC on the basis that it concerned committal proceedings.

[201] *R v H* [2004] 2 AC 134, HL.

Privilege

20

Key issues

- What is the justification for the rule that no one should be compelled to answer any question if the answer to it would have a tendency to expose him to a criminal charge ('the privilege against self-incrimination')?

- In what circumstances should the privilege be abrogated by statute?

- What is the justification for legal professional privilege, ie the rules that a client should be able to maintain the confidentiality of (a) communications between him and his lawyer made for the purposes of obtaining and giving legal advice ('legal advice privilege'); and (b) communications between him or his lawyer and third parties, such as potential witnesses, the dominant purpose of which was preparation for contemplated or pending litigation ('litigation privilege')?

- What exceptions should there be to legal professional privilege?

- If material is protected by legal professional privilege, for how long should the protection last?

- If someone other than the client, lawyer, or relevant third party obtains material protected by legal professional privilege, may she be compelled to produce it or give evidence about it?

- What is the justification for the rule that a party to civil proceedings should not be compelled to answer questions about what was said in the course of negotiations held with the other party to the proceedings and designed to settle their dispute ('without prejudice' privilege)?

- What exceptions should there be to 'without prejudice' privilege?

that there is reasonable ground to apprehend danger to the witness from his being called to answer...The danger to be apprehended must be real and appreciable with reference to the ordinary operation of law in the ordinary course of things; not a danger of an imaginary and unsubstantial character...[24]

It is not sufficient to ascertain that the claim was made on legal advice; the duty of the court is non-delegable and therefore it cannot simply adopt the conclusion of a solicitor advising the witness, whose conclusion may or may not be correct.[25] If necessary, the judge may hear the witness's explanation in camera. He must make due allowance for the possibility that apparently innocuous questions may, when combined with other material, give rise to damaging inferences.[26] Moreover, it is sufficient to support a claim that the answers sought might lead to a line of inquiry which would or might form a significant step in the chain of evidence required for a prosecution.[27] On the other hand, a claim to privilege will not succeed if the evidence against the witness is already so strong that if proceedings are to be taken at all they will be taken whether or not the witness answers. This is a question of fact for the judge, who should not ignore the possibility that although some evidence is already available to the authorities, additional evidence from the witness may increase the risk of proceedings being taken.[28] The triviality or staleness of the offence may lead the court to treat the likelihood of prosecution as too remote, but it remains to be seen whether protection can be refused on the *sole* ground that the charge, though likely to be brought, is a trivial one.[29]

Spouses, civil partners, strangers, and companies

In most cases the witness claiming privilege will do so because he fears prosecution himself. If he chooses not to claim the privilege or, in ignorance, fails to claim it—the judge may, but is not obliged to, remind him of his rights—no one else can claim it on his behalf.

A witness in either civil or criminal proceedings cannot claim privilege in respect of questions the answers to which would tend to incriminate strangers.[30] In civil proceedings, under s 14(1)(b) of the 1968 Act, the right of a person to assert the privilege 'shall include a like right to refuse any question or produce any document or thing if to do so would tend to expose

---

[24] Per Cockburn CJ at 330, approved in *Den Norske Bank ASA v Antonatos* [1998] 3 All ER 74, CA. See also *Dushkar Kanchan Singh v The Queen* [2010] NZSC 161. Cf *Triplex Safety Glass Co Ltd v Lancegaye Safety Glass (1934) Ltd* [1939] 2 KB 395: privilege may be claimed on the ground of exposure to criminal libel proceedings even though such proceedings are rare.

[25] *R (Crown Prosecution Service) v Bolton Magistrates' Court* [2004] 1 WLR 835, DC.

[26] Per Cockburn CJ in *R v Boyes* (1861) 1 B&S 311, QB at 330; see also *British Steel Corpn v Granada Television Ltd* [1981] AC 1096, HL, especially per Megarry V-C in the Chancery Division (at 1108).

[27] Per Beldam LJ in *Sociedade Nacional de Combustiveis de Angola UEE v Lundqvist* [1990] 3 All ER 283 at 297, CA, citing Lord Wilberforce in *Rank Film Distributors Ltd v Video Information Centre* [1982] AC 380 at 443.

[28] *Rio Tinto Zinc Corpn v Westinghouse Electric Corpn* [1978] AC 547. In *Khan v Khan* [1982] 2 All ER 60, CA a witness was required to answer questions about his use of the proceeds of a cheque. His conduct 'reeked of dishonesty' and evidence as to his use of the proceeds did not materially increase the risk of prosecution for theft of the cheque.

[29] See per Lord Fraser in *Rank Film Distributors Ltd v Video Information Centre* [1982] AC 380 at 445: the risk of prosecution for trivial offences under s 21 of the Copyright Act 1956 was not enough to establish the privilege, partly because the likelihood of prosecution was too remote, but also because it would be 'unreasonable to allow the possibility of incrimination of such offences to obstruct disclosure of information which would be of much more value to the owners of the infringed copyright than any protection they might obtain from s 21'.

[30] See *Ex p Reynolds* (1882) 20 Ch D 294, cited by Megarry V-C in *British Steel Corpn v Granada Television Ltd* [1981] AC 1096 at 1106, Ch D.

the spouse or civil partner of that person to proceedings for any such criminal offence or for the recovery of any such penalty'. However, the privilege remains that of the witness and, if he chooses to answer, the spouse or civil partner cannot complain. In criminal proceedings, however, it seems that a witness cannot claim privilege in respect of questions the answers to which would tend to incriminate his spouse.[31]

Because the privilege is a privilege against *self*-incrimination, office-holders, employees, or agents of a company may claim the privilege themselves, but cannot refuse to answer questions which would tend to incriminate the company or render it liable to a penalty under, for example, an EU regulation.[32] Equally, the company cannot refuse to answer questions which would tend to incriminate the office-holders.[33]

Statutory provisions

Statutory withdrawal of privilege

Pursuant to a variety of statutes and statutory instruments, specified persons in specified circumstances must answer questions for specified purposes notwithstanding that their answers may incriminate them. Some of the provisions abrogate the privilege expressly; others do so impliedly. However, clear language (express or by necessary implication) is required to show that Parliament intended to abrogate such a fundamental principle of the common law.[34] The true effect of any statutory withdrawal of privilege is also a matter of construction, but where a statute revokes the privilege without restricting the use that may be made of the answers, prima facie the answers may be used for any purpose for which they could have been used had the privilege never applied in the first place.[35] Thus if a witness is forced to make an incriminating admission, that admission cannot then be excluded at his own trial as being involuntary.[36] However, use of the answer in subsequent judicial proceedings may amount to a violation of the Art 6 right to a fair hearing, and in any event a criminal court may exclude the admission, in its discretion, if it would be oppressive to admit it.[37]

Compatibility with Article 6 of the European Convention on Human Rights

In *Saunders v UK*,[38] S was convicted of conspiracy, false accounting, and theft. At the trial, evidence was adduced of answers given by S to DTI inspectors appointed under the Companies Act 1985. Under s 434 of that Act, the inspectors could compel a person to answer their questions and the answers obtained could be used in evidence in any subsequent proceedings. The European Court of Human Rights was of the view that although not specifically mentioned in Art 6, the right to silence and the right not to incriminate oneself are 'generally recognized

---

[31] Per Lord Diplock in *Rio Tinto Zinc Corpn v Westinghouse Electric Corpn* [1978] AC 547 at 637 and, but only by inference, *R v Pitt* [1982] 3 All ER 63, CA. Contrast *R v All Saints, Worcester* (1817) 6 M&S 194.

[32] Per Lord Diplock in *Rio Tinto Zinc Corpn v Westinghouse Electric Corpn* [1978] AC 547 at 637–8.

[33] Per Beldam LJ in *Sociedade Nacional de Combustiveis de Angola UEE v Lundqvist* [1990] 3 All ER 283 at 300–1 and per Browne-Wilkinson V-C in *Tate Access Floors v Boswell* [1990] 3 All ER 303 at 314–15.

[34] *R (Malik) v Crown Court at Manchester* [2008] 4 All ER 403, DC at [73].

[35] *R v Scott* (1856) Dears&B 47.

[36] But if a judge wrongly denies a witness the protection of privilege, any admission thus compelled will be excluded in the trial of the witness as involuntary: *R v Garbett* (1847) 1 Den 236.

[37] See per French J in *Overseas Programming Co Ltd v Cinematographische Commerz-Anstalt and Iduna Film Gmbh* (1984) The Times, 16 May, QBD and per Ralph Gibson LJ in *Bank of England v Riley* [1992] 1 All ER 769, CA at 777.

[38] (1997) 23 EHRR 313 at para 68.

with carrying out the local authority's duties of investigation.[65] The purpose of s 98 is to protect a witness who is required to give evidence in relation to a child when such evidence would incriminate him or his spouse or civil partner. Thus s 98(2) will not prevent counsel for the accused from putting a 'statement or admission' to his spouse as a previous inconsistent statement in order to challenge her evidence or to attack her credibility.[66]

Section 2 of the Criminal Justice Act 1987

Under s 2, the Director of the Serious Fraud Office may require any person under investigation for a suspected offence involving serious or complex fraud, or any other person, to answer questions, furnish information, and produce documents, but under s 2(8) a statement in response to such a requirement may only be used in evidence against its maker (a) on a prosecution for an offence of knowingly or recklessly making a false or misleading statement (in purported compliance with a requirement under s 2); or (b) on a prosecution for some other offence where in giving evidence he makes a statement inconsistent with it. However, under s 2(8AA), the statement may not be used against its maker by virtue of (b) unless evidence relating to it is adduced or a question relating to it is asked, by him or on his behalf, in the proceedings arising out of the prosecution.

Section 434 of the Companies Act 1985

Under Pt XIV of the 1985 Act, officers and agents of a company and others possessing relevant information are obliged to answer questions put by Board of Trade inspectors appointed to investigate suspected fraud in the conduct or management of a company. However, under s 434(5A) and (5B) of the Act, in criminal proceedings in which the person who answered such a question is charged with an offence, other than an offence under s 2 or s 5 of the Perjury Act 1911 (false statements made on oath otherwise than in judicial proceedings or made otherwise than on oath), (a) no evidence relating to the answer may be adduced; and (b) no question relating to it may be asked, by or on behalf of the prosecution, unless evidence relating to it is adduced or a question relating to it is asked in the proceedings by or on behalf of the person charged.

Section 31(1) of the Theft Act 1968

Section 31(1) requires questions to be answered and orders to be complied with 'in proceedings for the recovery or administration of any property, for the execution of any trust or for an account of any property or dealings with property' notwithstanding that compliance may expose the witness or his spouse or civil partner to a charge for an offence under the Theft Act. The section goes on to provide that the answers may not be used in proceedings for any such offence.[67] However, neither the revocation of the privilege nor the restriction on the use of the answers applies to any other offences, a limitation which prompted Sir Nicolas Browne-Wilkinson V-C to express the hope that Parliament would urgently extend s 31 so as to remove the privilege in relation to all civil claims relating to property, including claims for damages, but on terms that the statements made in documents disclosed should not be admissible in *any* criminal proceedings.[68]

---

[65] See *Cleveland County Council v F* [1995] 2 All ER 236, Fam Div.
[66] See *Re K (minors)* [1994] 3 All ER 230, Fam Div.
[67] See also s 9 of the Criminal Damage Act 1971.
[68] *Sociedade Nacional de Combustiveis de Angola UEE v Lundqvist* [1990] 3 All ER 283 at 302–3.

In cases where there is a claim to privilege in respect of both a Theft Act offence and a non-Theft Act offence, the test, in each case, is whether to answer the question would create or increase the risk of proceedings for that offence. If the test is satisfied in the case of the Theft Act offence, s 31 will apply and prima facie the question must be answered. For the non-Theft Act offence, the test is whether to answer would create or increase the risk of proceedings for that offence, separate and distinct from its connection with the Theft Act offence. If the answer is in the negative, there is no privilege; but if in the affirmative, the privilege will subsist.[69]

Section 13 of the Fraud Act 2006

Section 13, modelled on s 31(1) of the Theft Act 1968, requires questions to be answered and orders to be complied with in 'proceedings relating to property', ie proceedings for the recovery or administration of any property, etc, notwithstanding that compliance may result in incrimination of an offence under the 2006 Act or a 'related offence', but prevents the answers from being used in evidence in proceedings for any such offence. 'Related offence' means conspiracy to defraud or 'any other offence involving any other form of fraudulent conduct or purpose'. In *Kensington International Ltd v Republic of Congo*[70] the Court of Appeal was reluctant to construe s 13 narrowly. First, it was held that 'proceedings relating to property' covers *Norwich Pharmacal* proceedings[71] brought to compel disclosure in aid of pending substantive proceedings relating to property, because the proceedings should be viewed as a whole so as to include the substantive proceedings. Second, it was held that the phrase 'any other offence involving any other form of fraudulent conduct or purpose' includes offences of offering or giving a bribe notwithstanding that they do not require proof of dishonesty. It also includes money laundering under s 328(1) of the Proceeds of Crime Act 2002.[72]

Section 72 of the Senior Courts Act 1981

The decision in *Rank Film Distributors Ltd v Video Information Centre*[73] that the privilege against self-incrimination applied to Anton Piller orders, now known as search orders, seriously undermined the effectiveness of that remedy, particularly in relation to breach of copyright, which often involves offences of fraud. Accordingly, the decision was rapidly reversed for the purposes of proceedings concerning intellectual property and passing off by s 72 of the Senior Courts Act 1981, the effect of which may be summarized as follows.[74] In proceedings brought to prevent any apprehended infringement of rights pertaining to any intellectual property (ie patent, trade mark, copyright, registered design, technical or commercial information, or other intellectual property)[75] or any apprehended passing off, questions must be answered and orders complied with even though the person complying may thereby expose himself or his spouse or civil partner to proceedings for a related offence or for the recovery of

---

[69] See *Renworth Ltd v Stephansen* [1996] 3 All ER 244 per Morritt LJ at 254, CA; but see also *Khan v Khan* [1982] 2 All ER 60, CA.

[70] [2007] EWCA Civ 1128.

[71] *Norwich Pharmacal Co v Commissioners of Customs & Excise* [1974] AC 133, HL.

[72] *JSC BTA Bank v Ablyazov* [2010] 1 Cr App R 131, CA.

[73] [1982] AC 380, HL.

[74] The terms of the section are complex and should be referred to for detail. See also *Universal City Studios v Hubbard* [1984] Ch 225, CA.

[75] Section 72(5). Commercially confidential information is 'commercial information': *Phillips v News Group Newspapers Ltd* [2012] 4 All ER 207, SC.

a related penalty. In proceedings for an infringement (or for passing off) which, it is alleged, has already occurred, or proceedings to obtain disclosure of information relating to such an infringement (or passing off), the privilege is withdrawn only in relation to (i) any offence committed by or in the course of the infringement (or passing off); (ii) offences of dishonesty or fraud committed in connection with the infringement (or passing off); and (iii) penalties incurred in connection with the infringement (or passing off). By s 72(3), answers compelled by reason of the withdrawal of privilege cannot be used in proceedings for the offence disclosed or for the recovery of any penalty liability to which was disclosed. Section 72 affects only proceedings for infringement of intellectual property rights and passing off: the decision in *Rank Film Distributors Ltd v Video Information Centre* still applies to the use of search orders for other purposes.

Substituted protection

In *AT & T Istel Ltd v Tully*,[76] a claim was made for damages and repayment of money obtained by fraud. A major police investigation was launched. The plaintiffs were granted a wide-ranging order for Mareva injunctions and disclosure, requiring the defendants to disclose all dealings regarding the money. Paragraph 33 of the order contained a condition that no disclosure made in compliance with it would be used as evidence in the prosecution of an offence alleged to have been committed by the person required to make that disclosure or by any spouse of that person. The order was subsequently varied and the plaintiffs appealed against the variation. Before the appeal, the Crown Prosecution Service (CPS) informed the plaintiffs that it did not seek to intervene in the civil proceedings, that it already had a large amount of potential evidence, and that it would not be prevented by para 33 from using that material or any other material obtained independently of the civil proceedings. The House of Lords restored the original order. Noting that the proceedings were not covered by any of the statutory modifications of the privilege, but were similar to situations in which Parliament had intervened, the House could see no reason why the defendants should blatantly exploit the privilege to deprive the plaintiffs of their civil rights and remedies. The courts were entitled to substitute a different protection in place of the privilege, provided it was adequate. The protection would be adequate if the CPS unequivocally agreed not to make use, directly or indirectly, of the material divulged in compliance with the order. Accordingly, a majority of the House held that, given the terms of para 33 and the clear indication by the CPS that it did not seek to use any of the material to be divulged in compliance with the order, the original order should stand.[77]

On the reasoning of the House, the principle of substituted protection is capable of application in many situations other than those which arose in *Re O* and *AT & T Istel v Tully*. However, those who, in the future, seek to confine the principle, will doubtless rely on the views of Lord Lowry, who emphasized that the decision of the House did not represent a breakthrough in relation to the privilege, being a decision on its own facts.[78]

---

[76] [1992] 3 All ER 523.

[77] See also *Re O* [1991] 2 WLR 475, CA, approved by the House of Lords in *AT & T Istel Ltd v Tully*, and *Re Thomas* [1992] 4 All ER 814, CA. An affidavit sworn by a person in compliance with such an order cannot be admitted in evidence against him in any subsequent criminal trial, but subject to proper directions from the judge may be used to show his inconsistency and impugn his credit: *R v Martin* [1998] 2 Cr App R 385, CA.

[78] [1992] 3 All ER 523 at 544.

Legal professional privilege

The nature of the privilege

The common law doctrine of legal professional privilege enables a client to maintain the confidentiality of (i) communications between him and his lawyer made for the purpose of obtaining and giving legal advice, the privilege in this case being known as 'legal advice privilege'; (ii) communications between him or his lawyer and third parties (such as potential witnesses and experts) the dominant purpose of which was preparation for contemplated or pending litigation, the privilege in this case being known as 'litigation privilege'; and (iii) items enclosed with or referred to in such communications and brought into existence for the purpose of obtaining legal advice, etc.[79]

Section 10 of the Police and Criminal Evidence Act 1984 (the 1984 Act), which is apparently intended to reflect the common law position,[80] provides that:

(1) Subject to subsection (2) below, in this Act 'items subject to legal privilege' means—
  (a) communications between a professional legal adviser and his client or any person representing his client made in connection with the giving of legal advice to the client;
  (b) communications between a professional legal adviser and his client or any person representing his client or between such an adviser or his client or any such representative and any other person made in connection with or in contemplation of legal proceedings and for the purposes of such proceedings; and
  (c) items enclosed with or referred to in such communications and made—
    (i) in connection with the giving of legal advice; or
    (ii) in connection with or in contemplation of legal proceedings and for the purposes of such proceedings, when they are in the possession of a person who is entitled to possession of them.

(2) Items held with the intention of furthering a criminal purpose are not items subject to legal privilege.

For the purposes of legal professional privilege, 'lawyer' includes, as well as solicitors and counsel, employed legal advisers[81] and overseas lawyers.[82] Internal communications by in-house lawyers are not protected by the privilege in relation to investigations into alleged infringements of EU competition law.[83] Nor does the privilege apply, at common law, in relation to

---

[79] For an excellent examination of the topic explicitly aimed more to generate questions than to provide answers, see Auburn, *Legal Professional Privilege: Law and Theory* (Oxford, 2000).

[80] See the majority view of the House of Lords in *Francis & Francis (a firm) v Central Criminal Court* [1988] 3 All ER 775, in this chapter, under **Legal professional privilege, Exceptions to the privilege, Fraud**, especially per Lord Goff at 797; and *R v R* [1994] 4 All ER 260, CA, in this chapter, under **Legal Professional Privilege, Communications with third parties—litigation privilege, Items enclosed with or referred to in communications**.

[81] *Alfred Crompton Amusement Machines Ltd v Customs and Excise Comrs (No 2)* [1974] AC 405; *AM & S Europe Ltd v EC Commission* [1983] QB 878, ECJ per Advocate General Sir Gordon Slynn at 914. It is possible that the privilege may also attach to communications between the police and the Director of Public Prosecutions, if they are seeking legal advice in circumstances analogous to a client approaching his solicitor for advice: per Moore-Bick J, obiter, in *Goodridge v Chief Constable of Hampshire Constabulary* [1999] 1 All ER 896, QBD at 903.

[82] *Re Duncan* [1968] P 306. The term 'proceedings' in this context includes proceedings in other jurisdictions: see *Re Duncan*. However, the fact that the advice given relates predominantly to English law is irrelevant: *IBM Corpn v Phoenix International (Computers) Ltd* [1995] 1 All ER 413, Ch D.

[83] *Akzo Nobel Chemicals Ltd v European Commission* [2010] EU ECJ C-550/07.

professionals other than solicitors, barristers, or appropriately qualified overseas lawyers, who have specialized knowledge of the law and advise on it, such as accountants who provide expert advice on tax law.[84] However, pursuant to statute a privilege parallel to legal professional privilege does apply to communications between a person and his patent agent,[85] trade mark agent,[86] or licensed conveyancer,[87] and individuals who are not solicitors or barristers but who are authorized persons for the purposes of providing advocacy, litigation, conveyancing, or probate services.[88]

The privilege survives the death of a client and vests in his personal representative or, once administration is complete, the person entitled to his estate,[89] and those persons are entitled to either claim or waive the privilege.[90]

The rationale of the privilege

The rationale of the rules of legal professional privilege is that they encourage those who know the facts to state them fully and candidly without fear of compulsory disclosure.[91] In *R v Derby Magistrates' Court, ex p B*[92] Lord Taylor CJ said:

> The principle...is that a man must be able to consult his lawyer in confidence, since otherwise he might hold back half the truth. The client must be sure that what he tells his lawyer in confidence will never be revealed without his consent. Legal professional privilege is thus much more than an ordinary rule of evidence....It is a fundamental condition on which the administration of justice as a whole rests.

In relation to litigation privilege, it is this confidentiality which enables lawyers to encourage strong cases and discourage weak ones, which is in the interests of the state.[93] However, in the absence of contemplated litigation, it is questionable whether there is any temptation for the client to be less than candid or 'to hold back half the truth',[94] and even if this is a real likelihood, it is equally questionable whether it should override the public interest that wherever possible the courts should reach their decisions on the basis of all relevant evidence. As Lord Phillips MR forcefully observed in *Three Rivers District Council v Governor and Company of the Bank of England (No 5)*:[95]

> The justification for litigation privilege is readily understood. Where, however, litigation is not anticipated it is not easy to see why communications with a solicitor should be privileged. Legal advice privilege attaches to matters such as the conveyance of real property or the drawing up of a will. It is not clear why it should. There would seem little reason to fear that, if privilege

---

[84] *R (Prudential plc) v Special Commissioner of Income Tax* [2013] 2 All ER 247, SC.

[85] Copyright, Designs and Patents Act 1988, s 280.

[86] Copyright, Designs and Patents Act 1988, s 284.

[87] Administration of Justice Act 1985, s 33.

[88] Legal Services Act 2007, s 190.

[89] *Bullivant v A-G for Victoria* [1901] AC 196, HL.

[90] *R v Malloy* [1997] 2 Cr App R 283, CA.

[91] See *Waugh v British Railways Board* [1980] AC 521, HL at 531–2 per Lord Wilberforce, and also at 535–6 per Lord Simon. As to the court's respect for other confidential relationships, see Ch 19, under **The scope of exclusion on grounds of public policy, Confidential relationships**.

[92] [1996] AC 487, HL at 507–8.

[93] See per Bingham LJ in *Ventouris v Mountain* [1991] 1 WLR 607 at 611.

[94] See Alexander, 'The Corporate Attorney–Client Privilege: A Study of the Participants' (1989) St John's L Rev 191.

[95] [2004] 3 All ER 168, CA at [39].

were not available in such circumstances, communications between solicitor and client would be inhibited.

Communications between lawyer and client—legal advice privilege

General

A client may, and his lawyer must (subject to the client's waiver) refuse to disclose written or oral communications between them made for the purpose of giving and receiving legal advice about any matter, whether or not litigation was contemplated at the time.[96] This applies whether the client or lawyer is a party to the litigation in which the question arises or a mere witness and it applies as much to the production of documents containing such communications as to oral evidence about them. It seems that receipt by the lawyer of a communication from the client is not necessary for the privilege to apply.[97]

The communication must have been confidential and, if not actually made in the course of a relationship of lawyer and client, must at least have been made with a view to the establishment of that relationship.[98] Provided that the communication was made in a professional capacity for the purposes of giving or receiving legal advice, the whole communication will be privileged, including any parts of it in which the solicitor conveyed to the client information which he had received in a professional capacity from a third party: such information cannot be hived off from the rest of what was said so as to become not privileged.[99] However, documents emanating from, or prepared by, independent third parties and then passed to the lawyer for the purposes of advice are not privileged. In *Three Rivers District Council v Governor and Company of the Bank of England*[100] it was held that legal advice privilege only protects direct communications between the client and the lawyer, and evidence of the content of such communications, and that in the case of a corporate client the privilege will only cover communications with those officers or employees expressly designated or nominated to act as 'the client'. Thus the privilege was held not to extend to documents prepared by other employees or ex-employees, even if prepared with the dominant purpose of obtaining legal advice, prepared at the lawyer's request, or sent to the lawyer. It is submitted that the 'designation' approach is too restrictive, not least because, as one commentator has pointed out, it operates in an unprincipled way to exclude other officers and employees with equivalent or greater authority to act 'as the client', such as, in the case in question, the Governor of the Bank.[101] Equally, however, the 'dominant purpose' test may be too wide and operate to prevent access to relevant facts. The answer may be to adopt the test used in the

---

[96] *Greenough v Gaskell* (1833) 1 My&K 98. If litigation does ensue, the standard form of words for claiming the privilege on disclosure is to refer to confidential correspondence, etc for the purpose of obtaining legal advice. This is a sufficient description of the documents: *Derby & Co Ltd v Weldon (No 7)* [1990] 3 All ER 161, Ch D.

[97] See *Three Rivers District Council v Governor and Company of the Bank of England* [2003] EWCA Civ 474, CA at [21].

[98] *Minter v Priest* [1930] AC 558. A client care letter is not privileged because it merely sets out the terms on which the solicitor is to act for the client: *Dickinson v Rushmer* (2002) 152 NLJ 58. Confidential information passed to a solicitor but not covered by the privilege may be protected from disclosure, but the protection may be overridden by other considerations: see, in the case of contact details supplied simply for the purposes of enabling communication, *JSC BTA Bank v Solodchenko* [2013] Ch 1, Ch D and Ch 19, under **The scope of exclusion on grounds of public policy, Confidential relationships**.

[99] *Re Sarah C Getty Trust* [1985] QB 956, QBD.

[100] [2003] QB 1556, CA.

[101] Loughrey, 'Legal advice privilege and the corporate client' (2005) 9 E&P 183. As to practical problems relating to pre-litigation risk management to which the approach gives rise, see Passmore, 'Watch what you say' (2006) NLJ 21 April 668.

United States,[102] which limits the corporate client to those who play a substantial role in deciding and directing the corporation's response to the legal advice given.[103]

Legal advice privilege extends to the instructions given by the client to his solicitor, or by the solicitor to the barrister, and counsel's opinion taken by a solicitor.[104] It does not extend to records of time spent with a client on attendance sheets, time sheets, or fee records, because they are not communications between client and legal adviser, or to records of appointments, because they are not communications made in connection with legal advice.[105] Similarly, such items as a conveyance or other legal document will not necessarily be protected by the privilege, unless made in connection with the giving of legal advice (or in connection with or in contemplation of legal proceedings and for the purposes of such proceedings).[106]

Communications between opposing parties

There is generally no protection for communications between opposing parties or their advisers, unless they can be treated as 'without prejudice' settlement negotiations.[107] Thus the privilege does not cover a solicitor's attendance note recording what took place in chambers or in open court, in the course of a hostile litigation, in the presence of the parties on both sides.[108] Similarly, if a solicitor has made an attendance note of a meeting or telephone conversation between the lawyers for each side, any subsequent communication by the lawyers to their respective clients, informing them about the discussion, advising them, and seeking further instructions, will be privileged, but the attendance note itself is not privileged. This remains the case, even if the discussion was 'without prejudice', although that may prevent the note from being given in evidence until the without prejudice ban has been removed.[109]

Solicitor instructed by two clients

In *Buttes Gas and Oil Co v Hammer (No 3)*[110] it was held that where a solicitor is instructed by two clients, communications between him and one of the clients will not be privileged against the other client insofar as they concern the subject matter in which they are jointly interested but, whether or not the communication is disclosed to the other client, they will be protected as against outsiders. Thus where two parties employ the same solicitor for a conveyancing transaction, communications between either of them and the solicitor, in his joint capacity,

[102] See *Upjohn Co v United States* 499, US 383, 101 SCt 677 (1981) at 684.
[103] For a good assessment of the implications of adopting the various tests, see Loughrey, 'Legal advice privilege and the corporate client' (2005) 9 E&P 183.
[104] *Bristol Corpn v Cox* (1884) 26 Ch D 678.
[105] *R v Crown Court at Manchester, ex p Rogers* [1999] 1 WLR 832, DC.
[106] *R (Faisaltex Ltd) v Preston Crown Court* [2009] 1 Cr App R 549, DC at [70], a decision under s 10 of the Police and Criminal Evidence Act 1984.
[107] *Grant v Southwestern and County Properties Ltd* [1975] Ch 185, Ch D: the plaintiff was obliged to produce on discovery a tape-recording of a discussion between the parties even though made for the purposes of instructing his solicitor in connection with contemplated litigation. However, if, after a meeting between opposing parties, one of them makes a record of the meeting for his solicitor, that record will be protected. 'Without prejudice' settlement negotiations are considered, in this chapter, under **Without prejudice negotiations, Settlement negotiations.**
[108] *Ainsworth v Wilding* [1900] 2 Ch 315.
[109] *Parry v News Group Newspapers Ltd* [1990] NLJR 1719, CA.
[110] [1981] QB 223, CA (reversed on other grounds, [1982] AC 888, HL), applied in *Guinness Peat Properties Ltd v Fitzroy Robinson Partnership (a firm)* [1987] 2 All ER 716, CA.

must be disclosed in favour of the other. Equally, if one of the parties is then adjudicated bankrupt, the other cannot assert the privilege as against a trustee in bankruptcy, because as the successor in title to the property in question, he should be treated as being in the same position as the bankrupt, and not in the position of a third party.[111] However, the waiver of privilege implied at the outset of a joint retainer ceases to apply in respect of communications made after the emergence of a conflict of interest between the two clients.[112] Similarly, the privilege cannot be claimed by the directors of a company against its shareholders, except in the case of communications made for the purposes of litigation between the company and the shareholders.[113]

Where there has been no joint retainer, but advice has been given to directors of a company by solicitors retained by the company, then, except in cases where the directors and the company are in reality one and the same, a director, in order to succeed in a claim of joint interest privilege, will need to establish that: he sought advice in an individual capacity; he made that clear to the lawyer; the lawyer knew or ought to have appreciated that he was communicating with the director on that basis; the company knew or ought to have appreciated the legal position; and the communication with the lawyer was confidential.[114]

Communications that do not specifically seek or convey legal advice

'Legal advice', for the purposes of legal advice privilege, does not mean advice given by a lawyer without more, but advice about legal rights and liabilities. However, some communications may enjoy privilege even if they do not specifically seek or convey legal advice. In *Balabel v Air-India*,[115] which concerned a conveyancing transaction, the privilege extended to communications between the appellants and their solicitors such as drafts, working papers, attendance notes, and memoranda. It was held that in most solicitor and client relationships, especially where a transaction involves protracted dealings, there will be a continuum of communications and meetings between the solicitor and client; and where information is passed between them as part of that continuum, the aim being to keep both informed so that legal advice may be sought and given as required, privilege will attach. Similarly, in *Nederlandse Reassurantie Groep Holding NV v Bacon & Woodrow (a firm)*[116] it was held that where a solicitor's advice relates to the commercial wisdom of entering into a transaction in respect of which legal advice is also sought, all communications between the solicitor and the client relating to the transaction will be privileged, even if they do not contain advice on matters of law or construction, provided that they are directly related to the performance by the solicitor of his professional duty as legal adviser.[117] According to *The Sagheera*,[118] the practical emphasis should

---

[111] *Re Konigsberg (a bankrupt)* [1989] 3 All ER 289, Ch D.

[112] *TSB Bank plc v Robert Irving & Burns (a firm)* [2000] 2 All ER 826, CA.

[113] *Woodhouse & Co (Ltd) v Woodhouse* (1914) 30 TLR 559; *CAS (Nominees) Ltd v Nottingham Forest plc* [2001] 1 All ER 954, Ch D.

[114] *R (Ford) v Financial Services Authority* [2012] 1 All ER 1238, QBD.

[115] [1988] Ch 317, CA.

[116] [1995] 1 All ER 976, QBD.

[117] See also *R v Crown Court at Inner London Sessions, ex p Baines and Baines* [1987] 3 All ER 1025, DC: privilege does attach to advice given in conveyancing transactions on factors serving to assist towards a successful completion, including the wisdom or otherwise of proceeding with it, the arranging of a mortgage and so on, but does not attach to the records of the conveyancing transaction itself.

[118] [1997] 1 Lloyd's Rep 160, QBD at 168.

be on the dominant purpose of the retainer. If it is to obtain and give legal advice, although in theory individual documents may fall outside that purpose, in practice it is most unlikely that they will. If, however, the dominant purpose is some business purpose, the documents will not be privileged, unless exceptionally advice is requested or given, in which case the relevant documents probably are privileged.

The leading authority is *Three Rivers District Council v Governor and Company of the Bank of England (No 6)*.[119] After the collapse of the Bank of Credit and Commerce International (BCCI) in 1991, Lord Justice Bingham was appointed to inquire into its supervision by the Bank of England, which had statutory responsibilities and duties in relation to UK banks. The Bank appointed a Bingham Inquiry Unit (BIU) to deal with all communications between the Bank and the inquiry and solicitors were retained to advise generally on all dealings with the inquiry. One of the main functions of the BIU was to prepare and communicate information and instructions to the Bank's solicitors. The solicitors gave advice as to the preparation and presentation of evidence to the inquiry and as to submissions to be made. After the publication of the inquiry report, depositors and BCCI, by its liquidators, brought proceedings against the Bank and sought the widest possible disclosure from the Bank. The Court of Appeal held that the only documents for which privilege could be claimed were communications between BIU and the solicitors seeking or giving advice as to legal rights and liabilities.

The House of Lords allowed the appeal of the Bank. Lord Scott accepted as correct the approach of Taylor LJ in *Balabel v Air India*,[120] who had said that for the purpose of attracting the privilege 'legal advice is not confined to telling the client the law; it must include advice as to what should prudently and sensibly be done in the relevant legal context' but that 'to extend privilege without limit to all solicitor and client communications upon matters within the ordinary business of a solicitor and referable to that relationship [would be] too wide'. Lord Scott said that if a solicitor became the client's 'man of business', responsible for advising him on matters such as investment and other business matters, the advice might lack a relevant legal context. The judge would have to ask whether it related to the rights, liabilities, obligations, or remedies of the client under either private or public law, and, if so, whether the communication fell within the policy underlying the justification for the privilege, the criterion being an objective one. It was held that although there may be marginal cases where the answer is not easy, the present case was not marginal. The preparation of the evidence to be submitted, and the submissions to be made, to the inquiry had been for the purpose of enhancing the Bank's prospects of persuading the inquiry that its discharge of its public law obligations was not deserving of criticism and had been reasonable. The presentational advice given for that purpose had been advice 'as to what should prudently and sensibly be done in the relevant legal context', namely, the inquiry and whether the Bank had properly discharged its public law duties, and fell squarely within the policy reasons underlying legal advice privilege.

Communications with third parties—litigation privilege

General

Litigation privilege is a creature of adversarial proceedings and cannot exist in the context of non-adversarial proceedings.[121] It covers communications between a client, or his lawyer, and

---

[119] [2005] 1 AC 610, HL.
[120] [1988] Ch 317 at 330–1.
[121] *Re L* [1997] AC 16, HL.

third parties—for example, statements from potential witnesses and experts—the dominant purpose of which was preparation for contemplated or pending litigation. The test is whether litigation was reasonably in prospect, which will not be satisfied if there is only a possibility of litigation, even if a distinct possibility, or a general apprehension of future litigation.[122] The privilege, which is a basic or fundamental right, also attaches to the identity and other details of witnesses intended to be called in adversarial litigation, civil or criminal, and whether or not their identity was the fruit of legal advice.[123] Claims to litigation privilege must set out the purpose for which the documents in question were produced, referring to contemporaneous material where possible. An affidavit in support will be conclusive unless (a) it is clear from the statements of the deponent that he has erroneously represented or misconceived the character of the document; (b) it is contradicted by the evidence of the person who, or the entity which, directed the creation of the document; or (c) there is other evidence before the court that it is incorrect or incomplete on the material points.[124]

The privilege covers documents 'brought into existence', that is created, by a party for the purpose of instructing the lawyer and obtaining his advice in the conduct of the litigation,[125] but not documents obtained by a party or his adviser for the purpose of litigation which did not come into existence for that purpose.[126] A copy or translation of an unprivileged document in the control of a party does not become privileged merely because the copy or translation was made for the purpose of the litigation,[127] but privilege will attach to a copy of an unprivileged document if the copy was made for the purpose of litigation and the original is not and has not at any time been in the control of the party claiming privilege.[128] Privilege will also attach where a solicitor has copied or assembled a selection of third party documents for the purposes of litigation, if its production will betray the trend of the advice he is giving his client,[129] but this principle does not extend to a selection of own client documents, or copies or translations representing the fruits of such a selection, made for the purposes of litigation.[130]

The dominant purpose test

The leading authority is *Waugh v British Railways Board*.[131] The plaintiff's husband, an employee of the defendant, was killed in a railway accident. In proceedings for compensation, the plaintiff sought discovery of routine internal reports prepared by the defendant regarding the accident. The House of Lords held that, in order to attract privilege, the dominant purpose of preparation of the reports must have been that of submission to a legal adviser for use in relation to anticipated or pending litigation. While this was undoubtedly one of the purposes of the

---

[122] *USA v Philip Morris Inc* [2004] EWCA Civ 330, CA.

[123] *R (Kelly) v Warley Magistrates' Court* [2008] 1 Cr App R 195.

[124] *West London Pipeline & Storage Ltd v Total UK Ltd* [2008] EWHC 1729 (Comm).

[125] Per James LJ in *Anderson v Bank of British Columbia* (1876) 2 Ch D 644 at 656. See also *Southwark and Vauxhall Water Co v Quick* (1878) 3 QBD 315, CA.

[126] *Ventouris v Mountain, The Italia Express* [1991] 1 WLR 607, CA.

[127] *Dubai Bank Ltd v Galadari* [1990] Ch 98, CA (copies) and *Sumitomo Corp v Credit Lyonnais Rouse Ltd* [2002] 1 WLR 479, CA.

[128] *The Palermo* (1883) 9 PD 6, CA and *Watson v Cammell Laird & Co Ltd* [1959] 1 WLR 702, CA.

[129] *Lyell v Kennedy (No 3)* (1884) 27 Ch D 1.

[130] *Sumitomo Corp v Credit Lyonnais Rouse Ltd* [2002] 1 WLR 479, CA.

[131] [1980] AC 521.

reports, it was not the dominant one, another equally important purpose being to inform the Board about the cause of the accident in order that steps could be taken to avoid recurrence. Accordingly, privilege could not be claimed and disclosure of the reports was ordered.

Although application of the dominant purpose test can give rise to difficulty, in many cases of accident investigation it will be possible to conclude that the major purpose was the prevention of recurrence. The courts will not be deterred from reaching such a conclusion, where appropriate, even if those under whose direction the report was prepared depose that its dominant purpose was submission to solicitors in anticipation of litigation and the report itself refers only to that purpose.[132] In *Neilson v Laugharne*[133] the plaintiff's demand for compensation for alleged police misconduct prompted the police to initiate the statutory complaints procedure. Statements taken for the purpose of that procedure were clearly obtained in anticipation of litigation but it was held that the dominant purpose was that of the complaints procedure. The statements therefore did not attract legal professional privilege in subsequent litigation against the police. In *Re Highgrade Traders Ltd*,[134] by contrast, it was held that the dominant purpose of the preparation of reports procured by an insurance company from specialists in fire investigations, in a case where arson was suspected, was to assess the strength of a claim which, if persisted in, would in all likelihood have resulted in litigation. The insurance company was primarily interested in questions of liability rather than prevention or recurrence. Oliver LJ made it clear that the privilege will attach to a document, whether it was 'brought into existence' before or after a decision was made to instruct a solicitor, provided that litigation was reasonably in prospect and the document was prepared for the sole or dominant purpose of enabling a solicitor to advise whether a claim should be made or resisted.

In *Guinness Peat Properties Ltd v Fitzroy Robinson Partnership (a firm)*[135] it was held that the dominant purpose of a document should be ascertained by an objective view of the evidence as a whole, having regard not only to the intention of its author, but also to the intention of the person or authority under whose direction it was procured. The plaintiffs, building developers, had notified the defendants, engaged by them to act as architects for the construction of a building, of an alleged design fault. The defendants, in order to comply with the condition of their insurance policy, which required immediate notification of claims, thereupon wrote a letter to their insurers enclosing relevant memoranda and expressing their own views on the merits of the claim. In the course of discovery in the action which ensued, the question arose whether the letter was privileged. The defendants conceded that it was not *their* purpose, in writing the letter, to obtain legal advice or assistance. The Court of Appeal held that it could look beyond that intention to the intention of the insurers who had procured its genesis. Their intention, in requiring an immediate written notice of claim, was to enable them to submit it, together with other relevant documentation, to their lawyers for advice on whether the claim should be resisted. The letter was therefore privileged.

In reaching this conclusion, the Court of Appeal distinguished *Jones v Great Central Rly Co*,[136] in which it was held that if a client communicates with a lawyer via a third party who is merely an agent for communication, privilege can be claimed, but that if the third party

---

[132] See *Lask v Gloucester Health Authority* (1985) 2 PN 96, CA.
[133] [1981] QB 736, CA.
[134] [1984] BCLC 151, CA.
[135] [1987] 2 All ER 716, CA.
[136] [1910] AC 4, HL.

has to make a preliminary decision on the matter, the privilege is lost. Accordingly, it was held that no privilege attached to information supplied by a dismissed employee to a trade union official for the purpose of enabling the latter to decide whether to refer the claim to the union's lawyers. This case was distinguished in the *Guinness Peat Properties* case on the grounds, inter alia, that the relationship between the trade union and the member was not the equivalent of that between the insurers and the insured where the insurers were, in all but name, the effective defendants to any proceedings. It was further held that since the insurers and the insured had a common interest and a common lawyer, the principle in *Buttes Gas and Oil Co v Hammer (No 3)*[137] applied: the letter was privileged in the hands of each of them as against all outsiders.

In *Re Barings plc*[138] Sir Richard Scott V-C doubted the correctness of the decisions in both *Re Highgrade Traders Ltd* and the *Guinness Peat Properties* case on the grounds that disclosure of the documents in those cases would not have impinged upon the inviolability of lawyer/client communications. In his view, the reason for extending the privilege to documents brought into existence for the dominant purpose of litigation is to prevent the disclosure of documents which will reveal the lawyer's view of his client's case or the advice he has given, and therefore there is no general privilege for such documents independent of the need to keep inviolate communications between client and legal adviser. Thus if the documents do not relate in some fashion to such communications, there is no element of public interest to override the ordinary rights of litigants on discovery. In *Re Barings plc* a report on the conduct of the directors of Barings Bank was prepared on behalf of administrators in compliance with their statutory duty to report to the Department of Trade and Industry, under s 7(3) of the Company Directors Disqualification Act 1986, where it appears to them that the conduct of directors makes them unfit to be concerned in the management of a company. In subsequent disqualification proceedings, the Secretary of State resisted inspection of the report on the grounds of privilege. The Vice-Chancellor held that the report was not privileged. *Re Highgrade Traders Ltd* and the *Guinness Peat Properties* case were distinguished on the basis that, whereas in those cases the makers of the documents had a choice whether to bring them into existence and it was therefore possible to investigate their purpose in doing so, the maker of a s 7(3) report is obliged by law to make the report, which is not procured by anyone. It was accepted that the statutory purpose underlying s 7(3) was to assist the Secretary of State to decide whether to commence disqualification proceedings, and that Parliament must have expected that the Secretary of State, in reaching his decision, would put the report before his legal advisers for their advice, but it was held that the question of privilege depended not on identifying this parliamentary purpose and expectation, but on whether there was a public interest requiring protection from disclosure sufficient to override the disclosure rights given to litigants. In the absence of any such public interest, it was ruled that the report was not protected from disclosure.

The rules on disclosure in civil cases

Despite the difficulties of the dominant purpose test, it is usually clear that proofs of evidence from potential witnesses and the written opinions of experts supplied for the purpose

[137] [1981] QB 223, CA; see, in this chapter, under **Legal professional privilege, Communications between lawyer and client—legal advice privilege, Solicitor instructed by two clients**.
[138] [1998] 1 All ER 673, Ch D.

European Court of Human Rights having said that the privilege is a fundamental human right which can be invaded only in exceptional circumstances.[169]

There are three other specific types of exception. The first, fraud, was referred to by Lord Lloyd in the *Derby Magistrates* case as 'a well-recognized exception'.[170] The second relates to reports by third parties prepared on the instructions of the client for the purposes of care proceedings under the Children Act 1989. The third concerns cases in which the instructions given or the advice received are themselves in issue in the litigation.[171]

Fraud

In *R v Cox and Railton*[172] it was held that if a client seeks legal advice intended to facilitate or guide him in the commission of a crime or fraud, the legal adviser being ignorant of the purpose for which the advice is sought, the communication between them is not privileged. The exception also applies if the solicitor *is* a party to the crime or fraud but not, it was held in *Butler v Board of Trade*,[173] if he merely volunteers a warning to the client that his conduct, if persisted in, may result in a prosecution.[174] The exception can only be relied on if there is prima facie evidence of the client's criminal purpose.[175] Although the court may look at the communications themselves, if necessary, to determine whether they came into existence in furtherance of such a purpose,[176] as a rule it should not do so; there should be some exceptional factor of real weight before the court looks at the communications, and the mere fact that the test is not satisfied by other non-privileged material is not such a factor.[177]

The exception is not confined to cases in which solicitors advise on or set up criminal or fraudulent transactions yet to be undertaken, but also covers criminal or fraudulent conduct undertaken for the purposes of acquiring evidence in or for litigation.[178]

There are a number of limitations on the scope of this exception. First, although not limited to crimes, it does not extend to communications concerning all intended legal wrongs. In *Crescent Farm (Sidcup) Sports Ltd v Sterling Offices Ltd*[179] Goff J said:[180]

> It is clear that parties must be at liberty to take advice as to the ambit of their contractual obligations and liabilities in tort and what liability they will incur whether in contract or tort by a

---

[169] See per Lord Hoffmann, obiter, in *R (Morgan Grenfell) v Special Commissioner of Income Tax* [2003] 1 AC 563 at [7] and [39], citing *Foxley v UK* (2000) 8 BHRC 571 at 581.

[170] [1995] 4 All ER 526 at 543.

[171] Although not creating an exception as such, see also *Edwards-Tubb v J D Wetherspoon plc* [2011] EWCA Civ 136, considered in Ch 18: the court may require a party to waive privilege as a condition of being permitted to rely on the evidence of a substitute expert.

[172] (1884) 14 QBD 153, CCR.

[173] [1971] Ch 680.

[174] However, the Board in that case were able to prove a letter since a copy of it had come into their hands and Goff J refused to grant an injunction to prevent such use: see, in this chapter, under **Legal professional privilege, Secondary evidence**.

[175] *O'Rourke v Darbishire* [1920] AC 581. But see also *Derby & Co Ltd v Weldon (No 7)* [1990] 3 All ER 161, Ch D: the court will be very slow to deprive a party of the privilege on an interlocutory application and will judge each case on its facts.

[176] *R v Governor of Pentonville Prison, ex p Osman* [1989] 3 All ER 701, QBD at 729–30.

[177] *BBGP Managing General Partner Ltd v Babcock & Brown Global Partners* [2011] 2 All ER 297, Ch D.

[178] *Dubai Aluminium Co Ltd v Al Alawi* [1999] 1 All ER 703, QBD.

[179] [1972] Ch 553.

[180] [1972] Ch 553 at 565.

proposed course of action without thereby in every case losing professional privilege. I agree that fraud in this connection is not limited to the tort of deceit and includes all forms of fraud and dishonesty such as fraudulent breach of contract, fraudulent conspiracy, trickery and sham contrivances, but I cannot feel that the tort of inducing a breach of contract or the narrow form of conspiracy pleaded in this case comes within that ambit.

Trespass and conversion are also outside the scope of the doctrine.[181] However, privilege will not attach to advice on a scheme, in breach of an employee's confidential duty of fidelity and involving the secret use of the employer's time and money, to take other employees (and the employer's customers) and to make profit from them in a competing business developed to receive them on leaving the employer's service.[182] Equally, if there is strong prima facie evidence that a transaction has been devised to prejudice the interests of a creditor by putting assets beyond his reach, privilege will not attach to legal advice on how to structure such a transaction.[183]

In *Kuwait Airways Corporation v Iraqi Airways Co*[184] it was confirmed that the fraud exception can apply to litigation privilege, as well as legal advice privilege. It was also held that whereas a prima facie case of fraud may suffice where the issue of fraud is not one of the very issues in the action, where it is such an issue then a very strong prima facie case of fraud is required. In *Chandler v Church*[185] the plaintiffs alleged that the defendant had fraudulently manipulated to his own advantage various share transactions. They sought discovery of communications between him and his solicitors on the basis of prima facie evidence showing that he had obtained their assistance to enable him to mislead the court by putting forward false documents and pretending that certain transactions were genuine. Hoffmann J held that although it does not matter whether the fraud concerns an earlier transaction or the conduct of the proceedings in question, disclosure at an interlocutory stage based on prima facie evidence of fraud in the conduct of the very proceedings in which the discovery is sought carries a far greater risk of injury to the party against whom discovery is sought, should he turn out to have been innocent, than disclosure of advice concerning an earlier transaction. The risk of injustice to the defendant in being required to reveal communications with his lawyers for the purpose of his defence, together with the damage to the public interest which the violation of such confidences would cause, outweighed the risk of injustice to the plaintiffs.[186]

The exception does not extend to the correspondence between a lawyer and an assignee or victim of a fraudsman. In *Banque Keyser Ullmann SA v Skandia (UK) Insurance Co Ltd*[187] insurance policies, issued to borrowers to cover banks against failure of the borrowers to repay, were assigned to the banks. The loans were not repaid and the banks claimed under the policies. The insurers denied liability on the grounds that the policies had been obtained by the fraud of the borrowers. The contention of the insurers that by reason of the borrowers' fraud no privilege attached to the correspondence passing between the banks and their lawyers was rejected.

---

[181] Per Rix J in *Dubai Aluminium Co Ltd v Al Alawi* [1999] 1 All ER 703 at 707.

[182] *Gamlen Chemical Co (UK) Ltd v Rochem Ltd* [1980] 1 All ER 1049.

[183] *Barclays Bank plc v Eustice* [1995] 4 All ER 511, CA.

[184] [2005] 1 WLR 2734, CA.

[185] [1987] NLJ Rep 451, Ch D.

[186] See also *R v Crown Court at Snaresbrook, ex p DPP* [1988] 1 All ER 315, QBD at 319. See also per Lord Goff in *Francis & Francis (a firm) v Central Criminal Court* [1988] 3 All ER 775, HL at 800.

[187] [1986] 1 Lloyd's Rep 336, CA.

prosecuting authorities, it is admissible in subsequent criminal proceedings against the party who made the admissions, subject to the discretion to exclude under s 78 of the 1984 Act, because the public interest in prosecuting crime is sufficient to outweigh the public interest in the settlement of disputes.[265]

The essential pre-condition for a claim to without prejudice privilege is the existence of a dispute. Thus in *Bradford & Bingley plc v Rashid*[266] the House of Lords held that the without prejudice rule had no application to open communications between a creditor and a debtor which dealt only with whether, when, and to what extent the debtor could meet his admitted liability. For a majority of their Lordships, since the debt was admitted, there was simply no dispute to be compromised.[267] Whether there is a dispute is sometimes a question of some nicety, as in *BNP Paribas v Mezzotero*.[268] While a grievance of M about perceived discrimination was being processed, the employer convened a without prejudice meeting, said to be independent of the grievance, at which M was advised that her job was no longer viable and an offer of a redundancy package was made. In a subsequent tribunal application claiming, inter alia, sex discrimination, it was held that M could rely on what was said at the meeting because there was no dispute at that time. Upholding this ruling, the Employment Appeal Tribunal held that there was no evidence of an employment dispute before the meeting. The grievance related to her continuing employment, not the threat of termination of employment, and therefore could not be treated as evidence of a dispute.

Conciliation and mediation schemes

The privilege attaches to any discussions that take place between actual or prospective parties with a view to avoiding litigation, including discussions within conciliation and mediation schemes.[269] The position as to confidentiality, privilege, and without prejudice privilege in relation to mediation proceedings is as follows. The proceedings are confidential as between the parties and as between the parties and the mediator and therefore even if the parties agree that the matters can be referred to outside the mediation, the mediator can enforce the confidentiality provision. The court will generally uphold the confidentiality, but not where it is necessary in the interests of justice for evidence to be given of the confidential matters. The proceedings are also covered by without prejudice privilege, which exists as between the parties and which they can waive; it is not a privilege of the mediator. If another privilege, eg legal professional privilege, attaches to documents which are produced by a party and shown to a mediator, that party retains the privilege and it is not waived by the disclosure or by waiver of the without prejudice privilege.[270]

Use or non-use of the expression 'without prejudice'

The fact that the expression 'without prejudice' is not actually used is 'not without significance',[271] but does not conclude the matter: provided that there is some dispute and an

---

[265] *R v K(A)* [2010] 1 Cr App R 44, CA. Cf s 54(3) of the Evidence Act 2006 (NZ).

[266] [2006] 1 WLR 2066, HL.

[267] Equally, the privilege will not protect correspondence designed to prevent a dispute arising: *Prudential Assurance Co Ltd v Prudential Insurance Co of America* [2002] EWHC 2809, Ch D.

[268] [2004] IRLR 508, EAT.

[269] See *Smiths Group plc v Weiss* [2002] EWHC 582, Ch D.

[270] *Farm Assist Ltd v Secretary of State for the Environment, Food and Rural Affairs (No 2)* [2009] EWHC 1102 (TCC). On the question whether there is a distinct privilege attaching to the mediation process, see [33] ff.

[271] *Prudential Assurance Co Ltd v Prudential Insurance Co of America* [2002] EWHC 2809, Ch D.

attempt is being made to settle it, the courts should be ready to infer that the attempt was without prejudice.[272] In order to decide whether or not a document was bona fide intended to be a negotiating document, the court has to look at the intention of the author and how the document would be received by a reasonable recipient. If the document is marked 'without prejudice' that is a factor that the court should take into account. It is an indication that the author intended it to be a negotiating document and, in many cases, a recipient would receive it on the understanding that the marking indicated that the author wished to attempt negotiation.[273] However, the heading 'without prejudice' does not conclusively or automatically render privileged a document so marked; if privilege is claimed for such a document but challenged, the court can look at it to determine its nature.[274] The privilege can attach to a document headed 'without prejudice' even if it is an 'opening shot', but the rule is not limited to documents which are offers; privilege attaches to all documents marked 'without prejudice' and forming part of negotiations, whether or not they contain offers, subject only to the recognized exceptions.[275]

Exceptions

There are a number of exceptions.[276] Without prejudice material is admissible if the issue is whether or not the negotiations resulted in an agreed settlement.[277] It is also admissible to show that a settlement agreement should be rectified.[278] Facts identified during the without prejudice negotiations which lead to a settlement agreement, which form part of its factual matrix or surrounding circumstances, and which but for the without prejudice rule would be admissible as an aid to construction of a settlement agreement, will also be admissible for that purpose.[279] The rule cannot be used to exclude an act of bankruptcy (such as a letter containing an offer to settle which also states the writer's inability to pay his debts as they fall due).[280] In *Ofulue v Bossert*[281] the House of Lords left open the question whether, and if so to what extent, a statement made in without prejudice negotiations would be admissible if 'in

---

[272] *Chocoladefabriken Lindt & Sprungli AG v Nestlé Co Ltd* [1978] RPC 287 at 288–9. If negotiations begin on a without prejudice basis, they remain so unless the party wishing to change them to an open basis makes this clear to the other party: *Cheddar Valley Engineering Ltd v Chaddlewood Homes Ltd* [1992] 4 All ER 942. However, open letters written after the negotiations and 'without prejudice' correspondence have finished and come to nothing, are not privileged: *Dixons Stores Group Ltd v Thames Television plc* [1993] 1 All ER 349.

[273] *Schering Corpn v Cipla Ltd* (2004) The Times, 10 Nov, Ch D.

[274] *South Shropshire District Council v Amos* [1987] 1 All ER 340.

[275] *South Shropshire District Council v Amos* [1987] 1 All ER 340, CA at 344.

[276] For a non-exhaustive, but nonetheless extensive, list of the exceptions, see per Robert Walker LJ in *Unilever plc v The Procter & Gamble Co* [2001] 1 All ER 783, CA at 791–3.

[277] *Walker v Wilsher* (1889) 23 QBD 335, CA at 337; *Tomlin v Standard Telephones and Cables Ltd* [1969] 3 All ER 201, CA. It is also admissible on the question whether a mediation resulted in an agreed settlement: *Brown v Rice* [2007] EWHC 625 (Ch).

[278] See *Pearlman v National Life Assurance Co of Canada* (1917) 39 OLR 141, *Butler v Countrywide Finance Ltd* (1992) 5 PRNZ 447 and per Lord Clarke in *Oceanbulk Shipping and Trading SA v TMT Asia Ltd* [2010] 4 All ER 1011, SC at [33].

[279] *Oceanbulk Shipping and Trading SA v TMT Asia Ltd*, [2010] 4 All ER 1011, SC. For critical commentary, see Zuckerman, 'Without prejudice interpretation—with prejudice negotiations: *Oceanbulk Shipping and Trading SA v TMT Asia Ltd*' (2011) 15 E&P 232.

[280] *Re Daintrey, ex p Holt* [1893] 2 QB 116.

[281] [2009] UKHL 16 at [92].

no way connected' with the issues in the case the subject of the negotiations. The privilege cannot be claimed when an agreement concluded between the parties during the negotiations should be set aside on the grounds of fraud or undue influence.[282] Negligent misrepresentations, however, will not prevent a claim to the privilege.[283] The privilege cannot be claimed if exclusion of the evidence would act as a cloak for perjury, blackmail, or other 'unambiguous impropriety',[284] but this exception should be applied only in the clearest cases of abuse.[285] As to perjury, the exception will apply in the case of a defendant who says that unless the case is withdrawn, he will give perjured evidence and will bribe other witnesses to perjure themselves.[286] However, the test is not whether there is a serious and substantial risk of perjury.[287] The exception will not apply where an admission is alleged to have been made that demonstrates that the pleaded case must be false[288] or where an admission is made that demonstrates that perjury has been committed in the past.[289] As to blackmail, the exception will apply where a claimant says that his claim is bogus and is being brought to 'blackmail' the defendant into a settlement of their real differences.[290] An example of other 'unambiguous impropriety' would be where an employer in dispute with a black employee says during discussions aimed at settlement, 'We do not want you here because you are black': such evidence should not be excluded from consideration by a tribunal hearing a subsequent complaint of race discrimination.[291]

Offers without prejudice except as to costs

CPR Pt 36 codifies the practice at common law whereby a party could make an offer in a letter headed 'without prejudice except as to costs', thereby reserving his right to refer to the letter, should the action proceed to judgment, on the question of costs. Under Pt 36, a written offer, called a 'Part 36 offer', may be made with a view to settling the whole or part of a claim. The offer may be made at any time, including before the commencement of the proceedings.[292] If it is an offer by a defendant to pay a sum of money in settlement of a claim, it must be an offer to pay a single sum of money.[293] If the offer is not accepted, normally the court must not be told about it until all questions of liability and quantum have been decided,[294] but if, at that stage, the judgment is no better than the offer, then normally, and unless the court considers it unjust to do so, it will order that the defendant is entitled to the costs that he has incurred

---

[282] *Underwood v Cox* (1912) 4 DLR 66.

[283] *Jefferies Group & Kvaerner International*, 19 January 2007, unreported.

[284] The expression used by Hoffmann LJ in *Forster v Friedland* [1992] CA Transcript 1052.

[285] *Forster v Friedland*, [1992] CA Transcript 1052 and *Fazil-Alizadeh v Nikbin* (1993) The Times, 19 Mar, CA.

[286] *Greenwood v Fitts* (1961) 29 DLR (2d) 260, BC CA.

[287] *Berry Trade Ltd v Moussavi* [2003] EWCA Civ 715.

[288] [2003] EWCA Civ 715.

[289] *Savings and Investment Bank Ltd v Fincken* [2004] 1 All ER 1125, CA.

[290] *Hawick Jersey International Ltd v Caplan* (1988) The Times, 11 Mar, QBD.

[291] Per Cox J in *BNP Paribas v Mezzotero* [2004] IRLR 508, EAT. See also per Smith LJ, obiter, in *Brunel University v Vaseghi* [2007] IRLR 592, CA at [32]; and cf *Brodie v Nicola Ward (t/a First Steps Nursery)* [2008] All ER (D) 115 (Feb), EAT, where, in proceedings for unfair constructive dismissal, the employee was prevented from using a without prejudice letter from the employer's solicitor which, she claimed, was the 'last straw' causing her to resign.

[292] Rule 36.3(2)(a).

[293] Rule 36.4(1). Special provision is made in personal injury claims in respect of future pecuniary loss: see r 36.5.

[294] Rule 36.13(2).

since the date of expiry of the 'relevant period',[295] which is usually a period of not less than 21 days specified in the Pt 36 offer.[296]

Matrimonial reconciliation cases

A privilege, similar to that which attaches to 'without prejudice' communications, has been developed to cover communications made in the course of matrimonial conciliation, matrimonial proceedings being in contemplation. In *D v NSPCC*[297] Lord Simon said:

> With increasingly facile divorce and a vast rise in the number of broken marriages, with their concomitant penury and demoralization, it came to be realized, in the words of Buckmill LJ in *Mole v Mole*:[298] 'in matrimonial disputes the state is also an interested party: it is more interested in reconciliation than in divorce'. This was the public interest which led to the application by analogy of the privilege of 'without prejudice' communications to cover communications made in the course of matrimonial conciliation (see *McTaggart v McTaggart*;[299] *Mole v Mole*;[300] *Theodoropoulas v Theodoropoulas*[301]) so indubitably an extension of the law that the textbooks treat it as a separate category of relevant evidence which may be withheld from the court. It cannot be classed, like traditional 'without prejudice' communications, as a 'privilege in aid of litigation...'.

In *Mole v Mole* it was established that the privilege applies to communications by a spouse not only with an official conciliator such as a probation officer but also with 'other persons such as clergy, doctors or marriage guidance counsellors to whom the parties or one of them go with a view to reconciliation, there being a tacit understanding that the conversations are without prejudice'.[302] In *Theodoropoulas v Theodoropoulas* Sir Jocelyn Simon P, having held that the same rule applied where a private individual is enlisted specifically as a conciliator, said:[303]

> Privilege [also] attaches to communications between the spouses themselves when made with a view to reconciliation. It also extends to excluding the evidence of an independent witness who was fortuitously present when those communications were made and who overheard or read them.[304]

The privilege is that of the spouses and can only be waived by them jointly. The intermediary cannot object to such waiver.

In proceedings under the Children Act 1989, evidence cannot be given of statements made by one or other of the parties in the course of meetings held, or communications made, for the purpose of conciliation. It is important to preserve a cloak over all attempts at settlements of disputes over children. However, an exception exists in the very unusual case where the statement clearly indicates that the maker has in the past or is likely in the future to cause serious harm to the well-being of a child. In these exceptional cases, it is for the trial judge to decide,

[295] Rule 36.14(1) and (2).
[296] See r 36.2(2)(c) and r 36.3(1)(c).
[297] [1978] AC 171 at 236–7.
[298] [1951] P 21, CA.
[299] [1949] P 94, CA.
[300] [1951] P 21, CA.
[301] [1964] P 311, CA.
[302] [1951] P 21 at 24 per Denning LJ.
[303] [1964] P 311 at 314.
[304] See also Law Reform Committee, 16th Report, *Privilege in Civil Proceedings*, Cmnd 3472 (1967), para 36.

in the exercise of his discretion, whether or not to admit the evidence, and he should do so only if the public interest in protecting the interests of the child outweighs the public interest in preserving the confidentiality of attempted conciliation.[305]

ADDITIONAL READING

Auburn, *Legal Professional Privilege: Law and Theory* (Oxford, 2000).

Loughrey, 'Legal advice privilege and the corporate client' (2005) 9 E&P 183.

MacCulloch, 'The privilege against self-incrimination in competition investigations: theoretical foundations and practical implications' (2006) 26(2) *Legal Studies* 211.

Passmore, 'Watch what you say' (2006) NLJ (21 April) 668.

Vaver, ' "Without Prejudice" Communications—Their Admissibility and Effect' [1974] U Br Col LR 85.

[305] *Re D (minors)* [1993] Fam 231, CA.

Judgments as evidence of the facts upon which they were based

21

Key issues

- When, and why, should the fact that a person has been convicted of an offence be admissible in evidence for the purpose of proving that he committed that offence (a) in subsequent civil proceedings; and (b) in subsequent criminal proceedings?

when the issue falls to be determined, he stands convicted of that offence shall be conclusive evidence that he committed that offence; and his conviction thereof shall be admissible in evidence accordingly.

(2) In any such action as aforesaid in which by virtue of this section the plaintiff is proved to have been convicted of an offence, the contents of any document which is admissible as evidence of the conviction, and the contents of the information, complaint, indictment or charge-sheet on which he was convicted, shall, without prejudice to the reception of any other admissible evidence for the purpose of identifying the facts on which the conviction was based, be admissible in evidence for the purpose of identifying those facts.

(2A) In the case of an action for libel or slander in which there is more than one plaintiff—

(a) the references in subsection (1) and (2) above to the plaintiff shall be construed as references to any of the plaintiffs, and

(b) proof that any of the plaintiffs stands convicted of an offence shall be conclusive evidence that he committed that offence so far as that fact is relevant to any issue arising in relation to his cause of action or that of any other plaintiff.

(3) For the purposes of this section a person shall be taken to stand convicted of an offence if but only if there subsists against him a conviction of that offence by or before a court in the United Kingdom or by a court-martial there or elsewhere.[25]

Previous findings of adultery and paternity

Section 12 of the 1968 Act not only reverses the rule in *Hollington v Hewthorn & Co Ltd* insofar as it applied to previous findings of adultery and paternity, but also creates a persuasive presumption in respect of such findings. Section 12 provides that:

(1) In any civil proceedings—

(a) the fact that a person has been found guilty of adultery in any matrimonial proceedings; and

(b) the fact that a person has been found to be the father of a child in relevant proceedings[26] before any court in England and Wales or Northern Ireland or has been adjudged to be the father of a child in affiliation proceedings before any court in the United Kingdom;

shall (subject to (3) below) be admissible in evidence for the purpose of proving, where to do so is relevant to any issue in those civil proceedings, that he committed the adultery to which the finding relates or, as the case may be, is (or was) the father of that child, whether or not he offered any defence to the allegation of adultery or paternity and whether or not he is a party to the civil proceedings; but no finding or adjudication other than a subsisting one shall be admissible in evidence by virtue of this section.

(2) In any civil proceedings in which by virtue of this section a person is proved to have been found guilty of adultery as mentioned in subsection (1)(a) above or to have been found or adjudged to be the father of a child as mentioned in subsection (1)(b) above—

(a) he shall be taken to have committed the adultery to which the finding relates or, as the case may be, to be (or have been) the father of that child, unless the contrary is proved; and

(b) without prejudice to the reception of any other admissible evidence for the purpose of identifying the facts on which the finding or adjudication was based, the contents of any document which was before the court, or which contains any pronouncement of

[25] As to the meaning of subsisting convictions, see, in this chapter, under **Civil proceedings, Previous convictions in civil proceedings generally—section 11 of the Civil Evidence Act 1968.**

[26] 'Relevant proceedings' means proceedings on complaints and applications made pursuant to a wide variety of statutory provisions: see s 12(5).

the court, in the other proceedings in question shall be admissible in evidence for that purpose.

(3) Nothing in this section shall prejudice the operation of any enactment whereby a finding of fact in any matrimonial or affiliation proceedings is for the purposes of any other proceedings made conclusive evidence of any fact.

Modelled as it is on s 11, s 12 of the 1968 Act calls for little comment. 'Matrimonial proceedings' are defined to include, inter alia, any matrimonial cause in the High Court or a county court in England and Wales and any appeal arising out of such cause.[27] Thus a finding of adultery in a magistrates' court would not be admissible under s 12. As in the case of previous convictions under s 11, the legal burden in relation to the finding of adultery or paternity admitted under s 12 is placed upon the party seeking to disprove that finding. The standard of proof required to discharge the burden is proof on a balance of probabilities.[28] A claimant who wishes to rely on evidence under s 12 of a finding or adjudication of adultery or paternity must include in his particulars of claim a statement to that effect and give details of the finding or adjudication and its date, the court which made it, and the issue in the claim to which it relates.[29]

Previous acquittals

In *Packer v Clayton*,[30] a case which pre-dates *Hollington v Hewthorn & Co Ltd*, Avory J was of the opinion that in affiliation proceedings, the respondent's acquittal of a sexual offence against the applicant would be admissible to show that the jury were not convinced by the latter's evidence. However, if the principle of *Hollington v Hewthorn & Co Ltd* applies to previous acquittals, they are inadmissible as evidence of innocence in subsequent civil proceedings. This conclusion may be justified on the grounds that an allegation which was not proved beyond reasonable doubt may be susceptible of proof on a balance of probabilities, as it was in *Loughans v Odhams Press*.[31] As a matter of policy, however, it may be argued that a person acquitted of an offence should be granted some measure of immunity from assertions to the contrary. Parliament has rejected the proposal that in defamation proceedings evidence of an acquittal should be conclusive evidence of innocence.[32] Whether, at common law, evidence of an acquittal is nonetheless *some*, albeit only prima facie, evidence of innocence, not only in defamation actions but also in civil proceedings generally, is, on the present state of the authorities, unclear.

Other previous findings

Subject to exceptions, the principle of *Hollington v Hewthorn & Co Ltd* would appear to apply in respect of judicial findings in previous *civil* proceedings. In *Secretary of State for Trade and Industry v Bairstow*,[33] the Secretary of State brought proceedings under the Company Directors Disqualification Act 1986, seeking a disqualification order against B. Prior to the proceedings,

---

[27] Section 12(5).

[28] *Sutton v Sutton* [1970] 1 WLR 183, PD.

[29] PD 16, para 8.1.

[30] (1932) 97 JP 14, DC.

[31] [1963] 1 QB 299, CA.

[32] See, in this chapter, under **Civil proceedings, Previous convictions in defamation proceedings—section 13 of the Civil Evidence Act 1968.**

[33] [2003] 3 WLR 841, CA.

B had been dismissed by the company of which he had been the managing director, his claim for wrongful dismissal against the company had been dismissed, and his appeal against that decision had failed. The Court of Appeal held that the principle of *Hollington v Hewthorn & Co Ltd* was not confined to cases in which the earlier decision was that of a court exercising a criminal jurisdiction and accordingly the judge's factual findings in the wrongful dismissal proceedings were inadmissible, in the proceedings under the 1986 Act, as evidence of the facts on which they were based.

The exceptions are findings of adultery and paternity, which, as we have seen, are now governed by s 12 of the 1968 Act. In the light of the somewhat novel observations of Lord Denning MR in *Hunter v Chief Constable of West Midlands*,[34] a decision on estoppel *per rem judicatam*, there is arguably a third exception. In that case, Lord Denning MR was of the opinion that a party to civil proceedings can only challenge a previous decision *against* himself by showing that it was obtained by fraud or collusion or by adducing fresh evidence which he could not have obtained by reasonable diligence before, to show conclusively that the previous decision was wrong. On this view, if a driver runs down two pedestrians, a finding of negligence against the driver in an action brought by one of the pedestrians could only be challenged in a subsequent action brought against him by the other in the limited way indicated. Applying the principle in *Hollington v Hewthorn & Co Ltd* to the same example, however, the earlier finding of negligence would be inadmissible as evidence of the driver's negligence in the subsequent proceedings.[35]

The principle of *Hollington v Hewthorn & Co Ltd* has been held to apply not only to judicial findings in previous civil proceedings, but also to the previous findings set out in the reports of inspectors under the Companies Act 1967 (see now Pt XIV of the Companies Act 1985),[36] to an arbitration award,[37] and to findings in extra-statutory reports.[38] Similarly, the principle of *Hollington v Hewthorn & Co Ltd* has been held to apply to findings of the Solicitors Disciplinary Tribunal that a solicitor has been dishonest.[39] However, in the earlier case of *Hill v Clifford*,[40] the Court of Appeal held that a finding by the General Medical Council that a dentist had been guilty of professional misconduct was admissible as prima facie evidence of such misconduct in subsequent civil proceedings concerning the dissolution of his partnership, a decision which may be explicable on the basis that the Council was under a statutory duty of inquiry.[41] However, in such a case the court is still entitled to reach its own view of the facts as previously found.[42]

---

[34] [1981] 3 All ER 727, HL, reported in the Court of Appeal as *McIlkenny v Chief Constable of West Midlands Police Force* [1980] 2 All ER 227 at 237–8. Although the views of Lord Denning MR in this respect were to some extent doubted when the case came before the House of Lords, Lord Diplock, giving the judgment of the House, found it unnecessary expressly to consider the topic of issue estoppel (at 732–3).

[35] In practice, problems of this kind are often avoided by virtue of the procedural provisions relating to joinder of parties and causes of action: see generally CPR Pts 19 and 20.

[36] *Savings and Investment Bank Ltd v Gasco Investments (Netherlands BV)* [1984] 1 WLR 271, Ch D.

[37] *Land Securities plc v Westminster City Council* [1993] 1 WLR 286.

[38] *Three Rivers District Council v Bank of England (No 3)* [2003] 2 AC 1, HL (the findings of Bingham LJ in relation to the collapse of the Bank of Credit and Commerce International).

[39] *Conlon v Simms* [2007] 3 All ER 802, CA.

[40] [1907] 2 Ch 236.

[41] See also *Faulder v Silk* (1811) 3 Camp 126 and *Harvey v R* [1901] AC 601 (inquisitions in lunacy as prima facie evidence of a person's unsoundness of mind).

[42] *Clifford v Timms* [1908] AC 12.

Criminal proceedings

Previous convictions

The application of the principle of *Hollington v Hewthorn & Co Ltd* in criminal cases meant that at the trial of a person charged with handling stolen goods, the previous conviction of the thief was inadmissible as evidence that the goods allegedly received were stolen.[43] Likewise, a woman's convictions for prostitution were inadmissible as evidence of her prostitution at the trial of a man charged with living off her immoral earnings.[44] A final example is *R v Spinks*,[45] where, as we have seen, the conviction of a principal was held to be inadmissible as evidence of his commission of the crime at the trial of the alleged accessory. The Criminal Law Revision Committee thought it was quite wrong, as well as being inconvenient, that in cases of this kind the prosecution should be required to prove again the guilt of the person concerned,[46] and recommended, in respect of convictions of persons other than the accused, a provision in criminal proceedings corresponding to s 11 of the 1968 Act. Section 74 of the 1984 Act not only gives effect to this recommendation but also makes similar provision in relation to the previous convictions of *the accused*: without affecting the law governing the admissibility of the accused's past misconduct, it provides that where evidence of the accused's commission of an offence *is* admissible, if the accused is proved to have been convicted of that offence, he shall be taken to have committed it unless the contrary is proved. Before considering the precise terms of s 74, it may first be noted that it is without prejudice to (i) the admissibility in evidence of any conviction which would be admissible apart from the section;[47] and (ii) the operation of any statutory provision whereby a conviction or finding of fact in criminal proceedings is made conclusive evidence of any fact for the purposes of any other criminal proceedings.[48]

Section 74 of the 1984 Act provides that:

(1) In any proceedings the fact that a person other than the accused has been convicted of an offence by or before any court in the United Kingdom or any other member State[49] or by a Service court outside the United Kingdom shall be admissible in evidence for the purpose of proving that that person committed that offence, where evidence of his having done so is admissible, whether or not any other evidence of his having committed that offence is given.

(2) In any proceedings in which by virtue of this section a person other than the accused is proved to have been convicted of an offence by or before any court in the United Kingdom or any other member State or by a Service court outside the United Kingdom, he shall be taken to have committed that offence unless the contrary is proved.

(3) In any proceedings where evidence is admissible of the fact that the accused has committed an offence, if the accused is proved to have been convicted of the offence—

(a) by or before any court in the United Kingdom or any other member State; or

---

[43] *R v Turner* (1832) 1 Mood CC 347 at 349.

[44] *R v Hassan* [1970] 1 QB 423, CA.

[45] [1982] 1 All ER 587, CA.

[46] 11th Report, Cmnd 4991 (1972), paras 217 ff.

[47] Section 74(4)(a): eg proof of a witness's conviction pursuant to s 6 of the Criminal Procedure Act 1865. See Ch 7.

[48] Section 74(4)(b). The saving appears to have been included not with any particular statute in mind but because of local and private enactments and the possibility of future public enactments: see Criminal Law Revision Committee, 11th Report, Cmnd 4991 (1972), Annex 2, 233.

[49] ie any other EU member state.

(b) by a Service court outside the United Kingdom, he shall be taken to have committed that offence unless the contrary is proved.

Section 75(1) of the 1984 Act provides that:

Where evidence that a person has been convicted of an offence is admissible by virtue of s 74 above, then without prejudice to the reception of any other admissible evidence for the purpose of identifying the facts on which the conviction was based—
(a) the contents of any document which is admissible as evidence of the conviction; and
(b) the contents of—
  (i) the information, complaint, indictment or charge-sheet on which the person in question was convicted, or
  (ii) in the case of a conviction of an offence by a court in a member State (other than the United Kingdom), any document produced in relation to the proceedings for that offence which fulfils a purpose similar to any document or documents specified in sub-paragraph (i),
shall be admissible in evidence for that purpose.[50]

Concerning the terminology of s 74, 'any proceedings' means any criminal proceedings.[51] A conviction, for the purposes of the section, includes a conviction in respect of which a probation order or absolute or conditional discharge was imposed,[52] but not an admission of an offence in a police caution.[53] A person is 'convicted' only if the conviction is 'subsisting'.[54] A subsisting conviction means either a finding of guilt that has not been quashed on appeal or a formal plea of guilt that has not been withdrawn; whether the accused has been sentenced or not is irrelevant.[55] A 'Service court' means a court-martial or a Standing Civilian Court.[56]

Foreign convictions, apart from convictions by Service courts outside the United Kingdom and convictions in other EU member states, are clearly not covered by s 74, but may be admissible under the bad character provisions of the Criminal Justice Act 2003[57] and, if admissible, may be proved under s 7 of the Evidence Act 1851.[58] The rule in *Hollington v Hewthorn & Co Ltd* does not apply, in criminal proceedings, to foreign convictions, since it has been treated as a rule 'governing the admissibility of evidence of bad character' and thus abolished by s 99(1) of the Criminal Justice Act 2003.[59]

Section 74(1) and (2): convictions of persons other than the accused

The question of relevance

Section 74(1) has an obvious application where proof of the commission of an offence by a person other than the accused is admissible to establish an essential ingredient of the offence

---

[50] Provision is also made for the admission of duly certified copies of such documents: s 75(2).

[51] Section 82(1).

[52] Section 75(3).

[53] *R v Olu* [2010] EWCA Crim 2975. Where evidence of such an admission is admitted, an accused may challenge it: *R v Olu* [2010] EWCA Crim 2975.

[54] Section 75(4).

[55] *R v Robertson; R v Golder* [1987] 3 All ER 231, CA. See also *R v Foster* [1984] 2 All ER 679, CA.

[56] Section 82(1).

[57] See Ch 17.

[58] *R v Kordasinski* [2007] 1 Cr App R 238, CA. Section 7 is considered in Ch 9.

[59] *R v Kordasinski* [2007] 1 Cr App R 238, CA. Section 99(1) is considered in Ch 17.

with which the accused is charged. Thus where A is seen transferring goods to B and they are jointly charged with handling the goods, A's guilty plea is admissible at B's trial to prove that the goods were stolen.[60]

In *R v Robertson; R v Golder*,[61] a decision under the original version of s 74(1), it was held that evidence of the commission of the offence may be relevant not only to an issue which is an essential ingredient of the offence charged, but also to less fundamental evidential issues arising in the proceedings. It was also held that the subsection is not confined to the proof of convictions of offences in which the accused on trial played no part; and that where the evidence is admitted, the judge should be careful to explain to the jury its effect and limitations.[62] In the case of Robertson, who was charged with conspiracy with two others to commit burglary, evidence that the others had been convicted of a number of burglaries was admissible because it could be inferred from their commission of these offences that there was a conspiracy between them and that was the very conspiracy to which the prosecution sought to prove that Robertson was a party. Golder was convicted of a robbery committed at garage X. Two of his co-accused pleaded guilty to that robbery and also to another committed at garage Y. The evidence against Golder consisted primarily of a confession statement, which he alleged to have been fabricated by the police, in which he referred to both robberies. It was held that evidence of the guilty pleas of the co-accused was admissible: proof of their commission of the offence at garage X was relevant because it showed that there had in fact been a robbery at that garage; and proof of the commission of both offences was relevant because it showed that the contents of the alleged confession were in accordance with the facts as they were known and therefore more likely to be true. *R v Robertson; R v Golder* was applied in *R v Castle*,[63] where C and F were charged with robbery and F pleaded guilty. At an identification parade, the victim said 'yes' in respect of C, 'possibly' in respect of F. Evidence of the guilty plea was admissible because it was relevant to the issue of the reliability of the identification of C: by confirming the correctness of the 'possible' identification of F, it also tended to confirm the correctness of the positive identification of C.[64]

Although in most cases s 74(1) has been relied on by the prosecution, in appropriate circumstances it may also be used by an accused to adduce evidence of the convictions of a co-accused which are relevant to an issue in the proceedings.[65]

The question of exclusion under section 78 of the Police and Criminal Evidence Act 1984

In *R v Robertson; R v Golder* it was stressed that s 74 should be used sparingly and not where, although the evidence is technically admissible, its effect is likely to be slight, particularly if there is any danger of contravening s 78 of the 1984 Act.[66] A judge, in deciding an application under s 78, should make a ruling, one way or the other, and if he decides to admit the evidence, should give a cogent reason for his decision.[67] If a conviction is admitted under s 74, an

---

[60] *R v Pigram* [1995] Crim LR 808, CA.

[61] [1987] 3 All ER 231, CA.

[62] See also per Staughton LJ in *R v Kempster* (1989) 90 Cr App R 14 at 22, CA and *R v Boyson* [1991] Crim LR 274, CA.

[63] [1989] Crim LR 567, CA.

[64] *R v Castle* was followed in *R v Gummerson and Steadman* [1999] Crim LR 680, CA, a case of *voice* identification. See also *R v Buckingham* (1994) 99 Cr App R 303, CA.

[65] See *R v Hendrick* [1992] Crim LR 427, CA where, on the facts, the convictions were irrelevant.

[66] See also *R v Skinner* [1995] Crim LR 805, CA.

[67] *R v Hillier* (1992) 97 Cr App R 349, CA.

appeal against a judge's ruling not to exclude it under s 78 will only succeed if no judge could reasonably have made it or it was made on a false basis.[68]

In *R v Kempster*[69] it was initially unclear whether the prosecution were relying on the evidence to prove the guilt of the accused or merely to prevent mystification of the jury. Although in the event the jury were encouraged to use the evidence to prove guilt, there was no clear or informed decision by the judge as to any adverse effect it might have had on the fairness of the proceedings. Quashing the convictions, the Court of Appeal highlighted the importance of ascertaining the purpose for which the evidence is adduced before deciding whether it should be excluded under s 78, and held that if the evidence is admitted, the judge should ensure that counsel does not seek to use it for any other purpose. Similarly, in *R v Boyson*[70] the Court of Appeal, *per curiam*, deprecated what it saw as the growing practice of allowing irrelevant, inadmissible, prejudicial, or unfair evidence to be admitted simply on the grounds that it is convenient for the jury to have 'the whole picture'.

Whether a conviction admissible under s 74 should be excluded under s 78 depends on the particular facts. In *R v Mattison*[71] M was charged in one count with gross indecency with D, and D, in another count, was charged with gross indecency with M. D pleaded guilty, M not guilty, his defence being a complete denial. It was held that evidence of the guilty plea was relevant to M's trial but the judge, given M's defence, should have exercised his discretion under s 78 to exclude it.[72] That decision falls to be compared with *R v Turner*.[73] T and L were driving separate cars. L overtook T, hit an oncoming vehicle and killed the passenger in his own car. The prosecution case was that the drivers were racing. L pleaded guilty to causing death by reckless driving. T, tried on the same charge, denied racing. It was held that the guilty plea was relevant, because the prosecution case was that L had been the principal, T the aider and abettor, but that it did not establish that L and T were racing, the essential issue at T's trial. The judge having made it clear that the evidence did not amount to an admission by L that he was racing, there was nothing unfair in admitting it.[74]

The question of exclusion under s 78 is of particular importance in conspiracy and related cases. In *R v O'Connor*[75] B and C were jointly charged in one count with conspiracy to obtain property by deception. B pleaded guilty, C not guilty. Evidence of the guilty plea was admitted, together with the details in the count against him, as permitted by s 75. It was held that the evidence should have been excluded under s 78 because B's admission that he had

---

[68] *R v Smith* [2007] EWCA Crim 215 and *R v Abdullah* [2010] EWCA Crim 3078.

[69] (1989) 90 Cr App R 14, CA.

[70] [1991] Crim LR 274, CA. See also *R v Hall* [1993] Crim LR 527, CA, *R v Mahmood and Manzur* [1997] 1 Cr App R 414, CA, and *R v Downer* [2009] 2 Cr App R 452, CA.

[71] [1990] Crim LR 117, CA.

[72] Where a co-accused pleads guilty but the prosecution do not seek to rely on s 74, it may be sufficient, depending on the circumstances, for the jury to be told that the guilty plea is not probative against the accused: see *R v Turpin* [1990] Crim LR 514, CA. In a case involving joint enterprise, it is insufficient for the judge to direct the jury that they must be sure that each of the accused was a party to the enterprise—they should be told that it is essential that they put the guilty plea of the co-accused out of their minds: *R v Betterley* [1994] Crim LR 764, CA. However, a warning will not suffice if the jury cannot properly consider the case of the accused in isolation from that of the co-accused, in which case the judge should discharge the jury and order a new trial: *R v Fedrick* [1990] Crim LR 403, CA. See also *R v Marlow* [1997] Crim LR 457, CA.

[73] [1991] Crim LR 57, CA.

[74] See also *R v Bennett* [1988] Crim LR 686, CA and *R v Stewart* [1999] Crim LR 746, CA.

[75] (1986) 85 Cr App R 298, CA.

conspired with C might have led the jury to infer that C, in turn, must have conspired with B. The same reasoning was applied in *R v Curry*.[76] C was convicted of conspiracy to obtain property by deception. She was charged with two others, W and H. H pleaded guilty. The prosecution case was that W drove the accused to the shops where C, with H's knowledge, used H's credit card to obtain the goods, H's intention being to report the card as stolen so as to avoid liability for payment. Evidence of the guilty plea was admitted to establish the existence of an unlawful agreement to deceive. The conviction was quashed on the basis that the evidence clearly implied as a matter of fact, albeit not law, that C had been a party to the conspiracy. The court said that s 74 should be used sparingly, especially in cases of conspiracy and affray, and should not be used where the evidence, expressly or by necessary inference, imports the complicity of the accused. *R v Lunnon*[77] was distinguished. That case also involved three accused jointly charged with conspiracy, but it was held that evidence of the guilty plea of one of them had been properly admitted to prove the existence of the conspiracy because the judge had separated for the jury two questions, whether there was a conspiracy and who was a party to it, and had made it clear that despite the evidence, they could acquit the accused.[78] In *R v Abdullah*[79] it was held that evidence of a guilty plea may be admitted if the count against the accused and former co-accused is amended to allege 'with others unknown', which enables the judge to direct the jury that the conviction does not help in any way on the question whether any of the co-accused on trial are guilty of conspiracy.

In deciding whether the guilty plea of a co-accused should be excluded under s 78, regard should be had not only to the interests of the accused, but to those of the prosecution and of justice as a whole.[80] On this basis, in the case of a joint enterprise, an initial decision to exclude the guilty plea may be reversed in order to avoid the jury being misled by the evidence of the accused.[81]

Section 78 may be invoked successfully on the basis that the prosecution, by relying on s 74, do not have to call the person convicted, thereby depriving the defence of the opportunity to challenge or test him in cross-examination.[82] The argument was rejected in *R v Robertson; R v Golder*[83] on the basis that R's name did not appear on any of the burglary counts to which the co-accused had pleaded guilty, and that even if the co-accused had given evidence in accordance with their pleas, R's counsel would have been unlikely to cross-examine them or, if he had, would have seriously prejudiced R. However, as Staughton LJ observed in *R v Kempster*,[84] although such cross-examination may be unlikely in some cases, or else turn out to be a disaster, one cannot always assume that.

An application under s 78 may succeed where a co-accused has pleaded guilty but the evidence was far from conclusive against him, on the basis that to allow the conviction to be

---

[76] [1988] Crim LR 527, CA.

[77] [1988] Crim LR 456, CA.

[78] Cf *R v Chapman* [1991] Crim LR 44, CA where C and seven others were charged with conspiracy to obtain by deception. It was held that a guilty plea by one of the others to two specific counts of obtaining by deception, incidents in which he was involved with C, were relevant and admissible and did not inevitably import the complicity of C. See also *R v Hunt* [1994] Crim LR 747, CA.

[79] [2010] EWCA Crim 3078.

[80] *R v Stewart* [1995] 1 Cr App R 441, CA.

[81] *R v Tee* [2011] EWCA Crim 462.

[82] This was part of the ratio in *R v O'Connor* (1986) 85 Cr App R 298, CA, see text at n 75.

[83] [1987] 3 All ER 231, CA.

[84] (1989) 90 Cr App R 14, CA at 22.

presumed fact, must be presumed. The party relying on the presumption bears the burden of establishing the basic fact. Once he has adduced sufficient evidence on that fact, his adversary bears the legal burden of disproving the presumed fact or, as the case may be, an evidential burden to adduce some evidence to rebut the presumed fact. The standard of proof to be met by the party seeking to rebut the presumed fact varies according to the presumption in question.[4] For example, there is a rebuttable presumption of law that a child proved or admitted to have been born or conceived during lawful wedlock (the basic facts) is legitimate (the presumed fact). A party seeking to rebut the presumed fact by evidence of, say, the husband's impotence, is, in civil proceedings, required to meet the ordinary civil standard of proof on a balance of probabilities.[5] Other examples to be considered in detail in this chapter are the presumptions of marriage, death, and, in testamentary cases, sanity, and the maxims *omnia praesumuntur rite esse acta* and *res ipsa loquitur*, the last-mentioned arguably being a presumption of fact.

Where a rebuttable presumption of law places a legal burden on the party against whom it operates, as does, for example, the presumption of legitimacy, it may be referred to as a 'persuasive' or 'compelling' presumption.[6] In such a case, the legal burden of disproving the presumed fact is on the party against whom the presumption operates. Where a rebuttable presumption of law operates to place an evidential burden on that party, as does, for example, the presumption of death, it may be referred to as an 'evidential' presumption.[7] In such a case, the legal burden of proving the presumed fact is borne by the party in whose favour the presumption operates. If he adduces prima facie evidence of the basic facts, an evidential burden is placed on his adversary. The adversary may discharge this burden in the usual way and, if he does so, the effect will be as if the presumption had never come into play at all; the party bearing the legal burden of proof must satisfy the tribunal of fact to the required standard of proof in the usual way. The terminology of 'persuasive' and 'evidential' presumptions is apposite only in civil proceedings. Subject to express or implied statutory exceptions and cases in which the accused raises the defence of insanity, in criminal proceedings the prosecution bears the legal burden of proving all facts essential to their case. It follows from this general rule that where a common law presumption operates in favour of the accused, the prosecution will always bear a *legal* burden (requiring them to disprove the presumed fact beyond reasonable doubt).[8] Likewise, although there are a number of statutory presumptions which operate to place on the accused a legal burden of proof (which may be discharged by the adduction of such evidence as might satisfy the jury on a balance of probabilities),[9] where a common law presumption operates in favour of the prosecution, the accused will never bear more than an *evidential* burden (which may be discharged by the adduction of such evidence as might leave a jury in reasonable doubt).

Irrebuttable presumptions of law

Where an irrebuttable presumption of law, sometimes referred to as a conclusive presumption, applies, on the proof or admission of a basic fact, another fact must be presumed and

---

[4] Unfortunately, as we shall see, the authorities are often in conflict as to the amount of evidence required to rebut certain presumptions.

[5] Section 26 of the Family Law Reform Act 1969, considered in this chapter, under **Presumptions, The presumption of legitimacy**.

[6] See Denning, 'Presumptions and Burdens' (1945) 61 LQR 380.

[7] See Glanville Williams, *Criminal Law (The General Part)* (2nd edn, London, 1961) 877 ff.

[8] See *R v Willshire* (1881) 6 QBD 366, in this chapter, under **Presumptions, Conflicting presumptions**, and *R v Kay* (1887) 16 Cox CC 292, both relating to the presumption of marriage.

[9] For examples, see Ch 4.

the party against whom the presumption operates is barred from adducing any evidence in rebuttal. Such presumptions amount to no more than rules of substantive law expressed, somewhat clumsily, in the language pertaining to presumptions. Indeed, there is no valid reason why the rather cumbersome phrase 'irrebuttable presumption of law' could not be applied to every rule of substantive law. The following examples may be given. Section 50 of the Children and Young Persons Act 1933 provides that: 'It shall be conclusively presumed that no child under the age of ten years can be guilty of an offence.' Under s 76 of the Sexual Offences Act 2003, in certain sexual cases, including cases of rape, if it is proved that the accused did the relevant act (intentional penetration of the vagina, anus, or mouth) and that he intentionally deceived the complainant as to the nature or purpose of the act, or intentionally induced the complainant to consent to it by impersonating a person known personally to the complainant, it is conclusively presumed that the complainant did not consent to the act and that the accused did not believe that the complainant consented to it. This is a somewhat convoluted way of saying that one of the ways in which rape may be committed is by intentional penetration and the intentional deceit or inducing of the kinds described (ie irrespective of whether the complainant consented and what the accused believed in that regard).[10]

Presumptions of fact

Where a presumption of fact applies, on the proof or admission of a basic fact, another fact *may* be presumed in the absence of sufficient evidence to the contrary. Presumptions of fact are sometimes referred to as 'provisional presumptions' to indicate that a party against whom they operate bears a provisional or tactical burden in relation to the presumed fact. Unlike rebuttable presumptions of law, establishment of the basic fact does not have the effect of placing either an evidential or a legal burden on that party. Thus presumptions of fact amount to nothing more than examples of circumstantial evidence. Certain facts or combinations of facts can give rise to inferences which the tribunal of fact *may* draw, there being no rule of law that such inferences *must* be drawn in the absence of evidence to the contrary. However, presumptions of fact can vary in strength and on the operation of a strong presumption of fact, if no evidence in rebuttal is adduced, a finding by the tribunal of fact against the existence of the presumed fact could, at any rate in civil proceedings, be reversed on appeal. Examples of circumstantial evidence which have recurred so frequently as to attract the label 'presumption of fact' include the presumptions of intention, guilty knowledge (in cases of possession of recently stolen goods), continuance of life, and seaworthiness.[11]

The presumption of intention

There is a presumption of fact that a man intends the natural consequences of his acts. In criminal proceedings, this presumption was treated as a presumption of fact[12] until the House of Lords in *DPP v Smith*[13] held that, in certain circumstances, it constituted a presumption of

---

[10] See also s 13(1) of the Civil Evidence Act 1968 (Ch 21); and s 15(2) and (3) of the Road Traffic Offenders Act 1988 and *Millard v DPP* (1990) 91 Cr App R 108, DC.

[11] See also *Re W (a minor)* (1992) The Times, 22 May, CA: there is a presumption of fact that a baby's best interests are served by being with the mother, although with children the situation might be different.

[12] See *R v Steane* [1947] KB 997 and per Lord Sankey in *Woolmington v DPP* [1935] AC 462 at 481.

[13] [1961] AC 290.

law. This conclusion was statutorily reversed by s 8 of the Criminal Justice Act 1967, the effect of which has been to re-establish the presumption as one of fact.[14] The section provides that:

A court or jury, in determining whether a person has committed an offence—
  (a) shall not be bound in law to infer that he intended or foresaw a result of his actions by reason only of its being a natural and probable consequence of those actions; but
  (b) shall decide whether he did intend or foresee that result by reference to all the evidence, drawing such inferences from the evidence as appear proper in the circumstances.

In civil proceedings it remains unclear whether the presumption of intention is one of fact or law.[15]

The presumption of guilty knowledge

Where an accused is found in possession of goods which have been recently stolen, an explanation is called for and if none is forthcoming the jury are entitled, but not compelled, to infer guilty knowledge or belief and to find the accused guilty of handling stolen goods. Where an explanation is given which the jury are convinced is untrue, likewise the jury are entitled to convict. However, if the explanation given leaves the jury in doubt as to whether the accused knew or believed the goods to be stolen, the prosecution have not proved their case and the jury should acquit.[16] This presumption may operate to the same effect in the case of theft.[17]

The presumption of continuance of life

Where a person is proved to have been alive on a certain date, an inference may be drawn, in the absence of sufficient evidence to the contrary, that he was alive on a subsequent date.[18] The strength of this presumption depends entirely upon the facts of the case in question. In *R v Lumley*,[19] on a woman's trial for bigamy, a question arose as to whether her husband was alive at the date of the second marriage. Lush J said:[20]

This is purely a question of fact. The existence of a party at an antecedent date may, or may not, afford a reasonable inference that he is living at the subsequent date. If, for example, it was proved that he was in good health on the day preceding the marriage, the inference would be strong, almost irresistible, that he was living on the latter day, and the jury would in all probability find that he was so. If, on the other hand, it were proved that he was then in a dying

---

[14] See *R v Wallett* [1968] 2 QB 367, CA; *R v Moloney* [1985] 1 All ER 1025, HL.

[15] See *Kaslefsky v Kaslefsky* [1951] P 38, CA; *Jamieson v Jamieson* [1952] AC 525, HL; *Lang v Lang* [1955] AC 402, PC; *Gollins v Gollins* [1964] AC 644, HL; and *Williams v Williams* [1964] AC 698, HL.

[16] See *R v Schama and Abramovitch* (1914) 11 Cr App R 45; *R v Garth* [1949] 1 All ER 773, CCA; *R v Aves* [1950] 2 All ER 330, CCA; and *R v Hepworth and Fearnley* [1955] 2 QB 600, CCA.

[17] In a case of handling, the prosecution are not obliged to adduce evidence that the goods were handled 'otherwise than in the course of the stealing' (see s 22(1) of the Theft Act 1968): the inference that in the proper case the jury are entitled to draw, namely that an accused was the guilty handler, includes the inference that he was not the thief. However, if the accused is in possession of property so recently after it was stolen that the inevitable inference is that he was the thief, as when he is found within a few hundred yards of the scene of the theft and within minutes after it took place, then if the charge is handling only, the jury should be directed that if they take the view that the accused was the thief, they should acquit him of the handling: *R v Cash* [1985] QB 801, CA, applied in *A-G of Hong Kong v Yip Kai-foon* [1988] 1 All ER 153, PC. See also *Ryan and French v DPP* [1994] Crim LR 457, CA.

[18] See *McDarmaid v A-G* [1950] P 218; *Re Peete, Peete v Crompton* [1952] 2 All ER 599; and *Chard v Chard* [1956] P 259.

[19] (1869) LR 1 CCR 196.

[20] (1869) LR 1 CCR 196 at 198. See also per Denman CJ in *R v Harborne Inhabitants* (1835) 2 Ad&El 540 at 544–5.

condition, and nothing further was proved, they would probably decline to draw that inference. Thus, the question is entirely for the jury.

The presumption of seaworthiness

Where a ship sinks or becomes unable to continue her voyage shortly after putting to sea, an inference may be drawn, in the absence of sufficient evidence to the contrary, that she was unseaworthy on leaving port. If, in these circumstances, a tribunal of fact were to find the contrary, it would be such a finding against the reasonable inference to be drawn that it would amount to a verdict against the evidence.[21]

Presumptions without basic facts

All of the presumptions defined in this chapter up to this point may be explained in terms of a basic fact on the proof or admission of which another fact may or must be presumed. Presumptions without basic facts come into operation without the proof or admission of any basic fact; they are merely conclusions which must be drawn in the absence of evidence in rebuttal. In other words, they are rules relating to the incidence of the legal and evidential burdens expressed in the language pertaining to presumptions. The following examples may be given. In criminal proceedings, reference is often made to the presumptions of innocence and sanity. Both are more meaningfully expressed in terms of the incidence of the burden of proof. The presumption of innocence is a convenient abbreviation of the rule that the prosecution bear the legal burden of proving any fact essential to their case.[22] Likewise, the presumption of sanity refers to the rule that the accused bears the legal burden of proving insanity when he raises it as a defence.[23] In *Bratty v A-G for Northern Ireland* two members of the House of Lords referred to 'the presumption of mental capacity'.[24] The reference was to the rule that the evidential burden in relation to the defence of non-insane automatism is borne by the accused.

A final example of a presumption without basic facts is the presumption that mechanical instruments of a kind that are usually in working order, were in working order at the time when they were used. This conclusion will be drawn by the court in the absence of evidence to the contrary, the party seeking to rebut the presumption bearing an evidential burden. The presumption has been applied in the case of speedometers,[25] traffic lights,[26] breath-test machines,[27] and public weighbridges.[28] The presumption, it is submitted, also applies in the case of computers, with the consequence that a party introducing computer-generated evidence need only produce evidence that the computer was working properly at the relevant time if his opponent introduces some evidence to the contrary.

[21] See per Brett LJ in *Pickup v Thames & Mersey Marine Insurance Co Ltd* (1878) 3 QBD 594, CA at 600. See also *Anderson v Morice* (1875) LR 10 CP 609 and *Ajum Goolam Hossen & Co v Union Marine Insurance Co* [1901] AC 362, PC.

[22] *Woolmington v DPP* [1935] AC 462. The presumption of innocence also applies when an allegation of criminal conduct is made in civil proceedings: see *Williams v East India Co* (1802) 3 East 192. Concerning the standard of proof to be met in these circumstances, see *Hornal v Neuberger Products Ltd* [1957] 1 QB 247, CA, Ch 4.

[23] *M'Naghten's case* (1843) 10 Cl & Fin 200. In testamentary cases, the presumption of sanity is not a presumption without basic facts but a rebuttable presumption of law: see, in this chapter, under **Presumptions, The presumption of sanity in testamentary cases.**

[24] [1963] AC 386 per Viscount Kilmuir LC at 407 and per Lord Denning at 413.

[25] *Nicholas v Penny* [1950] 2 KB 466.

[26] *Tingle Jacobs and Co v Kennedy* [1964] 1 All ER 888n, CA.

[27] *Castle v Cross* [1985] 1 All ER 87, DC.

[28] *Kelly Communications Ltd v DPP* [2003] Crim LR 479 and 875, DC.

The presumption of marriage

There are three discernible presumptions of marriage: a presumption of formal validity, a presumption of essential validity, and a presumption of marriage arising from cohabitation.

The presumption of formal validity

The formal validity of a marriage depends upon the *lex loci celebrationis*. A failure to comply with the formal requirements of the local law may make a marriage void. Under English law, a Church of England marriage (otherwise than by special licence) may be void because of irregularities such as failure duly to publish banns or to obtain a common licence. In the case of other marriages under English law, examples include cases of failure to give due notice to the superintendent registrar and cases in which a certificate and, where necessary, a licence have not been duly issued. However, on the proof or admission of the basic facts that a marriage was celebrated between persons who intended to marry, the formal validity of the marriage will be presumed in the absence of sufficient evidence to the contrary. The authorities almost always include among the basic facts the cohabitation of the parties following the ceremony of marriage[29] but the presumption has been held to apply to death-bed marriages,[30] which obviously suggests the opposite.

The leading case relating to an English marriage is *Piers v Piers*.[31] A marriage ceremony had been celebrated between two persons who had shown their intention, at the time, to marry. The ceremony was performed in a private house but there was no evidence that the bishop of the diocese had granted the necessary special licence. The House of Lords held that the marriage was formally valid.[32] An example of the application of the presumption to a foreign marriage is *Mahadervan v Mahadervan*.[33] Rejecting as irrational legal chauvinism an argument of counsel for the husband that there was no presumption in favour of a foreign marriage the establishment of which would invalidate a subsequent English one, Sir Jocelyn Simon P applied the presumption and held the foreign marriage to be formally valid.

In civil proceedings, the presumption operates as a persuasive presumption placing a legal burden on the party seeking to rebut formal validity.[34] The standard of proof to be met by that party is high. In *Piers v Piers* Lord Cottenham cited with approval the words of Lord Lyndhurst in *Morris v Davies*:[35] 'The presumption of law is not lightly to be repelled. It is not to be broken in upon or shaken by a mere balance of probabilities. The evidence for the purpose of repelling it must be strong, distinct, satisfactory, and conclusive.'[36] Lord Campbell said:[37] 'a presumption of this sort in favour of marriage can only be negatived by disproving every reasonable possibility'. In *Mahadervan v Mahadervan* Sir Jocelyn Simon P held that the presumption can only

---

[29] See, eg, per Barnard J in *Russell v A-G* [1949] P 391 at 394.

[30] See *The Lauderdale Peerage Case* (1885) 10 App Cas 692, HL and *Hill v Hill* [1959] 1 All ER 281.

[31] (1849) 2 HL Cas 331.

[32] See also *De Thoren v A-G* (1876) 1 App Cas 686, HL; *Re Shephard, George v Thyer* [1904] 1 Ch 456; and *Russell v A-G* [1949] P 391.

[33] [1964] P 233. See also *Spivack v Spivack* (1930) 46 TLR 243 and *Hill v Hill* [1959] 1 All ER 281.

[34] In criminal cases where the prosecution bear the legal burden of proving the validity of the marriage, the presumption operates to place an evidential burden on the accused: see *R v Kay* (1887) 16 Cox CC 292.

[35] (1837) 5 Cl&Fin 163 at 265.

[36] The word 'conclusive' hardly seems apposite and its use has been criticized: see Harman LJ in *Re Taylor* [1961] 1 WLR 9, CA.

[37] (1849) 2 HL Cas 331 at 380.

be rebutted by evidence which satisfies beyond reasonable doubt that there was no valid marriage.[38] In relation to matrimonial causes more generally, the authorities, although in conflict, tend to favour the ordinary civil standard[39] and it is likely that in future this lower standard will be applied. When Lord Cottenham in *Piers v Piers* adopted the words of Lord Lyndhurst in *Morris v Davies*, an authority on the presumption of legitimacy, the evidence in rebuttal of that presumption was required to meet a high standard of proof. The presumption of legitimacy is now rebuttable by evidence which satisfies the ordinary civil standard on a balance of probabilities.[40] It is submitted that the standard of proof to be met by the party seeking to rebut the presumption of marriage should also be the ordinary civil standard.

The presumption of essential validity

A marriage may be void on the grounds that the parties lacked the capacity to marry. Under English law, for example, the parties may lack the capacity to marry if they are related within the prohibited degrees or if either of them is under the age of 16 or already married. However, on the proof or admission of the basic fact that a formally valid marriage was celebrated, the essential validity of the marriage will be presumed in the absence of sufficient evidence to the contrary. In the words of Pilcher J in *Tweney v Tweney*,[41] 'The petitioner's marriage to the present respondent being unexceptionable in form and duly consummated remains a good marriage until some evidence is adduced that the marriage was, in fact, a nullity.' Although the matter is far from clear, in civil proceedings the presumption would appear to operate as a persuasive rather than evidential presumption, placing a legal burden on the party seeking to rebut it.[42] However, the standard of proof required to rebut the presumption is lower than that suggested by some of the authorities in the case of the presumption of formal validity. In *Gatty and Gatty v A-G*[43] it was held that evidence of a valid prior marriage sufficed. A similar conclusion was reached in *Re Peete, Peete v Crompton*.[44] A woman, W, made an application under the Inheritance (Family Provision) Act 1938 as the widow of Y. W had separated from her first husband X prior to 1916 and in 1919 went through a formally valid ceremony of marriage with Y. The question arose as to the essential validity of the subsequent marriage. The court held that the application failed. Although a presumption of essential validity arose in relation to the subsequent marriage, there was some evidence before the court, namely the existence of the first marriage, that in 1919 W lacked the capacity to marry Y. However, where the prior marriage is of doubtful validity, there is authority that the presumption is not rebutted.[45]

In most of the cases where the presumption of essential validity has fallen to be applied by the courts, one of the parties to a marriage has been married previously. The question has been whether the earlier marriage had terminated by the time of the subsequent ceremony. This issue may in turn require consideration of the presumption of death, the presumption of continuance of life, or even the presumption of essential validity in relation to the earlier marriage. Two

[38] [1964] P 233 at 246.

[39] *Blyth v Blyth* [1966] AC 643 and *Bastable v Bastable and Sanders* [1968] 1 WLR 1684.

[40] See s 26 of the Family Law Reform Act 1969, in this chapter, under **Presumptions**, **The presumption of legitimacy**.

[41] [1946] P 180 at 182.

[42] Cf *Axon v Axon* (1937) 59 CLR 395, High Court of Australia.

[43] [1951] P 444.

[44] [1952] 2 All ER 599, Ch D.

[45] *Taylor v Taylor* [1967] P 25. Cf *Monckton v Tarr* (1930) 23 BWCC 504, CA.

conflicting presumptions applied to the same facts in *Monckton v Tarr*.[46] A, a woman, married B in 1882. B deserted A in 1887. In 1895, at which time there was no evidence that B was alive, A married C. In 1913, at which time A was still alive, C married a woman, D. D made a claim for workmen's compensation as the widow of C. The employers alleged that the 1913 marriage was void because of the 1895 marriage. D replied that the 1895 marriage was void because of the 1882 marriage. D's claim was dismissed by the Court of Appeal. Although a presumption of essential validity arose in relation to the marriage of 1913, the same presumption applied to the marriage of 1895. These two presumptions cancelling each other out, it was for D to prove C's capacity to marry her and this she could only do by showing that B was alive at the date of the 1895 marriage, something which she had failed to do. A different approach was adopted, however, when a similar problem arose in *Taylor v Taylor*.[47] There was some weak evidence that a woman, W, had married X. Subsequently, in 1928, X married another woman, Y. Y left him and in 1942, when X was still alive, married Z. Z petitioned for a decree of nullity alleging that his marriage to Y was void because of the 1928 marriage. Y replied that the marriage of 1928 was void because of the earlier marriage between W and X. It might have been expected, on the reasoning employed in *Monckton v Tarr*, that the court would have held that the presumptions in favour of the 1928 and 1942 marriages effectively cancelling each other out, it was for Y to prove her capacity to marry Z and that she had failed to do this, the weak evidence adduced to show the marriage between W and X being insufficient for the purpose. However, Cairns J, expressing a preference for the preservation of existing unions, rather than their avoidance in favour of doubtful earlier and effectively dead ones, held that the marriage of 1942 was valid. The evidence of the earlier marriage of doubtful validity, that is the marriage of 1928, did not suffice to rebut the presumption of essential validity in relation to the marriage of 1942.[48]

The presumption of marriage arising from cohabitation

On the proof or admission of the basic fact that a man and woman have long cohabited as if man and wife and have acquired the reputation of being husband and wife, it is presumed, in the absence of sufficient evidence to the contrary, that they were living together in conse-quence of a valid marriage.[49] The authorities suggest that in civil proceedings this presump-tion operates as a persuasive presumption.[50] Evidence in rebuttal is required to meet a high standard of proof: it must be 'clear and firm'[51] or 'of the most cogent kind'.[52] In *Sastry Velaider Aronegary v Sembecutty Vaigalie*[53] the issue concerned the validity of a marriage ceremony

---

[46] (1930) 23 BWCC 504, CA.

[47] [1967] P 25.

[48] Cf, in this respect, the available evidence in rebuttal in *Re Peete, Peete v Crompton* [1952] 2 All ER 599, in text at n 44 in this chapter.

[49] In cases where, pursuant to local law, a valid marriage may come into existence by the consent of the par-ties without a formal ceremony, such consent is presumed: see *Breadalbane Case, Campbell v Campbell* (1867) LR 1 Sc&Div 182.

[50] In criminal proceedings in which the prosecution rely on this presumption, the authorities suggest that the presumption, by itself, is insufficient to discharge the evidential burden: see *Morris v Miller* (1767) 4 Burr 2057 and *R v Umanski* [1961] VLR 242. Proof or admission of cohabitation supported by the production of a marriage certificate does suffice for these purposes: *R v Birtles* (1911) 6 Cr App R 177.

[51] *Re Taylor* [1961] 1 WLR 9, CA.

[52] *Re Taplin, Watson v Tate* [1937] 3 All ER 105, Ch D. Some of the cases suggest an extremely high standard of proof: see, eg, *Re Shephard, George v Thyer* [1904] 1 Ch 456.

[53] (1881) 6 App Cas 364, PC.

which had taken place between Tamils in Ceylon. The Privy Council, of the opinion that the party in whose favour the presumption operated was under no obligation to prove that the ceremony had complied with the requisite customs, held the parties to be validly married. Although in that case evidence was given that a ceremony had taken place, it is clear that the presumption may apply in the absence of such evidence.[54] In *Al-Saedy v Musawi*[55] it was held that a party will succeed in rebutting the presumption if he can identify the only known ceremony or event which might have constituted a marriage and can show that it did not have that effect in English law.

The presumption of legitimacy

On the proof or admission of the basic fact that a child was born or conceived during lawful wedlock, it is presumed, in the absence of sufficient evidence to the contrary, that the child is legitimate. The presumption may be rebutted by evidence showing that the husband and wife did not have sexual intercourse as a result of which the child was conceived.[56] The evidence in rebuttal may be evidence of: non-access; the husband's impotence;[57] the use of reliable contraceptives; the blood groups of the parties; the results of a DNA test; the minimal nature of the husband's access to the wife; an admission of paternity by another man;[58] the wife's cohabitation with another man for an appropriate period of time before the birth of the child;[59] the results of a DNA test excluding the husband as the father combined with evidence of sexual intercourse with another man who refused to comply with an order for a blood test;[60] or the conduct of the wife and illicit partner to the child.[61] Evidence of adultery by the mother will not rebut the presumption in the absence of evidence that at the time of conception sexual intercourse between the husband and wife did not take place.[62]

Either birth or conception during wedlock suffices to give rise to the presumption. Thus where a child is born to a married woman so soon after the marriage ceremony that pre-marital conception is indicated, the presumption applies.[63] Likewise, the presumption applies where a child is born to a woman so soon after the termination of her marriage that conception during the marriage is indicated.[64] In *Re Overbury, Sheppard v Matthews*[65] the presumption was applied in such circumstances notwithstanding the remarriage of the mother prior to the birth of the child. Six months after her first husband's death a woman had remarried, giving birth to a girl

---

[54] *Re Taplin, Watson v Tate* [1937] 3 All ER 105. This remains the case even if the period of cohabitation was short: see *Re Taylor* [1961] 1 WLR 9, CA. Cf *Re Bradshaw, Blandy v Willis* [1938] 4 All ER 143. See also *Breadalbane Case, Campbell v Campbell* (1867) LR 1 Sc&Div 182.

[55] [2010] EWHC 3293 (Fam).

[56] See per Sir James Mansfield CJ in the *Banbury Peerage Case* (1811) 1 Sim&St 153. Under s 48(1) of the Matrimonial Causes Act 1973, the evidence of a husband or wife shall be admissible in any proceedings to prove that marital intercourse did or did not take place between them during any period.

[57] *Legge v Edmonds* (1855) 25 LJ Ch 125.

[58] *R v King's Lynn Magistrates' Court and Walker, ex p Moore* [1988] Fam Law 393, QBD.

[59] *Cope v Cope* (1833) 1 Mood&R 269 and *Re Jenion, Jenion v Wynne* [1952] Ch 454, CA.

[60] *F v Child Support Agency* [1999] 2 FLR 244, QBD.

[61] *Morris v Davies* (1837) 5 Cl&Fin 163 and *Kanapathipillai v Parpathy* [1956] AC 580.

[62] *R v Mansfield Inhabitants* (1841) 1 QB 444 and *Gordon v Gordon* [1903] P 141.

[63] *The Poulett Peerage Case* [1903] AC 395, HL.

[64] See *Maturin v A-G* [1938] 2 All ER 214 (termination by divorce) and *Re Heath, Stacey v Bird* [1945] Ch 417 (termination by death of husband).

[65] [1955] Ch 122, Ch D.

This statutory presumption is easier to raise than its common law counterpart. Apart from the continual absence, the only basic fact to be established relates to the belief of the petitioner, who must give evidence.[92] In *Thompson v Thompson*[93] the provision was construed by Sachs J to mean that during the period of seven years nothing should have occurred from which the petitioner could have reasonably concluded that his or her spouse was alive. The court left open the question whether the petitioner is required to have made all due inquiries appropriate to the circumstances, but it is submitted that a failure to do so could be relevant to the issue of the reasonableness of the petitioner's belief. The fact that the parties parted under a separation agreement does not prevent the operation of the presumption.[94]

The proviso to section 57 of the Offences Against the Person Act 1861

After defining the offence of bigamy, s 57 continues:

> Provided that nothing in this section contained shall extend…to any person marrying a second time whose husband or wife shall have been continually absent from such person for the space of seven years then last past, and shall not have been known by such person to be living within that time…

The prosecution, in order to prove bigamy, must show that the first spouse was alive at the date of the second marriage.[95] Where this has been done, the accused may rely upon the proviso, which amounts to a defence, to secure an acquittal.[96] The prosecution bear the legal burden of proving that the first marriage was valid and that the accused went through a second marriage knowing that the first spouse was alive. *R v Edwards*[97] suggests that the accused bears the legal burden of proving that the first spouse was continually absent for seven years[98] and that he or she did not know that the first spouse was living within that time. However, there is also authority that the prosecution bears the legal burden in relation to the accused's knowledge.[99]

Omnia praesumuntur rite esse acta

On the proof or admission of the basic fact that a public or official act has been performed, it is presumed, in the absence of sufficient evidence to the contrary, that the act has been regularly and properly performed. Likewise, persons acting in public capacities are presumed to have been regularly and properly appointed. In civil proceedings, the maxim operates as an evidential presumption and may be rebutted by some evidence of irregularity. The operation of the presumption may be illustrated by the following authorities. In *R v Gordon*[100] proof that

---

[92] *Parkinson v Parkinson* [1939] P 346.

[93] [1957] P 19.

[94] *Parkinson v Parkinson* [1939] P 346.

[95] Proof that the first spouse was alive before the second marriage may give rise to an inference that he or she was alive at the date of that marriage: see *R v Lumley* (1869) LR 1 CCR 196.

[96] In Australia, the proviso has been treated as a statutory presumption of death in relation to one party to a marriage on the remarriage of the other: see per Evatt J in *Axon v Axon* (1937) 59 CLR 395 at 413, HC of A and *Re Peatling* [1969] VR 214 (Supreme Court of Victoria).

[97] [1975] QB 27, Ch 4.

[98] See also *R v Jones* (1883) 11 QBD 118 and *R v Bonnor* [1957] VLR 227.

[99] *R v Curgerwen* (1865) LR 1 CCR 1.

[100] (1789) 1 Leach 515.

a police officer had acted as such was sufficient on a charge of assaulting a police officer in the course of his duty: evidence of due appointment was not required.[101] In *R v Roberts*,[102] on an indictment for perjury committed in the presence of a deputy county court judge, the judge was presumed, in the absence of evidence to the contrary, to have been duly appointed.[103] In *R v Langton*[104] the presumption applied to establish the due incorporation of a company which had acted as such. In *R v Cresswell*,[105] on proof that a marriage had been celebrated in a building some yards from a parish church, in which building several other marriages had also been celebrated, it was presumed that the building was duly consecrated. In *TC Coombs & Co (a firm) v IRC*[106] it was presumed, in the absence of evidence to the contrary, that a tax inspector, who had served notices under s 20 of the Taxes Management Act 1970 requiring delivery of documentary information relevant to tax liability, together with a General Commissioner, who had given his consent to the notices, had both acted within the limits of their authority, with honesty and discretion.

The authorities are in conflict as to the applicability of the presumption in criminal proceedings. Although there are cases in which the prosecution have relied on the presumption to establish part of their case,[107] in *Scott v Baker*,[108] on proof that a breathalyzer had been issued to the police, the court refused to presume that it had been officially approved by the Secretary of State. It was held that the presumption may not be used to establish an ingredient of a criminal office if the regularity and propriety of the matter in question is disputed at the trial.[109] However, there is also authority that it is insufficient merely to dispute regularity; evidence must be adduced.[110]

The presumption of sanity in testamentary cases

Although in criminal cases the presumption of sanity is a presumption without basic facts, a rule relating to the incidence of the burden of proof, in testamentary cases it operates as a rebuttable presumption of law casting an evidential burden on the party against whom it operates. On the proof or admission of the basic fact that a rational will has been duly executed, it is presumed, in the absence of sufficient evidence to the contrary, that the testator

---

[101] See also *Doe d Bowley v Barnes* (1846) 8 QB 1037.

[102] (1878) 14 Cox CC 101, CCR.

[103] See also *R v Verelst* (1813) 3 Camp 432. But there is no presumption that a court or tribunal has jurisdiction in relation to any given matter: see *Christopher Brown Ltd v Genossenschaft Oesterreichischer* [1954] 1 QB 8 per Devlin J at 13.

[104] (1876) 2 QBD 296.

[105] (1876) 1 QBD 446, CCR.

[106] [1991] 3 All ER 623, HL.

[107] See *Gibbins v Skinner* [1951] 2 KB 379, where it was held that on proof that speed limit signs had been placed on a road, the presumption could operate to establish the performance of a local authority's statutory duties pursuant to the Road Traffic Acts; and *Cooper v Rowlands* [1972] Crim LR 53, where a man in police uniform who administered a breath test was presumed to have been duly appointed.

[108] [1969] 1 QB 659, DC, approved by the Court of Appeal in *R v Withecombe* [1969] 1 WLR 84.

[109] See also *Dillon v R* [1982] AC 484, PC. *Scott v Baker* was distinguished in *Public Prosecution Service of Northern Ireland v Elliott* [2013] 2 Cr App R 180, SC, in the case of fingerprints taken using an electronic device that had not been, but should have been, officially approved, on the basis that whereas breath tests, like speed guns, are means of measuring something that cannot subsequently be re-measured, fingerprints can be reproduced subsequently and the accuracy of the initial readings, if disputed, can readily be checked by the provision of more samples.

[110] *Campbell v Wallsend Slipway & Engineering Co Ltd* [1978] ICR 1015, DC at 1025.

was sane. In *Sutton v Sadler*[111] the heir-at-law of a testator brought an action against the devisee alleging the insanity of the testator. The devisee produced the will, proved its due execution, and called witnesses to prove the competency of the testator. The plaintiff gave evidence of the testator's insanity. The trial judge directed the jury that the heir-at-law was entitled to succeed unless a will was proved but that on the production of a duly executed will he bore the burden of establishing the incompetency of the testator so that if they were left in doubt on the matter, the devisee would succeed. The jury found for the devisee. The Court of Common Pleas held that the jury had been misdirected. The devisee bore the legal burden of proving that he was the devisee under a duly executed will. Proof of the due execution of a rational will gave rise to the presumption of sanity placing an evidential burden on the heir-at-law, the legal burden of proving the competency of the testator resting with the devisee. Accordingly, if the heir-at-law had raised sufficient evidence for the issue of insanity to go before the tribunal of fact, they should have been directed to find against the devisee unless satisfied that he had discharged the legal burden by proving on a balance of probabilities that the testator was sane. A new trial was ordered.

Res ipsa loquitur

In the ordinary course of things bags of flour do not fall from warehouse windows,[112] stones are not found in buns,[113] cars do not mount the pavement,[114] and slippery substances are not left on shop floors[115] unless, in each case, those who have the management of the thing in question fail to exercise proper care. The normal rule, that in negligence actions the claimant bears the legal and evidential burden, is capable of causing injustice in cases such as these. Although the claimant is able to prove the accident, he cannot show that it was caused by the defendant's negligence, the true cause of the accident, in most cases, being known only to the defendant. In these circumstances, the claimant may be assisted by the principle of *res ipsa loquitur*.[116] Translating into the terminology of presumptions the statement of the principle given by Sir William Erle CJ in *Scott v London & St Katherine Docks Co*,[117] the presumption may be defined as follows: on the proof or admission of the basic facts that (i) some thing was under the management of the defendant or his servants; and (ii) an accident occurred, being an accident which in the ordinary course of things does not happen if those who have the management use proper care, it may or must be presumed, in the absence of sufficient evidence to the contrary, that the accident was caused by the negligence of the defendant. This definition allows for three possible classifications of the principle, as a presumption of fact, as an evidential presumption, or as a persuasive presumption, for each of which support may be found in the authorities.

---

[111] (1857) 3 CBNS 87.

[112] *Byrne v Boadle* (1863) 2 H&C 722.

[113] *Chaproniére v Mason* (1905) 21 TLR 633, CA.

[114] *Ellor v Selfridge & Co Ltd* (1930) 46 TLR 236.

[115] *Ward v Tesco Stores Ltd* [1976] 1 WLR 810, CA.

[116] This phrase has been used despite the strictures of the Court of Appeal in *Fryer v Pearson & Anor* (2000) The Times, 4 Apr: 'People should stop using maxims or doctrines dressed up in Latin which are not readily comprehensible to those for whose benefit they are supposed to exist.' The authors applaud the attempt to accommodate the lay client, but rather fear that some doctrines—eg estoppel *per rem judicatam*—will need explanation whatever language they are couched in.

[117] (1865) 3 H&C 596 at 601.

Some authorities suggest that the principle is no more than a presumption of fact: proof of the basic facts gives rise to an inference of negligence which the tribunal of fact may draw in the absence of evidence to the contrary. A party against whom the presumption operates bears the provisional or tactical burden in relation to negligence: if he adduces no evidence, he is not bound to lose but it is a clear risk that he runs and a finding by the tribunal of fact in his favour could be reversed on appeal.[118] Other authorities suggest that it is an evidential presumption: on proof of the basic facts, negligence must be presumed in the absence of evidence to the contrary, and the party against whom the presumption operates bears the evidential burden: he will lose unless he adduces some evidence but where, on all the evidence before the court, the probability of negligence is equal to the probability of its absence, he will succeed, the plaintiff having failed to discharge the legal burden of proving negligence.[119] Finally, there are authorities to suggest that the principle is a persuasive or compelling presumption: negligence must be presumed in the absence of evidence to the contrary, the party against whom the presumption operates bears the legal burden of disproving negligence, and he will lose not only where he adduces no evidence but also where on all the evidence before the court the probability of negligence is equal to the probability of its absence. To succeed, he must disprove negligence on a balance of probabilities. The evidence he adduces must either reveal the true cause of the accident and thereby convince the tribunal of fact that negligence is less probable than its absence or show that he used all reasonable care.[120]

It is submitted that there may be no anomaly in the fact that the courts have adopted such different approaches towards this presumption. Given that the facts calling for the application of the principle vary enormously from case to case so that in some the inference of negligence is slight, in others all but irresistible, efforts aimed at confining the principle to a single category seem ill-founded. At the risk of uncertainty, classification according to the facts of the case in question seems preferable. If the thing speaks for itself, it may do so with degrees of conviction. The hardship caused to the claimant may be remedied by placing the tactical, evidential, or legal burden on the defendant depending on the strength of the basic facts in question.

Conflicting presumptions

Where two presumptions apply to the facts of a case, the court may be required to draw two conclusions, the one conflicting with the other. If the two conflicting presumptions are of equal strength so that each operates to place a legal or, as the case may be, evidential or tactical burden on the party against whom it operates, one obvious and equitable solution is to treat the two presumptions as having cancelled each other out and to proceed, as if

---

[118] See, eg, per Greer LJ in *Langham v Wellingborough School Governors and Fryer* (1932) 101 LJKB 513 at 518 and per Goddard LJ in *Easson v London & North Eastern Rly Co* [1944] KB 421.

[119] See, eg, *The Kite* [1933] P 154 at 170. See also per Lord Porter in *Woods v Duncan* [1946] AC 401 at 434, HL; per Lord Pearson in *Henderson v Henry E Jenkins & Sons and Evans* [1970] AC 282 at 301, HL; per Lawton LJ in *Ward v Tesco Stores Ltd* [1976] 1 WLR 810 at 814, CA; and *Ng Chun Pui v Lee Chuen Tat* [1988] RTR 298, PC.

[120] See per Lords Simon, Russell, and Simmonds in *Woods v Duncan* [1946] AC 401, HL at 419, 425, and 439 respectively; per Asquith LJ in *Barkway v South Wales Transport Co Ltd* [1948] 2 All ER 460, CA at 471; *Walsh v Holst & Co Ltd* [1958] 1 WLR 800, CA; *Colvilles Ltd v Devine* [1969] 1 WLR 475, HL; the speeches of Lords Reid and Donovan in *Henderson v Henry E Jenkins & Sons and Evans* [1970] AC 282, HL; and, arguably, *George v Eagle Air Services Ltd* [2009] UKPC 21.

no presumption were involved, on the basis of the normal rules relating to the burden and standard of proof. As we have seen, this was the solution adopted in *Monckton v Tarr*,[121] where the same presumption of essential validity applied to two different ceremonies of marriage. However, when a similar conflict of presumptions arose in *Taylor v Taylor*,[122] Cairns J preferred to preserve an existing marriage rather than avoid it in favour of an earlier doubtful one. This approach suggests that the strength of a presumption may be gauged by reference to the comparative likelihood of the two presumed facts, or even to general considerations of public policy, as opposed to the nature of the burden placed on the party against whom it operates. Inherently imprecise, such an approach has the obvious advantage of flexibility compared to any set formula. In cases where the two presumptions are, by reference to the burden placed on the party against whom they operate, of unequal strength, there is a dearth of authority. To say that the presumption of greater strength should prevail is to acknowledge that the conflict is more apparent than real. Where, for example, the conflict is between a presumption of law and a presumption of fact,[123] the determinative factor is the incidence of the legal burden of proof; whether the presumption of law operates to place a legal or evidential burden on the party against whom it operates, the party bearing the legal burden of proof will lose on the issue in question if he fails to discharge it by adducing sufficient evidence to meet the required standard of proof. *R v Willshire*,[124] often cited as an example of conflicting presumptions, is, it is submitted, properly understood in this sense. The accused was convicted of bigamy, having married D in the lifetime of his former wife C. In fact he had gone through four ceremonies of marriage: with A in 1864; with B in 1868; with C in 1879; and with D in 1880. The prosecution, who bore the legal burden of proving the validity of the ceremony in 1879, relied upon the presumption of essential validity. The accused sought to show that the marriage of 1879 was void. He could prove that A was alive in 1868 by virtue of his earlier conviction of bigamy in that year (he married B in the lifetime of A) and he relied upon the presumption of fact as to the continuance of life to establish that A was still alive in 1879. The trial judge did not leave the question whether A was alive in 1879 to the jury but directed them that the defendant bore the burden of adducing other or further evidence of A's existence in 1879. On appeal, this was held to be a misdirection and the conviction was quashed. Lord Coleridge CJ, in the course of his judgment, referred to a conflict between the presumption of essential validity and the presumption of continuance of life. Although the judgment is consistent with the view that the two presumptions had cancelled each other out, it is equally consistent with the ordinary operation of both, the determinative factor being the incidence of the legal burden.[125] The prosecution bore the legal burden of proving the validity of the ceremony of 1879. Once they had proved the basic facts giving rise to the presumption of essential validity of that ceremony, the defendant bore an evidential burden to adduce some evidence in rebuttal.[126] He had successfully discharged this burden by relying on the presumption of the continuance of life and accordingly the jury should have been directed that they could only

[121] (1930) 23 BWCC 504, CA.

[122] [1965] 1 All ER 872.

[123] Or between a persuasive and an evidential presumption.

[124] (1881) 6 QBD 366, CCR.

[125] There is considerable variance in the reports of the judgment of Lord Coleridge CJ: see 6 QBD 366 and cf 50 LJMC 57.

[126] The presumption of essential validity operates as a *persuasive* presumption only in civil proceedings.

convict if the prosecution had satisfied them beyond reasonable doubt that the ceremony of 1879 was valid.[127]

Judicial notice

Judicial notice without inquiry

Certain facts are beyond serious dispute, so notorious, or of such common knowledge that they require no proof and are open to no evidence in rebuttal. In criminal and civil proceedings, a court may take judicial notice of such a fact and direct the tribunal of fact to treat it as established notwithstanding the absence of proof by evidence. To require proof of such facts, which in some cases could cause considerable difficulty, would be to waste both time and money and could result in inconsistency between cases in relation to which common sense demands uniformity. Any attempt at a compilation of the numerous facts of which judicial notice has been taken would be pointless. It will suffice to refer to the following examples: a fortnight is too short a period for human gestation;[128] the duration of the normal period of human gestation is about nine months;[129] the streets of London are crowded and dangerous;[130] a postcard is the sort of document which might be read by anyone;[131] flick-knives[132] and butterfly knives[133] are made for use for causing injury to the person; and reconstructed trials with a striking degree of realism are one of the popular forms of modern television entertainment.[134] A final example of general application is that the court is taken to know the meaning of any ordinary English expression.[135] In all of these examples, the doctrine of judicial notice was expressly applied, but more often than not judicial notice of a fact is taken without being stated. For example, when evidence is adduced that a burglar was found in possession of skeleton keys, judicial notice is tacitly taken of the fact that skeleton keys are frequently used in the commission of the crime of burglary; the fact is not required to be established by evidence but is taken as established as much as if express judicial notice had been taken of it. Judicial notice of certain facts is expressly required by statute. Most of these provisions require judicial notice to be taken of the fact that a document has been signed or sealed by the person by whom it purports to have been signed or sealed. This applies to any judicial or official document signed by certain judges,[136] and summonses and other documents issuing out of a county court and sealed or stamped with the seal of the court.[137] Judicial notice shall

---

[127] See also *Re Peatling* [1969] VR 214 (Supreme Court of Victoria): the presumption of validity can prevail over that of continuance by virtue of the greater strength of the former.

[128] *R v Luffe* (1807) 8 East 193.

[129] *Preston-Jones v Preston-Jones* [1951] AC 391, HL. A child born to a woman 360 days after the last occasion on which she had intercourse with her husband, cannot be his child (per Lord Morton).

[130] *Dennis v White* [1916] 2 KB 1.

[131] *Huth v Huth* [1915] 3 KB 32, CA.

[132] *R v Simpson* [1983] 1 WLR 1494, CA.

[133] *DPP v Hynde* [1998] 1 All ER 649, DC.

[134] *R v Yap Chuan Ching* (1976) 63 Cr App R 7, CA. Judicial notice of this fact related to the formulation by the court of the appropriate direction to be given to the jury on the standard of proof in criminal proceedings. Thus the fact judicially noticed was not a fact in issue but was relevant to the question of law which formed the subject of the appeal.

[135] *Chapman v Kirke* [1948] 2 KB 450 at 454.

[136] Section 2 of the Evidence Act 1845.

[137] Section 134(2) of the County Courts Act 1984.

and Drugs Act 1875, the issue was whether cocoa contained a quantity of foreign ingredients. Despite the absence of evidence to establish the matter, the justices, acting on the knowledge of the subject that some of them had acquired in the navy, found for the accused. Although Wills J observed that, in future, evidence should be heard,[174] the finding was not disturbed. In *Ingram v Percival*[175] the accused was convicted of unlawfully using a net secured by anchors for taking salmon or trout in tidal waters. The only issue being whether the place where the net was fixed was in tidal waters, the justices had acted on their own knowledge. Lord Parker CJ held that justices may and should take into consideration personal knowledge, particularly when it relates to local matters. In *Paul v DPP*[176] it was held that in a case of 'kerb crawling', justices, for the purpose of deciding whether or not the soliciting was 'such…as to be likely to cause nuisance to other persons in the neighbourhood',[177] were entitled to take into account their local knowledge that the area in question was a heavily populated residential area, often frequented by prostitutes, with a constant procession of cars at night.

When a judge takes judicial notice of a notorious fact, he is making use of his general knowledge. The extent to which a judge may make use of his personal knowledge of facts in issue or relevant to the issue is not clear from the authorities. In *Keane v Mount Vernon Colliery Co Ltd*[178] Lord Buckmaster held that 'properly applied, and within reasonable limits' it was permissible to use knowledge of matters within the common knowledge of people in the locality. Similarly, in *Reynolds v Llanelly Associated Tinplate Co Ltd*[179] Lord Greene MR said that whereas it is improper to draw on knowledge of a particular or highly specialized nature, the use of knowledge on matters within the common knowledge of everyone in the district is unobjectionable. These two cases and others cited in support of the same principle were all decided under the Workmen's Compensation Acts, under which the county court judges sat as arbitrators and could take into account, when assessing compensation, their own knowledge of the labour market, conditions of labour, and wages.[180] However, in *Mullen v Hackney London Borough Council*[181] the Court of Appeal has treated the principle as being of general application in any county court case. The judge in that case, in deciding the financial penalty to impose on the council for its failure to carry out an undertaking to the court to repair a council house, took account of the fact that the council had failed to honour previous undertakings to the court in similar cases. On appeal it was held that the judge was entitled to take judicial notice of his own knowledge of the council's conduct in relation to the previous undertakings, since even if not notorious or clearly established, it was clearly susceptible of demonstration by reference to the court records, and there was nothing to suggest that the judge had relied on his local knowledge improperly or beyond reasonable limits. It is submitted that this decision confuses and misapplies the separate principles relating to judicial notice and personal knowledge. As to judicial notice, the facts in question were clearly not notorious or of common knowledge, and bear no resemblance to the kinds of fact of which judicial notice has been held to have been properly taken after inquiry. As to personal knowledge, it appears to have

---

[174] (1895) 64 LJMC 158 at 159–60.

[175] [1969] 1 QB 548.

[176] (1989) 90 Cr App R 173, DC.

[177] See s 1(1) of the Sexual Offences Act 1985.

[178] [1933] AC 309 at 317.

[179] [1948] 1 All ER 140, CA.

[180] See Allen, 'Judicial Notice Extended' (1998) 2(1) E&P 37.

[181] [1997] 1 WLR 1103.

been used, without good reason, without notice, and to the unfair disadvantage of the council, as a substitute for evidence.

Formal admissions

It is important to distinguish between formal and informal admissions. An informal admission is a statement of a party adverse to his case and admissible as evidence of the truth of its contents, by way of exception to the rule against hearsay, subject to compliance with the relevant statutory conditions including, in civil cases, the notice procedure.[182] Unlike a formal admission, it is not conclusive: its maker may adduce evidence at the trial with a view to explaining it away. However, a fact which is formally admitted ceases to be in issue. Evidence of such a fact is neither required nor admissible. Thus a party who makes a formal admission, which is generally conclusive for the purposes of the proceedings, saves his opponent the trouble, time, and expense of proving the fact in question. A party who fails formally to admit facts about which there is no real dispute may be ordered to pay the costs incurred by his adversary in proving them. Legal advisers owe a duty to their clients to consider if any formal admissions can properly be made.

Civil cases

CPR r 14.1(1), (2), and (5) provide as follows:

(1) A party may admit the truth of the whole or any part of another party's case.
(2) He may do this by giving notice in writing (such as in a statement of case or by letter).[183]
(5) The permission of the court is required to amend or withdraw an admission.[184]

CPR r 14.1A(1) provides as follows:

(1) A person may, by giving notice in writing, admit the truth of the whole or any part of another party's case before commencement of proceedings (a 'pre-action admission').[185]

In civil proceedings, a fact may be formally admitted in a variety of additional ways: by an express admission in a defence,[186] by default, ie by a defendant failing to deal with an allegation,[187] or by either party in response to a notice to admit facts,[188] or in response to a written request, or court order, to give additional information.[189] Prior to the trial, formal admissions may also be made by letter written by a legal adviser acting on behalf of a client.[190] At the trial itself, a party or his legal adviser may admit facts, thereby rendering any evidence on the matter inadmissible.[191]

---

[182] As to criminal cases, see Ch 13. As to civil cases, see Ch 11, under **Evidence formerly admissible at common law**.

[183] Special provision has also been made for the making of admissions where the only remedy which the claimant is seeking is the payment of money: see CPR rr 14.1(3) and 14.4–14.7.

[184] Paragraph 7 of PD 14 contains a non-exhaustive list of factors to which the court must have regard when considering an application to withdraw a Pt 14 admission.

[185] Special provision is made for pre-action admissions made in proceedings falling within the pre-action protocol for personal injuries, for the resolution of clinical disputes, or for disease and illness claims: see r 14.1A(2)–(5).

[186] See CPR r 16.5(1)(c).

[187] See CPR r 16.5(5).

[188] See CPR r 32.18.

[189] See CPR rr 18.1 and 26.5(3), and PD 18.

[190] *Ellis v Allen* [1914] 1 Ch 904.

[191] *Urquhart v Butterfield* (1887) 37 Ch D 357, CA.

Criminal cases

Under s 10(1) of the Criminal Justice Act 1967, a formal admission may be made of 'any fact of which oral evidence may be given in any criminal proceedings', words which make it clear that the section covers only facts and therefore not the opinion of an expert,[192] and cannot be used to admit evidence which would otherwise fall to be excluded because, for example, it is inadmissible hearsay.[193] The admission, which may be made before or at the proceedings in question by or on behalf of the prosecutor or defendant, is conclusive evidence in those proceedings of the fact admitted. Ordinarily, it should be put before the jury, unless it contains material which should not be before them.[194] The admission is also treated as conclusive for the purposes of any subsequent criminal proceedings, including an appeal or retrial, relating to the same matter to which the original proceedings related.[195] The admission may, with the leave of the court, be withdrawn.[196] The making of an admission under the section is subject to certain protective restrictions: if made otherwise than in court, it shall be in writing;[197] if made in writing by an individual, it shall purport to be signed by the person making it (in the case of a body corporate the signature being required to be that of a director, manager, secretary, clerk, or other similar officer); if made on behalf of a defendant who is an individual, it shall be made by his counsel or solicitor; and if made at any stage before the trial by such a defendant, it must be approved by his counsel or solicitor (whether at the time it was made or subsequently) before or at the proceedings in question.[198] In the magistrates' court, where a party introduces in evidence a fact admitted by another party, or parties jointly admit a fact, then unless the court otherwise directs, a written record must be made of the admission.[199]

ADDITIONAL READING

Carter, 'Judicial Notice: Related and Unrelated Matters' in Campbell and Waller (eds), *Well and Truly Tried* (Sydney, 1982).

Zuckerman, *The Principles of Criminal Evidence* (Oxford, 1989) Chs 6 and 8.

---

[192] *R v Naylor* [2010] EWCA Crim 1188.

[193] See *R v Coulson* [1997] Crim LR 886, CA.

[194] *R v Pittard* [2006] EWCA Crim 2028.

[195] Section 10(3).

[196] Section 10(4).

[197] Section 10(2)(b). In court, counsel may admit a fact *orally: R v Lewis* [1989] Crim LR 61, CA. Cf *Tobi v Nicholas* [1987] Crim LR 774, DC.

[198] Section 10(2)(c)–(e).

[199] Rule 37.6, Criminal Procedure Rules 2013, SI 2013/1554.

INDEX